Rethinking the Color Line

6th Edition

This book is dedicated to my daughters Talia and Sophia. Their willingness to speak frankly, forcefully, and often about how teens see race and what parents miss has provided me with exceptional insight into contemporary issues of racism, identity construction, and racial inequality.

Rethinking the Color Line

Readings in Race and Ethnicity

6th Edition

Edited by

Charles A. Gallagher
La Salle University

Los Angeles | London | New Delhi
Singapore | Washington DC | Melbourne

FOR INFORMATION:

SAGE Publications, Inc.
2455 Teller Road
Thousand Oaks, California 91320
E-mail: order@sagepub.com

SAGE Publications Ltd.
1 Oliver's Yard
55 City Road
London, EC1Y 1SP
United Kingdom

SAGE Publications India Pvt. Ltd.
B 1/I 1 Mohan Cooperative Industrial Area
Mathura Road, New Delhi 110 044
India

SAGE Publications Asia-Pacific Pte. Ltd.
3 Church Street
#10-04 Samsung Hub
Singapore 049483

Printed in the United States of America

Library of Congress Cataloging-in-Publication Data

ISBN 978-1-5063-9413-8

Acquisitions Editor: Jeff Lasser
Editorial Assistant: Tiara Beatty
Production Editor: David C. Felts
Copy Editor: Liann Lech
Typesetter: Hurix Digital
Proofreaders: Jeff Bryant, Theresa Kay
Cover Designer: Janet Kiesel
Marketing Manager: Kara Kindstrom

This book is printed on acid-free paper.

18 19 20 21 22 10 9 8 7 6 5 4 3 2 1

CONTENTS

Race as Chameleon: How the Idea of Race Changes over Time and Place

Color-Blind America: Fact, Fantasy, or Our Future?

PART II • PREJUDICE, DISCRIMINATION, AND RACISM 151

Understanding Racism

How Space Gets Raced

Race and Romance: Blurring Boundaries

Living with Less Racism: Strategies for Individual Action

ABOUT THE EDITOR

 An old saying suggests that if you "scratch" at any creative endeavor you will uncover personal biography. The genealogy of *Rethinking the Color Line* reflects this adage. As a boy, I grew up in Overbrook Park, an all-white, working- and lower-middle-class neighborhood in Philadelphia. My world was a mix of first- and second-generation immigrants from Poland, Russia, Ireland, and Italy. Race was something I experienced when we left our completely self-contained, row house community and went "downtown." Race was typically presented to me in terms of geography: blacks lived in North and West Philly, Asians clustered in Chinatown, and Latinos resided off of N. Broad Street. The "race as geography" analogy was cemented as I got older and was taken on class trips to museums of art and natural history. The dioramas in the museums had each of the "major races of mankind" frozen in a variety of daily, primitive routines: some were engaged in tepee making, others were spearing fish or seals, farmers tended rice paddies, peasants worked the land. Typically there was a map that explained that black people were from this continent, brown people from there, and so on, until all the racial groups had been repatriated back to their "original" homeland.

I saw parallels to the representations of race I experienced as a boy and the textbooks available to me as a student teacher more than twenty years ago. Race and ethnicity readers and textbooks typically presented each group's history as discrete events that took place in a social vacuum, rather than weaving a narrative that reflects the constant interaction within and between racial and ethnic groups. Race relations play out in housing, the economy, criminal justice, schooling, love, culture, and politics. This perspective shows the social relations that link all racial and ethnic groups together, rather than an approach in which week four is dedicated to African Americans and week seven to American Indians. What I have attempted to do in this book is take the study of race out of the museum and into the spaces we live in and share across the color line.

PREFACE

When it comes to race and ethnic relations in the United States, we are two nations: the nation we imagine ourselves to be as depicted in the media and the nation we actually inhabit. The election of Barack Obama, the first black president of the United States, confirmed for many that we are a color-blind nation. If race still divided us, how is it possible that a black man could be elected president—twice?

Reflect for a moment about how race is depicted in popular culture. Turn on the television and you enter a fantasyland where whites, blacks, Latinos, and Asians gather together to shop, eat, work, and interact in spaces where race is meaningless. In this racial utopia, a car packed with young adults from every racial group drives through a Checkers fast-food takeout window as the hip-hop voice-over tells us "Ya gotta eat." Car commercials as well as advertisements for antacids, snack foods, soda, and fast-food restaurants routinely show an America that is integrated, assimilated, and color-blind. In this carefully manufactured racial utopia, television commercials depict actors of different races interacting in race-neutral environments like Chili's or Applebee's. In Hollywood's version of U.S. race relations, one of your best friends is always from a different race. In this racial nirvana, handsome, middle-class men of varying races relax in upper-middle-class living rooms backslapping and bonding over football, Coors beer, and Domino's pizza. America's racial "presentation of self" in the media is overwhelmingly depicted as an environment that is integrated, multiracial, and for the most part, color-blind. The media now present America as a kind of United Nations reunion party where everyone has equal social standing and equal opportunity, and everyone is middle class.

These representations of a color-blind America seriously misrepresent the extent to which race continues to shape the life chances of racial minorities in the United States. Consider, for example, racial diversity in corporate America. Significant movement into the upper ranks of top management would indicate that racial barriers have fallen. Progress has been made in the upper ranks of corporate America, but the proportion of racial minorities now in these positions is minuscule. In 2015, 94 percent of CEOs in Fortune 500 companies were white, and of them, 89 percent were white men.

Racial minorities make up 38 percent of the U.S. population. All things being equal, we should expect to see about 38 percent of the top jobs going to racial minorities. What we see, however, is that only 5 percent, not 38 percent, of senior managers at Fortune 1000 and Fortune 500 companies are members of racial minorities. What does this figure say about the notion that we are now a color-blind nation?

The U.S. Senate provides a rather good test of the fit between how groups are presented in television dramas like *CSI* or *The Walking Dead*, or in films at the multiplex, and the political power these groups have achieved. Since there are 100 members in the U.S. Senate and racial minorities in the United States account for about 38 percent of the population, all things being equal, the Senate should have about 38 members from racial minorities. When we look at the members of the 115th Congress, however, we find only ten racial minority members, which means that ninety senators are white. Since whites constitute about 70 percent of the population, proportional representation suggests that whites should hold seventy Senate seats, not ninety. There are currently no American Indians in the U.S. Senate. Although women comprise 52 percent of the adult population (which means we should see fifty-two women in the Senate), there are only twenty-one female U.S. senators.

It is difficult to think about life in America without directly confronting issues of race and ethnicity. Reflect for a moment on how recent events and trends both dominate and alter American social and cultural life. There has been a rise in right-wing, neo-Nazi hate groups often lumped under the umbrella term "alt-right" whose platform includes anti-immigrant, antiminority, and anti-Semitic rhetoric. At the same time, 85 percent of Millennials (those born between 1982 and 2004) support interracial marriage and 75 percent of this demographic group support gay marriage. Oprah Winfrey has a net worth of more than a billion dollars, while almost a quarter of the total black population lives below the poverty line; Latinos now outnumber the black population, yet each group is significantly underrepresented in Congress and in corporate America. The readings in *Rethinking the Color Line* will allow students to examine the contradictions of race and ethnicity and prepare them to live in an increasingly racially and ethnically diverse society.

Although the media have seized on a U.S. Census Bureau figure predicting that by the year 2060 whites will be outnumbered by Asians, blacks, Hispanics, and American Indians, this rather simplistic demographic forecast misses the conflicts, contradictions, and cultural convergences that currently define race and ethnic relations in the United States. *Rethinking the Color Line* is designed to help make sense of how race and ethnicity influence aspects of social life in ways that are often made invisible by culture, politics, and economics. This theoretically informed, empirically grounded reader uses a social constructionist perspective to frame and define the concepts of race and ethnicity in the United States. The selections should stimulate conversation in the classroom and allow students to think through solutions to what often seem intractable problems. As a pedagogical strategy, this text raises a number of questions in the part introductions that guide students through the readings by providing an overview of how each reading is conceptually linked to the others. Each chapter starts with "Questions to Consider,"

asking students to focus their attention on specific themes, issues, or questions raised in the reading. It is important to me that my students be exposed to the classic paradigms in the study of race and ethnic relations in the United States. However, just as important is my desire that students be exposed to and explore new theories and paradigms that are challenging, supplanting, and redefining the classic race and ethnicity canon, which itself changes over time. The biologically based, pseudoscientific assumptions that defined and guided race and ethnicity scholarship for much of this and the previous century have been debunked, discredited, and discarded. What has emerged in the past 30 years are competing narratives of what race and ethnic identity mean and the social pressures that shape those meanings. Postcolonial, postmodern, postethnic, class-based, and primordialist perspectives all claim to elucidate how race and ethnicity have been, and continue to be, thoroughly rethought.

The readings in the first part of this text provide students with the theoretical framework and analytical tools they will use throughout the book. Students come to understand what is meant by race and ethnicity as social constructions. The news, situation comedies, social media, and racial topography of neighborhoods all become subjects for sociological scrutiny. *Rethinking the Color Line* allows students to learn how race and ethnicity influence life in ways that many students routinely take for granted. It has been my experience that a majority of students who read these articles internalize a version of the "sociological imagination" that forever changes how they understand race and ethnic relations. Raising consciousness about how each of us influences and in turn is influenced by race and ethnic relations is an explicit goal of this book.

Over the past decade I have had the luxury of testing a large number of varied readings on hundreds of students in dozens of race and ethnic relations classes at large public universities as well as small, elite liberal arts colleges. The readings in this book represent the final outcome of classroom "hits and misses." I have used classroom experiences, the results of examinations, and how easily students were able to integrate the readings into research papers to gauge (1) the extent to which the reading contributed to students' understanding of a particular theory or concept, (2) whether the reading was intellectually engaging, and (3) whether it lent itself to active learning in the classroom. If a reading could pass these hurdles in at least three of my classes, then it made it into this book. Teaching at both public universities and private colleges also provided me with the opportunity to observe how students from different regions, class backgrounds, and racial and ethnic identities reacted to the assigned readings. The articles speak to, challenge, and find common ground among students from racially, ethnically, culturally, and economically diverse backgrounds. *Rethinking the Color Line* is a response to my students' calls for a book that was user-friendly but did not sacrifice intellectual or theoretical rigor.

This book has been designed to be relevant for students on an individual level while also helping them understand that race and ethnic relations are embedded in the institutions that structure their lives. The readings require students to constantly negotiate the tensions between individual agency and the often determined constraints of social structure. The common thread that links these readings is the ongoing debate about the relationship between agency and structure. It is this conceptual framework that will allow students to think about race and ethnicity in fluid rather than static terms.

CHANGES IN THE SIXTH EDITION

The sixth edition of *Rethinking the Color Line: Readings in Race and Ethnicity* contains eighteen new articles that explore a number of topics that are timely and topical, and that explore how the idea of race is being refashioned by various social, political, and cultural forces. The reason for the large number of new articles in the sixth edition reflects the seismic shifts that have taken place in race relations in the United States. In a relatively short amount of time we went from a national narrative about moving toward a post-race society to one where white nationalists, under the label of "alt-right," have moved into the political mainstream. Attitudes many Americans have about immigrants and new immigration policy are linked to and intertwined with issues of racial identity. The travel ban on visitors from eight primarily Muslim countries enacted in 2017 is linked to race because many from these countries would be defined as racial minorities here in the United States. Black Lives Matter, "taking a knee," and DACA (Deferred Action for Childhood Arrivals) have moved to the front page of our national dialogue on race relations. These new readings address these complicated issues.

John Iceland (reading 4) applies theories of human, social, and cultural capital to examine the tenacity of racial and ethnic inequality. Iceland asks and answers the question "To what extent does discrimination explain overall patterns of inequality today?" David R. Williams and Selina A. Mohammed (reading 6) examine the contributions sociologists have made to our understanding of race-based health disparities. They argue that "racism adversely affects the health of nondominant racial populations in multiple ways." In an update on their work on the racial wealth gap, Thomas Shapiro (reading 7) and his colleagues examine the root cause of the growing wealth gap between racial groups. Dina Okamoto and G. Cristina Mora (reading 10) map the ways in which the theory of panethnicity needs to be understood in relation to assimilation and racialization projects. Saher Selod and David G. Embrick (reading 11) examine the social and political factors that have resulted in the racialization of Arabs and Muslims. Kathleen J. Fitzgerald (reading 12) looks at how the popularity of DNA-based ancestry testing for both medical and genealogical reasons can be used to maintain the racial status quo. The use of skin-bleaching creams and cosmetic surgeries to "whiten" one's appearance is the focus of Margaret L. Hunter's article (reading 14). She argues that these actions should be viewed as a form of "racial capital" where one can ostensibly enhance his or her social standing by lightening one's skin or surgically altering one's body to look more "western" (read: white). New Orleans Mayor Mitchell J. Landrieu (reading 17) reframes the controversy surrounding the taking down of Confederate War monuments by asking why other aspects of the antebellum South weren't memorialized in the town square. Kathleen M. Blee and Elizabeth A. Yates (reading 19) look at how race and racist ideologies are both hidden and explicit in conservative and far-right social and political movements. In a rather ghoulish historical piece Daina Ramey Berry (reading 21) outlines how the black body had value even after death because there was a vibrant and lucrative underground market for the cadavers of formally enslaved people by doctors and medical schools. In reading 22 Douglas S. Massey and Jonathan Tannen provide an update on the extent to which neighborhoods remain racially segregated. While we tend to think of leisure pursuits as something quite individualistic, Jeff Wiltse (reading 26) shows that leisure, in this case having access to public swimming pools, was very much circumscribed by race and racism. Not only did blacks not have the same access to public swimming pools, but this exclusion had intergenerational and often deadly implications. Andrew Cohen (reading 27) compares the public response to the crack epidemic in the late 1980s to the heroin crisis roiling America today. He finds that the race of the user shaped how the public defined the problem and the solution to these epidemics. In the past five years there have been a number of high-profile cases where African American men were killed by police officers. Ronald Weitzer (reading 29) provides an overview of public reactions to these killings and what might be done to decrease these deadly interactions. In reading 37 Bhoomi K. Thakore examines how South Asian Americans are depicted in the media and what these often stereotypical depictions mean in terms of race relations. Evelyn Alsultany (reading 38) charts how the representation of Arabs and Muslims changed after 9/11, and subsequent political events have forever changed how many Americans view Arabs and Muslims. In reading 41 David Scott FitzGerald and David Cook-Martín show that from our country's very inception race, racism, and immigration have always been inextricably bound together. Finally, in reading 46 Gretchen Livingston and Anna Brown discuss the slow and steady increase in interracial marriages in the United States and which populations are more likely to marry outside of their racial group.

ACKNOWLEDGMENTS

SAGE gratefully acknowledges the contributions of the following reviewers: Katie Acosta, Georgia State University; Faye Allard, Community College of Philadelphia; Mary E. Campbell, Texas A&M University-College Station; Kimberly Fox, Bridgewater State University (fka Bridgewater State College); Rachel Head, The University of Texas at Tyler; Maria Johnson, University of Delaware; David Luke, University of Kentucky; Vania Penha-Lopes, Bloomfield College; Ralph Pyle, Michigan State University; Dwanna Lynn Robertson, Colorado College; Laura Simon, University of Nebraska-Lincoln; Christina Sue, Colorado at Boulder; and Kathryn Tillman, Florida State University.

RETHINKING THE COLOR LINE

Understanding How Boundaries Shift

THE TITLE *RETHINKING THE COLOR LINE* means that we will explore the contemporary meanings of race and ethnicity and examine how social, political, economic, and cultural forces shape those meanings.

This may seem like a straightforward task. It is not. Race and ethnicity are slippery concepts because they are always in a state of flux. Imagine for a moment the shape of the United States as analogous to a definition of race or ethnicity. It may appear that an outline or sketch of the U.S. border, like a definition of race or ethnicity, can be neatly described or mapped out; that is, just as we can imagine the borders of the United States, we can, with reasonable certainty, identify someone as black, white, Asian, or American Indian. We place people in these racial categories because we have been trained to focus on a combination of traits like skin color, hair texture, and eye shape. After we have placed individuals in racial categories, we typically use cultural markers, such as their ethnic background or ancestry, to further sort them. For instance, if a white person walks into a room, we see that individual's race. What happens when he or she starts talking and we pick up on an Irish brogue or a New York City accent or a southern dialect? What happens when the brown woman in front of us in the supermarket talks to the cashier and we recognize her accent as Jamaican or English? We tend to sort first by color and then by cultural background.

Since the founding of the United States more than two hundred years ago, the lines that have defined the nation's borders have been redrawn dozens of times. Just as there was no United States of America prior to 1776, the idea of race as it is currently understood did not exist until the Europeans colonized the Americas, Africa, and parts of Asia. The mental map we conjure up of the United States today is only about fifty years old. The map was last redrawn in 1959 when Hawaii was admitted into the Union as the fiftieth state. Previously, the map had been redrawn after the Louisiana Purchase of 1803 and again after the Missouri Compromise of 1820, as well as after the admittance of every new state to the Union. And we will have to redraw our mental map yet again if the Commonwealth of Puerto Rico votes to enter the Union as the fifty-first state.

The problem with definitions of race and ethnicity, as with the shape of the United States, is that the borders or contours that give form and meaning to these concepts change over time. A person defined as white in the year 2010 might have been defined as black or Irish or Italian at various times in American history. For example, around the turn of the twentieth century, Irish and Italian immigrants were not viewed as white when they first arrived in the United States. At that time, members of those groups did not easily fit into the existing racial hierarchy; they were in a racial limbo—not white, not black, not Asian. Their ethnic background—that is, the language, culture, and religious beliefs that distinguished these Irish and Italian immigrants from the dominant group—was used in various ways to define them as a racial group. Within a generation or two, these so-called Irish and Italian racial groups assimilated and were absorbed into the category we now know as white. The journey from being considered not white or racially ambiguous to white was rather swift. It may seem odd, and may even shock our racial sensibilities, to think of our Greek, Italian, or Irish grandparents as possibly being defined as nonwhite Italians or nonwhite Irish at different times in American history. But is a nonwhite Italian or nonwhite Irish any less curious an idea than a black-Irish American or an Asian-Italian American? If one's ethnic identity is subsumed or taken over by a racial identity, the question we need to ask as sociologists is, why?

Just as the shape of the United States has changed over time, so have the definitions of race and ethnicity. Do you think your view of race and ethnicity is different from that of your parents or grandparents? How you understand race and ethnicity reflects a definition specific to this moment in time, one that, in all likelihood, will look quite different in three or four decades. *Rethinking the Color Line* will provide you with a theoretical framework for understanding how and why definitions of race and ethnicity change over time, what sociological forces bring about these changes, and what these categories might look like in the future.

What these examples suggest, and what many of the readings in *Rethinking the Color Line*

consciously explore, is how race and ethnicity are socially constructed. When we say that something is "socially constructed," we mean that the characteristics deemed relevant to that definition are based on societal and cultural values. Race and ethnicity are social constructions because their meanings are derived by focusing on arbitrary characteristics that a given society deems important. Race and ethnicity are social products based on cultural values, not scientific facts.

Think for a moment about gravity. If you push this book off your desk, do you expect it to fall to the ground? Obviously, you do. If you lived in Brazil or South Africa or Puerto Rico, would you expect the same thing to happen to your book? Of course you would, because you know that gravity is a universal constant. However, someone defined as black in the United States could be defined as white in Brazil, Trigueno (intermediate) in Puerto Rico, and "coloured" in South Africa. Gravity is the same everywhere, but racial classifications vary across place and time because definitions of race and ethnicity are based on the physical traits a society chooses to value or devalue. Because each society's values are based on a different set of historical experiences, cultural circumstances, and political definitions, ideas about race and ethnicity can vary quite a bit, not only between countries but within them as well. For example, historically, it was not uncommon for someone to have been socially and legally defined as black in the southern part of the United States but to "pass" for white after migrating north. The beliefs and definitions that undergird the idea of race are very unstable and, as we will see in the readings, quite susceptible to political manipulation.

Racial and ethnic identity is culturally meaningful only because we define and understand it in that way. In other words, race exists because we say race exists. And because the characteristics that make up the idea of race and ethnicity reflect a social process, it is possible to imagine these concepts in a different way. Instead of looking at skin color, facial features, or hair texture as a way to sort individuals, we could create a racial category based on the size of people's feet. People with shoe sizes between 4 and 7 would be labeled the Petite Race, those with sizes 8–11 would be designated the Bigger Race, and the 12–15 shoe size crowd would be categorized as the Monster Foot Race. Those with feet smaller or larger than the existing categories would be the "Other" Race. Likewise, we could use eye color, height, glove size, or nose length to create racial categories. Because the physical markers we use to define race are arbitrary and have no basis in genetics, biology, anthropology, or sociology, using shoe size as the criterion to fashion a new definition of race would be just as valid as the system currently in place. Similarly, we could redefine ethnicity by changing the focus from language, culture, religion, or nationality as a method of sorting people and instead create categories of people based on the amount of meat they eat or the way they style their hair.

What complicates our ability to accurately and easily map these definitions of race and ethnicity is that the definitions are constantly changing. Are the almost 60 million Latinos in the United States (2018) an ethnic group because they are defined by the U.S. Census Bureau as such, or are Latinos a racial group? If the current census categories of white, black, Asian, and American Indian do not adequately reflect what Latinos experience or how Latinos are viewed by non-Latinos, should a "brown" category be added to the census? Would a newly created "brown" category link Puerto Ricans in New York City with Cuban Americans in Miami and Mexican Americans in San Diego? Why or why not? How should we define the race of a child whose father is Mexican-African American and whose mother is Japanese-Irish American? What is this child's ethnicity? For that matter, how and in what ways are race and ethnicity related?

In 1903, sociologist W.E.B. Du Bois wrote that "the problem of the twentieth century is the problem of the color-line." It appears that a key problem of the twenty-first century, while different in degree and context from the one Du Bois chronicled, will still be the color line. A topic or issue may not initially seem to be linked to race or ethnicity, but on closer sociological scrutiny, patterns often emerge that make it clear that race and ethnicity matter quite a bit. How do you see race and ethnicity being connected to who gets a good education or adequate health care, who is likely to be poor, where toxic waste sites are built, who gets hired or promoted, or who is more likely to be sentenced to death and executed? Race and ethnicity are intertwined in every aspect of our lives.

Rethinking the Color Line will provide you with the tools necessary to navigate the complicated and often contradictory meanings of race and ethnicity in the United States. The readings will take you on a sociological journey and explore how you, your classmates, your family, and your friends fit into the racial and ethnic mosaic of the United States. If you focus carefully on the readings, the "Questions to Consider" that introduce them, and the "Seeing the Big Picture" discussion at the end of most chapters, your perspective on race and ethnic relations in the United States will be changed forever.

SORTING BY COLOR

Why We Attach Meaning to Race

WHO TAUGHT YOU HOW TO "BE" BLACK or American Indian or white or Asian? Did you learn to "do" your race by watching sitcoms on television or by watching your peers in the schoolyard? Was it your parents or an older sibling or cousin who taught you how to act both your age and your race? In what social situations do you think about your racial identity? Is it only when you interact with an individual from a different racial background? Do you think about your race, about other racial groups, or about race relations when you watch football games or *CSI* or *Game of Thrones*? Do you think about your race while you are in your neighborhood or only when you drive through an area with a different racial population? Were you ever in a social setting in which you were the only person of your color? How did that make you feel?

How did you learn to "be" Korean or Jamaican or German? In what situations do you think about your ancestry? Is it during the holidays or when you spend time with your family? Or has your family been in the United States for so many generations that the family tree linking you to the homeland is unimportant, nonexistent, or untraceable? Does that mean you have a racial identity but not an ethnic identity? Or does "American" best mirror your social identity?

The readings in Part I answer these questions by exposing you to the social theories used to define and understand the dynamics of race and ethnicity. The first five readings, in Race and Ethnicity: Sociohistoric Constructions, examine how the natural variation in human skin color has been used as a way to sort people into groups, create a racial hierarchy, and justify exploitation based on skin color. Marvin Harris explains why gradations of color, from black to white, are "beautiful" sociocultural responses to the environment. Howard Zinn charts the evolution of the idea of race in early U.S. history and how the idea of racial categories was synonymous with who would be free and who would be enslaved. Michael Omi and Howard Winant explain the emergence of racial categories as a "sociohistoric" process they call racial formation; that is, the way we define ourselves racially reflects a political and social process that was hundreds of years in the making. John Iceland explains why and how racial discrimination seems to reinvent itself anew every generation. Eduardo Bonilla-Silva suggests that race, like class or gender, takes on a "life of its own," creating hierarchical social relations that are exploitive and coercive.

As you will see throughout the text, many of the articles in this reader draw on one or more of these theories to explain a particular aspect of racial inequality and race and ethnic relations.

The next two readings, in Race and Ethnicity: Contemporary Socioeconomic Trends, draw on theories outlined in the first section while emphasizing socioeconomic disparities between racial and ethnic groups. David Williams and Selina Mohammed examine racial and ethnic inequalities in health and how sociology's unique focus on social structure provides insight into the factors that lead to racial differences in disease. Not only are racial minorities worse off compared to whites on almost every health measure, but it is likely this gap will continue to grow as the United States limits access to public health care for the poor. Using national data on wealth, Thomas Shapiro and colleagues examine the racial dynamics of how transformative assets—the financial assistance one gets from families—shape life chances.

In Race as Chameleon: How the Idea of Race Changes over Time and Place, F. James Davis uses the "one-drop rule" to map the ever-changing definition of race by focusing on the various status and identity positions that emerged as groups mixed across the color line. What is important to note is that the definitions forced on mixed-race groups reflected power relations and the desire to fashion various social buffers that maintained white supremacy.

Readings by David Wilkins, and Dina Okamoto and Cristina Mora, demonstrate how, why, and in what situations racial and ethnic identities are used to organize politically. It is often the case that those in power thrust a racial identity upon a group even though there may be enormous cultural diversity within that group. Chinese, Japanese, and Koreans "became" Asian through the racialization process.

Throughout this book I will be arguing that the idea of race is not static. Saher Selod and David Embrick examine the social construction of race regarding Muslim Americans, and Kathleen Fitzgerald examines how the growth in the rise in DNA ancestry testing is not blurring the color line but making it more rigid. As these readings demonstrate, the creation of racial categories is as much a historical process as it is a political one.

The next three readings, in Color-Blind America: Fact, Fantasy, or Our Future?, focus on how different social conditions can exacerbate racial and ethnic relations and what might be done at both the macro and micro levels to ameliorate racial inequality. Professor Charles A. Gallagher notes that current trends in popular culture have blurred the color line by linking the consumption of products across racial groups to racial harmony. If groups from various races now share and consume the same products (rap/hip-hop, McDonald's, reality TV), Gallagher asks, has racial equality been achieved? Margaret Hunter explains how the use of new types of skin-bleaching creams is viewed by many as a way to enhance one's social standing, and Herbert Gans argues that a "beige-ing" of America is taking place that will incorporate some parts of the Latino and Asian populations but not blacks. The color line will shift, Gans argues, but not necessarily in a way that is inclusive. Each of these readings points to the various social, economic, and cultural barriers to racial equality and the rather lofty goal of becoming a truly color-blind nation.

1

HOW OUR SKINS GOT THEIR COLOR

Marvin Harris

The late **MARVIN HARRIS** spent a portion of his life teaching in the anthropology department at Columbia University, where he served as department chair. He published sixteen books, including *Cannibals and Kings; Culture, People, and Nature;* and *Our Kind.*

MOST HUMAN BEINGS ARE NEITHER VERY fair nor very dark, but brown. The extremely fair skin of northern Europeans and their descendants, and the very black skins of central Africans and their descendants, are probably special adaptations. Brown-skinned ancestors may have been shared by modern-day blacks and whites as recently as 10,000 years ago. Human skin owes its color to the presence of particles known as **melanin.** The primary function of melanin is to protect the upper levels of the skin from being damaged by the sun's ultraviolet rays. This radiation poses a critical problem for our kind because we lack the dense coat of hair that acts as a sunscreen for most mammals. . . . Hairlessness exposes us to two kinds of radiation hazards: ordinary sunburn, with its blisters, rashes, and risk of infection; and skin cancers, including malignant melanoma, one of the deadliest diseases known. Melanin is the body's first line of defense against these afflictions. The more melanin particles, the darker the skin, and the lower the risk of sunburn and all forms of skin cancer. This explains why the highest rates for skin cancer are found in sun-drenched lands such as Australia, where light-skinned people of European descent spend a good part of their lives outdoors

---

melanin The pigment that gives the skin its color. Melanin protects the skin from the ultraviolet rays associated with various skin cancers. Populations living near the equator have darker skin to protect them from the harsh effects of the sun.

Questions to Consider

Cultural anthropologist Marvin Harris links the variations in skin color one can observe in traveling around the world to the human body's ability to adapt physically to changes in exposure to solar radiation. How do you explain his assertion that "white was beautiful because white was healthy" and "black was beautiful because black was healthy"?

wearing scanty attire. Very dark-skinned people such as heavily pigmented Africans of Zaire seldom get skin cancer, but when they do, they get it on depigmented parts of their bodies—palms and lips.

If exposure to solar radiation had nothing but harmful effects, natural selection would have favored inky black as the color for all human populations. But the sun's rays do not present an unmitigated threat. As it falls on the skin, sunshine converts a fatty substance in the epidermis into vitamin D. The blood carries vitamin D from the skin to the intestines (technically making it a hormone rather than a vitamin), where it plays a vital role in the absorption of calcium. In turn, calcium is vital for strong bones. Without it, people fall victim to the crippling diseases rickets and osteomalacia. In women, calcium deficiencies can result in a deformed birth canal, which makes childbirth lethal for both mother and fetus.

Vitamin D can be obtained from a few foods, primarily the oils and livers of marine fish. But inland populations must rely on the sun's rays and their own skins for the supply of this crucial substance. The particular color of a human population's skin, therefore, represents in large degree a trade-off between the hazards of too much versus too little solar radiation: acute sunburn and skin cancer on the one hand, and rickets and osteomalacia on the other. It is this trade-off that largely accounts for the preponderance of brown people in the world and for the general tendency for skin color to be darkest among **equatorial populations** and lightest among populations dwelling at higher latitudes.

At middle latitudes, the skin follows a strategy of changing colors with the seasons. Around the Mediterranean basin, for example, exposure to the summer sun brings high risk of cancer but low risk for rickets; the body produces more melanin and people grow darker (i.e., they get suntans). Winter reduces the risk of sunburn and cancer; the body produces less melanin, and the tan wears off.

The correlation between skin color and latitude is not perfect because other factors—such as the availability of foods containing vitamin D and calcium, regional cloud cover during the winter, amount of clothing worn, and cultural preferences—may work for or against the predicted relationship. Arctic-dwelling Eskimo, for example, are not as light-skinned as expected, but their habitat and economy afford them a diet that is exceptionally rich in both vitamin D and calcium.

Northern Europeans, obliged to wear heavy garments for protection against the long, cold, cloudy winters, were always at risk for rickets and osteomalacia from too little vitamin D and calcium. This risk increased sometime after 6000 B.C., when pioneer cattle herders who did not exploit marine resources began to appear in northern Europe. The risk would have been especially great for the brown-skinned Mediterranean peoples who migrated northward along with the crops and farm animals. Samples of Caucasian skin (infant penile foreskin obtained at the time of circumcision) exposed to sunlight on cloudless days in Boston (42°N) from November through February produced no vitamin D. In Edmonton (52°N) this period extended from October to March. But further south (34°N) sunlight was effective in producing vitamin D in the middle of the winter. Almost all of Europe lies north of 42°N. Fair-skinned, nontanning individuals who could utilize the weakest and briefest doses of sunlight to synthesize vitamin D were strongly favored by **natural selection.** During the frigid winters, only a small circle of a child's face could be left to peek out at the sun through the heavy clothing, thereby favoring the survival of individuals with

---

equatorial populations Populations living near the equator.

natural selection In his 1859 book *The Origin of Species*, Charles Darwin describes the process by which nature "selects" the best-adapted varieties of animals for survival.

translucent patches of pink on their cheeks characteristic of many northern Europeans. (People who could get calcium by drinking cow's milk would also be favored by natural selection.)

If light-skinned individuals on the average had only 2 percent more children survive per generation, the changeover in their skin color could have begun 5,000 years ago and reached present levels well before the beginning of the Christian era. But natural selection need not have acted alone. **Cultural selection** may also have played a role. It seems likely that whenever people consciously or unconsciously had to decide which infants to nourish and which

to neglect, the advantage would go to those with lighter skin, experience having shown that such individuals tended to grow up to be taller, stronger, and healthier than their darker siblings. White was beautiful because white was healthy.

To account for the evolution of black skin in equatorial latitudes, one has merely to reverse the combined effects of natural and cultural selection. With the sun directly overhead most of the year, and clothing a hindrance to work and survival, vitamin D was never in short supply (and calcium was easily obtained from vegetables). Rickets and osteomalacia were rare. Skin cancer was the main problem, and what nature started, culture amplified. Darker infants were favored by parents because experience showed that they grew up to be freer of disfiguring and lethal malignancies. Black was beautiful because black was healthy.

---

cultural selection The idea that, in ways that mirror natural selection, society "selects" those cultural traits that will enhance the survival of a particular civilization.

2

DRAWING THE COLOR LINE

Howard Zinn

The late **Howard Zinn**, professor, activist, and author, dedicated his life to the notion that the knowledge of history is important to people's everyday lives and can be a powerful force for social change.

A BLACK AMERICAN WRITER, J. SAUNDERS Redding, describes the arrival of a ship in North America in the year 1619:

Sails furled, flag drooping at her rounded stern, she rode the tide in from the sea. She

was a strange ship, indeed, by all accounts, a frightening ship, a ship of mystery. Whether she was trader, privateer, or man-of-war no one knows. Through her bulwarks blackmouthed cannon yawned. The flag she flew was Dutch; her crew a motley. Her port of call, an English settlement, Jamestown, in the colony of Virginia. She came, she traded, and shortly afterwards was gone. Probably no ship in modern history has carried a more portentous freight. Her cargo? Twenty slaves.

There is not a country in world history in which racism has been more important, for so long a time, as the United States. And the problem of "the color line," as W.E.B. Du Bois put it, is still with us. So it is more than a purely historical question to ask: How does it start?—and an even more urgent question: How might it end? Or, to put it differently: Is it possible for whites and blacks to live together without hatred?

If history can help answer these questions, then the beginnings of slavery in North America—a continent where we can trace the coming of the first whites and the first blacks—might supply at least a few clues.

Some historians think those first blacks in Virginia were considered as servants, like the white **indentured servants** brought from Europe. But the strong probability is that, even if they were listed as "servants" (a more familiar category to the English), they were viewed as being different from white servants, were treated differently, and in fact were slaves. In any case, slavery developed quickly into a

Questions to Consider

In this reading, Howard Zinn chronicles the beginning of slavery in North America. How did law, custom, and culture reconcile the emergence of chattel slavery with Christian precepts, which reject the idea that one human can own or forcibly control another human being? What arguments were used to justify slavery? List which groups profited from the slave trade.

---

indentured servant Historically, a laborer under contract to an employer for some period of time, usually seven years, in exchange for travel, food, and accommodations. Servants often became indebted to their employer and were often subject to violence.

regular institution, into the normal labor relation of blacks to whites in the New World. With it developed that special racial feeling—whether hatred, or contempt, or pity, or patronization—that accompanied the inferior position of blacks in America for the next 350 years—that combination of inferior status and derogatory thought we call racism.

Everything in the experience of the first white settlers acted as a pressure for the enslavement of blacks.

The Virginians of 1619 were desperate for labor, to grow enough food to stay alive. Among them were survivors from the winter of 1609–1610, the "starving time," when, crazed for want of food, they roamed the woods for nuts and berries, dug up graves to eat the corpses, and died in batches until five hundred colonists were reduced to sixty.

In the *Journals* of the House of Burgesses of Virginia is a document of 1619 which tells of the first twelve years of the Jamestown colony. The first settlement had a hundred persons, who had one small ladle of barley per meal. When more people arrived, there was even less food. Many of the people lived in cavelike holes dug into the ground, and in the winter of 1609–1610, they were

driven thru insufferable hunger to eat those things which nature most abhorred, the flesh and excrements of man as well of our own nation as of an Indian, digged by some out of his grave after he had lain buried three days and wholly devoured him; others, envying the better state of body of any whom hunger has not yet so much wasted as their own, lay wait and threatened to kill and eat them; one among them slew his wife as she slept in his bosom, cut her in pieces, salted her and fed upon her till he had clean devoured all parts saving her head.

A petition by thirty colonists to the House of Burgesses, complaining against the twelve-year governorship of Sir Thomas Smith, said:

In those 12 years of Sir Thomas Smith, his government, we aver that the colony for the most part remained in great want and misery under most severe and cruel laws. . . .

The allowance in those times for a man was only eight ounces of meale and half a pint of peas for a day . . . mouldy, rotten, full of cobwebs and maggots, loathsome to man and not fit for beasts, which forced many to flee for relief to the savage enemy, who being taken again were put to sundry deaths as by hanging, shooting and breaking upon the wheel . . . of whom one for stealing two or three pints of oatmeal had a bodkin thrust through his tongue and was tied with a chain to a tree until he starved.

The Virginians needed labor, to grow corn for subsistence, to grow tobacco for export. They had just figured out how to grow tobacco, and in 1617 they sent off the first cargo to England. Finding that, like all pleasurable drugs tainted with moral disapproval, it brought a high price, the planters, despite their high religious talk, were not going to ask questions about something so profitable.

They couldn't force Indians to work for them, as Columbus had done. They were outnumbered, and while, with superior firearms, they could massacre Indians, they would face massacre in return. They could not capture them and keep them enslaved; the Indians were tough, resourceful, defiant, and at home in these woods, as the transplanted Englishmen were not.

White servants had not yet been brought over in sufficient quantity. Besides, they did not come out of slavery, and did not have to do more than contract their labor for a few years to get their passage and a start in the New World. As for the free white settlers, many of them were skilled craftsmen, or even men of leisure back in England, who were so little inclined to work the land that John Smith, in those early years, had to declare a kind of martial law, organize them into work gangs, and force them into the fields for survival.

There may have been a kind of frustrated rage at their own ineptitude, at the Indian superiority at taking care of themselves, that made the Virginians especially ready to become the masters of slaves. Edmund Morgan imagines their mood as he writes in his book *American Slavery, American Freedom*:

If you were a colonist, you knew that your technology was superior to the Indians'. You knew that you were civilized, and they were savages. . . . But your superior technology had proved insufficient to extract anything. The Indians, keeping to themselves, laughed at your superior methods and lived from the land more abundantly and with less labor than you did. . . . And when your own people started deserting in order to live with them, it was too much. . . . So you killed the Indians, tortured them, burned their villages, burned their cornfields. It proved your superiority, in spite of your failures. And you gave similar treatment to any of your own people who succumbed to their savage ways of life. But you still did not grow much corn.

Black slaves were the answer. And it was natural to consider imported blacks as slaves, even if the institution of slavery would not be regularized and legalized for several decades because, by 1619, a million blacks had already been brought from Africa to South America and the Caribbean, to the Portuguese and Spanish colonies, to work as slaves. Fifty years before Columbus, the Portuguese took ten African blacks to Lisbon—this was the start of a regular trade in slaves. African blacks had been stamped as slave labor for a hundred years. So it would have been strange if those twenty blacks, forcibly transported to Jamestown, and sold as objects to settlers anxious for a steadfast source of labor, were considered as anything but slaves.

Their helplessness made enslavement easier. The Indians were on their own land. The whites were in their own European culture. The blacks had been torn from their land and culture, forced into a situation where the heritage of language, dress, custom, family relations, was bit by bit obliterated except for the remnants that blacks could hold on to by sheer, extraordinary persistence.

Was their culture inferior—and so subject to easy destruction? Inferior in military capability, yes—vulnerable to whites with guns and ships. But in no other way—except that cultures that are different are often taken as inferior, especially when such a judgment is practical and profitable. Even militarily, while the Westerners could secure forts on the African coast, they were unable to subdue the interior and had to come to terms with its chiefs.

The African civilization was as advanced in its own way as that of Europe. In certain ways, it was more admirable; but it also included cruelties, hierarchical privilege, and the readiness to sacrifice human lives for religion or profit. It was a civilization of 100 million people, using iron implements and skilled in farming. It had large urban centers and remarkable achievements in weaving, ceramics, sculpture.

European travelers in the sixteenth century were impressed with the African kingdoms of Timbuktu and Mali, already stable and organized at a time when European states were just beginning to develop into the modern nation. In 1563, Ramusio, secretary to the rulers in Venice, wrote to the Italian merchants: "Let them go and do business with the King of Timbuktu and Mali and there is no doubt that they will be well-received there with their ships and their goods and treated well, and granted the favours that they ask."

A Dutch report, around 1602, on the West African kingdom of Benin, said: "The Towne seemeth to be very great, when you enter it. You go into a great broad street, not paved, which seemeth to be seven or eight times broader than the Warmoes Street in Amsterdam. . . . The Houses in this Towne stand in good order, one close and even with the other, as the Houses in Holland stand."

The inhabitants of the Guinea Coast were described by one traveler around 1680 as "very civil and good-natured people, easy to be dealt with, condescending to what Europeans require of them in a civil way, and very ready to return double the presents we make them."

Africa had a kind of **feudalism,** like Europe based on agriculture, and with hierarchies of lords and vassals. But African feudalism did not come, as did Europe's, out of the slave societies of Greece

---

feudalism A medieval European political system in which land was leased through the king to barons and knights who engaged serfs to work the land in return for military protection. The system was based on military, social, and economic obligations and enforced through law, custom, and religion.

and Rome, which had destroyed ancient tribal life. In Africa, tribal life was still powerful, and some of its better features—a communal spirit, more kindness in law and punishment—still existed. And because the lords did not have the weapons that European lords had, they could not command obedience as easily.

In his book *The African Slave Trade,* Basil Davidson contrasts law in the Congo in the early sixteenth century with law in Portugal and England. In those European countries, where the idea of private property was becoming powerful, theft was punished brutally. In England, even as late as 1740, a child could be hanged for stealing a rag of cotton. But in the Congo, communal life persisted, the idea of private property was a strange one, and thefts were punished with fines or various degrees of servitude. A Congolese leader, told of the Portuguese legal codes, asked a Portuguese once, teasingly: "What is the penalty in Portugal for anyone who puts his feet on the ground?"

Slavery existed in the African states, and it was sometimes used by Europeans to justify their own slave trade. But, as Davidson points out, the "slaves" of Africa were more like the serfs of Europe—in other words, like most of the population of Europe. It was a harsh servitude, but they had rights which slaves brought to America did not have, and they were "altogether different from the human cattle of the slave ships and the American plantations." In the Ashanti Kingdom of West Africa, one observer noted that "a slave might marry; own property; himself own a slave; swear an oath; be a competent witness and ultimately become heir to his master. . . . An Ashanti slave, nine cases out of ten, possibly became an adopted member of the family, and in time his descendants so merged and intermarried with the owner's kinsmen that only a few would know their origin."

One slave trader, John Newton (who later became an antislavery leader), wrote about the people of what is now Sierra Leone:

The state of slavery, among these wild barbarous people, as we esteem them, is much milder than in our colonies. For as, on the one hand, they have no land in high cultivation, like our West India plantations, and therefore no call for that excessive, unintermitted labour, which exhausts our slaves: so, on the other hand, no man is permitted to draw blood even from a slave.

African slavery is hardly to be praised. But it was far different from plantation or mining slavery in the Americas, which was lifelong, morally crippling, destructive of family ties, and without hope of any future. African slavery lacked two elements that made American slavery the most cruel form of slavery in history: the frenzy for limitless profit that comes from capitalistic agriculture; the reduction of the slave to less than human status by the use of racial hatred, with that relentless clarity based on color, where white was master, black was slave.

In fact, it was because they came from a settled culture, of tribal customs and family ties, of communal life and traditional ritual, that African blacks found themselves especially helpless when removed from this. They were captured in the interior (frequently by blacks caught up in the slave trade themselves), sold on the coast, then shoved into pens with blacks of other tribes, often speaking different languages.

The conditions of capture and sale were crushing affirmations to the black African of his helplessness in the face of superior force. The marches to the coast, sometimes for 1,000 miles, with people shackled around the neck, under whip and gun, were death marches, in which two of every five blacks died. On the coast, they were kept in cages until they were picked and sold. One John Barbot, at the end of the seventeenth century, described these cages on the Gold Coast:

As the slaves come down to Fida from the inland country, they are put into a booth or prison . . . near the beach, and when the Europeans are to receive them, they are brought out onto a large plain, where the ship's surgeons examine every part of everyone of them, to the smallest member, men and women being stark naked. . . . Such

as are allowed good and sound are set on one side . . . marked on the breast with a red-hot iron, imprinting the mark of the French, English, or Dutch companies. . . . The branded slaves after this are returned to their former booths where they await shipment, sometimes 10–15 days.

Then they were packed aboard the slave ships, in spaces not much bigger than coffins, chained together in the dark, wet slime of the ship's bottom, choking in the stench of their own excrement. Documents of the time describe the conditions:

The height, sometimes, between decks, was only eighteen inches; so that the unfortunate human beings could not turn around, or even on their sides, the elevation being less than the breadth of their shoulders; and here they are usually chained to the decks by the neck and legs. In such a place the sense of misery and suffocation is so great, that the Negroes . . . are driven to frenzy.

On one occasion, hearing a great noise from below decks where the blacks were chained together, the sailors opened the hatches and found the slaves in different stages of suffocation, many dead, some having killed others in desperate attempts to breathe. Slaves often jumped overboard to drown rather than continue their suffering. To one observer a slave-deck was "so covered with blood and mucus that it resembled a slaughter house."

Under these conditions, perhaps one of every three blacks transported overseas died, but the huge profits (often double the investment on one trip) made it worthwhile for the slave trader, and so the blacks were packed into the holds like fish.

First the Dutch, then the English, dominated the slave trade. (By 1795 Liverpool had more than a hundred ships carrying slaves and accounted for half of all the European slave trade.) Some Americans in New England entered the business, and in 1637 the first American slave ship, the *Desire,* sailed from Marblehead. Its holds were partitioned into racks, 2 feet by 6 feet, with leg irons and bars.

By 1800, 10 to 15 million blacks had been transported as slaves to the Americas, representing perhaps one-third of those originally seized in Africa. It is roughly estimated that Africa lost 50 million human beings to death and slavery in those centuries we call the beginnings of modern Western civilization, at the hands of slave traders and plantation owners in Western Europe and America, the countries deemed the most advanced in the world.

In the year 1610, a Catholic priest in the Americas named Father Sandoval wrote back to a church functionary in Europe to ask if the capture, transport, and enslavement of African blacks was legal by church doctrine. A letter dated March 12, 1610, from Brother Luis Brandaon to Father Sandoval gives the answer:

> Your Reverence writes me that you would like to know whether the Negroes who are sent to your parts have been legally captured. To this I reply that I think your Reverence should have no scruples on this point, because this is a matter which has been questioned by the Board of Conscience in Lisbon, and all its members are learned and conscientious men. Nor did the bishops who were in Sao Thome, Cape Verde, and here in Loando—all learned and virtuous men—find fault with it. We have been here ourselves for forty years and there have been among us very learned Fathers . . . never did they consider the trade as illicit. Therefore we and the Fathers of Brazil buy these slaves for our service without any scruple.

With all of this—the desperation of the Jamestown settlers for labor, the impossibility of using Indians and the difficulty of using whites, the availability of blacks offered in greater and greater numbers by profit-seeking dealers in human flesh, and with such blacks possible to control because they had just gone through an ordeal which if it did not kill them must have left them in a state of psychic and physical helplessness—is it any wonder that such blacks were ripe for enslavement?

And under these conditions, even if some blacks might have been considered servants, would blacks be treated the same as white servants?

The evidence, from the court records of colonial Virginia, shows that in 1630 a white man named Hugh Davis was ordered "to be soundly whipt . . . for abusing himself . . . by defiling his body in lying with a Negro." Ten years later, six servants and "a negro of Mr. Reynolds" started to run away. While the whites received lighter sentences, "Emanuel the Negro [was] to receive thirty stripes and to be burnt in the cheek with the letter R, and to work in shackle one year or more as his master shall see cause."

Although slavery was not yet regularized or legalized in those first years, the lists of servants show blacks listed separately. A law passed in 1639 decreed that "all persons except Negroes" were to get arms and ammunition—probably to fight off Indians. When in 1640 three servants tried to run away, the two whites were punished with a lengthening of their service. But, as the court put it, "the third being a negro named John Punch shall serve his master or his assigns for the time of his natural life." Also in 1640, we have the case of a Negro woman servant who begot a child by Robert Sweat, a white man. The court ruled "that the said negro woman shall be whipt at the whipping post and the said Sweat shall tomorrow in the forenoon do public penance for his offense at James citychurch."

This unequal treatment, this developing combination of contempt and oppression, feeling and action, which we call "**racism**"—was this the result of a "natural" antipathy of white against black? The question is important, not just as a matter of historical accuracy, but because any emphasis on "natural" racism lightens the responsibility of the social system. If racism can't be shown to be natural, then it is the result of certain conditions, and we are impelled to eliminate those conditions.

We have no way of testing the behavior of whites and blacks toward one another under favorable conditions—with no history of subordination, no money incentive for exploitation and enslavement, no desperation for survival requiring forced labor. All the conditions for black and white in

---

racism The assigning of attitudes, behaviors, and abilities to individuals or groups based on skin color; includes the institutional arrangements that privilege one group over another and the ideological apparatus that perpetuates and makes those arrangements possible.

seventeenth-century America were the opposite of that, all powerfully directed toward antagonism and mistreatment. Under such conditions even the slightest display of humanity between the races might be considered evidence of a basic human drive toward community.

Sometimes it is noted that, even before 1600, when the slave trade had just begun, before Africans were stamped by it—literally and symbolically— the color black was distasteful. In England, before 1600, it meant, according to the *Oxford English Dictionary*: "Deeply stained with dirt; soiled, dirty, foul. Having dark or deadly purposes, malignant; pertaining to or involving death, deadly; baneful, disastrous, sinister. Foul, iniquitous, atrocious, horribly wicked. Indicating disgrace, censure, liability to punishment, etc." And Elizabethan poetry often used the color white in connection with beauty.

It may be that, in the absence of any other overriding factor, darkness and blackness, associated with night and unknown, would take on those meanings. But the presence of another human being is a powerful fact, and the conditions of that presence are crucial in determining whether an initial prejudice, against a mere color, divorced from humankind, is turned into brutality and hatred.

In spite of such preconceptions about blackness, in spite of special subordination of blacks in the Americas in the seventeenth century, there is evidence that where whites and blacks found themselves with common problems, common work, common enemy in their master, they behaved toward one another as equals. As one scholar of slavery, Kenneth Stampp, has put it, Negro and white servants of the seventeenth century were "remarkably unconcerned about the visible physical differences."

Black and white worked together, fraternized together. The very fact that laws had to be passed after a while to forbid such relations indicates the strength of that tendency. In 1661 a law was passed in Virginia that "in case any English servant shall run away in company of any Negroes" he would have to give special service for extra years to the master of the runaway Negro. In 1691, Virginia provided for the banishment of any "white man or woman being free who shall intermarry with a negro, mulatoo, or Indian man or woman bond or free."

There is an enormous difference between a feeling of racial strangeness, perhaps fear, and the mass enslavement of millions of black people that took place in the Americas. The transition from one to the other cannot be explained easily by "natural" tendencies. It is not hard to understand as the outcome of historical conditions.

Slavery grew as the plantation system grew. The reason is easily traceable to something other than natural racial repugnance: the number of arriving whites, whether free or indentured servants (under four to seven years' contract), was not enough to meet the need of the plantations. By 1700, in Virginia, there were 6,000 slaves, one-twelfth of the population. By 1763, there were 170,000 slaves, about half the population.

Blacks were easier to enslave than whites or Indians. But they were still not easy to enslave. From the beginning, the imported black men and women resisted their enslavement. Ultimately their resistance was controlled, and slavery was established for 3 million blacks in the South. Still, under the most difficult conditions, under pain of mutilation and death, throughout their two hundred years of enslavement in North America, these Afro-Americans continued to rebel. Only occasionally was there an organized insurrection. More often they showed their refusal to submit by running away. Even more often, they engaged in sabotage, slowdowns, and subtle forms of resistance which asserted, if only to themselves and their brothers and sisters, their dignity as human beings.

The refusal began in Africa. One slave trader reported that Negroes were "so wilful and loth to leave their own country, that they have often leap'd out of the canoes, boat and ship into the sea, and kept under water till they were drowned."

When the very first black slaves were brought into Hispaniola in 1503, the Spanish governor of Hispaniola complained to the Spanish court that fugitive Negro slaves were teaching disobedience to the Indians. In the 1520s and 1530s, there were slave revolts in Hispaniola, Puerto Rico, Santa Marta, and what is now Panama. Shortly after those rebellions, the Spanish established a special police for chasing fugitive slaves.

A Virginia statute of 1669 referred to "the obstinacy of many of them," and in 1680 the Assembly took note of slave meetings "under the pretense of feasts and brawls" which they considered of "dangerous consequence." In 1687, in the colony's Northern Neck, a plot was discovered in which slaves planned to kill all the whites in the area and escape during a mass funeral.

Gerald Mullin, who studied slave resistance in eighteenth-century Virginia in his work *Flight and Rebellion,* reports:

> The available sources on slavery in 18th-century Virginia—plantation and county records, the newspaper advertisements for runaways—describe rebellious slaves and few others. The slaves described were lazy and thieving; they feigned illnesses, destroyed crops, stores, tools, and sometimes attacked or killed overseers. They operated blackmarkets in stolen goods. Runaways were defined as various types, they were truants (who usually returned voluntarily), "outlaws" . . . and slaves who were actually fugitives: men who visited relatives, went to town to pass as free, or tried to escape slavery completely, either by boarding ships and leaving the colony, or banding together in cooperative efforts to establish villages or hide-outs in the frontier. The commitment of another type of rebellious slave was total; these men became killers, arsonists, and insurrectionists.

Slaves recently from Africa, still holding on to the heritage of their communal society, would run away in groups and try to establish villages of runaways out in the wilderness, on the frontier. Slaves born in America, on the other hand, were more likely to run off alone, and, with the skills they had learned on the plantation, try to pass as free men.

In the colonial papers of England, a 1729 report from the lieutenant governor of Virginia to the British Board of Trade tells how

> a number of Negroes, about fifteen . . . formed a design to withdraw from their Master and to fix themselves in the fastnesses of the neighboring Mountains. They had found means to get into their possession some Arms and Ammunition, and they took along with them some Provisions, their Cloths, bedding and working Tools. . . . Tho' this attempt has happily been defeated, it ought nevertheless to awaken us into some effectual measures.

Slavery was immensely profitable to some masters. James Madison told a British visitor shortly after the American Revolution that he could make $257 on every Negro in a year, and spend only $12 or $13 on his keep. Another viewpoint was of slaveowner Landon Carter, writing about fifty years earlier, complaining that his slaves so neglected their work and were so uncooperative ("either cannot or will not work") that he began to wonder if keeping them was worthwhile.

Some historians have painted a picture—based on the infrequency of organized rebellions and the ability of the South to maintain slavery for two hundred years—of a slave population made submissive by their condition; with their African heritage destroyed, they were, as Stanley Elkins said, made into "Sambos," "a society of helpless dependents," or as another historian, Ulrich Phillips, said, "by racial quality submissive." But looking at the totality of slave behavior, at the resistance of everyday life, from quiet noncooperation in work to running away, the picture becomes different.

In 1710, warning the Virginia Assembly, Governor Alexander Spotswood said:

> freedom wears a cap which can without a tongue, call together all those who long to shake off the fetters of slavery and as such an Insurrection would surely be attended with most dreadful consequences so I think we cannot be too early in providing against it, both by putting our selves in a better posture of defence and by making a law to prevent the consultations of those Negroes.

Indeed, considering the harshness of punishment for running away, that so many blacks did run away must be a sign of a powerful rebelliousness. All through the 1700s, the Virginia slave code read:

> Whereas many times slaves run away and lie hid and lurking in swamps, woods, and other obscure places, killing hogs, and commiting other injuries to the inhabitants . . . if the slave does not immediately return, anyone what soever may kill or destroy such slaves by such ways and means as he . . . shall think fit. . . . If the slave is apprehended . . . it shall . . . be lawful for the county court, to order such punishment for the said slave, either by dismembering, or in any other way . . . as they in their discretion shall think fit, for the reclaiming any such incorrigible slave, and terrifying others from the like practices.

Mullin found newspaper advertisements between 1736 and 1801 for 1,138 men runaways, and 141 women runaways. One consistent reason for running away was to find members of one's family—showing that despite the attempts of the slave system to destroy family ties by not allowing marriages and by separating families, slaves would face death and mutilation to get together.

In Maryland, where slaves were about one-third of the population in 1750, slavery had been written into law since the 1660s, and statutes for controlling rebellious slaves were passed. There were cases where slave women killed their masters, sometimes by poisoning them, sometimes by burning tobacco houses and homes. Punishments ranged from whipping and branding to execution, but the trouble continued. In 1742, seven slaves were put to death for murdering their master.

Fear of slave revolt seems to have been a permanent fact of plantation life. William Byrd, a wealthy Virginia slave owner, wrote in 1736:

> We have already at least 10,000 men of these descendants of Ham, fit to bear arms, and these numbers increase every day, as well by birth as by importation. And in case there should arise a man of desperate fortune, he might with more advantage than Cataline

kindle a servile war . . . and tinge our rivers wide as they are with blood.

It was an intricate and powerful system of control that the slaveowners developed to maintain their labor supply and their way of life, a system both subtle and crude, involving every device that social orders employ for keeping power and wealth where it is. As Kenneth Stampp puts it:

> A wise master did not take seriously the belief that Negroes were natural-born slaves. He knew better. He knew that Negroes freshly imported from Africa had to be broken into bondage; that each succeeding generation had to be carefully trained. This was no easy task, for the bondsman rarely submitted willingly. Moreover, he rarely submitted completely. In most cases there was no end to the need for control—at least not until old age reduced the slave to a condition of helplessness.

The system was psychological and physical at the same time. The slaves were taught discipline, were impressed again and again with the idea of their own inferiority to "know their place," to see blackness as a sign of subordination, to be awed by the power of the master, to merge their interest with the master's, destroying their own individual needs. To accomplish this there was the discipline of hard labor, the breakup of the slave family, the lulling effects of religion (which sometimes led to "great mischief," as one slaveholder reported), the creation of disunity among slaves by separating them into field slaves and more privileged house slaves, and finally the power of law and the immediate power of the overseer to invoke whipping, burning, mutilation, and death. Dismemberment was provided for in the Virginia Code of 1705. Maryland passed a law in 1723 providing for cutting off the ears of blacks who struck whites, and that for certain serious crimes, slaves should be hanged and the body quartered and exposed.

Still, rebellions took place—not many, but enough to create constant fear among white planters. The first large-scale revolt in the North American colonies took place in New York in 1712. In New York, slaves were 10 percent of the population, the highest proportion in the northern states, where economic conditions usually did not require large numbers of field slaves. About twenty-five blacks and two Indians set fire to a building, then killed nine whites who came on the scene. They were captured by soldiers, put on trial, and twenty-one were executed. The governor's report to England said: "Some were burnt, others were hanged, one broke on the wheel, and one hung alive in chains in the town." One had been burned over a slow fire for eight to ten hours—all this to serve notice to other slaves.

A letter to London from South Carolina in 1720 reports:

> I am now to acquaint you that very lately we have had a very wicked and barbarous plot of the designe of the negroes rising with a designe to destroy all the white people in the country and then to take Charles Town in full body but it pleased God it was discovered and many of them taken prisoners and some burnt and some hang'd and some banish'd.

Around this time there were a number of fires in Boston and New Haven, suspected to be the work of Negro slaves. As a result, one Negro was executed in Boston, and the Boston Council ruled that any slaves who on their own gathered in groups of two or more were to be punished by whipping.

At Stono, South Carolina, in 1739, about twenty slaves rebelled, killed two warehouse guards, stole guns and gunpowder, and headed south, killing people in their way and burning buildings. They were joined by others, until there were perhaps eighty slaves in all and, according to one account of the time, "they called out Liberty, marched on with Colours displayed, and two Drums beating." The militia found and attacked them. In the ensuing battle perhaps fifty slaves and twenty-five whites were killed before the uprising was crushed.

Herbert Aptheker, who did detailed research on slave resistance in North America for his book *American Negro Slave Revolts,* found about 250 instances where a minimum of ten slaves joined in a revolt or conspiracy.

From time to time, whites were involved in the slave resistance. As early as 1663, indentured white servants and black slaves in Gloucester County, Virginia, formed a conspiracy to rebel and gain their freedom. The plot was betrayed, and ended with executions. Mullin reports that the newspaper notices of runaways in Virginia often warned "ill-disposed" whites about harboring fugitives. Sometimes slaves and free men ran off together, or cooperated in crimes together. Sometimes, black male slaves ran off and joined white women. From time to time, white ship captains and watermen dealt with runaways, perhaps making the slave a part of the crew.

In New York in 1741, there were ten thousand whites in the city and two thousand black slaves. It had been a hard winter and the poor—slave and free—had suffered greatly. When mysterious fires broke out, blacks and whites were accused of conspiring together. Mass hysteria developed against the accused. After a trial full of lurid accusations by informers, and forced confessions, two white men and two white women were executed, eighteen slaves were hanged, and thirteen slaves were burned alive.

Only one fear was greater than the fear of black rebellion in the new American colonies. That was the fear that discontented whites would join black slaves to overthrow the existing order. In the early years of slavery, especially, before racism as a way of thinking was firmly ingrained, while white indentured servants were often treated as badly as black slaves, there was a possibility of cooperation. As Edmund Morgan sees it:

> There are hints that the two despised groups initially saw each other as sharing the same predicament. It was common, for example, for servants and slaves to run away together, steal hogs together, get drunk together. It was not uncommon for them to make love together. In Bacon's Rebellion, one of the last groups to surrender was a mixed band of eighty negroes and twenty English servants.

As Morgan says, masters, "initially at least, perceived slaves in much the same way they had always perceived servants . . . shiftless, irresponsible, unfaithful, ungrateful, dishonest." And "if freemen with disappointed hopes should make common cause with slaves of desperate hope, the results might be worse than anything Bacon had done."

And so, measures were taken. About the same time that slave codes, involving discipline and punishment, were passed by the Virginia Assembly,

> Virginia's ruling class, having proclaimed that all white men were superior to black, went on to offer their social (but white) inferiors a number of benefits previously denied them. In 1705 a law was passed requiring masters to provide white servants whose indenture time was up with ten bushels of corn, thirty shillings, and a gun, while women servants were to get 15 bushels of corn and forty shillings. Also, the newly freed servants were to get 50 acres of land.

Morgan concludes: "Once the small planter felt less exploited by taxation and began to prosper a little, he became less turbulent, less dangerous, more respectable. He could begin to see his big neighbor not as an extortionist but as a powerful protector of their common interests."

We see now a complex web of historical threads to ensnare blacks for slavery in America: the desperation of starving settlers, the special helplessness of the displaced African, the powerful incentive of profit for slave trader and planter, the temptation of superior status for poor whites, the elaborate controls against escape and rebellion, the legal and social punishment of black and white collaboration.

The point is that the elements of this web are historical, not "natural." This does not mean that they are easily disentangled, dismantled. It means only that there is a possibility for something else, under historical conditions not yet realized. And one of these conditions would be the elimination of that class exploitation which has made poor whites desperate for small gifts of status, and has prevented that unity of black and white necessary for joint rebellion and reconstruction.

Around 1700, the Virginia House of Burgesses declared:

> The Christian Servants in this country for the most part consists of the Worser Sort of the people of Europe. And since . . . such numbers of Irish and other Nations have been brought in of which a great many have been soldiers in the late warrs that according to our present Circumstances we can hardly governe them and if they were fitted with Armes and had the Opertunity of meeting together by Musters we have just reason to fears they may rise upon us.

It was a kind of **class consciousness,** a class fear. There were things happening in early Virginia, and in the other colonies, to warrant it.

---

class consciousness Karl Marx argued that the working classes were not conscious of the ways in which the ruling class oppressed them. Class consciousness refers to the ability of the laboring class (the proletariat) to challenge the reasons given to them by economic elites as to why they were impoverished.

3

RACIAL FORMATIONS

Michael Omi and Howard Winant

MICHAEL OMI is a professor in the Department of Ethnic Studies at the University of California, Berkeley, and the co-author of *Racial Formation in the United States from the 1960s to the 1980s* (1986). He has also written about racial theory and politics, right-wing political movements, Asian Americans and race relations, and race and popular culture. In 1990, he was the recipient of Berkeley's Distinguished Teaching Award. **HOWARD WINANT** is a professor of sociology at the University of California, Santa Barbara. He is the author of numerous books and articles, including *Racial Formation in the United States from the 1960s to the 1990s* (1994) (with Michael Omi), *Racial Conditions: Politics, Theory, Comparisons* (1994), and *Stalemate: Political Economic Origins of Supply-Side Policy* (1988).

IN 1982–83, SUSIE GUILLORY PHIPPS unsuccessfully sued the Louisiana Bureau of Vital Records to change her racial classification from <u>black</u> to white. The descendant of an eighteenth-century white planter and a black slave, Phipps was designated "black" on her birth certificate in accordance with a 1970 state law which declared anyone with at least one-thirty-second "Negro blood" to be black. The legal battle raised intriguing questions about the concept of **race,** its meaning in contemporary society, and its use (and abuse) in public policy. Assistant Attorney General Ron Davis defended the law by pointing out that some type of racial classification was necessary to comply with federal record-keeping requirements and to facilitate programs for the prevention of genetic diseases.

Phipps's attorney, Brian Begue, argued that the assignment of racial categories on birth certificates was unconstitutional and that the one-thirty-second designation was inaccurate. He called on a retired Tulane University professor who cited research indicating that most whites have one-twentieth "Negro" ancestry. In the end, Phipps lost. The court upheld a state law which quantified racial identity, and in so doing affirmed the legality of assigning individuals to specific racial groupings.[1]

---

race Sociologists view race as a social concept because the idea of race has changed over time, the categories of race are not discrete (they blend into one another), and the definition of race changes from country to country. We tend to think about race in terms of skin color, but the reason we place human beings into skin color categories is as arbitrary as grouping individuals by height, blood type, weight, eye color, or finger length.

The Phipps case illustrates the continuing dilemma of defining race and establishing its meaning in institutional life. Today, to assert that variations in human physiognomy are racially based is to enter a constant and intense debate. *Scientific* interpretations of race have not been alone in sparking heated controversy; *religious* perspectives have done so as well.[2] Most centrally, of course, race has been a matter of *political* contention. This has been particularly true in the United States, where the concept of race has varied enormously over time without ever leaving the center stage of U.S. history.

WHAT IS RACE?

Race consciousness, and its articulation in theories of race, is largely a modern phenomenon. When European explorers in the New World "discovered" people who looked different than themselves, these "natives" challenged then-existing conceptions of the origins of the human species and raised disturbing questions as to whether *all* could be considered in the same "family of man."[3] Religious debates flared over the attempt to reconcile the Bible with the existence of "racially distinct" people. Arguments took place over creation itself, as theories of polygenesis questioned whether God had made only one species of humanity ("monogenesis"). Europeans wondered if the natives of the New World were indeed human beings with redeemable souls. At stake were not only the prospects for conversion, but the types of treatment to be accorded them. The expropriation of property, the denial of political rights, the introduction of slavery and other forms of coercive labor, as well as outright extermination, all presupposed a worldview which distinguished Europeans—children of God, human beings, etc.—from "others." Such a worldview was needed to explain why some should be "free" and others enslaved, why some had rights to land and property while others did not. Race, and the interpretation of racial differences, was a central factor in that worldview.

In the colonial epoch science was no less a field of controversy than religion in attempts to comprehend the concept of race and its meaning. Spurred on by the classificatory scheme of living organisms devised by Linnaeus in *Systema Naturae,* many scholars in the eighteenth and nineteenth centuries dedicated themselves to the identification and ranking of variations in humankind. Race was thought of as a *biological* concept, yet its precise definition was the subject of debates which, as we have noted, continue to rage today. Despite efforts ranging from Dr. Samuel Morton's studies of cranial capacity[4] to contemporary attempts to base racial classification on shared gene pools,[5] the concept of race has defied biological definition. . . .

Attempts to discern the *scientific meaning* of race continue to the present day. Although most physical anthropologists and biologists have abandoned the quest for a scientific basis to determine racial categories, controversies have recently flared in the area of genetics and educational psychology. For instance, an essay by Arthur Jensen arguing that hereditary factors shape intelligence not only revived the "nature or nurture" controversy, but raised highly volatile questions about racial equality itself.[6] Clearly the attempt to establish a *biological* basis of race has not been swept into the dustbin of history, but is being resurrected in various scientific arenas. All such attempts seek to remove the concept of race from fundamental social, political, or economic determination. They suggest instead that the truth of race lies in the terrain of innate characteristics, of which skin color and other physical attributes provide only the most obvious, and in some respects most superficial, indicators.

RACE AS A SOCIAL CONCEPT

The social sciences have come to reject biologistic notions of race in favor of an approach which regards race as a *social* concept. Beginning in the eighteenth century, this trend has been slow and uneven, but its direction clear. In the nineteenth century Max Weber discounted biological explanations for racial conflict and instead highlighted the social and political factors which engendered such conflict.[7] The work of pioneering cultural anthropologist Franz Boas was crucial in refuting the scientific racism of the early twentieth century by rejecting the connection between race and culture, and the assumption of a continuum of "higher" and "lower" cultural groups. Within the contemporary social science literature, race is assumed to be a variable which is shaped by broader societal forces.

Race is indeed a pre-eminently *sociohistorical* concept. Racial categories and the meaning of race are given concrete expression by the specific social relations and historical context in which they are embedded. Racial meanings have varied tremendously over time and between different societies.

In the United States, the black/white color line has historically been rigidly defined and enforced. White is seen as a "pure" category. Any racial intermixture makes one "nonwhite." In the movie *Raintree County*, Elizabeth Taylor describes the worst of fates to befall whites as "havin' a little Negra blood in ya'— just one little teeny drop and a person's all Negra."[8] This thinking flows from what Marvin Harris has characterized as the principle of *hypo-descent*:

> By what ingenious computation is the genetic tracery of a million years of evolution unraveled and each man [sic] assigned his proper social box? In the United States, the mechanism employed is the rule of hypo-descent. This descent rule requires Americans to believe that anyone who is known to have had a Negro ancestor is a Negro. We admit nothing in between. . . . "Hypo-descent" means affiliation with the subordinate rather than

the superordinate group in order to avoid the ambiguity of intermediate identity. . . . The rule of hypo-descent is, therefore, an invention, which we in the United States have made in order to keep biological facts from intruding into our collective racist fantasies.[9]

The Susie Guillory Phipps case merely represents the contemporary expression of this racial logic.

By contrast, a striking feature of race relations in the lowland areas of Latin America since the abolition of slavery has been the relative absence of sharply defined racial groupings. No such rigid descent rule characterizes racial identity in many Latin American societies. Brazil, for example, has historically had less rigid conceptions of race, and thus a variety of "intermediate" racial categories exist. Indeed, as Harris notes, "One of the most striking consequences of the Brazilian system of racial identification is that parents and children and even brothers and sisters are frequently accepted as representatives of quite opposite racial types."[10] Such a possibility is incomprehensible within the logic of racial categories in the U.S.

To suggest another example: the notion of "passing" takes on new meaning if we compare various American cultures' means of assigning racial identity. In the United States, individuals who are actually "black" by the logic of hypo-descent have attempted to skirt the discriminatory barriers imposed by law and custom by attempting to "pass" for white.[11] Ironically, these same individuals would not be able to pass for "black" in many Latin American societies.

Consideration of the term "black" illustrates the diversity of racial meanings which can be found among different societies and historically within a given society. In contemporary British politics the term "black" is used to refer to all nonwhites. Interestingly this designation has not arisen through the racist discourse of groups such as the National Front. Rather, in political and cultural movements, Asian as well as Afro-Caribbean youth are adopting the term as an expression of self-identity.[12] The wide-ranging meanings of "black" illustrate the manner in which racial categories are shaped politically.

The meaning of race is defined and contested throughout society, in both collective action and personal practice. In the process, racial categories themselves are formed, transformed, destroyed and reformed. We use the term **racial formation** to refer to the process by which social, economic and political forces determine the content and importance of racial categories, and by which they are in turn shaped by racial meanings. Crucial to this formulation is the treatment of race as a *central axis* of social relations which cannot be subsumed under or reduced to some broader category or conception.

RACIAL IDEOLOGY AND RACIAL IDENTITY

The seemingly obvious, "natural" and "common-sense" qualities which the existing racial order exhibits themselves testify to the effectiveness of the racial formation process in constructing racial meanings and racial identities.

One of the first things we notice about people when we meet them (along with their sex) is their race. We utilize race to provide clues about *who* a person is. This fact is made painfully obvious when we encounter someone whom we cannot conveniently racially categorize—someone who is, for example, racially "mixed" or of an ethnic/racial group with which we are not familiar. Such an encounter becomes a source of discomfort and momentarily a crisis of racial meaning. Without a racial identity, one is in danger of having no identity.

Our compass for navigating race relations depends on preconceived notions of what each specific racial group looks like. Comments such as, "Funny, you don't look black," betray an underlying image of what black should be. We also become disoriented when people do not act "black," "Latino," or indeed "white." The content of such stereotypes reveals a series of unsubstantiated beliefs about who these groups are and what "they" are like.[13]

---

racial formation The process in which race operates as a central axis of social relations, which then determine social, economic, and political institutions and practices.

In U.S. society, then, a kind of "racial etiquette" exists, a set of interpretive codes and racial meanings which operate in the interactions of daily life. Rules shaped by our perception of race in a comprehensively racial society determine the "presentation of self,"[14] distinctions of status, and appropriate modes of conduct. "Etiquette" is not mere universal adherence to the dominant group's rules, but a more dynamic combination of these rules with the values and beliefs of subordinated groupings. This racial "subjection" is quintessentially ideological. Everybody learns some combination, some version, of the rules of racial classification, and of their own racial identity, often without obvious teaching or conscious inculcation. Race becomes "common sense"—a way of comprehending, explaining, and acting in the world.

Racial beliefs operate as an "amateur biology," a way of explaining the variations in "human nature."[15] Differences in skin color and other obvious physical characteristics supposedly provide visible clues to differences lurking underneath. Temperament, sexuality, intelligence, athletic ability, aesthetic preferences, and so on are presumed to be fixed and discernible from the palpable mark of race. Such diverse questions as our confidence and trust in others (for example, clerks or salespeople, media figures, neighbors); our sexual preferences and romantic images; our tastes in music, films, dance, or sports; and our very ways of talking, walking, eating, and dreaming are ineluctably shaped by notions of race. Skin color "differences" are thought to explain perceived differences in intellectual, physical and artistic temperaments, and to justify distinct treatment of racially identified individuals and groups.

The continuing persistence of racial ideology suggests that these racial myths and stereotypes cannot be exposed as such in the popular imagination. They are, we think, too essential, too integral, to the maintenance of the U.S. social order. Of course, particular meanings, stereotypes and myths can change, but the presence of a *system* of racial meanings and stereotypes, of racial ideology, seems to be a permanent feature of U.S. culture.

Film and television, for example, have been notorious in disseminating images of racial minorities which establish for audiences what people from these groups look like, how they behave, and "who they are."[16] The power of the media lies not only in their ability to reflect the dominant racial ideology, but in their capacity to shape that ideology in the first place. D. W. Griffith's epic *Birth of a Nation,* a sympathetic treatment of the rise of the Ku Klux Klan during Reconstruction, helped to generate, consolidate and "nationalize" images of blacks which had been more disparate (more regionally specific, for example) prior to the film's appearance.[17] In U.S. television, the necessity to define characters in the briefest and most condensed manner has led to the perpetuation of racial caricatures, as racial stereotypes serve as shorthand for scriptwriters, directors and actors, in commercials, etc. Television's tendency to address the "lowest common denominator" in order to render programs "familiar" to an enormous and diverse audience leads it regularly to assign and reassign racial characteristics to particular groups, both minority and majority.

These and innumerable other examples show that we tend to view race as something fixed and immutable—something rooted in "nature." Thus we mask the historical construction of racial categories, the shifting meaning of race, and the crucial role of politics and ideology in shaping race relations. Races do not emerge full-blown. They are the results of diverse historical practices and are continually subject to challenge over their definition and meaning.

RACIALIZATION: THE HISTORICAL DEVELOPMENT OF RACE

In the United States, the racial category of "black" evolved with the consolidation of racial slavery. By the end of the seventeenth century, Africans whose specific identity was Ibo, Yoruba, Fulani, etc., were rendered "black" by an ideology of exploitation based on racial logic—the establishment and maintenance of a "color line." This of course did not

occur overnight. A period of indentured servitude which was not rooted in racial logic preceded the consolidation of racial slavery. With slavery, however, a racially based understanding of society was set in motion which resulted in the shaping of a specific *racial* identity not only for the slaves but for the European settlers as well. Winthrop Jordan has observed: "From the initially common term *Christian,* at mid-century there was a marked shift toward the terms *English* and *free.* After about 1680, taking the colonies as a whole, a new term of self-identification appeared—white."[18]

We employ the term **racialization** to signify the extension of racial meaning to a previously racially unclassified relationship, social practice, or group. Racialization is an ideological process, a historically specific one. Racial ideology is constructed from pre-existing conceptual (or, if one prefers, "discursive") elements and emerges from the struggles of competing political projects and ideas seeking to articulate similar elements differently. An account of racialization processes that avoids the pitfalls of U.S. ethnic history[19] remains to be written.

Particularly during the nineteenth century, the category of "white" was subject to challenges brought about by the influx of diverse groups who were not of the same Anglo-Saxon stock as the founding immigrants. In the nineteenth century, political and ideological struggles emerged over the classification of Southern Europeans, the Irish and Jews, among other "nonwhite" categories.[20] Nativism was only effectively curbed by the institutionalization of a racial order that drew the color line *around,* rather than *within,* Europe.

By stopping short of racializing immigrants from Europe after the Civil War, and by subsequently allowing their assimilation, the American racial order was reconsolidated in the wake of the tremendous challenge placed before it by the abolition of racial slavery.[21] With the end of Reconstruction in 1877, an effective program for limiting

---

racialization The social process by which a racial identity is attached to a group and that group is placed in a race-based social hierarchy. Upon their arrival in America, for example, Europeans labeled the hundreds of indigenous tribal populations "Indians" and placed them in a single group in a racial hierarchy.

the emergent class struggles of the later nineteenth century was forged: the definition of the working class *in racial terms*—as "white." This was not accomplished by any legislative decree or capitalist maneuvering to divide the working class, but rather by white workers themselves. Many of them were recent immigrants, who organized on racial lines as much as on traditionally defined class lines.[22] The Irish on the West Coast, for example, engaged in vicious anti-Chinese race-baiting and committed many pogrom-type assaults on Chinese in the course of consolidating the trade union movement in California.

Thus the very political organization of the working class was in important ways a racial project. The legacy of racial conflicts and arrangements shaped the definition of interests and in turn led to the consolidation of institutional patterns (e.g., segregated unions, dual labor markets, exclusionary legislation) which perpetuated the color line *within* the working class. Selig Perlman, whose study of the development of the labor movement is fairly sympathetic to this process, notes that

> the political issue after 1877 was racial, not financial, and the weapon was not merely the ballot, but also "direct action"—violence. The anti-Chinese agitation in California, culminating as it did in the Exclusion Law passed by Congress in 1882, was doubtless the most important single factor in the history of American labor, for without it the entire country might have been overrun by Mongolian [sic] labor and *the labor movement might have become a conflict of races instead of one of classes.*[23]

More recent economic transformations in the U.S. have also altered interpretations of racial identities and meanings. The automation of southern agriculture and the augmented labor demand of the postwar boom transformed blacks from a largely rural, impoverished labor force to a largely urban, working-class group by 1970.[24] When boom became bust and liberal welfare statism moved rightwards, the majority of blacks came to be seen, increasingly, as part of the "underclass," as state "dependents." Thus the particularly deleterious effects on blacks of global and national economic shifts (generally rising unemployment rates, changes in the employment structure away from reliance on labor intensive work, etc.) were explained once again in the late 1970s and 1980s (as they had been in the 1940s and mid-1960s) as the result of defective black cultural norms, of familial disorganization, etc.[25] In this way new racial attributions, new racial myths, are affixed to "blacks."[26] Similar changes in racial identity are presently affecting Asians and Latinos, as such economic forces as increasing Third World impoverishment and indebtedness fuel immigration and high interest rates, Japanese competition spurs resentments, and U.S. jobs seem to fly away to Korea and Singapore.[27] . . .

Once we understand that race overflows the boundaries of skin color, super-exploitation, social stratification, discrimination and prejudice, cultural domination and cultural resistance, state policy (or of any other particular social relationship we list), once we recognize the racial dimension present to some degree in *every* identity, institution, and social practice in the United States—once we have done this, it becomes possible to speak of *racial formation.* This recognition is hard-won; there is a continuous temptation to think of race as an *essence,* as something fixed, concrete, and objective, as (for example) one of the categories just enumerated. And there is also an opposite temptation: to see it as a mere illusion, which an ideal social order would eliminate.

In our view it is crucial to break with these habits of thought. The effort must be made to understand race as *an unstable and "decentered" complex of social meanings constantly being transformed by political struggle.*

RACE AND ETHNICITY IN AMERICA

John Iceland

John Iceland is a Professor of Sociology and Demography at Penn State University.

THEORIES EXPLAINING RACIAL AND ETHNIC INEQUALITIES

In a column critical of black civil rights leaders Jesse Jackson and Al Sharpton, *Wall Street Journal* columnist Jason Riley argues, "What we have left today as civil-rights leaders are second- and third-tier types striving for relevance in an era when the biggest barrier to black progress is no longer white racism but black anti-social behavior and counterproductive attitudes toward work, school, marriage and so forth."[1] In a succinct manner Riley clearly articulates the view that culture matters: black disadvantage can be blamed on harmful attitudes and behaviors among blacks today.

In contrast, in an article that makes a case for racial reparations, writer Ta-Nehisi Coates argues that not only have slavery, Jim Crow laws, and past discriminatory behavior contributed to black economic disadvantage, but so has present-day discrimination, such as in the housing market:

In 2010, the Justice Department filed a discrimination suit against Wells Fargo alleging that the bank had shunted blacks into predatory loans [loans with very high interest rates] regardless of their creditworthiness. This was not magic or coincidence or misfortune. It was racism reifying itself. According to *The New York Times*, affidavits found loan officers referring to their black customers as "mud people" and to their subprime products as "ghetto loans."

"We just went right after them," Beth Jacobson, a former Wells Fargo loan officer, told *The Times*. "Wells Fargo mortgage had an emerging markets unit that specifically targeted black churches because it figured church leaders had a lot of influence and could convince congregants to take out subprime loans."

In 2011, Bank of America agreed to pay $355 million to settle charges of discrimination against its Countrywide unit. The following year, Wells Fargo settled its discrimination suit for more than $175 million.[2]

This indicates that discrimination is not dead. But is this an unusual instance? To what extent does discrimination explain overall patterns of inequality today?

Questions to Consider

When you look through the appendix in this book, what is made abundantly clear is that quality of life indicators like wealth, health, and educational attainment vary by race. It is also the case in most instances that racial minorities experience more socioeconomic inequality than whites. John Iceland asks the question, why is this so? Is the reason for such disparities the result of discrimination? How and in what ways might the role of human capital, social capital, culture assimilation, racism, and discrimination play in creating and maintaining racial inequality?

The root causes of inequality among other groups are also frequently contested. Do low levels of education among Hispanics, for example, reflect discrimination, poor quality of schools in Hispanic neighborhoods, or the fact that Hispanic immigrants typically come to the United States with low levels of education, and it takes at least a couple of generations for their progeny to catch up to the American mainstream? Conversely, what explains relatively high levels of education and income among Asian families? Does it again have something to do with the immigration process (Asian immigrants come with relatively high levels of education), with a culture that emphasizes hard work, or something else? In the following section I systematically review different theories typically used to explain patterns of racial and ethnic inequality today. Specifically, I discuss the role of human capital, social capital, culture, assimilation, and racism and discrimination in turn.

Human Capital Theory

Economists are fond of discussing the role of *human capital* in affecting people's economic well-being. Human capital refers to people's knowledge, skills, personality, and experiences that help them attain good jobs and move ahead in their careers. Most studies of human capital focus on the importance of educational attainment and on-the-job experience in determining one's earnings and future productivity. Indeed, the evidence is very strong that people who invest in their education can expect higher incomes. The median weekly earnings of people with less than a high school diploma in 2013 was $472, far less than the median weekly earnings of people with a bachelor's degree ($1,108) and less yet with someone with an advanced professional degree ($1,714).[3]

Educational attainment can affect earnings in a number of ways. For one, people learn a variety of skills in school, such as analytical thinking, writing acumen, computer programming, accounting, and so on. In addition, a degree provides a credential that acts as a screening device by sending a signal to employers that a person is productive, even in the absence of information about specific skills.[4] For example, a degree from Harvard University may signal that a person is smart and capable and thus highly employable.

Human capital may affect racial differentials in earnings and wealth if there are significant differences in educational attainment and work experience across different groups. While I carefully evaluate this argument by examining patterns and trends in education in detail in the coming chapters, suffice it to say here that there are some basic differences across groups in, for example, attending college. In 2013, 32 percent of people twenty-five years and older had completed four years or more of college in the United States. Among non-Hispanic whites, this figure was a little higher at 35 percent, while the corresponding percentages were 22 percent for blacks and 15 percent for Hispanics. In contrast, 53 percent of Asians had completed four years or more of college.[5] Thus, holding other factors equal, we would expect for earnings to be higher among whites, and especially Asians, than blacks and Hispanics. Likewise, there are significant differences in levels of unemployment across groups, and this affects work experience and earnings both in the current period and over one's lifetime. The average unemployment rate among men sixteen years and older in 2013 was 7.6 percent, with a low of 5.6 percent among Asians, 6.8 percent among whites, 8.8 percent among Hispanics, and a high of 14.2 percent among blacks.[6] High black incarceration rates (black men are eight times more likely to be incarcerated than white men) means that a higher proportion of young black men enter the labor force with a criminal record, which further dampens their employability.[7]

Educational attainment is affected by other factors related to racial inequality. The quality of public schooling in different neighborhoods can affect the probability of one attending college later on. Schools in poor and minority neighborhoods often have inferior resources and fewer enrichment programs than schools in higher-income, mostly white, neighborhoods. High neighborhood poverty rates are strongly correlated with lower student test scores.[8] In addition, if people feel that their education won't pay off because of obstacles in the labor market (including discrimination), they may be less likely to make additional investments in their education. This can in turn further reinforce racial differences in socioeconomic achievement.

Social Capital Theory

Sociologists Pierre Bourdieu and Loic Wacquant define social capital as "the sum of the resources, actual or virtual, that accrue to an individual or a group by the virtue of possessing a durable network of more or less institutionalized relationships of mutual acquaintance and recognition."[9] In other words, social capital refers to the resources people have due to their social networks. These networks can be used as a vehicle for upward mobility. Many people, for example, find a job through word of mouth through friends and neighbors. If one has wealthy, well-connected neighbors, then one might have a leg up on finding a job than an otherwise similarly qualified person (in terms of skills and education) without such connections.

Racial differences in socioeconomic achievement, then, might not just reflect differences in human capital, but also differences in social capital. Economist

Glenn Loury has argued that African Americans have less access to—or are often excluded from—useful social relationships, leading to lower levels of social capital often crucial to achieving economic success.[10] White men are undoubtedly overrepresented in the proverbial **"old boys' network"** in many industries, such as finance, which might make it harder for minorities and women to make the connections to get a job, even if there is no intentional racial or gender bias.

High levels of black-white residential segregation both reflect and reinforce differences in social networks, and this could further contribute to black-white socioeconomic inequality. A significant proportion of Asians and Hispanics are immigrants or children of immigrants who live in or near ethnic communities. Immigrant and ethnic networks can help group members secure a job. But whether this leads to higher earnings over the long run could depend on the nature and quality of these networks and social contacts. For example, while employers in ethnic enclaves might provide jobs to new immigrants, they might also exploit these newcomers.[11] Thus, one's social networks can at times be harmful rather than helpful.

Cultural Theories

Sociologists typically define *culture* as the beliefs, values, customs, behaviors, and other characteristics that are shared and accepted by a group of people. The connection between culture and racial inequality is hotly debated. Culture has sometimes been used to blame poor people and minorities for their own disadvantage. For example, some people believe that cultural values and lifestyles, such as a weak work ethic, childbearing outside of marriage, criminal behavior, and drug use inhibit upward mobility among some groups.[12] Empirically, labor force participation rates are lower, and out-of-wedlock childbearing and crime and victimization are higher among African Americans than others, and these attributes are highly correlated with poverty and disadvantage.[13] Asians have the lowest

old boys' network Informal system where men, typically of similar class and racial backgrounds, use their position and influence to help promote one another.

levels of childbearing outside of marriage of any group, including whites.[14]

Much of the sociological work examining the link between culture, race, and poverty comes from ethnographies that provide detailed portraits of how people live and why they behave the way they do. Elijah Anderson's *Code of the Street: Decency, Violence, and the Moral Life of the Inner City,* for example, describes how low-income African Americans navigate public spaces in poor neighborhoods and the importance of an individual's ability to command respect through the use of violence if necessary. Another example is Kathryn Edin and Maria Kefalas's book, *Promises I Can Keep: Why Poor Women Put Motherhood before Marriage,* which describes how poor women value and aspire to marriage but feel that stable and rewarding marriages are nearly unattainable. Instead, having children provides meaning to their lives, and it is something that they can do on their own.[15]

The books often provide a structural context that helps explain behavior that may seem unproductive and self-defeating to the eye of middle- and upper-class Americans. In the case of *Code of the Street,* the lack of economic opportunities in the inner city and discrimination against black youth mean that many young men adopt a form of masculinity that emphasizes verbal boasts, sexual prowess, and violence in the quest for pride and respect. In the case of *Promises I Can Keep,* the declining economic opportunities for less educated men (of all races)—a result of globalization, deindustrialization, and the disappearance of high-paying blue-collar jobs—mean that there are fewer "marriageable" men who can help provide a stable basis for partnerships than in the past. This leads to greater rates of single parenthood, which has been linked to numerous negative outcomes, including higher poverty and lower levels of child well-being, as measured by school completion, and other social, cognitive, and behavioral outcomes.[16]

Culture has also been invoked by some as a possible explanation for relatively high levels of educational attainment among Asian Americans. The thinking here is that Asian Americans highly value education and its potential to foster upward mobility and communicate this to their children, who put more effort into their schoolwork than their white and other non-Asian peers.[17] These high levels of education translate into good jobs with high earnings. Asian American families likewise have particularly low levels of single parenthood and high levels of cohesiveness, and this also helps explain relatively low levels of Asian poverty.[18]

A related concept is *cultural capital,* which has been defined in a variety of ways, such as possessing the knowledge of high-status culture or, a bit more broadly, as "widely shared, legitimate culture made up of high status cultural signals (attitudes, preferences, behaviors, and goods) used in direct or indirect social exclusion."[19] The French sociologist Pierre Bourdieu argues that such capital helps perpetuate economic advantages across generations, as children with cultural capital might be better prepared to master academic material and communicate with teachers and other high-status adults who can potentially help them get ahead in life.[20] For example, there are certain expectations on how to act in most kinds of job interviews, such as shaking hands at the outset, providing some eye contact, and generally appearing open and friendly. The extent that white and minority students have different levels of cultural capital, then, could affect their levels of socioeconomic achievement.

Finally, while there has been excellent sociological work exploring the role of culture in shaping attitudes and behaviors and outcomes, we know much less about the exact *magnitude* of its impact on racial inequality. The concept of culture has a multitude of dimensions—it can refer to different kinds of attitudes and behaviors—and even attributing such attitudes and behaviors to culture alone, as opposed to, for example, structural conditions with which they can interact, is challenging and problematic.

Assimilation Theory

Assimilation refers to the reduction of differences between ethnic groups over time. Assimilation has been traditionally thought to occur when immigrant groups adopt mainstream attitudes, culture, and educational and work experiences. Assimilation theorists today emphasize that assimilation need not be a one-way street, where minority members become more like majority group members. Rather, assimilation involves a general convergence of social, economic, and cultural patterns.[21] The extent to which assimilation occurs affects racial and ethnic disparities.

Richard Alba and Victor Nee, in their discussion of assimilation theory, explain how assimilation is not necessarily a universal outcome for all groups. Moreover, assimilation is a lengthy process that typically spans generations:

> To the extent that assimilation occurs, it proceeds incrementally as an intergenerational process, stemming both from individuals' purposive action and from the unintended consequences of their workaday decisions. In the case of immigrants and their descendants who may not intentionally seek to assimilate, the cumulative effect of pragmatic decisions aimed at successful adaptation can give rise to changes in behavior that nevertheless lead to eventual assimilation.[22]

Descendants of European immigrants of the nineteenth and early twentieth centuries have largely assimilated into U.S. society. Groups once viewed as outsiders now view themselves, and are viewed by others, as part of the American mainstream. But just because white immigrants of the previous wave of immigration assimilated does not mean that post-1965 immigrants will experience the same. Asians, black immigrants, and darker-skinned Hispanics are all "visible minorities," so they may not be able to blend into what is sometimes referred to as the white mainstream. Immigrants themselves also differ in their characteristics, and this can affect levels of achievement and the pace of assimilation. Asian immigrants, for example, tend to have higher levels of education on average than immigrants from Latin America, and this likely affects other important outcomes, such as their earnings and the quality of neighborhoods in which they live, and subsequently the outcomes of their children.

One of the key aspects of the theory is that it is important not just to look at the well-being of immigrants themselves but rather how the next generations are faring. Thus, it is important to ask, Are the children of immigrants experiencing upward mobility? Are they less likely to live in ethnic enclaves than their parents? Are they more likely to intermarry with nongroup members? If so, then this is strong evidence that assimilation is occurring.

The Role of Racism and Discrimination

Perhaps the most invoked explanation for racial and ethnic inequality in the United States is racism and discrimination. In the context of today's sensibilities, the country has a very disturbing history of racial violence and oppression, including the annexation of land from American Indians, the institution of slavery and subsequent Jim Crow oppression against blacks, and the internment of more than a hundred thousand Japanese Americans in California and other western states during World War II, to name but a few.

The term *racism* refers to the linking of groups with alleged biological abilities and behaviors to assert the superiority of one racial group over another. Racism has taken on many forms over time and place. As discussed earlier, African Americans were typically thought of as inferior to whites in many respects through much of U.S. history. Jews were considered a degenerate and almost subhuman race in Nazi Germany, which made it easier to justify extinguishing them in Nazi-controlled countries during World War II. Likewise, the genocide of Tutsi by the Hutu majority in Rwanda in the 1990s was grounded in the legacy of Western colonialism, contemporary political conflict, and an inflammatory racist ideology that emphasized distinctions between the two groups.[23]

Racism goes hand in hand with *prejudice,* which can be defined as an "attitudinal system of negative beliefs, feelings, and action-orientations regarding a certain group or groups of people."[24]

Discrimination goes beyond attitudes and beliefs and into action. It is the differential and unequal treatment of other groups based on some usually observable trait such as race and ethnicity but also gender, sexual orientation, and religion, among other possible characteristics. One can hold many prejudices about the inferiority of other groups but might still refrain from discriminatory behavior. Discrimination itself can represent the actions of individuals or social institutions, such as in the form of Jim Crow laws that enforced segregation.

The Civil Rights Act of 1964, one of the crowning achievements of the civil rights movement, prohibited discrimination based on race, color, religion, sex, or national origin. The tools for enforcing the act were initially weak but were strengthened with the passage of additional legislation over time. While these laws have reduced the incidence of racial discrimination, this does not mean that prejudice and discrimination are relics of the past. We hear of plenty of news stories where people feel that they have been mistreated because of their race, and some of these cases end up in the courts, ranging from the settlement in 2013 of a $160 million racial discrimination suit brought against Merrill Lynch by African American brokers to the nearly $100 million settlement in 2014 of a lawsuit by 1,500 black and Hispanic applicants against the Fire Department of New York.

While overt racism is undoubtedly less common today than in the past, there is considerable debate about the extent to which it impedes the socioeconomic mobility of minority groups today. Some argue that nonracial factors, including those reviewed earlier, drive persisting social inequities. Others counter that whites in the United States often benefit from *colorblind privilege*. According to this theoretical perspective, we live in a society that celebrates a color-blind ideology: race is skin deep, people of all hues and backgrounds should be treated equally, and racism is an individual problem, in that discrimination is a product of the actions of misguided individuals.[25]

The problem with color-blind ideology, according to this perspective, is that it masks deep-rooted racial inequalities. Thus, sociologist Charles Gallagher argues that "color blindness maintains white privilege by negating racial inequality. Embracing a post-race, color-blind perspective provides whites with a degree of psychological comfort by allowing them to imagine that being white or black or brown has no bearing on an individual's or group's relative place in the socioeconomic hierarchy."[26] Entrenched racial inequality, however, comes in the form of persisting differences in wealth, which can affect whether someone attends college or purchases a house.[27] It is also reflected in the differential treatment of blacks by law enforcement and employers.[28] This perspective further argues that whites often don't recognize these systemic inequalities and thus don't acknowledge the privileges they enjoy by the virtue of being white and blame the disadvantaged position of many minorities on their own poor choices and wayward values.

As Lani Guinier and Gerald Torres argue, one of the negative consequences of this colorblind ideology is that it "inhibit[s] racialized minorities from struggling against their marginalized status. . . . It gives those who have enjoyed little power in our society no mechanisms for understanding and challenging the systemic nature of their oppression. . . . The way race has been used both to distribute resources and to camouflage the unfairness in that distribution remains invisible. . . . And the political space, where groups come together to give voice to their collective experience and mobilize to engage in fundamental social change, vanishes."[29]

Differing perceptions of systemic inequality drive many race-based controversies today. Was the shooting of Trayvon Martin by George Zimmerman symptomatic of the stereotypes people have about the criminality of young black men? Similarly, were the 2014 riots in Ferguson, Missouri, after the shooting of an unarmed young black man, Michael Brown, by a white police officer a result of criminal profiling? Or was it an isolated instance of an officer shooting a not-so-innocent man (who had stolen a box of cigarillos from a convenience store earlier in the day) during an unfortunate confrontation? Were supporters of Michael Brown playing the "race card" in a situation that didn't have much to do about race per se, or were the incident and the subsequent mishandling of the situation (e.g., the body was left in the street for hours and the police provided very little information about the situation even as tensions rose in the following days) and the manhandling of protestors a manifestation of deep institutional racism that African Americans face every day?

CONCLUSION

Through much of the twentieth century the stark black-white color line, perpetuated and reinforced by white racism, defined the American racial landscape. But American society has changed in some important ways over the past few decades. The civil rights movement overturned the legal framework that supported the unequal treatment of blacks, and there has been a gradual change in racist attitudes against minorities. Multiethnic perspectives on racial and ethnic inequality have also risen in prominence in recent years, spurred by growing racial and ethnic diversity. So the question arises, what is the trajectory of the American color line? How are various groups faring, and what explains their advantage or disadvantage? Are we seeing the softening of racial lines altogether?

If we find, for example, that the relatively low median household income among Hispanic families is mainly a function of the immigration process—whereby new immigrants have low incomes, but by third generation we see growing parity with whites—then this suggests a softening of the color line between Hispanics and others. But if we see persistent Hispanic disadvantage across generations, this speaks to the intransigence of broad social divisions based on race and ethnicity that may not change for the foreseeable future.

5

RACIALIZED SOCIAL SYSTEM APPROACH TO RACISM

Eduardo Bonilla-Silva

EDUARDO BONILLA-SILVA is professor of sociology at Duke University. He is best known for his 1997 piece in the *American Sociological Review* titled "Rethinking Racism: Toward a Structural Interpretation." He is the author of three books: *White Supremacy and Racism in the Post-Civil Rights Era* (2001), *Racism Without Racists: Color-Blind Racism and the Persistence of Racial Inequality in the United States* (2003), and *Whiteout: The Continuing Significance of Racism* (with Ashley Doane, 2003).

IN ORDER TO CAPTURE THE SOCIETY-WIDE, organized, and institutional character of racism I build my alternative theory around the notion of **racialized social systems.**[1] This term refers to societies in which economic, political, social, and ideological levels are partially structured by the placement of actors in racial categories or races. Races typically are identified by their phenotype, but (as we see later) the selection of some human traits to designate a racial group is always socially rather than biologically based.

These systems are structured partially by race because modern social systems incorporate two or more forms of hierarchical patterns. Although

Questions to Consider

Eduardo Bonilla-Silva argues that "after a society becomes racialized, racialization develops a life of its own." What does this mean? How does society become "racialized," and how is it possible that the idea of race can develop a "life" of its own? How, according to the author, is the United States characterized by racialized social systems?

---

racialized social systems The idea that society is organized along racial lines and that economic, political, social, and even psychological rewards differ according to one's placement in a racial hierarchy. Once established, the system of racial hierarchy takes on a life of its own.

processes of racialization are always embedded in other forms of hierarchy, they acquire autonomy and have independent social effects. This implies that the phenomenon that has been conceived as a free-floating ideology in fact has its own structural foundation.

In all racialized social systems the placement of actors in racial categories involves some form of hierarchy[2] that produces definite social relations among the races. The race placed in the superior position tends to receive greater economic remuneration and access to better occupations and prospects in the labor market, occupies a primary position in the political system, is granted higher social estimation (e.g., is viewed as "smarter" or "better looking"), often has the license to draw physical (segregation) as well as social (racial etiquette) boundaries between itself and other races, and receives what W.E.B. Du Bois called a "psychological wage."[3] The totality of these racialized social relations and practices constitutes the racial structure of a society.

Although all racialized social systems are hierarchical, the particular character of the hierarchy, and, thus, of the racial structure, is variable. For example, the domination of blacks in the United States was achieved through dictatorial means during slavery, but in the post-civil rights period this domination has been *hegemonic*—that is, in the Gramscian sense of the term, achieved through consent rather than coercion.[4] Similarly, the form of securing domination and white privilege is variable too. For instance, the racial practices and mechanisms that kept blacks subordinated changed from overt and eminently racist in the Jim Crow era to covert and indirectly racist in the contemporary period. The unchanging element of these systems is racial inequality—that the subordinated races' life chances are significantly lower than those of the dominant race. This is the feature that ultimately distinguishes this form of hierarchical social organization. Generally, the higher the level of racial inequality, the more racialized the social system, and vice versa.

Because the races receive different social rewards at all levels, they develop different interests, which can be detected in their struggles to either transform or maintain a particular racial order. These interests are collective rather than individual, are based on relations among races rather than on particular group needs, and are practical; that is, they are related to concrete struggles. Although one race's general interest may ultimately lie in the complete elimination of a society's racial structure, its array of alternatives may not include that possibility. For instance, the historical struggle against chattel slavery led not to the development of race-free societies but to the establishment of social systems with a different kind of racialization. Race-free societies were not among the available alternatives because the nonslave populations had the capacity to preserve some type of racial privilege. The historical "exceptions" occurred in racialized societies in which the nonslaves' power was almost completely superseded by that of the slave population.[5]

A simple criticism of the argument I have advanced so far is that it ignores the internal divisions of the races along class and gender lines. Such criticism, however, does not deal squarely with the issue at hand. The fact that not all members of the dominant race receive the same level of rewards and (conversely) that not all members of the subordinate race or races are at the bottom of the social order does not negate the fact that races, as social groups, are in either a superordinate or a subordinate position in a social system. Historically the racialization of social systems did not imply the exclusion of other forms of oppression. In fact, racialization occurred in social formations also structured by class and gender. Hence, in these societies, the racialization of subjects is fragmented along class and gender lines. The important question—Which interests move actors to struggle?—is historically contingent and cannot be ascertained a priori.[6] Depending on the character of racialization in a social order, class interests may take precedence over racial interests as in contemporary Brazil, Cuba, and Puerto Rico. In other situations, racial interests may take precedence over class interests as in the case of blacks throughout most of U.S. history.

In general, the systemic salience of class in relation to race increases when the economic, political, and social inequality among the races decreases substantially. Yet this broad argument generates at least one warning: The narrowing of within-class differences among racial actors usually causes *more* rather than *less* racial conflict, at least in the short run, as the competition for resources increases.[7] More significantly, even when class-based conflict becomes more salient in a social order, this cannot be interpreted as prima facie evidence that race has subsided as a social factor. For instance, because of the way in which Latin American racial formations rearticulated race and racial discourse in the nineteenth-century postemancipation era,[8] these societies silenced from above the political space for public racial contestation. Yet more than 100 years after these societies developed the myth of racial democracy, they have more rather than less racial inequality than countries such as the United States.[9]

Because racial actors are also classed and gendered (that is, they belong to class and gender groups), analysts must control for class and gender to ascertain the material advantages enjoyed by a dominant race. In a racialized society such as the United States, the independent effects of race are assessed by analysts who (1) compare data between whites and nonwhites in the *same* class and gender positions, (2) evaluate the proportion as well as the general character of the races' participation in some domain of life, and (3) examine racial data at all levels—social, political, economic, and ideological—to ascertain the general position of racial groups in a social system.

The first of these procedures has become standard practice in sociology. No serious sociologist would present racial statistics without controlling for gender and class (or at least the class of persons' socioeconomic status). By doing this, analysts assume they can measure the unadulterated effects of "discrimination" manifested in unexplained "residuals." Despite its usefulness, however, this technique provides only a partial account of the "race effect" because (1) a significant amount of racial data cannot be retrieved through surveys and (2) the technique of "controlling for" a variable neglects the obvious—why a group is over- or underrepresented in certain categories of the control variables in the first place.[10] Moreover, these analysts presume that it is possible to analyze the amount of discrimination in one domain (e.g., income, occupational status) "without

analyzing the extent to which discrimination also affects the factors they hold constant."[11] Hence to evaluate "race effects" in any domain, analysts must attempt to make sense of their findings in relation to a race's standing in other domains.

But what is the nature of races or, more properly, of racialized social groups? Omi and Winant state that races are the outcome of the racialization process, which they define as "the extension of racial meaning to a previously racially unclassified relationship, social practice, or group."[12] Historically the classification of a people in racial terms has been a highly political act associated with practices such as conquest and colonization; enslavement; peonage; indentured servitude; and, more recently, colonial and neocolonial labor immigration. Categories such as "Indians" and "Negroes" were invented in the sixteenth and seventeenth centuries to justify the conquest and exploitation of various peoples.[13] The invention of such categories entails a dialectical process of construction; that is, the creation of the category "Other" involves the creation of a category "Same." If "Indians" are depicted as "savages," Europeans are characterized as "civilized"; if "blacks" are defined as natural candidates for slavery, "whites" are defined as free subjects.[14] Yet although the racialization of peoples was socially invented and did not override previous forms of social distinction based on class or gender, it did not lead to imaginary relations but generated new forms of human association with definite status differences. After the process of attaching meaning to a "people" is instituted, race becomes a real category of group association and identity.[15]

Because racial classifications partially organize and limit actors' life chances, racial practices of opposition emerge. Regardless of the form of racial interaction (overt, covert, or inert), races can be recognized in the realm of racial relations and positions. Viewed in this light, races are the effect of racial practices of opposition ("we" versus "them") at the economic, political, social, and ideological levels.[16]

Races, as most social scientists acknowledge, are not biologically but socially determined categories of identity and group association. In this regard, they are analogous to class and gender.[17] Actors in racial positions do not occupy those positions because they are of X or Y race, but because X or Y has been socially defined as a race. Actors' **phenotypic** (i.e., biologically inherited) characteristics, such as skin tone and hair color and texture, are usually, although not always, used to denote racial distinctions.[18] For example, Jews in many European nations and the Irish in England have been treated as racial groups.[19] Also, Indians in the United States have been viewed as one race despite the tremendous phenotypic and cultural variation among nations. Because races are socially constructed, both the meaning and the position assigned to races in the racial structure are always contested. Who is to be black or white or Indian reflects and affects the social, political, ideological, and economic struggles among the races. The global effects of these struggles can change the meaning of the racial categories as well as the position of a racialized group in a social formation.

This latter point is illustrated clearly by the historical struggles of several "white ethnic" groups in the United States in their efforts to become accepted as legitimate whites or "Americans."[20] Neither light-skinned nor, for that matter, dark-skinned immigrants necessarily came to this country as members of X or Y race. Light-skinned Europeans, after brief periods of "not-yet white," became "white" but did not lose their "ethnic" character.[21] Their struggle for inclusion had specific implications: racial inclusion as members of the white community allowed Americanization and class mobility. On the other hand, among dark-skinned immigrants from Africa, Latin America, and the Caribbean, the struggle was to avoid classification as "black." These immigrants challenged the reclassification of their identity for a single reason: in the United States, "black" signified a subordinate status in society. Hence many of these groups struggled to keep their own ethnic or cultural identity, as denoted in expressions such as "I am not black; I am Jamaican," or "I am not black; I am Senegalese."[22] Yet eventually many of these groups resolved this contradictory situation by accepting the duality of their situation: in the United States, they were classified socially as black yet they retained and nourished their own cultural or ethnic heritage—a heritage deeply influenced by African traditions.

Although the content of racial categories changes over time through manifold processes and struggles, race is not a secondary category of group association. The meaning of black and white, the "racial formation," changes within the larger racial structure. This does not mean that the racial structure is immutable and completely independent of the action of racialized actors. It means only that the social relations among the races become institutionalized (form a structure as well as a culture) and affect social life whether or not individual members of the races want it to. In Frederick Barth's words, "Ethnic identity implies a series of constraints on the kinds of roles an individual is allowed to play [and] is similar to sex and rank, in that it constrains the incumbent in all his activities."[23] For instance, free blacks during the slavery period struggled to change the meaning of "blackness," specifically to dissociate it from slavery. Yet they could not escape the larger racial structure that restricted their life chances and their freedom.[24]

The placement of a group of people in a racial category stemmed initially[25] from the interests of powerful actors in the social system (e.g., the capitalist class, the planter class, and colonizers). After racial categories were employed to organize social relations in societies, however, race became an independent element of the operation of the social system.

What are the dynamics of racial issues in racialized systems? Most important, after a social formation is racialized, its "normal" dynamics always include a racial component. Societal struggles based on class or gender contain a racial component because both of these social categories are also racialized; that is, both class and gender are constructed along racial lines. In 1922, for example, white South African workers in the middle of a strike inspired by the Russian revolution rallied under the slogan "Workers of the world unite for a white South Africa." One of the state's "concessions" to this "class" struggle was the passage of the Apprenticeship Act of 1922, "which prevented Black workers acquiring apprenticeships."[26] In another example, the struggle of women in the

---

phenotype A biological term that refers to how we look (skin color, facial features, hair texture, etc.).

United States to attain their civil and human rights has always been plagued by deep racial tensions.[27]

Nonetheless, some of the strife that exists in a racialized social formation has a distinct racial character; I call such strife *racial contestation*— the struggle of racial groups for systemic changes regarding their position at one or more levels. Such a struggle may be social (Who can be here? Who belongs here?); political (Who can vote? How much power should they have? Should they be citizens?); economic (Who should work, and what should they do? They are taking our jobs!); or ideological (Black is beautiful!).

Although much of this contestation is expressed at the individual level and is disjointed, sometimes it becomes collective and general and can effect meaningful systemic changes in a society's racial organization. The form of contestation may be relatively passive and subtle (e.g., in situations of fundamental overt racial domination such as slavery and apartheid) or more active and overt (e.g., in quasi-democratic situations such as the contemporary United States). As a rule, however, fundamental changes in racialized social systems are accompanied by struggles that reach the point of overt protest.[28] This does not mean that a violent, racially based revolution is the only way of accomplishing effective changes in the relative position of racial groups. It is simply an extension of the argument that social systems and their supporters must be "shaken" if fundamental transformations are to take place.[29] On this structural foundation rests the phenomenon labeled racism by social scientists.

I reserve the term *racial ideology* for the segment of the ideological structure of a social system that crystallizes racial notions and stereotypes. Racial ideology provides the rationalization for social, political, and economic interactions among the races. Depending on the particular character of a racialized social system and on the struggles of the subordinated races, racial ideology may be developed highly (as in apartheid) or loosely (as in slavery) and its content expressed in overt or covert terms.

Although racial ideology originates in race relations, it acquires relative autonomy in the social system and performs practical functions.[30] In Paul Gilroy's words, racial ideology "mediates the world

of agents and the structures which are created by their social praxis."[31] Racism crystallizes the changing "dogma" on which actors in the social system operate and becomes "common sense"; it provides the rules for perceiving and dealing with the Other in a racialized society. In the United States, for instance, because racial notions about what blacks and whites are or ought to be pervade their encounters, whites still have difficulty in dealing with black bankers, lawyers, professors, and doctors.[32] Thus, although racist ideology is ultimately false, it fulfills a practical role in racialized societies.

At this point it is possible to sketch the framework of the racialized social system. First, racialized social systems are societies that allocate differential economic, political, social, and even psychological rewards to groups along racial lines, lines that are socially constructed. After a society becomes racialized, a set of social relations and practices based on racial distinctions develops at all societal levels. I designate the aggregate of those relations and practices as the racial structure of a society. Second, races historically are constituted according to the process of racialization; they become the effect of relations of opposition among racialized groups at all levels of a social formation. Third, on the basis of this structure, a racial ideology develops. This ideology is not simply a "superstructural" phenomenon (a mere reflection of the racialized system) but becomes the organizational map that guides actions of racial actors in society. It becomes as real as the racial relations it organizes. Fourth, most struggles in a racialized social system contain a racial component, but sometimes they acquire or exhibit a distinct racial character. Racial contestation is the logical outcome of a society with a racial hierarchy. A social formation that includes some form of racialization will always exhibit some form of racial contestation. Finally, the process of racial contestation reveals the different objective interests of the races in a racialized social system.

CONCLUSION

My central argument in this [reading] is that the commonsense understanding of racism, which is not much different than the definition developed by mainstream social scientists or even by many critical analysts, does not provide an adequate theoretical foundation for understanding racial phenomena. With notable exceptions,[33] analysts in academia are still entangled in ungrounded ideological interpretations of racism. Lacking a structural view, they tend to reduce racial phenomena to a derivation of the class structure (as Marxist interpreters do) or the result of an irrational ideology (as mainstream social scientists do).

In the racialized social system framework, I suggest, as do Omi and Winant, that racism should be studied from the viewpoint of racialization. I contend that after a society becomes racialized, racialization develops a life of its own.[34] Although racism interacts with class and gender structurations in society, it becomes an organizing principle of social relations in itself. Race, as most analysts suggest, is a social construct, but that construct, like class and gender, has independent effects in social life. After racial stratification is established, race becomes an independent criterion for vertical hierarchy in society. Therefore different races experience positions of subordination and superordination in society and develop different interests. This framework has the following advantages over traditional views of racism:

Racial phenomena are regarded as the "normal" outcome of the racial structure of a society. Thus we can account for all racial manifestations. Instead of explaining racial phenomena as deriving from other structures or from racism (conceived of as a free-floating ideology), we can trace cultural, political, economic, social, and even psychological racial phenomena to the racial organization of that society.

The changing nature of what analysts label "racism" is explained as the normal outcome of racial contestation in a racialized social system. In this framework, changes in racism are explained rather than described. Changes are due to specific struggles at different levels among the races, resulting from differences in interests. Such changes may transform the nature of racialization and the global character of racial relations in the system (the racial structure). Therefore, change is viewed as a normal component of the racialized system.

The racialized social system framework allows analysts to explain overt as well as covert racial behavior. The covert or overt nature of racial contacts depends on how the process of racialization is manifested; this in turn depends on how race originally was articulated in a social formation and on the process of racial contestation. This point implies that rather than conceiving of racism as a universal and uniformly orchestrated phenomenon, analysts should study "historically-specific racisms."[35] This insight is not new: Robert Park, Oliver Cox, Pierre van den Bergue, and Marvin Harris described varieties of "situations of race relations" with distinct forms of racial interaction.

Racially motivated behavior, whether or not the actors are conscious of it, is regarded as "rational"—that is, based on the given race's individual interests.[36] This framework accounts for Archie Bunker–type racial behavior as well as for more "sophisticated" varieties of racial conduct. Racial phenomena are viewed as systemic; therefore all actors in the system participate in racial affairs. Some members of the dominant racial group tend to exhibit less virulence toward members of the subordinated races because they have greater control over the form and outcome of their racial interactions. When they cannot control that interaction—as in the case of revolts or blacks moving into "their" neighborhood—they behave much like other members of the dominant race.

The reproduction of racial phenomena in contemporary societies is explained in this framework not by reference to a long-distant past but in relation to its contemporary structure. Because racism is viewed as systemic (possessing a racial structure) and as organized around the races' different interests, racial aspects of social systems today are viewed as fundamentally related to hierarchical relations among the races in those systems. Elimination of the racialized character of a social system entails the end of racialization, and hence of races altogether. This argument clashes with social scientists' most popular policy prescription for "curing" racism, namely, education. This "solution" is the logical outcome of defining racism as a belief. Most analysts regard racism as a matter of individuals subscribing to an irrational view, thus the cure is educating them to realize that racism is wrong. Education is also the choice pill prescribed by Marxists for healing workers from racism. The alternative theory offered here implies that because the phenomenon has structural consequences for the races, the only way to cure society of racism is by eliminating its systemic roots. Whether this can be accomplished democratically or only through revolutionary means is an open question, and one that depends on the particular racial structure of the society in question.

A racialization framework accounts for the ways in which racial and ethnic **stereotypes** *emerge, are transformed, and disappear.* Racial stereotypes are crystallized at the ideological level of a social system. These images ultimately indicate—although in distorted ways—and justify the stereotyped group's position in a society. Stereotypes may originate out of (1) material realities or conditions endured by the group; (2) genuine ignorance about the group; or (3) rigid, distorted views on the group's physical, cultural, or moral nature. Once they emerge, however, stereotypes must relate—although not necessarily fit perfectly—to the group's true social position in the racialized system if they are to perform their ideological function. Stereotypes that do not tend to reflect a group's situation do not work and are bound to disappear. For example, notions of the Irish as stupid or of Jews as athletically talented have all but vanished since the 1940s, as the Irish moved up the educational ladder and Jews gained access to multiple routes of social mobility. Generally, then, stereotypes are reproduced because they reflect a group's distinct position and status in society. As a corollary, racial or ethnic notions about a group disappear only when the group's status mirrors that of the dominant racial or ethnic group in the society.

The framework of the racialized social system is not a universal theory explaining racial phenomena in societies. It is intended to trigger a serious discussion of how race shapes social systems. Moreover, the important question of how race interacts and intersects with class and gender has not yet been addressed satisfactorily. Provisionally I maintain that a nonfunctionalist reading of the concept of social system may give us clues for comprehending societies *structured in dominance,* to use Stuart Hall's term. If societies are viewed as systems that articulate different structures (organizing principles on which sets of social relations are systematically patterned), it is possible to claim that race—as well as gender—has both individual and combined (interactive) effects in society.

To test the usefulness of the racialized social system framework as a theoretical basis for research, we must perform comparative work on racialization in various societies. One of the main objectives of this comparative work should be to determine the specific mechanisms, practices, and social relations that produce and reproduce racial inequality at all levels—that is, uncover the society's racial structure. Unlike analysts who believe that "racism" has withered away, I argue that the persistent inequality experienced by blacks and other racial minorities in the United States today is due to the *continued* albeit *changed* existence of a racial structure. In contrast to race relations in the Jim Crow period, however, racial practices that reproduce racial inequality in contemporary America are (1) increasingly covert, (2) embedded in normal operations of institutions, (3) void of direct racial terminology, and (4) invisible to most whites.

---

stereotype A simplfied picture we paint of an entire group of people. The tendency is to generalize about everyone in that group based on ignorance, limited information, or prejudice. Examples of racial stereotypes: all Asians are good at math, white people can't jump, and all black people have rhythm.

Seeing the Big Picture   The Social Construction of Race, 1790–2000

The appendix provides the official racial definitions used by the U.S. Census. Figure 1 shows how racial and ethnic categories changed from 1790 to 2000. How do these changing definitions reflect the idea that race is a "social construction"?

INSTITUTIONAL RACISM AND HEALTH

David R. Williams[1,2,3] and Selina A. Mohammed[4]

DAVID R. WILLIAMS is a Public Health Professor at Harvard University and **SELINA A. MOHAMMED** is Professor of Nursing and Associate Dean for the School of Health Sciences and Nursing at the University of Washington, Bothell.

IN THE UNITED STATES, as in other racialized countries in the world, racially stigmatized and disenfranchised populations have worse health than their more advantaged counterparts (D. Williams, 2012). The poorer health of these racial minority populations is evident in higher rates of mortality, earlier onset of disease, greater severity and progression of disease, and higher levels of comorbidity and impairment. In addition, disadvantaged racial populations tend to have lower levels of access to medical care and to receive care that is poorer in quality. In U.S. data, these patterns tend to be evident for African Americans (or Blacks), American Indians (or Native Americans), Native Hawaiians and other Pacific Islanders, and economically disadvantaged Hispanic (or Latino) and Asian immigrants with long-term residence in the United States (D. Williams, 2012). These striking disparities are persistent over time and, although reduced, are evident at every level of income and education (Braveman, Cubbin, Egerter, Williams, & Pamuk, 2010; D. Williams, 2012). In recent years, increased attention has been given to the role of racism as a determinant of these patterns of racial inequality in health.

This [reading] describes the complex nature of contemporary racism in the United States. To identify the leverage points for intervention, it outlines the multiple ways in which racism can affect health. First, it provides a brief overview of the empirical evidence that reveals that institutional racism

Questions to Consider

The authors argue that although most Americans hold fewer negative attitudes toward racial minorities, racism is still thoroughly embedded in American institutions. This article examines the extent to which "racism adversely affects the health of nondominant racial populations in multiple ways," specifically institutional and cultural racism. How might race and health outcomes be linked?

shapes socioeconomic status (SES) and opportunities in a variety of ways. Next, it shows that research reveals that cultural racism, with its associated negative images, stereotypes, and prejudice, can be damaging to health. Finally, it highlights the research indicating that interpersonal discrimination is a potent psychosocial stressor that has pervasive negative effects on health.

OVERVIEW OF THE NATURE OF RACISM AND ITS PERSISTENCE

Racism is an organized system premised on the categorization and ranking of social groups into races, and it devalues, disempowers, and differentially allocates desirable societal opportunities and resources to racial groups regarded as inferior (BonillaSilva, 1996; D. Williams, 2004). Racism often leads to the development of negative attitudes (prejudice) and beliefs (stereotypes) toward nondominant, stigmatized racial groups and differential treatment (discrimination) of these groups by both individuals and social institutions. These multiple dimensions of racism do not always co-occur. For example, it is possible for racism to exist in institutional structures and policies without the presence of racial prejudice or negative racial stereotypes at the individual level.

Despite progress in the reduction of explicit public support of racism in the United States, there is also strong evidence of its persistence. National data on the racial attitudes of Whites reveal positive changes over time in support of the principle of racial equality (Schuman, Steeh, Bobo, & Krysan, 1997). For example, the percentage of Whites supporting the view that "White people should have the first chance at any kind of job" fell from 55% in 1944 to 3% in 1972. At the same time, support for laws and policies to achieve equality lags behind the support for the principle of equality (Schuman et al., 1997). For example, in spite of increased support for the principle of equality and the advent of laws that prohibit discrimination, Whites' support for the federal government's efforts to ensure that Black people get fair treatment in jobs declined from 38% in 1964 to 28% in 1996.

Several lines of evidence support the notion that racism persists in contemporary society. First, many Americans believe that racism remains a problem in the United States. At the time of President Obama's inauguration in 2009, 85% of Blacks and 71% of Whites saw racism as a somewhat big (41% vs. 49%, respectively) or big (44% vs. 22%, respectively) problem in the United States (Washington Post Company, 2009). A 2012 national survey found that 67% of Whites and 90% of Blacks agreed that Blacks and Hispanics currently experience discrimination in the United States, and 74% of Blacks and 31% of Whites indicated that they had personally experienced racial discrimination (Schoen, 2012). At the same time, other national data reveal that Whites now believe that they are more likely to be victims of racial discrimination than Blacks (Norton & Sommers, 2011).

Documenting the persistence of racism is a challenge because the nature of racism in contemporary society has also changed in ways that make it not readily recognizable to most adults. Scientific evidence indicates that in addition to conscious, deliberate cognitive processes, humans also engage in implicit (unconscious), effortless, automatic, evaluative processes in which they respond to a stimulus based on images stored in their memory (Dovidio & Gaertner, 2004). For example, Americans manifest high levels of negative feelings and beliefs about Blacks, Latinos, obese people, and homosexuals (Nosek et al., 2007). *Aversive racism* is one of the terms used to characterize contemporary racism (Dovidio & Gaertner, 2004). An aversive racist lacks explicit racial prejudice (that is, has sympathy for those who were victimized by injustice in the past and is committed to principles of racial equality) but has implicit biases that favor Whites over Blacks. Research suggests that almost 70% of Americans have implicit biases that favor Whites over Blacks (Nosek et al., 2007). The pattern is most pronounced among Whites but is also evident for Asians, Hispanics, and American Indians. These high levels of implicit bias suggest that discrimination is likely to be commonplace in American society, with much of it occurring through behaviors that the perpetrator does not experience as intentional (Dovidio & Gaertner, 2004).

Discrimination

Second, racial discrimination persists in contemporary society, with Whites continuing to self-report that they discriminate against minorities (Pager & Shepherd, 2008). In addition, there is considerable high-quality scientific evidence documenting the persistence of racial discrimination. A recent review of audit studies—those in which researchers carefully select, match, and train individuals to be equally qualified in every respect but to differ only in race—provide striking examples of contemporary racial discrimination (Pager & Shepherd, 2008). For example, audit studies in employment document that a White job applicant with a criminal record is more likely to be offered a job than a Black applicant with an otherwise identical résumé whose record was clean. Similarly, job applicants with distinctively Black names (e.g., Aisha, Darnell) are less likely to get callbacks for job interviews than applicants with identical résumés who have distinctively White names (e.g., Alison, Brad). Other audit studies reveal racial discrimination in renting apartments, purchasing homes and cars, obtaining mortgages and medical care, applying for insurance, and hailing taxis. Research has also found that even the price of a fast food meal increases with the percentage Black of a zip code (Pager & Shepherd, 2008). Minority homebuyers and residential

areas were also explicitly targeted for subprime and predatory loans (Pager & Shepherd, 2008). Between 1993 and 2000, 78% of the new housing loans in minority neighborhoods and 72% of the increase in refinancing to Blacks were from subprime lenders.

Institutional Racism

Third, racial discrimination also persists in institutional mechanisms and processes. Residential segregation by race is a prime example (Massey & Denton, 1993). *Segregation* refers to the physical separation of the races in racially distinctive neighborhoods and communities that was developed to ensure that Whites were safeguarded from residential closeness to Blacks (Cell, 1982). This enforced residence in separate areas developed in both northern and southern urban areas in the late 19th and early 20th centuries and has remained strikingly stable since then but with small declines in recent years (Glaeser & Vigdor, 2001; Lieberson, 1980; Massey & Denton, 1993). Although segregation has been illegal since the Fair Housing Act of 1968, it is perpetuated today through an interlocking set of individual actions, institutional practices, and governmental policies. In the 2010 Census, residential segregation was at its lowest level in 100 years, and declines in segregation were evident in all of the nation's largest metropolitan areas (Glaeser & Vigdor, 2012). However, recent declines in segregation have been driven by a few Blacks moving to formerly all-White census tracts but have had little impact on the very high percentage of Black census tracts, the residential isolation of most African Americans, and the concentration of urban poverty (Glaeser & Vigdor, 2001). The forced removal and relocation of American Indians to reservations is another example of institutionalized isolation of a marginalized racial population.

The high level of incarceration of Blacks and other minorities is another example of institutional racism. The United States imprisons a higher proportion of its population than any other country in the world. Racial disparities in the criminalization and investigation of certain behaviors combined with discrimination in prosecution and sentencing have led to the inordinately high levels of incarceration of minorities in the United States (Alexander,

2010). Immigration policy in the United States, historically and currently, has been another form of institutional racism (Gee & Ford, 2011). These policies have ranked racial groups; excluded, segregated, and incarcerated some racial populations; and limited the rights and privileges of those deemed dangerous or undesirable.

Cultural Racism

The persistence of institutional and interpersonal discrimination is driven by the racism that remains deeply ingrained in American culture. Ideas of Black inferiority and White superiority have historically been embedded in multiple aspects of American culture, and many images and ideas in contemporary popular culture continue to devalue, marginalize, and subordinate non-White racial populations (Dirks & Mueller, 2007). Moreover, anti-Black ideology and representation are distinctive because they are typically the benchmarks to which other groups are compared. Findings from surveys and studies employing experimental or quasi-experimental design have found that greater exposure to TV programs that describe Blacks negatively was associated with higher levels of racial prejudice toward Blacks (Mutz & Goldman, 2010). Although Blacks and other minorities appear more frequently on TV than in the past, a recent study that examined characters in 11 popular TV programs found that more negative nonverbal behavior (facial expressions and body language) is directed toward Black characters than toward status-matched White characters and that exposure to nonverbal bias increased viewers' bias—even though viewers were not consciously aware of patterns of nonverbal behavior (Weisbuch, Pauker, & Ambady, 2009). Another study documented that a dehumanizing bias that associates Blacks with apes persists and that this dehumanization matters (Goff, Eberhardt, Williams, & Jackson, 2008). The study found that newspaper stories of defendants convicted of capital crime over a 20-year period were more likely to describe Black convicts than White ones with *ape*like words (e.g., *beast, brute, monster, prowl*). Importantly, adjusting for defendant SES, victim SES, crime severity, aggravating circumstances, and mitigating circumstances, researchers found that Blacks implicitly portrayed as

more ape-like were more likely to be executed than those whose lives were spared (Goff et al., 2008). A similar trend was evident for Whites.

Blacks and other minorities are also negatively stereotyped in the United States. The 1990 General Social Survey (GSS) found that 29% of Whites viewed Blacks as unintelligent, 45% saw them as lazy, 57% believed that Blacks prefer to live off welfare, and 51% believed that Blacks are prone to violence (Davis & Smith, 1990). Questions were asked on a 7-point scale from a positive to a negative stereotype, with 4 on the scale representing agreeing with neither side. Strikingly, one in five Whites or fewer saw Blacks as intelligent (21%), hardworking (17%), preferring to be self-supporting (13%), and not prone to violence (14%). Across the various stereotypes, Whites viewed Blacks, Hispanics, and Asians more negatively than themselves, with Blacks viewed the most negatively and Hispanics twice as negatively as Asians.

Data available in the GSS for two of the stereotypes since 1990 show very limited change over time (Smith, Marsden, & Hout, 2011). In 2010, 32% of Whites agreed that Blacks were lazy, down from 45% in 1990. However, the percentage of Whites endorsing the view that Blacks were hardworking changed from 17% in 1990 to 16% in 2010, with a higher proportion of Whites endorsing the *neither* category (49% vs. 34%). Some progress was evident on the intelligence stereotype, with the rate of Whites who viewed Blacks as unintelligent declining from 29% in 1990 to 13% in 2010 and that of Whites agreeing that Blacks were intelligent increasing from 21% in 1990 to 27% in 2010. The percentage of Whites endorsing the neutral response increased from 44% to 56%.

A recent study documents that negative stereotypes of Blacks are commonplace in American culture. The BEAGLE (Bound Encoding of the Aggregate Language Environment) Project constructed a database of about 10 million words from a sample of books, newspapers, and other materials that is a good representation of American culture and equivalent to what the average college-level student would read in his or her lifetime (Verhaeghen, Aikman, & Van Gulick, 2011). Statistical analysis of the associative strength between pairs of words revealed the following order of the frequency of the pairing of the word *Black* with these 10 words in American culture: *poor, violent, religious, lazy, cheerful, dangerous, charming, merry, ignorant,* and *musical.* Thus, the negative stereotypes of Blacks in the GSS (violent, lazy, dangerous, and unintelligent) probably reflect how often Americans have seen or heard these words paired with *Black* in their lifetime.

MECHANISMS BY WHICH RACISM CAN AFFECT HEALTH AND EVIDENCE OF HEALTH EFFECTS

Figure 1 outlines the multiple pathways by which racism can affect health. It indicates that racism is one of several fundamental or basic determinants of health, and it gives emphasis to institutional and cultural racism (D. Williams, 1997). The model emphasizes the importance of distinguishing basic causes from surface or intervening causes (proximal pathways). Whereas changes in fundamental causes lead to changes in outcomes, interventions in the intermediate or proximal pathways, without corresponding changes in fundamental causes, are unlikely to produce long-term improvements in population health. The model argues that race and other social status categories, such as SES, gender, age, and marital status, are created by the larger macro forces in society and are linked to health through several intervening mechanisms. Racism and other fundamental causes operate through multiple mechanisms to affect health, and the pathways through which distal causes affect health can change over time. Institutional and cultural racism can adversely affect health through stigma, stereotypes, prejudice, and racial discrimination. These aspects of racism can lead to differential access to SES and to a broad range of societal resources and opportunities. Racism is not the only determinant of intervening mechanisms, but its presence as a fundamental cause in a society can alter and transform other social factors and can exacerbate the negative effects of other risk factors for health. For example, stress is posited as one of the intervening pathways. Racism creates some types of stressors, such as discrimination and historical trauma, but it can also affect the levels, clustering, and impact of stressors, such as unemployment, neighborhood violence, or physical and chemical exposures in residential and occupational environments.

The model acknowledges that social inequalities in knowledge and communication play an insufficiently recognized role in contributing to and exacerbating social inequalities in health (Viswanath, 2006). Much of the contemporary disease burden is linked to behaviors that are potentially modifiable with the appropriate opportunities and access to preventive care and health information. Communication factors that shape health knowledge, attitudes, and behavior, such as access to and the use of various media sources, attention to health information, trust in the sources of information, and the processing of information, all vary by race-ethnicity and SES. Moreover, members of stigmatized racial groups are less able to act on and benefit from relevant health knowledge because they often lack the necessary resources to do so.

Much research on the determinants of health focuses on the responses (behavioral, psychological, physiological) to the proximal pathways. Figure 1 reminds us that these responses can be optimally understood and contextualized in the light of the upstream factors that initiate and sustain the conditions that population groups are responsive to. It also indicates that attention should be given to both individual and collective resistance and resilience. For example, some recent research suggests that some unhealthy behaviors of minority populations may reflect everyday resistance—an effort to express opposition to the larger society, assert independence, and reject the dominant society's norms (Factor, Williams, & Kawachi, 2013).

Institutional Racism and Health

Residential segregation is a potent institutional legacy of racism that is a driver of the persistence of racial economic inequality and thus racial inequities in health (D. Williams & Collins, 2001). Segregation

FIGURE 1 ■ A Framework for the Study of Racism and Health

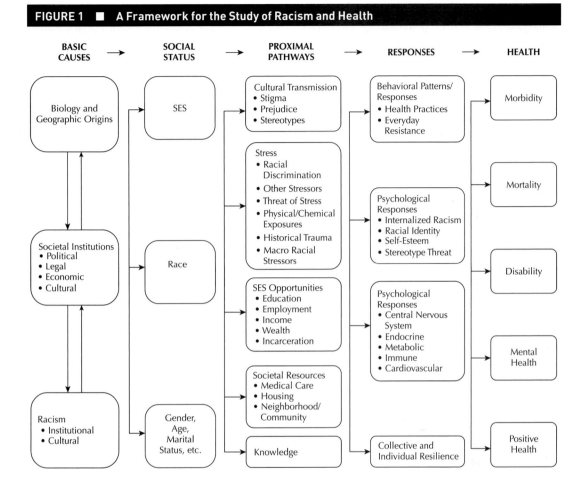

was one of the most successful domestic policies of the 20th century in the United States (Cell, 1982), and it can affect health through multiple pathways (D. Williams & Collins, 2001). First, it restricts socioeconomic mobility by limiting access to quality elementary and high school education, preparation for higher education, and employment opportunities. For example, segregated schools are unequal on multiple dimensions, including teacher quality; educational resources; per-student spending; and neighborhood violence, crime, and poverty (Orfield, Frankenberg, & Garces, 2008). Segregation also reduces access to employment opportunities. It has facilitated the exodus of low-skill, high-pay jobs from areas of minority concentration, and it has

facilitated discrimination based on place of residence (Pager & Shepherd, 2008; Wilson, 1987). One study found that the elimination of segregation would erase Black-White differences in earnings, high school graduation rate, and unemployment and reduce racial differences in single motherhood by two thirds (Cutler & Glaeser, 1997).

Segregation is also associated with residence in poorer-quality housing and in neighborhood environments that are deficient in a broad range of resources that enhance health and well-being, including medical care. The concentration of poverty in segregated environments can lead to exposure to elevated levels of chronic and acute stressors. A recent study documented, for example, that compared to Whites, Blacks and U.S.-born Latinos had higher exposure to a broad range of psychosocial stressors and greater clustering of multiple stressors (Sternthal, Slopen, & Williams, 2011). This stress exposure accounted for some of the residual effect of race on health after income and education were controlled. In addition, segregation leads minorities to have higher risk of exposure to toxic chemicals at the individual, household, and neighborhood level (Morello-Frosch & Jesdale, 2006). Research also reveals that segregation directly and indirectly contributes to lower access and poorer quality of health care across the entire continuum of care from prevention services through end-of-life care (White, Haas, & Williams, 2012). The poor health of minorities is further exacerbated by these racial differences in access and quality of care.

Segregation in the United States is also a fundamental cause of the high rates of violent crime and homicide for African Americans. Differences at the neighborhood level, driven by segregation, in the availability of jobs (especially for males), opportunities for marriage, concentrated poverty, family structure, and the supervision of adolescent males are the key determinants of elevated risk of violent crime and homicide (Sampson, 1987). These factors lead to the concentration of urban violence in a few "hot spots." Research in Boston documented that 3% of street segments and intersections accounted for more than 50% of all gun violence incidents (Braga, Papachristos, & Hureau, 2010). A study in Seattle found that most crime was concentrated in a few street segments, and 84% of these segments had stable concentrations of crime over a 14-year period, with increases in crime in a very few street segments accounting for overall city trends in crime (Weisburd, Bushway, Lum, & Yang, 2004).

Incarceration has a range of adverse impacts on the health of incarcerated people and of the communities to which they return after their release (Dumont, Brockmann, Dickman, Alexander, & Rich, 2012). When incarcerated individuals return to their communities, their access to public and private housing, employment opportunities, voting rights, welfare- and food-assistance programs, health services, and financial aid for higher education is limited (N. Williams, 2006). Most incarcerated adults are parents of children younger than 18 years of age, and these children are at increased risk for social and emotional difficulties and for engaging in criminal behavior in the future (Travis & Waul, 2003). When a parent is imprisoned, families often suffer from financial instability and social stigma and are deprived of social and caregiving support of the incarcerated parent (Travis & Waul, 2003). High rates of incarceration also adversely affect communities by reducing the availability of male partners for marriage.

Although institutional racism is arguably the most important mechanism by which racism adversely affects health, it is challenging to capture in traditional epidemiological research, and we have not fully quantified the impact of institutional racism on health. Some studies have found a positive association between area-level measures of residential segregation and infant and adult mortality rates, and other health outcomes, after adjusting for demographic and socioeconomic variables (Kramer & Hogue, 2009). A recent analysis estimated that segregation is responsible for 176,000 deaths annually (Galea, Tracy, Hoggatt, DiMaggio, & Karpati, 2011). Efforts have also been made, with limited success, to operationalize other aspects of institutional racism in epidemiological studies (e.g., Gee, 2002; Mendez, Hogan, & Culhane, 2012; Wallace, 2011). Recent reviews have provided a roadmap for the needed research to better conceptualize and measure the complex ways in which segregation can affect health and health care (Kramer, Cooper, Drews-Botsch, Waller, & Hogue, 2010; Osypuk & Acevedo-Garcia, 2010; White et al., 2012; White & Borrell, 2011). Implementing these recommendations is an important priority. Similar research attention needs to be given to other aspects of institutional racism.

Cultural Racism and Health

Research is needed to fully understand the multiple ways in which representations of race in popular culture affect persons who are exposed to them, but there is growing evidence that these effects can be decisive for the thoughts, feelings, and behavior of both dominant and subordinate groups. Cultural racism is likely to be a major contributor to negative racial stereotypes and the absence of positive emotion for stigmatized racial groups that can shape the policy preferences of the larger society and contribute to the lack of political will to address racial inequalities in society, including those in health. The absence of positive emotions has been identified as an important component of subtle prejudice (Pettigrew & Meertens, 1995). Research indicates that emotions have a large impact on decision making in general and on race-related attitudes and policy in particular. A recent meta-analysis found that emotional prejudice was twice as strongly predictive of discriminatory behavior as racial beliefs and stereotypes (Talaska, Fiske, & Chaiken, 2008). A study in Germany, the Netherlands, France, and the United Kingdom found that the absence of positive emotions (measured by two items that captured the absence of feelings of sympathy and admiration toward the out-group) was a strong predictor of opposition to policies regarding immigrant out-groups (Pettigrew & Meertens, 1995). Similarly, a study of Detroit-area Whites found that a two-item measure that assessed the lack of sympathy and admiration for Blacks was the strongest predictor of opposition to affirmative action in employment and to an active role of government in reducing racial inequalities (D. Williams et al., 1999). Moreover, recent research reveals that racial prejudice is a driver of opposition to President Obama's health care reform legislation, with the racial divide in attitudes toward health care being 20 percentage points larger now than it was for President Clinton's plan back in the early 1990s (Tesler, 2012).

One response of stigmatized racial populations to the pervasive negative racial stereotypes in the culture is to accept as true the dominant society's beliefs about their biological and/or cultural inferiority. This internalized racism or self-stereotyping is one mechanism by which negative stereotypes about race in the larger society can adversely affect health. By fostering the endorsement of beliefs about the innate deficiencies of one's self and one's group, internalized racism can lead to lower selfesteem and psychological well-being, which in turn could adversely affect health and health behavior in multiple ways (Kwate & Meyer, 2011). A recent review of existing research found that internalized racism was positively associated with alcohol consumption, psychological distress, being overweight, abdominal obesity, blood pressure, and fasting glucose (D. Williams & Mohammed, 2009). It has also been suggested that internalized stereotypes could also indirectly affect health by decreasing motivation for socioeconomic attainment (Kwate & Meyer, 2011).

However, the health consequences of internalized racism have received very limited research attention, and there are many unanswered questions. We currently have limited understanding of which groups are most vulnerable, the range of outcomes most affected, and how internalized racism combines with other aspects of racism to affect health. Some limited research has found that internalized racism is adversely related to cardiovascular risk factors for females but not males, and we do not have a clear understanding of the determinants of these gender differences (Chambers et al., 2004; Tull, Cort, Gwebu, & Gwebu, 2007). A recent study found a positive association between internalized racism and violence and delinquent behavior among adolescents (Bryant, 2011), suggesting that it may be a risk factor for a broad range of outcomes. Another recent study found that internalized racism interacted with perceived discrimination to affect cardiovascular disease risk (Chae, Lincoln, Adler, & Syme, 2010).

The term *stereotype threat* refers to the activation of negative stereotypes among stigmatized groups that creates expectations, anxieties, and reactions that can adversely affect social and psychological functioning (Fischer et al., 1996; Steele, 1997). U.S. research indicates that when a stigma of inferiority is activated for African Americans in experimental conditions, performance on an examination is adversely affected (Steele, 1997). Similarly, women who were told that they perform more poorly than men, and White men who were told that they do worse than Asians, had lower scores on an examination than control groups (Fischer et al., 1996; Steele, 1997). Research indicates that stereotype threat occurs only when a group is stereotype vulnerable. The activation of negative stereotypes about Blacks enhances academic performance for Black Caribbean immigrants who were not socialized in America's racism-filled culture, but it reduces it for the children of Caribbean Black immigrants (Deaux et al., 2007).

Similarly, for Asian American women, making gender salient reduces academic performance, but making their race salient enhances it (Shih, Pittinsky, & Ambady, 1999).

There has been little systematic attention to the direct effects of stereotype threat on health. However, existing research suggests the plausibility of two pathways. First, the psychological stress created by stereotype threat could lead to physiological arousal. One experimental study found that the activation of the stigma of inferiority led to increases in blood pressure for African American but not White students (Blascovitch, Spencer, Quinn, & Steele, 2001). Other limited evidence indicates that stereotype threat can increase anxiety, reduce self-regulation, and impair decision-making processes in ways that can increase aggressive behavior and overeating (Inzlicht & Kang, 2010). Second, stereotype threat can adversely affect the patient–provider relationship. In clinical encounters, stereotype threat can impair patients' communication abilities, leading to discounting of information from the provider, delays, or failure to obtain needed medical care and lower levels of adherence (Aronson, Burgess, Phelan, & Juarez, 2013; Burgess, Warren, Phelan, Dovidio, & van Ryn, 2010).

Cultural racism can trigger unconscious bias that can lead to unequal access to health-enhancing economic opportunities and resources. Many Whites have automatic, rapid, and unconscious emotional and neural reactions to Blacks, noticing an individual's race and whether he or she is trustworthy in less than 100 ms (Fiske, Bergsieker, Russell, & Williams, 2009). Research indicates that when one holds a negative stereotype about a group and meets someone who fits the stereotype, he or she will discriminate against that individual (van Ryn et al., 2011). This stereotype-linked unconscious or unthinking bias can occur among persons who are not prejudiced and is activated automatically (without intent) with individuals being unaware of its activation and the impact on their behavior (van Ryn et al., 2011). Cultural racism also undergirds the findings from the audit studies reviewed earlier that documented the pervasive societal presence of discrimination that leads to reduced opportunities for socioeconomic advancement, higher costs of goods and services, and poorer quality of life. For

example, the discrimination in mortgage lending noted earlier that led to a high level of subprime loans for minorities has contributed to the marked losses in home equity for these populations during the recent housing crisis. Between 2005 and 2009, the median wealth of White households declined by 16% compared to 53% for Black and 66% for Hispanic households (Pew Research Center, 2011). The median wealth of Whites is now 20 times that of Blacks and 18 times that of Hispanics. Wealth is a critical component of SES that has been shown to affect health over and above income and education (Pollack et al., 2007). Thus, the declining wealth of racial minorities is likely to have had adverse health consequences.

Unconscious (as well as conscious) bias can also lead to unequal access to high-quality medical care. A 2003 report from the Institute of Medicine concluded that across virtually every therapeutic intervention, ranging from high-technology procedures to the most basic forms of diagnostic and treatment interventions, Blacks and other minorities receive fewer procedures and poorer-quality medical care than Whites (Smedley, Stith, & Nelson, 2003). Strikingly, these differences persist even after statistical adjustment for variations in health insurance, SES, stage and severity of disease, co-occurring illness, and the type of health care facility are taken into account. Analyses of data from a large, volunteer, and nonrepresentative sample of persons who took the Implicit Association Test (IAT) reveal that physicians have an implicit preference for Whites over Blacks, similar to the pattern observed for other professionals (lawyers and others with PhDs) and the general population (Sabin, Nosek, Greenwald, & Rivara, 2009). Research reveals that higher implicit bias scores among physicians are associated with biased treatment recommendations in the care of Black patients (van Ryn et al., 2011), although the pattern is not uniform (Haider et al., 2011). This highlights the importance of research to better understand the conditions under which these biases are likely to occur. In addition, provider implicit bias is also associated with poorer quality of patient–provider communication and lower patient evaluation of the quality of the medical encounter, including provider nonverbal behavior (Cooper et al., 2012; van Ryn et al., 2011). Research is needed to identify optimal strategies of raising health providers' awareness of subtle, unconscious discrimination and providing them with strategies to minimize its occurrence.

EXPERIENCES OF DISCRIMINATION

Individuals are aware of at least some of the experiences of discrimination created by institutional and cultural racism. Research reveals that these subjective experiences of discrimination are psychosocial stressors that adversely affect a very broad range of health outcomes and health risk behaviors (Pascoe & Richman, 2009; D. Williams & Mohammed, 2009). For example, Tené Lewis and colleagues have shown that chronic, everyday discrimination is positively associated with coronary artery calcification (Lewis et al., 2006), C-reactive protein (Lewis, Aiello, Leurgans, Kelly, & Barnes, 2010), blood pressure (Lewis et al., 2009), giving birth to lower-birth-weight infants (Earnshaw et al., 2013), cognitive impairment (Barnes et al., 2012), subjective and objective indicators of poor sleep (Lewis et al., 2012), visceral fat (Lewis, Kravitz, Janssen, & Powell, 2011), and mortality (Barnes et al., 2008).

Research on discrimination has also shed light on some puzzles in the literature. For example, prior research reveals that African Americans are more likely than Whites to manifest no blood pressure decline or a blunted blood pressure decline during sleep, a pattern that has been associated with increased risk for mortality and cardiovascular outcomes (Profant & Dimsdale, 1999). Recent studies reveal that exposure to discrimination contributes to the elevated levels of nocturnal blood pressure among Blacks (Brondolo et al., 2008; Tomfohr, Cooper, Mills, Nelesen, & Dimsdale, 2010). Decreases in blood pressure dipping during sleep have

also been associated with low SES and other psychosocial stressors (Tomfohr et al., 2010). Prior research has also found lower levels of health care seeking and adherence behaviors among racial minorities, and research on discrimination now documents that racial bias is a contributor to these patterns. Moreover, research in the United States, South Africa, Australia, and New Zealand reveals that discrimination makes an incremental contribution over SES in accounting for racial disparities in health (D. Williams et al., 2008; D. Williams & Mohammed, 2009).

Many questions remain unanswered. Research suggests that across multiple societal contexts, perceptions of unfair treatment, regardless of whether they are attributed to race or other social reasons, are adversely related to health for both racial minorities and Whites (D. Williams & Mohammed, 2009). However, it is unclear whether the occasional experiences of discrimination by Whites are truly equivalent with the insidious and systematic experiences reported by stigmatized minority populations. Moreover, some studies find a more adverse impact of discrimination on mental health for Whites compared to Blacks (Kessler, Mickelson, & Williams, 1999; D. Williams, Yu, Jackson, & Anderson, 1997). One recent study found that discrimination was associated with a flatter (less healthy) diurnal slope of cortisol for Whites than for Blacks, with the healthier cortisol profile being more evident for low-SES Blacks than for their higher-SES counterparts (Fuller-Rowell, Doan, & Eccles, 2012). This highlights the importance of understanding the conditions under which specific aspects of discrimination are pathogenic for particular social groups as well as the extent to which socialization experiences, resilience resources, coping strategies, and co-occurring exposures may modify the relationship between exposure to discrimination and health.

Seeing the Big Picture　　**How Race Can Be Hazardous to Your Health**

Look at Section III in the appendix on race and health. What trends do you observe? Why do certain diseases affect one group more than others? Are you able to discern the role of race and class in these health disparities?

AUTHOR BIOGRAPHIES

David R. Williams is the Norman Professor of Public Health, African and African American Studies and Sociology at Harvard University. He is also Honorary Professor, Department of Psychiatry and Mental Health, University of Cape Town, South Africa. His research focuses on the ways in which socioeconomic status, race, stress, racism, and religious involvement can affect health. He is the author of over 300 scholarly papers and is an elected member of the Institute of Medicine and the American Academy of Arts and Sciences. In 2008, he was ranked as the Most Cited Black Scholar in the Social Sciences.

Selina A. Mohammed is an Associate Professor in Nursing and Health Studies at the University of Washington Bothell. Her research interests include examining the impact of racialized discrimination and other structural disadvantages on health, and using critical research methodologies to explore how historical, sociocultural, political, and economic contexts contribute to health inequities, particularly for American Indians. Dr. Mohammed holds a Master of Science in Nursing from the University of Michigan, Master of Public Health from the University of Washington, and Doctor of Philosophy in Nursing Science from the University of Washington.

THE ROOTS OF THE WIDENING RACIAL WEALTH GAP

Explaining the Black-White Economic Divide

Thomas Shapiro, Tatjana Meschede, and Sam Osoro

THOMAS SHAPIRO is Pokross Professor of Law and Social Policy and Director, Institute on Assets and Social Policy at Brandeis University, and **Tatjana Meschede** and **Sam Osoro** are senior research scholars at Brandeis University.

GROWING CONCERNS ABOUT WEALTH INEQUALITY and the expanding racial wealth gap have in recent years become central to the debate over whether our nation is on a sustainable economic path. This report provides critical new information about what has fueled the racial wealth gap and points to policy approaches that will set our country in a more equitable and prosperous direction.

All families need wealth to be economically secure and create opportunities for the next generation. Wealth—what we own minus what we owe—allows families to move forward by moving to better and safer neighborhoods, investing in businesses, saving for retirement, and supporting their children's college aspirations. Having a financial cushion also provides a measure of security when a job loss or other crisis strikes. The Great Recession of 2007–2009 devastated the wealth of all families except for those with the most. The unprecedented wealth destruction during that period, accompanied by long-term high unemployment, underscores the critical importance wealth plays in weathering emergencies and helping families move along a path toward long-term financial security and opportunity.

Extreme wealth inequality not only hurts family well-being, it hampers economic growth in our communities and in the nation as a whole. In the U.S. today, the richest 1 percent of households owns 37 percent of all wealth. This toxic inequality has historical underpinnings but is perpetuated by policies and tax preferences that continue to favor the affluent. Most strikingly, it has resulted in an enormous wealth gap between white households and households of color. In 2009, a representative survey of American households revealed that the median wealth of white families was $113,149 compared with $6,325 for Latino families and $5,677 for black families.[1]

Questions to Consider

There is a saying that the color of America is green (money!). But using income as a way to measure the relative success of racial groups does not, according to these authors, paint an accurate portrait of social inequality or who is likely to achieve the American Dream. In this article the authors look at the racial wealth gap over the past twenty-five years and provide an explanation of why this gap has grown over time. Why do you think the racial wealth gap is so hard to erase?

KEY FINDINGS

1. Tracing the same households over 25 years, the total wealth gap between white and African-American families nearly triples, increasing from $85,000 in 1984 to $236,500 in 2009.

2. The biggest drivers of the growing racial wealth gap are:

   - Years of homeownership

   - Household income

   - Unemployment, which is much more prominent among African-American families

   - A college education

   - Inheritance, financial supports by families or friends, and preexisting family wealth

3. Equal achievements, such as income gains, yield unequal wealth rewards for whites and African-Americans.

Looking at the *same set of families* over a 25-year period (1984–2009), our research offers key insight into how policy and the real, lived experience of families in schools, communities, and at work affect wealth accumulation. Tracing the same households during that period, the total wealth gap between white and African-American families nearly triples, increasing from $85,000 in 1984 to $236,500 in 2009[2] (see Figure 1). To discover the major drivers behind this dramatic $152,000 increase, we tested a wide range of possible explanations, including family, labor market, and wealth characteristics. This allowed us, for the first time, to identify the primary forces behind the racial wealth gap. Our analysis found little evidence to support common perceptions about what underlies the ability to build wealth, including the notion that personal attributes and behavioral choices are key pieces of the equation. Instead, the evidence points to policy and the configuration of both opportunities and barriers in workplaces, schools, and communities that reinforce deeply entrenched racial dynamics in how wealth is accumulated and that continue to permeate the most important spheres of everyday life.

Data for this analysis derived from the Panel Study of Income Dynamics (PSID), a nationally representative longitudinal study that began in 1968. We followed nearly 1,700 working-age households from 1984 through 2009. Tracking these families provides a unique opportunity to understand what happened to the wealth gap over the course of a generation and the effect of policy and institutional decision making on how average families accumulate wealth. Unfortunately, there were not enough data that tracked wealth information in a sufficient number of Latino, Asian American, or immigrant households to include in this report. As a result, the specific focus here is on black-white differences. Yet, while each group shares different histories and experiences, we believe this examination captures important dynamics that can be applied across communities of color.

The wealth trends depicted in Figure 1 beg the question of what caused such dramatic racial wealth inequities. With a gap of close to a quarter of a million dollars, virtually every possible explanation will have some degree of accuracy, no matter how minuscule a factor. The challenge is to identify the major evidence-based factors affecting the growing racial wealth gap. To discover the major drivers behind the $152,000 increase in the racial wealth gap, we tested a wide range of possible explanations

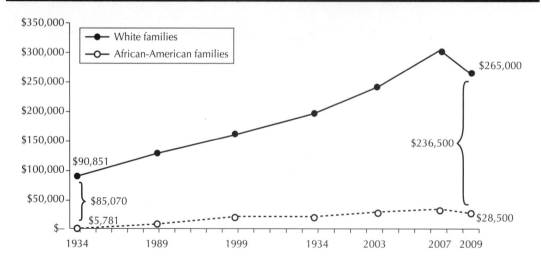

FIGURE 1 ■ Median Net Worth by Race, 1984–2009

that included family, labor market, demographic, and wealth characteristics, and we have determined how different factors affect the widening racial wealth gap over a generation. The compelling evidence-based story is that policy shaping opportunities and rewards where we live, where we learn, and where we work propels the large majority of the widening racial wealth gap.

THE FOUNDATIONS OF INEQUALITY

We started our analysis with an overriding question: Why has economic inequality become so entrenched in our post–Civil Rights era of supposed legal equality? The first step was to identify the critical aspects of contemporary society that are driving this inequality (Figure 2).[3] Next, we sought to determine whether equal accomplishments are producing equal wealth gains for whites and African-Americans (Figure 3).[4] This approach allows for an evidence based examination of whether the growing racial wealth gap is primarily the result of individual choices and cultural characteristics or policies and institutional practices that create different opportunities for increasing wealth in white and black families.

Among households with positive wealth growth[5] during the 25-year study period, as shown in Figure 2, the number of years of homeownership accounts for 27 percent of the difference in relative wealth growth between white and African-American families, the largest portion of the growing wealth gap. The second largest share of the increase, accounting for 20 percent, is average family income. Highly educated households correlate strongly with larger wealth portfolios, but similar college degrees produce more wealth for whites, contributing 5 percent of the proportional increase in the racial wealth gap. Inheritance and financial support from family combine for another 5 percent of the increasing gap. How much wealth a family started out with in 1984 also predicts a portion (3 percent) of family wealth 25 years later.

Unemployment, the only significant factor that depleted wealth since it forced families to draw upon their nest eggs, explains an additional 9 percent of the growing racial wealth gap. In addition to continuing discrimination, labor market instability affects African-Americans more negatively than whites.

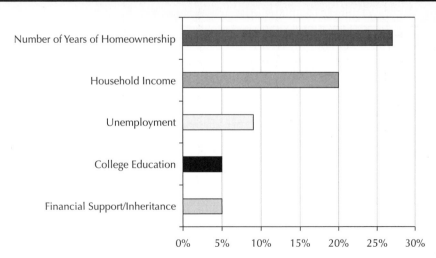

FIGURE 2 ■ What's Driving the Increasing Racial Wealth Gap

The evidence we present to examine the racial wealth gap points to institutional and policy dynamics in important spheres of American life: homeownership, work and increased earnings, employment stability, college education, and family financial support and inheritance. Together, these fundamental factors account for nearly two-thirds (66 percent) of the proportional increase in the wealth gap. In the social sciences, this is a very high level of explanatory power and provides a firm foundation for policy and reform aimed at closing the gap.

THE $152,000 QUESTION: WHAT DROVE THE GROWING GAP?

Having identified the major drivers of the racial wealth gap, we now can dig deeper into each one—homeownership, income, college education, inheritance, and unemployment—to determine how similar accomplishments grow wealth *differentially by race.* Figure 3 provides a close look at how these factors, as well as marriage, which we will discuss later, translate into differences in wealth accumulation for black and white families. We know that wealth increases through accomplishments such as job promotions, pay increases, or the purchase of a home, as well as important life and family events including receiving an inheritance and getting married. Figure 3 highlights how similar accomplishments and life events lead to unequal wealth gains for white and African-American families. The result is that while wealth grew for African-Americans as they achieved life advances, that growth is at a considerably lower rate than it is for whites experiencing the same accomplishments. This leads to an increase in the wealth gap.

Homeownership

The number of years families owned their homes was the largest predictor of the gap in wealth growth by race (Figure 2). Residential segregation by government design has a long legacy in this country and underpins many of the challenges African-American families face in buying homes and increasing equity. There are several reasons why home equity rises so much more for whites than African-Americans:

- Because residential segregation artificially lowers demand, placing a forced ceiling on home equity for AfricanAmericans who own homes in non-white neighborhoods[6];

FIGURE 3 ■ How Wealth Is Accumulated*		
	White Wealth Growth**	**Black Wealth Growth**
Each $1 in Income Increase Yields	$5.19	.69
Each $1 in Inheritance Yields	.91	.20
Each $1 in Family Financial Support Yields	.35	.51
Years of Homeownership	No Significant Impact	Significant Impact
Marriage	Significant Impact	No Significant Impact

*This table shows how key life advances and events (an increase in income, inheritance, family financial support, homeownership and marriage) translate into the ability to increase wealth. Even with equal advances, wealth grows at far lower rates for black households, who typically need to use financial gains for everyday needs rather than long-term savings and assets.

**Regression estimates at the median change in wealth over the 25-year study period conducted separately for white and black households.

- Because whites are far more able to give inheritances or family assistance for down payments due to historical wealth accumulation, white families buy homes and start acquiring equity an average eight years earlier than black families[7];

- Because whites are far more able to give family financial assistance, larger up-front payments by white homeowners lower interest rates and lending costs; and

- Due to historic differences in access to credit, typically lower incomes, and factors such as residential segregation, the homeownership rate for white families is 28.4 percent higher than the homeownership rate for black families.[8]

Homes are the largest investment that most American families make and by far the biggest item in their wealth portfolio. Homeownership is an even greater part of wealth composition for black families, amounting to 53 percent of wealth for blacks and 39 percent for whites.[9] Yet, for many years, redlining, discriminatory mortgage-lending practices, lack of access to credit, and lower incomes have blocked the homeownership path for African-Americans while creating and reinforcing communities segregated by race. African-Americans, therefore, are more recent homeowners and more likely to have high-risk mortgages, hence they are more vulnerable to foreclosure and volatile housing prices.

Figure 1 shows households losing wealth between 2007 and 2009 (12 percent for white families, 21 percent for African-American families), which reflects the destruction of housing wealth resulting from the foreclosure crisis and imploded housing market. Overall, half the collective wealth of African-American families was stripped away during the Great Recession due to the dominant role of home equity in their wealth portfolios and the prevalence of predatory high-risk loans in communities of color. The Latino community lost an astounding 67 percent of its total wealth during the housing collapse.[10]

Unfortunately the end to this story has yet to be written. Since 2007, 10.9 million homes went into foreclosure. While the majority of the affected families are white, borrowers of color are more than twice as likely to lose their homes. These higher foreclosure rates reflect a disturbing reality: borrowers of color were consistently more likely to receive high-interest risky loan products, even after accounting for income and credit scores.[11]

Foreclosures not only have a direct impact on families, they also result in severe collateral damage to surrounding neighborhoods. One report estimates that this collateral destruction led to nearly $2 trillion in lost property wealth for communities across the country. More than half of this loss is associated with communities of color, reflecting concentrations of high-risk loans, subsequent higher foreclosure rates, and volatile housing prices.[12]

While homeownership has played a critical role in the development of wealth for communities of color in this country, the return on investment is far greater for white households, significantly contributing to the expanding racial wealth gap shown in Figure 1. The paradox is that even as homeownership has been the main avenue to building wealth for African-Americans, it has also increased the wealth disparity between whites and blacks.

Income and Employment

Not surprisingly, increases in income are a major source of wealth accumulation for many US families. However, income gains for whites and African-Americans have a very different impact on wealth. At the respective wealth medians, every dollar increase in average income over the 25-year study period added $5.19 wealth[13] for white households (see Figure 3), while the same income gain only added 69 cents of wealth for African American households.

The dramatic difference in wealth accumulation from similar income gains has its roots in long-standing patterns of discrimination in hiring, training, promoting, and access to benefits that have made it much harder for AfricanAmericans to save and build assets. Due to discriminatory factors, black workers predominate in fields that are least likely to have employer-based retirement plans and other benefits, such as administration and support and food services. As a result, wealth in black families tends to be close to what is needed to cover emergency savings while wealth in white families is well beyond the emergency threshold and can be saved or invested more readily.

The statistics cited above compare change in wealth over the 25 years at the median wealth for typical white and black households. Yet we already know that the average white family starts out with abundantly more wealth and significantly higher incomes than the average black family. When whites and blacks start off on an equal playing field with a similar wealth portfolio, their wealth returns from similar income gains narrow considerably.[14] Black families under this scenario see a return of $4.03 for each dollar increase in income—a considerable closing of the wealth breach.

This analysis also captured the devastation of unemployment on wealth accumulation. Unemployment affects all workers but due to the discriminatory factors listed above, black workers are hit harder, more often, and for longer periods of time. With much lower beginning wealth levels and unequal returns on income, it is a greater challenge for African-Americans to grow their family wealth holdings in the face of work instability.

Inheritance

Most Americans inherit very little or no money, but among the families followed for 25 years whites were five times more likely to inherit than African-Americans (36 percent to 7 percent, respectively). Among those receiving an inheritance, whites received about ten times more wealth than African-Americans. Our findings show that inheritances converted to wealth more readily for white than black families: each inherited dollar contributed to 91 cents of wealth for white families compared with 20 cents for African-American families. Inheritance is more likely to add wealth to the considerably larger portfolio whites start out with since blacks, as discussed above, typically need to reserve their wealth for emergency savings.

College Education

In the 21st century, obtaining a college degree is vital to economic success and translates into substantially greater lifetime income and wealth. Education is supposed to be the great equalizer, but current research tells a different story. The achievement and college completion gaps are growing, as family financial resources like income and wealth appear to be large predictors of educational success. While current research identifies a narrowing black-white achievement gap, race and class intersect to widen the educational opportunity deficit at a time when workers without higher-level skills are increasingly likely to languish in the job market.

College readiness is greatly dependent on quality K–12 education. As a result of neighborhood segregation, lower-income students—especially students of color—are too often isolated and concentrated in lower-quality schools. Neighborhoods have grown more segregated, leaving lower-income students—especially students of color—isolated and concentrated in lower-quality schools, and less academically prepared both to enter and complete college. Further, costs at public universities have risen 60 percent in the past two decades, with many low-income and students of color forced to hold down jobs rather than attend college full time and graduating in deep debt. Average student debt for the class of 2011 was $26,600. Student debt is an issue that affects most graduates, but black graduates are far more vulnerable: 80 percent of black students graduate with debt compared with 64 percent of white students.[15] More blacks than whites do not finish their undergraduate studies because financial considerations force them to leave school and earn a steady income to support themselves and their families.[16]

The context of broad class and race educational inequity helps us better understand why a college education produces more wealth for white than black households, accounting for a 5 percent share of the widening racial wealth gap (see Figure 2). In the past 30 years, the gap between students from low- and high-income families who earn bachelor's degrees has grown from 31 percent to 45 percent.[17] Although both groups are completing college at higher rates today, affluent students (predominantly white) improved much more, widening their already sizable lead. In 1972, upper-income Americans spent five times as much per child on college as low-income families. By 2007, the difference in spending between the two groups had grown to nine to one; upper-income families more than doubled how much they spent on each child, while spending by low-income families grew by just 20 percent.[18]

Social and Cultural Factors

As part of this analysis we set out to test notions about the role social and cultural factors play in widening or closing the racial wealth gap. To determine how these factors might affect wealth, we zeroed in on the role of marriage in perpetuating the racial wealth gap. We find that getting married over the 25-year study period significantly increases the wealth holdings for white families by $75,635 but has no statistically significant impact on African-Americans. Single whites are much more likely to possess positive net worth, most likely due to benefits from substantial family financial assistance, higher paying jobs, and homeownership. Hence, marriages that combine modest wealth profiles seem to move whites past emergency-level savings to opportunities to invest and build wealth.

By contrast, marriage among African-Americans typically combines two comparatively low-level wealth portfolios and, unlike white households, does not significantly elevate the family's wealth. While the number of household wage earners bringing in resources does correlate to higher wealth, the impact of marriage is not statistically significant for blacks and the reality is that most do not marry out of the racial wealth gap.

CLOSING THE RACIAL WEALTH GAP

Public policy can play a critical role in creating a more equitable society and helping all Americans build wealth. College loans, preferential homeownership, and retirement tax policies helped build opportunities and wealth for America's middle class. Medicare and Social Security have protected that wealth. While the bold vision of policymakers, advocates, and others interested in social and racial justice is needed to develop a precise policy agenda,

we believe the following broad public policy and institutional changes are critical to closing the gap:

- **Homeownership**—The data in this report clearly target homeownership as the biggest driver of the racial wealth gap. We need to ensure that mortgage and lending policies and fair housing policies are enforced and strengthened so that the legacy of residential segregation no longer confers greater wealth opportunities to white homeowners than it does to black homeowners. As our nation moves towards a majority people of color population, increasingly diverse neighborhoods must deliver equitable opportunities for growing home equity.

- **Income**—This report identifies the importance of stable, family-supporting jobs and increasing incomes as a prime avenue for building wealth. To address the gap caused by income disparity, proven tools should be fully implemented at the national, state, and local levels, including raising the minimum wage, enforcing equal pay provisions, and strengthening employer-based retirement plans and other benefits.

- **Education**—It is clear that differential educational opportunities and rewards are further widening the racial wealth gap. We need to invest in affordable high-quality childcare and early childhood development so every child is healthy and prepared for school. We need to support policies that help more students from low- and moderate-income families and families of color attend college and graduate. And we need to value education as a public good and invest in policies that do not leave students strapped with huge debt or a reason to drop out.

- **Inheritance**—Due to the unearned advantages it transmits across generations, inheritance widens inequality and is a key driver of the racial wealth gap. If we truly value merit and not unearned preferences, then we need to diminish the advantages passed along to a small number of families. Preferential tax treatment for large estates costs taxpayers and provides huge benefits to less than 1 percent of the population while diverting vital resources from schools, housing, infrastructure, and jobs. Preferential tax treatment for dividends and interest is weighted toward wealthy investors as are the home mortgage deduction and tax-shielding benefits from retirement savings.

It is time for a portfolio shift in public investment to grow wealth for all, not just a tiny minority. Without that shift the wealth gap between white and black households has little prospect of significantly narrowing. A healthy, fair, and equitable society cannot continue to follow such an economically unsustainable trajectory.

Seeing the Big Picture   The Color of Money

Section VI in the appendix lists households making more than $250,000 and those in poverty, which the government defined in 2018 as $24,600 for a family of four. Using these two income categories as your reference points and the categories discussed by the authors, explain how racial intergenerational economic disparities continue.

RELATED IASP PUBLICATIONS

"The Racial Wealth Gap Increases Fourfold," May 2010, by Thomas Shapiro, Tatjana Meschede, and Laura Sullivan

"The Crisis of Economic Insecurity for African-American and Latino Seniors," September 2011, by Tatjana Meschede, Laura Sullivan, and Thomas Shapiro

"Severe Financial Insecurity Among African-American and Latino Seniors," May 2010, by Tatjana Meschede, Thomas Shapiro, Laura Sullivan, and Jennifer Wheary

SPECIAL ACKNOWLEDGMENT

A special thanks to the Ford Foundation for their continued partnership and dedication to worldwide social change and to Amy Saltzman, Anand Subramanian, Anne Price, Solana Rice, and Milly Hawk Daniel for their insightful contributions to this research brief.

8

DEFINING RACE

Comparative Perspectives

F. James Davis

F. JAMES DAVIS is professor emeritus of sociology at Illinois State University. Dr. Davis conducted research for the Air Force at the University of Washington during the years 1951–1952. He is the author of the classic work *Who Is Black? One Nation's Definition*, as well as *Society and the Law*, *Social Problems*, and *Minority-Dominant Relations*.

A BLACK PERSON IN THE UNITED STATES HAS long been defined as a person with any known African black ancestry, no matter how little or how distant. The aphorism for this so-called one-drop rule is that "one drop of black blood makes you black." So deeply rooted in the American psyche is this rule that a person can have predominantly white ancestry and even look white, yet unquestionably be defined as black. Such people as Halle Berry, Lena Horne, Julian Bond, or Muhammad Ali come to mind. Is it any wonder that foreign visitors and television viewers have trouble understanding why we define such people as black? No other nation defines blacks in this way, and our one-drop rule does not apply to any minority other than African Americans.

Walter White, president of the National Association for the Advancement of Colored People (NAACP) from 1931 to 1955, had blue eyes, blond hair, and fair skin, and his ancestry was no more than one sixty-fourth African black (Ottley 1943). He had been raised in Georgia in the black community and had been subjected to white discrimination and violence (White 1948). He passed as white in order to investigate lynchings in the Jim Crow South. White's second marriage, to a brunette white woman, provoked outrage from the black press for his betrayal. He had married outside the black community, across the ethnic barrier. When the White family made an international goodwill tour and were publicized as an interracial couple, White was often asked how he happened to marry a black woman (Cannon 1956).

A former law professor, now a university president, grew up in a white, middle-class neighborhood in Virginia and had always thought he was white until he was ten years old. He certainly looks white. His father, after a financial collapse and a broken marriage, took him and his younger brother to live in his home community in Muncie, Indiana, in the 1950s. While en route there by bus, their father told the boys that he had passed as white and they would be living in a black neighborhood. There the boys were discriminated against and harassed by both whites and blacks. Against all odds, this older brother's abilities, both in the classroom and in athletics, enabled him to achieve outstanding success. When asked why he does not pass as white, he answers that he has been taught through bitter experience that in the United States he is black (G. H. Williams 1995).

Although there are average differences in visible physical traits in human populations, there are no pure races. When I use the term "unmixed African black," I mean someone whose entire ancestry derives from populations in sub-Saharan Africa. Originally the term "mulatto" meant half African black and half white, but it came to mean any degree of mixture. Often people now say that a child of an African American and a white is "half and half," which correctly describes the child's racial background. However, one such child may have a parent whose ancestry is three-fourths African, whereas another's is one-fourth. The ancestry of the first child would be three-eighths black, the second one-eighth. Regardless of the ancestral fractions and physical appearances, both children are black under the American one-drop rule. Due to strong social conditioning, most light-hued African Americans identify themselves as black, but as we shall see, some do not.

Because of the one-drop rule, mixed offspring with any African ancestry are assigned to the black community. The result of over 350 years of **miscegenation** in the United States is a "new people," derived predominantly from African black populations but with a large infusion of genes from European whites and a substantial amount from Native Americans (Reed 1969; Williamson 1980). Estimates of the number of African Americans who have some white ancestry range from three-fourths to above 90 percent, and as many as one-fourth

Questions to Consider

For most of U.S. history the "one-drop" rule defined someone as black if he or she had a single "drop" of black blood—that is, any African ancestry. This "rule" was designed to maintain white supremacy by keeping the color line rigid and guaranteed there would be a constant source of slaves even after the importation of enslaved Africans was banned in 1808 (slavery wouldn't end until 1865). Professor F. James Davis makes the point that for many in the United States the law of hypodescent placed individuals within the black community even if they did not phenotypically "look" black. What Professor Davis brings to light is that there are many other identities (he outlines six) that mixed-race individuals occupy. Are these categories still relevant today?

---

miscegenation The social and intimate "mixing" of different racial groups and the children resulting from such unions.

have Native American ancestry. The color spectrum in the black community ranges from ebony to lighter than most whites, and other visible physical traits show a similar range of variation.

The one-drop rule is unique in the world because it has resulted from our particular experiences with slavery and racial segregation in the United States. The social statuses and identities of racially mixed people are determined by group power dynamics, just as those of their parent groups are. The varying social structures and histories of societies around the globe have produced sharply contrasting status positions and terms of identity for mixed-race people. Seven different status positions are identified here to help readers gain perspective on current issues of racial identity in the United States. First, we need to examine further the development and effects of the one-drop rule.

THE HYPODESCENT STATUS

Anthropologists call our one-drop rule a hypodescent rule because mixed black/white children are assigned the status position of the lower status parent group—that of blacks. Evidently this first occurred in the mid-1600s in the Chesapeake area of Maryland and Virginia, where miscegenation between white indentured servants and slaves from Africa became widespread. The mixed persons generally were assigned the status of slaves and the same racial identity as African blacks (Williamson 1980). By the early 1700s, the one-drop rule had become the social definition of a black person in the upper South, and from there it spread southward.

Also in the 1600s, a competitor to the one-drop rule emerged. In Louisiana and South Carolina, free mulattoes came to have an in-between, buffer status. These free mulattoes were allied with whites and not considered to be blacks (Williamson 1980). Until the 1840s in South Carolina, mulattoes could become white by behavior and reputation and could marry into white families (Catterall 1926–1937). Louisiana also rejected the one-drop rule, accepting

miscegenation and the intermediate status of mulattoes until 1808, when the Louisiana Civil Code prohibited "free people of color" from marrying either whites or blacks (Dominguez 1986).

In a number of states before the Civil War, there were court cases in which persons who had as much African ancestry as one-fourth were declared to be white. The United States had not yet lined up solidly behind the one-drop rule. Finally in the 1850s, in order to preserve slavery, the South came together in firm support of the one-drop rule (Williamson 1980). Although the competing rule was put down, for several decades there were statutes and court decisions that limited the definition of a black person to at least one-fourth, one-eighth, or some other fraction of ancestry.

The Civil War and Reconstruction accelerated the alienation of mulattoes from whites, who made it clear that mulattoes of all shades would be defined as blacks. The one-drop rule gained support in the North as well as the South and was further strengthened at the turn of the twentieth century by the passage of Jim Crow laws in the southern states. These segregation laws were reinforced by extralegal threats and terrorism. Light blacks were as likely as darker ones to pay the ultimate price for alleged violations of the master-servant etiquette for "getting out of their place" (Vander Zanden 1972). The lynching of blacks peaked from 1885 to 1909, and the peak of passing also occurred during this period, although most of those who could pass permanently did not do so (Burma 1946; Eckard 1947). By World War I, the one-drop rule was backed uniformly by US whites.

The one-drop rule was crucial to maintaining Jim Crow segregation, in which widespread miscegenation, not racial "purity," prevailed. The racial double standard of sexual relations gave white men access to black women but protected white women from black men. The entire system of white domination would be threatened by a mixed child living in a white home. Mixed children fathered by white males, defined as black by the one-drop rule, stayed with the mother in the black community (Blaustein and Ferguson 1957; Myrdal, Sterner, and Rose 1944; Rose 1956). US senator Theodore Bilbo of Mississippi trumpeted in a 1947 book that protecting white women from black men was preventing "**mongrelization**," keeping the white race pure (Bilbo 1947).

By 1925, the African American community had fully accepted the one-drop rule and was giving it strong support. The black community had developed a vested interest in a rule used for centuries to preserve slavery and legalized segregation. The rule had forced all shades of mixed persons into the black community, where, over time, white oppression and other common experiences created a common culture and a sense of ethnic unity and pride. Lighter mulattoes, discriminated against and terrorized by whites, allied themselves more firmly than ever with blacks. Many leaders of the Harlem Renaissance of the 1920s, including Langston Hughes and A. Philip Randolph, were light mulattoes.

The civil rights movement of the 1950s and 1960s put an end to the Jim Crow laws and saw major civil rights legislation passed in Washington, D.C. At the same time, white backlash to the movement strengthened African American support for the one-drop rule. In the 1960s, lighter blacks often felt heavy pressure to affirm their blackness (Williamson 1980). In 1972, the National Association of Black Social Workers (NABSW) strongly endorsed the one-drop rule by passing a resolution against the adoption of black children by white parents (Day 1979). Rejecting the terms "biracial" and "racially mixed," the Association insisted that mixed children be taught to acknowledge their blackness and raised to survive as blacks (Ladner 1977). By the mid-1970s, "cross-racial" adoption had almost stopped, and by 1987, thirty-five or more states had a policy against it. Although the issue has been revived, the NABSW has not changed its position.

In general the one-drop rule has had the support of law. The rule was challenged often in court in the nineteenth century and earlier but not much in the twentieth. State laws defining who is black in terms of fractions of ancestry, or an explicit one-drop rule, have generally been rescinded in recent decades. However, the courts have not invalidated

the one-drop rule. In 1983, the rule was upheld by a district court in Louisiana in a lawsuit brought by Susie Phipps (*Jane Doe v. Louisiana*), whose application for a passport was denied because she checked "white" as her race. She looks white, had always lived as white, and thought she was white (Trillin 1986). Lawyers for the state produced evidence that Mrs. Phipps was three thirty-seconds black, and by a 1970 statute, one thirty-second was enough. Before 1970, a "traceable amount" was enough in Louisiana. In 1986 the US Supreme Court refused to review this decision on the ground that no substantial federal question was involved (107 Sup.Ct.Reporter, interim ed. 638). Louisiana has abolished the one thirty-second criterion, but its courts have not ruled against the one-drop rule.

Despite the general support for the one-drop rule by both whites and blacks, there are long-standing examples of rejection of it in both communities (Daniel 1992). Some of the African American children adopted by whites and some children of mixed marriages are socialized to reject the black-only identity. Many Creoles of color in New Orleans and vicinity still reject both the black and the white identity (Dominguez 1986: 163–164). Many Hispanic Americans with some black ancestry resist the rule if they can and embrace a Latino identity. Although a majority of Puerto Rican immigrants have some African ancestry, few of them were identified as black when they were still on the island (Jorge 1979).

Native Americans with some African ancestry generally try to avoid the one-drop rule, usually by staying on a reservation (Bennett 1962). Those who leave the reservation are often treated as blacks. In Virginia, persons who are one-fourth or more Native American and less than one-sixteenth African black have been defined as Indians while on the reservation but as blacks when they leave (Berry 1965). States and tribes differ in their definitions of who is Indian. Some 200 small triracial communities have long evaded the rule by remaining isolated (Berry 1963).

The most common response to deviations from the rule in both the black and the white communities is to condemn the deviations and affirm the rule. Deviant acts and rhetoric call attention to a violated rule and can strengthen the consensus

---

mongrelization Used as a pejorative, a blending of different populations as a result of widespread miscegenation.

that supports it (Durkheim 1960). For most African Americans of all hues, apparently, the rule gets such constant reinforcement that it provides a clear sense of black ethnic identity. After the US Census Bureau offered respondents the opportunity to designate their own race in 1960, the percentage who checked "black" did not decline significantly.

Problems engendered by the rule, some of them painfully distressing, are borne primarily by the black community. Public concern about these problems does not rise very high because the one-drop rule is so taken for granted by both blacks and whites. All the problems stem from defining as black a mixed population with a rainbow of physical characteristics. The ambiguity of the racial identity of very light blacks often leads to everyday strains and embarrassments, even to traumatic experiences and deep dilemmas of identity.

The rule has other costs, including conflicts in black families and communities over differences in color, hair, and other traits. Darker and "nappier" blacks often receive stinging criticism of their appearance, and the lightest ones are also often harassed and humiliated (Gwaltney 1980). As filmmaker Spike Lee has shown in *School Daze* and later in *Jungle Fever,* intense conflicts among blacks over color and hair accompany dating, sexual relations, and marriage. Color discrimination among blacks also occurs in the workplace, in the media, and elsewhere (Russell, Wilson, and Hall 1992). Is discrimination based on racial traits not a violation of civil rights laws?

Among still other problems are collective anxieties of whites about "invisible blackness" (Williamson 1980) and of blacks about persons who "deny their color." Many white parents of mixed children worry about the suppression of their white ancestry. There is profound anxiety about the rare resort to passing to gain opportunities. There are complex administrative and legal problems in implementing the one-drop rule. The rule causes gross misperceptions of the racial classification of very large populations in Asia, the Middle East, Latin America, and elsewhere. It poses problems of sampling and interpretation in medical and scientific research on racial differences (Davis 1991).

Elsewhere in the world, persons whose ancestry is part African black are perceived as mixed, not as just black. However, the status positions of mixed-race persons vary greatly from one society to another, reflecting different group power dynamics. We now examine six other status and identity positions.

THE IN-BETWEEN STATUS

Remember that the one-drop rule assigns to mixed-race persons the identical status position occupied by the lower status parent group. A second rule assigns persons of mixed heritage a status between that of the parent groups, as occupied by the mulattoes of South Carolina and Louisiana before 1850. Such groups are seen as marginal to both parent groups, but often there is a firmer tie with one than the other. Some middle groups develop a strong separate identity.

Many, if not most, in-between minorities, whether racial hybrid groups or not, meet special occupational needs the dominant community is unable or unwilling to meet. "Middleman minorities," as the economists call them, may or may not have had previous experience with such work. Often the work is onerous, highly stigmatized, or very risky, or it involves long hours. This in-between group serves as a buffer between the groups above and below it. Political and economic changes, especially when they eliminate the group's special occupations, can have drastic consequences for the middle minority. When crises come, the dominant group rarely protects the middle group from the animosity of lower-status groups (Blalock 1967). The vulnerability of the middle minority is especially great when it is occupied by a mixed-race group because of special problems with identity and group acceptance.

Under the apartheid system in the Republic of South Africa, there were two buffer groups between the dominant whites and the native blacks: the Asians and the Coloureds. This system of fourfold segregation was legalized in 1948 (Van den Berghe 1971) and lasted for half a century. During the prolonged crisis that preceded the downfall of the system and of white domination in 1994, the two buffer groups experienced much harassment and violence. Major adjustments in group statuses in recent years are complex and have been proceeding with much less conflict than was expected.

The definitions of the four "race groups" in South Africa remain essentially as they were under the apartheid system. Blacks are unmixed Africans. South African whites often explain who the Coloureds are by saying they are not black and not Asian. Coloureds are any "mixed-blood" persons, including children and descendants of black/Asian and white/Asian unions, not just those of black/white and black/Coloured unions. The bulk of the Coloureds are mulattoes, ranging from very dark to very light, and thus are very similar to most African Americans. Under apartheid, both legal and informal controls were designed to prevent or punish all white/nonwhite sexual contacts, not just those involving white women. There was no double standard. White men were punished as severely for white/nonwhite sexual contacts as black, Asian, and Coloured men were.

Under apartheid, passing as white was facilitated by the infinite gradations of racial traits among the Coloureds, with many mixed persons appearing white. However, far from being secret as in the United States, passing was open, legalized, and administered by a complex bureaucracy. Passing required official reclassification to a different "racial" category, usually from Coloured to white. Some individuals and couples were reclassified more than once, and different members of a family were sometimes classified differently (Watson 1970). Such reclassification could not occur under a one-drop rule.

BOTTOM OF THE LADDER

By a third rule, persons of mixed race are assigned a status lower than that of either parent group. Not accepted on equal terms by either of the parent race groups, such people are defined as a separate and lowly people, as outcasts. In East Africa, mulattoes among the Ganda peoples of Uganda are regarded with condescension and contempt by the Ganda and not accepted by the English or other whites. For a time there was discussion of a plan to remove all the mulattoes to an island in Lake Victoria where they could be completely isolated (Berry 1965). A

similar position is occupied by the metis in Canada, the Anglo-Indians in India, Korean Americans in Korea, and Vietnamese Americans in Vietnam.

The metis population originated in the seventeenth century from unions in the Canadian wilderness between Indian women and French and Scottish trappers. At first, the children were called metis if they spoke French, or "half-breeds" if they spoke English, but eventually all racial hybrids were known as metis. They were regarded as neither white nor Indian. They felt superior to the Indians and would not marry them. They became valued middlemen—buffalo hunters, interpreters, and transporters of supplies and furs by canoe or carts. They plummeted from middle to bottom-of-the-ladder status when white settlement and the coming of the railroads in the latter half of the nineteenth century ended the need for their special occupations.

After the metis rebelled against the Canadian government in 1879 and 1884, they dispersed throughout the Canadian West, despised by whites and Indians alike. Some managed to get accepted on Indian reservations, but most lived as outcasts in poor, isolated areas or moved to towns and cities to become an urban underclass. There may be as many as 750,000 metis now in Canada, more than the number of full Indians. They remain a broken, desperately poor people.

Similarly, the mixed Anglo-Indian population in India went from a relatively secure middle minority status under British colonial rule to a precarious and lowly position, especially after India became independent in 1947 (Gist and Dean 1973). Anthropologists classify South Asians as "Hindu Caucasoids," but the British consider all dark-skinned "native peoples" to be nonwhite, and race is what people believe it to be. There is no place for "mixed-blood" people in the Hindu caste tradition (Ballhatchet 1980). Many Anglo-Indians fled to Australia or England as Indian nationalism grew (Berry 1965), but around a quarter of a million remain in India. Caste has been legally abolished, but the traditions still have force, and the Eurasians remain a despised out-group.

Thousands of Korean American children were born to women in Korea during the Korean War, some fathered by white servicemen and some by African Americans, and many more have been born since. Mixed children face extreme difficulties in Korea, where there is a strong prejudice against marrying someone of a different racial or ethnic group. Citizenship there is paternal, so the mixed children have been defined not as Koreans but as Americans. Children of American males are not granted US citizenship if born out of wedlock outside the United States. The great majority of the children thus have had no country and have been denied the rights of Korean citizens. These children are seen as debased and polluted, and some Korean families have refused to accept them. Mixed children under fifteen years of age can be adopted if the mothers give them up and register them with the Korean government as orphans.

The 80,000 or so mixed children fathered in Vietnam by white and black American military personnel during the war there are called the "dust of life" and treated with contempt. They are virtual outcasts in their own society, where, as in Korea, the child's identity and citizenship rights derive from the father. The US approach to this contrasts sharply with that of the French, who took 25,000 mixed children with them when they left in 1954 and offered them French citizenship. In 1982, the United States began allowing the mixed children to emigrate, provided that Americans adopt the younger ones and sponsor the older ones. Although many of these mixed children in both Vietnam and Korea have been adopted in the United States in recent years, most of them and their descendants remain lowly outcasts (Valverde 1992).

TOP OF THE LADDER

Sometimes racially mixed people have achieved a higher status than that of either parent group, as experienced by the mulattoes of Haiti, Liberia, and Namibia, and the mestizos of Mexico (Nicholls 1981; Stoddard 1973). The two examples discussed here required a successful political revolution. In the wealthy French colony on Saint Domingue (Hispaniola), later called Haiti, a slave named Toussaint L'Ouverture began a revolution in 1791 that ended slavery. Previously there had been some 30,000 whites exercising extremely harsh control over half a million black slaves, with about 24,000 free blacks and mulattoes occupying an in-between status. After the rebels achieved independence in 1804, the mulattoes emerged as the economically and politically dominant elites and retained their ascendancy for more than a century and a half. They maintained tight kinship ties among mulatto families, preventing intermarriage with both whites and African blacks. They looked down on both unmixed Africans and the small white population, although the Lebanese, Syrians, and other whites performed valuable middle minority commercial functions (Nicholls 1981). The mulattoes lost control to the Duvalier regime in 1957, later regained it, and lost it again, and the volatile struggle for political power goes on.

The Spanish ruled Mexico for three centuries. During the long colonial period, there was massive miscegenation between the Spanish and Indian populations and some that involved African blacks. At first the term "mestizo" meant half-Spanish and half-Indian, but it came to refer to the entire mixed population, regardless of the degree of mixture. Under Spanish rule, mestizos occupied a middle status position, with Indians on the bottom. The mestizos took pride in their Spanish ancestry and played down their Indian backgrounds (Stoddard 1973). Mestizos became the rulers when Spanish control was overthrown in 1821, and today they are by far the largest group in Mexico. Some Spanish and other whites have retained considerable wealth and influence, but political power remains chiefly in mestizo hands. The overwhelming size of the mestizo group would appear to be a major factor in its political dominance, yet in Haiti the mulatto elites retained control for a long time with relatively small numbers.

HIGHLY VARIABLE STATUS: LATIN AMERICA

Under a fourth rule, mixed-race persons are assigned a status that may vary from quite low to very high, depending more on education and wealth than on color or other racial traits. In Brazil and lowland Latin America generally, the upper class is called white, but it also includes light mulattoes and mestizos. The middle class is a long ladder with many rungs and is composed mainly of mulattoes, although in some countries it also includes many mestizos. The lower class includes most of the unmixed blacks and Indians, along with a few whites and some mulattoes and mestizos.

Race influences class placement, but it is only one factor, and it may be overcome by wealth and education. A plethora of terms is used for the innumerable gradations of racial mixture, but the color designations depend more on the place on the class ladder than on actual racial traits. As people use educational and economic success to climb the class ladder, their racial designations often change. No secrecy is needed to "pass" to another racial identity (Wagley 1963).

Latin Americans can accept light mulattoes and mestizos as whites, referring to any visible traces of African traits in such euphemistic terms as "brunette" or "a little mulatto" (Solaun and Kronus 1973). In Brazil it is class rather than racial discrimination that is pervasive, sharp, and persistent, even involving class-segregated public facilities and a class-based master–servant etiquette (Harris 1964). The expression "money whitens" indicates that class can have more weight than physical traits in determining racial classification. Census estimates of the number of people in different racial categories can be very misleading when compared with the estimates in the United States or other nations.

In Puerto Rico, as in Latin America generally, miscegenation of whites, native Indians, and African blacks has produced the entire range of skin color and other racial features. A substantial proportion of the mixed population is considered white, including many who are quite dark. Individuals are allowed some choice and room to negotiate for a racial identity (Dominguez 1986). Around 10 percent of Puerto Rican migrants to the United States are unmixed blacks, and half or more of the remainder have some African ancestry. Therefore, some three-fifths of the migrants are perceived as black in the United States, whereas on the island most of them were known either as whites or by one of the many color designations

other than black. It comes as a shock to the majority of the migrants to be defined as black in the United States. Some manage to become known as Hispanic whites by emphasizing their Spanish language and heritage, but others fail. Parents in the Puerto Rican immigrant community pressure their young to "whiten" the family in order to succeed, which puts them in conflict with the African American community.

On the Caribbean islands colonized by the Spanish and Portuguese, Iberian whites have readily married lighter mulattoes with visible African traits. Iberian colonists brought with them an ideal image of beauty known as Morena (meaning Moorish) and the acceptance of marriage with mulattoes. By contrast, whites on the Caribbean islands colonized by the English, French, and Dutch have accepted intermarriage only with those mulattoes who look white (Hoetink 1967). It is appearance that counts, however, not known African ancestry, so there is no one-drop rule. The Iberian approach seems to be the general rule in southern Europe and the Near and Middle East. The intermarriage rule on the English, French, and Dutch islands was brought from northern Europe. The one-drop rule is not inherent in British culture, then, or in northwestern Europe generally. It emerged on US soil.

EGALITARIAN PLURALISM FOR THE RACIALLY MIXED: HAWAI'I

As in Latin America, the status of mixed-race people in Hawai'i can range from quite low to very high, depending on educational and economic achievement. However, color and other racial traits do not affect the class placement in Hawai'i as they do to some extent in Latin America. There is no preoccupation with race in Hawai'i and no color ladder with a preferred hue at the top. Hawai'i has a long tradition of treating the racially mixed in an egalitarian manner that contrasts sharply with the hypodescent status on the US mainland. Despite the eventual wresting of political and economic power from the original Hawaiians by US economic interests in the 1890s, the competitive struggles and occasional conflicts have essentially been those of class and ethnicity, not race.

The Polynesian settlers in the Hawaiian Islands some 1,500 years ago were probably a racial blend of Mongoloid peoples from Southeast Asia and Caucasoid stocks from Indonesia and South Asia (Howard 1980). Further miscegenation with many different peoples began when the first **haoles** (non-Polynesians) came. Captain Cook found in 1778 that Hawaiian hospitality included openness to sexual relations and marriage with outsiders. The haoles never stopped coming, first for a way station for the fur trade; next for sandalwood; then for whales; then for sugarcane, pineapples, and other agricultural products; and finally as tourists. Many white traders and planters took Hawaiian wives, and eventually some of the children of Congregational missionaries from New England took native Hawaiian wives.

The demand for sugarcane workers escalated in the 1850s, and large numbers were brought from China and later from Portugal, other European countries, and Japan. By 1900 the Japanese were the largest ethnic group in Hawai'i. Migrants then came from Puerto Rico, Korea, and the Philippines. Still later, more came from South and East Asia, other Pacific Islands, Mexico, the Middle East, Europe, the United States, and elsewhere. Miscegenation never stopped. By 1930 there were more part-Hawaiians than unmixed ones, and by 1960 nine times as many. By the 1970s, Hawaiians and part-Hawaiians (one-eighth or more) were not quite one-fifth of the population, behind whites and Japanese (Howard 1980: 449–451). Native chiefs had made overly generous trade concessions and had lost much of their land. Revival of traditional culture began in the 1970s, along with charges of past and present discrimination against Hawaiians and part-Hawaiians by wealthy whites and other haole groups. This has been an ethnic and class protest, not a racial one. Clearly the native Hawaiians have been badly exploited, but the basis for it has been greed, not racism. The rhetoric of racist ideology is absent.

There has been no systematic racial segregation and discrimination, either de jure or de facto, and the various peoples in Hawai'i generally are scornful of anyone who exhibits racial prejudice. Many of the Pacific Island peoples are relatively dark-skinned, and the class status of the mixed people in Hawai'i seems to be unaffected by color or other racial traits. Ethnic and racial intermarriages are common, and many people can identify ancestry in several groups. It is considered bad manners to express disapproval of miscegenation. The tolerant, egalitarian balance of pluralism and assimilation extends to racially mixed persons, whose status is no lower or higher than that of the parent groups involved. The first racial hybrids in Hawai'i were highly respected, and this model has had a lasting impact (Adams 1969; Berry 1965).

ASSIMILATING MINORITY STATUS

The seventh rule accounts for the status of persons in the United States who are partly descended from racial minorities other than African American. The children of the first generation of miscegenation may experience ambiguity or be identified as members of the minority group. However, when the proportion of minority ancestry becomes one-fourth or less in the next generation of mixture, the children are accepted unambiguously as assimilating Americans. There is no need for them to "pass" in order to hide the minority background. In fact, they can be proud of having ancestry that is part Native American, Mexican, Chinese, Japanese, Filipino, Vietnamese, or other Asian, and they find little opposition to intermarriage with whites. There is no one-drop rule to deter their further miscegenation and full assimilation into the dominant Anglo-American community.

For many decades, Chinese immigrants in the United States were despised and did not have the benefit of the status of an assimilating minority. Neither did the earlier Japanese Americans, especially during the days of their relocation to prison camps as enemy aliens during World War II. The operating rule was that everyone with one-eighth or more Japanese ancestry was to be removed to the

---

haoles The Hawaiian word for whites.

camps. Since the Japanese had been immigrating to the United States only since 1885, this one-eighth criterion was a sure way to intern everyone with any known Japanese ancestry (T. K. Williams 1996). During the war years, then, what was in effect a one-drop rule was used for Japanese Americans.

The foregoing comparative discussion dramatizes the uniqueness of America's one-drop rule. It also shows that the status occupied by mixed-race people in a society can change in response to major shifts in racial group power relations. Experiences in other societies can provide valuable perspective on current issues about racial identity and the one-drop rule. They also suggest the need for caution in extrapolating to other societies the findings on the dynamics of the personal identity of mixed-race people in the United States.

THE MULTIRACIAL IDENTITY MOVEMENT

In recent years, new challenges to the one-drop rule have emerged. In the 1980s and 1990s, a movement to allow mixed-race persons to adopt a biracial or multiracial identity rapidly gained momentum. Campus groups were organized at many colleges and universities. A national organization called the Association of Multiethnic Americans (AMEA) was created to coordinate groups in thirty or more cities (Grosz 1989). The emphasis, rather than a frontal attack on the one-drop rule, has been on the freedom to acknowledge all of one's ancestries, including black (Nakashima 1992). The movement includes all racial blends, not just those with African black ancestry.

Mixed-race people with no black ancestry, although not subject to a one-drop rule, have been well aware that the rule for blacks has been responsible for the "check only one" instruction. Until the 2000 census, this rendered persons with Native American, Mexican, Asian, or Pacific Islander forebears unable to acknowledge two or more ancestries. Mexican Americans, the majority of whom are mestizos, had to check "black," "white," or "other." In 1990, 48 percent of them checked "other," and 97 percent of all Americans who checked "other" were Hispanics, who may be of any race or blend.

The marked increase in interracial marriages, although still a small proportion of all marriages, is one argument for recognizing the multiracial identity. The trend that began in the 1960s has accelerated, especially since the *Loving* case, in which the US Supreme Court in 1967 held the Virginia statute prohibiting interracial marriage to be unconstitutional. From 1970 to 1991, mixed-race marriages in the United States tripled. During this same period, births for one black and one white parent increased more than fivefold, and increases almost this large occurred in marriages involving one white and one Asian-American parent (Page 1996).

The vast majority of black/white sexual unions over 350 years have not had the benefit of marriage and have involved white males and black females. By contrast, a large majority of black/white marriages in recent decades have been between a black man and a white woman. One estimate is that at least 30 percent of these couples want to identify their children as biracial or multiracial. Many of these wives do not want their children to have to deny their mother's ancestry.

The multiracial identity movement has faced determined opposition. Many blacks fear that persons who want to affirm their European, Native American, or Asian ancestry want to deny their African roots. There is also fear that the movement will divide the black community, reduce its numbers, weaken black political power, and undermine civil rights remedies (Daniel 1992). Some fear that whites want to create a buffer class with a status above that of blacks or a system of "colorism" like the one in lowland Latin America.

Despite the opposition, the movement has had some successes. PROJECT RACE (Reclassify All Children Equally) has persuaded a number of states to require the multiracial option on some official forms, and school districts in several states have added the option (Graham 1995). In 1993, both PROJECT RACE and the AMEA testified in favor of the multiracial option before the Subcommittee on Census, Statistics, and Postal Personnel of the US House of Representatives. These organizations later gave similar testimony to the US Office of Management and

Budget (OMB), which defines racial categories for all levels of government in the country, including the public schools (Fernandez 1995).

The policy debate centered mainly on the possible use of the multiracial category on the Census Bureau forms for 2000, an option strongly opposed by the NAACP and other black leaders (Daniel 2000). The OMB decided to reject the multiracial category but to change the traditional instruction, "check only one," to "check one or more." This compromise was approved by the NAACP, the Urban League, the Congressional Black Caucus, and other black groups (Daniel 2000). Although it was only a partial victory for the multiracial identity movement, the federal government had finally acknowledged the reality of multiple racial ancestries. To counter the fears of civil rights leaders, the OMB instruction was that persons who check "white" and any minority race are to be counted as members of that minority for the purpose of enforcing civil rights laws. Also, the term "multiracial" was not to be used in interpreting the responses. The plan received unanimous support from thirty federal agencies and was adopted for the collection of all governmental data on race, not just census data (Lew 2000).

The percentage of Americans who checked more than one race in the 2000 census was 2.3. That percentage varies according to age group, however. Among African Americans over the age of fifty, 2.3 percent checked more than one race. However, for blacks eighteen years of age or younger, the percentage was 8.3. This age difference is probably due in part to the increase in the number of young interracial parents, in part to the multiracial identity movement, but also to the public rejection of the one-drop rule by a number of black celebrities. These rejections have been a prominent part of the increased publicity about mixed-race experiences in the past two decades. Issues of identity have been featured in books, articles, films, and newscasts and on talk shows.

One of the most dramatic news stories of the 1990s was the DNA testing that showed the high likelihood that Thomas Jefferson was the father of the last son of his slave Sally Hemmings (Foster 1998). Alex Haley's 1976 book *Roots* and the television series based on it had demonstrated how fully both African Americans and whites accept the one-drop rule. It seemed perfectly natural for Haley to pursue his African roots. In his 1993 book *Queen,* however, Haley focused on his white-appearing grandmother, played by Halle Berry in the television series. In 1990, when Renee Tenison was hailed as the first black woman to be Playboy's "Playmate of the Year," she protested that it was unfair for her to have to deny her white mother (Russell, Wilson, and Hall 1992). When Chelsi Smith was portrayed as the first black winner of the Miss USA pageant in 1995, she insisted that she is both black and white. (The first black winner was actually Carole Gist, in 1990.) It seems unlikely that such celebrities would so publicly reject the one-drop rule without the encouragement of the multiracial identity movement and the heightened awareness in the media.

Shirley Haizlip and her book *The Sweeter the Juice* (1994) were featured on the *Oprah Show* in 1994. The family members on the show all looked white, but some had passed while others had not. The author appeared on the show to explain how this can happen. In subsequent years, there have been other *Oprah* shows featuring similar experiences with the color line.

When Tiger Woods won the Masters Championship in 1997 and sports reporters asked how it felt to be the first black winner, he replied that he is not only black. He pointed out that his mother is from Thailand. Evidently he is one-fourth Thai, one-fourth Chinese, one-fourth black, one-eighth Native American, and one-eighth white. In the fall of 2003 in South Africa, US television reporters repeatedly referred to both Tiger and Vijay Singh as blacks. Tiger says he checks "Asian" on forms calling for race, and Singh is from India, not Africa. In South Africa, Tiger would be defined as Coloured, Singh as Asian, and neither one as black.

WHITHER THE ONE-DROP RULE?

Do the successes of the multiracial identity movement, along with the increased media attention, foreshadow the end of the one-drop rule? Or will they join the several patterned deviations that point to the rule and reinforce it? Some states that have passed statutes to legitimate a multiracial category are finding them difficult to implement. It remains to be seen how much the states will follow the OMB's instruction to "check one or more" in collecting governmental data. Evidently it will take a lot to convince most African Americans that they have more to gain than to lose by backing away from the one-drop rule, especially in the face of continuing prejudice and discrimination.

Exceptions can become so blatant, however, that a rule becomes conspicuously obsolete. Significant further changes might be a long time coming, yet the fall of the apartheid system in South Africa in 1994 shows that momentum sometimes builds to a point at which major change can occur very fast. Increasing global awareness puts a spotlight on the US one-drop rule and its uniqueness in the world. Since national origins immigration quotas were abolished in the 1960s, the United States has increasingly become a multiracial, multiethnic society. How rapidly might the view grow that persons with partly black ancestry have a human right to have both or all of their racial backgrounds recognized?

If and when the one-drop rule loses its hold, what then? Of the six other status positions for mixed-race people discussed here, which one might incur the least opposition from most whites and most blacks? Is there one that would be accompanied by problems that are less serious than those resulting from the one-drop rule? Some of the six alternatives could not possibly fit conditions in the United States, especially the bottom-of-the-ladder and the top-of-the-ladder statuses. The idea of a return to the in-between, buffer status would arouse intense hostility in the black community. Light mulatto leaders are highly valued and are held tightly in the embrace of black pride. African Americans also disdain the "colorism" of the Latin American pattern, and most whites would abhor very frequent intermarriage between whites and persons with visibly African traits.

The northern European status for mixed-race people would appear to be the closest alternative to the US hypodescent position. To some whites, marriage with persons with known black ancestry but who look white might seem but a limited and beneficial exception to the one-drop rule. After all, "white blacks" carry very few genes from African ancestors, and many common beliefs about miscegenation are false and racist. Other whites, however, would be dominated by irrational fears of massive miscegenation, widespread passing, and "invisible blackness." As for the black community, few would likely consider it a good thing that those wishing to be assimilated could do so without having to pass secretly and abandon their black families and community. It would require the belief that very few persons would be lost to the white community and that black unity would not be impaired. This leap of faith seems highly unlikely so long as fully equal treatment of blacks is still an elusive goal.

Opposition to the assimilating minority status for the racially mixed would no doubt be very strong. That alternative would require acceptance of widespread intermarriage between whites and persons with one-fourth or less African ancestry. This process has helped visible minorities other than blacks to climb the class ladder and achieve equal treatment. To many, if not most, whites, it would probably seem to be an extreme departure from the one-drop rule, which has been designed to prevent total assimilation of persons with invisible as well as visible black ancestry.

Most blacks want equal treatment and economic and political integration, not total assimilation. Some barriers to opportunities have been lowered, but there is still considerable opposition by both whites and blacks to more informal contacts. Churches are as segregated as ever, urban housing segregation has been increasing, and pressures for black unity have limited social contacts between blacks and whites. Neither the black nor the white community exhibits any enthusiasm for complete assimilation.

Unlikely as it may now seem, the mainland United States might someday move toward the Hawaiian approach as most feasible. Mainlanders who move to Hawai'i have seemed able to accept the island pattern, different though it is, within a few months (Adams 1969). The implicit rule for mixed-race status in Hawai'i is consistent with egalitarian pluralism, an outcome that African Americans and Hispanics generally prefer to full assimilation (Davis 1995). Although that may not be the road taken sooner or even later, we have seen that the status of racially mixed people can be changed by shifts in group power relations. Deeply rooted as it has been, then, the one-drop rule may not be perpetuated forever.

Seeing the Big Picture   **What Was Your Race in 1890?**

Look at Figure 1 in the introduction of the appendix. What parallels do you see between the six "status and identity" positions described by F. James Davis and the changing categories used by the U.S. Census? What do you make of the census categories in 1790 and 2000? Why are they so different?

A TOUR OF INDIAN PEOPLES AND INDIAN LANDS

David E. Wilkins

DAVID E. WILKINS is an associate professor of American Indian studies, political science, and law at the University of Minnesota, Twin Cities Campus. He has authored several books and a number of articles dealing with the political/legal relationship between indigenous nations and the United States and state governments. His most recent book is *American Indian Politics and the American Political System* (2002).

> One of the greatest obstacles faced by the Indian today in his desire for self-determination . . . is the American public's ignorance of the historical relationship of the United States with Indian tribes and the lack of general awareness of the status of the American Indian in our society today.
> —American Indian Policy Review Commission, 1977[1]

Questions to Consider

Why has it been so difficult to find a political and cultural definition of who is an American Indian, what constitutes a tribe, and what criteria need to be met to claim tribal membership? How are race, culture, identity, and politics linked in Wilkins's discussion of American Indians?

THIS [READING] PROVIDES DESCRIPTIONS, definitions, and analysis of the most important concepts necessary for a solid foundation for the study of Indian politics. I will attempt to clarify how indigenous peoples, variously grouped, are defined, and discuss why such definitions are necessary. I will then analyze how the term Indian is defined and discuss what constitutes a reservation or Indian Country. Finally, I will conclude the [reading] with a description of the basic demographic facts and socioeconomic data that apply throughout Indian lands.

WHAT IS AN INDIAN TRIBE?

American Indians, tribal nations, Indian **tribes,** indigenous nations, Fourth World peoples, Native American peoples, aboriginal peoples, First Nations, and native peoples—these are just a sample of current terms that are used to refer to indigenous peoples in the continental United States in a collective sense. Alaska Natives, including Aleuts, Inuit, and Indians, and Native Hawaiians are the indigenous people of those respective territories. While I will provide some descriptive details about Alaska Natives, I will have less to say about Native Hawaiians because their legal status is unique among aboriginal peoples of the United States.[2]

tribe A social unit organized around ancestry, ethnicity, race, or a common culture.

This was brought to light in the Supreme Court's 2000 ruling in *Rice v. Cayetano*.[3] In that case, the Court struck down restrictions that had allowed only persons with Native Hawaiian blood to vote for the trustees of the Office of Hawaiian Affairs, a state agency created to better the lives of Hawaii's aboriginal people. While *Cayetano* did not specifically address the political relationship of the Native Hawaiians to the federal government, it called into question the status of the more than 150 federal statutes that recognize that Hawaii's native peoples do, in fact, have a unique legal status.

The Departments of the Interior and Justice issued a preliminary report of August 23, 2000, that recommended that Congress "enact further legislation to clarify Native Hawaiians' political status and to create a framework for recognizing a government-to-government relationship with a representative Native Hawaiian governing body."[4] If Congress acts to create such a framework, and a bill was introduced on July 20, 2000 (S. 2898), by Senator Daniel K. Akaka (D-HI), then Hawaii's Natives would have a political relationship with the federal government similar to that of federally recognized tribes. The sovereignty movement in Hawaii is very complex, however, and some segments of the population desire more than mere federal recognition of their status because of their nation's preexisting sovereign status.[5]

Indigenous communities expect to be referred to by their own names—Navajo or Dine, Ojibwe or Anishinabe, Sioux or Lakota, Suquamish, or Tohono O'odham—since they constitute separate political, legal, and cultural entities. In fact, before Europeans arrived in the Americas, it is highly doubtful whether any tribes held a "conception of that racial character which today we categorize as 'Indian.' People recognized their neighbors as co-owners of the lands given to them by the Great Spirit and saw themselves sharing a basic status within creation as a life form."[6] However, when discussing Indian people generically, *American Indian tribes* and *Native Americans* remain the most widely used terms despite the inherent problems with both. For instance, America's indigenous people are not *from* India, and the term *Native American* was "used during the nativist (anti-immigration, anti-foreign) movement (1860s–1925) and the anti-black, anti-Catholic, and anti-Jewish Ku Klux Klan resurgence during the early 1900s."[7]

There is no universally agreed upon definition of what constitutes an Indian tribe, in part because each tribal community defines itself differently and because the U.S. government in its relations with tribes has operated from conflicting sets of cultural and political premises across time. Although no universal definition exists, many statutes give definitions for purposes of particular laws, federal agencies like the Bureau of Indian Affairs generate their own definitions, numerous courts have crafted definitions, and the term *tribe* is found—though not defined—in the Constitution's commerce clause.

For example, the Indian Self-Determination Act of 1975 (as amended) defines an Indian tribe as "any Indian tribe, band, nation, or other organized group or community . . . which is recognized as eligible for the special programs and services provided by the United States to Indians because of their status as Indians." By contrast, the Supreme Court in *Montoya v. United States* (1901) even more ambiguously said that "by a 'tribe' we understand a body of Indians of the same or a similar race united in a community under one leadership or government, and inhabiting a particular though sometimes ill-defined territory."[8]

Broadly, the term *tribe* can be defined from two perspectives—**ethnological** and *political-legal*.[9] From an ethnological perspective, a tribe may be defined as a group of indigenous people connected by biology or blood; kinship, cultural, and spiritual values; language; political authority; and a territorial land base. But for our purposes, it is the political-legal definition (since there is no single definitive legal definition) of tribe, especially by the federal government, which is crucial since whether or not a tribal group is *recognized* as a tribe by the federal government has important

political, cultural, and economic consequences, as we shall see shortly.

FEDERALLY RECOGNIZED TRIBAL AND ALASKA NATIVE ENTITIES

The extension of federal recognition by the United States to a tribal nation is the formal diplomatic acknowledgment by the federal government of a tribe's legal status as a sovereign. This is comparable to when the United States extended "recognition" to the former republics of the Soviet Union after that state's political disintegration. It is the beginning point of a government-to-government relationship between an indigenous people and the U.S. government.[10] The reality is that an American Indian tribe is not a legally recognized entity in the eyes of the federal government unless some explicit action by an arm of the government (i.e., congressional statute, administrative ruling by the BIA, presidential executive order, or a judicial opinion) decides that it exists in a formal manner.

Federal recognition has historically had two distinctive meanings. Before the 1870s, "recognize" or "recognition" was used in the cognitive sense. In other words, federal officials simply acknowledged that a tribe existed, usually by negotiating treaties with them or enacting specific laws to fulfill specific treaty pledges.[11] During the 1870s, however, "recognition," or more accurately, "acknowledgment," began to be used in a formal jurisdictional sense. It is this later usage that the federal government most often employs to describe its relationship to tribes. In short, federal acknowledgment is a formal act that establishes a political relationship between a tribe and the United States. It affirms a tribe's sovereign status. Simultaneously, it outlines the federal government's responsibilities to the tribe.

More specifically, federal acknowledgment means that a tribe is not only entitled to the immunities and privileges available to other tribes, but is also subject to the same federal powers, limitations, and other obligations of recognized tribes.

---

ethnology The branch of anthropology that compares human cultures; includes the study of the origin and history of racial groupings.

What this means, particularly the "limitations" term, is that "acknowledgment shall subject the Indian tribe to the same authority of Congress and the United States to which other federally acknowledged tribes are subjected."[12] In other words, tribes are informed that they are now subject to federal plenary power and may, ironically, benefit from the virtually unlimited and still largely unreviewable authority of the federal government. For example, recognized tribes have exemptions from most state tax laws, enjoy sovereign immunity, and are not subject to the same constitutional constraints as are the federal and state governments.

Until 1978, federal recognition or acknowledgment was usually bestowed by congressional act or presidential action. But in 1978 the BIA, the Department of the Interior agency primarily responsible for carrying out the federal government's treaty and trust obligations to tribal nations, published regulations which contained specific criteria that unacknowledged or nonrecognized tribal groups had to meet in order to be formally recognized by the United States. The set of guidelines was based mainly on confirmation by individuals and groups outside the petitioning tribe that members of the group were Indians. The mandatory criteria were the following: the identification of the petitioners "from historical times until the present on a substantially continuous basis, as 'American Indian' or 'Aboriginal' by the federal government, state or local governments, scholars, or other Indian tribes; the habitation of the tribe on land identified as Indian; a functioning government that had authority over its members; a constitution; a roll of members based on criteria acceptable to the secretary of the interior; not being a terminated tribe; and members not belonging to other tribes."[13]

These criteria largely were designed to fit the **"aboriginal"** or "mythic" image of the western and already recognized tribes. They were problematic for many eastern tribes who sought recognition,

---

aboriginal Usually refers to the first people to inhabit a particular region; often used as shorthand for native groups who were geographically displaced, mistreated, or slaughtered by settlers, as in the case of the indigenous population of Australia.

since they paid little heed to the massive historical, cultural, economic, and legal barriers those tribes had to endure merely to survive as tribes into the late twentieth century, lacking any semblance of federal support or protection.

Since the late 1970s there has been tension between those who support BIA or administrative recognition versus those who believe that only the Congress has authority to recognize tribes. The debate over administrative versus legislative recognition rages on, with some advocates from each camp asserting their exclusive right to extend or withhold recognition. This raises an important question: Is there a qualitative difference between the two types of recognition? There are two important differences. First, tribes that opt for administrative variety must meet the formalized set of criteria mentioned earlier. Tribes that pursue congressional recognition, provided they can muster enough proof that they are a legitimate group composed of people of Indian ancestry, have only to make a compelling case to the congressional representative(s) of the state they reside in. The congressional sponsor(s) then make(s) the case for the tribe via legislation.

The second major difference involves the administrative law component known as "subordinate delegation." The major grant of authority the Congress has delegated to the secretary of the interior is located in title 25—*Indians*—of the *U.S. Code*. Section 1 states that the head of Indian affairs, formerly the commissioner of Indian Affairs, today the assistant secretary of Indian Affairs, is "appointed by the President, by and with the advice and consent of the Senate."[14] In section 2, the head is authorized to "have the management of all Indian affairs and of all matters arising out of Indian relations."[15] As William Quinn states, this law "would arguably not authorize the Secretary or Commissioner to establish a perpetual government-to-government relationship via federal acknowledgment with an Indian group not already under the Department's aegis."[16] Nevertheless, Quinn asserts that the secretary of the interior, with the U.S. Supreme Court's approval, has historically exercised the authority to "recognize" tribes "when a vacuum of responsibility existed over decades, resulting in a gradual and unchallenged accretion of this authority."[17]

The problem, however, is not that the secretary is usurping unused congressional authority; instead, it is the manner and degree to which secretarial discretion and interpretation of federal laws have been discharged by BIA officials. As Felix Cohen said more than forty years ago, "Indians for some decades have had neither armies nor lawyers to oppose increasingly broad interpretations of the power of the Commissioner of Indian Affairs, and so little by little 'the management of all Indian affairs' has come to be read as 'the management of all the affairs of Indians.'"[18] This statement has relevance today, notwithstanding the federal government's policy of Indian self-determination and the more recent policy of tribal self-governance.

The Congress's track record is problematic as well. Generally speaking, however, tribes with explicit congressional acknowledgment have found their status less subject to the whims of BIA officials, though even that is no guarantee of smooth affairs, because BIA oversees and administers most of the government's political relationship with tribes.

A prime example involves the Pascua Yaqui tribe of southern Arizona. The Yaqui were legislatively recognized in 1978. However, in the late 1980s, when they solicited the approval of the BIA on some changes in their constitution, they were informed by bureau officials that they were limited in what governmental powers they could exercise because they were not a "historic tribe," but were instead merely a "created adult Indian community":

A historic tribe has existed since time immemorial. Its powers derive from its unextinguished, inherent sovereignty. Such a tribe has the full range of governmental powers except where it has been removed by Federal law in favor of either the United States or the state in which the tribe is located. By contrast, a community of adult Indians is composed simply of Indian people who reside together on trust land. A community of adult Indians may have a certain status which entitles it to certain privileges and immunities. . . . However, that status is derived as a necessary scheme to benefit Indians, not from some historical inherent sovereignty.[19]

The bureau's attempt to create two categories of recognized tribes, a novel and disturbing approach to determining tribal identity, was halted by Congress, which declared that no department or agency of the government could develop regulations that negated or diminished the privileges and immunities of any federally recognized tribes.[20] The Congress has, moreover, in recent years tried to reassert its constitutional authority in the field by introducing legislation that would transfer administrative and congressional consideration of applications for federal recognition to an independent commission.[21]

Congress's actions, along with the increasing politicization of the administrative recognition process because of Indian gaming operations and state concerns, compelled Kevin Gover, the assistant secretary of Indian Affairs (head of the BIA), in May 2000 to testify before Congress that his agency was no longer able to do the job of recognizing tribes. Gover admitted that he had been unable to streamline the recognition process, which in some cases had taken years to resolve, but he placed larger blame on the fact that Indian gaming revenues had enabled some groups to wage protracted legal battles that often involved nonrecognized tribes, non-Indian citizens and towns, and recognized tribes.[22]

As of 2001, the Department of the Interior officially recognizes 561 indigenous entities—332 are Indian nations, tribes, bands, organized communities, or Pueblos in the lower forty-eight states; 229 are Alaska Native villages or corporations—on a list annually prepared by the BIA. These constitute the indigenous people eligible for special programs and services provided by the United States to indigenous communities because of their status as Indians or Alaska Natives.

The situation of Alaska Native villages and corporations is complicated not only by distinctive ethnological differences but also by their unique political and legal status. Although Alaska Natives are eligible to receive services from the BIA, their political sovereignty as self-governing bodies has been questioned and at times constrained by the federal government. A recent Supreme Court case, *Alaska v. Native Village of Venetie Tribal Government* (1998),[23] cast some doubts on the sovereign status of Alaskan villages. *Venetie* dealt with the jurisdictional status of Alaska Native villages and whether or not lands owned in fee simple by these communities—a type of ownership defined by the Alaska Native Claims Settlement Act of 1971—constituted "Indian Country."

In a major victory for Alaskan state authorities and a blow to the sovereignty of the village of Venetie, an Alaskan community of some 350 people, Justice Clarence Thomas for a unanimous court held that Venetie's 1.8 million acres of fee-simple lands did not qualify as "Indian Country" because they had not been set aside by the federal government for tribal use and were not "under federal supervision." Thus, the tribal government lacked the inherent authority to impose a 5 percent business tax on a contractor building a state-funded school in the village. In denying Venetie, and by extension every other Alaskan village, the power to tax, this ruling called into question what the actual political status of these villages was.

In addition, the indigenous people of Hawaii, who prefer to be called Hawaiians, Hawaiian Natives, or Native Hawaiians, although they are treated as Native Americans for some legal purposes, are not on the Department of the Interior's list of federally recognized tribal entities and have a unique status under federal law.[24]

But there are other indigenous people in the United States who are *not federally recognized*, who had their recognized status *terminated* by the federal government, or who have *state recognition* only. I will discuss these three categories briefly.

Nonrecognized or Unacknowledged Groups

These are groups exhibiting a tremendous degree of racial, ethnic, and cultural diversity. In some cases, they are descendants of tribes who never fought the United States, had no resources desired by the federal government, or lived in geographic isolation and were simply ignored, and hence may never have participated in a treaty or benefited from the trust relationship which forms the basis of most contemporary recognized tribes' status. Despite these circumstances, some of these groups retain their aboriginal language, hold some lands in common, and in some cases have retained some degree of traditional structures of governance. These groups feel entitled to recognition status and have petitioned the United States to be so recognized.[25]

In other cases, groups have questionable genealogical connections to legitimate historical tribes but, for varying reasons, have chosen to self-identify as particular tribes and desire to be recognized by the federal government.[26] As of 2000, the BIA had received a total of 237 letters of intent and petitions for federal recognition. The acknowledgment process, established in 1978 and administered by the Branch of Acknowledgment and Research (BAR) in the BIA, proved to be an extremely slow, expensive, and politicized process that required excessive historical documentation and was greatly influenced by already recognized tribes who were reluctant to let other groups, regardless of their historical legitimacy, gain politically recognized status.[27] Because of these and other problems, the bureau surrendered its power to administratively recognize tribal groups in the fall of 2000. Between 1978 and 2000, the BIA officially recognized only fifteen tribes (e.g., Grand Traverse Band of Ottawa & Chippewa and Jamestown S'Klallam) and denied the petitions of fifteen groups (e.g., Lower Muscogee Creek Tribe east of Mississippi, Kaweah Indian Nation, Southeastern Cherokee Confederacy).[28]

Terminated Tribes

From 1953 to the mid-1960s, the federal government's Indian policy was called "termination" because the United States wanted to sever the trust relationship and end federal benefits and support services to as many tribes, bands, and California rancherias as was feasible in an effort to expedite Indian assimilation and to lift discriminatory practices and policies that negatively affected indigenous peoples.[29] This policy was exemplified by House Concurrent Resolution No. 108, passed in 1953. This measure declared that,

> Whereas it is the policy of Congress, as rapidly as possible, to make the Indians within the territorial limits of the United States subject to the same laws and entitled to the same privileges and responsibilities as are applicable to other citizens of the United States, to end their status as wards of the United States, and to grant them all the rights and prerogatives pertaining to American citizenship; and Whereas the Indians within the territorial limits of the United States should assume their full responsibilities as American citizens: Now, therefore, be it resolved . . . that it is declared to be the sense of Congress that, at the earliest possible time, all of the Indian tribes and the individual members thereof located within the States of California, Florida, New York . . . should be freed from Federal supervision and control and from all disabilities and limitations specially applicable to Indians.[30]

Over one hundred tribes, bands, and California rancherias—totaling a little more than eleven thousand Indians—were "terminated" and lost their status as "recognized" and sovereign Indian communities. Termination thus subjected the tribes and their members to state law, their trust assets were usually individualized and either sold or held by the banks, and they were no longer eligible for the other benefits and exemptions recognized tribes enjoy.

The terminated tribes, other tribes faced with termination, and Indian and non-Indian interest groups began to lobby Congress to end this disastrous policy because of the economic and political hardships it was causing. By the mid-1960s, the policy was stifled. Gradually, terminated tribes began to push for "restoration" of their recognized status. The first tribe terminated, the Menominee of Wisconsin (terminated in 1954), was also the first tribe to be legislatively "restored," in 1973.

Although discredited as policy by the mid-1960s, and rejected by Presidents Nixon and Reagan in their Indian policy statements, termination was not officially rejected by Congress until 1988 in a largely symbolic gesture that declared that "the Congress hereby repudiates and rejects HCR 108 of the 83rd Congress and any policy of unilateral termination of federal relations with any Indian nation."[31]

State-Recognized Tribes

Some Indian tribes have been recognized by their host states since the colonial era (e.g., Pamunkey Tribe of Virginia), although others have been recognized by state decrees (governor's action or state statute) in contemporary times. There are currently over fifty state-recognized tribes in Alabama, Connecticut, Georgia, Louisiana, Massachusetts, Michigan, Montana, New Jersey, North Carolina, New York, Oklahoma, Virginia, Washington, and West Virginia. See Table 1 for a list of these tribes. Depending on the policy established by the individual state, state recognition may or may not depend on prior federal recognition. Importantly, state recognition is not a prerequisite for federal recognition, although a long-standing relationship with a state is one factor in the federal recognition criteria that the BIA weighs in its determination of whether a group has historical longevity in a particular place.

For example, the Lumbee Tribe of North Carolina was legislatively recognized by the state in 1953.[32] Confident, the Lumbee leadership two years later asked Representative Frank Carlyle (D-NC) to introduce a bill before Congress that would extend federal recognition to the Lumbee. On June 7, 1956, the Congress passed an act which provided a measure of recognition to the Lumbee Nation[33] without giving them the full range of benefits and services other federally recognized tribes received because federal policy at the time was focused on terminating the unique trust relationship between tribes and the United States. To date, the Lumbee Tribe is still not considered a federally recognized tribe by the BIA or the Indian Health Service, though they qualify for and receive other federal services as a recognized tribe.[34]

WHO IS AN AMERICAN INDIAN?

Having established the complexity of determining what an Indian tribe is from a legal-political perspective, we now turn to a brief but necessary examination of the equally if not more cumbersome question of "Who is an Indian?" This is important, as McClain and Stewart note, because "the question of who is an Indian is central to any discussion of American Indian politics."[35] The political relationship that exists between tribes and the federal government, bloated with issues of disparate power, **cultural biases**, and race and ethnicity, makes this so. Of course, like the concept of "Indian tribe," before Columbus arrived in 1492 there were no peoples in the Americas known as "Indians" or "Native Americans." Each indigenous community had its own name relating to the character of its people and the lands they inhabited.

With the political status of Indian nations defined, the question of deciding just "who is an Indian" would not appear to be a difficult one to answer. The decision rests with the tribal nations who retain, as one of their inherent sovereign powers, the power to decide who belongs in their nation. Unless this right has been expressly ceded in a treaty, it remains probably the most essential component of self-government. If tribes were to lose the right to decide who their citizens/members were, then it would logically follow that any government could dictate or influence what the tribe's membership should entail.

Since the identification of individuals as Indians depends upon or coincides with their association in a unique body politic and distinctive cultural and linguistic systems, historically, at least, "allegiance rather than ancestry per se [was]

---

cultural bias The assumption that one's own cultural practices or beliefs are better and as such should be the norm by which other cultures are measured.

the deciding factor" in determining who was an Indian.[36] In other words, historically, to be considered an Indian one had to meet certain basic tribally defined criteria, including the social, cultural, linguistic, territorial, sociopsychological, and ceremonial. These criteria, of course, varied from tribal nation to tribal nation. However, as the federal government's power waxed by the late nineteenth century, with the corresponding waning of tribal power, indigenous cultural-social-territorial-based definitions of tribal identity were sometimes ignored and replaced by purely legal and frequently race-based definitions often arbitrarily articulated in congressional laws, administrative regulations, or court cases.

Congress, in particular, began to employ and still uses ethnological data, including varying fractions of blood quantum. In fact, blood quantum remains one of the most important criteria used by the federal government and tribal governments to determine Indian status, despite the fact that its continued use "poses enormous conceptual and practical problems" since blood is not the carrier of genetic material and cultural traits as was thought in the nineteenth century.[37]

When blood quantum was first used in the Indian context in the early part of the twentieth century as a mechanism to reduce federal expenditures for Indian education, it "was meant to measure the amount of Indian blood possessed by an individual. Because racial blood types could not be observed directly, Indian blood quantum was inferred from the racial backgrounds of parents. If both parents were reputed to have 'unadulterated' Indian blood, then the blood quantum of their children was fixed at 100 percent. For children of racially mixed parents, their Indian blood quantum might be some fractional amount such as ¾, ½, or ⅛."[38]

The federal government's principal function in formulating definitions of "Indian," since like the concept "tribe" there is no single constitutional or universally accepted definition, is to "establish a test whereby it may be determined whether a given individual is to be excluded from the scope of legislation dealing with Indians."[39] The most widely accepted "legal" definition of "Indian" is from Felix Cohen, who wrote in 1943 that:

TABLE 1 ■ State-Recognized Tribes

Alabama

Echota Cherokee

Northeast Alabama Cherokee

MaChis Lower Creek

Southeast Alabama Cherokee

Star Muscogee Creek

Mowa Band of Choctaw

Georgia

Georgia Eastern Cherokee

Cherokee of Georgia

Lower Muskogee Creek

Tama Tribal Town

New Jersey

Nanticoke Lenni-Lanape

Powhatan Renape

Ramapough Mountain

Michigan

Burt Lake Band of Ottawa & Chippewa Indians

Gun Lake Band of Grand River Ottawa Indians

Grand River Band of Ottawa Indians

Swan Creek Black River Confederated Tribes

North Carolina

Coharie Intra-Tribal Council

Haliwa-Saponi Tribe

Lumbee

Meherrin Tribe

Person County Indians

Waccamaw-Siouan Tribe

Virginia

Chickahominy Indian Tribe

Eastern Chickahominy Indian Tribe

Mattaponi Indian Tribe

Monacan Indian Tribe

Nansemond Indian Tribe

Pamunkey Indian Tribe

United Rappahannock Tribe

Upper Mattaponi Indian Tribe

West Virginia

Appalachian American Indians of West Virginia

Connecticut

Golden Hill Paugussett

Paucatuck Eastern Pequot

Schagticoke

Louisiana

Choctaw-Apache of Ebarb

Caddo Tribe

Clifton Choctaw

Four Winds Cherokee

United Houma Nation

New York

Shinnecock

Poospatuk

Montana

Little Shell Tribe of Chippewa

Oklahoma

Delaware Tribe of East Oklahoma

Loyal Shawnee Tribe

Yuchi Tribe

Washington

Chinook Indian Tribe

Duwamish Tribe

Kikiallus Indian Nation

Marietta Band of Nooksack Indians

Steilacoom Indian Tribe

Snohomish Tribe of Indians

Source: The Spike, The Original Newsletter on East Coast American Indian Events, http://www.thespike.com/tablest.htm

The term "Indian" may be used in an ethnological or in a legal sense. Ethnologically, the Indian race may be distinguished from the Caucasian, Negro, Mongolian, and other races. If a person is three-fourths Caucasian and one-fourth Indian, it is absurd, from the ethnological standpoint, to assign him to the Indian race. Yet legally such a person may be an Indian. From a legal standpoint, then, the biological question of race is generally pertinent, but not conclusive. Legal status depends not only upon biological, but also upon social factors, such as the relation of the individual concerned to a white or Indian community. . . . Recognizing the possible diversity of definitions of "Indianhood," we may nevertheless find some practical value in a definition of "Indian" as a person meeting two qualifications: (a) That some of his ancestors lived in America before its discovery by the white race, and (b) That the individual is considered an "Indian" by the community in which he lives.[40]

Because of the Constitution's silence on the issue of who is an Indian, Congress, the BIA, and the federal courts have had great latitude in developing specific meanings for specific situations which only sometimes reflect the definitions of particular tribes. But because of the plenary power doctrine and the trust doctrine, these federal actors, but especially the Congress, have vested themselves with the right to define "who an Indian is" for purposes relating to legislation and have sometimes established base rolls which actually identify who a tribe's members are. This was done in the case of the so-called Five Civilized Tribes of present-day Oklahoma. Congress, in 1893, enacted a law that all but secured to the federal government the right to determine membership of these tribes.[41]

Over thirty "legal" definitions have been promulgated by various agencies, departments, and congressional committees and subcommittees that explain who is and is not an Indian eligible for federal services.[42] These definitions can be grouped into six categories. First, and most common, are those definitions that require a specific blood quantum, with one-fourth being the most widely accepted fraction. Second, there is a set of definitions clustered under the requirement that the individual be a member of a federally recognized indigenous community.

A third category includes definitions that mandate residence "on or near" a federal Indian reservation. A fourth class includes definitions grouped under descendancy. These entail definitions that extend eligibility not only to tribal members but also to their descendants up to a specified degree. For example, the definition of Indian found in a 1998 bill, Indian Trust-Estate Planning and Land Title Management Improvement Act, declares that "the term 'Indian' means any individual who is a member, or a descendant of a member, of a North American tribe, band, pueblo, or other organized group of natives who are indigenous to the continental U.S., or who otherwise has a special relationship with the U.S. through a treaty, agreement, or other form of recognition." The bill's sponsors described an "Alaska Native" as "an individual who is an Alaskan Indian, Eskimo, Aleut, or any combination thereof, who are indigenous to Alaska."

Under the fifth grouping are several definitions that rely on self-identification. The U.S. Census Bureau, for example, allows individuals to simply declare that they are Indian. Finally, the sixth class is a miscellaneous category that includes definitions which do not easily fit in the other categories.[43]

Defining "Indian" and "tribe" are not simple tasks in part because of the political and economic resources involved and because of the number and power of the respective actors: tribal governments, individual Indians, Congress, the president, the Department of the Interior, the BIA, federal courts and, increasingly, state governments and the various agencies and individuals who constitute those sovereigns. But who does the defining and how these emotionally laden terms are defined are crucial in expanding our understanding of the politics of individual tribes, intertribal relations, and intergovernmental relations.

For example, in terms of identity, high out-marriage rates, steadily decreasing federal dollars, and an intensified tribal-state relationship have prompted questions about "whether the rules defining Indianness and tribal membership should be relaxed or tightened—that is, made more inclusionary or more exclusionary."[44] For instance, some tribes are eliminating blood quantum and adopting descent criteria, while others are pursuing an "ethnic purification strategy" by adopting a stricter set of **blood quantum** rules concerning tribal enrollment. These decisions impact tribes and their political relationship with the federal government.

While tribes retain the right to establish their own membership criteria, the BIA in August 2000 published proposed regulations on the documentation requirements and standards necessary for Indians to receive a "certificate of degree of Indian blood" (CDIB), which is the federal government's way of determining whether individuals possess sufficient Indian blood to be eligible for certain federal programs and services provided exclusively to American Indians or Alaska Natives.[45]

But a number of Indian leaders, like W. Ron Allen, chairman of the Jamestown S'Klallam Tribe of Washington, charged that the federal government should not be in the business of determining who is Indian. The proposed regulations, he argued, by requiring applicants to show a relationship to an enrolled member of a federally recognized tribe, would potentially exclude members or descendants of terminated tribes, state-recognized tribes, and non-recognized tribes.

Since the BIA's standard blood quantum is one-fourth, and with the high rates of out-marriage, Russell Thornton, an anthropologist, suggests that sometime in this century the proportion of the Indian population with less than one-fourth blood quantum will rise to 60 percent. If this trend is correct, from the federal government's standpoint "decreasing blood quanta of the total Native American population may be perceived as meaning that the numbers of Native Americans to whom it is obligated have declined."[46] This will not mean the extinction of Indian tribes, but it will mean a new form of federal termination of Indians who are eligible for federal aid and services.

---

blood quantum The idea of counting the percentage of racial heritage, which comes from racist laws that were used to place American Indians on reservations. The laws asked the question, in terms of a percentage, how black, or Indian, or white you were.

Questions around whether a tribe is federally recognized, state-recognized, nonrecognized, or terminated have direct bearing on the internal and external political dynamics of tribes, and directly affect intergovernmental relations, since only recognized tribes may engage in gaming operations that are not directly subject to state law, may exercise criminal jurisdiction over their members and a measure of civil jurisdiction over nonmembers, and are exempt from a variety of state and federal taxes.

WHAT ARE INDIAN LANDS?

The first and most obvious difference between Indian peoples and all other groups in the United States is that Indians were here before anyone else. All the land in the continental United States, Alaska, and Hawaii was inhabited and revered by the over six hundred distinctive indigenous peoples who dwelt here. Gradually, however, from 1492 forward, various foreign nations—Russia, Holland, Spain, Great Britain, France, Sweden, and later the United States—competed for an economic foothold in North America. For the three most dominant European states, France, Spain, and Great Britain (and later the United States, as Britain's successor), this usually included efforts to secure title to indigenous lands through formal treaties, which were sometimes coercive and occasionally fraudulent, while some were fairly negotiated.[47]

When the United States declared independence in 1776, it wisely opted to continue the policy of negotiating treaties with tribes, which it continued to do until 1871, when Congress unilaterally declared that "hereafter no Indian nation or tribe within the territory of the United States shall be acknowledged or recognized as an independent nation, tribe, or power with whom the United States may contract by treaty."[48] However, this stance proved unworkable and within a short period the United States was again negotiating *agreements* with tribal nations that were often referred to and accorded the legal status of treaties. The negotiation of agreements continued until 1912.

Many of these documents were primarily viewed as land cession arrangements by the federal government, in which the United States purchased varying amounts of tribal lands in exchange for monies, goods, and services. In addition, tribes "reserved" their remaining lands, or agreed to relocate to new lands, which were usually designated as reservations. These reserved lands were to be held "in trust" by the United States on behalf of the tribe(s), who were deemed the beneficiaries. As the tribes' "trustee," the federal government theoretically exercised the responsibility to assist the tribes in the protection of their lands, resources, and cultural heritage and pledged that it would hold itself to the highest standards of good faith and honesty in all its dealings with the tribes.

For example, article 1 of a treaty the Kickapoo signed on October 24, 1832, contained a cession of land:

> The Kickapoo tribe of Indians, in consideration of the stipulations hereinafter made, do hereby cede to the United States, the lands assigned to them by the treaty of Edwardsville, and concluded at St. Louis . . . and all other claims to lands within the State of Missouri.[49]

The second article, however, described the lands the tribe had secured for their land cessions:

> The United States will provide for the Kickapoo tribe, a country to reside in, southwest of the Missouri river, as their permanent place of residence as long as they remain a tribe . . . [and] it is hereby agreed that the country within the following boundaries shall be assigned, conveyed, and forever secured . . . to the said Kickapoo tribe.[50]

In this case the Kickapoo agreed to relocate to a little over 700,000 acres of new lands in Kansas that were to serve as their permanent "reservation."

In short, a reservation is an area of land—whether aboriginal or new—that has been reserved for an Indian tribe, band, village, or nation. Generally, the United States holds, in trust for the tribe, legal title to the reserved territory. The tribe in these instances holds a beneficial title to the lands, or, in other words, an exclusive right of occupancy. Of course, reservations were not all created by treaty. Congress established a number of reservations by statute.

The president, through the use of executive order power, established many other reservations. For instance, the state of Arizona has twenty-one reservations—twenty of which were created by presidents. The core foundation of the Navajo Reservation (the largest in the country) was treaty-established in 1868, though the many additions to it were mostly by executive orders. In 1919, Congress forbade the president from establishing any more reservations via executive order. Finally, the secretary of the interior is empowered under the 1934 Indian Reorganization Act to establish, expand, or restore reservations.

As of 1998, there were 314 reservations and other restricted and trust lands in the United States. These reserved lands are located in thirty-one states, mostly in the West. There are also twelve state-established reservations in Connecticut, Massachusetts, Michigan, New York, New Jersey, South Carolina, Georgia, and Virginia. Despite the large number of federally recognized Alaska Native groups, there is only one reservation, the Annette Island Indian Reserve.[51]

At present, the indigenous land base in the United States, including Alaska, is approximately 100 million acres—fifty-six million in the continental United States, forty-four million in Alaska. This represents approximately 4 percent of all lands in the United States. Map 1 graphically shows the rapid and enormous loss of aboriginal territory to the United States from the birth of the American republic to the present day.

The roughly 100 (per previous paragraph) million acres constitutes territory over which tribal governments and Alaska Native villages and corporations exercise varying amounts of governmental jurisdiction, and where state laws are generally inapplicable, with exceptions.

In 1999, 1,397,931 Indians were identified in a BIA report out of the total U.S. Indian population in 2000 of 2,475,956 (individuals self-identifying as single race American Indian or Alaska Native).

MAP 1 ■ American Indian Land Losses

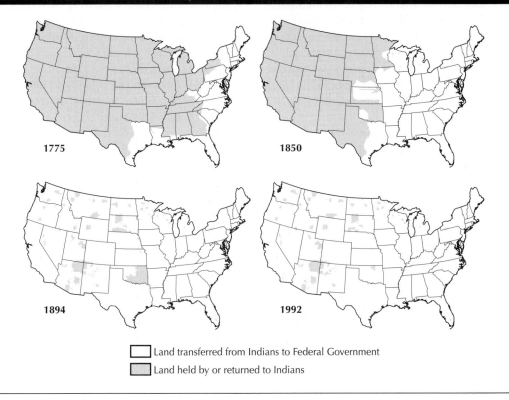

1775

1850

1894

1992

☐ Land transferred from Indians to Federal Government

▨ Land held by or returned to Indians

WHAT IS INDIAN COUNTRY?

For an indigenous government to be able to exercise criminal or civil jurisdiction over their territory, their own members, and, in some limited cases, non-Indians, the land in question must be designated as *Indian Country*. In the colonial era, Indian Country encompassed all the lands beyond the frontier lands "populated by tribes and bands of Indians who rejected contact with 'civilized' populations."[52] Today, however, the concept "has been elevated by federal law above other ideas because it transcends mere geographical limitations and represents that sphere of influence in which Indian traditions and federal laws passed specifically to deal with the political relationship of the United States to American Indians have primacy."[53]

INDIAN COUNTRY: BEYOND THE RESERVATION

Broadly, the term "Indian Country" means land within which Indian laws and customs and federal laws relating to Indians are generally applicable. But it is also defined as all the land under the supervision and protection of the federal government that has been set aside primarily for the use of Indians. Federal law defines it, first, as all land within the boundaries of an Indian reservation, whether owned by Indians or non-Indians. Second, it includes all "dependent Indian communities" in the United States. These are lands—pueblos of New Mexico, Oklahoma Indian tribal lands, and California rancherias—previously recognized by European nations and now by the successor government, the United States, as belonging to the tribes or as set aside by the federal government for use and benefit of the Indians.

Pueblo lands, because they were previously recognized as belonging to the pueblos under Spanish, Mexican, and later U.S. law, are not, strictly speaking, reservations, but are considered Indian lands and are held in trust by the federal government because they are held in communal ownership with fee-simple title residing in each pueblo. Some Pueblo Indian lands are held in equitable ownership by various pueblos, with the United States holding legal title. These lands include reservations created by congressional statute and executive order reservations established by the president.

Oklahoma's numerous Indian tribes also have a distinctive history, though their lands also constitute Indian Country. It is important to note that the tribes in the eastern part of the state, what was called "Indian Territory," home of the Five Civilized Tribes, have a somewhat different history from tribes in the western part of the state, or what was called "Oklahoma Territory," home of the Cheyenne, Arapaho, Kiowa, Comanche, etc. Although the BIA and the Bureau of the Census have asserted that there are no Indian reservations in Oklahoma, except for the Osage, John Moore argues that the reservation status of Oklahoma tribes persists, notwithstanding allotment and other policies designed to terminate Indian communal land holdings.[54]

Some California tribes, because of heavy Spanish influence dating from 1769, live on rancherias, a Spanish term meaning "small reservation" and originally applied to Indians who had not been settled in Christian mission communities. The history of death and dispossession visited upon California's indigenous population may well be the worst of any aboriginal peoples in the United States. From a population of well over 300,000 at the time of contact, California Indians experienced a staggering rate of decline from diseases, outright **genocide**, and displacement.[55] That they have retained any lands at all is a remarkable testimony to their fortitude.

Finally, the Indian Country designation includes all individual Indian allotments (I will discuss the allotment policy shortly) that are still held in trust or restricted status by the federal government—whether inside or outside an Indian reservation.[56]

For political and legal purposes, the designation of Indian Country is crucial because the reach of a tribal nation's jurisdiction is generally restricted to lands so designated. And it is Indian Country where most jurisdictional disputes arise between tribes and their members; tribes and non-Indians; and tribes and the local, county, state, or federal governments.

For example, this was the central question in the recent U.S. Supreme Court case involving indigenous people, *Alaska v. Native Village of Venetie Tribal Government* (1998). In this case, the court had to decide whether the village of Venetie constituted Indian Country. If so, then the tribal government had the right to impose a tax on a construction company; if not, then it lacked such taxing power. In a harmful ruling for Alaska Native sovereignty, the Supreme Court held that the village's fee-simple lands did not constitute Indian Country, thus depriving Alaska villages and corporations of the power to exercise a number of governmental powers that tribal nations in the lower forty-eight states exercise routinely. The Supreme Court, however, need not have relied so exclusively on the question of whether or not Venetie constituted "Indian Country" since the statutes articulating this concept clearly did not encompass Alaska at the time they were enacted.

---

genocide The systematic, wholesale killing of individuals because of their race, religion, ethnicity, or political affiliation. The idea behind genocide is the total eradication of a group, motivated by hatred.

DEMOGRAPHY AND INDIAN COUNTRY

According to a report, *Changing America,* prepared by the Council of Economic Advisers for President Clinton's Race Initiative in 1998, the population of the United States is increasingly diverse. In recent years the four major racial/ethnic minority groups—Latinos, Asian Americans, African Americans, and American Indians—have each grown faster than the population as a whole. Whereas in 1970 the combination of these four groups represented only 16 percent of the entire population, by 1998 this had increased to 27 percent.[57] The Bureau of the Census, the report noted, projects that by 2050, these groups will account for "almost half of the U.S. Population." Early data from the 2000 U.S. census, which shows a total population of 281,421,906, indicate the continuing transformation of race and ethnicity in America. While the categories of white (211,460,626),

Hispanic or Latino (35,305,818), black or African American (34,658,190), American Indian or Alaska Native (2,475,956), Asian (10,242,998), and Native Hawaiian or other Pacific Islander (398,835) were familiar, for the first time in history individuals could choose self-identify as having more than one race. Some 6,826,228 people, 2.4 percent of the total population, claimed affiliation with two or more races.[58]

While this projected growth has potentially staggering political and economic implications, the fact is that the total indigenous population, despite the large number of indigenous nations—561 and counting—is comparatively quite small (see Figures 1-5). In 2000, there were a reported 2,475,956 self-identified Indians and Alaska Natives, a 26 percent increase since 1990. This is a drastic decline from pre-European figures of over seven million, but it is far more than the nadir of perhaps only 250,000 around 1900.[59] The 2000 figure represents only 0.9 percent of the total U.S. population of 281,421,906.

FIGURE 1 ■ American Indian Population, 1890–1990 (thousands)

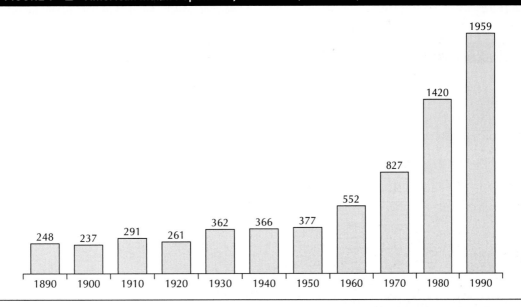

Source: Shinagawa, Larry Hajime & Michael Jang, *Atlas of American Diversity.* Reprinted with permission from Alta Mira Press.

Notes: 1900, partially estimated; 1940 Eskimo and Aleut populations are based on 1939 counts.

Although the overall population of self-identi-fied American Indians and Alaska Natives is still quite small, because of the new category allow-ing individuals to identify as belonging to more than one race (sixty-three racial options were possible), the 2000 census data are not directly comparable with data from the 1990 census or previous censuses. Thus, while approximately 2.5 million individuals identified themselves as Amer-ican Indian and Alaska Native alone, an additional 1.6 million people reported themselves as being indigenous and belonging to "at least one other race." Within this group, the most common combi-nations were "American Indian and Alaska Native *and* White" (66 percent of the population reported this); "American Indian and Alaska Native *and* Black or African American" (11 percent of the pop-ulation); and "American Indian and Alaska Native *and* White *and* Black or African American" (7 percent). In sum, approximately 4.1 million people reported themselves as being American Indian and Alaska Native "alone or in combination with one or more other races."[60] The wide diversity within this population will be discussed in greater detail in forthcoming census reports not yet available.

Suffice it to say, the amount of racial mixing acknowledged in the American Indian context is extreme when compared to that of other racial/ethnic groups. As Russell Thornton, a Cherokee anthropologist, noted in his analysis of the 2000 cen-sus data, American Indians have a racial mixture of 37 percent, which "far exceeds percentages for other

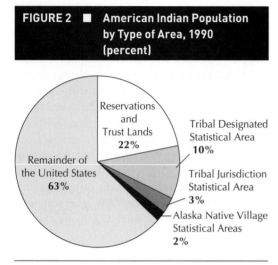

FIGURE 2 ■ American Indian Population by Type of Area, 1990 (percent)

Source: Shinagawa, Larry Hajime & Michael Jang, *Atlas of American Diversity.* Reprinted with permission from Alta Mira Press.

FIGURE 3 ■ States with the Ten Largest American Indian Populations, 2000 (thousands)

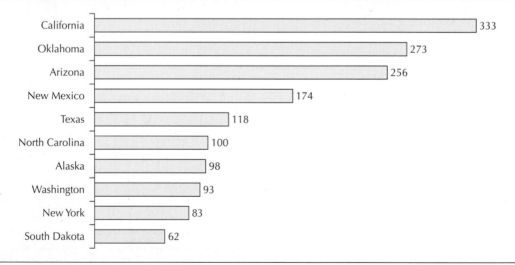

Source: www.census.gov/do/www/redistricting.html (no longer available) Revised Source: U.S. Census Bureau, Census 2000 Summary File 1; 1990 Census of Population, General Population Characteristics (1990 CP-1).

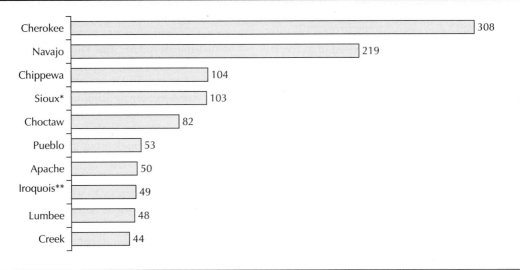

FIGURE 4 ■ Ten Largest American Indian Tribes, 1990 (thousands)

Cherokee	308
Navajo	219
Chippewa	104
Sioux*	103
Choctaw	82
Pueblo	53
Apache	50
Iroquois**	49
Lumbee	48
Creek	44

Source: Shinagawa, Larry Hajime & Michael Jang, *Atlas of American Diversity.* Reprinted with permission from Alta Mira Press.

*Any entry with the spelling "Siouan" was miscoded to Sioux in North Carolina.

**Reporting and/or processing problems have affected the data for this tribe.

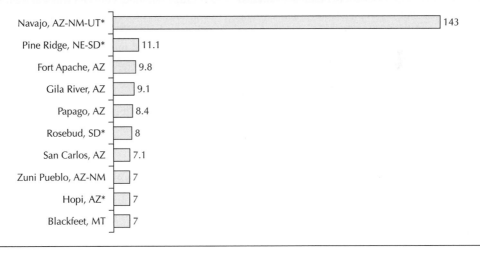

FIGURE 5 ■ Reservations with the Largest Numbers of American Indians, 1990 (thousands)

Navajo, AZ-NM-UT*	143
Pine Ridge, NE-SD*	11.1
Fort Apache, AZ	9.8
Gila River, AZ	9.1
Papago, AZ	8.4
Rosebud, SD*	8
San Carlos, AZ	7.1
Zuni Pueblo, AZ-NM	7
Hopi, AZ*	7
Blackfeet, MT	7

Source: Shinagawa, Larry Hajime & Michael Jang, *Atlas of American Diversity.* Reprinted with permission from Alta Mira Press.
*Includes trust lands.

groups." Thornton noted that only about 5 percent of African Americans reported mixed ancestry.[61]

In Alaska, there is only one small reservation, Annette Island Reserve, though for census purposes lands are designated as "Alaska Native Village Statistical areas" that are inhabited and recognized as indigenous areas. Approximately 47,244 Alaska Natives live on these lands. In sum, more than

60 percent, over one million, of all Indian people do not live on Indian reservations.[62] A majority of indigenous peoples, in fact some 56.2 percent, live in metropolitan or suburban areas. And roughly half of all urban Indians can be found in as few as sixteen cities, largely as a result of the 1950s and 1960s termination, relocation, and educational programs of the federal government.

In the early days of relocation, the BIA generally helped send Indians to Chicago, Los Angeles, Denver, or Salt Lake City. By 1990, Indians had migrated to a number of other metropolitan areas. Cities with the largest Indian populations in 1990 were Tulsa, Oklahoma (48,348); Oklahoma City, Oklahoma (46,111); Los Angeles-Long Beach, California (43,689); Phoenix, Arizona (38,309); and Seattle-Tacoma, Washington (32,980).[63] The vast majority of Indians still live in the western half of the United States.

The states with the ten largest indigenous populations are shown in Figure 3. The District of Columbia had the fewest Indians, 1,466.

There is also great variation in the population of individual tribes (see Figure 5). The largest tribe is the Cherokee Nation of Oklahoma, with 369,035 members. The smallest tribes have fewer than one hundred members. The indigenous population is also a young population, with more than 35 percent younger than age seventeen. In fact, the median age for reservation Indians is more than ten years younger than that of the general U.S. population. The Indian population, like that of the Jews and the Japanese Americans in Hawaii, is also one that experiences an extremely high level of intergroup marriage (marriage between persons of different races). Although intergroup marriage couples accounted for only 4 percent of all married couples in the United States in 1990, American Indians had a 53 percent intergroup marriage rate. Potentially, this figure could have severe cultural and political implications for indigenous nations.[64]

As Snipp mused:

> The extraordinarily high level of racial intermarriage for American Indians provides a good reason to expect that growing numbers of American Indians and their descendants will choose non-Indians for spouses and to a greater or lesser degree become absorbed

into the dominant culture. Some of these Indians will abandon their cultural heritage altogether, while others may make only minor accommodations as a result of having a non-Indian spouse. This raises a question that is extremely controversial within many quarters of the American Indian community: Are American Indians assimilating so quickly through racial intermarriage that they will eventually, in the not too distant future, marry themselves out of existence?[65]

Predicting the future is an impossible task and I will not hazard a guess as to whether this intermarriage rate will continue. Suffice it to say, this is viewed as a serious predicament by some tribes and raises some important questions. For instance, will Indians, like many intermarried Jews, be able to show a propensity for combining extensive intermarriage with a surge in ethnic and religious pride? For while the rate of Jewish intermarriage is higher today than at any other point, American Jewish culture and community life appear to be flourishing, including a resurgent interest in Yiddish.[66]

Other questions confront tribes as well. Will they continue to use blood quantum as their primary definitional criteria? Will the federal government claim that its legal and moral obligations to Indians dissipate if a tribal nation's blood quantum falls below a certain percentage? Will tribes be able to exercise jurisdiction over a multiracial citizenry? These are questions some tribes are beginning to address as we begin the new millennium.

CONCLUSION

The power to define—what is a tribe, who is an Indian, what constitutes Indian Country, which group gets recognized—along with the power to decide whether or not to act in a colonial capacity in relation to indigenous nations are important means by which the federal government has gained and retains a dominant position vis-à-vis tribal groups. While on one hand supporting the right of indigenous polities to exercise self-determination, the United States on the other hand still insists that it has the power and the right to trump important tribal governmental decisions regarding identity and has shown throughout its history that it will so act if it deems it necessary to further its own economic, political, and cultural interests.

The demographic data presented glaringly show that diversity and uncertainty are hallmarks of Indian Country, with more than half the indigenous population living off reservations and Indians outmarrying at increasing rates. What the impact of such movement and marriage rates will be on tribal national identity, federal Indian policy, and the government-to-government relationship is, however, impossible to predict.

Seeing the Big Picture   **From Riches to the "Res" (Reservation System)**

Map 1 in this reading shows land held by Indians in 1775 and 1992. Glance at the quality-of-life indicators in the appendix. Do you believe that socioeconomic standing and the loss of Indian lands are connected? How?

PANETHNICITY

Dina Okamoto[1] and G. Cristina Mora[2]

Dina Okamoto is a professor of sociology at Indiana University and **G. Cristina Mora** is an associate professor of sociology at UC Berkeley.

INTRODUCTION

The development of panethnic identities is a salient phenomenon within multiethnic societies and is an integral part of the social and political landscape in the United States. Scholars have used the term panethnicity to describe when different ethnic or tribal groups cooperate, organize, and build institutions and identities across ethnic boundaries (Cornell 1988, Espiritu 1992, Keyes 1981, Lopez & Espiritu 1990). Historically, this boundary shifting occurred in colonial settings as a response to the efforts of administrations that grouped native tribes

[1]Department of Sociology, Indiana University, Bloomington, Indiana 47405; email: dokamoto@indiana.edu
[2]Department of Sociology, University of California, Berkeley, California 94720–1980; email: cmora@berkeley.edu

Questions to Consider

Most non-Asian Americans have the tendency to "lump" Asians into a single, culturally homogeneous racial category. As many non-Asians see it, Chinese people are more or less no different from Vietnamese people or Koreans. Many non-Latinos think in the same monolithic way; Mexicans, Salvadorans, and Brazilians are lumped into one undifferentiated ethnic and/or racial group. These groups are, however, quite diverse culturally, religiously, and linguistically. Complicating perceptions of these groups is that a significant number of individuals in these categories have been here for many generations and have undergone extensive assimilation, while others, much larger in number, have arrived in the past few decades. Why do these groups get "lumped" together? Is forging a panethnic identity helpful, and if so, how? What are the implications of having new and old immigrants sharing social space and navigating the politics of race?

and enslaved populations into panethnic categories (Anderson 1991, Cornell 1990, Horowitz 1985). More recently, it has taken place among immigrant groups who have entered host societies with regional, national origin, and language differences and, over time, have come together and developed panethnic identities (Itzigsohn 2004; Mora 2014a; Oboler 1995; Okamoto 2003, 2006, 2014; Padilla 1985).

The vast majority of past research on panethnicity has been based upon single case studies. Scholars have documented how census surveys, birth certificates, school enrollment forms, and identification card applications routinely ask Americans to identify with panethnic Asian, Hispanic/Latina, or Native American categories (Nobles 2000, Rodríguez 2000). Research has also examined how

activists create slogans, such as "yellow power" or "red nation," to build panethnic social movements and bring attention to social inequality within minority communities (Cornell 1990, Maeda 2009, Nagel 1995, Rosales 2000, Wei 1993). Additionally, studies have detailed how ethnic media entrepreneurs develop commercials, comedies, and dramas that convey messages about the cultural bonds uniting Latino or Asian immigrant groups (Dávila 2012, Mora 2014b, Rodriguez 1999).

Panethnicity, however, is not simply an American phenomenon; it is also present across the globe. The Kikuyu in Kenya, the Moro in the Philippines, the Igbo in Nigeria, and the Malay in Malaysia were formed from smaller distinct groups on the basis of caste, region, ancestral place of origin, and religion (Horowitz 1985, Nagata 1981, Nnoli 1978, Wimmer 2008, Young 1976). Likewise, the Roma community is broadly composed of persons who hail from Romania, Spain, Bulgaria and other European nations (Csepeli & Simon 2004, Ladányi & Szelényi 2006, Prieto-Flores & Sordé-Martí 2011). Moreover, several national identities, such as Singaporean, Chinese, and Indian, are certainly panethnic as they represent a conglomeration of different ethnic identities (Eriksen 2002, Hill & Fee 1995). In each of these cases, ethnic or tribal groups came together long ago to form broader groupings, and today they share kin, interests, or cultural traditions across these lines.

The majority of our review focuses on three main subjects: (a) the issue of panethnic identification; (b) the conditions under which panethnic boundaries are constructed at the state, organizational, and local levels; and (c) new directions in research on panethnicity. We draw mainly on US research, but when possible, we incorporate international research that documents panethnic processes, even though it might not label them as such, i.e., research on census classification in Russia, intertribal unity in Nigeria, and work on Europeanness. We posit that panethnicity is characterized by an acknowledgment of subgroup diversity as well as a broader sense of solidarity. These aspects distinguish the concept from other forms of ethnic expression and influence how panethnicity should be understood in relation to ethnic processes, such as assimilation and racialization projects.

DEFINING THE CONCEPT AND APPROACH

Panethnicity refers to the construction of a new categorical boundary through the consolidation of ethnic, tribal, religious, or national groups. It is often misunderstood as simply synonymous with race, ethnicity, or national identity. Conceptually, we argue that panethnicity is uniquely defined by an inherent tension derived from maintaining subgroup distinctions while developing a sense of metagroup unity. The maintenance of subgroup identities is necessary for the success and longevity of broader-based panethnic groupings. Diversity is thus inherently a part of panethnicity. The Yoruba category exists only because it is comprised of different tribes, each with its own set of customs and rituals (Laitin 1986). The emblems of Latino and Asian American organizations, for example, are often snapshots of several different national flags (Espiritu 1992, Mora 2014b). Accordingly, one can feel panethnically European only if one has an ethnic attachment to a European country (Bruter 2005).

This recognition of ethnic diversity helps to sustain panethnic groups because it addresses fears about co-optation or unequal representation. For their movements to survive, panethnic leaders understand that they must balance the needs of different groups lest they disintegrate amid subgroup conflict. As such, leaders stress the multiethnic nature of their organizations and create narratives about the distinct ways that subgroups contribute to the panethnic whole. Moreover, an emphasis on diversity helps deflect arguments about the way that panethnic labels are imposed on communities. Panethnic leaders recognize that individuals are often, though not always, more attached to their subgroup identity than they are to their panethnic identity (see Jones-Correa & Leal 1996, Wong et al. 2011). Rather than force individuals to choose whether they are Mexican or Hispanic, for example, they exalt diversity and claim that panethnic identities are complementary to subgroup ones (Mora 2014b).

The need to manage diversity while promoting an image of cohesion and solidarity creates an inherent tension, we contend, within panethnic movements and categories. This differs from racial or ethnic forms of distinction where internal differences are often subsumed for the sake of producing a united, homogeneous front. When ethnic and racial movements recognize diversity, it is often to acknowledge the way that class or gender differences divide their constituents (Cornell & Hartmann 2007). Within panethnic movements, these forms of difference are secondary to ethnic subgroup ones.

In effect, panethnicity can be conceptualized as a group formation strategy based not simply on an argument of commonality, but also on one of internal diversity—whether ethnic, national, linguistic, or religious. Whereas researchers focused on race and ethnicity in the United States might emphasize group cohesion and elaborate on interracial relations, those focused on panethnicity begin by analyzing how different subgroups, comprising a broader identity or category view, interact and relate to one another. The study of panethnicity fundamentally steers researchers toward questions and issues based on intragroup dynamics, such as (a) the ways in which countervailing subgroup interests and identities must be negotiated and at times muted for the panethnic good and (b) how subgroup relationships might complicate the influence of political and economic contexts on group formation processes.

PANETHNIC IDENTIFICATION

Despite the persistence of ethnic and national identities, panethnic identification in the United States is on the rise. Early reports on Latino panethnicity, for example, showed that about 40% of Mexican Americans, Puerto Ricans, Cuban Americans, and others identified with panethnic labels (Jones-Correa & Leal 1996). By 2008, the percentage had doubled to over 80% (Fraga et al. 2012). Asian American identity has also increased such that in 2001 60% accepted the panethnic term as part of their identification (Lien et al. 2003).

Panethnic identification, however, has had an uneven rise across Latino and Asian populations. Studies conducted in the late 1980s and 1990s on Latino panethnicity found that the second generation and those with higher levels of education and income were more likely to identify as Latino or Hispanic (De La Garza 1992, Jones-Correa & Leal 1996, Portes & MacLeod 1996, Tienda & Ortiz 1986). Today, however, those correlations are weakening as many more first-generation immigrants are identifying panethnically (Fraga et al. 2009). Nonetheless, Cuban Americans are still significantly less likely than Mexican Americans and Puerto Ricans to identify as Hispanic or Latino (Fraga et al. 2012), and more recent research has attributed some of the differences in Latino panethnic identification to experiences of racial discrimination (Golash-Boza & Darity 2008). Class and education differences and experiences of discrimination have also marked panethnic identification trends within the Asian community, with the middle class most likely to be linked into panethnic networks developed in college settings (Kibria 2003, Lee 2004, Lien et al. 2003, Masuoka 2006, Wong et al. 2011; also see Read 2008). Among Asian Americans, Koreans are most likely to identify with a panethnic label and Japanese the least likely (Wong et al. 2011).

Recent work on European panethnic identification has demonstrated an increase over the past four decades (Bruter 2005), which has been most prominent among the middle class (Bruter 2003a, Fligstein 2009). This rise in panethnic identification is likely because the professional and middle classes have more resources for travel, more extended networks with Europeans in other countries, and more education—all of which expose them to broader arguments concerning European unity. However, there are also ethnic differences within the European middle class, with those from Denmark and Sweden being most likely, and those from the United Kingdom and Greece being least likely, to identify panethnically (Bruter 2003a).

To understand the meanings of panethnic identities, researchers have primarily drawn upon interviews with the sons and daughters of immigrants in the United States and have found that panethnic identities are understood in cultural terms, as a shared worldview or set of values and experiences, rather than in political terms (Kibria 2003, Louie 2012, Park 2008, Portes & MacLeod 1996, Tuan 1998). For example, Kibria (2003) found that most second-generation Chinese and Korean Americans referred to a panethnic identity based on shared orientations toward education, family, and hard work, as well as their common experiences of race, rather than a shared political community built upon the struggles emanating from the Asian American movement of the 1960s and 1970s. In contrast, studies exploring Muslim panethnic identity suggest that youth define Muslim panethnic identity as both cultural (especially religious) and political (Pew Res. Cent. 2007; see also Sirin et al. 2008). Additionally, research drawing upon survey data has demonstrated that identification with a panethnic label is strongly associated with a sense of linked fate—the belief that what happens to other ethnic groups in the panethnic category affects one's own life (Wong et al. 2011).

For some children of immigrants, the boundaries of the panethnic community only include second- and later-generation others, as there is a clear divide between native- and foreign-born in terms of shared culture (De Genova & Ramos-Zayas 2003, Kibria 2003). This indicates that, although panethnic labels are becoming more popular, understandings of what panethnicity actually means and who is included might differ by generation. These feelings might be most prominent in panethnic groups consisting of different linguistic groups. Thus, second-generation Asian Americans who are bonded by the English language might see more commonalities and more ties to one another than the first generation, for which language differences might create communication barriers (Espiritu 1992).

Research also shows that ethnic group members choose panethnic identities not only to signify who they are, but also to indicate who they are not. Some ethnic group members identify in panethnic terms to actively reject the labels of black, white, or American (Itzigsohn & Dore-Cabral 2000, Oropesa et al. 2008, Verkuyten & Yildiz 2007). For example, Ajrouch & Jamal (2007) found that, for those of Arab and Chaldean descent in the Detroit area, the adoption of a panethnic Arab American identity was consistent with rejecting a white identity. Massey & Sanchez (2010) discovered a similar pattern among Latin American immigrants: The vast majority chose a Latino identity characterized by hard work, devotion to friends and family, and an interest in helping others, which they defined in opposition to an American identity. And among Nigerians in the United States and the United Kingdom, "African" has emerged as a panethnic identity associated with high educational attainment and strong religious values that the second generation has adopted to distinguish themselves from African Americans and Caribbean immigrants (O. Imoagene, unpublished manuscript). This work reminds us that identities, like boundaries, are constructed vis-à-vis groups.

Despite the increase in panethnic identification, most research on the issue has found that individuals hold panethnicity as secondary to national identity. When provided with the option of identifying as Mexican or Latino, for example, most individuals preferred to identify with their national origin group (Fraga et al. 2009, Jones-Correa & Leal 1996). Among some communities, however, panethnicity has been rejected because it is seen as competing with nationality (Dhingra 2007, Hein 2006, Kibria 2003). For example, Cubans in Miami circulated bumper stickers and signs with the phrase "Don't Call Me Hispanic, I'm Cuban" to underscore their disdain for panethnic labels (Croucher 1997). And at one point, Chicano activist groups in the US Southwest viewed Hispanic and Latino labels as threats to their nationalist projects (Martinez 1990, Rodríguez 1998).

Among some black immigrant groups, the rejection of panethnicity often stems from a resistance to racialization. Instead of adopting a panethnic black identity, West Indian immigrants often choose ethnic identities, such as Haitian or Jamaican, to distance themselves from black Americans, owing to the negative attitudes and stereotyping associated with native-born blacks (Waters 1994, 1999). And in Britain, northern Sudanese immigrants rejected what they felt was an all-encompassing, racializing black label that glossed over important religious and ethnic traditions of Sudan (Nagel 2002). These instances of rejection and resistance to panethnicity beg the question of how the concept can be understood in relation to other processes, such as assimilation and racialization. We focus on this issue below.

PANETHNIC BOUNDARY CONSTRUCTION

Because panethnicity entails a consolidation of different groups, much of the literature has attempted to construct a theoretical framework for explaining panethnic solidarity. Although earlier scholars thought about panethnicity as simply an extension of a primordial ethnicity, Lopez & Espiritu (1990) contended that panethnic groups with structural similarities would display more solidarity and cohesion than those only with shared cultural affinities, such as a common language or religion. Comparing the cases of African Americans and Indian Americans, Cornell (1990) affirmed a structural argument and explained that panethnic group formation emanated from state-imposed economic and political systems, such as slavery and the reservation system, which ultimately shaped intergroup relations and the agency of ethnic groups to assert their own notions of identity and groupness. This research also elaborated on the importance of political strategy in bringing diverse groups together by constructing shared common interests (see also Trottier 1981, Nagata 1979). Padilla (1985) and Espiritu (1992) later argued that a group of leaders and a set of organizations were needed to create and sustain panethnic solidarity.

More recent research has theorized about panethnicity using US-based racialization and assimilation frameworks. Standard accounts of panethnicity suggest that racialization, or the process through which ethnic, cultural, and language groups are ascribed to racial categories, has led to the emergence of panethnic identities (Espiritu 1992, Itzigsohn & Dore-Cabral 2001, Laó-Montes

& Dávila 2001, Oboler 1995, Vo 2004). This categorization process, whereby diverse ethnic groups are treated as homogeneous with little or no recognition of differences in tribe, ethnicity, national origin, immigration history, and culture, has been a key influence on panethnic self-identification and group formation (Barth 1969; Cornell & Hartmann 2007; Jenkins 1994, 2008; Omi & Winant 1994; Winant 2000). Scholars have noted that when the larger society has lumped Asian ethnic groups together, activists and community leaders have responded by taking up the category of Asian American as their own and developing a pan-Asian narrative about a shared history of immigration and discrimination in the United States (Espiritu 1992, Liu et al. 2008, Zia 2000). Past research has emphasized the importance of the same racialization process for the emergence of other panethnic groups, such as Latinos and Native Americans (Calderon 1992, Nagel 1995, Padilla 1985).

The assimilation framework has been another way in which scholars have understood panethnicity. Some scholars in this tradition suggest that assimilation is the master trend among contemporary immigrants and interpret the development of panethnicity as a key part of this process (Alba & Nee 2003). When ethnic group members identify as Latina/Hispanic instead of Cuban or Mexican, this is interpreted as an indication that ethnic distinctions are waning and that assimilation will ensue. For other scholars who understand assimilation as a segmented process, when group members lose their ethnic distinctiveness and adopt panethnic identities, they are at risk of being downwardly mobile (Portes & Rumbaut 2001, Portes & Zhou 1993, Waters 1999). We contend that panethnicity is not simply part of the assimilation process but potentially an additional pathway that immigrants and the second generation can take as they continue to adapt to American society.

Although the process of racialization and models of immigrant incorporation can illuminate the concept of panethnicity and our understanding of it, they are limited. Ethnic distinctions matter, and we cannot simply apply assimilation models to panethnicity because such models presume that

when group boundaries expand to include others—here, when the dominant group expands to include new groups—this signals a decline in ethnic distinctions (see Okamoto 2014). The same cannot be said for panethnicity; its hallmark or defining characteristic is the inherent tension between smaller group boundaries that are based on ethnicity, culture, language, or religion and the larger panethnic group boundary.

Similarly, the explanation of racialization as a consolidating force that generates new group formations and identities is powerful, yet it presumes that all group members will identify along panethnic lines. It essentially overpredicts the extent of panethnicity and does not take into account the classification struggle or the ways in which factors like the state (policies, practices); institutions/organizations (churches, civic organizations, professional groups, lobbying groups); and local contexts legitimate panethnic categories and create shared interests among different ethnic and national origin groups. We argue that linking the findings from these studies helps us understand the conditions and processes that encourage panethnicity.

Specifically, we argue that structural conditions such as state classification schemes and racially segregated labor markets, as well as cultural narratives created and reinforced by organizations, community leaders, and the media, generate a social context where panethnic identities resonate with group members. We turn to a discussion of this literature next and highlight the advances made in understanding how panethnicity is formed and sustained.

State and Classification

Research on the state reveals much about how governing bodies construct and reinforce panethnicity. In this section, we cull from three literatures—writings on intergovernmental organizations, studies on nationalism, and research on the census and social policy—to show how the state forms and legitimates panethnic categories.

Intergovernmental organizations promote regional panethnic identities with the aim of fostering unity among nations and encouraging policy change. The Organization for African Unity, for example, draws on a narrative of pan-Africanism to encourage the adoption of common human rights laws throughout the region (Naldi 1999), and the Association for Caribbean States stresses that member states share a common history of colonialism (Elbow 1997). The European Union has perhaps been the most effective at shifting policy changes and developing panethnic claims. Over the past several decades, the organization has spearheaded the development of several new policies across Europe, including the formation of a common European market and the opening of national borders (Sandholtz & Stone Sweet 1998). Moreover, the European Union has attempted to foster panethnic unity by developing a European flag, currency, and even an anthem (Shore 2000; see Smith 1992). Through this work, the European Union and other organizations convey that member states hold certain histories, values, or traditions in common, and they attempt to promote a shared sense of belonging that surpasses national borders. Further research on the subject, especially on the relationship between participation in supranational organizations and panethnic identification, can improve our understanding about the effects of these institutions.

Individual states also carry out panethnic projects. Research on nationalism shows that governments promote national identities, such as American or Canadian, which encourage groups within their borders to see themselves as part of a larger community. Policies that confer the same rights to all citizens, for example, allow subgroups to view themselves as equal, contributing members of the nation-state (Eriksen 2002). And it is primarily when citizens hold an allegiance to a nation that they become invested in defending and upholding the functions of the state (Gellner 2009). Indeed, panethnic national identities effectively help governments to better carry out state-building projects, such as forming an army or creating a taxation system (Smith 2010).

In the American context, several states have developed offices for Asian or Hispanic affairs, which create policies and programs along panethnic lines. In turn, communities have come together to promote panethnic identities for resource mobilization purposes (Espiritu 1992; Nagel 1986; Padilla 1985, 1986). Moreover, contemporary states also endorse panethnic cultural symbols, events, and narratives

(Anderson 1991, Sommers 1991). Federally sponsored events like Hispanic Heritage week and Asian Pacific American Heritage month, for example, provide opportunities for government officials to convey the common traditions, rituals, and values that unite panethnic groups (see Sommers 1991).

Institutions and Organizations

Institutional and local contexts are also important in legitimizing and encouraging panethnic identities. In particular, panethnic political organizations reinforce state categorization processes by providing narratives that help to obscure the role of the state (Hanson 1997). In the United States, mosques serve to connect Muslim immigrants from across the Middle East, emphasizing the way that Islamic practices unite them as one community (Jamal 2005). Catholic churches help do the same for Latino immigrants (Ricourt & Danta 2003). In these organizations, different groups are taught to see their religious identity as one that unites and can overcome ethnic differences.

The establishment of panethnic political and religious organizations can also lead to the rise of panethnic civic and professional organizations, as political leaders and activists branch off to form social services and other types of more specialized panethnic groups (Haddad 2004), providing additional resources to build panethnic communities. Espiritu (1992), for example, found that Asian American political leaders went on to form pan-Asian social service, community, and professional organizations (see Shiao 1998). Additionally, Mora (2014b) documented how Hispanic activists in the United States helped to encourage the rise of Hispanic nonprofits and foundations. This broader panethnic organizational infrastructure helps to create interethnic partnerships and provides opportunities for people to work across ethnic and linguistic lines to solve community problems (Okamoto 2014, Okamoto & Gast 2013).

Yet the literature also shows that it is difficult to maintain panethnicity within organizations because the needs and interests of individual ethnic groups are not always effectively represented (Espiritu & Ong 1994, Otis 2001, Shankar & Srikanth 1998, Vo 2004). Panethnic groups can even face difficulties if one subgroup dominates the panethnic agenda and overshadows other groups. Research on Asian Americans shows how Filipinos objected to the disproportionate influence that Chinese and Japanese groups had in Asian organizations (Espiritu 1992). Similar sentiments about inequality exist with regard to the influence of Mexican American groups in Latino political organizations (De Genova & Ramos-Zayas 2003). Differences based on national origin, citizenship status, generation, and social class complicate the construction of an all-encompassing group where all group members are deemed to have equal weight.

Panethnic leaders are a key part of the panethnicity process, as they develop strategies to assuage intergroup tensions and maintain harmony within the panethnic group. A popular strategy involves making groups issue focused. When Latino political leaders realized that the issue of foreign policy threatened to cause rifts between Mexican Americans and Cuban Americans, they began to emphasize domestic issues to bring the groups together (Mora 2014b). Another strategy involves organizing a loose coalition of one subset of the panethnic group— Caribbean groups that target English-speaking Dominicans and Trinidadians (Vargas Ramos 2011) or Ecuadoran indigenous groups that only include Quichua-speaking tribes (Pallares 2002). Both of these strategies are imperfect, however, and are vulnerable to accusations of favoritism and inequality.

The media also help to institutionalize panethnicity by uniting audiences across borders or simply generating stories about the existence of a panethnic identity (Bruter 2003b). More than 500 Arabic channels (Albizu 2007) and scores of Spanish-language channels (Sinclair 1998) reach audiences throughout the globe, and they play an especially important role in replenishing a panethnic identity among immigrants in Europe and the United States (Harb & Bessaiso 2006, Roth 2012). For example, Georgiu (2012) notes that Arab soap operas allow Arab immigrants in London to connect with one another, fostering topics for communication that cross ethnic lines. Likewise, Rodriguez (1999) argues that Latino panethnic television portrays issues about the immigrant experience and thus encourages Latin Americans in the United States to see themselves as part of the same immigrant community.

On the one hand, media serve as a platform for state, political, and civic actors to broadcast their messages about panethnicity. For example, census officials and Hispanic political leaders in the 1980s often appeared on Spanish-language television to speak about the importance of panethnic identification (Mora 2014b). English-language newspapers that targeted the second generation also helped Asian American leaders spread their message about Asian political solidarity (Wei 1993). Additionally, Arab public affairs programming provided opportunities for political leaders to emphasize the important role of religion in Arab panethnic identification (Rinnawi 2012).

On the other hand, media create their own strategies for conveying panethnicity, which is typically accomplished by developing programs that provide generic images of the panethnic community (Dávila 2012). With respect to Latino television, the specific nationality of characters and other media personalities is deliberately omitted, and actors and broadcasters tone down their accents to produce a generic panethnic sound (Rodriguez 1999). Panethnicity is also produced through linking together stories about different groups, creating a multicultural potpourri. For example, throughout the 2000s, pan-Arab news broadcast stations brought together stories about the Israeli/Palestinian conflict with news about the Iraq war and events in Lebanon and other Middle Eastern countries (Rinnawi 2012; see also Mellor et al. 2011).

Local/Structural Contexts

Once state categories exist, they are further institutionalized by the formation of panethnic organizations and legitimated by panethnic narratives deployed by organizations, community leaders, and the media. But simply because the state, organizations, leaders, and the media deploy panethnic categories and narratives, this does not necessarily mean that individuals and groups will identify panethnically and engage in panethnic organizing. Structural conditions can also affect the salience of panethnic identities and the extent to which distinct groups cooperate and organize under a panethnic category or label.

The demographic composition and current social structures in regions, cities, and neighborhoods can shape the ways that groups interact, which give rise to panethnic forms. In particular, research has demonstrated that urban contact resulting from migration can contribute to greater contact among diverse ethnic, cultural, and language groups. Cornell (1988, 1990) pointed out that it was not until Native Americans moved to cities where they could freely interact across tribal lines that a pan-Indian movement and identity were forged. Over time, as members of different tribes built up social networks and trust, they came to see themselves as sharing interests, especially in relation to out-groups that were more distinctive in terms of status, culture, and lived experiences (also see Espiritu 1992, Nagel 1995). This process of urban contact among different cultural and language groups also encouraged the greater recognition of shared commonalities among the Shona in Zimbabwe in the 1920s, when they began to work in townships, mines, and farmlands owned by Europeans (Burgess 1981).

Existing or emergent economic and social structures, such as labor markets and neighborhoods, can also give significance to panethnic boundaries (Cornell 1996, Cornell & Hartmann 2007, Nagel 1995, Sanders 2002, Yancey et al. 1976). These shared spatial locations can increase social interaction, help build social networks, and heighten perceptions of sameness (Kim & White 2010). Research has found that ethnic group members will develop and maintain strong ethnic attachments when they participate in similar market activities, especially when these activities are located in the same geographic area (Bonacich 1973, Min 2006, Reitz & Ashton 1980, Waldinger 2000) and when life chances are increasingly determined by ethnic group membership (Cornell & Hartmann 2007, Hechter & Levy 1994, Hechter 2000). This same principle holds for panethnic groups. In an analysis of panethnic organizing over the post-civil rights era, Okamoto (2003, 2006) found that when Asian Americans were segregated from whites and other racial groups in local labor markets, this led to higher rates of panethnic organizing. Racial segregation encouraged interaction between Asian ethnic groups and contributed to the development of interethnic trust and new commonalities, which resulted in panethnic solidarity (see Mettam & Williams 1998, Peled 1998 for non-US examples).

Similarly, geographic concentration in neighborhoods can encourage and even reflect the formation of panethnic identities, as neighbors interact, share experiences, and come to depend upon one another (Sanders 2002, Yancey et al. 1976). Using census data, Kim & White (2010) discovered that ethnic groups sharing a panethnic category (i.e., black, white, Asian, Latino) exhibited greater residential proximity than those that did not share a panethnic boundary. Past research has also demonstrated that Asian and Latino national origin groups living in panethnic neighborhoods tend to adopt broader-based identities and even take on the issues of others within the same panethnic category at a higher rate compared to those residing in areas with lower levels of panethnic concentration (Okamoto 2010, Ricourt & Danta 2003).

Simple demographics, such as the size of one's ethnic group, can also influence panethnic identities. The sizes of different ethnic groups can define whether or not they will be useful vehicles for political competition (see Hannan 1979). For example, when an ethnic or national origin group has sufficient numbers to mobilize collectively on its own, panethnic group interests are unlikely to be realized (Chai 2005, Chandra 2007, Espiritu 1992, Posner 2004). This principle of group size also applies to panethnic affiliations, such as friendships and intermarriage, where individuals are less likely to enter into panethnic affiliations if the size of one's ethnic group is relatively large (Kao & Joyner 2006, Okamoto 2007, Qian et al. 2001, Rosenfeld 2001). The assumption is that individuals will first search for coethnic partners, and if that pool is relatively large, they will not venture outside of ethnic boundaries.

Additionally, the level of ethnic and racial diversity in local areas plays a role in shaping panethnic outcomes. For the most part, living in areas with diverse Asian or Hispanic populations is associated with panethnic identification, affiliation, and organizing (Okamoto 2006, Oropesa et al. 2008). In such areas, ethnic group members are likely to have more intergroup contact, which may help break down interethnic barriers and encourage group members to see themselves as part of a larger grouping (see Blau 1977, Hewstone 1996, Pettigrew & Tropp 2011). However, the influx of new immigrant groups—another indicator of diversity—can also encourage group members to assert a panethnic identity. Established ethnic groups may feel threatened by newcomers and engage in panethnic efforts in an attempt to construct difference and maintain dominance over community resources (Hannan 1979; Olzak 1992, 2004). For example, in Malaysia, colonial authorities assigned ethnic groups, such as the Celebes, Borneo, Java, and Acehnese, to the Malay category in the mid-1800s, but a panethnic identity based on an adherence to Islam and knowledge of the Malay language only emerged after Chinese immigration dramatically increased in the early 1900s (Nagata 1981).

Finally, the literature has emphasized that local contexts characterized by exclusionary action, threats, or discrimination directed toward ethnic, linguistic, or cultural groups activate panethnic identities and group formation (Espiritu 1992, Massey & Sanchez 2010, Partes & Rumbaut 2001). A hostile environment can influence individuals and groups to develop interests with others who have similar characteristics or are treated similarly. As an example, Massey & Sanchez (2010) discovered that an increasingly hostile context of reception faced by immigrants and the accumulation of discriminatory experiences in the United States reinforced an emergent Latino panethnic identity among Latin American immigrants. Likewise, when the highland populations in Vietnam experienced conflicts with the state over territory and autonomy in the 1950s, members of distinct ethnic and language groups formally organized on a panethnic basis in response, and a panethnic Montagnard identity became meaningful at the local level (Tefft 1999; also see Fournier 2002, Gause 2011).

Yet alone, economic and social structures, and even contexts characterized by threats, do not operate in a vacuum to create panethnicity. State categories and panethnic narratives from leaders and organizations play key roles in generating panethnicity. Taken together, cultural narratives, processes of legitimacy, the roles of leaders, and structural conditions are important factors in generating panethnicity.

CONCLUSION

The consolidation of national, ethnic, tribal, or religious communities into a broader categorical group is a process and an outcome that is central to the study of race, ethnicity, and nation. Indeed, the issue of panethnicity directly addresses the question of how groups emerge, endure, become legitimated, and even disintegrate over time. As an approach, it forces researchers to think about the conditions that lead differing peoples to identify as part of a larger group and lead to categorical stability rather than simply subgroups in and of themselves. Although studies about panethnicity in the United States have proliferated, the field would benefit from moving beyond the case study model by employing an international and comparative framework. It is only when we are able to generate a discussion about panethnicity that engages US and international researchers alike that we will be best able to discern the processes and mechanisms that uphold panethnicity and undergird its global spread.

Seeing the Big Picture **Panethnic Fortunes: Riches and Rags**

Look at Asians relative to other groups in Sections VI (Income, Wealth and Poverty), VII (Employment), and VIII (Occupations) in the appendix. Might panethnic identity formation as a political strategy explain the relative success of Asians? How?

DISCLOSURE STATEMENT

The authors are not aware of any affiliations, memberships, funding, or financial holdings that might be perceived as affecting the objectivity of this review.

ACKNOWLEDGMENTS

We thank Michael Hechter and Doug Massey for their comments on earlier versions of this reading.

11

RACIALIZATION AND MUSLIMS

Situating the Muslim Experience in Race Scholarship

Saher Selod and David G. Embrick

SAHER SELOD is an assistant professor at Simmons College and DAVID G. EMBRICK is an Associate Professor of Sociology and Africana Studies at the University of Connecticut.

INTRODUCTION

The US race scholarship within sociology has yet to critically engage with issues surrounding immigration.

As the American landscape has changed, newer theories of race are required in order to reflect these changes. While the field of race and ethnicity has made strong advances in some areas, other areas

Questions to Consider

In the past decade scholars have examined how and under what conditions Muslim and Muslim Americans have been racialized. That is, being a Muslim, for many Americans, is like being a member of a distinct racial category like being African-American or white. The category Muslim is not a race but a religion. Imagine saying that Catholics or Protestants were distinct races. Arab is also *not* a race but is both a linguistic and a regional construct. One can be racially white, black, or Asian and define themselves as being an Arab. Many Arabs are Muslims and fewer than 15 percent of Muslims are Arabs. So how, then, did color, religion, and region get jumbled together? Selod and Embrick explain the social factors that have resulted in the racialization of this group.

remain underdeveloped. For example, race scholars need to theoretically explain how some cultural traits, like religious identity, have become essentialized and thus impact individual experiences with discrimination. Our aim in this review is to advocate for research that explores Muslim and Muslim Americans within race scholarship. We suggest that the concept of "racialization" is a useful theoretical tool which allows scholars the needed language to talk about the Muslim or Muslim American experience as racial.

Antiquated theories of race were primarily concerned with biological explanations for differences between Blacks and Whites in the United States (Turner 1978). As African American sociologists, such as W.E.B. Du Bois (1989) and Frazier (1968a, 1968b), began to theorize about race, they debunked many of the racist theories used to justify the oppression of African-Americans. Assimilation theories became popular after Robert Park (1950) introduced the stages in the cycle of race relations. Assimilationists were interested in how White ethnic immigrants were able to become a part of the mainstream, while

Blacks were still economically, politically, and socially disempowered. The majority of race scholarship in the early- to mid-20th century derived from a need to understand the experiences of African-Americans in society primarily because of their history with slavery and segregation in the United States. Although Native Americans were living in the United States at the time, their racialized experiences have not garnered the same amount of attention in sociology race scholarship as African-Americans.

In the middle of the 20th century, the Immigration and Nationality Act of 1965 lifted restrictions on immigration from non-European countries such as those from Asia, Africa, and the Middle East resulting in a new racial, ethnic, and religious landscape. As a consequence of this, current race scholarship has begun to look at the ways new racial paradigms can explain the experiences of these newer immigrant groups in the United States by understanding the social construction of race. One theory that has become influential is racial formation (Omi and Winant 1994), which argues racial categories laden with racial meaning are the result of the social, political, and economic influences of the time. Thus, racial and ethnic categories are constantly forming, evolving, and being maintained in society at the institutional and individual level of society. In the same vein, race theories such as the Latin Americanization Thesis (Bonilla-Silva 2004) attempt to racially classify American society into three (or more) strata determined primarily (although not necessarily) by skin tone, phenotype, hair texture, eye color, culture, education, class, and pigmentocracy: Whites, honorary Whites, and collective Blacks. These new classifications were created with the intent to move beyond binary racial theories that explained only Black/White relationships to ones that could include the racial experiences of newer racial and ethnic groups who migrated to the United States after the passage of the Immigration and Nationality Act of 1965. There are a few contributions these newer racial paradigms produced: a new language to explain how groups acquire racial meaning when they migrate to the United States and space to understand how racial meanings change due to political, economic, and social contextual shifts. Additionally, race scholarship is moving toward incorporating other types of racism, moving beyond skin tone. For example, ethnoracism (Aranda and Rebollo-Gil 2004) is a concept that incorporates cultural markers, such as clothing, language, and beliefs, as the basis for racism. Thus, cultural racism has become more prominent in understanding the complexity of racism for newer immigrant populations both in the United States and Europe (Modood 2005; Bonilla-Silva 2010). Modood (2005) argues that cultural traits are subjected to "othering" explaining how Muslims have become racialized, while Bonilla-Silva (2010) found newer forms of racism include essentializing cultures of minorities. Although there are differences in the way the two define cultural racism, both highlight the need for the examination of the importance of cultural traits in understanding race and racism.

This movement in race theory away from what often were phenotypical explanations of race creates space for a discussion of Muslim experiences within race scholarship. Rana (2011) relies on racial formation to examine the racialization of Muslims. He uncovers how historically religion was once used to differentiate Muslims and Jews from Christians into second-class citizens (Rana 2011). Muslims were once excluded from membership in European societies because they were viewed as inherently different from Christians because of their religious identity. This ideology justified colonization and imperialism against Muslim populations. It is important to revisit this history in order to understand the similarities between the past and the present in the current racialization of Muslims.

In the rest of this article, we do the following: First, we examine how religion was once used as a way to place individuals into social hierarchies prior to a system of race based on biological differences. The historical relationship of religion to race informs current discussions of the inclusion of Muslims in contemporary race dialog. Next, we unpack the concept of "racialization" and discuss why we believe it to be a useful (and more accurate) tool for understanding Muslim and Muslim American identity in America. Third, we provide an extended review of how racialization has been used by scholars to theorize about Arabs and Muslims in the United States. These scholars examined the impact of 9/11 on an

Arab racial identity and argue that Arabs are no longer an invisible minority but are rather a visible one (Naber 2008; Shyrock 2008; Tehranian 2008). As a result, much of the scholarship on 9/11 that incorporates a racial paradigm focused on the Arab experience. Thus, it is important to first understand how racialization has been used to talk about Arabs and race before exploring its application to Muslims. We also demonstrate how applying racialization to Muslims requires an analysis of gender. Too often, gender and race are treated as separate entities, even though our identities of gender, class, race, and sexuality intersect. We show that Muslim men and women are racialized differently. Finally, we conclude with suggestions as to how researchers might address some of the shortcomings we outlined above.

RELIGIOUS DISCRIMINATION: CREATING SOCIAL HIERARCHIES BASED ON RELIGIOUS DIFFERENCES

Prior to imperialist classifications of race, religious identities were used to organize people into social, economic, and political hierarchies. Religious discrimination toward non-Christians was prevalent in Europe; non-Christians were seen as inferior to Christians, which justified imperialism, and in many instances genocide. In Europe, after the expulsion of the Ummayyad dynasty (a Muslim population) from Spain, non-Christian society was differentiated into two types of people—those who were viewed as godless and those with the "wrong" religion. African slaves and Native Americans fell into the former category (Grosfoguel and Mielants 2006). Debate circulated about whether the indigenous people who were seen as godless were also without a soul. One school of thought perpetuated the belief that people without a soul could be enslaved since they were not human, while another view posited that these were humans who, rather than be enslaved, should be converted to Christianity (Wallerstein 2006). Thus, groups without a god were exposed to harsher forms of discrimination, such as violence and enslavement. Those with the wrong god were treated as if they could be saved, although they were still treated as less than human because of their religious differences. Religion was used to create a hierarchy very similar to a racial one, where some groups were seen as potentially assimilable, and others were treated as if they were incapable of being part of the human race.

Muslims, along with Jews, were placed in the latter category as individuals with the wrong religion and were deemed biologically inferior to Christians (Grosfoguel and Mielants 2006; Rana 2011). The term "purity of blood" was used to differentiate Jews, Muslims, and Christian converts from true Christians (Goldschmidt 2004). The prevailing ideology was that in order to be considered a "real" Christian, one had to have pure Christian blood. Religious identity had a biological component to it and was not simply based on cultural differences. It was believed that Muslims were inherently and innately inferior to Christians due to perceived biological differences. Consequently, Christians were placed at the top of the hierarchy in society, while Jews and Muslims were given second-class status.

Even though Muslims have been denied basic rights because of their religious identity for hundreds of years (especially in Europe), anti-Muslim discrimination has been largely ignored or minimized within academic scholarship. Rana (2007) argues prominent race theorists like Omi and Winant (1994) affirm anti-Semitism as a form of racism but ignore anti-Muslim prejudices that have been prominent in European history. For example, the term *Muselmann* was used during World War II to refer to Jews in concentration camps close to dying from starvation and exhaustion, whose listlessness and lack of expression were likened to that of a prostrate Muslim in prayer.

This final description attempts to undo the entanglement of Jews and Muslims in their history of shared racialization by referring to Muslims as Orientals and supplicants with a rigid disposition. This is itself an older description of Muslims that relies on

European stereotypes of the Turk and Moor in terms of bodily comportment. Hence this conflation of the Jew-as-Muslim refers to a projection of a racialized mutability of a religious state that is not only a religious practice but somehow an essential character (Rana 2007: 158).

Here, Jews are further dehumanized through an association with Muslims. Anti-Muslim and anti-Islamic sentiments have been closely connected to anti-Semitism, even though this has been largely ignored in research on race (Kalmar 2009).

This history is important to revisit because it incorporates the complexities of how individuals were historically situated as the "other." Religion was one of the many factors used to differentiate between groups of people based on biological differences, relying on the notion that you could have Christian or non-Christian blood. Parallels between the "one-drop" rule and this can be drawn. For example, imperialists created imagined racial and religious differences between populations in order to justify the genocide and colonization of Asia, Africa, and the Middle East. In a post-9/11 society, imperialism is once again being sold to the American public under the guise of the "war on terror." Wide acceptance of socially constructed notions of Muslims and Arabs as terrorists who are inherently opposed to democracy, freedom, and Western values attracts public support and allows for justification of illegal or irrational wars such as the US invasion of Iraq and Afghanistan (Razack 2008; Cainkar 2009; Rana 2011). This creation of the Muslim as the "other" is a racial project and should be situated within race scholarship. Racialization is a theoretical tool scholars can use to understand the creation, maintenance, and changing nature of racial meanings and experiences. In the next section, we review this theoretical approach.

RACIALIZATION

Racialization is not a new concept. European scholars have been defining and redefining racialization for the past few decades.[1] For example, Fanon (2004) used the term to talk about the "racialization of thought" in order to describe the way Africans who were colonized by Europeans adopted a colonized way of thinking about their national identities (Murji and Solomos 2005). Banton (1977) wrote about racialization as the process where European imperialists applied racial categories to individuals from colonized nations. According to Banton, this process is tied to race-making which is a product of misclassifications of humans based on imagined biological difference. In the United States, Omi and Winant (1986) employ the term to talk about shifting and changing meanings associated with race within the United States. "The concept of racialization signifies the extension of racial meaning to a previously racially unclassified relationship, social practice, or group" (Omi and Winant 1986:64).[2] Their definition of racialization is largely tied to racial classifications as they employ racialization as a process of racial formation, the process where racial categories are formed, occupied, transformed, and dismantled. While Banton (1977) and Omi and Winant (1986) view racialization as tied to an actual race, Miles (1993) argues that racial meaning can be given to various forms of difference such as ideological and cultural traits allowing for a discussion of the racialization of some groups without relying on phenotypical differences. By using Miles' application of the concept, "racialization" can be used to better understand how racial meanings are assigned to groups that were racially classified as White but were not afforded the privileges associated with whiteness, such as Jews and Irish (Kushner 2005; Garner 2009). Scholars can use racialization to identify how cultural traits of White ethnics were assigned racial meaning resulting in their rejection from a White identity, even if their skin tone was white. This framework has created some debate and controversy because of its capability of moving beyond discussions of phenotypical differences in a discussion of race and racism. Cohen (1994) contends it is impossible to talk about racial experiences without racial classification based on phenotypical differences. Another major critique of racialization is that as a concept, it becomes too broad and can incorporate a myriad of differences, such as gender

or sexuality, that are not inherently racial (Barot and Bird 2001; Goldberg 2005).

The critiques of racialization are problematic for a few reasons. First, it privileges biological definitions of race. Race scholars who insist race has to be tied to phenotype or pigmentation ignore the nuances of racism by reducing it to skin tone. Scholars can use racialization to understand how African immigrants who migrate to the United States acquire a new racial classification of Black or African-American due to their shared pigmentation, but they can also employ it to explain how signifiers such as language, religion, clothing, etc. acquire racial meanings. Racialization as a concept reflects the changing meanings of race within different political, social, and economic contexts, producing a more expansive and complex discussion of race. Applying racialization provides a more complex analysis of how Irish and Jews in the United States experienced de facto racism and were denied the privileges associated with whiteness (Ignatiev 1996; Brodkin 1998). It also explains how some White ethnic groups were able to vacillate in and out of whiteness. Scholars' use of racialization would provide a multifaceted and accurate understanding of White ethnic experiences, situating it within the appropriate social, political, and cultural contexts as opposed to trying to make sense of their experiences by comparing them with Blacks in the United States, a contextually incomparable comparison.

Scholars of racialization are able to bridge the gap between scholarship on immigration and race. Because race theories in the United States were used to understand Black/White experience, attempting to apply these frameworks to groups that were socially, politically, and economically contextually distinct is irresponsible. For example, Pakistani and Indian immigrants who migrated immediately after the passage of the Immigration and Nationality Act of 1965 were educated professionals (Smith 1999). Their economic status requires attention when analyzing the status of each group in relation to whiteness as well as the privileges they have access to and the ones they are denied. Although Pakistani and Indian immigrants have never been considered white, their experiences are not identical to African-Americans regardless of some similarities in pigmentation. Indian and Pakistani professionals gained access into White communities due to a combination of factors. They migrated with professional degrees to the United States after segregation was legally dismantled and therefore were granted opportunities denied to Blacks. Although they were provided economic opportunities, Pakistani and Indian immigrants and their offspring have not been fully accepted as Americans due to cultural, religious, and physical differences because they are perpetually viewed as foreigners. Thus, due to reasons for migration, their experiences do not mirror African-Americans, and due to their physical appearance and cultural traits, their experiences are not comparable with White ethnics. Because race is a fluid concept and not static, it is imperative to understand that racism does not only affect one group but also uniquely impacts racial and ethnic groups. Those who employ racialization are able to provide a space where race theory can move beyond a Black/White paradigm in order to discuss new racial meanings and new racisms experienced in new political, cultural, and economic contexts. Racialization is the needed language race scholars need to talk about the issues that are often ignored, such as immigration. The next two sections provide a review of how racialization has been used to theorize about Arabs and Muslims.

RACIALIZATION OF ARABS, ARAB AMERICANS, MUSLIMS, AND MUSLIM AMERICANS

Arabs and Arab Americans

After 9/11, the status of Arabs in the United States was viewed as tenuous. Many academics argued that negative attitudes and discrimination toward Arabs increased after the attacks on the World Trade Center. Notwithstanding, such arguments increasingly supported the fact that Arabs

were becoming a "visible" as opposed to an "invisible" minority (Alsultany 2012; Naber 2008; Tehranian 2008; Cainkar 2009). Because Arabs are racially classified as White, their experiences with discrimination are often overlooked or denied as racist. As a result, there was an increase in research that situated the Arab experience within race scholarship (Bayoumi 2006; Cainkar 2008; Jamal 2008; Naber 2008). When Arab cultural traits are essentialized as inferior, barbaric, disloyal, patriarchal, and a potential terrorist, Arab bodies are rejected from whiteness regardless of their assigned racial classification. Scholars use racialization in this case to demonstrate the porous boundaries of whiteness, where the social, political, and economic contexts influence inclusion and exclusion from racial categories (Jamal 2008; Naber 2008; Shyrock 2008). This application of racialization to Arab bodies should be questioned because it does not accurately reflect or represent all Arab experiences. It is important to clarify the specific factors which result in an Arab population being stripped of privileges associated with whiteness and whether or not this universally impacts the entire Arab population. Thus, some Arabs are viewed and treated as White in society and enjoy the privileges associated with whiteness, while others do not. In other words, utilizing racialization to talk about Arabs in the United States requires a more thorough examination of the specific characteristics that result in differential experiences with race and racism.

Shyrock's (2008) analysis of the 2003 Detroit Area Arab Study (DAAS) revealed that religion is an important factor in whether or not Arabs self-identify as White or not. Shyrock (2008) found 73 percent of Christians identified themselves as White compared with 50 percent of Muslims, highlighting that religion influenced how Arabs racially identified themselves. Another study on Arabs and psychological stress showed Arab Muslims were more likely to experience increased levels of stress due to discrimination compared with Arab Christians (Amer and Hovey 2007). These studies demonstrate the salience of religion in the racialization of Arabs as well as its influence on Arab experiences with racism. Although a Muslim identity contributes to the exclusion from whiteness, situating anti-Muslim experiences within race scholarship has been difficult. Attempting to fit the Muslim experience into the existing paradigms of race becomes hard to do because Muslims are not a monolithic group racially, ethnically, or economically. Thus, they do not comprise one racial category but are members of many existing racial groups. Rather than abandon efforts to situate Muslim experiences within a racial framework, race scholars need to find newer tools and paradigms that accurately reflect the changing nature of race and racism.

More race scholars are finding the concept of racialization useful in analyzing the Muslim experience in the US context (Kibria 2011; Rana 2011). As the result of increased levels of discrimination and prejudice against Muslims in the United States (Pew Research Center for the People and the Press 2009), there has been an elevated interest in anti-Muslim racism and Islamophobia. This requires investigating how religious signifiers acquire racial meaning. The next section summarizes this newer trend of applying racialization to Muslim experiences.

Muslims and Muslim Americans

The term Islamophobia is frequently used to describe the negative images and feelings that exist toward Islam. Runnymede Trust Commission's report, *Islamophobia: A Challenge for Us All* (1997), defines Islamophobia as the view of Islam as a separate, aggressive, violent, sexist political ideology promoting military advancement. Halliday (1999) problematizes the utilization of Islamophobia as a framework because of its overreliance on attitudes toward a religion rather than acts toward individuals. Islamophobia and racism are not mutually inclusive terms. Rather, Islamophobia is conceptualized as a form of phobia toward a religion rather than a label for discriminatory actions against Muslims. In a post-9/11 society, however, a new framework is necessary that allows for an examination of the experiences of people with anti-Muslim racism.

A Muslim identity, although diverse, can trigger certain shared experiences regardless of one's racial or ethnic background exemplified by

the public and state scrutinizing of Muslims in Europe and North America (Cole 2003; Razack 2008; Cainkar 2009; Meer and Modood 2010; Peek 2011; Rana 2011). Muslim men and women experience racialization in different ways because of their gender. Because some Muslim women wear one of the most recognizable symbols of Islam, the hijab, they are easily identifiable as a Muslim (Williams and Vashi 2007) and have become targets for verbal abuse by the public (Cainkar 2009). Muslim men, on the other hand, are viewed as potential terrorists and a threat to homeland security (Cainkar 2009; Rana 2011). For example, immediately after the terrorist attacks, the United States waged the "war on terror" by invading Afghanistan and Iraq, and domestically through laws and policies implemented to monitor non-citizens as well as citizens. The first step in this war was to define the enemy, which resulted in the widespread acceptance of the socially constructed terrorist as a Muslim (Rana 2011). This stereotype was not a new one, but one that has been in existence for decades. This association of Muslims as a terrorist and violent has been deeply ingrained in the psyche of many Americans prior to 9/11 through Orientalist stereotypes in the media (Mandel 2001; Calvert 2007; Gottschalk and Greenberg 2007; Shaheen 2008). Thus, it was easy for Muslims to become suspects and targets of the policies and laws passed in order to protect society from the enemy living within. An example of one law passed in 2001 is the USA PATRIOT Act, Uniting and Strengthening America by Providing Appropriate Tools Required to Intercept and Obstruct Terrorism, which attacked the civil liberties of Muslim immigrants and citizens in the United States by making secret searches and wire-taps without probable cause legal and allowing the deportation of noncitizens for associations with unfavorable political organizations (Cole 2003). The National Security Entry-Exit Registration System (NSEERS or more widely referred to as the Special Registration Program), enacted in June of 2002, required non-citizen men over the age of 16 from twenty-four Muslim countries to undergo fingerprinting and interrogations (Cainkar 2009;

Maira 2009). Islam as a religion became synonymous with terrorism, and as a result, Muslim men were criminalized (Rana 2011). Thus, gender plays a significant role in how Muslims are racialized. Muslim men are targeted by the state as potential threats to national security. They become the terrorist. The combination of laws and policies in addition to the internalization of existing stereotypes created the political and social contexts for the treatment of Muslim men as the "other."

The experiences of Muslim women vary from that of Muslim men. Muslim women have not been treated as if they were a national threat but rather are viewed as if they are a cultural threat to society. Indeed, Razack (2008) demonstrates how Muslim women are viewed as imperiled by Muslim men. This rationale has then been used to justify imperialism and war against Muslim nations. In the United States, the hijab has often been associated with inequality and the subordination of women rather than evidence of women's agency (Williams and Vashi 2007). Second, women who are identifiable as Muslim are viewed as a cultural threat to Western ideals of feminism and equality of the sexes (Ahmed 1992; Razack 2008). Thus, a Muslim identity racializes women as subordinate, oppressed, and powerless women in relation to violent and aggressive Muslim men.

European scholars are also employing racialization to understanding the Muslim experience in Europe. Meer and Modood (2010), for example, argue that social hierarchies of individuals were once based on religious differences. Hence, perceived differences of human bodies due to religion preceded biological racism in Europe, resulting in the horrific treatment of Muslims and Jews. They argue the ethnic cleansing of Bosnian Muslims represents a return to this ideology. Cultural racism incorporates religious difference as a way to differentiate individuals into deserving and undeserving of certain rights and privileges.

 Current Muslim experiences with racism illustrate a return to essentializing religious differences to differentiate between the deserving and undeserving in America as well as in a global society. When cultural traits are racialized, this enables an understanding of how Muslim experiences with discrimination are racial in nature (Rana 2011). Muslim signifiers and symbols have become riddled with essentialized racial meanings such as foreign, violent, aggressive, and misogyny. Taken together, these stereotypes result in the belief that a Muslim body is incapable of upholding democratic or Western ideals and values. This justifies the surveillance of Muslims because they are viewed as a disloyal population that is a threat to national security. It also justifies military action against Muslim populations around the world.

One of the few scholars in the United States who has thoroughly engaged with racialization of Muslims is anthropologist Junaid Rana. Rana (2011) makes the case that Muslims have become a new racial category in his study on Pakistani labor migrants. He argues this is not a new phenomenon, but one that is situated in a history of nationalism, racism, sexism, and the exploitation of migrant laborers. According to Rana, the racialization of Muslims is situated within a "global racist system." In a post-9/11 world, the Muslim terrorist body derives from an imagined Muslim nation through the conflation of South Asian and Arab countries. "The conceptual history of Islamophobia is based in a theory of racial ascription of bodily comportment, superimposition, and dissimulation—that is the assorted ways to define 'race' based on visual attributes such as skin color and phenotype, as well as customs and costumes. The process of racializing Muslims involves placing biological and cultural determinism in a contradictory logic purporting that race is immutable and essential but simultaneously mutable and fluid" (Rana 2011:28). He argues the creation of the Muslim terrorist is how migrant laborers are criminalized and controlled in a global economy. When labor demands are exceeded or no longer needed, Pakistani migrants are criminalized as a threat to society and are deported or threatened with deportation. By unveiling the complex relationship of labor, immigration, racism, gender, and nationalism, Rana successfully demonstrates how a Muslim identity has become racialized as a threat to national security resulting in Pakistani labor migrants' precarious status within a global racial system.

While Rana makes a compelling case for employing racialization as a theoretical tool to analyze Muslim experiences with racism, his research had some noteworthy limitations. Rana's research assumes a homogeneous understanding of Muslim experiences. Although Rana (2011) shows the importance of gender when Muslim immigrant men's bodies are racialized as terrorists, his study does not include the experiences of American citizens, Muslim immigrants who do not migrate as unskilled laborers, or the impact of racialization on Muslim women's experiences. Arguing that a Muslim is becoming a new racial category based on his study of labor migrants is interesting, but he does not address how all migrants acquire a racial category once they come to the United States. In a racialized social system, all individuals are assigned a racial identity, and resources are allocated based on race (Bonilla-Silva 2001). Thus, Muslims are already racially classified in the United States, and to argue they have moved into a new racial category assumes that religion is the only factor in one's racialization. Rana fails to reveal how religion intersects with skin tone, gender, language, and nation of origin in further racializing individuals. Ultimately, Rana's argument is compelling and a contribution to studies on racialization.

DISCUSSION: THE FUTURE OF RACIALIZATION

There is a need for race scholars to work toward further conceptualizing racialization. For example, race scholars could use racialization to understand how boundaries of whiteness are maintained. As scholars begin to further develop this concept, it will allow for a broader understanding of race that can include immigrant experiences. Therefore, racialization should not be exclusively viewed as the process in which new racial categories are created (although it can be used to explain this process for African immigrants migrating to the United States) but should be used to understand how groups are rejected from whiteness and how race and racisms mutate and change depending on the social and historical context. In a post-9/11 society, Muslim civil liberties are not protected when their experiences with discrimination either by the state or their fellow citizen are viewed as necessary or acceptable in order to promote national security. This simply reinforces the notion that a Muslim is inherently dangerous to society. Furthermore, if the Muslim experience is divorced from racism, collective action and public outcry will be minimal. It is necessary to create race language that enables scholars to advance race scholarship. In order to make racialization a comprehensive tool, it cannot be utilized without an analysis of the intersection of other variables such as skin tone, gender, language, sexuality, and nation of origin. Racialization enables the intersection of gender and race that is so often missing from discussions of race. Racialization provides the appropriate language to talk about the details of how racial meanings are applied to Muslim men and women's bodies. It is the responsibility of race scholars to create new ways to talk about newer racial relationships in the United States. Until they do, this anti-Muslim discrimination, as well as other forms of racism, will be dismissed and ignored.

Seeing the Big Picture   **America's New Public Enemy**

The statistics on hate crimes in the appendix (Section IV) show patterns that are analogous to the attacks on Arab Americans and Muslims in the United States. How is the disproportionate number of hate crimes committed against racial minorities similar to what has happened to Arab Americans and Muslims in the past decade?

SHORT BIOGRAPHIES

Saher Selod is an assistant professor of sociology at Simmons College.

Dr. David G. Embrick is an associate professor in the Sociology Department Latino/as Section. He is also the current chair of the Society for the Study of Social Problems' Racial/Ethnic Minorities Division as well as the vice-president of publications for the Association of Humanist Sociology and the vice-president of the Southwestern Sociological Association. He has been invited to give talks on his work in a wide range of venues both academic and public to include University of Missouri at Columbia, Indiana University Purdue University at Fort Wayne, University of Illinois at Chicago, Chicago Commission on Human Relations, Chicago United, University of Oklahoma, Southeastern Louisiana State University, Duke University, Stonehill College, Roosevelt University, and, most recently, Transylvania University.

THE CONTINUING SIGNIFICANCE OF RACE

Racial Genomics in a Postracial Era

Kathleen J. Fitzgerald

KATHLEEN J. FITZGERALD is professor of sociology at The University of New Orleans.

THE RESURGENCE OF BIOLOGICAL NOTIONS OF RACE in the form of racial genomics is both unanticipated and predictable. It is unanticipated because in 2000, when the success of the Human Genome Project was initially announced, scientists declared the idea of race as genetic or biologically based to be dead. After all, the mapping of the Human Genome found that humans were 99.9 percent similar. However, within five short years, these same scientists shifted their analysis; instead of focusing on the overwhelming similarity among people, the focus shifted to the minor differences between humans, resulting in a new search for the biological meaning of race (Bliss 2012). It is also surprising because this shift occurred simultaneously as claims of a postracial society and colorblindness reigned in mainstream society. "At the very moment that race consciousness is intensifying at the molecular level, it is fading at the social level" (Roberts 2011: xi).

The resurgence of biological notions of race is predictable if this shift is understood to be an extension of racial science, which has been an integral part of racial domination. As legal scholar Dorothy Roberts argues, "the speedy resuscitation of biological concepts of race seems less surprising if we consider the intimate marriage of race and science that has lasted more than three centuries" (2011:26). Roberts argues that we need to understand "racial science" as more than eugenics and "scientific racism," or illegitimately using science to support racist ideas. Instead, she argues that we must understand race as essential to science because "the belief that race is natural has always been validated by mainstream—not aberrational—scientific theories and methods" (2011:28). Scientists created race, as the very idea of race is rooted in the science of zoology (Krimsky 2011). Scientists historically extended great effort to find evidence supporting notions of racial inferiority and superiority and, thus, helped reproduce white racial dominance. In fact, Roberts (2011:27) argues, "Science is the most effective tool for giving claims about human difference the stamp of legitimacy."

KEYWORDS

Race, Genomics, Group Position, Postraciality, White Dominance

One of the earliest examples of science being used in the name of racial domination involved the work of scientist Samuel Morton. In the early 1800s, Morton began collecting, measuring, and categorizing human skulls from across the world in order to prove his hypothesis that the racial hierarchy could be objectively established through evidence of physical distinctiveness along racial lines, primarily brain size. Perhaps not surprisingly, he concluded that Caucasians had the largest cranial capacity, and thus the highest intellectual endowment, followed by "Mongolians" and Native Americans, while Ethiopians had the smallest cranial capacity (Jackson and Weidman 2006; Roberts 2011). Morton eventually became a leading voice among American polygenists, the idea that the human races were actually separate species.

What is the significance of the reemergence of race science in the form of racial genomics for not only the sociological understanding of race and ethnicity as social constructs, but for the discipline itself? How does this impact how sociologists teach the social construction of race as common understandings of race are reified through simplified media portrayals of racial genomics?

While there have always been difficulties getting people to understand race as a social construct rather than as something biological, in an era where racial genomics is receiving increasing attention, sociologists are faced with an even

---

Questions to Consider

The results from a home-administered DNA ancestry kit told me that I was 0.2% North African. In the United States, the one-drop rule meant that having *any* black ancestors defined you as black and, by extension, defined you as an enslaved person. Does this trace amount of North African ancestry mean I'm black even though I have lived my life and am seen as a white man? Can I tell people I am mixed race? Are my children mixed race? How might ancestry testing challenge conventional notions of racial categories? Professor Fitzgerald examines the uses and misuses of DNA tests and what these tests mean in terms of US race relations.

greater challenge. Getting people to understand race as a social construction, when the idea of race as biological seemed so self-evident, has always been difficult. The problem today is no different, except that the idea of race as biological is pervasive in our culture. Research finds that the idea of race as biology is again alive and well in high school biology textbooks (Morning 2008, 2011). Mainstream media reproduce the notion of race as biology in TV shows such as Gates' *Finding Your Roots* and *African American Lives,* in which genetic ancestry testing is used to presumably identify the racial makeup of people or to identify what region of Africa one's ancestors descended from. The media also reproduce biological understandings of race through news reports about race-specific drugs like BiDil, a drug marketed to African Americans for congestive heart failure, and through popular news stories on the search for ancestry through the use of genetic genealogy, among other things. For instance, findings that President Obama is related to African slaves in the United States—through his white mother's ancestral line (challenging the idea that Obama had no direct links to slavery)—generated national media attention (Thompson 2012). Similar media attention surrounded research findings that Michelle Obama is a descendant of both slaves and slave owners (Swarns 2012).

While some argue that social scientists are naive in their resistance to viewing race as having any biological essence at all and that we need to understand race both as a social construction and as biologically based (Bliss 2012; Shiao et al. 2012; Walsh and Yun 2011), in this article, I argue sociology can help us understand the resurgence of race as biologically based. To do so, I rely on Herbert Blumer's classic argument on race as group position to understand the emergence of racial genomics. In other words, I argue that the return of biological notions of race is a response to the current threats to the racial hierarchy and white privilege.

The specific threats to white racial dominance that I focus on in this article are the original interpretation of the Human Genome Project that claimed there was no scientific basis for race, the electoral wins of President Barack Obama and the ensuing claim that we are a postracial society, and the increase in interracial relationships and biracial/multiracial identities. As Hochschild, Weaver, and Burch (2012) note, "The American racial order is unsettled . . . It used to be easy to identify groups' relative positions. On a vertical dimension of more to less, Whites held the overwhelming share of desirable resources and statuses and Blacks were at the bottom of most distributions" (p. 6). In the current era, identifying groups' relative position has become more difficult, claims to group identity have become more fluid, and white dominance is perceived by many whites as threatened. White perception of a threat to their social dominance exists despite the fact that on no empirical indicator are whites disadvantaged compared to people of color. In response, we see a return to science to remake race as biological, as science remains one of those ways racial dominance is perpetuated in a seemingly nonracial way (Bonilla-Silva 2013).

FROM SOCIAL CONSTRUCTIONISM TO RACIAL GENOMICS

While there is a long history of racial science supporting the understanding of race as biologically based, most extremely in the case of eugenics, the idea of race as a social construction eventually became the prevailing scientific view over the past century. At the turn of the twentieth century, social scientists, particularly anthropologists such as Franz Boas and his students, Margaret Mead, Ruth Benedict, and Ashley Montagu, among others, began arguing for understanding race as a social construction. Sociologists of the Chicago School, such as Robert Ezra Park, challenged biological notions of race, albeit while simultaneously reifying problematic notions of black cultural inferiority (Steinberg 2007). By 1950, United Nations Educational, Scientific, and Cultural Organization issued their landmark Statement on Race, which declared race to be a social myth rather than a biological reality, at least partially in response to the horrors of the Holocaust. Later, the findings of geneticist Richard Lewontin (1972), which showed that 85 percent of genetic variation exists within so-called racial groups, seemed to confirm the social constructionist arguments. Despite the scientific shift toward understanding race as a social construction, the idea of race as biological, of course, still resonated to a certain degree with the general public primarily because "race is a political system that will not be brought down with scientific evidence alone" (Roberts 2011:79).

Racial genomics, the current approaches to understanding race as biological, is the latest version of racial science and can be understood as a hidden mechanism of race, as fostering institutional practices that allow for structural racism to remain in a society that calls itself postracial. As sociologist Ann Morning emphasizes, "the historical record shows that when racial essentialism comes under attack, it survives by making its way to newer and more authoritative areas of inquiry . . . Today DNA offers the most compelling evidence" (2008:S129).

Population geneticists look to the nonrecombining DNA (DNA that stays the same over generations and does not split, such as the Y chromosome or mitochondria) to understand the history of genetic lineages and to try to understand a people's origins and migrations. Mitochondria provides all of us with a record of our maternal ancestry and the Y chromosome is passed intact from father to son, providing a record of a man's paternal ancestry. Human genome research has identified differences in allele frequencies, variant forms of a gene, which are referred to as single nucleotide polymorphisms. These minor genetic variations in human alleles correspond to the major continentally based population groups, which some scientists claim is roughly equivalent to race and argue that race is not merely a social construct but instead has a biological basis (Abraham 2006; Leroi 2005; Risch et al. 2002; Rosenberg et al. 2002; Wade 2006).

There is by no means consensus among natural scientists, much less social scientists, on this conflation of major continentally based population groups and race and many scientists have challenged this interpretation (e.g., Duster 2011; Roberts 2011; Graves 2005). For instance, since race is a construct that has changed across time and place, to say these allele frequencies vary along population lines that correspond to race leads to the obvious question, whose understanding of race? The racial categorization of what era or of what country? Since all human beings originate on the continent of Africa, where do we draw the line associating a particular race with a particular continent or region? The racial categorization system ultimately chosen by population geneticists is hardly objective science; it is a social decision, not a biological or natural one, and is intimately related to colonialism, imperialism, and nation building.

The problem with conflating race with major continental groups is best exemplified by exploring the current state of Jewish genetic genealogy. Jewish ancestry has been the most consistently identifiable in terms of allele frequencies, for the obvious reason that people "mate with their neighbors," as Smedley (2007) says, and thus are likely to share certain alleles with their neighbors. Jews, both through choice and coercion, have experienced relatively isolated reproduction and have been more endogamous than most human groups, and thus tend to share more genetic similarities. Yet, "Jew" is not a race as we currently understand the concept of race (although, certainly in different times and places, Jews have been defined as a distinct race) nor can Jews be considered to correspond with a major continental population. Additionally, even with the consistencies in allele frequencies that scientists find among Jews, Lewontin (2012) points out that none of the genetic elements found are characteristic of all or even a large majority of Jews. He argues that

> the closest thing to a 'Jewish gene' is an element on the Y chromosome of males that has been passed down at least for several millennia in the male line of the Cohanim family, and whose presence in a man's genome is evidence of descent from the priestly class. The frequency of this 'CMH'

(Cohanim Modal Haplotype) is around 50 percent among members of the Cohen line. It is [also] found in some other Middle Eastern groups in frequencies of around 20 percent. (Lewontin 2012)

Some social scientists have sought a middle ground on the issue: acknowledging that race is both socially constructed and biologically based (Bliss 2012; Shiao et al. 2012; Walsh and Yun 2011). Viewing the debate between social constructionists and racial essentialists as futile, sociologist Catherine Bliss (2012) has argued for understanding the scientific shift from focusing on the genetic similarity of humans to the minute genetic differences between humans through a notion of anti-racist racialism. With this notion, she suggests recognizing racial categories while not embracing a racial hierarchy, stating, "there is no rank to races but that there are nevertheless discrete populations worth studying" (2012:15). She is correct in an abstract sense that it is not the mere categorization of humans into discrete groups that is problematic but instead is the fact that we turn racial categories into a racial hierarchy that results in inequality. Haney-Lopez (2011) would argue, however, that one cannot separate race from the racial hierarchy because they are necessarily interrelated; races were created in order to establish white racial group dominance. In fact, he argues that one of the ways postracialism operates to obscure ongoing racism is by recognizing race while simultaneously ignoring the asymmetric group hierarchy. Race as a social, historical, and political creation was designed to allow one group to control access to resources and deny those resources to other groups; thus, the racial hierarchy cannot be separated from cultural understandings of race.

Other social scientists avoid using racial terminology, while accepting the understanding that human populations exhibit some level of genetic diversity that distinguishes human groups from one another. Walsh and Yun (2011) argue that social scientists should accept the genetic evidence of race, yet dispense with the term race, replacing it with "population" or "ethnic group," claiming

that the "essentialist versus constructivist" debate is really one of the terminology rather than empirical reality. While their acceptance of biological notions of race is problematic, their solution to use the term "ethnic group" in place of race has its own dilemmas. Particularly in light of the shift to what sociologists refer to as color-blind racism or laissez-faire racism, where racial inequality is viewed as a result of cultural deficiencies of minority groups (Bobo and Kluegel 1993; Bonilla-Silva 2010), simply shifting the terminology to "ethnic group" will do nothing to distance the idea from the baggage associated with race/ethnicity. It will still allow for a racial/ethnic hierarchy to exist and be perpetuated and it will still fuel notions of racial inferiority and superiority, only it will do so by linking cultural deficiencies to genetic deficiencies of populations.

Shiao et al. (2012) also proposes changing the terminology as a way to avoid the context, meaning, and consequences of using racial terminology. Rather than using the term "race," they argue for using the notion of clinal classes to understand the clustering of alleles, similar to the way the term "class" is used among social scientists today. Terminology taken from biology, clines refer to species that exhibit gradual genetic phenotypic differences over a geographic area. They argue that

> clinal classes are a complementary measure of ancestry in terms of how both physical geography and mating restrictions have produced clusters in human genetic variation . . . clinal classes assume a common evolutionary history, possess extensive genetic similarities, and coexist with clinal variations both within each class and across classes. (Shiao et al. 2012:72)

It is clear that science is still in the "race business," and racial genomics is just the latest version of race science. Much like Morton's use of cranial measurements to support the racial hierarchy during the 1800s, racial genomics is seemingly objective science. Racial genomics challenges notions of the social construction of race in new and problematic ways because genetics is treated as objective science, in ways social science is not, and because race is being marketed to people in new ways. For instance, genetic ancestry testing companies sell racial identity and even target particular racial/ethnic audiences with their services: Jewish people, African Americans, and Native Americans as well as people of European ancestry. "Race is continually being remade, and it is being refashioned today as genetic genealogy tests, race-targeted pharmaceuticals, and high school textbooks make clear. When the race concept has been challenged . . . Americans have reworked and thus preserved it, often by recalibrating its relationship to science" (Morning 2008: S130).

RACIAL GENOMICS AND BLUMER'S "RACE AS GROUP POSITION"

I argue that we can understand the resurgence of biological notions of race through revisiting Blumer's (1958) classic argument that race is about group position. This argument was one of the first to emphasize race as structural rather than individual, which, of course, is a foundational idea for most of the major sociological perspectives on race today, including Feagin's (2009) white racial frame and Bonilla-Silva's (2010) understanding of "racism without racists" and color-blind racism.

In order to explain racial prejudice as a sense of group position, Blumer identifies four key criteria. One is that the dominant racial group feels a sense of superiority over subordinate racial groups. The second is that subordinate racial groups are perceived by the dominant racial group as intrinsically different and even alien from them. His third criterion involves dominant group claims to privilege. He expands on this by claiming, "it is the feeling on the part of the dominant group of being entitled to either exclusive or prior rights in many important areas of life" (Blumer 1958:4), a prescient point that predates the sociological interrogation of white privilege by at least four decades. The fourth key aspect of his argument is that "a fear and suspicion

that the subordinate race harbors designs on the prerogatives of the dominant race," or more to the point, that the subordinate racial group threatens the privileged status of the dominant racial group results in racial prejudice and discrimination (Blumer 1958:4). The dominant group is not necessarily concerned about subordinate racial groups per se, as they are deeply concerned about their own position in relation to subordinate groups. Finally, Blumer emphasizes that the sense of group position held by the dominant group reflects more about how things ought to be than what actually is. Ultimately, "race prejudice lies in a felt challenge to this sense of group position" (Blumer 1958:5).

Others have extended Blumer's argument to an understanding of "the role that group identity plays in the reproduction of racial inequalities" (Perry 2007:375) and that threats to group identity are threats to the ontological security of whites (Perry 2007). Still other research has relied on Blumer's notion of race as a sense of group position to document the links between white racism and threats to white privilege (Bobo 1988; Bobo and Hutchings 1996; Bobo, Kleugel, and Smith 1997; Bonilla-Silva 1997, 2010; Gallagher 1995, 2003; Jackman 1994; Wellman [1977] 1993).

CHALLENGES TO THE RACIAL HIERARCHY

If the resurgence of race as biology in the form of racial genomics is a response to threats to dominant group privilege, what are those threats? The U.S. racial hierarchy has faced unprecedented challenges in the last 20 years by a number of factors such as the original interpretation of the Human Genome Project that found human beings to be 99.9 percent similar, the electoral wins of President Barack Obama, the claim that we are a postracial society, and the increasing numbers of interracial relationships and biracial/multiracial identities. Such trends can be understood as threats to whites' sense of superiority, to their dominant group position, and to white privilege.

Human Genome Project and Race

A significant threat to white dominance was the initial interpretation of the Human Genome Project results in which humans were declared to be 99.9 percent similar. Population geneticists Cavalli-Sforza, Menozzi, and Piazza (1994), in their foundational book *The History and Geography of Human Genes,* claimed that trying to classify people into races based upon genetics was a futile exercise. As a species, *homo sapiens* is a highly homogeneous species according to geneticists. At a press conference in 2000, President Clinton famously declared, "I believe one of the great truths to emerge from this triumphant expedition inside the human genome is that in genetic terms, all human beings, regardless of race, are more than 99.9 percent the same" (Roberts 2011). Bobo (1999) has argued that "dominant group members must make an affectively important distinction between themselves and subordinate group members" (p. 449), a job made that much more difficult by this finding. Ultimately, racial subordination requires the ability to distinguish between groups of people in some way. Thus, seeking genetic evidence of race operates to reestablish these once taken for granted distinctions between human groups.

Electoral Wins of President Obama

With the election of Barack Obama in 2008, for the first time in U.S. history, the face of political power was not white, presenting at least a symbolic challenge to whiteness. However, more is going on. As Tea Party rhetoric exposes, many whites believe themselves to be racially disadvantaged relative to minorities by the policies of the Obama administration. Of course, this is not true. Sociologist Lawrence Bobo states, "the point is not that these perceptions are accurate. Rather, it is that many people see themselves and other groups with whom they identify as losing ground to members of a racial minority group" (1999:459). While the economic recession that began in 2008 has hit the white middle class hard, on most socioeconomic indicators, African Americans have actually lost ground during the Obama era (Smiley and West 2012).

Claims of Postraciality

The notion of a postracial society, a term that sociological research challenges but which became part of the mainstream discourse after the election of President Obama in 2008, also presents a symbolic challenge to the racial hierarchy. The term "postracial" signifies a society in which racial differences are no longer significant (Love and Tosolt 2010). If the idea that the United States is postracial is widely believed by whites to be real, it represents a threat to white privilege. Privilege and disadvantage are relational statuses; one cannot exist without the other. The rhetoric of "postracialism" implies that barriers formerly faced by racial minorities are no longer obstacles. What remains unsaid, however, is what postracialism means for the dominant group. It clearly implies a lessening of privilege, as the obstacles racial minorities faced were the very privileges whites counted on to benefit them, consciously or not.

Increases in Interracial Relationships and Biracial/Multiracial Identities

Finally, we look to the increase in interracial relationships and biracial/multiracial identities as another threat to white dominance, as encroaching on "whiteness," thus threatening whites' sense of dominance and white privilege. Sociologists have long looked to rates of interracial marriage in a society as a barometer of the ongoing significance of race. The data on interracial intimacies show that the United States is not a color-blind society. However, attitudes toward interracial marriages have changed enormously since World War II. In 1958, when Gallup first asked Americans whether or not they approved of marriage between blacks and whites, only 4 percent approved. By 1983, 50 percent of people surveyed still disapproved of interracial marriage. As of 2007, only 17 percent of Americans disapproved of black–white intermarriage and 77 percent of Americans approved (Romano 2003).

These changes are often viewed as racial progress, but they can also be understood as a threat to white dominance. As Jacobson (1998) points out, the policing of sexual boundaries—the defense against hybridity—is precisely what keeps a racial group a racial group . . . from the perspective of white supremacism interracial liaisons 'resulted in mixed race progeny who slipped back and forth across the color line and defied social control.' Thus sexuality is one site at which all the economic advantages, political privileges, and social benefits inhering in a cultural invention like Caucasian converge and reside. (1998:3)

In the United States, people tend to adhere to the norm of endogamy, meaning they tend to become intimately involved with people similar to themselves, thus, rates of interracial marriage in the United States are quite low. As of 2010, only about 7.6 percent of all marriages were interracial, and this statistic includes all possible interracial marriage combinations: Asian white, Latino black, Native American white, black–white marriages, and so on. However, interracial marriage rates have more than doubled since 1980. In 2008, a record 14.6 percent of all new marriages, defined as individuals who married within 12 months of being surveyed, were interracial. Even if rates of interracial marriage appear low, it is clear that there has been a dramatic shift in the past 40 years on the issue, paralleling changes in attitudes toward interracial marriage over the same period.

Rates of interracial marriage do vary by group, for instance, Hispanic–white marriages are the most common, while black–white marriages are the least common. Black–white marriages have increased in the last 30 years, but they have increased at a slower rate than interracial unions that do not involve a black spouse (Root 2001). White–other marriages, which refer to unions between a white and an Asian American or a Native American spouse, have more than doubled since 1980.

Interracial intimacies may be the most significant barometer of societal assimilation, but looking at the fluid racial identities claimed by biracial/multiracial people allows us to explore another challenge to white dominance. Biracial/multiracial people have always recognized the problematic nature of racial categorization since they never fit neatly into discrete, socially constructed racial categories, however, as long as the "one-drop rule" reigned, they found themselves forced to accept racial categories as at least a political reality (Rockquemore and Brunsma 2002). Biracial/multiracial people gained a certain amount of legitimacy with the 2000 census when, for the first time, people were allowed to check more than one racial category. In 2000, approximately 2.4 percent of the population marked more than one race (Saulny 2011). According to the 2010 Census, nine million people, or about 3 percent of the population, reported more than one race.

There is nothing new about biracial/multiracial people; what is new is that so many of these people are claiming a biracial/multiracial identity rather than being constrained in their racial identity choices to being black, as the one-drop rule prescribed. People who grew up in the pre–Civil Rights era were more likely to identify as black, while those born in the post–Civil Rights era show more fluidity in their racial identity—at different points in their lives identifying as black, biracial, and sometimes even white (Harris and Khanna 2010; Rockquemore and Brunsma 2002). Some argue that they are rejecting the color lines that have long defined our nation (Saulny 2011).

Many argue that the increasing presence of people claiming biracial/multiracial identities does not really challenge our existing racial order because it does not challenge whiteness (Dalmage 2004; Spencer 2011). Spencer (2011), for instance, argues that we are merely adding new nonwhite categories, which in no way challenges the racial hierarchy where whites are in a position of privilege and blacks remain on the lowest rungs of the hierarchy. However, while the increasing numbers of people claiming biracial/multiracial identities may or may not disrupt the racial hierarchy, the multiracial idea does disrupt notions of race as fixed and biological, which is a powerful challenge to our racial ideology, our racial hierarchy, and, ultimately, white privilege.

DISCUSSION

Using Blumer's notion of race as a sense of group position, the previous four examples can be understood as threats to white dominance. Blumer's first point, that the dominant group feels a sense of superiority over the subordinate group, is threatened by the election of Obama, twice, to the presidency and the perception among many whites that this represents a disadvantage for whites. Ultimately, this contributes to white perceptions of subordinate racial groups "getting out of place" (Bobo 1999).

His second point, that the dominant racial group views subordinate racial groups as intrinsically alien and different from them, was clearly threatened by the initial interpretation of the results of the Human Genome Project that there was no significant genetic difference between humans and that humans are, essentially, all the same. The increase in and legitimation of biracial and multiracial identities also challenges the sense dominant racial groups have of subordinate groups being intrinsically different from them because it treats race as fluid rather than discrete. Discrete racial categories allow one to more easily see someone as different or alien, whereas fluid racial categorizations make such assumptions problematic.

Blumer's third point pertained to dominant group privilege. The rhetoric of postraciality surrounding Obama's electoral wins was that the United States was now a postracial society, which threatened dominant group privilege because without race, a racial hierarchy on which whites are advantaged could not exist. The increase in interracial marriages, while still accounting for a small percentage of U.S. marriages overall, can also be understood as a threat to dominant group privilege. The fastest growing rates of interracial marriage are between Latinos and whites and Asian Americans and whites, and the least common are black–white intermarriages. Bonilla-Silva (2010) argues that this is evidence of his Latin Americanization thesis, or the shift to a triracial system rather than the erosion of the U.S. racial hierarchy. Under this new racial hierarchy, whites remain at the top and blacks remain on the bottom, while an emerging category of "honorary whites" exists in the middle. The "honorary white" category consists of some Latinos and Asian Americans, such as light-skinned Latinos, Japanese Americans, Korean Americans, Asian Indians, Chinese Americans and Middle Eastern Americans, and acts as a buffer between whites and blacks, helping to protect white privilege and to preserve white racial dominance. Increasing rates of interracial marriage threaten white privilege, unless whiteness is expanded and a buffer category such as that of "honorary whites" is implemented, which could still be perceived as a threat to dominant group privilege by whites.

All four of these trends fit with the final tenet of Blumer's argument, which is that racial prejudice is the result of the dominant racial group feeling that their status is threatened by the subordinate racial group or groups. As Perry argues, "contemporary white culture and identity, though no longer wedded to blatant expressions of white racial superiority, are nonetheless still shaped by colonial discourses of self-other/universal-particular that invoke and underhandedly sustain notions of white supremacy" (2007:380). Ultimately, she continues, "identity, in itself, addresses a need for ontological security—knowing one's 'group position' on the scope of being and existence" (Perry 2007:377).

In the face of such challenges to white racial dominance, racial genomics emerges as a way to keep our notions of race alive. This is particularly true in the ways race is reified in the marketing of genetic ancestry testing to individuals. There are at least 15 companies that offer consumers genetic genealogy services and many of these specifically target their clientele along racial lines. For instance, most of the companies offer Y chromosome and mitochondrial DNA (mtDNA) tests which identify patterns of mutations that are thought to show European ancestry. One company claims to be able to help people find out where their ancestors came from in Africa. Many companies claim to offer genetic ancestry testing specifically for so-called Native American DNA markers (Tallbear 2008). Another company offers to test for Jewish ancestry, specifically offering the "Cohanim chromosome" test (Greely 2008).

Since 2002, almost a half-million people have pursued genetic genealogy testing (Duster 2011). Some journalists have found DNA ancestry testing to be much more common among African Americans, primarily due to the limitations placed upon them in pursuing traditional genealogical research due to the slave trade and the erasure of much of African culture in America (Duster 2011; Greely 2008; Nelson 2008). Many Jews have also embraced this technology since genetic genealogy can provide clues about a people's origins and migrations, and some genetic markers indicating migration patterns have been discovered. Many people who believe they have Native American ancestry are unable to provide adequate evidence of this to gain tribal membership (Fitzgerald 2007). Thus, however flawed the science, genetic ancestry testing holds some appeal to people who have no other way to prove their Native American ancestry (Tallbear 2008; Golbeck and Roth 2012). This has placed some pressure on Native American tribes to include these new "genetic cousins" as official tribal members, despite the fact that such people do not qualify for tribal membership through traditional methods.

While most of these prior examples do not involve the dominant racial group, whites, genetic ancestry companies are still reifying race and whiteness no matter who their target audience is. First, by claiming to find evidence of a biological basis of racial group membership (black, Native American, or Jewish in most examples), "white" is also being created, as racial categories are relational and hold no meaning in isolation. Second, most genetic ancestry testing companies offer plenty of information on European lineage for their white consumers. While genetic ancestry testing is being aggressively marketed to racial/ethnic minorities, it is hard not to notice the Eurocentrism of the haplogroups (a DNA haplogroup is defined by differences or mutations in human mtDNA) relied on by genetic genealogy companies. For example, Sykes' (2001) book *The Seven Daughters of Eve* argues that all modern Europeans fall into one of the seven ancestral lines and share a common ancestor known as Mitochondrial Eve. Additionally, in my observations of a genetic genealogy online discussion board, I have found that while genetic genealogy results almost always indicate admixture, which refers to evidence of the breeding between two or more previously isolated populations, how people interpret their findings is another matter. They overwhelmingly focus on rather narrow conceptions of their whiteness rather than having admixture results challenge how they understand race (Fitzgerald 2013).

Certainly, there is the hope that genetic ancestry testing can challenge the racial hierarchy and the notion of discrete races. Some researchers emphasize the "potential of new genetic knowledge to transform long-standing notions of social coherence and belonging" (Brodwin 2005:139). Hackstaff (2009) argues that genetic genealogy can "transform our racial 'common-sense' by reconstituting our social histories" (p. 191). However, as it stands, these companies seem to be reifying twentieth-century racial categorizations rather than transforming our understanding of race. A significant problem with the design of genetic ancestry testing is that they begin with existing racial categories and work backward from there, which biases their findings. In other words, they begin with existing racial categories that were socially and politically constructed to assist colonial and imperialist agendas, and then apply those categories to different times and places as if they are somehow universal, an assumption that runs counter to everything we know about race.

Genetic ancestry tests compare a sample of a customer's DNA with DNA samples from Western Europe, West Africa, East Asia, and indigenous Americans—to see if they match Ancestry Information Markers from those populations. The results of these DNA searches have been interpreted as a measure of racial makeup (results claim that someone is 48 percent African, for instance). However, assessing the probability that someone comes from a particular region of the world is not the same as discovering one's racial ancestry or, by extension, their current racial makeup.

An additional problem with genetic ancestry testing is that these companies begin with an assumption of racial purity, which is problematic. As sociologist Duster (2011:105) explains, "the process relies excessively on the idea of 100-percent purity, a condition that could never have existed in human populations." Population geneticists treat races as pure (one can be "African" or "American Indian" or "European") and then explain genetic ancestry as admixture, the mixing of these otherwise pure races (Roberts 2011).

Why is racial genomics appealing to scientists who had once discarded biological understandings of race? While the average person may have struggled with understanding race as socially constructed and as NOT biological, most scientists throughout the twentieth century had accepted that race was a social construction. Bonilla-Silva (2010) emphasizes that color-blind racism perpetuates white privilege and white dominance without whites having any discernible hostility or resentment toward minorities. Roberts argues that racial genomics works in the same way in that scientists are able to "create a new racial science that claims to divide the human species into natural groups without the taint of racism" (2011:54).

However, this new science of race goes even farther than that. Not only do scientists working in racial genomics appear to lack hostility and resentment toward minorities, but they actually view their attention to race as a form of antiracism. Bliss (2012) argues that the paradigm shift in science from treating race as a social construction to viewing it as having at least some genetic basis was a result of several significant factors and has, ultimately, been what she calls "race positive." One is the shift toward minority inclusion in scientific and biomedical research, such as efforts to include minority participants and women in pharmaceutical testing, for instance. This shift is also due to scientists' reflecting on their own life experiences concerning race and many "personalize their participation in this new science of race" (Bliss 2012:6). Bliss finds that for current scientists, understanding race as biological is part of their commitment to racial justice and scientific ethics, rather than a perpetuation of the racial hierarchy.

Without doubting the sincerity of the scientists and their intentions behind reviving race as biology through racial genomics, it is still fair to question how realistic their position is. Scientists are members of the society they study, not separate from it, as those working within the sociology of knowledge remind us. When Gould ([1981] 1996) offered his critique of Morton's work in *The Mismeasure of Man* based upon his systematic replication of Morton's study, he argued that he found

> no evidence of conscious fraud. . . . Conscious fraud is probably rare in science. It is also not very interesting for it tells us little about the nature of scientific activity. . . . The prevalence of unconscious finagling, on the other hand, suggests a general conclusion about the social context of science. For if scientists can be honestly self-deluded to Morton's extent, then prior prejudice may be found anywhere. (pp. 86–88)

Thus, today's scientists' casual conflation of "major continental groups" with common understandings of "race" are just as much a product of a society with an entrenched racial hierarchy as they are anything else. It is also about more than how scientists understand clusters of alleles; it is how these are portrayed in the media and interpreted by nonscientists. We know that both conservatives who cling to a "color-blind ideology and liberals who believe in a postracial America have embraced . . . the science validating racial difference at the genetic level" (Roberts 2011:288).

Finally, the validation of racial genomics by the public at large should give us pause, as "the public expects biology to provide the objective truth apart from social influences. Geneticists and the public should realize that the science of genetics is often closely intertwined with social attitudes and political considerations" (Provine, quoted in Smedley 2007:329). Bonilla-Silva (2013) is more forthright in his critique, and refers to racial genomics as problematic, calling on "Foundations and government agencies alike . . . [to] sponsor work to debunk so-called 'genetic' explanations of racial inequality. And if they continue funding this work in the name of science, we must challenge them vigorously as sponsors of racism" (p. 39).

COLOR-BLIND AMERICA
Fact, Fantasy, or Our Future?

COLOR-BLIND PRIVILEGE

The Social and Political Functions of Erasing the Color Line in Post-Race America

Charles A. Gallagher

CHARLES A. GALLAGHER is professor and chair of the Department of Sociology, Social Work and Criminal Justice at La Salle University in Philadelphia. His research focuses on racial and social inequality, immigration, urban sociology, and the ways in which the media, the state, and popular culture construct, shape, and disseminate ideas of race. He has published articles on the sociological functions of color-blind political narratives, how racial categories expand and contract within the context of interracial marriages, race theory, racial innumeracy, and how one's ethnic history shapes perceptions of privilege.

INTRODUCTION

An adolescent white male at a bar mitzvah wears a FUBU[1] shirt while his white friend preens his tightly set, perfectly braided corn rows. A black model dressed in yachting attire peddles a New England yuppie boating look in Nautica advertisements. It is quite unremarkable to observe whites, Asians, or African Americans with dyed purple, blond, or red hair. White, black, and Asian students decorate their

Questions to Consider

The dominant view in the United States is that we are now a color-blind nation. Rap and hip-hop are thoroughly mainstream commodities available for sale in every mall across the country. Celebrities, CEOs, high-level politicians, and opinion makers are drawn from every racial and ethnic group. Race, the mainstream media would have us believe, no longer matters. Charles A. Gallagher argues that the story of color blindness promoted in the mass media disguises a more troubling reality: continued racial inequality. How does presenting the United States as a color-blind nation serve various political, ideological, and social functions?

bodies with tattoos of Chinese characters and symbols. In cities and suburbs, young adults across the color line wear hip-hop clothing and listen to white rapper Eminem and black rapper Jay-Z. A north Georgia branch of the NAACP installs a white biology professor as its president. The music of Jimi Hendrix is used to sell Apple Computers. Du-Rag kits, complete with bandana headscarf and elastic headband, are on sale for $2.95 at hip-hop clothing stores and family-centered theme parks like Six Flags. Salsa has replaced ketchup as the best-selling condiment in the United States. Companies as diverse as Polo, McDonald's, Tommy Hilfiger, Walt Disney World, MasterCard, Skechers sneakers, IBM, Giorgio Armani, and Neosporin antibiotic ointment have each crafted advertisements that show a balanced, multiracial cast of characters interacting and consuming their products in a post-race, color-blind world.[2]

Americans are constantly bombarded by depictions of race relations in the media which suggest that discriminatory racial barriers have been dismantled. Social and cultural indicators suggest that America is on the verge, or has already become, a truly color-blind nation. National polling data indicate that a majority of whites now believe discrimination against racial minorities no longer exists. A majority of whites believe that blacks have as good a chance as whites in procuring housing and employment or achieving middle-class status while a 1995 survey of white adults found that a majority of whites (58%) believed that African Americans were better off finding jobs than whites.[3] Much of white America now sees a level playing field, while a majority of black Americans see a field which is still quite uneven. Best-selling books like *The End of Racism*[4] and *Color-Blind: Seeing Beyond Race in a Race-Obsessed World* suggest the United States is not very far from making **color blindness** a social and political reality.[5] The color-blind or race neutral perspective holds that in an environment where institutional racism and discrimination have been replaced by equal opportunity, one's qualifications, not one's color or ethnicity, should be the mechanism by which upward mobility is achieved. Whites and blacks differ significantly, however, on their support for affirmative action, the perceived fairness of the criminal justice system, the ability to acquire the "American Dream," and the extent to which whites have benefited from past discrimination.[6]

This article examines the social and political functions color blindness serves for whites in the United States. Drawing on information compiled from interviews and focus groups with whites around the country, I argue that color blindness maintains white privilege by negating racial inequality. Embracing a post-race, color-blind perspective provides whites with a degree of psychological comfort by allowing them to imagine that being white or black or brown has no bearing on an individual's or a group's relative place in the socioeconomic hierarchy. My research included interviews with seventeen focus groups and thirty individual whites around the country. While my sample is not representative of the total white population, I used personal contacts and snowball sampling to purposively locate respondents raised in urban, suburban, and rural environments. Twelve of the seventeen focus groups were conducted in a university setting,

---

color blindness This term can be understood in two ways: the idea that we *should* live in a society where people are treated equally regardless of their skin color, or the belief that we *are now* a color-blind society where race no longer shapes life chances.

one in a liberal arts college in the Rocky Mountains and the others at a large urban university in the Northeast. Respondents in these focus groups were selected randomly from the student population. The occupational range for my individual interviews was quite eclectic and included a butcher, construction worker, hair stylist, partner in a prestigious corporate law firm, executive secretary, high school principal, bank president from a small town, retail workers, country lawyer, and custodial workers. Twelve of the thirty individual interviews were with respondents who were raised in rural and/or agrarian settings. The remaining respondents lived in suburbs of large cities or in urban areas.

What linked this rather disparate group of white individuals together was their belief that race-based privilege had ended. As a majority of my respondents saw it, color blindness was now the norm in the United States. The illusion of racial equality implicit in the myth of color blindness was, for many whites, a form of comfort. This aspect of pleasure took the form of political empowerment ("what about whites' rights") and moral gratification from being liberated from "oppressor" charges ("we are not responsible for the past"). The rosy picture that color blindness presumes about race relations and the satisfying sense that one is part of a period in American history that is morally superior to the racist days of the past is, quite simply, a less stressful and more pleasurable social place for whites to inhabit.

THE NORM OF COLOR BLINDNESS

The perception among a majority of white Americans that the socioeconomic playing field is now level, along with whites' belief that they have purged themselves of overt racist attitudes and behaviors, has made color blindness the dominant lens through which whites understand contemporary race relations. Color blindness allows whites to believe that segregation and discrimination are no longer an issue because it is now illegal for individuals to be denied access to housing, public accommodations, or jobs because of their race. Indeed, lawsuits alleging institutional racism against companies like Texaco, Denny's, Coca-Cola, and Cracker Barrel validate what many whites know at a visceral level is true; firms which deviate from the color-blind norms embedded in **classic liberalism** will be punished. As a political ideology, the commodification and mass marketing of products that signify color but are intended for consumption across the color line further legitimate color blindness. Almost every household in the United States has a television that, according to the U.S. Census, is on for seven hours every day.[7] Individuals from any racial background can wear hip-hop clothing, listen to rap music (both purchased at Wal-Mart) and root for their favorite, majority black, professional sports team. Within the context of racial symbols that are bought and sold in the market, color blindness means that one's race has no bearing on who can purchase an SUV, live in an exclusive neighborhood, attend private schools, or own a Rolex.

The passive interaction whites have with people of color through the media creates the impression that little, if any, socioeconomic difference exists between the races. Research has found that whites who are exposed to images of upper-middle-class African Americans, like the Huxtable family in *The Cosby Show*, believe that blacks have the same socioeconomic opportunities as whites.[8] Highly visible and successful racial minorities like Secretary of State Colin Powell and National Security Advisor Condoleezza Rice are further proof to white America that the nation's efforts to enforce and promote racial equality have been accomplished. Reflecting on the extent to which discrimination is an obstacle to socioeconomic advancement and the perception of seeing African Americans in leadership roles, Tom explained:

> If you look at some prominent black people in society today, and I don't really see [racial discrimination], I don't understand how they can keep bringing this problem onto themselves. If they did what society would want them to, I don't see that society is making problems for them. I don't see it.

---

classic liberalism A school of thought stressing individual freedom and limited government.

The achievement ideology implicit in the color-blind perspective is also given legitimacy and stripped of any racist implications by black neoconservatives like anti-affirmative action advocate Ward Connerly, Shelby Steele, and Clarence Thomas, and Asian American Secretary of Labor Elaine Chou.[9] Each espouses a color-blind, race neutral doctrine that treats race-based government programs as a violation of the sacrosanct belief that American society only recognizes the rights of individuals. These individuals also serve as an important public example that in a post-race, color-blind society climbing the occupational ladder is now a matter of individual choice.

The new color-blind ideology does not, however, ignore race; it acknowledges race while ignoring racial hierarchy by taking racially coded styles and products and reducing these symbols to commodities or experiences which whites and racial minorities can purchase and share. It is through such acts of shared consumption that race becomes nothing more than an innocuous cultural signifier. Large corporations have made American culture more homogeneous through the ubiquity of fast food, television, and shopping malls, but this trend has also created the illusion that we are all the same through consumption. Most adults eat at national fast-food chains like McDonald's; shop at mall anchor stores like Sears and J. C. Penney's; and watch major league sports, situation comedies, or television dramas. Defining race only as cultural symbols that are for sale allows whites to experience and view race as nothing more than a benign cultural marker that has been stripped of all forms of institutional, discriminatory or coercive power. The post-race, color-blind perspective allows whites to imagine that depictions of racial minorities working in high-status jobs and consuming the same products, or at least appearing in commercials for products whites desire or consume, is the same as living in a society where color is no longer used to allocate resources or shape group outcomes. By constructing a picture of society where racial harmony is the norm, the color-blind perspective functions to make white privilege invisible while removing from public discussion the need to maintain any social programs that are race-based.

How then is color blindness linked to privilege? Starting with the deeply held belief that America is now a meritocracy, whites are able to imagine that the socioeconomic success they enjoy relative to racial minorities is a function of individual hard work, determination, thrift, and investments in education. The color-blind perspective removes from personal thought and public discussion any taint or suggestion of white supremacy or white guilt while legitimating the existing social, political, and economic arrangements that whites are privileged to receive. This perspective insinuates that class and culture, and not institutional racism, are responsible for social inequality. Color blindness allows whites to define themselves as politically progressive and racially tolerant as they proclaim their adherence to a belief system that does not see or judge individuals by the "color of their skin." This perspective ignores, as Ruth Frankenberg puts it, how whiteness is a "location of structural advantage societies structured in racial dominance."[10] Frankenberg uses the term "color and power evasiveness" rather than color blindness to convey how the ability to ignore race by members of the dominant group reflects a position of power and privilege. Color blindness hides white privilege behind a mask of assumed meritocracy while rendering invisible the institutional arrangements that perpetuate racial inequality. The veneer of equality implied in color blindness allows whites to present their place in the racialized social structure as one that was earned.

Given the pervasiveness of color blindness, it was not surprising that respondents in this study believed that using race to promote group interests was a form of racism.

Joe, a student in his early twenties from a working-class background, was quite adamant that the opportunity structure in the United States did not favor one racial group over another.

I mean, I think that the black person of our age has as much opportunity as me, maybe he didn't have the same guidance and that might hurt him. But I mean, he's got the same opportunities that I do to go to school, maybe even more, to get more money. I can't get any aid. . . . I think that blacks have the same opportunities as whites nowadays and I think it's old hat.

Not only does Joe believe that young blacks and whites have similar educational experiences and opportunity but it is his contention that blacks are more likely or able to receive money for higher education. The idea that race matters in any way, according to Joe, is anachronistic; it is "old hat" in a color-blind society to blame one's shortcomings on something as irrelevant as race.

Believing and acting as if America is now color-blind allows whites to imagine a society where institutional racism no longer exists and racial barriers to upward mobility have been removed. The use of group identity to challenge the existing racial order by making demands for the amelioration of racial inequities is viewed as racist because such claims violate the belief that we are a nation that recognizes the rights of individuals, not rights demanded by groups. Sam, an upper-middle-class respondent in his twenties, draws on a pre- and post-civil rights framework to explain racial opportunity among his peers:

I guess I can understand my parents' generation. My parents are older, my dad is almost sixty and my mother is in her mid-fifties, ok? But the kids I'm going to school with, the minorities I'm going to school with, I don't think they should use racism as an excuse for not getting a job. Maybe their parents, sure, I mean they were discriminated against. But these kids have every opportunity that I do to do well.

In one generation, as Sam sees it, the color line has been erased. Like Sam's view that there are opportunities for all, there is, according to Tara, a reason to celebrate the current state of race relations.

I mean, like you are not the only people that have been persecuted—I mean, yeah, you have been, but so has every group. I mean, if there's any time to be black in America, it's now.

Seeing society as race neutral serves to decouple past historical practices and social conditions from present-day racial inequality. A number of respondents viewed society this way and pointed out that job discrimination had ended. Michelle was quite direct in her perception that the labor market is now free of discrimination, stating that "I don't think people hire and fire because someone is black and white now." Ken also believed that discrimination in hiring did not occur since racial minorities now have legal recourse if discrimination occurs.

I think that pretty much we got past that point as far as jobs. I think people realize that you really can't discriminate that way because you will end up losing . . . because you will have a lawsuit against you.

Critical race theorist David Theo Goldberg sees this narrative as part of the "continued insistence on implementing an ideal of color blindness [that] either denies historical reality and its abiding contemporary legacies, or serves to cut off any claims to contemporary entitlements."[11] It also means that whites can picture themselves as victims of reverse discrimination and racism, as Anne, a woman in a focus group, explained:

Why is it so important to forget about, you know, white people's rights? I mean, not that, not being racist or anything, but why is it such a big deal that they have to have it their way or no way when it should be a compromise between the two, and the whites should be able to voice their opinions as much as the blacks do.

There is the belief that whites have been silenced by race politics and as Jodie explains, "The tables have turned where they're getting more rights than we have. Like it never balanced out."

The logic inherent in the color-blind approach is circular; since race no longer shapes life opportunities in a color-blind world, there is no need to take race into account when discussing differences in outcomes between racial groups. This approach erases America's racial hierarchy by implying that social, economic, and political power and mobility are equally shared among all racial groups.

Ignoring the extent or ways in which race shapes life opportunities validates whites' social location in the existing racial hierarchy while legitimating the political and economic arrangements that perpetuate and reproduce racial inequality and privilege.

COLOR IS NOW A MATTER OF CHOICE

Leslie Carr suggests "the roots of color-blind ideology are found in classic liberal doctrines of freedom—the freedom of the individual created by the free capitalist marketplace."[12] Within the context of a free-market model, color blindness has come to mean that ignoring or attending to one's racial identity is a matter of individual choice, much like the ways in which whites can choose whether or not to emphasize part of their ethnic background. Many whites, for example, claim to be Irish on St. Patty's Day. Some Italian Americans feel purchasing a meal at the Olive Garden Restaurant is an ethnic dining experience that reconnects them to their immigrant past or fictive ethnic family tree. Some whites don kilts at Highlander Fairs or dress as medieval artisans or knights at Renaissance Festivals. These individuals experience their ethnicity as an option. There is no social cost to "being ethnic" for a day, nor does this voluntary behavior circumscribe opportunities in life. The color-blind narrative holds that affirming racial identity is, like whites who have the luxury of an **optional ethnicity**, an individual, voluntary decision.[13] If pride in one's ethnicity and by extension one's color is a matter of choice, then race no longer matters as an independent force which organizes social life, allocates resources, or creates obstacles to upward mobility.[14] In **post-race**, color-blind

---

optional ethnicity A form of ethnicity that one can pick and choose. There is little or no social cost to engaging in optional ethnicity, as in someone being "Irish" on St. Patrick's Day even though this person does not think about being Irish during the rest of the year.

post-race The notion that race is no longer relevant in politics, culture, or economics. The post-race perspective posits that racism no longer shapes individuals' life chances.

America, one can now consume images and products for, from, and about any racial or ethnic group. Racial styles, like clothing fashion, food choices, or musical preferences, are like interchangeable, mix-and-match commodities for sale at the mall.

The color-blind narrative allows racial identity to be acknowledged in individual and superficial ways, but using race to assert group demands violates the cherished notion that as a nation we recognize the rights of individuals rather than group rights. Within the color-blind perspective, it is understood that one does not choose one's race, but one should be conscious, or at least cautious, not to make race more than background cultural information. In a post-race, color-blind world, race can be seen, but pointing out race-based inequities should not be heard. The idea of identity, race, and the fluidity of individual choices was part of Jeff's explanation of race relations:

> It just seems like a gap's been bridged, where people don't have like separate things. You know, like in past generations there were things that each group had to itself, but now it's like there are plenty of things you can find in, like, black people that white people do. You know, there's music; rap music is no longer, . . . it's not a black thing anymore. . . . When it first came out, it was black music, but now it's just music. It's another choice, just like country music can be considered like white hick music or whatever. You know, it's just a choice.

Tom makes the point that race categories exist, but assimilation allows any individual to become an American, if they so choose:

> Blacks don't seem, poor blacks seem like they're more immigrant than we are.
>
> Interviewer: In what way?
>
> Because they try to keep pushing the differences. You know, like I said, the Asians just meld in a little bit better than the

blacks. . . . Why do they have to be caught up in being African American? They've been in America all their lives. They were born here. They're not African Americans. That's just separate.

There was the perception that Asians did not embrace identity politics or use their racial identity to promote group rights. As Mike, a young white man in a focus group told me:

It's just becoming like really, really popular for black students to be black and proud and racist. But with Asians, it's not that way. I mean there is a magazine Ebony for strictly black people—I've never really read it. I mean there is no magazine for just Asian people. There's nothing saying, like, "Asian power."

Comedian Chris Rock points to how erasing the color line and color blindness are linked when he asked rhetorically, "What does it say about America when the greatest golfer in the world [Tiger Woods] is black and the greatest rapper [Eminem] is white." Rock's message is clear: No role or occupation (at least in sports and music) is now determined by skin color. By allowing anyone to claim ownership of racial styles, color-blind narratives negate the ways in which race continues to circumscribe opportunities in life. The color-blind approach requires that these preferences, while racially bracketed, be available to all for purchase or consumption. At its core, the color-blind philosophy holds that racial minorities can succeed if they rid themselves of any notion that their race entitles them to special treatment. Racial identity can still be expressed or acknowledged, but one's race should mean nothing more than a tendency towards individualistic expressions, like music, foods, or clothes.

Within the color-blind perspective, it is not race per se which determines upward mobility, but how much an individual *chooses* to pay attention to race that determines one's fate. According to this perspective, race is only as important as you allow it

to be, as Kevin, a 33-year-old white male custodial worker in Colorado, told me:

I never really look at anyone as a color, you know. Your skin's a color, but that doesn't mean, . . . I don't know, I never look at someone being black or Chinese. Yeah, you're Chinese because of the way your eyes are slanted, but you talk just like me. You're just like me. I don't look at you any different than you being me. You know, that's how I've always looked at it. You know.

Implicit in this expression of color blindness is that color does not matter as long as blacks and Chinese assimilate to the point where they are "just like" Kevin. As a member of the dominant group, Kevin has the privilege of defining color blindness as the expectation that racial minorities will mirror his own cultural and social experiences while denying how racism shapes the experiences of racial minorities.[15]

When racial identity shifts from being an individual expression to one that is used to organize politically or make group-based grievances, whites view it as racist. Mary believes that race is used to force whites to think about color and inequality:

I think that they are making it worse for themselves. I think that anybody can see in this country—I think it's you [blacks]. It doesn't matter what color you are. I mean, sure there are black things but why put it on a T-shirt? Why not just have a plain black T-shirt? Why would you have to make such a big statement that pushes people away, that threatens people. I would never want to threaten anybody.

As Mary's comments make clear, embracing racial symbols that serve to socially isolate and challenge the racial status quo is a "threat." Implicit in this exchange is that it is not very pleasurable for Mary to interact with those who would use race to promote a political agenda.

The respondents below were bothered by what they saw as a double standard concerning beauty pageants; blacks could have their own pageant but whites could not. Their anger is based, at least in part, on an understanding that the norm of color blindness has been violated. Jodie lamented that:

> You know, it's amazing. Like, even, like even, like the Miss America pageants. There's a black Miss America pageant. But there's also black contestants in the Miss America pageant and then there's a separate pageant for blacks only. And if we had a separate pageant for whites only I just think that things would be . . . more hell would be raised.

Michelle was also bothered by her perception that the idea of race was taken too seriously by blacks:

> You know, it just seems, even for silly things, even the fact that you have to have black women in the Miss America pageant but then they have their own Miss Black America pageant. You know, like that type of thing, and it's like, come on. . . .

John, a 22-year-old male from New Jersey, also felt that whites were held to a different set of social expectations than blacks:

> I watch Miss America and we've had what, a black Miss America three out of the last five years, yet they do have a black Miss America [contest]. They don't have white contestants, they only have black contestants. Now, I'm not saying that a black person can't enter the white contest, but it's just kind of ironic that here a black woman enters a predominately white contest and, you know, usually a Miss America's supposed to be representative of the whole population, yet only 12% of the population is black. . . . It just kind of seems strange that if a white person tried to enter a black contest, forget it, you'd have mayhem.

Viewed within the color-blind perspective, the Miss Black America pageant is a form of institutional racism because it denies all racial groups full access to participation. The Miss Black America pageant is, as suggested above, racist for excluding whites because of the color of their skin. The long history of racial minorities being excluded from white organizations and institutions as the reason behind why black, Latino, and Asian organizations were formed in the first place is now only viewed as irrelevant.

Like the anger expressed over what was perceived as a racial double standard concerning the Miss America pageant, Malcolm X also came to represent challenges to the color-blind perspective, which were viewed as illegitimate because they advocate group solutions to race-based inequities. As one respondent told me about Malcolm X:

> He got into Buddha [sic] and changed his violence. When he was younger, I think that's when he was violent but in the years before he was killed I think he definitely went towards peace, like Martin Luther King. I don't know why they can't wear Martin Luther King hats [instead of Malcolm X hats].

Color blindness has emerged as America's newest racial mythology because it provides a level-playing-field narrative that allows whites to inhabit a psychological space that is free of racial tension. This new era of color blindness is a respite from the racial identity movements which often result in white guilt, defensiveness, or the avoidance of racially charged issues. Color blindness provides whites with the belief that they live in an era that is free of racism. Convinced that these racist attitudes and practices are over, whites today are able to define themselves as racially progressive and tolerant. Within this universe where racial differences are almost meaningless, whites are able to claim that their privileged social position relative to racial minorities reflects individual achievement rather than the fruits of white supremacy. The constant barrage of color-blind messages and messengers reinforces and confirms that the egalitarian and meritocractic norms that undergird American culture are intact. Embracing color blindness allows whites to be blind to or ignore the fact that racial and ethnic minorities lag behind whites on almost every measure of quality of life. Color-blind pleasure means whites are able to think about contemporary race relations as a clean slate where the crimes of slavery, Jim Crow, institutional racism, and white privilege have been ended and the racist sins of their grandparents have been erased.

OUR SURVEY SAYS— "COLOR-BLIND NATION"

National survey data suggest that a majority of whites view race relations through the lens of color blindness. A 1997 Gallup poll found that a majority of whites believe that blacks have "as good a chance as whites" in their community in procuring employment (79%).[16] A Kaiser Family Poll (1997) found that a majority of whites believe that blacks are doing at least as well or better than whites in income and educational attainment. The poll found that "almost two-thirds (64%) of whites do NOT believe that whites have benefited from past and present discrimination against African Americans."[17] In their study on racial attitudes, Schuman and associates found that when white Americans are asked to account for black disadvantage, the most popular explanation is that of black people's lack of motivation or willpower to get ahead.[18] These surveys suggest a majority of whites view the opportunity structure as being open to all, regardless of color. Not only do whites see parity compared to blacks in access to housing, employment, education, and achieving a middle-class lifestyle, but where differences do exist, whites attribute racial inequities to the individual shortcomings of blacks.

Reflecting on affirmative action, Monica articulates an all-is-now-equal argument as to why color should no longer matter in hiring decisions or school admissions:

I think all the backgrounds have come a long way to where they don't need it any more.

Basically everyone has equal opportunity to get a certain job, to get into a certain school, and now it should be based on your performance and not for what you are.

Drawing on an ideology of egalitarianism and meritocracy, Monica believes, as most white Americans do, that color is no longer a factor in obtaining employment or a quality education. Given the premise that racial equality has now been achieved, Monica is able to argue that achievement and not skin color should shape the allocation of resources. In other words, since the playing field is now level, any group claims to address real or imagined inequities are illegitimate. Joan voiced the anger that whites should in some way be held accountable for past or present racial inequities.

That's what bothers me. They say "we" have been oppressed. They have not. The students here at the university right now have not been oppressed. They did not experience the Watts riot, they didn't experience physically being hosed down by police. Granted, the white population was responsible for that, but we are not. We are not responsible. Therefore, we should not be put out because of that. We didn't do it. We're not doing it now, therefore they have no right to say, well, we've been oppressed.

Neither Joan, nor the white race, should be "put out" for past racist practices. The color-blind perspective is a historical rendering of the actions of the near and distant past as events which are disconnected from contemporary racial inequality.

James expresses a number of the trends found in the surveys cited earlier. After stating that "hey, everybody's got the same opportunity" when asked about what his views were on the idea of white privilege, James countered that:

They say that I have white privileges. Uh, and if they say it's like because where I live, I live in a big house or something like that, they're wrong, because that's not a privilege.

That's something my parents worked for. And if they don't live in a big fancy house that's something that their parents didn't work for. And if they want to change that . . . I've got black people living across from me. Uh, they're no different than me. They're different from the black people down here because they worked for what they wanted. These people [blacks in a poor segregated part of the city], they don't have to live here. There's no one holding them back. They can get into school as well as everybody else can. I was lucky my parents could pay for school and I didn't need financial aid. . . . You know, the opportunity is there. You've just got to take hold of it.

James suggests that when class background is taken into account whites and blacks are the same. The blacks who are unable to leave poor, segregated neighborhoods reflect individual shortcomings on the part of blacks, not structural obstacles. Rob implies that it is hard work and individual merit, not one's skin color that matters. Examining his own mobility, Rob remarks, "I don't know if their situation is any different than mine. I mean, I can only gauge on the fact that I've been busting my ass for the last ten years to get to where I want to be."

HOW COLOR-BLIND A NATION?

The beliefs voiced by whites in national survey data and my own interviews raise an empirical question: to what extent are we now a color-blind nation? If educational opportunity, occupational advancement, health, upward mobility, and equal treatment in the public sphere can be used as indicators of how color-blind we are as a nation, then we have failed. U.S. census figures present a picture of America that is far from color-blind. In 1999, over 73% of white households owned their own homes compared to 46% for blacks, 45% for Hispanics, 53% for Asians, and 56% for American Indians.[19]

In 1993, whites had about ten times more in assets than blacks or Latinos.[20] Median family income in 1998 was $42,439 for whites, $25,351 for blacks, $27,330 for Latinos, and $46,637 for Asians. In 1997, almost 25% of whites over the age of 25 had four years of college or more compared to less than 14% for blacks and Latinos. In 1997, 8.6% of whites compared to 26.5% of blacks, 27% of Latinos, and 14% of Asians lived at or below the poverty line.[21] A national study found that even after controlling for individual credit history, blacks in 33 states were charged more for car loans than whites.[22] Health statistics tell a similar tale. Whites have lower rates of diabetes, tuberculosis, pregnancy-related mortality, and sudden infant death syndrome (SIDS), and are more likely to have prenatal care in the first trimester than blacks, Latinos, or Asians. In 1997, 15% of whites did not have public or private health care coverage compared to 21.5% for blacks, 34% for Latinos, and 20.7% for Asians.[23]

In 1998, blacks and Latinos were also underrepresented as lawyers, physicians, professors, dentists, engineers, and registered nurses. A Glass Ceiling study commissioned by the federal government found that when one reaches the level of vice president and above at *Fortune* 1000 industrial companies and *Fortune* 500 service industries, 96.6% of the executives are white males. Nationally, white men comprise 90% of the newspaper editors and 77% of television news directors.[24] In 1999, the Department of Justice found that blacks and Latinos were twice as likely as whites to be subject to force when they encounter a police officer, were more likely to be subjected to car searches during a traffic stop, and were more likely to be ticketed than whites. Although blacks and whites are just as likely to use drugs, almost two-thirds of those convicted on drug charges are black.[25] Congress does not represent the racial and ethnic diversity of this country. In 2000, blacks were 13% of the population, Asians and Pacific Islanders 4%, and Latinos 12%. Yet the House of Representatives was only 9% black, 4% Latino, and 0.9% Asian. The U.S. Senate was 97% white and only 2% Asian and 1% American Indian, and therefore had no black or Latino members.[26] In early 2003, there were no black or Latino governors. According to another report, if you were black and living in Florida, you were four times as likely as whites to have your ballot invalidated in the 2000 presidential election.[27] We are not now, nor have we ever been, a color-blind nation.

THE COST OF RACIALIZED PLEASURES

Being able to ignore or being oblivious to the ways in which almost all whites are privileged in a society cleaved on race has a number of implications. Whites derive pleasure in being told that the current system for allocating resources is fair and equitable. Creating and internalizing a color-blind view of race relations reflects how the dominant group is able to use the mass media, immigration stories of upward mobility, rags-to-riches narratives, and achievement ideology to make white privilege invisible. Frankenberg argues that whiteness can be "displaced," as is the case with whiteness hiding behind the veil of color blindness. It can also be made "normative" rather than specifically "racial," as is the case when being white is defined by white respondents as being no different than being black or Asian.[28] Lawrence Bobo and associates have advanced a theory of laissez-faire racism that draws on the color-blind perspective. As whites embrace the equality of opportunity narrative they suggest that

> laissez-faire racism encompasses an ideology that blames blacks themselves for their poorer relative economic standing, seeing it as a function of perceived cultural inferiority. The analysis of the bases of laissez-faire racism underscores two central components: contemporary stereotypes of blacks held by whites, and the denial of societal (structural) responsibility for the conditions in black communities.[29]

As many of my respondents make clear, if the opportunity structure is open ("It doesn't matter what color you are"), there must be something inherently wrong with racial minorities or their culture that explains group-level differences.

Leslie Carr argues "that color blindness is not the opposite of racism; it is another form of racism."[30] I would add that the form color blindness takes as the nation's hegemonic political discourse is a variant of laissez-faire racism. Historian David Roediger contends that in order for the Irish to have been absorbed into the white race in the mid-nineteenth century "the imperative to define themselves as whites came from the particular public and psychological wages whiteness offered" these new immigrants.[31] There is still a "wage" to whiteness, that element of ascribed status whites automatically receive because of their membership in the dominant group. But within the framework of color blindness the imperative has switched from whites overtly defining themselves or their interests as white, to one where they claim that color is irrelevant; being white is the same as being black, yellow, brown, or red. Some time ago, Ralph Ellison asked this important question about race relations that continues to go unanswered:

> What, by the way, is one to make of a white youngster who, with a transistor radio glued to his ear, screaming a Stevie Wonder tune, shouts racial epithets at black youngsters trying to swim at a public beach . . . ?[32]

My interviews with whites around the country suggest that in this post-race era of color-blind ideology Ellison's keen observations about race relations need modification. The question now is what are we to make of a young white man from the suburbs who listens to hip-hop, wears baggy hip-hop pants, a baseball cap turned sideways, unlaced sneakers, and an oversized shirt emblazoned with a famous NBA player who, far from shouting racial epithets, lists a number of racial minorities as his heroes? It is now possible to define oneself as not being racist because of the clothes you wear, the celebrities you like, or the music you listen to while believing that blacks or Latinos are disproportionately poor or overrepresented in low-pay, dead-end jobs because they are part of a debased, culturally deficient group. Having a narrative that smooths over the cognitive dissonance and ofttimes schizophrenic dance that whites must do when they navigate race relations is likely an invaluable source of pleasure.

BUYING RACIAL CAPITAL

Skin-Bleaching and Cosmetic Surgery in a Globalized World

Margaret L. Hunter

MARGARET L. HUNTER is the Fletcher Jones Professor of Sociology at Mills College. Her research interests include skin tone stratification in the African American and Latino communities, colorblind racism and discourse, and race and gender politics in hip-hop. Her publications include *Race, Gender, and the Politics of Skin Tone* (2005, Routledge), "If You're Light You're Alright: Skin Color as Social Capital for Women of Color" in *Gender & Society,* and "Women of Color in Hip Hop: The Pornographic Gaze" in *Race, Gender, & Class.*

ABSTRACT

The merging of new technologies with old colonial ideologies has created a context where consumers can purchase "racial capital" through skin-bleaching creams or cosmetic surgeries. The use of skin-bleaching creams is on the rise throughout Africa and the African Diaspora, and cosmetic surgery has increased dramatically among people of color in wealthy countries. Public discourse, however, is fraught with tension over these manipulations of the body. This [reading] examines three competing discourses: 1) the beauty discourse, based on the mass-marketing of cosmetic whitening products; 2) the public health discourse, designed to dissuade

Questions to Consider

It is said that beauty is in the eye of the beholder; however, beauty standards reflect the cultural values of a given society. What does it say about beauty (and racism) when millions of people around the world use skin-bleaching creams in an effort to "whiten" their skin color? Why would someone engage in elective cosmetic surgery to create a more "Western" (read "white") look? Professor Hunter looks at how and why skin-bleaching has become a worldwide phenomenon.

potential skin-bleachers by exposing health risks; and 3) the cosmetic surgery discourse, created to market cosmetic procedures to the new and growing "ethnic" market. Through analysis of advertisements and public health campaigns, this [reading] demonstrates that the focus on individual attitudes in all three discourses obfuscates color-based discrimination and encourages the purchase of racial capital.

A cursory search on any Internet search engine reveals hundreds of skin-lightening[1] websites that provide information for would-be consumers about the "best" skin-lightening products and strategies. Lighterskin.org, whiterskin.com, skinwhitening.org, skin-whitening-product.com, and skin-whiteningexperts.com all purport to share with readers the newest information on, and reviews of, skinlightening products. How is information about skin-lightening conveyed today, and how do competing discourses frame the nature of skin-lightening differently? This [reading] investigates three discursive frameworks on skin-lightening around the globe: the beauty discourse, the public health discourse, and the new cosmetic surgery discourse. Each discourse frames skin-lightening, body manipulation, and social actors in different and important ways, revealing much about the global beauty industry, neo-colonial and post-colonial racial ideologies, and the ongoing role of women of color's bodies as the battleground for these conflicts.

Skin-lightening, or bleaching, has reached epidemic levels in scores of nations around the globe, and especially in many African nations, including Ghana, Kenya, Tanzania, Senegal, Mali, South Africa, and Nigeria (Adebajo, 2002; Blay, 2009; Harada et al., 2001; Lewis et al., 2009; Mahe et al., 1993; Mahe, Ly, & Gounongbe, 2004; Olumide et al., 2008). Although both men and women engage in skin-whitening practices of various sorts, women generally have higher rates of skin-whitening than men, and women also sometimes apply skin-whitening products to their children (Counter & Buchanan, 2004; Fokuo, 2009). This [reading] will investigate why women bleach, and why men and women in Africa and the African Diaspora encourage women to bleach their skin.

The benefits of light skin, although not universal, are widespread around the globe, particularly in countries formerly colonized by Europe or with a significant U.S. presence (Glenn, 2008; Hunter, 2005; Mire, 2001; Rondilla & Spickard, 2007; Telles, 2006). Throughout Africa, Asia, and Latin America, skinbleaching is a common practice as people try to acquire lighter skin and the social and economic status that goes with it (Perry, 2006). Although people in some cultures have tried to lighten their skin for centuries, recent data suggest that skin-bleaching is on the rise, particularly among educated, urban women in the Global South[2] (del Giudice & Yves, 2002; Ntshingla, 2005). What accounts for this recent shift? Glenn (2008) suggests that while historic, European colonial ideologies still have an effect on people, the rise of skin-bleaching around the globe can also be attributed to the constant, current mass-marketing of contemporary images of white beauty. Charles (2009a) suggests that hegemonic representations of white skin are thoroughly rooted in multiple social institutions including education, religion, mass media, and popular culture. Wealthy nations like the United States, Japan, and many European nations create many of the global images of white (or light) beauty (Burke, 1996). In turn, these same nations are also home to the cosmetics companies that produce some of the topselling skin-bleaching creams, including L'Oreal, Unilever, Shiseido, and others.

Images of white beauty do not simply rely on white women with blonde hair and light eyes to sell products. Images of white beauty sell much more than beauty ideals or fashions for women around the globe. Taken as a whole, images of white beauty sell an entire lifestyle imbued with racial meaning (Burke, 1996; Saraswati, 2010). The lifestyle that is communicated through these ads sells whiteness, modernity, sophistication, beauty, power, and wealth (Leong, 2006; Mahe, Ly, & Gounongbe, 2004). The mass-marketing of these images of white beauty and a "white lifestyle" build on the long-standing European colonial ideologies that valorize white beauty, European culture, and white aesthetics (Mire, 2001).

"Yearning for whiteness" (Glenn, 2008) has long been present in nations formerly colonized by Europe, but today, those old ideologies combine with new mass media and communication technologies to compound the message that "white is right" (Thomas, 2009). For example, the largest social networking application, Facebook, launched a new "app," sponsored by cosmetics giant Vaseline, that allows users to lighten their skin tone in their profile pictures. By dragging a vertical bar across their pictures they can create instant before-and-after images devised to sell more of Vaseline's best-selling product, "Healthy White: Skin Lightening Lotion." This [reading] will investigate how the age-old cultural practice of skin-bleaching has evolved as competing discourses from the beauty industry, public health officials, and the cosmetic surgery industry vie to control the way we think about race, the body, colonialism, and power.

The increase in skin-bleaching around the globe is a result of the merger between old ideologies of colonialism and race, and new technologies of the body (Hunter, 2005). The racist ideologies of race and color were an integral part of the European colonial experience (Charles, 2003). However, new transnational neocolonial ideologies now continue and elaborate these old belief systems (Leonardo, 2002). Images from the U.S. and Europe lead the way in valorizing white/light beauty around the world. Japan's influence is particularly strong throughout Asia and is evidenced in their best-selling beauty products marketed as "specially designed for Asian skin" (Ashikari, 2005). White/light beauty is communicated through mass advertising, television shows, film, Internet images, billboards, and celebrity culture (Baumann, 2008; Saraswati, 2010; Winders, Jones, & Higgins, 2005).

The quest for white beauty is very important because white or light skin is a form of "racial capital" gaining its status from existing racial hierarchies. Racial capital is a resource drawn from the body that can be related to skin tone, facial features, body shape, etc. I use the term "racial capital" to describe the role that white/Anglo bodies play in the status hierarchy. Both Anglo bodies and light or white skin confer status on people of color in an individualistic way. Light skin tone can be transformed into social capital (social networks), symbolic capital (esteem or status), or even economic capital (high-paying job or promotion) (Bourdieu, 1984; Hunter, 2005). Blay (2009) found that women in Ghana who used bleaching products were trying to attain beauty vis a vis light skin. She argues that light skin and beauty were the vehicles through which women attempted to gain social capital (Blay, 2009). The concept of "racial capital" is distinct from racial identity. Racial capital is more closely related to phenotype and how others perceive an individual, rather than how that individual defines him- or herself.

Racial capital only makes sense in a racist society where light skin and Anglo bodies are valued over dark skin and African or Indian/Indigenous bodies. The concept of racial capital is connected to the larger systems of racism and colorism. Racism operates at the level of racial category where people in a given category experience institutional discrimination regardless of phenotype, and colorism operates within the system of racism and differentiates how subordinate groups experience racism according to the tone of their skin (Hunter, 2002). Colorism is broadly evidenced in many societies today and helps explain why lighter-skinned and darker-skinned people of the same race have different experiences with regard to discrimination (Glenn, 2009).

Racial capital only exists in a social context that views the body as a commodity. Women's bodies have been dismembered and marketed in advertising for several decades now (Cortese, 1999), but the merging of technologies of the body, the 24-hour multi-media cycle, the increased importance of beauty for women, and the explosion of pornography culture (where women's bodies are routinely commodified and manipulated for a viewing audience) has created a perfect storm, resulting in an explosion of cosmetic procedures for women's bodies.

It is now normative in many societies to view the body as a "work in progress" (Davis, 1995). People no longer view the human body as "given," but increasingly see it as changeable (Davis, 1995). For example, in a recent interview with a major U.S. news corporation, a Senegalese woman said, "Women bleach their skin to come across as modern women who can modify their skin tone as they wish" (Barnier, 2009). The interviewee describes the connection between "modernity" and the use of cosmetics to alter the body. Her statement also reflects the notion that women make individual choices to suit their own aesthetic preferences. Sophisticated women can modify their skin tones "as they wish" (Barnier, 2009). The connection between modernity and body manipulation is distinctive from the centuries-old trend of "decorating or ornamenting" the body, and is really about reshaping the body to present a new body as "natural." In this way, the body is not adorned (through jewelry, painting, or scarring, for example), but is "recreated" as if original. Although publicly discussing one's cosmetic surgeries is more common in some places than others, the modified body must still be presented as "natural" or "normal" in order to garner the status of an "ideal female body" (Blum, 2005). Similarly, criticisms of women who bleach are often based on the idea that bleaching women are trying to get something that is not naturally theirs.

THE BEAUTY DISCOURSE: THE POWER OF MARKETING AND CELEBRITY

Sales of skin-lightening products are on the rise and their global demand has never been higher (Perry,

2006). In a post-colonial world, and some suggest a post-racial era, how can we make sense of this surge in the demand for skinwhitening? The global beauty industry has reinvented itself in recent years in the image of multiculturalism (Hunter, 2005). Many cosmetics companies that once exclusively featured white women have added light-skinned women of color to their advertisements and as spokespersons for their products. I call this maneuver the "illusion of inclusion" (Hunter, 2005). The illusion of inclusion is a seductive marketing strategy to draw in women of color who might otherwise feel alienated from products marketed exclusively with images of white beauty. By including a few light-skinned, Anglo-looking women of color, cosmetics companies appear to be inclusive of people of color, without disrupting their message that white bodies are beautiful. The inclusion of fair-skinned women of color like Halle Berry of the U.S. (Revlon), Aishwarya Rai of India (L'Oreal), Genevieve Nnaji of Nigeria (Lux soap), or Terry Pheto of South Africa (L'Oreal) is designed to lull women of color consumers into buying these products and believing that their bodies and beauty are being valued (Osuri, 2008).

Ironically, as the marketing strategies have added a veneer of inclusion, there has simultaneously been a boom of products offered that all claim to lighten, brighten, or whiten the skin. Skin-lightening products are readily available from major cosmetics companies, from local mom-and-pop stores and widely over the Internet. The most lucrative skin-lightening products are increasingly likely to have celebrity endorsements. Celebrity endorsements serve two important purposes: 1) When celebrities endorse a particular product, the public is more likely to believe in its effectiveness and purchase the product, and 2) When celebrities endorse skin-lightening products they also endorse the act of skin-lightening itself, suggesting that their own beauty is attainable and that skin-lightening is a mainstream, culturally acceptable act. The latter point is particularly important because skin-lightening is still shameful in some cultures either because one should "naturally" have light skin, not chemically derived light skin, or because some believe that lightening the skin implies a shame of one's race or ethnic identity (Charles, 2003).

Overcoming these powerful narratives of "natural beauty" and "racial pride" are crucial for the success of cosmetics companies.

In fact, organizers in Ivory Coast have gone so far as to create a new and controversial beauty pageant called "Miss Authentica." The Miss Authentica Pageant was designed to speak back to the white beauty regime, raise awareness about the dangers of skin-bleaching, and highlight "natural" African beauty (James, 2009). The important criterion for participation in this pageant is natural, non-bleached skin. Although this pageant has taken a creative approach to revaluing African aesthetics, it has not eliminated the premise that women should be valued for their bodies and their physical beauty. White beauty is a discourse of white supremacy and patriarchy. So, while efforts like Miss Authentica are an important critique of racial beauty regimes, their reliance on the beauty discourse limits their ability for social transformation.

In order to appeal to the powerful discourse of "natural beauty" in many societies, most products claim to *restore* the natural beauty of skin (if it is lost), *reveal* the natural beauty of skin (if it is hidden), or *create* a natural beauty (if the consumer never had it to begin with). All of these claims are supported with compelling before and after photos and promises backed with the discourse of science in phrases like, "clinically tested" (see www.super-skinlightener.com) or "scientifically developed" (see www.blackskinlightening.com). Ads use copy such as, "reveal your natural beauty" (see www.fixderma.com/face.html) to appeal to consumers' need to feel like their achieved light skin is theirs by birthright.

One of the most controversial celebrity endorsements came in 2007 when mega-successful Bollywood actor Shah Rukh Khan endorsed the skin-lightening product, "Fair and Handsome." Created by the British company, Unilever, and marketed as the masculine companion product to best-selling Fair & Lovely, Fair and Handsome became the first major skin-lightening product mass-marketed exclusively to men. Khan's endorsement was read by the Indian public as an endorsement of skin-bleaching itself and as an endorsement of a strongly colorbased system of privilege in India (Parameswaran & Cardoza, 2009).

Similarly, U.S. baseball star Sammy Sosa, originally of the Dominican Republic, recently attracted international media attention when he appeared at the Latin Grammy Awards with notably lighter skin than he had during his career in Major League Baseball (Mitchell, 2009). Sosa has suggested that he is negotiating an endorsement deal with the cosmetic company that manufactured his skin-lightening cream (which he has refused to name in public) (Mitchell, 2009). His de facto celebrity endorsement of skin-bleaching elicited significant feedback including a televised ridiculing from former NBA basketball star Charles Barkley. Despite the media furor, Sosa's actions reinforce the idea that skinbleaching is a mainstream route to building racial capital.

Skin-bleaching products are marketed in a number of ways and with a variety of different product names. In some countries "bleaching" carries a negative stigma so products are marketed instead as skin-evening creams, skin-lighteners, skin-brighteners, skin-whiteners, skin-toners, fading creams, or fairness creams. Despite these euphemisms, the names of the products themselves are often overt and clear about the intended outcomes. The following is a small sampling of skin-whitening products marketed around the globe at a variety of price ranges: Porcelana's Skin-Lightening Cream, Cosmetic Surgeon in a Jar's Illuminator Brightening Complexion, Darphin's Clear White Brightening and Soothing Serum, Sekkisei's White Powder Wash, Fair and White's So White! Skin Perfector Brightening Cream, Clinique's DermaWhite, Shiseido's White Lucent, Loreal's White Perfect, Ambi Fade Cream, and India's best-selling Fair & Lovely (for women) and Fair and Handsome (for men) are all readily available in shops around the globe.

The names of these products reveal the racial hierarchies in which they are situated. The majority of skin-lightening products use the word "white" in their name. This practice reveals the strong desire by consumers to achieve aesthetic whiteness, if not a white identity. The racial capital of whiteness is now something consumers can buy. It is not necessarily the case that consumers of skin-whitening products want to be white per se, but the huge demand for these products suggests that many people want to look white, or at least light, relative to other people in their racial or ethnic group. Scholars have established that there are many motivating factors for bleaching, including trying to attract a spouse, increased job market competitiveness, higher self-esteem, and even fashion (Blay, 2009; Fokuo, 2009; Charles, 2009b). Although skin-bleachers' motivations cannot summarily be characterized as "wanting to be white," much of the motivation to whiten takes place in a larger context of white supremacy. It is the global context of white supremacy that I am investigating in this article and how it shapes a growing market for the purchase of racial capital. The global context of white supremacy is so insidious that many bleaching creams are marketed with the word "white" in their names or product descriptions.

Products are also available in a variety of price ranges from a few cents per ounce to over one hundred U.S. dollars per ounce. In addition to these more expensive products created by multinational cosmetics companies, many small mom-and-pop vendors offer local products in informal markets throughout the Global South and in smaller markets catering to immigrant communities in the West. These products, often created and sold outside of formal regulatory channels, frequently contain active ingredients illegal in many nations, or legal chemicals in illegal doses (Mire, 2005). Many skin-whitening products with dangerous chemical ingredients are manufactured in Europe or the United States, sent to Nigeria, and then distributed throughout Africa in both formal and informal markets (Barnett & Smith, 2005). The bleaching products often make their way back to Europe and the United States for sale to the African and Asian immigrant communities there (Barnett & Smith, 2005).

THE PUBLIC HEALTH DISCOURSE: A MISSED OPPORTUNITY

In response to the growing numbers of women and men using skin-bleaching creams in Africa and throughout the Diaspora, many governments have spoken out through their ministers of health to dissuade people from using the products. Often leading government officials will release a formal statement, hold a press conference, and sometimes launch a nation-wide public health campaign informing people of the dangers of the skin-bleaching products. Because these state-sponsored messages come largely from public health entities within the government or NGOs, their focus tends to be on the physical dangers of using such products. The most dangerous ingredients found in many skin-lightening products are hydroquinone, corticosteroids, and mercury. Despite strict regulation of these chemicals in many Western nations, they are still found in many products sold throughout the world (Mire, 2005). In fact, a recent study of skin-lightening products in the U.S. revealed that several contained mercury and others contained illegally high doses of hydroquinone, despite tight regulations from the Food and Drug Administration (Gabler & Roe, 2010). The most dangerous side effects of mercury, hydroquinone, and topical steroid usage include, but are not limited to, damage to the adrenal glands, kidney failure, liver failure, and skin cancer. For these reasons, several governments have launched public service announcements and public health campaigns to educate the public on the risks of using these products.

The Jamaican government recently launched its widely publicized "Don't Kill the Skin" campaign. This public health campaign was designed to both raise awareness about the dangers of bleaching and outlaw the sale of many skin-whitening products. In an interview about the campaign, Dr. Clive Andersen, a Jamaican dermatologist, commented on the widespread practice of skin-bleaching in Jamaica.

"It is very worrying because a lot of persons know that they are doing severe damage to the skin and persist in it. Some of this damage is reversible; a lot of it is not reversible. We need to realize that when we use these products, we are doing our skin immeasurable harm. There is no advantage to lightening our skin colour and at the same time damaging our skin. Beautiful skin really is healthy skin, whatever the colour" ("Campaign to Rid," 2007).

This quotation exemplifies a common theme in public health campaigns: all women have the potential to be beautiful regardless of skin color. As the dermatologist above states, "beautiful skin really is healthy skin." This quotation highlights a shortcoming of the public health discourse—its focus on attitudes as opposed to discrimination. Moreover, women are often the target of these campaigns because officials describe the problems as many women's "misconceptions" about beauty. Women are under the false impression, they argue, that only light skin is beautiful and they go to "dangerous lengths" to achieve that look. But are women really under a "false impression"? In fact, beauty is still defined in Jamaica, and elsewhere, in relation to white and European aesthetics, including light skin and Anglo facial features, thus the elevation of the "browning" (Charles, 2003). The public health discourse constructs women as "getting it wrong" by mistakenly believing that lighter skin is viewed as more beautiful and higher status. In fact, women have read their social cues exactly right, the skin-bleaching creams may be risky, but the payoffs are potentially high if lighter skin attracts a higher status husband or a better-paying job. Public health officials have not acknowledged the social and political reality of the benefits of light skin, so their message about "misconceptions" only makes women appear vain and pathological, instead of savvy, if risk-taking.

For example, the Ghana Health Service asks, why do women bleach? "It is centred on vanity" they argue ("Skin-Bleaching," 2005). Purchasing racial capital is an option more available than ever before,

and the growing middle class in the Global South is poised to seize the opportunity (Pierre, 2008). With increasing purchasing power and disposable income, the rapidly growing middle class in countries such as South Africa, Nigeria, India, and China is increasingly looking to compete for jobs with professionals from the United States, Europe, and Japan. The ascendance of the new global middle class has made white aesthetics increasingly desirable in a competitive global job market (Glenn, 2008).

Perhaps public health campaigns avoid talking about the larger social context of colorism because it seems like an intractable problem, difficult to fix through public policy. Or, government officials of African countries and other black and brown nations may not want to publicly admit that cultural aesthetics of the body still mimic European or white norms, generations after the colonial experience. The public health discourse, then, has the effect of maintaining silence around the structural benefits of light skin and pathologizing women for taking "unnecessary risks" with their health, and sometimes, the health of their children. Although women bear the brunt of the health costs associated with bleaching (although some men bleach, too), women have been constructed as villains in this national discourse, at fault for succumbing to vain beliefs about beauty and risking their health to attain these standards.

A psychology professor from Uganda draws on the public health discourse in a similar fashion. When asked to comment on why people continue to use such dangerous bleaching products, he explained, "Such a person lacks self-esteem, has low self-efficacy and a perception that she or he looks ugly . . . It is common among women who are not educated" (quoted in Kisule, 2008). Another psychologist in Uganda says, "Do something positive to counter [your low self-esteem]. Take advantage of the good parts of your body or talents" (Calistas as quoted in Kisule, 2008). The public health professionals in Jamaica and Uganda employ a discourse common among other government agencies in other nations. They argue that skin-bleaching can be combated largely by altering individuals' attitudes. They assert that many people have misguided beliefs that light skin is better and higher in status, but that this is not actually true. The inability of many public health professionals to publicly acknowledge the real benefits of light skin, especially for women, has hampered their effectiveness.

Urban, educated women in countries such as Nigeria, Jamaica, South Africa, and other post-colonial nations are engaged with the global job market and have an acute awareness of competing for jobs with people from other racial and ethnic groups. This global job competition is one motivating factor for skin-bleaching among this population (Perry, 2006). More exposed to beauty images from Europe and the U.S. than their more rural counterparts, the educated and urban women of these nations may be motivated to lighten their skin (with highend cosmetics) in order to effectively compete with whites, Latinos, Asians and others from around the globe (Glenn, 2008). Moreover, the elites of the African Diaspora also see the real benefits to light skin and Anglo features in the global job market. It is evident that leaders in business, politics, education, and even government are often lighter-skinned with more Anglo facial features. The reality of color-based discrimination is one motivating factor in the skin-lightening trend among elites.

The public health discourse on skin-bleaching regularly overlooks this reality. It appears to the consumer that the government officials standing before the microphones during their press release are living in another reality, one where merit trumps race or color. In fact, the inability of the public health discourse to incorporate an acknowledgement of the "pigmentocracy" at work in many countries and around the globe makes their pleas not to bleach impotent.

Not only do public health officials avoid discussing light-skinned privilege, they also typically avoid acknowledging discrimination against dark-skinned men and women. For example, in nations like Brazil, with one of the largest black populations outside of Africa or the United States, discrimination against dark-skinned people is rampant, but publicly denied. Many job descriptions still require a "clean" appearance which is often coded language for middle class and light-skinned or white

(Caldwell, 2007). Practices like these drive the skin-bleaching market around the globe.

Finally, the public health discourse is remarkably similar to the beauty discourse of skin-bleaching in that it, too, focuses on the individual as the site of the problem. For example, the Public Health Partnership Forum in Zambia urged the government to ban the sale of skin-bleaching creams. The publicity secretary of the organization said, "skin-bleaching, being a psycho-socio and health problem, needs to be addressed with interventions aimed at changing the users' perceptions of themselves and educating people on its consequences" ("Zambia: Ban," 2010). Skin-bleaching is defined as an individual problem that can be solved with education and a new attitude. Sentiments such as this are common throughout the discourse emblematic of an individualist, attitude-oriented perspective on bleaching. This discourse is less effective, in part, because it avoids discussions of structural discrimination or institutionalized white supremacy.

THE COSMETIC SURGERY DISCOURSE: THE NEW "ETHNIC" MARKET

Although skin-lightening is a centuries-old practice, the cosmetic surgery industry is a new invention. Globally, cosmetic surgery is on the rise and is most practiced in nations such as China, Brazil, India, Mexico, and the United States (ISAPS, 2009). White women comprise the vast majority of all clients in the U.S. cosmetic surgery industry, but rates among people of color are rising dramatically (ASAPS, 2000–2008). In fact, from 2000 to 2008 the number of cosmetic surgeries done on whites in the United States increased 31%, while that number increased 145% for African Americans, 240% for Latinos, and 290% for Asian Americans (ASAPS, 2000–2008). These data reveal startlingly high increases in people of color's willingness to have cosmetic surgical procedures in the United States. Boodman (2007) argues in the *Washington Post* that the rapid growth of this industry has led to the "bourgeoning field called 'ethnic plastic surgery.'"

The broad reach of global white supremacy has not stopped with the billion dollar industry of skin-whitening products, but in fact extends into manipulations of the entire body. While skin-bleaching is notably less common in the United States than in other countries, people of color in the U.S. are much more likely to go under the knife to reshape their bodies, often in ways that Anglicize their facial features and body types. The cosmetic surgery industry sells racial capital as well, in the forms of Anglo noses, Anglo eyes, and more. Racial capital can be purchased this way, too, although the prices are higher and the risks more dangerous. In the United States, cosmetic surgery is becoming increasingly mainstream and part of the cultural norm. In the recent past, a small minority of people approved of cosmetic surgery, but by 2009 over half of all Americans approved of cosmetic surgery (ASAPS, 2009). Approval is also linked to dimensions of inequality such as class, gender, and race. The more income one has, the more likely he or she is to approve of cosmetic surgery, with 63% of people earning over $75,000 approving of cosmetic surgery (ASAPS, 2009). Approving of cosmetic surgery is different from considering it for oneself, but even these numbers are on the rise. In 2009, nearly twice as many women (37%) as men (19%) would consider cosmetic surgery for themselves (ASAPS, 2009). And in terms of race, 30% of whites and 22% of people of color would consider cosmetic surgery for themselves now or in the future (ASAPS, 2009).

CONCLUSION

The pursuit of racial capital is enabled by the social context of global media, technologies of the body, global economies and job markets, and persistent racism and sexism. Multinational cosmetics companies market skin-whitening products around the world, and especially to women (and men) of the Global South. Urban, educated women in Africa, Asia, and Latin America are especially poised to increase their market share of expensive skin-lightening products as they anticipate competing in a global job market often dominated by the West.

The competing discourses around skin-bleaching and cosmetic surgery provide an opportunity to examine how the voices for and against bleaching have more in common than one might think. Both the beauty discourse and the public health discourse evade the realities of skin color hierarchies and instead focus on self-improvement themes. While the beauty discourse suggests that self-improvement via skin-lightening is a pathway to a happier personal and professional life, the public health discourse suggests that self-improvement via one's attitude is all that is necessary to realize that dark skin is beautiful, too. Both discourses miss the systematic and institutional aspect of skin color hierarchies that are manifest both nationally and globally. By focusing on individuals and attitudes, leading voices from both sides of the debate have ignored the larger social context in which bleaching occurs.

15

THE POSSIBILITY OF A NEW RACIAL HIERARCHY IN THE TWENTY-FIRST-CENTURY UNITED STATES

Herbert J. Gans

HERBERT J. GANS is emeritus professor of sociology at Columbia University. He received his PhD from the University of Pennsylvania. He has worked as a research planner for public and private agencies, and prior to coming to Columbia taught at the University of Pennsylvania, MIT, and Teachers College of Columbia University. He is the author of nine books and more than 160 articles. His first book was *The Urban Villagers* (1962). Recent works include *War Against the Poor* (1995), *Making Sense of America* (1999), and *Democracy and the News* (2003).

OVER THE LAST DECADE, A NUMBER OF social scientists writing on race and ethnicity have suggested that the country may be moving toward a new racial structure (Alba 1990; Sanjek 1994; Gitlin 1995). If current trends persist, today's multiracial hierarchy could be replaced by what I think of as a dual or bimodal one consisting of "nonblack" and "black" population categories, with a third, "residual," category for the groups that do not, or do not yet, fit into the basic dualism.[1]

More important, this hierarchy may be based not just on color or other visible bodily features, but also on a distinction between undeserving and deserving, or stigmatized and respectable, races.[2] The hierarchy is new only insofar as the old white-nonwhite dichotomy may be replaced by a nonblack-black one, but it is hardly new for blacks, who are likely to remain at the bottom once again. I fear this hierarchy could develop even if more blacks achieve educational mobility; obtain professional and managerial jobs; and gain access to middle-class incomes, wealth, and other "perks." Still, the hierarchy could also end, particularly if the black distribution of income and wealth resembles that of the then-dominant races, and if interracial marriage eliminates many of the visible bodily features by which Americans now define race.

Since no one can even guess much less model the many causal factors that will influence the future, the observations that follow are not intended to be

Questions to Consider

In a timely and provocative article, Herbert Gans suggests that racial categories, as currently understood, are undergoing fundamental changes. He argues that the current racial hierarchy will collapse into two categories: black and nonblack. How will this happen? Which racial and ethnic groups will be placed in each of these two categories, and why?

read as a prediction but as an exercise in speculative analysis. The weakness of such an analysis is its empirical reliance on the extrapolation of too many current trends and the assumed persistence of too many current phenomena. The analysis becomes a justifiable exercise, however, because it aims only to speculate about what future "scenarios" are possible, and what variables might shape these.

Obviously, the observations about such a hierarchy are not meant to suggest that it is desirable. Indeed, I wrote the [reading] with the hope that if such a future threatens to become real, it can be prevented.

The remainder of this [reading] elaborates the basic scenario, adds a set of qualifications, and considers the variables and alternative scenarios now most likely to be significant for the future. The [reading] concludes with observations about the contemporary construction of race in the United States raised by my analysis about a possible future.

THE DUAL RACIAL HIERARCHY

Before what is now described, somewhat incorrectly, as the post-1965 immigration, the United States was structured as a predominantly Caucasian, or white, society, with a limited number of numerically and otherwise inferior races, who were typically called Negroes, Orientals, and American Indians—or blacks, yellows, and reds to go with the pinkish-skinned people called whites. There was also a smattering of groups involving a huge number of people who were still described by their national or geographic origins rather than language, including Filipinos, Mexicans and Puerto Ricans, Cubans, etc.[3]

After 1965, when many other Central and Latin American countries began to send migrants, the Spanish-speaking groups were all recategorized by language and called Hispanics. Newcomers from Southeast Asia were classified by continental origin and called Asians, which meant that the later Indian, Pakistani, and Sri Lankan newcomers had to be distinguished regionally, and called South Asians.

At the end of the twentieth century, the country continues to be dominated by whites. Nevertheless, both the immigrants who started to arrive after the end of World War II and the political, cultural, and racial changes that took place in the wake of their arrival have further invalidated many old racial divisions and labels. They have also set into motion what may turn out to be significant transformations in at least part of the basic racial hierarchy.

These transformations are still in an early phase, but one of the first has been the elevation of a significant, and mostly affluent, part of the Asian and Asian-American population into a "**model minority**" that also bids to eradicate many of the boundaries between it and whites. Upward socio-economic mobility and increasing intermarriage with whites may even end up in eliminating the boundary that now constructs them as a separate race. Thus, one possible future trend may lead to all but poor Asians and Asian-Americans being perceived and even treated so much like whites that currently visible bodily differences will no longer be judged negatively or even noticed, except when and where Asians or Asian-Americans threaten

---

model minority A minority ethnic or racial group that has been socioeconomically successful relative to other racial minorities. The media typically frame this group as a "model" that other racial and ethnic groups should emulate.

white interests (e.g., Newman 1993). The same treatment as quasi whites may spread to other successfully mobile and intermarrying immigrants and their descendants, for example Filipinos and white Hispanics.[4]

What these minorities have in common now with Asians, and might have in common even more in the future, is that they are all nonblack, although not as many are currently as affluent as Asians. Nonetheless, by the middle of the twenty-first century, as whites could perhaps become, or will worry about becoming, a numerical minority in the country, they might cast about for political and cultural allies.[5] Their search for allies, which may not even be conscious or deliberate, could hasten the emergence of a new, nonblack racial category, whatever it is named, in which skin color, or in the case of "Hispanics," racially constructed ethnic differences, will be ignored, even if whites would probably remain the dominant subcategory.

The lower part of the emerging dual hierarchy will likely consist of people classified as blacks, including African-Americans, as well as Caribbean and other blacks, dark-skinned or black Hispanics, Native Americans, and anyone else who is dark skinned enough and/or possessed of visible bodily features and behavior patterns, actual or imagined, that remind nonblacks of blacks. Many of these people will also be poor, and if whites and other nonblacks continue to blame America's troubles on a low-status scapegoat, the new black category will be characterized as an undeserving race.

In effect, class will presumably play nearly as much of a role in the boundary changes as race, but with some important exceptions. For example, if a significant number of very poor whites remain as the twenty-first-century equivalent of today's "white trash," they will probably be viewed as less undeserving than equally poor blacks simply because they are whites.[6]

Furthermore, the limits of class are indicated, at least for today, by the continued stigmatization of affluent and otherwise high-status blacks, who suffer some of the same indignities as poor blacks (Feagin and Sykes 1994).[7] So, of course, do moderate and middle-income members of the working class, who constitute the majority of blacks in America even if whites do not know it. The high visibility of "black" or Negroid physical features renders class position invisible to whites, so that even affluent blacks are suspected of criminal or pathological behavior that is actually found only among a minority of very poor blacks.

Despite continuing white hatreds and fears of blacks that continue almost 150 years after the Civil War, racial classification systems involving others have been more flexible. When the first Irish immigrants came to New York, they were so poor that they were perceived by Anglo-Saxon whites as the black Irish and often treated like blacks. Even so, it did not take the Irish long to separate themselves from blacks, and more important, to be so separated by the city's Anglo-Saxons. A generation later, the Irish were whites (Roediger 1991; Ignatiev 1995).

Perhaps their new whiteness was reinforced by the arrival of the next set of newcomers: people from Eastern and Southern Europe who were often described as members of "swarthy races." Even though the word *race* was used the way we today use *ethnicity,* the newcomers were clearly not white in the Anglo-Saxon sense, and Southern Italians were sometimes called "guineas" because of their dark skin. Nonetheless, over time, they too became white, thanks in part to their acculturation, their integration into the mainstream economy, and after World War II, their entry into the middle class. Perhaps the disappearance of their swarthiness was also reinforced by the arrival in the cities of a new wave of Southern blacks during and after World War II.

A less typical racial transformation occurred about that time in Mississippi, where whites began to treat the Chinese merchants who provided stores for poor blacks as near whites. As Loewen (1988) tells the story, increased affluence and acculturation were again relevant factors. Although whites neither socialized nor intermarried with the Chinese, they accorded them greater social deference and political respect than when they had first arrived. They turned the Chinese into what I previously called a residual category, and in the process created an early version of the nonblack-black duality that may appear in the United States in the next century.

As the Mississippi example suggests, changes in racial classification schemes need not require racial or class equality, for as long as scarce resources or positions remain, justifications for discrimination also remain and physical features that are invisible in some social settings can still become visible in others. **Glass ceilings** supply the best example, because they seem to change more slowly than some other hierarchical boundaries. Even ceilings for Jews, non-Irish Catholics, and others long classified as whites are still lower than those for **WASPs** in the upper reaches of the class and prestige structures.

I should note that the racial hierarchy I have sketched here, together with the qualifications that follow, are described both from the perspective of the (overtly) detached social scientist, and also from the perspective of the populations that end up as dominant in the structure. A longer [reading] would analyze how very differently the people who are fitted into the lower or residual parts of the hierarchy see it.[8]

QUALIFICATIONS TO THE DUAL HIERARCHY

Even if the country would someday replace its current set of racial classifications, the result would not be a simple dual structure, and this model needs to be qualified in at least three ways.

Residuals

The first qualification is the near certainty of a residual or middle category that includes groups placed in a waiting position by the dominant population until it becomes clear whether they will be allowed to become nonblack, face the seemingly permanent inferiority that goes with being black, or become long-term residuals.

If such a structure were to develop in the near future, those likely to be placed in a residual category would include the less affluent members of today's Asian, Hispanic and Filipino, Central and South American Indian, and mixed Indian-Latino populations. The future of the dark-skinned members of the South Asian newcomers is harder to predict. Indeed, their treatment will become an important test of how whites deal with the race-class nexus when the people involved are very dark skinned but are not Negroid—and when their class position is so high that in 1990 it outranked that of all other immigrants (Rumbaut 1997, table 1.4).[9]

Who is classified as residual will, like all other categorizations, be shaped by both class and race. To borrow Milton Gordon's (1964) useful but too rarely used notion of "ethclass," what may be developing are "race-classes," with lower-class members of otherwise racially acceptable groups and higher-class members of racially inferior ones being placed in the residual category.

It is also possible for two or more residual categories to emerge, one for nonwhite and Hispanic populations of lower- and working-class position, and another for nonwhites and Hispanics of higher-class position, with the latter more likely to be eligible eventually to join whites in the nonblack portion of a dual hierarchy. Yet other variations are conceivable, however, for white America has not yet given any clues about how it will treat middle-class Latinos of various skin colors and other bodily features. Perhaps today's ad hoc solution, to treat nonblack Hispanics as a quasi-racial ethnic group that is neither white nor black, may survive for another generation or more, particularly if enough Hispanics remain poor or are falsely accused of rejecting linguistic Americanization.

Being placed in a residual classification means more than location in a middle analytic category; it is also a socially enforced, even if covert, category, and it will be accompanied by all the social, political, and emotional uncertainties that go with being placed in a holding pattern and all the pains these create (Marris 1996). True, residuals may not

---

glass ceiling A situation in which the advancement of a qualified person within the hierarchy of an organization is curtailed at a particular point due to sexist or racist discrimination. One is able to "see" the corporate path to the top but hits an imaginary "glass ceiling" where advancement stops.

WASP White Anglo-Saxon Protestant.

know they are waiting, but then the second-generation white ethnic "marginal men" identified by Stonequist (1937) did not know they were waiting for eventual acculturation and assimilation.

Multiracial

A second qualification to the dual model is created by the emergence of biracials or multiracials that result from the rising intermarriage rates among Asian, Hispanic, and black and white immigrants as well as black and white native-born Americans.[10] Interracial marriages increased from 1 percent of all marriages in 1960 to 3 percent in 1990 (Harrison and Bennett 1995, 165).[11] They are expected to increase much faster in the future, particularly Asian-white ones, since even now, about a third of all Asian marriages, and more than half of all Japanese ones, are intermarriages.[12] If Hispanic-white marriages were also counted, they would exceed all the rest in current number and expected growth, but these are usually treated as ethnic rather than racial intermarriages.

Another set of recruits for a residual position includes the light-skinned blacks, once called mulattos, who today dominate the African-American upper class, some of whom may be sufficiently elite and light skinned to be viewed as nonblack. Even now, the most prominent among the light-skinned black-white biracials, including business and civic leaders, celebrities and entertainers, are already treated as honorary whites, although many refuse this option and take special pride in their blackness and become "race leaders."[13]

Meanwhile, "multiracial" is in the process of slowly becoming a public racial category, and someday it could become an official one codified by the U.S. Census.[14] At this writing, however, many people of mixed race are not ready to define themselves publicly as such, and those who can choose which racial origin to use are sometimes flexible on instrumental grounds, or may choose different racial origins on different occasions.[15] How people of various racial mixtures construct themselves in the longer run is impossible to tell, since issues of their identification and treatment by others; their own identity; and the social, occupational, financial, and political benefits and costs involved cannot be predicted either.

As far as the country's long-term future racial structure is concerned, however, what matters most is how whites will eventually view and treat multiracial people. This will be affected by the variations in class and visible physical features among multiracial people—for example, how closely they resemble whites or other deserving races. Another question is the future of the traditional identification of race with "blood," which counts all nonwhites in halves, quarters, or even eighths, depending on how many and which ancestors intermarried with whom.[16] If the late-twentieth-century belief in the power of genes continues, blood might simply be replaced by genes someday.

Mixed race is a particularly complex category, for several reasons. In any racial intermarriage with more than one offspring, each sibling is likely to look somewhat different racially from the others, ranging from darker to lighter or more and less nonwhite. Thus, one black-white sibling could be viewed as black and another as nonblack—even before they decide how they view themselves. What happens in subsequent generations is virtually unimaginable, since even if mixed-race individuals marry others of the same mixture, their children will not resemble their grandparents and some may barely resemble their parents. Eventually, a rising number will be treated as, and will think of themselves as, white or nonblack, but this is possible only when people of multiracial origin can no longer bear children who resemble a black ancestor.

Empirical evidence about the effects of racial intermarriage from countries where it has taken place for a long time is unfortunately not very relevant. The closest cases, the Caribbean islands, are for the most part, tiny. They are also former plantation societies, with a small number of white and light-skinned elites, and a large number of nonwhites—and a differential conception of white and nonwhite from island to island.[17] Caribbean nonwhites appear to intermarry fairly freely but skin color does count, and the darkest-skinned peoples are invariably lowest in socioeconomic class and status (Mintz 1989; Rodriguez 1989).

The only large country, Brazil, also began as a plantation society, and it differs from the United States particularly in that the Brazilian state eschewed racial legislation. As a result, Brazil never passed Jim Crow laws, but as of this writing (January 1998) it has not passed civil rights legislation either. Racial stratification, as well as discrimination and segregation, has persisted nonetheless, but it has been maintained through the class system. Drastic class inequalities, including a high rate of illiteracy among the poor, have enabled whites to virtually monopolize the higher class and status positions.

The absence of state involvement has given Brazil an undeserved reputation as a society that encourages intermarriage but ignores racial differences, a reputation the state has publicized as "racial democracy." The reality is not very different from that of the United States, however, for while there has been more intermarriage, it appears to have taken place mainly among blacks and black-white biracials, who together make up about half the country's population. Moreover, biracials gain little socioeconomic advantage from their lighter skins, even as the darkest-skinned blacks are kept at the bottom, forced into slums and prisons as in the United States.[18]

In effect, the Brazilian experience would suggest an empirical precedent for my hypothesis that blacks will remain a separate, and discriminated-against, population in the United States of the future. Indeed, in just about every society in which blacks first arrived as slaves, they are still at the bottom, and the political, socioeconomic, and cultural mechanisms to keep them there remain in place. Although blacks obtain higher incomes and prestige than Asians or white Hispanics in a number of American communities, the descendants of nonblack immigrants are, with some notable exceptions, still able to overtake most blacks in the long run.

Since parts of the United States were also a plantation society in which the slaves were black, the leftovers of the racial stratification pattern will likely continue here as well. Thus, children of black-white intermarriages who turn out to be dark skinned are classified as blacks, even if the United States is on the whole kinder to light-skinned biracials than Brazil.

The future of Asian-white biracials remains more unpredictable, in part because no empirical data exist that can be used to shore up guesses about them. The same observation applies to the endless number of other multiracial combinations that will be created when the children of multiracial parents intermarry with yet other multiracials. There will be few limits to new variations in bodily features, though which will be visible or noticed, and which of the latter will be stigmatized or celebrated as exotic cannot be guessed now.[19] Most likely, however, the larger the number of multiracials and of multiracial variations, the more difficult it will be for nonblacks to define and enforce racial boundaries, or to figure out which of the many darker-skinned varieties of multiracials had black ancestors. In that case, an eventual end to racial discrimination is possible.

If future racial self-identification patterns will also resemble today's ethnic ones, the racial equivalent of today's voluntary white ethnicity and its associated lack of ethnic loyalty may mean that many future triracial, quadriracial, and other multiracial people may eventually know little, and care even less, about the various racial mixtures they have inherited. It is even conceivable that this change will extend to black multiracials, and should race become voluntary for them as well, the possibility of an end to racial discrimination will be increased. Unfortunately, at the moment such extrapolations are far closer to utopian thinking than to sociological speculation.

Regional Variations

A third qualification to the dual model is that the portrait I have drawn is national, but given the regional variations in old racial groups and new immigrant populations, it fits no single U.S. region. Moreover, some parts of the country are now still so devoid of new immigrants, with the exception of the handful who come to establish "ethnic" restaurants, that the present racial hierarchies, categories, and attitudes, many of them based on stereotypes imported from elsewhere, could survive unchanged for quite a while in such areas. Furthermore, some areas that have experienced heavy immigration from Asia and Latin America are currently seeing an outmigration of whites, especially lower-income ones (Frey 1996). Thus, even current patterns in the racial makeup of U.S. regions could change fairly quickly.

In addition, regional differences remain in the demography of the lowest strata. The racial hierarchy of the Deep South will probably continue to bear many direct marks of slavery, although the de facto black experience elsewhere in the country has so far not been totally different. Moreover, in some regions, Latin American and other poor nonblack immigrants have already been able to jump over the poor black population economically and socially, partly because whites, including institutions such as banks, are less hostile—or less necessary—to them than they are to blacks.

In the Southwest, Mexicans and other Hispanics remain at the socioeconomic bottom, although in California, they may be joined by the Hmong, Laotians, and other very poor Asians. And Native Americans still occupy the lowest socioeconomic stratum in the handful of mostly rural parts of the country where they now live, although tribes with gambling casinos may be able to effect some changes in that pattern.

Even though some of the new immigrants can by now be found just about everywhere in America, the Los Angeles and New York City areas not only remain the major immigrant arrival centers but also contain the most diverse populations. As a result, a number of the issues discussed in this [reading] will be played out there, even as they are barely noticeable in the many smaller American cities that may have attracted only a handful of the newcomers. Since these two cities are also the country's prime creators of popular culture, however, their distinctive racial and ethnic characteristics will probably be diffused in subtle ways through the country as a whole.

ALTERNATIVE SCENARIOS

Speculating about the future also requires some explicit consideration of the variables that could affect the guesses I have made here, which in turn could lead to alternative scenarios. Generally speaking these variables are macrosociological—major changes in the economy, demographic patterns including internal migration and immigration, as well as political realignments and racial divisions of labor, among others. These in turn can result in changes in racial and ethnic relations as well as in classification systems.

As noted earlier, dominant groups can alter racial categories and constructions. Model minorities are "chosen" by the dominant population precisely because they appear to share, and thereby to uphold, that population's behavior or values. If new behavior or values need to be upheld, new model minorities may be recruited. Scapegoats are populations that can be blamed for social problems, although the dominant populations choose, or even create, the social problems for which scapegoats will be blamed. Scapegoats, or targets for blame, generally come in two varieties: *higher* scapegoats, usually recruited from higher status minority groups that can be blamed for obtaining too much economic or cultural power; and *lower* ones, typically the undeserving poor, who can be accused of deviant behavior or values said to hold back economic growth, require public expenditures that could bankrupt governmental budgets, threaten familial and sexual norms, or impair the moral fabric of the rest of society. Blaming both types of scapegoats is a politically easy way of responding to a crisis, particularly one for which immediate and feasible solutions are lacking.

During the long Cold War, the Soviets and other foreign scapegoats could be blamed for American problems, but now, domestic scapegoats have again become the primary target. While illegal and even legal American immigrants are once again joining poor blacks as the country's principal lower scapegoats, only a few states have sufficient immigrants to serve as targets for blame, which may help to explain why conservative politicians, particularly Republicans, have more often demonized poor blacks.

The most likely candidates for change in current racial categories, other than of model minorities, are the people whites now call Hispanics, as well as descendants of some now officially nonwhite populations in the new immigration. They will have to be allowed into the higher-status occupations in larger number if and when the supply of whites runs out, and in that case, today's forms of racial and ethnic discrimination against them, particularly those shaped by class considerations, would have to give way. In fact, by the middle of the twenty-first century, demographers and journalists may be amazed that fifty years earlier, whites expected to be swamped in 2050 by an aggregate of diverse peoples then all called Hispanics.

Two macrosocial factors are probably most important in thinking about alternative scenarios. One is the set of geopolitical and economic demographics that can be produced by cross-national population movements, including the one that has fueled the immigration from Central and Latin America, as well as Russia, Asia, and now Africa, during the last half century. These movements were controlled at least in part by U.S. government legislation, but world catastrophes could take place that could force even the United States to open its borders to much larger numbers of people who might alter the racial distribution significantly.

National demographics can also be changed by domestic political considerations, however, which could lead to a new search for white—and non-Hispanic—immigrants. The United States found its late-nineteenth-century industrial workforce in white Europe rather than among the newly freed slaves in the South. Likewise, Australia has recently looked for European immigrants to discourage the arrival of further Asians.

The second major factor is the state of the domestic economy. If late-twentieth-century trends in the world economy and on Wall Street continue in their present forms, the further disappearance of American firms, jobs, and high wages, as well as related changes in the country's economy, would persist too.

Suppose, for example, that unemployment, or the decline of real income, or both, worsened in the first quarter of the twenty-first century, and Americans in large numbers conclude that the country's economy can never again supply full-time jobs paying a living wage for everyone. While the descendants of the poorer immigrants would be the first to experience what I once called "second generation decline" (Gans 1992), other immigrants can also be dispatched into persistent poverty when not enough jobs are available, with the appropriate racial stereotypes invented or reinvented to justify their downward mobility. Even some middle-class descendants of Asian, Russian, and other newcomers could be transformed into lower scapegoats. Then, the dual racial hierarchy I have described would look very different or might not come to pass at all.

Should economic crises result in political crises as well, or raise religious and culture "wars" to more feverish pitches, the current movement toward a dual racial structure could also end quickly. Then, a modern version of the nineteenth-century American monoracial pattern might reappear, with the children of white newcomers joining older white ethnics and WASPs as the only acceptable race. Some members of the newly scapegoated races would probably react in turn, inaugurating political protest, intensifying identity politics and slowing down on intermarriage and other forms of acculturation and assimilation. Some descendants of today's newcomers might return to the old country.

What if a very different economic scenario were assumed, involving a return of old-style economic growth accompanied by a stronger U.S. position in the global economy, a shortage of domestic workers, and an upward trend in real income? In that case, the trend toward a dual structure might be hastened, and the erosion of perceived racial differences speeded up as well.

At that point, the now still visible bodily differences of Asian-Americans and their descendants might no longer be noticed, and these groups would repeat the post–World War II pattern by which Southern and Eastern European "races" were redefined as "ethnic groups." The reclassification of Hispanics, including the treatment of third-generation Central and Latin Americans, would probably move in the same direction.

The fate of blacks is more difficult to imagine. If the economy created a seller's market for people with job skills at all levels from blue collar to professional and managerial, all poverty would decline sharply, including that of blacks. Moreover, blacks would be able to enter the upper middle and middle classes in such numbers as to disturb white America's long association of poverty with blackness. Indeed, in an economy with enough decent jobs for all, private and public affirmative action policies to assure the spread of blacks at all levels of the occupational and socioeconomic structure would be likely as well.

Under such conditions, those aspects of white racism due to fear of and anger at black poverty would begin to decline, and if the federal government was committed to fight racial discrimination and segregation, so would the construction of blacks as an undeserving race. Black-white intermarriage rates might also rise more quickly.

If the prosperity were long term, and it as well as other events in the society and the world reduced the country's resort to domestic scapegoats, a dual racial hierarchy might be replaced by the beginnings of a multiracial structure in which the boundaries of all races would become fuzzier and weaker. Since now-stigmatized visible bodily differences would then lose their negative connotations, they might not only be ignored but even come to be celebrated as positive contributions to American diversity, just as current ethnic differences among Europeans provide the country with nonthreatening cultural diversities.

Prosperity alone does not necessarily solve a society's other problems, however, and political, cultural, and religious conflicts could remain, encouraging dominant groups to choose and stigmatize an undeserving race, even if it is not a poor one. Anti-Semitic activities, for example, have occurred in prosperous times and societies, and in nations with minuscule Jewish populations.

Likewise, more economic prosperity and other positive economic tendencies alone do not necessarily produce more acculturation and assimilation of immigrants. Even the acculturation of large numbers of immigrants and their descendants does not automatically preclude identity politics, for today's college and university campuses are rife with rapidly acculturating newcomers who nevertheless feel strongly enough about their racial identity to become active in identity politics.

It is even possible that in a multiracial America, some latter-day descendants of WASPs and white ethnics will resort to identity politics as an attempt to retain or restore their political and cultural dominance.[20] And if a global economy also produced pressures toward global cultural and political homogeneities, nation-states or their successors might develop now unimagined forms of national identity politics or cultural revivals to maintain some kind of national distinctiveness. Immigrants and their descendants might be victimized by such developments more than blacks, however.

THREE TENDENCIES IN THE CONTEMPORARY CONSTRUCTION OF RACE

Biological Constructions

The first tendency is the continuing construction of race from biological as well as social building blocks. Most scientific experts agree that there are no biologically definable races, and that race is therefore not a useful biological concept. The lay public, however, which is not ready to accept expert opinion, sees differences in visible bodily features, mostly facial, between people and treats them as racial differences caused by differences in "blood." People also racialize differences in personality traits such as "soul"—and national character in the case of immigrants.

The visible bodily differences are not imaginary, for people do differ by skin color, and the shapes or other characteristics of various body parts, including heads, eyelids, noses, hair, and others. To cite just a few examples, even in third-generation white ethnic America, one can find Irish and Welsh (or "Celtic") faces, southern Italian and Sicilian ones, and Slavic as well as Scandinavian ones.

What people notice are not scientifically defined races or subraces, but the descendants of once-isolated peoples who had been inbreeding for centuries.[21] Since most have now stopped doing so as a result of rural to urban and other migrations, their distinctiveness is disappearing with each new generation, but it has by no means disappeared.

Some of the variations in personality and social characteristics that laypeople correlate with race or "blood" can undoubtedly be traced in part to the societies and economies, as well as the racial hierarchies, in which these once-isolated peoples lived. The occupational and other social roles that immigrants play in their new societies also play a part, one reason why immigrant shopkeepers in "middlemen" roles are often seen as "clannish" by the populations they serve, for example.

Some visible bodily features that distinguish people are noticed and judged; some are noticed but not judged one way or another; and yet others are not even noticed, seeming to be virtually invisible. Although how features are judged can be traced in part to the popular Darwinisms of the last two centuries, in general, the bodily features of the most prestigious peoples are usually adopted as ideals of physical perfection, while features found among the lower social classes are judged pejoratively.[22]

Variations in skin color, as well as in head shapes, noses, eyes, lips, and hair, have been noticed in many societies, but differences in some bodily parts have been ignored, for example, the size of fingers and the shapes of ears and earlobes.[23] Yet other bodily features are not noticed because they are hidden by clothes; while a few are not noticed because people wear clothes to hide them. These often spur fantasies, for example about black penis size and other imagined racial differences in reproductive and other organs.[24]

A major ingredient of the social construction of race is the determination of which visible bodily features are noticed and used to delineate race and which remain unnoticed. In the process shaping that construction, various social constructors, including laypersons, experts, and, when relevant, commercial and political decision makers, take part. Unless explicit ideological, commercial, or political reasons are involved, the constructors may not be aware of the process in which they are involved, or the causes that shape the final determination. Usually, whites

are the major constructors, but increasingly, representatives of the racial minorities to be constructed participate when they can politicize the process, or can frighten manufacturers or advertisers of national consumer goods.[25]

Strictly speaking, a biological construction should make racial characteristics and classifications relatively fixed, but lay biological construction is almost as flexible as social construction. The reason for the lack of fixity is not hard to find, for the choice of which visible bodily features are to be noticed has almost nothing to do with race and everything to do with stratification.

As the Brazilian and United States experiences indicate, the race of the lowest class became the lowest race because slaves were almost by definition the lowest class and race. That captured blacks were the only population economically and otherwise powerless to prevent their becoming enslaved in recent centuries led whites to use their distinguishable skin color and facial features to translate their class inferiority into a racial one (Fields 1990). Similarly, the stigmatization of "yellow" skin resulted from the serflike status of Chinese "coolies" on railroad construction gangs; the stigmatization of "swarthiness" followed from the low status of the Southern and Eastern European newcomers; and a century later, white Hispanic immigrants are sometimes called a race because of their low class position.[26] That the ancestors of now-respected Americans were once damned for their swarthy skins has been quietly forgotten, both among their descendants and among the peoples who "invented" the original stigma.

Ethnicity as Racial

The second, and related, tendency is the continuing lay practice of identifying ethnic and national differences as racial, particularly in private self-naming. Census analysts have discovered that in the 1990 census, respondents to open-ended questions claimed membership in nearly three hundred races or ethnic groups, including seventy Hispanic categories (Morganthau 1995, 64). In many instances, they equated their race with their nationality—or with their tribes in the case of Native Americans.[27] As Eleanor Gerber and

Manuel de la Puente pointed out in reporting on a study of test questions for the 2000 census: "Most respondents recognized the term 'ethnic group' but ... would indicate it was 'the same thing' as race ... [and] often coined the term 'ethnic race' during our discussions" (Gerber and de la Puente 1996, 21).

The two Bureau of Census researchers suggest lack of education as the causal factor in this conflation, indicating that only the college educated could distinguish ethnic group from race. However, as long as Americans notice visible bodily differences among people of the same official race, they will hold on to *private* constructions of race that differ from the official definitions.[28] Even among the third- and fourth-generation white multiethnics whose "ethnic options" Mary Waters (1990) studied, some chose their ethnicities on the basis of racial conceptions of national origin.[29] In effect, ethnicity continues to be a matter of "blood."[30]

Racial Tolerance

The third and perhaps most important tendency is the apparently increasing white tolerance for racial differences, except with respect to blacks. At the same time, whites seem to use race less often as an indicator of class, except when they are considering poor blacks. This trend may become more widespread as racial intermarriage among people of similar class increases further. Today, class homogamy is apparently outranking racial homogamy among college-educated young people (Kalmijn 1991).

If this pattern spreads to other Americans of the same age, and if it becomes permanent, and if whites were willing and able to see that their hatreds and fears of blacks and other very poor nonwhites are so often reactions to their extreme and persistent poverty rather than their race, class could become more important and more overt as a boundary and a principle of stratification in the future. If Americans could also realize that class is more than a matter of "lifestyle" differences among near equals, class stratification might someday become a matter of general public discussion. In that case, the myth of a classless America might eventually be laid to rest.[31]

Even a more modest increase in awareness of class would be desirable, because class is, after all,

an achieved status, while race is not, even in its reasonably flexible lay construction. However, the shift from race to class would also require Americans to develop a more fundamental understanding of the United States and to invent a new conception of the American dream and its underlying myth to replace that of the classless society. So far, there is no indication of this happening.

In fact, it would probably not happen until events in the political economy make it possible to achieve a drastic reduction of joblessness and poverty, so that the correlation of poverty with blackness is significantly lowered. If and when blacks become roughly equal economically to nonblacks, blacks can no longer be treated as an undeserving race.

If poverty and inequality are not lessened, however, and if more poor blacks are condemned to work for nothing but their welfare benefits, they could be treated as an ever more undeserving race, and other populations who cannot enter, or stay in, the middle class, including poor Hispanics and Asians, might join them. In that case, the racial hierarchy of the next century's United States would look very different from the one I have sketched here.

CONCLUSION

A society's reconstruction of racial categories appears to require at least the following conditions: (1) an influx of immigrants who do not fit the existing racial categories and their associated class backgrounds; (2) a healthy economy with sufficient opportunity for upward mobility even for poorer immigrants; (3) a lack of demand for new lower (and higher) racial scapegoats; and (4) an at least temporary demand for model minorities.

If these conditions are met, existing racial definitions and categories will be altered, sometimes even quickly if there is a proliferation of interracial marriages. However, in a society with a history of slavery, one possible effect is a dual racial hierarchy, in which one part consists mostly of ex-slaves. However, since even the effects of slavery should eventually be eliminated, at least in theory, the

United States could become a predominantly interracial or multiracial society someday.

Even then, the more prestigious racial mixtures are apt to remain somewhat whiter for a while than the rest, and the less prestigious ones darker. But if the country's racial mixing ever became so thorough that skin color and other currently used bodily features were sufficiently unrecognizable or no longer of sufficient interest to be noticed, race would no longer be associated with social ranking. If Americans then still needed to rank each other, new criteria would have to be found.

Seeing the Big Picture   **Color-Blind or Blind to Color?**

Briefly glance through the appendix. Based on your observations of statistics on race in this section, can you make an argument that the United States is now color-blind? How might you reconcile the ideal of colorblindness with the trends in the data?

PREJUDICE, DISCRIMINATION, AND RACISM

IMAGINE YOU ARE A 57-YEAR-OLD WHITE vice president with Friendly Bank. You earn a considerable amount of money, have a large mortgage and car payments, and support four kids, two of whom are in college. You are the primary breadwinner in your family. At lunch, your boss asks you about the new manager you will be hiring. He hints to you in a subtle way, a way you could never prove in court, that he has had bad experiences working with Asian Americans and would be extremely upset if one was hired. You are not racist toward Asians. In fact, one of your best friends is an Asian American. You do, however, need this job, your family needs to eat, two of your children are in college, and you are at an age at which moving from one job to another would be very difficult and extremely costly. Of the three hundred people who apply for this position, several Asian American candidates appear to be highly qualified, and one unquestionably would make an excellent bank manager. Would you turn a blind eye to the résumés of the Asian Americans, or would you hire the most qualified person, even if that meant hiring an Asian American and being marginalized or conveniently downsized by your boss?

How do feelings of antipathy toward or dislike of a group of people because of their skin color, ethnicity, or religion culminate in actions against members of that group? As the preceding example indicates, individuals may act in discriminatory ways and not be prejudiced or racist. Conversely, someone may be prejudiced and racist toward a group and not discriminate. The Asian or black shoe salesperson who does not like whites may still sell a white customer a pair of shoes in order to earn a commission.

Prejudice and **discrimination** are linked in complicated ways. Since World War II, whites' views on integration, interracial marriage, voting for nonwhite politicians, and sharing social space with blacks and Asians suggest that whites are gradually embracing the idea of a color-blind society. However, things, particularly attitudes through surveys, are not always as they seem. Such survey findings are encouraging only if you believe that respondents' answers are an accurate reflection of

prejudice To "prejudge"; having preconceived notions, attitudes, or negative beliefs about a group.

discrimination The denial of goods or services to an individual or group for arbitary reasons, such as a person's race, religion, or nationality.

what they really think or feel. Perhaps these trends reflect pressure to conform to what respondents believe is a socially desirable attitude. Typically, individuals want to present themselves to others in a positive way. This pressure to conform may lead respondents to conveniently forget or tightly monitor racist or prejudiced beliefs. Are answers to questions about racial attitudes merely a reflection of what takes place in the abstract, unnatural interview setting, or are these responses a valid and reliable window into Americans' racial attitudes? Frankly, social scientists are not always sure. To further complicate matters, it's not clear what connection, if any, exists between attitudes and action or between prejudice and discrimination. Demonstrating a strong, consistent causal link between attitudes and actions has proved elusive in the social sciences. The proposition that actions flow from attitudes may seem straightforward, but as we will see in the readings, it is not. It seems logical that individuals would behave in a manner consistent with their attitudes, opinions, or beliefs about a particular topic. If, for example, you define yourself as not being racist, you would not engage in racial discrimination. But as the example about the vice president of Friendly Bank suggests, various social and economic pressures mediate what we would like to do, what we should do, and what we actually do.

Prejudice and discrimination take many forms. The first five readings, in Understanding Racism, examine those forms and the way certain social and structural conditions can create an environment in which prejudice and discrimination are likely to emerge. In an insightful and classic piece of sociology, Herbert Blumer explains race prejudice (racism) as a reflection of how individuals place themselves in a racial hierarchy relative to other racial groups they encounter; that is, individuals attempt to maintain privilege and status by reserving the "prerogatives" of their racial group, even if they are not consciously aware of it. Many believe that race-based discrimination is a part of our nation's past. New Orleans's Mayor Mitchell

Landrieu explains how our nation's past of racism in the form of slavery lives on in the Confederate memorials that occupy town squares throughout our nation. Robert Merton provides examples of the social context in which a nonprejudiced individual like our vice president at Friendly Bank might act in a discriminatory fashion. Like Blumer, Merton outlines how prejudice and discrimination are often rooted in efforts to maintain privileges or advantages that accrue to individuals because of their skin color. Kathleen Blee and Elizabeth Yates explain how hate and right-wing, neo-Nazi movements can move from the political margins to the center of political life. Their research and insights are particularly important given the United States and Europe have witnessed a rise in right-wing, anti-immigrant hate groups. George Lipsitz chronicles how racism by the federal government in housing, bank lending, and huge subsidies to spur suburbanization (and white flight from the cities) after World War II should be understood as institutional practices that resulted in substantial long-term, intergenerational "investments" in the white population. In what can only be described as the most ghoulish form of institutional racism, Professor Berry chronicles how the cadaver trade was organized selling dead black bodies. While there were laws about desecration of dead bodies, racism and the pursuit of profit excluded blacks from these legal protections.

The five articles in How Space Gets Raced reveal a nation highly segregated by race and ethnicity. Douglas Massey and Jonathan Tannen argue that residential segregation results in a loss of occupational and educational mobility for racial minorities and cuts off communities from "mainstream" America. Elijah Anderson explains how many poor, young African Americans use fear and intimidation as a way to gain respect among their peers. Robert Bullard details how poor and nonwhite neighborhoods are disproportionately exposed to toxic waste, perhaps the most obvious way in which social space gets raced to the detriment of a racial minority.

The Reverend Dr. Martin Luther King, Jr., commented, "The church is the most segregated institution in America . . . and Sunday service is the most segregated hour in the nation." Michael Emerson asks why this is the case and, perhaps more important, what the social characteristics are of racially integrated congregations. Finally, Jeff Wiltse shows that leisure spaces were racialized by examining how and why public swimming pools were segregated, and the long-term effects of that practice.

16

RACE PREJUDICE AS A SENSE OF GROUP POSITION

Herbert Blumer

The late **HERBERT BLUMER** spent most of his professional career at the University of Chicago and the University of California, Berkeley. Blumer established symbolic interactionism as a major sociological perspective in American sociology.

IN THIS [READING] I AM PROPOSING AN APPROACH to the study of race prejudice different from that which dominates contemporary scholarly thought on this topic. My thesis is that race prejudice exists basically in a sense of group position rather than in a set of feelings which members of one racial group have toward the members of another racial group. This different way of viewing race prejudice shifts study and analysis from a preoccupation with feelings as lodged in individuals to a concern with the relationship of racial groups. It also shifts scholarly treatment away from individual lines of experience and focuses interest on the collective process by which a racial group comes to define and redefine another racial group. Such shifts, I believe, will yield a more realistic and penetrating understanding of race prejudice.

There can be little question that the rather vast literature on race prejudice is dominated by the idea that such prejudice exists fundamentally as a feeling or set of feelings lodged in the individual. It is usually depicted as consisting of feelings such as antipathy, hostility, hatred, intolerance, and aggressiveness. Accordingly, the task of scientific inquiry becomes two-fold. On one hand, there is a need to identify the feelings which make up race prejudice—to see how they fit together and how they are supported by other psychological elements, such as mythical beliefs. On the other hand, there is need of showing how the feeling complex has come into being. Thus, some scholars trace the complex feelings back chiefly to innate dispositions; some trace it to personality composition, such as authoritarian personality; and others regard the feelings of prejudice as being

Questions to Consider

Herbert Blumer writes, "to characterize another racial group is, by opposition, to define one's own group." How does a "sense of group position" shape how we see other racial and ethnic groups? Have you ever defined your racial group membership in such a way as to heighten your group's status at the expense of another? What was the context?

formed through social experience. However different may be the contentions regarding the makeup of racial prejudice and the way in which it may come into existence, these contentions are alike in locating prejudice in the realm of individual feeling. This is clearly true of the work of psychologists, psychiatrists, and social psychologists, and tends to be predominantly the case in the work of sociologists.

Unfortunately, this customary way of viewing race prejudice overlooks and obscures the fact that race prejudice is fundamentally a matter of relationship between racial groups. A little reflective thought should make this very clear. Race prejudice presupposes, necessarily, that racially prejudiced individuals think of themselves as belonging to a given racial group. It means, also, that they assign to other racial groups those against whom they are prejudiced. Thus, logically and actually, a scheme of racial identification is necessary as a framework for racial prejudice. Moreover, such identification involves the formation of an image or a conception of one's own racial group and of another racial group, inevitably in terms of the relationship of such groups. To fail to see that racial prejudice is a matter (a) of the racial identification made of oneself and of others, and (b) of the way in which the identified groups are conceived in relation to each other, is to miss what is logically and actually basic. One should keep clearly in mind that people necessarily come to identify themselves as belonging to a racial group; such identification is not spontaneous or inevitable but a result of experience. Further, one must realize that the kind of

picture which a racial group forms of itself and the kind of picture which it may form of others are similarly products of experience. Hence, such pictures are variable, just as the lines of experience which produce them are variable.

The body of feelings which scholars, today, are so inclined to regard as constituting the substance of race prejudice is actually a resultant of the way in which given racial groups conceive of themselves and of others. A basic understanding of race prejudice must be sought in the process by which racial groups form images of themselves and of others. This process, as I hope to show, is fundamentally *a collective process*. It operates chiefly through the public media in which individuals who are accepted as the spokesmen of a racial group characterize publicly another racial group. To characterize another racial group is, by opposition, to define one's own group. This is equivalent to placing the two groups in relation to each other, or defining their positions vis-à-vis each other. It is the *sense of social position* emerging from this collective process of characterization which provides the basis of race prejudice. The following discussion will consider important facets of this matter.

I would like to begin by discussing several of the important feelings that enter into race prejudice. This discussion will reveal how fundamentally racial feelings point to and depend on a positional arrangement of the racial groups. In this discussion I will confine myself to such feelings in the case of a dominant racial group.

There are four basic types of feeling that seem to be always present in race prejudice in the dominant group. They are (1) a feeling of superiority, (2) a feeling that the subordinate race is intrinsically different and alien, (3) a feeling of proprietary claim to certain areas of privilege and advantage, and (4) a fear and suspicion that the subordinate race harbors designs on the prerogatives of the dominant race. A few words about each of these four feelings will suffice.

In race prejudice there is a self-assured feeling on the part of the dominant racial group of being naturally superior or better. This is commonly shown in a disparagement of the qualities of the subordinate racial group. Condemnatory or debasing traits, such as laziness, dishonesty, greediness, unreliability, stupidity, deceit and immorality, are usually imputed to it. The second feeling, that the subordinate race is an alien and fundamentally different stock, is likewise always present. "They are not of our kind" is a common way in which this is likely to be expressed. It is this feeling that reflects, justifies, and promotes the social exclusion of the subordinate racial group. The combination of these two feelings of superiority and of distinctiveness can easily give rise to feelings of aversion and even antipathy. But in themselves they do not form prejudice. We have to introduce the third and fourth types of feeling.

The third feeling, the sense of proprietary claim, is of crucial importance. It is the feeling on the part of the dominant group of being entitled to either exclusive or prior rights in many important areas of life. The range of such exclusive or prior claims may be wide, covering the ownership of property such as choice lands and sites; the right to certain jobs, occupations or professions; the claim to certain kinds of industry or lines of business; the claim to certain positions of control and decision-making as in government and law; the right to exclusive membership in given institutions such as schools, churches and recreational institutions; the claim to certain positions of social prestige and to the display of the symbols and accoutrements of these positions; and the claim to certain areas of intimacy and privacy. The feeling of such proprietary claims is exceedingly strong in race prejudice. Again, however, this feeling even in combination with the feeling of superiority and the feeling of distinctiveness does not explain race prejudice. These three feelings are present frequently in societies showing no prejudice, as in certain forms of feudalism, in caste relations, in societies of chiefs and commoners, and under many settled relations of conquerors and conquered. Where claims are solidified into a structure which is accepted or respected by all, there seems to be no group prejudice.

The remaining feeling essential to race prejudice is a fear or apprehension that the subordinate racial group is threatening, or will threaten, the position of the dominant group. Thus, acts or suspected acts that are interpreted as an attack on the natural superiority of the dominant group, or an intrusion into their sphere of group exclusiveness, or an encroachment on their area of proprietary claim are crucial in arousing and fashioning race prejudice. These acts mean "getting out of place."

It should be clear that these four basic feelings of race prejudice definitely refer to a positional arrangement of the racial groups. The feeling of superiority places the subordinate people *below;* the feeling of alienation places them *beyond;* the feeling of proprietary claim excludes them from the prerogatives of position; and the fear of encroachment is an emotional recoil from the endangering of group position. As these features suggest, the positional relation of the two racial groups is crucial in race prejudice. The dominant group is not concerned with the subordinate group as such but it is deeply concerned with its position vis-à-vis the subordinate group. This is epitomized in the key and universal expression that a given race is all right in "its place." The sense of group position is the very heart of the relation of the dominant to the subordinate group. It supplies the dominant group with its framework of perception, its standard of judgment, its patterns of sensitivity, and its emotional proclivities.

It is important to recognize that this sense of group position transcends the feelings of the individual members of the dominant group, giving such members a common orientation that is not otherwise to be found in separate feelings and views. There is likely to be considerable difference between the ways in which the individual members of the dominant group think and feel about the subordinate group. Some may feel bitter and hostile, with strong antipathies, with an exalted sense of superiority and with a lot of spite; others may have charitable and protective feelings, marked by a sense of piety and tinctured by benevolence; others may be condescending and reflect mild contempt; and others may be disposed to politeness and considerateness with no feelings of truculence. These are only a few of many different patterns of feeling to be found among members of the dominant racial group. What gives a common dimension to them is a sense of the social position of their group. Whether the members be humane or callous, cultured or unlettered, liberal or reactionary, powerful or impotent, arrogant or humble, rich or poor, honorable or dishonorable—all are led, by virtue of sharing the sense of group position, to similar individual positions.

The sense of group position is a general kind of orientation. It is a general feeling without being reducible to specific feelings like hatred, hostility or antipathy. It is also a general understanding without being composed of any set of specific beliefs. On the social psychological side it cannot be equated to a sense of social status as ordinarily conceived, for it refers not merely to vertical positioning but to many other lines of position independent of the vertical dimension. Sociologically it is not a mere reflection of the objective relations between racial groups. Rather, it stands for "what ought to be" rather than for "what is." It is a sense of where the two racial groups *belong*.

In its own way, the sense of group position is a norm and imperative—indeed a very powerful one. It guides, incites, cows, and coerces. It should be borne in mind that this sense of group position stands for and involves a fundamental kind of group affiliation for the members of the dominant racial group. To the extent they recognize or feel themselves as belonging to that group they will automatically come under the influence of the sense of position held by that group. Thus, even though given individual members may have personal views and feelings different from the sense of group position, they will have to conjure with the sense of group position held by their racial group. If the sense of position is strong, to act contrary to it is to risk a feeling of self-alienation and to face the possibility of ostracism. I am trying to suggest, accordingly, that the locus of race prejudice is not in the area of individual feeling but in the definition of the respective positions of the racial groups.

The source of race prejudice lies in a felt challenge to this sense of group position. The challenge, one must recognize, may come in many different ways. It may be in the form of an affront to feelings of group superiority; it may be in the form of attempts at familiarity or transgressing the boundary line of group exclusiveness; it may be in the form of encroachment at countless points of proprietary claim; it may be a challenge to power and privilege; it may take the form

of economic competition. Race prejudice is a defensive reaction to such challenging of the sense of group position. It consists of the disturbed feelings, usually of marked hostility, that are thereby aroused. As such, race prejudice is a protective device. It functions, however short-sightedly, to preserve the integrity and the position of the dominant group.

It is crucially important to recognize that the sense of group position is not a mere summation of the feelings of position such as might be developed independently by separate individuals as they come to compare themselves with given individuals of the subordinate race. The sense of group position refers to the position of group to group, not to that of individual to individual. Thus, vis-à-vis the subordinate racial group the unlettered individual with low status in the dominant racial group has a sense of group position common to that of the elite of his group. By virtue of sharing this sense of position such an individual, despite his low status, feels that members of the subordinate group, however distinguished and accomplished, are somehow inferior, alien, and properly restricted in the area of claims. He forms his conception as a representative of the dominant group; he treats individual members of the subordinate group as representative of that group.

An analysis of how the sense of group position is formed should start with a clear recognition that it is an historical product. It is set originally by conditions of initial contact. Prestige, power, possession of skill, numbers, original self-conceptions, aims, designs and opportunities are a few of the factors that may fashion the original sense of group position. Subsequent experience in the relation of the two racial groups, especially in the area of claims, opportunities and advantages, may mold the sense of group position in many diverse ways. Further, the sense of group position may be intensified or weakened, brought to sharp focus or dulled. It may be deeply entrenched and tenaciously resist change for long periods of time. Or it may never take root. It may undergo quick growth and vigorous expansion, or it may dwindle away through slow-moving erosion. It may be firm or soft, acute or dull, continuous or intermittent. In short, viewed comparatively, the sense of group position is very variable.

However variable its particular career, the sense of group position is clearly formed by a running process in which the dominant racial group is led to define and redefine the subordinate racial group and the relations between them. There are two important aspects of this process of definition that I wish to single out for consideration.

First, the process of definition occurs obviously through complex interaction and communication between the members of the dominant group. Leaders, prestige bearers, officials, group agents, dominant individuals and ordinary laymen present to one another characterizations of the subordinate group and express their feelings and ideas on the relations. Through talk, tales, stories, gossip, anecdotes, messages, pronouncements, news accounts, orations, sermons, preachments and the like definitions are presented and feelings are expressed. In this usually vast and complex interaction separate views run against one another, influence one another, modify each other, incite one another and fuse together in new forms. Correspondingly, feelings which are expressed meet, stimulate each other, feed on each other, intensify each other and emerge in new patterns. Currents of view and currents of feeling come into being; sweeping along to positions of dominance and serving as polar points for the organization of thought and sentiment. If the interaction becomes increasingly circular and reinforcing, devoid of serious inner opposition, such currents grow, fuse and become strengthened. It is through such a process that a collective image of the subordinate group is formed and a sense of group position is set. The evidence of such a process is glaring when one reviews the history of any racial arrangement marked by prejudice.

Such a complex process of mutual interaction with its different lines and degrees of formation gives the lie to the many schemes which would lodge the cause of race prejudice in the makeup of the individual—whether in the form of innate disposition, constitutional makeup, personality structure, or direct personal experience with members of the other race. The collective image and feelings in race prejudice are forged out of a complicated social process in which the individual is himself shaped and organized. The scheme, so popular today, which would trace race prejudice to a so-called authoritarian personality shows a grievous misunderstanding of the simple essentials of the collective process that leads to a sense of group position.

The second important aspect of the process of group definition is that it is necessarily concerned with *an abstract image* of the subordinate racial group. The subordinate racial group is defined as if it were an entity or whole. This entity or whole—like the Negro race, or the Japanese, or the Jews—is necessarily an abstraction, never coming within the perception of any of the senses. While actual encounters are with individuals, the picture formed of the racial group is necessarily of a vast entity which spreads out far beyond such individuals and transcends experience with such individuals. The implications of the fact that the collective image is of an abstract group are of crucial significance. I would like to note four of these implications.

First, the building of the image of the abstract group takes place in the area of the remote and not of the near. It is not the experience with concrete individuals in daily association that gives rise to the definitions of the extended, abstract group. Such immediate experience is usually regulated and orderly. Even where such immediate experience is disrupted the new definitions which are formed are limited to the individuals involved. The collective image of the abstract group grows up not by generalizing from experiences gained in close, first-hand contacts but through the transcending characterizations that are made of the group as an entity. Thus, one must seek the central stream of definition in those areas where the dominant group as such is characterizing the subordinate group as such. This occurs in the "public arena" wherein the spokesmen appear as representatives and agents of the dominant group. The extended public arena is constituted by such things as legislative assemblies, public meetings, conventions, the press, and the printed word. What goes on in this public arena attracts the attention of large numbers of the dominant group and is felt as the voice and action of the group as such.

Second, the definitions that are forged in the public arena center, obviously, about matters that are felt to be of major importance. Thus, we are led to recognize the crucial role of the "big event" in developing a conception of the subordinate racial group. The happening that seems momentous, that touches deep sentiments, that seems to raise fundamental questions about relations, and that awakens strong feelings of identification with one's racial group is the kind of event that is central in the formation of the racial image. Here, again, we note the relative unimportance of the huge bulk of experiences coming from daily contact with individuals of the subordinate group. It is the events seemingly loaded with great collective significance that are the focal points of the public discussion. The definition of these events is chiefly responsible for the development of a racial image and of the sense of group position. When this public discussion takes the form of a denunciation of the subordinate racial group, signifying that it is unfit and a threat, the discussion becomes particularly potent in shaping the sense of social position.

Third, the major influence in public discussion is exercised by individuals and groups who have the public ear and who are felt to have standing, prestige, authority and power. Intellectual and social elites, public figures of prominence, and leaders of powerful organizations are likely to be the key figures in the formation of the sense of group position and in the characterization of the subordinate group. It is well to note this in view of the not infrequent tendency of students to regard race prejudice as growing out of the multiplicity of experiences and attitudes of the bulk of the people.

Fourth, we also need to perceive the appreciable opportunity that is given to strong interest groups in directing the lines of discussion and setting the interpretations that arise in such discussion. Their self-interests may dictate the kind of position they wish the dominant racial group to enjoy. It may be a position which enables them to retain certain advantages, or even more to gain still greater advantages. Hence, they may be vigorous in seeking to manufacture events to attract public attention and to set lines of issue in such a way as to predetermine interpretations favorable to their interests. The role of strongly organized groups seeking to further special interest is usually central in the formation of collective images of abstract groups. Historical records of major instances of race relations, as in our South, or in South Africa, or in Europe in the case of the Jew, or on the West Coast in the case of the Japanese, show the formidable part played by interest groups in defining the subordinate racial group.

I conclude this highly condensed [reading] with two further observations that may throw additional light on the relation of the sense of group position to race prejudice. Race prejudice becomes entrenched and tenacious to the extent the prevailing social order is rooted in the sense of social position. This has been true of the historic South in our country. In such a social order race prejudice tends to become chronic and impermeable to change. In other places the social order may be affected only to a limited extent by the sense of group position held by the dominant racial group. This I think has been true usually in the case of anti-Semitism in Europe and this country. Under these conditions the sense of group position tends to be weaker and more vulnerable. In turn, race prejudice has a much more variable and intermittent career, usually becoming pronounced only as a consequence of grave disorganizing events that allow for the formation of a scapegoat.

This leads me to my final observation which in a measure is an indirect summary. The sense of group position dissolves and race prejudice declines when the process of running definition does not keep abreast of major shifts in the social order. When events touching on relations are not treated as "big events" and hence do not set crucial issues in the arena of public discussion; or when the elite leaders or spokesmen do not define such big events vehemently or adversely; or where they define them in the direction of racial harmony; or when there is a paucity of strong interest groups seeking to build up a strong adverse image for special advantage—under such conditions the sense of group position recedes and race prejudice declines.

The clear implication of my discussion is that the proper and fruitful area in which race prejudice should be studied is the collective process through which a sense of group position is formed. To seek, instead, to understand it or to handle it in the arena of individual feeling and of individual experience seems to me to be clearly misdirected.

Seeing the Big Picture   **Racism: Group Position or Individual Belief?**

Blumer explains that four "feelings" make up race prejudice. Are you able to come up with an example of each of these four feelings for a specific racial or ethnic group? Are you convinced by his argument that racism is "a fundamental matter of relationship between racial groups" rather than individual-level feelings of animosity?

"TRUTH: REMARKS ON THE REMOVAL OF CONFEDERATE MONUMENTS IN NEW ORLEANS"

Mayor Mitchell J. Landrieu
City of New Orleans

MITCH J. LANDRIEU is mayor of New Orleans.

The soul of our beloved City is deeply rooted in a history that has evolved over thousands of years; rooted in a diverse people who have been here together every step of the way—for both good and for ill.

It is a history that holds in its heart the stories of Native Americans—the Choctaw[1], Houma Nation[2], the Chitimacha[3].

Of Hernando de Soto[4], Robert Cavelier, Sieur de La Salle[5], the Acadians[6], the Islenos[7], the enslaved people from Senegambia[8], Free People of Color[9], the Haitians[10], the Germans[11], both the empires of France[12] and Spain[13]. The Italians[14], the Irish[15], the Cubans[16], the south and central Americans[17], the Vietnamese[18] and so many more.[19, 20]

You see—New Orleans is truly a city of many nations—a melting pot—a bubbling cauldron of many cultures.

There is no other place quite like it in the world that so eloquently exemplifies the uniquely American motto: e pluribus unum—out of many we are one.

But there are also other truths about our city that we must confront.

New Orleans was America's largest slave market: a port where hundreds of thousands of souls were brought, sold and shipped up the Mississippi River to lives of forced labor, of misery, of rape, of torture[21].

America was the place where nearly 4000[22] of our fellow citizens were lynched, 540[23] alone in Louisiana; where the courts enshrined "separate but equal"[24]; where Freedom riders coming to New Orleans were beaten to a bloody pulp.[25]

So when people say to me that the monuments in question are history, well, what I just described is real history as well, and it is the searing truth.

And it immediately begs the questions, why there are no slave ship monuments, no prominent markers on public land to remember the lynchings or the slave blocks; nothing to remember this long chapter of our lives; the pain, the sacrifice, the shame . . . all of it happening on the soil of New Orleans.

So for those self-appointed defenders of history and the monuments, they are eerily silent on what amounts to this historical malfeasance, a lie by omission.

There is a difference between remembrance of history and reverence of it.

For America and New Orleans, it has been a long, winding road, marked by great tragedy and great triumph. But we cannot be afraid of our truth.

As President George W. Bush said at the dedication ceremony for the National Museum of African American History & Culture, "A great nation does not hide its history. It faces its flaws and corrects them."[26]

So today I want to speak about why we chose to remove these four monuments to the **Lost Cause of the Confederacy,** but also how and why this process can move us towards healing and understanding of each other.

So, let's start with the facts.

The historic record[27, 28] is clear, the Robert E. Lee, Jefferson Davis, and P.G.T. Beauregard statues were not erected just to honor these men, but as part of the movement which became known as The Cult of the Lost Cause.

This "cult" had one goal—through monuments and through other means—to rewrite history to

Questions to Consider

Over the past few years, dozens of statues commemorating Confederate War soldiers have been removed from town squares around the country. Some see these as monuments to slavery and glorifying a time when African-Americans were routinely lynched and treated as second-class citizens. Others argue that these memorials are "about heritage not hate," and that these memorials merely reflect a Southern culture. Heritage or hate—which is it? Mayor Landrieu, a Southerner himself, casts this discussion within the context of Southern history why those particular monuments were chosen to represent Southern culture.

hide the truth, which is that the Confederacy was on the wrong side of humanity.

First erected over 166 years[29] after the founding of our city and 19 years[30] after the end of the Civil War, the monuments that we took down were meant to rebrand the history of our city and the ideals of a defeated Confederacy.

It is self-evident that these men did not fight for the United States of America, they fought against it. They may have been warriors, but in this cause they were not patriots.

These statues are not just stone and metal. They are not just innocent remembrances of a benign history.

These monuments purposefully celebrate a fictional, sanitized Confederacy; ignoring the death, ignoring the enslavement, and the terror that it actually stood for.

After the Civil War, these statues were a part of that terrorism as much as a burning cross on someone's lawn; they were erected purposefully to send a strong message to all who walked in their shadows about who was still in charge in this city.

Should you have further doubt about the true goals of the Confederacy, in the very weeks before the war broke out, the Vice President of the Confederacy—Alexander Stephens—made it clear that the Confederate cause was about maintaining slavery and white supremacy.

He said in his now famous "cornerstone speech" that the Confederacy's *"cornerstone rests upon the great truth, that the negro is not equal to the white man; that slavery—subordination to the superior race—is his natural and normal condition. This, our new government, is the first, in the history of the world, based upon this great physical, philosophical, and moral truth."*[31]

Now, with these shocking words still ringing in your ears . . .

I WANT TO TRY TO GENTLY PEEL FROM YOUR HANDS THE GRIP ON A FALSE NARRATIVE OF OUR HISTORY THAT I THINK WEAKENS US, AND MAKE STRAIGHT A WRONG TURN WE MADE MANY YEARS AGO—SO WE CAN MORE CLOSELY CONNECT WITH INTEGRITY TO THE FOUNDING PRINCIPLES OF OUR NATION AND FORGE A CLEARER AND STRAIGHTER PATH TOWARD A BETTER CITY AND A MORE PERFECT UNION.

Last year, President Barack Obama echoed these sentiments about the need to contextualize and remember all our history.

He recalled a piece of stone, a slave auction block engraved with a marker commemorating a single moment in 1830 when Andrew Jackson and Henry Clay stood and spoke from it.

President Obama said, "Consider what this artifact tells us about history . . . on a stone where day after day for years, men and women . . . bound and bought and sold and bid like cattle on a stone worn down by the tragedy of over a thousand bare feet. For a long time the only thing we considered important, the singular thing we once chose to commemorate as history with a plaque were the unmemorable speeches of two powerful men."[32]

A piece of stone—one stone.

Both stories were history.

One story told.

One story forgotten or maybe even purposefully ignored.

As clear as it is for me today . . . for a long time, even though I grew up in one of New Orleans' most diverse neighborhoods, even with my family's long, proud history of fighting for civil rights . . . I must have passed by those monuments a million times without giving them a second thought.

So I am not judging anybody, I am not judging people. We all take our own journey on race. I just hope people listen like I did when my dear friend Wynton Marsalis helped me see the truth.

He asked me to think about all the people who have left New Orleans because of our exclusionary attitudes.

Another friend asked me to consider these four monuments from the perspective of an African American mother or father trying to explain to their fifth-grade daughter who Robert E. Lee is and why he stands atop of our beautiful city.

Can you do it?

Can you look into that young girl's eyes and convince her that Robert E. Lee is there to encourage her? Do you think she will feel inspired and hopeful by that story?

Do these monuments help her see a future with limitless potential? Have you ever thought that if her potential is limited, yours and mine are too?

We all know the answer to these very simple questions.

When you look into this child's eyes is the moment when the searing truth comes into focus for us. This is the moment when we know what is right and what we must do.

We can't walk away from this truth.

And I knew that taking down the monuments was going to be tough, but you elected me to do the right thing, not the easy thing, and this is what that looks like. So relocating these Confederate monuments is **not** about taking something away from someone else. This is **not** about politics, this is not about blame or retaliation.

This is **not** a naïve quest to solve all our problems at once.

THIS IS HOWEVER ABOUT SHOWING THE WHOLE WORLD THAT WE AS A CITY

AND AS A PEOPLE ARE ABLE TO ACKNOWL-EDGE, UNDERSTAND, RECONCILE, AND MOST IMPORTANTLY, CHOOSE A BET-TER FUTURE FOR OURSELVES MAKING STRAIGHT WHAT HAS BEEN CROOKED AND MAKING RIGHT WHAT WAS WRONG.

Otherwise, we will continue to pay a price with discord, with division, and yes, with violence.

TO LITERALLY PUT THE CONFEDERACY ON A PEDESTAL IN OUR MOST PROMINENT PLACES OF HONOR IS AN INACCURATE RECITATION OF OUR FULL PAST, IT IS AN AFFRONT TO OUR PRESENT, AND IT IS A BAD PRESCRIPTION FOR OUR FUTURE.

History cannot be changed. It cannot be moved like a statue. What is done is done. The Civil War is over, and the Confederacy lost and we are better for it. Surely we are far enough removed from this dark time to acknowledge that the cause of the Confederacy was wrong.

And in the second decade of the 21st century, asking African Americans—or anyone else—to drive by property that they own; occupied by reverential statues of men who fought to destroy the country and deny that person's humanity seems perverse and absurd.

Centuries-old wounds are still raw because they never healed right in the first place.

Here is the essential truth—we are better together than we are apart.

Indivisibility[33] is our essence.

Isn't this the gift that the people of New Orleans have given to the world?

We radiate beauty and grace in our food, in our music, in our architecture, in our joy of life, in our celebration of death; in everything that we do.

We gave the world this funky thing called jazz—the most uniquely American art form that is developed across the ages from different cultures[34].

Think about second lines, think about Mardi Gras, think about muffaletta, think about the Saints, gumbo, red beans and rice.

By God, just think.

All we hold dear is created by throwing everything in the pot; creating, producing something better; everything a product of our historic diversity.

We are proof that out of many we are one— and better for it! Out of many we are one—and we really do love it!

And yet, we still seem to find so many excuses for not doing the right thing. Again, remember President Bush's words, "A great nation does not hide its history. It faces its flaws and corrects them."[35]

We forget, we deny how much we really depend on each other, how much we need each other.

WE JUSTIFY OUR SILENCE AND INAC-TION BY MANUFACTURING NOBLE CAUSES THAT MARINATE IN HISTORICAL DENIAL.

We still find a way to say "wait"—not so fast, but like Dr. Martin Luther King Jr. said, "wait has almost always meant never."[36]

We can't wait any longer. We need to change. And we need to change now. No more waiting. This is not just about statues, this is about our attitudes and behavior as well.

If we take these statues down and don't change to become a more open and inclusive society, this would have all been in vain.

While some have driven by these monuments every day and either revered their beauty or failed to see them at all, many of our neighbors and fellow Americans see them very clearly.

Many are painfully aware of the long shadows their presence casts; not only literally but figuratively.

And they clearly receive the message that the Confederacy and the cult of the lost cause intended to deliver.

Earlier this week, as the cult of the lost cause statue of P.G.T. Beauregard came down, world-renowned musician Terence Blanchard stood watch[37], his wife Robin and their two beautiful daughters at their side.

Terence went to a high school[38] on the edge of City Park named after one of America's greatest heroes and patriots, John F. Kennedy.

But to get there he had to pass by this monument to a man who fought to deny him his humanity.

He said, "I've never looked at them as a source of pride . . . its always made me feel as if they were put there by people who don't respect us.

"This is something I never thought I'd see in my lifetime. It's a sign that the world is changing."[39]

Yes, Terence, it is, and it is long overdue.

Now is the time to send a new message to the next generation of New Orleanians who can follow in Terence and Robin's remarkable footsteps.

A message about the future, about the next 300 years and beyond; let us not miss this opportunity, New Orleans, and let us help the rest of the country do the same.

Because now is the time for choosing.

Now is the time to actually make this the City we always should have been, had we gotten it right in the first place.

We should stop for a moment and ask ourselves—at this point in our history—after Katrina, after Rita, after Ike, after Gustav, after the national recession, after the BP oil catastrophe and after the tornado—if presented with the opportunity to build monuments that told our story or to curate these particular spaces . . . would these monuments be what we want the world to see? Is this really our story?

We have not erased history; we are becoming part of the city's history by righting the wrong image these monuments represent and crafting a better, more complete future for all our children and for future generations.

And unlike when these Confederate monuments were first erected as symbols of white supremacy, we now have a chance to create not only new symbols, but to do it together, as one people.

In our blessed land we all come to the table of democracy as equals.

We have to reaffirm our commitment to a future where each citizen is guaranteed the uniquely American gifts of life, liberty, and the pursuit of happiness.

That is what really makes America great, and today it is more important than ever to hold fast to these values and together say a self-evident truth that out of many we are one. That is why today we reclaim these spaces for the United States of America.

Because we are one nation, not two; indivisible with liberty and justice for all . . . not some.

We all are part of one nation, all pledging allegiance to one flag, the flag of the United States of America.

And New Orleanians are in . . . all of the way.

It is in this union and in this truth that real patriotism is rooted and flourishes.

Instead of revering a 4-year brief historical aberration that was called the Confederacy we can celebrate all 300 years of our rich, diverse history as a place named New Orleans and set the tone for the next 300 years.

After decades of public debate[40], of anger, of anxiety, of anticipation, of humiliation and of frustration.

After public hearings and approvals from three separate community-led commissions[41].

After two robust public hearings and a 6-1 vote by the duly elected New Orleans City Council.

After review by 13 different federal and state judges[42].

The full weight of the legislative[43], executive[44] and judicial[45, 46, 47] branches of government has been brought to bear and the monuments in accordance with the law have been removed.

So now is the time to come together and heal and focus on our larger task. Not only building new symbols, but making this city a beautiful manifestation of what is possible and what we as a people can become.

Let us remember what the once exiled, imprisoned, and now universally loved Nelson Mandela and what he said after the fall of apartheid.

"If the pain has often been unbearable and the revelations shocking to all of us, it is because they indeed bring us the beginnings of a common understanding of what happened and a steady restoration of the nation's humanity."[48]

So before we part let us again state the truth clearly.

The Confederacy was on the wrong side of history and humanity. It sought to tear apart our nation and subjugate our fellow Americans to slavery. This is the history we should never forget and one that we should never again put on a pedestal to be revered.

As a community, we must recognize the significance of removing New Orleans' Confederate monuments.

It is our acknowledgment that now is the time to take stock of, and then move past, a painful part of our history.

Anything less would render generations of courageous struggle and soul searching a truly lost cause.

Anything less would fall short of the immortal words of our greatest President Abraham Lincoln, who with an open heart and clarity of purpose calls on us today to unite as one people when he said:

"With malice toward none, with charity for all—with firmness in the right—as God gives us to see the right—let us strive on to finish the work we are in—to bind up the nation's wounds . . .—to do all which may achieve and cherish—a just and lasting peace among ourselves and with all nations."[49]

Thank you.

18

DISCRIMINATION AND THE AMERICAN CREED

Robert K. Merton

The late **ROBERT K. MERTON** was an eminent sociological theorist and a well-known defender of sociology as a genuine science. His publications include *On the Shoulders of Giants: A Shandean Postscript* (1965) and *The Sociology of Science: Theoretical and Empirical Investigations* (1973).

THE PRIMARY FUNCTION OF THE SOCIOLOGIST is to search out the determinants and consequences of diverse forms of social behavior. To the extent that he succeeds in fulfilling this role, he clarifies the alternatives of organized social action in a given situation and of the probable outcome of each. To this extent, there is no sharp distinction between pure research and applied research. Rather, the difference is one between research with direct implications for particular problems of social action and research which is remote from these problems. Not infrequently, basic research which has succeeded only in clearing up previously confused concepts may have an immediate bearing upon the problems of men in society to a degree not approximated by applied

Questions to Consider

Have you ever been in a situation in which social, economic, or peer pressure forced you to treat someone from a different racial group in an inappropriate way? Robert Merton suggests that individuals who are *not* prejudiced often act in bigoted and discriminatory ways. How and why does this happen? Is it possible to live our lives in the category Merton calls the "unprejudiced non-discriminator"?

research oriented exclusively to these problems. At least, this is the assumption underlying the present [reading]: clarification of apparently unclear and confused concepts in the sphere of race and ethnic relations is a step necessarily prior to the devising of effective programs for reducing intergroup conflict and for promoting equitable access to economic and social opportunities. . . .

THE AMERICAN CREED: AS CULTURAL IDEAL, PERSONAL BELIEF AND PRACTICE

The American **creed** as set forth in the Declaration of Independence, the preamble of the Constitution and the Bill of Rights has often been misstated. This part of the cultural heritage does *not* include the patently false assertion that all men are created equal in capacity or endowment. It does *not* imply that an Einstein and a moron are equal in intellectual capacity or that Joe Louis and a small, frail Columbia professor (or a Mississippian Congressman) are equally endowed with brawny arms harboring muscles as strong as

---

creed In the context of this reading, the belief system that a people share.

iron bands. It does *not* proclaim universal equality of innate intellectual or physical endowment.

Instead, the creed asserts the indefeasible principle of the human right to full equity—the right of equitable access to justice, freedom and opportunity, irrespective of race or religion or ethnic origin. It proclaims further the universalist doctrine of the dignity of the individual, irrespective of the groups of which he is a part. It is a creed announcing full moral equities for all, not an absurd myth affirming the equality of intellectual and physical capacity of all men everywhere. And it goes on to say that though men differ in innate endowment, they do so as individuals, not by virtue of their group memberships.

Viewed sociologically, the creed is a set of values and precepts embedded in American culture, to which Americans are expected to conform. It is a complex of affirmations, rooted in the historical past and ceremonially celebrated in the present, partly enacted in the laws of the land and partly not. Like all creeds, it is a profession of faith, a part of cultural tradition sanctified by the larger traditions of which it is a part.

It would be a mistaken sociological assertion, however, to suggest that the creed is a fixed and static cultural constant, unmodified in the course of time, just as it would be an error to imply that as an integral part of culture, it evenly blankets all subcultures of the national society. It is indeed dynamic, subject to change and in turn promoting change in other spheres of culture and society. It is, moreover, unevenly distributed throughout the society, being institutionalized as an integral part of local culture in some regions of the society and rejected in others.

. . . Learned men and men in high public positions have repeatedly observed and deplored the disparity between ethos and behavior in the sphere of race and ethnic relations. In his magisterial volumes on the American Negro, for example, Gunnar Myrdal called this gulf between creed and conduct "an American dilemma," and centered his attention on the prospect of narrowing or closing the gap. The President's Committee on Civil Rights, in their report to the nation, and . . . President [Truman] himself, in a message to Congress, have called public attention to this "serious gap between our ideals and some of our practices."

But as valid as these observations may be, they tend so to simplify the relations between creed and conduct as to be seriously misleading both for social policy and for social science. All these high authorities notwithstanding, the problems of racial and ethnic inequities are not expressible as a discrepancy between high cultural principles and low social conduct. It is a relation not between two variables, official creed and private practice, but between three: first, the cultural creed honored in cultural tradition and partly enacted into law; second, the beliefs and attitudes of individuals regarding the principles of the creed; and third, the actual practices of individuals with reference to it.

Once we substitute these three variables of cultural ideal, belief and actual practice for the customary distinction between the two variables of cultural ideals and actual practices, the entire formulation of the problem becomes changed. We escape from the virtuous but ineffectual impasse of deploring the alleged hypocrisy of many Americans into the more difficult but potentially effectual realm of analyzing the problem in hand.

To describe the problem and to proceed to its analysis, it is necessary to consider the official creed, individuals' beliefs and attitudes concerning the creed, and their actual behavior. Once stated, the distinctions are readily applicable. Individuals may *recognize* the creed as part of a cultural tradition, *without having any private conviction of its moral validity or its binding quality.* Thus, so far as the beliefs of individuals are concerned, we can identify two types: those who genuinely believe in the creed and those who do not (although some of these may, on public or ceremonial occasions, profess adherence to its principles). Similarly, with respect to actual practices: conduct may or may not conform to the creed. But, and this is the salient consideration: *conduct may or may not conform with individuals' own beliefs concerning the moral claims of all men to equal opportunity.*

Stated in formal sociological terms, this asserts that attitudes and overt behavior vary independently.

Prejudicial attitudes need not coincide with discriminatory behavior. The implications of this statement can be drawn out in terms of a logical syntax whereby the variables are diversely combined, as can be seen in the following typology.

By exploring the interrelations between prejudice and discrimination, we can identify four major types in terms of their attitudes toward the creed and their behavior with respect to it. Each type is found in every region and social class, though in varying numbers. By examining each type, we shall be better prepared to understand their interdependence and the appropriate types of action for curbing ethnic discrimination. The folk labels for each type are intended to aid in their prompt recognition.

Type I: The Unprejudiced Non-Discriminator or All-Weather Liberal

These are the racial and ethnic liberals who adhere to the creed in both belief and practice. They are neither prejudiced nor given to discrimination. Their orientation toward the creed is fixed and stable. Whatever the environing situation, they are likely to abide by their beliefs: hence, the *all-weather* liberal.

This is, of course, the strategic group which *can* act as the spearhead for the progressive extension of the creed into effective practice. They represent the solid foundation both for the measure of ethnic equities which now exist and for the future enlargement of these equities. Integrated with the creed in both belief and practice, they would seem most motivated to influence others toward the same democratic outlook. They represent a reservoir of culturally legitimatized goodwill which can be channeled into an active program for extending belief in the creed and conformity with it in practice.

Most important, as we shall see presently, the all-weather liberals comprise the group which can so reward others for conforming with the creed, as to transform deviants into conformists. They alone can provide the positive social environment for the other types who will no longer find it expedient or rewarding to retain their prejudices or discriminatory practices.

But though the ethnic liberal is a *potential* force for the successive extension of the American creed, he does not fully realize this potentiality in actual fact, for a variety of reasons. Among the limitations on effective action are several fallacies to which the ethnic liberal seems peculiarly subject. First among these is *the fallacy of group soliloquies.* Ethnic liberals are busily engaged in talking to themselves. Repeatedly, the same groups of like-minded liberals seek each other out, hold periodic meetings in which they engage in mutual exhortation and thus lend social and psychological support to one another. But however much these unwittingly self-selected audiences may reinforce the creed among themselves, they do not thus appreciably diffuse the creed in belief or practice to groups which depart from it in one respect or the other.

More, these group soliloquies in which there is typically wholehearted agreement among fellow-liberals tend to promote another fallacy limiting effective action. This is *the fallacy of unanimity.* Continued association with like-minded individuals tends to produce the illusion that a large measure of consensus has been achieved in the community at large. The unanimity regarding essential cultural axioms which obtains in these small groups provokes an overestimation of the strength of the movement and of its effective inroads upon the larger population which does not necessarily share these creedal axioms. Many also mistake participation in the groups of like-minded individuals for effective action. Discussion accordingly takes the place of action. The reinforcement of the creed for oneself is mistaken for the extension of the creed among those outside the limited circle of ethnic liberals.

Arising from adherence to the creed is a third limitation upon effective action, the *fallacy of privatized solutions* to the problem. The ethnic liberal, precisely because he is at one with the American creed, may rest content with his own individual behavior and thus see no need to do anything about the problem at large. Since his own spiritual house is in order, he is not motivated by guilt or shame to work on a collective problem. The very freedom of the liberal from guilt thus prompts him to secede from any *collective* effort to set the national house in order. He essays a *private* solution to a *social* problem. He assumes that numerous individual adjustments will serve in place of a collective adjustment. His outlook, compounded of good moral philosophy but poor sociology, holds that each individual must put his own house in order and fails to recognize that privatized solutions cannot be effected for problems which are essentially social in nature. For clearly, if each person *were* motivated to abide by the American creed, the problem would not be likely to exist in the first place. It is only when a social environment is established by conformists to the creed that deviants can in due course be brought to modify their behavior in the direction of conformity. But this "environment" can be constituted only through collective effort and not through private adherence to a public creed. Thus we have the paradox that the clear conscience of many ethnic liberals may promote the very social situation which permits deviations from the creed to continue unchecked. Privatized liberalism invites social inaction. Accordingly, there appears the phenomenon of the inactive or passive liberal, himself at spiritual ease, neither prejudiced nor discriminatory, but in a measure tending to contribute to the persistence of prejudice and discrimination through his very inaction.

The fallacies of group soliloquy, unanimity and privatized solutions thus operate to make the potential strength of the ethnic liberals unrealized in practice.

It is only by first recognizing these limitations that the liberal can hope to overcome them. With some hesitancy, one may suggest initial policies for curbing the scope of the three fallacies. The fallacy of group soliloquies can be removed only by having ethnic liberals enter into organized groups not comprised merely by fellow-liberals. This exacts a heavy price on the liberal. It means that he faces initial opposition and resistance rather than prompt consensus. It entails giving up the gratifications of consistent group support.

The fallacy of unanimity can in turn be reduced by coming to see that American society often provides large rewards for those who express their ethnic prejudice in discrimination. Only if the balance of rewards, material and psychological, is modified will behavior be modified. Sheer exhortation and propaganda are not enough. Exhortation verges on a belief in magic if it is not supported by appropriate changes in the social environment to make conformity with the exhortation rewarding.

Finally, the fallacy of privatized solutions requires the militant liberal to motivate the passive liberal to collective effort, possibly by inducing in him a sense of guilt for his unwitting contribution to the problems of ethnic inequities through his own systematic inaction.

One may suggest a unifying theme for the ethnic liberal: goodwill is not enough to modify social reality. It is only when this goodwill is harnessed to social-psychological realism that it can be used to reach cultural objectives.

Type II: The Unprejudiced Discriminator or Fair-Weather Liberal

The fair-weather liberal is the man of expediency who, despite his own freedom from prejudice, supports discriminatory practices when it is the easier or more profitable course. His expediency may take the form of holding his silence and thus implicitly acquiescing in expressions of ethnic prejudice by others or in the practice of discrimination by others. This is the expediency of the timid: the liberal who hesitates to speak up against discrimination for fear he might lose status or be otherwise penalized by his prejudiced associates. Or his expediency may take the form of grasping at advantages in social and economic competition deriving solely from the ethnic status of competitors. This is the expediency of the self-assertive: the employer, himself not an anti-Semite or Negrophobe, who refuses to hire Jewish or Negro workers because "it might hurt business"; the trade union leader who expediently advocates racial discrimination in order not to lose the support of powerful Negrophobes in his union.

In varying degrees, the fair-weather liberal suffers from guilt and shame for departing from his own effective beliefs in the American creed. Each deviation through which he derives a limited reward from passively acquiescing in or actively supporting discrimination contributes cumulatively to this fund of guilt. He is, therefore, peculiarly vulnerable to the efforts of the all-weather liberal who would help him bring his conduct into accord with his beliefs, thus removing this source of guilt. He is the most amenable to cure, because basically he wants to be cured. His is a split conscience which motivates him to cooperate actively with those who will help remove the source of internal conflict. He thus represents the strategic group promising the largest returns for the least effort. Persistent re-affirmation of the creed will only intensify his conflict; but a long regimen in a favorable social climate can be expected to transform the fair-weather liberal into an all-weather liberal.

Type III: The Prejudiced Non-Discriminator or Fair-Weather Illiberal

The fair-weather illiberal is the reluctant conformist to the creed, the man of prejudice who does not believe in the creed but conforms to it in practice through fear of sanctions which might otherwise be visited upon him. You know him well: the prejudiced employer who discriminates against racial or ethnic groups until a Fair Employment Practice Commission, able and willing to enforce the law, puts the fear of punishment into him; the trade union leader, himself deeply prejudiced, who does away with Jim Crow in his union because the rank-and-file demands that it be done away with; the businessman who forgoes his own prejudices when he finds a profitable market among the very people he hates, fears or despises; the timid **bigot** who will not express his prejudices when he is in the presence of powerful men who vigorously and effectively affirm their belief in the American creed.

---

bigot Someone deeply committed to his or her own prejudices, distortions, or biases regarding other people. Bigots are intolerant of difference.

It should be clear that the fair-weather illiberal is the precise counterpart of the fair-weather liberal. Both are men of expediency, to be sure, but expediency dictates different courses of behavior in the two cases. The timid bigot conforms to the creed only when there is danger or loss in deviations, just as the timid liberal deviates from the creed when there is danger or loss in conforming. *Superficial similarity in behavior of the two in the same situation should not be permitted to cloak a basic difference in the meaning of this outwardly similar behavior,* a difference which is as important for social policy as it is for social science. Whereas the timid bigot is under strain when he conforms to the creed, the timid liberal is under strain when he deviates. For ethnic prejudice has deep roots in the character structure of the fair-weather bigot, and this will find overt expression unless there are powerful countervailing forces, institutional, legal and interpersonal. He does not accept the moral legitimacy of the creed; he conforms because he must, and will cease to conform when the pressure is removed. The fair-weather liberal, on the other hand, is effectively committed to the creed and does not require strong institutional pressure to conform; continuing interpersonal relations with all-weather liberals may be sufficient.

This is the one critical point at which the traditional formulation of the problem of ethnic discrimination as a departure from the creed can lead to serious errors of theory and practice. Overt behavioral deviation (or conformity) may signify importantly different situations, depending upon the underlying motivations. Knowing simply that ethnic discrimination is rife in a community does not, therefore, point to appropriate lines of social policy. It is necessary to know also the distribution of ethnic prejudices and basic motivations for these prejudices as well. Communities with the same amount of overt discrimination may represent vastly different types of problems, dependent on whether the population is comprised by a large nucleus of fair-weather liberals ready to abandon their discriminatory practices under slight interpersonal pressure or a large nucleus of fair-weather illiberals who will abandon discrimination only if major changes in the local institutional setting can be effected. Any statement of the problem as a gulf between creedal ideals and prevailing practice is thus seen to be overly simplified in the precise sense of masking this decisive difference between the type of discrimination exhibited by the fair-weather liberal and by the fair-weather illiberal. That the gulf-between-ideal-and-practice does not adequately describe the nature of the ethnic problem will become more apparent as we turn to the fourth type in our inventory of prejudice and discrimination.

Type IV: The Prejudiced Discriminator or the All-Weather Illiberal

This type, too, is not unknown to you. He is the confirmed illiberal, the bigot pure and unashamed, the man of prejudice consistent in his departure from the American creed. In some measure, he is found everywhere in the land, though in varying numbers. He derives large social and psychological gains from his conviction that "any white man (including the village idiot) is 'better' than any nigger (including George Washington Carver)." He considers differential treatment of Negro and white not as "discrimination," in the sense of unfair treatment, but as "discriminating," in the sense of showing acute discernment. For him, it is as clear that one "ought" to accord a Negro and a white different treatment in a wide diversity of situations, as it is clear to the population at large that one "ought" to accord a child and an adult different treatment in many situations.

This illustrates anew my reason for questioning the applicability of the unusual formula of the American dilemma as a gap between lofty creed and low conduct. For the confirmed illiberal, ethnic discrimination does *not* represent a discrepancy between *his* ideals and *his* behavior. His ideals proclaim the right, even the duty, of discrimination. Accordingly, his behavior does not entail a sense of social deviation, with the resultant strains which this would involve. The ethnic illiberal is as much a conformist as the ethnic liberal. He is merely conforming to a different cultural and institutional pattern which is centered, not about the creed, but about a doctrine of essential inequality of status ascribed to those of diverse ethnic and racial origins. To overlook this is to overlook the well-known fact that our national culture is divided into a number of local subcultures which are not consistent among themselves in all respects. And again, to fail to take this fact of different subcultures into account is to open the door for all manner of errors of social policy in attempting to control the problems of racial and ethnic discrimination.

This view of the all-weather illiberal has one immediate implication with wide bearing upon social policies and sociological theory oriented toward the problem of discrimination. The extreme importance of the social surroundings of the confirmed illiberal at once becomes apparent. For as these surroundings vary, so, in some measure, does the problem of the consistent illiberal. The illiberal, living in those cultural regions where the American creed is widely repudiated and is no effective part of the subculture, has his private ethnic attitudes and practices supported by the local mores, the local institutions and the local power structure. The illiberal in cultural areas dominated by a large measure of adherence to the American creed is in a social environment where he is isolated and receives small social support for his beliefs and practices. In both instances, the *individual* is an illiberal, to be sure, but he represents two significantly different *sociological types*. In the first instance, he is a *social conformist,* with strong moral and institutional reinforcement, whereas in the second, he is a *social deviant,* lacking strong social corroboration. In the one case, his discrimination involves him in further integration with his network of social relations; in the other, it threatens to cut him off from sustaining interpersonal ties. In the first cultural context, personal change in his ethnic behavior involves alienating himself from people significant to him; in the second context, this change of personal outlook may mean fuller incorporation in groups meaningful to him. In the first situation, modification of his ethnic views requires him to take the path of greatest resistance whereas in the second, it may mean the path of least resistance. From all

this, we may surmise that any social policy aimed at changing the behavior and perhaps the attitudes of the all-weather illiberal will have to take into account the cultural and social structure of the area in which he lives. . . .

IMPLICATIONS OF THE TYPOLOGY FOR SOCIAL POLICY

. . . In approaching problems of policy, two things are plain. First, these should be considered from the standpoint of the militant ethnic liberal, for he alone is sufficiently motivated to engage in positive action for the reduction of ethnic discrimination. And second, the fair-weather liberal, the fair-weather illiberal and the all-weather illiberal represent types differing sufficiently to require diverse kinds of treatment.

Treatment of the Fair-Weather Liberal

The fair-weather liberal, it will be remembered, discriminates only when it appears expedient to do so, and experiences some measure of guilt for deviating from his own belief in the American creed. He suffers from this conflict between conscience and conduct. Accordingly, he is a relatively easy target for the all-weather liberal. He represents the strategic group promising the largest immediate returns for the least effort. Recognition of this type defines the first task for the militant liberal who would enter into a collective effort to make the creed a viable and effective set of social norms rather than a ceremonial myth. . . .

Since the fair-weather liberal discriminates only when it seems rewarding to do so, the crucial need is so to change social situations that there are few occasions in which discrimination proves rewarding and many in which it does not. This would suggest that ethnic liberals self-consciously and deliberately seek to draw into the social groups where they constitute a comfortable majority a number of the "expedient discriminators." This would serve to counteract the dangers of self-selection through which liberals come to associate primarily with like-minded individuals. It would, further, provide an interpersonal and social environment for the fair-weather liberal in which he would find substantial social and psychological gains from abiding by his own beliefs, gains which would more than offset the rewards attendant upon occasional discrimination. It appears that men do not long persist in behavior which lacks social corroboration.

We have much to learn about the role of numbers and proportions in determining the behavior of members of a group. But it seems that individuals generally act differently when they are numbered among a minority rather than the majority. This is not to say that minorities abdicate their practices in the face of a contrary-acting majority, but only that the same people are subjected to different strains and pressures according to whether they are included in the majority or the minority. And the fair-weather liberal who finds himself associated with militant ethnic liberals may be expected to forgo his occasional deviations into discrimination; he may move from category II into category I. . . .

Treatment of the Fair-Weather Illiberal

Because his *beliefs* correspond to those of the full-fledged liberal, the fair-weather liberal can rather readily be drawn into an interpersonal environment constituted by those of a comparable turn of mind. This would be more difficult for the fair-weather illiberal, whose beliefs are so fully at odds with those of ethnic liberals that he may, at first, only be alienated by association with them. If the initial tactic for the fair-weather liberal, therefore, is a change in interpersonal environment, the seemingly most appropriate tactic for the fair-weather illiberal is a change in the institutional and legal environment. It is, indeed, probably this type which liberals implicitly have in mind when they expect significant changes in behavior to result from the introduction of controls on ethnic discrimination into the legal machinery of our society.

For this type—and it is a major limitation for planning policies of control that we do not know his numbers or his distribution in the country—it would seem that the most effective tactic is the institution of legal controls administered with strict efficiency. This would presumably reduce the amount of *discrimination* practiced by the fair-weather illiberal, though it might *initially* enhance rather than reduce his *prejudices*. . . .

A second prevalent tactic for modifying the prejudice of the fair-weather illiberal is that of seeking to draw him into interethnic groups explicitly formed for the promotion of tolerance. This, too, seems largely ineffectual, since the deeply prejudiced individual will not enter into such groups of his own volition. As a consequence of this process of self-selection, these tolerance groups soon come to be comprised by the very ethnic liberals who initiated the enterprise.

This barrier of self-selection can be partially hurdled only if the ethnic illiberals are brought into continued association with militant liberals in groups devoted to significant common values, quite remote from objectives of ethnic equity as such. Thus, as our Columbia-Lavanburg researches have found, many fair-weather illiberals *will* live in interracial housing projects in order to enjoy the rewards of superior housing at a given rental. And some of the illiberals thus brought into personal contact with various ethnic groups under the auspices of prestigeful militant liberals come to modify their prejudices. It is, apparently, only through interethnic collaboration, initially enforced by pressures of the situation, for immediate and significant objectives (other than tolerance) that the self-insulation of the fair-weather illiberal from rewarding interethnic contacts can be removed.

But however difficult it may presently be to affect the *prejudicial sentiments* of the fair-weather illiberal, his *discriminatory practices* can be lessened by the uniform, prompt and prestigeful use of legal and institutional sanctions. The critical problem is to ascertain the proportions of fair-weather and all-weather illiberals in a given local population in order to have some clue to the probable effectiveness or ineffectiveness of anti-discrimination legislation.

Treatment of the All-Weather Illiberal

It is, of course, the hitherto confirmed illiberal, persistently translating his prejudices into active discrimination, who represents the most difficult problem. But though he requires longer and more careful treatment, it is possible that he is not beyond change. In every instance, his social surroundings must be assiduously taken into account. It makes a peculiarly large difference whether he is in a cultural region of bigotry or in a predominantly "liberal" area, given over to verbal adherence to the American creed, at the very least. As this cultural climate varies, so must the prescription for his cure and the prognosis for a relatively quick or long delayed recovery.

In an unfavorable cultural climate—and this does not necessarily exclude the benign regions of the Far South—the immediate resort will probably have to be that of working through legal and administrative federal controls over extreme discrimination, with full recognition that, in all probability, these regulations will be systematically evaded for some time to come. In such cultural regions, we may expect nullification of the law as the common practice, perhaps as common as was the case in the nation at large with respect to the Eighteenth Amendment, often with the connivance of local officers of the law. The large gap between the new law and local mores will not *at once* produce significant change of prevailing practices; token punishments of violations will probably be more common than effective control. At best, one may assume that significant change will be fitful, and excruciatingly slow. But secular changes in the economy may in due course lend support to the new legal framework of control over discrimination. As the economic shoe pinches because the illiberals do not fully mobilize the resources of industrial manpower nor extend their local markets through equitable wage payments, they may slowly abandon some discriminatory practices as they come to find that these do not always pay—even the discriminator. So far as discrimination is concerned, organized counteraction is possible and some small results may be expected. But it would seem that wishes father thoughts, when one expects basic changes in the immediate future in these regions of institutionalized discrimination.

The situation is somewhat different with regard to the scattered, rather than aggregated, ethnic illiberals found here and there throughout the country. Here the mores and a social organization oriented toward the American creed still have some measure of prestige and the resources of a majority of liberals can be mobilized to isolate the illiberal. In these surroundings, it is possible to move the all-weather illiberal toward Type III—he can be brought to conform with institutional regulations, even though he does not surrender his prejudices. And once he has entered upon this role of the dissident but conforming individual, the remedial program designed for the fair-weather illiberal would be in order.

THE PLACE OF RACE IN CONSERVATIVE AND FAR-RIGHT MOVEMENTS

Kathleen M. Blee and Elizabeth A. Yates

KATHLEEN M. BLEE is a professor of sociology and Bettye J. and Ralph E. Bailey Dean of the Kenneth P. Dietrich School of Arts and Sciences and the College of General Studies at the University of Pittsburgh. **ELIZABETH A. YATES** is completing her PhD at the University of Pittsburgh.

RACE IS IMPLICATED IN A RANGE of contemporary rightist movements in the United States. This is most obvious in far-right movements that promote overtly racist agendas, but race also is salient in conservative mobilizations that disavow racial motives or consequences. In both cases, the place of race is not fully captured by examining how movements frame their intentions and agendas to their supporters and audiences. Understanding race in rightist politics requires attention to the range of factors identified in social movement studies and the sociology of race and ethnicity.

We take the opportunity in this reading to provide an overview on race in contemporary U.S. right-wing movements and suggest directions for future research. Since the literature on rightist movements is vast, we focus on two broad movements in which race is significant, but in different ways. One is conservative mobilizations whose members are mostly white and in which racial themes and agendas are largely implicit. These movements are the product of a dual political legacy, forged in the fiscal conservatism and anticommunism of the mid-twentieth century Old Right (Ribuffo 1983) and the social conservatism of the New Christian Right (Blee and Creasap 2010; Diamond 1998; McGirr 2001). Our focal movements are just one segment of modern conservatism, a broader category that also includes multiracial movements to oppose same-sex marriage and abortion; movements that preach racial reconciliation and the need for whites to expunge the "sin" of racism (Allen 2000; Bartkowski 2004); and movements that mostly ignore race, such as

Questions to Consider

It is easy to identify hate groups when individuals give a Nazi salute, wear Ku Klux Klan robes and hoods, or parade behind a Confederate flag. However, it is much more difficult to define political movements when they outwardly reject racist statements but have agendas that are implicitly racist. Blee and Yates compare and contrast white majority conservative movements and far-right movements to see where and how these groups overlap in terms of how they achieve their racial goals. At what point do political and social movements move from making legitimate claims around grievances to ones motivated by racial animosity?

those opposing climate-change research or seeking bans on the inclusion of sexuality or evolution in public school curricula (Irvine 2002; Lewis 2005; Lienesch 2007; McCright and Dunlap 2003; Smith 2008).[1] As an example of a primarily-white conservative mobilization, we look at the Tea Party, a large and loosely affiliated network of activists who advocate a mixture of libertarian and traditional conservative opposition to taxation and government-sponsored social welfare; participate in Republican electoral campaigns; and mobilize supporters through mass media, social networks, and direct recruiting (Skocpol and Williamson 2012).

Our second focus is far-right movements that explicitly promote racist ideologies and, for some, goals of violent racial terrorism. Their racial targets vary but generally include African Americans; Jews; Muslims; Latinos/as; and immigrants from Africa, South Asia, and Latin America. In the last decades, such movements generally have reflected the political legacies of either World War II–era German Nazism and/or American traditions of organized racism and xenophobia (Durham 2000, 2007). As such, they include groups that seek an international alliance with pro-Aryan groups around the world as well as intense nationalists who want to establish a white homeland in the United States (Blee 2002; Dobratz and Shanks-Meile 2000). Not all far-right movements are explicitly racist; for example, some radical anti-abortion movements advocate violence that is not attached to a racial agenda, while vigilante, patriot, and militia groups generally disavow racism even if their anti-immigrant, anti-state, and pro-gun stances attract racist members (Rydgren 2007; Shapira 2013; Stern 1996; Zeskind 2009). As an example of a far-right movement, we look at U.S. neo-Nazis, who advocate the violent overthrow of the government because of its supposed accommodation to the interests of Jews and people of color. Unlike popular conservative movements, the neo-Nazi movement is tiny and, to minimize infiltration by the police or antiracist groups, recruits largely through direct personal contacts made in the subculture of white power music shows, parties, rallies, and gatherings.

To orient scholars of race and ethnicity to the particular issues of studying rightist movements, we begin by summarizing the theoretical trends and methodological challenges that have characterized this scholarship. Here, we draw special attention to differences in how scholars have analyzed right-wing and progressive movements and the implications for understanding the place of race on the right. Next, we explore a set of issues that has commanded considerable scholarly attention. For white-dominated conservative movements which generally insist that they are not racially defined, we show how scholars have explored the extent to which racial factors are operative in movement practices and the beliefs of their participants and how these movements address accusations that they are racist. For far-right movements that openly proclaim racist agendas, we show how scholars examine the complexities in how these movements define and enact racial agendas. We conclude with ideas for additional research on the place of race in rightist movements.

SCHOLARLY APPROACHES TO THE STUDY OF RIGHTIST MOVEMENTS

Scholarship on rightist movements has gone through two distinct conceptual stages. Until the 1990s, these movements were understood through the lens of psychology, even as this framework had been largely abandoned for studies of progressive social movements. Through a psychological lens, rightist movements were viewed as the product of the personality deficits, problematic familial upbringing, and stunted emotional responses of their members and supporters. By focusing on prejudices, rigidity, and scapegoating, this scholarship left race essentially unanalyzed except to the extent that rightist politics reflected the irrational racial schemas and animus of its adherents.

More recently, studies of the right have adopted the social-structural lens commonly used to study other social movements. This approach assumes that rightist movements are motivated by the rational concerns of their members, advancing beyond theories of individual irrationality to identify the social structures and dynamics that generate group interests, such as economic competition and racial domination (e.g., Cunningham 2012b; McVeigh 2009; McVeigh and Cunningham 2012; van Dyke and Soule 2002). This approach has been extended by scholars who argue that movements are not the product of the immediate and obvious interests of their adherents, but rather that participants' interests are shaped by cultural factors and moral valuations (Polletta 2006; Smith 2003).

An area of considerable attention today is the effect of rightist movements on their members. Rather than assuming that people join rightist movements because they are confused (irrationality lens) or because they regard such movements as vehicles to promote their interests (rationality-structural lens), this scholarship questions how racial beliefs and perceived self-interests are transformed in rightist politics, a question that lies at the intersection of microlevel processes of individual mobilization and mesolevel factors of group dynamics and organization. These studies have found that fan-right movements typically intensify the racial commitments of their members, especially by introducing them to conspiratorial logics, such as the idea that Jews are engineering world-wide racial conflict or that the white race is on the brink of racial suicide (Barkun 1994; Blee 2010; Hughey 2012; Simi and Futrell 2010). There is less work using this approach to study race in conservative movements, although it is possible that the racial rhetoric in conservative movements may reinforce members' associations of crime, poverty, and social dysfunction with racial minorities (Hardisty 1999).

Scholars who investigate the place of race in rightist movements confront unique challenges of access that shape what can effectively be investigated. Conservative movements often are reluctant to grant unrestricted access to their organizational materials or members to university-based researchers since they suspect that these scholars will seek to elicit racist statements from members or depict the movement in a negative light. Conservative movements that are heavily funded by corporate elites or right-wing foundations or tied to politicians and elected officials are especially reluctant to disclose information that could be racially sensitive. Far-right movements pose even more profound difficulties to scholars of race. Some hide themselves from public view, fearing infiltration by antiracist activists or police informants. Others make themselves visible but attempt to threaten or intimidate researchers who are critical, as illustrated in the libel case brought against a historian by a major figure in the Holocaust-denial movement (Emory University n.d.).

In all rightist movements, the perceived racial category of the researcher has a significant effect on access to groups and members. Scholars seen as nonwhite or Jewish face the danger of personal violence at the hands of far-right racist activists who regard them as enemies, although a few scholars have effectively used their enemy status to elicit important information on these movements (Ezekiel 1996; Shapira 2013). In parts of the far-right in which the sense of racial loyalty is surprisingly elastic, even scholars perceived as white and non-Jewish may be regarded as race traitors and targeted for violence (Blee 2002, 2000; Twine and Warren 2000). The racial dynamics between researchers and participants are less studied for conservative movements, although nonwhite scholars likely would have limited access to majority white groups, especially for studies that probe issues of race. Despite these hurdles, some scholars have been remarkably successful in gaining permission to interview and observe the internal racial dynamics of conservative and far-right movements and analyzing how such movements frame their racial ideas to the public (Adams and Roscigno 2005; Hughey 2012; Miller-Idriss 2012; Simi and Futrell 2010).

THE PLACE OF RACE IN CONSERVATIVE MOVEMENTS

The debate over race in conservative movements engages both movement spokespersons and scholars, particularly on three issues. One is whether conservative ideologies are inherently racist. A few conservative movements use explicitly racist appeals, as for instance depicting Latinos/as, Native Americans, and African Americans as lazy, satisfied to rely on the largess of government benefits, or perpetrators of voter fraud (Collins 2000). However, such open racism is increasingly stigmatized in the larger society, and most contemporary conservative movements insist that they do not engage in racial politics but simply favor equal treatment for all, including whites. This claim is a conservative twist on the widespread color-blind ideology that regards racism as relevant only in an individual, discriminatory context (Bonilla-Silva 2009). By ignoring how racial privileges and subordination are embedded in the social structures and patterns of everyday life, color-blind ideology fits conservative efforts to eliminate government policies that address structural

racism or benefit racial minorities as a group, such as affirmative action or equal opportunity laws (Bonilla-Silva 2009; Feagin 2006). Moreover, by insisting that the cultural and moral failures of poor communities hinder the achievements of their members, conservative movements argue that their opposition to social welfare programs and guarantees of racial equity (such as same-day voting registration, equal opportunity policies, and immigration reform) is a race-neutral position (Ansell 1997).

Another issue is whether individual conservative activists are motivated by racist animus, irrespective of the stated ideology of their organization or the ideological claims they make directly (Parker and Barreto 2013). This is a contentious issue among conservatives who, like others who embrace color-blind ideologies, consider as racist only expressions of individual racial prejudice (Feagin 2006). Meanwhile, conservative movements often use cultural symbols to mobilize sympathizers based on cultural identities that are not exclusively, and likely not overtly, race-based (McVeigh 2014). Moreover, emphasizing the racism of conservative activists can obscure the pervasive nature of racism across political boundaries (Burke 2013; Hughey 2010). For example, there is some evidence that conservative movements attract those with racial grievances, particularly downwardly mobile or working and lower middle class whites who regard racial minorities as unfairly benefiting from liberal policies in competition for economic and political power (Kimmel 2013). Elite whites, however, also often support conservative movements without being cast as racists (Lassiter 2007).

A third issue is how conservative movements manage accusations of racism, through efforts that may be authentic, strategic, or both. Some conservative leaders promote the visibility of racial minority members to demonstrate that their movement is not racist as well as to present models of racial minorities who have been successful through individual effort rather than by depending on government policies and programs (Burghart and Zeskind 2010; Dillard 2001; Hardisty 1999). Other leaders address charges of racism by preventing members from making racist statements in public (Prior 2014). And many conservative movements use ideological frames borrowed from racial equality movements such as the civil rights movement to present whites as victims of current social policies, arguing that whites are subject to reverse discrimination in the workplace, deprived of their rights, and accused of being racist simply for wanting equal treatment in society (Lassiter 2007; Lio, Melzer, and Reese 2008; Lowndes 2011). Such efforts have had some success, as evidenced by the conservative African American and Latino candidates who have found support among white activists at the grassroots level (Brennan and Sullivan 2011; Vozella 2013).

The Conservative Tea Party Movement

The Tea Party movement began in 2009 to oppose U.S. federal government intervention in the fiscal crisis and the federal healthcare mandate. Over time, its agenda has broadened to support strict fiscal policies and dramatically reduced government regulation and public investment. Initially organized by conservative elites, the Tea Party quickly developed a broad grassroots base, with more than 800 local groups and as many as 200,000 participants in 2011 (Skocpol and Williamson 2012); recent analysis shows its continuing strength at the grassroots level (Burghart 2014). At the national level, Tea Party-affiliated politicians, candidates, and organizations lobby Congress to maintain tax deductions for the wealthy while slashing federal funding for social services. These national leaders operate separately from local Tea Party groups, the latter of which hold regular meetings with conservative speakers, provide members with information on how to campaign for conservative candidates, educate the public on conservative issues, and lobby local and state officials on behalf of fiscally conservative policies (Yates 2014).

There is considerable debate about the racial nature of Tea Party support. On one hand, some evidence suggests that racial animosity fueled the emergence of the Tea Party immediately after the inauguration of America's first nonwhite president, Barack Obama. Indeed, analysts consistently find

that Tea Party supporters and activists are overwhelmingly white, and polling data show that Tea Party supporters express greater resentment toward racial minorities than do non-Tea Party supporters, other Republicans, and whites overall. For example, a 2010 survey examining racial and political attitudes among citizens primarily in battleground electoral states found that 73% of Tea Party supporters believe that African Americans merely need to "try harder" to obtain equal status as whites as compared with 56% of whites overall. A full 88% of Tea Party supporters said that African Americans should do so "without special favors," compared with 70% of whites (Parker and Barreto 2013; Parker and Towler 2010; see also Abramowitz 2011).

On the other hand, scholars caution against according too much importance to racial animosity in Tea Party mobilization, arguing that racial issues are complicated by anxieties about wider social changes that affect many social groups. Theda Skocpol and Vanessa Williamson (2012) found that Tea Party activists essentially differentiated between broad categories of "deserving" and "undeserving" citizens, a distinction that is often racialized but also is frequently applied to distinguish among nonracial groups, such as older and younger people. Yet as Lisa Disch (2011) emphasized, the Tea Party's valorization of hard-working, tax-paying citizens ignores the greater benefits that whites have derived from government services and benefits compared with nonwhites. In that sense, its activists draw from what Meghan Burke (2013:101) described as a "continuum of knowledge" in which racialized political beliefs are shaped by genuine economic, political, and social concerns as well as by racial ideologies promulgated by conservative media and social networks.

THE PLACE OF RACE IN FAR-RIGHT MOVEMENTS

Unlike conservative movements, far-right groups openly advocate white and/or Aryan supremacism; some seek to harm, even exterminate, their racial enemies. Despite these extremist goals, such movements often mix mainstream and extremist frames in messages to supporters and the public, both adopting language from the civil rights movement to mobilize whites as a racial interest group (White Americans) and declaring whites to be on the verge of "race suicide" (Berbrier 2000; Fleming and Morris 2014).

Far-right movements have used different understandings of race over time. Until recently, most extreme racist groups relied on essentialist definitions of race, insisting that biological differences account for racial disparities in social life. Far-right activists thus regarded policies such as equal employment laws as both objectionable and futile since they insisted that whites were biologically superior. These activists also saw race as stable and starkly dichotomous: People were purely white, descended from northern Europeans, or they were not (Durham 2007; Gardell 2003; Ignatiev 2008; Nagel 2003).

In the last few decades, far-right movements that aspire to recruit larger numbers have shifted to a cultural definition of race they consider more compatible with mainstream beliefs. These movements continue to defend white supremacy but trace it to a racial culture that values perseverance, achievement, and adherence to the rule of law. Moreover, some far-right adherents use a fluid sense of race. They regard as white only those who work toward white supremacism, so whites who do not support white superiority are considered to be essentially nonwhite. Oddly, the reverse can be true as well. People who appear nonwhite can be considered white if they support white supremacism and its activists (Blee 2002).

The groups deemed enemies of the white race vary somewhat among far-right groups. African Americans and Jews are the most commonly regarded as enemies. Yet, whether Jews or African Americans are considered to be the most pernicious group changes over time. For example, the original Ku Klux Klan (KKK) of the post–Civil War South directed its malevolence toward African Americans and the political allies of former slaves such as white supporters of the Reconstruction state (Chalmers

1987). In its next incarnation in the 1920s, the KKK attacked both African Americans and Jews, along with Catholics (Blee 1991; McVeigh 2009). Klans of the 1960s returned to a focus on African Americans as their racial enemies, drawing on the racial tensions of desegregation conflicts across the nation (Cunningham 2012a). The most recent Klans, influenced by neo-Nazi doctrines, have mainly targeted Jews as the antagonistic racial category, viewing people of color as inferior but manipulated by Jewish conspirators (Durham 2007).

The Neo-Nazi Movement

A variety of groups that espouse Nazi ideologies have emerged in recent decades, including racist skinhead gangs; the Aryan Brotherhood and related prison networks; Nazi-oriented white supremacists; and Christian Identity networks that regard Jews as the literal, biological descendants of Satan (Barkun 1994; Zeskind 2009). All neo-Nazis identify Jews as the central racial enemy, and most describe the U.S. government, especially at the federal level, as Jewish-controlled or ZOG (Zionist Occupied Government). They vary in the extent to which they express ultranationalist and xenophobic sentiments, especially toward immigrants, or seek to participate in a global project of pan-Aryanism with neo-Nazis in Europe and other regions. In the United States, neo-Nazi groups attract substantial numbers of women, especially to the younger segments of the movement such as skinheads (Blee 2002). Outside the United States, neo-Nazi groups have been disproportionately male, although this is beginning to change in European groups (Blee and Linden 2012; Miller-Idriss 2012).

Racist ideas are not necessarily what bring people into neo-Nazism. Indeed, research finds that recruits to such groups were not necessarily more racist or anti-Semitic than similarly situated others prior to joining. Rather, many learned these beliefs by participating in racist groups. In that sense, racist beliefs can be as much effects as causes of participating in neo-Nazism. One reason is that neo-Nazism exists in an intense culture of violence that can be a powerful lure to potential recruits, especially young people, by suggesting that such groups confer both protection and empowerment. Recruits enter for the violence and learn the racism. The other reason is that neo-Nazism today is highly conspiratorial. Only when recruits are brought into its "secret knowledge" about race are they given details of supposed Jewish domination, African American criminality, and immigrant depravity (Blee 2002).

In neo-Nazism there can be a substantial gap between the stated doctrines of the movement and the beliefs of even its most dedicated adherents. The propaganda and internal documents of neo-Nazi groups promote racial ideas that are little changed from those of World War II–era German Nazism. Most either applaud Hitler's attempt to exterminate European Jews as justified by the degenerate culture of Jews or claim that Holocaust accusations are false, part of an effort by contemporary Jews to extract monetary reparations from Aryan Europeans and promote the interests of the state of Israel (Blee 2002; Zeskind 2009). Even in their daily practices, neo-Nazis make frequent reference to the twentieth-century German Nazi movement. They greet each other by signaling 88, a coded reference to the eighth letter of the alphabet, for "Heil Hitler," and display the swastika on their bodies, websites, and documents.

Yet, at least some ardent neo-Nazis express quite different racial beliefs in private, even expressing skepticism about the movement's claims of Jewish atrocity or German military victories. They value the comradeship of these groups but often have a thin commitment to their racial ideals. Moreover, individual neo-Nazis often know little about the history they are dedicated to repeating. Young skinheads cannot explain why they wear brown shirts or carve "SS" or iron cross tattoos on themselves (Blee 2002).

It is clear that race has a place in rightist movements, even in those that deny involvement in racial issues. As the preceding discussion indicates, scholars have made significant advances in understanding how race is understood in conservative and far-right activism and how racial appeals can advance rightist agendas.

Compare the processes of demobilization and deradicalization for both movements and activists. Do racist movements that are in decline (demobilizing) become more radical by disproportionately shedding their more moderate members (della Porta 2013)? Do individual racist activists become more dangerous as they leave racist groups and operate as lone wolves?

These suggestions are presented as a starting point for extending the productive intellectual exchanges between scholars of the sociology of race and those working within the framework of social movement studies.

Seeing the Big Picture   Hate Crimes in America

The statistics of hate crimes in the appendix show that certain racial and religious minorities are routinely targeted. How have these patterns changed over time? Do you see any connection to increasing rates of immigration and the increase of hate crimes?

20

THE POSSESSIVE INVESTMENT IN WHITENESS

Racialized Social Democracy

George Lipsitz

GEORGE LIPSITZ researches racialization in U.S. society, including the racialization of space, urban culture, collective memory, and movements for social change. He is the author of *American Studies in a Moment of Danger* (2001) and *The Possessive Investment in Whiteness: How White People Profit from Identity Politics* (1998).

SHORTLY AFTER WORLD WAR II, A FRENCH reporter asked expatriate Richard Wright his opinion about the "Negro problem" in the United States. The author replied "There isn't any Negro problem; there is only a white problem."[1] By inverting the reporter's question, Wright called attention to its hidden assumptions—that racial polarization comes from the existence of blacks rather than from the behavior of whites, that black people are a "problem" for whites rather than fellow citizens entitled to justice, and that unless otherwise specified "American" means whites.[2] But Wright's formulation also placed political mobilization by African Americans in context, attributing it "to the systemic practices of aversion, exploitation,

denigration, and discrimination practiced by people who think of themselves as white."

Whiteness is everywhere in American culture, but it is very hard to see. As Richard Dyer argues, "white power secures its dominance by seeming not to be anything in particular."[3] As the unmarked category against which difference is constructed, whiteness never has to speak its name, never has to acknowledge its role as an organizing principle in social and cultural relations.[4]

To identify, analyze, and oppose the destructive consequences of whiteness, we need what Walter Benjamin called "presence of mind." Benjamin wrote that people visit fortune-tellers not so much out of a desire to know the future but rather out of a fear of not noticing some important aspect of

Questions to Consider

What does George Lipsitz mean by a "possessive investment in whiteness"? How is it possible that being a member of a particular racial group could confer social and economic privileges (or disadvantages) that are both institutional and intergenerational? How many specific programs does Lipsitz identify as being party to institutional racism?

the present. "Presence of mind," he argued, "is an abstract of the future, and precise awareness of the present moment more decisive than foreknowledge of the most distant events."[5] In our society at this time, precise awareness of the present moment requires an understanding of the existence and the destructive consequences of "white" identity.

In recent years, an important body of American studies scholarship has started to explore the role played by cultural practices in creating "whiteness" in the United States. More than the product of private prejudices, whiteness emerged as a relevant category in American life largely because of realities created by slavery and segregation, by immigration restriction and Indian policy, by conquest and colonialism. A fictive identity of "whiteness" appeared in law as an abstraction, and it became actualized in everyday life in many ways. American economic and political life gave different racial groups unequal access to citizenship and property, while cultural practices including Wild West shows, minstrel shows, racist images in advertising, and Hollywood films institutionalized racism by uniting ethnically diverse European-American audiences into an imagined community—one called into being through inscribed appeals to the solidarity of white supremacy.[6] Although cross-ethnic identification and pan-ethnic antiracism in culture, politics, and economics have often interrupted and resisted racialized white supremacist notions of American identity, from colonial days to the present, successful political

coalitions serving dominant interests have often relied on exclusionary concepts of whiteness to fuse unity among otherwise antagonistic individuals and groups.[7]

In these accounts by American studies scholars, cultural practices have often played crucial roles in prefiguring, presenting, and preserving political coalitions based on identification with the fiction of "whiteness." Andrew Jackson's coalition of the "common man," Woodrow Wilson's "New Freedom," and Franklin D. Roosevelt's New Deal all echoed in politics the alliances announced on stage and screen by the nineteenth-century minstrel show, by D. W. Griffith's cinema, and by Al Jolson's ethnic and racial imagery.[8] This impressive body of scholarship helps us understand how people who left Europe as Calabrians or Bohemians became something called "whites" when they got to America and how that designation made all the difference in the world.

Yet, while cultural expressions have played an important role in the construction of white supremacist political alliances, the reverse is also true (i.e., political activity has also played a constitutive role in racializing U.S. culture). Race is a cultural construct, but one with sinister structural causes and consequences. Conscious and deliberate actions have institutionalized group identity in the United States, not just through the dissemination of cultural stories but also through systematic efforts from colonial times to the present to create a possessive investment in whiteness for European Americans. Studies of culture too far removed from studies of social structure leave us with inadequate explanations for understanding racism and inadequate remedies for combatting it.

From the start, European settlers in North America established structures encouraging possessive investment in whiteness. The colonial and early-national legal systems authorized attacks on Native Americans and encouraged the appropriation of their lands. They legitimated racialized chattel slavery, restricted naturalized citizenship to "white" immigrants, and provided pretexts for exploiting labor, seizing property, and denying the franchise to Asian Americans, Mexican Americans,

Native Americans, and African Americans. Slavery and "Jim Crow" segregation institutionalized possessive identification with whiteness visibly and openly, but an elaborate interaction of largely *covert* public and private decisions during and after the days of slavery and segregation also produced a powerful legacy with enduring effects on the racialization of experience, opportunities, and rewards in the United States. Possessive investment in whiteness pervades public policy in the United States past and present—not just long ago during slavery and segregation but in the recent past and present as well—through the covert but no less systematic racism inscribed within U.S. social democracy.

Even though there has always been racism in American history, it has not always been the same racism. Political and cultural struggles over power shape the contours and dimensions of racism in any era. Mass mobilizations against racism during the Civil War and civil rights eras meaningfully curtailed the reach and scope of white supremacy, but in each case reactionary forces then engineered a renewal of racism, albeit in new forms, during successive decades. Racism changes over time, taking on different forms and serving different social purposes in different eras.

Contemporary racism is not just a residual consequence of slavery and **de jure segregation** but rather something that has been created anew in our own time by many factors including the putatively race-neutral liberal social democratic reforms of the past five decades. Despite hard-fought battles for change that secured important concessions during the 1960s in the form of civil rights legislation, the racialized nature of social democratic policies in the United States since the Great Depression has, in my judgment, actually increased the possessive investment in whiteness among European Americans over the past half-century.

The possessive investment in whiteness is not a simple matter of black and white; all racialized minority groups have suffered from it, albeit to different degrees and in different ways. Most of my argument here addresses relations between European Americans and African Americans because they contain many of the most vivid oppositions and contrasts, but the possessive investment in whiteness always emerges from a fused sensibility drawing on many sources at once—on antiblack racism to be sure, but also on the legacies of racialization left by federal, state, and local policies toward Native Americans, Asian Americans, Mexican Americans, and other groups designated by whites as "racially other."

During the New Deal, both the Wagner Act and the Social Security Act excluded farm workers and domestics from coverage, effectively denying those disproportionately minority sectors of the work force protections and benefits routinely channeled to whites. The Federal Housing Act of 1934 brought home ownership within reach of millions of citizens by placing the credit of the federal government behind private lending to home buyers, but overtly racist categories in the Federal Housing Administration's (FHA's) "confidential" city surveys and appraisers' manuals channeled almost all of the loan money toward whites and away from communities of color.[9] In the post–World War II era, trade unions negotiated contract provisions giving private medical insurance, pensions, and job security largely to the mostly white workers in unionized mass-production industries rather than fighting for full employment, universal medical care, and old age pensions for all or for an end to discriminatory hiring and promotion practices by employers.[10]

Each of these policies widened the gap between the resources available to whites and those available to aggrieved racial communities, but the most damaging long-term effects may well have come from the impact of the racial discrimination codified by the policies of the FHA. By channeling loans away from older inner-city neighborhoods and toward white home buyers moving into segregated suburbs, the FHA and private lenders after World War II aided and abetted the growth and development of increased segregation in U.S. residential neighborhoods. For example, FHA appraisers denied

---

de jure segregation Segregation that is imposed by law; versus de facto segregation, which exists "in fact" or practice but is not specified by law.

federally supported loans to prospective home buyers in the racially mixed Boyle Heights neighborhood of Los Angeles because it was a "**'melting pot'** area literally honeycombed with diverse and subversive racial elements."[11] Similarly, mostly white St. Louis County secured five times as many FHA mortgages as the more racially mixed city of St. Louis between 1943 and 1960. Home buyers in the county received six times as much loan money and enjoyed per capita mortgage spending 6.3 times greater than those in the city.[12]

In concert with FHA support for segregation in the suburbs, federal and state tax monies routinely provided water supplies and sewage facilities for racially exclusive suburban communities in the 1940s and 1950s. By the 1960s, these areas often incorporated themselves as independent municipalities in order to gain greater access to federal funds allocated for "urban aid."[13] At the same time that FHA loans and federal highway building projects subsidized the growth of segregated suburbs, urban renewal programs in cities throughout the country devastated minority neighborhoods.

During the 1950s and 1960s, federally assisted urban renewal projects destroyed 20 percent of the central city housing units occupied by blacks, as opposed to only 10 percent of those inhabited by whites.[14] Even after most major urban renewal programs had been completed in the 1970s, black central city residents continued to lose housing units at a rate equal to 80 percent of what had been lost in the 1960s. Yet white displacement declined back to the relatively low levels of the 1950s.[15] In addition, the refusal first to pass, then to enforce, fair housing laws has enabled realtors, buyers, and sellers to profit from racist collusion against minorities without fear of legal retribution.

During the decades following World War II, urban renewal helped construct a new "white" identity in the suburbs by helping destroy ethnically specific European-American urban inner-city neighborhoods. Wrecking balls and bulldozers

eliminated some of these sites, while others became transformed by an influx of minority residents desperately competing for a declining number of affordable housing units. As increasing numbers of racial minorities moved into cities, increasing numbers of European-American ethnics moved out. Consequently, ethnic differences among whites became a less important dividing line in American culture, while race became more important. The suburbs helped turn European Americans into "whites" who could live near each other and intermarry with relatively little difficulty. But this "white" unity rested on residential segregation and on shared access to housing and life chances largely unavailable to communities of color.[16]

During the 1950s and 1960s, local "progrowth" coalitions led by liberal mayors often justified **urban renewal** as a program designed to build more housing for poor people, but it actually destroyed more housing than it created. Ninety percent of the low-income units removed for urban renewal were never replaced. Commercial, industrial, and municipal projects occupied more than 80 percent of the land cleared for these projects, with less than 20 percent allocated for replacement housing. In addition, the loss of taxable properties and tax abatements granted to new enterprises in urban renewal zones often meant serious tax increases for poor, working-class, and middle-class home owners and renters.[17] Although the percentage of black suburban dwellers also increased during this period, no significant desegregation of the suburbs took place. From 1960 to 1977, four million whites moved out of central cities, while the number of whites living in suburbs increased by twenty-two million.[18] During the same years, the inner-city black population grew by six million, but the number of blacks living in suburbs increased by only 500,000 people.[19] By 1993, 86 percent of suburban whites still lived in places with a black population below

---

melting pot The blending or "melting" of different racial, cultural, and ethnic groups into a new configuration.

urban renewal Also known as slum clearance, these policies attempted to renew blighted urban areas by redeveloping the land. Many have viewed these policies as a way to dislocate the urban poor and working classes, seize the land, and create development opportunity for the elites.

1 percent. At the same time, cities with large numbers of minority residents found themselves cut off from loans by the FHA; in 1966, because of their growing black and Puerto Rican populations, Camden and Paterson, New Jersey, received no FHA-sponsored mortgages between them.[20]

Federally funded highways designed to connect suburban commuters with downtown places of employment destroyed already scarce housing in minority communities and often disrupted neighborhood life as well. Construction of the Harbor Freeway in Los Angeles, the Gulf Freeway in Houston, and the Mark Twain Freeway in St. Louis displaced thousands of residents and bisected previously connected neighborhoods, shopping districts, and political precincts. The process of urban renewal and highway construction set in motion a vicious cycle: population loss led to decreased political power, which made minority neighborhoods more likely to be victimized by further urban renewal and freeway construction, not to mention more susceptible to the placement of prisons, waste dumps, and other projects that further depopulated these areas.

In Houston, Texas—where blacks make up slightly more than one-quarter of the local population—more than 75 percent of municipal garbage incinerators and 100 percent of the city-owned garbage dumps are located in black neighborhoods.[21] A 1992 study by staff writers for the *National Law Journal* examined the Environmental Protection Agency's response to 1,177 toxic waste cases and found that polluters of sites near the greatest white population received penalties 500 percent higher than penalties imposed on polluters in minority areas—an average of $335,566 for white areas contrasted with $55,318 for minority areas. Income did not account for these differences—penalties for low-income areas on average actually exceeded those for areas with the highest median incomes by about 3 percent. The penalties for violating all federal environmental laws about air, water, and waste pollution in minority communities were 46 percent lower than in white communities. In addition, **Superfund** remedies left minority communities with longer waiting times for being placed on the national priority list, cleanups that begin from 12 to 42 percent later than at white sites, and a 7 percent greater likelihood of "containment" (walling off a hazardous site) than cleanup, while white sites experienced treatment and cleanup 22 percent more often than containment.[22]

Urban renewal failed as a program for providing new housing for the poor, but it played an important role in transforming the U.S. urban economy away from factory production and toward producer services. Urban renewal projects subsidized the development of downtown office centers on land previously used for residences, and they frequently created buffer zones of empty blocks dividing poor neighborhoods from new shopping centers designed for affluent commuters. In order to help cities compete for corporate investment by making them appealing to high-level executives, federal urban aid favored construction of luxury housing units and cultural centers, such as symphony halls and art museums, over affordable housing for workers. Tax abatements granted to these producer-services centers further aggravated the fiscal crisis that cities faced, leading to tax increases on existing industries, businesses, and residences.

Workers from aggrieved racial minorities bore the brunt of this transformation. Because the 1964 Civil Rights Act came so late, minority workers who received jobs because of it found themselves more vulnerable to seniority-based layoffs when businesses automated or transferred operations overseas. Although the act initially made real progress in reducing employment discrimination, lessened the gaps between rich and poor and black and white, and helped bring minority poverty to its lowest level in history in 1973, that year's recession initiated a reversal of minority progress and a reassertion of white privilege.[23] In 1977, the U.S. Civil Rights Commission reported on the disproportionate impact of layoffs on minority workers. In cases where minority workers made up only 10 to 12 percent of the work force in their area,

---

Superfund Aid to communities for cleanup and abatement of the effects of living near abandoned industrial waste sites.

they accounted for from 60 to 70 percent of those laid off in 1974. The principle of seniority, a social democratic triumph, in this case worked to guarantee that minority workers would suffer most from technological changes because the legacy of past discrimination by their employers left them with less seniority than white workers.[24]

When housing prices doubled during the 1970s, white home owners who had been able to take advantage of discriminatory FHA financing policies received increased equity in their homes, while those excluded from the housing market by earlier policies found themselves facing higher costs of entry into the market in addition to the traditional obstacles presented by the discriminatory practices of sellers, realtors, and lenders. The contrast between European Americans and African Americans is instructive in this regard. Because whites have access to broader housing choices than blacks, whites pay 15 percent less than blacks for similar housing in the same neighborhood. White neighborhoods typically experience housing costs 25 percent less expensive than would be the case if the residents were black.[25]

A recent Federal Reserve Bank of Boston study showed that minority applicants had a 60 percent greater chance of being denied home loans than white applicants with the same credit-worthiness. Boston bankers made 2.9 times as many mortgage loans per one thousand housing units in neighborhoods inhabited by low-income whites than they did to neighborhoods populated by low-income blacks.[26] In addition, loan officers were far more likely to overlook flaws in the credit records of white applicants or to arrange creative financing for them than they were with black applicants.[27]

A Los Angeles study found that loan officers more frequently used dividend income and underlying assets criteria for judging black applicants than they did for whites.[28] In Houston, the NCNB Bank of Texas disqualified 13 percent of middle-income white loan applicants but disqualified 36 percent of middle-income black applicants.[29] Atlanta's home loan institutions gave five times as many home loans to whites as to blacks in the late 1980s. An analysis of sixteen Atlanta neighborhoods found

that home buyers in white neighborhoods received conventional financing four times as often as those in black sections of the city.[30] Nationwide, financial institutions get more money in deposits from black neighborhoods than they invest in them in the form of home mortgage loans, making home lending a vehicle for the transfer of capital away from black savers and toward white investors.[31] In many locations, high-income blacks were denied loans more often than low-income whites.[32]

Federal home loan policies have placed the power of the federal government behind private discrimination. Urban renewal and highway construction programs have enhanced the possessive investment in whiteness directly through government initiatives. In addition, decisions about the location of federal jobs have also systematically supported the subsidy for whiteness. Federal civilian employment dropped by 41,419 in central cities between 1966 and 1973, but total federal employment in metropolitan areas grew by 26,558.[33] While one might naturally expect the location of government buildings that serve the public to follow population trends, the federal government's policies in locating offices and records centers in suburbs helped aggravate the flight of jobs to suburban locations less accessible to inner-city residents. Since racial discrimination in the private sector forces minority workers to seek government positions disproportionate to their numbers, these moves exact particular hardships on them. In addition, minorities who follow their jobs to the suburbs generally encounter increased commuter costs because housing discrimination makes it harder and more expensive for them to relocate than for whites.

The racialized aspects of fifty years of these social democratic policies became greatly exacerbated by the anti-social democratic policies of neoconservatives in the Reagan and Bush administrations during the 1980s and 1990s. They clearly contributed to the reinforcement of possessive investments in whiteness through their regressive policies in respect to federal aid to education and their refusal to challenge segregated education, housing, and hiring, as well as their cynical cultivation of an antiblack, counter-subversive consensus through attacks on affirmative action and voting rights legislation. In the U.S. economy, where 86 percent of available jobs do not appear in classified advertisements and where personal connections provide the most important factor in securing employment, attacks on affirmative action guarantee that whites will be rewarded for their historical advantages in the labor market rather than for their individual abilities or efforts.[34]

Yet even seemingly race-neutral policies supported by both neoconservatives and social democrats in the 1980s and 1990s have also increased the absolute value of being white. In the 1980s, changes in federal tax laws decreased the value of wage income and increased the value of investment income—a move harmful to minorities who suffer from an even greater gap between their total wealth and that of whites than in the disparity between their income and white income. Failure to raise the minimum wage between 1981 and 1989 and the more than one-third decline in value of Aid for Families with Dependent Children payments hurt all poor people, but they exacted special costs on nonwhites facing even more constricted markets for employment, housing, and education than poor whites.[35]

Similarly, the "tax reforms" of the 1980s made the effective rate of taxation higher on investment in actual goods and services than it was on profits from speculative enterprises. This encouraged the flight of capital away from industrial production with its many employment opportunities and toward investments that can be turned over quickly to allow the greatest possible tax write-offs. Consequently, government policies actually discouraged investments that might produce high-paying jobs and encouraged investors to strip companies of their assets in order to make rapid short-term profits. These policies hurt almost all workers, but they exacted particularly high costs from minority workers who, because of employment discrimination in the retail and small business sectors, were overrepresented in blue-collar industrial jobs.

On the other hand, while neoconservative tax policies created incentives for employers to move their enterprises elsewhere, they created

disincentives for home owners to move. Measures such as California's Proposition 13 granting tax relief to property owners badly misallocate housing resources because they make it financially unwise for the elderly to move out of large houses, further reducing the supply of housing available to young families. While one can well understand the necessity for protecting senior citizens on fixed incomes from tax increases that would make them lose their homes, the rewards and punishments provided by Proposition 13 are so extreme that they prevent the kinds of generational succession that have routinely opened up housing to young families in the past. This reduction works particular hardships on those who also face discrimination by sellers, realtors, and lending institutions.

Subsidies to the private sector by government agencies also tend to reward the results of past discrimination. Throughout the country, tax increment redevelopment programs give tax-free, low-interest loans to developers whose projects use public services, often without having to pay taxes to local school boards or county governments. Industrial development bonds resulted in a $7.4 billion tax loss in 1983, a loss that ordinary tax payers had to make up through increased payroll taxes. Compared to white Americans, people of color, who are more likely to be poor or working class, suffer disproportionately from these changes as tax payers, as workers, and as tenants. A study by the Citizens for Tax Justice found that wealthy Californians spend less than eleven cents in taxes for every dollar earned, while poor residents of the state paid fourteen cents out of every dollar in taxes. As groups overrepresented among the poor, minorities have been forced to shoulder this burden in order to subsidize the tax breaks given to the wealthy.[36] While holding property tax assessments for businesses and some home owners to about half of their market value, California's Proposition 13 deprived cities and counties of $13 billion a year in taxes. Businesses alone avoided $3.3 billion to $8.6 billion in taxes per year under this statute.[37]

Because they are ignorant of even the recent history of the possessive investment in whiteness— generated by slavery and segregation but augmented by social democratic reform—Americans produce largely cultural explanations for structural social problems. The increased possessive investment in whiteness generated by disinvestment in America's cities, factories, and schools since the 1970s disguises the general problems posed to our society by deindustrialization, economic restructuring, and **neoconservative** attacks on the welfare state as *racial* problems. It fuels a discourse that demonizes people of color for being victimized by these changes, while hiding the privileges of whiteness by attributing them to family values, fatherhood, and foresight—rather than to favoritism.

The demonization of black families in public discourse since the 1970s is particularly instructive in this regard. During the 1970s, the share of low-income households headed by blacks increased by one-third, while black family income fell from 60 percent of white family income in 1971 to 58 percent in 1980. Even when adjusting for unemployment and for African-American disadvantages in life-cycle employment (more injuries, more frequently interrupted work histories, confinement to jobs most susceptible to layoffs), the wages of full-time year-round black workers fell from 77 percent of white workers' income to 73 percent by 1986. In 1986, white workers with high school diplomas earned three thousand dollars per year more than African Americans with the same education.[38] Even when they had the same family structure as white workers, blacks found themselves more likely to be poor.

Among black workers between the ages of twenty and twenty-four, 46 percent held blue-collar jobs in 1976, but that percentage fell to only 20 percent by 1984. Earnings by young black families had reached 60 percent of the amount secured by white families in 1973, but by 1986 they fell back to 46 percent. Younger African-American families experienced a 50 percent drop in real earnings between 1973 and 1986, with the decline in black male wages particularly steep.[39]

---

neoconservatism A response to the liberalism of the 1960s, this political philosophy is an attempt to return to the conservatism of the 1950s. The movement is characterized by privatizing public goods, nation building through military intervention abroad, and minimum government regulation.

Many recent popular and scholarly studies have explained clearly the causes for black economic decline over the past two decades.[40] Deindustrialization has decimated the industrial infrastructure that formerly provided high-wage jobs and chances for upward mobility to black workers. Neoconservative attacks on government spending for public housing, health, education, and transportation have deprived African Americans of needed services and opportunities for jobs in the public sector. A massive retreat from responsibility to enforce anti-discrimination laws at the highest levels of government has sanctioned pervasive overt and covert racial discrimination by bankers, realtors, and employers.

Yet public opinion polls conducted among white Americans display little recognition of these devastating changes. Seventy percent of whites in one poll said that African Americans "have the same opportunities to live a middle-class life as whites."[41] Nearly three-fourths of white respondents to a 1989 poll believed that opportunities for blacks had improved during the Reagan presidency.[42]

Optimism about the opportunities available to African Americans does not necessarily demonstrate ignorance of the dire conditions facing black communities, but, if not, it then indicates that many whites believe that blacks suffer deservedly, that they do not take advantage of the opportunities offered them. In the opinion polls, favorable assessments of black chances for success often accompanied extremely negative judgments about the abilities, work habits, and character of black people. A National Opinion Research Report in 1990 disclosed that more than 50 percent of American whites viewed blacks as innately lazy and less intelligent and less patriotic than whites.[43] Furthermore, more than 60 percent of whites questioned in that survey said that they believed that blacks suffer from poor housing and employment opportunities because of their own lack of willpower. Some 56.3 percent of whites said that blacks preferred welfare to employment, while 44.6 percent contended that blacks tended toward laziness.[44] Even more important, research by Mary and Thomas Byrne Edsall indicates that many whites structure nearly all of their decisions about housing, education, and politics in response to their aversions to black people.[45]

The present political culture in this country gives broad sanction for viewing white supremacy and antiblack racism as forces from the past, as demons finally put to rest by the passage of the 1964 Civil Rights Act and the 1965 Voting Rights Act.[46] Jurists, journalists, and politicians have generally been more vocal in their opposition to "quotas" and to "reverse discrimination" mandating race-specific remedies for discrimination than to the thousands of well-documented incidents every year of routine, systematic, and unyielding discrimination against blacks.

It is my contention that the stark contrast between black experiences and white opinions during the past two decades cannot be attributed solely to ignorance or intolerance on the part of individuals but stems instead from the overdetermined inadequacy of the language of liberal individualism to describe collective experience.[47] As long as we define social life as the sum total of conscious and deliberate individual activities, then only *individual* manifestations of personal prejudice and hostility will be seen as racist. Systemic, collective, and coordinated behavior disappears from sight. Collective exercises of group power relentlessly channeling rewards, resources, and opportunities from one group to another will not appear to be "racist" from this perspective because they rarely announce their intention to discriminate against individuals. But they work to construct racial identities by giving people of different races vastly different life chances.

The gap between white perceptions and minority experiences can have explosive consequences. Little more than a year after the 1992 Los Angeles rebellion, a sixteen-year-old high school junior shared her opinions with a reporter from the *Los Angeles Times*. "I don't think white people owe anything to black people," she explained. "We didn't sell them into slavery, it was our ancestors. What they did was wrong, but we've done our best to make up for it."[48] A seventeen-year-old senior echoed those comments, telling the reporter:

> I feel we spend more time in my history class talking about what whites owe blacks than

just about anything else when the issue of slavery comes up. I often received dirty looks. This seems strange given that I wasn't even alive then. And the few members of my family from that time didn't have the luxury of owning much, let alone slaves. So why, I ask you, am I constantly made to feel guilty?[49]

More ominously, after pleading guilty to bombing two homes and one car, to vandalizing a synagogue, and attempting to start a race war by murdering Rodney King and bombing Los Angeles's First African Methodist Episcopal Church, twenty-year-old Christopher David Fisher explained that "sometimes whites were picked on because of the color of their skin. . . . Maybe we're blamed for slavery."[50] Fisher's actions were certainly extreme, but his justification of them drew knowingly and precisely on a broadly shared narrative about the victimization of innocent whites by irrational and ungrateful minorities.

The comments and questions raised about the legacy of slavery by these young whites illumine broader currents in our culture that have enormous implications for understanding the enduring significance of race in our country. These young people associate black grievances solely with slavery, and they express irritation at what they perceive as efforts to make them feel guilty or unduly privileged in the present because of things that happened in the distant past. Because their own ancestors may not have been slave owners or because "we've done our best to make up for it," they feel that it is unreasonable for anyone to view them as people who owe "anything" to blacks. On the contrary, Fisher felt that his discomfort with being "picked on" and "blamed" for slavery gave him good reason to bomb homes, deface synagogues, and plot to kill black people.

Unfortunately for our society, these young whites accurately reflect the logic of the language of liberal individualism and its ideological predispositions in discussions of race. They seem to have no knowledge of the disciplined, systemic, and collective *group* activity that has structured white identities in American history. They are not alone in their ignorance; in a 1979 law journal article, future Supreme

Court Justice Antonin Scalia argued that affirmative action "is based upon concepts of racial indebtedness and racial entitlement rather than individual worth and individual need" and is thus "racist."[51]

Yet liberal individualism is not completely color-blind on this issue. As Cheryl I. Harris demonstrates, the legacy of liberal individualism has not prevented the Supreme Court from recognizing and protecting the group interests of *whites* in the Bakke, Croson, and Wygant cases.[52] In each case, the Court nullified affirmative action programs because they judged efforts to help blacks as harmful to whites: to white expectations of entitlement, expectations based on the possessive investment in whiteness they held as members of a group. In the Bakke case, for instance, neither Bakke nor the court contested the legitimacy of medical school admissions standards that reserved five seats in each class for children of wealthy donors to the university or that penalized Bakke for being older than most of the other applicants. The group rights of not-wealthy people or of people older than their classmates did not compel the Court or Bakke to make any claim of harm. But they did challenge and reject a policy designed to offset the effects of past and present discrimination when they could construe the medical school admission policies as detrimental to the interests of whites as a group—and as a consequence they applied the "strict scrutiny" standard to protect whites while denying that protection to people of color. In this case, as in so many others, the language of liberal individualism serves as a cover for coordinated collective group interests.

Group interests are not monolithic, and aggregate figures can obscure serious differences within racial groups. All whites do not benefit from the possessive investment in whiteness in precisely the same way; the experiences of members of minority groups are not interchangeable. But the possessive investment in whiteness always affects individual and group life chances and opportunities. Even in cases where minority groups secure political and economic power through collective mobilization, the terms and conditions of their collectivity and the logic of group solidarity are always influenced and intensified by the absolute value of whiteness in American politics, economics, and culture.[53]

In the 1960s, members of the Black Panther Party used to say that "if you're not part of the solution, you're part of the problem." But those of us who are "white" can only become part of the solution if we recognize the degree to which we are already part of the problem—not because of our race, but because of our possessive investment in it. Neither conservative **"free market"** policies nor liberal social democratic reforms can solve the "white problem" in America because both of them reinforce the possessive investment in whiteness. But an explicitly antiracist pan-ethnic movement that acknowledges the existence and power of whiteness might make some important changes. Pan-ethnic, antiracist coalitions have a long history in the United States—in the political activism of John Brown, Sojourner Truth, and the Magon brothers, among others—but we also have a rich cultural tradition of panethnic antiracism connected to civil rights activism of the kind detailed so brilliantly in rhythm and blues musician Johnny Otis's recent book, *Upside Your Head! Rhythm and Blues on Central Avenue.*[54] These efforts by whites to fight racism, not out of sympathy for someone else but out of a sense of self-respect and simple justice, have never completely disappeared; they remain available as models for the present.[55]

Walter Benjamin's praise for "presence of mind" came from his understanding of how difficult it may be to see the present. But more important, he called for presence of mind as the means for implementing what he called "the only true telepathic miracle"—turning the forbidding future into the fulfilled present.[56] Failure to acknowledge our society's possessive investment in whiteness prevents us from facing the present openly and honestly. It hides from us the devastating costs of disinvestment in America's infrastructure over the past two decades

---

free market A system of exchange in which buyers and sellers come to agreement about pricing with no outside influences. The idea of a free market is that there is little or no government intervention in the private transactions of individuals.

and keeps us from facing our responsibilities to reinvest in human capital by channeling resources toward education, health, and housing—and away from subsidies for speculation and luxury. After two decades of disinvestment, the only further disinvestment we need is to disinvest in the ruinous pathology of whiteness that has always undermined our own best instincts and interests. In a society suffering so badly from an absence of mutuality, an absence of responsibility, and an absence of simple justice, presence of mind might be just what we need.

Seeing the Big Picture   **Race as an Investment**

How do rates of homeownership (Section II in the appendix) and occupations by race (Section VIII) point to historic investments that have privileged one group over another?

THE COST OF A BLACK CORPSE

The Racism in the Cadaver Trade

Average Value of Cadavers: $0-$30 [$881 in 2014][1]

Daina Ramey Berry

DAINA RAMEY BERRY is an Associate Professor of History and African and African Diaspora Studies and the Oliver H. Radkey Regents Fellow in History at the University of Texas at Austin.

Richard H. Whitehead's University of North Carolina School of Medicine anatomy student during a dissection staged outdoors, Raleigh, circa 1890. Notice the African American janitor sits on a bucket in front of an African American man who is being dissected.

Source: North Carolina Collection, University of North Carolina Library at Chapel Hill.

Do tell me, what is the cost of a fine, stiff [n _____ r]?

—Fran Bowen to Dr. Wyman,
Richmond Medical College, 1845[2]

It makes me feel very bad when I think of the way the graves of
my race have been desecrated.

—Jim Burrell, janitor,
Jefferson Medical College[3]

On a cold New York winter night, February 25, 1836, an audience of fifteen hundred people filled the City Saloon, anxiously anticipating the main attraction. Some had come from miles away and all had gladly paid the 50-cent admission fee for a show that promised to be like no other. Some arrived hoping to satisfy their long-held curiosity and wondered whether their theories would prove true. Others arrived not knowing what to expect. The saloon had been converted into a makeshift operating room for this special occasion, and the lights centered on a table in the middle of the stage.

The central figure in this drama, a deceased elderly enslaved woman named Joice Heth, lay atop the elevated table. She had died six days prior; her public autopsy was the main event that evening. The people surrounding her were Dr. David L. Rogers of Barclay Street Hospital, students, clergymen, *New York Sun* editor Richard Adams Locke, and lawyer Levi Lyman, who served as her "agent," along with

the infamous showman P. T. Barnum. Nearly everyone present was male, and some reports suggest that the entire procedure was distasteful, described as a "bloodily invasive circus."[4]

While still alive, Heth had spent her last year on tour, advertised as a purportedly 161-year-old enslaved woman and the former nurse of George Washington. Barnum made $1,500 per week displaying her at halls and facilities throughout the mid-Atlantic and Northeast. She told stories and sang hymns as part of Barnum's "Freak Show": In seven months, he made roughly $42,000 from this orchestrated public spectacle. In contemporary times, that would be equivalent to $1,102,336.[5] As Barnum's property, Heth made nothing. Now, less than a week after her death, Barnum organized his last show, a public autopsy to determine her cause of death and true age. People who paid to see her while living marveled at the old soul. Barnum claimed she had lived a century and a half and although she was blind, she remembered seeing the Red Coats during

Questions to Consider

Enslaved people were commodities that could be bought, sold, traded, used as collateral, and willed to family members. Slavery and Jim Crow were institutions that are permanent moral and ethical scars of our nation's history. One would think in death that enslaved people, at least in a transcendental sense, could finally have a dignified rest. For many, however, this was not to be. Before the Civil War and for decades afterwards there was a robust and lucrative demand by doctors and medical schools for cadavers. Deceased enslaved people were sold once again to medical schools to teach students human anatomy through dissection. Professor Berry looks at the cadaver trade, the "respected" institutions that bought the dead, and the list of individuals who profited from this racist and unethical practice.

the American Revolution. She was also paralyzed and had use of only her right arm.

On stage, doctors and medical students felt the crevices of her wrinkles, gazed into her sunken eye sockets, and marveled at her internal organs. When Dr. Rogers cut her open, he and his team of medical professionals from the New York College of Physicians and Surgeons expected to see extreme ossification of the arteries near her heart if she was as old as Barnum claimed. Instead, however, she had the internal organs of a woman in her seventies and not older than eighty. Immediately, Barnum went on the defensive, blaming Heth for deceiving him. Local newspapers covered the autopsy; there was significant outrage that Barnum had deceived the public. Barnum had made a great deal of money off Heth when she was alive and even managed to collect fees for her very public display after she died.[6]

Organized autopsies differed from mob dissections, like those of Nat Turner and Shields Green. Although both autopsies and dissections educated medical students about pathologies in the human body, the former were typically state or locally sanctioned and often sought the cause of death in the case of alleged foul play. Determining the cause of death became a significant development that paralleled medical professionalization. In the nineteenth century, "The examination of the anatomy of very aged persons" was believed to be "one of the most curious and instructive studies in science."[7]

Physicians began publicly asserting their "expertise" in the field of medical jurisprudence in the opening decades of the nineteenth century at the New York College of Physicians and Surgeons (which eventually became a part of Columbia University), because physicians' findings were used in legal cases. Decades later, in 1853, medical practitioners in Gonzales, Texas, for example, performed a "post-mortem examination" of an enslaved boy named Jack to try to understand his cause of death. Approximately "13 hours after death," Drs. J.B. Logue, William Craig, F.M. Lyle, and W.T. Lockridge examined Jack's heart and found "a fibro adipose substance" or cyst in the "cavity of the right ventricle." They also found a second growth on "the left side of the heart extending 5 or 6 inches down the aorta." They noted that Jack had been "sick about 5 or 6 days" and complained about having "shortness of breath." In the end, the autopsy allowed them to determine that Jack had suffered from heart disease for "about 3 years standing." In another case, from 1857, a Dr. Bennett of Bridgeport, Connecticut, conducted a postmortem on "a stout, healthy negro, eighteen years of age." We do not know if this man was ever enslaved, but we know that he suffered a traumatic injury after being stabbed with a "dirk-knife." Although it seemed as if he could recover from the injury, he died a few days later. During Dr. Bennett's postmortem exam, he discovered that the deceased man had a wound that was "sufficiently large to have produced instant death." Had the deceased rested as instructed and not climbed two flights of stairs, he would have had a chance of survival.[8]

These autopsies, which span from the 1830s to the eve of the Civil War, confirm the growing interest in cause of death, but they also illustrate the medical curiosity for understanding the human body (the heart, in particular). This curiosity was apparent in life and death. Measured examinations of the heart differed from the bodily dismemberment that occurred at the hands of mob violence. Mob dissections typically involved vigilante groups that took the law into their own hands, lynching, dissecting, and mauling the body of the deceased as a form of punishment.[9]

In the 1930s, when some of the last living formerly enslaved people were interviewed about their experiences under enslavement, they too recalled the medical curiosities of their bodies expressed in the form of "soundness." Once enslaved, Barney Stone of Kentucky noted that some doctors accompanied buyers on the eve of sales "to examine the slave's heart." If they were pronounced "sound," the "buyer would make an offer to the owner and if the amount was satisfactory, the slave was sold."[10]

Heth's public autopsy clearly gave new meaning to the monetary value of the dead. We know from the bellies of enslaved pregnant women that the financial value of their "future increase" was projected, but very little consideration has been given to the value of enslaved bodies after death, until now. Considering this topic brings us into a direct study of nineteenth-century medicine, medical education, the history of anatomy, and slavery.[11]

Dr. Rogers had students and colleagues standing by his side, watching his every move when he cut open Heth's body. Hands-on training was as important to medical education then as it is today, particularly at teaching hospitals. But historian of medicine Michael Sappol reminds us that "dissection for the purposes of medical instruction" had a completely different meaning than an autopsy. Typically, autopsies fell under the category of "medical jurisprudence," when questions surrounding the cause of death resulted in a hearing. Such procedures were "performed in a private room" with physicians who served as jurors; medical students could not weigh in on the case.[12] Perhaps people's curiosity about Heth's age justified their desire to

pay for and watch the dissection. Some of the same individuals who paid to see her while she was living likely also paid to see her after death.

Dissections in public settings such as this, and in medical facilities for higher learning, occurred regularly in the nineteenth century, and the dissections of enslaved and formerly enslaved people represented a unique way to extend the profits of slavery beyond the grave. Heth arrives in the historical record as an aged woman loaned and purchased for display in popular cultural settings such as fairs, circuses, and live performances. Some argue that this was not only the result of her physical appearance but also her coerced complicity in her own exploitation. Clearly she participated in the public spectacle Barnum and Lyman created. She told stories and sang songs to entertain her audiences, and Barnum aided with publicity by sending anonymous letters to local newspapers before their shows. When Heth became ill, a Boston woman cared for her until she died on February 19, 1836. Her postmortem journey brought her corpse about 233 miles via carriage to the New York home of Barnum, where he allegedly "stored her" in a hallway for a few days and then hosted one final public performance in which Heth was the attraction. In addition to attending the autopsy, people paid for the newspapers that described the event, discussing Heth for months and years after she departed. Similar to the contemporary story of Henrietta Lacks, Heth's afterlife contributed to medical education.

This chapter examines the postmortem journeys of deceased enslaved people [and] unknown cadavers, who were on display at medical schools for the benefit of higher learning. Because they were dead, the voices of the enslaved are barely represented here. Instead, I rely heavily on the perspective of physicians who handled their bodies. What follows is the story of the corpses of the enslaved bodies after death, bodies that became part of a clandestine cadaver trade that I believe paralleled other illegal forms of human trafficking. Formerly enslaved people and many others (black, white, and free) experienced a postmortem journey that few scholars consider. As one of the first to trace this history, with a particular focus on enslaved people and their cadaver journeys, I think that we have much more to learn about the life cycles of the enslaved. Their bodies experienced commodification after death. The fiscal values of their cadavers became tradable goods that were part of a clandestine traffic in bodies used for anatomical education.

IDENTIFYING THE DOMESTIC CADAVER TRADE

Procuring bodies for medical instruction created an unusual problem for university faculty between the 1830s and 1880s. They needed bodies for dissection, but in most states, there were no legally sanctioned sources (aside from the gallows).

However, between 1760 and 1876, medical students likely participated in anywhere from an estimated 4,200 to 8,000 dissections. These statistics are more revealing when one considers that the only legal candidates for medical dissection were often unclaimed executed criminals and enslaved people with their enslaver's consent. This raises questions about where the bodies came from, and the role of enslavers in this process.

Some enslavers had the bodies of enslaved people dug up and sold. . . . Other enslavers passively allowed the bodies of their deceased enslaved people to be harvested or exhumed. An unknown number of enslavers were also medical doctors who took the cadavers directly to the dissection table because they considered them their personal property. A number of corpses entered this market when stolen from burial grounds or the sites of enslavement on which they died. But not all enslavers supported this traffic, making this history difficult to trace. My focus here is on the cadavers in circulation, even when I cannot fully determine how they ended up on the dissection table. I know that a large number of medical specimens were obtained illegally, and that a significant proportion of them were of African descent; arguably many had once been enslaved.

Parts of the illegal activity involved purchasing cadavers through a clandestine market. In this setting, bodies sold for a range of prices, from $5 in most places to $30 in "Ohio and other states." Bodies were cheaper if it was easier "to procure the necessary supply of subjects," and they were more expensive when "it is difficult."[13] Just as in the domestic slave trade, in the cadaver trade, importing and exporting states depended on the enslaved population, the willingness of traders, and the ability to transport this unusual merchandise. Thus, before the passage of most statewide anatomy acts in the 1880s, "teachers of anatomy were driven to the undignified and illegal practice of encouraging and rewarding grave-robbing as the sole means of supplying the dissecting room." Some were directly involved in this practice, and others relied on professional 'resurrectionists,' who stole fresh bodies from cemeteries at night and served as medical school janitors during the day. Dr. Daniel Drake, a physician from Kentucky, noted that "the 'resurrectionist' (grave robber) might be the college or hospital janitor, although often it was the student himself or even the professor of anatomy."[14] From this "material" taken by university janitors in the middle of the night, medical students learned "the structure of the [human] body."[15]

Tracing the origins, routes, and agents, I find that the traffic in enslaved bodies modeled itself after the transatlantic and domestic slave trade and is comparable to modern forms of human trafficking. In order to understand this network, however, we must consider the value of deceased people, outlined in previous chapters through ghost values, and the key people involved in facilitating "a traffic of dead bodies."[16] From private and public autopsies to an illegal cadaver trade, I will address the valuation and sale of formerly enslaved and some free black people after death.[17] Most of the cadavers were once enslaved, and neither death nor burial freed them from additional commodification and exploitation. Corpses of formerly enslaved people were technically the property of enslavers, institutions, or state agencies at the time of death, making it difficult or impossible for enslaved and free family members to claim the rights to their relative and ensure proper burial, or to prevent tampering after a body was laid to rest.

Cultivating a Corpse

The domestic cadaver trade was a highly organized transportation system. One way to understand it is to consider how it paralleled agricultural production. For this traffic to happen, a body had to be planted, harvested, and transported.

The cadaver trade functioned on a cyclical calendar, much as enslaved people's lives were governed by an agricultural calendar. As laborers, the life cycle of the enslaved followed the crop schedule. As cadavers, the lifespan of a body followed a decomposition schedule; proper preservation was important.

Like other forms of involuntary migration, the domestic cadaver trade was seasonal. The majority of body snatching occurred in the summer, fall, and early winter, just as coffles were transferred from the Upper South to markets in the Deep South, and as transatlantic ships made their voyages during specific months depending on the location, weather, and crop.[18] African merchants waited until harvest was done and crops were stored before they "sold enslaved farmers and provisions to coastal middlemen, who in turn, sold these captives to ship captains" headed to New World plantation communities in North and South America as well as the Caribbean.[19] Fall weather proved ideal for domestic travel and for grave digging, before frozen ground revealed snow-tracked footsteps and such work became nearly impossible. Brisk fall nights offered suitable temperatures for preserving corpses; the summer months were challenging because hot weather sped up decomposition. Thus, most bodies were stolen, sold, and prepared for dissection during cooler months. Anatomy demonstrations that involved dissections often occurred during the winter and concluded at the onset of spring.

These rather unusual trading systems make sense when understood through the metaphor of cultivating crops and corpses. In January, agricultural laborers working with cotton prepared the fields for planting. Cadavers were also prepared before being placed in the ground, but this work, often done by family members or close associates, occurred throughout the year, as people died daily.[20] In March, enslaved laborers put cotton seeds in the ground; after planting came the "lay by" stage, in which the crop was given time to incubate and grow. Burial represented the planting phase of a cadaver, but in order to cultivate a corpse, it had to be exhumed. In other words, the "lay by" season for a cadaver was less than seventy-two hours after burial because it took seven to ten days to completely "anatomize" a corpse before "the body became too decomposed to be useful for study."[21] Harvesting marked the next important stage for cotton crops and cadavers. The cotton harvest lasted from the summer to the early fall. Cadavers were often harvested or exhumed in late summer, fall, and the early winter months. Following the harvest, the crop or, in this case, cadaver had to be packaged and prepared for the market. The process of producing a good crop or cadaver involved highly specialized packaging. These "products" had to make it to their destinations intact, well preserved, and ready for the process that turned a corpse into a specimen. Cotton bales and bags protected fibers by keeping them clean. Cadaver bags, also made of cotton, functioned the same way for short transports, but for further distances that involved shipping, bodies were placed in large casks filled with preservation liquids such as whiskey or brine. At the market, planters and brokers sold the raw crops and the smuggled cadavers. When the "fresh" body arrived at a medical college, it was removed from its packaging, set on a table-like assembly line, "manufactured" as a specimen, and used for dissection until complete decomposition ended the cycle.

The causes of death of an enslaved person varied, and so did the way their bodies entered the market. Some were executed, sold, or stolen, others buried and exhumed, and some were unclaimed and legal candidates for dissection. The once-enslaved body now had a different purpose; it was manufactured into a valuable commodity that would be used to train medical professionals in the halls of some of America's leading institutions, including Dartmouth College, Harvard University, Northwestern University, the University of Chicago, the University of Virginia, the University of Maryland, and Virginia Commonwealth University.[22] At these colleges, the harvest process was completed and the corpse was fully manufactured for anatomical education. Just as the raw cotton produced by enslaved people was manufactured into cloth, and then transformed into aprons covered with rubber and worn by physicians and their students in the dissecting rooms, the once-enslaved body underwent a similar process as a way for medical professionals to better understand the human body.

Schools were dependent on cadavers, whether formerly enslaved or not. However, given the illegal nature of the trade in the early to mid-nineteenth century, members of the medical community proceeded with caution and participated in an underground market to obtain these unusual goods. In their opinion, they had no alternative, because "the number of legally available corpses was woefully inadequate."[23] It was, however, legal to dissect executed criminals and unclaimed persons, so almshouses, hospitals, and prisons worked closely with physicians.[24] Although denied humanity while enslaved, after cultivation and manufacturing the corpse-turned-specimen was now more human than before as it was used to understand the intricacies of the human body. This ghost value enabled the bodies of the enslaved to generate money for enslavers after death. Determining the racial identity and social status of the cultivated corpses is difficult; however, it is clear through the historical record that the majority were African Americans.[25]

Major medical men in the United States played key roles in the domestic cadaver trade. They were the orchestrators of this grand symphony, while enslaved and free janitors served as the conductors. These men were of great medical stature and were well known in their communities as local physicians and leaders. They were also men who encouraged and participated in an illegal trade in deceased people. Their training overlapped and so did their methods. Rather than operating in a triangular trade, the doctors involved in the domestic cadaver trade created an intricate web that had recognizable patterns. First, many of them were trained at the same institutions; second, they relied on European methods of dissection; and finally, they recognized that an ample supply of cadavers was crucial to anatomical training. Some early American physicians did part of their training in Europe, where members of the upper-class elite killed and dissected poor citizens who had few legal avenues of protection. This web of doctors appears in the historical literature.[26]

By tracing physicians and their protégés' academic genealogies, the trade in dead bodies becomes clear. The point here is not to demonize these medical practitioners, but to paint a historical picture based on the records.[27] Thus, when placed in the context of the global history of anatomical education, the cadaver trade functioned along familiar routes, and the advancement of higher learning served as the primary object. The value of cadavers to nineteenth-century medical education clearly supports the idea that ghost values were a necessary part of the trade. Physicians were not always trying to obstruct justice; many were doing as their mentors had trained them. Yet the disrespect of African American life, as well as the lives of the poor and disadvantaged, also comes to the fore.

Body Snatching

In 1839, the Medical College of Georgia in Augusta purchased $100 worth of cadavers from a New York source. Anatomical "subjects" at that time cost approximately 75 cents each; therefore, it is likely that the school received 130 cadavers through this transaction. The subjects were "shipped in casks of brine or whiskey" and placed on a "coastal steamer" to Charleston, along the same routes as shipments of living enslaved people. Three years later in 1842, Dr. Newton, the demonstrator of anatomy, took a trip to Baltimore "to secure subjects for the coming year." He probably traveled the Atlantic seaboard along the same shipping lanes as domestic and transatlantic slave ships. These ships would have been outfitted with a small crew and raw goods being sent north for manufacturing. To take such a voyage, Newton had to make arrangements in advance, and the items he purchased had to be prepared for transportation. He would need casks to transport the bodies and whiskey or lime for preservation. He also knew that popular sentiment did not support dissection, so he used discretion in conversations with enslavers and "next of kin."[28] Some enslavers in Norfolk, nearly two hundred miles from the University of Virginia, did not want their enslaved people's graves tampered with; others simply did not care. The same patterns existed in Georgia.[29]

From 1848 to 1852, the Medical College of Georgia used "resurrection slaves named Joe, King, Peter, Jackson, John and Edmund" to rob graves from local cemeteries. It brought in sixty-four subjects for dissection, equivalent to "16 subjects per term."[30] These enslaved men were given wages or modest fees for their services, which included grave robbing and then reinterment after the medical students and faculty were finished with the dissection. They acquired bodies in South Carolina and Georgia.

Eventually, by the 1850s, the Medical College of Georgia (MCG) faculty relied on one enslaved man to conduct this business. On January 6, 1852, seven members of the medical faculty purchased Grandison Harris from a Charleston, South Carolina, auction block. Known as a member of the Gullah community, the thirty-six-year-old Harris was bought for $700, and valued at $753, equivalent to $22,125 in 2014. Faculty members each owned one-seventh of his person and could sell their share if they left the school.[31] His official title was "porter," but the faculty purchased him for one purpose: to supply the school with subjects for dissection. Those who knew him said he "was good." We do not know the race and status of all those he procured; some were free blacks. Members of the African American community had mixed feelings about him.[32] We do know that he stole bodies from Cedar Grove Cemetery, which was reserved for poor and black residents; the cemetery was not fenced. Harris learned to read and write, searched obituaries for potential subjects, and sat in on anatomy lectures. Some referred to him as a "teaching assistant," and "students respected his expertise." He became knowledgeable about dissections and, over time, perfected his craft. One scholar described him as being responsible for all the preparations necessary for acquiring, preparing, displaying, and disposing of human specimens.[33]

Once he identified a potential corpse, he went to Cedar Grove Cemetery at night and dug "down to the upper end of the box"; then he smashed it "with an axe" and drew the subject out, placed it in a sack, and carted it to the college. By employing Harris, the Medical College of Georgia saved money, because it no longer had to hire enslaved people to do this work, nor did it have to purchase cadavers

from sources in South Carolina, Maryland, New York, and Massachusetts, as they had done before Harris's arrival.[34]

Harris was fully integrated into MCG, and he appears frequently in school records. Faculty made note of his activities, including his wages, room and board, supplies, and payments for acquiring dissection subjects from 1853 through 1857. At a glance, he appears in about 25 percent of the faculty account records. Harris received $6.75–$10.00 in monthly wages from the college.[35] Over this four-year period, he was paid a total of $412 for forty-one subjects collected. He likely needed supplies for his clandestine activities, so in December 1854, the faculty paid $4 for "containing subjects and cover" and, on another occasion, purchased a wheelbarrow. Likewise, on January 17, 1856, the school paid $66.67 for whiskey, which was probably used to preserve cadavers.[36]

After years of collecting subjects for dissection, Harris had also been traveling back and forth to South Carolina to see his family. In 1858, the dean of the college returned to the Charleston auction block and purchased Harris's wife, Rachel, and son, George, for a total cost of $1,250, equivalent to $37,083 in 2014.[37] Again, this represented another financial decision, because owning the entire family "kept Grandison Harris off the railroad between Augusta and Charleston," a journey that cost the school twelve dollars each time. Rachel worked as a cook and laundress, while George learned about his father's business. Although we do not know much about Rachel and George, we can speculate that she washed the sheets, blankets, aprons, and rags used in the dissecting rooms. Postslavery photographs of black laundresses at medical colleges show unnamed women with brooms behind medical students performing dissections. We know, from the testimonies of medical students themselves, that the smells and substances involved were not pleasant. We can only imagine that George aided his parents in their work, which was customary at the time. In a photo of the MCG anatomy class taken in the early twentieth century, an unidentified African American adolescent is present. Could this be Grandison and Rachel's son George? The family spent their lives at the college where they lived and worked.[38]

Recognizing the domestic cadaver trade allows us to connect the overt and covert medical education in nineteenth-century United States to contemporary forms of organ and human trafficking. Through the cultivation and processing of bodies 150 to 200 years ago, we learn that the orchestrators of this web were men of distinction. Well-trained physicians, many who knew one another, corresponded through letters and publications in college circulars and medical journals. They discussed the illegal acquisition of bodies, many formerly enslaved people and free blacks. However, they could not do their work without help from janitors, students, or professional grave robbers. These individuals, like Grandison Harris, Chris Baker, and Albert Wilson Monroe, aided in acquiring "subjects for dissection" and completed a host of janitorial tasks at their respective institutions. Also known as "night prowlers," these men were highly skilled and respected by medical practitioners. They mastered the craft of grave robbing and were publicly acknowledged in life and in death.

Harris, Baker, and Monroe, along with an Irishman named Frank in Baltimore and William Watson in Philadelphia, cultivated corpses and facilitated traffic in dead bodies. This cadaver trade continues today in the form of underground organ markets.[39]

The public outcry over dissection in England in the 1830s resulted in the British 1832 Anatomy Act. US physicians outside Massachusetts continued the practices for fifty more years until US legislation restricted anatomical dissection. After a series of arrests of doctors and body snatchers in the 1880s, other states passed legislation and joined Massachusetts (1831) in passing anatomy acts, clarifying the avenues for procuring legal subjects for dissection under specific circumstances. Such legislation occurred in states including Pennsylvania (1883), Virginia (1884), and Georgia (1887).

Today, people can choose to donate their organs, but fees are involved. For example, Mercer University in Macon, Georgia, covers "the costs for transportation, embalming and cremation" if the donor lives within a fiftymile radius. Those who live outside this perimeter are "responsible for costs of transport[ing]" cadavers "to the Mercer University School of Medicine." Just as Dr. Davis of the University of Virginia negotiated freight charges in Virginia with Drs. Minor and Wyman, Mercer University provides a formula to estimate transportation costs. On its website, the university suggests that the family of the deceased "multiply the distance from the location to Macon in miles by \$2.25/mile."[40] At least the fees are now clearly publicized, and family and friends can rest assured that their loved ones' wishes have been granted. This was not true for the enslaved, free blacks, and poor whites.

Even in graves, the souls and spirits of the enslaved rested lightly. Would they be exhumed, reburied, and/or removed? Enslaved and free blacks worried about their corpses being disturbed after death. Returning to the story of Joice Heth in her final hours, we learn that she was buried in a mahogany casket, one that Barnum felt was honorable. This was certainly a more respectable, better-quality type of wood for a casket than a pine box. We know nothing of her funeral, except that Barnum stated in his autobiography that her remains were removed to Bethel, Connecticut, and buried "respectably."[41] What did he mean by "respectably" given her exploitation in life and death? She had already been dissected. Was she truly at rest?

The contemporary case of Henrietta Lacks, whose cancerous cells were taken without her consent, confirms that even after death, bodies and body parts are still sometimes in circulation. Lacks's HeLa cells continue to advance medical research in human and animal bodies. Today, we can try to determine whether our bodies or body parts will continue to serve medical research or the life of another human being by checking "donor" on our driver's license. However, the Lacks case confirms that we are still not in complete control of our bodily materials, particularly blood after it is drawn or "waste" after surgery. We simply do not know how it's used, recycled, or disposed. We can thank medical research for showing us possibilities, and we can acknowledge the unknown, unnamed, enslaved, and free blacks, and poor whites, who aided in this process. Despite the fact that enslavers made a spectacle of the deaths of the enslaved, we can still lay them to rest. We do so by honoring their memories and tracing their postmortem journeys. The stories in this chapter remind us that the circle of life exceeds time and space, and that the life cycle of the enslaved is much longer than we realized. May the bodies and souls uncovered here rest in peace.

22

A RESEARCH NOTE ON TRENDS IN BLACK HYPERSEGREGATION

Douglas S. Massey and Jonathan Tannen

DOUGLAS S. MASSEY is Professor of Sociology at the Woodrow Wilson School of Public and International Affairs at Princeton University. JONATHAN TANNEN is a demographer.

ABSTRACT

In this note, we use a consistently defined set of metropolitan areas to study patterns and trends in black hypersegregation from 1970 to 2010. Over this 40-year period, 52 metropolitan areas were characterized by hypersegregation at one point or another, although not all at the same time. Over the period, the number of hypersegregated metropolitan areas declined by about one-half, but the degree of segregation within those areas characterized by hypersegregation changed very little. As of 2010, roughly one-third of all black metropolitan residents lived in a hypersegregated area.

KEYWORDS

Residential, Segregation, Hypersegregation, Spatial isolation, African Americans, Dissimilarity

Published online: 20 March 2015 © Population Association of America 2015

INTRODUCTION

It has been nearly four decades since Pettigrew (1979) identified black residential segregation as the "structural linchpin" of American race relations, and evidence in support of this hypothesis has only grown stronger over time. In the 1980s, Wilson (1987) pointed to the rising concentration of poverty in black neighborhoods and argued that this condition perpetuated disadvantage among African Americans, isolating them from jobs, alienating them from mainstream norms, and generating a scarcity of employed, "marriageable" males. Massey (1990) directly connected concentrated black poverty to racial segregation by developing a simulation model to show how rising rates of black poverty interact with high levels of black segregation to concentrate poverty in black neighborhoods. Massey and Denton (1993) went on to argue that by concentrating poverty and its negative correlates, segregation created a uniquely harsh and disadvantaged social environment for African Americans.

Massey and Fischer (2000) later showed that the concentration of black poverty was exacerbated by class segregation among African Americans. More recently, Quillian (2012:354) demonstrated both mathematically and empirically that black poverty concentration actually stems from a more complex interaction between poverty and three types of segregation: racial segregation, poverty-status

segregation within race, and segregation of blacks from high- and middle-income members of other racial groups. Although the poverty-by-segregation interaction proved to be more complicated than originally posited by Massey (1990), Quillian (2012:370) nonetheless concluded that given conditions prevailing in metropolitan America, "Massey's theoretical argument is correct: segregation and poverty concentration interact for the reasons Massey's simulation model made clear."

Subsequent research has confirmed the close connection between black segregation and spatially concentrated disadvantage, as well as the strong negative influence of concentrated disadvantage on black life chances (Massey and Brodmann 2014; Sharkey 2013). Owing primarily to racial segregation, black and white distributions of average neighborhood income barely overlap (Sampson 2012). As a result, the most affluent African Americans routinely experience levels of neighborhood disadvantage that are rarely faced even by the poorest whites (Massey and Brodmann 2014; Peterson and Krivo 2010). According to Sharkey, one-half of all African Americans have lived in the poorest quartile of urban neighborhoods for at least two consecutive generations, compared with just 7% of whites; and "the reason children end up in neighborhood environments similar to those of their parents is not that their parents have passed on a set of skills, resources, or abilities to their children. . . . Instead, parents pass on the place itself to their children" (Sharkey 2013:21).

Owing to the important role that it plays in concentrating poverty, therefore, segregation is critical to understanding racial stratification in the United States today. The concentration of neighborhood poverty is particularly high in "hypersegregated" areas such as Chicago (Sampson 2012). Whenever a group is highly segregated along multiple geographic dimensions it is said to be hypersegregated. In their analysis of 1980 census data, Massey and Denton (1989) found that in 16 metropolitan areas, African Americans were highly segregated on at least four of the five characteristic dimensions of segregation. Using 1990 census data, Denton (1994) expanded the list of black hypersegregated metropolitan areas to 29; and in their analysis of 2000 census data, Wilkes and Iceland (2004) also

Questions to Consider

Massey and Tannen point out that almost all racial and ethnic groups in the United States are highly segregated. This has been true for decades. What is most disturbing in their analysis is that as of 2010, "roughly one-third of all black metropolitan residents lived in hypersegregated areas." Why is residential segregation the norm rather than the exception, and why is it that black residential segregation is consistently the most severe?

identified 29 hypersegregated areas, although not necessarily the same ones identified by Denton.

Here we update prior work on hypersegregation using data from the 2010 census. Rather than restricting our attention to just one census year, however, we place the subject in a broader historical context by analyzing trends across a large set of consistently defined metropolitan areas from 1970 to 2010. We begin by describing our data and methods, and then proceed to document changes in the number of hypersegregated areas and average levels of segregation observed across five dimensions over the past four decades. Turning our attention to 2010, we identify 21 metropolitan areas where African Americans remain hypersegregated and then analyze trends and patterns of segregation in these metropolitan areas to assess the extent to which African Americans continue to be hypersegregated more than four decades after the passage of the Fair Housing Act.

DATA AND METHODS

As noted earlier, the concept of hypersegregation was developed by Massey and Denton (1989) to describe metropolitan areas in which African Americans were highly segregated on at least four of the five dimensions of segregation they had identified in an earlier analysis (Massey and Denton 1988). *Unevenness* is the degree to which blacks and whites are unevenly distributed across neighborhoods in a metropolitan area; *isolation* is the extent to which African Americans live in predominantly black neighborhoods; *clustering* is the degree to which neighborhoods inhabited by African Americans are clustered together in space; *concentration* is the relative amount of physical space occupied by African Americans within a given metropolitan environment; and *centralization* is the degree to which blacks reside near the center of a metropolitan area.

For this study, we drew on census tract data compiled by Logan and Stults (2011) for 287 consistently defined metropolitan areas from 1980 to 2010, and for 1970, we extracted tract data for the same set of metropolitan areas using the professional version of Social Explorer (www.socialexplorer.com). Following the procedures of Massey and Denton (1989),

we measured unevenness using the black-white dissimilarity index, isolation using the P* black isolation index, clustering using the black-white spatial proximity index, concentration using the relative concentration index, and centralization using the absolute centralization index. Using census tracts to indicate "neighborhoods," we computed all five indices for African Americans in each metropolitan area during each census year. Readers are referred to Massey and Denton's (1988) original article for formal definitions, formulae, and detailed discussion of the five measures. Here we offer brief conceptual descriptions of the indices and what they measure.

The dissimilarity index gives the relative number of blacks and whites who would have to exchange neighborhoods to achieve an even residential distribution (Duncan and Duncan 1955), and the P* isolation index states the percentage of African Americans living in the neighborhood of the average black resident (Lieberson 1981). The spatial proximity index assesses the differential clustering in space of blacks and whites and equals 0 if there is no difference in clustering and 100 when all blacks are clustered together in a set of contiguous black neighborhoods and all whites are clustered together in a set of contiguous white neighborhoods (White 1983). The final two indices derive from work by Duncan et al. (1961). The concentration index compares the total amount of physical space occupied by blacks and whites and takes a value of 0 when two groups occupy the same amount of space and 100 when blacks occupy the smallest amount of physical space possible compared with whites. The centralization index gives the proportion of blacks who would have to change neighborhoods to achieve an even distribution around the geographic center of the metropolitan area.

FOUR DECADES OF BLACK HYPERSEGREGATION

Over the period from 1970 to 2010, 52 metropolitan areas satisfied the criteria for black hypersegregation at one point or another. These metropolitan areas are listed in alphabetical order in Table 1. When it comes

TABLE 1 ■ Metropolitan Areas Ever Hypersegregated, 1970–2010

Albany, GA	Dayton, OH	Las Vegas, NV	Richmond, VA
Amarillo, TX	Denver, CO	Louisville, KY	Roanoke, VA
Asheville, NC	Detroit, MI	Milwaukee, WI	Rochester, NY
Atlanta, GA	Flint, MI	Mobile, AL	Saginaw, MI
Baltimore, MD	Fort Wayne, IN	Monroe, LA	Savannah, GA
Birmingham, AL	Gadsden, AL	Muncie, IN	Springfield, MA
Boston, MA	Grand Rapids, MI	Nashville, TN	St. Louis, MO
Buffalo, NY	Hartford, CT	New Orleans, LA	Syracuse, NY
Chattanooga, TN	Houston, TX	New York, NY-NJ	Toledo, OH
Chicago, IL	Indianapolis, IN	Oklahoma City, OK	Washington, DC
Cincinnati, OH	Jacksonville, FL	Omaha, NE-IA	Wichita, KS
Cleveland, OH	Kansas City, MO	Philadelphia, PA	Winston-Salem, NC
Columbus, OH	Lakeland, FL	Pittsburgh, PA	York, PA

to the hypersegregation of African Americans, the South historically has led the way, with 22 entries on the list, followed by 18 in the Midwest and 12 in the Northeast, but only two in the West: Denver and Las Vegas. The list obviously contains many exemplars of well-known segregated black ghetto communities. In the Northeast, the list includes New York and Philadelphia; in the Midwest, Chicago, Cleveland, and Detroit; and in the South, Baltimore, the District of Columbia, and New Orleans.

At no point between 1970 and 2010 were all 52 metropolitan areas hypersegregated at the same time, however. Over the four decades, segregation in some areas intensified to meet the criteria for hypersegregation, while in other areas segregation moderated to drop out of that classification. Figure 1 shows trends in the number of hypersegregated areas from 1970 through 2010, along with average segregation scores computed across the five dimensions. In 1970, just after the 1968 Fair Housing Act banned racial discrimination in the sale or rental of homes—but before the 1974 Equal Credit Opportunity Act and the 1977 Community Reinvestment Act had outlawed lending discrimination against black individuals and neighborhoods—40 metropolitan areas satisfied the criteria for black hypersegregation. In the wake of the civil rights legislation of the 1960s and 1970s, however, the number dropped to 35 in 1980; but the number changed little over the next two decades, remaining at 33 in 2000. It was only after 2000 that the number of hypersegregated areas substantially declined to reach 21 in 2010.

Figure 1 also shows the trend in average segregation across five dimensions to reveal the very slow pace of integration in hypersegregated areas. The average segregation score remained at roughly 75 from 1970 to 1990 before declining to 73 in 2000 and then to 70 in 2010; still, 70 is a very high level of segregation by any standard. Despite the modest decline in segregation within hypersegregated metropolitan areas by 2010, however, the drop in the *number* of hypersegregated areas nonetheless reduced African Americans' exposure to extreme segregation over the period. Figure 2 presents bar charts to indicate the relative number of blacks who

FIGURE 1 ■ Number of Metropolitan Areas Where African Americans Were Hypersegregated and Average Level Five-Dimensional Segregation

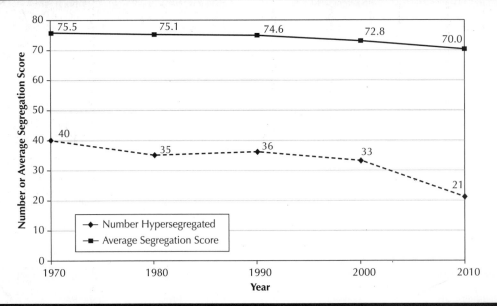

FIGURE 2 ■ Percentage of African Americans Living in Hypersegregated Metropolitan Areas

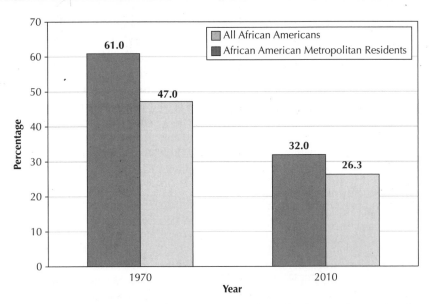

experienced hypersegregation in 1970 and 2010. Among all African Americans living in the United States in 1970, nearly one-half (47%) lived in a hypersegregated metropolitan area, a figure that fell to 26% by 2010 (data on total black populations come from the decennial census). Likewise, among black metropolitan residents, 61% were hypersegregated in 1970 compared with 32% in 2010. Clearly, then, some progress toward residential desegregation has been made over the past four decades.

BLACK HYPERSEGREGATION IN 2010

In Figure 3, we consider the overall exposure of metropolitan African Americans to segregation in the present day by classifying African Americans into five categories based on the degree of segregation prevailing in the metropolitan areas where they lived in 2010. The first category, Hypersegregated 5, includes metropolitan areas where African Americans are highly segregated across all five dimensions simultaneously. It accounts for 14% of all black metropolitan residents. These are the most racially segregated metropolitan areas in America. Another 18% of black metropolitan residents live in Hypersegregated 4 areas, where blacks are segregated on four of the five geographic dimensions. The 21% of black urban dwellers classified as living in High Segregation metropolitan areas live in areas that have a dissimilarity index of 60 or greater but do not satisfy the criteria for hypersegregation. Adding across these three categories, we see that more than one-half of all metropolitan African Americans continued to live under conditions of high segregation or hypersegregation in 2010.

Moderate Segregation is defined as living in a metropolitan area where the black-white dissimilarity index varies from 30 to 60, and 46% of all black metropolitan residents live under such circumstances, leaving just 0.8% of all black metropolitan residents who live in an area characterized by Low Segregation (a dissimilarity index less than 30). By way of contrast, in 2010, 94% of Asians and 74% of Hispanics lived in metropolitan areas characterized by moderate residential segregation, and 6% of the former and 2% of the latter live in areas characterized by low segregation. Therefore, whereas low-to-moderate segregation is experienced by a minority of African Americans, these residential circumstances are experienced by all Asians and three quarters of Hispanics, underscoring the continued distinctiveness of black segregation in metropolitan America.

FIGURE 3 ■ Percentage of Metropolitan African Americans Living at Different Levels of Racial Segregation in 2010

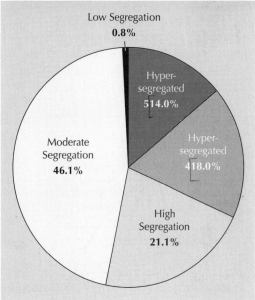

Low Segregation 0.8%

Hypersegregated 5 14.0%

Hypersegregated 4 18.0%

Moderate Segregation 46.1%

High Segregation 21.1%

Table 2 lists the specific metropolitan areas where African Americans were still hypersegregated in 2010. The top panel shows areas where black segregation was high across all five dimensions, and the bottom panel shows areas where black segregation was high on just four dimensions. With two exceptions, the top panel is dominated by older manufacturing centers in the Midwest (Chicago, Cleveland, Detroit, Flint, and St. Louis); and the two metropolitan areas from the South, Baltimore and Birmingham, are among the most industrial areas in that region. The bottom panel includes two Midwestern areas (Dayton and Kansas City), as well as six industrial areas in the Northeast (Boston, Hartford, New York, Philadelphia, Rochester, and Syracuse). The five remaining five hypersegregated areas are all in the South (Chattanooga, Gadsden, Mobile, Monroe, and Winston-Salem).

A cursory perusal of the average scores computed for each dimension at the bottom of each panel reveals that segregation levels are

TABLE 2 ■ Hypersegregated Metropolitan Areas in 2010						
	Unevenness	Isolation	Clustering	Concentration	Centralization	Average
High Score on All Five Dimensions						
Baltimore	64.3	62.4	62.6	79.1	79.1	69.5
Birmingham	65.2	62.6	78.3	68.3	79.3	70.7
Chicago	75.2	64.8	86.3	79.1	79.6	77.0
Cleveland	72.6	64.7	80.6	85.4	81.9	77.0
Detroit	74.0	70.0	82.6	86.2	74.6	77.5
Flint	67.3	61.7	84.2	80.1	84.1	75.5
Milwaukee	79.6	65.5	100.0	87.1	91.2	84.7
St. Louis	70.6	62.0	75.9	87.3	91.2	77.4
Average	71.1	64.2	81.3	81.6	82.6	76.2
High Score on Four Dimensions						
Boston	61.5	31.1	64.8	75.2	79.2	62.4
Chattanooga	63.0	48.6	66.8	78.8	62.6	64.0
Dayton	63.3	55.1	63.4	70.4	76.7	65.8
Gadsden	66.4	47.0	67.2	81.7	81.4	68.7
Hartford	62.3	35.4	80.5	71.1	70.7	64.0
Kansas City	58.6	43.3	52.1	86.5	88.1	65.7
Mobile	59.0	62.2	42.0	68.4	72.6	60.8
Monroe	63.4	66.7	62.6	51.7	71.6	63.2
New York	76.9	51.3	78.6	80.6	83.6	74.2
Philadelphia	67.0	55.8	85.0	69.7	70.0	69.5
Rochester	63.0	40.3	98.9	75.7	78.6	71.3
Syracuse	64.6	37.5	69.0	83.7	87.5	68.5
Winston-Salem	56.1	43.4	55.4	74.8	81.2	62.2
Average	63.5	47.5	68.2	74.5	77.2	66.2

generally higher in metropolitan areas where African Americans remain highly segregated across all five dimensions. With respect to unevenness, the average black-white dissimilarity score is 71.1 in the top panel but 63.5 in the bottom panel. In terms of black isolation indices, the respective numbers are 64.2 and 47.5. Isolation is the dimension on which metropolitan areas most commonly fall short of inclusion in the Hypersegregation 5 category. On the remaining three dimensions, the top and bottom averages are generally closer, with respective figures of 81.3 and 68.2 for clustering, 81.6 and 74.5 for concentration, and 82.6 and 77.2 for centralization.

Considering segregation scores averaged for each metropolitan area across all five dimensions (the last column), by far the most segregated metropolitan area in the United States is clearly Milwaukee, with an average five-dimensional score of around 85—some 9% greater than its next closest competitor, Detroit, at 78. After Detroit, the next highest scores occur in St. Louis, Cleveland, and Chicago, each with a score around 77. Flint comes in at 75; New York, at 74; and Rochester and Birmingham, at 71. Philadelphia and Baltimore are tied for 10th place, with an average score of around 70. A casual perusal of the research literature reveals that these metropolitan areas, as well as the rest of those on the list, continue to account for a disproportionate share of the nation's neighborhoods of concentrated disadvantage and poverty (see Jargowsky 1997; Peterson and Krivo 2010; Sampson 2012; Sharkey 2013; Small 2004).

Inspection of trends in average five-dimensional segregation scores reveals little evidence of decline in segregation in these urban centers (not shown). Segregation increased in some metropolitan areas and declined in others, but scores converged on a narrow range above 60. In those areas that were highly segregated on all five dimensions, average scores fell in the range of 71 to 86 by 2010; by contrast, in areas segregated on four dimensions, scores fell in the range of 61 to 74. Of the six metropolitan areas where average segregation levels increased from 1970 to 2010, five were in the South (Birmingham, Chattanooga, Gadsden, Mobile, and Monroe). As Massey and Denton (1993) noted, when the social segregation of Jim Crow broke down in the wake of the Civil Rights Era, it was replaced increasingly by residential segregation.

CONCLUSION

Until the civil rights era of the 1960s, high segregation was almost universal across U.S. metropolitan areas. In 1970, 61% of all black urbanites lived in one of 40 hypersegregated metropolitan areas, constituting nearly half the total black population of the United States. Over the ensuing four decades, some metropolitan areas ceased being hypersegregated but others became hypersegregated, yielding a total of 52 areas that experienced the condition at some point over the period. The total number of hypersegregated areas nonetheless fell over time, slowly before 2000 and more rapidly thereafter; but the average level of multidimensional segregation within hypersegregated areas changed relatively little. Although the number of such areas was almost cut in half from 1970 to 2010, falling from 40 to 21, average segregation within hypersegregated areas fell by only 8%, going from 75.5 to 70. Nonetheless the share of black metropolitan residents living under conditions of hypersegregation dropped to around one-third by 2010.

Despite evidence of progress in many metropolitan areas, therefore, the United States has not become a race-blind society. Because of segregation, race continues to matter a great deal in determining the fate of African Americans (Sharkey 2013). Research shows that black neighborhoods were specifically targeted for predatory lending during the housing boom (Hartman and Squires 2013) and that the level of black-white segregation was the strongest single predictor of the number and rate of foreclosures across metropolitan areas during the housing bust (Rugh and Massey 2010). Whereas mortgages to white borrowers were issued mainly for the purchase of homes, those issued to blacks were predominantly home equity loans, often to borrowers whose homes were paid off (Rugh et al. forthcoming). As a result, African Americans experienced a far greater loss of wealth than whites during the housing bust (Kochhar et al. 2011).

Although hypersegregation may have become less common in recent years, it hasn't disappeared, but has instead become centered in a subset of metropolitan areas containing some of the nation's largest black communities. It is perhaps no coincidence that as of this writing, Ferguson, MO, a predominantly black suburb in the hypersegregated St. Louis metropolitan area is under National Guard occupation to prevent rioting in the wake of a police shooting, putting it at the center of discussions about the meaning of race in the Age of Obama. Although the United States may have been able to elect a black President, it has not been able to eradicate hypersegregation from its urban areas, and we can continue to expect a disproportionate share of the nation's racial conflicts and disturbances to occur within these intensely segregated landscapes.

ACKNOWLEDGMENTS

The authors thank Jacob Rugh for sharing his data and saving us time and effort.

Seeing the Big Picture   **How Integrated Is Your Neighborhood?**

The index of dissimilarity is a measure of how residentially segregated one population is from another. A score of 0 would mean groups are randomly distributed throughout a particular area while a score of 100 would mean groups share no social space with one another. What do the index of dissimilarity numbers in Section II of the appendix tell us about residential segregation in the United States?

23

THE CODE OF THE STREETS

Elijah Anderson

ELIJAH ANDERSON is William K. Lanman, Jr. Professor of Sociology at Yale University. He is the author of *Streetwise: Race, Class and Change in an Urban Community* (1990) and *The Code of the Streets* (1999).

OF ALL THE PROBLEMS BESETTING THE POOR inner-city black community, none is more pressing than that of interpersonal violence and aggression. It wreaks havoc daily with the lives of community residents and increasingly spills over into downtown and residential middle-class areas. Muggings, burglaries, carjackings, and drug-related shootings, all of which may leave their victims or innocent bystanders dead, are now common enough to concern all urban and many suburban residents. The inclination to violence springs from the circumstances of life among the ghetto poor— the lack of jobs that pay a living wage, the stigma of race, the fallout from rampant drug use and drug trafficking, and the resulting alienation and lack of hope for the future.

Simply living in such an environment places young people at special risk of falling victim to aggressive behavior. Although there are often forces in the community which can counteract the negative influences, by far the most powerful being a strong, loving, "decent" (as inner-city residents put it) family committed to middle-class values, the despair is pervasive enough to have spawned an oppositional culture, that of "the streets," whose norms are often consciously opposed to those of mainstream society. These two orientations—decent and street—socially organize the community, and their coexistence has important consequences for residents, particularly children growing up in the inner city. Above all, this environment means that even youngsters whose home lives reflect mainstream values—and the majority of homes in the community do—must be able to handle themselves in a street-oriented environment.

This is because the street culture has evolved what may be called a code of the streets, which amounts to a set of informal rules governing interpersonal public behavior, including violence. The rules prescribe both a proper comportment and a proper way to respond if challenged. They regulate the use of violence and so allow those who are inclined to aggression to precipitate violent encounters in an approved way. The rules have been established and are enforced mainly by the street-oriented, but on the streets the distinction between street and decent is often irrelevant; everybody knows that if the rules are violated, there are penalties. Knowledge of the code is thus largely defensive; it is literally necessary for operating in public. Therefore, even though families with a decency orientation are usually opposed to the values of the code, they often reluctantly encourage their children's familiarity with it to enable them to negotiate the inner-city environment.

At the heart of the code is the issue of respect— loosely defined as being treated "right," or granted the deference one deserves. However, in the troublesome public environment of the inner city, as people increasingly feel buffeted by forces beyond their control, what one deserves in the way of respect becomes more and more problematic and uncertain. This in turn further opens the issue of respect to sometimes intense interpersonal negotiation. In the street culture, especially among young people, respect is viewed as almost an external entity that is hard-won but easily lost, and so must constantly be guarded. The rules of the code in fact provide a framework for negotiating respect. The person whose very appearance—including his clothing, demeanor, and way of moving—deters transgressions feels that he possesses, and may be considered by others to possess, a measure of respect. With the

Questions to Consider

In "The Code of the Streets," Elijah Anderson chronicles how an individual's environment can create a set of expectations that is at odds with the "dominant" culture. How is "oppositional culture" often detrimental to children and young adults in these communities? How is oppositional culture linked to Anderson's discussion of "street" and "decent" families?

right amount of respect, for instance, he can avoid "being bothered" in public. If he is bothered, not only may he be in physical danger but he has been disgraced or "dissed" (disrespected). Many of the forms that dissing can take might seem petty to middle-class people (maintaining eye contact for too long, for example), but to those invested in the street code, these actions become serious indications of the other person's intentions. Consequently, such people become very sensitive to advances and slights, which could well serve as warnings of imminent physical confrontation.

This hard reality can be traced to the profound sense of alienation from mainstream society and its institutions felt by many poor inner-city black people, particularly the young. The code of the streets is actually a cultural adaptation to a profound lack of faith in the police and the judicial system. The police are most often seen as representing the dominant white society and not caring to protect inner-city residents. When called, they may not respond, which is one reason many residents feel they must be prepared to take extraordinary measures to defend themselves and their loved ones against those who are inclined to aggression. Lack of police accountability has in fact been incorporated into the status system: the person who is believed capable of "taking care of himself" is accorded a certain deference, which translates into a sense of physical and psychological control. Thus the street code emerges where the influence of the police ends and personal responsibility for one's safety is felt to begin. Exacerbated by the proliferation of drugs and easy access to guns, this volatile situation results in the ability of the street-oriented minority (or those who effectively "go for bad") to dominate the public spaces.

DECENT AND STREET FAMILIES

Although almost everyone in poor inner-city neighborhoods is struggling financially and therefore feels a certain distance from the rest of America,

the decent and the street family in a real sense represent two poles of value orientation, two contrasting conceptual categories. The labels "decent" and "street," which the residents themselves use, amount to evaluative judgments that confer status on local residents. The labeling is often the result of a social contest among individuals and families of the neighborhood. Individuals of the two orientations often coexist in the same extended family. Decent residents judge themselves to be so while judging others to be of the street, and street individuals often present themselves as decent, drawing distinctions between themselves and other people. In addition, there is quite a bit of circumstantial behavior—that is, one person may at different times exhibit both decent and street orientations, depending on the circumstances. Although these designations result from so much social jockeying, there do exist concrete features that define each conceptual category.

Generally, so-called decent families tend to accept mainstream values more fully and attempt to instill them in their children. Whether married couples with children or single-parent (usually female) households, they are generally "working poor" and so tend to be better off financially than their street-oriented neighbors. They value hard work and self-reliance and are willing to sacrifice for their children. Because they have a certain amount of faith in mainstream society, they harbor hopes for a better future for their children, if not for themselves. Many of them go to church and take a strong interest in their children's schooling. Rather than dwelling on the real hardships and inequities facing them, many such decent people, particularly the increasing number of grandmothers raising grandchildren, see their difficult situation as a test from God and derive great support from their faith and from the church community.

Extremely aware of the problematic and often dangerous environment in which they reside, decent parents tend to be strict in their child-rearing practices, encouraging children to respect authority and walk a straight moral line. They have an almost obsessive concern about trouble of any kind and remind their children to be on the lookout for people and situations that might lead to it. At the same time, they are themselves polite and considerate of others, and teach their children to be the same way. At home, at work, and in church, they strive hard to maintain a positive mental attitude and a spirit of cooperation.

So-called street parents, in contrast, often show a lack of consideration for other people and have a rather superficial sense of family and community. Though they may love their children, many of them are unable to cope with the physical and emotional demands of parenthood, and find it difficult to reconcile their needs with those of their children. These families, who are more fully invested in the code of the streets than the decent people are, may aggressively socialize their children into it in a normative way. They believe in the code and judge themselves and others according to its values.

In fact the overwhelming majority of families in the inner-city community try to approximate the decent-family model, but there are many others who clearly represent the worst fears of the decent family. Not only are their financial resources extremely limited, but what little they have may easily be misused. The lives of the street-oriented are often marked by disorganization. In the most desperate circumstances people frequently have a limited understanding of priorities and consequences, and so frustrations mount over bills, food, and, at times, drink, smoke cigarettes, and do drugs. Some tend toward self-destructive behavior; many street-oriented women are crack-addicted ("on the pipe"), alcoholic, or involved in complicated relationships with men who abuse them. In addition, the seeming intractability of their situation, caused in large part by the lack of well-paying jobs and the persistence of racial discrimination, has engendered deep-seated bitterness and anger in many of the most desperate and poorest blacks, especially young people. The need both to exercise a measure of control and to lash out at somebody is often reflected in the adults' relations with their children. At the least, the frustrations of persistent poverty shorten the fuse in such people—contributing to a lack of patience with anyone, child or adult, who irritates them.

In these circumstances a woman—or a man, although men are less consistently present in children's lives—can be quite aggressive with children, yelling at and striking them for the least little infraction of the rules she has set down. Often little if any serious explanation follows the verbal and physical punishment. This response teaches children a particular lesson. They learn that to solve any kind of interpersonal problem one must quickly resort to hitting or other violent behavior. Actual peace and quiet, and also the appearance of calm, respectful children conveyed to her neighbors and friends, are often what the young mother most desires, but at times she will be very aggressive in trying to get them. Thus she may be quick to beat her children, especially if they defy her law, not because she hates them but because this is the way she knows to control them. In fact, many street-oriented women love their children dearly. Many mothers in the community subscribe to the notion that there is a "devil in the boy" that must be beaten out of him or that socially "fast girls need to be whupped." Thus much of what borders on child abuse in the view of social authorities is acceptable parental punishment in the view of these mothers.

Many street-oriented women are sporadic mothers whose children learn to fend for themselves when necessary, foraging for food and money any way they can get it. The children are sometimes employed by drug dealers or become addicted themselves. These children of the street, growing up with little supervision, are said to "come up hard." They often learn to fight at an early age, sometimes using short-tempered adults around them as role models. The street-oriented home may be fraught with anger, verbal disputes, physical aggression, and even mayhem. The children observe these goings-on, learning the lesson that might makes right. They quickly learn to hit those who cross them, and the dog-eat-dog mentality prevails. In order to survive, to protect oneself, it is necessary to marshal inner resources and be ready to deal with adversity in a hands-on way. In these circumstances physical prowess takes on great significance.

In some of the most desperate cases, a street-oriented mother may simply leave her young children alone and unattended while she goes out. The most irresponsible women can be found at local bars and crack houses, getting high and socializing with other adults. Sometimes a troubled woman will leave very young children alone for days at a time. Reports of crack addicts abandoning their children have become common in drug-infested inner-city communities. Neighbors or relatives discover the abandoned children, often hungry and distraught over the absence of their mother. After repeated absences, a friend or relative, particularly a grandmother, will often step in to care for the young children, sometimes petitioning the authorities to send her, as guardian of the children, the mother's welfare check, if the mother gets one. By this time, however, the children may well have learned the first lesson of the streets: survival itself, let alone respect, cannot be taken for granted; you have to fight for your place in the world.

CAMPAIGNING FOR RESPECT

These realities of inner-city life are largely absorbed on the streets. At an early age, often even before they start school, children from street-oriented homes gravitate to the streets, where they "hang"—socialize with their peers. Children from these generally permissive homes have a great deal of latitude and are allowed to "rip and run" up and down the street. They often come home from school, put their books down, and go right back out the door. On school nights eight- and nine-year-olds remain out until nine or ten o'clock (and teenagers typically come in whenever they want to). On the streets they play in groups that often become the source of their primary social bonds. Children from decent homes tend to be more carefully supervised and are thus likely to have curfews and to be taught how to stay out of trouble.

When decent and street kids come together, a kind of social shuffle occurs in which children have a chance to go either way. Tension builds as a child comes to realize that he must choose an orientation.

The kind of home he comes from influences but does not determine the way he will ultimately turn out—although it is unlikely that a child from a thoroughly street-oriented family will easily absorb decent values on the streets. Youths who emerge from street-oriented families but develop a decency orientation almost always learn those values in another setting—in school, in a youth group, in church. Often it is the result of their involvement with a caring "old head" (adult role model).

In the street, through their play, children pour their individual life experiences into a common knowledge pool, affirming, confirming, and elaborating on what they have observed in the home and matching their skills against those of others. And they learn to fight. Even small children test one another, pushing and shoving, and are ready to hit other children over circumstances not to their liking. In turn, they are readily hit by other children, and the child who is toughest prevails. Thus the violent resolution of disputes, the hitting and cursing, gains social reinforcement. The child in effect is initiated into a system that is really a way of campaigning for respect.

In addition, younger children witness the disputes of older children, which are often resolved through cursing and abusive talk, if not aggression or outright violence. They see that one child succumbs to the greater physical and mental abilities of the other. They are also alert and attentive witnesses to the verbal and physical fights of adults, after which they compare notes and share their interpretations of the event. In almost every case the victor is the person who physically won the altercation, and this person often enjoys the esteem and respect of onlookers. These experiences reinforce the lessons the children have learned at home: might makes right, and toughness is a virtue, while humility is not. In effect they learn the social meaning of fighting. When it is left virtually unchallenged, this understanding becomes an ever more important part of the child's working conception of the world. Over time the code of the streets becomes refined.

Those street-oriented adults with whom children come in contact—including mothers, fathers, brothers, sisters, boyfriends, cousins, neighbors, and friends—help them along in forming this understanding by verbalizing the messages they are getting through experience: "Watch your back." "Protect yourself." "Don't punk out." "If somebody messes with you, you got to pay them back." "If someone disses you, you got to straighten them out." Many parents actually impose sanctions if a child is not sufficiently aggressive. For example, if a child loses a fight and comes home upset, the parent might respond, "Don't you come in here crying that somebody beat you up; you better get back out there and whup his ass. I didn't raise no punks! Get back out there and whup his ass. If you don't whup his ass, I'll whup your ass when you come home." Thus the child obtains reinforcement for being tough and showing nerve.

While fighting, some children cry as though they are doing something they are ambivalent about. The fight may be against their wishes, yet they may feel constrained to fight or face the consequences—not just from peers but also from caretakers or parents, who may administer another beating if they back down. Some adults recall receiving such lessons from their own parents and justify repeating them to their children as a way to toughen them up. Looking capable of taking care of oneself as a form of self-defense is a dominant theme among both street-oriented and decent adults who worry about the safety of their children. There is thus at times a convergence in their child-rearing practices, although the rationales behind them may differ.

SELF-IMAGE BASED ON "JUICE"

By the time they are teenagers, most youths have either internalized the code of the streets or at least learned the need to comport themselves in accordance with its rules, which chiefly have to do with interpersonal communication. The code revolves around the presentation of self. Its basic requirement is the display of a certain predisposition to violence. Accordingly, one's bearing must send the unmistakable if sometimes subtle message to "the next person" in public that one is capable of violence and mayhem when the situation requires it, that one can take care of oneself. The nature of this communication is largely determined by the demands of the circumstances but can include facial expressions, gait, and verbal expressions—all of which are geared mainly to deterring aggression. Physical appearance, including clothes, jewelry, and grooming, also plays an important part in how a person is viewed; to be respected, it is important to have the right look.

Even so, there are no guarantees against challenges, because there are always people around looking for a fight to increase their share of respect—or "juice," as it is sometimes called on the street. Moreover, if a person is assaulted, it is important, not only in the eyes of his opponent but also in the eyes of his "running buddies," for him to avenge himself. Otherwise he risks being "tried" (challenged) or "moved on" by any number of others. To maintain his honor he must show he is not someone to be "messed with" or "dissed." In general, the person must "keep himself straight" by managing his position of respect among others; this involves in part his self-image, which is shaped by what he thinks others are thinking of him in relation to his peers.

Objects play an important and complicated role in establishing self-image. Jackets, sneakers, gold jewelry, reflect not just a person's taste, which tends to be tightly regulated among adolescents of all social classes, but also a willingness to possess things that may require defending. A boy wearing a fashionable, expensive jacket, for example, is vulnerable to attack by another who covets the jacket and either cannot afford to buy one or wants the added satisfaction of depriving someone else of his. However, if the boy forgoes the desirable jacket and wears one that isn't "hip," he runs the risk of being teased and possibly even assaulted as an unworthy person. To be allowed to hang with certain prestigious crowds, a boy must wear a different set of expensive clothes—sneakers and athletic suit—every day. Not to be able to do so might make him appear socially deficient. The youth comes to covet such items—especially when he sees easy prey wearing them.

In acquiring valued things, therefore, a person shores up his identity—but since it is an identity based on having things, it is highly precarious. This very precariousness gives a heightened sense of urgency to staying even with peers, with whom the person is actually competing. Young men and women who are able to command respect through their presentation of self—by allowing their possessions and their body language to speak for them—may not have to campaign for regard but may, rather, gain it by the force of their manner. Those who are unable to command respect in this way must actively campaign for it—and are thus particularly alive to slights.

One way of campaigning for status is by taking the possessions of others. In this context, seemingly ordinary objects can become trophies imbued with symbolic value that far exceeds their monetary worth. Possession of the trophy can symbolize the ability to violate somebody—to "get in his face," to take something of value from him, to "dis" him, and thus to enhance one's own worth by stealing someone else's. The trophy does not have to be something material. It can be another person's sense of honor, snatched away with a derogatory remark. It can be the outcome of a fight. It can be the imposition of a certain standard, such as a girl's getting herself recognized as the most beautiful. Material things, however, fit easily into the pattern. Sneakers, a pistol, even somebody else's girlfriend, can become a trophy. When a person can take something from another and then flaunt it, he gains a certain regard by being the owner, or the controller, of that thing. But this display of ownership can then provoke other people to challenge him. This game of who controls what is thus constantly being played out on inner-city streets, and the trophy—extrinsic or intrinsic, tangible or intangible—identifies the current winner.

An important aspect of this often violent give-and-take is its zero-sum quality. That is, the extent to which one person can raise himself up depends on his ability to put another person down. This underscores the alienation that permeates the inner-city ghetto community. There is a generalized sense that very little respect is to be had, and therefore everyone competes to get what affirmation he can of the little that is available. The craving for respect that results gives people thin skins. Shows of deference by others can be highly soothing, contributing to a sense of security, comfort, self-confidence, and self-respect. Transgressions by others which go unanswered diminish these feelings and are believed to encourage further transgressions. Hence one must be ever vigilant against the transgressions of others or even *appearing* as if transgressions will be tolerated. Among young people, whose sense of self-esteem is particularly vulnerable, there is an especially heightened concern with being disrespected. Many inner-city young men in particular crave respect to such a degree that they will risk their lives to attain and maintain it.

The issue of respect is thus closely tied to whether a person has an inclination to be violent, even as a victim. In the wider society people may not feel required to retaliate physically after an attack, even though they are aware that they have been degraded or taken advantage of. They may feel a great need to defend themselves *during* an attack, or to behave in such a way as to deter aggression (middle-class people certainly can and do become victims of street-oriented youths), but they are much more likely than street-oriented people to feel that they can walk away from a possible altercation with their self-esteem intact. Some people may even have the strength of character to flee, without any thought that their self-respect or esteem will be diminished.

In impoverished inner-city black communities, however, particularly among young males and perhaps increasingly among females, such flight would be extremely difficult. To run away would likely leave one's self-esteem in tatters. Hence people often feel constrained not only to stand up and at least attempt to resist during an assault but also to "pay back"—to seek revenge—after a successful assault on their person. This may include going to get a weapon or even getting relatives involved. Their very identity and self-respect, their honor, is often intricately tied up with the way they perform on the streets during and after such encounters. This outlook reflects the circumscribed opportunities of the inner-city poor. Generally people outside the ghetto have other ways of gaining status and regard, and thus do not feel so dependent on such physical displays.

BY TRIAL OF MANHOOD

On the street, among males these concerns about things and identity have come to be expressed in the concept of "manhood." Manhood in the inner city means taking the prerogatives of men with respect to strangers, other men, and women—being distinguished as a man. It implies physicality and a certain ruthlessness. Regard and respect are associated with this concept in large part because of its practical application: if others have little or no regard for a person's manhood, his very life and those of his loved ones could be in jeopardy. But there is a chicken-and-egg aspect to this situation: one's physical safety is more likely to be jeopardized in public *because* manhood is associated with respect. In other words, an existential link has been created between the idea of manhood and one's self-esteem, so that it has become hard to say which is primary. For many inner-city youths, manhood and respect are flip sides of the same coin; physical and psychological well-being are inseparable, and both require a sense of control, of being in charge.

The operating assumption is that a man, especially a real man, knows what other men know—the code of the streets. And if one is not a real man, one is somehow diminished as a person, and there are certain valued things one simply does not deserve. There is thus believed to be a certain justice to the code, since it is considered that everyone has the opportunity to know it. Implicit in this is that everybody is held responsible for being familiar with the code. If the victim of a mugging, for example, does not know the code and so responds "wrong," the perpetrator may feel justified even in killing him and may feel no remorse. He may think, "Too bad, but it's his fault. He should have known better."

So when a person ventures outside, he must adopt the code—a kind of shield, really—to prevent others from "messing with" him. In these circumstances it is easy for people to think they are being tried or tested by others even when this is not the case. For it is sensed that something extremely valuable is at stake in every interaction, and people are encouraged to rise to the occasion, particularly with strangers. For people who are unfamiliar with the code—generally people who live outside the inner city—the concern with respect in the most ordinary interactions can be frightening and incomprehensible. But for those who are invested in the code, the clear object of their demeanor is to discourage strangers from even thinking about testing their manhood. And the sense of power that attends the ability to deter others can be alluring even to those who know the code without being heavily invested in it—the decent inner-city youths. Thus a boy who has been leading a basically decent life can, in trying circumstances, suddenly resort to deadly force.

Central to the issue of manhood is the widespread belief that one of the most effective ways of gaining respect is to manifest "nerve." Nerve is shown when one takes another person's possessions (the more valuable the better), "messes with" someone's woman, throws the first punch, "gets in someone's face," or pulls a trigger. Its proper display helps on the spot to check others who would violate one's person and also helps to build a reputation that works to prevent future challenges. But since such a show of nerve is a forceful expression of disrespect toward the person on the receiving end, the victim may be greatly offended and seek to retaliate with equal or greater force. A display of nerve, therefore, can easily provoke a life-threatening response, and the background knowledge of that possibility has often been incorporated into the concept of nerve.

True nerve exposes a lack of fear of dying. Many feel that it is acceptable to risk dying over the principle of respect. In fact, among the hard-core street-oriented, the clear risk of violent death may be preferable to being "dissed" by another.

The youths who have internalized this attitude and convincingly display it in their public bearing are among the most threatening people of all, for it is commonly assumed that they fear no man. As the people of the community say, "They are the baddest dudes on the street." They often lead an existential life that may acquire meaning only when they are faced with the possibility of imminent death. Not to be afraid to die is by implication to have few compunctions about taking another's life. Not to be afraid to die is the quid pro quo of being able to take somebody else's life—for the right reasons, if the situation demands it. When others believe this is one's position, it gives one a real sense of power on the streets. Such credibility is what many inner-city youths strive to achieve, whether they are decent or street-oriented, both because of its practical defensive value and because of the positive way it makes them feel about themselves. The difference between the decent and the street-oriented youth is often that the decent youth makes a conscious decision to appear tough and manly; in another setting—with teachers, say, or at his part-time job—he can be polite and deferential. The street-oriented youth, on the other hand, has made the concept of manhood a part of his very identity; he has difficulty manipulating it—it often controls him.

GIRLS AND BOYS

Increasingly, teenage girls are mimicking the boys and trying to have their own version of "manhood." Their goal is the same—to get respect, to be recognized as capable of setting or maintaining a certain standard. They try to achieve this end in the ways that have been established by the boys, including posturing, abusive language, and the use of violence to resolve disputes, but the issues for the girls are different. Although conflicts over turf and status exist among the girls, the majority of disputes seem rooted in assessments of beauty (which girl in a group is "the cutest"), competition over boyfriends, and attempts to regulate other people's knowledge of and opinions about a girl's

behavior or that of someone close to her, especially her mother.

A major cause of conflicts among girls is "he say, she say." This practice begins in the early school years and continues through high school. It occurs when "people," particularly girls, talk about others, thus putting their "business in the streets." Usually one girl will say something negative about another in the group, most often behind the person's back. The remark will then get back to the person talked about. She may retaliate or her friends may feel required to "take up for" her. In essence this is a form of group gossiping in which individuals are negatively assessed and evaluated. As with much gossip, the things said may or may not be true, but the point is that such imputations can cast aspersions on a person's good name. The accused is required to defend herself against the slander, which can result in arguments and fights, often over little of real substance. Here again is the problem of low self-esteem, which encourages youngsters to be highly sensitive to slights and to be vulnerable to feeling easily "dissed." To avenge the dissing, a fight is usually necessary.

Because boys are believed to control violence, girls tend to defer to them in situations of conflict. Often if a girl is attacked or feels slighted, she will get a brother, uncle, or cousin to do her fighting for her. Increasingly, however, girls are doing their own fighting and are even asking their male relatives to teach them how to fight. Some girls form groups that attack other girls or take things from them. A hard-core segment of inner-city girls inclined toward violence seems to be developing. As one thirteen-year-old girl in a detention center for youths who have committed violent acts told me, "To get people to leave you alone, you gotta fight. Talking don't always get you out of stuff." One major difference between girls and boys: girls rarely use guns. Their fights are therefore not life-or-death struggles. Girls are not often willing to put their lives on the line for "manhood." The ultimate form of respect on the male-dominated inner-city street is thus reserved for men.

"GOING FOR BAD"

In the most fearsome youths such a cavalier attitude toward death grows out of a very limited view of life. Many are uncertain about how long they are going to live and believe they could die violently at any time. They accept this fate; they live on the edge. Their manner conveys the message that nothing intimidates them; whatever turn the encounter takes, they maintain their attack—rather like a pit bull, whose spirit many such boys admire. The demonstration of such tenacity "shows heart" and earns their respect.

This fearlessness has implications for law enforcement. Many street-oriented boys are much more concerned about the threat of "justice" at the hands of a peer than at the hands of the police. Moreover, many feel not only that they have little to lose by going to prison but that they have something to gain. The toughening-up one experiences in prison can actually enhance one's reputation on the streets. Hence the system loses influence over the hard core who are without jobs, with little perceptible stake in the system. If mainstream society has done nothing *for* them, they counter by making sure it can do nothing *to* them.

At the same time, however, a competing view maintains that true nerve consists in backing down, walking away from a fight, and going on with one's business. One fights only in self-defense. This view emerges from the decent philosophy that life is precious, and it is an important part of the socialization process common in decent homes. It discourages violence as the primary means of resolving disputes and encourages youngsters to accept nonviolence and talk as confrontational strategies. But "if the deal goes down," self-defense is greatly encouraged. When there is enough positive support for this orientation, either in the home or among one's peers, then nonviolence has a chance to prevail. But it prevails at the cost of relinquishing a claim to being bad and tough, and therefore sets a young person up as at the very least alienated from street-oriented peers and quite possibly a target of derision or even violence.

Although the nonviolent orientation rarely overcomes the impulse to strike back in an encounter, it does introduce a certain confusion and so can prompt a measure of soul-searching, or even profound ambivalence. Did the person back down with his respect intact or did he back down only to be judged a "punk"—a person lacking manhood? Should he or she have acted? Should he or she have hit the other person in the mouth? These questions beset many young men and women during public confrontations. What is the "right" thing to do? In the quest for honor, respect, and local status—which few young people are uninterested in—common sense most often prevails, which leads many to opt for the tough approach, enacting their own particular versions of the display of nerve. The presentation of oneself as rough and tough is very often quite acceptable until one is tested. And then that presentation may help the person pass the test, because it will cause fewer questions to be asked about what he did and why. It is hard for a person to explain why he lost the fight or why he backed down. Hence many will strive to appear to "go for bad," while hoping they will never be tested. But when they are tested, the outcome of the situation may quickly be out of their hands, as they become wrapped up in the circumstances of the moment.

AN OPPOSITIONAL CULTURE

The attitudes of the wider society are deeply implicated in the code of the streets. Most people in inner-city communities are not totally invested in the code, but the significant minority of hardcore street youths who are have to maintain the code in order to establish reputations, because they have—or feel they have—few other ways to assert themselves. For these young people the standards of the street code are the only game in town. The extent to which some children—particularly those who through upbringing have become most alienated and those lacking in strong and conventional social support—experience, feel, and internalize racist rejection and contempt from mainstream society may strongly encourage them to express contempt for the more conventional society in turn. In dealing with this contempt and rejection, some youngsters will consciously invest themselves and their considerable mental resources in what amounts to an oppositional culture to preserve themselves and their self-respect. Once they do, any respect they might be able to garner in the wider system pales in comparison with the respect available in the local system; thus they often lose interest in even attempting to negotiate the mainstream system.

At the same time, many less alienated young blacks have assumed a street-oriented demeanor as a way of expressing their blackness while really embracing a much more moderate way of life; they, too, want a nonviolent setting in which to live and raise a family. These decent people are trying hard to be part of the mainstream culture, but the racism, real and perceived, that they encounter helps to

legitimate the oppositional culture. And so on occasion they adopt street behavior. In fact, depending on the demands of the situation, many people in the community slip back and forth between decent and street behavior.

A vicious cycle has thus been formed. The hopelessness and alienation many young inner-city black men and women feel, largely as a result of endemic joblessness and persistent racism, fuel the violence they engage in. This violence serves to confirm the negative feelings many whites and some middle-class blacks harbor toward the ghetto poor, further legitimating the oppositional culture and the code of the streets in the eyes of many poor young blacks. Unless this cycle is broken, attitudes on both sides will become increasingly entrenched, and the violence, which claims victims black and white, poor and affluent, will only escalate.

ENVIRONMENTAL JUSTICE IN THE 21ST CENTURY

Race Still Matters

Robert D. Bullard

ROBERT D. BULLARD is Ware Professor of Sociology and director of the Environmental Justice Resource Center at Clark Atlanta University. He is the author of numerous articles, monographs, and scholarly papers that address environmental justice and public participation concerns. His book, *Dumping in Dixie: Race, Class and Environmental Quality* (1990, 1994, 2000), has become a standard text in the environmental justice field.

HARDLY A DAY PASSES WITHOUT THE MEDIA discovering some community or neighborhood fighting a landfill, incinerator, chemical plant, or some other polluting industry. This was not always the case. Just three decades ago, the concept of environmental justice had not registered on the radar screens of environmental, civil rights, or social justice groups.[1] Nevertheless, it should not be forgotten that Dr. Martin Luther King, Jr., went to Memphis in 1968 on an environmental and economic justice mission for the striking black garbage workers. The strikers were demanding equal pay and better work conditions. Of course, Dr. King was assassinated before he could complete his mission.

Another landmark garbage dispute took place a decade later in Houston, when African-American homeowners in 1979 began a bitter fight to keep a sanitary landfill out of their suburban middle-income neighborhood.[2] Residents formed the Northeast Community Action Group or NECAG. NECAG and their attorney, Linda McKeever Bullard, filed a class-action lawsuit to block the facility from being built. The 1979 lawsuit, *Bean v. Southwestern Waste Management, Inc.,* was the first of its kind to challenge the siting of a waste facility under civil rights law.

The landmark Houston case occurred three years before the environmental justice movement was catapulted into the national limelight in the rural and mostly African-American Warren County, North Carolina. The environmental justice movement has come a long way since its humble beginning in Warren County, North Carolina, where a PCB landfill ignited protests and over 500 arrests. The Warren County protests provided the impetus for a U.S. General Accounting Office study, *Siting of Hazardous Waste Landfills and Their Correlation with Racial and Economic Status of Surrounding Communities.*[3] That study revealed that three out of four of the off-site, commercial hazardous waste landfills in Region 4 (which comprises eight states in the South) happen to be located in predominantly African-American communities, although African Americans made up only 20 percent of the region's population. More important, the protesters put "environmental racism" on the map. Fifteen years later, the state of North Carolina is required to spend over $25 million to clean up and detoxify the Warren County PCB landfill.

The Warren County protests also led the Commission for Racial Justice to produce *Toxic Wastes and Race,*[4] the first national study to correlate waste facility sites and demographic characteristics. Race was found to be the most potent variable in predicting where these facilities were located—more powerful than poverty, land values, and home ownership. In 1990, *Dumping in Dixie: Race, Class, and Environmental Quality* chronicled the convergence of two social movements—social justice and environmental movements—into the environmental justice movement. This book highlighted African Americans' environmental activism in the South, the

Questions to Consider

Where is the trash dump, the water treatment plant, or the power plant in your community? In this reading, Robert Bullard argues that in all likelihood these environmental dangers are in low-income, black and brown neighborhoods. Why do some communities get "dumped on" while others remain free of any toxic waste sites?

same region that gave birth to the modern civil rights movement. What started out as local and often isolated community-based struggles against toxics and facility siting blossomed into a multi-issue, multiethnic, and multiregional movement.

The 1991 First National People of Color Environmental Leadership Summit was probably the most important single event in the movement's history. The Summit broadened the environmental justice movement beyond its early antitoxics focus to include issues of public health, worker safety, land use, transportation, housing, resource allocation, and community empowerment.[5] The meeting also demonstrated that it is possible to build a multiracial grassroots movement around environmental and economic justice.[6]

Held in Washington, DC, the four-day Summit was attended by over 650 grassroots and national leaders from around the world. Delegates came from all fifty states including Alaska and Hawaii, Puerto Rico, Chile, Mexico, and as far away as the Marshall Islands. People attended the Summit to share their action strategies, redefine the environmental movement, and develop common plans for addressing environmental problems affecting people of color in the United States and around the world.

On September 27, 1991, Summit delegates adopted 17 "Principles of Environmental Justice." These principles were developed as a guide for organizing, networking, and relating to government and nongovernmental organizations (NGOs). By June 1992, Spanish and Portuguese translations of the Principles were being used and circulated by NGOs and environmental justice groups at the Earth Summit in Rio de Janeiro.

In response to growing public concern and mounting scientific evidence, President Clinton on February 11, 1994 (the second day of the national health symposium), issued Executive Order 12898, "Federal Actions to Address Environmental Justice in Minority Populations and Low-Income Populations." This Order attempts to address environmental injustice within existing federal laws and regulations.

Executive Order 12898 reinforces the 35-year-old Civil Rights Act of 1964, Title VI, which prohibits discriminatory practices in programs receiving federal funds. The Order also focuses the spotlight back on the National Environmental Policy Act (NEPA), a twenty-five-year-old law that set policy goals for the protection, maintenance, and enhancement of the environment. NEPA's goal is to ensure for all Americans a safe, healthful, productive, and aesthetically and culturally pleasing environment. NEPA requires federal agencies to prepare a detailed statement on the environmental effects of proposed federal actions that significantly affect the quality of human health.

The Executive Order calls for improved methodologies for assessing and mitigating impacts, health effects from multiple and cumulative exposure, collection of data on low-income and minority populations who may be disproportionately at risk, and impacts on subsistence fishers and wildlife consumers. It also encourages participation of the impacted populations in the various phases of assessing impacts—including scoping, data gathering, alternatives, analysis, mitigation, and monitoring.

The Executive Order focuses on "subsistence" fishers and wildlife consumers. Everybody does not buy fish at the supermarket. There are many people who are subsistence fishers, who fish for protein, who basically subsidize their budgets, and their diets, by fishing from rivers, streams, and lakes that happen to be polluted. These subpopulations may be underprotected when basic assumptions are made using the dominant risk paradigm.

Many grassroots activists are convinced that waiting for the government to act has endangered the health and welfare of their communities. Unlike the federal EPA, communities of color did not first discover environmental inequities in 1990. The federal EPA only took action on environmental justice concerns in 1990 after extensive prodding from grassroots environmental justice activists, educators, and academics.[7]

People of color have known about and have been living with inequitable environmental quality for decades—most without the protection of the federal, state, and local governmental agencies. Environmental justice advocates continue to challenge the current environmental protection apparatus and offer their own framework for addressing environmental inequities, disparate impact, and unequal protection.

AN ENVIRONMENTAL JUSTICE FRAMEWORK

The question of environmental justice is not anchored in a debate about whether or not decision makers should tinker with risk management. The framework seeks to prevent environmental threats before they occur.[8] The environmental justice framework incorporates other social movements that seek to eliminate harmful practices (discrimination harms the victim) in housing, land use, industrial planning, health care, and sanitation services. The impact of redlining, economic disinvestments, infrastructure decline, deteriorating housing, lead poisoning, industrial pollution, poverty, and unemployment are not unrelated problems if one lives in an urban ghetto or barrio, rural hamlet, or reservation.

The environmental justice framework attempts to uncover the underlying assumptions that may contribute to and produce unequal protection. This framework brings to the surface the ethical and political questions of "who gets what, why, and how much." Some general characteristics of the framework include:

1. *The environmental justice framework incorporates the principle of the "right" of all individuals to be protected from environmental degradation.* The precedents for this framework are the Civil Rights Act of 1964, Fair Housing Act of 1968 and as amended in 1988, and Voting Rights Act of 1965.

2. *The environmental justice framework adopts a public health model of prevention (elimination of the threat before harm occurs) as the preferred strategy.* Impacted communities should

not have to wait until causation or conclusive "proof" is established before preventive action is taken. For example, the framework offers a solution to the lead problem by shifting the primary focus from treatment (after children have been poisoned) to prevention (elimination of the threat via abating lead in houses).

Overwhelming scientific evidence exists on the ill effects of lead on the human body. However, very little action has been taken to rid the nation of childhood lead poisoning in urban areas. Former Health and Human Services Secretary Louis Sullivan tagged this among the "number one environmental health threats to children."[9]

The Natural Resources Defense Council, NAACP Legal Defense and Educational Fund, ACLU, and Legal Aid Society of Alameda County joined forces in 1991 and won an out-of-court settlement worth $15–20 million for a blood-lead testing program in California. The *Matthews v. Coye* lawsuit involved the State of California not living up to the federally mandated testing of some 557,000 poor children for lead who receive Medicaid. This historic agreement triggered similar actions in other states that failed to live up to federally mandated screening.[10]

Lead screening is an important element in this problem. However, screening is not the solution. Prevention is the solution. Surely, if termite inspections can be mandated to protect individual home investment, a lead-free home can be mandated to protect public health. Ultimately, the lead abatement debate, public health (who is affected) vs. property rights (who pays for cleanup), is a value conflict that will not be resolved by the scientific community.

3. *The environmental justice framework shifts the burden of proof to polluter/dischargers who do harm, discriminate, or who do not give equal protection to racial and ethnic minorities, and other "protected" classes.* Under the current system, individuals who challenge polluters must "prove" that they have been harmed, discriminated against, or disproportionately impacted. Few impacted communities have the resources to hire

lawyers, expert witnesses, and doctors needed to sustain such a challenge.

The environmental justice framework would require the parties that are applying for operating permits (landfills, incinerators, smelters, refineries, chemical plants, etc.) to "prove" that their operations are not harmful to human health, will not disproportionately impact racial and ethnic minorities and other protected groups, and are nondiscriminatory.

4. *The environmental justice framework would allow disparate impact and statistical weight, as opposed to "intent," to infer discrimination.* Proving intentional or purposeful discrimination in a court of law is next to impossible, as demonstrated in *Bean v. Southwestern Waste.* It took nearly a decade after *Bean v. Southwestern Waste* for environmental discrimination to resurface in the courts.

5. *The environmental justice framework redresses disproportionate impact through "targeted" action and resources.* This strategy would target resources where environmental and health problems are greatest (as determined by some ranking scheme but not limited to risk assessment). Reliance solely on "objective" science disguises the exploitative way the polluting industries have operated in some communities and condones a passive acceptance of the status quo.

Human values are involved in determining which geographic areas are worth public investments. In the 1992 EPA report, *Securing Our Legacy,* the agency describes geographic initiatives as "protecting what we love."[11]

The strategy emphasizes "pollution prevention, multimedia enforcement, research into causes and cures of environmental stress, stopping habitat loss, education, and constituency building."[12] Geographic initiatives are underway in the Chesapeake Bay, Great Lakes, Gulf of Mexico programs, and the U.S.-Mexican Border program. Environmental justice targeting would channel resources to "hot spots," communities that are overburdened with more than their "fair" share of environmental and health problems.

The dominant environmental protection paradigm reinforces instead of challenges the stratification of people (race, ethnicity, status, power, etc.); place (central cities, suburbs, rural areas, unincorporated areas, Native American reservations, etc.); and work (i.e., office workers are afforded greater protection than farm workers). The dominant paradigm exists to manage, regulate, and distribute risks. As a result, the current system has (1) institutionalized unequal enforcement; (2) traded human health for profit; (3) placed the burden of proof on the "victims" and not the polluting industry; (4) legitimated human exposure to harmful chemicals, pesticides, and hazardous substances; (5) promoted "risky" technologies such as incinerators; (6) exploited the vulnerability of economically and politically disenfranchised communities; (7) subsidized ecological destruction; (8) created an industry around risk assessment; (9) delayed cleanup actions; and (10) failed to develop pollution prevention as the overarching and dominant strategy.[13]

The mission of the federal EPA was never designed to address environmental policies and practices that result in unfair, unjust, and inequitable outcomes. EPA and other government officials are not likely to ask the questions that go to the heart of environmental injustice: What groups are most affected? Why are they affected? Who did it? What can be done to remedy the problem? How can the problem be prevented? Vulnerable communities, populations, and individuals often fall between the regulatory cracks.

IMPETUS FOR A PARADIGM SHIFT

The environmental justice movement has changed the way scientists, researchers, policy makers, and educators go about their daily work. This bottom-up movement has redefined environment to include where people live, work, play, go to school, as well as how these things interact with the physical and natural world. The impetus for changing the dominant environmental protection paradigm did not come from within regulatory agencies, the polluting industry, academia, or the "industry" that has been built around risk management. The environmental justice movement is led by a loose alliance of grassroots and national environmental and civil rights leaders who question the foundation of the current environmental protection paradigm.

Despite significant improvements in environmental protection over the past several decades, millions of Americans continue to live, work, play, and go to school in unsafe and unhealthy physical environments.[14] During its 30-year history, the U.S. EPA has not always recognized that many of our government and industry practices (whether intended or unintended) have an adverse impact on poor people and people of color. Growing grassroots community resistance emerged in response to practices, policies, and conditions that residents judged to be unjust, unfair, and illegal. Discrimination is a fact of life in America. Racial discrimination is also illegal.

The EPA is mandated to enforce the nation's environmental laws and regulations equally across the board. It is also required to protect all Americans—not just individuals or groups who can afford lawyers, lobbyists, and experts. Environmental protection is a right, not a privilege reserved for a few who can vote with their feet and escape or fend off environmental stressors that address environmental inequities.

Equity may mean different things to different people. Equity is distilled into three broad categories: procedural, geographic, and social equity.

Procedural equity refers to the "fairness" question: the extent that governing rules, regulations, evaluation criteria, and enforcement are applied uniformly across the board and in a non-discriminatory way. Unequal protection might result from nonscientific and undemocratic decisions, exclusionary practices, public hearings held in remote locations and at inconvenient times, and use of English-only material as the language to communicate and conduct hearings for non-English-speaking publics.

Geographic equity refers to location and spatial configuration of communities and their proximity to environmental hazards, noxious facilities, and locally unwanted land uses (LULUs) such as landfills, incinerators, sewer treatment plants, lead smelters, refineries, and other noxious facilities. For example, unequal protection may result from land-use decisions that determine the location of residential amenities and disamenities. Unincorporated, poor, and communities of color often suffer a "triple" vulnerability of noxious facility siting.

Social equity assesses the role of sociological factors (race, ethnicity, class, culture, life styles, political power, etc.) on environmental decision making. Poor people and people of color often work in the most dangerous jobs, live in the most polluted neighborhoods, and their children are exposed to all kinds of environmental toxins on the playgrounds and in their homes.

The nation's environmental laws, regulations, and policies are not applied uniformly—resulting in some individuals, neighborhoods, and communities being exposed to the elevated health risks. A 1992 study by staff writers from the *National Law Journal* uncovered glaring inequities in the way the federal EPA enforces its laws. The authors write:

> There is a racial divide in the way the U.S. Government cleans up toxic waste sites and punishes polluters. White communities see faster action, better results and stiffer penalties than communities where blacks, Hispanics and other minorities live. This unequal protection often occurs whether the community is wealthy or poor.[15]

These findings suggest that unequal protection is placing communities of color at special risk.

The *National Law Journal* study supplements the findings of earlier studies and reinforces what many grassroots leaders have been saying all along: not only are people of color differentially impacted by industrial pollution, they can expect different treatment from the government. Environmental decision-making operates at the juncture of science, economics, politics, special interests, and ethics.

This current environmental model places communities of color at special risk.

THE IMPACT OF RACIAL APARTHEID

Apartheid-type housing, development, and environmental policies limit mobility, reduce neighborhood options, diminish job opportunities, and decrease choices for millions of Americans.[16] The infrastructure conditions in urban areas are a result of a host of factors including the distribution of wealth, patterns of racial and economic discrimination, redlining, housing and real estate practices, location decisions of industry, differential enforcement of land use and environmental choices, and diminished job communities for African Americans.

Race still plays a significant part in distributing public "benefits" and public "burdens" associated with economic growth. The roots of discrimination are deep and have been difficult to eliminate. Housing discrimination contributes to the physical decay of inner-city neighborhoods and denies a substantial segment of the African-American community a basic form of wealth accumulation and investment through home ownership.[17] The number of African-American homeowners would probably be higher in the absence of discrimination by lending institutions.[18] Only about 59 percent of the nation's middle-class African Americans own their homes, compared with 74 percent of whites.

Eight out of every ten African Americans live in neighborhoods where they are in the majority. Residential segregation decreases for most racial and ethnic groups with additional education, income, and occupational status. However, this scenario does not hold true for African Americans. African Americans, no matter what their educational or occupational achievement or income level, are exposed to higher crime rates, less effective educational systems, higher mortality risks, more dilapidated surroundings, and greater environmental threats because of their race. For example, in the heavily populated South Coast air basin of the Los Angeles area, it is estimated that over 71 percent of African Americans and 50 percent of whites live in highly polluted areas.[19]

It has been difficult for millions of Americans in segregated neighborhoods to say "not in my backyard" (NIMBY) if they do not have a backyard.[20] Nationally, only about 44 percent of African Americans own their homes compared to over two-thirds of the nation as a whole. Homeowners are the strongest advocates of the NIMBY positions taken against locally unwanted uses or LULUs such as the construction of garbage dumps, landfills, incinerators, sewer treatment plants, recycling centers, prisons, drug treatment units, and public housing projects. Generally, white communities have greater access than people-of-color communities when it comes to influencing land use and environmental decision making.

The ability of an individual to escape a health-threatening physical environment is usually related to affluence. However, racial barriers complicate this process for many Americans.[21] The imbalance between residential amenities and land uses assigned to central cities and suburbs cannot be explained by class factors alone. People of color and whites do not have the same opportunities to "vote with their feet" and escape undesirable physical environments.

Institutional racism continues to influence housing and mobility options available to African Americans of all income levels—and is a major factor that influences the quality of neighborhoods they have available to them. The "web of discrimination" in the housing market is a result of action and inaction of local and federal government officials, financial institutions, insurance companies, real estate marketing firms, and zoning boards. More stringent enforcement mechanisms and penalties are needed to combat all forms of discrimination.

Uneven development between central cities and suburbs combined with the systematic avoidance of inner-city areas by many businesses have heightened social and economic inequalities. For the past two decades, manufacturing plants have been fleeing central cities and taking their jobs with them. Many have moved offshore to Third World countries where labor is cheap and environmental regulations are lax or nonexistent.

Industry flight from central cities had left behind a deteriorating urban infrastructure, poverty, and pollution. What kind of replacement industry can these communities attract? Economically depressed communities do not have a lot of choices available to them. Some workers have become so desperate that they see even a low-paying hazardous job as better than no job at all. These workers are forced to choose between unemployment and a job that may result in risks to their health, their family's health, and the health of their community. This practice amounts to "economic blackmail." Economic conditions in many people-of-color communities make them especially vulnerable to this practice.

Some polluting industries have been eager to exploit this vulnerability. Some have even used the assistance of elected officials in obtaining special tax breaks and government operating permits. Clearly, economic development and environmental policies flow from forces of production and are often dominated and subsidized by state actors. Numerous examples abound where state actors have targeted cities and regions for infrastructure improvements and amenities such as water irrigation systems, ship channels, road and bridge projects, and mass transit systems. On the other hand, state actors have done a miserable job in protecting central city residents from the ravages of industrial pollution and nonresidential activities valued as having a negative impact on quality of life.[22]

Racial and ethnic inequality is perpetuated and reinforced by local governments in conjunction with urban-based corporations. Race continues to be a potent variable in explaining urban land use, streets and highway configuration, commercial and industrial development, and industrial facility siting. Moreover, the question of "who gets what, where, and why" often pits one community against another.[23]

ZONING AND LAND USE

Some residential areas and their inhabitants are at a greater risk than the larger society from unregulated growth, ineffective regulation of industrial toxins, and public policy decisions authorizing industrial facilities that favor those with political and economic clout.[24] African Americans and other communities of color are often victims of land-use decision making that mirrors the power arrangements of the dominant society. Historically, exclusionary zoning (and rezoning) has been a subtle form of using government authority and power to foster and perpetuate discriminatory practices.

Zoning is probably the most widely applied mechanism to regulate urban land use in the United States. Zoning laws broadly define land for residential, commercial, or industrial uses, and may impose narrower land-use restrictions (e.g., minimum and maximum lot size, number of dwellings per acre, square feet and height of buildings, etc.). Zoning ordinances, deed restrictions, and other land-use mechanisms have been widely used as a "NIMBY" tool, operating through exclusionary practices. Thus, exclusionary zoning has been used to zone against something rather than for something. With or without zoning, deed restrictions or other devices, various groups are unequally able to protect their environmental interests. More often than not, people-of-color communities get short-changed in the neighborhood protection game.

In Houston, Texas, a city that does not have zoning, NIMBY was replaced with the policy of PIBBY (place in black's back yard).[25] The city government and private industry targeted landfills, incinerators, and garbage dumps for Houston's black neighborhoods for more than five decades. These practices lowered residents' property values, accelerated physical deterioration, and increased disinvestment in the communities. Moreover, the discriminatory siting of landfills and incinerators stigmatized the neighborhoods as "dumping grounds" for a host of other unwanted facilities, including salvage yards, recycling operations, and automobile "chop shops."[26]

The Commission for Racial Justice's landmark *Toxic Wastes and Race* study found race to be the single most important factor (i.e., more important than income, home ownership rate, and property values) in the location of abandoned toxic waste sites.[27] The study also found that (1) three out of five African Americans live in communities with abandoned toxic waste sites; (2) sixty percent of African Americans (15 million) live in communities with one or more abandoned toxic waste sites; (3) three of the five largest commercial hazardous waste landfills are located in predominately African American or Latino communities and account for 40 percent of the nation's total estimated landfill capacity; and (4) African Americans are heavily overrepresented in the population of cities with the largest number of abandoned toxic waste sites, which include Memphis, St. Louis, Houston, Cleveland, Chicago, and Atlanta.

Waste facility siting imbalances that were uncovered by the U.S. General Accounting Office (GAO) in 1983 have not disappeared.[28] The GAO discovered three out of four of the off-site commercial hazardous waste landfills in Region IV (Alabama, Florida, Georgia, Kentucky, Mississippi, North Carolina, South Carolina, and Tennessee) were located in predominately African-American communities. African Americans still made up about one-fifth of the population in EPA Region IV. In 2000, 100 percent of the off-site commercial hazardous waste landfills in the region is dumped in two mostly African-American communities.

ENVIRONMENTAL RACISM

Many of the differences in environmental quality between black and white communities result from institutional racism, which influences local land use; enforcement of environmental regulations; industrial facility siting; and where people of color live, work and play. The roots of institutional racism are deep and have been difficult to eliminate. Discrimination is a manifestation of institutional racism and causes life to be very different for

whites and blacks. Historically, racism has been and continues to be a major part of the American sociological system, and as a result, people of color find themselves at a disadvantage in contemporary society.

Environmental racism is real. It is just as real as the racism found in the housing industry, educational institutions, the employment arena, and the judicial system. What is environmental racism and how does one recognize it? *Environmental racism refers to any policy, practice, or directive that differentially affects or disadvantages (whether intended or unintended) individuals, groups, or communities based on race or color.* Environmental racism combines with public policies and industry practices to provide benefits for whites while shifting costs to people of color.[29] Environmental racism is reinforced by government, legal, economic, political, and military institutions.

Environmental decision making and policies often mirror the power arrangements of the dominant society and its institutions. Environmental racism disadvantages people of color while providing advantages or privileges for whites. A form of illegal "exaction" forces people of color to pay costs of environmental benefits for the public at large. The question of who pays and who benefits from the current environmental and industrial policies is central to this analysis of environmental racism and other systems of domination and exploitation.

Racism influences the likelihood of exposure to environmental and health risks as well as accessibility to health care.[30] Many of the nation's environmental policies distribute the costs in a regressive pattern while providing disproportionate benefits for whites and individuals who fall at the upper end of the education and income scale. Numerous studies, dating back to the seventies, reveal that people of color have borne greater health and environmental risk burdens than the society at large.[31]

Elevated public health risks are found in some populations even when social class is held constant. For example, race has been found to be independent of class in the distribution of air pollution,[32] contaminated fish consumption,[33] location of municipal landfills and incinerators,[34] toxic waste dumps,[35] cleanup of superfund sites,[36] and lead poisoning in children.[37]

Lead poisoning is a classic example of an environmental health problem that disproportionately impacts children of color at every class level. Lead affects between 3 million and 4 million children in the United States—most of whom are African-Americans and Latinos who live in urban areas. Among children 5 years old and younger, the percentage of African-American children who have excessive levels of lead in their blood far exceeds the percentage of whites at all income levels.

In 1988, the federal Agency for Toxic Substances Disease Registry (ATSDR) found that for families earning less than $6,000, 68 percent of African-American children had lead poisoning, compared with 36 percent for white children. In families with income exceeding $15,000, more than 38 percent of African-American children suffer from lead poisoning compared with 12 percent of whites. The average blood-lead level has dropped for all children with the phasing out of leaded gasoline. Today, the average blood-lead level for all children in the U.S. is under 6 µg/dl.[38] However, these efforts have not had the same positive benefits on all populations. There is still work to be done to address the remaining problem. The lead problem is not randomly distributed across the nation. The most vulnerable populations are low-income African-American and Hispanic-American children who live in older urban housing.[39]

Figures reported in the July 1994 *Journal of the American Medical Association* on the Third National Health and Nutrition Examination Survey (NHANES III) revealed that 1.7 million children (8.9 percent of children aged 1 to 5) are lead poisoned, defined as blood-lead levels equal to or above 10 µg/dl.[40] Lead-based paint (chips and dust) is the most common source of lead exposure for children. Children may also be exposed through soil and dust contamination built up from vehicle exhaust, lead concentration in soils in urban areas, lead dust brought into the home on parents' work clothes, lead used in ceramics and pottery, folk medicines, and lead in plumbing.

THE RIGHT TO BREATHE CLEAN AIR

Urban air pollution problems have been with us for some time now. Before the federal government stepped in, issues related to air pollution were handled primarily by states and local government. Because states and local governments did such a poor job, the federal government set out to establish national clean air standards. Congress enacted the Clean Air Act (CAA) in 1970 and mandated the U.S. Environmental Protection Agency (EPA) to carry out this law. Subsequent amendments (1977 and 1990) were made to the CAA that form the current federal program. The CAA was a response to states' unwillingness to protect air quality. Many states used their lax enforcement of environmental laws as lures for business and economic development.[41]

Central cities and suburbs do not operate on a level playing field. They often compete for scarce resources. One need not be a rocket scientist to predict the outcome between affluent suburbs and their less affluent central city competitors.[42] Freeways are the lifeline for suburban commuters, while millions of central-city residents are dependent on public transportation as their primary mode of travel. But recent cuts in mass transit subsidies and fare hikes have reduced access to essential social services and economic activities. Nevertheless, road construction programs are booming—even in areas choked with automobiles and air pollution.[43]

The air quality impacts of transportation are especially significant to people of color who are more likely than whites to live in urban areas with reduced air quality. National Argonne Laboratory researchers discovered that 437 of the 3,109 counties and independent cities failed to meet at least one of the EPA ambient air quality standards.[44] Specifically, 57 percent of whites, 65 percent of African Americans, and 80 percent of Hispanics live in 437 counties with substandard air quality. Nationwide, 33 percent of whites, 50 percent of African Americans, and 60 percent of Hispanics live in the 136 counties in which two or more air pollutants exceed standards. Similar patterns were found for the 29 counties designated as nonattainment areas for three or more pollutants. Again, 12 percent of whites, 20 percent of African Americans, and 31 percent of Hispanics resided in the worse nonattainment areas.

Asthma is an emerging epidemic in the United States. The annual age-adjusted death rate from asthma increased by 40 percent between 1982 and 1991, from 1.34 to 1.88 per 100,000 population,[45] with the highest rates being consistently reported among blacks aged 15–24 years of age during the period 1980–1993.[46] Poverty and minority status are important risk factors for asthma mortality.

Children are at special risk from ozone.[47] Children also represent a considerable share of the asthma burden. It is the most common chronic disease of childhood. Asthma affects almost 5 million children under 18 years. Although the overall annual age-adjusted hospital discharge rate for asthma among children under 15 years old decreased slightly from 184 to 179 per 100,000 between 1982 and 1992, the decrease was slower compared to other childhood diseases,[48] resulting in a 70 percent increase in the proportion of hospital admissions related to asthma during the 1980s.[49] Inner-city children have the highest rates for asthma prevalence, hospitalization, and mortality.[50] In the United States, asthma is the fourth leading cause of disability among children aged less than 18 years.[51]

The public health community has insufficient information to explain the magnitude of some of the air pollution-related health problems. However, they do know that persons suffering from asthma are particularly sensitive to the effects of carbon monoxide, sulfur dioxide's particulate matter, ozone, and nitrogen oxides. Ground-level ozone may exacerbate health problems such as asthma, nasal congestion, throat irritation, respiratory tract inflammation, reduced resistance to infection, changes in cell function, loss of lung elasticity, chest pains, lung scarring, formation of lesions within the lungs, and premature aging of lung tissues.[52]

Nationally, African Americans and Latino Americans have significantly higher prevalence of asthma than the general population. A 1996 report from the federal Centers for Disease Control shows hospitalization and death rates from asthma increasing for persons twenty-five years or less.[53] The greatest increases occurred among African Americans. African Americans are two to six times more likely than whites to die from asthma.[54] Similarly, the hospitalization rate for African Americans is three to four times the rate for whites.

A 1994 CDC-sponsored study showed that pediatric emergency department visits at Atlanta Grady Memorial Hospital increased by one-third following peak ozone levels. The study also found that the asthma rate among African American children is 26 percent higher than the asthma rate among whites.[55] Since children with asthma in Atlanta may not have visited the emergency department for their care, the true prevalence of asthma in the community is likely to be higher.

EXPLOITATION OF LAND, ENVIRONMENT, AND PEOPLE

Environmental decision making and local land-use planning operate at the juncture of science, economics, politics, and special interests that place communities of color at special risk.[56] This is especially true in America's Deep South. The Deep South has always been thought of as a backward land based on its social, economic, political, and environmental policies. By default, the region became a "sacrifice zone," a dump for the rest of the nation's toxic waste.[57] A colonial mentality exists in the South where local government and big business take advantage of people who are politically and economically powerless. Many of these attitudes emerged from the region's marriage to slavery and the plantation system—a brutal system that exploited humans and the land.[58] The Deep South is stuck with this unique legacy—the legacy of slavery, Jim Crow, and white resistance to equal justice for all. This legacy has also affected race relations and the region's ecology. Southerners, black and white, have less education, lower incomes, higher infant mortality, and lower life expectancy than Americans elsewhere. It should be no surprise that the environmental quality that Southerners enjoy is markedly different from that of other regions of the country.

The South is characterized by "look-the-other-way environmental policies and giveaway tax breaks."[59] It is our nation's Third World where "political bosses encourage outsiders to buy the region's human and natural resources at bargain prices."[60] Lax enforcement of environmental regulations has left the region's air, water, and land the most industry-befouled in the United States.

Toxic waste discharge and industrial pollution are correlated with poorer economic conditions. Louisiana typifies this pattern. Nearly three-fourths of Louisiana's population—more than 3 million people—get their drinking water from underground aquifers. Dozens of the aquifers are threatened by contamination from polluting industries.[61] The Lower Mississippi River Industrial Corridor has over 125 companies that manufacture a range of products including fertilizers, gasoline, paints, and plastics. This corridor has been dubbed "Cancer Alley" by environmentalists and local residents.[62] Ascension Parish typifies what many people refer to as a toxic "sacrifice zone." In the two parish towns of Geismer and St. Gabriel, 18 petrochemical plants are crammed into a nine-and-a-half-square-mile area. Petrochemical plants discharge millions of pounds of pollutants annually into the water and air.

Louisiana citizens subsidize this corporate welfare with their health and the environment. Tax breaks given to polluting industries have created a few jobs at high cost. Nowhere is the polluter-welfare scenario more prevalent than in Louisiana. The state is a leader in doling out corporate welfare to polluters. A 1998 *Time Magazine* article reported that in the 1990s, Louisiana wiped off the books $3.1 billion in property taxes to polluting companies.[63] The state's top five worst polluters received $111 million dollars over the past decade.

GLOBAL DUMPING GROUNDS

There is a direct correlation between exploitation of land and exploitation of people. It should not be a surprise to anyone to discover that Native Americans have to contend with some of the worst pollution in the United States.[64] Native American nations have become prime targets for waste trading.[65] More than three dozen Indian reservations have been targeted for landfills, incinerators, and other waste facilities.[66] The vast majority of these waste proposals were defeated by grassroots groups on the reservations. However, "radioactive colonialism" is alive and well.[67] The legacy of institutional racism has left many sovereign Indian nations without an economic infrastructure to address poverty, unemployment, inadequate education and health care, and a host of other social problems. In 1999, Eastern Navajo reservation residents filed suit against the Nuclear Regulatory Commission to block uranium mining in Church Rock and Crown Point communities.

Hazardous waste generation and international movement of hazardous waste pose some important health, environmental, legal, and ethical dilemmas. It is unlikely that many of the global hazardous waste proposals can be effectuated without first addressing the social, economic, and political context in which hazardous wastes are produced (industrial processes); controlled (regulations, notification and consent documentation); and managed (minimization, treatment, storage, recycling, transboundary shipment, pollution prevention, etc.). The "unwritten" policy of targeting Third-World nations for waste trade received international media attention in 1991. Lawrence Summers, at the time he was chief economist of the World Bank, shocked the world and touched off an international scandal when his confidential memorandum on waste trade was leaked. Summers writes: "'Dirty' Industries: Just between you and me, shouldn't the World Bank be encouraging MORE migration of the dirty industries to the LDCs?"[68]

Consumption and production patterns, especially in nations with wasteful "throw-away" life styles such as the United States, and the interests of transnational corporations create and maintain unequal and unjust waste burdens within and between affluent and poor communities, states, and regions of the world. Shipping hazardous wastes from rich communities to poor communities is not a solution to the growing global waste problem. Not only is it immoral, but it should be illegal. Moreover, making hazardous waste transactions legal does not address the ethical issues imbedded in such transactions.[69] The practice is a manifestation of power arrangements and a larger stratification system where some people and some places are assigned greater value than others.

In the real world, all people, communities, and nations are not created equal. Some populations and interests are more equal than others. Unequal interests and power arrangements have allowed poisons of the rich to be offered as short-term remedies for poverty of the poor. This scenario plays out domestically (as in the United States where low-income and people-of-color communities are disproportionately impacted by waste facilities and "dirty" industries) and internationally (where hazardous wastes from OECD states flow to non-OECD states).

The conditions surrounding the more than 1,900 maquiladoras, assembly plants operated by American, Japanese, and other foreign countries, located along the 2,000-mile U.S.-Mexico border may further exacerbate the waste trade.[70] The industrial plants use cheap Mexican labor to assemble imported components and raw material and then ship finished products back to the United States. Nearly a half million Mexican workers are employed in the maquiladoras.

A 1983 agreement between the United States and Mexico required American companies in Mexico to return waste products to the United States. Plants were required to notify the federal EPA when returning wastes. Results from a 1986 survey of 772 maquiladoras revealed that only 20 of the plants informed the U.S. EPA that they were returning waste to the United States, even though 86 percent of the plants used toxic chemicals in their manufacturing process. Much of the wastes end up being illegally dumped in sewers, ditches, and the desert. All along the Lower Rio Grande River Valley maquiladoras dump their toxic wastes into the river, from which 95 percent of the region's residents get their drinking water.[71]

The disregard for the environment and public safety has placed border residents' health at risk. In the border cities of Brownsville, Texas, and Matamoras, Mexico, the rate of anencephaly—babies born without brains—is four times the national average. Affected families have filed lawsuits against 88 of the area's 100 maquiladoras for exposing the community to xylene, a cleaning solvent that can cause brain hemorrhages, and lung and kidney damage.

Contaminated well and drinking water looms as a major health threat. Air pollution has contributed to a raging asthma and respiratory epidemic. The Mexican environmental regulatory agency is understaffed and "ill-equipped to adequately enforce its environmental laws."[72] Only time will tell if the North American Free Trade Agreement (NAFTA) will "fix" or exacerbate the public health, economic, and environmental problems along the U.S.-Mexico border.

SETTING THE RECORD STRAIGHT

The environmental protection apparatus is broken and needs to be fixed. The environmental justice movement has set out clear goals of eliminating unequal enforcement of environmental, civil rights, and public health laws. Environmental justice leaders have made a difference in the lives of people and the physical environment. They have assisted public decision makers in identifying "at-risk" populations, toxic "hot spots," research gaps, and action models to correct existing imbalances and prevent future threats. However, impacted communities are not waiting for the government or industry to get their acts together. Grassroots groups have taken the offensive to ensure that government and industry do the right thing.

Communities have begun to organize their own networks and force their inclusion into the mainstream of public decision making. They have also developed communication channels among environmental justice leaders, grassroots groups, professional associations (i.e., legal, public health, education, etc.), scientific groups, and public policy makers to assist them in identifying "at-risk" populations, toxic "hot spots," and research gaps, and work to correct imbalances.

In response to growing public concern and mounting scientific evidence, President Clinton signed Executive Order 12898. The Executive Order is not a new law. It only reinforces what has been the law of the land for over three decades. Environmental justice advocates are calling for vigorous enforcement of civil rights laws and environmental laws.

The number of environmental justice complaints is expected to escalate against industry, government, and institutions that receive funds. Citizens have a right to challenge discrimination— including environmental discrimination. It is a smokescreen for anyone to link Title VI or other civil rights enforcement to economic disinvestment in low-income and people-of-color communities. There is absolutely no empirical evidence to support the contention that environmental justice hurts **brownfield** redevelopment efforts.

The **EPA** has awarded over 200 brownfield grants. In 1998, the agency had received some

---

brownfield An industrial or commercial site that is idle or underused because of real or perceived environmental pollution.

EPA U.S. Environmental Protection Agency. The EPA's Brownfields Program provides direct funding for brownfields assessment, cleanup, revolving loans, and environmental job training.

five dozen Title VI complaints. It is worth noting that not a single Title VI complaint involves a brownfield site. On the other hand, two decades of solid empirical evidence documents the impact of racial redlining on African American and other communities of color. Racial redlining by banks, savings and loans, insurance companies, grocery chains, and even pizza delivery companies thwarts economic vitality in black communities—not enforcement of civil rights laws. Racial redlining was such a real problem that Congress passed the Community Reinvestment Act in 1977.

States have had three decades to implement Title VI of the Civil Rights Act of 1964. Most states have chosen to ignore the law. States need to do a better job assuring nondiscrimination in the application and the implementation of permitting decisions, enforcement, and investment decisions. Environmental justice also means sharing in the benefits. Governments must live up to their mandate of protecting all people and the environment. Anything less is unacceptable. The solution to environmental injustice lies in the realm of equal protection of all individuals, groups, and communities. No community, rich or poor, urban or suburban, black or white, should be allowed to become a "sacrifice zone" or the dumping ground.

Hazardous wastes and "dirty" industries have followed the "path of least resistance." Poor people and poor communities are given a false choice of "no jobs and no development" versus "risky low-paying jobs and pollution." Industries and governments (including the military) have often exploited the economic vulnerability of poor communities, poor states, poor regions, and poor nations for their "risky" operations.

25

RACE, RELIGION, AND THE COLOR LINE (OR IS THAT THE COLOR WALL?)

Michael O. Emerson

MICHAEL O. EMERSON is the Allyn and Gladys Cline Professor of Sociology and the Funding Director of the Center on Race, Religion, and Urban Life at Rice University. He has authored many papers and several books on the relationships between race and religion, as well as on neighborhood segregation and immigration issues.

A COUPLE OF YEARS AGO, BISHOP FRED CALDWELL, pastor of Shreveport, Louisiana's Greenwood Acres Full Gospel Baptist Church, a large African-American congregation, offered a unique proposal. He was offering to *pay* nonblacks to attend his church. So adamant was he that his church should not be segregated, Bishop Caldwell said that for at least one month he would pay nonblacks five dollars per hour to attend the multiple-hour Sunday morning service, and ten dollars an hour to attend the church's Thursday night service. And he would pay this money out of his own pocket. Bishop Caldwell told the Associated Press, "This idea is born of God. God wants a rainbow in his church." He said the inspiration came to him during a sermon. "The most segregated hour in America is Sunday morning at 11 o'clock. The Lord is tired of it, and I'm certainly tired of it. This is not right."[1]

Questions to Consider

Michael O. Emerson points out that among the most segregated institutions in the United States are our houses of worship. How much racial separation is there in American religion? Why? Does this racial separation matter, and if so, how? What do we know about multiracial congregations? Why are these racially integrated congregations of interest for understanding race in the United States?

This story was first reported in the local Shreveport, Louisiana, newspaper, but was soon picked up by papers across the country. The day the story appeared in *USA Today*, ten people sent me online links to the article, often with an e-mail subject heading like "You've got to see this!" The story was soon the talk on radio airwaves and television outlets. Internet chat rooms were talking about it, and people were debating it at the proverbial water cooler.

Pay people to attend worship services? To many, paying people to worship seemed outrageous. Others thought the idea was brilliant, highlighting the racial segregation in houses of worship across the nation. Still others thought the bishop should not focus on the race of those who attended his church, but merely minister to whoever attended. They found his "religious affirmative action" deeply troubling. Discussion spread beyond this simple offer to pay people to attend one church, and turned to whether the racial makeup of congregations matters.

Shortly after this story hit the national news, I was a guest on a two-hour radio call-in show in Baltimore. The show's hosts opened by discussing Bishop Caldwell's offer to pay nonblacks to come to his church, and featured the more general topic of congregational segregation. The issue touched a hot button among the listeners. The hosts kept commenting that their lines were lit up, jammed full. I could hear and feel that the callers were passionate about this topic.

When the first "post-pay-to-attend-offer" Sunday service was held, reporters were eager to see the results. The headlines told the story: "Few take pastor up on offer," said one headline. A year later, a small bit of change had happened. According to a report in one magazine, a year after the offer, about two dozen whites were attending this congregation of thousands, and five whites had become members.[2]

HOW SEGREGATED ARE RELIGIOUS CONGREGATIONS?

For a long time, when people studied race relations and inequality, they did not think of religion. But when well over 100 million Americans are attending religious congregations each week, and when

90 percent of Americans say they have a religious faith and believe in a higher being, it seems like a gross oversight not to consider the role of religion. It seems even more of a mistake given that the early giants in the field, such as W. E. B. Du Bois, thought it so important that they actually wrote books about it. And like Bishop Caldwell, Martin Luther King, probably the best known advocate for racial equality, called religion the most segregated institution in the nation.

I wanted to piggyback on these giants, so I have spent a number of years researching the relationship between religion and race, and I am delighted to share some of what has been learned with you. One of my first questions was: How segregated are religious congregations? This question did not have an answer other than "very." So my colleagues and I set out to find a more precise answer.

To do so, we decided to study the segregation in two ways. First, we defined homogeneous congregations (80 percent or more of a congregation is of the same race) and mixed-race congregations (no one racial group is 80 percent or more of the congregation). We used this cutoff of 80 percent because research done on other organizations—such as businesses—has found that until another group or groups make up 20 percent or more of an organization, they lack the critical mass to make any significant changes in the organization.

Armed with this definition, we used data collected from a national random sample of congregations. We found that *more than 90 percent* of congregations are racially homogeneous (Figure 1). You have to look hard to find a racially mixed congregation in the United States.

But where you look is important. As Figure 2 shows, the faith tradition matters. Because of the sample size, unfortunately I had to combine all non-Christian congregations—such as Buddhist temples, Muslim mosques, and Jewish synagogues—into one category. When I do that, more than a quarter of all non-Christian congregations are racially mixed. Among Catholic congregations, 15 percent of them are mixed, and among Protestants, just 5 percent are mixed. Why this variation? We found that the larger the

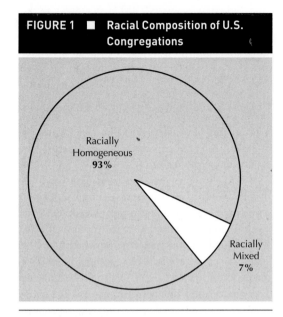

FIGURE 1 ■ Racial Composition of U.S. Congregations

Racially
Homogeneous
93%

Racially
Mixed
7%

Source: National Congregations Study. "Percentage of Congregations that are racially mixed by faith tradition." This study was directed by Dr. Mark Chaves of the University of Arizona, Tucson.

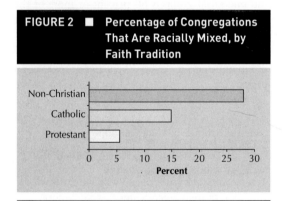

FIGURE 2 ■ Percentage of Congregations That Are Racially Mixed, by Faith Tradition

Non-Christian

Catholic

Protestant

0   5   10   15   20   25   30

Percent

Source: National Congregations Study. "Percentage of Congregations that are racially mixed by faith tradition." This study was directed by Dr. Mark Chaves of the University of Arizona, Tucson.

religious tradition—the number of people involved in that faith and the number of congregations to choose from—the more segregated it is. To put it most bluntly, the more choices people have of where to worship, the more they choose to be with people who are racially similar to themselves.

We have a more sophisticated way to study the level of congregational segregation. Instead of just studying whether a congregation is or is not racially mixed, we can ask how diverse congregations are by asking: *What is the probability that any two randomly selected people in the congregation will be of different races?* In other words, if you were to walk into a congregation, write the name of each person in attendance on a little slip of paper, put those slips of paper into your hat, mix them up, and then, with your eyes closed, draw out two names, how often would those two people be of different socially defined racial groups? Fifty percent of the time, perhaps, or maybe 30 percent of the time?

Rather than using a hat and slips of paper, we did this process with a statistical formula and a computer. We found that the average (median) diversity of a congregation in the United States is *just .02.* That means that the probability that any two randomly selected people in a congregation will be of different races is only 2 percent.

To put that number in context, we did the same calculations for the nation's neighborhoods and schools, both of which are highly segregated, and found that religious congregations are *10 times less diverse* than the neighborhoods in which they reside, and *20 times less diverse* than the nation's public schools. When Martin Luther King said that religious congregations are the most segregated institution in the United States, he wasn't kidding. Forget the color line. When it comes to religion in the United States, we have a color wall. Just as China has its great wall, so too does the United States.[3]

SO WHAT IF RELIGIOUS CONGREGATIONS ARE SEGREGATED?

Having found out more precisely how segregated religious congregations are, I wondered if it made any difference for race relations and inequality. It does, dramatically so.

Religion has much potential for mitigating racial division and inequality. Most religions teach love, respect, and equality of all peoples. They usually teach of the errors inherent in racial prejudice and discrimination. They often proclaim the need to embrace all people. They speak of the need for fairness and justice. They often teach that selfishness and acting in self-interested ways are counter to the will of the divine.

In the United States, religious faith motivated the fight against slavery. It played an essential role in the Civil Rights movement. It currently is motivating many believers to attempt to reduce the racial divide and injustice. It directs people to value openness and diversity. It guides some to vote in ways that will overcome racial inequality. It motivates others to volunteer in groups working against racial hate and discrimination. For still others, it motivates them to form organizations intent on reducing inequality and strengthening justice. Others are motivated to donate money to such organizations.

Stories of positive actions of religious people and organizations to combat racial division and inequality abound. But in this section, focusing on the structural arrangement of racially segregated religious congregations, I demonstrate the powerful countervailing influences of religion on racialization.

To reflect on this issue properly, let's keep in mind the distinction between macro and micro effects. Part of the irony of religion's role is that in strengthening micro bonds between individuals, religion contributes to within-group sameness, heightens isolation from different groups, and reduces the opportunity to form macro bonds—that is, bonds between groups that serve to integrate a society. The lack of social ties between religious groups across race inhibits movement between them, increasing the importance of group boundaries and social differences. This means that racially segregated congregations lower the probability of intergroup mobility (such as through intermarriage) and heighten the importance of racial boundaries, separate racial identities, and other differences between groups. So though many in the religious community call and work for an end to racial division, the organization of religion into segregated congregations often undercuts their efforts.

The separate groups that are reproduced through religious division result in categorization, for separate groups must be categorized by something—in this case, by race and often by religious and other views. According to scholars Hamilton and Trolier, categorization has important implications:

> The social categories we develop are more than convenient groupings of individuals that simplify the actual diversities among the people we observe and encounter. They are also categories that can bias the way we process information, organize and store it in memory, and make judgments about members of those social categories.[4]

We all consistently engage in social comparison (Am I smart? Who is good-looking? Who has money?), and research links categorization to at least seven biases:

1. Our brains exaggerate the similarities of ingroup members and their differences from outgroup members.

2. Because people know the outgroup by its perceived differences, outgroup members are identified by these differences, overly homogenizing them.

3. Ingroup favoritism: Even when performing exactly the same actions, ingroup members are evaluated more positively and outgroup members more negatively.

4. We attribute positive behavior of ingroup members to internal traits such as intelligence, and negative behavior to external causes such as a poor home life. We do the exact opposite for outgroup members.

5. Cognitive psychologists find that we have better memories for negative outgroup behaviors than for negative ingroup behaviors.

6. Because our brains tend to overly homogenize outgroups, a negative behavior of an outgroup member is likely to be

perceived as characteristic of the entire outgroup. We appear to make the leap from James of Group X shoplifted to people of Group X shoplift.

7. Once people have preconceived stereotypes of an outgroup, they tend to recall only information that confirms their stereotypes, while contradictory evidence is dismissed as an exception. A relative of mine, for example, knew for sure that African Americans were lazy, shiftless, and liars, even though one of my relative's closest friends was African American. My relative's explanation? Her friend was not like other African Americans; she was the exception.[5]

Religion contributes to racial division and inequality, then, in that it increases racial categorization, which is a by-product of congregational segregation.

Given human limitations, racially exclusive identities and congregations necessitate another bias. We can call this the ethical paradox of group loyalty. The paradox is that even if made up of loving, unselfish individuals, the group transmutes individual unselfishness into group selfishness.

What does that mean in English? Imagine two groups. Each member of each group is a deeply committed religious person, full of love and concern for others, and has even developed a friendship or two with people of other groups. For historical reasons, one group has more social goods—income, wealth, education, power—than the other group. Despite being made up entirely of unselfish individuals, the two groups will continue to be divided and unequal. How can this be?

Reinhold Niebuhr explored this question way back in 1932 in his book *Moral Man and Immoral Society*.[6] For one thing, he wrote, direct contact with members of other groups is limited, always less than with members of one's own group. People thus know the members of their own group and their needs more deeply, fully, and personally than the members and needs of other groups. Therefore, they attend to the needs of their own group first, precisely because they are moral and

loving. How can they turn their backs on the needs of their own group in favor of another group? At the individual level, selfishness is usually considered negative, but at the group level, it is considered moral and just. Indeed, at the group level, it is not selfishness, but morality, service, sacrifice, and loyalty.

We find evidence of this every day. Consider the family. Although we are selfish if we always look out for our individual needs first, it is considered wrong and immoral if we do not consider the needs of our family first, ahead of other families. Your parents would be considered immoral if they did not help pay for their own children's college first. Only if they had extra money (at college prices today, that would be rare!) would they even consider helping other children, but even then, there would be so many other family needs to be met.

So, the approximately 350,000 congregations in the United States are busy creating group identity and forming moral persons. Those moral persons, acting morally, are aware of and help their families and the members of their own congregations first, making sure those needs are met before looking to help elsewhere. Because of segregation, this means we help people of our own race—whites helping whites, African Americans helping African Americans, Asians helping Asians, Latinos helping Latinos, and so on.

The problem with this pattern is that the inequality between groups is maintained. Members of groups with the most share it with others of their group. Members of groups with the least are busy trying to meet the needs of others in their group, which, because the group has less, are typically bigger needs, trying to be met with less. It is a nasty cycle, even though the people involved are themselves not acting nasty.

We also have another problem, according to Niebuhr. Because the members of a group cannot understand and feel the needs of another group as completely and deeply as those of their own group, reliance on love, compassion, and persuasion to overcome group divisions and inequalities is practically impossible. For this reason, relations between groups are always mainly political rather than ethical or moral (wow, reflect on this statement—it's a doozy). As Niebuhr says, "They will always be determined by the proportion of power which each group possesses at least as much as by any rational and moral appraisal of the comparative needs and claims of each group."[7]

The facts just considered have considerable implications for the perpetuation of racial inequality and stratification. The logic is straightforward: (1) In the United States there is racial inequality in access to valued resources. (2) Access to valued resources—such as jobs, prestige, wealth, and power—is gained in significant part through social ties.[8] (3) For reasons such as social categorization, comparison, and the paradox of ingroup loyalty, people have positive bias for their ingroup and negative bias for outgroups. These three facts suggest that, other factors being equal, any social structure or process that both increases the saliency of group boundaries and reduces interracial ties necessarily reproduces racial inequality. Because the organization of religion in the United States heightens the salience of racial boundaries and reduces interracial ties, it necessarily reproduces racial inequality.[9]

CAN WE FIND A SOLUTION?

So is that it? Must we then conclude that religion really can only entrench and amplify the racial divisions and inequalities that already exist? For the millions of religious people, that would be a pretty disappointing conclusion. But that is not it. If you give it some thought, how could religion change to actually move toward reducing racial division and inequality?

If the whole edifice of evidence against positive effects of religion is built upon the foundation of segregated congregations, what if congregations were not segregated? Could positive changes for racial division and inequality result?

My colleagues and I spent a number of years trying to figure this out. We did so by studying multiracial congregations (those 7 percent of congregations from Figure 1) and, for comparative purposes, racially homogeneous congregations. We conducted telephone interviews, mail surveys, and face-to-face interviews, and we spent lots of time in congregations across the country. I even spent nearly six years in one congregation as it transformed from an all-white congregation to one that no longer had a majority racial group and had people from well over forty nations in attendance.

Social Ties

The first difference we noticed in studying these congregations was the extensive amount of friendships across race that people in these racially mixed congregations had. As an African American woman from Chicago who was a member of a multiracial congregation called Crosstown told us:

> I grew up in a predominantly black church and neighborhood. Crosstown has taught me about other races of people. [The diversity at Crosstown] helped me to develop relationships with people outside my race where I felt they were my friend and we share Christ in our life and that they have the same struggles as I do. . . . I've gotten to know other people on that more personal level.

To test whether this is true more systematically, we conducted a national survey and asked people several questions about the racial composition of their friends and acquaintances. We classified Americans into three groups: those attending racially homogeneous congregations, those attending racially mixed congregations, and those not attending any congregation. One of the questions we asked them was to think of their circle of friends, those people they like to spend time with and keep in regular contact (whether friends from their congregation, neighborhood, work, childhood, etc.). Were all, most, about half, some, or none of their circle of friends the same race as them?

What did we find? Of those attending racially homogeneous congregations, 83 percent said that most or all of their friends were the same race as them. Among those not attending any congregation, 70 percent said most or all of their friends were the same race as them. Here we see a general pattern I often find in my studies. Religion typically serves to intensify general patterns in the larger society. If society is segregated, religion can intensify that segregation through a variety of ways, but most certainly by providing yet another plane of segregation—its congregations.

What is the case, though, for people attending racially mixed congregations? We found a dramatic difference not only from people attending racially homogeneous congregations, but from people not attending congregations. Whereas 83 percent and 70 percent of those two groupings said most or all of their friends were the same race as them, only 36 percent of people attending racially mixed congregation said most or all of their friends were the same race as them. And we found that those 36 percent who did say most of their friends were the same race as them were relatively recent arrivals to their racially mixed congregation.

We found this same pattern for every question we asked about relationships with other people. People not attending congregations are more likely to be interracially married, have best friends who are of a different race, and have more diverse social networks than are those who attend racially homogeneous congregations. But both groups' level of racial diversity in relationships greatly pales compared to that of people in racially mixed congregations.

In terms of creating holes in the color wall, racially mixed congregations seem a promising avenue. But we cannot get ahead of ourselves. For all we know at this point, the folks attending these types of congregations formed their friendships before they started attending their mixed congregation. In fact, perhaps they ended up in such congregations precisely because they had racially diverse friendships to begin with.

So my colleagues and I again set out to find the answer. We went around the country and interviewed about two hundred people attending racially mixed congregations and, for comparison,

people attending racially homogeneous congregations. We found two answers. People who attend racially mixed congregations are somewhat more likely to have at some time in their lives attended a racially mixed school or lived in a racially mixed neighborhood. But more than 80 percent of the people in racially mixed congregations said that most of the racial diversity in their friendships came *because of* their involvement in their racially mixed congregation. Indeed, when we did a fancy statistical analysis called logistic regression, we found that by far the most important factor in people's having racially diverse relationships is whether they attend a racially mixed congregation. Representative of this finding, a Salvadoran immigrant living in Los Angeles and attending a racially mixed congregation said that perhaps 10 percent of the people she knew before she started attending her church were of different races, but now, "since I have been at this church the majority of my friends are of different races."

This pattern happens for a couple of reasons. First, of course, people make friends with others in their racially mixed congregation. But the diversity effect of these types of congregations goes even further. After making interracial friends in their congregation, people were often introduced to others in their new friends' networks. For example, Chanel, an African American who attends a racially mixed congregation in the South, met Rosita, a Latina who attends the same congregation, through a women's group at the congregation. They soon became friends. Over time, Rosita would invite Chanel over to her place, for birthday parties or other gatherings, where Chanel would meet and get to know an extended network of other Hispanics. And vice versa. Chanel would invite Rosita to her place for family gatherings, where Rosita met and became friends with an extended network of other African Americans. Their children too became fast friends, and so they often got together so their children could play. And we found that this sort of pattern made people more confident and comfortable getting to know still others of different racial groups. As one man from the Northeast who attends a racially mixed congregation said: "Being in this church has really opened me up to people of all different backgrounds. Now when I meet people of different races at work, I don't just say hello and move on. I am comfortable to get to know them. I've made new friends at work this way."

Attitudes

At a celebration service culminating a weekend of youth events at a Baptist church in the Deep South, families and friends of the youths who had attended were invited for the service. Chase, white, 16 years of age, and due to an accident, in a wheelchair for life, was in attendance that weekend. Not attending any congregation prior to this event, he was invited to this youth weekend by a white classmate who did belong to the church. That Sunday, moved by what he had experienced over the past few days of the youth event, he shared with the congregation that he had found a purpose in this congregation—he had made friends with youth of many different races, and who didn't seem to care at all that he was in a wheelchair. Having talked it over with his parents the day before, he announced, through tears, that he had found a home and that he wanted to become a member of the congregation.

Also in attendance that day were his parents and his brother, Tre. Tre was a longtime devout skinhead. His head shaved nearly clean, he had swastika tattoos all around his upper arms. He had a skinhead symbol tattooed on his chest. And he had a noose tattooed on the full length of this left thigh. He didn't at all like nonwhites: "they're whiners, they steal jobs that belong to us, they're lazy, steal, and they have the government always givin' 'em stuff." He was particularly upset at this church he had come to in support of his brother, Chase. The senior pastor was African American, the associate pastor Hispanic. The entire congregation, in fact, was, in his view, a sickening mix of the different races—black, Hispanic, Asian, and worst of all, whites. What are whites doing here with these people? he thought. He felt ill at the sight. Why hadn't his brother told him who was at this church? And now there was his brother, up front, saying he wanted to become part of this God-forsaken place,

even with the support of his parents. Unbelievable! he thought. He was angry, feeling claustrophobic. He just wanted out of this place. But as he described it to me, something happened, something broke inside of him.

Seein' the people all come up to hug my brother, seein' his happy face, seein' all these different people singin' together, feelin' the power in that, it was somethin' I ain't never seen or felt before. Not sure how to describe it, just that it felt real, like it was the way things was supposed to be. I felt like some real bad stuff broke inside of me that day. These people weren't all bad people. They were carin' for my brother.

Two weeks later, through tears of his own, Tre joined the church as well, and asked if the African American pastor would come with him later that week to get his white supremacy tattoos removed.

Few stories of change in racial attitudes are as dramatic as this one. But we found a strong pattern of change in the direction of more positive racial attitudes of people that attend these mixed congregations. We found change in all racial groups, but especially among whites. They were the ones who most often had significant changes in their views, and they are the ones who differ the most from their white peers not in mixed-race congregations. These changes in attitudes seemed to come about as a result of the newly formed friendships, through preaching and teaching, and through observing those of different races involved in common tasks.

We found these differences across religious traditions. At a multiracial mosque in the Midwest, they had a serious problem. The mosque had people from nations who thought you must *always* remove your shoes when entering the mosque, and people from others nations who thought you must *never* insult Allah by removing your shoes when entering the mosque. Pretty easy to see we've got a problem here. Folks take the shoe issue very seriously, because it is tied to their religion and the proper way to worship. And because the shoe issue was related to nationality, ethnicity, and race, the problem quickly became destructive. People took such offense at the other groups that the mosque leaders decided to put up a screen to divide the shoe removers from the shoe wearers, even though this also divided people by ethnicity and race. But they did not intend to keep it there permanently. After they put it up, the imam began to teach that Allah calls all Muslims to be together, across race, ethnicity, and worship approach. They therefore must find a way to do so in their mosque. Either they would all have to remove their shoes or all wear their shoes, or, the solution he proposed, they would have to accept that whichever people do, they do it out of reverence for Allah, not as a reflection of an inferior ethnicity or culture. Reverence for Allah is what must unite them. Over time, the worshippers came to accept this view, and the screen was eventually removed, even though some continued to remove their shoes, and some continued to wear their shoes. Friendships across cultures formed, and attitudes about the different groups became more favorable.

Raised Status

This leads to yet another difference we found in these mixed congregations. The congregation I spent years studying made a commitment to go on mission and service trips to each of the nations that members of the congregation were from. When they went on these trips, the appointed leaders were always the people from that country. As the senior pastor of the congregation told me, this worked wonders on the views of his congregants. A Guatemalan cleaning lady who can barely speak English is easy to marginalize in the U.S. context, but when she was the leader on the trip to Guatemala, when she became the person who was fluent in the language, who knew the lay of the land, who had the social connections, who knew what to eat and what to avoid, she came to be seen, this pastor and his congregants told me, in a substantially new light. She was important, she had skills they did not have, and they were dependent upon her. Through evening discussions while on these trips, the congregants came to conclude that social context, not

a person's essence, shapes views of their worth and skills. Multiracial congregations, we found, often raise the status of racially different others in the eyes of their members.

As you will recall, segregated congregations contribute to socioeconomic inequality. But we found a different pattern in many mixed-race congregations. Because of the social ties between people and changed attitudes, the average education, income, and occupational status of people in these congregations—especially for marginalized groups—were higher than their counterparts not in such congregations. Again, was this the case before or after they came to the congregation? We found that a great deal happened in these congregations that led to increased socioeconomic status after they arrived. Connections were made, child care was provided, and funding was often found that allowed for further schooling. People were hired into jobs that they otherwise might never have known about or had a chance at, because of their connections to others in the congregation well placed in the labor market. It also seems that such congregations help people accrue resources that can gain them access to better heath care, neighborhoods, schools, and other social goods. Mixed-race congregations, then, seem to actually reduce the racial divide in inequality.

Bridge Organizations and Sixth Americans

Mixed-race congregations are what I call bridge organizations; that is, they gather and facilitate cross-race social ties, creating a "natural" setting where people of different racial groups meet and form relationships, pursuing a common purpose (if you have ever studied contact theory, these types of congregations meet well the conditions necessary for forming friendships and reducing prejudice). So different is the average person in a mixed-race congregation compared to the average American outside of these congregations that I call them Sixth Americans. The United States, writes David Hollinger, is really five melting pots;[10] that is, people come from hundreds if not thousands of ethnic backgrounds, but in the United States, they are expected to meld into one of five racial groupings: Indian/Native American, African American/Black, White/Caucasian, Hispanic/Latino/a, or Asian/Asian American.

But people in mixed-race congregations, although phenotypically often part of one of these five melting pots, seem to operate outside of their melting pot in most aspects of their social relations. Sixth Americans live in multiple melting pots simultaneously. Minorities among Americans to be sure, Sixth Americans live in a world of primary relationships and associations that are racially diverse. Like other Americans, the Sixth American may work in a racially diverse setting, see racially different others at the grocery store, or perhaps have a friend of a different race. But unlike other Americans, the Sixth American's "world of racial diversity" does not stop here. It is not a racially homogeneous world with some diversity sprinkled in; the Sixth American's world is a racially diverse world with some homogeneity sprinkled in. In my book, *People of the Dream,* I argue that these Sixth Americans are a different kind of American. And their congregations, where they gather together to worship, serve, and support one another, despite the failures along the way (which I detail in Chapter 6 of the book), may be harbingers of what is to come.[11]

CONCLUSION

Religion in the United States is divided by a vast, thick, massive color wall. That color wall has had and has severe implications for racial division and racial stratification. We have ignored the impact of religion on race for too long. Through studying not segregated congregations, but the small percentage of congregations that are racially mixed, I found that despite risks, the overall trends work to reduce racial division and inequality. These findings serve to further amplify the deleterious effects that segregated congregations have on American race relations.

Changing the organization of American religion is not the sole answer to destructive race relations, but it is part of the answer. To that end, several scholars are now pursuing studies of how multiracial congregations form, how to minimize costs and accentuate positives, and how people come to be in these congregations. If you are interested, we invite you to read further by searching out books and other articles on this topic. Humans create their social structures, so change is possible when humans decide their current social structures will no longer do. Will enough decide to make a change, and put enough holes in the color wall to eventually collapse it? Time will tell.

26

THE BLACK-WHITE SWIMMING DISPARITY IN AMERICA

A Deadly Legacy of Swimming Pool Discrimination

Jeff Wiltse

JEFF WILTSE is professor of history at the University of Montana.

INTRODUCTION

On August 2, 2010, several families gathered for a barbecue picnic along the banks of the Red River outside Shreveport, Louisiana. Upon arriving, some of the kids in the group entered the shallow water near the shoreline. Suddenly, 15-year-old DeKendrix Warner slipped off a ledge into much deeper water. He did not know how to swim and screamed for help. Instinctively, his siblings and cousins rushed out to save him. But they did not know how to swim either. One by one, JaTavious Warner, JaMarcus Warner, Takeitha Warner, Litrelle Stewart, LaDairus Stewart, and Latevin Stewart dropped off into the same deep water. Thrashing their arms, they screamed "help me, help me, somebody please help me." Their parents watched helplessly from the shore, for none of them could swim either. A short distance away, Christopher Patlan was hanging

out with friends and heard the screams. Patlan did know how to swim, having taken lessons as a child. He ran to the scene, plunged out into the water, and grabbed the nearest body, which turned out to be DeKendrix Warner. By the time Patlan had pulled him to safety, the six others had sunk beneath the surface and were drowning. Their bodies were found hours later at the bottom of the river. "Six Teens Drown in La. River: No One Knew How to Swim," read one newspaper headline (Robertson, 2010; "Six Teens Drown in La. River," 2010; Stengle, 2010).

The Red River tragedy was widely reported in the news media and focused public attention on the troubling disparity in swimming and drowning rates between Blacks and Whites in the United States. All six teens who drowned were African Americans, and no one among the several families at the picnic knew how to swim. In an effort

242

Questions to Consider

It seems almost far fetched that the likelihood one would learn how to swim or the statistical probability of drowning would be predicated on one's race. Professor Wiltse's research found exactly this link. The racist and discriminatory practice of barring blacks from public swimming pools in the past set in motion a deadly chain of events that continues today. How and in what ways do race and class play a role in access to public swimming pools?

to explain how that could be, major news outlets such as ABC World News, the BBC, NPR, and CNN highlighted two startling statistics: Black children are half as likely to know how to swim as White children and 3 times more likely to drown.[1] And, they posed the obvious questions: Why are Black Americans less likely to swim than Whites? Why are Black Americans so much more likely to drown? (Claiborne & Francis, 2010; James, 2010; Rohrer, 2010; "Six Teens Drown in Shreveport's Red River," 2010).

While it took the Red River deaths to bring all this to the public's attention, these are not new questions. In fact, the perception that Blacks cannot swim is a long-standing racial stereotype. In the past, it was believed that Blacks had inherent physical characteristics that hindered them from swimming. A 1969 study titled "The Negro and Learning to Swim," for example, concluded that Black men had low capacity for swimming because their bodies were "less buoyant than Caucasians" and their muscles functioned poorly in cold water (Allen & Nickel, 1969, pp. 408–409). More recently, scholars have mostly abandoned genetic and physical explanations for swimming disparities and pointed to social and cultural factors instead.[2] In a study funded by USA Swimming, researchers at the University of Memphis concluded that low swimming rates among Black Americans result

from the lack of parental encouragement, widespread fear of drowning, concerns about damaging one's hair, and the perception that swimming is something White people do (Irwin, Irwin, Martin, & Ross, 2010).

The second question—why Black Americans are more likely to drown than Whites—has not been thoroughly researched. Many scholars and doctors surmise that Black children suffer from comparatively high drowning rates in part because they are less likely to know how to swim, but no published studies have conclusively established the connection.[3] An unpublished article by Samuel L. Myers, Jr. and Ana Cuesta suggests a correlation between the relatively low number of competitive Black swimmers and the high drowning rates among Black Americans generally, but the findings have not been scrutinized by outside reviewers (Myers & Cuesta, 2012). A report published by the American Academy of Pediatrics in 2010 encapsulated the current state of research knowledge this way:

> The reasons that black children and teenagers are more likely to drown are not clear, but poor parental swimming skills, lack of early training, poor swimming ability, and lack of lifeguards at motel/hotel pools [where black children swim more commonly] may be important factors. (Weiss, 2010)

The Red River deaths anecdotally corroborate this set of explanations. The six deaths resulted because none of the teens could swim, their parents did not know how to swim and thus could not rescue them, and they were playing in water not supervised by a lifeguard.

This reading does not propose to offer a definitive answer to the second question; that would require a major, well-funded study. Rather, it accepts the general premise that lack of swimming ability contributes to drowning deaths and then attempts to provide a more historically informed answer to the first question—why Black Americans are so much less likely to know how to swim than White Americans. This article contends that past discrimination in the provision of and access to swimming pools is largely responsible for the current swimming disparity and thus indirectly responsible, at least in part, for the current drowning disparity.

During much of the 20th century, Black Americans faced widespread discrimination that severely limited their access to swimming pools and swim lessons. The most consequential discrimination occurred at public swimming pools and took three basic forms. Public officials and White swimmers denied Black Americans access to pools earmarked for Whites. Cities provided relatively few pools for Black residents, and the pools they did provide were typically small and dilapidated. And, third, cities closed many public pools in the wake of desegregation, just as they became accessible to Black Americans. Black Americans also faced restricted access to Young Men's Christian Association (YMCA) pools and YMCA swim lessons—especially during the critical period of 1920 to 1940, when swimming first became popularized in the United States. Finally, Black Americans were systematically denied access to the tens of thousands of suburban swim clubs opened during the 1950s and 1960s. These pools spurred a second great leap forward in the popularity of swimming, but only for the millions of White families that were able to join.

This past discrimination casts a long shadow. As a result of limited access to swimming facilities and swim lessons and the unappealing design of most pools earmarked for Blacks, swimming did not become integral to the recreation and sports culture within African American communities. Some Black Americans learned to swim but relatively few. By contrast, swimming became broadly popular among Whites and developed into a self-perpetuating recreational and sports culture precisely because they generally had convenient access to appealing swimming pools. Successive generations of White parents took their children to swimming pools and taught them to swim, because that is what they did as children. No such broad, self-perpetuating swim culture developed among Black Americans, however, because they were largely denied access to the pools at which swimming became popularized during the 20th century.

In this way, the swimming disparity created by past discrimination persists into the present.

The same blatant forms of racial discrimination do not exist today, but Americans nonetheless still have unequal access to swimming pools.[4] The inequality now, however, cuts primarily along class lines. Over the past several decades, cities have opened comparatively few new public pools and closed many existing ones. At the same time, the number of private club and backyard pools has increased rapidly. As a result, poor and working-class Americans—who rely more on public recreation facilities—have generally less access to swimming facilities and swim lessons than middle- and upper-class Americans, who can afford to swim at private pools. Studies have already shown the emergence of a class-based swimming gap in the United States, and that gap will likely widen unless the current trend toward privatization is reversed (Irwin, Drayer, Irwin, Ryan, & Southall, 2008).

THE PARADOX OF POSTWAR DESEGREGATION

Public swimming pools were racially desegregated in the United States after World War II. Desegregation occurred first in the North and West, where social protests and court orders broke down segregation during the late 1940s and early 1950s (Wiltse, 2007). Desegregation took longer in the South, where many public pools remained officially segregated well into the 1960s (Kuettner, 1963). Desegregation might have significantly narrowed the swimming gap between Blacks and Whites by giving Black Americans equal access to all public pools, but that is not what happened. Blacks did gain access to some additional pools, but their opportunities to swim remained limited due to a wave of pool closures that followed desegregation and by the racially segregated geography of northern cities.

Southern cities generally shut down their public pools in response to desegregation. When a federal judge ordered Montgomery, West Virginia, to open its municipal pool to Black residents in 1948, city officials drained the pool and locked the gates. For 14 years, the empty pool stood as a conspicuous reminder that racial prejudice was preventing Blacks and Whites in Montgomery from being able to swim (Wiltse, 2007). Birmingham, Alabama, closed all eight of its municipal pools in 1962 after a federal judge ordered them desegregated ("Birmingham Keeps Parks Closed," 1962). Canton, Mississippi, closed its two public swimming pools in 1965 in response to integration efforts by local Black residents. For the next 23 years, Canton operated no public pools. It finally reopened one of the pools in 1988. "It was a long time coming," commented Alderman Jewel Williams. "It was something we had to do and was needed. We had pools, and they were closed. That should never have happened" ("Pool Reopened After 23 Years," 1988). But it did happen, and it happened in cities throughout the South ("Close 4 Fla. Pools Over Race Issue," 1961; "Close Pool to Avoid Integration," 1961; "Jackson Case Ruling," 1971; Kuettner, 1963). And so, even after desegregation, the large number of African Americans living in the South had access to few swimming pools.

The response to racial desegregation in more northern cities was not as blunt, but the effects were similar. For one, residential segregation limited Black Americans' access to public swimming pools, even after the pools were desegregated. In most northern cities, Blacks lived clustered in segregated neighborhoods, commonly referred to as "black belts" (Hirsch, 1983; Sugrue, 1996). Dating all the way back to the late 19th century, public officials had purposefully located most public pools in thoroughly White neighborhoods (Wiltse, 2007). During the postwar period, the existing pools were still located mostly in these neighborhoods far removed from concentrated areas of Black settlement. For Blacks living in most northern cities to take advantage of desegregation and access pools previously off-limits to them, they had to travel into a White neighborhood and swim with the locals. Prospective Black swimmers typically faced varying degrees of hostility that intimidated them from

using these pools. Desegregation enabled northern Blacks to gain access to some additional pools, but, as the examples of Pittsburgh and Baltimore show, many pools located in thoroughly White sections of cities remained inaccessible.

At the start of the postwar period in 1945, Black residents of Pittsburgh had access to one small outdoor pool, whereas Whites could swim in more than 20 pools scattered throughout the city, including a giant resort pool in Highland Park ("Need for Democracy Cited Here," 1945). After a 6-year struggle, the local NAACP finally desegregated Highland Park Pool in 1951 ("5,000 Negroes Used Highland Park Pool This Year," 1952). A year later, after additional protests, the city promised to ensure Black swimmers safe access to a second public pool located near an African American neighborhood ("Minor Incidents at Paulson Pool to be Stopped," 1953). It seemed that the city's history of racially segregated pool use was coming to an end. But that was not to be the case. For many years after 1952, most city pools remained the exclusive domain of Whites precisely because they were located within thoroughly White neighborhoods, and residents of those neighborhoods did not welcome Black swimmers. In 1962, for example, a sign placed outside West Penn Swimming Pool read, "No dogs or niggers allowed" ("Bigots Hurl Insults at Race Swimmer," 1962).

The story of desegregation in Baltimore was much the same. In 1953, the city operated seven outdoor pools—six for Whites and one for Blacks. The Whites-only facilities were distributed throughout the city and offered large pools, concrete sun decks, and grassy lawns. The city's only pool for Blacks, by contrast, was "quite small," according to the Baltimore Department of Recreation, and provided virtually no leisure space (Pangburn & Allen, 1943, p. 97; "Six Outdoor Pools for Whites Only," 1953). A federal appeals court forced the city to end segregation at its pools starting in 1956 (*Dawson v. Mayor and City Council of Baltimore,* 1955). The city obeyed the court order and stopped enforcing official segregation, but Black residents did not gain access to all the city pools. Three pools that had previously been for Whites only (but were located near Black residential neighborhoods) became accessible to Black swimmers: Druid Hill Park Pool no. 1, Clifton Park Pool, and Gwynn's Falls Park Pool. As a result of having access to these additional pools, Black residents' use of city pools increased 39% the first summer after desegregation ("1 Druid Hill Park City Pool Closed," 1956). And yet, just as was the case in Pittsburgh, Blacks in Baltimore still had less access to public pools than did Whites. For many years after 1956, the three pools located within predominately White neighborhoods—Riverside Park, Roosevelt Park, and Patterson Park—remained off-limits to Black swimmers ("Attendance Relatively Small as City's Public Pools Open," 1956; "Baltimore Arrests 13 in Racial Dispute," 1962). In 1963, for example, Floyd Stevens, director of the Clyburn Home for Orphans, brought a group of parentless children to swim at Roosevelt Park Pool. As the group approached, swimmers began to shout, "Nigger, get out of here." Two of the children—a 10-year-old boy and a 13-year-old girl—were Blacks. Stevens let the White orphans enter the pool but took the Black boy and girl back to the orphanage. As a newspaper account of the incident explained, "municipal pools in Baltimore have been declared integrated, but the one visited by the orphans has been used only by whites" ("2 Negro Orphans Jeered Out of Baltimore Pool," 1963).

While desegregation enabled northern Blacks to gain access to some public pools that had previously been off-limits, their use of these pools set off a chain of events that eventually led to many of them being closed. When Blacks began using pools that had previously been earmarked for Whites, White swimmers often abandoned them en masse. In the summer of 1948, prior to the desegregation of St. Louis's Fairgrounds Pool, the city recorded 313,000 swims, all by Whites. In the years after desegregation, the number of swims per year plummeted to 20,000 and almost all the swimmers were now Blacks (St. Louis Division of Parks and Recreation, 1949, 1954). "It appears likely," the city's parks and recreation division explained with considerable understatement, "that the failure of the large outdoor pools to draw the huge number of swimmers

that were attracted in the past may be a reflection of passive resistance to inter-racial swimming" (p. 18). In Baltimore, the total number of swims by Whites in city pools dropped by 62% after desegregation, but that figure actually understates White resistance to mixed-race swimming. Almost all the swims recorded by Whites took place at the three pools that remained off-limits to Blacks: Riverside, Roosevelt, and Patterson. At the previously Whites-only pools that Black Americans began using after desegregation, White attendance dropped by over 95%. "The white people in Druid Hill Park and Clifton Park areas have deserted [these pools]," noted Director of Parks and Recreation R. Brooke Maxwell, "because of the integration policy" ("Baltimore Reports Attendance Drop at Integrated Pools," 1956; "Integrated Baltimore Pool Shut," 1956).

When White attendance dwindled, public swimming pools became much less a priority than they had been previously. For one, cities opened few new pools during the period of desegregation. New York City and Washington, D.C., for example, opened a combined 19 new pools during the 1930s, but no new pools between 1945 and 1960 (Wiltse, 2007). Kansas City likewise built no new pools between 1945 and 1957, even though it operated only three at the time ("Grove Pool Is Closed," 1957). In addition to not building new pools, many cities closed existing pools—especially those serving minority swimmers—rather than pay for costly maintenance and repairs. St. Louis closed Fairgrounds Park Pool in 1956, 6 years after it was desegregated and abandoned by White swimmers (St. Louis Division of Parks and Recreation, 1958). In Washington, D.C., local officials let McKinley Pool fall into disrepair after it was desegregated in 1950 and its use changed from exclusively White to "predominately" Black. By 1960, the "pipes were corroded," the drainage system backed up, and the filtration system did not work properly. Rather than repair it, which is what local Black residents wanted, the federal government decided to close it ("McKinley Pool in Bad Condition," 1962; "Pickets Ask Reopening of Closed Pool," 1963). Public officials in Kansas City closed one of its pools in 1957 for similar reasons. After Grove Pool was desegregated in 1954, attendance plummeted because most Whites stopped using it. City officials then began to view the pool as a financial burden. Rather than pay the yearly operating deficit of US$6,000, the city closed the facility even though it operated only two other pools ("Adieu to Grove Pool," 1957; "Grove Pool Is Closed," 1957). Swimming pools were no longer the high public priority they had been during the period of segregation.

SUBURBAN POOLS AND THE POSTWAR SWIMMING BOOM

The decline of municipal pools during the postwar period did not affect all Americans equally. At the same time that cities built few new pools and closed many existing pools, private swim clubs sprouted in the nation's suburbs like crabgrass during a wet spring. In 1950, there were approximately 1,200 private swim clubs nationally, whereas the National Swimming Pool Institute counted 10,550 such pools in 1959 and more than 23,000 in 1962 ("Data on Swimming Pools," 1952; "Large Splash Being Made by Pool Clubs," 1962). These suburban club pools sparked another massive surge in the popularity of swimming. They attracted millions of families as members and served as the center of summertime social life in the nation's burgeoning suburbs. The clubs offered regular swimming lessons and formed swim teams, which propelled competitive swimming to new heights of popularity. And yet, in a repetition of the past, racial minorities were almost entirely excluded from these pools where the postwar swimming boom occurred. They could not access the swim lessons, they could not join the swim teams, and they could not spend their summer days swimming and socializing at these suburban oases. This time, though, Black Americans were not alone. The suburban location of the swim clubs and the relatively high cost of membership effectively excluded poor and working-class Whites as well.

Suburban Washington, D.C., exemplifies the rapid growth of private swim clubs during the 1950s and 1960s. As tens of thousands of people moved into the D.C. suburbs following World War II, they found an inadequate supply of swimming pools. A small number of country club pools existed, but the many new subdivisions lacked pools. Beginning in the early 1950s, neighborhood families joined together to organize private swim clubs. Each family typically contributed between US$150 and US$200 for an ownership share, which covered the initial construction cost, and then paid yearly dues of US$40 to US$75 for upkeep and operating expenses ("The Cooperative Family Swim Club," 1959; Murray, 1959). By 1958, 125 club pools were operating in the Washington, D.C., area with a combined membership of 40,000, and several dozen more swim clubs were under construction ("Use of District Pools Cut in Half Since '48," 1959). The building spree continued unabated during the 1960s, with new clubs being built in Fort Washington, College Park, Calverton, London Towne, and many more Washington suburbs ("Calverton Will Have New Pool," 1965; "Community Pool Opens," 1960; "New Pool Group Lets Contract," 1962; "Pool Under Way at London Towne," 1969).

The tens of thousands of private swim clubs opened throughout the country further expanded the popularity of swimming. In many suburbs, swim clubs became the center of summertime social and recreational life. Kids in particular frequented the clubs day after day, often for hours at a time. They swam in the pools, sunbathed on the concrete decks, and played games on the grassy lawns. Families gathered at the clubs for evening barbecues and weekend recreation (Donihi, 1963). Swim clubs also offered swimming lessons, which meant that new members and young children had ample opportunity to learn ("How a Swim Club Was Born This Year," 1964). Some clubs even required children to demonstrate the ability to swim two lengths of the pool before they were allowed to use the diving board or enter the deep end (Harvey, 1962). Suburban swim clubs also became the seedbeds for the explosion of swimming as a participatory sport. Most clubs had swim teams that practiced several days a week and then competed against other area clubs. Just in the Washington, D.C., area, more than 200 swim club teams—involving 15,000 swimmers—participated in various suburban leagues in 1972. "Area swim teams are being deluged with applicants and are expanding to . . . unimaginable numbers," reported the *Washington Post* (Attner, 1972).

In addition to the many club pools opened during the 1950s and 1960s, suburbanites also built hundreds of thousands of backyard pools. By one count, there were only 2,500 residential pools nationwide in 1950 ("Data on Swimming Pools," 1952). Ten years later that number had grown to more than 150,000, and, by 1970, there were approximately 800,000 ("Buyers Plunge to Get Into Swim as Installation of Pools Widens," 1960; "Swimming Pool Sales Making a Bigger Splash," 1971). Nearly all these residential pools were located in suburbs and satisfied several desires that were common among the nation's burgeoning suburban middle class. They advertised financial success and upward mobility, enabled owners to control their social environment, and provided an ideal setting for family recreation and at-home entertaining (Wiltse, 2007). Backyard pools and swim clubs became so ubiquitous during this period that swimming and pool play became a common, almost everyday, part of suburban life.

This was a life, however, that few Black Americans could access. For one, few Black Americans lived in suburbs at the time, which meant that most were physically (and financially) cut off from backyard pools and private swim clubs (on the racial composition of postwar suburbs, see Jackson, 1985; Wiese, 2005). But even in cases where Blacks lived in or near suburbs and could afford the cost of membership at a private club, they were still excluded. The Washington, D.C., area had an unusually large Black middle class at the time and therefore provides a useful example of the racial discrimination at suburban swim clubs. The swim clubs located close to downtown Washington, including those in Chevy Chase and Bethesda, passed bylaws when they first opened in the 1950s that explicitly limited membership to White persons ("Chevy Chase Club Explains Stand on Membership," 1962; "Fairfax

Club Affirms Barring of Negro Family," 1965; "Integration Vote Fails at Bethesda Swim Club," 1966). Swim clubs further removed from downtown relied, at least initially, on the racial exclusivity of their neighborhood to prevent Black families from joining. One club in suburban Maryland, for example, passed a residency requirement in 1958 mandating that members live within three fourths of a mile of the pool. The club did not receive a membership application from a Black family until 1968. When that first Black family applied, the club rejected its application, and members quickly voted not to allow any Black members. As the club could no longer rely on residential segregation to protect the racial composition of its membership, it now needed an explicit policy (*Tillman v. Wheaton-Haven Recreation Association*, 1973). Many other swim clubs in suburban Washington similarly passed explicit bylaws in the mid-to-late 1960s that barred Blacks from becoming members ("Club in New Carrollton Excludes Negro Family," 1968; "Integration Effort Fails at Virginia City Pool," 1966).

As a result of residential segregation and discriminatory membership policies, Black Americans simply did not have access to private swim clubs during this period. In 1968, for example, the Montgomery County (Maryland) Swimming League organized swim meets between 42 different swim clubs. Not one of the participating clubs had a single identifiably Black member (Feinberg, 1968). Noting the pervasive discrimination against Black Americans at club pools generally, a Washington, D.C., judge lamented,

> I suppose like many people I really didn't believe when the issue had to be faced that intelligent, well-educated, financially secure suburban middle-class people would effectively exclude a neighbor from a community [swimming pool] solely on the basis of race. ("Club in New Carrollton Excludes Negro Family," 1968)

And yet they did. Once again, swimming boomed in popularity at pools that were inaccessible to Black Americans.

"GIANT-SIZED URINALS"

During the late 1960s, there was a short burst of municipal-pool building, in which public officials suddenly prioritized providing swimming pools for urban Black Americans. The spark that ignited the pool-building spree was Chicago's 1966 race riot. The riot began on a hot mid-July day after police attempted to arrest Donald Henry for defiantly opening a fire hydrant located in the heart of the city's West Side Black belt. As the officers moved to detain Henry, onlookers began throwing rocks at them. Fifteen more police cars quickly rushed to the scene, and the angry crowd greeted them with a barrage of rocks, bottles, and bricks. The fire-hydrant dispute sparked 3 days of intense rioting on Chicago's West Side. In the end, three people were killed, countless injured, and 300 were arrested. The property damage was extensive ("1500 Troops Go to Area Ready to Shoot," 1966; "Police Get 12-Hour Duty in Westside Uproar," 1966).

The fire-hydrant confrontation did not merely precipitate the riot—it hinted at an underlying cause of it as well. Black Chicagoans seethed with anger in part because they lacked summertime recreation opportunities, especially swimming pools. "Hell, it's so God Damn hot," explained one man. "I'll cool my ass anywhere I want to. They ought to take some of that poverty money and put a swimmin' pool over here." The *Chicago Defender* agreed, noting that "a swimming pool may be the most immediate need the community faces" ("Police Get 12-Hour Duty in Westside Uproar," 1966). There were three municipal pools located within a mile of the riot flashpoint, but they were inaccessible to Black residents. The pools were located within White enclaves, where, according to one Westside resident, Blacks "can't go there without being beaten" ("Here's How a Westsider Explains the Outbreak," 1966). Even city officials acknowledged that the pools were not "readily available to Negroes because of hostility in the white community" ("The Pools Inadequate? The West Side Picture," 1966). A few years earlier, for

example, 750 Whites attacked a group of Black swimmers with bricks and stones as they left the South Side's Bessemer Park Pool ("Race Riot in Chicago," 1960).

The 1966 Chicago riot prompted public officials to redress the historically inadequate provision of public pools for Black Americans. During the riot, Martin Luther King, Jr., met with Chicago mayor Richard Daly and advised him that swimming pools would help alleviate some of the tensions that caused the riot. Three days later, the city purchased 10 small, pre-fabricated pools and quickly set them up in the "troubled neighborhoods" ("Guard Patrol Is Cut in Chicago Ghetto," 1966). Daly then announced a long-range plan to build more than 100 "neighborhood" pools in Chicago ("Goal: A Pool for Every Neighborhood," 1967). The federal government also became concerned about the lack of swimming pools for urban Blacks. Four days after the Chicago riot ended, President Lyndon Johnson announced that federal "anti-poverty" grants would be used to fund swimming pools for "disadvantaged youth" across the country. Within a month, the federal government had disbursed pool money to 40 metropolitan areas, including Chicago, New York, Philadelphia, Washington, and Atlanta ("Program Rushed for Slum Youth," 1966). Providing summer recreation for urban Blacks had suddenly become a national priority.

Most of the municipal pools opened during this late-1960s building spree, however, did not provide viable recreation or encourage actual swimming. Overall, 70 of the 84 pools opened in New York, and all but 2 of the 32 pools eventually opened in Chicago were "mini-pools," measuring only 20 by 40 ft and uniformly 3 ft deep. The pools were usually too crowded for swimming, so youngsters mostly stood in the water splashing. Nor did the mini-pools provide any leisure space. The tanks were surrounded by a narrow concrete perimeter and enclosed by a chain-link fence. Most did not have changing rooms either, so swimmers traveled to the pools in their swimsuits. Children in one New York neighborhood dubbed them "giant-sized urinals" ("32 New Pools to Help Chicago Keep Its Cool,"

1968; "Cool Minipools for the Hot Summer," 1968; "Lindsay Smiles His Way Through City," 1971). Such pools were not the type of facilities that would help popularize swimming among Black Americans. Nor did cities typically offer swimming instruction at the mini-pools (Brozan, 1976; "Feelings Vary on Swim Lessons," 1976).

POOL CLOSINGS IN RECENT TIMES

The "mini-pool" building spree of the late 1960s was short lived. Whereas urban public pools had briefly been a national priority, pool building stalled in the 1970s. The primary reasons were economic. Ballooning budget deficits and the threat of bankruptcy forced many cities to abandon plans for future pools and put off costly maintenance and repairs on the existing pools. As a result, municipal pools deteriorated and came to reflect the poverty of urban America at the time. "Boards have replaced broken windows. The water fountain is broken. Walls are smeared with graffiti. The ground is littered and a burned car sits in the parking lot" ("Troubled Waters," 1989). Although a bit extreme, this description of an abandoned Detroit swimming pool captures the general state of municipal pools during the 1970s and 1980s, especially in northern cities.

The fate of municipal pools in Youngstown, Ohio, exemplifies the general decline of public pools in the urban north. Youngstown operated eight public pools as of the early 1980s. Historically, the city's pools had registered more than 200,000 swims per summer, but, by 1984, the pools recorded only 43,000 swims. The breakdown of de facto racial segregation and the deteriorating condition of the pools largely account for the decline. Beginning in 1985, city officials began closing pools, citing the low attendance and the city's financial woes as the reasons. The city closed four pools between 1985 and 1988 and two more in 1991. Thereafter, Youngstown operated only

two municipal pools and the annual attendance plummeted all the way down to 10,000 (Wiltse, 2007). The story in other cities was much the same. Between 1996 and 2004, Pittsburgh permanently closed 20 of its 32 pools in an effort to reduce its ballooning budget deficit. Some members of the city council complained that pools should be one of the last city services suspended, but most did not agree. As a result of the closings, Pittsburgh offered residents fewer municipal pools in 2005 than it had in 1925 (Wiltse, 2007). Even rapidly growing metropolitan areas reduced their provision of public pools during this period. The city and county of Los Angeles operated 87 public pools in 1975, when their combined population was 7.1 million ("City Pools Open," 1974; "County Swimming Pools to Be Free," 1975; "Los Angeles County Population Growth," 2000). By 2005, when the population had grown to 9.8 million, the city and county operated 81 pools (City of Los Angeles Department of Parks and Recreation, 2006; County of Los Angeles Department of Parks and Recreation, 2005–2006; "Estimated Population of Los Angeles County," 2005).

The economic recession that began in 2008 caused a new wave of pool closures. As Jeffrey Collins explained in a 2011 Associated Press article, "From New York City to Sacramento, Calif., pools now considered costly extravagances are being shuttered, taking away a rite of summer for millions" (Collins, 2011). Sacramento closed 9 of its 12 public pools during the recession. Cincinnati closed 11 of its 39 pools. Phoenix shuttered almost one third of its pools but did reopen them in 2012. Residents of Tucson were not so lucky. The city "temporarily" closed 17 of its 27 pools in 2010, but 11 never reopened (Collins, 2011; O'Dowd, 2010; Sexton, 2012). Other cities—including Atlanta, Baltimore, Houston, and Philadelphia—closed some pools and struggled to keep others open by reducing hours, shortening the summer season, and relying on last-minute corporate donations (McKinley, 2011; Skwine, 2009). In assessing the provision of public swimming pools nationwide in 2011, Bill Beckner, the research manager for the National Park and

Recreation Association, concluded, "There's some [cities] treading water, and some [that] are sinking" (McKinley, 2011).

These waves of pool closures have affected poor and working-class Americans most severely. Whereas middle- and upper-class Americans— especially those living in suburbs—have ample access to private swimming pools, the urban poor rely primarily on public recreation facilities. When a public pool closes in their neighborhood, they often have no alternative place to swim. During the midst of the pool closures in Youngstown, for example, city officials considered closing North Side Pool, one of the few pools that remained open. Local councilwoman Darlene Rogers objected, pointing out that it was one of the only recreation spaces available to children in the area. "My concern is that it is the only pool left on the North Side. If we close the pool, there won't be any place for those kids to swim. And we don't have many other recreation activities for them" ("Youngstown May Close Second Pool," 1989). Ed Gonzalez, a city councilman in Houston, expressed the same point in 2009 after the city closed Independence Heights pool, which was located in a historically Black neighborhood with many poor and working-class residents. In an interview with the *New York Times,* Gonzalez emphasized that the loss of a public pool in this neighborhood was much more consequential than the loss of a pool in a well-to-do neighborhood. "There are no other true community assets out there. Your neighborhood park and your pools are the only real amenities that some of these communities have" (McKinley, 2011). The more municipal pools close, the less opportunity the urban poor has to swim. As Collins points out in his AP article on the recent pool closings, the poor "can't afford a membership to [a] private pool or fitness club and don't live in a neighborhood where they can befriend someone with a backyard pool" (Collins, 2011).

To the extent to which Black Americans are over-represented among the urban poor, public pool closings reinforce the longstanding swimming disparity between Blacks and Whites. But the decline of public pools has also created a class-based swimming disparity. In recent times, middle- and upper-class Americans have learned to swim in high proportion to their overall numbers because they have easy access to swimming pools and can afford to pay for swim lessons. Access to swimming pools and swim lessons for poor and working-class Americans is far more variable. Some are fortunate to live near an affordable pool, which enables them to swim regularly. Many others, however, are not so fortunate. They do not have easy access to an appealing and affordable pool or to swim lessons. As a result, poor and working-class Americans of all racial identities are less likely to know how to swim than middle- and upper-class Americans (Irwin et al., 2008). Whereas the current racial disparity in swimming and drowning is largely a product of what happened in the past, this class-based disparity is largely a product of what is happening now and will likely widen in the future unless the nation reprioritizes the funding of public swimming pools.

Seeing the Big Picture   Racialized Public Spaces: From Church to Pool

Look through the appendix and see if you are able to locate any social spaces where you think it would be likely that individuals interact in a sustained way across the color line. What are these situations? If you can't find any, why not?

AUTHOR BIOGRAPHY

Jeff Wiltse is associate professor of history at the University of Montana, Missoula and author of *Contested Waters: A Social History of Swimming Pools in America* (UNC Press, 2007). He is currently at work on a study of the role music played in the public life of American cities, tentatively titled *In and Out of Harmony: Public Music in American Cities, 1840–1930*.

RACIALIZED OPPORTUNITY IN SOCIAL INSTITUTIONS

Answer the questions that follow.

1. As of 2018, what percentage of the U.S. population do you think was:

   a. Black _____%

   b. White _____%

   c. Asian _____%

   d. American Indian _____%

   e. Latino _____%

2. Who are your three best friends? 1) _____
   2) _____ 3) _____

3. Does the unemployment rate in the United States vary by color or ethnicity? _____

Each of your answers, whether you realize it or not, reflects how you have been shaped by social institutions. Compare your answers on item 1 to the correct percentages as enumerated by the U.S. Bureau of the Census in 2016: 13.3 percent black, 61 percent non-Hispanic white, 5.7 percent Asian/ Pacific Islander, 1.3 percent American Indian, and 17.8 percent Latino.

Did your estimates of the size of these groups differ from the actual numbers? If you said that the black population was around 30 percent or that the Asian population was 10 percent, your answer was similar to the average American response. How do you explain the fact that most people in the United States almost triple-count the black and Asian population? From a sociological perspective, what does the overcounting of the nonwhite population mean?

Item 2 asked you to list your three best friends. How many of the people you listed are from a different race? How many are the same sex as you? If you don't have any best friends who are from a racial background different from your own, why not? Is it that you do not like people from other races? Does this mean you are a racist? Do you only have friends of the same sex? Why?

With regard to item 3, the unemployment rate in the United States does vary by color or ethnicity, with blacks and Latinos twice as likely as whites to be unemployed. How is the unemployment rate linked to how close people live to areas of high job growth, and how are both of these factors linked to race and ethnicity?

The answers to these questions reflect the ways in which institutions shape how we view the world. Your beliefs, opinions, and attitudes, and the "commonsense" knowledge that guides your moment-to-moment understanding of the world—all may seem to be highly individualistic. Upon closer sociological inspection, however, we see that institutions and other social arrangements influence, mediate, and structure how we think about and come to understand the world in which we live. Think for a moment about your answers to the preceding questions. People of all colors typically overestimate the nonwhite population and underestimate the white population. Perhaps you overestimated the nonwhite population because you live in an all-black or all-Latino neighborhood. When you look out the window or walk down the street, you see that everyone in your neighborhood is like you. That local information is then used to make a judgment about the rest of the United States. But what if you are white and you overestimated the nonwhite population? How do you explain doubling or tripling the black or Asian population? Do you get your information about other racial groups secondhand, from watching television? Might there be a difference between the media's portrayal of race and ethnic relations and what is actually taking place in society? Do you watch professional sports, music videos, or the local television news? Might your estimates reflect something about your television viewing habits? If you live in a racially segregated neighborhood, might that explain why your best friends are all the same color as you? Do you think you might have close friends from different racial backgrounds if your high school or neighborhood were racially integrated? Why is it that compared to white areas or the suburbs, jobs are often not as plentiful or as well paying in black or Latino neighborhoods?

In Part III, we focus on how race and ethnic identity intersect with the criminal justice system,

the labor market, where individuals live and why, and how the media shape our views on race and ethnic relations. The four readings in Race and Criminal Justice: Oxymoron or an American Tragedy? examine the influence of race and class on the American justice system.

Andrew Cohen compares the crack epidemic of the late 1980s to the opioid epidemic playing out right now and how these events were framed by politicians and the media. It seems that the race of addicts plays a part in how society responds to a crisis. Should we be punitive and throw more people in jail, or should we define a drug epidemic as a public health situation? Who is likely to live or die, controlling for the type of crime committed, varies by race. Michelle Alexander examines the disproportionate impact government policies like the "War on Drugs" and "Three Strikes and You're Out" have had on communities of color. She does not see these trends as the unintended consequences of poorly designed public policy but rather a continuation of Jim Crow laws of the past that ultimately resulted in the control and incarceration of male black and brown populations. Ronald Weitzer provides insight into why there have been so many deaths of unarmed black men by police and the reforms that could make these interactions less deadly. Finally, what Devah Pager found is almost incomprehensible—that white men with a prison record were more likely to get a call back for a job than black men who had no criminal record.

The next section, How Race Shapes the Workplace, examines the sociological reasons why economic and occupational outcomes vary by race and ethnicity. The short research summary by Amy Braverman details how a name can signal racial identity and how employers use this information. Roger Waldinger provides historical and contemporary examples of how employment opportunities have changed over time by examining the different occupational niches that ethnic and racial groups occupied in New York City and the conditions that allowed upward mobility for some and economic stagnation for others. Katherine Newman and Catherine Ellis document the work strategies used by fast-food workers in Harlem. The

"McJob" experiences of two hundred black and brown respondents in their study challenge a number of "commonsense" assumptions about work at a fast-food restaurant and workers' attitudes about upward mobility. Xiaolan Bao chronicles the ways in which two newly arrived immigrant groups, Chinese laborers in the sweatshops of New York City, are part of an unregulated and exploited workforce that is becoming all too common.

The third section, Race, Representations, and the Media, explores how the media shape our views on race and ethnicity. In the first subsection Racism and Popular Culture, Danielle Dirks and Jennifer Mueller discuss how racist images are articulated and "consumed" by the public through the media. Marci Bounds Littlefield uses the theory of racialization discussed in an earlier reading to frame how sexist and racist images are a staple in the media but are uncontested because many individuals believe these stereotypes to be true. Bhoomi Thakore explores the depictions of South East Asians in the media and how and in what ways stereotypes creep into the roles for these actors. Evelyn Alsultany points out that both positive and negative depictions of Arabs and Muslims appear on television, but the net effect is to cement negative stereotypes of these two groups. These readings ask us to consider how representations of race and ethnicity in the nightly news or in situation comedies shape our worldview.

The final section, Crazy Horse Malt Liquor and Athletes: The Tenacity of Stereotypes, takes two examples of stereotypes that refuse to go away: the image of the savage Indian and the violent black athlete. Debra Merskin deconstructs the meaning of American Indians in popular culture and the consequences of such stereotypical and racist imagery. Finally, Jeremy Adam Smith and Dacher Keltner discuss the social and political context of athletes "taking a knee" to protest police brutality and why many people saw this not as a form of social protest but as an action disrespectful to the flag.

27

HOW WHITE USERS MADE HEROIN A PUBLIC-HEALTH PROBLEM

Andrew Cohen

ANDREW COHEN is a writer for *The Atlantic* magazine.

HEROIN USE AND ABUSE IN AMERICA has dramatically increased over the past decade. Between 2006 and 2013, federal records reveal that the number of first-time heroin users doubled from 90,000 to 169,000. Some of those users, no doubt, already are gone. The Centers for Disease Control and Prevention announced last month that the rate of deadly heroin overdoses nearly quadrupled between 2002 and 2013.

These troubling figures, and a spate of more recent stories and daunting statistics, have prompted officials across the country to implement bold new policies and practices designed to reduce the harm of heroin use. Although there has been some push to enhance criminal sanctions to combat the surge, much of the institutional reaction to the renewed popularity of the drug has sounded in the realm of medicine, not law.

Questions to Consider

The Centers for Disease Control and Prevention reported that there were 64,000 drug overdose deaths in 2016, of which 15,446 were deaths from heroin overdoses. The United States is in the midst of an opioid epidemic. In the late 1980s, the United States was in the throes of another epidemic that involved crack cocaine, but the response was quite different than what is taking place around the current opioid crisis. The crack epidemic was met by greater and more punitive legal measures while the opioid epidemic is being framed as a public health issue. Many writers argue that the only real difference between these two epidemics was the race of the populations. Andrew Cohen looks at the racial implications of how society responded to these two national emergencies. What are the long-term implications of how society responded to these emergencies?

One public official after another, in states both "red" and "blue," has pressed in recent years to treat increased heroin use as a public-safety problem as opposed to a criminal-justice matter best left to police, prosecutors, and judges. This is good news. But it forms a vivid contrast with the harsh reaction a generation ago to the sudden rise in the use of crack cocaine, and from the harsh reaction two generations ago to another heroin epidemic.

What accounts for the differences? Clearly policymakers know more today than they did then about the societal costs of waging a war on drugs, and dispatching low-level, nonviolent drug offenders to prison for decades. The contemporary criminal-justice system places more emphasis on treatment and reform than it did, say, during the Reagan years or when New York's draconian "Rockefeller laws" were passed in the 1970s. But there may be another explanation for the less hysterical reaction, one that few policymakers have been willing to acknowledge: race.

Some experts and researchers see, in the different responses to these drug epidemics, further proof of America's racial divide. Are policymakers going easier today on heroin users (white and often affluent) than their elected predecessors did a generation ago when confronted with crack addicts who were largely black, disenfranchised, and economically bereft? Can we explain the disparate response to the "black" heroin epidemic of the 1960s, in which its use and violent crime were commingled

in the public consciousness, and the white heroin "epidemic" today, in which its use is considered a disease to be treated or cured, without using race as part of our explanation?

Marc Mauer, the executive director of the Sentencing Project, a group that targets racial disparities in the criminal-justice system, has been following this issue closely for decades. He agrees there is strong historical precedent for comparing the crises through the prism of race:

The response to the rise in heroin use follows patterns we've seen over decades of drug scares. When the perception of the user population is primarily people of color, then the response is to demonize and punish. When it's white, then we search for answers. Think of the difference between marijuana attitudes in the "reefer madness" days of the 1930s when the drug was perceived to be used in the "racy" parts of town, and then the 1960s (white) college town explosion in use.

It is now axiomatic that although the crack epidemic of the 1980s devastated communities of color, the legal and political responses to the crisis compounded the tragedy. Crack was an inner-city drug, a street-corner drug, a drug of gangs and guns that white America largely experienced from a distance. Powder cocaine, the more expensive version of the drug, found its way to more affluent users. The federal Anti-Drug Abuse Act, passed in 1986, imposed mandatory-minimum sentences that were far harsher on users of crack cocaine than on those found with the drug in powdered form. The Fair Sentencing Act of 2010 reduced that disparity in sentencing from 100:1 to 18:1, but that remains a striking gap.

Indeed, the harsh, punitive reaction to the crack era was the result of mythology about its use, and its users, that later turned out to be false, says Jeffrey Fagan, a Columbia University professor who has long studied the intersection of criminal justice and race. "It was instantly

FIGURE 1 ■ Opioid Overdose Deaths by Race/Ethnicity: White, Non-Hispanic & Black, Non-Hispanic & Hispanic, 1999–2015

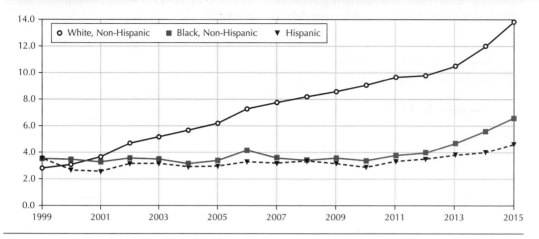

Source: Kaiser Family Foundation's State Health Facts.

addictive, it created 'superpredators,' you became a sexual deviant, especially if you were a woman, it destroyed maternal instincts," he said. All of that nonsense led to the draconian sentencing laws associated with crack use in the 1980s, Fagan told me.

And that, Fagan says, was the sequel to another criminal-justice crackdown that had taken place decades earlier. A surge in heroin use among blacks in the 1960s was blamed for a rise in violent crime, and provoked a harsh response.

By contrast to those earlier drug crises, the heroin epidemic of the 21st century is largely a white person's scourge. The Centers for Disease Control says the cheap, easily accessible drug is attracting affluent suburbanites and women. Nearly 90 percent of the people who tried heroin for the first time in the past decade are white, according to a study published in JAMA Psychiatry in July 2014, and there is no reason to believe the trend has eased since then. Said the researchers:

> Heroin use has changed from an inner-city, minority-centered problem to one that has a more widespread geographical distribution, involving primarily white men and women

in their late 20s living outside of large urban areas.

The cause for *this* may be simple. White people addicted to prescription opiates, the sorts of drugs they could conveniently get from a friendly doctor or pharmacist, are finding heroin an obvious (and cheap) substitute now that law-enforcement officials have cracked down on those opiates. The hottest fronts in this war now can be seen in rural states like Vermont and in suburban areas that largely missed the ravages of the crack craze.

And politicians on both sides of the aisle clearly are paying attention to what researchers diplomatically call the "changing face of heroin use." According to the Pew Charitable Trusts, lawmakers in at least 24 states and the District of Columbia have enacted laws in the past few years that make naloxone, a prescription drug that helps counter the effect of a heroin overdose, more broadly available. Just three weeks ago, Ohio Governor John Kasich, a Republican presidential candidate, signed emergency legislation to make naxolone available without a prescription.

His neighbor in Kentucky, Senator Rand Paul, another Republican running for the White House, introduced the Recovery Enhancement for Addiction Treatment Act earlier this year. It would make it easier for doctors to treat heroin users with a drug called buprenorphine. Nearly two-dozen states have also passed laws that protect "good Samaritans" who alert doctors or nurses to heroin overdoses.

Such public-health responses were not necessarily unthinkable during the crackcocaine wave of the 1980s or the heroin epidemic of the 1960s. But the limited public-health measures adopted during those eras were overshadowed by more punitive responses to those crises. Can you imagine the Congress and the White House of 1985 debating a "Recovery Enhancement for Addiction Act" for crack users? Mauer remembers instead the brutal mandatory-sentencing laws of that era sweeping toward passage in Congress in near-record time. What accounts for the difference? "I don't think that's only because we are more thoughtful today," Mauer said.

Seeing the Big Picture   **Race, Drugs, and Death**

In Section III (Figure 11B) a chart shows that all racial groups have been adversely affected by drug overdose deaths, but this trend has hit white Americans particularly hard. Why is this the case?

ABOUT THE AUTHOR

ANDREW COHEN is a contributing editor at *The Atlantic*. He is a legal analyst for *60 Minutes* and CBS Radio News, a fellow at the Brennan Center for Justice, and commentary editor at The Marshall Project.

THE NEW JIM CROW

Michelle Alexander

MICHELLE ALEXANDER won the 2005 Soros Justice Fellowship and holds a joint appointment at the Kirman Institute for the Study of Race and Ethnicity and is a Professor of Law at Ohio State University.

THE LAW AND ORDER PERSPECTIVE, FIRST introduced during the peak of the Civil Rights Movement by rabid segregationists, had become nearly hegemonic two decades later. By the mid-1990s, no serious alternatives to the War on Drugs and "get tough" movement were being entertained in mainstream political discourse. Once again, in response to a major disruption in the prevailing racial order—this time the civil rights gains of the 1960s—a new system of racialized social control was created by exploiting the vulnerabilities and racial resentments of poor and working-class whites. More than 2 million people found themselves behind bars at the turn of the twenty-first century, and millions more were relegated to the margins of mainstream society, banished to a political and social space not unlike **Jim Crow**, where discrimination in employment, housing, and access to education was perfectly legal, and where they could be denied the right to vote. The system functioned relatively automatically, and the prevailing system of racial meanings, identities and ideologies already seemed natural. Ninety percent of those admitted to prison for drug offenses in many states were black or Latino, yet the mass incarceration of communities of color was explained in race-neutral terms, an adaptation to the needs and demands of the current political climate. The New Jim Crow was born.

Questions to Consider

If one were to look at who is incarcerated in the United States for drug crimes, one might conclude that black and Latino men are more likely to carry, use, and distribute illegal drugs. What we learn from Michelle Alexander, however, is that national studies on drug use find that whites are in fact more likely to carry and use drugs like cocaine, marijuana, and heroin. If it is the case that whites have more contact with illegal drugs, why are African Americans and Latinos overrepresented in our prisons? Why is it that certain racial and ethnic groups are more likely to be stopped, searched, or arrested by the police? How might the very act of policing be linked to rates of incarceration?

Jim Crow Laws put in place throughout the United States, but particularly in the South in the 19th century that institutionalized racism and discrimination toward blacks.

Imagine you are Erma Faye Stewart, a thirty-year-old, single African American mother of two who was arrested as part of a drug sweep in Hearne, Texas.[1] All but one of the people arrested were African American. You are innocent. After a week in jail, you have no one to care for your two small children and are eager to get home. Your court-appointed attorney urges you to plead guilty to a drug distribution charge, saying the prosecutor has offered probation. You refuse, steadfastly proclaiming your innocence. Finally, after almost a month in jail, you decide to plead guilty so you can return home to your children. Unwilling to risk a trial and years of imprisonment, you are sentenced to ten years' probation and ordered to pay $1,000 in fines, as well as court and probation costs. You are also now branded a drug felon. You are no longer eligible for food stamps; you may be discriminated against in employment; you cannot vote for at least twelve years; and you are about to be evicted from public housing. Once homeless, your children will be taken from you and put in foster care.

A judge eventually dismisses all cases against the defendants who did not plead guilty. At trial, the judge finds that the entire sweep was based on the testimony of a single informant who lied to the prosecution. You, however, are still a drug felon, homeless, and desperate to regain custody of your children.

Now place yourself in the shoes of Clifford Runoalds, another African American victim of the Hearne drug bust.[2] You returned home to Bryan,

Texas, to attend the funeral of your eighteen-month-old daughter. Before the funeral services begin, the police show up and handcuff you. You beg the officers to let you take one last look at your daughter before she is buried. The police refuse. You are told by prosecutors that you are needed to testify against one of the defendants in a recent drug bust. You deny witnessing any drug transaction; you don't know what they are talking about. Because of your refusal to cooperate, you are indicted on felony charges.

After a month of being held in jail, the charges against you are dropped. You are technically free, but as a result of your arrest and period of incarceration, you lose your job, your apartment, your furniture, and your car. Not to mention the chance to say good-bye to your baby girl.

This is the War on Drugs. The brutal stories described above are not isolated incidents, nor are the racial identities of Erma Faye Stewart and Clifford Runoalds random or accidental. In every state across our nation, African Americans—particularly in the poorest neighborhoods—are subjected to tactics and practices that would result in public outrage and scandal if committed in middle-class white neighborhoods. In the drug war, the enemy is racially defined. The law enforcement methods described [earlier] have been employed almost exclusively in poor communities of color, resulting in jaw-dropping numbers of African Americans and Latinos filling our nation's prisons and jails every year. We are told by drug warriors that the enemy in this war is a thing—drugs—not a group of people, but the facts prove otherwise.

Human Rights Watch reported in 2000 that, in seven states, African Americans constitute 80 percent to 90 percent of all drug offenders sent to prison.[3] In at least fifteen states, blacks are admitted to prison on drug charges at a rate from twenty to fifty-seven times greater than that of white men.[4] In fact, nationwide, the rate of incarceration for African American drug offenders dwarfs the rate of whites. When the War on Drugs gained full steam in the mid-1980s, prison admissions for African Americans skyrocketed, nearly quadrupling in three years, and then increasing steadily until it reached

in 2000 a level *more than twenty-six times* the level in 1983.[5] The number of 2000 drug admissions for Latinos was twenty-two times the number of 1983 admissions.[6] Whites have been admitted to prison for drug offenses at increased rates as well—the number of whites admitted for drug offenses in 2000 was eight times the number admitted in 1983—but their relative numbers are small compared to blacks' and Latinos'.[7] Although the majority of illegal drug users and dealers nationwide are white, three-fourths of all people imprisoned for drug offenses have been black or Latino.[8] In recent years, rates of black imprisonment for drug offenses have dipped somewhat—declining approximately 25 percent from their zenith in the mid-1990s—but it remains the case that African Americans are incarcerated at grossly disproportionate rates throughout the United States.[9]

There is, of course, an official explanation for all of this: crime rates. This explanation has tremendous appeal—before you know the facts—for it is consistent with, and reinforces, dominant racial narratives about crime and criminality dating back to slavery. The truth, however, is that rates and patterns of drug crime do not explain the glaring racial disparities in our criminal justice system. People of all races use and sell illegal drugs at remarkably similar rates.[10] If there are significant differences in the surveys to be found, they frequently suggest that whites, particularly white youth, are more likely to engage in illegal drug dealing than people of color.[11] One study, for example, published in 2000 by the National Institute on Drug Abuse reported that white students use cocaine at seven times the rate of black students, use crack cocaine at eight times the rate of black students, and use heroin at seven times the rate of black students.[12] That same survey revealed that nearly identical percentages of white and black high school seniors use marijuana. The National Household Survey on Drug Abuse reported in 2000 that white youth aged 12–17 are more than a third more likely to have sold illegal drugs than African American youth.[13] Thus the very same year Human Rights Watch was reporting that African Americans were being arrested and imprisoned at unprecedented rates, government data revealed that blacks were no more likely to be guilty of drug crimes than whites and that white youth were actually the *most likely* of any racial or ethnic group to be guilty of illegal drug possession and sales. Any notion that drug use among blacks is more severe or dangerous is belied by the data; white youth have about three times the number of drug-related emergency room visits as their African American counterparts.[14]

The notion that whites comprise the vast majority of drug users and dealers—and may well be more likely than other racial groups to commit drug crimes—may seem implausible to some, given the media imagery we are fed on a daily basis and the racial composition of our prisons and jails. Upon reflection, however, the prevalence of white drug crime—including drug dealing—should not be surprising. After all, where do whites get their illegal drugs? Do they all drive to the ghetto to purchase them from somebody standing on a street corner? No. Studies consistently indicate that drug markets, like American society generally, reflect our nation's racial and socioeconomic boundaries. Whites tend to sell to whites; blacks to blacks.[15] University students tend to sell to each other.[16] Rural whites, for their part, don't make a special trip to the 'hood to purchase marijuana. They buy it from somebody down the road.[17] White high school students typically buy drugs from white classmates, friends, or older relatives. Even Barry McCaffrey, former director of the White House Office of National Drug Control Policy, once remarked, if your child bought drugs, "it was from a student of their own race generally."[18] The notion that most illegal drug use and sales happen in the ghetto is pure fiction. Drug trafficking occurs there, but it occurs everywhere else in America as well. Nevertheless, black men have been admitted to state prison on drug charges at a rate that is more than thirteen times higher than white men.[19] The racial bias inherent in the drug war is a major reason that 1 in every 14 black men was behind bars in 2006, compared with 1 in 106 white men.[20] For young black men, the statistics are even worse. One in 9 black men between the ages of twenty and thirty-five was behind bars in 2006, and far more

were under some form of penal control—such as probation or parole.[21] These gross racial disparities simply cannot be explained by rates of illegal drug activity among African Americans.

What, then, does explain the extraordinary racial disparities in our criminal justice system? Old-fashioned racism seems out of the question. No politicians and law enforcement officials today endorse racially biased practices, and most of them fiercely condemn racial discrimination of any kind. When accused of racial bias, police and prosecutors—like most Americans—express horror and outrage. Forms of race discrimination that were open and notorious for centuries were transformed in the 1960s and 1970s into something un-American—an affront to our newly conceived ethic of color-blindness. By the early 1980s, survey data indicated that 90 percent of whites thought black and white children should attend the same schools, 71 percent disagreed with the idea that whites have a right to keep blacks out of their neighborhoods, 80 percent indicated they would support a black candidate for president, and 66 percent opposed laws prohibiting intermarriage.[22] Although far fewer supported specific policies designed to achieve racial equality or integration (such as busing), the mere fact that large majorities of whites were, by the 1980s, supporting the antidiscrimination principle reflected a profound shift in racial attitudes. The margin of support for color-blind norms has only increased since then.

This dramatically changed racial climate has led defenders of mass incarceration to insist that our criminal justice system, whatever its past sins, is now largely fair and nondiscriminatory. They point to violent crime rates in the African American community as a justification for the staggering number of black men who find themselves behind bars. Black men, they say, have much higher rates of violent crime; that's why so many of them are locked in prisons.

Typically, this is where the discussion ends.

The problem with this abbreviated analysis is that violent crime is *not* responsible for the prison boom. As numerous researchers have shown, violent crime rates have fluctuated over the years and bear little relationship to incarceration rates—which have soared during the past three decades regardless of whether violent crime was going up or down.[23] Today, violent crime rates are at historically low levels, yet incarceration rates continue to climb.

Murder convictions tend to receive a tremendous amount of media attention, which feeds the public's sense that violent crime is rampant and forever on the rise. But like violent crime in general, the murder rate cannot explain the prison boom. Homicide convictions account for a tiny fraction of the growth in the prison population. In the federal system, for example, homicide offenders account for 0.4 percent of the past decade's growth in the federal prison population, while drug offenders account for nearly 61 percent of that expansion.[24] In the state system, less than 3 percent of new court commitments to state prison typically involve people convicted of homicide.[25] As much as a third of state prisoners are violent offenders, but that statistic can easily be misinterpreted. Violent offenders tend to get longer prison sentences than nonviolent offenders, and therefore comprise a much larger share of the prison population than they would if they had earlier release dates. The uncomfortable reality is that convictions for drug offenses—not violent crime—are the single most important cause of the prison boom in the United States, and people of color are convicted of drug offenses at rates out of all proportion to their drug crimes.

These facts may still leave some readers unsatisfied. The idea that the criminal justice system discriminates in such a terrific fashion when few people openly express or endorse racial discrimination may seem far-fetched, if not absurd. How could the War on Drugs operate in a discriminatory manner, on such a large scale, when hardly anyone advocates or engages in explicit race discrimination? That question is the subject of this [reading]. As we shall see, despite the **color-blind rhetoric** and fanfare of recent years, the design of the drug war effectively guarantees that those who are swept into the nation's new undercaste are largely black and brown.

---

color-blind rhetoric The tendency by the news media and Hollywood to define racism as a problem of the past.

This sort of claim invites skepticism. Nonracial explanations and excuses for the systematic mass incarceration of people of color are plentiful. It is the genius of the new system of control that it can always be defended on nonracial grounds, given the rarity of a noose or a racial slur in connection with any particular criminal case. Moreover, because blacks and whites are almost never similarly situated (given extreme racial segregation in housing and disparate life experiences), trying to "control for race" in an effort to evaluate whether the mass incarceration of people of color is really about race or something else—anything else—is difficult. But it is not impossible.

A bit of common sense is overdue in public discussions about racial bias in the criminal justice system. The great debate over whether black men have been targeted by the criminal justice system or unfairly treated in the War on Drugs often overlooks the obvious. What is painfully obvious when one steps back from individual cases and specific policies is that the system of mass incarceration operates with stunning efficiency to sweep people of color off the streets, lock them in cages, and then release them into an inferior second-class status. Nowhere is this more true than in the War on Drugs.

The central question, then, is how exactly does a formally color-blind criminal justice system achieve such racially discriminatory results? Rather easily, it turns out. The process occurs in two stages. The first step is to grant law enforcement officials extraordinary discretion regarding whom to stop, search, arrest, and charge for drug offenses, thus ensuring the conscious and unconscious racial beliefs and stereotypes will be given free rein. Unbridled discretion inevitably creates huge racial disparities. Then, the damning step: Close the courthouse doors to all claims by defendants and private litigants that the criminal justice system operates in a racially discriminatory fashion. Demand that anyone who wants to challenge racial bias in the system offer, in advance, clear proof that the racial disparities are the product of intentional racial discrimination—i.e., the work of a bigot. This evidence will almost never be available in the era of color-blindness, because everyone knows—but does not say—that the enemy in the War on Drugs can be identified by race. This simple design has helped to produce one of the most extraordinary systems of racialized social control the world has ever seen.

RACE AS A FACTOR

The dirty little secret of policing is that the Supreme Court has actually granted the police license to discriminate. This fact is not advertised by police departments, because law enforcement officials know that the public would not respond well to this fact in the era of colorblindness. It is the sort of thing that is better left unsaid. Civil rights lawyers—including those litigating racial profiling cases—have been complicit in this silence, fearing that any acknowledgment that race-based policing is authorized by law would legitimate in the public mind the very practice they are hoping to eradicate.

The truth, however, is this: At other stages of the criminal justice process, the Court has indicated that overt racial bias necessarily triggers strict scrutiny—a concession that has not been costly, as very few law enforcement officials today are foolish enough to admit bias openly. But the Supreme Court has indicated that in policing, race can be used as a factor in discretionary decision making. In *United States v. Brignoni-Ponce* the Court concluded it was permissible under the equal protection clause of the Fourteenth Amendment for the police to use race as a factor in making decisions about which motorists to stop and search. In that case, the Court concluded that the police could take a person's Mexican appearance into account when developing reasonable suspicion that a vehicle may contain undocumented immigrants. The Court said that "the likelihood that any person of Mexican ancestry is an alien is high enough to make Mexican appearance a relevant factor."[26] Some commentators have argued that *Brignoni-Ponce* may be limited to the immigration context; the Court might not apply the same

principle to drug-law enforcement. It is not obvious what the rational basis would be for limiting overt race discrimination by police to immigration. The likelihood that a person of Mexican ancestry is an "alien" could not be significantly higher than the likelihood that any random black person is a drug criminal.

The Court's quiet blessing of race-based traffic stops has led to something of an Orwellian public discourse regarding racial profiling. Police departments and highway patrol agencies frequently declare, "We do not engage in racial profiling," even though their officers routinely use race as a factor when making decisions regarding whom to stop and search. The justification for the implicit doublespeak—"we do not racial-profile; we just stop people based on race"—can be explained in part by the Supreme Court's jurisprudence. Because the Supreme Court has authorized the police to use race as a factor when making decisions regarding whom to stop and search, police departments believe that racial profiling exists only when race is the *sole* factor. Thus, if race is one factor but not the only factor, then it doesn't really count as a factor at all.

The absurdity of this logic is evidenced by the fact that police almost never stop anyone because of race. A young black male wearing baggy pants, standing in front of his high school surrounded by a group of similarly dressed black friends, may be stopped and searched because police believe he "looks like" a drug dealer. Clearly, race is not the only reason for that conclusion. Gender, age, attire, and location play a role. The police would likely ignore an eighty-five-year-old black man standing in the same spot surrounded by a group of elderly black women.

The problem is that although race is rarely the sole reason for a stop or search, it is frequently a *determinative* reason. A young white male wearing baggy pants, standing in front of his high school and surrounded by his friends, might well be ignored by police officers. It might never occur to them that a group of white kids might be dealing dope in front of their high school. Similarly situated people inevitably are treated differently when police are granted permission to rely on racial stereotypes when making discretionary decisions.

Equally important, though, the sole-factor test ignores the ways in which seemingly race-neutral factors—such as location—operate in a highly discriminatory fashion. Some law enforcement officials claim that they would stop and search white kids wearing baggy jeans in the ghetto (that would be suspicious)—it just so happens they're rarely there. Subjecting people to stops and searches because they live in "high crime" ghettos cannot be said to be truly race-neutral, given that the ghetto itself was constructed to contain and control groups of people defined by race.[27] Even seemingly race-neutral factors such as "prior criminal history" are not truly race-neutral. A black kid arrested twice for possession of marijuana may be no more of a repeat offender than a white frat boy who regularly smokes pot in his dorm room. But because of his race and his confinement to a racially segregated ghetto, the black kid has a criminal record, while the white frat boy, because of his race and relative privilege, does not. Thus, when prosecutors throw the book at black repeat offenders or when police stalk ex-offenders and subject them to regular frisks and searches on the grounds that it makes sense to "watch criminals closely," they are often exacerbating racial disparities created by the discretionary decision to wage the War on Drugs almost exclusively in poor communities of color.

Defending against claims of racial bias in policing is easy. Because race is never the only reason for a stop or search, any police officer with a fifth-grade education will be able to cite multiple nonracial reasons for initiating an encounter, including any number of the so-called "indicators" of drug trafficking discussed [previously], such as appearing too nervous or too calm. Police officers (like prosecutors) are highly adept at offering race-neutral reasons for actions that consistently disadvantage African Americans. Whereas prosecutors claim they strike black jurors not because of their race but because of their hairstyle, police officers have their own stock excuses—e.g., "Your honor, we didn't stop him because he's black; we stopped him because he failed to use his turn signal

at the right time," or "It wasn't just because he was black; it was also because he seemed nervous when he saw the police car." Judges are just as reluctant to second-guess an officer's motives as they are to second-guess prosecutors'. So long as officers refrain from uttering racial epithets and so long as they show the good sense not to say "the only reason I stopped him was because he's black," courts generally turn a blind eye to patterns of discrimination by the police.

Studies of racial profiling have shown that police do, in fact, exercise their discretion regarding whom to stop and search in the drug war in a highly discriminatory manner.[28] Not only do police discriminate in their determinations regarding where to wage the war, but they also discriminate in their judgments regarding whom to target outside of the ghetto's invisible walls.

The most famous of these studies were conducted in New Jersey and Maryland in the 1990s. Allegations of racial profiling in federally funded drug interdiction operations resulted in numerous investigations and comprehensive data demonstrating a dramatic pattern of racial bias in highway patrol stops and searches. These drug interdiction programs were the brainchild of the DEA, part of the federally funded program known as Operation Pipeline.

In New Jersey, the data showed that only 15 percent of all drivers on the New Jersey Turnpike were racial minorities, yet 42 percent of all stops and 73 percent of all arrests were of black motorists—despite the fact that blacks and whites violated traffic laws at almost exactly the same rate. While radar stops were relatively consistent with the percentage of minority violators, discretionary stops made by officers involved in drug interdiction resulted in double the number of stops of minorities.[29] A subsequent study conducted by the attorney general of New Jersey found that searches on the turnpike were even more discriminatory than the initial stops—77 percent of all consent searches were of minorities. The Maryland studies produced similar results: African Americans comprised only 17 percent of drivers along a stretch of I-95 outside of Baltimore, yet they were 70 percent of those who were stopped and searched. Only 21 percent of all drivers along that stretch of highway were racial minorities (Latinos, Asians, and African Americans), yet those groups comprised nearly 80 percent of those pulled over and searched.[30]

What most surprised many analysts was that, in both studies, whites were actually *more likely* than people of color to be carrying illegal drugs or contraband in their vehicles. In fact, in New Jersey, whites were almost twice as likely to be found with illegal drugs or contraband as African Americans, and five times as likely to be found with contraband as Latinos.[31] Although whites were more likely to be guilty of carrying drugs, they were far less likely to be viewed as suspicious, resulting in relatively few stops, searches, and arrests of whites. The former New Jersey attorney general dubbed this phenomenon the "circular illogic of racial profiling." Law enforcement officials, he explained, often point to the racial composition of our prisons and jails as a justification for targeting racial minorities, but the empirical evidence actually suggested the opposite conclusion was warranted. The disproportionate imprisonment of people of color was, in part, a product of racial profiling—not a justification for it.[32]

In the years following the release of the New Jersey and Maryland data, dozens of other studies of racial profiling have been conducted. A brief sampling:

- In Volusia County, Florida, a reporter obtained 148 hours of video footage documenting more than 1,000 highway stops conducted by state troopers. Only 5 percent of the drivers on the road were African American or Latino, but more than 80 percent of the people stopped and searched were minorities.

- In Illinois, the state police initiated a drug interdiction program known as Operation Valkyrie that targeted Latino motorists. While Latinos comprised less than 8 percent of the Illinois population and took fewer than 3 percent of the personal vehicle trips in Illinois, they comprised

approximately 30 percent of the motorists stopped by drug interdiction officers for discretionary offenses, such as failure to signal a lane change.[33] Latinos, however, were significantly less likely than whites to have illegal contraband in their vehicles.

- A racial profiling study in Oakland, California, in 2001 showed that African Americans were approximately twice as likely as whites to be stopped, and three times as likely to be searched.[34]

Pedestrian stops, too, have been the subject of study and controversy. The New York Police Department released statistics in February 2007 showing that during the prior year its officers stopped an astounding 508,540 people—an average of 1,393 per day—who were walking down the street, perhaps on their way to the subway, grocery store, or bus stop. Often the stops included searches for illegal drugs or guns—searches that frequently required people to lie face down on the pavement or stand spread-eagled against a wall while police officers aggressively groped all over their bodies while bystanders watched or walked by. The vast majority of those stopped and searched were racial minorities, and more than half were African American.[35]

The NYPD began collecting data on pedestrian stops following the shooting of Amadou Diallo, an African immigrant who died in a hail of police bullets on the front steps of his own home in February 1999. Diallo was followed to his apartment building by four white police officers—members of the elite Street Crime Unit—who viewed him as suspicious and wanted to interrogate him. They ordered him to stop, but, according to the officers, Diallo did not respond immediately. He walked a bit further to his apartment building, opened the door, and retrieved his wallet—probably to produce identification. The officers said they thought the wallet was a gun, and fired forty-one times. Amadou Diallo died at the age of twenty-two. He was unarmed and had no criminal record.

Diallo's murder sparked huge protests, resulting in a series of studies commissioned by the attorney general of New York. The first study found that

African Americans were stopped six times more frequently than whites, and that stops of African Americans were less likely to result in arrests than stops of whites—presumably because blacks were less likely to be found with drugs or other contraband.[36] Although the NYPD attempted to justify the stops on the grounds that they were designed to get guns off the street, stops by the Street Crime Unit—the group of officers who supposedly are specially trained to identify gun-toting thugs—yielded a weapon in only 2.5 percent of all stops.[37]

Rather than reducing reliance on stop-and-frisk tactics following the Diallo shooting and the release of this disturbing data, the NYPD dramatically *increased* its number of pedestrian stops and continued to stop and frisk African Americans at grossly disproportionate rates. The NYPD stopped five times more people in 2005 than in 2002—the overwhelming majority of whom were African American or Latino.[38]

In Los Angeles, mass stops of young African American men and boys resulted in the creation of a database containing the names, addresses, and other biographical information of the overwhelming majority of young black men in the entire city. The LAPD justified its database as a tool for tracking gang or "gang-related" activity. However, the criterion for inclusion in the database is notoriously vague and discriminatory. Having a relative or friend in a gang and wearing baggy jeans is enough to put youth on what the ACLU calls a Black List. In Denver, displaying any two of a list of attributes—including slang, "clothing of a particular color," pagers, hairstyles, or jewelry—earns youth a spot in the Denver Police's gang database. In 1992, citizen activism led to an investigation, which revealed that eight out of every ten people of color in the entire city were on the list of suspected criminals.[39]

THE END OF AN ERA

The litigation that swept the nation in the 1990s challenging racial profiling practices has nearly vanished. The news stories about people being stopped and searched on their way to church or work or school have faded from evening news. This is not because the problem has been solved or because the experience of being stopped, interrogated, and searched on the basis of race has become less humiliating, alienating, or demoralizing as time has gone by. The lawsuits have disappeared because, in a little noticed case called *Alexander v. Sandoval,* decided in 2001, the Supreme Court eliminated the last remaining avenue available for challenging racial bias in the criminal justice system.[40]

Sandoval was not, on its face, even about criminal justice. It was a case challenging the Alabama Department of Public Safety's decision to administer state driver's license examinations only in English. The plaintiffs argued that the department's policy violated Title VI of the Civil Rights Act of 1964 and its implementing regulations, because the policy had the effect of subjecting non-English speakers to discrimination based on their national origin. The Supreme Court did not reach the merits of the case, ruling instead that the plaintiffs lacked the legal right even to file the lawsuit. It concluded that Title VI does not provide a "private right of action" to ordinary citizens and civil rights groups, meaning that victims of discrimination can no longer sue under the law.

The *Sandoval* decision virtually wiped out racial profiling litigation nationwide. Nearly all of the cases alleging racial profiling in drug-law enforcement were brought pursuant to Title VI of the Civil Rights Act of 1964 and its implementing regulations. Title VI prohibits federally funded programs or activities from discriminating on the basis of race, and the regulations employ a "disparate impact test" for discrimination—meaning that plaintiffs could prevail in claims of race discrimination without proving discriminatory intent. Under the regulations, a federally funded law enforcement program or activity is unlawful if it has a racially discriminatory impact and if that impact cannot be justified by law enforcement necessity. Because nearly all law enforcement agencies receive federal funding in the drug war, and because drug war tactics—such as pretext stops and consent searches—have a grossly discriminatory impact and are largely ineffective, plaintiffs were able to argue persuasively that the tactics could not be justified by law enforcement necessity.

In 1999, for example, the ACLU of Northern California filed a class action lawsuit against the California Highway Patrol (CHP), alleging that its highway drug interdiction program violated Title VI of the Civil Rights Act because it relied heavily on discretionary pretext stops and consent searches that are employed overwhelmingly against African American and Latino motorists. During the course of the litigation, the CHP produced data that showed African Americans were twice as likely, and Latinos three times as likely, to be stopped and searched by its officers as were whites. The data further showed that consent searches were ineffective; only a tiny percentage of the discriminatory searches resulted in the discovery of drugs or other contraband, yet thousands of black and brown motorists were subjected to baseless interrogations, searches, and seizures as a result of having committed a minor traffic violation. The CHP entered into a consent decree that provided for a three-year moratorium on consent searches and pretext stops statewide and the collection of comprehensive data on the race and ethnicity of motorists stopped and searched by the police, so that it would be possible to determine whether discriminatory practices were continuing. Similar results were obtained in New Jersey, as a result of landmark litigation filed against the New Jersey State Police. After *Sandoval,* these cases can no longer be brought under Title VI by private litigants. Only the federal government can sue to enforce Title VI's antidiscrimination provisions—something it has neither the inclination nor

the capacity to do in most racial profiling cases due to its limited resources and institutional reluctance to antagonize local law enforcement. Since the War on Drugs, private litigants represented by organizations such as the ACLU have been at the forefront of racial profiling litigation. Those days, however, have come to an end. The racial profiling cases that swept the nation in the 1990s may well be the last wave of litigation challenging racial bias in the criminal justice system that we see for a very long time.

The Supreme Court has now closed the courthouse doors to claims of racial bias at every stage of the criminal justice process, from stops and searches to plea bargaining and sentencing. The system of mass incarceration is now, for all practical purposes, thoroughly immunized from claims of racial bias. Staggering racial disparities in the drug war continue but rarely make the news. The Obama administration has indicated it supports abolition of the hundred-to-one disparity in sentencing for crack versus powder cocaine—the most obvious and embarrassing example of racial bias in a system that purports to be colorblind. But that disparity is just the tip of the iceberg. This system depends primarily on the prison label, not prison time. What matters most is who gets swept into this system of control and then ushered into an undercaste. The legal rules adopted by the Supreme Court guarantee that those who find themselves locked up and permanently locked out due to the drug war are overwhelmingly black and brown.

AMERICAN POLICING UNDER FIRE

Misconduct and Reform

Ronald Weitzer

RONALD WEITZER is Professor of Sociology at George Washington University.

ABSTRACT

A cluster of recent police killings of African American men has sparked an unprecedented amount of public debate regarding policing in the United States. Critics and protesters have made sweeping allegations about the police; a presidential commission has been formed to study police misconduct; and reforms are being debated. These events provide a backdrop for this [reading's] review of recent poll data and discussion of research regarding police relations with African Americans, Latinos, and whites.

KEYWORDS

Law enforcement; Race; Mass media; Police reform

POLICING IN AMERICA COULD NOT BE a hotter topic than it is now. Several incidents, in a relatively short time span, have rattled public confidence in the police and sparked fresh debate on reforms. This is a fairly unique moment in American history, surpassing the level of outrage that followed other high-profile incidents a decade or two ago (Lawrence 2000).

Questions to Consider

On the heels of some very high-profile cases involving unarmed black men being killed by police officers, police departments and policing procedures around the country have come under increased scrutiny. Professor Weitzer examines the factors in play that lead to such deadly encounters. What do you think these factors might be, and what reforms might you put in place to make such encounters less lethal?

Published online: 25 August 2015 © Springer Science+Business Media New York 2015

Research shows that public confidence in the police typically erodes after a controversial incident is heavily publicized in the news media. Two weeks after the 1991 videotaped beating of Rodney King in Los Angeles, confidence in the city's police department plummeted to 31% for Latino residents and 14% for African Americans.[1] Over time, however, public opinion typically rebounds (Weitzer 2002). In Los Angeles, approval ratings reverted to their pre-King level 4 years after his beating (May 1995), eroded again after a major scandal in 1999–2000, and rebounded again a decade later.[2]

Recent events, however, may have a longer-term impact than those in previous decades. A series of incidents that occur in a compressed time period and gain massive traction in the media can tarnish the image not only of the police in the cities where the incidents took place but can also damage the reputation of the police nationwide (Weitzer 2002). This contamination-by-association is occurring today in a cumulative manner—with each incident pollinating subsequent ones—in part because activists and the media are drawing connections between them (see Table 1). And this perfect storm gained added momentum with the creation in December 2014 of the President's Task Force on 21st Century Policing, which signals to the public that recent incidents are much more serious than a sum of their parts.

Each of the incidents has been politicized—interpreted according to diametrically opposed frames—by activists and pundits on the one hand and law enforcement officials on the other. Time and again, we have seen protestors on the streets and commentators in the media (1) operating with a presumption of guilt toward the officer or officers involved; (2) asserting that misconduct is widespread and systemic, not confined to a few rogue cops; and (3) imputing racial animus as a motive. When it was announced that charges would not be brought against the officer who killed Tony Robinson in Madison, Wisconsin, one protestor filmed on the street shouted, "This is not what democracy is about," which clearly presumes that the officer should have been indicted. For their part, the police often circle the wagons after such incidents. More often than not, the department is slow to provide the public with information about the incident, and the police union (if not the chief of police) typically jumps to the defense of the accused officer (Baker 2015).

All victims were black males except Zambrano-Montes. At the time of the contact with police officers Tamir Rice was displaying a toy gun, Freddie Gray had a knife in his pocket, and Eric Harris was trying to sell a gun to undercover officers. All other victims were unarmed.

TABLE 1 ■ Recent High-Profile Killings			
Date	**City**	**Victim**	**Outcome**
July 2014	New York, NY	Eric Garner	No charges
August 2014	Ferguson, MO	Michael Brown	No charges
November 2014	Cleveland, OH	Tamir Rice	In progress
February 2015	Pasco, WA	Antonio Zambrano-Montes	In progress
March 2015	Madison, WI	Tony Robinson	No charges
April 2015	North Charleston, SC	Walter Scott	Murder charges
April 2015	Tulsa, OK	Eric Harris	Manslaughter charges
April 2015	Baltimore, MD	Freddie Gray	Multiple charges

Whether politicized or not, incidents of apparent police misconduct gain added significance when they resonate with other factors that condition individuals' perceptions of and experiences with the police.

SOME UNDERLYING FACTORS

Americans' attitudes toward the police are shaped by several factors, including the dynamics of face-to-face encounters and structural factors beyond media reporting. At the interactional level, it is now well established that procedural justice during encounters can make a big difference in citizens' willingness to cooperate with officers, in their evaluation of the contact, and in their overall opinion of the police (Tyler and Huo 2002; Wiley and Hudik 1974). Procedural justice takes place when officers give citizens a reason for a stop, treat them courteously, allow them to explain their actions, and demonstrate that police procedures are fair. When a person is verbally demeaned, given no reason for being stopped, told to "shut up," detained in public for a long time, subjected to excessive force, or given a "rough ride" in a police van, it is almost guaranteed that he or she will define this treatment as unjust and that these experiences will spill over and color the citizen's general opinion of the police.

But procedural injustice at the micro level is only part of the equation. Having a good interaction with an officer does not necessarily enhance one's general opinions of the police (Jacob 1971; Skogan 2006). People are also influenced by their "vicarious experiences": the narratives of friends, family members, neighbors, or remote others (as portrayed in the media) that are indirectly experienced by an individual. Latinos and African Americans are much more likely than whites to hear about instances of officer mistreatment from people in their social networks and to internalize these experiences (Weitzer and Tuch 2006). And proactively, there has been a long tradition among African Americans of elders taking pains to

transmit "proper" conduct norms to young people in the hope of preventing them from having altercations with police officers (Brown 2009; Brunson and Weitzer 2011). These norms include keeping hands in full view, speaking softly and respectfully, avoiding sudden movements, and complying with officer commands. There is no evidence that white parents caution their children in this way.

Police-citizen relations are also influenced by neighborhood socioeconomic conditions. In middle-class and affluent communities, a police presence is typically episodic and, on the rare occasions when officers are called to the neighborhood, they are likely to treat residents with a measure of respect (Mastrofski et al. 2002; Sykes and Clark 1975; Weitzer 1999). In disadvantaged communities, irrespective of their racial composition, police are less likely to show respect toward residents. In addition, some residents of these neighborhoods engage in unconventional survival practices (e.g., selling loose cigarettes, drug dealing), which is correlated with aggressive law enforcement and stops that are essentially fishing expeditions (Epp et al. 2014; Fagan et al. 2010). A minor infraction, such as walking in the middle of the street (e.g., Michael Brown in Ferguson), can serve as a pretext for a stop and interrogation whose real purpose is to discover other types of wrongdoing (drug or gun possession, stolen goods, an outstanding warrant, etc.). Young black and Latino men and women who live in these neighborhoods are not only uniquely vulnerable to being stopped and questioned by the police,[3] but are also much more likely than their white counterparts to be stopped *repeatedly* (ACLU 2015; Epp et al. 2014; Weitzer and Tuch 2006). There is thus an interaction between (1) high neighborhood-level poverty and unemployment; (2) residents' involvement in illicit survival strategies (including victimless and property crime); and (3) aggressive police practices—each of which contributes to popular alienation from and avoidance of the police, if not outright hostility toward them. This syndrome is more fundamental than the popular assertion that officers' racial animus is the main problem.

This hardly means that racial bias is a thing of the past, however. It is clear that at least some officers, irrespective of racial background, hold overtly racist views toward people of color (e.g., Christopher Commission 1991; Moskos 2008), whereas, for others, racial stereotypes may be more latent, albeit quite consequential. Regarding police-involved killings, 6 out of 10 whites, but only one-fifth of blacks, believe that "race does not affect police use of deadly force," according to a poll conducted a few days after Michael Brown was killed in Ferguson (New York Times 2014). Data on 771 incidents recorded in the U.S. Police Shootings Database suggest that race may indeed be a factor: Not only are armed and unarmed black and Hispanic individuals shot by police at much higher rates, in most counties, than their armed and unarmed white counterparts, but in some counties unarmed blacks are shot at significantly higher rates than armed white civilians (Ross 2014; cf. Kindy 2015). The *Guardian* newspaper maintains its own database on police-involved killings, which shows that such killings vary from one to eight per day in the U.S. and that African American shooting victims are twice as likely as whites to have been unarmed.[4] Unfortunately, neither database contains complete details for all killings, so caution is needed in drawing conclusions about the role of race in police shootings. But if these statistics approximate reality, they would be consistent with experimental laboratory findings on how implicit racial bias affects the decision to shoot (Correll 2007).

REFORMS

One positive outcome of the events in the cities listed in Table 1 is that the mass media are now seriously debating a host of reforms in policing. This rarely happened in the past, as Regina Lawrence (2000) demonstrated in her study of news coverage of policing in the 1980s and 1990s. The reforms being discussed today may, if implemented, help to reduce police misconduct and enhance police professionalism. I discuss a few of these reforms here.

During the past year, reporters and commentators have almost universally assumed that racial diversification of police departments will reduce misconduct. The issue dates back to the 1967 President's Commission on Law Enforcement and the Administration of Justice, which considered the lack of minority officers one of the central problems in policing at that time. Almost 50 years later, the interim report of President Obama's policing task force similarly recommended diversification, but offered little to justify it. Behaviorally, the available evidence shows that the vast majority of police officers are "blue," meaning that their occupational training and on-the-job socialization by fellow officers trumps racial background vis-à-vis their treatment of citizens. It appears that the police subculture is relatively autonomous from incremental change in the direction of demographic inclusiveness (racial or gender). A few studies have documented some differences among white and black officers working in a particular city,[5] but for the most part the literature points to overall similarities in police behavior irrespective of officers' racial background (National Research Council 2004). Unfortunately, Latino and Asian officers have not been included in the few studies that have examined this question (Weitzer 2014).

At the macro level, however, there may be important symbolic dividends to having a police department that reflects the composition of its city. A department like Ferguson's, where 50 out of 53 officers are white in a city that is two-thirds black, is a glaring mismatch and is almost guaranteed to lead at least some black residents to racialize their encounters with officers. Another example is Hartford, Connecticut, where 66% of the police department but only 16% of the population is white. At the same time, several big-city police departments are majority-black or majority-Hispanic and led by police chiefs and/or mayors from those communities (e.g., Atlanta, Baltimore, Birmingham, Detroit, Washington, Miami, Santa Fe, El Paso). There is very little research on whether a shift to a majority-black or -Latino department leads to any appreciable change in the pre-existing police subculture or in department-wide behavior patterns (Howell et al. 2004; Weitzer et al. 2008). It is difficult, in a comparative study, to separate the police-composition variable from other city-level variables that might conceivably influence aggregate levels of police treatment of citizens. But this task remains crucial for determining whether a major transition in departmental demographics, from minority to majority, has an impact on the police subculture and behavior patterns.

Irrespective of how officers behave on the ground, racial diversification of police departments in multi-racial cities can enhance the overall reputation of a department. Such diversification is not a sufficient condition for building public confidence, but it can be considered a necessary condition—providing a foundation on which to build trust, coupled with other needed reforms. A diverse police force can also help decrease the sense that individuals are being stopped and questioned solely because of their race. This clearly applies when the officers and citizens are of the same race, but even encounters between white officers and minority citizens may be perceived as less racialized when the department has a critical mass of minority officers. And Americans overwhelmingly endorse racial diversification: in one poll, more than 70% of whites, blacks, and Latinos believed that a city's police department should have a similar racial complexion to that of the city (Weitzer and Tuch 2006). Unfortunately, the recent string of highly-publicized incidents and street protests makes the job of recruiting minority officers even harder than it normally is.

In addition to racial diversification as a type of reform, the past year has seen countless news reports and talk shows discussing body cameras, sensitivity training, community policing, demilitarization, use of external prosecutors, civilian review boards, and abandoning zero-tolerance and stop-and-frisk policies. Such debate is refreshing, but it should be noted that each of these corrective measures has been advocated for decades. Even the newest of these remedies—police cameras—has been proposed for years (Reaves 2010; Weitzer and Tuch 2006).

The public overwhelmingly supports each of these reforms. Regarding civilian review boards—responsible for reviewing citizen complaints against officers—63% of whites, 72% of Hispanics, and 80% of African Americans believe that creation of such a board would improve policing in their city (Weitzer and Tuch 2006). Similar or even higher proportions of all three groups endorse equipping officers with video cameras, creating early-warning systems to flag and monitor rogue officers, appointment of outside prosecutors to investigate police-involved killings, demilitarization, and various types of community policing (New York Times 2014; Washington Post 2014; Weitzer and Tuch 2006). What is especially noteworthy here is the cross-racial consensus on the value of these reforms.

But perhaps strangely, whites' support for reforms does not mean that they believe there are indeed problems to be corrected! Although a large majority of whites support the reforms mentioned above, 63% of them are "confident" that the police treat blacks and whites "equally," compared to 40% of Latinos and 21% of blacks (Washington Post 2014). And 60% of whites believe that the recent killings of unarmed black men were "isolated incidents," not "a sign of broader problems," whereas 45% of Hispanics and only 18% of blacks subscribe to the isolated-incidents view (Washington Post 2014). Whites are also much more likely than the other two groups to be "confident" that police officers are adequately trained to avoid using excessive force and that officers who engage in misconduct are held accountable. Another poll confirmed the racial gap on accountability: 70% of blacks think that police departments do a poor job in holding officers accountable for misconduct, while only 27% of whites agree (Pew Research Center 2014).

There is racial polarization in sentiment regarding more robust policing as well: Over one-third of whites and Hispanics nationwide favor police "stopping and searching more people on the streets," compared to about one-fifth of African Americans (Weitzer and Tuch 2006), and in New York City, 50% of whites but only 30% of Latinos and 20% of blacks want the city's intrusive stop-and-frisk practice to continue (Wall Street Journal 2013).

Despite the impression that American policing is at a crossroads and that meaningful reforms may be on the horizon, there are reasons to be pessimistic that this is a pivotal moment in policing. First, it is not known how many police chiefs are learning lessons from the cities where police are now embroiled in controversy. How many are reviewing their own practices and considering new measures to curb misconduct and enhance accountability among their officers? How many of them have read the consent decrees and settlements that the Justice Department has entered into with the 20+ departments it has investigated for "pattern or practice" misconduct in the past 20 years? How many of them have thoroughly institutionalized community policing as a philosophy and practice in their departments, rather than simply giving it lip service or marginalizing it in a "community relations" unit? A majority of departments mention community policing in their mission statements, give officers some training in community policing, and have a specialized community affairs unit (Reaves 2010, 2015). But these superficial indicators cannot be used to measure department-wide institutionalization of community policing as a policy and practice, which appears to be the exception rather than the rule. We do know, however, that at least a few police departments have made substantial changes in the recent past in the direction of a more community-oriented model (e.g., Chanin 2015; Greene 1999; Lowery 2015; Stone et al. 2009; Zernikeaug 2014).

Second, even when reforms are initiated, social scientists know just how hard it is to make them "stick"—institutionalizing them in training, codes of conduct, performance evaluations, and rewards and punishments, and being embraced in the police subculture (Chanin 2015; Skogan 2008; Walker 2012). The record is mixed for departments that have undergone a Justice Department pattern-or-practice investigation and then introduced the mandated reforms (Chanin 2015; Walker 2012). Some of the departments that have complied and instituted reforms have made clear progress, while others have had difficulty sustaining the reforms after the period of DOJ oversight has ended. This is partly due to resistance to change from patrol officers, mid-level managers, and police unions (Skogan 2008), but mostly because of the very nature of policing on the ground. It is axiomatic that patrol officers enjoy a substantial amount of discretionary authority, which can be curbed only to a limited extent by any reform. And most officers patrol alone, unfettered by the checks that a fellow officer or supervisor might provide. For these reasons we should expect more officer misconduct in the future, including unjustified killings. And we should also expect a growing public perception that misconduct is dramatically increasing, even if this is simply an artifact of greater reporting of altercations, including footage from video recordings. The increasing display of visual images gives the impression, as one woman at a protest in Baltimore exclaimed, that police brutality is a "skyrocketing epidemic." Scholars would challenge this claim by pointing out that misconduct was simply more hidden, and more prevalent, in the twentieth century. Overall, policing has become more professional in recent decades (National Research Council 2004), yet, as recent events illustrate, such progress has not been uniform across the country.

CONCLUSION

The current debate about policing has neglected a central fact: variation among police departments. Media representations and assertions by protestors and pundits give the impression that police brutality and racism are pervasive throughout the country. Rarely do we get a more nuanced, polymorphous picture—recognizing that there are 18,000 law enforcement agencies in the United States and cautioning against sweeping generalizations. Police departments differ significantly in their size, resources, composition, leadership, accountability mechanisms, and so forth. And, although extremely difficult to measure—given the invisibility of most police-citizen interactions—there is evidence that both cities and neighborhoods vary in rates of police misconduct (e.g., Fagan et al. 2010; Greene 1999; Kane 2002; Terrill and Reisig 2003). In the public square today, these important contextual distinctions have too often been replaced with blanket indictments of "the police" nationwide—claims that may have a cumulative long-term effect in eroding public confidence in law enforcement agencies, even for people whose local department has a fairly clean record.

Regarding the future, the creation of a national task force on policing is a rare opportunity for federal engagement and promotion of "best practices" nationally. Responding to recent incidents, several state legislatures have passed bills that seek to enhance police accountability (Wilson 2015). But it remains to be seen whether these developments will have an appreciable effect on improving officer behavior on the ground and in helping to rebuild public trust in the police.

ABOUT THE AUTHOR

Ronald Weitzer is Professor of Sociology at George Washington University. He has conducted research on police-minority relations in Israel, Northern Ireland, South Africa, and the United States and is the author of *Race and Policing in America* (Cambridge University Press, 2006) and *Policing under Fire: Ethnic Conflict and Police-Community Relations in Northern Ireland* (SUNY Press, 1995).

30

THE MARK OF A CRIMINAL RECORD

Devah Pager

DEVAH PAGER is an associate professor of sociology and faculty associate of the Office of Population Research at Princeton University. Her research focuses on institutions affecting racial stratification, including education, labor markets, and the criminal justice system. Pager's current research has involved a series of field experiments studying discrimination against minorities and ex-offenders in the low-wage labor market.

AMONG THOSE RECENTLY RELEASED FROM prison, nearly two-thirds will be charged with new crimes and 40 percent will return to prison within three years. Those who are not reincarcerated have poorer employment and incomes than those without criminal records. But there is strong disagreement over the reasons that ex-offenders do so poorly after release. Does incarceration itself actually lead to lower employment and income? Or do the poor outcomes of ex-offenders merely arise from the environmental and personal histories that sent them to prison in the first place—the broken families, the poor neighborhoods, the lack of education and absence of legitimate opportunities, the individual tendencies toward violence or addiction?[1]

Questions to Consider

The rate of recidivism (convicts who return to jail) is extremely high in the United States. Poverty, a lack of formal education, and the disappearance of employment opportunities in the inner city that pay a living wage create conditions that researchers believe are linked to criminal activity. How difficult is it for someone with a criminal record—a "mark," as this author describes it—to secure employment? Furthermore, how might race play out among those with and without a criminal "mark"? Devah Pager's research findings are shocking.

Survey research has consistently shown that incarceration is linked to lower employment and income. Many hypotheses have been proposed for this relationship: the labeling effects of criminal stigma, the disruption of social and family networks, the loss of human capital, institutional trauma, and legal barriers to employment. It is, however, difficult, using survey data, to determine which of these mechanisms is at work and whether, for any given mechanism, the results are due to the effect of imprisonment or to preexisting characteristics of people who are convicted. A further issue, given racial disparities in imprisonment rates, is whether the effect of a criminal record is more severe for African American than it is for white ex-offenders.

In the research reported here I sought to answer three primary questions about the mechanisms driving the relationship between imprisonment and employment.[2] First, to what extent do employers use information about criminal histories to make hiring decisions? Second, does race, by itself, remain a major barrier to employment? Its continued significance has been questioned in recent policy debates.[3] Third, does the effect of a criminal record differ for black and white applicants? Given that many Americans hold strong and persistent views associating race and crime, does a criminal record trigger a more negative response for African American than for white applicants?

THE EMPLOYMENT AUDIT

Just as a college degree may serve as a positive credential for those seeking employment, a prison term attaches a "negative credential" to individuals, certifying them in ways that may qualify them for discrimination or social exclusion. Using an experimental audit design, I have been able to isolate that institutional effect, holding constant many background and personal characteristics that otherwise make it very difficult to disentangle cause and effect.[4]

In an employment audit, matched pairs of individuals ("testers") apply for real job openings to see whether employers respond differently to applicants on the basis of selected characteristics. The methodology combines experimental methods with real-life contexts. It is particularly valuable for those with an interest in discrimination, and has primarily been used to study characteristics such as race, gender, and age that are protected under the Civil Rights Act.

Several states, including Wisconsin, have expanded fair employment legislation to protect individuals with criminal records from discrimination by employers, because of their concern about the consequences of the rapid expansion and the skewed racial and ethnic composition of the ex-offender population over the last three decades. Under this legislation, employers are warned that past crimes may be taken into account only if they closely relate to the specific duties required by the job—as, for example, if a convicted embezzler applies for a bookkeeping position, or a sex offender for a job at a day care center. Because of the Wisconsin legislation barring discrimination on the basis of a criminal record, we might expect circumstances to be, if anything, more favorable to the employment of ex-offenders than in states without legal protections.

This audit was conducted between June and December, 2001, in Milwaukee, Wisconsin, which in population, size, racial composition, and employment rate is typical of many major American cities. At the time, the local economy was moderately strong and unemployment rates ranged between 4 percent and 5.2 percent.[5]

I used two audit teams of 23-year-old male college students, one consisting of two African Americans and the other of two whites. All were bright and articulate, with appealing styles of self-presentation. Characteristics that were not already identical, such as education and work experience, were made to appear identical for the purposes of the audit. Within each team, one auditor was randomly assigned a "criminal record" for the first week; then week by week auditors took turns playing the ex-offender role. The "criminal record" consisted of

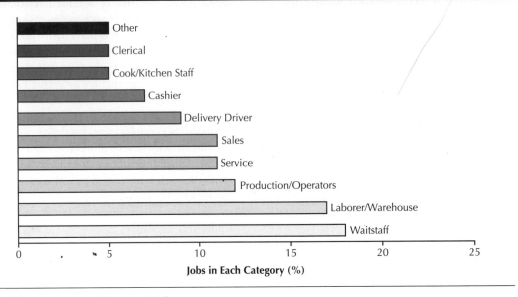

FIGURE 1   ■   The Jobs in the Milwaukee Audit Sample

Jobs in Each Category (%)

Categories (top to bottom): Other, Clerical, Cook/Kitchen Staff, Cashier, Delivery Driver, Sales, Service, Production/Operators, Laborer/Warehouse, Waitstaff

Original Source: Data from U.S. Bureau of the Census.
Revised Source: "The mark of a criminal record," Devah Pager, Focus Vol. 23, No. 2, Summer 2004.

a nonviolent felony drug conviction (possession of cocaine with intent to distribute). If the employment application did not request information about previous convictions, ways were found to include that information—for example, by reporting work experience in the correctional facility and citing a parole officer as a reference.

The audit teams applied to separate sets of jobs drawn from the Sunday classified section of the city's major daily newspaper, the *Milwaukee Journal Sentinel,* and from Jobnet, a state-sponsored Web site for employment listings. Since nearly 90 percent of state prisoners have no more than a high school diploma, the job openings chosen were for entry-level positions requiring no previous experience and no education beyond high school (see Figure 1). All openings were within 25 miles of downtown Milwaukee; a majority were in the suburbs or surrounding counties.[6] The survey audited 350 employers, 150 by the white audit team and 200 by the black team.

The audit study focused only on the first stage in the employment process—the stage most likely to be affected by the barrier of a criminal record. Auditors visited the employers, filled out applications, and went as far as they could during that first interview. They did not return for a second visit. Thus our critical variable of interest was the proportion of cases in which employers called the applicant after the first visit. Reference checks were included as an outcome, in the belief that it would be important to have a former employer or parole officer vouch for applicants with criminal records. As it turned out, employers paid virtually no attention to references; only 4 out of 350 actually checked.

Even though employers are not allowed to use criminal background information to make hiring decisions, about three-quarters of employers in this sample explicitly asked if the applicant had ever been convicted of a crime and, if so, for details. A much smaller proportion, just over a quarter, indicated that they would perform a background check (employers are not required to say if they intend to, and this doubtless represents a lower-bound estimate). The use of background checks by employers has been increasing steadily, however, because of greater ease of access to criminal history information and growing concerns over security.

To what extent are applicants with criminal backgrounds dropped at the beginning of the process? For answers, we turn to the results of the audit.

THE EFFECTS OF A CRIMINAL RECORD AND RACE ON EMPLOYMENT

Given that all testers presented nearly identical credentials, the different responses they encountered can be attributed fully to the effects of race and criminal background.

The results in Figure 2 suggest that a criminal record has severe effects. Among whites, applicants with criminal records were only half as likely to be called back as equally qualified applicants with no criminal record.

The second question involved the significance of race, by itself, in shaping black men's employment prospects, and here too the audit offered an unequivocal answer (Figure 2). The effect of race was very large, equal to or greater than the effect of a criminal record. Only 14 percent of black men

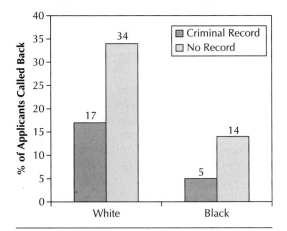

FIGURE 2 ■ The Effect of a Criminal Record in the Milwaukee Audit Sample

Original Source: Data from U.S. Bureau of the Census.
Revised Source: "The mark of a criminal record," Devah Pager, Focus Vol. 23, No. 2, Summer 2004.

without criminal records were called back, a proportion equal to or less than even than the number of whites *with* a criminal background. The magnitude of the race-effect found here corresponds very closely to effects found in previous audit studies directly measuring racial discrimination.[7] Since 1994, when the last major audit was reported, very little has changed in the reaction of employers to minority applicants, at least in Milwaukee.

In addition to the strong independent effects of race and criminal record, evidence suggests that the combination of the two may intensify the negative effects: black ex-offenders are one-third as likely to be called as black applicants without a criminal record. It seems that employers, already reluctant to hire blacks, are even more wary of those with proven criminal involvement. None of our white testers was asked about a criminal record before submitting his application, yet on three occasions black testers were questioned. Our testers were bright, articulate young men, yet the cursory review that entry-level applicants receive leaves little room for these qualities to be noticed.

In some cases, testers reported that employers' levels of responsiveness changed dramatically once they had glanced down at the criminal record questions. Employers seemed to use the information as a screening mechanism, without probing further into the context or complexities of the applicant's situation. But in a few circumstances employers expressed a preference for workers who had recently been released from prison because (in one case) "they tend to be more motivated and are more likely to be hard workers" and (in the case of a janitorial job) the job "involved a great deal of dirty work." Despite these cases, the vast majority of employers were reluctant to take a chance on applicants with a criminal record.

The evidence from this audit suggests that the criminal justice system is not a peripheral institution in the lives of young disadvantaged men. It has become a dominant presence, playing a key role in sorting and stratifying labor market opportunities for such men. And employment is only one of the domains affected by incarceration. Further research is needed to understand its effects on housing, family formation, and political participation, among others, before we can more fully understand its collateral consequences for social and economic inequality.

| Seeing the Big Picture | The Link between Race, Education, and Crime |

In the appendix, look at the unemployment statistics by race in Section VII, the bachelor's degrees conferred by race in Section I, and the crime statistics in Section IV. How do you think these trends are linked?

HOW RACE SHAPES THE WORKPLACE

31

KRISTEN V. AISHA; BRAD V. RASHEED

What's in a Name and How It Affects Getting a Job

Amy Braverman

AMY BRAVERMAN is a reporter for *The University of Chicago Magazine*.

COULD THE NAME AT THE TOP OF A RESUME prompt racial discrimination? According to Marianne Bertrand, associate professor in the Graduate School of Business, and MIT economist Sendhil Mullainathan, it can. Answering more than 1,300 help-wanted ads in Boston and Chicago, the researchers sent four resumes—two higher quality, two lower quality,

FIGURE 1 ■ Why Brad and Kristen Beat Out Jermaine and Ebony

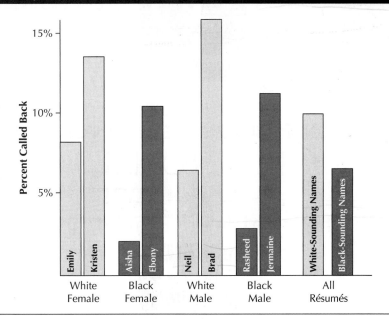

Source: "Why Brad and Kristen Beat Out Jermaine and Ebony" by Amy Braverman Puma and Allen Carroll. Reprinted by permission of University of Chicago Magazine.

Questions to Consider

We tend to think of racial discrimination as the denial of rights or opportunities to someone because of his or her race. Is it possible that race discrimination could also include denying someone employment opportunities because that person has a black-sounding name?

one of each with a black-sounding name—to companies seeking sales, administrative-support, clerical, and customer-service employees. Overall, "white" applicants were called back 50 percent more often than "black" applicants. Brad and Kristen were the top performing white-sounding names, while Jermaine and Ebony got the most callbacks among black-sounding names. Neil, Emily, Rasheed, and Aisha received the fewest callbacks.

32

WHEN THE MELTING POT BOILS OVER

The Irish, Jews, Blacks, and Koreans of New York

Roger Waldinger

ROGER WALDINGER is a professor of race/ethnic/minority relations, urban sociology, and migration and immigration at the University of California, Los Angeles. He is the author of *Still the Promised City? New Immigrants and African-Americans in Post-Industrial New York* (1996) and *Ethnic Los Angeles,* co-edited with Medhi Bozorgmehr (1996).

ASSIMILATION IS THE GRAND THEME OF American immigration research. The classic sociological position provided an optimistic counter to the dim assessments of the new immigrants prevalent at the early part of the century. Notwithstanding the marked differences that impressed contemporaries, Robert Park, Ernest Burgess, W. I. Thomas, and others contended that the new immigrant groups would lose their cultural distinctiveness and move up the occupational hierarchy. Milton Gordon's now classic volume distilled the essence of the sociological view: immigrant-ethnic groups start at the bottom and gradually move up; their mobility takes place through individual advancement, not group collective action; in the process of moving up, ethnic groups lose their distinctive social structure; and as ethnics become like members of the core group, they become part of the core group, joining it in neighborhoods, in friendship, and eventually in marriage.

But the image of immigrants moving onward and upward is hard to reconcile with the darker, conflictual side of American ethnic life. Conflict, often of the fiercest kind, runs like a red thread through the history of American ethnic groups. Certainly New Yorkers evince an extraordinary propensity to come to blows over racial and ethnic differences. The latest conflicts pitting blacks against Hasidim and Koreans in Brooklyn or Chinese against Puerto Ricans in Manhattan are but the latest episodes in a longer saga, extending

Questions to Consider

Roger Waldinger makes a number of astute observations about how racial and ethnic groups get sorted into certain occupations. How and in what ways does the historical timing of a group's entry (for example, Irish, Jews, Italians, and Afro-Caribbeans) into the United States affect its economic and social mobility? How does one group come to monopolize one trade or occupation? How are race, ethnicity, upward mobility, and control of local politics linked to upward mobility?

from the anti-Catholic crusades of the 1850s to the school conflicts of the 1890s, to the controversies engendered by the Coughlinites and the German Bund of the 1930s, to the school integration struggles of the 1960s, right up to this day.

The contradiction between ethnic assimilation and ethnic conflict is more apparent than real. Where the classic sociological model goes wrong is not in its depiction of an upward trajectory, but rather in its individualistic assumptions about the process of ethnic change. The story of ethnic progress in America can be better thought of as a collective search for mobility, in which the succession of one migrant wave after another ensures a continuous competitive conflict over resources. Groups move up from the bottom by specializing in and dominating a particular branch of economic life; that specialization goes unchallenged as long as the newest arrivals are content to work in the bottom-level jobs for which they were initially recruited. This [reading] develops the story in the form of brief episodes from the New York experience of four ethnic groups—Irish, Jews, African Americans, and Koreans. Each group is associated with the four successive waves of migration that have swept over New York in the past two hundred years.

THE IRISH

Nearly one and a half million Irish flocked to the United States between 1846 and 1855 in flight from famine; they converged on the eastern port cities of Boston, Philadelphia, and New York, where, lacking resources, about a quarter stayed. Low levels of education, lack of exposure to industrial or craft work, and lack of capital led the Irish into the lower ranges of manual work, with women taking domestic work and men engaging in insecure, low-paid itinerant employment, especially in construction. Irish progress from the bottom proceeded at a slow pace.

By 1900, however, the Irish had already established themselves in public employment. At the time, the public sector provided relatively few jobs, but this was soon to change. Irish employment in New York City government almost quadrupled between 1900 and 1930, increasing from just under 20,000 to 77,000, while the total number of city workers climbed from 54,000 to 148,000, less than a factor of three.[1]

Irish penetration into the public sector reflected the growing political power of the Democratic machine, which remained Irish dominated. But the machine's hold on local government was met by opposition from WASP reformers. Seeking to break the machine's power by severing the link between political activity and government employment, the reformers installed a civil service system—to little avail. The Irish encountered few effective competitors for city jobs. There was never any serious threat that WASPs would dislodge the Irish. Moreover, the increasingly numerous Poles, Jews, Italians, and others who were just off the boat had little chance of doing well in essay-type exams against the Irish, who were, after all, native English speakers.

The liabilities of the new immigrants lasted hardly a generation; with the Jews' rapid educational and occupational advancement, another competitor entered the scene. But as long as the Irish, through Tammany Hall's grip over city government, could control municipal hiring, inter-ethnic competition posed little threat. Competition was structured in such a way as to minimize the value of Jews' educational advantages. The patronage system functioned unencumbered throughout Tammany's dominance between 1917 and 1933.

The depression severely challenged Irish control over public jobs; LaGuardia's election in 1933 delivered the coup de grace. Keeping control of City Hall required LaGuardia to undermine the material base of Tammany's power and consolidate his support among groups not firmly under Tammany's tow— the most important of which were the Jews, who had split between LaGuardia and his Tammany opponent in 1933. Both goals could be accomplished in the same way, namely pursuing the administrative changes long championed by the reformers.[2]

The depression and LaGuardia's reforms made city jobs more attractive to highly educated workers, which, under the circumstances, mainly meant Jews. One door at which Jewish competitors knocked was teaching, previously an Irish reserve (as the 1900 statistics show). If Jewish entrance into teaching produced antagonism, far more explosive was the situation in the police force. Twenty-nine thousand men sat for the exam held in April 1939, from whom three hundred were selected to enter the department in 1940. Of these, over one-third were Jews. Not surprisingly, this class of 1940 constituted the first significant proportion of Jews to enter the police.[3]

Jewish-Irish competition produced some other episodes, but conflict between them abated, thanks to the prosperity of the postwar era and the new opportunities it provided. Outmigration to the suburbs and the Sun Belt and mobility into the middle class depleted the ranks of the city's Irish population. By the late 1950s, as Nathan Glazer and Daniel Moynihan noted, so profound was the sense of displacement that the remaining Irish New Yorkers reminded themselves, "There are still some of us left."[4]

Those who are left have kept up the long-established Irish occupational ways. Although the commissioners of the police and fire departments are black and Puerto Rican, respectively, the top brass retains a strongly Irish cast, as does the rank and file. Indeed, the fire department presents a glimpse of New York gone by, with a workforce that is 93 percent white and 80 percent Catholic. Some unions still have a distinctly Irish makeup.[5]

In the 1980s, some of the old niches at last gained new blood, as an influx of new, illegal Irish immigrants fled unemployment in the Republic of Ireland for better times in New York. Whereas black Americans still found the doors of construction unions closed, the new arrivals, dubbed "JFK carpenters," were warmly welcomed by their aging compatriots. Women also retraced the steps of the past, as could be seen from the classified pages of the *Irish Echo,* with its columns of ads for nannies, babysitters, and housekeepers.

THE JEWS

Although the Jewish presence in New York extends far back, almost to the city's founding, Jews did not become an important, visible element in the city's economic life until the 1880s. Rising anti-Semitism, combined with the pressures of modernization, led to a huge outflow of Jews from Eastern Europe. By 1920, New York, with two million Jews, had become the world's largest Jewish city.

The new arrivals came just when the demand for factory-made clothing began to surge. Many had been tailors in the old country, and although most had worked with needle and thread, they quickly adapted themselves to machine production. As the various components of the clothing industry grew in synergistic fashion, the opportunities for mobility through the ethnic economy multiplied. Through rags, some immigrants found riches; the sweatshop workers who moved to contracting and then to manufacturing, or possibly careers in retailing, filled the newly formed ranks of New York's *alrightniks.*[6]

The Jewish concentration in commerce and clothing manufacture defined their initial place in the ethnic division of labor. Jewish specializations seldom overlapped with the Irish: domestic service and general labor were rarities among the Russians but were common Irish pursuits; by the same token, tailoring and retailing, whether by merchant or peddler, were far more likely to engage Russians than Irish.

As Jews sought to move beyond the ethnic economy, interethnic competition and antagonism grew more intense. The relatively rapid educational progress of younger immigrants and of the second generation prepared them to work outside the ethnic economy, but gentile employers were rarely eager to hire Jews. One study, completed just before the Great Depression, found that the doors of New York's large, corporate organizations—"railroads, banks, insurance companies, lawyers' offices, brokerage houses, the New York Stock Exchange, hotels . . . and the home offices of large corporations of the first rank"—were infrequently opened to Jews.[7] The surge into the schools, and through the schools into the professions, met with resistance from the older, largely Protestant population that dominated these institutions.

In the 1930s, depression and discrimination outside the ethnic economy led many second-generation Jews to seek an alternative in public employment. Although the quest for government jobs, and in particular teaching positions, had started earlier, the straitened circumstances of the 1930s accelerated this search. The quality and quantity of Jews vying for government employment increased, heightening the competitive pressure on the Irish and yielding the antagonism we've already observed.

Jewish-Irish conflict reached its height in the late 1930s; it gradually subsided, replaced by a more explosive, deeply antagonistic relationship with blacks. Although black occupations were more similar to those of the Irish than they were to the Jews', the economic pursuits of Jews put them at odds with blacks on various counts. The Jews dominated small retail activity throughout the city and were particularly prominent in Harlem. The Jewish storeowners in Harlem sold to blacks but preferred not to employ them until protests in the mid-1930s finally forced them to relent. Antagonism toward Jewish shopkeepers in Harlem rose during the 1930s, fueled by the depression and by Jews' broader role as middlemen in the Harlem economy. Frustration boiled over in the riot of 1943, when black Harlemites burned down the stores of Jews in a fury that presaged events to come.[8] Hostility simmered thereafter, reaching the boiling point during the 1960s.

The transformation of the ethnic economy also engendered black-Jewish conflict. Rapid Jewish social mobility meant a dwindling Jewish working class; the diminishing supply of Jewish workers had a particularly notable effect on the garment industry, where Jewish factory owners were forced to hire outsiders in growing numbers—first Italians, then blacks. In World War II, desperate for workers, Jewish employers hired blacks in great numbers. By 1950, there were 25,000 African American garment workers, 20,000 more than were working in clothing factories ten years before.[9]

But relations between blacks and Jews proved uneasy. Blacks moved into less-skilled, poorer-paying positions, from which mobility into better-remunerated positions proved difficult. Although the garment unions made explicit efforts to organize black workers and integrate them into union structures, few blacks moved up to elected offices, and none high up in the union hierarchy. To protect jobs from southern competitors, the unions adopted a policy of wage restraint, which inevitably meant a softened stance on union employers at home—much to the dismay of black New York garment workers.[10]

The garment business was the Jewish enclave of the past; Jewish mobility into the middle class had made teaching the Jewish niche of the mid-1960s. As the schools came to serve a growing black population, their role was increasingly contested by black students, parents, and protest organizations. The complaints were various, and not all directly linked to the Jews' prominent role in the school system; but the situation in which so many Jews were teachers and so many schools in black neighborhoods were staffed by Jews inevitably led to conflict. In 1968, a black-dominated school board in Brooklyn dismissed a group of white, largely Jewish teachers and replaced them with a mainly black staff; these actions set off a three-month-long strike by the Jewish-led teachers' union. Although the union eventually won, its victory was pyrrhic, at least concerning black-Jewish relations. Memory of the strike and the resentments it fueled have not significantly changed, even a generation later.[11]

What has altered, however, is the economic position of the Jews. The ethnic economy of the immigrant days remains, but in vestigial form. Although Jews are still active in the garment industry, they mainly concentrate in the designing and merchandising ends. "Goldberg" no longer runs clothing factories; his place has been taken by "Kim" and "Wong," who only employ compatriots, not blacks. The same transformations have changed the face of petty retailing and small landlording—the older flash points of black-Jewish conflict. The Jewish presence in the public sector is also fading fast: working as a city engineer or accountant used to be a Jewish occupation; now these careers engage far many more Patels than Cohens.[12] Only in teaching and in higher education do the Jewish concentrations of the past remain in full force.[13]

A distinctive Jewish role in New York's economy still lives on. It is to be found in the professions, in the persistently high rate of Jewish self-employment, in the prominence of Jews in law, real estate, finance, and the media. But the current Jewish pursuits differ crucially from the older ethnic economy in that they are detached from the dynamics of interethnic composition that characterized earlier periods. In a sense, the material basis that underlay anti-Semitic currents in New York for most of the twentieth century is gone. But its legacy and the many other resources around which groups can compete—status, politics, and territory—ensure continued conflict between Jews and their ethnic neighbors.

THE BLACKS

In 1890, the black share of the New York population was 1.6 percent—just about what it had been on the eve of the Civil War. But in the 1890s the South started losing blacks due to outmigration, and that loss quickly translated into New York's gain. By 1920, New York housed 150,000 black residents—who, although only 3 percent of the city's population, made New York the country's largest black urban concentration. In the next twenty years, as European immigration faltered and then stopped, and bad conditions in the rural South provided additional reasons to leave, the number of black New Yorkers tripled. Postwar prosperity and

a new wave of mechanization down South launched a final, massive flow northward: by 1960, the African American population of New York numbered 1,088,000, of whom approximately 320,000 had moved to the city from other areas (mainly the South) in the previous ten years.[14]

It was not until 1940 that black New Yorkers moved out of the peripheries of the New York economy. At the turn of the century, blacks mainly found work in domestic labor, with 90 percent of black women and 55 percent of black men working in some type of domestic service occupation. Blacks' confinement to domestic service reflected, in part, the unfavorable terms of competition with immigrants, who had evicted them from trades where they had previously been accepted. The continued expansion of New York's economy slowly opened doors in a few manufacturing industries; the shutoff of immigration during World War I and its permanent demise after 1924 further accelerated dispersion into other fields.[15]

But the depression largely put an end to these gains. By 1940, 40 percent of blacks still worked in personal service—a far greater proportion than among the workforce overall.[16] With the advent of World War II doors to other jobs were finally unlocked; manufacturing, in particular, saw very large black employment gains. Yet unlike the case in Chicago or Detroit, the black sojourn in New York's manufacturing sector proved short-lived. Lacking auto factories or steel mills, New York's goods-producing sector was a concentration of low-wage jobs; white workers remained ensconced in the better-paying, more skilled positions. Opportunities for blacks were more easily found in the burgeoning service sector—for example, health care—and in government; hence, blacks quickly dispersed into other fields.

Government, where 35 percent of native-born black New Yorkers worked in 1990,[17] has become the black niche par excellence. The history of black employment in the public sector provides yet another example of the continuing, interethnic competitive conflicts over jobs and economic resources in which New York's ethnic groups have been engaged.

In the early years of the twentieth century, local government, like most other New York employers, closed its doors to blacks: in 1911, the city only employed 511 blacks, almost all of whom were laborers. In the early 1920s, Tammany installed the leader of its black client organization, the United Colored Democracy, as a member of the three-person Civil Service Commission, but black access to public jobs changed marginally. By the late 1920s, the city counted 2,275 black workers on its payroll of whom 900 were in laboring jobs and an additional 700 were in other noncompetitive or per diem positions.[18] The reform regime did more for blacks, pushing black employment above parity by 1940.[19] But these effects occurred as a result of the government's burgeoning payrolls, and they were mainly felt in the black concentrations of hospitals, sanitation, and public works, where more than 80 percent of the city's black job holders worked in 1935.[20] Moreover, blacks remained vulnerable to discriminatory practices, as in the city-owned subway system, where blacks only worked as porters, with the exception of a few stations in Harlem. Most important, the employment system that emerged during the depression put blacks at a structural disadvantage in competition with whites. Lacking the educational skills and credentials needed to qualify for most city jobs, blacks and Puerto Ricans found themselves channeled into noncompetitive positions, of which the single largest concentration was found in the municipal hospital system. From here there were few routes of movement upward, as these bottom-level positions were disconnected from the competitive system, which promoted from within.

Race didn't reach the top of the government's agenda until 1965, when John Lindsay arrived in office, the first reformer elected mayor since LaGuardia.[21] Elected with the votes of liberals and minorities, Lindsay lacked his predecessors' commitments to the interests of the largely white, civil service workforce and pledged to increase black and Puerto Rican employment in city agencies. But the new mayor quickly discovered that the civil service structure was not easily amenable to change. Lindsay gradually made progress in reducing the inflated eligibility requirements inherited from the depression, but resistance proved severe when his reforms threatened established white ethnic workers in the better-paid ranks.

Lindsay's main focus, in contrast to earlier reform administrations, was to evade the civil service system and its unionized defenders. The Lindsay administration created new, less-skilled positions for which minority residents could be more easily hired. But this approach never involved large numbers and, more important, left existing eligibility requirements unchallenged, shunting minority recruits into dead-end jobs, where they were marooned.

Lindsay backed off from his confrontations with the civil service system and its defenders in the aftermath of the disastrous 1968 teachers' strike. Where the mayor could both accommodate the unions and pursue his earlier goals of increasing minority employment, he did—mainly by tripling the number of exempt workers and shifting them from agency to agency to avoid the requirement of taking an examination. But in other instances, pressure from civil service interests proved overwhelming. With Abraham Beame's accession to City Hall in 1973, followed in 1977 by Edward Koch, mayoral support for black employment gains vanished for the next sixteen years.

The 1970s and 1980s nevertheless saw dramatic gains in black government employment. Like earlier white ethnic groups that had developed a concentration in public jobs, blacks benefited from simultaneous shifts in the structure of employment and in the relative availability of competing groups.

Changes in the structure of employment came from a variety of sources. The Equal Employment Opportunity (EEO) Act of 1972 prohibited discrimination in local government. By requiring local governments to maintain records on all employees by race and gender and to submit them to the Equal Employment Opportunity Commission, with the clear expectation that governments would show improvement over time, the act also led to institutional changes. As EEO functions were established in each city agency, recruitment and personnel practices changed in ways that benefited previously excluded groups, as recruitment became focused on minority and immigrant communities.

Moreover, the 1972 act provided minority employees with levers to act on more recalcitrant agencies, which they used with greatest effectiveness in the uniformed services. For example, in 1973 the Vulcan Society (the organization of black firefighters) successfully challenged the results of a 1971 exam, leading to an imposition of a 1:3 quota for the duration of that list (1973–79). In 1979, the Guardians and the Hispanic Society challenged the 1979 police officer's exam; court findings of disparate impact led to the imposition of a 33.3 percent minority quota for the duration of the list.

While the advent of affirmative action helped increase access for blacks and other minorities, other changes on the supply side hastened the growth of black employment. Although the city's attraction to its traditional white ethnic labor force had begun to diminish by the 1960s, the fiscal crisis of the mid-1970s decisively exacerbated and extended the city's recruitment difficulties among its traditional workforce. By the time large-scale hiring resumed in the early 1980s, public employment had become a less attractive option than before. Moreover, municipal salaries and benefits took a severe beating during the fiscal crisis; although compensation edged back upward during the 1980s, real gains never recaptured the losses endured during the 1970s. The strength enjoyed by New York's private sector during the 1980s pulled native white workers up the hiring queue and out of the effective labor supply for many city agencies.[22]

In a situation where "the City was hiring a great deal and not turning away anyone who was qualified," as one deputy commissioner told me in an interview, the disparity in the availability of minority and white workers led to rapid recruitment of minority workers. Minorities had constituted only 40 percent of the new workers hired in 1977, making up the majority in only two low-paid occupational categories. By 1987, minorities made up 56 percent of all hires, dominating the ranks of new recruits in five out of eight occupational categories.[23]

Thus, the Koch years of 1977 to 1989 saw the ethnic composition of the municipal workforce completely transformed, notwithstanding the mayor's opposition to affirmative action and the disfavor with which minority leaders greeted his hiring policies. By 1990, whites constituted 48 percent of the 375,000 people working for the city and just slightly more—50 percent—of the 150,000 people working in the agencies that the mayor directly controlled.[24] The declining white presence in municipal employment chiefly benefited blacks. Blacks constituted 25 percent of the city's population and a still smaller proportion of residents who were older than eighteen and thus potentially employable, but made up 36 percent of the city's total workforce and 38 percent of those who worked in the mayoral agencies. Although blacks were still underrepresented in some of the city's most desirable jobs, the earlier pattern of concentration at the bottom was overcome. The municipal hospital system, which employed two-thirds of the city's black employees in the early 1960s, in 1990 employed less than one-fifth, reflecting the dispersion of blacks throughout the municipal sector. And higher-level jobs showed clusters of considerable black overrepresentation as well, with blacks accounting for 40 percent of the administrators and 36 percent of the professionals employed in the direct mayoral agencies.

By 1990, when David Dinkins became New York's first black mayor, the phase of black-for-white succession in municipal employment was nearly complete. Blacks held just over 35 percent of all city jobs; although unevenly represented among the city's many agencies, they were often a dominant presence, accounting for more than 40 percent of employment in six of the ten largest agencies, and more than 50 percent of employment in three of the largest ten.

The comparison with Latinos underlines blacks' advantage in the new ethnic division that has emerged in city government. Whereas the city's Latino and black populations are equal in number, Latinos hold one-third as many municipal jobs as do blacks. The discrepancies are even greater as one moves up the occupational hierarchy into the ranks of managers and professionals. And blacks have been far more successful than Latinos in gaining new permanent civil service jobs, rather than the provisional appointments on which Latinos have mainly relied. The disparity has not gone unnoticed, as the Commission on Hispanic Concerns pointed out in a 1986 report.[25] Of course, other answers might be invoked to explain Latinos' municipal jobs deficit relative to blacks'. But whatever the precise explanation, Mayor Dinkins's continuing conflicts with the Hispanic community suggest that earlier patterns of interethnic competition over municipal jobs remain alive and well.

THE KOREANS

In the mid-1960s, just when New York could no longer retain its native population, it reverted back to its role as an immigrant mecca. Immigrants began flocking to New York immediately after the liberalization of U.S. immigration laws in 1965. Their arrival has been the principal driving force of demographic and ethnic change in New York ever since—and will continue to be for the foreseeable future.

In 1965, what no one expected was the burgeoning of Asian immigration. The reforms tilted the new system toward immigrants with kinship ties to permanent residents or citizens. Since there had been so little Asian immigration in the previous fifty years, how could Asian newcomers find settlers with whom to seek reunification? The answer is that kinship connections were helpful, but not essential. The 1965 reforms also created opportunities for immigrants whose skills—as engineers, doctors, nurses, pharmacists—were in short supply. Along with students already living in the United States and enjoying easy access to American employers, these professionals made up the first wave of new Asian immigrants, creating the basis for the kinship migration of less well-educated relatives.

Thus, well-educated, high-skilled immigrants have dominated the Korean influx to the United States and to New York in particular. Although

Koreans constitute a small portion of New York's new immigrants—rarely more than 3 percent of the eighty thousand to ninety thousand legal immigrants who come to New York each year—they play an important and very visible role. As middle-aged newcomers with poor English-language skills and often lacking professional licenses, relatively few Koreans have managed to steer a route back into the fields for which they trained. Instead they have turned to small business, setting up new businesses at a rate that few other groups can rival.

Koreans started in fruit and vegetable stores, taking over shops in all areas of the city, regardless of neighborhood composition or customer clientele. From there, Koreans moved on to other retail specialties—dry cleaning, fish stores, novelty shops, and nail salons. By 1980, a third of New York Korean males were already self-employed. The *1991 Korean Business Directory* provides a ready indicator of commercial growth over the 1980s, listing over 120 commercial specialties in which Korean firms are to be found.[26]

The roots of the Korean ethnic economy are found in several sources. The competitive field was open. By the middle to late 1960s, the sons and daughters of Jewish and Italian storekeepers had better things to do than mind a store, and their parents, old, tired, and scared of crime, were ready to sell out to the newcomers from Korea. By the 1980s, the supply of new, native-born white entrepreneurs had virtually dried up. One survey of neighborhood businesses in Queens and Brooklyn found that almost half of the white-owned shops were run by immigrants and that most white businesses were long-established entities, in contrast to the newly founded Korean shops with which they competed.[27]

Another spur to growth came from within the ethnic community. Koreans, like every other immigrant group, have special tastes and needs that are best served by an insider: the growth of the Korean population has created business for Korean accountants, doctors, brokers, hair stylists, and restaurant owners. Although the Korean community is too small to support a huge commercial infrastructure oriented to ethnic needs, the community has utilized its ethnic connections to Korea to develop commercial activities oriented toward non-Korean markets. Active trade relations between South Korea and the United States have provided a springboard for many Korean-owned import-export businesses, of which 119 are listed in the *1991 Korean Business Directory.*

Finally, the social structure of the Korean community itself generates advantages for business success that few other immigrant groups share. Many Koreans emigrate with capital, and those who are cash poor can raise money through rotating credit associations known as *gae*. Because Koreans migrate in complete family units, family members provide a supply of cheap and trusted labor. The prevalence of self-employment means that many Koreans have close ties to other business owners, who in turn are a source of information and support, and the high organizational density of the Korean community—which is characterized by an incredible proliferation of alumni clubs, churches, businessmen's associations—provides additional conduits for the flow of business information and the making of needed contacts. These community resources distinguish the Koreans from their competitors, who are less likely to be embedded in ethnic or family ties that can be drawn upon for help with business information, capital assistance, or staffing problems.

The Koreans have discovered that conflict *need not* be interethnic; there are other sources of threat, and in the 1980s they mobilized Korean merchants on a considerable scale. Like other small business owners, Koreans were unhappy with local government, usually with something that government was doing or was threatening to do. Fruit and vegetable store owners felt that sanitation officials were too conscientious about sidewalk cleanliness, especially since the result of the officials' demands was often a fine that the Korean store owner had to pay. Pressuring the city to relax inspections became a high priority for Korean organizations. In the late 1980s, as the city's fiscal crisis led it to search for new sources of revenue, fiscal planners thought of placing a special tax on dry cleaners. So Korean dry cleaners entered an unusual coalition with the white owners of commercial laundries, and the union that represented the laundry workers, to roll back the planned tax. Like other small business owners, Korean merchants could also become dissatisfied with government's *failure* to act. The prosperity of the 1980s gave commercial landlords license to raise rents to the maximum, much to the distress of small business owners throughout the city. Koreans joined with their non-Korean counterparts to push for commercial rent control—to no avail.

Although Italians and Jews have largely deserted petty retail trade, they have remained in wholesaling, where the businesses are larger and profits more sizable. Thus Jewish and Italian fruit and vegetable or fish wholesalers have acquired a substantial Korean trade. The encounter has not always been a happy one, as Illsoo Kim recounted in his pathbreaking book: "Especially in their first years of emergence into the fruit and vegetable business, Koreans reported many incidents at the Hunts Point [wholesale] Market. The incidents ranged from unfair pricing and sale of poor-quality produce by the Italian and Jewish wholesalers, to physical threats and beatings administered by competing white retailers."[28] Such conflicts sparked the first mass demonstration by Koreans ever in New York. Although Kim reports that Koreans were subsequently accepted by the wholesaling community, there have been continued incidents and protests, including a recent boycott by Koreans of one of the city's largest fish wholesalers.[29]

In New York, as in almost every other major American city, black neighborhoods have provided new immigrants from Asia and the Middle East with an important economic outlet. To some extent, Koreans and other immigrants have simply replaced older white groups that had long sold to blacks and were now eager to bail out of an increasingly difficult and tense situation. By opening stores in black neighborhoods Koreans were also filling the gap left by the departure of large, nonethnic chain stores, which were steadily eliminating the low-margin, high-cost operations involved in serving a ghetto clientele. Selling to black customers proved fraught with conflict. Small protests erupted in the late 1970s. In 1981 a boycott erupted along 125th Street, Harlem's main commercial thoroughfare, with black leaders calling Korean shop owners "vampires" who came to Harlem to "suck black consumers dry."[30]

Repeated security problems as well as more organized clashes led Korean store owners to establish neighborhood prosperity associations, in addition to those organizations that grouped merchants in a particular retail branch. Thus, alongside groups like the Korean Produce Association or the Korean Apparel Contractors Associations, one finds neighborhood groups like the Korean Merchant Association of the Bronx or the Uptown Korean Merchants Association, which seek "to improve Korean merchants' relations with local residents or communities" while lobbying local police for more effective support.[31]

In 1990 antagonism between black shoppers and Korean merchants erupted in picket lines set up in front of two Korean stores in the Flatbush section of Brooklyn. The clash started with a dispute between a Korean store owner and a black Haitian customer who charged assault; that claim then provoked black activist groups—of fairly dubious repute[32]—to establish a boycott that targeted not only the offending owner, but a neighboring Korean merchant against whom no injury was ever charged.

The boycott lasted for months, choking off business at both stores. Although customers disappeared, the two stores were kept alive by contributions from the organized Korean community, which perceived a broader danger to its economic viability should the boycott succeed. As time went

on, government officials were inevitably involved. The boycott became a crisis for Mayor Dinkins, who was widely criticized for not actively seeking an end to the dispute.

The boycott ground to a halt, and a court threw out the legal suit brought by the aggrieved Haitian shopper. Other, fortunately short-lived boycotts were started in New York even while the Flatbush dispute lingered on. A clash in a nearby Brooklyn area between blacks and a small group of Vietnamese refugees—possibly mistaken for Koreans—showed how quickly tensions generated in one arena could move to another.

CONCLUSION

The story of New York's Irish, Jews, blacks, and Koreans is richer and more complicated than the occupational histories I've recounted in the preceding pages. But if the [reading's] deliberately one-sided focus provides only a partial account, it reminds us of ethnicity's continuing importance, and not simply because of feelings for one's own kind or animosities toward outsiders. Rather, ethnicity's centrality stems from its role as the mechanism whereby groups of categorically different workers have been sorted into an identifiably distinct set of jobs. In this sense, the ethnic division of labor has been the central division of labor in modern New York. Now, as in the past, distinctive roles in the ethnic division of labor impart a sense of "we-ness" and group interest—ensuring the persistence of ethnic fragmentation and conflict.

Seeing the Big Picture   **Who's Got the "Good" Jobs and Why?**

Look at Section VIII on occupations in the appendix. Which racial and ethnic groups monopolize which occupations? How might these trends reflect Waldinger's thesis concerning control of occupations and upward mobility?

"THERE'S NO SHAME IN MY GAME"

Status and Stigma among Harlem's Working Poor

Katherine S. Newman and Catherine Ellis

KATHERINE S. NEWMAN is professor and director of Princeton's Institute for International and Regional Studies. Her 1999 book, *No Shame in My Game: The Working Poor in the Inner City*, won both the Sidney Hillman Book Prize and the Robert F. Kennedy Book Award. **CATHERINE ELLIS** is a consulting producer for American RadioWorks®, the documentary unit of American Public Media. She holds a PhD in anthropology from Columbia University.

I N THE EARLY 1990s, THE MCDONALD'S corporation launched a television ad campaign featuring a young black man named Calvin, who was portrayed sitting atop a Brooklyn stoop in his Golden-Arches uniform while his friends passed by to hard-time him about holding down a "McJob." After brushing off their teasing with good humor, Calvin is approached furtively by one young black man who asks, sotto voce, whether Calvin might help him get a job. He allows that he too could use some earnings and that, despite the ragging he has just given Calvin, he thinks the uniform is really pretty cool—or at least that having a job is pretty cool.

Questions to Consider

Katherine Newman and Catherine Ellis ask us to imagine what life is like working a "McJob." How do individuals maintain self-respect working at a job that provides little in the way of social status? Is it possible for these workers to find employment that pays a living wage (about $16 an hour in New York City)? What does "No Shame in My Game" mean, and what does this phrase suggest about our attitude toward work?

Every fast-food worker we interviewed for this study knew the Calvin series by heart: Calvin on the job; Calvin in the street; Calvin helping an elderly woman cross the street on his way to work; Calvin getting promoted to management. They knew what McDonald's was trying to communicate to young people by producing the series in the first place. Fast-food jobs are burdened by a lasting stigma, but one that can be overcome in time. Eventually, so the commercial suggests, the public "dissing" will give way to private admiration as the value of sticking with a job eclipses the stain of a burger flipper's lowly reputation.

One of the moral maxims of American culture is that work defines the person. We carry around in our heads a rough tally that tells us what kinds of jobs are worthy of respect or of disdain, a pyramid organized by the income attached to a particular job, the educational credentials it demands, and the social characteristics of an occupation's incumbents. We use this system of **stratification** (ruthlessly at times) to boost the status of some and humiliate others.[1]

Given our tradition of equating moral value with employment, it stands to reason that the most profound dividing line in our culture is that which separates the working person from the unemployed.[2] Only after this line has been crossed do we begin to make the finer gradations that distinguish a white-collar worker from his blue-collar counterpart, a CEO from a secretary. A whole host of moral virtues—discipline, personal responsibility, pragmatism—are ascribed to those who have found and kept a job, almost any job, while those who have not are dismissed in public discourse as slothful and irresponsible.[3]

We inhabit an unforgiving culture that fails to acknowledge the many reasons some people cross that employment barrier and others are left behind. We may remember, for a time, that unemployment rates are high; that particular industries have downsized millions of workers right out of their jobs; or that racial barriers or negative attitudes toward teenagers make it harder for some people to get jobs than others. Yet in the end American culture wipes out these background truths in favor of a simpler dichotomy: the worthy and the unworthy, the working folk and the lazy deadbeats.

For those on the positive side of the divide, those who work for a living, the rewards are far greater than a paycheck. The employed enter a social world in which their identities as mainstream Americans are shaped, structured, and reinforced. The workplace is the main institutional setting—and virtually the only one after one's school career is over—in which individuals become part of the collective American enterprise that lies at the heart of our culture: the market. We are so divided in other domains—race, geography, family organization, **gender roles**, and the like—that common ground along almost any other lines is difficult to achieve. For our diverse and divided society, participation in the world of work is the most powerful source of social integration.

It is in the workplace that we are most likely to mix with those who come from different backgrounds, are under the greatest pressure to subordinate individual idiosyncrasy to the requirements of an organization, and are called upon to contribute to goals that eclipse the personal. All workers have these experiences in common, even as segregation constrains the real mix of workers; conformity is imposed on some occupations more than others; and the goals to which we must subscribe are often elusive, unreachable, or at odds with personal desire.

The creation of a workplace identity is rarely the task of the self-directed individualist, moving along some preordained path. It is a miracle worked by organizations, firms, supervisors, fellow workers, and by the whole long search that leads from the desire to find a job to the endpoint of landing one. This transformation is particularly fraught for ghetto youth and adults, for they face a difficult job market, high hurdles in convincing employers to take a chance on them, and relatively poor rewards—from a financial point of view—for

---

stratification How a society ranks its members within a social hierarchy. In the United States, class, power, and social status are the primary sorting mechanisms.

gender roles Beliefs, attitudes, expectations, and behaviors that a society links to one's sex.

their successes. But the crafting of an identity is an important developmental process for them, just as it is for their more privileged counterparts.

Powerful forces work to exclude African Americans, Latinos, and other minorities from full participation in American society. From the schools that provide a substandard education for millions of inner-city kids, to an employment system rife with discrimination, to a housing market that segregates minority families, there is almost no meaning to the notion that Americans all begin from the same starting line.[4] Precisely because this is the case, blasting one's way through the job barrier and starting down that road of acquiring a common identity as mainstream worker is of the greatest importance for black and brown youth in segregated communities. It may be one of the few accessible pipelines into the core of American society and the one with the greatest payoff, symbolic and material.

This [reading] draws upon a two-year study of fast-food workers and job seekers in central and northern Harlem. Two hundred African American and Latino workers participated in this study by participating in face-to-face interviews. Sixty of them completed extensive life histories, and a smaller group contributed yearlong personal diaries and permitted the members of our research group to spend extensive periods of time with them, their family members, and their friends. We draw upon all of these data here to explore the nature of values among the working poor in the inner city.

THE SOCIAL COSTS OF ACCEPTING LOW-WAGE WORK

While the gainfully employed may be honored over those who stand outside the labor force, all jobs are not created equal. Fast-food jobs, in particular, are notoriously stigmatized and denigrated. "McJob" has become a common epithet meant to designate work without redeeming value. The reasons for this

heavy valence are numerous and worthy of deconstruction, for the minority workers who figure in this study have a mountain of stigma to overcome if they are to maintain their self-respect. Indeed, this is one of the main goals of the organizational culture they join when they finally land a job in the restaurant chain we will call "Burger Barn."

Fast-food jobs epitomize the assembly line structure of deskilled service jobs: they are highly routinized and appear to the untutored observer to be entirely lacking in discretion—almost military in their scripted nature. The symbolic capital of these routinized jobs can be measured in negative numbers. They represent the opposite of the autonomous entrepreneur who is lionized in popular culture (from *BusinessWeek* to hip-hop).

Burger Barn workers are told that they must, at all cost to their own dignity, defer to the public. Customers can be unreasonably demanding, rude, and demeaning, and workers must count backward from one hundred in an effort to stifle their outrage. Servicing the customer with a smile is music to management's ears because making money depends on keeping the clientele happy, but it can be an exercise in humiliation for inner-city teenagers. It is hard for them to refrain from reading this public nastiness as another instance of society's low estimation of their worth. But if they want to hold on to these minimum-wage jobs, they soon realize that they have to tolerate comments that would almost certainly provoke a fistfight outside the workplace.

It is well known among ghetto consumers that fast-food crew members have to put up with whatever verbiage comes across the counter. That knowledge occasionally prompts nasty exchanges designed explicitly to anger workers, to push them to retaliate verbally. Testing those limits is an outlet for customers down on their luck, and a favorite pastime of teenagers in particular. This may be the one opportunity they have to put someone else down in public, knowing there is little the worker can do in return.

It is bad enough to be on the receiving end of this kind of abuse from adults, especially white adults, for that has its own reading along race lines. It is, in some respects, even worse to have to contend with it from minority peers, for there is much more personal honor at stake, more pride to be lost, and an audience whose opinion matters more. This no doubt is why harassment is a continuous problem for fast-food workers. It hurts. Their peers, with plenty of anger bottled up for all kinds of reasons extraneous to the restaurant experience, find counterparts working the cash register convenient targets for venting.

Roberta Sampson[5] is a five-year veteran of Burger Barn who has worked her way up to management. A formidable African American woman, Roberta has always prided herself on her ability to make it on her own. Most of Roberta's customers have been perfectly pleasant people; many have been long-time repeat visitors to her restaurant. But she has also encountered many who radiate disrespect.

> Well, I had alcoholics, derelicts. People that are aggravated with life. I've had people that don't even have jobs curse me out. I've dealt with all kinds.
>
> Sometimes it would get to me. If a person yelled out [in front of] a lobby full of people, "Bitch, that's why you work at Burger Barn," I would say [to myself], "I'm probably making more than you and your mother." It hurts when people don't even know what you're making and they say those things. Especially in Harlem, they do that to you. They call you all types of names and everything.

Natasha Robins is younger than Roberta and less practiced at these confrontations. But she has had to contend with them nevertheless, especially from age-mates who are (or at least claim to be) higher up the status hierarchy than she is. Hard as she tries, Natasha cannot always control her temper and respond the way the firm wants her to:

> It's hard dealing with the public. There are good things, like old people. They sweet. But the younger people around my age are always snotty. Think they better than you because they not working at Burger Barn. They probably work at something better than you.

How do you deal with rude or unfriendly customers? They told us that we just suppose to walk to the back and ignore it, but when they in your face like that, you get so upset that you have to say something. . . . I got threatened with a gun one time. 'Cause this customer had threw a piece of straw paper in the back and told me to pick it up like I'm a dog. I said, "No." And he cursed at me. I cursed at him back and he was like, "Yeah, next time you won't have nothing to say when I come back with my gun and shoot your ass." Oh, *excuse* me.

Ianna Bates, who had just turned sixteen the summer she found her first job at Burger Barn, has had many of the same kinds of problems Natasha Robins complains of. The customers who hard-time her are just looking for a place to vent their anger about things that have nothing to do with buying lunch. Ianna recognizes that this kind of thing could happen in any restaurant, but believes it is a special problem in Harlem, for ghetto residents have more to be angry about and fewer accessible targets for one-upmanship. Cashiers in fast-food shops catch the results:

> What I hate about Burger Barn is the customers, well, some of them that I can't stand. . . . I don't want to stereotype Harlem . . ., but since I only worked in Harlem that's all I can speak for. Some people have a chip on their shoulders. . . . Most of the people that come into the restaurant are black. Most of them have a lot of kids. It's in the ghetto. Maybe, you know, they are depressed about their lifestyles or whatever else that is going on in their lives and they just . . . I don't know. They just are like *urff!*
>
> And no matter what you do you cannot please them. I'm not supposed to say anything to the customer, but that's not like me.

I have a mouth and I don't take no short from nobody. I don't care who it is, don't take anybody's crap.

Despite this bravado, Ianna well knows that to use her mouth is to risk her job. She has had to work hard to find ways to cope with this frustration that do not get her into trouble with management:

I don't say stuff to people most of the time. Mostly I just look at them like they stupid. Because my mother always told me that as long as you don't say nothin' to nobody, you can't never get in trouble. If you look at them stupid, what are they going to do? If you roll your eyes at somebody like that, I mean, that's really nothing [compared to] . . . cursing at them. Most of the time I try to walk away.

As Ianna observes, there is enough free-floating fury in Harlem to keep a steady supply of customer antagonism coming the way of service workers every day of their work lives. The problem is constant enough to warrant official company policies on how Burger Barn's crew members should respond to insults, what managers should do to help, and the evasive tactics that work best to quell an incendiary situation without losing business.[6] Management tries to minimize the likelihood of such incidents by placing girls on the registers rather than boys, in the apparent belief that young men will attract more abuse and find it harder to quash their reactions than their female counterparts.

Burger Barn does what it can to contend with these problems on the shop floor. But the neighborhood is beyond its reach and there, too, fast-food workers are often met with ridicule from the people they grew up with. They have to learn to defend themselves against the criticism that they have lowered themselves in taking these jobs coming from people they have known all their lives. Stephanie Harmon, who has worked at Burger Barn for over a year, explains that here, too, she leans on the divide between the worker and the do-nothing:

People I hang out with, they know me since I was little. We all grew up together. When they see me comin', they laugh and say, "Here come Calvin, here come Calvin sister." I just laugh and keep on going. I say, "You're crazy. But that's OK cause I got a job and you all standing out here on the corner." Or I say, "This is my job, it's legal." Something like that. That Calvin commercial show you that even though his friends tease him and he just brushed them off, then he got a higher position. Then you see how they change toward him.

As Stephanie indicates, the snide remarks of peers and neighbors when a worker first dons a Burger Barn uniform are often replaced with requests for help in getting hired and a show of respect when that worker sticks with the job, shows up with money in her pockets and, best of all, moves into management. Still, the scorn is a burden to endure.

Tiffany Wilson, also a teen worker in a central Harlem Burger Barn, thinks she knows why kids in her community who don't work give her such a hard time. They don't want her to succeed because if no one is making it, then no one needs to feel bad about failing. But if someone claws their way up and looks like they have a chance to escape the syndrome of failure, it must mean everyone could, in theory, do so as well. The teasing, a thinly veiled attempt to enforce conformity, is designed to push would-be success stories back into the fold:

What you will find in any situation, more so in the black community, is that if you are in the community and you try to excel, you will get ridicule from your own peers. It's like the "crab down" syndrome. . . . If you put a bunch of crabs in a big bucket and one crab tries to get out, what do you think the other crabs would do now? According to my thinking, they should pull him up or push him or help him get out. But the crabs pull him back in the barrel. That's just an analogy for what happens in the community a lot.

Keeping everyone down prevents any particular person from feeling that creeping sense of despair that comes from believing things could be otherwise but aren't.

Swallowing ridicule would be a hardship for almost anyone in this culture, but it is particularly hard on minority youth in the inner city. They have already logged several years' worth of interracial and cross-class friction by the time they climb behind a Burger Barn cash register. More likely than not, they have also learned from peers that no self-respecting person allows themselves to be "dissed" without striking back. Yet this is precisely what they must do if they are going to survive on the shop floor.

This is one of the main reasons why these jobs carry such a powerful stigma in American popular culture: they fly in the face of a national attraction to autonomy, independence, and the individualist's right to respond in kind when their dignity is threatened. In ghetto communities, this stigma is even more powerful because—ironically—it is in these enclaves that this mainstream value of independence is elaborated and embellished. Film characters from the Superfly variety to the political version (e.g., Malcolm X), rap stars, and local idols base their claims to notoriety on standing above the crowd, going their own way, being beyond the ties that bind ordinary mortals. There are white parallels, to be sure, but this is a powerful genre of icons in the black community, not because it is a disconnected subculture, but because it is an intensified version of a perfectly recognizable American middle- and working-class fixation.

It is therefore noteworthy that thousands upon thousands of minority teens, young adults, and even middle-aged adults line up for jobs that will subject them, at least potentially, to a kind of character assassination. They do so not because they start the job-hunting process with a different set of values, one that can withstand society's contempt for fast-food workers. They take these jobs because in so many inner-city communities, there is nothing better in the offing. In general, they have already tried to get better jobs and have

failed, landing instead at the door of Burger Barn as a last resort.

The stigma of these jobs has other sources beyond the constraints of enforced deference. Low pay and poor prospects for mobility matter as well. Fast-food jobs are invariably minimum-wage positions.[7] Salaries rise very little over time, even for first-line management. In ghetto areas, where jobs are scarce and the supply of would-be workers chasing them is relatively large, downward pressure keeps these jobs right down at the bottom of the wage scale.[8]

The public perception (fueled by knowledge of wage conditions) is that there is very little potential for improvement in status or responsibility either. Even though there are Horatio Algers in this industry, there are no myths to prop up a more glorified image. As a result, the epithet "McJob" develops out of the perception that a fast-food worker is not likely to end up in a prestigious position as a general manager or restaurant owner; she is going to spend her whole life flipping burgers.

As it happens, this is only half true. The fast-food industry is actually very good about internal promotion. Shop floor management is nearly always recruited from the ranks of entry-level workers. Carefully planned training programs make it possible for people to move up, to acquire transferable skills, and to at least take a shot at entrepreneurial ownership. Industry leaders, like McDonald's, are proud of the fact that half of their present board of directors started out on the shop floor as crew members. One couldn't say as much for most other Fortune 500 firms.

Nevertheless, the vast majority of workers never even get close to management. The typical entry-level worker cycles through the job in short order, producing an industry average job tenure of less than six months. Since this is just an average, it suggests that a large number of employees are there and gone in a matter of weeks. It is this pattern, a planned operation built around low skills and high turnover, that has given fast-food jobs such a bad name. Although it is quite possible to rise above the fray and make a very respectable living in fast-food management, most crew members remain at the entry level and leave too soon to see much upward movement. Observing this pattern on such a large scale—in practically every town and city in the country—Americans naturally conclude that there is no real future in a job of this kind, and anyone with more on the ball wouldn't be caught dead working behind the counter.

The stigma also stems from the low socioeconomic status of the people who hold these jobs. This includes teenagers, immigrants who often speak halting English, those with little education, and (increasingly in affluent communities afflicted with labor shortages) the elderly. To the extent that the prestige of a job refracts the social characteristics of its average incumbents, fast-food jobs are hobbled by the perception that people with better choices would never purposively opt for a McJob. We argue that entry-level jobs of this kind don't merit this scorn: a lot more skill, discretion, and responsibility are locked up in a fast-food job than meets the public eye. But this truth hardly matters where public perception is concerned. There is no faster way to indicate that a person is barely deserving of notice than to point out that they hold a "chump change" job in Kentucky Fried Chicken or Burger King. We "know" this is the case just by looking at the age, skin color, or educational credentials of the people already on the job: the tautology has a staying power that even the most expensive public relations campaign cannot shake.

It is hard to know the extent to which this stigma discourages young people in places like central Harlem from knocking on the doors of fast-food restaurants in search of employment. It is clear that the other choices aren't much better and that necessity drives thousands, if not millions, of teens and older job seekers to repudiate the stigma associated with fast-food work or learn to live with it.[9] But no one comes into the central Harlem job market without having to contend with the social risks to their identity that come with approaching stigmatized ground.

Tiffany Wilson started working in the underground economy bagging groceries when she was little more than ten years old because her mother was having trouble supporting the family, "checks weren't coming in," and there was "really a need for food" in the family. She graduated to summer youth by the time she was fourteen and landed a job answering phones in a center that dealt with domestic violence cases, referring terrified women to shelters. By the time she was sixteen, Tiffany needed a real job that would last beyond the summertime, so she set about looking—everywhere. As a black teenager, she quickly discovered there wasn't a great deal open to her. Tiffany ended up at Burger Barn in the Bronx, a restaurant two blocks from her house and close enough to her high school to make afterschool hours feasible.

> The first Burger Barn I worked at was because nobody else would take me. It was a last resort. I didn't want to go to Burger Barn. You flip burgers. People would laugh at you. In high school, I didn't wanna be in that kind of environment. But lo and behold, after everything else failed, Martin Paints, other jobs, Burger Barn was welcoming me with open arms. So I started working there.

Tiffany moved to Harlem when she finished high school and found she couldn't commute back to the Bronx. Reluctant to return to the fast-food business, Tiffany tried her luck at moving up, into a service job with more of a white-collar flavor. She looked everywhere for a position in stores where the jobs are free of hamburger grease and hot oil for French fries, stores where clerks don't wear aprons or hair nets. Nothing panned out, despite her best efforts:

> I'm looking at Lerners and Plymouth [clothing stores] and going to all these stores and lo and behold Burger Barn is there with open arms because I had two years of experience by then.

The new Burger Barn franchise was right in the middle of Harlem, not far from the room she rents over a storefront church. It had the additional appeal of being a black-owned business, something that mattered to Tiffany in terms of the "more cultural reasons why [she] decided to work there." But she confesses to a degree of disappointment that she was not able to break free of entry-level fast-food jobs. With a high-school diploma in hand, Tiffany was hoping for something better.

William Johnson followed a similar pathway to Burger Barn, graduating from summer youth jobs in the middle of high school and looking for something that would help pay for his books and carfare. The Department of Labor gave him a referral to Burger Barn, but he was reluctant at first to pursue it:

> To go there and work for Burger Barn, that was one of those real cloak-and-dagger kind of things. You'll be coming out [and your friends say], "Yo, where you going?" You be, "I'm going, don't worry about where I'm going." And you see your friends coming [to the restaurant] and see you working there and now you be [thinking], "Now, the whole [housing] project gonna know I work in Burger Barn." It's not something I personally proclaim or pride and stuff. . . . If you are a crew member, you really aren't shit there. . . . You got nothing there, no benefits, nothing. It was like that [when I was younger] and it's like that now.

William tried every subterfuge he could think of to conceal his job from the kids he knew. He kept his uniform in a bag and put it on in the back of the restaurant so that it would never be visible on the street. He made up fake jobs to explain to his friends where his spending money was coming from. He took circuitous routes to the Barn and hid back by the gigantic freezer when he spotted a friend coming into the store. The last thing William wanted was to be publicly identified as a shift worker at Burger Barn.

In this, William was much like the other teen and young adult workers we encountered. They are very sensitive to stigma, to challenges to their status, and by taking low-wage jobs of this kind they have positioned themselves to receive exactly the kind of insults they most fear. But the fact is that they do take these risks and, in time, latch on to other "narratives" that undergird their legitimacy.

BREAKING THE STIGMA

One of the chief challenges of an organization like Burger Barn is how to take people who have come to them on the defensive and turn them into workers who at least appear on the surface, if not deep in their souls, to enjoy their work. Customers have choices; they can vote with their feet. If ordering french fries at Burger Barn requires them to run a gauntlet of annoyance, rudeness, or diffidence from the person who takes their order, they can easily cross the street to a competitor the next time. It is clearly in the company's interest to find ways to turn the situation around. Ideally, from the industry's viewpoint, it would be best if the whole reputation of these jobs could be reversed. This is what McDonald's had in mind when it launched the Calvin series. But for all the reasons outlined earlier in this [reading], that is not likely to happen, for the conditions that give rise to the stigma in the first place—low wages, high turnover, enforced deference—are not likely to change. Beyond publicizing the opportunities that are within reach, much of which falls on deaf ears, there is little the industry can do to rehabilitate its workers in the eyes of the public and thereby dampen the tension across the counter.

Yet behind the scenes, managers and workers, and peers working together in restaurant crews, do build a moral defense of their work. They call upon timeless American values, values familiar to many, including conservatives, to undergird their respectability. Pointing to the essential virtues of the gainfully employed, Burger Barn workers align themselves with the great mass of men and women who work for a living. "We are like them," they declare, and in so doing separate themselves from the people in their midst who are not employed.

They have plenty of experience with individuals who don't work, often including members of their own families: beggars who come around the restaurants looking for handouts every day; fast-talkers who come into Burger Barn hoping for free food; and age-mates who prefer to deal drugs. In general, these low-wage workers are far less forgiving, and far less tolerant, of these people than are the liberals who champion the cause of the working poor. Since they hold hard, exhausting, poorly paid jobs, they see little reason why anyone ought to get a free ride. What the indigent should do, on this account, is to follow their example: get a job, any job.

Ianna Bates is an articulate case in point. She has had to confront the social degradation that comes from holding a "low job" and has developed a tough hide in response. Her dignity is underwritten by the critique she has absorbed about the "welfare dependent":

> I'm not ashamed because I have a job. Most people don't and I'm proud of myself that I decided to get up and do something at an early age. So as I look at it, I'm not on welfare. I'm doing something.
>
> I'm not knocking welfare, but I know people that are on it that can get up and work. There's nothing wrong with them. And they just choose not to. . . . They don't really need to be on [welfare]. They just want it because they can get away with it. I don't think it's right because that's my tax dollars going for somebody who is lazy, who don't wanna get up. I can see if a woman had three children, her husband left her and she don't have no job cause she was a housewife. OK. But after a while, you know, welfare will send you to school. Be a nurse assistant, a home attendant, something!
>
> Even if you were on welfare, it should be like, you see all these dirty streets we have? Why can't they go out and sweep the streets, clean up the parks? I mean, there is so much stuff that needs to be done in this city. They can do that and give them their money. Not just sit home and not do anything.

Patricia Hull, a mother of five children in her late thirties, couldn't agree more. Patty has worked at Burger Barn for five years now, having pulled herself off of welfare by the sheer determination to be a decent role model for her children. One might imagine that she would be more tolerant of **AFDC** recipients, since she has been there. She moved up to the Big Apple from Tennessee after her husband walked out on her, hoping to find more job opportunities than the few that were available in the rural south. It took a long time for her to get on her feet, and even Patty would agree that without "aid" she would not have made it this far. Still, having finally taken the hard road to a real job, she sees no reason why anyone else should have an easier ride:

> There's so much in this city; it's always hiring. It may not be what you want. It may not be the pay you want. But you will always get a job. If I can work at Burger Barn all week and come home tired and then have to deal with the kids and all of that, and be happy with $125 a week, so can you. Why would I give quarters [to bums on the street]? My quarter is tax-free money for you! No way.

Or, in a variation on the same theme, Larry Peterson reminds us that any job is better than no job. The kids who would dare to hard-time Larry get nothing but a cold shoulder in return because Larry knows in his soul that he has something they don't have: work for which he gets paid.

> I don't care what other people think. You know, I just do not care. I have a job, you know. It's my job. You ain't puttin' *no* food on my table; you ain't puttin' *no* clothes on my back. I will walk tall with my Burger Barn uniform on. Be proud of it, you know.

These views could have come straight from the most conservative Republicans in the country, bent on justifying draconian cuts in the welfare budget. For they trade on a view held by many of the ghetto-based working poor: that work equals dignity and no one deserves a free ride. The difference between them is simply that the working

---

AFDC Aid to Families with Dependent Children: assistance provided by the federal government to families in economic need.

poor know whereof they speak: they have toiled behind the hot grease pits of french-fry vats, they have stood on their feet for eight or nine hours at a stretch, all for the magnificent sum of $4.25 an hour. Virtually all they have to show for their trouble is the self-respect that comes from being on the right side of that gaping cavern that separates the deserving (read working) and the undeserving (read nonworking) poor (Katz 1989).

Other retorts to status insults emerge as well. Flaunting financial independence often provides a way of lashing back at acquaintances who dis young workers for taking Burger Barn jobs. Brian Gray, born in Jamaica but raised in one of Harlem's tougher neighborhoods, knows that his peers don't really think much of his job. "They just make fun," he says. "Ah, you flipping burgers. You gettin' paid $4.25. They'd go snickering down the street." But it wasn't long after Brian started working that he picked up some serious money, serious at least for a teenager in his neighborhood.

> What I did was made Sam [the general manager] save my money for me. Then I got the best of clothes and the best sneakers with my own money. Then I added two chains. Then [my friends] were like, "Where you selling drugs at?" And I'm like, "the same place you said making fun of me, flipping burgers. That's where I'm getting my money from. Now, where are you getting yours from?" They couldn't answer.

Contrary to public perception, most teenagers in Harlem are afraid of the drug trade and won't go near it. They know too many people who are six feet under, in jail, or permanently disabled by the ravages of drugs. If you aren't willing to join the underground economy, where are you going to get the money to dress yourself, go out on the town, and do the other things teens throughout the middle class do on Mom and Dad's sufferance? Most of Harlem's youth cannot rely on their parents' financial support to meet these needs. Indeed, this is one of the primary pressures that pushes young people out into the labor market in the first place, and at

an early age. Most workers we interviewed had their first job by the age of fourteen.

What Brian does, then, is to best his mates at their own game by showing them that he has the wherewithal to be a consumer, based on his own earnings. He derives no small amount of pleasure from turning these tables, upending the status system by outdoing his friends on style grounds they value as much as he does.

It might be comforting to suggest that these hardworking low-wage workers were, from the very beginning, different from their nonworking counterparts, equipped somehow to withstand the gauntlet of criticism that comes their way when they start out on the bottom of the labor market. It would be comforting because we would then be able to sort the deserving, admirable poor (who recognize the fundamental value of work and are willing to ignore **stigma**) from the undeserving (who collapse in the face of peer pressure and therefore prefer to go on the dole). This is too simplistic. Burger Barn workers of all ages and colors fully admit that their employment is the butt of jokes and that it has subjected them to ridicule. Some, like Larry Peterson, argue that they don't care what other people think, but even these brave souls admit that it took a long time for them to build up this confidence.

Where, then, does the confidence come from? How do ghetto residents develop the rejoinders that make it possible to recapture their dignity in the face of peer disapproval? To some degree, they can call on widely accepted American values that honor working people, values that float in the culture at large.[10] But this is not enough to construct a positive identity when the reminders of low status—coming from customers, friends, and the media—are abundant. Something stronger is required: a workplace culture that actively works to overcome the negatives by reinforcing the value of the work ethic. Managers and veteran employees on the shop floor play a critical role in the reinforcement process by counseling new workers distressed by bad-mouthing.

---

stigma A social mark of disgrace that prevents a person from entering mainstream society. For example, society stigmatizes ex-felons and pedophiles.

Kimberly Sampson, a twenty-year-old African American woman, began working at Burger Barn when she was sixteen and discovered firsthand how her "friends" would turn on her for taking a low-wage job. Fortunately, she found a good friend at work who steadied her with a piece of advice:

Say it's a job. You are making money. Right? Don't care what nobody say. You know? If they don't like it, too bad. They sitting on the corner doing what they are doing. You got to work making money. You know? Don't bother with what anybody has to say about it.

Kim's advisor, a workplace veteran who had long since come to terms with the insults of his peers, called upon a general status hierarchy that places the working above the nonworking as a bulwark against the slights. His point was later echoed by Kim's manager in the course of a similar episode, as she explained:

Kids come in here . . . they don't have enough money. I'll be like, "You don't have enough money; you can't get [the food you ordered]." One night this little boy came in there and cursed me out. He [said], "That's why you are working at Burger Barn. You can't get a better job. . . ."

I was upset and everything. I started crying. [My manager] was like, "Kim, don't bother with him. I'm saying, *you got a job.* You know. It is a *job.*"

Absorbing this defensive culture is particularly important for immigrant workers in Harlem who often find fast-food jobs the first venue where they have sustained interaction with African Americans who resent the fact that they have jobs at all, much less jobs in their community. Marisa Gonzalez, a native of Ecuador, had a very difficult time when she first began working as a hostess at Burger Barn. A pretty, petite nineteen-year-old, she was selected for the job because she has the kind of sparkle and

vivaciousness that any restaurant would want customers to see. But some of her more antagonistic black customers saw her as an archetype: the immigrant who barely speaks a word of English who snaps up a job some native-born English speaker ought to have. Without the support of her bilingual, Latino manager, she would not have been able to pull herself together and get on with the work:

I wasn't sent to the grill or the fries [where you don't need to communicate with customers]. I was sent to the cash register, even though the managers knew I couldn't speak English. That was only one week after my arrival in the United States! So I wasn't feeling very well at all. Three weeks later I met a manager who was Puerto Rican. He was my salvation. He told me, "Marisa, it's not that bad." He'd speak to me in English, even though he knows Spanish. He'd tell me, "Don't cry. Dry off those tears. You'll be all right, you'll make it." So he encouraged me like no other person in that Burger Barn, especially when the customers would curse at me for not knowing English. He gave me courage and after that it went much better.

Among the things this manager taught Marisa was that she should never listen to people who give her a hard time about holding a job at Burger Barn. Having been a white-collar clerical worker in her native country, it did bother Marisa that she had slipped down the status hierarchy—and it still does. She was grateful, nevertheless, to have a way to earn money and her family was desperate for her contribution. When customers would insult her, insinuating that someone who speaks limited English was of lowly status, she turned to management for help. And she found it in the form of fellow Latino bosses who told her to hold her head up because she was, after all, working, while her critics on the whole were not.

Once these general moral values are in place, many Burger Barn workers take the process one step further: they argue their jobs have hidden virtues that make them more valuable than most people credit. Tiffany Wilson, the young black woman who reluctantly settled for a Burger Barn job when none of the clothing stores she wanted to work for would take her, decided in the end that there was more substance to her job than she credited initially:

When I got in there, I realized it's not what people think. It's a lot more to it than flipping burgers. It's a real system of business. That's when I really got to see a big corporation at play. I mean, one part of it, the foundation of it: cashiers, the store, how it's run. Production of food, crew workers, service. Things of that nature. That's when I really got into it and understood a lot more.

Americans tend to think of values as embedded in individuals, transmitted through families, and occasionally reinforced by media images or role models. We tend not to focus on the powerful contribution that institutions and organizations make to the creation and sustenance of beliefs. Yet it is clear that the workplace itself is a major force in the creation of a rebuttal culture among these workers. Without this line of defense it would be very hard for Burger Barn employees to retain their dignity. With the support of fellow workers, however, they are able to hold their heads up, not by defining themselves as separate from society, but by calling upon the values they hold in common with the rest of the working world.

This is but one of the reasons why exclusion from the society of the employed is such a devastating source of social isolation. We could hand people money, as various guaranteed income plans of the past thirty years have suggested. But we can't hand out honor. For a majority of Americans, honor comes from participation in this central setting in our culture and from the positive identity it confers.

Franklin Roosevelt understood this during the Great Depression and responded with the creation of thousands of publicly funded jobs designed to put people to work building the national parks, the railway stations, the great highways that criss-cross the country, and the murals that decorate public walls from San Francisco to New York. Social scientists studying the unemployed in the 1930s showed convincingly that people who held **WPA** jobs were far happier and healthier than those who were on the dole, even when their incomes did not differ significantly. WPA workers had their dignity in the midst of poverty; those on the dole were vilified and could not justify their existence or find an effective cultural rationale for the support they received.

This historical example has its powerful parallels in the present. Joining the workforce is a fundamental, transforming experience that moves people across barriers of subculture, race, gender, and class. It never completely eradicates these differences, and in some divisive settings it may even reinforce consciousness of them—through glass ceilings, discriminatory promotion policies, and the like. But even in places where pernicious distinctions are maintained, there is another, overarching identity competing with forms that stress difference: a common bond within the organization and across the nation of fellow workers. This is what makes getting a job so much more than a means to a financial end. It becomes a crucial developmental hurdle, especially for people who have experienced exclusion before, including minorities, women, the elderly, and teenagers. Any experience that can speak back to the stigma that condemns burger flippers as the dregs, resurrecting them as exemplars of the American work ethic, has extraordinary power.

Those who choose to earn a living in the legitimate job market receive few material rewards for their effort, but they can claim moral legitimacy from the traditional American work ethic. They can't flash large rolls of cash before the eyes of their neighbors, but they can pride themselves on "doing the right thing," avoiding the dangers of the drug trade and the sloth of welfare recipients. While they understand that some people have a legitimate need to receive government assistance, they don't see the payoff of dealing drugs, and this is not an opinion

---

WPA Works Progress Administration: a New Deal program from the 1930s to provide jobs for the unemployed.

they keep to themselves. Workers with friends or family in the drug trade often implore them to get out, warning them of the dangers, and reasoning that they each make about the same amount of money in a week, while the one involved with drugs has to work longer hours.

Nadine Stevens has worked at Burger Barn since graduating from high school five years ago. By all accounts she lives in one of the most dangerous neighborhoods in Harlem. Her apartment building is the home of an active drug trade and, indeed, the mailboxes were recently removed from the building by police because they were being used for drug transactions. She knows most of the drug dealers who sit on her stoop every day and night, having grown up with them. She and her mother and sister, whose ground-floor apartment faces the street, have seen many young women they know wasted by drugs, and young men killed in their hallway.

Nadine tries to convince the dealers she knows to get out of the trade, and to shoot for getting into management at Burger Barn. She and her sister, Rachael, with whom she works at Burger Barn, recently accosted a young teen they knew on the street whom they suspected of drug running. They told her that if she was desperate for money they'd get her a job at Burger Barn. Sensing the girl's reluctance, Nadine cried, "There's no shame in my game! Come work with me."

The dealers they know argue that the Burger Barn employee is working in a poorly paid, demeaning job and that, furthermore, they couldn't get hired there if they tried. Although their work is dangerous, illegal, and despised by neighbors, they brandish the accoutrements of success glorified in the United States: expensive cars, stylish clothes, and lots of cash. Their honor is measured in dollars, a common American standard that competes for the attention of people otherwise destined to earn little more than the minimum wage.

Anthony Vallo has had to choose on which side of the law to work and, once he secured his Burger Barn job, had to decide what to do about his friends and acquaintances who chose the wrong side. Two of his best friends are in jail. Another friend is dealing drugs and probably isn't far from a jail term

himself. What Anthony does is try to maintain a cordial relationship with these guys, but to put as much distance between himself and them as he can without giving offense:

> This friend of mine is selling and stuff like that, but he's my friend. We used to go to school back then. He was like, "Damn, you still doin' that Burger Barn shit? I can get you a real job!" I think he respects me; at least he don't criticize me behind my back. But I try to avoid him, you know.

Drug dealers are not the only problem cases with which Harlem workers must contend. At least until welfare reform began to force women on AFDC back into the labor force, many young mothers working low-wage jobs were faced with the fork in the road that led either to a job at a place like Burger Barn or public assistance. Since most know a fair number of women who have elected, or had no choice but to opt for, the latter, it takes no small amount of fortitude to go for a minimum-wage job.[11] Indeed, given that AFDC offered greater financial benefits—when health coverage, food stamps, and subsidized housing are part of the package—than these jobs provide, it takes a strong attachment to the work ethic and a willingness to sacrifice elements of one's financial well-being in favor of the dignity that goes with holding a real job.

THE IMPORTANCE OF GOING TO WORK

Although having a well-paid, respected career is prized above all else in the United States, our culture confers honor on those who hold down jobs of any kind over those who are outside of the labor force. Independence and self-sufficiency—these are virtues that have no equal in this society. But there are other reasons why we value workers besides the fact that their earnings keep them above water and therefore less in need of help from government, communities, or charities. We also value workers because they share certain common views, experiences, and expectations. The work ethic is more than an attitude toward earning money—it is a disciplined existence, a social life woven around the workplace.

For all the talk of "family values," we know that in the contemporary period, family often takes a backseat to the requirements of a job, even when the job involves flipping burgers. What we are supposed to orient toward primarily is the workplace and its demands. This point could not be made more forcefully than it is in the context of the welfare reform bills of 1996. Public policy in the late 1990s makes clear that poor women are now supposed to be employed even if they have young children. With a majority of women with children, even those under a year of age, in the labor force, we are not prepared to cut much slack to those who have been on welfare. They can and should work like the rest of us, or so the policy mantra goes. This represents no small change in the space of a few decades in our views of what honorable women and mothers should do. But it also reflects the growing dominance of work in our understanding of adult priorities.

We could think of this increasingly work-centered view of life as a reflection of America's waning economic position, a pragmatic response to wage stagnation, downsizing, and international competition: we must work harder. And this it may be. But it is also part of a secular transformation that has been ongoing for decades as we've moved away from home-centered work lives in the agricultural world to employment-centered lives outside the domestic sphere altogether. The more work departs from home, the more it becomes a social system of its own, a primary form of integration that rivals the family as a source of identity, belonging, and friendship. Women like Antonia Piento are not content only to take care of children at home. They want a life that is adult centered, where they have peers they can talk to. Where they might once have found that company in the neighborhood, now they are more likely to find it on the shop floor. Those primary social ties are grounded in workplace relations, hence to be a worker is also to be integrated into a meaningful community of fellow workers, the community that increasingly becomes the source of personal friends, intimate relations, and the worldview that comes with them.

Work is therefore much more than a means to a financial end. This is particularly the case when the work holds little intrinsic satisfaction. No one who gets paid for boiling french fries in hot oil thinks they are playing a world-shattering role. They know their jobs are poorly valued; they can see that in their paychecks, in the demeanor of the people whom they serve across the counter, even among some managers. But what they have that their nonworking counterparts lack is both the dignity of being employed and the opportunity to participate in a social life that increasingly defines their adult lives. This community gives their lives structure and purpose, humor and pleasure, support and understanding in hard times, and a backstop that extends beyond the instrumental purposes of a fast-food restaurant. It is the crucible of their values, values that we have argued here are decidedly mainstream.

The working poor sit at the bottom of the occupational structure and feel the weight of disapproval coming down upon their shoulders from better paid, more respectable employees. Yet they stand at the top of another pyramid and can look down the slope toward people they know well who have taken another pathway in the world.

34

SWEATSHOPS IN SUNSET PARK

A Variation of the Late-Twentieth-Century Chinese Garment Shops in New York City

Xiaolan Bao

The late **XIAOLAN BAO** was a professor of history at California State University Long Beach. She is the author of *Holding up More Than Half the Sky: Chinese Women Garment Workers in New York City, 1948–1992.*

ON MARCH 12, 1995, THE *NEW YORK TIMES* carried a report on the Chinese garment shops in the Sunset Park area of Brooklyn, a neighborhood that houses the new Chinese garment production center in New York City. Unlike most of the Chinatown garment shops in Manhattan, many of the Chinese shops in Sunset Park are not unionized. The weak influence of organized labor and law enforcement agencies in the area had virtually turned the industry there into a safety valve for some Chinese employers to extract quick profits while not complying with any labor laws. Incidents of exploitation increased with the expansion of the Chinese garment shops in the area.

The report in the *New York Times,* written by reporter Jane H. Lii, largely confirmed the above observation. The vivid description of life in the shops, based on the reporter's firsthand experience, gripped the hearts of its readers. According to Lii, the shop she worked in for an entire week was "typical of the small, new shops outside Manhattan":

> The steel doors opened into a dim, dusty warehouse. Red and blue rags covered the four windows, shutting out all natural light. Bundles of cut cloth sat piled in haphazard mounds, some stacked taller than a worker. Under fluorescent lights swinging from chains, rows of mid-aged Chinese women hunched over sewing machines, squinting and silent.

Were the working conditions there as horrific as those that splashed across the headlines in city newspapers? Lii's reply indicated that there was "something more complex at work." What, then, was the complexity? Lii reported that the owner of the shop was "actually benevolent, albeit in a harsh way." "She does not pay minimum wage, but she

Questions to Consider

Imagine working twelve hours a day, seven days a week, under physical conditions that are brutal: exposure to lint, physical confinement, sleep deprivation, and chemicals that constantly burn your throat. Your take-home pay at the end of an eighty-four-hour week is about $55. This is not a Jacob Riis description of New York City in 1890 but New York City one hundred years later in the 1990s. Bao's ethnography documents the modern sweatshop and the new immigrants who supply the labor and large profits to the entrepreneurs who are quick to take advantage of young women new to the United States. How and in what ways are sweatshop conditions today similar to or different from sweat shops in 1900? How is it possible that the horrific sweatshop conditions of yesterday can be found in clothing factories throughout the United States today?

to supplement their incomes. It was said that their mothers wanted to instill in them a work ethic by allowing them to do so.

Lii reported that both the employer and her workers considered American labor laws ideal and laudable, but impractical. The workers considered their employer a good boss "precisely because she was willing to violate labor laws and allow their children to work by their sides." The situation was, therefore, "a miserable complicity born of necessity in an insular, immigrant world" or, simply, "a grim conspiracy of the poor," as the reporter concluded. No wonder that the result of working at Sunset Park was pitiful:

> Seven days later, after 84 hours of work, I got my reward, in the form of a promise that in three weeks I would be paid $54.24 or 65 cents an hour (minimum wage is $4.25). I also walked away from the lint-filled factory with aching shoulders, a stiff back, a dry cough and a burning sore throat.

How representative is Lii's seven-day experience in the shops, and how valid is her analysis? In what ways are the conditions in the Sunset Park Chinese shops similar to the union shops in Manhattan's Chinatown, the hub of the Chinese industry in New York City? In what ways are they different? To what extent are the conditions in Sunset Park similar to those of the city's garment shops at the turn of the twentieth century? What are the factors that have led to these similarities and differences? In the era of globalization, what can the conditions in Sunset Park Chinese garment shops tell us about the impact of globalization in the United States? This study attempts to answer these questions.

This article is primarily based on the author's historical research of the Chinese garment industry in New York City over the last ten years, her visits to a number of shops in Sunset Park in the late 1990s, and her interviews with several dozen workers in the area.[1] It gives a brief account of the working conditions in the shops and discusses several highly controversial issues in the Sunset Park Chinese community that relate to the garment industry.

serves her workers tea. She makes them work until midnight, but she drives them home afterward. She uses child laborers, but she fusses over them, combing their ponytails, admiring their painted fingernails, even hugging them." According to Lii, the boss had opened the business only to save her family's honor, for her brother had, among many things, absconded with close to $80,000 owed to his workers in back wages. The shop also was reopened, according to its present owner, in order to provide jobs for those who came from the same region in China and whom she called "our people."

As Lii reported, the situation of the workers in the shop was also complicated. They "sewed virtually nonstop" because they wanted to make money and had no other alternatives without speaking English. They brought their children into the shop to care for them while working. Several children, however, toiled by their mothers' sides

By presenting a more differentiated picture of the industry, it argues that while labor organizing and law enforcement remain important ways to address labor abuse in the industry, it is imperative for law enforcement agencies, organized labor, and all concerned individuals to understand the complexity embedded in the highly competitive structure of the garment industry, the multidimensional impact of labor legislation and law enforcement, and the need to develop new forms of labor organizing that are informed and responsive to the challenges of the time. Without such an understanding, any effort to curb the sweating phenomenon is likely to be sporadic and without lasting effect on the industry.

WORKING ENVIRONMENTS

The shop where Jane Lii worked and reported is, in large part, typical of the Chinese garment shops in the Sunset Park area. Many of them are housed in former warehouses or converted garages. Because these shops are often hidden behind a steel door and have no sign on the front, one can hardly tell from the outside the nature of the activities inside the shops or, simply, whether there is any activity at all.

Sunset Park offers the Chinese garment industry many advantages. First, the former warehouses and the converted garages there are spacious. Even though they do not provide comfortable working conditions, they offer much more production space than industrial lofts in Manhattan's Chinatown.[2] The 1983 Chinatown Garment Industry Study reports that in 1981, Chinese shops with about 30 sewing machines occupied an average of 6,070 square feet in Soho. These shops were and are still the largest garment shops in the Chinatown area.[3] However, shops in Sunset Park with a similar number of sewing machines can cover as much as 10,000 square feet.[4] The spacious environment of the shops not only allows an effective flow of production, but also provides shop owners with enough space to expand their businesses.

In addition, rents and maintenance fees for buildings in Sunset Park are relatively inexpensive.

In the spring of 1998, for example, the owner of a shop, located between Fort Hamilton Parkway and 43rd Street and covering more than 10,000 square feet, told me that she paid only $2,500 a month for a space that accommodates forty workers. For the same money, she could afford only a 4,000-square-foot shop in Manhattan's Chinatown. Maintenance fees are also low. For an additional yearly payment of $100 to $200, the gas and other equipment and utility lines would be checked by the building owner.[5]

There are, however, many characteristics that Sunset Park shops share with their counterparts in Manhattan's Chinatown. Besides bundles of cut cloth piled up in haphazard mounds in almost any open floor space, there are severe problems with ventilation. Shops that were converted from former warehouses and garages have very few or virtually no windows at all. Conditions are even worse when the employers cover the few windows with rags or newspapers or simply lock the main entrance to conceal operations. In these shops the air is stifling and filled with lint and dust, while workers sew under fluorescent lights in the daytime.[6]

However, unlike Chinatown shops that generally suffer from space limitations, the physical size and working conditions of Sunset Park shops are not all the same. There are shops that have more than thirty workers and cover a space of over 10,000 square feet. There are also shops packed with a dozen sewing machines and piles of cut garments but covering less than 4,000 square feet. These small and big shops are located side by side. However, regardless of the differences, they have something in common. Like their counterparts in Manhattan's Chinatown, there is virtually no space reserved for workers' activities other than sewing. Even in the relatively spacious shops, workers eat their lunch at their sewing machines or at the desks where they work.

DIVISION OF LABOR

Although the shops in Sunset Park, like those in Manhattan's Chinatown, work on various lines of garments from manufacturers or other contractors, workers mostly produce sportswear and other low-priced women's apparel. The division of labor in the shops varies according to the size of the shop and the line of the garments they produce, but there are in general five kinds of workers on the floor: the sorter, the foreperson, machine operators, pressers, and floor workers.

Garment production starts with the sorter, who separates the cut-up fabrics according to the style of the garments and decides where the work should begin. The cut fabrics are then sent to the machine operators for either sewing or hemming. Machine operators include those workers who sew minor parts of the garments, such as zippers, collars, cuffs, and pockets. The garment then passes to the hands of the foreperson, who checks the quality of the sewed or hemmed garments. A quality garment will be sent to buttoners and trimmers who attach buttons, sew buttonholes, and trim extra threads. In its final stage, the garment will be sent to floor workers who hang tags, eliminate irregularities, and put the garments in a transparent plastic bag for shipping.

Like its counterparts elsewhere in the city, the Chinese garment industry in Sunset Park is characterized by its gender hierarchy. The rationale used to justify it is always inconsistent and contradictory. For example, the sorter and pressers, the two highest paid jobs on the shop floor, are almost invariably men. Trimmers, the lowest paid workers, are virtually all women. This arrangement is said to have its basis in women's lack of physical strength to move the bundles of cut-up materials around, and women's intellectual inability to sort the cut-up pieces and to lay out a workable schedule for production. Women are also believed to be too weak to operate the heavy pressing machines and endure the heat generated by them. As a result, they are denied the opportunity to work as a sorter or a presser. What is forgotten in this ungrounded rationale for the gender division of labor on the floor is the duration of strength, which the Chinese call *yin li,* and the extraordinary wisdom to figure out the way to sew the garments with their ever-changing styles. Both of these are necessary qualities of machine operators, who are overwhelmingly women.

It is said that women constitute the majority of machine operators in the shops because the flexible work hours, made possible by the piece-rate system and the larger number of operators in the shops, allow them to fulfill their family responsibilities while working in the shops. This justification ignores the highly competitive environment among the large number of machine operators that is generated by the piece-rate system. Since garment production is seasonal and work tends to be limited in most of the shops, in order to make ends meet, women workers are most likely to utilize every minute available to compete with one another in seizing work and to produce as many garments as they can. This work atmosphere is likely to deprive them of the flexibility that the piece-rate system is supposed to offer.

In addition, as known in the shops, workers' earnings depend not only on the piece rates and the speed at which they work, but also on the kind of work they do. The more mechanical and simple the work is, the faster they can produce, and the more money they can earn. There is no denying that pressers work under extremely stressful conditions, because there are usually only two or three of them in a shop of thirty or more machines and they have to press all the finished garments within a given time. However, their work is simpler than that of machine operators, so they can easily speed up their work after they become used to the structure of the garments and thus increase their incomes. Because there are only a few pressers in a shop, they are protected from the frenetic competition that is a routine part of the lives of machine operators.[7]

Unlike the pressers, machine operators' incomes fluctuate a great deal. Since styles are transient due to the unpredictable nature of fashion, it tends to take much longer for machine operators to get familiar with their work before they can speed up their production. The unpredictable nature of their work also creates more opportunities for their employers to keep wages low by constantly changing their piece rates, which are allegedly based on styles.

Family wages are always invoked to justify not only the higher pay of some traditionally men's work, but also the special payment arrangements in such sections as buttoning and bagging (putting the finished garments into bags). Since piece rates in these two sections are much lower than other sections, employers would subcontract the entire workload to one or two married male workers and allow them to complete the work with the assistance of their families. It used to be said that this arrangement was made to help the men fulfil their traditional gender roles as "rice winners" and to respect Chinese traditional culture. However, this rationale was cast aside in the early 1990s when the male workers left for higher paying jobs and women replaced them in these sections.

As Nancy Green and Susan Glenn have cogently argued, the gender division of labor in the garment industry has never been static.[8] Take the operation of sewing machines, for example. Although most sewing machine operators are women, an increasing number of undocumented male workers have taken over these positions in Sunset Park over the last few years. Gender remains at work, however. The recently arrived men could easily take over the traditionally female jobs from women, but the gender identity of their jobs continued to subject them to a position inferior to those in the traditionally men's sections. They are generally believed to be less skilled, physically weak, and hence less manly than the rest of the male workers in the shops.

Fluidity between class and gender lines, generated by the structural flexibility of the garment industry, does not preclude opportunities for upward mobility for female as well as male workers, albeit in different ways and to different degrees. Although most Chinese employers are men and had been workers themselves, an increasing number of women workers have become owners of the garment shops in recent years. This was the case in the shop where reporter Lii worked. Many women employers learned English by attending the free language classes offered by their union or other public institutions. Speaking from fair to good English, they operate their businesses successfully, without the assistance of men. Their past experience as workers and their gender identity may enable them to better understand their women employees. However, this does not guarantee that they will be benevolent bosses, as implied in Lii's report. Recent cases of labor law violations in the Chinese garment shops owned by women have demonstrated that, situated

in a highly competitive and marginal position in the city's industry, women employers can be as unscrupulous as their male counterparts.[9]

WAGES AND HOURS

Workers' wages in the Sunset Park garment shops fluctuate greatly, contingent upon the type of work they produce, the level of skill, and the quality and adequacy of work their employer provides. A new hand may earn practically nothing for the first day, while a skilled long-stitch machine operator can earn as much as $600 a week in the high season. In general, as in the case of most Chinatown shops in Manhattan, the sorter, the foreperson, the cleaner(s), and the floor workers are paid by the hour. My interviews show that in 1998 a full-time foreperson or a sorter earned an average of more than six dollars per hour, and the finished garment checkers and cleaners, about three dollars. The rest of the workers in the shops are paid at piece rates. Their incomes vary greatly, ranging from weekly averages of $600 to $700 for a presser; $400 to $500 for a hemmer; $300 to $400 for a single machine operator and buttoner; $250 to $300 for a general machine operator; and $150 to $200 for a trimmer. Compared with the union's minimum wages, the above wages of the Sunset Park Chinese garment workers may appear desirable. However, most of these weekly wages are in fact the result of workers' working ten to twelve hours a day. Their work hours are even longer during the busy seasons, with competition mounting in recent years.

Forms of payment are also factors that affect workers' incomes. Like their counterparts in Manhattan's Chinatown, most employers in Sunset Park issue payments in a combination of checks and cash. The portion of the payment received by check is determined by the worker's status or need. For union members, whose number is small in the area, employers tailor the amount of their checks strictly according to the union minimum income requirement for benefit eligibility. However, for nonunion workers, who form the overwhelming majority of the workforce in Sunset Park, the amounts of their checks are either kept below the poverty threshold so that they can maintain eligibility for welfare benefits, or kept in line with the U.S. Immigration and Naturalization Service's basic requirement for financial eligibility for sponsoring the immigration of their family members or relatives into the United States. Working underground, undocumented workers are paid invariably by cash.

Chinese employers argue that workers themselves request various forms of payment. However, my interviews reveal that all workers, regardless of their status, are forced to accept a reduction in their wages, because checks are issued with a deduction of a five to seven percent "handling fee." The same is true for cash payments. Furthermore, piece rates are often not announced before the completion of work and in some shops employers reserve their rights to reduce workers' wages if they consider the wages to be too high.

Researcher Mark Levitan reports that in 1990, 72 percent of the reported incomes of less-skilled blue-collar workers, apparel workers included, were below the poverty threshold for a family of four ($12,674).[10] Underreporting might be a factor in leading to the low-income status of some workers' families. However, what Levitan reported did not appear to be far from reality in the case of Chinese garment workers in New York. My interviews suggest that in the late 1990s the actual average annual income of most Sunset Park Chinese garment workers was only about $20,000.[11] To sustain their families, many have to work long hours, in violation of U.S. labor laws.

In the shops where the employers still bother to concern themselves with the investigations of law enforcement agencies, workers were required to punch their work cards to show that they were working eight hours a day, even before they start their day's work. My interviews, however, reveal that 90 percent of the workers employed in Sunset Park are working ten to twelve hours a day. During the busy seasons or when orders have to be rushed out, it is not unusual for workers to work unusually long hours, or as Lii indicated, even labor around the clock.

Long hours of work, coupled with the hazardous environment of the shops, severely damages workers' health. What happened to Bao Zhi Ni is, indeed, not an isolated case. Her written testimony at a public hearing held by the New York State Assembly Subcommittee on Sweatshops on October 2, 1997, is illustrative of workers' situations:

My name is Bao Zhi Ni. I am a garment worker. I have worked in the garment factories for close to ten years. For many long hours, I work without proper safety equipment, and under filthy conditions. I work at least ten to twelve hours everyday, but because the bosses depress the wages so low we can only make $20, $30 a day, even though we're working over ten hours . . .

For many long hours I sit at the sewing machine repeating the same motions. I also have to handle heavy bundles of garments every day. Each day at work is an exhausting day. My eyes are tired, and my vision is blurry. My fingers, wrists, shoulders, neck, back, spine, all these parts of my body are inflicted with pain. I started feeling the pain in my lower back five years ago, but I continued to work in the sweatshops. I have no medical benefits.

My shoulders and back hurt constantly. Because I have been forced to work for such long hours, the cartilage between the bones in my back has rubbed away, and I have a pinched nerve. With the pain and the numbness in my left leg, I know that I have muscular and nervous problems. My fingers and wrists hurt. Now, even after just one or two hours of work, my back aches so much that I can barely stand straight. . . . In order to make a living I have no choice but to force myself to work through this pain. Sometimes I can't do it, but I have no choice but to take one or two days off.

Sometimes I have to take one or two weeks off. When I take this time off to heal just a little, my boss gets angry. The boss will call my house to scold me and say that I'm lazy, tell me that I must go back to work as soon as possible.[12]

My interviews reveal that almost all the garment workers who worked in the industry for more than five years have various health problems. Deng Ying Yi, a longtime labor activist at the Workers Center in Brooklyn run by the Union of Needletrades, Industrial and Textile Employees (UNITE!), is virtually disabled after working in the garment industry for more than ten years, with her nervous system partially damaged. Her case is not unique among workers in Sunset Park. However, most of these nonunionized workers are not covered by any form of health insurance.

To survive in their new homeland, nonunionized workers have to develop their own system to cope with the situation. Many rely heavily on their family ties and community networks. The experience of a Mr. Zhang, who had been a middle-rank official in Guangzhou but who became a finished garment checker in a Sunset Park Chinese garment shop, is indicative of this phenomenon:

I was already fifty-two when I immigrated to this country. I worked in a garment shop as *chayi* (Cantonese: a finished garment checker) and my wife *jin sin* (Cantonese: a trimmer). Together, we earned an average of less than $400 a week and we still had to raise a daughter, our youngest daughter who was in her teens and was eligible to come with us when we immigrated to this country. She had to eat, to dress and to go to school. In addition, we had to save money in order to sponsor our two older children to come to the United States. How did we manage to do all this? Well, we relied on our family. . . .

I came with my other five siblings under the sponsorship of a brother. Each of us came with his or her own family. Altogether, it was more than twenty of us who came to New York City on the same day on the same plane. We rented three two-bedroom apartments in this part of Brooklyn because the brother who came earlier told us that rents are much less expensive in this area. Each apartment was shared by two families. My family and my brother's family shared a two-bedroom apartment and we paid a total of $700 for rent and utilities but we ate separately. My family spent a little more than $100 each month on groceries. How did we manage to do this? We bought the cheapest possible food at the market, say, the thirty-nine-cent-a-pound chicken on sale at Key Foods and the four-head-for-one-dollar broccoli at the street stands in this neighborhood. In addition, my wife and I also picked up empty soda cans and other stuff on our way home from work. If we were lucky, the monthly income from that part of our labor could cover our groceries for an entire week.

For eight years after we came to this city, we never ate out and never stopped working, eleven to twelve hours a day and seven days a week. Whenever we did not have work to do in our shop my wife and I went to work in another shop.[13]

While family ties are important resources for immigrant workers who came with their families, community networks are the most important assets for undocumented immigrant workers, most of whom did not come with their families. For example, undocumented workers from Wenzhou have contributed money to establish their own "mutual funds." These funds can be used by any member in time of need. This practice has proved to be the most effective way for these workers to survive in time of adversity, since they are denied any social services and benefits in the United States.

As elsewhere in the world, the gendered definitions of roles in the Sunset Park Chinese garment shops, their hierarchical order, and the rationale applied to justify them are shaped by the flexible but highly competitive structure of the garment industry, and have been inherently unstable. This fluidity generates dynamics in the industry, but has also taken a toll on those who labor in the industry. It is by exhausting human resources among the workers and in their community that the nonregulated segment of the garment industry has managed to thrive. Sunset Park is a case in point.

"CO-ETHNIC CONSPIRACY?"

One major aspect of the Chinese garment industry in New York that has generated great interest among some scholars is its co-ethnic nature. Although in recent years more and more garment shops in New York have employers and workers who do not share the same ethnic identity, this is not the case with many of the Chinese garment shops in Manhattan's Chinatown and Brooklyn's Sunset Park. Most Chinese employers continue to hire only workers from major Chinese settlements.

As many studies have pointed out, this co-ethnic nature of the industry has benefited both workers and management.[14] Like their Eastern European counterparts at the turn of the twentieth century, Chinese workers do not have to learn to speak or understand English to work in a garment shop. They can also learn the trade on site and from scratch. In truth, without the industry, many working-class Chinese immigrant families may not have been able to survive.

The co-ethnic nature of the industry is also said to have simplified and humanized management of the shops. Many studies have discussed the particular recruitment pattern of the Chinese shops. Although in recent years a growing number of new immigrant workers have begun to seek employment through advertisements in community newspapers or the help-wanted signs posted in the front of the shops, most employers continue to rely on the recommendations of their workforce for new recruits, and most new immigrant workers obtain their first jobs through their families, friends, and relatives. Some employers also hire job applicants on the spot, without giving them much of a background check. New recruits, especially those who are employed with the recommendations from workers already in the shop, are allowed to use the facilities in the shop to receive on-site training.

Workers can maintain their cultural practices at their workplaces. They celebrate major Chinese festivals in the shops. They also share Chinese food and cooking with one another, listen to the blasting of the closed-circuit Chinese radio broadcasts, and share news about their homeland while working. As Lii noted, although employers in most Chinese shops do not offer their employees overtime payments when they expect workers to work long hours or on weekends, they offer them free rice and water, or even tea in some shops, to eat and drink with their lunch. They also provide lunch or afternoon tea to compensate workers' working on weekends. It is also widely known that most employers in Sunset Park will drive their employees home if their work ends after 11:00 p.m.

Workers who are unfamiliar with the labor laws and their rights in the United States feel obligated to work hard for their employers if their employers are willing to accommodate their needs. The undocumented workers feel particularly grateful to their employers if their employers have offered them any form of protection during immigration or other law enforcement raids. Employers in Sunset Park are known to cover workers up with piles of cut garments scattered on the floor, or allow them to use the ladder in the shop to climb to the skylight. These gestures foster gratitude on the workers' part, which they feel obligated to reciprocate.

Many workers find it easy to identify with their employers if they are immigrants and have been workers themselves. Workers who desire upward social mobility look up to their employers as role models, a mirror of their future in the land of opportunity. Workers' empathy with their employers' situation, generated by a mixture of gratitude, fear, and admiration, has often led to their acquiescence to their employers' unscrupulous practices on the shop floor. In some cases this relationship of empathy has become so entrenched that law enforcement agents from outside the Chinese community and Chinese union organizers find it difficult to break. No wonder observers of the industry, like reporter Lii, do not hesitate to call the Sunset Park shop "a miserable complicity born of necessity in an insular, immigrant world." However, this conspiracy theory is too simplistic to explain the complex interdependent relationship between the workers and their employers in the ethnic enclave economy of the United States. It also fails to highlight the imbalance of power embedded in this relationship. Failing to locate the ultimate beneficiaries of this relationship, this theory cannot explain fully the causes of sweated labor in the shops.

Clearly, employers' various forms of accommodation benefit themselves rather than the workers. Let's take the special form of recruitment, for example. Since workers' incomes are based on the work they have accomplished, it will only hurt the new recruits if they are slow to learn their routine of work. However, on-site training allows employers to strengthen their personal ties with the newly hired as well as those who are already in the shop. Paying wages in a mixture of cash and checks or simply by cash also enables the employers to avoid paying taxes, the amounts of which are likely to be much larger than their workers'. A closer investigation of the situation in the industry also reveals that accommodations offered by employers are not unconditional. They are given only to workers who follow the rules they set. Those who refuse to do so are fired, blacklisted, physically assaulted, or subjected to other forms of retaliation.

Most Chinese employers do not force their workers to work long hours. However, production is organized in such a way that workers who do not stay as long as the rest will find themselves in an extremely disadvantageous position. Since there is no limit on work hours in most of the shops and workers who are willing to maximize their work hours can work as long as they wish, those who refuse to do so will end up having only "pork neckbones" (a slang term in the Chinatown garment industry, referring to garments difficult to sew), or simply no garments to work on the next morning when they return.

Similar situations occur if a worker is ill and takes sick leave, or refuses to work on Sunday. Employers will hire a replacement worker almost immediately after a laborer fails to show up. Employers will also distribute "chickens in soy sauce" (another slang term in the Chinatown garment industry, referring to work easy to sew) or paychecks on Sunday. Under these situations, workers who take a sick day are likely to lose their jobs, and those who do not work on Sunday will miss not only an important

opportunity to increase their incomes, but also to get paid in a timely manner. Since workers' wages tend to be withheld by their employers for months in Sunset Park, failing to be present on payday will mean another indefinitely long delay in getting paid. It's no wonder that workers in Sunset Park tend to lament, "We have the option to die but we don't have the option to take a sick day or a rest."

Some employers have also blatantly taken advantage of their workers' acquiescence to maximize their profit. Instances of *zhen jia lao ban* (real and fake bosses) and *yi guo liang zhi* (one country, two systems), stories told by labor activist Deng Ying Yi, are indications of how far employers would go.[15] As Deng recalled, one day workers of a shop came to the UNITE! Workers' Center to seek assistance in collecting their wages. It turned out that their employer had closed the shop after owing them several hundred thousands of dollars in back wages and had vanished without a trace. However, when the State Department of Labor finally undertook this case, the department found it difficult to file charges against the real owner of the shop. The owner, an undocumented immigrant himself, had registered the shop with the name and social security number of an elderly worker and had been signing all the legal documents under this worker's name without informing him. Filing charges against the owner of the shop would mean charges against this worker, who was not the real owner of the shop.[16]

The story of "one country, two systems" is about a peculiar phenomenon in some unionized shops in Sunset Park. According to Deng, although union contracts stipulate that all workers in a union shop are union members and entitled to union benefits, employers of some unionized shops refuse to register their new recruits as union members and keep their wages in the books. Consequently, there are both union and nonunion members in the same shop who are working under very different systems of employment.

My interviews further reveal other forms of discrimination on the floor. For example, some employers offer different piece rates to workers of different immigration status and from different regions in China. Cantonese immigrant workers, who form the majority of the workforce, tend to receive higher piece rates and work relatively regular hours, while non-Cantonese or undocumented workers are denied all these "privileges." Discriminatory treatments have taken a different form in a small number of shops that hire several skilled workers from other ethnic groups. The non-Chinese workers are offered wages and other working conditions that comply with labor laws, while their Chinese fellow workers, who work side by side with them, have to struggle against the grim reality of low pay and long hours of work.[17]

Chinese employers have been so reckless in exploiting workers in their own community that it reinforces the stereotypical image of Chinese workers as the docile "willing slaves" in the Sunset Park area. This image of the workers subjects them to exploitation not only by Chinese employers, but also by shop owners of other ethnic groups. In 1997, the *Sing Tao Daily* reported that seven Chinese workers from a Jewish-owned garment shop came to seek help from the UNITE! Workers' Center. They complained that they had been discriminated against by their Jewish employer who had closed the shop and refused to pay them according to labor laws, as he did to his Hispanic workers.[18]

The most common problem workers face, however, is the failure to receive compensation for their work in a timely manner. Employers benefit tremendously from withholding their workers' wages. Community labor activists estimate that a shop of average size in Sunset Park has thirty-five workers, and the lowest wage of garment workers in the area is about $150 per week. If the owner of a shop withholds his/her employees' wages for eight weeks, which is not uncommon in the area, the employer will have more than $40,000 in hand by the end of the eighth week, even if workers in the shop earned the lowest wage in the area. With this $40,000, an employer can open another shop without having to pay interest as they would if borrowing money from a bank.

Regrettably, as union organizers and law enforcement agencies have pointed out, workers tend not to take any legal action against their employers until their employers close down the shops. The reasons are varied. One major reason is the workers' lack of knowledge about their rights and the political operation in their new homeland. With few employment alternatives, many immigrant workers fear that any form of cooperation with law enforcement agencies or organized labor will cost them their jobs. This was particularly the situation before the signing of the Hot Goods Bill by the New York State governor in 1996.[19] Prior to the adoption of this bill, law enforcement agencies had difficulty in helping workers retrieve their back wages if a shop was closed and the employer was hard to locate. As a result, the longer wages were withheld, the more reluctant workers were to report their cases. They feared that their reporting would lead their employers to close the shop for good.

Workers' reluctance to report labor violations on the floor is also compounded by a lack of understanding about the U.S. income tax system. Many are afraid that the amount of money they receive will be reduced by paying taxes if they seek assistance from law enforcement agencies and have to report their back wages to the Internal Revenue Service. Understandably, undocumented workers have additional concerns. Working underground, they fear that a visit from the Department of Labor to their work place will bring in a raid by the Immigration and Naturalization Service.

While workers are often reluctant to take action against their employers, employers are not hesitant to take advantage of workers' fear. According to longtime observers of the community, many employers in the garment industry engage in speculative financial activities with the money they have withheld from their workers, such as gambling or buying high-return but high-risk stocks. Since most of these activities will not lead to their expected outcomes, the employers close down their shops to avoid payments they owe their employees.

There are also employers who simply try to extract larger profits by closing down operations, absconding with the money they have withheld from their employees, and reopening their business under a different name. This was the case where reporter Lii worked. Hence, labor violations are widespread and the turnover rate of many Sunset Park Chinese garment shops is at a record high.[20] This highly unstable situation makes it even more difficult to enforce labor laws in the area, especially in recent years when most of these agencies are understaffed.

Tensions and exploitation in many Chinese garment shops in Sunset Park lay bare the limits of ethnic solidarity in the garment industry. Relegated to the same ethnic economic sector, Chinese employers have to rely on workers in their own community to run their businesses and accommodate workers' needs. However, situated in a marginal position of a highly competitive industry, many employers also do not hesitate to exploit their community ties to maintain their competitive edge in the industry. As in the case with their predecessors in the city's industry, the garment industry offers new Chinese immigrant workers many advantages in working among their own, but it also makes them more vulnerable to exploitation by management on all levels. The degree of labor violation in many Chinese garment shops demonstrates not only the limits of ethnic solidarity but also the devastating impact of the frenetic search for cheap labor on the Chinese community. This impact, as well as the limited nature of ethnic solidarity, will be further explored in the following section.

"THE CANTONESE VS. THE FUJIANESE"?

One major issue that surfaced constantly during my interviews with workers is their concern about the increasing number of undocumented workers in the industry, most of whom are believed to be from Fuzhou, a major city in the province of Fujian in southeastern China. These newcomers, who speak their own dialect, are often blamed for worsening labor conditions on the shop floor and deteriorating living standards in Sunset Park. They also are charged with undermining workers' solidarity in the industry. Many Cantonese workers believe that there is no way for them to get along well with the Fujianese.

In the course of interviewing workers in Sunset Park, however, I came to know many Cantonese and Fujianese workers who are good friends. I also came to see that although a large number of undocumented workers came from Fuzhou, Fuzhou is not the only place that has sent undocumented Chinese immigrants to the United States. Undocumented Chinese workers also come from Wenzhou, Guangdong, and almost all the coastal areas of China. There are also some from Malaysia and other Southeast Asian countries. Nevertheless, there is a pronounced tendency in New York's Chinese community to identify all undocumented workers as Fujianese. Stories about how fanatically hardworking they are became a recurring theme in the narratives of almost all the non-Fujianese workers. Fujianese workers were said to be so money-crazy that they would bring their rice cookers to the shops, cook and eat there while working, and even spend the night in the shops if they found any work there.

These undocumented workers are also blamed for having eroded the image of the Chinese in the Sunset Park area. It is said that since they spend so many hours at work, they could even do without a place to stay. It is a general belief in the Sunset Park Chinese community that several dozen immigrants from Fuzhou would share a single one-bedroom apartment, either only spending the night there or using it just for bathing and other purposes while spending their nights in the garment shops. I heard little sympathy for their plight in my interviews with non-Fujianese workers.

Anecdotal as these stories are, recycled repeatedly, they have fostered a profound prejudice against workers from Fuzhou. This prejudice is so prevalent that it often blinds non-Fujianese workers to class conflicts on the shop floor. For example, I came across a group of Cantonese workers who had just been fired by their employer for refusing to work as many hours as he wanted. Rather than blaming their unscrupulous employer, they blamed their unemployment on the workers from Fuzhou whom their employer had hired for lower rates and longer hours of work.

Although all prejudices are unjustified, factors that have contributed to the prejudice against

Fujianese workers are worth exploring. My conversation with a Mrs. Deng, a Taishanese worker and a staunch opponent of "those hateful Fujianese," is revealing:[21]

A: As you know, the Chinese garment shops in Sunset Park have a bad name as sweatshops these days. Our lives are miserable. It was all because of those hateful Fujianese. They have taken our jobs. The bosses love them because they don't have family responsibilities and can work twenty-four hours a day in the shop. They are very greedy. What is in their eyes is only money, money, money. Recently we Cantonese have been losing ground in my shop. The Fujianese are taking over. They are everywhere in my shop.

Q: Could you tell me how many workers from Fuzhou are exactly in your shop?

A: Well, I never counted them, but, never mind, let me try. There are a total of about forty machine operators in my shop, one, two, three, yes, three are Cantonese, three are Mandarin speaking from Shanghai and Wuhan, and . . . [It turned out that only eight out of a total of thirty-five workers in her shop were from Fuzhou and only five out of the nine undocumented workers in her shop came from Fuzhou.]

Q: So the majority in your shop is not Fujianese and the undocumented workers in your shop are not all from Fuzhou.

A: Yes, you are right. My impression was wrong. But still I am nervous about them. Let me tell you something, actually, there are also undocumented workers from Taishan. A village in Taishan is now almost empty, you know, because they had a smuggler in that village, and he had connections with those snakeheads in New York City. The conditions of the undocumented workers from that village are deplorable. I always think that

my situation is already miserable enough. [She was collecting welfare benefits at the time of this interview. Her husband just had surgery and could not work and she had four schoolchildren to raise.] But theirs are even worse. However, I have been told that compared with those from Fuzhou, they seem to be doing fine because many of them have family members or relatives in New York. Those from Fuzhou don't seem to have this advantage and they owe the snakeheads much more money than those from Taishan. Anyway, I should admit that I don't know very much about them because I don't talk to them and they don't talk to me either.

Q: What then made you so angry with them?

A: They work too hard! Whenever there is some work in the shop, especially the easy jobs, they are there. Very often we don't have any work left when we return in the morning. They have finished all the work at night! But we can't do this. We have to go home at night to take care of our families and to have a little rest. We are human beings, you know. But work is money. They have taken away all our money. They are so hateful!

Q: Did your boss ever close the door of the shop at a time like that?

A: No, how could you expect them to do so? Of course not; for the bosses, the sooner they can get the work done the better. So they love those illegal immigrants from Fuzhou. In the past, many garment shop owners had signs on the gates of their shops, saying "Cantonese only," because they were afraid that they would be harassed by the Fujianese gangsters, who are well known for their fearlessness, if they had Fujianese workers in their shops. But now they don't care. They need workers who can work twenty-four hours a day. So the sign on their gates has also changed. It reads "Fujianese only."

The situation has made me really mad. To be honest, who doesn't need money? I too wish that I could work around the clock, if I did not have a family to take care of. I need money too. I don't mind working hard. I was a peasant in China. Rain or shine, I worked outdoors, under conditions much worse than sewing in a garment shop. I wish I could make more money for my family.

But, wait a minute, I sense something wrong with myself in answering your questions. Haven't I somewhat misjudged those undocumented workers from Fuzhou? Yes, I think I have.

Obviously, tension among the workers, ignited by the highly competitive nature of garment organization and accelerated by the manipulation of management, has led to their misjudgment of reality in the shop.

Ungrounded as the stories about undocumented workers from Fuzhou are, generated by a mixture of myth and reality, they take a toll on all workers from the same place. This can be seen in the response of a Ms. Wong:

I think we immigrants from Fuzhou have been treated very unfairly by our own Chinese community. I am not an illegal immigrant. I came with all the papers as a legal immigrant. In addition, unlike the majority of illegal immigrants from the Fuzhou area, I came from the city and with my family. But still, I am looked at as an illegal immigrant because I came from Fuzhou.

I don't speak Cantonese, so I could not find a job in a restaurant or other place. That's how I ended up working in a garment shop.

My husband and I had a hard time looking for a place for our family to stay when we first came. Landlords from other parts of China refused to rent to us, because we are from Fuzhou. People in the community said we lived like pigs, with several dozen people usually packed in one apartment but registered under only one or two names. So the landlords were scared. Landlords from Fuzhou did not treat us well either. They charged us much higher rents because they knew that we had no choice.

My husband and I finally got to rent this place because we decided to speak Mandarin and pretended to be from other parts of China when we first met our landlady, who is Cantonese. Yes, now she knows that we are from Fuzhou but she doesn't care anymore because we have become very good friends, and she says we are the best tenants she has ever had.[22]

Many immigrant workers from Fuzhou whom I interviewed shared her experience. Although almost all immigrant workers from Fuzhou have been affected by the prejudice against them, the undocumented ones among them are the most victimized. A Mr. Dong's response was typical:

I don't understand why we should be treated like this! We are human beings too! Yes, we work very hard, because we need money to pay back our debts! Yes, many of us share an apartment, because we want to save money. Do we enjoy our lives in this country? Of course not. We are separated from our families and working underground. We are bullied by our bosses, even including those from Fuzhou. They make us work long hours but pay us much less than other workers in the shops. I don't think anyone would like to live a life like ours! But, still, we are not going to give up because we are working for a better life for our families.

My family lives in a village along the Ming River, and I was a fisherman in the village before I came to the United States. I left my home village because the water there was so seriously polluted that there were no edible fish left. I could not make a living for my family by fishing.

Some people ask, "Why don't you go home if life is so hard for you?" But can we? My family has borrowed a lot of money to send me here. My wife and my kids have pinned their hopes on me, yearning for me to bring them to *meiguo* [the beautiful land, which refers to the United States].

In addition, what will folks in my village say if I return home penniless? I remember when I was in the village, I envied those who returned home from the United States. They looked so successful, squandering money like dirt. I wished I could be like them one day. Of course, after I came to the United States, I got to know that many of them too had been working in a sweatshop, as I do now. If they can make it, I can make it, too. So, I work hard. It is none of anyone's business if I don't eat, don't sleep, and work nonstop.[23]

The strong desire to improve the well-being of their families, reinforced by a degree of vanity for a glamorous return, led the undocumented workers to leave their native land and fall prey to the sweating system in the United States. Although the living conditions of their native land have "pushed" them out of China, it was the underground economy in the United States that has "pulled" them in and lured them to violate U.S. immigration laws.

The experience of the Fujianese garment workers in Sunset Park reminds one of what has happened to each group of newcomers in New York's garment industry. While the constant search for cheap labor brings in different groups of ethnic workers at different points in history, newcomers are always blamed for the cutthroat competition in the industry. This "finger pointing" takes place even within the same ethnic group. As national characteristics were used in the past as a convenient way of explaining the deterioration of working conditions, today regional and dialectal differences, immigration status, and even the location of one's family have become indexes in the Chinese garment industry for differentiating the old from the new, the "human" from the "inhuman," and thereby the excusers from the excused.[24] Labor solidarity in the community is thus undermined by conflicts of interest among workers, as well as elements in the cultural repertoire of the community.

WILL TOO MUCH LAW ENFORCEMENT KILL THE CHINESE GARMENT INDUSTRY IN NEW YORK CITY?

In the late 1990s, a number of Chinese employers in Sunset Park began to react strongly when the New York State Apparel Industry Task Force carried out its mission to enforce labor laws in the city's garment industry. In October 1996, after the task force completed its investigation and charged many Chinese garment shops with labor violations, Chinese employers in Sunset Park launched a massive demonstration to protest the state operation. They called it "adding salt to the wound." Claiming that the law enforcement agency had unjustly labeled all Chinese shops as "sweatshops," Chinese employers held the state investigation accountable for causing the further decline of the Chinese garment industry in the city by providing manufacturers with the justification for withdrawing their work from the Chinese community.

According to the Chinese employers, manufacturers should be blamed for the deteriorating working conditions in the Chinese shops. Since they suppressed piece rates to such an intolerable degree and demanded such quick production and delivery of finished garments, Chinese employers were forced to reduce the piece rates they offered to their workers and expect them to work longer hours in order to remain competitive. In addition, since manufacturers frequently delayed payments for finished work, Chinese employers had to withhold wages to their own workers. Labor law enforcement will kill the Chinese garment industry, they asserted, because only by reducing wages and extending work hours could the industry survive in the highly competitive environment of garment production in New York.[25]

The Chinese employers' accusation against manufacturers is not entirely groundless, given manufacturers' frantic efforts to reduce the costs of labor in recent years. However, as many concerned individuals in the community have rightly pointed out, even though the Chinese garment industry has been hit hard by the outflow of garment production from the city, the sweatshop conditions in the industry are what allow the manufacturers to put a human face on their move from the city.[26]

What has happened since the State Department of Labor established its Apparel Industry Task Force in 1987? Did the efforts of the Task Force lead to the decline of the Chinese garment industry in New York City? Did the industry really decline?

Statistics show that despite the shrinking of the city's share in the U.S. garment industry, the absolute numbers of Chinese shops and their workforce in the past decade or more did not suggest any sign of decline; indeed, they grew. In the early 1980s, there were approximately 500 Chinese shops in the city, largely concentrated in Manhattan's Chinatown and employing an estimated 25,000 Chinese workers. In 1998, there was an estimate of more than 800 Chinese shops, scattered in various parts of the city and employing more than 30,000 Chinese workers.[27]

One specific segment of the Chinese garment industry has declined significantly in recent years, however. It is the number of the unionized shops in Manhattan's Chinatown. Between 1992 and 1997 the number of garment shops in Manhattan's Chinatown dropped from 608 to 555 and employment declined from 21,015 to 14,887, a loss of more than 6,000 jobs.[28] The decline in Manhattan's Chinatown garment industry coincided with the rapid growth of Chinese garment shops in other parts of the city, in particular, Sunset Park in Brooklyn. Although Manhattan's Chinatown remains the center of the Chinese garment industry in New York, with about 500 Chinese shops still clustered in this area, its importance has been significantly reduced by the rapid growth of the Chinese garment industry in other boroughs.

The decline of Manhattan's Chinatown shops has also led to the weakening of union influence on the entire Chinese garment industry in New York City. In the early 1980s, when shops in Chinatown represented an overwhelming majority of the Chinese garment shops in New York City, more than 90 percent of them were unionized. By the end of the 1990s, it is estimated that the UNITE! Local 23-25 represented only half of the Chinese garment shops in the city.[29] The union's influence has declined even in Manhattan's Chinatown, with the percentage of Chinese union shops dropping from more than 90 percent in the early 1980s to fewer than 80 percent by 1997.[30] As a result, membership of the UNITE! Local 23-25—the largest local of the union, with an 85 percent Chinese membership—dropped from 28,083 in 1992 to 22,995 in 1996, a loss of more than 5,000 members.[31]

Despite problems embedded in the unionization of the Chinatown garment industry in earlier years, there are still many significant differences in working conditions between union and nonunion shops. The shrinking percentage of union shops in the Chinese garment industry indicates that more and more Chinese garment workers have been deprived of the benefits and protection to which union members are entitled. It should, therefore, come as no surprise that labor violations are rampant in many nonunion Chinese shops, which have, in turn, undercut working conditions in the union shops.

There is little doubt that manufacturers and retailers should be held accountable for the deteriorating working conditions in the city's garment industry. However, many individuals in the community are also correct in pointing out that it is the sweating system in some Chinese garment shops that has provided them with the most convenient excuse to pull production out of New York City. This is particularly true when politicians of all stripes have recognized a political advantage in promoting the elimination of sweatshops in the U.S., and manufacturers and retailers have also been pressured by consumer groups as well as labor to distance themselves from contract shops labeled as sweatshops.

The Chinese employers' argument that "too much law enforcement will kill the Chinese garment industry in New York City" reminds one of the situations at the turn of the twentieth century. As Nancy Green has noted, during that time when progressive reformers, labor leaders, and state legislators endeavored to improve labor conditions by passing new legislation and enforcing laws, manufacturers also argued that too many constraints would make the landscape of the garment industry disappear altogether from the city.[32] However, the garment industry remains in New York City, and so will the Chinese garment industry, at least for the decade to come.

SOME REFLECTIONS

Driven by the search for cheap nonunion labor, runaway shops and sweated labor are not unique to the Chinese garment industry, nor are they new in the history of the city's industry. As early as the 1920s the dispersion of garment shops from Manhattan into various parts of the city already became a peculiar aspect in the landscape of New York's garment industry.[33] The Chinese garment industry, as a major part of the city's industry, is no exception in these regards.

The experience of Chinese workers is in many ways similar to that of their predecessors in the city's garment industry, but there are also differences. Particularly in the 1980s and 1990s, these differences were caused by the challenge of the times rather than simply by the cultural characteristics of the Chinese workers. Garment workers in the first half of the twentieth century were able to enjoy improved working conditions, thanks to the strong influence of labor unions and the continuous growth of the city's garment industry. However, Chinese workers in the late twentieth century were increasingly subjected to abusive labor conditions as the city's industry declined rapidly. Their union, plagued by its entrenched bureaucratic culture, could hardly respond to their needs.

As in the case of the city's garment industry in the early twentieth century, law enforcement and labor organizing remain the two most powerful ways to address the problems in the Chinese garment industry. Both law enforcement agents and labor organizers face the challenge of how to understand the complex reality of the garment industry beyond the highly politicized representations of it in political arenas. However, they also have to address different issues in their own realms.

As Mark Levitan has aptly put it, one of the major factors that has undermined significantly the efforts to eliminate sweated labor in the city is that "there are not enough cops on the beat." Despite the growth of sweated labor in the city's garment industry and the politicians' highly emotional pledges to eliminate it, both New York State and federal investigation teams are severely understaffed. According to Levitan, in 1998, there were only twenty-three investigators in the federal office of the Wage and Hour Division that had responsibility for the entire New York City metropolitan area, and only twenty-three out of thirty-four positions in New York City's Apparel Industry Task Force were filled.[34] As a result, in addition to improving their understanding of the dynamics generated by the highly competitive structure of the garment industry, the history and culture of each ethnic group, and the multifaceted impact of their operations, law enforcement agents still have to battle the shortage of hands in carrying out their tasks, a difficult situation that is indeed not of their own making.

Organized labor faces another type of challenge. Never before has UNITE!, the major labor union of the U.S. garment industry, been under so much pressure to reform itself. The parochialism and the culture of business unionism that UNITE! shares with other traditional trade unions have proved to be impotent in this new age of the global economy. Today, with the impressive growth of the community-based labor organizations in New York's Chinatown and other ethnic communities, the question UNITE! faces is no longer whether it is willing to change but whether the change is adequate to maintain its legitimacy as a labor union in the industry.[35] In this era when capital has already globalized its search for inexpensive labor, how can we develop effective organizing strategies that are not only responsive to the needs of U.S. workers but also allow them to join forces with workers in other parts of the world? This is a question very much on the agendas of trade unions as well as concerned individuals in the Chinese community and the city.

RACISM AND POPULAR CULTURE[1]

Danielle Dirks and Jennifer Mueller

DANIELLE DIRKS is a doctoral candidate at the University of Texas at Austin. **JENNIFER MUELLER** is a doctoral candidate at Texas A&M.

> Exemplifying the ill will, oppression, and domination of blacks by whites, the merchants of popular culture have used these icons to shackle our psyches as deftly as enslavers once used real chains to shackle our bodies.
>
> —Turner, 1994, xv

> To pretend (as we all do from time to time) that film or television, for example, is a neutral vessel, or contentless, mindless, or unpersuasive, is sheer denial. It is, for better and frequently for worse, one of the major forces in the shaping of our national vision, a chief architect of the modern American sense of identity.
>
> —Williams, 1996, 194

IN 2002, THE BOARD GAME GHETTOPOLY WAS released, promising "playas" the amusement of "buying stolen properties, pimpin' hoes, building crack houses and projects, paying protection fees, and getting car jacked" (Ghettopoly, 2002). Invoking stereotypical images that implicitly implicate the cultural deficiency of African Americans, the game pieces included a pimp, a hoe, a machine gun, a 40-ounce malt liquor beverage, a marijuana leaf, a basketball, and a piece of crack rock. The game garnered significant positive attention, advertised as a great way to entertain and introduce "homies,"

Questions to Consider

It is easy to think that we have moved beyond the extremely racist images that were a mainstay of television's early years. The mammy stereotype of Aunt Jemima selling pancakes, the Mexican Frito Bandito criminal advertising corn chips, and the heavily accented Chinese dry cleaner selling laundry soap seem like antiquated relics of television's past. Dirks and Mueller argue that although the extremely offensive racist imagery once so common on television may have been discarded, it has been replaced with equally problematic images that in turn shape how individuals view popular culture. What is more problematic is that many of these racist and stereotypical images are now so ingrained in popular culture that they appear to be normal representations of these groups. Think for a moment of the shows, sports mascots, television characters, or advertisements that draw on stereotypes to convey a particular message. To what extent are those images now such a part of popular culture that these stereotypes seem to be an accurate depiction of an entire group?

coworkers, and children to "ghetto life." Yet, this game must be grasped beyond simple considerations of entertainment or play. Ghettopoly must be added to the wide array of popular culture productions that exist as contemporary reflections of the continual distortion and misappropriation of so-called blackness by dominant groups in the United States. In this paper, we seek to illustrate the many ways in which racist popular culture images persist today, and how their continued existence reflects a white thirst for blackness that seems unquenchable. We adopt the view that marks popular culture as pedagogical and, against the backdrop of this assumption, consider what the racial lessons are that we learn from popular culture.

The concept of race in American social life is a concept under constant contestation, giving it no single fixed meaning in defining racial boundaries, hierarchies, and images (Guerrero, 1993). Despite this fluidity, both historically and today, ideas about race have dictated notions about white superiority as much as they have about black inferiority. Although ideas about race are, in their rawest forms, fictions of our collective imagination, they have real and meaningful consequences—economic, psychological, and otherwise. Popular culture has had a centuries-old history of communicating racist representations of blackness in Western societies, giving it the power to distort, shape, and create reality, often blurring the lines between reality and fiction (Baudrillard, 1981, 1989; Pieterse, 1992). We argue that these productions do not exist without consequences—they permeate every aspect of our daily lives.

Popular culture has served as part of the ideological and material apparatus of social life for as long as it has existed. Most cultural theorists today disavow the polarities of popular culture as merely pure and innocent entertainment or as an uncontested instrument for executing top-down domination, adopting instead, as Kellner (1995) does, the model of media cultural texts as complex artifacts that embody social and political discourses. The power of popular culture lies in its ability to distort, shape, and produce reality, dictating the ways in which we think, feel, and operate in the social world (Kellner). And while popular culture certainly exists in many ways as a contested terrain in the sense that Kellner asserts, it has been frequently used hegemonically, as an effective pedagogical tool of dominant classes in Western culture, supporting the lessons that keep structural inequalities safely in place (hooks, 1996).

As theorists like Kellner (1995) and Guerrero (1993) have asserted, this is the promise and predicament of popular culture. Contemporary media culture certainly provides a form for the reproduction of power relations based in racism (and classism and sexism), yet its very fluidity and contestation provide some space and resource for struggle and resistance. This is the sole reason why challenging racist representations—in their various recycled and newer transformations—is crucial if we are truly, vigorously devoted to making social change a reality.

HISTORICAL BACKGROUND

In the United States, popular culture has assisted in the maintenance of a white supremacist racial hierarchy since its American inception. We provide a brief history of American popular culture's racist past to show that there is nothing creative about present-day images, ideas, or material goods manufactured by today's merchants of culture. Antiblack images are central to our historical analysis because, as Guerrero (1993) has contended, "Blacks have been subordinated, marginalized, positioned, and devalued in every possible manner to glorify and relentlessly hold in place the white-dominated order and racial hierarchy of American society" (p. 2). This is certainly not to deny a long history of exploitation and domination for other groups in the United States, particularly among popular culture ideas and images; yet we see antiblack ideology and iconography as structurally embedded in every aspect of American social life—historically and today. In many respects, this ideology contains the racial "yardstick" by which other groups have been and continue to be measured, and elevated or devalued. We hope to show that contemporary popular cultural ideas and images are recycled products and remnants of dominant ideologies past—ideologies that exploited, distorted, and oppressed people of color historically and continue to do so today. As popular culture is constantly reinventing itself under the guise of innovation, a historical understanding of these ideas and images is crucial to deconstructing their continued existence today as simply reformations of such deeply rooted ideologies, rather than truly novel inventions.

Contemptible Collectibles

Although the sale of actual African Americans ended in 1865 with the official demise of the state-supported U.S. slavery system, the consumption of blackness through popular culture ideas, images, and material goods marked an easy, if figurative, transition in the postbellum South. From black-faced caricatures found on postcards, children's toys, and household items to 19th-century minstrelsy, these examples provide only a smattering of the racist iconography and ideology found throughout Western culture. As such, images of coons, pickaninnies, mammies, bucks, and Uncle Toms were born, to live out lives distorting the image of black Americans for centuries to come.

In the United States, popular racist stereotypes of the Jim Crow era easily became the faces of mass-produced lawn ornaments, kitchen items, postcards, and children's toys such as noisemakers, dolls, and costumes. Many of the material goods depicting black personas from this time, such as the mammy or pickaninny, have been mistakenly called "Black Americana," suggesting that these items come from the creative endeavors of black Americans themselves. However, this description is as incorrect as it is insulting, leading one author to more accurately describe them as "contemptible collectibles" (Turner, 1994). Perversely, these items have become immensely popular among collectors, with some originals of the era fetching several thousands of dollars apiece.

Manufacturers of everything from coffee, hair products, and detergents plastered the insidious iconography on virtually every type of household product available. Particularly prevalent was the image of the "coon," who, in addition to being depicted as unreliable, lazy, stupid, and child-like, was known for his "quaking," superstitious nature, making him an ideal target. Similar characterizations included the wide-eyed pickaninny and the image of the mammy (Skal, 2002). Mammy—the rotund, smiling, benevolent, uniformed black woman—is by far the most popularly disseminated contemptible collectible of all. Today she continues to happily oversee our pancakes and waffles as Aunt Jemima. For all of her popularity, no other image has been so historically identified as a fiction of white imagination than she. Social historians have pointed out that the existence of any "real" mammies in the antebellum South would have been very few and far between; her being overweight would be equally implausible given the severe rationing of food for slaves (Clinton, 1982; Turner, 1994). Yet the image of this obsequious and docile black woman has survived only to become immortalized through the mass production (and reproduction) of thousands of household and kitchen items made for "sufficiently demented homemakers" (Turner, 42).

Postcards depicting black Americans in various states of childishness and need have provided some of the most interesting snapshots of white thinking and imagination of the time. As if it were an aesthetic rule, adults and children were regularly depicted in print media coupled with watermelons. Even more disturbing is the vast collection of alligator-themed postcards and "artwork" depicting small black children and infants being chased or ready to be devoured by the toothy creatures. Apparently both alligators and their white American counterparts have an insatiable appetite for distorted images of society's most vulnerable members. Consumption here, in the Freudian and an all-too-literal sense, cannot be understated among this genre of "memorabilia."

Racist artifacts of the time were not limited to the enjoyment of adults, however, as children's toys represent some of the more pernicious forms of transmission of racist thought and belief. Dress-up items for children allowed them to "play at being a 'Negro,'" including wigs, masks, and a "Negro make-up outfit," described in a 1912 Sears display as "the funniest and most laughable outfit ever sold" (Wilkinson, 1974, 105). Indeed, blackface Halloween masks and costumes are among the numerous racist artifacts created and marketed during the 19th-century Jim Crow era, and popularly collected as Americana memorabilia today (Pilgrim, 2001).

The Only True American Drama

Many 19th-century Americans proudly boasted of minstrelsy as the first distinct form of American entertainment, laying claim to it as "our only original American institution" (Pilgrim, 2000; Toll, 1974, v). In many respects, it might be considered the earliest form of American popular culture. Despite the romantic sound of such historicized ideas, to most people such entertainment was more simply referred to as "nigger minstrelsy" or "coon shows." The typical minstrel show was put on by a troupe of white men in burnt cork blackface makeup, performing song, dance, and comedy claiming to be authentically "Negro." Such minstrels created extreme caricatures through heavy mocking dialect, bulging eyes, and gaping lips, easily reinforcing and popularizing beliefs that blacks were inherently lazy, dim-witted, subhuman, inferior, and unworthy of integration, to their almost exclusively white audiences (Feagin, 2000; Pilgrim, 2000; Toll, 1974).

Minstrel shows swept the nation in the 1840s, even performing for the "Especial Amusement of the President of the United States" (including Abraham Lincoln and John Tyler's inauguration), making them one of the most popular forms of entertainment in the country for over half a century (Roediger, 1991; Toll, 1974).

Toward the latter half of the 19th century, black Americans began replacing white minstrels in order to make a living on the stage, blackening their own faces and engaging in similarly exaggerated performances. This tragic and ironic twist greatly enhanced the credibility of minstrel images of black Americans, as white audiences perceived black minstrels as "genuine Negroes" displaying what were simply "natural impulses" (Toll, 1974, 202). Clearly, the degrading and dehumanizing minstrel portrayals set up ideas that were as much about whiteness as blackness, highlighting white virtue against the clear contrast of the inferior black (Feagin, 2000). As Toll explains, characterizations of blacks as indolent, improvident, immature, and unintelligent were "the very antithesis of what white men liked to believe about themselves," and as such served not only as "ego-boosting scapegoats for whites" but also as confirmation that blacks could not play a constructive role in society and should remain segregated (p. 71).

Historical Images Today

In 1987, independent filmmaker Marlon Riggs completed *Ethnic Notions,* an award-winning documentary on contemptible collectible objects and other minstrelsy media with the premise that: "Contained in these cultural images is the history of our national conscience: a conscience striving to reconcile the paradox of racism in a nation founded on human equality—a conscience coping with this profound contradiction through caricature" (Riggs, 1987). It begs an answer to the questions, why did such images exist in the first place? Who made them, and why have they enjoyed such immense popularity both historically and continuing into contemporary society? And, what does their continued popularity say about racial relations in the United States today?

During early American history, popular culture reflected and supported an ideology that sought to romanticize conditions of slavery—particularly when its eradication came into focus. As people worked to dismantle the U.S. slavery system, the rise of dehumanizing images such as the contented Sambo and coon served to whitewash the depravity of plantation life and ease white consciences. These caricatures mirrored the prevailing belief that slaves were not human, therefore not deserving of full and free citizenship. Over time researchers have assigned additional functions to the continually expanding dehumanizing characterizations, suggesting, for instance, that they assuaged white male economic insecurity or created solidarity for the KKK by asserting the image of black male rapist (Gayle, 1976; Guerrero, 1993).

In probing the historical rationales underlying the creation and maintenance of such racist iconography, it is highly significant to consider the continued popularity of their original forms during an age where blacks are no longer slaves or noncitizens. These images continue to be manufactured, and the reproduction and sale of contemptible collectibles are in full swing. Our own eBay search using the terms "nigger" and "mammy" in the early weeks of 2006 found thousands of items—original and reproduction—of jolly nigger banks, mammy salt and pepper shakers, and postcards with watermelons and pickaninnies in every shape and style imaginable. Apparently, as Turner (1994) writes, "We still live in a world eager to develop new reasons and rationales for commodifying African Americans—past and present" (p. 30).

Indeed, other authors have turned to identifying what they consider contemporary examples of recycled racial themes. For instance, Grindstaff (2004) points to daytime talk shows, and Lhamon (1998), hip hop, as examples of modern-day minstrelsy. Similarly, Bogle (2000 [1973]), in tracing black representations in movies from 1903's *Uncle Tom's Cabin* through the end of the 20th century, notes the regular resurfacing of the old racial stereotypes among contemporary characters, even in the face of seeming progress.

PRESENT-DAY REALITIES

Despite the advances made during the Civil Rights movement, we live in a post–Civil Rights era where social progress has been co-opted to help deny the existence of racism today. We view contemporary forms of racist popular culture as dangerous not only for the same reasons they were in the past, but also because we live in a slippery, self-congratulatory era where we can easily look back at popular images of the past with such disdain that it temporarily blinds most from its subtle, yet equally egregious, forms today. Delgado and Stephancic (1992) suggest that "We acquiesce in today's version with little realization that it is wrong, that a later generation will 'How could they?' about us. . . . [Racism] of our own time strikes us, if at all, as unexceptionable, trivial, or well within literary license" (p. 1278).

Yet racism in popular culture has not gone uncontested, and in recent years well-organized and successful protests have risen up in various forms against corporations, athletic organizations, and other purveyors of racialized popular media. However, for as many successful protests, decades-long battles continue today to end the dehumanizing portrayals of marginalized groups in the United States. We begin by focusing on some recent successes gained in fighting against distorted and dangerous images as exemplary of the context of contestation that has and can exist in contemporary media culture. As others have asked, if future generations are to look back on the images and iconography current today, what will they have to say? And what we will say about our own roles in rallying against them?

Contested Images

Corporate entities, in their push for profits, have misappropriated images of the Other for as long as they have existed. Yet these images have not gone uncontested, and social organizing around these movements has been swift and well-organized, despite severe corporate foot dragging in recent decades. One example comes from Frito-Lay's 1967 introduction of the Frito Bandito—a greasy, pudgy character who would steal Anglos' Frito corn chips at gunpoint (Noriega, 2000). The company launched several commercials depicting the corporate mascot singing: "Ayiee, yie-yie-yieeee/I am dee Frito Bandito/I love Frito's Corn Chips/I love dem I do/I love Frito's Corn Chips/I take dem from you."

Chicano groups such as the National Mexican-American Anti-Defamation Committee and Involvement of Mexican Americans in Gainful Endeavors organized and appealed to Frito-Lay on moral grounds to remove the negative image and replace it with a more positive one. In response, Frito-Lay "sanitized" the *bandito*, deciding to remove his gun and his gold tooth, making him less grimacing—an utter disregard for the moral pleas that the image was damaging to Mexican Americans. It was only after the threat of a class action anti-defamation lawsuit on behalf of the 6.1 million Mexican Americans in the United States at the time that Frito-Lay dropped the corporate mascot, after four years of immense profiteering (Carrillo, 2003; Noriega, 2000).

More recently, in 2003, retail giant Abercrombie and Fitch launched a line of T-shirts featuring screen-printed images of slant-eyed, smiling caricatures donning rice hats. Shirts with slogans such as "Wong Brothers Laundry Service: Two Wongs Make It White" led to swift online activism and organizing among Asian American and student groups across the United States. In response to the massive protests—both online letter and petition campaigns and on-site protesting across American shopping malls—Abercrombie and Fitch finally agreed to pull the shirts from stores. However, this reluctant action was taken with a weak non-apology by the company spokesperson: "We personally thought Asians would love this T-shirt. We are truly and deeply sorry we've offended people. . . . We never single out any one group to poke fun at. We poke fun at everybody, from women to flight attendants to baggage handlers, to football coaches, to Irish Americans to snow skiers. There's really no group we haven't teased" (Strasburg, 2002). An explanation such as this reveals an utter disregard for persons of Asian descent by attempting to level the racial playing field, effectively dismissing the exploited and often tragic existence of Asian Americans in the United States. By providing a list of groups also allegedly targeted (openly revealing sexist and classist notions), it suggests that any group who takes offense simply cannot take a joke, deflecting any wrongdoing away from the company itself. Yet this attempt at racial innocence became even more thinly veiled in 2005, when the company was ordered to pay $40 million in a class action settlement for the company's widespread racial, ethnic, and gender hiring discrimination (Lieff, Cabraser, Heimann, & Bernstein, 2005).

Some of the most widely contested and long-standing controversies over dehumanizing and degrading images are those surrounding athletic team mascots. American Indians have been widely targeted with the naming of teams, such as the Washington Redskins, Cleveland Indians, and Atlanta Braves. Images of so-called Indian-ness are inaccurate and inappropriate cultural fictions of the white imagination that are disturbing on several levels. First, these images continue today despite decades-long fights over their use. Second, like blackface, they perpetuate a perverse means by which whites can "play Indian" during halftime spectacles (Deloria, 1998). Third, these images relegate Native Americans to the "mascot slot," denying them a meaningful sociopolitical identity in American public life (Strong, 2004; Trouillot, 1991). Overall, the continued existence of these racist representations—despite other images that have been resisted and retired—indicate that white America is so deeply invested in these cultural inventions that they are unconcerned if the images bear any resemblance to reality as long as they can still "participate" in the mythologized dances, rituals, and movements they have come to love so dearly. Whites' resistance reflects an unjust sense of entitlement to "owning" these images, as well as their devotion to profit from the continued use of these racist representations.

Social movements against Native American mascot images remain some of the most visible and arguably most successful examples of American Indian activism and sociocultural resurgence, and over 1,000 mascot images have been retired as a result (King & Springwood, 2001). Much of this protest has invoked comparison among other marginalized groups, stating that groups such as the "Pittsburgh Negroes, the Kansas City Jews, and the San Diego Caucasians" would cause outrage, asking why these logos continue to exist for Native Americans (Strong, 2004, 81). Using this logic, a University of Northern Colorado intramural basketball team called themselves "The Fighting Whities," in protest of a local high school team, The Fighting Reds. In one year, they raised over $100,000 for scholarships for American Indians, selling clothing items with their name and mascot, a 1950s-style caricature of a middle-aged white man in a suit, bearing the phrase "Every thang's gonna be all white!" (Rosenberg, 2002).

Despite these successes, there is clear evidence that the critical evaluation and challenge of racist representations is more often the exception than the rule—both in real life as well as on screen. In the next section, we trace the twisted fate depicted in Spike Lee's film *Bamboozled* (2000) and the tumultuous, real-life events leading to the demise of black comedian Dave Chappelle's wildly successful Comedy Central sketch show. We offer this examination because their deep connection provides an excellent example of the boundaries of reality colliding and blurring with fiction.

Satire Appropriated: Bamboozled and Chappelle's Show

Released in 2000, Spike Lee's *Bamboozled* satirically restages minstrelsy to show that contemporary white America has no interest in seeing black Americans portrayed on television as anything more than buffoons.[2] Lee's film challenges modern racial ideology that encourages the belief that we have progressed far beyond the days of black-faced minstrel shows. The film is posthumously narrated by the main character, Pierre Delacroix, an African American television network executive "**buppie**" recklessly determined to get fired from his job at a major network where they are looking to improve a ratings slump by creating something "dope, sexy, and funny." Seeking to be laid off, he pitches what he thinks is an outrageously offensive and racist pilot, *Mantan: The New Millennium Minstrel Show,* to his white boss, Thomas Dunwitty. To his surprise, Dunwitty jumps on the idea, quickly turning the pilot into a show about "two real coons" who are "keepin' it real."

Dunwitty, who boasts being blacker than Delacroix because he has an African American wife and two biracial children, sets *Mantan: The New Millennium Minstrel Show* in a watermelon (or "nigger apple") patch with a house band, The Alabama Porch Monkeys. The show, like its historical minstrel predecessors, chronicles the dull-witted and unlucky antics of tap-dancing Mantan and his sidekick, Sleep 'n' Eat. The live-audience sitcom garners a wildly successful following across America, and by the end of the film, audience members of all races don blackface, exclaiming they are "real niggers." Quickly the satire is lost—if it ever existed—and Delacroix is loved by all for his "creative genius" and the fact that "the show can't be racist because he's black." Finally unshackled to laugh freely at some of the most degrading images of black Americans of all time, America becomes obsessed with *Mantan,* delighting in and restaging a nostalgic era where "a man could be a man, a woman could be a woman, and a nigger knew his place."

Buppie Black Urban Professional.

Interestingly, before *Bamboozled* had been released, *The New York Times* blocked its ad of a watermelon-eating pickaninny, perhaps over concern that the satire would be lost on its readers. Blending real life with fiction, the allure of *Bamboozled* is its seamless juxtaposition of historical reality with a fictional sociopolitical future fantasy. Weaving images of *Ethnic Notions* (1987) throughout, *Bamboozled* reminds its viewers that these racist icons from the not-so-distant past can, and have been, resurrected with relative ease. Ironically, if not surprisingly, *Bamboozled*'s art-imitating-life approach was brought to fruition with the tremendous success of African American comedian Dave Chappelle's Comedy Central Network program, *Chappelle's Show* (2003).

With sketches like "The Racial Draft," "The Niggar Family," and "The Life of Clayton Bigsby" (a blind white supremacist unaware that he is a black man), *Chappelle's Show* tackled American racial issues head-on with satire and humor—enjoying two wildly successful seasons of episodes dealing with race, sex, and celebrity. Having signed a $50 million contract with Comedy Central, fans were shocked when the third season was delayed indefinitely in early 2005 amidst rumors that Chappelle had become drug addicted and mentally unstable. During this time of delay and uncertainty, it became clear how much white America had come to "love"—and *need*—*Chappelle's Show*. To be sure, *Chappelle's Show* enjoyed a multiracial audience, and white fans were not the only ones bemoaning its absence. Chappelle's smart satire provided black Americans an outlet for expressing common racial frustration. White audiences had an arguably different attraction to the material, however, as the program not only provided white America with the license to play out their black alter egos while exclaiming, "I'm Rick James, bitch!" but also finally created a space where white Americans could safely—and openly—laugh at some of their most inner thoughts on race and racism.[3]

Perhaps, then, it is unsurprising to learn that these were the precise reasons Chappelle had come to question his role in bringing sharp-witted satire into millions of white American homes only to have the message destroyed upon delivery. In a revealing interview done to dismiss rumors of his disappearance, Chappelle described one of his last tapings, where he played the role of a black-faced pixie trying to get other black pixies to act in stereotypical ways. Discussing his reaction to one spectator, a white man laughing too loudly, Chappelle revealed, "When he laughed, it made me uncomfortable. As a matter of fact, that was the last thing I shot . . . because my head almost exploded" (Farley, 2005).

Comedy Central and Chappelle's long-time, white writing partner, Neal Brennan, failed to understand the underlying reasons for concern over how the show was being received. Brennan said, "We'd write it. He'd love it, say, 'I can't wait to do it.' We'd shoot it, and then at some point he'd start saying, 'This sketch is racist, and I don't want this on the air.' And I was like, 'You like this sketch. What do you mean?' There was this confusing contradictory thing: he was calling his own writing racist." Similar to the fate of *Bamboozled*'s Delacroix, white America renders black artists incapable of determining the artistic or problematic merits of their own work. White America takes on a paternalistic role in deciding what is racist and not and is least likely to make these types of judgments fairly and without its own best interests—psychological or economic—at heart. The fictional Delacroix and the real Dave Chappelle both clearly came to understand the difficult lesson pinpointed by critical film analyst, Armond White (1995): "A Black filmmaker can take nothing for granted" (p. 62).

To be sure, this lesson extends to people of color in most if not all genres of popular media production. And ultimately, as Chappelle himself noted, in the multinational media outlet, those not willing to toe the line are replaceable when it is the message, and perhaps more importantly, the dollar hanging in the balance. Reflecting on the end of the second season, the actor portended his own fate: "I was replaceable. I'm still replaceable now. That's what's so crazy about show business." In *Bamboozled*, when Mantan and Sleep 'n' Eat finally decide to walk away from the degrading show, their characters are quickly replaced by another desperate actor waiting in the wings, Honey Cut. Comedy Central, too, has attempted to fill the gap left by Chappelle with a new show, *Mind of Mencia.* This program features Latino comic Carlos Mencia, who shares his own brand of racial humor with the Comedy Central audience. As the show's Web page promises, consumers can "enter Carlos Mencia's mind and immerse themselves in his unique, unflinching take on the world." While *Mind of Mencia* attempts to work within the racial satire formula that made Chappelle famous, its execution is much less analytical and nuanced, relying on blatant stereotypes to make fun of everyone from Mexican immigrants to the disabled. And, indeed, this show appeals to the fans of *Chappelle* who missed the point of his smart satire.

Beyond *Mencia,* at the time of this writing, Comedy Central had promised its viewers a third season of *Chappelle's Show*—with or without Chappelle (who traditionally introduced each show to a live audience following a monologue), highlighting yet again the economic interests at stake. Literally scrapping together pieces from unused filming from the previous two seasons, the network is giving the show a life of its own to feed the Chappelle-hungry white audiences. Here, we see the fates of *Mantan* and *Chappelle's Show* end the same: the show taking on a life of its own, supported only by a white thirst for the laughter and the expense at which it tolls black Americans in real life, even in the absence of its creators. With or without Chappelle, it appears as if he will be just fine, reflecting, "I want to make sure I'm *dancing and not shuffling.* . . . Your soul is priceless" (Farley, 2005).

Addressing Race in Film

Analysts like Bogle (2000 [1973]), Kellner (1995), Vera and Gordon (2003), White (1995), and others have each taken on the important task of critically addressing the varied ways in which race is portrayed, often problematically, in the popular media of film. While it is beyond the scope of this paper to recite their important contributions here, we wish to consider two very recent examples of race in film that present arguably new formats for conveying recycled ideas. For many years following the

Civil Rights movements of the 1960s, a politically correct discourse pushed frank talk about race into the corners of popular culture. This was precisely what made the classic *Guess Who's Coming to Dinner?* (Kramer, 1967) such a seemingly groundbreaking work for its time. In many respects, and as *Chappelle's Show* demonstrated for TV media, it appears that we have moved into a new post–Civil Rights era where it has become fashionable to talk about race as a more "genuine" proof that we are a progressive society. In this way, 2005's feature film *Crash* is for movies what *Chappelle's Show* is for television.

The Oscar award-winning motion picture drama *Crash* (Haggis, 2005) was hailed by critics and audiences alike for its seemingly forthright treatment of race in America. It marked itself unafraid to take on the explicit bigotry of whites, from the heinous abuses of a racist white cop to the purse-clutching prejudices of a wealthy white woman. Perhaps more important, however, was *Crash's* seeming equal-opportunity-racism message—not only were the white characters regular espousers of racist dialogue, but the many characters of color were as well. Nearly all the characters in this movie, including African Americans, Latino Americans, Asian Americans, and Arab Americans, participated in interpersonal interactions that are traditionally labeled racist. The net effect is a leveling of the racial playing field. White moviegoers certainly made uncomfortable by the white characters' forthrightness with their prejudices can be comforted in the notion that racism is not a white problem, but rather a human problem. We all must fight against our tendencies to stereotype—whites are no longer the lonely oppressors, but rather engaged in a common struggle against the detached evil of racism.

While *Crash* undoubtedly addresses race in a more candid way than is traditionally done in Hollywood, it is precisely its claim of being progressive that marks it dangerous. What appears to be an enlightened take is in many respects a new form of whitewashing. Liberal whites, in particular, will feel validated by their brave willingness to face the uncomfortable. In another 2005 film, we see the same ideas offered through humor. The remake of *Guess Who's Coming to Dinner* (1967) offers a racial role reversal in *Guess Who*. Similar to its predecessor, *Guess Who* portrays a middle-class black family unwilling to accept their daughter's white boyfriend.

Laughter is the vehicle that makes this film—and its messages about race—appear innocuous at best, hardly as controversial as its predecessor. Yet, with the portrayal of a black father unwittingly prejudiced against a white boyfriend, it levels the racial playing field—teaching us that black people are just as racist and prejudiced as white people, a problematic message that resonates well among those who believe that "reverse discrimination" and "reverse racism" are alive and well. Here, historical issues regarding racism are shallowly presented and go unchallenged (Vera & Gordon, 2005). Films like *Crash* and *Guess Who* that focus on interpersonal interactions, and present equal-opportunity-racism themes, effectively dismiss the long, structured, systemic legacy of white supremacy in the United States. These new forms of erasure make certain histories—and people—invisible, and this is particularly problematic for the future of racial relations not only in the United States, but globally as well.

Something Old, Something New, Something Borrowed, Something...

Under critical historical examination, images of "blackness" found in popular culture today have shifted very little from their historical counterparts. Yet, as Patricia Hill Collins (2004) explains, "In modern America, where community institutions of all sorts have eroded, popular culture has increased in importance as a source of information and ideas" (p. 121). This is particularly problematic for black American youth, as popular culture has come to authoritatively fill the void where other institutions that could "help them navigate the challenges of social inequality" are beginning to disappear (p. 121).

Although whites have appropriated black popular culture throughout history, in recent decades it has reached new heights of global commodification—circulating problematic ideas about race, class, gender, and sexuality domestically and globally. Black women's roles in popular culture have been limited to mammies, matriarchs, jezebels, or welfare queens, yet we have seen these images being repackaged for contemporary consumption and global exportation (Collins, 2001). Contemporary hip hop portrays black women—lyrically and visually—as gold diggers and sexualized bitches who like to "get a freak on," an updated form of the jezebel (Collins, 2004).

Sexualized images of black men have also been repackaged for contemporary popular consumption as well, being touted as a way of life for many black American young men. bell hooks (2004) writes that, "Gangsta culture is the essence of patriarchal masculinity. Popular culture tells young black males that only the predator will survive" (p. 27). Today's *criminal-blackman* is not much different from the historical stereotype of bucks who are "always big, baadddd niggers, oversexed and savage, violent and frenzied as they lust for white flesh" (Bogle, 2000 [1973], 13; Russell, 2001). Currently, sexualized images of black femininity and black masculinity have become highly marketable yet remain historically rooted in an intersectional racialized sexism. "These controlling images are designed to make racism, sexism, poverty, and other forms of injustice appear to be natural, normal, and inevitable parts of everyday life" (Collins, 2001, 69). Such lessons are not only learned all too well domestically, but globally as well, with their continued popularity and exportation.

THE FUTURE OF RACISM AND POPULAR CULTURE

Pieterse (1992) tells us, "The racism that [has] developed is not an American or European one, but a Western one" (p. 9). With the global exportation of Western popular culture, it is no surprise that racist Western iconography and ideology have enjoyed immense popularity as well. The Hollywood film industry is a prime example of this problematic globalization of images, with U.S. studios controlling three-quarters of the distribution market outside the United States (Movie Revenues, 2006). When Disney's Uncle Remus tale, *Song of the South* (1946), was highly contested for its "this is how the niggers sing" jubilant portrayal of plantation life, its distribution was blocked in the United States after serious protest (Bernstein, 1996; Neupert, 2001; Schaffer, 1996; Vera & Gordon, 2003). However, the film was quickly made available for global distribution, making it the highest-grossing film in 1946 with $56.4 million in worldwide sales (World Wide Box Office, 2006).

Not to let the fantastic lore of Uncle Remus's tales be forgotten, in 1992 Walt Disney World resurrected Critter Country to create the animated roller coaster ride Splash Mountain (Schaffer, 1996). Children and adults 40 inches and taller from all over the world can "hop a hollowed-out log to follow Brer Rabbit's mischievous escapades as he tries to flee the clutches of Brer Fox and Brer Bear until you plunge five stories off Chick-a-pin Hill! 'It's the truth. It's actual. Everything is satisfactual. It's a zip a dee doo dah day!'" (Walt Disney World, 2006). Like other stories manufactured under the Disney-fication project, *Song of the South* and Splash Mountain serve to disguise the horrors of American slavery from visitors to Disney World and Disneyland in the United States, but also from visitors to Tokyo Disneyland and, in 2006, Hong Kong Disneyland (Walt Disney World, 2006; Wasko, 2001). While the antebellum American South may be far off the radars of visitors to such spectacles, *Song of the South* and Splash Mountain represent the height of Baudrillard's (1992) sense of whitewashed and sanitized American **simulacra**, to be sure.

Global recycling of contested antiblack images and ideas has been found in numerous other examples. In 2003, the Bubble Sisters, an all-female quartet in Korea, made headlines when they used a "blackface gimmick" to gain popularity among pop music fans. Performing in black-face makeup, afros, and grotesquely caricatured rubber lips, and dancing in pajamas, the group received airtime

from several sources, including MTV Korea, leading to swift protests against the Bubble Sisters and their producers (Hodges, 2003). In response, Bubble Sister Seo Seung-hee explained the group "loved music by black people," and "we happened to have black makeup. With the makeup we felt good, natural, free and energized. In taking the real album cover photos, we finally decided to go for it" (KOCCA, 2003). Similar to other contemporary examples of people who have reported "accidentally" donning blackface, blackface appears to just spontaneously happen to people.[4] After severe backlash, their manager reported, "To the 1 percent of people who were offended by this, we're really sorry. . . . We won't be performing with black faces" (Hodges, 2003).

In Japan, *Chikibura Samba* (or "Little Black Sambo" in English), a children's book with a long history of controversy over its racial caricatures and stereotypes, was re-released in 2005, 17 years after Japanese booksellers agreed to pull it from shelves following a U.S.-led campaign against its racist imagery and language. Its contemporary re-release sold over 100,000 copies, making it a national bestseller in Japan. The book publisher's president, Tomio Inoue, announced that, "Times have changed since the book was removed. Black people are more prominent in politics and entertainment, so I don't think this book can be blamed for supporting racial stereotypes. We certainly had no intention of insulting black people" (McCurry, 2005). Like other corporate apologies, this one invokes a colorblind racial story of progress to try to minimize their actions in the name of profits. And this apology does not appear to address whether this racial progress has occurred in the United States or Japan (a country with an even smaller population of black persons), and still delineates black people's roles to entertainers, a stereotypical post invoked to cite progress among the entire population of black people.

With new technologies and the continued globalization of American popular culture, we can only imagine that these images will find their way into more and more spaces—problematically defining blackness across the globe. As one study found

---

simulacra a diluted or superficial representation of something else (e.g., Main Street in Disney World).

with interviews of rural Taiwanese who had never traveled to the United States, they "knew" about race and black Americans in the United States from watching U.S. movies. Like other immigrants who come to the United States, their exposure to U.S. movies undoubtedly shaped their stereotypical views and acceptance of racist ideas about black Americans. As popular culture's global audience grows, so do the lessons it provides about race and racism in the United States today. Without a critical resistance against these images, we can have no hope for racial equality in the United States or globally.

CONCLUSION

On any typical day, one could feasibly rise and dress in their Abercrombie and Fitch "Wok n Bowl" T-shirt, eat breakfast with Aunt Jemima. Get ready for lunch with, "Yo quiero Taco Bell!" Have dinner with Uncle Ben, before retiring to the television to watch the Indians, Redskins, or Braves (and don't forgot to throw down your "tomahawk chop" in an important moment of collective consciousness). After a leisurely game of "Ghettopoly" before

heading to bed, you finally watch the late night news to get a daily dose of Arab and Muslim terrorists and criminal-blackmen bedtime stories.

As Noriega (2001) has argued, race in popular culture is in many ways a paradox—its representation has become regular in our media culture, while the profound ways it affects the real-life chances of individuals and groups remain hidden. And indeed, as Noriega notes, while popular media cannot be implicated as the "cause" of racism, neither does it offer a value-free medium for the exchange of ideas and information. The problem with the stranglehold popular culture has over dictating the way that the populace "knows" people of color is that for people who have very little real, interpersonal experience with individuals from these groups, they can believe in an essentialist vision composed of every stereotype and myth promoted. In today's world of mass information, it is easy to see how the very ubiquity of such images makes keeping pace with them nearly impossible. As addressed above, this is the promise and predicament of popular culture. The deep need for a critical cultural studies is clear, one that seeks to understand the tools available, how they have been used in support of the dominant ideology, and how they might challenge such ideologies and offer countercultural solutions.

THE MEDIA AS A SYSTEM OF RACIALIZATION

Exploring Images of African American Women and the New Racism

Marci Bounds Littlefield

MARCI BOUNDS LITTLEFIELD is an assistant professor of sociology at Indiana University–Purdue University, Indianapolis.

HISTORICALLY, THE MEDIA PERPETUATE IDEAS about race and ethnicity that place African American women at a clear disadvantage. Beginning with the welfare queen image during the Reagan administration and moving to the porno chick represented in current videos, society views a daily discourse on race, gender, and class that continues to reproduce dominant and distorted views of African American womanhood and sexuality. The overabundance of this portrayal in popular culture raises serious implications associated with linking sexual promiscuity to the nature and identity of African American women. These popular representations of African American women and men are mostly unchallenged by larger society and the African American community. This [reading] discusses the media as a system of racialization and proposes to challenge this system as a method of social justice and social change.

As a society, America was fashioned and born out of binary ethnocentric, oppressive, sexual notions of race. These notions of race informed the early colonists; they described Africans as beasts with animal passions prone to lasciviousness (Jordan, 1968). The initial reactions of the colonists to the Africans foreshadowed the experience of Africans in American society, and the sexual depictions of the African women functioned as a catalyst igniting the politics of race. American society became the living epitome of hypocrisy as it struggled with creating a pluralistic society.

Pluralism, a pattern of racial integration, represented the American ideology—a nation that would accept and celebrate racial and ethnic differences while affirming its allegiance to the larger society (Schaefer, 2005). In practice, American pluralism enforced Anglo conformity and created an American identity that excludes all groups outside

Questions to Consider

In this reading, Littlefield makes the point that "the media produce and circulate images that determine our beliefs and attitudes and that inform our behaviors." What might the link be between our attitudes toward race, gender, and sexuality and the sexist and racist ways individuals behave toward women and racial minorities? Is it possible that how the media present black women in rap videos shapes the way these women are treated? How might negative images of women of color translate in their objectification or result in discrimination? Could one argue that these images are merely entertainment and have no bearing on how women are treated?

the norm and realm of Whiteness. This binary distinction among the races created a hierarchy in which Anglo perceptions about race and ethnicity dominated the social structure, and other non-White groups were placed in the Other category, which translated into inferior social status. Rather than fashion a society that embraces difference, we instead live in one that punishes, dehumanizes, and alienates difference in every form of social life.

In theory, racial and ethnic difference should create the impetus and premise for a just society. However, this difference in American society translates into social policies, laws, customs, and norms that justify all forms of oppression and a social structure that promotes inequality and domination based on class, race, and gender. The prevalent and permanent systems of racialization that inform our lived experiences as a society and divide us in spite of civil rights, affirmative action, and diversity initiatives are multiple. These systems of racialization must be interrogated to disrupt a society that has developed and prospered at the expense of the oppressed. Although many vehicles inform the hegemonic social structure, the media are the

primary agent of socialization in which participants are seduced, educated, and transformed by ideas concerning race, gender, and class on a global level, and these ideas often support White supremacist capitalist patriarchy.[1]

As I scrutinize the profound impact of the media in their transformative possibilities, it is disturbing to witness the popular portrayal of the values of our youth, which do not extend beyond sex, drugs, and money, as portrayed in the ever-so-popular hip-hop videos. This genre has been referred to as the voice of the youth but, today, clearly represents the impact of a capitalist White patriarchal society that supports images that degrade minorities to sell music. Thus, like slavery, the bodies, talent, and potential of minority youth are commodified and objectified to promote an industry that marginally benefits the artists but continues to send the message that race is a defining factor in American society.

On first glance, it appears that American society is accepting of its minorities: Popular representations of youth culture are represented in a variety of media outlets, diversity initiatives are supported in most government agencies, and businesses embrace ideas about multiculturalism. International viewers have sufficient examples to conclude that minorities have obtained a piece of the American dream, given the representation of African Americans in politics, sports, and music. This, however, is the logic behind the *new racism,* which Collins (2004) describes as being predicated on inclusion and containment, which hides behind the notion of a color-blind society. This new racism assumes that the social changes that took effect during the civil rights movement benefited African Americans and that, consequently, America has lived up to its promise of equality. Current strategies that highlight diversity initiatives but do not single out problems faced by Black Americans dilute the real issues and needs of African Americans. Therefore, any social justice paradigm has to include an analysis of the hegemonic structure of American society and the role of the media as an agent that enforces historical ideas about African American sexuality and perpetuates inequality. This [reading] analyzes the concomitant effects of the media as a system of racialization and proposes a social justice framework that interrogates this system and proposes methods for change.

MASS MEDIA

The media have historically perpetuated ideas about race and ethnicity that place African American women at a clear disadvantage. The overabundant portrayal of the African American woman stereotype, as **Jezebel** in popular culture, raises serious questions concerning the state of race in America and the persistence of linking sexual promiscuity to the nature and identity of African American women. Despite the changes and understanding of race as a social concept with no biological meaning, race is still a factor in the lives of African American women who, since slavery, have been consistently portrayed as the sexual prowler. The media perpetuate this image, popularize it, and present it as the defining characteristic of African American women, thus leaving our communities with images that are damaging, demeaning, and injurious to race relations.

Although the idea of race and its definition are constantly changing, the effects of race are still present and so persist in the areas of employment, education, poverty, and health care, to name a few. Although this is clearly the nature of social stratification in American society, the systems that perpetuate racism are not definitively identified as a factor in perpetuating the hegemonic ideas concerning race and gender. Consequently, popular representations of African American women in videos and the acceptance of these representations by the African American community and larger society suggest that African American women are still society's sexual scapegoat. These popular representations of African American women and men go largely unchallenged by larger society and by the

African American community, which accepts these images without recognizing their power to disrupt an oppressive cycle of commodification.

The media have transformed the ways that we are able to communicate as a society, and these methods of communication make it easy to transfer ideas in a global context. The media strategically remake our picture of reality by controlling the images and the information that we receive. This process of selective reporting affects the ability of the populace to make objective, informed decisions because the information presented is biased and controlled (Murray, Schwartz, & Lichter, 2001). The media serve as a tool that people use to define, measure, and understand American society. For that reason, the media serve as a system of racialization in that they have historically been used to perpetuate the dominant culture's perspective and create a public forum that defines and shapes ideas concerning race and ethnicity. This is clearly evident in the representation of African Americans in various media. The power of the media to define and create attitudes that inform behavior is a crucial strategy of the new racism because the media are used to reproduce and disseminate the ideologies needed to justify racism (Collins, 2004).

Scholars suggest that the media produce and circulate images that determine our beliefs and attitudes and that inform our behaviors (Collins, 1991; Schiller, 1973). This is evident in studies that draw a correlation between television and violence/aggression in children (Baker & Ball, 1969) and infer television as an agent of socialization (Berger & Luckmann, 1967), and as a source for providing role models that affect children's attitudes, beliefs, and behavior (Comstock, Chaffee, Katzman, McCombs, & Roberts, 1978). The media are also suggested as being a factor in shaping, processing, and defining self-identity for young viewers (Milkie, 1999), whereas the media's negative stereotypical images may damage young girls' self-image as well (McRobbie, 1982). Symbolic interactionist approaches consider how viewers interpret media representations. They are concerned with how meaning is created, and this meaning varies according to the viewers' social, cultural, and historical

---

Jezebel A racist stereotype depicting black women as hypersexual and promiscuous.

group perspective (Blumer, 1969). This group perspective is shared among members of the same *interpretive community* because of similar cultural experiences that may not be shared by different groups (Fish, 1980). Therefore, the way that African Americans interpret popular media representations and the way that they believe other groups perceive these representations can be an important factor in shaping their identity.

Again, the context in which the media shape our ideas concerning race is an important discussion as we consider the current generation. Born in the eighties and afterward, this generation has been bombarded with negative controlling images of African Americans. Beginning with the welfare queen image during the Reagan administration to the strip-club porno chick represented in current videos, the media of the new generation broadcast a daily discourse on race, gender, and class that continues to reproduce dominant and distorted views of African American womanhood and sexuality. Thus, the media have historically operated as an agent constructing racial ideology.

Historical Representations

Historical representations of African American women help us to see the permanence and persistence of stereotypical images that justify the treatment of African American women as society's Other. African American women were described by English slave traders as "hot constitution's ladies' . . . making no scruple to prostitute themselves to the Europeans . . . so great is their inclination to white men" (Jordan, 1968, p. 35). These notions of African American women as sexual predators defined their sexuality in the 16th and early 17th century and became the standard by which they were measured. Slavery defined African American women as society's Other, which placed them in a category different from that of White women and suggested that they were not true women. Consequently, a number of stereotypes emanated, one of which depicted African American women as the Jezebel, an insatiable sexual being unable to control her sexuality (Collins, 1991). These images

created a context for African American women that defined their sexuality and made it impossible to violate their identity. African American women were described as lustful and impudent, and this became a justification for the rape and commodification of their bodies in the 19th century. This commodification during slavery objectified African American women, and this objectification continues to be defined by the media in music videos and in other popular representations of African American culture.

During the era of King Cotton, early American culture produced a society in which race defined social interactions with African Americans. The slave trade and the cultural ethos of slavery defined African American women in pluralistic terms of property, commodities, breeders, concubines, servants, and laborers (Collins, 1991, 2004).

This view of African American women represented the interpretation of the hegemonic culture, and it was maintained through a system of educational, psychological, economic, and physical degradation. This system insisted that these women not consider themselves as women but as sexual animals whose purpose was to satisfy the needs of the oppressor. Hence, the stereotypes used to justify racial oppression included lazy, unintelligent, sexual, and sinister, and African American men and women were both viewed in this context.

Early Portrayal of African American Women in the Media

The stereotypical representation of Blacks in the media began with the release of W. Griffith's film *The Birth of a Nation* in 1915. This film was released during reconstruction, and it played on Southern fears of racial equality. Southerners believed that equality for African Americans would ultimately lead to miscegenation and political disaster. In response, the film fed Southern racism by using common stereotypes of African Americans as savages. *Birth of a Nation* ran for 44 consecutive weeks, sparked the revival of the KKK, and fueled the lynching campaign (*Slavery and the Making of America,* 2004). African American men and women were represented in spaces that relegated them to a persona of servitude, crime, savagery, inferiority, and animalism (Diawara, 1993). Through this forum, the media participated in a public discourse on race that had a direct impact on the lives of African Americans. This film also led to further representations of African Americans in the public sphere that summarized the context in which African Americans had been defined since slavery.

Portraying stereotypical images of African American women in a way that dehumanizes them is not a new one; it stems from a societal need to place a group of people in the Other category, which objectifies their existence and suggests that they are not really human and so deserve the unfair treatment that they receive (Collins, 2004). Relegating African American women to the Other category set historical precedence for viewing them through a prism of difference, whereas everyone outside that prism is viewed as normal. Collins (1991) suggests that this binary relationship is a natural part of human society's tendency to make distinctions, which attributes good and bad in its schematic arrangement and to which African American women have consistently been placed in the Other category. Thus, maintaining images of African American women as the Other provides ideological justification for race, gender, and class oppression. DuCille (1996) labels this constant portrayal of African American women in the Other category as the "occult of true Black womanhood."

The portrayal of African Americans in the media in these representations served to perpetuate the racial inferiority that was part of the Southern mentality and transformed into an American way of thinking about African Americans. This ideology posited African Americans as inferior beings who did not warrant any social justice and were deserving of their ill treatment. Earlier attempts to rectify social injustice during reconstruction were superseded by the country's desire to pacify the South and restore to it a measure of autonomy and power that the Civil War undermined. African Americans were relegated to an inferior position, and the historic ***Plessy v. Ferguson*** case of 1896, the

Black codes, and the lynching campaign ensured that African Americans would not experience equal opportunity. As such, the ideas about race were developed during this era, and the media disseminated an ideology of African American inferiority.

Current Representations

Today, the images of African American women carry an almost identical resemblance to their original characterizations as sexually insatiable creatures. The most recent objections include the "Tip Drill" video, which displays African American women as nameless objects whose sexuality is for sale. The alarming image of Nelly swiping his credit card through the buttocks of a African American woman serves as a rallying cry for the community of students, scholars, and others to open a public debate concerning the pornographic and misogynist representations of African American women in music videos and the meaning of these representations for the viewers. As this debate continues, this video is one of many popular representations of African American women that perpetuate an age-old ideology that their sexuality and their bodies should be used for public profit. Accordingly, the media perpetuate these controlling images and inform African American women's reality by creating stereotypical images that perpetuate a system of domination that links sex, race, and gender to the sexuality of African American women.

The crucial problem with the negative images of African American women in today's society is not merely the overabundance of these images but rather the absence of equal amounts of alternative, positive images. These images are damaging because they limit African American women's choices by excluding other options. Therefore, the representations of these women in the music videos depict the oversexual, deviant image of the African American woman which society crafted during slavery and has systematically perpetuated. When considering

---

Plessy v. Ferguson The U.S. Supreme Court decision that held that blacks and whites could be legally segregated as long as both were treated equally. Commonly known as the separate but equal doctrine.

the popular representation of these women in the media and especially in the music industry, the question becomes, are there enough positive images to combat the sexually insatiable representations of African American women that inundate our culture?

When these images were first presented in the early 19th century, African American club women sought to influence and redefine the images of African American women through public work centered on racial uplift and through education and public service (Pough, 2004). The 19th century bore African American women as social leaders in the public sphere and challenged the common representations of African American women as sexual deviants. Women such as Maria Stewart, Mary Shad Clary, Margaret Murray Washington, and Anna Julia Cooper ensured that African American women were viewed in ways that uplifted the race and presented African American women in a positive light. Scholars suggest that a few female rappers are the modern-day equivalent of these 19th-century female revolutionaries—that is, they are willing to challenge the male space that has consumed the rap industry and in doing so present an alternative female voice (Emerson, 2002; Pough, 2004; Rose, 1994). Although this argument may have some merit, the limited examples of positive women rappers are not sufficient to alter the negative representations of African American women; unlike the club women, current female rappers do not appear to have a real purpose, a group perspective, or a common goal.

Today the media inundate the populace with the body politics of African American womanhood, where women's bodies are exploited as they were for cheap labor during slavery—in each case, the institution reinforces the images of African women as hypersexual workhorses used for profit whether by slave owners or recording producers. These sexually insatiable images are detrimental for the African American woman because they have a life of their own and take shape and meaning to viewers of these images. Although images alone cannot create behavior, they can certainly inform behavior (which is essentially what happened

during reconstruction) and become the fabric of an American way of life. According to Collins (1991), stereotypes of African American women create barriers for them to succeed in areas of employment outside the traditional occupations relegated to them. The idea that African American women are not capable of intellectual thought and direction has become the way of thinking about African American women. Today the continued use of their bodies for profit makes rape and other forms of violence against women an acceptable norm.

NEW RACISM

When we see images of African American sexuality portrayed in the media, they are viewed through this new lens of difference, which suggests that diversity exists but denies the context for which racial definitions and categorizations create social inequality. On one hand, our society accepts racial labels and distinctions, but it does not accept policies initiated to create a just society and, in reality, does not foster real inclusion of minority groups. This new racism is precisely the context in which the melting pot metaphor originally defined American society as a pluralistic society that professes racial justice and egalitarian principles of equality while, in practice, promoting Anglo conformity.

Clearly, the state of American society in the 19th century and the obvious need to join in the battle for racial uplift defined the social agenda of African Americans. Today the need to participate in a racial uplift campaign is unclear. As of 2007, this agenda is not clearly defined and has been represented as a class problem and not a race problem. Inequality has been redefined to discuss issues around class, whereas race is presented as an issue that has been "solved" by the civil rights movement, by affirmative action, and by the legal precedents that have favored African Americans. This is the crux of the new racism that has convinced the populace that multiculturalism, diversity, and equality have been accounted for in American society. The African American distinction becomes no more meaningful than any other minority distinction, and

African Americans continue to experience institutional discrimination and live in communities with disparities that affect their life chances. Meanwhile, oversexed depictions of African American women justify the problems that overwhelmingly affect the African American community—namely, the increase in unwed childbirths, AIDS, teenage pregnancy, decline in marriage among African Americans—and thus create the same paradigm of blaming the victim that has characterized dominant-minority relations in the United States.

PEDAGOGY AND SOCIAL JUSTICE

Any social justice strategy that seeks to understand and respond to the current issues surrounding the media as a system of racialization has to first address methods of pedagogy. As educators, we have to address the pedagogy of how people define the continuing effects of racism and understand the extent of the hegemonic domination as part of our social structure that permeates and controls the minds of the oppressed. Any social justice paradigm has to include an understanding of the system and the current context in which all actors have a role in promoting misogynist ideology.

In the African American community, there seems to be an overall resistance to the reality of its resident sexism. Accordingly, when it views music videos and other media representations of African American women and men, its conclusion is that the youth have gone astray and that the missing value structure defines their decisions, rather than a comprehensive understanding of the oppressive social structure, which is committed to patriarchy and capitalism. Consequently, the decisions of music artists are seen in a vacuum, outside a social context, which dismisses the community's role in not addressing the issues. Hence, an attention to community education that educates young Black women, Black men, and the overall community is the only context that will have any meaning for social justice. Every actor in the social system must take responsibility

for the way that he or she perpetuates the media as a source of racialization by directly participating in the music industry and by not demanding change. As a result, change is possible only when all participants understand their own agency and respond. As long as the traditional blame-the-victim scenario defines our understanding of popular culture and the media, then the actors will never be challenged to change or make different choices.

There has to be a cultural context for African American men to think differently about gender and a reason to reject the hypermasculine images presented in popular culture that reward sexual violence, criminality, and deviant lifestyles. African American men need to understand their role in replicating an ideology that dehumanizes African American women and uses their talent as a way to make an industry richer at their expense. African American women have to understand the impact of the choices that they make in playing in stereotypical roles. The women who are portrayed in the videos are explained away by "choice," by free will, which places the blame solely on the women who supposedly make this free choice. However, there is no discussion of the social context in which this choice is made, and there is no consideration that African American women's bodies have historically been used to economically prosper in the capitalist system of social inequality. During slavery, African American women were stripped of their agency, and their bodies were commodified in a way in which choice never existed. Many African American women protested this lack of choice: Some killed their babies and performed abortions; others ran away. True freedom did not exist under slavery. Today this free choice is still diluted because ideas about sexuality and how sex is used in the African American community create a paradigm that defines the reality of African Americans. Unfortunately, what is absent is a forum to have these conversations, which would educate young African American women and thus create a new way of thinking about media images and choices.

Community organizations and other businesses need to develop alternate choices for young men and women—an alternative to buying into the stereotypical images portrayed by the media necessary to make it in the world of music and television. The old ideas of self-help that defined the social context for African Americans in the early 20th century created a generation of people who left a strong legacy for African Americans in business, education, and other industries who did not allow a capitalist social system to define their choices and their life chances. Alternative methods of "making it" have to be considered so that our youth will have other viable choices.

Popular and expressive culture can create a space for resisting stereotypical images and for creating a context source of racialization and an agent of racism. Ideas about race and ethnicity are transferred to the public through images and public presentations of racial groups, and until these presentations are filtered and challenged, racial identity and understanding will constantly be viewed through the lens of capitalism. That is, until minority groups play an active role in self-definition and reject the presentations of minorities by producers who are motivated by the dollar, then media representations will continue to define minority groups. Until African American women and men understand their respective roles in the portrayal of race and are challenged to make different choices, then we will always need public spaces to define and discuss racial issues.

MUST-SEE TV

South Asian Characterizations in American Popular Media

Bhoomi K. Thakore[*]

BHOOMI K. THAKORE is chair and assistant professor of sociology at Elmhurst College.

Why are there so many Indians on TV all of a sudden?

—Nina Shen Rastogi (2010)

INTRODUCTION

In June 2010, Rastogi pondered the above question in her article, "Beyond Apu: Why Are There Suddenly So Many Indians on Television?" for the online magazine, *Slate*. The increasing number of Indians and South Asians[1] in American popular television has been hard not to notice.[2] For example, among *TV Guide*'s top 15 television shows of 2010 (the year Rastogi wrote this article), four had a South Asian character or actor—*Community, Glee, The Good Wife,* and *Parks and Recreation*. Since then, more characters have entered the fold—including those in such shows as *The Big Bang Theory, Royal Pains, Outsourced,* and *The Mindy Project*.

As Rastogi (2010) noted, the popularity of the 2008 film *Slumdog Millionaire* helped propel Indians to become a noteworthy ethnic group in popular media. These days, South Asian characters tend to be presented as the minority alongside majority-white characters. South Asians are also a good stand-in for Arab and Muslim characters in this post-9/11 reality of fear (Alsultany 2012; Nacos and Torres-Reyna 2007).

Contemporary South Asian media characters tend to reflect the characteristics of one of the two South Asian demographic groups. In the 1960s and 1970s, highly educated South Asians were allowed to immigrate to the United States after the passage of the 1965 Immigration and Nationality Act (Prashad 2000; Takaki 1998; Wu 2002). Soon after that, less educated family members of these immigrants arrived in the United States and worked in service positions, including behind the counters of convenience stores, franchises, and motels (Dhingra 2012; Prashad 2000; Rangaswamy 2007). To date, there has been relatively little scholarship addressing the reasons behind this increasing trend of South Asian characters in the media and, more specifically, the ways in which these characters have been created, written, and produced. In this review, I discuss these representations by bridging the gaps between discussions in the fields of immigration studies, race/ethnicity studies, and critical media studies. In my discussion, I identify the concept of "(ethnic) characterization" and illustrate how studying the media representations of this ethnic group are in line with the concerns of sociology. As I suggest, scholarship in the disciplines of sociology and critical media studies is relevant, one to the other, particularly when understanding these ethnic media characterizations.

SOUTH ASIAN IMMIGRATION AND ASSIMILATION

The immigration and assimilation experiences of South Asians are relevant when understanding their influence on the representation of South Asians in American media. Those ethnic characteristics that media producers (and most Americans) know as "South Asian characteristics" will be used in the media characterization of these characters. This is evident in those media examples of South Asian characters that rely on overt stereotypes of this group, such as convenience store clerks or cab drivers. Thus, it is important to understand how South Asians, as a new and growing demographic, have assimilated in their new society and negotiated their own hyphenated-American identity.

Questions to Consider

In the past decade, there has been a significant increase in the number of Indians and South Asians in American television. Why is this the case, and how are members of these groups cast when they appear on television shows? Professor Thakore explores the reasons for the growing representation of South Asian characters on television and the extent to which actors are typecast into particular types of roles because of their ethnic and/or racial background. Can you think of other ethnic or racial groups where stereotypes lead to typecasting?

Like all other immigrant and ethnic groups before them, Indians and South Asians have experienced an uphill battle in conceptualizing their identity in the United States and claiming their place in the American racial hierarchy. After President Johnson signed the Immigration and Nationality Act in 1965 that allowed technical professionals from Asia to immigrate to the United States, most South Asians immigrated in order to achieve financial and professional success. Many were able to experience upward social mobility as a result of the educational capital they brought with them. Additionally, their success influenced the success of their children and proceeding generations.

Experiences of assimilation are particularly salient for the second-generation American-born children of first-generation South Asian immigrants, many of whom are portrayed in American media, and also happen to be the actors of these media characters. As Alba and Nee (2003) argued, while immigrants of the late 20th century overall have equal chances for social success as compared to their non-immigrant counterparts, the experiences of these immigrants collectively are not always the same. Their experiences are influenced by the various forms of capital a particular first- or second-generation immigrant possesses, and the extent to which that capital can be useful within economic and labor markets. These experiences of segmented assimilation explain not only differences in the social mobility of immigrant groups, but also the differences by individuals within an immigrant group.

Segmented assimilation, as it relates to the social mobility between first-generation parents and second-generation children, is noteworthy for all post-1965 South Asian immigrant families in the United States today (e.g. Alba and Nee 2003; Haller et al. 2011; Zhou and Xiong 2007). Additionally, it is important to note that the characterizations of South Asians in American media do not occur in a vacuum, but are informed in large part by the extent to which they assimilate into American society. However, traditional theories of assimilation fail to take into account the everyday experiences of racism that occur in the labor market and throughout society. These experiences inform the level at which ethnic groups can integrate into their new society, which in turn inform their acceptance by mainstream (white) Americans. Both dynamics are influenced by ideologies inherent in the pre-existing US racial hierarchy.

THE RACIALIZATION OF SOUTH ASIANS

In the history of the United States, race relations have been fluid in order to serve particular political or social interests. The extent to which immigrants are able to assimilate into mainstream American culture will influence their place within the American racial hierarchy. Their place within the American racial hierarchy will also determine their social success in American society. As I argue, racial perceptions play a significant role in the characterization of South Asians in the media.

Some contemporary race scholars have argued that the U.S. racial hierarchy is developing into a three-tiered system consisting of Whites at the top, Blacks at the bottom, and (South) Asians as honorary Whites in the middle (Bonilla-Silva 2004; Feagin 2001; Kim 1999). As Kim (1999) argued, Asian Americans are triangulated between Blacks and Whites in terms of perceived superiority but outside of both groups for their perceived foreignness. Tuan (1999) identified these physical differences as the "forever foreigner" syndrome that Asians in the United States are subjected to regardless of their immigrant or citizenship status. However, as Bonilla-Silva (2004) argued, light skin tone and high class can help "whiten" the position and experiences of South Asians in the United States. These dynamics are particularly influential when considering the "types" of South Asian characters found in American popular media.

Historically, immigrants and racial minorities (including South Asians) have been subjected to a fluid racial hierarchy in the United States. As Omi and Winant (1994) suggested, these racial formations are the result of social, political, and economic forces that determine the social status of racial and ethnic minorities. These statuses have formed over time and are dependent on various social and historical circumstances. Examples of such racial formations include everything from Jim Crow slavery to changes in immigration policy.

Racial formations are further influenced by the level of racialization that immigrants and minorities experience. Racialization is the process by which individuals are categorized into racial groups based on their physical appearance. Additionally, these racial categorizations are then used as units of analysis to explain social relations (Webster 1992). Bonilla-Silva (1997) develops upon the idea of racialization in his racialized social systems theory, which supposes that political, economic, and social structures are dependent on a racialized society and the racialization of individuals into it.

As South Asian scholars have argued, the racialization of Indian and South Asian Americans tends to be a negative process, specifically through the perpetuation of those negative stereotypes and assumptions associated with this group (Desai 2004, 2005; Kibria 1998; Kim 1999; Sharma 2010; Selod and Embrick 2013). While slavery and Jim Crow shaped the racialization of African-Americans in the United States, immigration and legislative policy have shaped the racialization of South Asians and determined the extent to which they compare to Whites in America (Koshy 2002). Contemporary ideologies, including the post-9/11 rhetoric in America and the global West, have contributed to a racialization of South Asians that portray them in popular media as foreigners and "others." These dynamics are further intersected by overt racialized perceptions that use obvious differences in skin color, religion, and ethnicity as markers of difference (Desai 2005).

According to Sharma (2010), Whites "commit" racialization of South Asians through the negative, stereotypical, and secondary ways in which they perceive them. Not only are they seen as "others" in American society, but they are also seen as "less than" in the American racial hierarchy. As Purkayastha (2005) suggested, racialization exists separate from the segmented assimilation based on skin color and class to which South Asians are

subjected. Racialization is a process imposed upon all Indians and South Asians as another way to maintain the perceptions of this group as outside of American norms. As Kiblia (1998) suggested, the development of such hyphenated umbrella identities as "South Asian American" is a result of racialization and these racialized experiences.

South Asian media characterizations are informed by the degree to which South Asians are racialized in society. This is evident in the examples of South Asian characters that are characterized solely around overt stereotypes. As I argue in the next section, these stereotypes not only serve the purpose of maintaining the perception of South Asians as foreigners in society, but are used consciously by media producers in their characterizations and ultimately reflect how South Asians are already perceived in the United States.

SOUTH ASIAN CHARACTERIZATIONS IN AMERICAN POPULAR MEDIA AND SOCIETY

Racial and ethnic minorities have historically been stereotyped in American popular media (Gray 2004; Hall 1997; Ono and Pham 2009; Rodriguez 1997; Vera and Gordon 2003, among others). While these representations have generally improved in recent years, insofar as there are significantly fewer examples of overt stereotypes, reflections of covert and subtle stereotypes remain. As I argue, the characterization of South Asians and other minorities in the media is informed by an intentional characterization that is dependent in large part on the racial ideologies that are reproduced in the representations. This is evident in the historical trajectory of South Asian characterizations in American popular media.

South Asian media characters began appearing sporadically in films throughout the 20th century (Davé 2013; Jones 1955). These early examples generally consisted of savage Indians in India who were defeated by the White star and savior (e.g. Vera and Gordon 2003). What was unique about these early representations was the location of the story itself—most were represented as Indians in India. During the 1980s, Indian and South Asian characters began appearing sporadically as tertiary or non-speaking characters cast in an American, usually urban, environment. Examples of representations included the generic and stereotypical cab driver, convenience store owner, and high-achieving student.

On the one hand, this stereotype of South Asians as a low-level service employee runs counter to the historical realities of South Asian demographics in the United States. Immigrants who arrived from South Asia in the 1960s and 1970s were highly educated. As Prashad (2000) noted, 83% of Indian immigrants between 1966 and 1977 had backgrounds in the STEM fields, including approximately 20,000 science PhDs, 40,000 engineers, and 25,000 physicians. However, after these early migrants and their immediate families were settled, many chose to invest in franchises and small businesses, including fast food stores, convenience stores, and motels (Dhingra 2012; Rangaswamy 2007). Once these businesses became established, Indian American owners took advantage of family reunification immigration policies of the 1970s and 1980s to bring over relatives to work for them. As more and more extended family members were able to settle in the United States, these individuals with few skills took other blue-collar jobs working in factories or driving taxi cabs.

Media producers in positions to create media characterizations do so based on their personal experiences. While they may have been less likely to run into South Asians who were scientists, professors, or even doctors, they were more likely to run into South Asians who were behind the counter of a local convenience store or driving their cab in an urban city. Additionally, such representations proved useful to them in the context of the stories they were producing—well-to-do White American characters encountering bumbling, foreign, South Asian immigrants working in jobs most identifiable to viewers, often with ensuing hilarity. These stereotypes proved useful for the story and for the characterization of South Asian characters. As

critical media studies scholars argue, White media executives have total control over the major media outlets and consciously reproduce upper-class ideologies, which in turn subjugate racial minorities (Bagdikian 2004; Bourdieu 1999; Hall 1997; McChesney 2004, 2008; Mistry 1999).

In the early 21st century, there were more noteworthy examples of Indian and South Asian media characters that were cast in such roles as highly skilled scientists or medical professionals. It is difficult to identify what led to this change, but it is likely due to the increased awareness of the high economic capital possessed by South Asian Americans, thus identifying them as a group to be coveted by advertisers (the financiers of network television). These new representations were more in line with the "model minority" stereotype, which was originally used in the 1960s to characterize East Asians in the United States (Kitano and Daniels 2001; Takaki 1998; Wu 2002, among others). While it is assumed that the model minority stereotype is a positive one, many scholars have identified its problematic nature. The assumption that Asian Americans are the model minority presupposes that they experience no discrimination in the United States. In fact, South Asians are subjected to the same discriminatory experiences of not being White as are other ethnic minorities in the United States.

One key example of such discrimination is through skin tone, particularly for women. All women of color deal with hegemonic skin tone ideologies in their racial/ethnic communities, with lighter skin tone and Caucasian facial features considered more appealing and attractive (Collins 2004; Glenn 2008; Hunter 2005). As media scholars have argued, these same beauty ideals are also reproduced in the media (e.g. Beltran 2005; Chito Childs 2009; Jefferson and Stake 2009; Rodriguez 1997; Wilson et al. 2003). This is evident in the examples of South Asian women in the media, particularly those created and cast by White, American producers.[3] As media producers favor casting women who are attractive, so too do the same media producers favor casting women of color who are attractive in terms of their proximity to White physical characteristics. Not only is this another reproduction of hegemonic ideology that favors one particular type of physical appearance over others, but it creates a social assumption around what an attractive South Asian can "look like."

In popular media, particularly through online magazines, the increasing examples of South Asian characters and actors in American film and television have been of much interest. In the article discussed at the beginning of this paper, Nina Shen Rastogi (2010) wrote,

> Yes, there are lots and lots of doctors and the occasional cab driver. But there's also a low-level government worker; a middle-American high-school principal; and a tough-talking, leather-boot-wearing, possibly bisexual Chicago investigator. If that's not progress, I don't know what is.

By referencing such examples as those characters in *Parks and Recreation, Glee,* and *The Good Wife,* respectively, Rastogi is making a point about this variety in South Asian representation. In the last few years, there have been many other articles published online, particularly those covering the TV show *Outsourced* and Mindy Kaling's latest TV show, *The Mindy Project* (e.g. Jacobs 2012; Lizardi 2011; Stewart 2013). Thus, while academic research on these contemporary South Asian characters is lacking, the interest in these shows, characters, and phenomenon itself is enough to fuel coverage from many online journalists and bloggers.

In order to incorporate these arguments into the field of sociology, it is important to acknowledge a few points. First, ethnic media characterizations are intentional decisions made by media producers. These characterizations reflect hegemonic ideologies and also reproduce commonly understood stereotypes. These stereotypes are the by-products of the US racial hierarchy. The racial hierarchy in turn is developed alongside immigration and assimilation trends, which further determine the qualities that an individual needs to become "American." All of these dynamics inform and influence 21st-century representations in American popular media.

38

ARABS AND MUSLIMS IN THE MEDIA AFTER 9/11

Representational Strategies for a "Postrace" Era

Evelyn Alsultany

EVELYN ALSULTANY is the Arthur F. Thurnau Professor and Associate Professor in the Department of American Culture and Director of Arab and Muslim American Studies at the University of Michigan.

AFTER 9/11 A STRANGE THING HAPPENED: there was an increase in sympathetic portrayals of Arabs and Muslims on US television. If a TV drama or Hollywood film represented an Arab or Muslim as a terrorist, then the story line usually included a "positive" representation of an Arab or Muslim to offset the negative depiction. Dozens of TV dramas portrayed Arab and Muslim Americans as the unjust target of hate crimes or as patriotic U.S. citizens. President George W. Bush was sure to distinguish between Arab and Muslim "friends" and "enemies," stating "the enemy of America is not our many Muslim friends; it is not our many Arab friends. Our enemy is a radical network of terrorists, and every government that supports them."[1] News reporters interviewed Arab and Muslim Americans, seemingly eager to include their perspectives on the terrorist attacks,

careful to point out their experiences with hate crimes.

Yet at the same time that sympathetic portrayals of Arab and Muslim Americans proliferated on U.S. commercial television in the weeks, months, and years after 9/11, hate crimes, workplace discrimination, bias incidents, and airline discrimination targeting Arab and Muslim Americans increased exponentially. According to the FBI, hate crimes against Arabs and Muslims multiplied by 1,600 percent from 2000 to 2001.[2] In just the first weeks and months after 9/11, the Council on American-Islamic Relations, the American-Arab Anti-Discrimination Committee, and other organizations documented hundreds of violent incidents experienced by Arab and Muslim Americans and people mistaken for Arabs or Muslims, including several murders. Dozens of airline passengers

Questions to Consider

Professor Alsultany argues that after 9/11, instead of the creation and casting of *all* Arab or Muslim characters on television as terrorists or enemies of the United States, some representations were "positive," depicting patriotic Arabs or Muslims to offset the Arab or Muslim who was a terrorist. She argues, however, that these "positive" representations had some unintended and negative consequences. What were they? How is it that a positive depiction of these groups could justify mistreatment against Arabs or Muslims?

perceived to be Arab or Muslim were removed from flights. Hundreds of Arab and Muslim Americans reported discrimination at work, receiving hate mail, and physical assaults, and their property, mosques, and community centers vandalized or set on fire.[3] In the decade after 9/11, such discriminatory acts have persisted.

In addition to individual citizens taking the law into their own hands, the U.S. government passed legislation that targeted Arabs and Muslims (both inside and outside the United States) and legalized the suspension of constitutional rights.[4] The government's overt propaganda of war was palatable to many citizens on edge and regarded with suspicion by others as the government passed the USA PATRIOT Act, initiated war in Afghanistan and later in Iraq, and explained the terrorist attacks to the public by stating "they hate us for our freedom."

Given that Arabs and Muslims have been stereotyped for over a century, given that 9/11 was such an opportune moment for further stereotyping, given that the U.S. government passed domestic and foreign policies that compromised the civil and human rights of Arabs and Muslims, and given that demonizing the enemy during times of war has been commonplace, why would sympathetic portrayals appear during such a fraught moment? As overt war propaganda has become increasingly transparent

and ineffective over the decades since World War II and the Cold War, the production and circulation of "positive" representations of the "enemy" have become essential to projecting the United States as benevolent, especially in its declaration of war and passage of racist policies. Positive representations of Arabs and Muslims have helped form a new kind of racism, one that projects antiracism and multiculturalism on the surface but simultaneously produces the logics and affects necessary to legitimize racist policies and practices.[5] It is no longer the case that the other is explicitly demonized to justify war or injustice. Now the other is portrayed sympathetically in order to project the United States as an enlightened country that has entered a postrace era.

The representational mode that has become standard since 9/11 seeks to balance a negative representation with a positive one, what I refer to as "simplified complex representations." These are strategies used by television producers, writers, and directors to give the impression that the representations they are producing are complex, yet they do so in a simplified way. These predictable strategies can be relied on if the plot involves an Arab or Muslim terrorist, but are a new standard alternative to (and seem a great improvement on) the stock ethnic villains of the past. I argue that simplified complex representations are the representational mode of the so-called postrace era, signifying a new standard of racial representations. These representations often challenge or complicate earlier stereotypes yet contribute to a multicultural or postrace illusion. Simplified complex representations have taken numerous forms in TV dramas and news reporting, some of which I outline here to highlight the various mechanisms through which positive imagery of Arabs and Muslims can operate to justify discrimination, mistreatment, and war against Arabs and Muslims.

SIMPLIFIED COMPLEX REPRESENTATIONS IN TV DRAMAS

Watching dozens of television shows between 2001 and 2009, it becomes evident that writers have increasingly created "positive" Arab and Muslim characters to show that they are sensitive to negative stereotyping. Such positive representations have taken several forms, such as a patriotic Arab or Muslim American, an Arab or Muslim who is willing to help the United States fight terrorism, or an innocent Arab or Muslim American who is the victim of post-9/11 hate crimes. If an Arab/Muslim terrorist is represented in the story line of a TV drama or film, then a "positive" representation of an Arab, Muslim, Arab American, or Muslim American is typically included, seemingly to subvert the stereotype of the terrorist.

Examples of patriotic Arab or Muslim American characters who assist the U.S. government in its fight against terrorism, either as a government agent or civilian, include Mohammad "Mo" Hassain, an Arab American Muslim character who is part of the USA Homeland Security Force on the show *Threat Matrix,* and Nadia Yassir, a dedicated member of the Counter Terrorist Unit on season 6 of 24.[6] In *Sleeper Cell* the "good" Muslim is the lead African American character, Darwyn Al-Sayeed, an undercover FBI agent who proclaims to his colleagues that terrorists have nothing to do with his faith and cautions them not to confuse the two.[7] This strategy challenges the notion that Arabs and Muslims are not American and/or un-American. Judging from the numbers of these patriots, it appears that writers have embraced this strategy as the most direct method to counteract potential charges of stereotyping.

Multiple stories appeared on TV dramas with Arab or Muslim Americans as the unjust targets of hate—as victims of violence and harassment. The viewer is nearly always positioned to sympathize with their plight. In an episode of *The Practice,* the government detains an innocent Arab American without due process or explanation and an attorney steps in to defend his rights.[8] On another episode of *The Practice,* an Arab American man is barred from being a passenger on an airplane, and it is debated in court whether airlines have the right to discriminate in a post-9/11 world in which Arab and Muslim identities are considered a security threat.[9] This emphasis on victimization and sympathy challenges long-standing representations of

Arabs and Muslims as terrorists that have inspired a lack of sympathy and even a sense of celebration when the Arab or Muslim character is killed.[10]

However, many of these sympathetic portrayals of Arabs and Muslims do the ideological work of justifying discriminatory policies. For example, a TV drama that portrays an Arab American as the unjust victim of post-9/11 discrimination often appears in a story line that concludes that it is unfortunate but inevitable that Arabs and Muslims will have to deal with discrimination because of the exceptional national security crisis. So, on the one hand, we have unusually sympathetic portrayals of Arabs and Muslims on network television. And on the other, the image often appears in a narrative that justifies discrimination against them. Furthermore, the inclusion of positive representations of Arabs and Muslims comes in limited forms: patriotic Americans and victimized Americans.

In addition to Arab and Muslim patriots and victims, TV dramas use numerous devices to circumvent the charge of stereotyping, including flipping the enemy and fictionalizing the country of the enemy. "Flipping the enemy" involves leading the viewer to believe that Muslim terrorists are plotting to destroy the United States, and then revealing that those Muslims are merely pawns or a front for Euro-American or European terrorists. The enemy's identity is thus flipped: viewers discover that the terrorist is not Arab, or they find that the Arab or Muslim terrorist is part of a larger network of international terrorists. During season 2 of *24,* Counter Terrorism Unit agent Jack Bauer spends the first half of the season tracking down a Middle Eastern terrorist cell, ultimately subverting a nuclear attack. In the second half of the season, we discover that European and Euro-American businessmen are behind the attack, goading the United States to declare a war on the Middle East in order to benefit from the increase in oil prices.[11] By including multiple terrorist identities, this strategy seeks to challenge the idea that terrorism is an Arab or Muslim monopoly.

It has become increasingly common for the country of the terrorist characters in television dramas to go unnamed. This strategy rests on the assumption that leaving the nationality of the villain blank eliminates potential offensiveness; if no particular country or ethnicity is named, then there is less reason for any particular group to be offended by the portrayal. In season 4 of *24*, the terrorist family is from an unnamed Middle Eastern country. They are possibly from Turkey, but where exactly is never stated; it is, we assume, intentionally left ambiguous.[12] In *The West Wing*, the fictional country "Qumar" is a source of terrorist plots; in season 8 of *24*, it is "Kamistan." Fictionalizing the country of the terrorist can give a show more latitude in creating salacious story lines that might be criticized if identified with an actual country.

Despite the shift away from the more blatant stereotypes of previous decades, Arab and Muslim identities are still understood and evaluated primarily in relation to terrorism. This binary focus, in turn, overpowers the strategies described above. Though some television writers and producers might desire to create innovative shows, devoid of stereotypes, such efforts are overwhelmed by the sheer momentum of the current representational scheme. Representations of Arab and Muslim identities in contexts that have nothing to do with terrorism remain strikingly unusual in American commercial media.[13]

SIMPLIFIED COMPLEX REPRESENTATIONS IN NEWS REPORTING

Versions of simplified complex representations that commonly appear in news reporting include the use of disclaimers and native informants, often found in stories about oppressed Muslim women. An examination of representations of Arab and Muslim women in the commercial news media after 9/11 reveals an overwhelming number of stories about the oppression of Muslim women. Within a year after 9/11, headlines often read as follows: "Lifting the Veil," "Free to Choose," "Unveiling Freedom," "Under the Veil," "Beneath the Veil," and "Unveiled Threat."[14] Journalists promised to take viewers "behind the veil" to reveal a secret,

hidden, mysterious world that would shed light on why Arabs/Muslims are terrorists. The oppression of women is framed as providing insight, a vital clue, into why terrorism occurs. What is revealed "behind the veil"? An assault of evidence is then presented, testifying to the oppressive and backward nature of Islam, especially when it comes to women. Story after story chronicles Muslim women dying in "honor killings"; facing female genital mutilation; being beaten on the streets of Afghanistan and Saudi Arabia for violating the dress code; sentenced to death for adultery and being buried alive in the ground or stoned to death; beaten for disobeying their husbands; raped by male family members; and being unable to get a divorce or child custody rights.[15]

A November 2001 article in *Time* magazine, "The Women of Islam," by Lisa Beyer, is one example of how journalists use simplified complex representational strategies while advancing a monolithic image of Islam as brutal, violent, and oppressive.[16] The article's subtitle reads: "The Taliban perfected subjugation. But nowhere in the Muslim world are women treated as equals." The article begins with a few concessions, stating that the prophet Muhammad was a feminist who improved the status of women in the seventh century. The author also writes:

> While it is impossible, given their diversity, to paint one picture of women living under Islam today, it is clear that the religion has been used in most Muslim countries not to liberate but to entrench inequality. The Taliban, with its fanatical subjugation of the female sex, occupies an extreme, but it nevertheless belongs on a continuum that includes, not so far down the line, Saudi Arabia, Kuwait, Pakistan and the relatively moderate states of Egypt and Jordan. Where Muslims have afforded women the greatest degree of equality—in Turkey—they have done so by overthrowing Islamic precepts in favor of secular rule. As Riffat Hassan, professor of religious studies at the University of Louisville, puts it, "The way Islam has been

practiced in most Muslim societies for centuries has left millions of Muslim women with battered bodies, minds and souls."[17]

Journalists often begin with a disclaimer—"It is impossible to capture the diversity of the Muslim world," or "These are not Islamic practices"—before presenting an onslaught of evidence to prove the brutality of Islam. The disclaimer signals that the journalist is aware of the diversity of Muslim lived experiences and is making an effort to present a semblance of sensitivity and awareness. While lip service is paid to diversity and complexity, the vast majority of evidence supports the opposite idea.

In addition to using disclaimers to signal that the news media do not intend to contribute to a monolithic portrait of Islam, and selectively including and excluding particular aspects of the context to understand the oppressed Muslim woman, another important simplified complex representational strategy is the use of native informants. This is evident in how the above quote by the Islamic feminist scholar Riffat Hassan is used. Several Muslim women, including Nonie Darwish, Wafa Sultan, and Ayaan Hirsi Ali, have made successful careers as women who have defected from Islam and become spokespersons for its inherent backwardness. While the oppressed Muslim woman narrative has cross-ideological appeal and has been taken up as a cause by both the Right and the Left, these native informants collaborate with right-wing agendas that aim not only to help oppressed women but also to denounce Islam entirely. Darwish, an Egyptian, is the founder of Arabs for Israel, the director of Former Muslims United, and the author of two books arguing that Islam is a retrograde religion.[18] Sultan, a Syrian, claims that Islam promotes violence; she is the author of a book titled *A God Who Hates*.[19] Hirsi Ali, a Somali, embraced atheism after 9/11; she has written numerous books in which she argues that Islam is incompatible with democracy.[20]

In a guest appearance on CNN's *Anderson Cooper 360*, Hirsi Ali commented on a case in which a woman in Saudi Arabia was raped and punished with two hundred lashes. In response to a question about what life is like for women in Saudi Arabia, Hirsi Ali said:

> For all women, the reality is stay in the house unless you have a pressing need to go outside. If you have a pressing need to go out you must wear the veil. If you marry, your husband can say three times, "I divorce you," and you are divorced. The other way around is not possible. The problem of child brides in Saudi Arabia is as common as drinking espresso coffee in Italy. It is because the Prophet Muhammad married a nine-year-old girl, every man in Saudi Arabia feels that he can marry a minor or he can marry off his daughter who is underage. You will be stoned, flogged if you commit or give the impression that you may have committed adultery. It is not nice being a woman in Saudi Arabia.[21]

Hirsi Ali's insider status authenticates her narrative. Moustafa Bayoumi argues that these Muslim women commentators are modern-day neo-orientalists who narrate stories about Islam for Western consumption. The stories they tell are about Islam as a system of tyranny that defeats human liberty and the subsequent need to either renounce or drastically reform Islam to be more like Christianity, Judaism, or even atheism.[22] These female native informants are a version of the "good Muslim" who confirms to Western viewers that Islam poses a threat to women and to the West. Sunaina Maira writes, "By definition, 'good' Muslims are public Muslims who can offer first-person testimonials, in the mode of the native informant, about the oppression of women in Islam, . . . and the hatred, racism, and anti-Semitism of Arabs and Muslims. These Muslim spokespersons are the darlings of the Right-wing and mainstream media, publish widely distributed books, and have slick websites."[23] While there are male Muslim spokespersons, it is the women specifically who authenticate a Western feminist narrative about Islam. These female spokespersons are often regarded and praised by the news media as "moderate Muslims."[24]

My point here is not that we should not feel outrage at human rights abuses and injustice. Rather, my point is that pity for the oppressed Muslim woman has been strategically used to advance U.S. imperialism. This highly mediated evocation of outrage for the plight of the oppressed Muslim woman inspires support of U.S. interventions in Arab and Muslim countries. It is no coincidence that inspiring outrage at the impact of U.S. foreign policies—from sanctions in Iraq that killed approximately five hundred thousand children to the ongoing wars in Iraq and Afghanistan that have killed over one hundred thousand civilians to the detention of hundreds of Muslims at Guantánamo Bay prison without being charged—is not part of the regular news cycle. Sympathy for Muslim women operates to justify withholding sympathy for Muslim men because they presumably deserve to be in Guantánamo or Abu Ghraib.

Arab and Muslim victims emerge as particularly important to simplified complex representations because they allow viewers to *feel* for "the enemy." The growth of this affect in turn comes to symbolize multicultural progress. Rather than demonize all Arabs and Muslims, having sympathy for some of them reflects an enlightened culture that can distinguish between the "good" and "bad" ones. The continued support of the U.S. empire after 9/11 has been made possible partly through the use of disclaimers, native informants, and other simplified complex representations that signal that the United States has achieved a postrace society that no longer discriminates.

Seeing the Big Picture **Television's Interracial Images: Some Fact, Mostly Fiction**

Section VIII in the appendix shows that racial minorities are underrepresented in most white-collar occupations. Think for a moment about some of your favorite television shows. Are racial minorities over- or underrepresented as lawyers or doctors or CEOs on television? Are the facts in the appendix regarding occupations by race consistent with what you see on television? What are the social implications of having racial minorities over- or underrepresented in the media?

PROJECT MUSE*

Arabs and Muslims in the Media after 9/11: Representational Strategies for a "Postrace" Era

Evelyn Alsultany

American Quarterly, Volume 65, Number 1, March 2013, pp. 161–169 (Article)

Published by The Johns Hopkins University Press

DOI: 10.1353/aq.2013.0008

➔ For additional information about this article http://muse.jhu.edu/journals/aq/summary/v065/65.1.alsultany.html

CRAZY HORSE MALT LIQUOR AND ATHLETES
The Tenacity of Stereotypes

WINNEBAGOS, CHEROKEES, APACHES, AND DAKOTAS

The Persistence of Stereotyping of American Indians in American Advertising and Brands

Debra Merskin

DEBRA MERSKIN is an associate professor at the University of Oregon. Her research interests focus on the representation of women and minorities in media, historical studies, and the social influences of the media.

FROM EARLY CHILDHOOD ON, WE HAVE all learned about "Indianness" from textbooks, movies, television programs, cartoons, songs, commercials, fanciful paintings, and product logos.[1] Since the turn of the century, American Indian images, music, and names have been incorporated into many American advertising campaigns and product images. Whereas patent medicines of the past featured a "coppery, feather-topped visage of the Indian" (Larson, 1937, p. 338), butter boxes of the present show the doe-eyed, buckskin-clad Indian "princess." These stereotypes are pervasive, but not necessarily consistent—varying over time and place from the "artificially idealistic" (noble savage) to present-day images of "mystical environmentalists or uneducated, alcoholic bingo-players confined to reservations" (Mihesuah, 1996, p. 9). Yet today a trip down the grocery store aisle still

Questions to Consider

Driving your Winnebago recreational vehicle (fully loaded 2001 Chieftain model) with Jeep Cherokee in tow, you pull into the Navajo National Park in New Mexico for your much-needed vacation. You sit down, light up a Natural American Spirit Cigarette, open a forty-ounce bottle of Crazy Horse Malt Liquor, and get ready to watch the World Series match between the Atlanta Braves (with their "Tomahawk Chop") and the Cleveland Indians. Each of these products draws on extremely stereotypical imagery of American Indians. Why, according to Debra Merskin, do these stereotypes continue, and what effect do these images have on the way individuals view American Indians?

reveals ice cream bars, beef jerky, corn meal, baking powder, malt liquor, butter, honey, sour cream, and chewing tobacco packages emblazoned with images of American Indians. Companies that use these images of Indians do so to build an association with an idealized and romanticized notion of the past through the process of branding (Aaker & Biel, 1993). Because these representations are so commonplace (Land O' Lakes maiden, Jeep Cherokee, Washington Redskins logo), we often fail to notice them, yet they reinforce long-held stereotypical beliefs about Native Americans.

Trade characters such as Aunt Jemima (pancake mix), Uncle Rastus (Cream of Wheat), and Uncle Ben (rice) are visual reminders of the subservient occupational positions to which blacks often have been relegated (Kern-Foxworth, 1994). Similarly, Crazy Horse Malt Liquor, Red Chief Sugar, and Sue Bee Honey remind us of an oppressive past. How pictorial metaphors on product labels create and perpetuate stereotypes of American Indians is the focus of this study. McCracken's (1993) Meaning Transfer Model and Barthes's (1972) semiotic analysis of brand images serve as the framework for

the analysis of four national brands. The following sections discuss how stereotypes are constructed and how they are articulated in, and perpetuated through, advertising.

To understand how labels on products and brand names reinforce long-held stereotypical beliefs, we must consider beliefs already in place that facilitated this process. Goings (1994), in his study of African American stereotypes, points out that "Racism was not a byproduct of the Civil War; it had clearly been around since the founding of the nation" (p. 7). Similarly, anti-Indian sentiments did not begin with the subjugation and dislocation efforts of the 1800s. Racial and ethnic images, part of American advertising for more than a century, were created in "less enlightened times" but have become a part of American popular culture and thought (Graham, 1993, p. 35) and persist today. The system of representation thereby becomes a "stable cultural convention that is taught and learned by members of a society" (Kates & Shaw-Garlock, 1999, p. 34).

Part of the explanation for the persistent use of these images can be found in the power and persuasiveness of popular culture representations. Goings's (1994) analysis of black collectibles and memorabilia from the 1880s to the 1950s is a useful analogy for understanding the construction of Native American stereotypes in popular culture. He suggests that "collectible" items such as salt and pepper shakers, trade cards, and sheet music with images of happy Sambos, plump mammies, or wide-eyed pickaninnies served as nonverbal articulations of racism made manifest in everyday goods. By exaggerating the physical features of African American men and women, and making them laughable and useable in everyday items, these household objects reinforced beliefs about the place of Blacks in American society. Aunt Jemima, the roly-poly mammy, and Uncle Rastus, the happy slave chef (ironically, both remain with us today), helped make Whites feel more comfortable with, and less guilty about, maintenance of distinctions on the basis of race well after Reconstruction. These items were meant for daily use, hence constantly and subtly reinforcing stereotypical beliefs.

Similarly, Berkhofer (1979) suggests that "the essence of the white image of the Indian has been the definition of American Indians in fact and in fancy as a separate and single other. Whether evaluated as noble or ignoble, whether seen as exotic or downgraded, the Indian as image was always alien to white" (p. xv). White images of Native Americans were similarly constructed through children's games, toys, tales, art, and theater of the 1800s. Whereas "Little Black Sambo" tales reinforced the construction of racist beliefs about Blacks, songs such as "Ten Little Indians" or "cowboy and Indian" games similarly framed Indian otherness in the White mind. Goings (1994) makes an important point about the source of the construction of objects that represent this way of thinking:

> It is important to note that Black memorabilia are figures from white American history. White Americans developed the stereotypes; white Americans produced the collectibles; and white American manufacturers and advertisers disseminated both the images and the objects to a white audience. (p. xix)

The maintenance of these kinds of beliefs satisfies the human need for psychological equilibrium and order, finding support and reinforcement in ideology. Defined as "typical properties of the 'social mind' of a group" (van Dijk, 1996, p. 56), ideologies provide a frame of reference for understanding the world. *Racist* ideologies serve several social functions operating to reproduce racism by legitimating social inequalities, thereby justifying racially or ethnically constructed differences. Racist ideology is used to (1) organize specific social attitudes into an evaluative framework for perceiving otherness, (2) provide the basis for "coordinated action and solidarity among whites," and (3) define racial and ethnic identity of the dominant group (van Dijk, 25–27). These beliefs and practices are thereby articulated in the production and distribution of racist discourse.

To every ad they see or hear, people bring a shared set of beliefs that serve as frames of reference for understanding the world around them. Beyond their obvious selling function, advertising images are about making meaning. Ads must "take into account not only the inherent qualities and attributes of the products they are trying to sell, but also the way in which they can make those properties mean something to us" (Williamson, 1978, p. 12).

Barthes (1972) describes these articulations as myth, that is, "a type of speech" or mode of signification that is conveyed by discourse that consists of many possible modes of representation including, but not limited to, writing, photography, publicity, and advertising. Myth is best described by the process of semiology (Barthes, 1972). Semiology "postulates a relation between two terms, a signifier and a signified" (Barthes, 1972, p. 112). The correlation of the terms *signifier, signified,* and *sign* is where associative meaning is made. What we see in an advertisement or product label, at first glance, are basic elements composed of linguistic signs (words) and iconic signs (visuals). Barthes (1972) uses a rose, for example, as a symbol of passion. Roses are not passion per se, but rather the roses (signifier) + concept of passion (signified) = roses (sign). He states that "the signifier is empty, the sign is full, it is a meaning" (Barthes, 1972, p. 113). Another example that involves race is the use of Aunt Jemima for maple syrup. We see the representation of a bandana-clad black woman who suggests the mammy of the Deep South (signified). When placed on the bottle of syrup (sign), meaning is transferred to the otherwise ambiguous product—care giving, home cooking, and food sharing. The sign is formed at the intersection between a brand name and a meaning system that is articulated in a particular image. Quite simply, a sign, whether "object, word, or picture," has a "particular meaning to a person or group of people. It is neither the thing nor the meaning alone, but the two together" (Williamson, 1978, p. 17).

McCracken (1993, p. 125), who defines a brand as a "bundle or container of meaning," expanded on the Barthesian analysis and developed a framework for understanding the cultural relationship that brands have within society. His anthropological model illustrates the meanings of brands. McCracken shows how brands assume meaning through advertising, combined with consumption behavior, and the nature of common knowledge that consumers bring to this system. The present study expands on this process by adding a reinforcement loop from consumer back to the culture where stereotypes are experienced and recirculated through the system.

A brand can have gendered meaning (maleness/femaleness), social standing (status), nationality (country meaning), and ethnicity/race (multicultural meaning). A brand can also stand for notions of tradition, trustworthiness, purity, family, nature, and so on. McCracken (1993) uses the Marlboro man as an example of these components with which a simple red and white box came to signify freedom, satisfaction, competence, maleness, and a quintessentially American, Western character. The product becomes part of the constellation of meanings that surrounds it and thereby "soaks up" meanings. When the rugged Marlboro man is situated on his horse, on the open plain, almost always alone, the meanings of the constellation become clear—freedom, love of the outdoors, release from the confines of industrialized society—he is a "real man," self-sufficient and individualistic. These meanings become part of a theme made up of prototypical content while simultaneously being "idealizations and not reality itself" (Schmitt & Simonson, 1997, p. 124).

Advertisements are created in such a way as to boost the commodity value of brand names by connecting them to images that resonate with the social and cultural values of a society. These images are loaded with established ideological assumptions that, when attached to a commodity, create the commodity sign. Tools of branding are thereby used to create a particular image in the mind of the consumer. According to van Dijk (1996), this pattern often serves to present an U.S. versus THEM dichotomy, with U.S. being white, "positive, tolerant, modern," and THEM being minorities who are "problematic, deviant and threatening" (pp. 26–27). Hence, attitudes, beliefs, and behavior that are racist serve to support a dominant ideology that focuses on difference and separatism.

These ideas and values are articulated through the construction, maintenance, and perpetuation of stereotypes. Stereotypes are overgeneralized beliefs that

> get hold of the few simple, vivid, memorable, easily grasped, and widely recognized

characteristics about a person, reduce everything about the person to those traits, exaggerate and simplify them, and fix them without change or development to eternity. (Hall, 1997, p. 258)

An example is the way the "Indian problem" of the 1800s has been shown in "cowboy and Indian" films. In his analysis of the representation of Indians in film, Strickland (1998, p. 10) asks, "What would we think the American Indian was like if we had only the celluloid Indian from which to reconstruct history?" (Strickland, 1998, p. 10). The cinematic representation includes the Indian as a

> bloodthirsty and lawless savage; the Indian as enemy of progress; the Indian as tragic, but inevitable, victim; the Indian as a lazy, fat, shiftless drunk; the Indian as oil-rich illiterate; the Indian as educated half-breed unable to live in either a white or Indian world; the Indian as nymphomaniac; the Indian as noble hero; the Indian as stoic and unemotional; the Indian as the first conservationist. (Strickland, 1998, p. 10)

Champagne's (1994) analysis of Indians in films and theater suggests that the longevity of James Fenimore Cooper's *Last of the Mohicans*, evidenced by its many film treatments, demonstrates that "Hollywood prefers to isolate its Indians safely within the romantic past, rather than take a close look at Native American issues in the contemporary world" (p. 719).

Natty Bumppo, in James Fenimore Cooper's *Deer-slayer*, is a literary example of the male who goes from a state of "uncultured animality" to a state of "civilization and culture" (Green, 1993, p. 327). Larson (1937) describes how this stereotype was translated into a tool for marketing patent medicines:

> No sooner had James Fenimore Cooper romanticized the Indian in the American imagination in his novels than patent-medicine manufacturers, quick to sense and take advantage of this new enthusiasm, used the red man as symbol and token for

a great variety of ware. How the heart of the purchaser—filled, like as not, with the heroic exploits of Cooper's Indians—must have warmed as he gazed at the effigy, symbolic of "Nature's Own Remedy." (p. 338)

The female savage becomes an Indian princess who "renounces her own family, marries someone from the dominate culture and assimilates into it" (Green, 1993, p. 327), for example, Pocahontas. From this perspective, Indians are thought of as childlike and innocent, requiring the paternalistic care of Whites; that is, they are tameable. In her study of Indian imagery in *Dr. Quinn, Medicine Woman,* Bird (1996, p. 258) suggests that what viewers see is a white fantasy filled with white concerns around "guilt and retrospective outrage." Green's (1993) analysis of the use of male Indian images in ads posits that Natives continue to be portrayed according to stereotypical images: (1) noble savage (the stoic, innocent, child of nature); (2) civilizable savage (redeemable, teachable); and (3) bloodthirsty savage (fierce, predatory, cultureless, animalistic). Taken together, these studies suggest that historically constructed images and beliefs about American Indians are at the essence of stereotypical thinking and are easily translated into product images.

To study the articulation of racist ideology in brand images, four currently available national products (Land O' Lakes butter, Sue Bee Honey, Big Chief [Monitor] Sugar, and Crazy Horse Malt Liquor) were analyzed according to Barthes's (1972) semiotic analysis. First, the material object was identified (signifier); second, the associative elements were identified (signified); and, third, these were brought together in what we as consumers recognize as the sign. Company Web sites, press releases, and product packages were used for visual and textual information. Several attempts to communicate directly with the companies yielded no response. Through this method of analysis we can see how these meanings are transferred to the different products on the basis of both race and gender.

The following section presents a descriptive analysis of Land O' Lakes, Sue Bee Honey, Big Chief (Monitor) Sugar, and Crazy Horse Malt Liquor brand images.

LAND O' LAKES

Although not the first national manufacturer to draw on the mystique of Indianness (that honor goes to Red Man Tobacco in 1904), Land O' Lakes is certainly one of the more prominent. In 1921, the Minnesota Cooperative Creameries Association opened for business in Arden Hills, Minnesota. This company served as the central shipping agent for a small group of small, farmer-owned dairy cooperatives (Morgan, 1986, p. 63). In 1924, the group wanted a different name and solicited ideas from farmers. Mrs. E. B. Foss and Mr. George L. Swift came up with the winning name—Land O' Lakes, "a tribute to Minnesota's thousands of sparkling lakes" (p. 63). The corporate Web site opens with a photograph of a quiet lake amid pine trees and blue sky. The copy under the photograph reads:

> Welcome to Land O' Lakes. A land unlike anywhere else on earth. A special place filled with clear, spring-fed lakes. Rivers and streams that dance to their own rhythms through rich, fertile fields. It's the land we call home. And from it has flowed the bounty and goodness we bring to you, our neighbors and friends. (Land O' Lakes, 2000)

In addition, "The now famous Indian maiden was also created during the search for a brand name and trademark. Because the regions of Minnesota and Wisconsin were the legendary lands of Hiawatha and Minnehaha, the idea of an Indian Maiden took form" (Land O' Lakes, 2000). A painting was sent to the company of an Indian maiden facing the viewer, holding a butter carton with a background filled with lakes, pines, flowers, and grazing cows.

At the Land O' Lakes corporate Web site, the director of communications includes a statement about the maiden image, where he agrees that the logo, the "Indian Maiden," has powerful connotations (Land O' Lakes). Hardly changed since its introduction in the 1920s, he says that Land O' Lakes has built on the "symbolism of the purity of the products" (Burnham, 1992). The company "thought the Indian maiden would be a good image. She represents Hiawatha and the Land of Gitchygoomee and the names of Midwest towns and streets that have their roots in the American Indian population" (Burnham, 1992).

The signifier is thereby the product, be it butter, sour cream, or other Land O' Lakes products. The Indian woman on the package is associated with youth, innocence, nature, and purity. The result is the generic "Indian maiden." Subsequently, the qualities stereotypically associated with this beaded, buckskinned, doe-eyed young woman are transferred to the company's products. Green's "noble savage" image is extended to include the female stereotype.

SUE BEE HONEY

The Sioux Honey Association, based in Sioux City, Iowa, is a cooperative of honey producers, yielding 40 million pounds of honey annually (Sioux Honey Association, 2000). Corporate communications describe a change of the product name in 1964 from Sioux Bee to Sue Bee, "to reflect the correct pronunciation of the name" (Sioux Honey Association, 2000). The brand name and image are reinforced on trucks (both real and toys), on the bottles and jars in which the honey is sold, and through collectibles such as coffee mugs and recipe books.

Sue Bee Honey also draws upon the child-of-nature imagery in an attempt to imbue qualities of purity into their products. If we were to view Sue Bee in her full form (as she is shown on many specialty items such as mugs, glasses, and jars) we would see that she is an Indian maiden on top, with braided hair and headband, and a bee below the waist. Changing the spelling of her name from "Sioux Bee" to "Sue Bee" could be interpreted in a variety of ways—possibly simply as a matter of pronunciation, as the company asserts, or as an effort to draw attention away from the savage imagery stereotypically attributed to members of this tribe and more toward the little girlishness of the image. In this case, the product is honey, traditionally associated with trees and forests and

natural places. This association works well with the girl–child Indian stereotype. By placing the girl bee on the package of honey, consumers can associate the innocence, purity, and naturalness attributed to Native American females with the quality of the product.

In the tradition of Pocahontas, both the Land O' Lakes and the Sue Bee maidens symbolize innocence, purity, and virginity—children of nature. The maiden image signifies a female "Indianness." She is childlike, as she happily offers up perhaps honey or butter (or herself) that "is as pure and healthy as she is" (Dotz & Morton, 1996, p. 11). The maiden's image is used to represent attempts to get back to nature, and the association is that this can be accomplished through the healthy, wholesome products of Land O' Lakes. Both images are encoded with socially constructed meanings about female Indian sexuality, purity, and nature.

MONITOR SUGAR COMPANY

Founded in 1901, the Monitor Sugar Company processes approximately 4% of U.S. beet production into sugar (granulated, powdered, brown, and icing; Monitor Sugar Company, 2000). For 60 years, the company has been producing sugar from beets, relying on the image of an American Indian in full headdress to sell the sugar goods. The products are available on grocery store shelves and in bulk for institutions, delivered by trucks with the Big Chief logo emblazoned on the sides.

So, who is this Chief said to represent? Is he a bona fide tribal leader or a composite Indian designed to communicate naturalistic characteristics associated with Indians with the sugar? Green's (1993) savage typology suggests that this individual is a combination of the noble savage (natural) and the bloodthirsty savage (ferocious). He is proud, noble, and natural and yet he is wearing a ceremonial headdress that communicates strength and stoicism.

CRAZY HORSE MALT LIQUOR

A 40-ounce beverage that is sold in approximately 40 states (Metz & Thee, 1994), Crazy Horse Malt Liquor is brewed by the Heilman Brewing Company of Brooklyn, New York. Crazy Horse Malt Liquor employs the image of Tasunke Witko (Crazy Horse) on the label of its malt liquor. On the front of the bottle is an American Indian male wearing a headdress that appears to be an eagle feather bonnet, and there is a symbol representing a medicine wheel—both sacred images in Lakota and other Native cultures (Metz & Thee, 1994).

Image analysis shows that the sign is that of an actual Indian chief. Signified, however, are beliefs about Indians as warriors, westward expansion, how mighty the consumer might be by drinking this brand, and wildness of the American Western frontier.

This brand, perhaps more than any other, has come under public scrutiny because it is the image of a particular person. A revered forefather of the Oglala Sioux tribe of South Dakota, Crazy Horse died in 1877 (Blalock, 1992). The labels feature the prominent image of Chief Crazy Horse, who has long been the subject of stories, literature, and movies. Larger than life, he has played a role in American mythology.

Signifying Green's (1993) bloodthirsty savage image, Crazy Horse Malt Liquor makes use of American myths through image and association. Ironically, Crazy Horse objected to alcohol and warned his nation about the destructive effects of liquor (Specktor, 1995). As a sign, Crazy Horse represents a real symbol of early American life and westward expansionism. He was, according to the vice president of the Oglala Sioux Tribe, a "warrior, a spiritual leader, a traditional leader, a hero who has always been and is still revered by our people" (Hill, 1992; Metz & Thee, 1994, p. 50). This particular image brings together some interesting aspects of branding. Not only is the noble and bloodthirsty savage stereotype brought together in a proud, but ultimately defeated, Indian chief, but

also this is an image of a real human being. The association of alcohol with that image, as well as targeting the Indian population, draws on assumptions of alcohol abuse.[2]

Although there are dozens of possible examples of Native images on product labels, ranging from cigarette packages to sports utility vehicles, the examples discussed above illustrate the principles behind semiotics. The four presented here are significant examples of national brands employing stereotypical representations. When people are made aware of these products, they see how these images are consistently found in many products that employ Indian stereotypes either in product names or in their logos.

Many of these signs and symbols have been with us so long we no longer question them. Product images on packages, in advertisements, on television, and in films are nearly the only images non-Indians ever see of Native Americans. The covers of romance novels routinely feature Indian men sweeping beautiful non-Indian women off their feet as their bodices are torn away. These stereotypical representations of American Indians deny that they are human beings, and present them as existing only in the past and as single, monolithic Indians (Merskin, 1998).

American Indians are certainly not the only racial or ethnic group to be discriminated against, overtly or covertly. Aunt Jemima and Rastus certainly have their origins in dehumanizing, one-dimensional images based on a tragic past. Yet, like Betty Crocker, these images have been updated. Aunt Jemima has lost weight and the bandana, and the Frito Bandito has disappeared (Burnham, 1992). But the Indian image persists in corporate marketing and product labeling.

These are highly visible and perhaps more openly discussed than images that appear on the products we see in grocery store aisles. An Absolut Vodka ad shows an Eskimo pulling a sled of vodka and a GreyOwl Wild Rice package features an Indian with braids, wearing a single feather, surrounded by a circle that represents (according to GreyOwl's distribution manager) the "oneness of nature" (Burnham, 1992). A partial list of others includes

Apache helicopter, Jeep Cherokee, Apache rib doormats, Red Man Tobacco, Kleek-O the Eskimo (Cliquot Club ginger ale), Dodge Dakota, Pontiac, the Cleveland Indians, Mutual of Omaha, Calumet Baking Powder, Mohawk Carpet Mills, American Spirit cigarettes, Eskimo pies, Tomahawk mulcher, Winnebago Motor Homes, Indian Motorcycles, Tomahawk missiles, many high school sports teams, and the music behind the Hamm's beer commercials that begins "From the land of sky blue waters." And the list goes on.

Change is coming, but it is slow. For one thing, American Indians do not represent a significant target audience to advertisers. Representing less than 1% of the population, and the most economically destitute of all ethnic minority populations, American Indians are not particularly useful to marketers. Nearly 30% live below the official poverty line, in contrast with 13% of the general U.S. population (Cortese, 1999, p. 117). Without the population numbers or legal resources, it is nearly impossible for the voices of Natives to be heard, unlike other groups who have made some representational inroads. According to Westerman (1989), when minority groups speak, businesses are beginning to listen: "That's why Li'l Black Sambo and the Frito Bandito are dead. They were killed by the very ethnic groups they portrayed" (p. 28).

Not only does stereotyping communicate inaccurate beliefs about Natives to whites, but also to Indians. Children, all children, are perhaps the most important recipients of this information, for it is during childhood that difference is first learned. If, during the transition of adolescence, Native children internalize these representations that suggest that Indians are lazy, alcoholic by nature, and violent, this misinformation can have a life-long impact on perceptions of self and others. As Lippmann (1922/1961) wrote,

> The subtlest and most pervasive of all influences are those which create and maintain the repertory of stereotypes. We are told about the world before we see it. We imagine most things before we experience them. (p. 89)

By playing a game of substitution, by inserting other ethnic groups or races into the same situation, it becomes clear that there is a problem. Stereotypical images do not reside only in the past, because the social control mechanisms that helped to create them remain with us today.

Future research should continue to examine how the advertising and marketing practice of branding contributes to the persistent use of racist images on product labels. This study adds to the sparse literature on media representations of Native Americans in general and adds to Green's (1993) typology by including female counterparts to the male savage stereotypes. Future research could explore more images of Native Americans in ads and on products. Qualitative research with members of different tribes would add depth to this area of study.

Seeing the Big Picture   **The Tomahawk Chop: Racism in Image and Action**

Look through the appendix and notice the relative quality-of-life measures of American Indians. What is the link between this group's socioeconomic standing and the way they are portrayed in the media?

TAKING A KNEE

Jeremy Adam Smith and Dacher Keltner

JEREMY ADAM SMITH is the editor of *Greater Good* magazine which is published by the University of California, Berkeley Greater Good Science Center. DACHER KELTNER is professor of psychology at the University of California, Berkeley.

WHAT DOES IT MEAN TO KNEEL? What emotions and beliefs does this action communicate? Does your culture or group membership affect how you see gestures like kneeling?

Those are some of the scientific questions raised when San Francisco 49ers quarterback Colin Kaepernick decided last year to kneel, instead of stand, for "The Star-Spangled Banner" before a preseason game. Teammate Eric Reid joined him. Their cause? Police violence against unarmed black people.

His knee unleashed a movement—and triggered a chain of events that culminated last week in the president of the United States calling a player who kneels a "son of a bitch." Over the following days, dozens of NFL players—including entire teams—"took the knee" before their games. In response, crowds booed.

To some, Kaepernick and the players who kneel with him are "unpatriotic," "ungrateful," "disrespectful," "degenerate," to quote just a few of the descriptions hurled their way. To others,

Kaepernick's act—for which he may have paid dearly, as he is now unsigned—makes him a hero.

What's going on?

At first glance, research into emotion and nonverbal communication suggests that there is nothing threatening about kneeling. Instead, kneeling is almost always deployed as a sign of deference and respect. We once kneeled before kings and queens and altars; we kneel to ask someone to marry, or at least men did in the old days. We kneel to get down to a child's level; we kneel to beg.

While we can't know for sure, kneeling probably derives from a core principle in mammalian nonverbal behavior: make the body smaller and look up to show respect, esteem, and deference. This is seen, for example, in dogs and chimps, who reduce their height to show submissiveness. Kneeling can also be a posture of mourning and sadness. It makes the one who kneels more vulnerable. In some situations, kneeling can be seen as a request for protection—which is completely appropriate in Kaepernick's case, given the motive of his protest.

As sports protests go, taking the knee might not seem nearly as subversive or dangerous as thrusting a black-power fist into the air, as Tommie Smith and John Carlos did during their medal ceremony at the 1968 Summer Olympics in Mexico City. Researchers David Matsumoto and Jess Tracy show that even blind athletes from over 20 countries thrust their arms in the air in triumph after winning, which reveals the deep-seated urge to signal power with that body-expanding gesture. You can also find power in the fist. In the Darwinian sense, the fist is the antithesis of the affiliative, open hand, but when we combine a raised arm with a fist it becomes something more communicative—a rallying cry. It's a gesture that seeks to bring one group together while warning another away.

None of that should be too surprising. But there is an important point of similarity in the raised black-power fist—which makes bodies bigger—and the bended knee, which makes us smaller. Both Carlos and Smith bowed their heads in Mexico City, in a sign of respect and humility that accompanies their social signal of strength and triumph. That mix of messages makes the black-power salute one of the most famous, complex, effective nonverbal protests in our lifetimes—one that we can see echoed on today's football field.

Which returns us to the kneel. Kneeling is a sign of reverence, submissiveness, deference—and sometimes mourning and vulnerability. But with a single, graceful act, Kaepernick invested it with a double meaning. He didn't turn his back as the anthem was played, which would have been a true sign of disrespect. Nor did he rely on the now-conventionalized black-power fist.

Rather, he transformed a collective ritual—the playing of the national anthem—into something somber, a reminder of how far we still have to go to realize the high ideal of equal protection under the law that the flag represents. The athletes who followed him are showing reverence for the song and the flag, but they are simultaneously deviating from cultural norms at the moment their knees hit the grass.

By transforming this ritual, the players woke us up. Our amygdalae activate as soon as our brains spot deviations from routine, social norms, and in-group tendencies. We want to know what's happening and why. We need to know if the deviation poses a threat to us or our group. This may start to explain why so many Americans reacted with such fear and rage to a few athletes kneeling on the field in the midst of a national ritual.

But there's a lot more to it than that.

"Group membership affects interpretation of body language because groups develop norms and expectations around behavior, language, and life," says our UC Berkeley colleague Rodolfo Mendoza-Denton, an expert on intergroup communication. "Breaking these norms is used intentionally to signal disagreement with the norms, as well as to signal that one is not conforming. It sparks strong emotion and backlash precisely because of its symbolic meaning—a threat to the status quo."

It matters that most of the athletes are black and much of the audience is white, that the ancestors of one group were brought here as slaves and the ancestors of the other were their owners. That's why, when the Pittsburgh Steelers stayed in the locker room as the anthem played, one Pennsylvania fire chief called their coach a "no good n*****" on Facebook, amplifying the racial themes of the debate. That's why Michigan's police director called them "degenerates."

When you mix power differences with intergroup dynamics, more factors come into play. Our lab has found that high-power people (say, the president or members of the numerical majority) are more likely to misinterpret nonverbal behavior. The experience of having power makes us less accurate in reading suffering on the faces of strangers and emotions in static photos of facial expressions. Powerful people are less able to take the perspective of others; they're quicker to confuse friendliness with flirtatiousness. This is the empathy deficit of people in power, one found in many kinds of studies.

Thus, we should not be surprised that many white people misread the meaning of "taking the knee" and fail to see the respect, concern, and even vulnerability inherent in kneeling. Of course, it is also the case that some white people may want to see black people terrorized by police and politically disenfranchised. Any effort by African Americans, no matter how deferential, to raise these issues will incite anger from those who benefit—emotionally or materially—from America's racial hierarchy.

But from a psychological perspective, that political elucidation still doesn't quite explain the specific inability of a majority of white football fans to interpret taking the knee according to universal human norms. And why would they take the misperception further, to actually see this humble posture as an act of aggression against America?

There is some evidence from Princeton's Susan Fiske and Penn State's Theresa Vescio that high-power people, in not attending carefully to others, are more likely to stereotype others, and more likely to miss individual nuances in behavior. This means that some white-majority football fans may be falling victim to the stereotype of African Americans—particularly large, well-muscled, pro football players—as violent and aggressive. In fact, as we've discussed, kneeling is actually the opposite of an aggressive signal.

What's the way forward from here? One of us (Dacher Keltner) has co-authored a paper with colleague Daniel Cordaro that examines the expression of 20 emotions across five cultures. We found that while most outward emotional expressions are shared or partially shared, a quarter are not. It's in that non-shared space that intercultural conflict flares up—but that conflict can sometimes lead to cross-pollination, as people come to comprehend each other and synchronize their gestures.

Will Americans one day look back on Kaepernick's symbolic act as a moment when we started to understand each other just a little bit better? When many kinds of people were galvanized to work concretely on the problems of police brutality and racial bias in the criminal justice system, instead of discounting the concerns of African Americans?

Perhaps. Such a time seems very distant from where we are right now, as our society's leaders foster racial antagonism and people cannot seem to recognize the emotion and belief behind even the gentlest of gestures. Change happens, but it doesn't happen all by itself. Sometimes, you need to kneel to conquer.

HOW AMERICA'S COMPLEXION CHANGES

A NATIONALLY DISTRIBUTED, FULL-PAGE magazine advertisement placed by IBM depicts nine of its employees at a business meeting. The employees, presumably managers, are focusing on a white-haired man who is pointing to a chart. The activity depicted is rather mundane—meetings of this type take place thousands of times every business day. What makes this ad exceptional is what it is selling. In large letters across the top of the page, the text of the ad announces "Diversity Works." The employees shown in the hand-drawn advertisement consist, in order, of an older white woman, a black woman, an Asian woman, a white man, an older black man with white hair, two men of ambiguous racial identity, and a white woman in a wheelchair. The racial and ethnic makeup of the cartoon characters in this ad is intended to convey to readers that IBM, as the supporting text tells us, "values individual differences." What is particularly interesting is the lack of white men in this rendering of the inner workings of a large corporation.

IBM may indeed value diversity, but the reality is that the upper ranks of corporate management are still the domain of white men. About 4% of the Fortune 500 companies are run by people of color (19 out of 500). How corporate America presents its workforce to the public and how diverse the organization actually is, especially as one moves up the occupational ranks, is a contradiction. Perhaps there is a reason this advertisement was a drawing and not an actual photograph of a diverse work environment. What occupations or organizations can you name in which high-status positions reflect the racial, ethnic, and gender composition of the United States? Think about the racial and ethnic composition of members of Congress, or the CEOs of the Fortune 500 companies, or the fifty state governors, or tenured college professors. What is the race and gender of your university or college president? What about the racial or ethnic background of sports or entertainment celebrities? What patterns emerge, and what do they mean?

We are an incredibly diverse nation. We are reminded of this by advertisements promoting diversity from corporations like Microsoft, Apple, McDonald's, Texaco, Denny's, and Ford. We are reminded of this when we are repeatedly told that by the year 2050, about half of U.S. residents will be white and the other half will be black, Asian, and Latino. We are reminded of this when we debate the relative merits of affirmative action, bilingual education, or immigration quotas.

In the public imagination, the idea of ethnic and racial diversity seems to be simultaneously celebrated, feared, and reviled. The United States is promoted as the land of opportunity, but some groups have had more opportunity than others. Why? The United States is defined as a country of immigrants, yet many citizens are fearful that the "new wave" of immigrants will radically change "American" culture. Why? The United States is proclaimed as a color-blind nation, yet inequities based on race and ethnicity are still the norm for a sizable part of the population. If we are a color-blind nation, why is it very likely you will marry someone from the same racial background?

The readings in Part IV examine these contradictions. The five readings in the first section of Part IV, Race, Ethnicity, and Immigration, focus on the changing complexion of the United States. David Scott FitzGerald and David Cook-Martín point out that race and racism have always been the central framing mechanism for American immigration policy. Stephen Steinberg calls into question the assertion that the United States is a melting pot by pointing out that some groups have never been "melted" into the stew because they were not allowed in the pot. John Logan documents the rise of black immigrants from Africa and the Caribbean and the unique immigration experiences of these groups. This exceptionally diverse group often gets "lumped" by the media with African Americans or Latinos, but Logan demonstrates that such groupings would be a mistake. Michael Suleiman examines a community that until very recently received very little attention from the mainstream media. Suleiman describes the ebb and flow of Arab immigrants to the United States and their socioeconomic success relative to other immigrant groups. Mary Waters examines mobility and racial identity construction to explore how race, ethnicity, and opportunity shape the experiences of Afro-Caribbeans in New York City.

The second section, Race and Romance: Blurring Boundaries, explores historical and contemporary trends in interracial marriage. Gretchen Livingston and Anna Brown detail current trends, which are on the upswing, of interracial marriage.

Law Professor Randall Kennedy uses popular representations of interracial couples in the media to examine just how much progress we have made in the area of interracial romance. Heather Dalmage explains how and why "racial borders" are patrolled in order to promote racial endogamy.

Kimberly McClain DaCosta examines how the color line is being redrawn within the context of the rise of multiracial families and individuals who define themselves as occupying more than one racial identity.

The last section, Living with Less Racism: Strategies for Individual Action, suggests ways individuals can think about addressing racial inequality at the level of public policy and in everyday interactions with those around them. Meizhu Lui and associates discuss which social policies could ameliorate racial inequality, while Charles Gallagher suggests ten things we can do to ameliorate racism as we go about our day.

RACE, ETHNICITY, AND IMMIGRATION

CULLING THE MASSES

The Democratic Origins of Racist Immigration Policy in the Americas

David Scott FitzGerald and David Cook-Martín

DAVID SCOTT FITZGERALD is Theodore E. Gildred Chair in U.S.-Mexican Relations, professor of sociology, and co-director of the Center for Comparative Immigration Studies. DAVID COOK-MARTÍN is a professor of sociology at Grinnell College and assistant vice-president of global education.

THE UNITED STATES

Paragon of Liberal Democracy and Racism

The United States is the world's oldest continuous democracy and has often been described as a global beacon—"the only example of a true liberal democracy that the rest of the world would emulate."[1] The United States was also the first independent country in the Americas to introduce racial selection in policies of naturalization (1790) and immigration (1803) and late to end racial discrimination in policies of naturalization (1952) and immigration (1965). What explains the paradox of a liberal democracy culling newcomers by race while proclaiming that all men are created equal? It is one facet of a deep contradiction in U.S. history—the promise of democracy in the midst of slavery and exclusions of a long list of groups—that has perplexed observers since Alexis de Tocqueville.[2]

Questions to Consider

We like to tell the world that the United States is a "nation of immigrants." While there is certainly some truth to this claim, the reality is that most of the immigrants who came to the United States were at some point mistreated, stereotyped, persecuted, marginalized, or subject to prejudice and discrimination. What the authors explore is the extent to which the negative perceptions of immigrants got codified into law and the role race played in this process. What parallels do you see with the historic mistreatment of immigrants in the early twentieth century and how immigrants are treated today?

White Naturalization

Within a decade of winning independence, the United States reserved naturalization for whites. Aside from backward steps for free blacks between 1857 and 1866 and the muddled court cases and bureaucratic regulations defining whether various groups of Asians were white in the early twentieth century, there was a slow, episodic widening of racial eligibility to naturalize until all restrictions had fallen by 1952. The internal dynamics of liberalism did not drive this opening. With the important exception of the inclusion of blacks following the Union victory in the Civil War, the expanding foreign policy interests of the U.S. government in Latin America and Asia explain the widening circle of eligibility.

Security interests guided immigration and nationality policy during the colonial period. Britain's colonies in North America were sandwiched between Catholic French and Spanish rivals. The British parliament's naturalization act of 1740 accepted Jews but excluded Catholics.[3] Many British colonies charged head taxes on immigrating Catholics and offered positive inducements only to

TABLE 1 ■ Principal U.S. Laws of Immigration and Nationality Selecting by Ethnicity	
1790	Naturalization restricted to free whites[1]
1803	Restriction of black immigration[2]
1862	Ban on Chinese "coolie" migration[3]
1870	Naturalization allowed for persons of African descent[4]
1875	Ban on subjects from "China, Japan, or any other oriental country" coming for "lewd or immoral purposes"[5]
1882	Exclusion of Chinese labor immigration[6]
1907–08	"Gentlemen's Agreement" restricts Japanese[7]
1917	Creation of Asiatic Barred Zone and literacy tests[8]
1921	Quota system favoring northwestern Europeans[9]
1924	Quota system further favoring northwestern Europeans and banning aliens ineligible to citizenship[10]
1940	Naturalization allowed for "descendants of races indigenous to the Western Hemisphere"[11]
1943	Repeal of Chinese exclusion; Chinese become eligible to naturalize[12]
1952	End of racial prerequisites to naturalization; symbolic Asian quotas[13]
1965	End of national-origins quotas; caps on annual preference visas per country for Eastern Hemisphere[14]
1968	Caps on annual preference visas for Western Hemisphere take effect[15]
1976	Applies the annual caps on preference visas per country to the Western Hemisphere[16]
1978	Single worldwide preference visa cap[17]

| 1986 | Mass legalization program; small NP-5 program favoring citizens of countries "adversely affected" by the 1965 act[18] |
| 1990 | "Diversity visa" program[19] |

1. 1790 Uniform Rule of Naturalization, 1 Stat. 103, Sec. 1.

2. Act of Feb. 28, 1803, ch. 10, 2 Stat. 205.

3. 1862 Act to Prohibit the "Coolie Trade" by American Citizens in American Vessels, 12 Stat. 340.

4. Naturalization Act of 1870, 16 Stat. 254, Sec. 7.

5. 1875 Page Law, 18 Stat. 477.

6. 1882 Chinese Exclusion Act, 22 Stat. 58.

7. 1908 Root-Takahira Agreement.

8. 1917 Immigration Act, 39 Stat. 874.

9. 1921 Emergency Quota Law, 42 Stat. 5.

10. 1924 Immigration Act, 43 Stat. 153.

11. 1940 Nationality Act, 54 Stat. 1137.

12. 1943 Magnuson Act, 57 Stat. 600.

13. 1952 Immigration and Nationality Act, 66 Stat. 163.

14. 1965 Immigration and Nationality Act, 79 Stat. 911.

15. 1965 Immigration and Nationality Act, 79 Stat. 911.

16. 1976 Eilberg Act, 90 Stat. 2703.

17. Act of October 5, 1978, 92 Stat. 907.

18. 1986 Immigration Reform and Control Act, 100 Stat. 3359.

19. Immigration and Nationality Act, 104 Stat. 4978.

Protestants.[4] Some colonies, such as Georgia, banned Catholic immigration outright. Pennsylvania and Rhode Island discriminated by assessing special taxes on immigrants from outside Great Britain.[5] Exceptions to allow the widespread immigration of Germans are explained by Germany's absence as a colonial competitor in the Americas. As in Cuba, colonists in the South sought black slaves for the plantation economy while fearing that blacks would threaten whites if their percentage of the population grew too high. The colonists' solution was to tax the slave trade to subsidize white immigration. For example, Carolina's Act of 1751 mandated that three-fifths of government revenue raised by slave duties be used over the next five years to pay six pounds to every qualified "poor foreign protestant" from Europe.[6]

British authorities began to sharply restrict immigration to North America in the late 1760s and early 1770s, primarily because they feared that a larger population would be tempted to secede and compete economically with Britain. The Declaration of Independence (1776) condemned George III's "absolute Tyranny" in matters of immigration and naturalization. "He has endeavored to prevent the population of these States; for that purpose obstructing the Laws for Naturalization of Foreigners; refusing to pass others to encourage their migrations hither, and raising the conditions of new Appropriations of Lands," the seventh of 27 charges against the king declared.[7]

When the United States became independent, the 1787 Northwest Ordinance opened citizenship in the Northwest Territory to French Catholics, free blacks, and Native Americans, as well as European Protestants.[8] The expansiveness of the ordinance reflected the colonists' interests in increasing their population to achieve military security and economic growth, as well as recognizing the crucial military assistance of Catholic France in the rebel campaign.[9] The promise of equality implicit in the ordinance dissipated, however, when Congress established systematic naturalization requirements three years later. The 1790 Uniform Rule of Naturalization restricted eligibility to naturalize to free whites,[10] a provision that seemed so obvious to lawmakers that the whiteness requirement passed without debate. Zolberg points out that even with this racial requirement, the 1790 act was comparatively expansive in that it allowed full citizenship for Jews (a year before revolutionary France) and Catholics (nearly half a century before the United Kingdom).[11] Opening eligibility to all whites allowed for the demographic and military expansion of a country with a tenuous toehold on a continent populated by rival powers and indigenous groups.

The 1790 act did not define who was white at a time when elite notions of whiteness could be quite narrow. Benjamin Franklin's 1751 essay on population argued that "white excludes not only the black and tawny, but also Europeans of a 'swarthy complexion' such as Spaniards, Italians, Russians, Swedes, and most Germans."[12] Legally, however, white was understood to be "European" rather than exclusively Anglo-Saxon, an interpretation that gave a critical advantage to Irish, southern European, and Jewish immigrants. Even though these groups were not socially considered fully white when they arrived, they remained eligible for naturalization and became socially white over time.[13]

A contradictory series of fifty-two court cases from 1878 to 1952 gradually defined who was *not* white, even though these cases never positively defined who *was* white. From 1878 to 1909, eleven of twelve cases deciding racial prerequisites to naturalize ruled against their plaintiffs, thus declaring people from China, Japan, Burma, and Hawaii to be nonwhite.[14] Despite the U.S. Attorney General's 1906 instruction that Japanese not be considered white, a rule extended to Asian Indians the following year, several hundred Japanese and Asian Indians were able to naturalize during the 1900s and 1910s.[15] The Supreme Court eventually declared in 1922 in *Ozawa v. United States* that regardless of their degree of cultural assimilation, Japanese were not eligible for naturalization because of their Japanese race.[16] The courts often ruled inconsistently on the whiteness of particular groups. Syrians were ruled nonwhite in 1913 and 1914 but white in 1909, 1910, and 1915. Between 1909 and 1923, Armenians were declared white despite their origins in Asia. Filipinos were not considered white, but they could naturalize if they immigrated to the United States and served in the U.S. military in World War I.[17] Asian Indians were ruled white in 1910, 1913, 1919, and 1920 but were ruled nonwhite in 1909 and 1917. The Supreme Court's 1923 ruling in *U.S. v. Bhagat Singh Thind* definitively categorized Indians as nonwhite and established that "common usage," rather than "scientific terminology," was the legal basis for racial categorization.[18] The variation in decisions about the whiteness of these groups suggests a high degree of judicial autonomy regarding Asians and Pacific Islanders.

For Mexicans, however, the definition of who was legally white became intertwined with U.S. treaties and the bilateral relationship. The 1897 *In re Rodriguez* case upheld the right of a Mexican immigrant to naturalize. Even though the judge found that "if the strict scientific classification of the anthropologist should be adopted, [Rodriguez] would probably not be classified as white," he ruled that the United States had to accept the naturalization of Mexicans due to its obligations in the 1848 Guadalupe Hidalgo and 1853 Gadsden treaties with Mexico. The foreign relations commitments of the U.S. government thus ensured that Mexicans would be treated as white in the law, even if in daily practice Mexicans were typically racialized as an inferior population.[19] Diplomatic considerations about not offending a large neighbor on the horizontal plane trumped popular sentiment on the vertical plane.

Black Restriction

Most accounts date racial selection in U.S. immigration law to the 1882 Chinese exclusion, even though explicit discriminations against black immigrants began in 1803. During the antebellum period, states in the U.S. South and northern states such as Illinois banned the migration of free blacks. The targets of these prohibitions were primarily blacks living in other states, but in some cases included the immigration of blacks from abroad. White plantation owners were especially afraid of blacks from Haiti, where slaves revolted in 1791 and established a black republic.[20] The states with bans on black admission enlisted federal support to enforce their immigration laws, resulting in an 1803 act prohibiting the importation into those states of "any negro, mulatto, or other person of colour, not being a native, a citizen, or registered seaman, of the United States, or seamen, natives of countries beyond the Cape of Good Hope."[21] While this ban did not apply to states that allowed black in-migration, it is an important milestone in the racialization of federal immigration policy that is all but forgotten in the historiography.

Following the Union's victory in the Civil War, Reconstructionists imposed the 1866 Civil Rights Act and 1868 Fourteenth Amendment that established citizenship for all persons born in the United States regardless of their racial categorization. This overturned the Supreme Court's 1857 *Dred Scott v. Sandford* decision that had stripped all blacks, including free blacks, of their U.S. citizenship.[22] During debates over the Naturalization Act of 1870, Reconstructionist Senator Charles Sumner (R-MA) proposed that naturalization should be open to any race, but opponents who wanted to exclude American Indians and Chinese defeated the Sumner amendment by a vote of 26 to 12.[23] The bill's final language extended eligibility to naturalize "to aliens of African nativity and to persons of African descent," along with whites.[24]

The end of restrictions on black naturalization was not meant to encourage black immigration [to the United States]. On the contrary, President Lincoln and many abolitionists, both black and white, supported schemes for U.S. blacks to immigrate to Liberia, Central America, and Haiti.[25] Extending eligibility to naturalize to blacks was a byproduct of the main project of granting full citizenship (at least on paper) to the black population already in the country. It was not the result of American liberalism purifying itself of racism *tout court*. Indeed, just as the door symbolically opened to blacks, it slammed shut on the Chinese.

Chinese Exclusion

The Chinese were the targets of the first federal restriction on the immigration of a particular racial group to anywhere in the country. For the U.S. president, steering between the Scylla of domestic restrictionism and the Charybdis of international pressure to ease restriction would prove to be a difficult course. The linkage between trade and immigration moderated the degree of Chinese exclusion by allowing in merchants and motivating bilateral treaties that were less degrading to China. It was only when immigration became linked to deeper military and diplomatic interests that exclusion was overturned. When the United States needed China in its existential fight against the Axis in World War II, the vertical interests demanding restriction yielded to the horizontal exigencies of foreign policy.

An estimated 110,000 to 300,000 Chinese, mostly men, entered the United States between 1850 and 1882. The vast majority worked in California, where they comprised a third of the adult male population. California farmers saw the Chinese as cheap labor, and in 1852, the governor proposed granting land to the Chinese to induce further immigration. Companies building the transcontinental railroad in the 1860s recruited Chinese migrants, whom they paid lower wages than whites and sometimes used as strikebreakers. The Chinese on the West Coast quickly established ethnic niches in mining, laundries, and domestic service. In Louisiana, a handful of sugarcane plantation owners recruited Chinese workers from Cuba to replace the slaves who had been freed by the Union victory.[26]

Opposition to Chinese immigration soared in the 1850s. Vernon Briggs and Charles Price emphasize the material interests that explain organized labor's hostility to Chinese immigrants, while Andrew Gyory asserts that politicians on the East Coast scapegoated Chinese to distract workers from genuine national problems.[27] In Alexander Saxton's classical account, economic and ideological interests overlapped. Employers generally opposed the initial attempts at Chinese exclusion but were not any less racist than workers. Business interests wanted a reserve labor army of cheap Chinese labor, not Chinese neighbors or fellow citizens. For intellectuals, the supposed servility of the Chinese evidenced by their willingness to accept low wages was an indicator that they were unfit for citizenship. A California statewide referendum in 1879 on whether Chinese immigration should be allowed received 883 votes in favor and 154,638 opposed.[28] The fact that the exclusionary position came to be held by a broad coalition cutting across classes and was virulently racist in its rhetoric suggests that ideology, more than class interests, drove exclusion.

California led the movement toward restricting Chinese admissions and discriminating against residents. In 1855, the state assembly imposed a head tax for arriving ship passengers who were not eligible for citizenship.[29] The assembly went on to pass a Chinese Exclusion Law preventing admissions of Chinese or Mongolians.[30] A new state constitution in 1879 banned government and businesses from hiring Chinese, delegated to cities and towns the authority to segregate Chinese, and urged an end to further Chinese immigration.[31] In 1891, the state assembly passed a racialized ban on all Chinese immigration regardless of the applicant's nationality.[32] San Francisco, home to the largest Chinese population in the country, passed an ordinance that confined Chinese residences and businesses to a segregated slum—the Chinatown so loved by modern tourists.

Japanese Restriction

Around 30,000 Japanese contract laborers worked in Hawaii from the 1880s to 1894, when the Japanese government ended contract migration and signed a treaty with the United States allowing for mutual rights of residence for their nationals. In California, the Japanese population soared from 1,000 to 41,000 between 1890 and 1910. A cross-class consensus against Japanese immigration quickly developed. San Francisco labor unions began an anti-Japanese campaign in 1900 that culminated in the 78,000 members of the Asiatic Exclusion League calling for a ban on Japanese, Korean, and Asian Indian immigration. The national American Federation of Labor (AFL) joined in demanding an end to Japanese immigration. Conservative businessmen united with the anti-Asian crusade, thus creating a white consensus around exclusion. Both houses of the California legislature passed a unanimous resolution in 1905 calling for a limit on Japanese immigration. As with Chinese immigrants, the Japanese were excluded from integrating and then blamed for refusing to assimilate. The resolution's litany of complaints against Japanese laborers included their "race habits," "mode of living," refusal to assimilate, lack of regard for "republican institutions," loyalty to their country of origin, and servile work as near-slaves that drove out white labor unwilling to accept such low wages. The following year, the San Francisco Board of Education forced the Japanese to join the Chinese in a segregated Oriental School.[33]

The Japanese government reacted angrily to the segregation of the Japanese. While privately sympathetic to restricting the Japanese, whom he saw as part of an "Oriental invasion" of white countries, President Roosevelt and Secretary of State Elihu Root feared that their outright exclusion would provoke a serious diplomatic crisis that might even lead to armed confrontation.[34] In his December 1906

State of the Union address, Roosevelt denounced segregation in San Francisco and warned that hostility toward the Japanese threatened "the gravest consequences to the nation." He told Congress that in the wake of the Russo-Japanese War (1904–1905), "Japanese soldiers and sailors have shown themselves equal in combat to any of whom history makes note." The president urged restraint and called for a bill allowing Japanese immigrants to be eligible to naturalize.[35]

To resolve the crisis, in a way that allowed the Japanese government to avoid the humiliation of explicit discrimination against the Japanese, U.S. and Japanese diplomats exchanged a series of notes between 1907 and 1908 known as the Root-Takahira or "Gentlemen's Agreement." It allowed the Japanese to remain in regular California public schools; banned the entry of Japanese laborers coming from Hawaii, Canada, and Mexico; and charged Japan with stopping labor migration to the continental United States through its own exit controls.[36] President Roosevelt issued a proclamation on March 14, 1907, that banned Japanese or Korean laborers from entering through Mexico, Canada, or Hawaii. There was never a formal treaty based on the Gentlemen's Agreement, and Congress did not ratify its terms. The presidency used its executive powers to respond to vertical demands in a way that would minimize damage on the horizontal field.

Ten years later, the Immigration Act (1917) banned labor immigration from the "Asiatic Barred Zone" defined by lines of latitude and longitude. While the Philippines and Guam geographically fell in the zone, they were under U.S. jurisdiction and thus exempt from its immigration ban. Parts of China, Japan, and Korea were not excluded in the barred zone, but Chinese were already excluded under laws dating back to 1882, and Koreans were under Japanese colonial control and thus treated under the 1907–1908 Gentlemen's Agreement restricting immigration from Japan.

Filtering "Scum from the Melting-Pot"

While the U.S. government was establishing controls on black and Asian immigration in the nineteenth century, why did it not also select Europeans by ethnicity, given that many groups were seen as only liminally white and/or politically threatening? In the 1850s, the Know-Nothing Party and its 1 million members demanded restrictions on Irish and German Catholics, whom they portrayed as papists bent on undermining the republic.[37] By the late nineteenth century, southern and eastern immigrants were widely seen as agents of anarchism, socialism, and violent radicalism that culminated in events such as the Haymarket Riot of 1886. Federal immigration policy nevertheless remained open to almost all Europeans. Minor regulation of shipping companies began in 1819 followed by bans on the immigration of criminals in 1875; lunatics, idiots, and those likely to become a public charge in 1882; contracted labourers in 1885; and carriers of contagious disease in 1891.[38] Despite the steady expansion of grounds of inadmissibility, the U.S. Immigration Service excluded only 1 percent of the 25 million Europeans who landed between 1880 and World War I.[39]

It was not until the republic had become firmly established that policymakers had the luxury of restricting particular groups of Europeans.[40] Scientific racism gave a new shine to the old argument that certain races should be barred. Intellectuals in Europe and European settler societies circulated scientific papers and popularized works warning of the perils of race mixing. The most influential ideas originated in France, Germany, and Britain and spread through cultural emulation.[41] In the United States, blacks and Asians were considered to be completely inassimilable, and discussion centered on how much the mixing of different European groups threatened national demographic health. Groups such as Celts and Alpines were considered different "races" with distinctive phenotypes and inherited social and behavioral characteristics.[42]

Racism cut across the class divide on questions of immigration. By the 1880s, the Knights of Labor supported preferences for northern Europeans and restrictions on new sources from southern and eastern Europe. Business interests split. The National Association of Manufacturers opposed restriction, even as Protestant businessmen joined workers in the 2 million-strong American Protective Association that called for anti-Catholic and anti-immigrant measures in the 1890s. Irish and German ethnic lobbies fought against restriction, as did some social reformers.[43]

Literacy tests became the preferred technique for restricting the entry of southern and eastern Europeans.[44] Literacy tests were already an established model for racially neutral restrictions with racist goals, and proponents of tests for immigrants explicitly explained their motivation in racist terms. Mississippi already had adopted literacy tests at the polls to disenfranchise black voters, who were disproportionately illiterate.[45] The Immigration Restriction League founded by Boston intellectual elites promoted a literacy test in the 1896 immigration bill. Senator Henry Cabot Lodge, a prominent member of the League, explained its goals: "The literacy test will bear most heavily upon the Italians, Russians, Poles, Hungarians, Greeks, and Asiatics, and very light, or not at all upon English-speaking emigrants or Germans, Scandinavians, and French." He invoked the warnings of French racist Gustave Le Bon, whose writings Lodge had encountered on a trip to France the previous year, that racial assimilation between superior and inferior groups would only progress if the numbers of the inferior group were small.[46] President Grover Cleveland vetoed the literacy test bill primarily on the grounds that the test was a "pretext for exclusion."[47] Congress passed literacy test bills again in 1913, 1915, and 1917, but Presidents Taft and Wilson vetoed them.[48] Congress finally overrode the veto in 1917 and a test requiring immigrants to prove their literacy in any language was instituted at Ellis Island.[49] To the consternation of nativists, most immigrants from southern and eastern Europe passed the tests and gained admission.

During the debates over the national-origins quota laws, Rep. Johnson summarized the supposed dangers that the innate qualities of new immigrants posed for democracy.

Today, instead of a nation descended from generations of freemen bred to knowledge of the principles and practices of self-governments, of liberty under law, we have a heterogeneous population no small proportion of which is sprung from races that, throughout the centuries, have known no liberty at all, and no law save the decrees of overlords and princes. In other words, our capacity to maintain our cherished institutions stands diluted by a stream of alien blood with all its inherited misconceptions respecting the relationships of the governing power to the governed.[50]

A broad coalition for restriction formed around security, ideological, and economic interests. Writing in the *American Journal of Sociology* on his proposal to rid the country of "Scum from the Melting-Pot," Edwin Grant called for "a systematic deportation" that "eugenically cleanses America."[51] Various Europeans were blamed for the assassination of President McKinley in 1901, a bombing campaign against government officials in 1919, and other violence. The Bolshevik Revolution in 1917 exacerbated fears of foreign radicalism that culminated in the Red Scare of the early 1920s. At the same time, a revitalized Ku Klux Klan of 3 million members demanded the exclusion of Catholics and Jews.[52] Opponents of quotas for Europeans were generally limited to politicians and organizations whose constituents were targeted for restriction.

Discrimination in Action

While nationals of the Western Hemisphere enjoyed preferences on the books, in practice, U.S. officials sometimes restricted Latin Americans and Caribbean blacks while avoiding the diplomatic problems of overt exclusion. When the State Department eventually agreed to limit Mexican immigration in January 1929 (before the Wall Street crash in October), it used administrative discretion rather than quotas. The department instructed American consuls in Mexico to strictly enforce existing laws that prohibited the admission of contracted laborers,

illiterates, and immigrants likely to become public charges. As Divine explains the interview process for an immigrant visa at U.S. consulates in Mexico, "When an applicant was asked about his financial status, if he replied he had a job waiting for him in the United States, he was ruled out on the contract labor provision, while if he answered that he had no job in sight, he was rejected as likely to become a public charge."[53] Admissions of Mexican immigrants fell by 50 percent in April 1929 and 80 percent by February 1930. Senator Carl Hayden (D-AZ) pointed to the effectiveness of this technique on the floor of the Senate to defend the exemption of the Western Hemisphere from the quota system in 1930.[54] Federal and local governments used deportations and repatriations to remove an estimated 400,000 Mexicans from the United States during the Great Depression, including many who were U.S. citizens by virtue of their birth on U.S. territory. No other national-origin group was singled out for this harsh treatment. The Border Patrol, founded in 1924, used its discretion to target Mexicans as well.[55]

Discrimination in Practice?

While ethnic discrimination has been erased from the law on the books, immigration policy unquestionably affects ethnic groups differently. Immigration law will always differentially impact ethnic groups because socioeconomic characteristics are unevenly distributed among potential migrants. Even a hypothetical policy of open borders would benefit those with the resources to travel and social networks already linking them to the United States. Policies favoring high-skilled immigration in practice disproportionately attract high-skilled individuals from particular places—countries with lower wages such as China and India. Language requirements clearly favor native speakers of those tongues, but languages can also be learned, and there is no shortage of people other than native speakers who would likely enjoy the advantages of an English-speaking preference.

42

THE MELTING POT AND THE COLOR LINE

Stephen Steinberg

STEPHEN STEINBERG is the assistant chair of day studies and a sociologist in the Urban Studies Department at Queens College.

"EVERY NATION, UPON EXAMINATION, TURNS out to have been a more or less successful melting pot." So wrote Robert Park, the founder of the famed Chicago School of Sociology, in 1930. It is a testament to Park's prescience that he was able to imagine the melting pot at a time when the United States was ethnically more diverse, and more fragmented, than ever before. During the previous half-century, the nation had absorbed some 24 million immigrants, mostly from Eastern and Southern Europe. These "new immigrants"—Italians, Poles, Russian Jews, Ukrainians, Hungarians, and others, far removed geographically and culturally from the people who settled the United States during its first century—were widely believed to be "unassimilable." In Chicago, for example, 70 percent of the population consisted of immigrants and the children of immigrants, and the city was divided into a patchwork of ethnic neighborhoods. In 1921 and 1924, Congress responded with legislation that cut the volume of immigration and instituted national quotas biased against further immigration from Southern and Eastern Europe.

Against this background, Park's dictum provided reassurance that the intermingling of peoples was a universal process and that America's ethnic discord would resolve itself over time. This optimism was shared by Chicago sociologists W. Lloyd Warner and Leo Srole, who conducted field studies of immigrant communities in the 1940s. Warner and Srole argued that appearances were deceptive, that the ethnic enclave, though it seemed to nurture isolation and separatism, actually functioned as a decompression chamber, helping immigrants adjust to their new surroundings and preparing the next generation to venture into the mainstream. Whatever its original raison d'être, the ethnic community actually functioned as an instrument of assimilation.

But if early sociologists were confident about assimilation, a later generation rejected the idea of the melting pot. Ironically, many of these scholars were themselves children of immigrants who have risen to the top of the academic ladder. Their revisionist view of the melting pot can be seen as part of a broader trend among second-generation immigrants: assimilation breeds

Questions to Consider

According to the theory of the melting pot, diverse ethnic and racial groups will be thrown together and meld into a new American amalgam that represents the finest cultural aspects of each community. Food is perhaps the easiest way to understand the melting pot perspective. Salsa, not ketchup, is now the number one condiment. There are almost 64,000 pizzerias, almost 7,000 Taco Bells, and 30,000 Asian restaurants in the United States, according to experts in the food industry. But as sociologist Stephen Steinberg argues, not everyone has been allowed into the pot. He suggests "America's melting pot has been inclusive of everybody but blacks." Is his statement about black exclusion from the melting pot justified when we consider African American contributions to popular culture?

nostalgia. First-generation immigrants, who are most authentically steeped in ethnic culture, tend to throw it away, often with both hands, as they pursue the opportunities that led them to come to America in the first place. Decades later, their largely assimilated children engage in desperate, but usually futile, efforts to recover the very culture that their parents relinquished. As the children of immigrants entered the ranks of social science, they brought this same nostalgia to their analysis of ethnic trends.

The turning point came with the publication of *Beyond the Melting Pot* in 1970. Scholars Nathan Glazer and Daniel Patrick Moynihan, who had each ascended from immigrant poverty to the ivory tower, concluded from their study of New York City that "the most important thing about the melting pot was that it did not happen." The syntax of this much-quoted passage warrants a moment's reflection. To

say that the melting pot "did not happen" is not the same as saying that it was not happening. After all, Park and other theorists of assimilation never claimed that the melting pot was a fait accompli; nor did they project a deadline for the completion of this evolutionary process. Nevertheless, the book's title and argument found a receptive audience. Aside from selling over half a million copies, *Beyond the Melting Pot* marked the beginning of a paradigm shift in the study of ethnicity.

Other books soon appeared that trumpeted the survival of ethnicity over the sinister forces of assimilation. Their titles celebrated *The Decline of the WASP* (1971) and *The Rise of the Unmeltable Ethnics* (1971). A year later, an article in the *New York Times Magazine* proclaimed, "America Is NOT a Melting Pot." Indeed, these writers contended that the United States was undergoing an "ethnic revival" that would resuscitate immigrant cultures. Again, there is a striking historical irony. When ethnic groups were intact and cultural differences pronounced, leading sociologists held that assimilation was inevitable. Several decades later, when these groups had undergone profound transformation, forsaking major elements of their ancestral cultures and assuming comfortable identities as Americans, the prevailing view was that the melting pot had "never happened."

But such attempts to turn back the clock of assimilation would prove difficult. With the exception of Native Americans, ethnic groups in America are transplanted peoples, far removed in time and space from their original homelands. The necessity of adapting to life in America made assimilation, in Park's words, "progressive and irreversible." By the late 1970s, a number of scholars, myself among them, had begun to argue that the so-called ethnic revival was in fact a symptom of decline, a dying gasp of ethnic consciousness. In fact, all the long-term trends suggested that the melting pot was working as predicted: during the twentieth century, immigrants largely lost their original language and culture, ethnic enclaves dispersed as economic and occupational mobility increased, and the rate of ethnic and religious intermarriage accelerated.

melting pot - a place where a variety of race, cultures

It may be that some observers deny the evident fact of assimilation simply because of the ambiguous terminology that we use to describe it. "Melting pot" conjures up an image of a bubbling cauldron into which immigrants descend—whether they jump or are pushed is another matter—and are quickly dissolved into oblivion. Though rhetorically effective, this imagery obscures the evolutionary nature of assimilation. Correctly understood, it is a process that occurs incrementally across generations. To argue that ethnicity is still an active force in American life—as Glazer and Moynihan did in 1970 and other scholars have repeated ever since—is to beg the crucial question. Just because assimilation isn't complete doesn't mean that it isn't taking place.

How we view assimilation also depends on our conception of culture. Revisionists argue that the melting pot theory is based on a static view in which the original culture of an immigrant's homeland is simply replaced by American culture. Such critics concede that Italian Americans, for example, bear little resemblance to Italians in Italy, but they argue that Italian Americans are nevertheless a distinct community, forged on American soil, complete with its own identity and subculture.

Yet melting pot theorists also realize that immigrant cultures evolve and take new forms as newcomers adapt to life in America. The crucial issue is not whether change occurs, but rather the direction and the end result of that change. The key question is this: will the ethnicity of formerly hyphenated Americans endure, or is it merely a transitional stage in a long-term assimilation? My position has long been that, even if we assume a greater tolerance for diversity than actually exists in American society, the conditions were never promising for a genuine and lasting pluralism.

. . .

Today there is an emerging consensus that the descendants of the great waves of European immigration have reached an advanced stage of assimilation. The most striking evidence is provided by the soaring rates of intermarriage across ethnic lines. According to a 1990 study by sociologist Richard Alba, the percentage of white ethnics aged twenty-five to thirty-four who married outside their own groups was as follows: Germans, 52 percent; Irish, 65 percent; English, 62 percent; Italians, 73 percent; French, 78 percent; Scots, 82 percent; Poles, 84 percent. Even in the case of Jews, for whom intermarriage was historically low, the figure is now thought to approach 50 percent. The conclusion seems inescapable that the melting pot, in the most literal sense, is a reality for groups of European ancestry.

Indeed, sociologists now lump these groups together under the rubric of "Euro-American," thus resolving with a single word the assimilation question that was debated for half a century. It is now conceded that the various nationalities of European descent have become simply "white." As a result, ethnic pluralists and opponents of the melting pot have retreated to a new position: the melting pot does exist, but it is "for whites only." On this view, the common "whiteness" of the Irish, Italians, Poles, Jews, and other groups destined them to "melt," even though they were once regarded as distinct races whose cultural and genetic differences rendered them unassimilable. A new genre of "whiteness studies" has documented the process through which these erstwhile pariahs were incorporated into the white majority. The core argument is encapsulated in the titles of several recent books, including *How the Irish Became White, How Jews Became White Folks,* and *Whiteness of a Different Color.*

But this argument goes on to hold that the current wave of immigrants, composed mainly of "people of color" from Asia, Latin America, and the Caribbean, will not be able to follow in the footsteps of the white ethnics. The fault line dividing ethnic groups in America is no longer nationality or religion, but race. Indeed, a number of scholars have declared that "assimilation theory is dead," since its Eurocentric bias renders it useless for understanding the condition and destiny of people of color.

Aside from racism, the new ethnic pluralists cite several positive factors that, they argue, will spare the new immigrants from the dreaded melting pot. Today's immigrants enter a society that is far more tolerant of ethnic diversity. The ideology of multiculturalism extols ethnic difference and provides institutional mechanisms, such as bilingual education, for the preservation of immigrants' language and culture. As a result, the Asians, Latinos, and Caribbeans who make up the new immigration have formed cohesive ethnic communities with flourishing economies and foreign-language media, including cable television, that provide institutional anchorage for language and culture. Furthermore, compared to earlier immigrants, the new immigrants have easy access to their homelands, thanks to telecommunications and cheap airfare. And finally, many new immigrants arrive with education and skills, and often capital as well, and therefore are not forced to compromise their ethnic identities for the sake of economic survival. Indeed, in today's global economy, it is not a handicap but an asset to be multilingual and multicultural.

These are all valid points. The question is whether they add up to the conclusion that assimilation is dead, and that the new immigrants will not "melt" as did their predecessors from Europe. It must be conceded that this is a possible scenario, given what we know about racism as a divisive force in American history. One cannot immediately discount the argument that the melting pot is "for whites only," and that today's immigrants will be prevented from assimilating.

In fact, however, this proposition receives little empirical support from the large body of research on today's immigrants. Indeed, the most compelling evidence leads to the conclusion that, notwithstanding their racial difference, the new immigrants are not only assimilating but are doing so at an even faster rate than did earlier immigrants from Europe.

In retrospect, an early indicator of the eventual assimilation of European immigrants was the rapidity with which they lost their native languages. A pattern emerges with stubborn consistency. Immigrants, of course, retained their native tongues; their children typically were bilingual; and by the third generation, the vast majority were monolingual in English. The virtual eradication of languages in only two generations shows just how fragile culture is, at least once it loses its "survival value" and is severed from the institutions that nourish it. Needless to say, immigrants and their bilingual children were not indifferent to the snuffing out of their native language. But the lesson of history is that sentiment—even passionate loyalty—is not enough to withstand the powerful forces of assimilation.

This process is being reenacted—if anything, at an accelerated pace—among the new immigrants. In a study of Los Angeles based on 1990 census data, David Lopez found that, among Asians, the shift to English monolingualism was nearly universal by the third generation. Consider what this means for family relations. Unless the immigrant grandparents acquire a basic fluency in English, which often is not the case, then grandchildren cannot converse with their grandparents except through the mediation of their bilingual parents.

The picture is somewhat more complex among Latinos, though the overall pattern is still one of rapid language loss. If retention of Spanish were to occur anywhere in the United States, it would be in Los Angeles. Not only do most L.A. Latinos live in predominantly Latino neighborhoods, but the city also has a thriving ethnic press and electronic media. Furthermore, Los Angeles has had an official policy of promoting multiculturalism, including bilingual education and bilingual ballots. Yet Lopez found that 57 percent of third-generation Latinos spoke only English at home. Closer examination of the data revealed that Spanish was retained mainly in households where a foreign-born person—presumably that all-important immigrant grandparent—was present. In the case of Mexican American youth living in households with no immigrants, only 20 percent spoke Spanish at home.

A study of Cubans in South Florida also found that most young people preferred to speak English at home, even when they were bilingual. Nor was this true only of the middle classes. Among second-generation youth who classified themselves as working class or poor, three-quarters preferred to speak English. Clearly, even though today's society is nominally more conducive to language retention, the new immigrants are moving very rapidly to English monolingualism.

If loss of a native language marks the beginning of the assimilation process, marriage across ethnic lines represents the last (or next to last) stage. Here again, the data do not support either the assumptions or the hopes of the new ethnic pluralists. A study based on the 1990 census found that 40 percent of Asians born in the United States married non-Asians—and these are mostly the children, not even the grandchildren, of immigrants. The figures ranged from 22 percent among Vietnamese to 31 percent among Japanese, 38 percent among Asian Indians, 46 percent among Chinese, 65 percent among Filipinos, and 72 percent among Koreans. These figures are so high that they call into question the very category of race in describing Asian-Americans. Indeed, the level of marriage between Asians of different nationalities is strikingly low, suggesting that they do not see themselves as members of a pan-ethnic Asian "race." Rather, most Asians who intermarry do so with whites, giving rise to speculation that Asians are in the process of "becoming white."

Rates of intermarriage for Latinos are lower than for Asians, but they are high nevertheless. Almost one-third of U.S.-born Hispanics between the ages of twenty-five and thirty-four are married to non-Hispanic whites. Indeed, marriage across racial lines has become so commonplace that some commentators have raised the possibility of a "mestizo America"—a racial mixture that blurs the boundaries among ethnic groups. On this view, it is not a question of minorities being absorbed into the white majority, but rather of a fusing of these diverse peoples into a new amalgam. This is the literal meaning of a "melting pot," and a fulfillment of Robert Park's prescient observation that every nation is a "more or less successful melting pot." Like it or not, and the dissent of the ethnic pluralists is clear, assimilation does appear to be progressive and irreversible, the inexorable by-product of forces put into motion by the very act of immigrating.

. . .

Admittedly, this sweeping conclusion, while it captures the main thrust of American ethnic history, does not tell the whole story: in particular, it does not account for the African American experience.

Here we speak of a group that came to America in slave ships, not immigrant steamers. While successive waves of immigrants flowed into the country, first to settle the land and later to provide labor for burgeoning industries, blacks were trapped in the South in a system of feudal agriculture. Even in the North, a rigid color line excluded them from the manufacturing sector. In short, the Industrial Revolution was "for whites only," depriving blacks of the jobs and opportunities that delivered Europe's huddled masses from poverty.

This was the historic wrong that was supposed to be remedied by landmark civil rights legislation in the 1960s. But by the time most blacks arrived in Northern cities, the manufacturing sector was undergoing a permanent decline, reflecting the impact of labor-saving technology and the export of jobs to low-wage countries. Not only did blacks encounter far less favorable opportunities than did immigrants, not only did they suffer from the economic consequences of past discrimination, and not only did they encounter pervasive racism in the world of work, but they also experienced intense labor competition from yet another huge wave of immigrants, which began in the 1960s and continues to this day.

Though these new immigrants are conspicuous for their "racial" difference, they are not subjected to the all-encompassing system of racial discrimination that was the legacy of slavery. Furthermore, many of these immigrants arrived with education and skills—and sometimes capital as well—that accelerated their mobility and social integration. As noted earlier, Asians and Latinos already display a far greater degree of "residential assimilation" than blacks. And at a time when marriage across racial lines is soaring for Asians and Latinos, it has inched up only slightly for blacks, again indicating that a fundamentally different dynamic is at work. The conclusion is unavoidable: America's melting pot has been inclusive of everybody but blacks.

This is not to deny the obvious fact that there has been enormous progress over the past half-century. Jim Crow is a thing of the past, thanks largely to the black protest movement. The emergence of a large black middle class is another encouraging development, though in my view this does not reflect the deracialization of labor markets so much as the favorable impact of affirmative action policy over several decades. Finally, there has been an unmistakable shift in America's fundamental attitudes toward race. The prominence of blacks among the nation's elites, as well as its pantheon of folk heroes, is stark proof that skin color is no longer a badge of inferiority.

Nevertheless, ours is still a society riven by race. Claims of "progress" invariably depend on comparing the situation today to a retrograde past. The problem here, as James Baldwin observed, is that the crimes of the past are used to gloss over the crimes of the present. When comparisons are made between blacks and whites today, a far less sanguine picture emerges. For example, blacks today earn only three-fifths as much as whites. Furthermore, although the income gap between blacks and whites closed somewhat in the 1960s, there has been little or no progress since the mid-1970s. So long as nearly a quarter of blacks, and half of black youth, live below the poverty line, these class factors will continue to engender and reinforce racial division.

Even more germane to the question of whether America is a melting pot, black and white Americans are as residentially segregated as ever. Nor is this true only of inner-city blacks. Middle-class blacks also encounter pervasive discrimination in housing, and their arrival into white suburbs usually triggers white flight, resulting in resegregation. It is a mark of the melting pot's failure that African Americans, whose roots go back to the founding of the nation, are more segregated than even recent immigrants from Asia and Latin America.

In short, despite "progress," ghettoization is still a fact of life. And here we confront a great historical paradox—for these ghettos, the enforced "home" of the nation's racial pariahs, also nourished a vibrant African American subculture. As sociologist Bob Blauner has observed, while immigrant ghettos "functioned as way stations on the road to acculturation and assimilation," the black ghetto has been permanent, "a continuing crucible for ethnic development and building." And unlike immigrants, who clung to vestiges of cultures ripped from their moorings in distant places, black culture evolved out of the lived experience of black people in America. Instead of isolated fragments selected precisely because they did not interfere with mainstream American culture, black culture is an integral part of the everyday lives of black people. As a result, black culture displays a vitality and dynamism that is generally lacking among the ossifying cultures of the nation's immigrant groups.

Ironically, generations of sociologists have taken precisely the opposite position, on the one hand celebrating the cultures of the nation's immigrant groups and, on the other, holding that blacks were merely "white Americans in black skin," lacking a culture of their own. In the same book where they declared that the melting pot "never happened," Glazer and Moynihan wrote that "it is not possible for Negroes to view themselves as other ethnic groups viewed themselves because—and this is the key to much in the Negro world—the Negro is only an American and nothing else. He has no values and culture to guard and protect." Under a barrage of criticism, Glazer subsequently explained that he meant blacks had *no foreign* culture to guard or protect. However, this only compounds the error, since these foreign cultures—and precisely because they were foreign—were destined to a gradual but inexorable decline. On the other hand, as an indigenous product of the American experience, black culture continues not only to thrive in segregated black communities but also to exert a powerful influence on mainstream American culture.

. . .

Throughout this essay, I have emphasized that the melting pot is still at work and that, like past immigrants, today's immigrants from outside the Western Hemisphere will also be fully assimilated at some indeterminate point in the future. The problem, of course, is that we live in the present. It may be our national destiny to become a melting pot, but today the United States is a remarkably polyglot society in which ethnicity flourishes. Despite an overriding trend toward assimilation, ethnic loyalties and attachments remain strong even among segments of older immigrant groups. New immigrants, freshly arrived on American soil, are only at the early stages of the assimilation process. To turn a blind eye to these realities by focusing on long-term trends runs the risk of blotting out the lives and sensibilities of entire communities.

Nor does this warning apply only to ideologues on the political right who, in the name of the melting pot, have waged a relentless crusade against bilingualism, multicultural education, and affirmative action. In recent years, a left discourse has emerged that looks "beyond race" and "beyond ethnicity," imagining a post-ethnic future where people are not defined by genes or ancestry. This vision promotes intermarriage across racial and ethnic lines as a way of eliminating, once and for all, the dissonances and conflicts attending racial and ethnic diversity.

For example, historian Gary Nash, a pioneer of multicultural education, has published an essay titled "The Hidden History of Mestizo America," in which he argues that we "need new ways of transcending America's Achilles' heel of race, now that a certain amount of progress has been achieved in living up to our own credo." Like Nash, sociologist Orlando Patterson advocates miscegenation as the ultimate solution to America's intractable race problem. Never mind that African Americans—not to speak of other ethnic groups—may not wish to miscegenate themselves out of existence. Never mind that it would take generations, if not centuries, to produce the hybrid nation that they envision. Instead of confronting the urgent problems of race in America and addressing the challenges of a multicultural society, these visionaries are throwing in the towel. They use a utopian vision of the melting pot as a façade for moral capitulation.

Let me be clear. There is compelling evidence that the United States will one day become a melting pot, and that this day is approaching faster than ethnic pluralists are willing to acknowledge. From a moral standpoint, however, it is imperative that this melting pot evolve through the operation of historical forces rather than through public policy interventions. It is wrong—to continue the metaphor—to turn up the temperature under the melting pot, or to nudge, cajole, or push people into the bubbling cauldron. Any use of state power to undermine ethnicity or to force assimilation is incompatible with democratic principles and violates the rights of ethnic minorities to hold on to their languages and cultures.

The irony of the matter is that, like earlier waves of immigrants, today's newcomers will find their way to the melting pot in due course. So, presumably, will African Americans, but not until the structures of American apartheid are thoroughly dismantled and the persistent inequalities are resolved. These groups will pursue the personal and social integration that is the promise of the melting pot. But they must do so of their own accord, and not on somebody else's timetable. Here we can take another lesson from history: the carrot, not the stick, has always been the more effective instrument of assimilation.

Seeing the Big Picture   Who Is Allowed to "Melt" in the Pot? Who Wants to?

In Section X of the appendix, do rates of intermarriage support the assertion that the United States is a melting pot? What does the popularity of hip-hop and rap say about the theory of the melting pot?

43

WHO ARE THE OTHER AFRICAN AMERICANS?

Contemporary African and Caribbean Immigrants in the United States

John R. Logan

JOHN R. LOGAN is professor of sociology at Brown University. Dr. Logan is co-author, along with Harvey Molotch, of *Urban Fortunes: The Political Economy of Place*. His most recent, edited book, *The New Chinese City: Globalization and Market Reform*, was published by Blackwell in 2001.

AS QUICKLY AS THE HISPANIC AND ASIAN populations in the United States have grown, there has been nearly equal growth among black Americans with recent roots in Africa and the Caribbean. The number of black Americans born in sub-Saharan Africa nearly tripled during the 1990s. The number identifying a Caribbean ancestry increased by over 60 percent. Census 2000 shows that Afro-Caribbeans in the United States number over 1.5 million—more than some more visible national-origin groups, such as Cubans and Koreans. Africans number over six hundred thousand. In some major metropolitan regions, these "new" black groups amount to 20 percent or more of the black population. And, nationally, nearly 25 percent of the growth of the black population between 1990 and 2000 was due to people arriving from Africa and the Caribbean.

This [reading] summarizes what is known about these "new" black Americans: their numbers, social backgrounds, and residential locations in metropolitan areas. It makes the following key points:

- It is well known that the socioeconomic profile of non-Hispanic blacks is unfavorable compared to whites and Asians. There is also striking variation within America's black population. The social and economic profile of Afro-Caribbeans and Africans is far above that of African Americans and even better than that of Hispanics.

Questions to Consider

The national narrative on immigration usually focuses on immigrants from Mexico and Central and South America, but there has been a sizable increase in the number of black immigrants from Africa and the Caribbean. There is also a tendency to lump the socio-economic status and life experiences of new black immigrants from Africa and the Caribbean with African Americans. Professor Logan's research shows that there are some similarities between these populations (e.g., levels of segregation from whites), but these groups are exceptionally diverse. How and in what ways do the experiences of these new groups differ from those of African Americans? Is it the case that the experiences of black African and Caribbean immigrants are similar to those of Latinos? Why and how?

- Afro-Caribbeans are heavily concentrated on the East Coast. Six out of ten live in the New York, Miami, and Ft. Lauderdale metropolitan regions. More than half are Haitian in Miami; Haitians are well represented, but outnumbered by Jamaicans, in New York and Ft. Lauderdale.

- America's African population, on the other hand, is much more geographically dispersed. The largest numbers are in Washington, D.C., and New York. In both places, the majority are from West Africa, especially Ghana and Nigeria. East Africa, including Ethiopia and Somalia, is the other main region of origin.

- Like African Americans, Afro-Caribbeans and Africans are highly segregated from whites. But these black ethnic groups overlap only partly with one another in the neighborhoods in which they live. Segregation among black ethnic groups reflects important social differences among them.

- In the metropolitan areas where they live in largest numbers, Africans tend to live in neighborhoods with a higher median income and education level than African Americans and Afro-Caribbeans. In these metro areas, Afro-Caribbeans tend to live in neighborhoods with a higher percentage of homeowners than either African Americans or Africans.

COUNTING NON-HISPANIC BLACKS IN AMERICA

The Census Bureau provides different ways of identifying these black populations, depending on the data source that is used.

For data on individuals, the 1990 5 percent Public Use Microdata Sample (1990 PUMS) data files and the Census 2000 1 percent Public Use Microdata Sample (2000 PUMS) make it possible to count the number of African Americans, Afro-Caribbeans, and Africans by combining information on their race, birth, and ancestry. Among non-Hispanic blacks, this study classifies those reporting their ancestry, country of birth, or both in the predominantly black islands of the Caribbean (including such places as Jamaica and Trinidad, but not Guyana) as "Afro-Caribbean." . . .

THE SIZE AND REGIONAL DISTRIBUTION OF THE BLACK POPULATION

Census 2000 counted over 35 million non-Hispanic blacks, as shown in Table 1. This represents over 12 percent of the U.S. population. The non-Hispanic black population grew by over 6 million people, a growth rate of almost 21 percent, since the last

	Population		Percentage of Black Population		Percentage of Total Population		Growth
Group	**1990**	**2000**	**1990**	**2000**	**1990**	**2000**	**1990–2000**
African American	28,034,275	33,048,095	96.0	93.9	11.3	11.7	17.9
Afro-Caribbean	924,693	1,542,895	3.2	4.4	0.4	0.5	66.9
African	229,488	612,548	0.8	1.7	0.1	0.2	166.9
Non-Hispanic white	188,013,404	194,433,424			75.6	69.1	3.4
Non-Hispanic black	29,188,456	35,203,538			11.7	12.5	20.6
Hispanic	21,836,851	35,241,468			8.8	12.5	61.4
Asian	6,977,447	10,050,579			2.8	3.6	44.0
United States Total	248,709,873	281,421,906			100.0	100.0	13.2

TABLE 1   ■   Composition and Growth of the Non-Hispanic Black Populations of the U.S., 1990–2000

Source: Courtesy of Lewis Mumford Center for Comparative Urban and Regional Research, University of Albany.

decennial census. More than nine out of ten of these were African American (based on our classification of persons using 2000 PUMS), but the percentage of other black groups is growing rapidly (from 4 percent in 1990, based on 1990 PUMS data, to 6.1 percent in 2000).

Over 1.5 million blacks can now be classified as Afro-Caribbeans, and over 600,000 can be classified as African. The Afro-Caribbean population grew by more than 618,000 (almost 67 percent), and Africans grew by more than 383,000 (a growth rate of almost 167 percent, approaching a tripling of the African population). These two groups combined, despite being much smaller than the African American population, contributed about 17 percent of the 6-million-person increase in the non-Hispanic black population during the 1990s. Although not an often recognized part of the American ethnic mosaic, both of these groups are emerging as large and fast-growing populations. Afro-Caribbeans now outnumber and are growing faster than such well-established ethnic minorities as Cubans and Koreans.

Analysis of all 331 metropolitan regions reveals distinct residential patterns for African Americans, Afro-Caribbeans, and Africans. Consider the ten metropolitan regions with the largest representation of the latter two groups. These are listed in Tables 2 and 3. New York, Boston, Washington, D.C., and Atlanta are the metros represented in both tables.

Like African Americans, who are present in large numbers in many metro areas, Africans are dispersed throughout the country. Only a quarter of Africans live in one of the ten largest metropolitan regions, and these metro areas are geographically dispersed. This dispersion, in combination with their smaller numbers, may help explain the "invisibility" of African immigrants in the United States (Arthur 2000). In contrast, Afro-Caribbeans are heavily concentrated in just a few metro areas, all on the East Coast. Six out of ten live in the New York, Miami, and Ft. Lauderdale metro areas; nearly six hundred thousand live in New York alone.

All of the top ten metro regions for Afro-Caribbean populations show growth rates of at least 40 percent since 1990, but four metro areas more than doubled the size of this population. Atlanta saw a fourfold increase in its Afro-Caribbean population, while Orlando nearly tripled its population of this group. With the exceptions of Washington, D.C., and Atlanta, the percentage of the non-Hispanic black population accounted for by Afro-Caribbeans in these top metropolitan regions is quite striking. For instance, over one-quarter of the non-Hispanic black population in the New York and Boston metro areas is Afro-Caribbean.

Jamaicans and Haitians are the two major sources of Afro-Caribbeans in all ten areas shown in Table 2. A majority in Miami (61 percent), West Palm Beach (62 percent), and Boston (57 percent), and a near majority in Newark (49.8 percent), are of Haitian ancestry. Jamaicans are the larger group in Ft. Lauderdale (46 percent), New York (40 percent), Nassau–Suffolk (39 percent), Washington, D.C. (49 percent), and Atlanta (53 percent).

Washington, D.C., and New York have the largest African-born populations (80,281 and

73,851, respectively). The 1990–2000 growth rates exceed 100 percent in all the top metro areas for this population (save Los Angeles–Long Beach at 53.5 percent). Minneapolis–St. Paul saw a 628.4 percent increase in its African population, largely due to refugees from East Africa. In Minneapolis–St. Paul, Africans contribute over 15 percent of the non-Hispanic black population; in Boston, Africans account for nearly 10 percent of non-Hispanic blacks.

In the ten metro areas in Table 3, most Africans were born in West Africa (mainly Nigeria and Ghana) or East Africa (Ethiopia or Somalia). East Africans are the larger source in Minneapolis (61 percent), and they approximately equal West Africans in Los Angeles–Long Beach (37 percent) and Dallas (40 percent). Elsewhere, West Africans predominate: Washington, D.C. (53 percent), New York (69 percent), Atlanta (48 percent), Boston (60 percent), Houston (61 percent), Chicago (58 percent), and Philadelphia (53 percent).

TABLE 2 ■ Metros with Largest Afro-Caribbean Population, 2000							
	Afro-Caribbean		Percentage of Black Total		Percentage of Metro Total		Growth
Metro Area	1990	2000	1990	2000	1990	2000	1990–2000
New York, NY	403,198	566,770	20.3	25.7	4.7	6.1	40.6
Miami, FL	105,477	153,255	28.5	34.4	5.4	6.8	45.3
Fort Lauderdale, FL	55,197	150,476	29.6	43.4	4.4	9.3	172.6
Boston, MA-NH	40,825	62,950	20.6	25.6	1.3	1.8	54.2
Nassau–Suffolk, NY	32,210	60,412	17.7	25.5	1.2	2.2	87.6
Newark, NJ	29,818	55,345	7.3	12.1	1.6	2.7	85.6
West Palm Beach–Boca Raton, FL	20,441	49,402	19.8	30.3	2.4	4.4	141.7
Washington, DC-MD-VA-WV	32,440	48,900	3.1	3.7	0.8	1.0	50.7
Orlando, FL	14,872	42,531	10.4	18.4	1.2	2.6	186.0
Atlanta, GA	8,342	35,308	1.1	2.9	0.3	0.9	323.3

Source: Courtesy of Lewis Mumford Center for Comparative Urban and Regional Research, University of Albany.

TABLE 3 ■ Metros with Largest African-Born Population, 2000

Metro Area	African Born 1990	African Born 2000	Percentage of Black Total 1990	Percentage of Black Total 2000	Percentage of Metro Total 1990	Percentage of Metro Total 2000	Growth 1990–2000
Washington, DC-MD-VA-WV	32,248	80,281	3.0	6.1	0.8	1.6	148.9
New York, NY	31,532	73,851	1.6	3.4	0.4	0.8	134.2
Atlanta, GA	8,919	34,302	1.2	2.9	0.3	0.8	284.6
Minneapolis–St. Paul, MN-WI	3,788	27,592	4.3	15.4	0.1	0.9	628.4
Los Angeles–Long Beach, CA	16,826	25,829	1.8	2.7	0.2	0.3	53.5
Boston, MA-NH	11,989	24,231	6.0	9.8	0.4	0.7	102.1
Houston, TX	9,882	22,638	1.6	3.1	0.3	0.5	129.1
Chicago, IL	8,738	19,438	0.6	1.2	0.1	0.2	122.5
Dallas, TX	7,373	19,134	1.8	3.6	0.3	0.5	159.5
Philadelphia, PA-NJ	5,098	16,344	0.6	1.6	0.1	0.3	220.6

Source: Courtesy of Lewis Mumford Center for Comparative Urban and Regional Research, University of Albany.

SOCIAL AND ECONOMIC CHARACTERISTICS OF AMERICA'S BLACK POPULATIONS

We know that the socioeconomic profile of non-Hispanic blacks does not compare favorably to those of whites and Asians. Table 4 offers a comparison based on the 1990 and 2000 PUMS. Less recognized is the diversity within the black population. African Americans have lower educational attainment and median household income and higher unemployment and impoverishment than Afro-Caribbeans and Africans. Afro-Caribbeans and Africans generally compare favorably to America's Hispanic population, while African Americans fare worse. There has been considerable debate about the source of these differences (see, especially, Sowell 1978 and a review of critiques of Sowell's conclusions by James 2002). Thomas

Sowell suggests that they are due to cultural gaps, where the thrift and work ethic of immigrants operate in favor of the newer black groups. Mary Waters (1999) reports that Afro-Caribbean immigrants tend to agree with this thesis and that they often seek to distance themselves from an African-American identity; however, she also finds that employers favor Afro-Caribbean workers, in part because they are perceived to be more compliant and more willing to accept inferior wages and working conditions. Winston James (2002) argues that most differences in outcomes are due to immigrant selectivity (see also Takyi 2002a) and that black immigrants, like African Americans and unlike most other immigrant groups, are strongly affected by racial discrimination in the United States.

In sum, Table 4 makes the following points:

- *Nativity:* Over two-thirds of the Afro-Caribbean and nearly 80 percent of the African population is foreign born. The percentage of foreign born in these groups is higher than that of Asians. Not surprisingly,

TABLE 4 ■ Social and Economic Characteristics of Non-Hispanic Black Populations in Comparison with Major U.S. Racial and Ethnic Groups, 1990 and 2000

Group	Population	Foreign Born (%)	Years of Education	Median Household Income ($)	Unemployed (%)	Below Poverty (%)
1990						
African American	28,034,275	1.8	11.7	29,251	12.5	32.8
Afro-Caribbean	924,693	72.4	12.1	42,927	9.4	17.8
African	229,488	72.1	14.3	35,041	8.5	24.7
Non-Hispanic white	188,013,404	3.9	12.9	47,481	4.7	11.3
Non-Hispanic black	29,188,456	4.7	11.7	29,850	12.3	32.3
Hispanic	21,836,851	42.7	10.2	35,041	9.9	27.0
Asian	6,977,447	67.5	13.1	54,508	5.0	15.9
2000						
African American	33,048,095	2.2	12.4	33,790	11.2	30.4
Afro-Caribbean	1,542,895	68.3	12.6	43,650	8.7	18.8
African	612,548	78.5	14.0	42,900	7.3	22.1
Non-Hispanic white	194,433,424	4.2	13.5	53,000	4.0	11.2
Non-Hispanic black	35,203,538	6.4	12.5	34,300	11.0	29.7
Hispanic	35,241,468	40.9	10.5	38,500	8.8	26.0
Asian	10,050,579	66.5	13.9	62,000	4.6	13.9

Source: Courtesy of Lewis Mumford Center for Comparative Urban and Regional Research, University of Albany.

the percentage of foreign born among the group we define as African American is small.

- *Education:* Educational attainment of Africans (14.0 years) is higher than Afro-Caribbeans (12.6 years) or African Americans (12.4 years); indeed, it is higher even than that of whites and Asians.

- *Income:* Median household income of African Americans is lower than that of any other group in the table, lower even than that of Hispanics. Africans and Afro-Caribbeans

have much higher median incomes (about $43,000), though these are still well below those of whites and Asians.

- *Unemployment and poverty:* Africans and Afro-Caribbeans also have the lowest rates of unemployment and impoverishment among blacks, comparing favorably to Hispanics. Their position is substantially worse than that of Asians and whites, but Africans' unemployment is not far from that of these two groups.

The social and economic profile of all three black groups generally improved during the 1990s, though the gain in median household income of Afro-Caribbeans was marginal, and the average educational attainment of Africans slipped. Gains for African Americans somewhat diminished their gap with other non-Hispanic black populations. Very substantial differences in the average socioeconomic standing of these groups remain, though it is unclear how these various characteristics are interrelated. Some studies have shown, for example, that among employed males, there are no differences among black groups in work intensity and motivation to work (Dodoo 1999). There are also additional differences among Africans with different national origins (Takyi 2002b; Kollehlon and Eule 2003).

RESIDENTIAL PATTERNS WITHIN METROPOLITAN REGIONS

Another way to evaluate and compare the experiences of these black populations is to look at the degree to which their neighborhoods are segregated from those of other groups and from one another. It was shown above that the socioeconomic conditions of Afro-Caribbeans and Africans are different from those of African Americans; are their residential surroundings also distinct?

This question can be studied through the summary files in which Afro-Caribbeans are identified by ancestry and Africans by country of birth. The 1990 and 2000 population censuses provide the counts necessary to calculate levels of group isolation (the percentage of same-group members in the census tract where the average group member lives); exposure to all non-Hispanic blacks and exposure to whites (defined as the percentage of non-Hispanic blacks and non-Hispanic whites, respectively, in the census tract where the average group member lives); and segregation (the Index of Dissimilarity) from non-Hispanic whites and other black groups

(the scores show the percentage of a given group that would have to move to another tract in order for the two groups to be equally distributed). These are indicators of the extent to which a group has developed its own residential enclaves in metropolitan areas. These figures have been calculated by computing levels of isolation, exposure, and dissimilarity in every metropolitan area, then taking a weighted average, giving more weight to areas with more group members.

Table 1 showed that African Americans make up just under 12 percent of the population in the United States, while Afro-Caribbeans and Africans account for 0.5 percent and 0.2 percent, respectively. Thus, if these non-Hispanic black groups were distributed randomly (without regard to in-group preferences or discrimination), their isolation index values would be about 12, 0.5, and 0.2, respectively. Likewise, the exposure scores would match the population percentages of non-Hispanic blacks and whites in Table 1. Dissimilarity is a measure of evenness and thus captures how equally members of a given group are distributed across tracts compared to another group. A dissimilarity score of less than 30 is generally thought to indicate low segregation, scores between 30 and 55 indicate moderate segregation, and scores above 55 indicate high segregation.

Table 5 shows that exposure to whites is low and declining for each black group. Africans have the highest exposure to whites (in 2000, just under half of the people in the neighborhood where an average African person lived was white); Afro-Caribbeans now have the lowest exposure to whites (29.9 percent) among black groups. Conversely, dissimilarity scores indicate high, though slightly declining, segregation of all non-Hispanic black groups from whites. All dissimilarity scores from non-Hispanic whites are in excess of 60 percent.

The percentage of African Americans in the neighborhood where an average African American person lives declined from 54.3 percent in 1990 to 49.4 percent in 2000. Because of their smaller size, other black groups have much lower isolation scores, though these were on an upward trajectory in the

TABLE 5 ■ Segregation of Black Populations, National Metro Averages

		African Americans	Afro-Caribbeans	African Born
Exposure to whites	1990	33.4%	33.5%	56.7%
	2000	33.3	29.9	46.3
Segregation from whites	1990	68.6	74.1	69.6
	2000	65.0	71.8	67.8
Isolation (exposure to own group)	1990	54.3	12.5	1.8
	2000	49.4	15.3	3.3
Exposure to blacks	1990	56.1	47.3	23.3
	2000	51.8	47.3	28.3
Segregation from African Americans	1990	—	46.6	68.9
	2000	—	42.5	59.2
Segregation from Afro-Caribbeans	1990	62.3	—	66.7
	2000	56.3	—	60.3
Segregation from Africans	1990	75.8	66.1	—
	2000	66.7	60.0	—

Source: Courtesy of Lewis Mumford Center for Comparative Urban and Regional Research, University of Albany.

1990s. While they live in neighborhoods where their own group tends to be a small minority, Afro-Caribbeans' neighborhoods are, on average, close to 50 percent black. Africans, on the other hand, live in neighborhoods where blacks are outnumbered by whites (though they did increase their exposure to blacks from 23.3 percent to 28.3 percent).

Segregation of black groups from one another, as measured by the Index of Dissimilarity, is declining, but it is strikingly high. (Note that these average values are not symmetrical because the average segregation of group *x* from group *y* is weighted by the number of group *x* residents; segregation of group *y* from group *x* is weighted by the number of group *y* residents.) Caution should be exercised in interpreting these figures, however. Because Africans and Afro-Caribbeans are found in very small numbers in many metropolitan areas, the national averages

include many values for metro areas where the score is unreliable. It will be more revealing to assess dissimilarity scores among black groups in places like New York, Washington, D.C., and Atlanta, where all three are found in larger numbers. These data are shown in Tables 6 and 7.

Table 6 describes residential patterns for Afro-Caribbeans in the ten largest metropolitan areas for this population. Segregation from whites is very high in all of them, increasing in some areas, while declining in others. Exposure to whites, however, varies greatly—from living in neighborhoods that are less than a quarter white and majority black (New York, Miami, and Newark) to living in neighborhoods where whites make up as much as 40 percent of the population (Boston, West Palm Beach, and Orlando). Segregation from African Americans is only in the moderate

TABLE 6 ■ Segregation of the Ten Metro Regions with Largest Afro-Caribbean Population in Census 2000										
	Exposure to Whites		Segregation from Whites		Exposure to Blacks		Segregation from African Americans		Segregation from Africans	
Metro Area	1990	2000	1990	2000	1990	2000	1990	2000	1990	2000
New York, NY	15.4%	11.8%	81.8%	82.7%	62.2%	64.0%	40.2%	39.2%	62.6%	57.7%
Miami, FL	23.9	15.0	66.6	68.1	49.6	54.1	50.6	47.3	66.1	59.0
Fort Lauderdale, FL	52.8	36.6	56.1	57.2	36.3	43.6	44.4	34.6	69.8	67.5
Boston, MA-NH	42.7	40.7	76.4	73.2	42.8	39.3	41.3	34.9	63.4	54.5
Nassau–Suffolk, NY	45.5	36.7	76.8	75.2	38.0	38.7	40.8	36.4	68.7	48.8
Newark, NJ	26.2	22.9	79.8	78.0	60.8	60.0	40.5	37.8	59.7	47.7
West Palm Beach–Boca Raton, FL	46.1	47.3	69.7	60.2	41.5	34.6	42.7	44.0	83.0	74.4
Washington, D.C.-MD-VA-WV	40.8	34.6	67.0	64.6	43.0	43.3	55.2	48.4	44.9	42.5
Orlando, FL	62.8	42.4	52.9	58.1	26.0	32.6	49.1	40.2	67.3	65.4
Atlanta, GA	48.8	36.2	69.0	61.8	46.6	52.3	53.6	39.8	56.8	48.2

Source: Courtesy of Lewis Mumford Center for Comparative Urban and Regional Research, University of Albany.

range (35–45), indicating that Afro-Caribbeans' neighborhoods overlap substantially with those of African Americans. Segregation from Africans is substantially higher, though it remains within the moderate range. New York is the one case where both Afro-Caribbeans and Africans are present in large numbers, and segregation between these two groups is in the high range.

Table 7 shows segregation measures in the ten largest metropolitan areas for the African born. Exposure of Africans to whites declined significantly in all ten regions; it was extremely low in New York (17.0 percent) and near or above 50 percent only in Minneapolis–St. Paul, Boston,

Dallas, and Philadelphia. Segregation from whites is in the high range in all cases, though falling in some of them. At the same time, Africans' exposure to blacks is growing, though it is much lower for Africans than for Afro-Caribbeans.

The table generally confirms the national pattern in which Africans are surprisingly segregated from African Americans and Afro-Caribbeans, though these values generally declined during the last decade. Washington, D.C., and Atlanta offer the possibility that where their populations are larger, Africans' neighborhoods may overlap more with those of other blacks. However, the case of New York shows that such a tendency is not inevitable.

TABLE 7 ■ **Segregation of the Ten Metro Regions with Largest African-Born Population in Census 2000**

Metro Area	Exposure to Whites		Segregation from Whites		Exposure to Blacks		Segregation from African Americans		Segregation from Afro-Caribbeans
	1990	2000	1990	2000	1990	2000	1990	2000	1990	2000
Washington, D.C.-MD-VA-WV	47.7%	37.5%	62.7%	63.1%	34.6%	36.7%	62.9%	58.2%	44.9%	42.5%
New York, NY	29.9	17.0	71.6	78.0	38.4	47.0	62.1	48.5	62.6	57.7
Atlanta, GA	53.1	39.4	67.2	63.6	39.7	43.2	57.4	54.0	56.8	48.2
Minneapolis–St. Paul, MN–WI	78.0	59.2	73.0	68.4	11.2	21.9	66.1	50.0	79.3	73.5
Los Angeles-Long Beach, CA	44.7	34.4	59.4	59.9	17.1	19.9	68.3	60.6	65.8	61.1
Boston, MA-NH	55.5	47.5	68.2	63.7	22.4	26.6	64.7	48.9	63.4	54.5
Houston, TX	46.8	33.0	68.2	67.9	23.7	27.3	71.3	64.7	61.6	54.8
Chicago, IL	51.7	45.1	78.0	72.7	29.1	31.0	80.5	71.2	73.2	66.3
Dallas, TX	66.4	49.0	64.8	60.0	15.5	19.6	74.3	64.2	72.9	66.4
Philadelphia, PA-NJ	56.8	49.2	78.1	70.2	34.5	38.7	72.2	61.9	68.0	58.8

Source: Courtesy of Lewis Mumford Center for Comparative Urban and Regional Research, University of Albany.

BLACKS' NEIGHBORHOOD CHARACTERISTICS

Non-Hispanic black groups are residentially segregated from whites and from each other. Do they also live in neighborhoods of different quality? (For research on this same question in the 1970–1980 period, see Adelman et al. 2001.) This final section of this [reading] analyzes selected neighborhood characteristics for the average group member: the neighborhood's median household income (in constant dollars for 1990 and 2000), the percentage of group members who own their homes, and the percentage of residents (over age twenty-five) with a college education. These are characteristics of the neighborhoods in which an average group member

lives, rather than of the groups themselves (these were shown previously in Table 4).

Table 8 shows that non-Hispanic blacks, regardless of ethnicity, live in worse neighborhoods, on average, than do non-Hispanic whites, with one exception—Africans exceed whites in the educational attainment of their neighbors.

More relevant here are the differences among black populations:

- *Income:* The average African American lives in a census tract with a median income of $35,679, while the average Afro-Caribbean lives in a census tract with a median income of $41,328. Africans live in more advantaged neighborhoods with a median income of $45,567 (though this is still more than $7,000 below the neighborhood median income of an average non-Hispanic white).

- *Homeownership:* The average African American lives in a tract where 53.1 percent of the residents own their homes. This is higher than the other black groups, and to some extent it reflects the advantage of having lived for more generations in the United States. The average Afro-Caribbean lives in a tract where 49.8 percent of the residents own homes. Although lower than the national average for African Americans, this deficit is largely due to their concentration in the New York metro area, where this group is mainly found in inner-city neighborhoods. Regional comparisons of this neighborhood characteristic show that Afro-Caribbeans fare much better than African Americans in New York and somewhat better in Washington, D.C., and Atlanta. The average African lives in a tract where 47.2 percent of neighbors are homeowners.

- *Education:* The average African lives in a neighborhood where 29.3 percent of residents have a college education, compared to 29 percent for an average non-Hispanic white. This reflects the very high

educational attainment of the Africans who have been able to immigrate to the United States. By contrast, the average African American lives in a neighborhood where 17.5 percent of residents have a college education, while 20 percent of an average Afro-Caribbean person's neighbors have a college education.

Table 9 provides a closer look at the metro areas where Afro-Caribbeans are most numerous. Homeownership in their neighborhoods, as noted above, is especially low in New York (and Newark and Boston as well, where they also are concentrated in the inner city).

Their neighborhoods are relatively less affluent and less educated in New York. In other metro areas in the table, homeownership in their neighborhoods is actually well above the national average for African Americans. Afro-Caribbeans live in relatively affluent neighborhoods in Nassau–Suffolk (which is all suburban), Washington, D.C., and Atlanta and in neighborhoods with a relatively high education level in Washington, D.C., Atlanta, and Boston.

Similar information is given in Table 10 for the top ten metro areas of Africans. Their neighborhoods have especially high levels of education in Washington, D.C., but in several other metro areas, the percentage of neighbors with a college degree

TABLE 8 ■ Neighborhood Characteristics of the Average Group Member, National Metro Averages						
	Median Household Income ($)		Percentage Homeowners		Percentage College Educated	
Group	1990	2000	1990	2000	1990	2000
African American	31,548	35,679	49.8	53.1	14.0	17.5
Afro-Caribbean	39,970	41,328	44.1	49.8	17.5	20.3
African born	44,715	45,567	44.7	47.2	28.8	29.3
Non-Hispanic white	47,683	52,637	67.6	70.7	23.8	29.0

Source: Courtesy of Lewis Mumford Center for Comparative Urban and Regional Research, University of Albany.

TABLE 9 ■ Neighborhood Characteristics of the Average Afro-Caribbean Resident

Metro Area	Median Household Income ($)		Percentage Homeowners		Percentage College Educated	
	1990	2000	1990	2000	1990	2000
New York, NY	39,410	38,758	31.0	35.1	15.5	18.2
Miami, FL	33,665	33,873	53.8	58.1	13.9	15.0
Fort Lauderdale, FL	35,403	39,621	59.2	64.3	13.3	17.0
Boston, MA-NH	40,825	42,463	36.9	42.3	22.5	26.1
Nassau–Suffolk, NY	63,190	64,241	73.7	75.9	21.4	23.5
Newark, NJ	44,036	45,216	39.6	41.9	17.9	20.5
West Palm Beach–Boca Raton, FL	33,061	38,114	54.9	62.2	12.5	17.5
Washington, DC-MD-VA-WV	53,864	57,218	51.9	57.6	31.5	35.7
Orlando, FL	38,210	39,252	59.6	60.0	17.2	18.1
Atlanta, GA	46,267	50,911	57.9	61.9	27.1	29.9

Source: Courtesy of Lewis Mumford Center for Comparative Urban and Regional Research, University of Albany.

TABLE 10 ■ Neighborhood Characteristics of the Average African-Born Resident

Metro Area	Median Household Income ($)		Percentage Homeowners		Percentage College Educated	
	1990	2000	1990	2000	1990	2000
Washington, DC-MD-VA-WV	55,784	57,143	47.0	50.4	37.5	39.5
New York, NY	40,145	35,243	24.3	24.2	22.7	20.3
Atlanta, GA	43,049	48,614	45.1	49.8	30.0	30.5
Minneapolis–St. Paul, MN-WI	36,321	37,679	46.4	44.0	31.2	27.9
Los Angeles–Long Beach, CA	49,075	47,009	41.9	42.9	26.9	29.8
Boston, MA-NH	43,138	42,925	37.9	40.2	27.3	28.2
Houston, TX	41,298	46,531	39.2	48.8	30.9	30.9
Chicago, IL	40,700	45,509	41.0	47.4	30.7	34.3
Dallas, TX	45,671	49,347	38.2	43.6	35.0	33.1
Philadelphia, PA-NJ	43,811	41,647	60.2	60.7	25.4	23.1

Source: Courtesy of Lewis Mumford Center for Comparative Urban and Regional Research, University of Albany.

is higher than the national average for whites' neighborhoods: Atlanta, Los Angeles–Long Beach, Houston, Chicago, and Dallas. Exceptionally low are the education levels in New York and Philadelphia. Africans also live in especially affluent neighborhoods in Washington, D.C., with a median income of over $57,000—again, well above the national average for whites' neighborhoods. These income levels are lowest in New York and Minneapolis. Finally, Philadelphia stands out for high homeownership in Africans' neighborhoods (over 60 percent), while in New York, homeownership is exceptionally low (less than 25 percent).

CONCLUSION: THE INCREASING DIVERSITY OF AMERICA'S BLACK POPULATIONS

All of these analyses point in a similar direction. Black Americans of all ethnic backgrounds are highly segregated from whites and disadvantaged in comparison to them. Yet, beneath this communality born of the color line are substantial differences between the majority of blacks with historical origins in the United States and new, growing minorities from the Caribbean and Africa. Nearly 17 percent of recent growth in the black population is due to increases in these new groups. Particularly in metro areas where they constitute 20 percent or more of the black population, an increasingly urgent social and political question is whether common problems associated with race

will outweigh differences linked to national origins (Logan and Mollenkopf 2003). Scholars generally agree that the differences are substantial and that black immigrants have limited prospects of assimilation either into mainstream American society or into the African American minority (Kasinitz 1992; Ho 1991). In some places with a long history of black ethnic diversity, such as New York City, the differences have appeared to be divisive in political races (Rogers 2004). But some studies have shown that majority-black institutions are capable of successfully incorporating newcomers (Foerster 2004).

The newcomers have numerous advantages compared to African Americans. Their own education levels and incomes tend to be higher. Not only do they typically live in somewhat different neighborhoods, but in most metro areas, these neighborhoods have a higher socioeconomic standing.

Comparable diversity has been documented among Hispanics (particularly contrasting South Americans and Cubans with Mexicans, Central Americans, and Dominicans) and Asians (among whom Indians and Filipinos present a very different profile than Chinese or Koreans). The American public is used to thinking in terms of the broader racial and ethnic categories—Hispanic, Asian, black. Certainly in the history of black-white relations in this country, the distinctions between blacks of different social class or national origin have paled in comparison to their common treatment. We may nevertheless be moving into an era when those distinctions become more salient and when we must think not only in terms of majority and minority groups but in terms of a nation of many minorities.

THE ARAB IMMIGRANT EXPERIENCE

Michael W. Suleiman

MICHAEL W. SULEIMAN is University Distinguished Professor in the Department of Political Science at Kansas State University. He has written and co-edited numerous works in the field of Arab American studies, including *U.S. Policy on Palestine from Wilson to Clinton* and *Arab Americans: Continuity and Change.*

INTRODUCTION

In 1977, William E. Leuchtenburg, the prominent American historian, remarked, "From the perspective of the American historian, the most striking aspect of the relationship between Arab and American cultures is that, to Americans, the Arabs are a people who have lived outside of history."[1] Professor Leuchtenburg could have just as accurately made the same observation about Arabs in America.

Ignorance about Arab Americans among North Americans at large means that, before looking at more detailed accounts of the Arab American experience, we may benefit from a quick overview of Arab immigration to North America and what the Arab American communities here have been like.

There have been two major waves of Arab immigration to North America. The first lasted from the 1870s to World War II and the second from World War II to the present. Members of the two waves of immigrants had somewhat different characteristics and faced different challenges in the social and political arena. Any examination of the immigrant communities must take into account these differences. As we shall see, the two communities began to come together in the 1960s, especially after the 1967 Arab–Israeli war,[2] and this rapprochement must also be taken into account.

The term "Arab Americans" refers to the immigrants to North America from the Arabic-speaking countries of the Middle East and their descendants. The Arabic-speaking countries today include Algeria, Bahrain, Egypt, Iraq, Jordan, Kuwait, Lebanon, Libya, Mauritania, Morocco, Oman, pre-1948 Palestine and the Palestinians, Qatar, Saudi Arabia, Sudan, Syria, Tunisia, United Arab Emirates, and Yemen. Somalia and Djibouti are also members of The League of Arab States and have some Arabic-speaking populations. Most Arab immigrants of the first wave came from the Greater

Questions to Consider

Since 9/11, the media seem to have discovered the Arab American population in the United States, but this group has had significant presence in this country for almost 150 years. In this reading, Suleiman maps Arab migration to the United States and the "Americanization" process this group, like almost all immigrant groups to this country, has experienced. He suggests that an ambiguous racial status and racism were used to deny citizenship to Arab immigrants. How and why did this happen?

Syria region, especially present-day Lebanon, and were overwhelmingly Christian; later immigrants came from all parts of the Arab world, but especially from Palestine, Lebanon, Syria, Egypt, Iraq, and Yemen, and had large numbers of Muslims among them. Although most Muslim Arab immigrants have been Sunni (reflecting the population in the region), there is a substantial Shi'a minority. Druze started immigrating in small numbers late in the nineteenth century.

Immigrants from the Arabic-speaking countries have been referred to and have referred to themselves by different names at different times, including Arabs or Arabians, but until World War II the designation Syrian or Syrian-Lebanese was used most often. The changeability of the name may indicate the absence of a definite and enduring identity, an issue that is discussed later. For the purposes of this [reading], the various names are used interchangeably, but the community primarily is referred to as Arab or Arab American.[3]

It is impossible to determine the exact number of Arab immigrants to North America, because U.S. and Canadian immigration officials have at different times used different classification schemes. Until 1899 in the United States, for instance, immigration statistics lumped the Arabs with Greeks, Armenians, and Turks. For this and other reasons, only estimates can be provided.

According to U.S. immigration figures, which generally are considered to be low, about 130,000 Arabs had immigrated to the United States by the late 1930s.[4] Estimates of the size of the Arab American community by scholars and community leaders vary widely. A conservative estimate is that there were approximately 350,000 persons of Arab background in the United States on the eve of World War II.[5] In the 1990s, the size of the Arab community in the United States has been estimated at less than one million to the most frequently cited figure of 2 1/2 to 3 million.[6]

Numerous reasons have been given for the first wave of Arab immigration to America, which began in large numbers in the 1880s, but the reasons usually fall into two categories: push and pull factors, with the push factors accorded greater weight.

Most scholars argue that the most important reasons for emigration were economic necessity and personal advancement.[7] According to this view, although the economy in geographic or Greater Syria (a term encompassing the present-day countries and peoples of Syria, Lebanon, the Palestinians, Israel, Jordan, and possibly Iraq) registered some clear gains in the late nineteenth and early twentieth centuries, this progress was uneven in its impact and did not manifest itself in a sustained manner until "after emigration to the New World began to gather momentum."[8] The economy of Mount Lebanon suffered two major crippling blows in the mid-1800s. The first was the opening of the Suez Canal, which sidetracked world traffic from Syria to Egypt and made the trip to the Far East so easy and fast that Japanese silk became a major competitor for the Lebanese silk industry. The second blow came in the 1890s, when Lebanese vineyards were invaded by phylloxera and practically ruined.[9]

Also contributing to the economic stress in the Syrian hinterland was a rapid increase in population without a commensurate increase in agricultural or industrial productivity. Many families found that the subsistence economy could support only one child, who eventually inherited the farm or household. Other male children had to fend for themselves, and emigration to a New World of great wealth became an irresistible option.[10]

Many Lebanese Christians, who constituted most of the early Arab arrivals in North America, emphasize religious persecution and the lack of political and civil freedom as the main causes of their emigration from lands ruled by an oppressive **Ottoman** regime.[11] Under Ottoman rule, Christians in the Syrian province were not accorded equal status with their Muslim neighbors. They were subjected to many restrictions on their behavior and often suffered persecution. These oppressive conditions worsened and discriminatory actions occurred more often as the Ottoman rulers became weaker and their empire earned the title of the "Sick Man of Europe." As the power of the sultan declined, the local rulers began to assert greater authority and power, which they at times used to suppress and oppress further their subjects, particularly Christians. In part, this persecution took place in response to the increased power and prestige of "Christian" Europe and the encroachment of its rulers on Ottoman sovereignty. This effect, combined with the Christian population's desire for greater equality, threatened the Muslim public's sense of security. Like the "poor white trash" of the American South at the time of the Civil War and the Civil Rights Movement, the Muslim population in the Syrian province was poor and oppressed—but it still enjoyed a social status that was superior to that of the non-Muslims, particularly the Christians. The threat of losing that "high" status made many Muslims susceptible to suggestions from local Ottoman rulers that their Christian neighbors were the cause of rather than companions in their troubles. The worsened social and economic conditions in Syria in the mid-1800s and the beginning of the disintegration of feudalism, especially among the Druze, produced social turmoil that erupted in sectarian riots in which thousands of Christians perished.[12] Many Christian Lebanese, especially Maronites, cite the 1860 disturbances and massacres as the main factor contributing to the exodus from their homeland.

In addition to the economic, political, and social causes of the early Arab immigration to North America, some incidental factors should be cited. Among these are improved transportation and communication facilities worldwide, development of steam navigation that made the sea voyage safer and shorter, and aggressiveness of agents of the steamship companies in recruiting new immigrant passengers. Although American missionaries often actively discouraged Syrians or Arabs from migrating to the United States, their very presence as model Americans, their educational activities, and their reports about American life ignited a desire, especially among the graduates of American schools and colleges in Syria, to immigrate to America.

After the feasibility and profitability of immigration to the United States and to "America" in general were well established, chain migration became the norm, with immigrants making it possible for the ambitious and the disgruntled in the old homeland to seek newer horizons. Those wanting to escape military service in the Ottoman army and those craving freedom from oppression and the liberty to speak and publish without censorship or reprisal left their homeland quickly and stealthily and sought what they thought would be a temporary refuge in America.

THE EARLY ARAB COMMUNITY IN AMERICA

Before World War II, most Arabs in America were Christians who came from the Mount Lebanon region of geographic Syria. Especially until the turn of the century, these travelers were mainly poor, uneducated, and illiterate in any language. They were not trained for a particular profession. As unskilled workers, after they learned the rudiments of the English language, they could work in factories and mines. However, such jobs were taxing and monotonous and, most importantly, did not offer opportunities for the fast accumulation of wealth, which was the primary objective of these early Arab arrivals. Farming presented them with the added hardships of isolation, loneliness, and severe weather conditions. Peddling therefore was an attractive alternative. It did not require much

---

Ottoman Empire An empire covering parts of Europe, Asia, and Africa that dominated that region from the thirteenth century until World War I.

training, capital, or knowledge of English. With a few words of English learned on the run, a suitcase (*Kashshi*) full of notions (e.g., needles, thread, lace) provided by a better-established fellow Lebanese or other Arab supplier, probably a relative who helped bring them to the New World, many new arrivals often were on the road hawking their wares only a day or so after they landed in America. Success in peddling required thrift, hard work, very long hours, the stamina to endure harsh travel conditions (mostly walking the countryside on unpaved roads), and not infrequently, the taunting and insults from children or disgruntled customers. These conditions were made tolerable for most early Arab arrivals by their vision of a brighter economic future and the concomitant prestige they and their families would eventually acquire in the old country. When they could afford to do so, they switched to the "luxury" of a horse and buggy and later to a drygoods store.[13]

Before World War I, Arabs in North America thought of themselves as sojourners, as people who were in, but not part of, American society. Their politics reflected and emulated the politics of their original homeland in substance and style, because they were only *temporarily* away from home. In New York, *Kawkab America* (*Kawkab Amirka*), the first Arabic-language newspaper established in North America, declared in its very first issue its unequivocal support for the Ottoman sultan, whose exemplary virtues it detailed at length.[14] All other newspapers had to define in one way or another their attitude toward and their relationship with the Ottoman authorities. Although *Kawkab America* was pro-Ottoman, at least initially, *Al-Ayam* (*al-Ayyam*) was the most vehement opponent of the Ottoman authorities, a role it later shared with *Al-Musheer* (*al-Mushir*).[15] It excoriated the cruelty and corruption of Ottoman rulers, especially in the Mount Lebanon region. It also called for rebellion against the Turkish tyrants and urged its readers to exercise their freedom in America to call for freedom back home. Other newspapers, including *Al-Hoda* (*al-Huda*) and *Meraat-ul-Gharb* (*Mir'at al-gharb*), fell between these two extremes of total support or clear rejection of Ottoman authority.

The orientation of early Arab Americans toward their homeland meant that their political activities were also focused on issues that were important in their country or village of origin. There was communal solidarity, but the community was a collective of several communities. The sectarian and regional disputes that separated the Arabs back home were also salient in this "temporary" residence. The newspapers they established were in the main socializing agencies conveying the messages of their sectarian leadership. Because the Orthodox already had their *Kawkab America*, *Al-Hoda* was set up to represent and speak for the Maronites. Later, *Al-Bajan* (*al-Bajan*) proclaimed itself the newspaper of the Druze.[16] Within each community there were rivalries and competing newspapers, each claiming to be the best defender or representative of its sect.

World War I was a watershed event for Arabs in North America, cutting them off from their people back home. This separation from the homeland became almost complete with the introduction of very restrictive quota systems in the United States and Canada after World War I, which practically cut off emigration from Arab regions. These developments intensified the community's sense of isolation and separation, simultaneously enhancing its sense of solidarity. One consequence was a strengthening of the assimilationist trend—a trend already reinforced by the American-born children of these Arab immigrants.

The substance and style of the Arab community's politics changed after the war, with a clear realization that they had become part of American society. Intersectarian conflicts became less intense and fewer in number. Calls for unity were heeded more often. For instance, Syrian-Lebanese clubs formed regional federations that joined together to form a national federation.[17] A process of socialization into American politics resulted in greater participation in voting and party membership and in public and political service at local or state levels. "Syrian" Republican and Democratic Clubs were formed in the United States, and the arena for political competition changed as the Arab community became part of the American body politic. There also emerged a clear change in matters of style—generally for the better. By the 1930s and 1940s, conflicts became fewer and somewhat less personal, and the language of discourse became much less offensive.

Whereas first-generation Arabs in America managed as best they could in an alien environment, their children were thoroughly immersed in American society and culture—and their first or only language was English. Consequently, English-language newspapers and journals were established to cater to young Americans of Arab heritage.[18] Eastern churches began to translate some of the liturgy and conduct part of the services in English to prevent the loss of members,[19] although many members left the church nonetheless. Some intellectuals, including some of the most celebrated Arab American writers and poets, took advantage of the blessings of freedom and democracy in North America to attack the tyranny and corruption of the clergy, especially in the old homeland but also in America. Some also expressed atheistic or agnostic views, and others left their old churches and joined new ones.[20]

As Arabs assimilated in American society, they also worked harder for a better image of themselves and their people in the old homeland. More effort was spent on campaigns to inform Americans about the rich Arab heritage. In the political arena, especially in the United States, there were many, serious efforts to get the government to support foreign policy positions favored by the Arab community, especially in regard to Palestine. During World War I and its aftermath, the main political preoccupation of the Arabic-speaking groups in North America was to achieve the liberation of their homelands from Ottoman rule and to provide economic assistance to their starving relatives, especially in the Mount Lebanon region. To accomplish these objectives, their leaders set up relief committees, raised funds, and sent money and supplies whenever it was possible to do so. They also urged Arab young men in the United States to join the American armed forces to help their new country and to liberate their old homeland.[21] Leaders organized campaigns to have their people buy American Liberty bonds to help with the war effort.[22]

After the war, the Arabs in America were divided over the destiny of the regions liberated from Ottoman rule. In general, there was a strong sentiment among the Maronites to support French control over Syria and Lebanon under the League of Nations' Mandate.[23] Others argued for complete independence, viewing France as a new occupying power.[24] On the question of Palestine, there was general agreement in support of the Palestinian-Arab population and for eventual, if not immediate, independence. There was widespread opposition to Zionism as a movement bent on establishing a Jewish state there.[25] Arabs in America showed their support for the Palestinians through lectures, publications, fund raising, and political lobbying, especially with U.S. government officials.[26]

Until World War I, Arabs in North America may be considered sojourners exhibiting many traits of a middleman minority—a community whose members primarily engage in one particular specialized activity such as migrant farm work or peddling. Substantial numbers of Arabs in America engaged in commerce, most often beginning as peddlers commissioned by their own countrymen. Their objective was to make the greatest amount of money in the shortest possible time to help their families in the old country and eventually to retire in comfort in their village or neighborhood. In the meantime, they spent as little as possible of their income in America, often living in crowded tenements and, while on the road, in barns or shacks to avoid expensive hotel costs. They did not live rounded lives, allowing themselves no luxuries and finding contentment and solace in family life. Because they could pull up stakes anytime, they sought liquidity in their economic enterprises. Long-term investments were avoided. For that reason, in addition to other advantages, they preferred peddling, dry goods stores, restaurants, the professions, and a cottage industry in lace and needlework. In all of these activities, their primary contacts were with other Arab Americans, especially relatives or people from the same town, religious sect, or geographic region.[27] They developed few lasting relationships with "Americans." *Al-Nizala,* the term the Arab American community used to refer to itself, is a name that clearly describes its status and purpose. It means a temporary settlement, and it was used in contrast to "the Americans" to indicate the alien or stranger status of Arabs in America. At first, Arabs in America formed their own residential colonies, especially in New York and Boston. Even when they did not, they encouraged within-group marriage, frequently praising its virtues and especially pointing out the disadvantages of marrying "American" girls. In other words, they resisted assimilation, even after their intellectuals began to urge acculturation to life in America.[28]

Arabs in America, sharing an attitude common to other middleman or sojourner communities, were charged with being "clannish, alien, and unassimilable."[29] Such attitudes were fairly common among influential American journalists and public officials, who also viewed Arabs as inferior to whites. In the economic field, Arabs were sometimes seen as parasites because they allegedly did not engage in any productive industry, merely being engaged in trade. They were sometimes attacked as a drain on the American economy because they sent part of their income back home.[30]

THE PROCESS OF AMERICANIZATION

Arab immigrants soon found out that the land of opportunity was also strewn with hardship and an "unwelcome" mat. In response to insults and charges of inferiority, they did occasionally defend themselves.[31] However, to add injury to insult, the U.S. and Canadian authorities began to claim that Arabs had no right to naturalization and citizenship because they allegedly were Asian and did not belong to the white race.[32] This problem of racial identification and citizenship traumatized the Arabic-speaking community. In their attempt to resolve this crisis, the "Syrians" searched for their roots and found them in their *Arab* background, which ensured them Caucasian racial status and therefore eligibility for U.S. citizenship—or so they argued.[33] Beginning in 1909, Arabic-speaking individuals from geographic Syria began to be challenged in

their citizenship petitions. It was not until 1914, however, that George Dow was denied a petition to become a U.S. citizen because, as a "Syrian of Asiatic birth," he was not a free white person within the meaning of the 1790 U.S. statute.[34] In 1915, the Dow decision was reversed based on the argument that the pertinent binding legislation was not that of 1790 but the laws of 1873 and 1875, and in accordance with these, Syrians "were so closely related to Europeans that they could be considered 'white persons.'"[35] Despite this precise and authoritative language, "Syrians" in the United States continued to be challenged and to feel insecure about their naturalization status until the period of 1923 to 1924.[36]

Even during World War II, the status of Arabs remained unclear. In 1942, a Muslim Arab from Yemen was denied U.S. citizenship because "Arabs as a class are not white and therefore not eligible for citizenship," especially because of their dark skin and the fact that they are "part of the Mohammedan world," separated from Christian Europe by a wide gulf.[37] On the other hand, in 1944, an "Arabian" Muslim was granted citizenship status under the 1940 Nationality Act, because "as every schoolboy knows, the Arabs have at various times inhabited parts of Europe, lived along the Mediterranean, been contiguous to European nations and been assimilated culturally and otherwise by them."[38]

Apart from the legal battles to ensure they were allowed to reside in their new homelands, especially in the United States, Arabic-speaking persons had to figure out what identity best fit their indeterminate status. They knew who they were and had a very strong sense of personal identity centered first and foremost in the family. There were, however, other lesser but still important identities related to clan, village, or sect. Because these identities were strong, a "national" identity could remain amorphous or at least indeterminate, shifting from one orientation to another with relative ease and without much psychological dislocation. In practical terms, the Arabic-speaking people in North America functioned as a collective of communities whose bonds of solidarity beyond the family were mainly related to sect or country, such as Maronite, Orthodox, Muslim, Druze, and Palestinian affiliations. Before World War II, the primary or most acceptable designation for the group was "Syrian." However, when Lebanon emerged as a country in the 1920s, some Maronites, especially N. Mokarzel, the editor and publisher of *Al-Hoda,* spearheaded a campaign to get the community to change its name to Lebanese, because Lebanon was where most of its members originally came from.[39] The campaign was not a big success, although many of the clubs did change their name to Syrian-Lebanese.[40]

Another and more important identity crisis occurred when these peripatetic sojourners realized that they had to decide whether to become "settlers" or return to the old homeland. It had become increasingly difficult for them to function as temporary aliens. After World War I, it became clear to large numbers of Arabs in North America that it was not possible to go "home" again and that the United States and Canada were their homes.[41] This change from sojourner to permanent settler necessitated and was accompanied by other changes in the way Arabs in America thought and in the way they behaved. The substantial investments they had made in homes, property, and real estate in the old country lost their original purpose, and much more attention was paid to material improvements and investments in their new countries. In the United States, one manifestation was the migration by substantial numbers of the New York Arab community from the rundown and extremely crowded tenements of Manhattan to the nicer environment of South Ferry in Brooklyn and beyond.[42]

Arabs in America saw that they had to become full-fledged Americans. Assimilation became strongly and widely advocated, and citizenship training and naturalization were greatly encouraged. Although outmarriage was still not favored, some now claimed that success in such situations was possible if the American partner (usually female) was a "good" person who behaved in a conservative or traditional manner.[43] Along the same lines, Arab women were told to retain the modesty code of the old homeland.[44]

Although Arab women in America constituted a major asset to their kinfolk, they also presented the community with many difficulties, primarily related to issues of honor and modesty. This problem was most acute among the Druze, some of whom asked to restrict or totally ban the immigration of Druze women to America. Among Christians, women peddlers were a big concern. The complaints and areas targeted for reform included the act of peddling itself, the personal appearance and dress of the woman peddler, the distance she covered and whether she had to stay away from home overnight, and her demeanor or behavior. These problems were viewed as especially serious because large numbers had decided to stay in America and wanted to become "acceptable" to the host society. The preference was for Arab women to help their kinfolk by crocheting or sewing at home or by minding their family's store. Work in factories was also acceptable, although not favored, especially among the rising middle-class Arab Americans.[45]

The decision to settle in America meant setting a higher priority on children's education for boys and girls. This was viewed as more important than any contribution the children might make to the family's economic welfare. The result was a marked improvement in women's education and an increase in the number of male and female graduates from universities and professional institutions.

Another consequence of the decision to stay in America was that parents and children had to learn to be good Americans, and they flocked to citizenship classes. Parents attended English-language classes and studied the American governmental system in preparation for their new role as American citizens. Americanization was seen as a process of shedding old loyalties, the traditional culture, and the Arabic language. The children therefore grew up barely aware of their Arabic heritage.

Although the assimilationist approach began to gain favor and was encouraged by the leadership, it was not presented in ideological terms. Often, it took the form of a suggestion that Arabs should no longer feel like strangers in their new country and that they should make a positive contribution to American society.[46] Nevertheless, in the heyday of the melting pot approach to assimilation, the Arabs in America strove to remove any differences, except perhaps food and music, that separated them from the general American population. They also neglected or chose not to teach their children Arabic or to instill into them much pride of heritage.[47] The result was that, by World War II, Arabs in North America were, for all practical purposes, an indistinguishable group from the host society. It took a second wave of immigration and other developments to rekindle interest in their Arab heritage and to revive them as an ethnic community.

POST–WORLD WAR II IMMIGRATION

The second wave of Arab immigration brought to North America a much more diverse population, one that differed greatly from the early pioneering group. Whereas the first-wave immigrants came almost exclusively from the area of Greater Syria and were overwhelmingly Lebanese, the new immigrants came from all parts of the Arab world, including North Africa. Unlike early arrivals, who were predominantly Christian, the new immigrants were Christians and Muslims.

The two groups' reasons for immigration were also somewhat different. In addition to economic need and the attraction of a major industrial society, new immigrants often were driven out of their homes as a result of regional conflicts (e.g., Palestine–Israel, Arab–Israeli, Iraq–Iran, Iraq–Kuwait) or civil wars (e.g., Lebanon, Yemen) or as a consequence of major social and political changes in the homeland that made life difficult, especially for the wealthy or the middle class in Egypt, Iraq, Syria, and other countries. The search for a democratic haven, where it is possible to live in freedom without political or economic harassment and suppression by the government, was a strong motivation, even more so than during the earlier period, that affected much larger numbers of individuals. To these political and economic motivations can be added a psychological one. The great improvements in transportation and communication facilitated the process of immigration, and by making the world seem smaller, they made it much easier for people to accept the notion of migration to other parts of the world, especially to the United States and Canada.

Whereas the early Arab immigrants were mainly uneducated and relatively poor, the new arrivals included large numbers of relatively well-off, highly educated professionals: lawyers, professors, teachers, engineers, and doctors. Many of the new immigrants began as students at American universities who decided to stay, often as a result of lack of employment opportunities back home or because of the unstable political conditions in the homeland—conditions that often threatened imprisonment or death for returnees.[48] Besides these comparatively affluent immigrants, especially in the 1990s, relatively large numbers of semieducated Arabs, primarily engaged in commerce, came to North America as political refugees or as temporary residents to escape the wars and violence of the Middle East region.

An important difference between members of the two immigration waves is the way each group thought of itself in terms of American society and politics. First-wave immigrants were viewed and thought of themselves as mere sojourners staying in the United States on a temporary basis with the primary or sole purpose of making a fortune they could enjoy back home. This orientation remained dominant at least until World War I and probably well into the 1920s. Such a stance meant that they avoided participation in American society beyond taking care of basic needs such as commerce. They were "Syrians" or "Arabians" and sought to establish their own churches, clubs, or newspapers. They sought (and preached to their people) not to "meddle" in the affairs of the host society. They were anxious not to offend their hosts, not to break the law, and not to behave in a manner offensive to Americans, but they also tried not to imitate American social customs (i.e., Americanize), not to mix socially with Americans, and not to intermarry. Although most did not participate in politics much beyond voting, they nevertheless expressed pride in the occasional Arab who was able to make it as a city alderman, political party functionary, or a candidate for local political office.

The change from these conditions came slowly and as a result of changes in the world around them, especially World War I; the Ottomans' oppressive treatment of their subjects in the Syria–Lebanon region; and the success of Zionism in securing Western, especially British and American, support for its objective of establishing a Jewish homeland in Palestine.

Immigrants who arrived after World War II came with a well-defined view of democracy and the role of citizens in it—ideas they had learned in their homeland but that had originally been imported from Europe and America. Their higher level of education and social status gave them greater confidence about participating in American politics almost as soon as they arrived in their new country. Even when they thought about returning to their Arab homeland, they were anxious to live full and productive lives in the United States or Canada for themselves and their children. The Arab American community today constitutes a combination of the diversities of the early and more recent immigrants. In addition to the sectarian and mainly social clubs that the early immigrants formed, new political organizations were gradually established. In the United States, Syrian Democratic and Syrian Republican clubs were formed in the 1920s and 1930s. These were, as the Arab Democratic and Arab Republican clubs are today, adjuncts to the main two major parties designed to encourage political participation and to integrate Arabs into the American body politic. What was new and significant was the establishment of bona fide Arab American pressure groups and voluntary associations whose main function has been to protect themselves against harassment from private groups or public agencies and to influence policy in the United States and Canada concerning different parts of the Arab World or Middle East.

As World War I had marked a watershed for the early Arab immigrants, the 1967 Arab–Israeli war did for the entire community. The older and newer Arab American communities were shocked and traumatized by the 1967 war. In particular, they were dismayed and extremely disappointed to see how greatly one-sided and pro-Israeli the American communications media were in reporting on the Middle East.[49] The war itself also produced soul-searching on the part of many Arab

Americans, old and new, and often reinforced or strengthened their Arab identity. This group included many members already active in various Palestinian, Syrian, and Lebanese clubs, which were mainly social in nature.

By 1967, members of the third generation of the early Arab immigrants had started to awaken to their own identity and to see that identity as Arab, not "Syrian." Elements of this third generation combined with politically sophisticated immigrants to work for their ethnic community and the causes of their people in the old homelands. The result was establishment of the Association of Arab-American University Graduates (AAUG) in late 1967, which was the first post–World War II national, credible, nonsectarian organization seeking to represent diverse elements of the Arab American community and to advance an Arab rather than regional or country orientation.

To the AAUG, however, American hostility to "Arabs" and the concept of Arabism was so extreme and so widespread among policy makers and the general public that influencing the political process or public policy, especially in the United States, seemed futile. The Republican and Democratic parties were almost completely and solidly one-sided in their support of Israel and in their hostility to Arab causes, even though the United States had huge economic and military assets in the region and was on the friendliest terms with most leaders and countries of the Arab world. The AAUG sought support from or identified with other individuals and groups. Among these were a few politicians such as Senator William Fulbright and others who were courageous enough to voice criticism of U.S. policy in the Middle East, other minority or disenfranchised groups in American society, and some intellectuals who began to criticize the administration and its policies.

The AAUG's first priority was the need to provide accurate information about the Arab world and Arabs in North America and to distribute this literature to the public at large, wherever access was possible. It sought to educate the Arab countries and people about the true nature of the problems facing the region and to educate Arab intellectuals and political leaders about U.S. and Canadian policies and the American political process. While the AAUG sought mainly to inform and educate, it also performed other tasks, because no other organizations existed to perform them. Among the tasks to which the AAUG devoted some time and effort were political lobbying, attacks against defamation of and discrimination against Arabs and Arab Americans, and activism among Arab Americans to get them to participate in politics.

These ancillary tasks were later championed and performed by newer organizations. The National Association of Arab Americans (NAAA) was formed in 1972 in the United States to act as a political lobby to defend and advance Arab American interests and causes. In 1980, in response to the continuing slander and attacks against Arabs and Arab Americans, the American-Arab Anti-Discrimination Committee (ADC) was established and quickly drew widespread support from the varied elements of the Arab community. In 1985, the Arab American Institute (AAI) was formed, primarily to encourage Arab Americans to become active in the American political arena.[50]

BUILDING A NEW FUTURE

To get a feel for how the Arab community has fared in America, it is useful to review some of the challenges and concerns that Arabs have faced in their new homeland and how they have coped with building a new future. Among the most important issues with which Arabs in America have had to wrestle is the definition of who they are, their sense of identity as a people, especially as they encountered and continue to encounter bias and discrimination in their new homeland.

Although Arabs in the United States and Canada constitute an ethnic group, they were not an ethnic minority in their old homeland. Their new identity has been shaped by many factors but especially by continuing interactions between conditions in the old and new homelands and by the interplay between their perceptions of themselves and how others see them. The early immigrants spoke Arabic and came from a predominantly Arabic culture and heritage, but they did not think of themselves as "Arabs." The main bond of solidarity among them at that time was based on familial, sectarian, and village- or region-oriented factors. The plethora of names by which they were known in the New World reflects their lack of "national" identity and ignorance or confusion on the part of the host society. Another factor in this process was the American, especially U.S., obsession with the idea of race and the various attempts early in this century to classify every immigrant group, no matter how small, by its racial composition.[51] The early Arabic-speaking groups were called Asians, "other Asians," Turks from Asia, Caucasian, white, black, or "colored."

Although immigration officials and the general press looked down on Arabic-speaking peoples, they nevertheless viewed them as part of the "white race," at least for the first thirty years or so of their presence in North America. These authorities then decided those immigrants were not white. With their very identity questioned and maligned, the reaction of the early Arab Americans was to try to refute what they saw as demeaning and untrue charges. They argued that they were very much part of the white race.[52] Stung by accusations of inferiority in terms of scientific and technological accomplishments, Syrian–Arab Americans developed a two-cultures thesis long before C. P. Snow discussed it.[53] Their argument, which became popular in the community, especially among Arab literati, was that, although America was the most advanced country in the world in science, technology, and industrialization, the East was spiritually superior.[54] Coming from the Holy Land, they offered themselves as guides and instructors to Americans in their search for and desire to experience the life and times of Jesus—where he was born, preached, was crucified, and rose from the dead.[55] Arab Americans spoke and wrote about the "spiritual" East in terms that suggested perpetuity: it was always so and would always be so. By accident or not, these writers in essence condemned the

East to an absence of material progress and desire to produce such for all time.

The emphasis on Eastern spirituality, although useful in making Arabs feel good about themselves compared with "materialist" Americans, still left Arabs in America with little cultural heritage to offer their American-born children. The result often was to ignore their Arab heritage and, especially beginning in the 1920s, to emphasize almost full assimilation in American society. As the children grew up immersed in American society and culture while simultaneously exposed to a smattering of Arabic words at home and some Arabic food and music, they often found themselves experiencing an identity crisis of some kind, mainly resulting in rootlessness, ambiguity, and a fractionalized personality.[56] These were the reactions of some of the Arab American literati of the post–World War II period. The very culture of their own country denied them the privilege of being openly proud of their heritage. They sometimes dealt with this awkward situation by complaining about American prejudice and discrimination against Arabs and by simultaneously denigrating their own people and heritage—if only to ingratiate themselves with their readers, their fellow Americans.[57]

The 1967 war changed the situation radically. Israel, in the short period of seven days, defeated the Arab armies. The Arab people generally felt let down and humiliated. Arabs in America, both newcomers and third-generation descendants of the early pioneers, deeply resented the extreme partisanship America and Americans (especially the U.S. government and people) showed toward Israel and the occasional hostility toward Arabs. The consequence was for Arab Americans to shake off their malaise and to organize. Their first goal was to fight against the negative stereotyping of Arabs. Their second was to help modify American policy toward the Middle East and make it more balanced. In the process, sectors of the well-established older community de-assimilated. They began openly to call themselves Arab and to join political groupings set up to defend Arab and Arab American causes.[58] Arab Americans also began to organize conferences and publish journals and books in defense of their

cause. They wrote fiction, poetry, and memoirs declaring pride in and solidarity with Arabs and the Arab community in America.

Open Arab American pride in their heritage and activism on behalf of their cause does not, however, mean that prejudice against them ceased. On the contrary, many in the community feel that prejudice and discrimination have increased. Different reasons have been advanced to explain the prejudice and discrimination that Arabs encounter in North America, and different individuals and groups have emphasized what they believe to be the main cause or the one most pertinent to their situation.

The most popular explanation for the negative stereotypes Americans hold about Arabs is that they are ignorant of the truth because they have not read or have read inaccurate and false reports about Arabs and have not come into contact with Arabs. According to this view, the stereotypes are mainly the result of propaganda by and on behalf of Zionist and pro-Israeli supporters. The primary objective of this propaganda has been to deprive Arabs, especially Palestinians, from presenting their case to the American public and the American political leadership.[59]

In this view, the attempt to deny Arabs and Arab Americans a public voice also extends to the political arena. In this way, it becomes a "politics of exclusion" in an attempt to prevent debate on any issues that reflect poorly on Zionists or Israel. It also smears and defames Arab candidates for political office to defeat them and exclude them from effective participation in political decision making. This "political racism" is presumed to be ideological in nature and not necessarily directed against Arabs or Arab Americans as a people or as an ethnic community.[60]

Another view sees hostility and violence against Arabs and Arab Americans as anti-Arab racism. This hostility is seen as part of the native racist attitudes and is believed to be present in all sectors of American society, not just among fringe groups. Somewhat related to this view is "jingoistic racism," which is directed at whatever foreign enemy is perceived to be out there.[61] Because of the many recent conflicts in the Middle East in which the United

States directly or indirectly became involved and where incidents of hijacking and hostage taking occurred, many Americans reacted negatively against a vaguely perceived enemy next door, often not distinguishing between Arabs and Muslims or between Arabs and any foreigner who "looks" Arab.[62]

Still another view of negative Arab stereotypes, at least in the United States, argues that these ideas are "rooted in a core of hostile archetypes that our culture applies to those with whom it clashes."[63] According to this argument, most of the elements that constitute the Arab image in America are not unique to Arabs but also have been applied to other ethnic groups, especially blacks and Jews in the form of racism and anti-Semitism. These negative stereotypes have been transferred to a new group, the Arabs or Arab Americans.

Part of the negative stereotyping and hostility many Americans harbor toward Arabs is based on the latter's alleged mistreatment of their women. It is rather ironic, therefore, that Arab American women find themselves the subject of prejudice, discrimination, and hostility at the hands of American men and women. This is often the result of hostility based on race, color, or religion.[64]

Arab American women have had more problems than their male counterparts in defining an acceptable or comfortable identity. The problem is multifaceted and affects different sectors differently. Women who have come from the most traditional countries of the Arab world have experienced a greater restriction of their freedom in the United States. This is primarily the result of an inability on the part of traditional husbands, fathers, and brothers to deal with the nearly complete freedom accorded to women in American society. Just as important is the inability of the women to participate fully in the United States because they do not know the language, lack the necessary education, and are unfamiliar with American customs. They are not psychologically ready to countenance, let alone internalize, certain mores pertaining to the public display of affection and male–female interaction. Because many cannot drive and probably do not have a car, they find themselves much more isolated than they were back home, where they often

had a vibrant and full life, albeit within the confines of the family and female friends.[65]

Among middle-class, first-generation Arab American women, there is perhaps not much adjustment necessary. They usually follow the somewhat liberal mores they brought with them from the old homeland. On the other hand, Arab girls reaching their adolescence in the United States are likely to experience more problems as a result of the potential clash between traditional childrearing practices and the freer atmosphere found in North America.[66]

Among better-educated, young Arab American women, the issue of identity is both more subtle and more openly discussed. Like their male Arab American counterparts, these women suffer from and are offended by the hostility against Arabs and Arab Americans. They also find American views of how women are allegedly treated in the Arab world to be inaccurate and grotesque. Nevertheless, they would like to expand the rights of Arab women and to improve the quality of their lives. They resent and reject any attempt on the part of Arab American men to define what their role should be in maintaining Arab culture and mores in North America. In particular, they want to reject the notion that family honor resides in women and that the way a woman behaves, especially concerning her modesty and sexuality, can bring honor or dishonor to the family. They do not wish to be the conveyors or transmitters of tradition and culture—at least not as these are defined by men or as they prevail in the old homeland.[67]

Women and men in the Arab American community of the 1990s find that the "white" racial classification that the early Syrian-Arab community worked so hard to attain is flawed. In practical daily interactions, Arabs in America are often treated as "honorary whites" or "white but not quite."[68] In reaction to this situation, at least four different orientations have been advocated. For the majority, especially among the older and well-established Christian community, there is some disgruntlement but general passivity about the discrimination and the prejudice that accompany their "white but not quite" status, and they work to remove these negative attitudes. Others, especially the Arab American

Institute, have argued for a special designation of Arabs in the United States as a minority (e.g., the Hispanics) or as a specific census category encompassing all peoples of the Middle East.[69] Still others, especially some young, educated Arab American women, have expressed a preference for the designation "people of color."[70] This would place them as part of a larger category that includes most of the federally recognized minorities in the United States. There are also those who resent being boxed into one category. Their sense of identity is multifaceted; they are men or women; Arab, American, Muslim or Christian; white or dark skinned; and so on. They think of themselves in different ways at different times or in different contexts, and they argue for getting rid of such categories or for the use of more descriptive categories that recognize different aspects of their background, culture, or physical appearance.[71]

The search for an adequate or comfortable identity for Arabs in America has been guided and perhaps complicated by the need to feel pride in their heritage and simultaneously avoid prejudice and discrimination in their new homeland. For most, the search is neither successful nor final. They continue to experience marginality in American society and politics, and they try to overcome this in various ways. Some resort to ethnic denial; they de-emphasize their Arab or Islamic background by claiming a connection with what they believe is a more acceptable appearance in America. Instead of proclaiming their Arabism, for instance, they claim that they are Lebanese or Egyptian. Some may even deny their heritage altogether, claiming to be Greek or Italian. Some new arrivals instead choose ethnic isolation. They are unwilling to change themselves and do not believe they can change the host society.

Among those who want full integration or assimilation into American society, especially middle-class Arab Americans, many emphasize the strong cultural link between Arabs and Americans. They refuse to give up and continue to work hard to show where the dominant American view is wrong. For most, accommodation is the easiest and most comfortable stance. These men and women consciously or subconsciously act in ways that reduce their difference from the American dominant group. They attempt "to pass."[72] Others, especially those who seek material success, especially those who are in public professions (e.g., television, radio, movies), often give in and convert to the prevailing view. Not infrequently, the very individuals who are looked down on by the Arab American community are selected to speak for and represent the Arabs in America.[73]

THE ARAB AMERICAN COMMUNITY IN THE 1990S

After more than a century of immigration, it is clear that the basic reasons Arabs came are no different from those that drove or attracted other groups to come here. They came because of the promise of a quick fortune and a sense of adventure; the threat of war or economic disaster; education, training, technology; and the thrill of living in a free democratic system. Whatever their reasons, true integration and full assimilation have eluded them. In part, this is the result of the many developments leading to the debunking of the notion of a melting pot and the greater tolerance of a multicultural society. The more important reason, however, has been the hostility the host society has shown toward Arab immigrants.[74]

Nevertheless, Arabs in America have done very well. Since the 1960s, there has always been at least one representative of Arab background in the U.S. Congress (e.g, James Abourezk, Mary Rose Oakar, Mark Joe [Nick] Rahall II). Others have served as state governors (e.g., Victor Atiyeh, OR) or on the White House staff (e.g., John H. Sununu). Similarly, individuals of Arab descent have been elected to the Canadian parliament (e.g., Mac Harb, Mark Assad) and to provincial legislatures. Many of these individuals have faced difficulties in attaining their positions because they were of Arab background. Some have found it useful to de-emphasize or deny that background to get or maintain their positions. Most also have not been strong or vocal supporters of Arab or Arab nationalist causes.

Nonetheless, ethnic pride is more openly displayed by an increasing number of political candidates at local, state, and national levels.[75]

Arab Americans have done well and fared better economically than the general population average in many areas. The 1980 and 1990 U.S. census data show that Arab Americans reach a higher educational level than the American population as a whole. According to the 1990 census, 15.2 percent of Arab Americans have "graduate degrees or higher"—more than twice the national average of 7.2 percent. Household income among Arab Americans also tends to be higher than the average. Arab Americans have also done well in professional, management, and sales professions.[76]

Although many Arabs in America have reached the highest level of their profession in almost all professions,[77] the American media primarily highlight the negative achievements of Arabs and Muslims. Quite often, the media announce the Arab or Islamic origin or affiliation of anyone accused of a terrorist act—even before they know whether the perpetrator is Arab or Muslim. In the case of positive role models such as Michael DeBakey or Ralph Nader, the media often never mention their Arab background. One reason is that "some [too many] have found it necessary to hide their origins because of racism."[78] Lists of prominent Arab Americans occasionally are published in the press to inform the public about the community's accomplishments, but the fact that such lists are compiled indicates that Arab Americans feel the sting of negative stereotyping and try to correct the bad publicity. Despite the fact that Arabs have lived in America for more than a century and despite their major successes, they are still struggling to be accepted in American society. Full integration and assimilation will not be achieved until that happens.[79]

ETHNIC AND RACIAL IDENTITIES OF SECOND-GENERATION BLACK IMMIGRANTS IN NEW YORK CITY

Mary C. Waters

MARY C. WATERS is a professor of sociology at Harvard University. She is the author of *Ethnic Options: Choosing Identities in America* and the co-author of *From Many Strands: Ethnic and Racial Groups in Contemporary America.*

THE GROWTH OF NONWHITE VOLUN-TARY immigrants to the United States since 1965 challenges the dichotomy that once explained different patterns of American inclusion and assimilation—the ethnic pattern of assimilation of European immigrants and the racial pattern of exclusion of America's nonwhite peoples. The new wave of immigrants includes people who are still defined racially in the United States but who migrate voluntarily and often under an immigrant preference system that selects for people with jobs and education that put them well above their coethnics in the economy. Do the processes of immigration and assimilation for nonwhite immigrants resemble the processes for earlier white immigrants? Or do these immigrants and their children face very different choices and constraints because they are defined racially by other Americans?

This [reading] examines a small piece of this puzzle—the question of the development of an ethnic identity among the second generation of black immigrants from the Caribbean. While there has been a substantial amount of interest in the identities and affiliations of these immigrants, very little research has been conducted on the identities of their children. The children of black immigrants in the United States face a choice about whether to identify as black American or whether to maintain an ethnic identity reflecting their parents' national origins. First-generation black immigrants to the United States have tended to distance themselves from American blacks, stressing their national origins and ethnic identities as Jamaican or Haitian or Trinidadian, but they also face overwhelming pressures in the United States to identify only as blacks (Foner 1987; Kasinitz 1992; Stafford 1987; Sutton and Makiesky 1975; Woldemikael 1989). In fact, they have been described as "invisible immigrants," because rather than being contrasted with other immigrants (for example, contrasting how Jamaicans are doing relative to Chinese), they are compared with black Americans. The children of black immigrants, because they lack their parents' distinctive accents, can choose to be even more invisible as ethnics than their parents.

Questions to Consider

Based on her research of West Indians and Haitian Americans in New York City, Mary Waters found that first-generation black immigrants "tended to distance themselves from American blacks." Why? What does this "distancing" strategy say about the way American blacks are perceived by new immigrant groups? How is racism *within* a racial group possible?

Second-generation West Indians in the United States most often will be seen by others as merely "American"—and must actively work to assert their ethnic identities.

The types of racial and ethnic identities adopted by a sample of second-generation West Indians[1] and Haitian Americans in New York City are explored here, along with subjective understandings these youngsters have of being American, being black American, and being their ethnic identity. After a short discussion of current theoretical approaches to understanding assimilation among the second generation, three types of identities adopted by the second generation are described and the different experiences of race relations associated with these identities are traced. Finally, this [reading] suggests some implications for future patterns of identity development. . . .

Interviews with first-generation immigrants and their American coworkers reveal a great deal of tension between foreign-born and American-born blacks in both the working-class and the middle-class work sites. Long-standing tensions between newly arrived West Indians and American blacks have left a legacy of mutual stereotyping. (See Kasinitz 1992.) The immigrants see themselves as hardworking, ambitious, militant about their racial identities but not oversensitive or obsessed with race, and committed to education and family. They see black Americans as lazy, disorganized, and obsessed with racial slights and barriers, with a disorganized and laissez-faire attitude toward family life and child raising. American blacks describe the immigrants as arrogant, selfish, exploited in the workplace, oblivious to racial tensions and politics in the United States, and unfriendly and unwilling to have relations with black Americans. The first generation believes that their status as foreign-born blacks is higher than American blacks, and they tend to accentuate their identities as immigrants. Their accent is usually a clear and unambiguous signal to other Americans that they are foreign born.

The dilemma facing the second generation is that they grow up exposed to the negative opinions voiced by their parents about American blacks and to the belief that whites respond more favorably to foreign-born blacks. But they also realize that because they lack their parents' accents and other identifying characteristics, other people, including their peers, are likely to identify them as American blacks. How does the second generation handle this dilemma? Do they follow their parents' lead and identify with their ethnic identities such as Jamaican or Haitian or West Indian? Or do they try to become "American" and reject their parents' ethnic immigrant identities? . . .

THEORETICAL APPROACHES TO ASSIMILATION

Theories derived from the experiences of European immigrants and their children in the early twentieth century predicted that the more time spent in the United States, the more likely second-generation youths were to adopt an "American identity" and to reduce ties to the ethnic identities and culture of their parents. This "straight-line" assimilation model assumes that with each succeeding generation, the groups become more similar to mainstream Americans and more economically successful. For instance, Warner and Srole's (1945) study of ethnic groups in Yankee City (Newburyport, Massachusetts) in the early 1930s describes

the generational march from initial residential and occupational segregation and poverty to residential, occupational, and identificational integration and Americanization.

However, the situation faced by immigrant blacks in the 1990s differs in many of the background assumptions of the straight-line model. The immigrants do not enter a society that assumes an undifferentiated monolithic American culture but rather a consciously pluralistic society in which a variety of subcultures and racial and ethnic identities coexist. In fact, if these immigrants assimilate, they become not just Americans but black Americans. The immigrants generally believe that it is higher social status to be an immigrant black than to be an American black. Second, the economic opportunity structure is very different now from what it was at the beginning of the twentieth century. The unskilled jobs in manufacturing that enhanced job mobility for immigrants' children at the turn of the century have been lost as economic restructuring in the United States has shifted to a service economy (Gans 1992). The immigrants also are quite varied in the skills they bring with them. Some arrive with advanced educations and professional qualifications to take relatively well-paying jobs, which put them ahead of native American blacks (for example, Jamaican nurses). Others are less skilled and face difficulties finding work in the United States. Finally, the degree of residential segregation faced by blacks in the United States, whether foreign born or American born, has always been, and continues to be, of a much higher order than the segregation faced by foreign-born white immigrants (Lieberson 1980; Massey 1990). Thus, even with occupational mobility, it is not clear that blacks would be able to move into higher-status neighborhoods in the orderly progression that Warner and Srole (1945) describe in their Yankee City study of European ethnic succession. A further complication for the black second generation is that part of being a black American involves dealing with American racism. Because immigrants and black Americans report a large difference in the perception and expectation of racism in American society, part of becoming

American for the second generation involves developing a knowledge and perception of racism and its subtle nuances. . . .

PATTERNS IN THE SECOND GENERATION

The interviews suggest that while the individuals in this study vary a great deal in their identities, perceptions, and opinions, they can be sorted into three general types: identifying as Americans, identifying as ethnic Americans with some distancing from black Americans, or identifying as an immigrant in a way that does not reckon with American racial and ethnic categories.

A black American identity characterized the responses of approximately 42 percent of the eighty-three second-generation respondents interviewed. These youngsters identified with other black Americans. They did not see their "ethnic" identities as important to their self-image. When their parents or friends criticized American blacks or described what they perceived as fundamental differences between Caribbean-origin people and American blacks, these youngsters disagreed. They tended to downplay a national-origin identity and described themselves as American.

Another 30 percent of the respondents adopted a very strong ethnic identity that involved a considerable amount of distancing from American blacks. It was important for these respondents to stress their ethnic identities and for other people to recognize that they were not American blacks. These respondents tended to agree with parental judgments that there were strong differences between Americans and West Indians. This often involved a stance that West Indians were superior to American blacks in their behaviors and attitudes.

A final 28 percent of respondents had an immigrant attitude toward their identities, as opposed to American-identified youth or ethnic-identified youth. Most, but not all, of these respondents were more recent immigrants themselves. A crucial factor for these youngsters is that their accents and styles of clothing and behavior clearly signaled to others that they were foreign born. In a sense, their identity as an immigrant people precluded having to make a "choice" about what kind of American they were. These respondents had a strong identity, such as Jamaican or Trinidadian, but did not evidence much distancing from American blacks. Rather their identities were strongly linked to their experiences on the islands, and they did not worry much about how they were seen by other Americans, white or black.

A number of factors influence the type of identity the youngsters develop. They include the class background of the parents, the social networks in which the parents are involved, the type of school the child attends, and the family structure. All of these factors affect the ability of parents and other family members to shield children from neighborhood peer groups that espouse anti-school values.

The type of identity and outlook on American race and ethnic relations that the youngsters developed was strongly related to their social class and its trajectory. The ethnic-identified youngsters were most likely to come from a middle-class background. Of the eighty-three second-generation teens and young adults interviewed, 57 percent of the middle-class teens identified ethnically, whereas only 17 percent of the working-class and poor teens identified ethnically.[2] The poorest students were the most likely to be immigrant or American identified. Only one out of the twelve teens whose parents were on public assistance identified ethnically. The American identified, perhaps not surprisingly, were also more likely to be born in the United States—67 percent of the American identified were born in the United States, as opposed to only 13 percent of the immigrant identified and 42 percent of the ethnically identified.

Parents with more education and income were able to provide better schools for their offspring. Among the respondents, some of the middle class had moved from the inner-city neighborhoods they had originally settled in to middle-class neighborhoods in the borough of Queens or to suburban areas where the schools were of higher academic quality and more likely to be racially integrated.

Other middle-class parents sent their children to Catholic parochial schools or to citywide magnet schools such as Brooklyn Tech or Stuyvesant. Thus, the children were far more likely to attend schools with other immigrant children and with other middle-class whites and blacks, although some of the Catholic high schools were all black in enrollment.

The children of middle-class parents who did attend the local high schools were likely to be recent immigrants who had an immigrant identity. Because of their superior education in the West Indies, these students were the best in the local high schools, attended honors classes, and were bound for college. The children of middle-class parents who identified as American and were pessimistic about their own future opportunities and adopted anti-school ideologies were likely to have arrived early in their lives and to have attended New York City public schools in inner-city areas from an early age.

The social networks of parents also influenced the type of identity the children developed. Regardless of social class, parents who were involved in ethnic voluntary organizations or heavily involved in their churches seemed to instill a strong sense of ethnic identity in their children. Parents whose social networks transcended neighborhood boundaries seemed to have more ability to provide guidance and social contacts for their children.

The two neighborhood schools where we interviewed the teenagers were among the five most dangerous schools in New York City—they were inadequate facilities with crumbling physical buildings, high dropout rates, and serious problems with violence. Both schools were all minority, with over 90 percent of the student body composed of black students, both American and foreign born. The students who attended these schools and were not in the separate honors track (which was overwhelmingly filled with newly arrived immigrants) faced very limited future options, even if they managed to graduate.

Finally, the family structure and the experience of migration itself have a profound effect on the degree of control parents have over teenage children. Many families are composed of single

working mothers and children. These mothers have not been able to supervise their children as much as they would like, and many do not have any extended family or close friends available to help with discipline and control. Even families with two spouses present often have been apart for long periods because one spouse preceded the family in migration. Often children have been left in the islands or sent ahead with relatives to New York, with the parents often struggling to reassert authority after the family reunites. The generational conflict that ensues tends to create greater pressure for students to want to be "American" to differentiate themselves from parents.

ETHNIC RESPONSE

All of the teenage respondents reported comments by their parents about American blacks that were very similar to those recorded in our interviews with the first generation. The differences were in how the teens interpreted what their parents were saying. In general, the ethnic-identified teens agreed with their parents and reported seeing a strong difference between themselves and black Americans, stressing that being black is not synonymous with being black American. They accept their parents' and the wider society's negative portrayals of poor blacks and wanted to avoid any chance that they will be identified with them. They described the culture and values of lower-class black Americans as lacking discipline, a work ethic, good child-rearing practices, and respect for education. They contrast these failures with the values of their parents' ethnic groups, which include an emphasis on education, strict discipline for children, a strong work ethic, and social mobility. They try to impress that they are Jamaican or Haitian and most definitely not black American. This allows them less dissonance with their parents' negative views of American blacks. They do not reject their parents' culture and identities but rather reject the American social system that would identify them as black American and strongly reject the African American peer group culture to which they would be assigned by whites and others if they did not consciously transmit their ethnic identities.

Although society may define the second generation on the basis of skin color, the second-generation ethnic teens believed that being black American involves more than merely having black skin. One young woman criticized American blacks in this way:

Some of them [black Americans] think that their heritage includes not being able to speak correctly or walk correctly, or act loud and obnoxious to make a point. I don't think they have to do that. Just when I see black Americans, it depends on how I see you on the street. Walking down the street with that walk that moves a little bit too much. I would say, I'd think you dropped out of high school.

These teens also differentiated themselves from black Americans in terms of their sensitivity to racism, real or imagined. Some of the ethnic-identified second generation echo the feelings we heard from the first generation that American blacks are too quick to use race as an explanation or excuse for not doing well:

There was a time back in the 40s and 50s and 60s or whenever when people was actually trying to keep down black people and stuff like that. But, you know, some black people now, it's like they not actually trying to make it better, you know? Some are just like, people are like, oh, this place is trying to keep me down, and they sulk and they cry about it, and they're not really doing that much to help themselves.

. . . It's just like hyping the problem if they keep [saying] everything is racial, everything is racial.

The second-generation teens who are doing well try to understand how it is that they are so successful when black Americans are not—and often they chalk it up to family values. They say that

their immigrant families have close-knit family values that stress education. Aware of, and sometimes sharing, the negative images of black Americans that the whites they encounter believe, the second generation also perceives that whites treat them better when they realize they are not "just" black Americans. When asked if they ever benefited from their ethnicity, they responded "yes": "It seems white Americans don't tend to put you in the same category as black Americans." Another respondent said:

The West Indians tend to go that extra step because they, whites, don't usually consider them really black Americans, which would be working class. They don't consider them, I guess, as black. They see them as a person.

The dilemma for the second generation is that while they have a strong sense of their own identities as very different from black Americans, this was not clear to other people. Often both whites and blacks saw them as just black Americans and did not notice that they were ethnically different. When people did comment on their ethnic difference, it was often because of the way they talked and the way they walked. These two characteristics were cited as reasons that whites and other blacks gave for thinking those of the second generation were not "really black." Whites tend to let these children know that they think of them as exceptions to the rule, with the rule being that most blacks are not good people. However, these young people also know that unless they tell people of their ethnicity, most whites have no idea they are not black Americans.

Many of these teens coped with this dilemma by devising ways to telegraph their identities as second-generation West Indians or Haitians. One girl carried a Guyanese map as part of her key chain so that when people looked at her keys they would ask her about it and she could tell them that her parents were from Guyana. One young woman described having her mother teach her an accent so that she could use it when she applied for a job or a place to live. Others just try to work it into conversation when they meet someone. This means that their self-identification is almost always at odds with the identifications others make of them in impersonal encounters in American society and that, as a result, they must consciously try to accentuate their ethnic identity:

Q: When a form or survey asks for your race, what do you put down?

A: Oh boy, that is a tough one. It's funny because, you know, when we fill applications I never know what to check off, you know. I'm serious. 'Cause they have Afro-American, but they never have like Caribbean. They do have white, Chinese. To tell the truth, I would like to be called Caribbean, West Indian. Black West Indian.

The teens who were around many black Americans felt pressure from their peers to be part of the group and identify as black American. These teens would consciously talk about passing for American at some points and passing for Haitian or Jamaican at others by changing the way they talked or acted:

When I'm at school and I sit with my black friends and, sometimes I'm ashamed to say this, but my accent changes. I learn all the words. I switch. Well, when I'm with my friends, my black friends, I say I'm black, black American. When I'm with my Haitian-American friends, I say I'm Haitian. Well, my being black, I guess that puts me when I'm with black Americans, it makes people think that I'm lower class. . . . Then, if I'm talking like this [regular voice] with my friends at school, they call me white.

AMERICAN-IDENTIFIED SECOND GENERATION

The American-identified second-generation teenagers differed in how little they stressed their immigrant or ethnic identities to the interviewers. They follow a path that is more similar to the model posed in the straightline theory. They stress that they are American because they were born here, and they are disdainful of their parents' lack of understanding of the American social system. Instead of rejecting black American culture, it becomes their peer culture, and they embrace many aspects of it. This brings them in conflict with their parents' generation, most especially with their parents' understandings of American blacks. They most definitely assimilate to black America; they speak black English with their peers, they listen to rap music, and they accept the peer culture of their black American friends. They are aware of the fact that they are considered black American by others and that they can be accused of "acting white" if they don't speak black English and behave in particular ways. Most included their ethnic identities as background, but none of them adopted the stance that they were not, in a major sense, black American. When asked about ethnic background and how other people think of it, one respondent replied:

Q: What is your ethnic background?

A: I put down American because I was born up here. I feel that is what I should put down. . . .

Q: What do other people think you are?

A: Black American because if I don't say . . . like if they hear my parents talk or something they always think they are from Jamaica. . . . But they just think I am black American because I was born up here.

Many of these teens discuss how they do not control how others see them:

A: Some people just think I am American because I have no accent. So I talk like American people. I don't talk Brooklynese. They think I am from down south or something. . . . A lot of people say you don't look Haitian. I think I look Haitian enough. I don't know, maybe they are expecting us to look fresh off the boat. I was born here and I grew up here, so I guess I look American and I have an American accent.

Q: If people think you are black American, do you ever do anything about it?

A: No, I don't. If they ask me if I am American, I say yes. If they ask me where my parents are from, I tell them Haiti.

In fact, they imply that being a black American is more stylish and "with it" than being from the islands:

A: I consider myself a black American. When I think of a black American I don't think of them as coming from the West Indies.

Q: Any characteristics that come to mind?

A: I would not think of someone in a suit. I would think of a regular teenager. I would think of a regular person. I think of someone that is in style.

Q: What about someone from the islands?

A: Jamaicans. They dress with neon colors. Most of the girls wear gold and stuff like that.

Some of the young people told us that they saw little, if any, difference between the ethnic blacks and the American blacks. Many stressed the Caribbeanization of black New York and described how all the Americans were interested in being Caribbean now:

A: It used to be Jamaicans and American blacks did not get along because everyone was afraid of Jamaicans. But now I guess we are closer now. You tell an American that you are Jamaican and it is no big deal. Americans are acting more like Jamaicans. Jamaicans are acting like Americans.

Q: What do you mean by acting like each other?

A: Sure there are a lot of Americans out there speaking patois. And then all the Jamaicans are coming over here and they are like "Yo, what's up" and they are like that. Pretty soon you can't really tell who is Jamaican and who is American.

However, the parents of the American-identified teens have expressed to their children the same negative impressions of American blacks that the ethnic-identified teens reported. These teenagers report many negative appraisals of American blacks by their parents:

They always say Haiti is better in this way or in that way. They say the kids here have no respect. The kids here are brought up without any supervision. My father is always talking about they [American blacks] be hanging out on the corner. And he says you won't find Haitians doing that. My mom always says you will marry a Haitian. Why are you talking to those American boys?

This young Haitian American teen tries to disagree with her mother and to temper her mother's interpretations of American blacks:

Q: Are there any characteristics or traits that come to mind about Haitian Americans?

A: Not really. I don't really—cause most people are Haitian American if they are born here. . . . Like me, I don't know if I act like a Haitian or do I have Haitian characteristics, but I'm mostly—like everything I do or like is American. My parents, they do not like American blacks, but they feel that they are lazy. They don't want to work and stuff like that from what they see. And I feel that, um, I feel that way too, but sometimes it won't be that person's fault, so I try to stick up for them. And my mother is like, yeah, you're just too American.

In marked contrast to the ethnic-identified teens, though, the American-identified teens disagreed with their parents' statements about American blacks, reluctantly agreed with some of it but provided qualifications, or perhaps, most disturbingly, accepted the appraisals as true of American blacks in general and themselves as American blacks. This young Trinidadian American swallows her parents' stereotypes and applies them directly to herself:

Q: How close do you feel in your ideas about things to West Indians?

A: Not very close. My feelings are more like blacks than theirs. I am lazy. I am really lazy and my parents are always making comments and things about how I am lazy. They are always like, in Trinidad you could not be this lazy. In Trinidad you would have to keep on working.

The fact that the teens are identifying as American and that their parents have such negative opinions of Americans causes some conflict. The teens either adopt a negative opinion of themselves or disagree with their parents' assessments of American blacks. But it is not just their parents who criticize black Americans. These youngsters are very aware of the generalized negative view of blacks in the wider culture. In answer to the question, "Do whites have an image of blacks?" all of them responded that whites have a negative view of blacks, seeing them as criminal, lazy, violent, and uncaring about family. Many of the teenagers prefaced their remarks by saying that they did not know any whites but that they knew this is what whites thought through the mass media and through the behaviors of whites they encountered in buses, trains, and stores. This mostly involved incidents such as whites protecting their handbags when the teenagers arrived or store clerks following them and expecting them to shoplift. This knowledge that the society in which they live devalues them because of their skin color and their identity affected these teens deeply.

IMMIGRANT-IDENTIFIED TEENS

The more recently arrived young people who still identify as immigrant differed from both the ethnic- and the American-identified youth. They did not feel as much pressure to "choose" between identifying with or distancing from black Americans as did either the American or the ethnic teens. Strong in their national-origin identities, they were neutral toward American distinctions between ethnics and black Americans. They tended to stress their nationality or their birthplace as defining their identity. They also pointed to their experiences growing up and attending school in a different country. This young man had dreadlocks and a strong Jamaican accent. He stresses his African roots and lets his Jamaican origin speak for itself:

Q: What is your ethnicity? For example, when forms or surveys ask what your ethnic group or ancestry is, what do you put?

A: African.

Q: Do you ever put Jamaican or anything?

A: No, not really. Only where Jamaican comes up is if someone asks where you're from. I'll say I am from Jamaica.

Q: What do people usually think you are?

A: They say I am Jamaican.

Q: They know that immediately?

A: Yeah.

Q: How do they know?

A: I change my voice. I don't have to tell them. I think it's also because of my locks sometimes and the way I carry myself, the way I dress.

While an ethnic-identified Jamaican American is aware that she might be seen by others as American and thus actively chooses to present herself as Jamaican, an immigrant-identified Jamaican could not conceive of herself as having a choice, nor could she conceive of being perceived by others as American. While an ethnic-identified teen might describe herself as Jamaican American, for the immigrant teen Jamaican would be all the label needed. Most teens in this category were recent immigrants. The few U.S.-born teens classified as immigrant identified had strong family roots on the islands, were frequent visitors to the islands, and had plans to return to live there as adults. A crucial factor that allows these youngsters to maintain this identity is that their accents and styles of clothing and behavior clearly signaled to others that they were foreign born.

Q: How important is it to you that your friends think of you in terms of your ethnicity?

A: Oh, very important. You know, I try hard not to lose my roots, you know, when I come to the United States. A lot of people who come here try to lose their accent, you know. Even in the workplace, you know, because they fear what other people might think of them. Even in the workplace. Me, I never try to change, you know, the way I am. I always try to, you know, stay with them, the way of my culture.

Q: So it's something you want people to recognize?

A: Yeah, definitely, definitely, absolutely.

Q: Why?

A: Why? I'm proud of who I am, you know. I'm proud of where I'm from and I'm not going to change because somebody might not like the way I walk, talk or dress, you know.

The importance of birthplace was stressed repeatedly by the immigrant identified as they stressed their difference from American-born coethnics:

Q: What would you put on a form or survey that asked about your ethnicity?

A: I'll say I'm Jamaican. You gotta say where you come from.

Q: And do you think of yourself more as a Jamaican or more as an American?

A: I think of more of a Jamaican' 'cause it's, I wasn't born here. I was born in Jamaica and was there for fourteen years.

Q: And what about kids who are born in America, but their parents were born in Jamaica?

A: Well, you see that is the problem. You see, kids whose parents are Jamaican, they think that, well, they are Jamaican. They need to recheck that they're Americans 'cause they was born in the country and they wasn't born outside the country. So I think they should, you know, know more about American than Jamaican.

Some who adopt this strong identity with the immigrant country were born in the United States, but the combination of strong family roots on the island, frequent visits, and plans to go live there when they are older allows them to think of themselves as not really American at all. This is especially easy to do in the public high schools where there are large numbers of freshly arrived youngsters from the islands.

Q: What do you think your race is?

A: Well, I'm black. I consider myself black. I don't consider myself black American, Afro-American and stuff like that because it's hard to determine, you know, for a person as an individual to determine himself to be Afro-American. . . . I'll be more a Guyanese person because certain things and traditions that I am accustomed to back home, it's still within the roots of me. And those things have not changed for a long period of time, even though you have to adapt to the system over here in order to get ahead and cope with what is going on around you.

While the ethnics tended to describe people as treating them better when they described their ethnic origins, and the Americans tended to stress the antiblack experiences they have had and the lack of difference between the foreign born and the American, the immigrant teens spoke about anti-immigrant feelings and discrimination and responded with pride in their national origins.

CONTRASTING IDENTITIES

In some sense one can see each of these identities as an embrace of one identity and an opposition to another. The American-identified youth are assimilating, in fact, to the American black subculture in the neighborhood. They are adapting to American black cultural forms, and they do so in distinction to their parents' ethnic identities and the wider mainstream white identities. These students adopt some of the "oppositional" poses that American black teenagers show toward academic achievement, the idea of America, the idea of opportunity, and the wider society (Fordham 1988; Ogbu 1990; Portes and Zhou 1993). They also are opposed to their parents' outlooks and ideas, stressing that what worked as a life strategy and a child-raising technique in the islands does not work in the United States. These teens tend to adopt a peer culture of racial solidarity and opposition to school authorities. What is clear from the interviews is that this stance is in part a socialized response to a peer culture, but the vast majority of it comes about as a reaction to their life experiences. Most specifically, the teens respond to their experiences with racial discrimination and their perceptions of blocked social mobility. The lives of these youngsters basically lead them to reject their parents' immigrant dream of individual social mobility and to accept their peers' analysis of the United States as a place with blocked social mobility where they will not move far.

The American-identified teens do not seem aware of the scholarly literature and the perceptions among ethnic- and immigrant-identified youngsters that the foreign born are of higher social status than the American born. In the peer culture of the neighborhood and the school, these teenagers describe a situation in which being American offers higher social status than being ethnic. For instance, several youngsters described "passing" as black American in order not to be ridiculed or picked on in school:

> I used to be scared to tell people that I was Haitian. Like when I was in eighth grade there were lots of Haitians in the ESL classes, and people used to beat them up. They used to pick on them. I said to myself I am going to quiet down, say I am American.

When asked about the images others held of being from the islands, most of the teens described neutral attributes, such as styles of dress. However, many who identified as Americans also described negative associations with the immigrants' identities. The Jamaicans said most people thought of drug dealers when they thought of Jamaicans. A few of the teens also intimated that people from the islands were backward in not knowing how to live in a big city, both in appreciating the wonders of the city and being street smart to avoid crime and hassles with other people. In terms of the former attribute, the teens described people from the islands who were not accustomed to shopping in big malls or having access to a wide variety of consumer goods.

Not one of the American-identified teens voiced the opinion of the overwhelming majority of the ethnic teens that whites were more likely to like the foreign born. In part, this reflected the differences the groups had in their contact with whites. Most of the inner-city ethnic-identified teens had almost no contact with whites, except for teachers. They also are in schools where the vast majority of the students are foreign born or second generation. The larger number of middle-class teens who were ethnic-identified were more likely to have white classmates in citywide magnet high schools, in parochial schools, or in suburban schools or workplaces.

The inner-city American-identified teens also voiced more positive appraisals of black Americans than did the immigrant- or the ethnic-identified teens. Their descriptions reflect the reality of living in neighborhoods where there is crime and violence. A majority of the American-identified teens said that a good trait of black Americans is that they work hard and they struggle. These are the very same children whose parents describe black Americans primarily as lazy and unwilling to take advantage of the opportunities available to them. The children seem to be perceiving a reality that the parents cannot or will not.

Many of these teens live in neighborhoods that are all black and also attend schools that are all black. So, aside from teachers, these young people have almost no contact with white Americans. This does not stop them from absorbing the fact that whites have negative stereotypic views of blacks. But unlike the middle-class blacks who come in contact with whites who tell them that they are "good blacks," these youths live in the urban areas associated with crime, they dress like the typical black urban youth, and they talk with Brooklyn accents and black American slang. When they do encounter whites in public places, the whites do not ask about their parents' backgrounds.

Q: Have you ever experienced any discrimination or hostility in New York?

A: From being Trinidadian, no. But because of being black, you know, everybody stereotypes. And they say "blacks, they tend to steal, and stuff like that." So, like, if I am walking down the street and a white lady go by and they smile and I smile. They put their bag on the other side.

The parents of these teens grew up in situations where blacks were the majority. The parents do not want their children to be "racial" in the United States. They define "being racial" as being overly concerned with race and with using race as an excuse or explanation for lack of success at school or on the job. The first generation tends to believe that, while racism exists in the United States, it can be overcome or circumvented through hard work, perseverance, and the right values and attitudes.

The second generation experiences racism and discrimination constantly and develops perceptions of the overwhelming influence of race on their lives. These teens experience being hassled by police and store owners, not being given jobs, even being attacked on the streets if they venture into white neighborhoods. The boys adopt black American culture in their schools, wearing flattops, baggy pants, and certain types of jewelry. This contributes to the projection of the "cool pose," which in turn causes whites to be afraid of them. This makes them angry and resentful. The media also tell these youngsters that blacks are disvalued by American society. While parents tell their children to strive for upward mobility and to work harder in the face of discrimination, the American-identified teens think the rewards for doing so will be very slim.

This causes a wide gulf between the parents and their children. These parents are absolutely terrified of their children becoming Americans. For the children, to be American is to have freedom from the strict parental controls of the immigrant parents. This is an old story in the immigrant saga, one visible in novels and movies about conflicts between Jewish and Italian immigrants and their children. But the added dimension here is that these parents are afraid of the downward social mobility that becoming an American black represents to them. And this idea is reinforced constantly to these parents by whites who tell them that they are better than American blacks.

One question about how things had changed since the civil rights movement shows the different perceptions of the teens about race in American society. The ethnically identified gave answers I suspect most white Americans would give. They said that things are much better for blacks now. They state that blacks now can ride at the front of the bus and go to school with whites. The irony, of course, is that I was sitting in an all-black school when they told this story. The vast majority of the American-identified teens state that things are not better since the civil rights movement; the change is that discrimination now is "on the down low," covered up, more crafty. Some pointed out that we were in an all-black school. The result of these different world views is that the parents' view of an opportunity structure that is open to hard work is systematically undermined by their children's peer culture and, more important, by the actual experience of these teens.

On the other hand, the ethnic-identified teens, whose parents are more likely to be middle class and doing well or who attend parochial or magnet schools, see clearer opportunities and rewards ahead, despite the existence of racism and discrimination. Their parents' message that hard work and perseverance can circumvent racial barriers does not fall on unreceptive ears. The ethnic-identified youngsters embrace an identity derived directly from their parents' immigrant identity. Such an identity is in opposition to their peers' identities and in solidarity with their parents' identities. These youngsters stress that they are Jamaican Americans and that, while they may be proud of their racial identity as black, they see strong differences between themselves and black Americans. They specifically see their ethnic identities as keys to upward social mobility, stressing, for instance, that their parents' values of hard work and strict discipline help them to succeed in the United States when black Americans fail. This ethnic identity is very much an American-based identity—it is in the context of American social life that these youngsters base their assumptions of what it means to be Jamaican or Trinidadian. In fact, the pan-ethnic identities of Caribbean or West Indian often are the most salient label for these youngsters, as they see little differences among the groups and it is more important to differentiate themselves as second-generation Americans. The distancing that these teens show from black Americans often leads them to accept many negative stereotypes of black Americans. These youngsters tend to have ethnic friends from a West Indian background, white American friends, and very few, if any, black American friends.

The immigrant-identified teens are different from either of the other two because of how they think about who they are not as well as how they think about who they are. These teens have a strong identity as Jamaican or Trinidadian, but this identity tends to be related to their interactions with other Jamaicans or Trinidadians rather than their interactions with black or white Americans. These youngsters identify with their homelands or their parents' homelands, but not in opposition to black Americans or in opposition to white Americans. They tend to be immersed in the immigrant community, to have friends who are all the same ethnicity or from other islands. They tend to be more recent arrivals. Unlike the ethnically identified, however, they do not distance themselves from American blacks, and they have neutral or positive attitudes and relations with them. At the same time, they see themselves as different from, but not opposed to, black Americans.

These identities are fluid and change over time and in different social contexts. We found cases of people who describe identifying very strongly as black American when they were younger and who became more immigrant identified when they reached high school and found a large immigrant community. Most new arrivals to the United States start out as immigrant identified, and the longer they stay in the United States, the more they begin to think of themselves in terms of American categories. The kind of social milieu the child faces, especially the school environment, has a strong influence on the outcome. A school with many black Americans creates pressure to identify racially; likewise a neighborhood and school with many immigrants make it possible to avoid thinking much about American categories. In the face of much pressure not to follow the rules and not to succeed academically, youngsters who are doing well in school and do value education increasingly come to stress their ethnic backgrounds as an explanation for their ambition and success.

The American racial classification system that pushes toward an either/or—"black or white"—designation of people makes the immigrant option harder to hold on to. When others constantly identify the individual as black and refuse to make distinctions based on black ethnicity, pressure builds for the individual to adapt his or her identity to that outside identification—either to say "Yes, I am black," and to accept categorization with black Americans, or to resent the characterization and strongly make an ethnic identification as Trinidadian American. The American myopia about ethnic differences within the black community makes the middle-ground immigrant identity unstable. Because every young person is aware of the negative images held by whites and the wider society of black Americans, the acceptance of an American black identity also means the acceptance of the oppositional character of that identity. Oppositional identities, as Ogbu (1990) clearly argues, are self- and group-affirming identities for stigmatized groups—defining as good and worthy those traits and characteristics that are the opposite of those valued by the majority group. This tends to draw the aspirations of the teens downward.

IMPLICATIONS OF THE PATTERNS

Some of the distancing shown by the ethnic-identified teens vis-à-vis underclass black identity is the same as that exhibited by middle-class black Americans. Elijah Anderson (1990) has noted that middle-class blacks in a gentrifying neighborhood in Philadelphia use various verbal and nonverbal strategies to convey to others that they are not from the ghetto and that they disapprove of the ghetto-specific behaviors of the blacks who live there. Being an ethnic black in interactions with whites seems to be a shorthand way of conveying distance from the ghetto blacks. Thus, the second generation reserves their ethnic status for use as an identity device to stress their distance from poor blacks and to stress their cultural values, which are consistent with American middle-class values. This same use of an ethnic identity is present among first-generation immigrants of all social classes, even those in racially segregated poor neighborhoods in New York.

The second generation in the segregated neighborhoods, with little chance for social mobility, seems to be unaware that status as a black ethnic conveys higher social status among whites, in part because they have not had much contact with whites. The mass media convey to them the negative image of American blacks held by whites but do not convey to them the image among intellectuals, middle-class whites, and conservative scholars, such as Thomas Sowell, that they have cultural capital by virtue of their immigrant status. They do get the message that blacks are stereotyped by whites in negative ways, that the all-black neighborhoods they live in are violent and dangerous, and that the neighborhoods of whites are relatively safe. They also encounter a peer culture that values black American cultural forms. The immigrant culture of struggle, hard work, and educational success that their parents try to enforce is experienced in negative ways by these youngsters. They see their parents denying them privileges that their American peers enjoy and, unlike the middle-class youth, they do not automatically associate hard work, lack of dating and partying, and stress on scholastic achievement with social mobility. In the peer culture of the school, immigrant- and ethnic-identified teens tend to be the best students. In the neighborhood inner-city schools, newly arrived immigrants who have attended better schools in the islands tend to outperform the students who have spent their lives in substandard New York City public schools. This tends to reinforce the association between ethnicity and school success—and the more American-identified teens adopt an adversarial stance toward school.

Warner and Srole (1945), in their study of Yankee City in the 1930s, report that it is the socially mobile white ethnics whose ties to the ethnic group and the ethnic identity decline. In their work, those individuals stuck in the lower classes turned to their ethnic identities and groups as a sort of consolation prize:

> Our class system functions for a large proportion of ethnics to destroy the ethnic subsystems and to increase assimilation. The mobile ethnic is much more likely to be assimilated than the nonmobile one. The latter retains many of the social characteristics of his homeland. . . . Some of the unsuccessfully mobile turn hostile to the host culture, develop increasing feelings of loyalty to their

ethnic traditions, become active in maintaining their ethnic subsystems, and prevent others from becoming assimilated. But, generally speaking, our class order disunites ethnic groups and accelerates their assimilation. (p. 284)

It could be that the process will be exactly the opposite for black immigrants and black ethnics. In this case, the more socially mobile cling to ethnic identity as a hedge against their racial identity. The less mobile blacks see little advantage to stressing an ethnic identity in the social worlds in which they travel, which are shared mostly with black Americans. Stressing an ethnic identity in that context risks being described as "acting white," being seen as rejecting the race and accepting the white stereotypes, which they know through their everyday lives are not true.

The changes in race relations in the United States since the 1960s are very complicated and most surely involve a mixing of class and race. Some white Americans are trying to see the difference between ghetto inner-city blacks, whom they fear and do not like, and middle-class blacks, whom they do not fear and with whom they would like to have contact, if only to prove to themselves that they are not racist or, in a more formal sense, to meet their affirmative goals.

Middle-class blacks realize this and try to convey their class status in subtle and not so subtle ways (Feagin 1991). The immigrants also utilize the fact that New Yorkers tend to use foreign-born status as a proxy for the class information they are seeking. The white New Yorkers we interviewed do notice differences among blacks, and they use ethnic differences as clues for class differences. If the association found here between social class and ethnic identity is widespread, this perception could become a self-fulfilling prophecy. It could be that the children of poor parents will not keep an ethnic identity and the children whose parents achieve social mobility will keep the ethnic identity. This will reinforce the image in the minds of whites that the "island people" are "good blacks," thus giving the edge in employment decisions and the like to ethnic blacks over American blacks.

On the other hand, it remains to be seen how long the ethnic-identified second generation will continue to identify with their ethnic backgrounds. This also is related to the fact that whites tend to make racial judgments about identity when it comes to blacks. The second generation does not have an accent or other clues that immediately telegraph their ethnic status to others. They are aware that, unless they are active in conveying their identities, they are seen as black Americans, and that often in encounters with whites, the status of their black race is all that matters. It could be that by the time they have children, they will have decided that the quest not to be seen as a black American will be a futile one.

Seeing the Big Picture   **Is a Nonethnic Racial Identity Possible?**

The four readings in this section recall a saying appropriate to this material: "You can change your ethnicity, but you can't change your race." Is this expression true or false? Why?

46

INTERMARRIAGE IN THE U.S. 50 YEARS AFTER *LOVING V. VIRGINIA*

Gretchen Livingston and Anna Brown

GRETCHEN LIVINGSTON and ANNA BROWN are researchers at Pew Research Center.

ONE-IN-SIX NEWLYWEDS IS MARRIED TO SOMEONE OF A DIFFERENT RACE OR ETHNICITY

In 2015, 17% of all U.S. newlyweds had a spouse of a different race or ethnicity, marking more than a fivefold increase since 1967, when 3% of newlyweds were intermarried, according to a new Pew Research Center analysis of U.S. Census Bureau data.[1] In that year, the U.S. Supreme Court in the *Loving v. Virginia* case ruled that marriage across racial lines was legal throughout the country. Until this ruling, interracial marriages were forbidden in many states.

More broadly, one-in-ten married people in 2015—not just those who *recently* married—had a spouse of a different race or ethnicity. This translates into 11 million people who were intermarried. The growth in intermarriage has coincided with shifting societal norms as Americans have become more accepting of marriages involving spouses of different races and ethnicities, even within their own families.

The most dramatic increases in intermarriage have occurred among black newlyweds. Since 1980, the share who married someone of a different race or ethnicity has more than tripled from

Questions to Consider

It is hard to imagine that not very long ago, it was illegal in many states to marry across the color line. In *Loving v. Virginia* (1967), the U.S. Supreme Court ruled that antimiscegenation laws were unconstitutional. Simply put, the court argued that the federal government had no right to intervene in or prohibit matters of intimacy between consenting adults. The number of interracial marriages has grown, but only about 9% of all marriages are interracial. In 2015, however, 17% of newlyweds were interracial or interethnic couples. What does this say about how younger people think about interracial marriage?

5% to 18%. White newlyweds, too, have experienced a rapid increase in intermarriage, with rates rising from 4% to 11%. However, despite this increase, they remain the least likely of all major racial or ethnic groups to marry someone of a different race or ethnicity.

Asian and Hispanic newlyweds are by far the most likely to intermarry in the United States. About three-in-ten Asian newlyweds[2] (29%) did so in 2015, and the share was 27% among recently married Hispanics. For these groups, intermarriage is even more prevalent among the U.S. born: 39% of U.S.-born Hispanic newlyweds and almost half (46%) of U.S.-born Asian newlyweds have a spouse of a different race or ethnicity.

FOR BLACKS AND ASIANS, STARK GENDER DIFFERENCES IN INTERMARRIAGE

Among blacks, intermarriage is twice as prevalent for male newlyweds as it is for their female counterparts. While about one-fourth of recently married black men (24%) have a spouse of a different race or ethnicity, this share is 12% among recently married black women.

There are dramatic gender differences among Asian newlyweds as well, though they run in the opposite direction—Asian women are far more likely to intermarry than their male counterparts. In 2015, just over one-third (36%) of newlywed Asian women had a spouse of a different race or ethnicity, compared with 21% of newlywed Asian men.

In contrast, among white and Hispanic newlyweds, the shares who intermarry are similar for men and women. Some 12% of recently married white men and 10% of white women have a spouse of a different race or ethnicity, and among Hispanics, 26% of newly married men and 28% of women do.

A MORE DIVERSE POPULATION AND SHIFTING ATTITUDES ARE CONTRIBUTING TO THE RISE OF INTERMARRIAGE

The rapid increases in intermarriage rates for recently married whites and blacks have played an important role in driving up the overall rate of intermarriage in the United States. However, the growing share of the population that is Asian or Hispanic, combined with these groups' high rates of intermarriage, is further boosting U.S. intermarriage overall. Among all newlyweds, the share who are Hispanic has risen by 9 percentage points since 1980, and the share who are Asian has risen 4 points. Meanwhile, the share who are Asian has risen 4 points. Meanwhile, the share of newlyweds who are white has dropped by 15 points.

Attitudes about intermarriage are changing as well. In just seven years, the share of adults saying that the growing number of people marrying someone of a different race is *good* for society has risen 15 points, to 39%, according to a new Pew Research Center survey conducted February 28 through March 12, 2017.

The decline in opposition to intermarriage in the longer term has been even more dramatic, a new Pew Research Center analysis of data from the General Social Survey has found. In 1990 63% of nonblack adults surveyed said they would be very or somewhat opposed to a close relative marrying a black person; today the figure stands at 14%. Opposition to a close relative entering into an intermarriage with a spouse who is Hispanic or Asian has also declined markedly since 2000, when data regarding those groups first became available. The share of nonwhites saying they would oppose having a family member marry a white person has edged downward as well.

INTERMARRIAGE SOMEWHAT MORE COMMON AMONG THE COLLEGE EDUCATED

In 1980, the rate of intermarriage did not differ markedly by educational attainment among newlyweds. Since that time, however, a modest intermarriage gap has emerged. In 2015, 14% of newlyweds with a high school diploma or less were married to someone of a different race or ethnicity, compared with 18% of those with some college and 19% of those with a bachelor's degree or more.

The educational gap is most striking among Hispanics: While almost half (46%) of Hispanic newlyweds with a bachelor's degree were intermarried in 2015, this share drops to 16% for those with a high school diploma or less—a pattern driven partially, but not entirely, by the higher share of immigrants among the less educated. Intermarriage is also slightly more common among black newlyweds with a bachelor's degree (21%) than those with some college (17%) or a high school diploma or less (15%).

Among recently married Asians, however, the pattern is different—intermarriage is far more common among those with some college (39%) than those with either more education (29%) or less education (26%). Among white newlyweds, intermarriage rates are similar regardless of educational attainment.

OTHER KEY FINDINGS

- The most common racial or ethnic pairing among newlywed intermarried couples is one Hispanic and one white spouse (42%). Next most common are one white and one Asian spouse (15%) and one white and one multiracial spouse (12%).

- Newlyweds living in metropolitan areas are more likely to be intermarried than those in non-metropolitan areas (18% vs. 11%). This pattern is driven entirely by whites; Hispanics and Asians are more likely to intermarry if they live in non-metro areas. The rates do not vary by place of residence for blacks.

- Among black newlyweds, the gender gap in intermarriage increases with education: For those with a high school diploma or less, 17% of men vs. 10% of women are intermarried, while among those with a bachelor's degree, black men are more than twice as likely as black women to intermarry (30% vs. 13%).

- Among newlyweds, intermarriage is most common for those in their 30s (18%). Even so, 13% of newlyweds ages 50 and older are married to someone of a different race or ethnicity.

- There is a sharp partisan divide in attitudes about interracial marriage. Roughly half (49%) of Democrats and independents who lean to the Democratic Party say the growing number of people of different races marrying each other is a good thing for society. Only 28% of Republicans and Republican-leaning independents share that view.

47

CAPTAIN KIRK KISSES LIEUTENANT UHURA

Interracial Intimacies—The View from Hollywood

Randall L. Kennedy

RANDALL L. KENNEDY is a professor of law at Harvard Law School. His areas of research and interest include the intersection of racial conflict and legal institutions in American life. He is author of *Interracial Intimacies: Sex, Marriage, Identity and Adoption* (2003) and *Race, Crime, and the Law* (1997).

IN 1960 THERE WERE ABOUT 51,000 BLACK-WHITE married couples in the United States; in 1970, 65,000; in 1980, 121,000; in 1991, 213,000; and in 1998, 330,000. In other words, between 1960 and 2000, black-white mixed marriages increased more than sixfold. But not only are mixed marriages becoming more numerous; they are also becoming more common among people who are younger and more fertile. Previously, participants in such marriages tended to be older than other brides and grooms. Frequently they were veterans of divorce, embarking on second or third marriages. In recent years, though, interracial couples have been marrying at younger ages than their pioneering predecessors, and have shown a greater

inclination to raise children and pursue all of the other "normal" activities that married life offers.

Given the low historical baselines against which trends today are measured, it is easy to exaggerate the scope of black-white marital integration. It should therefore be stressed that mixed marriages remain remarkably rare, comprising a mere 6 percent of the total marriages in 1998, for instance, when 330,000 couples out of 55,305,000 overall had one black and one white partner. Moreover, blacks' racial isolation on the marriage market appears to eclipse that of other people of color. The percentages of Native Americans and Asian Americans marrying whites are much larger than the percentage of blacks doing the same.[1] Professor Nathan Glazer is correct, then,

Questions to Consider

How many television shows and movies can you name in which the love interests are interracial couples? Now list the number of those interracial couples that were a black man and a white woman. Is it still true, as law professor Randall Kennedy suggests, that the only way Hollywood would pair a black man, even a superstar like Denzel Washington, with a white woman would be for him to be "paralyzed from the waist down" as in the movie *The Bone Collector* (1999)?

in stating that "blacks stand out uniquely among the array of ethnic and racial groups in the degree to which marriage remains within the group." Among the complex reasons for this social isolation are aggregate subjective evaluations of marriageability, beauty, personality, comfort, compatibility, and prestige that favor certain groups over others. At the dawn of the twenty-first century, a wide array of social pressures continue to make white-black marital crossings more difficult, more costly, and thus less frequent than other types of interethnic or interracial crossings.

Still, even taking into account the peculiar persistence of the black-white racial divide, the trajectory of this form of **miscegenation** is clear: through turbulent times and in the face of considerable opposition, the number of black-white marriages has been increasing consistently (albeit slowly) for at least forty years. Reinforcing this growth is the fact that interracial marriage has become compatible with lofty ambitions across a variety of fields—not only entertainment but government service, scholarship, the philanthropic

miscegenation The "mixing" of different racial groups—that is, marrying, cohabiting, having sexual relations and children with a partner from outside of one's racially or ethnically defined group.

sector, business, and the professions. The Thomas-Lamp marriage is indicative of this trend. So, too, are the unions of William Cohen (former senator from Maine and secretary of defense in the Clinton administration) and his black wife, Peter Norton (inventor of widely used computer software) and his black wife,[2] and Franklin Raines (former director of the Office of Management and Budget and chief executive officer of Fannie Mae) and his white wife. Furthermore, despite the substantial influence of the black-power backlash, some African Americans whose positions make them directly dependent upon black public opinion have managed to marry whites without losing their footing. A good example is Julian Bond, the chairman of the board of directors of the NAACP, whose wife is white.

There are other signs, too, that black-white interracial romance has become more broadly accepted and even, in certain contexts, quite fashionable. One such indicator is advertising. Advertisers seek to persuade people to buy goods and services by increasing awareness of them and associating them with imagined pleasures. In the past, advertisers targeting general audiences with the lure of romance have typically—indeed, overwhelmingly—used couples of the same race. But these days, at least occasionally, interracial couples are being deployed as enticements to shop at Nordstrom's, Club Monaco, or Walmart, or to purchase furniture from IKEA, jeans from Guess, sweaters from Tommy Hilfiger, cologne from Calvin Klein, shampoo from Procter & Gamble, or watches from Gucci.

Television programming also signals important changes in sexual attitudes. Prior to the 1960s, portrayals or even insinuations of black-white interracial romance were virtually nonexistent on TV. The November 22, 1968, episode of the popular science-fiction series *Star Trek* marked a breakthrough in showing a kiss shared by the legendary (white) Captain James T. Kirk and (black) Lieutenant Uhura. Remarkably, however, the characters were not portrayed as actively *wanting* to kiss each other; instead, they *were forced* to do so by a villain who captured Kirk's vessel, the starship *Enterprise,* and usurped the will of its crew. Not until 1975 did network television portray a married black-white couple, Tom and Helen Willis, who occupied a prominent place on the popular sitcom *The Jeffersons.* The show, a spinoff of Norman Lear's *All in the Family,* was about an eponymous black family whose patriarch, the hardworking but obnoxious George Jefferson, was obsessed with upward mobility, or what the theme song referred to as "movin' on up." The Willises lived in the same expensive apartment building as the Jeffersons. Although George constantly taunted the couple, calling them zebras, the families ultimately merged when the Jeffersons' son married the Willises' daughter.[3] Since the 1970s, depictions of interracial intimacies have remained rare on commercial television, though they do surface occasionally. In 1989 the short-lived *Robert Guillaume Show* presented viewers with a romance between a divorced black marriage counselor and his white secretary. The following year, the upstart Fox television network reluctantly aired *True Colors,* a situation comedy centered on the marriage of a black dentist (with two teenage sons) and a white schoolteacher (with a live-in mother and a teenage daughter). According to the show's creator, executives at the three older networks (ABC, CBS, and NBC) expressly stated that they were afraid the interracial marriage would alienate potential advertisers and dissuade at least some local affiliates from broadcasting the program. Notwithstanding cold feet at the top, writers have in the last decade or so succeeded in convincing television executives to air more entertainment fare featuring, or at least noting the existence of, interracial intimacy. Indeed, several of the most popular and influential shows of the 1990s portrayed transracial romances. Sometimes the racial aspect of the relationship was highlighted, as in *L.A. Law's* dramatization of a black lawyer feeling that he must choose between his white lover and his job as an elected representative of a mainly black constituency. Sometimes it was ignored, as on *Ally McBeal,* where race matters seldom if ever arose in conversations between the white woman attorney and the black male physician with whom she was infatuated. On occasion, on-screen interracial relationships failed. The producers of *ER,* for example,

terminated a romance between a black male doctor and a white colleague, not in deference to viewer opposition but because the black actor involved objected. He complained that whereas his character had always been obnoxious in his dealings with black women, he was now being shown as sympathetic in his treatment of the white woman. On other programs, interracial romance was permitted to blossom. In 1994, for example, on *In the Heat of the Night,* the white sheriff of a town in the Deep South married a black woman onscreen,[4] and in 1997, a network production of *Cinderella* paired a black actress in the title role with a Filipino Prince Charming, to great popular acclaim.[5]

In some venues, nonfictional portrayals of interracial intimacy have been sensationally negative, as on confessional talk shows that, for a while at least, uniformly depicted transracial relationships as troubled, weird, or pathological.[6] In other contexts, however, television programs have acknowledged the gamut of personalities and emotions to be found among those who happen to be involved in interracial intimacies. In the fall of 1999, the Public Broadcasting System (PBS) aired *An American Love Story,* a ten-hour documentary film by Jennifer Fox that chronicled the lives of an interracial family: Bill Sims, a black man; Karen Wilson, a white woman; and their two daughters, Cecily and Chaney. Wilson and Sims first met in 1967, at a resort where he was playing piano in a rhythm-and-blues band and she was vacationing with her parents. He was the son of a cleaning woman and a steelworker who was also a Baptist minister; her father was a machinist, and her mother was a grocery clerk. When their courtship began, Bill was eighteen and Karen seventeen. Neither set of parents objected to the relationship, and both urged the couple to marry after Wilson got pregnant (though they in fact did not do so until the child was six years old).

Whites in Wilson's hometown of Prospect, Ohio, strongly condemned her romance with Sims. Her supposed friends ostracized the couple, and the local sheriff jailed Sims on several occasions for no other reason than to harass him. In 1972 they moved with their baby daughter to Columbus, but even in this larger, less isolated locale, they encountered overt hostility. They suspected bigots of killing their dog and setting their car afire in a successful campaign to frighten them away. They moved again, this time to Flushing, New York, where they hoped to find a more open-minded community.

Over the years, the Wilson-Sims family subsisted largely on Karen's reliable earnings as a manager, supplemented by Bill's spotty wages as, among other things, a carpenter, mail carrier, and musician. At the price of some tedium, *An American Love Story* shows its subjects engaged in all the quotidian tasks of daily life—cooking, cleaning, resting, seeking comfort, venting frustration—that have little or nothing to do with racial differences. It also shows them facing various nonracial crises, including Karen's hysterectomy and Bill's alcoholism. Almost inevitably, though, racial difficulties surface to menace the couple and their children. Among the most poignant segments of the series are wrenching scenes from Cecily's years as an undergraduate at Colgate College, where tyrannical black classmates tell her, essentially, that if she wants to be their friend, she must refuse to join a predominantly white sorority and, more generally, defer to their black-separatist sensibilities. She declines their terms, and they retaliate; she is hurt. Throughout, the television audience is privy to the conflict.[7]

The creators of *An American Love Story* wanted to document an interracial marriage that spanned the final decades of the twentieth century. Its subjects, for their part, wanted to change perceptions through education; this ambition constituted the principal explanation offered by the Sims-Wilson clan for permitting their family life to be examined in such a public manner. Education was also the primary aim cited by the program's director, Jennifer Fox, a white woman who credited her own love affair with a black man with opening her eyes to important areas of American life to which she had previously been blind.[8]

On the big screen, too, recent years have seen an increase in both the number and the quality of depictions of interracial intimacy. There was a time,

not so long ago, when the scarcity of such portrayals made keeping track of them easy; now, because of their increasing numbers and variety, that task is much more difficult. True, the fear of an adverse audience response can still cause cautious film producers to suppress interracial romance, not only through their choice of projects but even in their handling of plot points. In John Grisham's novel *The Pelican Brief* (1992), for instance, the protagonists become lovers, but in the screen version (1993), there is no romance; the relationship remains resolutely platonic. The reason for this alteration is obvious: the male lead is played by a black actor (Denzel Washington), and the female lead by a white actress (Julia Roberts). There are, moreover, scores of other examples of black actors apparently being singled out for Hollywood's cold shoulder treatment lest they mirror real-life interracial erotic excitement. Prominent among these desexualized roles are Will Smith's character in *Men in Black* (1997) and Wesley Snipes's in *Murder at 1600* (1997). This approach led one wag to remark, in reference to *The Bone Collector* (1999), that the only way Denzel Washington would ever be shown "getting the girl" was if he played a man paralyzed from the waist down. That being said, a number of major motion pictures released in the past decade have followed actors and actresses of all complexions in their pursuit of sexual pleasures across color lines, and have done so with a boldness that probably would not have been tolerated in the environment that generated *Guess Who's Coming to Dinner?* Examples include the explicit erotic grapplings of Lawrence Fishburne and Ellen Barkin in *Bad Company* (1995), Wesley Snipes and Natassia Kinski in *One Night Stand* (1997), Reese Witherspoon and Bookeem Woodbine in *Freeway* (1996), Warren Beatty and Halle Berry in *Bulworth* (1998), Tom Cruise and Thandie Newton in *Mission: Impossible 2* (2000), Julia Stiles and Sean Patrick Thomas in *Save the Last Dance* (2000), and Halle Berry and Billy Bob Thornton in *Monster's Ball* (2001).[9] In increasing numbers of films, moreover, interracial intimacy has been emerging as simply one part of a larger story in which racial difference is of little or no significance.

This is an important development because presuming the normalcy of interracial intimacy—treating it as "no big deal"—may be more subversive of traditional norms than stressing the racial heterodoxy of such relationships. Although examples of this presumption can be found in several films (e.g., *Pulp Fiction* [1994], *Cruel Intentions* [1999], and *Mystery Men* [1999]), the most significant was the blockbuster *The Bodyguard* (1992), which starred Kevin Costner and Whitney Houston.

. . .

Perhaps the most potent influence in creating new possibilities for interracial intimacy is that wielded by individuals engaged in (or born of) transracial dating, marriage, and parenting. This population, numbering in the hundreds of thousands, exhibits tremendous variety. One generalization that can properly be made about it, however, is that it is becoming increasingly vocal. There was a time, not so long ago, when the vast majority within this group sought invisibility; now, by contrast, many of its members seek recognition and are establishing or joining advocacy organizations devoted to publicizing their views and institutionalizing their presence. Announcing the formation of the Association of MultiEthnic Americans (AMEA) in November 1988, Carlos Fernandez declared:

> We who embody the melting pot . . . stand up, not merely as neutrals in interethnic conflicts, but as intolerant participants against racism from whatever quarter it may come. . . . We are the faces of the future. Against the travails of regressive interethnic division and strife, we can be a solid core of unity bonding the peoples of all cultures together in the common course of human progress.

People involved in interracial intimacies used to voice quiet requests for simple protection against intimidation and violence. Now their demands are becoming more ambitious. One of these has to do with racial labeling. Many interracial couples object to standardized forms that compel them to designate their children either merely "black" or merely "white." Similarly, many who identify themselves as "mixed"—or "mulatto" or "half-and-half" or

"multiracial"—bridle at classificatory regimes that impose singular racial identifications, as if everyone must be *only* white *or* black *or* Latino *or* Asian (etc., etc.). Prior to the census of 2000, the United States Census Bureau counted individuals according to that assumption. But after a good deal of prodding by AMEA and similar groups, the bureau decided to broaden the menu boxes available for indicating racial affiliation. Rather than being limited to only one box, respondents are now authorized to check whatever boxes they deem applicable, though the census bureau continues to decline to offer a separate "multiracial" box.[10] One complaint leveled against the traditional "check one box" regime is that it fosters confusion and inaccuracy—describing as "black," for example, people who are also partly white or partly Native American or partly Asian. Susan Graham, the (white) founder of Project RACE (Reclassify All Children Equally), notes that her "child has been white on the U.S. Census, black at school, and multiracial at home, all at the same time." Beyond the issue of statistical inaccuracy, the system has more personal ramifications, in that it compels mixed individuals to select for recognition only one aspect of their composite background, and thereby subordinate all the other aspects.

The census bureau's multiple-box-checking initiative addresses some but by no means all of the objections raised by critics.[11] Some contend that even the option of checking several boxes indicates, in effect, that multiracial individuals are only parts of other communities, rather than constituent members of a distinct multiracial community of their own. Some observers protest, moreover, the continuation of *any* racial scheme of classification, however it may be supplemented or repackaged. Whatever one may think of the ideas propounded by these various dissidents, it is clear that they are flexing their political muscles as never before and affecting hearts and minds in fundamental ways. They are not content to accept inherited conventions but insist instead on adding their own preferences to America's cultural mix. Professor Maria P. P. Root has demanded a Bill of Rights for racially mixed people, which would include the rights to identify one's race differently in different situations, to change one's racial identity over a lifetime (and more than once), to have loyalties to and identifications with more than one racial group, and to be able freely to choose whom to befriend and love. The winner of the 1995 Miss USA beauty pageant objected to being pegged as "black." "If people are going to know me," Chelsi Smith explained, "it's important for them to know that I'm black and white and that it hasn't been a disadvantage." Tiger Woods likewise does not enjoy being referred to as the first "black" or "African American" golf superstar, believing that those labels obscure other aspects of his ancestry that are just as important to him. He has therefore coined the term "'Cablinasian'—[for] Caucasian, Black, Indian, Asian"—to describe himself.[12] The coinage has proved controversial.[13] Many people, mainly blacks, have accused him of wanting to flee an African American identity that whites will impose upon him regardless of his preferences. ("When the black truck comes around," one observer quipped, "they're gonna haul his ass on it.") Such reactions notwithstanding, the real point here is that Root, Smith, Woods, and tens of thousands more like them have felt sufficiently self-assured to speak up, and have received substantial support in doing so. Their conduct mirrors and strengthens a new force in America: the will of people engaged in or born of multiracial relationships, who have begun to insist upon public recognition of the full complexity of their lives.

Across the country, scores of interracial support groups have sprung up, among them MOSAIC (Multiethnics of Southern Arizona in Celebration); A Place for Us (North Little Rock, Arkansas); I-Pride (Interracial Intercultural Pride, Berkeley, California); MASC (Multiracial Americans of Southern California, Los Angeles, California); F.C. (Families of Color) Communique (Fort Collins, Colorado); Interracial Family Alliance (Augusta, Georgia); Society for Interracial Families (Troy, Michigan); 4C (Cross Cultural Couples & Children, Plainsboro, New Jersey); the Interracial Club of Buffalo; the Interracial Family Circle of Washington, D.C.; and HONEY (Honor Our New Ethnic Youth, Eugene, Oregon). On college campuses, students can join organizations such as FUSION (Wellesley); Kaleidoscope (University of Virginia); Students of Mixed Heritage and Culture (SMHAC, Amherst); Half 'n' Half (Bryn Mawr); and Mixed Plate (Grinnell). These groups offer forums in which people can meet others in their situation, disseminate relevant information, debate, and organize. Although most of these organizations lack deep roots, many display a vigor and resourcefulness that suggest they will survive into the foreseeable future. They stem from and represent a community in the making. It is a community united by a common demand that the larger society respect and be attentive to people who either by descent or by choice fall outside the conventional racial groupings—people who are partners in interracial couples, parents of children whose race is different from their own, and children whose race differs from their parents'. The members of this community want whites to cease viewing them as products or agents of an alarming mongrelization. They want blacks to stop regarding them as inauthentic and unstable in-betweeners. They want security amid the established communities from which they have migrated. They want to emerge from what the writer Lise Funderberg has aptly called the "racial netherworld." They want to enjoy interaction with others without regret or fear, defensiveness or embarrassment. They want respect.

Seeing the Big Picture   Love May Be Blind, but It's Not Color-Blind

Look at Section X in the appendix. All things being equal, one would think that if people choose to marry across the color line, these unions would be randomly distributed—that is, we would observe similar marriage rates across racial categories. But we don't. What do these data suggest about intergroup relations?

48

DISCOVERING RACIAL BORDERS

Heather M. Dalmage

HEATHER M. DALMAGE is an associate professor of sociology at the School of Policy Studies at Roosevelt University, Chicago. She is the author of *Tripping on the Color Line: Black-White Multiracial Families in a Racially Divided World* (2000) and a national expert on interracial relationships. She is editor of *The Multiracial Movement: The Politics of Color* (2003).

BORDER PATROLLING

The belief that people ought to stick with their own is the driving force behind efforts to force individuals to follow prescribed racial rules. Border patrollers often think (without much critical analysis) that they can easily differentiate between insiders and outsiders. Once the patroller has determined a person's appropriate category, he or she will attempt to coerce that person into following the category's racial scripts. In *Race, Nation, Class: Ambiguous Identities,* Etienne Balibar and Immanuel Wallerstein observe that "people shoot each other every day over the question of labels. And yet, the very people who do so tend to deny that the issue is complex or puzzling or indeed anything but self-evident."[1] Border patrollers tend to take race and racial categories for granted. Whether grounding themselves in essentialist thinking or hoping to strengthen socially constructed racial categories, they believe they have

the right and the need to patrol. Some people, especially whites, do not recognize the centrality and problems of the color line, as evinced in color-blind claims that "there is only one race: the human race" or "race doesn't really matter any more." Such thinking dismisses the terror and power of race in society. These individuals may patrol without being aware of doing so. In contrast, blacks generally see patrolling the border as both problematic and necessary.

While border patrolling from either side may be scary, hurtful, or annoying, we must recognize that blacks and whites are situated differently. The color line was imposed by whites, who now have institutional means for maintaining their power; in contrast, blacks must consciously and actively struggle for liberation. Repeatedly, people in multiracial families have told me, "The one thing that David Duke and Louis Farrakhan agree on is that we should not exist." What is not analyzed are the different historical legacies that bring both men to the same conclusion. The only form of borderism in

Questions to Consider

Heather M. Dalmage explains how racial borders are "policed" to discourage individuals from falling in love across the color line. How and in what ways (if any) were racial borders enforced in your own life so that dating across the color line was not very likely to happen? How would your family react if your new romantic partner was from a racial category different from your own? Given that such unions are often stigmatized, what strategies do interracial couples employ, according to Dalmage, to dismiss such views and normalize their own relationship?

which blacks engage is border patrolling, although they can act on prejudicial feelings and discriminate. After centuries of systemic control, only whites can be racist. As Joe Feagin and Hernán Vera explain, "black racism would require not only a widely accepted racist ideology directed at whites, but also the power to systematically exclude whites from opportunities and rewards in major economic, cultural, and political institutions."[2] White and black border patrollers may both dislike interracial couples and multiracial families, but their dislike comes from different historical and social perspectives. Moreover, border patrolling tends to take place intraracially: whites patrol whites, and blacks patrol black and multiracial people.

White Border Patrolling

Despite the institutional mechanisms in place to safeguard whiteness, many whites feel both the right and the obligation to act out against interracial couples. If a white person wants to maintain a sense of racial superiority, then he or she must attempt to locate motives and explain the actions of the white partner in the interracial couple. A white person who crosses the color line threatens the assumption that racial superiority is essential

to whites. The interracially involved white person is thus often recategorized as inherently flawed—as "polluted."[3] In this way, racist and **essentialist** thinking remains unchallenged.

Frequently, white families disown a relative who marries a person of color, but several people have told me that their families accepted them again once their children were born. The need to disown demonstrates the desire to maintain the facade of a pure white family.[4] By the time children are born, however, extended family members have had time to shift their racial thinking. Some grant acceptance by making an exception to the "rule," others by claiming to be color-blind. Neither form of racial thinking, however, challenges the color line or white supremacy. In fact, both can be painful for the multiracial family members, who may face unending racist compliments such as "I'll always think of you as white."

The myth of purity is maintained by controlling white women's wombs. Thus, white women are patrolled more harshly than white men are. The regulations women face have not always been overtly displayed but have developed within the culture's conception of *the family ethic,* an ideal extant since the arrival of the early settlers that has influenced perceptions of proper work and home roles for white, middle-class family members.[5] The proper family should have a male breadwinner and patriarch and a female who makes her husband and obedient children her life's central work. According to Mimi Abramowitz, the family ethic "has made [women] the guardians of family and community morality, expected them to remain pious and chaste and to tame male sexuality, and defined them as weak and in need of male protection and control."[6] Ultimately, the family ethic has kept white women under the control of white men. In *Whiteness Visible: The Meaning of Whiteness in American Literature and Culture,* Valerie Babb notes that images depicting white women as helpless and in need of white men's protection grew against a

---

essentialism The false idea that individuals or groups have an immutable fundamental nature that exists outside of society. An essentialist statement would be that all women are nurturing.

backdrop of a developing patriarchy. White women faced particularly harsh regulations because the "loss of sexual purity through intercourse with other races endangers visible race difference, a key driving force behind an ideology of whiteness that gives political, economic, and social advantage to those with 'appropriate' race lineage."[7] The myth of white racial purity required white women to give birth to the offspring of white men—and only white men. Unfortunately, many white women have played active roles in maintaining this myth of purity. For instance, in 1897 one wrote: "If it takes lynching to protect women's dearest possession from drunken, ravening beasts, then I say lynch a thousand a week if it becomes necessary."[8] Today many white women who give birth to children of color give them up for adoption, fearing that as mothers of children of color they will become pariahs in their families and society at large.[9] Such complicity has worked to strengthen the color line and white-supremacist abuses.

It has been argued that white women should be protected because they are the gatekeepers of racial purity.[10] Any white woman who would trade in her white privilege and connections to white male power must be dismissed as unnaturally bad and bizarre. Julie, a white mother recently divorced from her black husband, has contended with white border patrolling and its underlying images. One incident (although not the only one) occurred while she was on a date with a white physician:

> He asked to see a picture of my daughter. I handed it to him. He was very clever; he asked, "Is her dad from the U.S.?"
>
> I think he was praying her dad was Spanish, and he could deal with that, anything but black. I could tell it bothered him, so I said, "Listen, I can see by the look on your face that there is obviously a problem here, so why don't we just talk about it right now."
>
> He said, "You want to know the truth? Well, I have a real problem with the fact that you slept with a black man." Then he went on

with the whole, "You're such a pretty and intelligent woman; why would you marry a black man?"

Her date was drawing on the interlocking imagery of race and sex and what it means to be a good white woman. In his attempt to explain away Julie's behavior, he searched for motives, implying that only unattractive, unintelligent white women sleep with and marry black men. Further, the fact that she slept with a black man removed her eligibility as a white woman. She is assumed to be fundamentally and essentially changed. Perhaps he feared that his white purity would be contaminated with blackness through this bad white woman. Perhaps he felt threatened because he could not immediately detect her racial flaw. He may have begun to discover the mutability of race, which could undermine his own sense of racial superiority. While all people of color face some form of racist imagery in a white racist society, Julie notes the centrality and power given to racist images directed specifically against black people and interracially involved whites and blacks: "I think he was praying her dad was Spanish, and he could deal with that, anything but black."

Black men are seen "as a constant threat" to patriarchal whiteness.[11] Abby Ferber writes: "A photograph of a white woman with an Asian American man, for example, does not have the same symbolic power. The image of interracial sexuality between a white woman and a black man is pregnant with meaning in the American imagery. Powerful enough to serve as a symbol of all interracial sexuality."[12] White women who enter into interracial relationships with black men are often treated as aberrant, misguided white trash who are in this relationship solely for sex or rebellion. Barbara gained forty pounds because she "got tired of being mistaken for a prostitute." She explains, "It's assumed that the only reason you're involved in the relationship is because you're sexually depraved . . . that you've got to be the dregs of society to get involved or you want to hurt somebody." Women may be explained away as money or status seekers.[13] often when we are out, people will ask Philip what he does for work. After learning he's an attorney, they don't bother to ask me what I do. This could be a gender issue; in a **patriarchal** world men are seen as the subjects, women the objects. But I often wonder how much it has do with assumptions about uncovering the motive behind our relationship—that I have traded my white status for his occupational and class status.[14]

The strength of racist images is manifested in the comments directed at women who are assumed to be good, upstanding white women. June, a businesswoman who is raising two biracial sons in suburban New Jersey, commented, "I think America still hates [white] women who sleep with black men. And when they see you with these children, they want to believe you adopted them, which is usually the first question people will ask: 'Did you adopt them?' I always just say, 'No, I slept with a black man.'" June's comments highlight a few issues. First, she does not specify who constitutes "America." Whites may hate these women because they threaten the color line that maintains white privilege and power. At the same time, blacks may hate them because they threaten the unity of African Americans. Second, several white women talked to me about the frequency of the adoption question—one more attempt to explain their behavior. If women who appear to be good turn out to be polluted, white border patrollers become nervous. Their inability to tell "us" from "them" calls into question their own racial identity. The more the border patroller clings to an identity of racial superiority, the more he or she looks for ways to explain away these aberrant white women. Third, like June, many interracially married white women resist allowing whites to recategorize them in an attempt to regain or maintain a sense of superiority. "No, I used the good-old fashioned method" is a common retort to such questioners.

Not all white women resist border patrollers. Many succumb to the hostility and end their relationships with black men. Several white women told me they had temporarily ended their interracial relationship, each citing border patrolling as

patriarchal Refers to a society organized so that men dominate women.

the reason. For instance, Barbara, the woman who gained forty pounds to avoid being seen as a prostitute, said:

> When I met my husband, he was the sweetest, kindest—he was a wonderful human being, everything I was looking for except for the color and at one point I was really apprehensive about it. The race thing really bothered me 'cause I didn't like being stared at and I didn't like people hating me. I didn't like how black women viewed me, and to white men I was a possession. It's like, "you crossed the line." You know the feeling, like you have to be the lowest of the low to be with an African American. "Who are you trying to hurt?" It was just really sick. So I went away for a while.

Although she did eventually marry this "wonderful human being," she needed time away to think about race on a more sophisticated level— time to question her internalization of racist images and the color line.

The stereotype of black male sexuality converges with the myth of the chaste and virtuous good white woman, making white female–black male relationships the ones most patrolled by whites.[15] White men contend with a different type of border patrolling in a society that privileges both whiteness and maleness. Historically, white men who interracially marry were reported to come from lower economic classes and were at times designated as crazy.[16] Today the more common image that white interracially married men face is of being in the relationship solely for sex. These men may be seen as committing an individual transgression but are not held responsible for protecting whiteness. In her study of white supremacist publications, Abby Ferber found that "while relationships between white women and black men are condemned, and described as repulsive, relationships between white men and black women were common and remain beyond condemnation."[17] The lack of imagery about white male–black female relations reflects a history of silence among whites concerning their complicity in the rape of black women. Moreover, in a society in which whiteness (and maleness) represents power, privilege, and unearned advantage, many white men view their privilege in the world as normal. They risk "outing" these taken-for-granted privileges when they talk about race.[18]

The white men with whom I spoke were split about the importance of—even the existence of—border patrolling. Unlike black men, black women, and white women, they did not consistently talk about the effects of racialized images. When I asked, "As an interracially married white man, how do you think others view you?" responses were split: half the men spoke of border patrollers; the other half denied the importance of race in their lives and society. The first few times I heard white men deny or disregard the importance of racism and border patrolling, I was surprised. It took me some time and several more interviews to make sense of this.

Joe, the first interracially married white man I interviewed, lived in a predominantly white, upper-class community about an hour from New York City. With his infant daughter on his lap and a tape recorder on the table, he began to unfold the details of his life. I asked how he thinks others view him. He responded, "I can't worry about what other people think. For a long time my wife worried, but once she got over that, we had a big wedding. . . . It took a lot to convince her that's how we should think about it, and I think she's more comfortable with that." He said that they do not have problems as an interracial couple, that everything is smooth. We were chatting after the interview when his wife walked into the room. She began to cite several problems they had faced because of their interracial relationship. When she referred to each incident, he nodded in agreement.

Several months later I interviewed Raymond, a white interracially married man living on Chicago's north side. Drinking coffee in a local cafe, he discussed the meaning of race in his life. When I asked him about how others view him, he replied staunchly, "I don't know, and I don't care. I never thought about it. I don't think about it. What do they think when they see my wife and me together?

Pardon my language, but I don't give a shit what they think; I just don't give a shit. I go for months, and that never occupies my mind."

These men may be proving masculinity through a show of strength, rugged individualism, and disinterest and thus verbally disregard border patrolling and racial images. Each, however, repeatedly claimed that race does not matter. Instead, they believed the focus "should be on ethnic backgrounds" or on the fact that "we are all Americans." Men who did not want to recognize racial images tended not to recognize the privilege associated with whiteness, drawing instead on notions of meritocracy. Whether or not they recognized differences, they did not recognize power. Nevertheless, they used their power as white males to create a racial discussion with which they felt comfortable. For instance, Joe's comfort came from not having to hear any racially derogatory comments: "If somebody would make a derogatory comment, I would just say, 'My wife is black.' Usually I wouldn't even have to say, 'I don't want to hear comments like that'—they would just stop." Whiteness is about privilege and power. It is a privilege to be able to set the parameters of racial discussions and expect that others will comply. Moreover, the power of these professional white men overrides the power that white border patrollers may have to influence them.

In addition to proving masculinity, these men may be attempting to downplay the prevalent stereotype that interracial couples are together for sexual reasons only. For instance, Raymond repeatedly stated that his relationship was not about "jungle fever," a phrase that filmmaker Spike Lee popularized to suggest that interracial couples are attracted only because of sexual curiosity. At the end of our interview I asked Raymond if there was anything else he wanted to say. He answered, "Let people know that this is not about jungle fever. Race does not matter. I love my wife." His repeated references to jungle fever reflected his awareness of border patrolling despite his claim of color blindness. Rather than critically thinking about race and the origins of such stereotypes, he defensively dismisses the significance of race.

Some white men did recognize and address the importance of racial images, border patrollers, and the relationship between race and power. The common thread for these men was that they had friendships and networks with black males before meeting their spouse. Through these male friends they began to recognize the privileges that remain invisible to so many other white men. The importance of friendships with black males cannot be understated. White men sit in a position of power because of both their race and sex. When sex differences are removed as a factor in their relationships, they can understand more clearly the ways in which race mediates power relations. This is not as obvious to white men who are introduced to blackness (and thus whiteness) through intimate relations with a woman.

Clancy, a fifty-year-old white man who grew up outside Chicago, had black roommates and friends in college. By the time he met his wife he understood from his buddies the effects of racism in society. He spoke in detail about the border patrolling he faced from the white teachers at the Chicago elementary school where he taught after getting married: "My wife and I walked into a meeting with the white teachers and the people from the neighborhood, and it sent those people into conniptions. I won't forget that. It was my first year teaching there, and from then on it was like, 'God have mercy on my soul,' I was a dead person in that school and that stayed with me for seventeen years—the whole time I was there." In this case, Clancy's teaching position was continually threatened by white border patrollers.

Peter, a white minister living on Chicago's South Side, had graduated from a black seminary in the southern United States. As the only white in many situations, he was immersed in black culture. The privileges and power bestowed on whites in a system of whiteness and the richness of black culture became visible to him. Like Clancy, he recognized and addressed the border patrolling he encountered from whites. In the following case, Peter had just been named the pastor of a white church in a white working-class neighborhood in Cleveland: "I had gotten moved to a white church. That turned out to

be two years from hell. The church did not want me to be appointed there. They actually had a special meeting after they got wind of who was coming; 95 percent of the church did not want me there because I was interracially married. The first church meeting I was at, the chair asked for further motions. One person said, 'I make a motion that the reverend resign from this church.'" Peter laughed about the absurdity of the situation and then continued: "The first sermon, attendance was over one hundred; everyone came out to see the show. From then on, attendance never got above sixty, so basically about forty people boycotted the whole time I was there. I had people who still attended but resigned all their offices." In addition, church members began a letter-writing campaign to the bishop accusing Peter of various wrongdoings—for example, claiming he had taken all the Bibles out of the church. Peter and his family eventually moved to a black church in Chicago. The Ohio church members who had resigned their offices returned to them after he left.

Privileges granted to people with white skin have been institutionalized and made largely invisible to the beneficiaries. With overwhelming power in society, why do individual whites insist on border patrolling? As economic insecurity heightens and demographics show that whites are losing numerical majority status, the desire to scapegoat people of color, especially the poor, also heightens. As whites lose their economic footing, they claim white skin as a liability. Far from recognizing whiteness as privilege, they become conscious of whiteness only when defining themselves as innocent victims of "unjust" laws, including affirmative action.[19] In their insecurity they cling to images that promote feelings of superiority. This, of course, requires a racial hierarchy and a firm essentialist color line. Border patrolling helps to maintain the myth of purity and thus a color line created to ensure that whites maintain privileges and power.

Black Border Patrolling

Some blacks in interracial relationships discover, for the first time, a lack of acceptance from black communities. Others experienced border patrolling before their marriage, perhaps because of hobbies and interests, class, politics, educational goals, skin tone, vernacular, or friendship networks. Patrolling takes on new proportions, however, when they go the "other way" and marry a white person. While all relationships with individuals not seen as black are looked down on, relationships with whites represent the gravest transgression. Interracially married black women and men often believe they are viewed as having lost their identity and culture—that they risk being seen as "no longer really black." Before their interracial marriage, most called black communities their home, the place from which they gained a sense of humanity, where they gained cultural and personal affirmation. During their interracial relationship many discovered black border patrolling. Cathy Cohen suggests that "those failing to meet indigenous standards of blackness find their life chances threatened not only by dominant institutions or groups, but also by their lack of access to indigenous resources and support."[20] Interracially involved blacks needed to carefully weigh their decision to cross the color line.

George, a black man, lives with his wife, Dorothy, a white woman, and their two young children in Montclair, New Jersey, a racially mixed suburb of New York City. I drove along the town's big, clean, tree-lined streets one Sunday morning to meet with George in his home. During our interview, he explained that he had dated a white girl in high school and was aware of how blacks and whites respond to such a relationship. Nonetheless, a recent event at his Manhattan workplace troubled him. Bill, a black male coworker, told him:

"I couldn't marry a white woman. How about you?"

I said, "I am married to a white woman."

"You joking me, George! Big strong handsome brother like you!"

I said, "Yo, man, I don't know what all that handsome stuff you comin' with."

He said, "All jokes aside, George, you telling me you went the other way?"

I said, "There's nothing wrong with that."

And he's like "Oh, George, I don't believe it."

He was just solemn after that and looked down, so I said, "Bill, does that mean we're not going to be friends anymore?"

He goes, "No, man, you still my man."

He gave me the ole handshake; I said, "Bill, no, man, you frontin' now."

He said, "I'm just surprised, you know. You never told me about your wife."

The implication here is that a "strong brother" would not sell out his community like this; only weak men would do that. Before this confrontation, George had been an integral part of many conversations at work about race, racism, and black culture. After it, he found "they'll be talking about something totally in the black culture. I come into the room and be listening; and when I would put my opinion in, the conversation would end—just like that. The room goes empty . . . because I'm married to a white woman, blacks figure my culture is gone; it's shot." He is accused of having lost connectedness to African Americans, being weak, and marrying a white woman to escape his blackness.

Blacks in interracial relationships defend themselves against accusations of weakness, neurosis, and betrayal. In *Black Skin, White Masks,* Frantz Fanon writes about black men in interracial relationships: "I marry white culture, white beauty, white whiteness. When my restless hands caress those white breasts, they grasp white civilization and dignity and make them mine."[21] In his psychoanalytic interpretation of the effects of **colonization** and racism, Fanon suggests that many black men who intermarry suffer from neurosis created in a world in which black men are not valued and thus do not value themselves. They think that a relationship with a white woman will validate them—that is, whiten them. Of black

---

colonization When one country controls another in order to seize resources, such as land, gold, timber, or ivory, or to enslave its population.

women, Fanon writes, "It is because the Negress feels inferior that she aspires to win admittance into the white world."[22] Without acknowledging the pain caused by border patrolling and the desire many interracially married blacks have to maintain strong ties with other blacks, Fanon labels black men and black women in interracial relationships as pathological and neurotic.

More recently, Paul Rosenblatt and his colleagues conducted a study of forty-two multiracial couples in the Minneapolis–St. Paul area. They conclude that many African Americans feel that "it is inappropriate to choose as a partner somebody from the group that has been oppressing African Americans."[23] Many black border patrollers have an overriding concern about loyalty to the race. If an individual is not being loyal, then he or she is explained away as weak, acting in ways that are complicit with the oppression of other black Americans. In "Essentialism and the Complexities of Racial Identity," Michael Eric Dyson suggests, "Loyalty to race has been historically construed as primary and unquestioning allegiance to the racial quest for freedom and the refusal to betray that quest to personal benefit or the diverting pursuit of lesser goals. Those who detour from the prescribed path are labeled 'sellouts,' 'weak,' 'traitors,' or 'Uncle Toms.'"[24] Thus, black men and women face differing social realities and forms of patrolling.

An overwhelming percentage of black-white couples involve a black male and a white female at a time when there are "more single women in the black community than single men."[25] Many black men are hindered by a racist educational system and job market that make them less desirable for marriage. Many others are scooped into the prison industrial complex. High-profile athletes and entertainers who marry white women confirm for many that black men who are educated and earn a good living sell out, attempting to buy white status through their interracial relationship.[26] Beyond issues of money and status, many black women see black male–white female interracial relationships "as a rejection of black women's beauty, [and] as a failure to acknowledge and reward the support that black women give black men."[27] In *Rooted against*

the Wind, Gloria Wade-Gayles writes about the pain and feeling of rejection that black women experience when they see black men with white women:

> We see them, and we feel abandoned. We feel abandoned because we have been abandoned in so many ways, by so many people, and for so many centuries. We are the group of women furthest removed from the concept of beauty and femininity which invades almost every spot of the planet, and as a result, we are taught not to like ourselves, or, as my student said, not to believe that we can ever do enough or be enough to be loved or desired.[28]

Black women and men may both feel a sense of rejection when they see an interracial couple, but for each that sense of rejection comes from a different place. In a society in which women's worth is judged largely by beauty—more specifically, **Eurocentric** standards of beauty—black women are presumed to be the farthest removed from such a standard. Men's worth is judged largely by their educational and occupational status, two primary areas in which black men are undermined in a racist system. Black men with few educational and job opportunities lack status in the marriage market. Thus, when black men see a black woman with a white man, they may be reminded of the numerous ways in which the **white-supremacist** system has denied them opportunities. The privilege and power granted to whites, particularly to white males, is paraded in front of them; and they see the black women in these relationships as complicit with the oppressor.

I met Parsia, a successful businesswoman and a black interracially married mother living in Connecticut, through a family friend. Having grown up in a close-knit African American community, she

---

Eurocentric The view that European culture is superior to all other cultures in the world; implies that European culture should be the yardstick by which all other cultures are measured.

white supremacist A person who believes in the supremacy of the white race.

was uncertain if she wanted to marry interracially and risk losing the support of that community. Now happily married and the mother of a beautiful little girl, she is still very aware of border patrolling. For this reason she prefers not to bring her husband to some areas in Harlem and to black-centered events:

> African Americans do view blacks in interracial relationships as turncoats. There is a pervasive belief in the African American community that it is much more difficult to maintain your identity in an interracial relationship. I believe that once blacks see me as part of an interracial couple, it changes their perception of me right away. They disrespect me as another black person, and then they just disregard my belonging to the community, and suddenly I become the outsider—an outsider because I am with him.

Her fears are not unfounded. One day she and her husband were walking in Philadelphia when a young black man accosted them:

> If I had been alone and this young brother was hassling me in any way, I would have stopped, turned around, and said, "Look, why are you bothering me? What's the deal here?" But I didn't feel at all that I could have this conversation with this young man. He was so hostile, and the source of his hostility was totally his perception of black-white relationships, and there was nothing I could say to change that perception.

This young border patroller may be responding to a belief that Parsia is a race traitor. She is no longer an insider worthy of respect but an outsider who signifies neurosis in the form of self-hate and community betrayal—perhaps the highest form of betrayal. The prospect of rejection by other African Americans is enough for many blacks to deny, hide, or avoid interracial relationships. Border patrolling from other blacks, racism from whites, and the prospect of struggling alone in a racist society seem

too high a price, so many who enter interracial relationships end them in a short time.

Today there are no longer legal sanctions against interracial marriage, but de facto sanctions remain. At times, family and friends exert pressure to end the interracial relationship; at other times, pressure may come from the border patrolling of strangers. Even if the relationship is clandestine, thoughts of how friends, family members, coworkers, employers, and the general public might respond can deter people from moving forward in a relationship. In each of the following cases the couples did get back together eventually, but all the black women took some time away from the relationship to make this choice.

Lisa met her white husband when she was a college student at a historically black college in the South.

> [I was] the only female in the jazz orchestra, [so] there were all these [black] guys saying, "Why are you with this white guy?" And one band member would make racial comments about "Don't marry whitey, don't trust whitey, don't do this for whitey." This guy in the band tried to talk me out of marrying Peter. I had some apprehension, so I broke up with him and told him I did not want to develop a relationship.

Parsia explains why she temporarily ended her relationship before finally deciding to marry her white husband, Joe:

> When I met Joe, I was really resistant to dating across racial lines. No way would I do that. It took me a very long time to get over that and deal with those feelings, biases, and expectations. I expected friends would feel very uncomfortable socializing with us. I still do believe that there is a certain language that blacks have when we are apart from other races, when we are alone socially. That's a very important part of my life, and I expected that I might lose that, and that was a very fearful thing for me. The more I felt

him getting closer, the more I started seeing the possibility of longevity in the relationship, the more afraid I got. I was terrified that I would be in an interracial relationship for the rest of my life, so I pulled back in a big way and we broke up. There was definitely a shame and a guilt I had to get over because I felt that by dating interracially I was betraying black men.

Her fear reflects her reliance on other African Americans for mutual support in a white-supremacist system. Moreover, her observation that "there is a certain language that blacks have when we are apart from other races" indicates a shared cultural identity that creates and demands the enforcement of borders.

In some cases parents and family reinforce reservations about crossing over. Quisha, like Parsia, broke up with her white boyfriend, Raymond, because she needed time to think about what life would be like in an interracial relationship. "I was really excited about him and told my mom, and she just had a heart attack because he was white. I totally did not expect this from her. She would call every day and was just hammering it into me to just forget this—and so I really badly and abruptly broke it off with Raymond. He was a real gentleman; he kept calling to find out what happened, and I totally blew him off." She explained her underlying fears as she discussed how she handles people staring at her: "I can feel my grandmother and my mother and my aunts disapproving in those stares, so that's intimidating." Lisa, Parsia, and Quisha all married the men they had left, but they needed time to think about risks, their own understandings of race and community, and what it means to be a black woman in the United States.

They are three of the many black women in interracial relationships who challenge the idea that white men are responsible for the low number of black female–white male interracial marriages. Theorists attempting to explain motives behind interracial marriages have often pointed to the low number of these marriages as evidence that white

men are choosing not to marry black women.[29] These theorists suggest that white men are least likely to intermarry with black women because they would gain nothing in these marriages: no money, no status. My research, however, demonstrates the power of black women. The stories they share directly challenge long-held motive myths that imply that black women would marry white men if only white men would choose them. On the contrary, in each of the relationships just discussed, the black woman instigated a breakup. Perhaps their understanding of what it means to be strong, dedicated, and connected to black communities is responsible for the lower numbers of black female–white male marriages.

Border patrolling plays a central role in life decisions and the reproduction of the color line. As decisions are made to enter and remain in an interracial relationship, the color line is challenged and racial identities shift. Many blacks spoke of the growth they experienced because of their interracial relationship and border patrolling. Parsia explains, "I used to be real concerned about how I would be perceived and that as an interracially married female I would be taken less seriously in terms of my dedication to African American causes. I'm not nearly as concerned anymore. I would hold my record up to most of those in single-race relationships, and I would say, 'Okay, let's go toe to toe, and you tell me who's making the biggest difference,' and so I don't worry about it anymore." Identities, once grounded in the presumed acceptance of other black Americans, have become more reflective. Acceptance can no longer be assumed. Definitions of what it means to be black are reworked. Likewise, because of border patrolling, many whites in interracial relationships began to acknowledge that race matters. Whiteness becomes visible in their claims to racial identity.

CONCLUSION

Unlike transracially adopted and multiracial people who are raised across the color line, people in interracial relationships discover borderism when they decide to cross the line. This unique form of discrimination, grounded in a racist and segregated society, is always at work even when multiracial family members are not present. Yet by examining the experiences of multiracial family members, we can see the myriad ways in which the color line is both reproduced and resisted. Because interracially married people are often raised in single-race worlds, they have internalized borderism. Thus, part of the decision to become involved interracially includes the need to overcome internalized borderist thoughts. Most of them begin questioning color-blind and essentialist perspectives and learn to understand race as more fluid and complex. Skin color and physical features become just one set of criteria used to think about community and belonging. Many of the people I interviewed referred to this growth process (although not all interracially married people accept the invitation to rethink race).

In a society that often rejects people who cross the color line, individuals involved in such relationships have much to consider before making a permanent commitment. Given the significance of race in our society, a basic choice that all couples contend with is whether or not to stay together in the face of borderism. A few individuals claimed that there was no decision; they fell in love, and that was it. For most others, however, a life across the color line and facing borderism did not look all that inviting and in fact was enough to cause some to terminate their relationships.[30] While the number of people involved in interracial relationships is not known, we do know that in 1995 the census bureau estimated that there were only 246,000 black-white interracial marriages in the United States.[31] This is quite a small percentage considering that in the same year there were more than 50 million total marriages.[32] Borderism and its various components are strong and painful enough to keep black-white interracial marriages the least common marriage pattern for both blacks and whites.

49

REDRAWING THE COLOR LINE?

The Problems and Possibilities of Multiracial Families and Group Making

Kimberly McClain DaCosta

KIMBERLY MCCLAIN DACOSTA is interested in the intersection of cultural ideas about race and the family and is currently completing a book on efforts to create a multiracial collective identity in the United States, based on interviews and fieldwork with members of organizations for interracial families and people of mixed descent. She is currently associate dean of students and an associate professor at the Gallatin School of Individualized Study at New York University.

It is my belief that the next generation's principal task will be the hard and painful one of destroying color-caste in the United States.

—W. LLOYD WARNER.[1]

AFTER TIGER WOODS WON THE 1997 MASTERS Tournament, he quickly became the poster boy of multiracialism—the well-adjusted, hugely successful, mixed race child with two devoted, loving, and *married* parents. Woods's rising public profile mirrored and symbolized the increasingly public profile of mixed descent persons. By the 1990s, multiracial families and multiracial identity were given more attention in the media, portrayed in such a positive way that one could be excused if one forgot the powerful stigma previously heaped upon intermarried couples and their families. Woods's success and embrace by the American public lent credibility to assertions that multiraciality was "old news"—that this had been going on for centuries (by which people usually meant interracial sex, not family), and that Americans were no longer shocked by this anymore.

Yet the emergence of multiracial families represents a significant historical shift, particularly when we consider the efforts made to prevent and conceal family ties across racial boundaries. The emergence of a multiracial identity as the expression of such family ties is a major shift as well. Given that race as a mark of identity (rather than an uncomplicated descriptor of a biological reality) only developed in the twentieth century, and that the major period of growth in marriages across racial categories did not begin until the 1960s, this shift has taken place in a relatively short period of time. In the last decade, the idea of "multiracial community" has developed a social and cultural presence in the United States. Since the struggle over the census in the 1990s, references to "multiracials" regularly appear in the popular press, in academic literature, and in the marketplace, and the creation of multiracial organizations has continued unabated. Due to the efforts of people in those organizations, in conjunction with increasing rates of intermarriage, the multiracial family is no longer a contradiction in terms. Rather than "melting" into traditional racial groups, people of mixed

race are elaborating a distinct sense of groupness as "multiracial." At the same time, they are asserting specific mixed ethnoracial identifications such as "Japanese and Mexican" or "black and Irish."

How then should we evaluate the impact and significance of multiracial group making? How is the color line being redrawn? The definition of race—a basic concept for describing social differences and inequalities in the United States—is in the process of changing. But in what ways and with what impact?

It is impossible to evaluate the impact of multiracial politics without attention to historical and social contexts. Without such contexts, it is tempting to conclude, as many have, that the collective efforts of multiracials are inherently progressive, inherently regressive, or even irrelevant. Appearing on the Oprah Winfrey show, for example, a black/white woman explains to the audience that as a multiracial person she can be a bridge to promote understanding between racial groups. In hearings over changes to racial classification, opponents to the possibility of the state enumerating mixed descent persons invoke the specter of **apartheid** South Africa, suggesting that new categories will create an escape hatch from blackness. At around the same time, some scholars claim that Asian outmarriage reflects Asian self-hatred and is an attempt to leave behind a stigmatized group. Still others state that the issue is "old news," not important enough to waste time commenting on it.

The social and historical contexts will allow us to make sense of what multiracials are doing today and that make such blanket assessments of multiracial politics less defensible. For the multiracial movement is about race and family—cultural categories, not static institutions—the meanings of which depend on context. This being the case, there can be no definitive answer to the question "Are multiracial politics progressive or regressive?" Such evaluations will differ according to individual identities and political intentions. More useful than evaluations of the logic of racial categories or

Questions to Consider

In 2000 the U.S. Census Bureau allowed individuals to check more than one racial category in the decennial census. Although there is a long history of "multiracials" in the United States, the effect of institutionalizing the mixed race or multiracial category has carved out a distinct social identity that challenges the way we typically think about racial categories. Within the context and acceptance of a multiracial movement, one can now claim, as Professor DaCosta points out, a "Japanese and Mexican" or a "black and Irish" identity. How might these "new" identities redraw the color line? How might you respond when someone explains to you they are "black, white, and a little bit Latina" or "Italian, Asian, and Puerto Rican"?

---

apartheid The state-sanctioned and legally enforced policy of racial segregation instituted by South Africa.

intermarriage in the abstract, then, are historically grounded and ethnographically parsed accounts that show us what is different between now and the past and that ask what these categories mean to the people who feel invested in organizing around them.

FAMILY MATTERS

According to Drake and Cayton (1993 [1945])," Social segregation is maintained, in the final analysis, by **endogamy**—the rule that Negroes must marry Negroes, and whites must marry whites—and by its corollary that when an intermarriage does 'accidentally' occur, the child must automatically be classed as a Negro no matter how white his skin color."[2]

In order to understand multiracial group making—its rise, shape, contents, and possible impact—one must not only denaturalize race but denaturalize the family, for the construction of the American family and race are joint historical and cultural processes that are mutually determinative. Racial classifications and antimiscegenation policies facilitated the creation of sharp divisions between social groups, defined them as racially different, and in so doing shaped the cultural common sense in which racial difference and the division of families along racial lines appears to be natural. Despite the possibility of legal marriage across racial boundaries, the normative family is still monoracial, and racial affiliation exacts a kind of loyalty that disqualifies intimate connections across racial categories. The realization that they are misfits in this context motivates multiracial actors to challenge the prevailing race/family nexus.

This struggle is apparent in the stories told by my respondents. While the interracial unions in my respondents' families were legally sanctioned, some struggled with the discretionary acts of disowning by their monoracial parents that mimicked the economic impacts that antimiscegenation laws

once had. For most intermarried couples and families, however, what is at stake lies in the terrain of relatedness, emotional connection, the sense of cultural loss and gain, and the recognized reflection of the self in one's child—all structured by the racial dimension of the normative family.

The legalization of intermarriage, along with popular representations of multiracial families as heterosexual and nuclear, leads to interpretations of multiracial families as an interesting "flavor" of the normative family. While it is clear that the heterosexual nuclear family is accorded material and social privilege in U.S. society, and that most of the contemporary discussion of multiracial families concerns heterosexual couplings, it misses the point to see multiracial families as an interesting variation on the theme of the heterosexual nuclear family. Rather, multiracial families—and multiracial politics broadly conceived—should be understood as part of an historical transformation in kinship, ideology, and social relations that has come about as the result of conflict, contradiction, and struggle.

Yet just how far we have come is a matter of debate. Although antimiscegenation laws are unconstitutional, intermarriage remains rare, especially so between blacks and whites. Moreover, a nontrivial percentage of people (of all racial groups) still disapprove of intermarriage. While the social climate for intermarried couples and families has certainly improved in the last several decades, Drake and Cayton's observations of Chicago in the 1930s describe all too well the state of intermarriage today, especially for blacks. They found that while blacks had made gains in governmental and economic areas, only "very moderate" gains had been made in "spatial and family relations." They concluded that while intermarriage is legally permitted, "it is generally discouraged." "[I]nformal social controls among both Negroes and whites," they wrote, "keep the number of such marriages small despite the fact there are no legal prohibitions against them" (1993 [1945], 127).

Of course, the same degree of separation is not found between Asians and whites and Latinos and whites. Intermarriage rates with whites for

---

endogamy The custom of marrying only within one's racial, ethnic, or social group.

Asians, Latinos, and Native Americans are comparable to those of Southern and Eastern European immigrants in the early twentieth century who, through intermarriage with American-born whites, expanded the definition of who is white. With each generation in the United States and as income and education levels rise, Latinos and Asians are more likely to marry whites. This has prompted Roger Sanjek (1994) to argue that we may be seeing a "race-to-ethnicity" conversion for Hispanics and Asians, but not for African Americans.

Despite very low intermarriage rates for blacks, which testify to a firmer racialized boundary separating blacks from other groups, assertions by multiracials—even those of African descent—that they are not "just black" confounds that once defining feature of the color line to which DuBois ([1903] 1996) referred a century ago. Multiracial activists' demand for a recognition of mixedness challenges the categorical nature of the American racial classification system which, until 1997, recognized membership in only one category. As such, it is in direct opposition to the logic of the one-drop rule—the key mechanism that maintained that color line. Moreover, their efforts disrupt what the one-drop rule firmly established, namely the racial basis of kinship in which relatedness across racial boundaries is not socially recognized.

In everyday life, not just in official categories, the definition of blackness (and consequentially of white, Asian, Indian, and Latino identities) is shifting as well. So while in the 1930s Drake and Cayton (1993 [1945]) observed that the "children of mixed matings" are "always defined as Negroes," an understanding that prevailed through the 1980s, this is no longer as certain as it once was. Mariah Carey, for example, is not understood (or marketed) as a black singer, despite being of African descent, just as respondents with an ambiguous physical appearance and who lack cultural credentials are not necessarily accepted by blacks as (authentically) black, nor are they necessarily seen as sharply different by nonblacks despite knowledge of their African ancestry.

RACIAL OPTIONS? CHOICE AND THE LIMITS OF CHOICE

Twenty-six years ago, in the conclusion of her study on the Lumbee Indians of Robeson County, North Carolina, Karen Blu stated that "there is no 'right' to choose one's 'racial' ancestry, as race is currently conceived, but if race and ethnicity become progressively intertwined in a new way, it is possible that being Black will, in years to come, be more a matter of individual choice and less a matter of assignment by others" (1980, 210). Students of race and ethnicity in the United States often note that a key difference between the ways Americans experience ethnic and racial identities is the degree of choice one has to identify (or not) in ethnic or racial terms. This distinction is based on the historical experience of European immigrants. As the voluntary and involuntary factors that held together European immigrant ethnic communities (for example, residential segregation, discrimination, prejudice, religious affiliation) have declined, so too has the salience of ethnicity in the lives of their descendants (Alba 1990; Gans 1979; Lieberson 1985; Waters 1990). For these white ethnics, ethnicity is chosen rather than ascribed and expressions of ethnic identity are largely symbolic in content.

In her often-cited book *Ethnic Options: Choosing Identities in America*, Mary Waters (1990) found that not only did her white respondents choose which ethnicity to be, but also whether to be ethnic *at all*. Moreover, ethnic identity held few negative consequences for her respondents. It did not limit whom they could marry, determine where they could live, their employment prospects, or who their friends were. In contrast, the literature is replete with examples showing the continued prevalence and salience of ethnoracial ascription for nonwhites. The third and fourth generation Japanese and Chinese Americans Mia Tuan studied report that "others consistently expect them to identify ethnically (e.g., as Chinese or Japanese) or racially as Asian and be knowledgeable about Chinese or Japanese 'things' and express dissatisfaction when they are not" (Tuan 1998, 156). Attributions of racial difference are consequential for African Americans whether or not they choose to assert a racial identity, even for middle-class blacks who conform to white middle-class norms of behavior (Bell 1992; Cose 1992; Fordham 1997).[3] Racial options—the ability to choose whether to identify or be identified in racial terms—have been elusive.

Events of the last decade, however, suggest that we need to revisit the question of whether or not "racial options" are in the making. The institutionalized option to choose multiple racial affiliations in official race counts represents a racial option "on paper." The flexibility exhibited by respondents in how they describe, display, and perform their ethnoracial identities makes clear that indeed racial identification and categorization are somewhat malleable. But how much can this be said to approximate the kind of symbolic ethnicity found among white ethnics?

In all the ways ethnic identity did not matter for Waters's respondents, racial identity *did* matter for mine. Regardless of how much they chose to identify themselves as mixed, they faced resistance from institutions, peers, and even family members. When they wished not to have to identify themselves in racial terms, others *did* classify them in racial terms, and not necessarily in the ways they wished to be classified. Moreover, *how* they looked mattered very much in what types of identity expressions were likely to be authenticated by others. The dark-skinned person who identifies as white—or even mixed—must still work very hard to get others to treat him as such. In other words, not all heritages can equally be chosen or discarded at will. That their efforts have been met with suspicion and resistance is telling of lingering opposition to treating what are considered racial distinctions as just another form of ethnicity.

A key aspect of the optional character of white ethnicity is its costlessness. Unlike the ethnic identifications of white ethnics, for my respondents "being" mixed race or marrying someone of a different race had significant costs. Some intermarried respondents were "disowned" by their parents. For others, racial difference within the family was sometimes a source of tension that distorted emotional connections between family members. Moreover, for mixed descent respondents, asserting a mixed racial identification threatened their belonging within ethnic communities.

Yet while racial identification for multiracials is not entirely voluntary or costless, there is a way in which multiracial identification looks like the symbolic ethnicity of whites. Waters (1990) explains the apparent paradox that while ethnicity is a matter of choice, relatively costless and inconsequential in her respondents' lives, her respondents "cling tenaciously to their ethnic identities." They do so, she argues, because symbolic ethnicity actually reconciles two contradictory impulses in the American character—the desire for both individuality *and* conformity. "Having an ethnic identity is something that makes you both special and simultaneously part of a community. It is something that comes to you involuntarily through heredity, and at the same time it is a personal choice. And it allows you to express your individuality in a way that does not make you stand out as in any way different from all kinds of other people" (Waters, 1990, 150).

Similarly, the idea that racial identity can be freely chosen appeals to the high value Americans place on individualism. The novelty of a mixed racial identity makes one stand out against dominant modes of identification. At the same time, the elaboration of a sense of multiracial group identity makes one feel as if one belongs to a community where one is, if only in one's perceived marginality, just like everyone else. The irony here is that while the discourse of choice in racial identification suggests we as individuals are determining for ourselves who we want to be, in fact we are "choosing" within a given set of epistemological, social, and political conditions that make only certain choices possible.

Scholars have sometimes described the trajectory of white ethnicity from a consequential group affiliation to a largely symbolic one as a transition from "being" to "feeling" ethnic (Bakalian 1993). "People desperately wish to 'feel' ethnic," Steinberg argues, "precisely because they have all but lost the prerequisites of 'being' ethnic" (1989, 63). In this respect, the multiracial example is perhaps best understood as a move in the opposite direction. Elaborations of multiracial collective identification represent an attempt to move *from* "feeling" *to* "being" multiracial. For some of my respondents, that feeling of being mixed race was largely a feeling of not fitting into any ethnoracial community. For others it was based on a feeling of being a part of both. The construction of multiracial organizations, the push for official designation of mixed race status—these are moves to make multiracials appear more real in a culture that elevates ethnicity and race as primary markers of personhood—to not only feel multiracial, but also to "be" multiracial in civic and social life.

The dividing line between what constitutes racial versus ethnic difference in the United States has always fallen fairly close to the line marking whom one would consider marrying and what ancestry one would publicly claim. Yet according to this barometer, some racialized distinctions—particularly American Indian status—have also been treated as "ethnic" ones—interesting "decorations" to the family tree that have little consequence in everyday life. Of course, the symbolic aspect of American Indian identity has only been inconsequential for persons of mixed background, whose native ancestry is generations removed, and who do not live on reservations. While to date visible non-European ancestry has been consequential, particularly for persons of African descent, one can certainly imagine a time in the not too distant future where being Asian, Mexican, and even black will increasingly be treated and *experienced* (much like American Indian ancestry is currently treated by whites who claim it)—symbolically. As this generation of mixed descent persons has children of their own, who may cross even more racialized boundaries, they are likely to encourage their children to "embrace" all of their ancestry. As such, the proliferation of racial identifiers that individuals use is likely to expand. The consequences of such racial identifications and the nature of the connections to those racialized communities, however, will largely depend on where they live, whom they live with, and what they look like.

THE FUTURE OF MULTIRACIAL GROUP MAKING

I have discussed in detail how the multiracial example draws our attention to the hegemonic, yet hidden assumptions about the American family—namely, that families are monoracial—and how racial homogeneity has been fundamental to how families are constructed. But what does the multiracial example teach us about ethnoracial group making? In the process of elaborating what they share with each other, and seeking public recognition for themselves, multiracials make the mixed position a socially recognizable one. As the idea that multiracials exist is further institutionalized, it is appropriate to evaluate in what sense this "group" will come to be like traditional ethnoracial groups.

Like panethnic formations among Latinos, Asian Americans, and American Indians in the United States, the construction of multiracial community is profoundly shaped by state policies. These panethnic formations arose out of a context in which the state "lumped" together groups who consider themselves to be distinct on some basis deemed salient (such as shared language or presumed racial similarity). In response, these distinct cultural and linguistic groups began to assert a common identification (Espiritu 1992; Nagel 1995; Omi and Winant 1994). Collective identification, generally speaking, followed categorization.

The assertion of a collective identification among "multiracials" emerges out of a different relationship to the state. Unlike Latinos, Asians, and American Indians, "multiracials" have not been lumped together for the purposes of racial classification or the administration of social policies. Neither were they counted separately in racial statistics nor was social policy developed to deal with them as a class of people. Multiracials began to coalesce in response to social and cultural pressures that defined them as misfits and that stigmatized interracial families. They *sought* a state classification as a remedy to those grievances.

Now that the state classifies mixed race people as such, one of the key factors motivating multiracial mobilization in the 1990s is no longer available. Additionally, the prejudice and stigma associated with interracial marriage and families have declined significantly. Even in the absence of those initial motivating factors, however, it seems likely that collective mobilization around multiracial identification will continue for the foreseeable future.

First, mixed race organizations have become increasingly institutionalized. The Mavin Foundation has professionalized what began as grassroots, minimally organized community building efforts. Matt Kelley, its founder and president, has assembled a paid staff that operates a Web site, runs community outreach activities, and acts as a kind of clearinghouse for information on mixed race people and issues of race and social justice. The foundation publishes a quarterly magazine (*Mavin: The Mixed Race Experience*), the production values of which rival those of most national monthlies—a far cry from the photocopied newsletters irregularly produced by local community organizations in the 1990s. Moreover, through its Campus Awareness and Compliance Initiative, sponsored jointly with HIF, AMEA, and the Level Playing Field Institute, it aims to ensure that the MOOM [mark one or more] option is fully institutionalized in federal agencies.[4]

Groups like Mavin, as well as campus organizations and academic classes, focused on mixed race people are manifestations of ongoing attempts to create and sustain mixed race community. Once established, people have vested interests in maintaining them, as they provide jobs, income, and a public platform for members. These venues for expressing and exploring multiracial identity are likely to thrive, as the "two or more races" population is expected to grow significantly in the next decade. Recent population

estimates show the "two or more races" population was the third fastest growing group between 2003 and 2004 (behind Hispanics and Asians) (Files 2005). While demographic statistics cannot predict whether multiracial collective identification will be meaningful to this population, the ongoing institutionalization of mixed race identity will encourage such an identification. For example, schools are required to ask students if they are "of two or more races," and given the opportunity to identify themselves this way, many people will. With statistics on this population, school administration will likely craft programs for such students, further encouraging such an identification. Indeed, this is already happening. In 1988, when students at Harvard formed a discussion group for mixed race students, they knew of no other such group. By 2005, the ninth annual Pan-Collegiate Mixed Race Conference took place while one of the largest professional associations of student affairs personnel inaugurated a standing committee on multiracial student affairs, alongside its committees for Asian, African American, Latino, and Native American students.[5]

While the educational arena will likely encourage multiracial identification, so too will the market. The juggernaut of consumer capitalism has taken up multiracialism. As long as mixed race retains its air of hipness and authenticity, marketers will continue to exploit it. As long as the population that identifies itself as mixed race continues to grow, business will court "it," developing products to meet its putative needs and helping to make multiracials in the process. Five years after Census 2000, multiracial community is increasingly translocal, Web based, and media driven. The advent of high-speed global communications technology in the 1990s has allowed those previously isolated by geography to "come together" virtually. These virtual communities are cheap to start up and to run and so will likely continue. Not incidentally, the low cost and wide reach of Web communications has greatly facilitated the creation of companies selling mixed race consumer products. Increasingly, mixed race organizations, Web communities, and entrepreneurs engage in a symbiotic relationship, with each Web site giving links to each other, and in so doing reinforcing their raison d'être.

While mixed racial identifications have become further institutionalized through state codification, it is not clear to what extent "multiracials" will make demands on the state on behalf of multiracials as a group. To date, self-appointed spokespersons for multiracials limit themselves to ensuring that federal agencies collect multirace data and to calls to investigate the extent to which multiracials have unique health care needs.[6] At this time, the multiple race population is not a protected class for the purposes of antidiscrimination efforts, which may be the next battle multiracial activists wage. The political commitments of younger organized multiracials, however, appear to be left leaning. Participants in Mavin, the leaders of Mixed Media Watch, and my respondents largely consider themselves to be politically progressive and antiracist. They are skeptical of the claims that race does not matter by conservatives who point to their multiple racial identifications as proof of its irrelevance. There is a strong impulse among these respondents to avoid essentializing a set of differences that distinguish multiracials from others. Yet through the debate over official classification and the organizations in which they explore what they share as a group, racial mixedness is constituted as an adequate principle upon which to act.

There is an inescapable irony of group making that in seeking to undermine the foundations of American racial thinking, they reaffirm racial thinking as well. While activists and parents describe their use of multiple terms for indicating their racial identity as "revolutionary" or simply "accurate," it is also true that the logic of mixed race stems from the same underlying logic that preceded it—that individuals have race, and when they combine sexually we get "racial mixture." Both ideas assume there is race, it is carried in the body, and it's mixed through sexual reproduction.

While those who fought official enumeration of mixed race status challenged the prevailing way that race was categorized, they stopped short of challenging the principle of racial classification itself. While seeming to challenge the racial state,

multiracial activists *affirmed* the right of the state to label individuals in racial terms by arguing that it has a *duty* to label them in ways that fully recognize the possibility of boundary crossing. This can only entrench the underlying notion that individuals are made of "racial stuff" (albeit of more than one type) and that their racial composition ought to be recognized by that ultimate symbolic agency—the state. Their activism recognizes, indeed *welcomes,* the right of the state to record a race for each of its members (even if individuals "self-identify"). This is a striking acceptance of the racial state, in and through which the category of race was created and through which it is reproduced.

Yet this irony is not limited to this movement. "The reproduction of ethnicity and the reinforcement of its pragmatic salience," writes Comaroff, "is as much a function of efforts directed at its erosion as it is of activities that assert its positive value" (Comaroff 1987, 315). If race is where you locate your difficulties, race is where you look for solutions. "Race" seems like an efficacious basis upon which to act.

The construction of multiracial community, like panethnic constructions and movements for ethnic renewal, is a flexible, sometimes strategic, and sometimes contradictory phenomenon. It creates new racial subjects while conforming to the preexisting U.S. racial order, as it provides a crucial consciousness-raising tool with which to make demands on the state. It undermines rigid modes of racial thinking in the United States while multiplying the available ways of naming racial difference. While mixed race people may identify *with* each other, they eschew the notions of racial sameness that racial identity usually entails. While a collective mixed race identity is potentially subversive, it may be readily absorbed into the existing racial order, in which multiraciality comes to be seen as simply another racial category, robbed of its critical content.[7] The meaning of multiracial will be affected by the political alignments, demographics, and economic pressures of all other groups.

Critics of the group-making project among multiracials claim that "the multiracial community" is a fabrication. After all, mixed race people come in a variety of "mixes." As such, as a group they share no ancestry in common. Nor do they necessarily share language, religion, or culture. They are not, in other words, a "real" ethnic group. Yet the fabricated aspect of multiracial group making that its critics find so troubling is precisely what makes studying this phenomenon so valuable. The notion of "fabrication" has a double meaning, signifying both an act of creation (which captures the constructed nature of groups) and a *deception,* in which the ways we tend to perceive groups in everyday life (as durable, real, substantial entities) masks the reality that groups do not exist as such, but rather are the products of a complex work of *group making.* All ethnoracial groups are constructed. In the project of making multiracials, however, the ways in which such construction proceeds are just more obvious.

The Family's Role in Racial Change

Multiracial activists have used the state as a means through which to gain symbolic recognition not only of their racial identity, but of their families as well. The multiracial family, some believe, serves as proof that America's racial problems can be overcome. I dub this the "family thesis," inspired by Benjamin DeMott's critique of contemporary racial politics. In his book, *The Trouble with Friendship,* DeMott (1998 [1995]) critiques what he calls "the friendship thesis" that underlies many putative solutions offered in culture and politics for healing racial division. According to DeMott, embedded within the "friendship thesis" is the "certainty that one-on-one, black-white relations can be relied on to resolve race problems." In a similar vein, the "family thesis" suggests that if we all just intermarried and had children together our problems would be resolved.

Historical and cross-cultural analyses show the problems with such an idea. First, rather than bringing about social equality, intermarriage tends to follow other indicators of social equality (such as educational achievement) between groups. But more to the point, it is questionable that personal relations can resolve what is wrought institutionally with the help of the state, no matter how intimate and caring those personal relations are. The hierarchies of relatedness that my respondents hold, which structure their sense of trust, affinity, and beliefs about others (despite growing up in interracial families), suggest that more than intimate and empathetic relations between individuals is needed to bring about social change. Empathy is limited in its capacities to bring about social change, since people can cultivate empathy for specific individuals while keeping intact their basic (negative) beliefs about the categories of people from which those individuals come. This is why assertions that people in intermarriages and multiracial individuals are less prejudiced natural bridges across the racial divide are problematic. It is easy to make exceptions for one's kin, marking them as the exception to the negative rule for others of a particular group, thus leaving the line of demarcation intact.

The complexities of interracial intimacy revealed through the stories of my respondents are cautionary tales with implications for how we interpret intermarriage statistics as barometers of racial change. In his influential study of white ethnicity Richard Alba writes, "By far the most impressive evidence of the diminishing power of ethnicity among whites is the rising tide of interethnic marriage. Marriage is a sensitive barometer of social integration because it involves great social intimacy" and links together members of families in regular contact (1990, 11–12). In contemporary interpretations of intermarriage patterns, families are assumed to engage in regular contact and to be intimate—to care for one another in a variety of ways (physically, financially, and emotionally). In the process, children are assimilated into one ethnic group (usually the dominant one) or act as bridges between those of their parents. This formulation imagines intermarriage as the sine qua non of assimilation: a cultural merger that produces children who embody that merging.

While interracial families are imagined as sites where racial differences meet and melt (away), racialized differences among family members create variable experiences for the members of such families. The family, as feminist scholars have argued for decades, is not a monolithic unit, and members within families have divergent and competing interests. For my respondents, race often formed the ground of those competing interests. In other words, while intermarriage may be common for some groups, it does not follow that it is either preferred or without controversy for either the partners in a marriage or their children, to say nothing of the ethnoracial communities with which they are engaged.

While invaluable for helping us understand changes in identification and marriage patterns, such statistics are very crude instruments for understanding meaning and tell us very little about practice—how and why people think of themselves in such terms and how they behave on the basis of them. When we rely on demographics to tell our stories we are merely recording and elaborating the preconstructed categories of the state and of social movements and are unable to say anything about whether and in what ways such categories are meaningful.

My point here is both methodological and epistemological. We need qualitative ethnographic work to understand meaning and process, and we also need to question on what basis the assortment of people who marked boxes on the census can be considered a social group. Analyzing the statistics on racial identification tells us about patterns, but before we begin to make inferences about what those patterns say about group boundaries, the existence of groups, or the "groupness" of groups, we need to know something about meaning and practice.

Family's Radical Potential

All this is not to say that interracial kinship lacks a radical *potential*. Though I am cautious about interpreting multiracial identification and rising rates of intermarriage as signs of fading ethnoracial boundaries, I do believe that these developments, along with a growing public discussion of interracial intimacy, reflect and signal significant changes in the nature of racial division in the United States.

The attempt to obtain some form of multiracial classification grew out of a desire to make visible those bonds that are easily elided—a recognition of not only a varied racial heritage, but of *relationships*. The MOOM option institutionalizes and records in statistical form a trace of those relationships.

For many of my respondents, parenting mixed race kids provided a powerful means through which they were able to extend their sense of obligation, empathy, and likeness beyond the circle of their ethnic group of origin. The notion that one can change one's people, to embrace the "other," is a potentially powerful tool to begin healing social divisions because it says that such social boundaries are artificial, and despite the very real consequences of those boundaries, through love and work they can be overcome.

The experience of living within interracial families allowed many of my respondents to overcome the racial categories that have almost always served to mark others outside one's moral domain, emphasizing the difference, and even the inhumanity, of the Other. It strikes me that the multiracial movement has its most radical potential in this vein. Presentations of multiracial family *as* families lessen the presumed distance across racial categories. Kinship symbolically bridges the imagined distance between racial groups. I am reminded of Patricia Williams's observation of a white woman suckling a black child. She writes:

> Is there not something unseemly in our society about the spectacle of a white woman mothering a black child? A white woman giving totally to a black child; a black child totally and demandingly dependent for everything, sustenance itself, from a white woman. The image of a white woman suckling a black child. . . . Such a picture says, there is no difference; it places the hope of continuous generation of immortality of the white self in a little black face.

Given the pitfalls of family imagery mentioned earlier, images of the family are only truly transformative if they extend the cultural obligation to care for and about others *outside* the limits of both genealogical relatives *and* racial groups. One respondent tried to put into words how he saw this potential:

> The way that a multiracial person sees the world—we come in so many different shades that I realize I can't look at someone and tell what they are any more. They could be black and white. They could be the same mixture that I am and look totally different or look very similar. So walking down the street, I can't look at someone and immediately conclude that I'm not related to them in some way, maybe not immediately but somewhere back in history we probably had some common ancestors, you know. Who knows? I really don't know. I can't say as a fact. So in a sense you start walking down the street and you look at everyone and see everyone as being related to you. Now, if you do that how can you discriminate against someone if you acknowledge that they're related to you? You can't discriminate against your brother or sister. What line, what rules—what lines of demarcation are you going to use to say this is us, this is them, these are the haves, these are the have-nots? You start to break them down. So the people can then start seeing or recognizing that—we are talking about the whole idea of one common humanity, you know, and I think that's a part of multiracial identity. The more you learn about multiracial people you just see multiracial people. This is what they look like. They're not so different as I thought. You know, so-and-so might not be so different. So that's why I really like to promote a multiracial outlook.

Seeing oneself in the other, as Jessica Benjamin (1988) argued, opposes the breakdown of mutual recognition that allows members of one category to see themselves as apart and above (or below) that leads to domination. It is this sense—that they are visible yet not seen—that motivates the action of the people who have been most involved in the multiracial movement. An acknowledgment of their social existence is something they understand to be crucial to eroding the color line. The issue is as much emotional as it is structural.

Understanding the emergence of multiracial families as a politicization of kinship helps clarify, if not the political implications of multiracial politics, then how multiracials understand the meaning of the actions in which they are engaged. The meaning of multiracial movement for its participants cannot be grasped merely at the cognitive level, where analysts of multiracial politics insist on grounding their critiques (for example, chastizing notions of racial accuracy or the use of fractional language as a reification of race). The notion of racial coherence put forth by respondents and evident in the idea that multiracial identification is expressive of a "whole self" should be understood not as a ground of politics, but as its effect—a response to the social conditions that create, sustain, and reproduce racial division.

The opposition between race and mixed race reaffirms boundaries between categories (white/black/Asian and so forth) even as the vocabulary of kinship brings together categories of bodies previously isolated outside of the sphere of family. So while multiracialism may reinscribe racial thinking by leaving intact the idea of race, it also calls attention to the peculiar history of the United States that denies social and sexual mixing across boundaries and helps us understand the role of such denial in supporting white domination.

The notion that one can choose one's racial identification disrupts the notion of genealogical descent as well. Such a notion says that people can choose *not* to identify with one of their ancestors' categories, or may choose to identify with a group to which none of their ancestors belonged, as did Mandy Rodriguez. Moreover, while some people might claim a multiracial identity, their children might not necessarily retain such an understanding of themselves.

While perhaps not revolutionary, the emergence of multiracial families as such represents a significant transformation in the logic (or illogic) underpinning dominant American racial discourse. The increasing prevalence and acceptance of intermarriage is a redefinition of permissible objects of sexual passion, as well as a redefinition of kinship. Multiracial families (and multiracial politics more broadly) do not necessarily challenge the biologistic and genealogical logic of race or family. Instead, they undercut the twin pillars of racial formation—hypodescent and antimiscegenation—creating the space by which the racialized family and familized notions of race are undermined.

While the multiracial family has long been a cultural contradiction in terms, that is no longer the case. The formation of collective organizations for multiracial families and their assertions that they are indeed families challenges a fundamental feature of American racial domination, yet its implications are not entirely clear. Intermarriage patterns and the political and cultural response to them and to mixed racial identity have always been linked to the broader system of racial domination that demarcates white from black (and less rigidly, white from other ethnoracial groups), and the fates of those of African descent (whether one is putatively "mixed" or not) have always been linked. While the possibility exists that the greater visibility of multiracial families will lead to more acceptability of all kinds of relations across racial boundaries—beginning with intimate and familial ones and corresponding with spatial and social ones—this does not mean, of course, that the problem that defined America in the twentieth century—the color line—has not followed us into the twenty-first.

Seeing the Big Picture | **Interracial Marriage and the Blurring of the Color Line**

Look at Figure 35, "Interracial Married Couples," in the appendix. Why is it that so few individuals marry across the color line? What would it take for these numbers to radically change?

50

POLICY STEPS TOWARD CLOSING THE GAP

Meizhu Lui, Barbara J. Robles, Betsy Leondar-Wright, Rose M. Brewer, and Rebecca Adamson

MEIZHU LUI is the executive director of United for a Fair Economy (UFE). BARBARA J. ROBLES taught Latino public policy at the LBJ School of Public Affairs at the University of Texas at Austin from 1998 to 2005. She has a PhD in economics from the University of Maryland at College Park. BETSY LEONDAR-WRIGHT is UFE's communications director. A longtime economic justice organizer and researcher, she is the author of *Class Matters: Cross-Class Alliance Building for Middle-Class Activists* (New Society Publishers, 2005). ROSE M. BREWER is associate professor and Morse Alumni Distinguished Teaching Professor of African American & African Studies at the University of Minnesota and a contributing editor to *Souls*, an interdisciplinary journal of the Institute for Contemporary Black History at Columbia. REBECCA ADAMSON, a Cherokee, is founder and president of First Nations Development Institute (1980) and founder of First Peoples Worldwide (1997).

THIS LIST IS BY NO MEANS COMPRE-HENSIVE, but perhaps it can spark more energy to tackle the issue of wealth building for communities of color, and for all those currently without economic security.

FIRST STEPS: HUMAN ASSETS

Education has been an important tool in creating white advantage. It was a crime to teach African slaves to read and write, Latinos have been disadvantaged by English-only classrooms, Native Americans were forced into assimilationist school settings, and Asians had to sue to go to school with whites.

In today's economy, more than ever, you need an education to get ahead. Even for a menial job, a high school diploma is often required. Current mechanisms for public school funding—largely local property taxes—enable wealthier families in white suburbs who pay more property taxes to have more dollars invested in their public schools. Disparity in funding produces disparities in educational outcomes and perpetuates a class and race divide. The infusion of federal dollars to invest

more in communities that are poor could help close the gap.

As unionized jobs in manufacturing have shrunk, higher education has become an even more important ticket to a job at a decent wage with benefits. Professor Hubie Jones, former dean of the Boston University School of Social Work and a longtime community activist, grew up with his single mom in Harlem, New York. Without the possibility and promise of free higher education at the City College, he says, he would not have had the motivation to work hard in school in order to get that ticket up and out. Gangs and drugs would have been the only option.

Free public universities came about in 1862, the same year as the Homestead Act, when the Morrill Act established land-grant colleges in every state. Their purpose was to provide knowledge and skills to the newly landed masses.[1] Public institutions of higher education were the ticket out of poverty for many people of color who could not afford tuition at private colleges. Today, affordable higher education is moving out of reach for many of our children.

The federal government spends $55 billion on student aid, but the mix has been changing. Seventy-seven percent of that aid is in loans, not grants, a reversal of past policies. With tax cuts mostly for the wealthy, and the resulting budget shortfalls, states have been spending less on their public colleges, and tuitions have been growing at a faster rate than family income. The new welfare policies set in 1996 have led to a decline in enrollment of low-income women in college. Before the Temporary Assistance for Needy Families (TANF) program, forty-two states allowed women to count college attendance as employment in order to qualify for benefits: after TANF, only twenty-six states still allowed this option.[2] We can change the mix back again, and raise new taxes to invest in public colleges. A well-educated populace is the cornerstone of democracy, and the cornerstone is crumbling.

For those who don't speak English as their first language, English classes are the first stepping stones to success. It is not possible to get a decent

---

Questions to Consider

The authors provide a number of proposals for achieving socioeconomic equality between the races. How and in what ways does everyone benefit from living in a society where there is greater social equality? As you read each suggestion, ask yourself if you believe that these calls for greater social justice are politically possible. Would most Americans sign on to these plans to create a more just society? If it seems as though their proposal might be too difficult to implement, what would you do to convince the public that achieving racial equality would benefit all of society?

job without English skills. Some immigrants are not literate in their native language and need extended classes. Some come with degrees from other countries and can learn English quickly. For all of them, long waiting lists for free or affordable classes prevent them from obtaining this skill so essential for entry of limited English speakers into the U.S. workforce. On the other hand, so that non-English speakers do not get cheated out of their assets, or miss out on the benefits of programs for which they qualify, English-only policies must be rejected.

One big health problem can wipe out a lifetime of savings. The cost of care for a premature baby in a neonatal intensive care unit can be $500,000. In 1999, one quarter of the families that filed for bankruptcy cited health problems and the related costs as the reason.[3]

A 2000 study found that people of color are more likely to be uninsured than non-Hispanic whites, and are less likely to have job-based health insurance.[4] Thirty percent of Latinos, 25 percent of African Americans, 20 percent of Asian Americans and Pacific Islanders, and 17 percent of Native Americans are uninsured.[5] (The relatively low percentage rate of uninsured Native Americans is mostly due to their access to Indian Health Services as opposed to private or Medicaid coverage.[6]) Medicaid, which cares for the poor in inner cities and rural areas, is increasingly underfunded, as states face budget crises.

Universal coverage is possible. In 1983, Hawaii received permission from the federal government to require all employers to provide insurance to employees. In 1993, they were able to pool all their public dollars to create one big statewide insurance system. Not only were they able to provide health, dental, and mental health coverage for all, but the system was also able to save public dollars through a competitive bidding system.[7]

HITTING A STRIDE: INCOME ASSETS

One of the main reasons that nonwhite people were shut out of asset building was because they were restricted to no wage or low-wage jobs. From African slaves in the South to Latino day laborers on the street corners of Los Angeles, people of color have been denied fair compensation for their labor power. They have been limited to jobs that whites did not and do not want, were excluded from unions, paid taxes to work, and have always been the last hired and the first fired.

Jobs are needed that provide the cash income to cover day-to-day needs, *with something left over to build savings,* the basis for financial wealth. Today, income disparity lays the groundwork for future wealth disparities. Thomas Shapiro, in *The Hidden Cost of Being African American: How Wealth Perpetuates Inequality,* analyzed the impact of income on wealth. Once basic living expenses are met, each additional dollar of annual income generates $3.26 in net worth over a person's lifetime. Wealth disparity grows because of differences in income. For example, the difference in net worth between someone making $30,000 a year and someone making $60,000 a year is nearly $100,000.[8] Income includes not just wages and salaries based on working, but cash supports for those who are unemployed, retired, or parents of small children.

In Barbara Robles's class at the LBJ school at the University of Texas in Austin, students simply did not believe her when she told them that the minimum wage means a family must live on $10,000 a year. Over 27 million workers make less than $8 an hour; of these workers, 16.8 million are adults twenty-five and over; more than 16 million are women; 22 million are white; 4.2 million are black; and more than 17.5 million work full-time.[9] The present federal minimum wage of $5.15 an hour translates into an annual income of $10,712. The Economic Policy Institute has done several studies that reveal that an increase in the minimum wage would primarily benefit full- and part-time workers of low-income families,[10] which are disproportionately headed by single women of color. It would require raising the minimum wage to at least $8.10 an hour as of 2004 for a family of four to move above the official poverty line.[11] Around the country, people are organizing for more than the minimum wage: they are demanding a living wage. Since the cost of living varies across the country, communities are calculating costs particular to their cities. For example, in San Francisco voters approved a city living wage of $8.50 an hour in 2003; this will put over $100 million per year into the pockets of roughly fifty-four thousand workers.

And what about a maximum wage? In most countries, the ratio of CEO pay to worker pay has been around 40 to 1. In the United States in 2004, the ratio of CEO pay to the average worker's pay was 431 to 1.[12] Rep. Martin Sabo of Minnesota wants to curb that excess. His Proposed Income Equity Act would prevent corporations from claiming tax deductions on any executive pay that totals over 25 times what a company's lowest paid workers are earning.

The poorest group in the United States is women of color and their children. As Miami resident Thelma Brown puts it, "[C]ertified nursing assistants in Miami start at $5.75 an hour with no benefits. Day care costs ninety to one hundred dollars every two weeks per kid; then you have to pay rent, electricity, food, and everything else. A single mom can't live on one job at that rate."[13] They require government help to survive. For many years, it was mainly white women who received welfare payments. Attieno Davis, a longtime African American activist, remembers how empowering it was for black women in the 1960s to realize that they were *entitled* to these benefits, too. Latinos also were underenrolled, since no outreach was conducted in Spanish, nor were there Spanish-speaking workers in welfare offices. However, President Reagan's caricature of "welfare queens," stereotyped as a woman of color, created backlash. In 1996, the program changed to Temporary Assistance to Needy Families. To quality for the meager payments, women cannot have assets of more than $1,000 in some states.

One positive tax provision for the poor is the Earned Income Tax Credit (EITC). It was born out of the welfare debates in the late 1960s and early 1970s. At the time, President Nixon was proposing a guaranteed income to all families with children, regardless of whether the parent(s) worked. It is amazing today to remember that Nixon was proposing such a progressive policy. But Democratic senator Russell Long of Louisiana felt that the Nixon proposal would discourage people from working. His alternate proposal provided tax relief to low-income workers, rather than guaranteed income for all. The EITC was passed in 1975. Its annual budget rose from $2 billion to $12 billion between 1980 and 1992. According to the 2001 Census, 43 million people were living in low-income working families with children, and two out of every three poor families with children had at least one parent working. The EITC has lifted more families with children out of poverty than any other government program.[14]

Low-wage workers use the money they receive from the EITC for investments in education and savings, as well as to help them pay daily living expenses.[15] In order to encourage savings, Ray Boshara from the New America Foundation suggests that a portion of EITC refunds could be channeled directly into a basic savings account.[16] The Center on Budget and Policy Priorities found that EITC funds are often spent locally, serving as an economic development tool for low-income neighborhoods.[17]

Decent pay and accumulation of assets are hard to come by if you are not allowed citizenship. As we have seen, immigrant status has been a major barrier to economic equality for people of color. Jeannette Huezo, a political refugee from El Salvador, has lived and worked in Boston for fifteen years. However, she had to leave four of her children behind when she fled, and they are not allowed to reunite; she has been sending money home to support them. Salvadorans in the United States send remittances back home that now amount to half of the Salvadoran economy. Being forced into low-paying jobs because of their tenuous legal status, coupled with the need to send money home, makes it difficult to build assets in either country. The National Coalition for Dignity and Amnesty developed a proposal for a federal Freedom Act.

It would legalize undocumented immigrants currently living in the United States and create a status of "temporary residency" for future migrants, who would be eligible for permanent residency after three years.

People of color should be hired into jobs for which they are qualified and [enabled] to rise to the level of their capabilities. Affirmative action, won through the Civil Rights Movement, did bring many more people of color into middle-income jobs where they could begin to save, buy homes, and build wealth. However, the gap is still not closed. Over their working lifetime, African Americans with a college degree can expect to earn $500,000 less than equally qualified white people.[18] Asians do fine getting in on the ground floor and moving up, but then encounter glass ceilings: an Asian with a college degree had median annual earnings in 1993 of $36,844; comparably qualified whites made $41,094.[19] The need for affirmative action and government enforcement of nondiscrimination laws is far from over.

GOING THE DISTANCE: FINANCIAL ASSETS

Over the course of history, the federal government has used public resources to create wealth-building starter kits as well as continuing subsidies for whites, and has removed assets from people of color and denied them the benefits given to whites. In recent years, the white middle class has taken a hit: overall, it's shrinking, and general economic inequality has reached the levels of the Gilded Age at the turn of the last century. As a result, more and more academics, advocates, foundations, and public officials are recognizing that income alone is not enough to lift a family out of poverty. While this attention is not mainly because of wide recognition of the racial wealth gap, there is an opportunity to bring race into the conversation.

It's not that there aren't federal asset policies currently in place. The government spends approximately $355 billion a year in direct outlays and tax expenditures (allowing tax breaks for certain kinds of income). However, they are not named as asset policies, and they disproportionately benefit those who already have assets.[20] As we have seen, the net worth of people of color is far below that of whites.

While there are many ways to group asset-building opportunities, the Asset Policy Initiative of California has designed a framework that is simple and user-friendly. They see that strategies in four areas are needed. *Asset accumulation* is about policy strategies that encourage families to save; *asset leveraging* policies help low-wealth families use their limited savings to get loans for larger assets such as home and business ownership. Unfortunately, if there are not *asset preservation* assistance programs, often low-wealth people lose everything they have to predatory lenders. And finally, "*asset creation*" goes beyond individual strategies; communities can gain control over development in their own neighborhoods and rural communities.

Asset Accumulation

New thinking on how to help low-income people save money has been inspired by Michael Sherradan's groundbreaking book *Assets and the Poor: A New American Welfare Policy*. Sherradan and others recognize that income-support programs do not foster asset accumulation.[21]

Individual Development Accounts (IDAs) are nontaxable matching funds savings accounts that can be used—and used *only*—toward purchasing a home, retirement, education, starting a business, or other asset-accumulating endeavors. The outside matching source comes either from the public or private sector. Generally, the program has been targeted to the working poor, those who have a low but stable income in which some money can be set aside. Foundations and local banks have both provided funding to augment savings on the part of the poor. There are about 250 neighborhoods participating in IDA programs across the country, many in communities of color. The National Council of La Raza and the First Nations Development Institute have developed projects for Latinos and Native peoples.

Pilot IDA programs funded privately have encouraged policy change. According to the Corporation for Enterprise Development (CFED), since 1993, twenty-nine states and the District of Columbia have passed laws in support of IDAs. Thirty-two states have included IDA initiatives in their welfare reform programs and seven states have instituted state-funded IDA programs. In 1998, a federal pilot program of savings incentives for the poor was enacted, with $125 million over five years set aside for matching individual savings. While on the one hand this legislation helps to make the IDA idea more visible, it is not on a scale to be truly transformative.[22]

Another promising idea involves investing in our future: our nation's children. It is every parent's dream to leave their child a nest egg. And wouldn't it be great if everyone could be born with a trust fund! An impossible dream? Just such a program was instituted in England, sponsored by Prime Minister Tony Blair's Labor Party. In 2003, the British Parliament established what has become known as "baby bonds," a small child trust fund for each newborn in the country. Modest amounts of public funds will be deposited and invested for each newborn infant, and made available for withdrawal at the age of eighteen. If a child is given an initial deposit of $1,000, and then the parent makes a yearly contribution of $500, matched by another $500 from an outside source, this would translate into $40,000 available to eighteen-year-olds to use toward education, starting a business, or putting a down payment on a home.[23]

In 2005, a bill to create a similar program was introduced in Congress by an unusual alliance of conservative Republicans and progressive Democrats. The America Saving for Personal Investment, Retirement, and Education Act (the ASPIRE Act of 2005) proposed that a $500 KIDS Account be established for every newborn child. Children in households earning below the national median income would be eligible for a supplemental government contribution of up to $500. Additional benefits would include tax-free earnings, matched savings for lower income families, and financial education. Here is a program that provides a double incentive for lower income people to save: no taxes on the savings account, and matched government contributions for the poor.

Whether such new asset subsidiary programs should be universal or targeted to people of color is a strategic question. In any case, additional resources for outreach, translation, and other mechanisms to ensure inclusion must be part of the program.

Asset Leveraging

When you have some savings, you can either keep them, or use them to leverage more assets through making bigger investments.

Rotating savings and credit associations (ROSCA) have been an important strategy utilized by immigrant households in order to start a small business, purchase a home, or pay for a child's education. This strategy has origins in many different ethnic groups from East Asia, Latin America, the Caribbean, the Near East, and Africa. The Vietnamese ROSCA is called a *hui,* the Ethiopian is *ekub,* Jamaican is *partners,* Dominican, *san,* Korean, *keh,* and Cambodian *tong-tine.*[24]

A ROSCA is formed among family members, friends, and kin groups. They require participants (usually five or more people) to pay in a monthly sum agreed upon by the group. A participant can make a request to borrow the month's pool of money, or there may be an agreed-upon sequence for withdrawal—tax- and interest-free, since these transactions take place outside of the mainstream economic structure. This continues until all members have had access to the funds. The system is based on trust and social pressure. Thus, if members do not return the money at some point, their reputation in the community is tainted, something they are usually not willing to risk.

A *Philadelphia Inquirer* reporter sat in on a ROSCA meeting. "A Vietnamese *hui* group listened as one member asked to break the payout schedule and let her have that month's collection. . . . [T]he group sat in judgment on her needs, then let her take the tax-free, no-interest pot of $14,000."

But because ROSCAs are part of an unregulated, unprotected financing system, they have no recourse in case of theft. While sometimes immigrants do not trust banks, banks also do not make it easy to deposit ROSCA dollars. They treat deposits as belonging to an individual or household, and have no category to accommodate this unique form of savings. They report any deposit of more than $10,000 to the Internal Revenue Service. Without a financial institution to hold the money, one member has to keep the mounting dollars under his or her bed. A policy that recognized ROSCAs as a micro lending system, and allowed the money to be banked and borrowed tax-free, would build on existing community customs and help rather than hinder these activities.

Another way to use your small savings to leverage larger loans without worrying about a financial institution charging excessive fees and interest is to join a community credit union. The credit union movement was essentially a response to mainstream financial institutions' neglect of marginalized groups. Community Development Credit Unions (CDCUs) provide basic financial services such as check cashing and small loans at fair rates to their members within a restricted area or community.[25] They are member based and member governed; some are based in churches or community organizations. One of the problems plaguing poor communities is that the meager resources present in poor communities tend to flow out of them.[26] In response to this problem, CDCUs keep local money in the community, as well as draw in outside money.[27] The resources accrued from CDCUs are then channeled back into the community and are used to respond to its various needs.

Usually, the first asset leveraged from savings is a home to live in. Expanding opportunities for home ownership are critical in closing the racial wealth divide. Home equity is one of the first building blocks for wealth, and is the most significant source of assets for people of color. For blacks, 62 percent of their net worth is held in homes; for Latinos, 51 percent. For white families, housing accounts for only 32 percent of their net worth. Given the history of federal subsidies for home ownership for whites, targeted funding for people and communities of color is now needed.

The Community Reinvestment Act of 1977 (CRA) came out of community struggles demanding access to banks and mortgage companies. Evidence was compiled showing that financial institutions engaged in discriminatory lending practices based on race, age, and location, instead of on an applicant's creditworthiness. These discriminatory practices had contributed to the decline of low-income and minority neighborhoods. The CRA required banks to lend in low-income communities, and federal banking regulators were mandated to maintain a close watch on financial institutions to ensure that they were meeting the needs of local communities. Communities of color were successful in getting the federal government to use its powers to stop private industry from providing affirmative action in lending to whites.

Through the CRA, significant strides were made during the 1990s as major banking institutions increased lending toward affordable housing and economic development to assist low-income people.[28] Over $20 billion has been invested in low-income neighborhoods and communities of color thanks to the CRA.[29]

Asset Preservation

Home ownership has been a double-edged sword for many homeowners of color. It is a struggle first to gain access to fair loan terms, and another to try and keep the home. If we were to dig beneath the home ownership figures, which provide only a snapshot in time, we would find a lot more turnovers of home ownership among people of color than among whites. Lending predators target the weak—those unfamiliar with the rules of the game.

ACORN's Mary Gaspar described her ordeal: "Here's how my nightmare started: I got a check in the mail from Household Finance with an offer to refinance our home. . . . Household was misleading and dishonest. I received my first bill and it was $13,000 more than I thought it was going to be! I have seen how Household preys on people who are economically desperate as well as middle-class people like us." ACORN (Association of Community Organizations for Reform Now) responded by putting public pressure on Household Finance by holding demonstrations at their annual shareholder meetings. They were joined in their efforts by members of United for a Fair Economy's Responsible Wealth project. Proxy votes given to ACORN members by Responsible Wealth members who owned shares allowed Mary to tell her story—*inside* the halls of wealth, usually barred to the people of color whose hard-earned homes were being stolen from them. Having shareholders and ACORN members speaking with one voice brought Household to the table to discuss changing its behavior.[30]

Mortgage foreclosure has been another impediment to maintaining home ownership. A report done by the Family Housing Fund in Minneapolis found that the major reason homeowners default on mortgage payments is job loss or a significant reduction in income; other causes include health emergencies and separation or divorce. While home ownership rates have increased, so have instances of foreclosure.

Foreclosure prevention is an important tool in stabilizing homeowners at risk of losing their homes and neighborhoods by preventing houses from becoming vacant and boarded up. Between 1991 and 1997, the Mortgage Foreclosure Program (MFP) carried out by the Family Housing Fund assisted close to seventeen hundred homeowners and helped to reinstate the mortgages of over half of them within the St. Paul and Minneapolis area.[31] Foreclosure prevention counseling provides a more affordable way for homeowners to stabilize their home ownership, compared to going through a mortgage insurer. It costs an average of $2,800 to help a homeowner reinstate a mortgage, while with a mortgage insurer it could cost $10,000 to $28,000, depending on the insurer and the location of the home.[32] Ana Moreno, a housing consultant who conducted the study, contends that "[p]rograms that promote home ownership for households with very low incomes need to be linked to the full continuum of homeownership support

services—pre-purchase education and counseling, financial assistance, post-purchase support, and delinquency and foreclosure prevention."[33]

Even with a home, you can spend your final years in poverty if you have no retirement account from which to draw. Social Security was invented to protect U.S. workers from this risk: it is the country's most successful insurance program. While 10 percent of those over age sixty-five live in poverty today, without Social Security that rate would be almost 50 percent.[34] Occupations held mostly by African Americans and Latinos were excluded initially, but all employment sectors were included beginning in 1950. Social Security was also expanded to include not only retirement benefits, but also benefits to disabled workers and the families of workers who have died.

Because people of color have less income from stock holdings or capital gains than whites, Social Security is especially important to them: it is the sole source of income for 40 percent of elderly African Americans. The shorter life span of African American men means that both survivor and disability benefits go disproportionately to African Americans. While African Americans make up 12 percent of the U.S. population, 23 percent of children receiving Social Security survivor benefits are African American, as are about 17 percent of disability beneficiaries.[35]

Private pension plans are also an important asset. They provide retirement income, often as an employment benefit. The loss of unionized manufacturing jobs in the 1990s led to the loss of this asset for many. Laid off from auto and steel jobs which opened up to them during World War II, African Americans in particular have had to shift to jobs in the low-wage service sector, which do not provide employer-sponsored pension plans. In 2001, the mean value of the retirement account of a black family was $12,247, compared to $10,206 for a Latino family and $65,411 for a white family.[36]

For those who are fortunate to have jobs with pensions, there has been a change from defined benefit plans, in which workers receive a defined percentage of their wages, based on age and years of service, to defined contribution plans, in which employers and/or employees contribute a defined amount of money into a plan, but they do not guarantee that the money will still be there when you retire. The risk has been shifted to the worker. The AFL-CIO news related the story of Wanda Chalk, an African American employee at Enron. She had worked at Enron for fifteen years and had stock options worth $150,000, which were to generate income for her retirement. But due to Enron's fraudulent dealings, when Enron crashed, so did she. She lost her job, her stock value dropped to zero, and her retirement security went up in smoke.

Privatizing Social Security could produce the same effect. Preservation of assets, not risky schemes that could fail when you need the money most, needs to remain the cornerstone of retirement plans. As a society, we should not revert to a pre-Depression system, where our elders are at risk of dying in poverty.

Asset Creation

Even if a few individuals of color hold greater assets, that will not be enough to close the racial wealth divide. Just because in 2004 Bill Cosby was worth $540 million in assets, and just because the Unanues, owners of Goya Foods, were worth $700 million, it doesn't help those members of their racial groups who are stuck at the bottom. Assets need to be utilized to expand wealth for the community as a whole.

For example, Native land was given away to railroad owners and, in 1887, tribal land was broken into individual plots. Over the years, more and more Native owners lost their plots, resulting in a checkerboard pattern of landownership in what should have been tribally owned territory. In 2002, the Northwest Area Foundation, funded by heirs of James J. Hill, head of the Great Northern Railroad, who grew rich from the displacement of Ojibwes in

Minnesota, made voluntary reparations. They gave $20 million in seed money for a buyback. Now millions of acres are back under tribal control.

In the 1970s, the inner city of Battle Creek, Michigan, became an economically depressed area due to the closing of a military base nearby; by 1990, there were fifty recognized crack houses within a mile of downtown. Battle Creek Neighborhoods Incorporated, a community development financial institution, stepped in. Their approach has been to focus on lending to people who are willing to buy particular community blocks rather than to buyers of housing units scattered throughout the city. Their loans come with a requirement to improve the property and to participate in improving the quality of life on the block. For example, they sponsor "best of neighborhood" contests—Best Front Porch, Best Back Yard, Best Group Effort—that encourage home maintenance and improvement. Brenda Sue Woods wasn't going to participate in the Porch contest at first, but then decided to try. When she took first place, "I was just screaming like I won something on The Price Is Right." The emphasis on neighborhoods will enable housing values to rise in the area.

The Hawai'i Alliance for Community-Based Economic Development, a statewide nonprofit organization, provides loans not to individuals, but to groups. For example, a group of young people put in a proposal with the goal of "reconnection with their elders." One of the ways they used the loan was for a community van to transport those elders to needed services.

In a variety of locations, nonprofit organizations and government entities are experimenting with wealth-creation frameworks that are "inclusive, community-driven, and action oriented, protecting community, cultural, and environmental concerns while shielding individual private rights."[37] These efforts are road signs to the future.

51

TEN THINGS YOU CAN DO TO IMPROVE RACE RELATIONS

Charles A. Gallagher

CHARLES A. GALLAGHER is professor and chair of the Department of Sociology, Social Work and Criminal Justice at La Salle University in Philadelphia. His research focuses on racial and social inequality; immigration; urban sociology; and the ways in which the media, the state, and popular culture construct, shape, and disseminate ideas of race. He has published articles on the sociological functions of color-blind political narratives, how racial categories expand and contract within the context of interracial marriages, race theory, racial innumeracy, and how one's ethnic history shapes perceptions of privilege.

THE STUDY OF RACE AND ETHNIC RELATIONS in the United States can be a rather depressing and disempowering undertaking. Ongoing institutional racism in education, employment, housing, lending, and law enforcement; continued wealth and income disparities between racial groups; and the persistence of racial prejudice and discrimination in most spheres of social life may leave one with the impression that nothing can be done to improve race relations. The modern civil rights movement was three hundred years in the making, and while movement toward racial equality has been substantial, racism and racial

inequality still infect our nation and poison civic life. Such prejudice and inequality persist in part because changing the institutional barriers that allocate occupational and educational opportunity is a slow and difficult task. Upward mobility for different racial and ethnic groups is typically measured in generations rather than decades or years. One is tempted to throw one's hands in the air and yell, "There is nothing I can do!!!" But there is. You have the power to influence your family, friends, and peers by discussing the topics raised in this class. At the individual, interpersonal, and community level you can engage in activities to promote equal

Questions to Consider

Photocopy and pass along my "Ten Things You Can Do to Improve Race Relations" to family, friends, teachers, spiritual leaders, brothers, and sisters. Please contact me with any additions you might have for my list. I can be reached at gallagher@lasalle.edu.

opportunity while building bridges between people from different racial backgrounds. Understanding the root causes of ethnic and racial inequality in the United States and examining in this class the facts, theories, evidence, and examples that pertain to such inequality will allow you to explain to others why racism and racial and ethnic inequality remain so stubbornly part of our culture. You now have the sociological tools to calmly, intelligently, and rationally engage in conversations with other adults about racism in America and what individuals, institutions, and the government *could* and *should* do to fashion a society where equal opportunity exists for all groups. Following are ten simple things you can do as you go about your day to raise your own and other people's consciousness about race relations and racial justice in America.

1. TALK TO YOUR FAMILY

Respectfully engage your friends and family in what you learned in this class. If you have family members that are racist or use stereotypes, ask them politely and nonjudgmentally why they harbor such animosity towards a whole group of people. Did they have a bad experience with someone from that group? Ask them if they have ever been the target of animosity or hatred because of their race, ethnic background, religion, or nationality. How did such an encounter make them feel? Were their parents or grandparents ever subject to such prejudice or discrimination? Why? Ask them if they think their

prejudice or racism violates the American creed of equal treatment and opportunity for all regardless of group membership. If they believe in the American creed, how do they reconcile their racism or prejudice? Ask them if they believe in the golden rule that states "do unto others as you would have them do unto you."

2. AVOID STEREOTYPICAL LANGUAGE

Be mindful that certain words or phrases typically mean the person is about to use stereotypes to describe a group. When you hear someone say "All black people do this . . .," or "Latinos always like to . . .," or "I never met a white person who could . . .," a red flag should go up that stereotypes are in use. Politely ask if they are referring to an individual encounter with someone from another group or if they mean to speak for 38 million blacks, 40 million Latinos, 10 million Asians, 200 million whites, or 2.5 million American Indians in this country. Ask the person if they really believe *all people* in that group actually share the same behaviors and attitudes. Is it possible that certain behaviors or beliefs only appear in one racial or ethnic group and not another?

3. RACISM ISN'T FUNNY

Don't tolerate racist jokes. If you hear a joke being told that disparages someone because of his or her group membership, stop the person from telling the joke. If they insist on finishing, ask them why they don't like black people or white people or Asians or Catholics or whomever they are ridiculing in their attempt at humor. You have many retorts to such simplistic and retrograde behavior. You might say, "Hey, I don't think putting down other people is funny," or "I have gay friends, I don't want to hear you trashing them," or "My brother-in-law is black (or white or Asian or Catholic or Jewish, etc.) and

I think he's great." Be willing to "take the stand" about what is appropriate public discourse. If you do not speak up and let the person know that such remarks are socially inappropriate, you are condoning their beliefs and behavior. Inaction is a form of action.

4. BE INTROSPECTIVE

Think back to reading 18, in which Robert Merton discussed the unprejudiced nondiscriminator. This person was not prejudiced, nor did she discriminate against anyone in any way. How can we live our lives so social or peer pressure does not push us toward racist, prejudiced, or bigoted beliefs or actions? If you find yourself being a prejudiced nondiscriminator (fair-weather illiberal) or an unprejudiced discriminator (fair-weather liberal), ask yourself how you got there. Be introspective and honest about why you acted or behaved a certain way toward someone from a different ethnic or racial group. What scared you about the situation that made you deviate from your core beliefs or values? Did you overreact? Were you defensive? If you could relive that experience, what would you do differently? Is it possible you were socialized or taught to react the way you did? What role did peer pressure play in your actions? The most important thing you can do is to think critically about the root causes of your anxieties, attitudes, and actions. Be introspective and be willing to change how you think about groups different from your own.

5. BE A GOOD CITIZEN—VOTE

Vote in every election. Take the time to find out candidates' positions on policies that have implications for race relations. Do not support a politician whose campaign rhetoric is racially divisive or attempts to win votes by manipulating racial (or class) fears. Knowing what the issues are (and are not) requires reading a newspaper every day.

6. TV, RAP, ROCK: APPEALS TO THE LOWEST COMMON DENOMINATOR

When you watch television, realize that you are under constant bombardment by the most simplistic and stereotypical images of ethnic and racial groups. Ask yourself which racial and ethnic groups are on prime time and how those groups are represented. Are whites, blacks, Asians, Latinos, or American Indians in a wide range of roles, or are some groups more likely to be maids, gangbangers, exotics, or lawyers? Why? What you watch on television is not just entertainment. The mass media provide the images, symbols, and narratives that shape the way we understand society. The media cement existing stereotypes and construct expectations about where groups should be placed in America's racial hierarchy. The television industry uses stereotypes to make racial inequality look like the "normal" order of society. How are you being manipulated by the programs you watch?

7. LEARN YOUR FAMILY'S HISTORY

Take time to talk to the elderly people in your life. Ask your parents, aunts and uncles, neighbors, and spiritual leaders in your community about how race relations have changed since they were children. Ask your parents, grandparents, and other relatives about the *Brown* decision, the Civil Rights movement, Martin Luther King Jr.'s assassination, the American Indian Movement (AIM), La Raza, and the L.A. riots. How do they explain these events? What were they doing as these monumental events unfolded? Your elders are resources. Talk to them about the past and the present.

8. TEACH THROUGH EXAMPLE

Be a positive role model to all the younger people in your life. If you are of college age or older, you probably have a number of children and young adults who look up to you for moral guidance. If they hear you use foul language, then in all likelihood they will too. If you speak and act in a racist manner, they will learn your racism. Explain to those who view you as a role model what it means to live in a multiracial, multiethnic society. Explain to them what the American creed and the "golden rule" mean.

9. STEP OUT OF YOUR COMFORT ZONE

Involve yourself in activities that place you in an environment where you will be exposed to people from different racial and ethnic backgrounds. Think about attending museums, music events, ethnic festivals, restaurants, supermarkets, shops, or any other public place where you will share space with people different from yourself.

10. KNOW THYSELF

Did you grow up in a community that was racially homogeneous? Was your house of worship pretty much composed of people who looked like you? Are your best friends all of the same race? Was your elementary school segregated? How about your high school? What did it look like in terms of racial composition? Do you think being raised in a segregated environment shapes racial attitudes? How? How do you think being the only racial minority in most social settings might shape a person's views of race relations? Have your ideas about race changed since you were fifteen years old? How and why? Reflect on these questions and write your answers as an essay. Circulate what you write to your friends and family. Set up a meeting to have a discussion on what you wrote and what their views on race relations in the United States are.

"If You're Not Part of the Solution, You're Part of the Problem."

APPENDIX

RACE BY THE NUMBERS

America's Racial Report Card

INTRODUCTION

How are the race categories used in Census 2010 defined?

"White" refers to people having origins in any of the original peoples in Europe, the Middle East, or North Africa. It includes people who indicated their race or races as "White" or wrote in entries such as Irish, German, Italian, Lebanese, Near Easterner, Arab, or Polish.

"Black or African American" refers to people having origins in any of the black racial groups of Africa. It includes people who indicated their race or races as "Black, African Am., or Negro" or wrote in entries such as African American, Afro American, Nigerian, or Haitian.

"American Indian and Alaska Native" refers to people having origins in any of the original peoples of North and South America (including Central America), and who maintain tribal affiliation or community attachment. It includes people who indicated their race or races by marking this category or writing in their principal or enrolled tribe, such as Rosebud Sioux, Chippewa, or Navajo.

"Asian" refers to people having origins in any of the original peoples of the Far East, Southeast Asia, or the Indian subcontinent. It includes people who indicated their race or races as "Asian Indian," "Chinese," "Filipino," "Korean," "Japanese," "Vietnamese," or "Other Asian," or wrote in entries such as Burmese, Hmong, Pakistani, or Thai.

"Native Hawaiian and Other Pacific Islander" refers to people having origins in any of the original peoples of Hawaii, Guam, Samoa, or other Pacific Islands. It includes people who indicated their race or races as "Native Hawaiian," "Guamanian or Chamorro," "Samoan," or "Other Pacific Islander," or wrote in entries such as Tahitian, Mariana Islander, or Chuukese.

"Some other race" was included in Census 2010 for respondents who were unable to identify with the five Office of Management and Budget race categories. Respondents who provided write-in entries such as Moroccan, South African, Belizean, or a Hispanic origin (for example, Mexican, Puerto Rican, or Cuban) are included in the Some other race category (U.S. Census 2010).

Compare total U.S. population to trends shown in appendix figures.

Compare the size of the total population at the bottom of the page to the trends observed in figures in the appendix. Is the group overrepresented?

The U.S. population is 76% white (including Latinos who define themselves as white). The total U.S. population comprises: non-Hispanic white, 61%; black, 13.3%; Latino, 17.8%; Asian 5.7%; American Indian, 1.3% (U.S. Census 2017).

For example, Figure 26 shows us that 89% of all lawyers are white, although whites make up 74% of the total U.S. population. Whites are overrepresented in the field of law. Or is it the case that a group is underrepresented? Figure 27 shows us that 5% of all physicians are Latinos, but Latinos make up 15% of the total U.S. population. Latinos are underrepresented as physicians.

FIGURE 1 ■ Changes to Race and Ethnicity Categories on the U.S. Census, 1790–2000		
Year	**Categories included**	**Categories eliminated**
1790	Free white male/female, non-taxed Indian, slaves (3/5 of a person)	
1870	White, black, mulatto, quadroon, octoroon, Indian	Non-taxed Indian, slaves, free white
1890	White, black, mulatto, quadroon, octoroon, Indian, Japanese, Chinese	
1900	Black, white, Japanese, Chinese, Indian	Mulatto, quadroon, octoroon
1910	Black, white, Japanese, Chinese, Indian, mulatto	
1930	White, black, Japanese, Chinese, Indian, Hindu, Korean, Mexican	Mulatto
1940	White, black, Japanese, Chinese, Indian, Hindu, Korean	Mexican
1950	White, black, Japanese, Chinese, American Indian	Hindu, Korean
1960	White, black, Japanese, Chinese, American Indian, Hawaiian, part-Hawaiian, Aleut, Eskimo	
1980	White, black or African American, American Indian and Alaska Native, Asian, Native Hawaiian and other Pacific Islander	
2000	"Check all that apply" system implemented	

Source: Dispatches from the Color Line: The Press and Multiracial America. SUNY Press, 2007, Catherine R. Squires.

The U.S. population is 76% white (including Latinos who define themselves as white). The total U.S. population comprises: non-Hispanic white, 61%; black, 13.3%; Latino, 17.8%; Asian 5.7%; American Indian, 1.3% (U.S. Census 2017).

FIGURE 2 ■ Population of the U.S. 2016 and Projected 2060

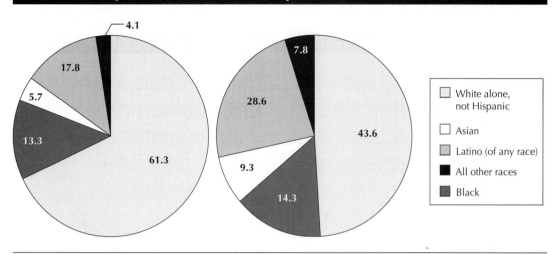

Source: Data from U.S. Census Bureau, 2016, "U.S. Interim Projections by Age, Sex, Race, and Hispanic Origin," http://www.census.gov/ipc/www/usinterimproj/.

FIGURE 3 ■ Fifteen Largest Ancestries

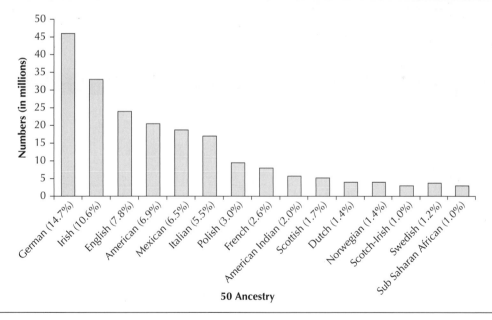

Source: Data from U.S. Census Bureau, Census 2015 special tabulation.

Note: Percent of total population in parentheses. Data based on sample.

The U.S. population is 76% white (including Latinos who define themselves as white). The total U.S. population comprises: non-Hispanic white, 61%; black, 13.3%; Latino, 17.8%; Asian 5.7%; American Indian, 1.3% (U.S. Census 2017).

SECTION I: EDUCATION

FIGURE 4 ■ High School Graduation Rates for 2013

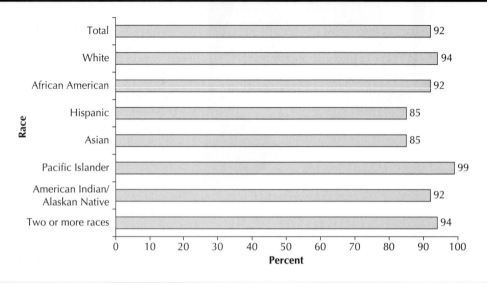

Source: Data from the *Status and Trends in the Education of Racial and Ethnic Groups 2016* report from the National Center for Education Statistics, a part of the United States Department of Education's Institute of Education Sciences.

FIGURE 5 ■ High School Dropout Rates for 2015

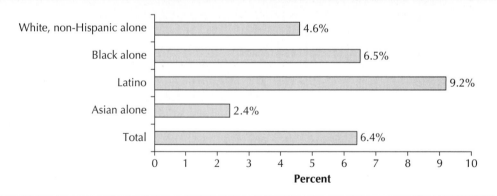

Source: Data from *The Condition of Education* report on Status Dropout Rates in April 2017 from the National Center for Education Statistics, a part of the United States Department of Education's Institute of Education Sciences.

The U.S. population is 76% white (including Latinos who define themselves as white). The total U.S. population comprises: non-Hispanic white, 61%; black, 13.3%; Latino, 17.8%; Asian 5.7%; American Indian, 1.3% (U.S. Census 2017).

FIGURE 6 ■ Racial Composition of Public and Private Schools

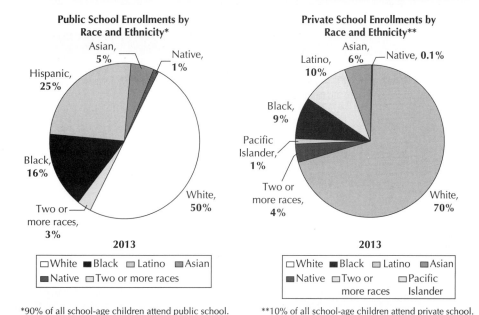

Public School Enrollments by Race and Ethnicity*

- Asian, 5%
- Native, 1%
- Hispanic, 25%
- White, 50%
- Black, 16%
- Two or more races, 3%

2013

□White ■Black ▨Latino ▨Asian
■Native □Two or more races

*90% of all school-age children attend public school.

Private School Enrollments by Race and Ethnicity**

- Asian, 6%
- Native, 0.1%
- Latino, 10%
- Black, 9%
- Pacific Islander, 1%
- Two or more races, 4%
- White, 70%

2013

□White ■Black ▨Latino ▨Asian
■Native □Two or more races □Pacific Islander

**10% of all school-age children attend private school.

Source: Data from the *Status and Trends in the Education of Racial and Ethnic Groups 2016* report from the National Center for Education Statistics, a part of the United States Department of Education's Institute of Education Sciences.

FIGURE 7 ■ Degrees Conferred

Racial/Ethnic Group	BA	MA	Law	MD	PhD
White	70.0	60.3	83.0	68.6	81.0
Black	8.7	7.8	4.4	6.7	7.0
Latino	6.3	4.4	6.6	6.4	5.0
Asian	6.2	4.8	7.4	15.6	6.0
Native American	0.7	0.5	0.5	1.4	<1

Source: Data from U.S. Department of Education, National Center for Education Statistics, Integrated Postsecondary Education Data System (IPEDS), Fall 2003, National Postsecondary Student Aid Study (NPSAS) (2000), and NSF/NIH/USED/USDA/NASA, Survey of Earned Doctorates by U.S. Citizens, 2003.

Note: These numbers have not changed significantly since 2003.

The U.S. population is 76% white (including Latinos who define themselves as white). The total U.S. population comprises: non-Hispanic white, 61%; black, 13.3%; Latino, 17.8%; Asian 5.7%; American Indian, 1.3% (U.S. Census 2017).

SECTION II: HOUSING

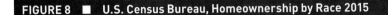

FIGURE 8 ■ **U.S. Census Bureau, Homeownership by Race 2015**

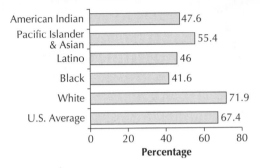

Source: Data from U.S. Bureau of the Census: Home Ownership Rates by Race and Ethnicity of Householder, Annual Statistics 2015.

FIGURE 9 ■ **Diversity Experienced in Each Group's Typical Neighborhood—National Metropolitan Average, 2010 Census**

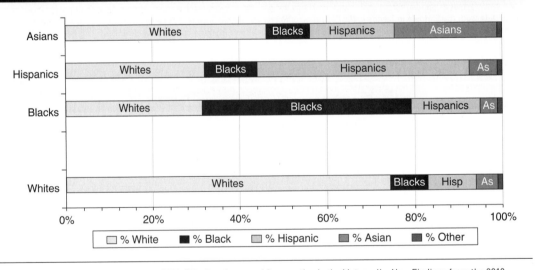

Source: John R. Logan and Brian Stults. 2011. "The Persistence of Segregation in the Metropolis: New Findings from the 2010 Census." Census Brief prepared for Project US2010. http://www.s4.brown.edu/us2010.

The U.S. population is 76% white (including Latinos who define themselves as white). The total U.S. population comprises: non-Hispanic white, 61%; black, 13.3%; Latino, 17.8%; Asian 5.7%; American Indian, 1.3% (U.S. Census 2017).

FIGURE 10 ■ Segregation from Whites in the Largest 10 Metropolitan Areas

Metropolitan Area	Population (millions)	Black	Latino	Asian
Los Angeles–Long Beach	9.5	67.5	63.2	48.3
New York	9.3	81.8	66.7	50.5
Chicago	8.3	80.8	62.1	44.4
Philadelphia	5.1	72.3	60.2	43.8
Washington, DC	4.9	63.1	48.4	39.0
Detroit	4.4	84.7	45.7	45.9
Houston	4.2	67.5	55.7	49.4
Atlanta	4.1	65.6	52.5	45.2
Dallas	3.5	59.4	54.1	45.0
Boston	3.4	65.7	58.8	44.9

Source: Data from John R. Logan, Brian Stults, and Reynolds Farley. 2004. "Segregation of Minorities in the Metropolis: Two Decades of Change," *Demography* 41: 1–22. For more information, see http://browns4.dyndns.org/cen2000_s4.

Note: A zero on this index would mean that racial groups are evenly integrated throughout a city. A score of 100 means complete racial segregation among groups.

The U.S. population is 76% white (including Latinos who define themselves as white). The total U.S. population comprises: non-Hispanic white, 61%; black, 13.3%; Latino, 17.8%; Asian 5.7%; American Indian, 1.3% (U.S. Census 2017).

SECTION III: HEALTH

FIGURE 11A ■ Health Disparities by Race					
	White	Black	Latino	Asian	American Indian/Native American
Heart disease (%)	26.9	40.1	27.7	5.4	n/a
Premature deaths (%)	14.7	31.5	23.5	n/a	36.0
High blood pressure (%)	31.1	43.2	18.6	16.3	20.7
Overweight and obesity rate (%)	55.3	65.8	57.6	35.9	61.6
Birthrate (births/1000)	11.7	16.1	22.6	16.5	13.8
Infant mortality (death/1000)	5.7	13.5	5.4	4.7	9.7
Rate of teen births (births/1000)	28.5	68.3	83.4	18.3	53.8
Cases of HIV (rates 100K)	12.3	18.4	39.7	8.6	16.9
Distribution of new AIDS cases (%)	31.1	48.2	18.5	1.3	0.5
Tuberculosis (rates 100K)	1.5	12.6	10.4	27.8	6.8
Cigarette smoking (%)	23.3	21.7	18.5	13.7	38.4

Source: Data from U.S. Bureau of the Census, updated July 2005.

Note: These numbers have not changed significantly since 2005.

FIGURE 11B ■ Overdose Deaths by Race in 2014 per 100,000 People

	HEROIN	OPIOIDS
White	4.4	7.9
Black	2.5	3.3
Hispanic of Latino	1.9	2.2
Native American	3.7	8.4
Asian	0.3	0.7

Source: Data from the Centers for Disease Control and Prevention.

The U.S. population is 76% white (including Latinos who define themselves as white). The total U.S. population comprises: non-Hispanic white, 61%; black, 13.3%; Latino, 17.8%; Asian 5.7%; American Indian, 1.3% (U.S. Census 2017).

FIGURE 12 ■ Percentage of Americans Uninsured by Race		
	Uninsured Non-Elderly	**Uninsured Children**
White	6.3%	4.1%
Black	10.5%	5.5%
Latino	16%	7.9%
Asian	7.6%	5%
USA	8.8%	5.4%

Source: Data from National Health Interview Survey, 2016.

SECTION IV: CRIME

FIGURE 13 ■ Percentage of Crime in the U.S. by Race and Ethnicity					
	White	**Black**	**Asian**	**Native American and Alaskan Native**	**Native Hawaiian and Other Pacific Islander**
Murder & non-negligent manslaughter	44.7	52.6	1.2	1.2	0.3
Forcible rape	67.6	29.1	1.7	1.3	0.4
Robbery	43.4	54.5	0.9	0.9	0.4
Aggravated assault	62.8	33.3	1.5	2.1	0.3
Burglary	68.4	29.1	1.2	1	0.3
Larceny-theft	69	27.7	1.2	1.8	0.2
Motor vehicle theft	66	30.7	1.3	1.5	0.5
Arson	72	23.3	1.5	2.8	0.3
Violent crime	59	37.5	1.4	1.8	0.3
Property crime	68.7	28.1	1.2	1.7	0.3

Source: Data from U.S. Bureau of Justice Statistics, 2016.

The U.S. population is 76% white (including Latinos who define themselves as white). The total U.S. population comprises: non-Hispanic white, 61%; black, 13.3%; Latino, 17.8%; Asian 5.7%; American Indian, 1.3% (U.S. Census 2017).

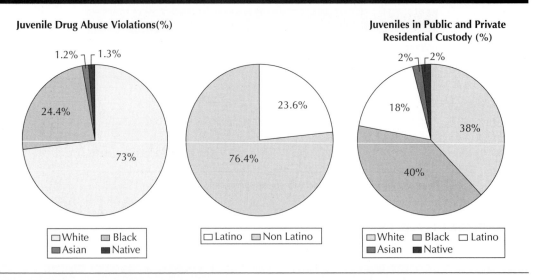

FIGURE 14 ■ Juvenile Crime Statistics

Juvenile Drug Abuse Violations(%)

1.2% 1.3%
24.4%
73%

☐White ☐Black
☐Asian ☐Native

23.6%
76.4%

☐Latino ☐Non Latino

**Juveniles in Public and Private
Residential Custody (%)**

2% 2%
18%
38%
40%

☐White ☐Black ☐Latino
☐Asian ☐Native

Source: Data from U.S. Bureau of Justice Statistics, 2016.

FIGURE 15 ■ Hate Crimes by Race

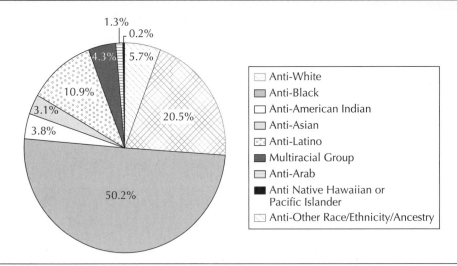

1.3%
0.2%
4.3% 5.7%
10.9%
3.1%
3.8%
20.5%
50.2%

☐ Anti-White
☐ Anti-Black
☐ Anti-American Indian
☐ Anti-Asian
☐ Anti-Latino
☐ Multiracial Group
☐ Anti-Arab
■ Anti Native Hawaiian or
   Pacific Islander
☐ Anti-Other Race/Ethnicity/Ancestry

Source: FBI's Uniform Crime Report, 2016.

The U.S. population is 76% white (including Latinos who define themselves as white). The total U.S. population comprises: non-Hispanic white, 61%; black, 13.3%; Latino, 17.8%; Asian 5.7%; American Indian, 1.3% (U.S. Census 2017).

FIGURE 16 ■ Lifetime Chances of Going to Prison

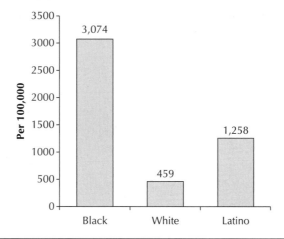

Source: Data from Paul Guerino, Paige M. Harrison, and William J. Sabol, "Prisoners in 2010," U.S. Bureau of Justice Statistics, 2010.

FIGURE 17 ■ Prison and Death Row Inmates

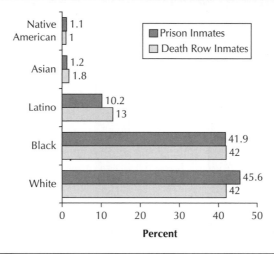

Source: Data from U.S. Department of Justice and Death Row USA Spring 2004.

The U.S. population is 76% white (including Latinos who define themselves as white). The total U.S. population comprises: non-Hispanic white, 61%; black, 13.3%; Latino, 17.8%; Asian 5.7%; American Indian, 1.3% (U.S. Census 2017).

FIGURE 18 ■ **Percent of Stopped Drivers Searched by Police by Race, 2011**

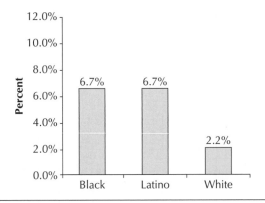

Source: Data from U.S. Bureau of Justice Statistics, 2011.

SECTION V: COMPUTERS, DESKTOP OR LAPTOP

FIGURE 19 ■ **Families Who Own Computers, Smartphones, and Cellphones (Income $15K–$30K, 2015)**

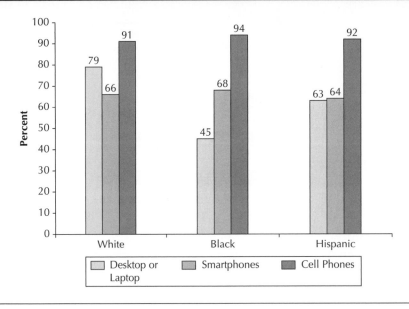

Source: Data from the Pew Research report *Technology Device Ownership: 2015* on The Demographics of Device Ownership.

The U.S. population is 76% white (including Latinos who define themselves as white). The total U.S. population comprises: non-Hispanic white, 61%; black, 13.3%; Latino, 17.8%; Asian 5.7%; American Indian, 1.3% (U.S. Census 2017).

FIGURE 20 ■ Computer Access and Use by Children 3–17 Years Old

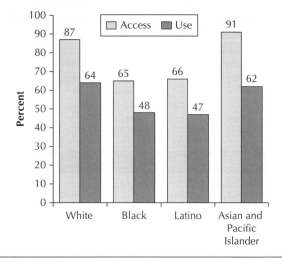

Source: Data from U.S. Bureau of the Census, 2013.

FIGURE 21 ■ Households with NO Internet Use at Home

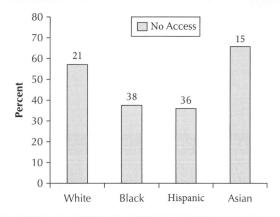

Source: Data from U.S. Bureau of the Census, Computer and Internet Access in the U.S. in 2012.

The U.S. population is 76% white (including Latinos who define themselves as white). The total U.S. population comprises: non-Hispanic white, 61%; black, 13.3%; Latino, 17.8%; Asian 5.7%; American Indian, 1.3% (U.S. Census 2017).

SECTION VI: INCOME, WEALTH, AND POVERTY

FIGURE 22 ■ Median Household Income, 2015			
White Non-Hispanic	**Black**	**Latino**	**Asian**
$62,950	$36,898	$45,148	$77,166

Source: Data from U.S. Bureau of the Census, 2015.

FIGURE 23 ■ Who Is Rich, Who Is Poor

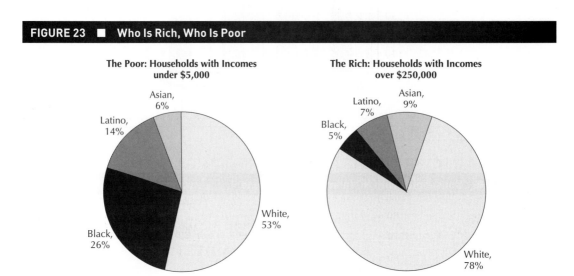

The Poor: Households with Incomes under $5,000

Asian, 6%
Latino, 14%
White, 53%
Black, 26%

The Rich: Households with Incomes over $250,000

Latino, 7%
Asian, 9%
Black, 5%
White, 78%

Source: U.S. Census current population survey, 2016.

FIGURE 24 ■ Poverty in the United States

	White	White Not Hispanic	Black	Hispanic, Any Race	Asian
% of population living in poverty (2016)	11%	8.8	22	19.4	10.1
Related kids under 18 in families living in poverty (2015)	12%	8.9	3.6	30	11
Working poor (%) (2014)		5.5	11.7	11.7	4.3
Poverty (%) (2003)		9.1	24	21	11.4

Source: Data from U.S. Bureau of the Census, 2015.

The U.S. population is 76% white (including Latinos who define themselves as white). The total U.S. population comprises: non-Hispanic white, 61%; black, 13.3%; Latino, 17.8%; Asian 5.7%; American Indian, 1.3% (U.S. Census 2017).

SECTION VII: EMPLOYMENT

FIGURE 25 ■ Unemployment Statistics

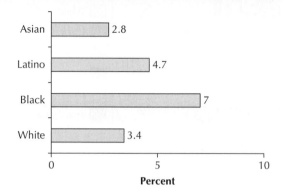

Source: U.S. Bureau of Labor Statistics, 2017.

SECTION VIII: OCCUPATIONS

FIGURE 26 ■ Resident Active Attorney Demographics

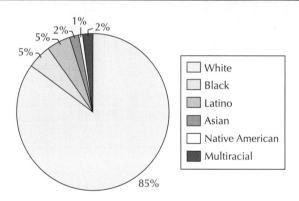

Source: Data from U.S. Census Bureau 1 Percent Public Use Microdata Sample Surveys, *201*, 2017.

Note: Numbers are the percent of the population.

The U.S. population is 76% white (including Latinos who define themselves as white). The total U.S. population comprises: non-Hispanic white, 61%; black, 13.3%; Latino, 17.8%; Asian 5.7%; American Indian, 1.3% (U.S. Census 2017).

FIGURE 27 ■ Physicians and Surgeons by Race and Ethnicity

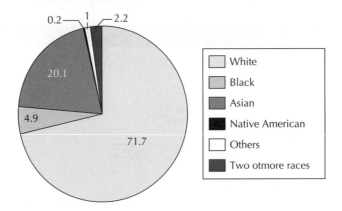

Source: Data from U.S Census Bureau 1 Percent Public Use Microdata Sample Surveys, *201*, 2015.

Note: Numbers are the percent of the population.

FIGURE 28 ■ Washington, D.C., National Press Corps Reporters and Editor by Race and Ethnicity

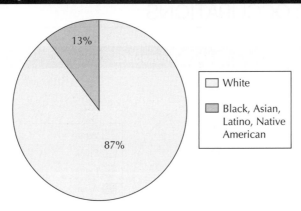

Source: Data from ASNE, 2014.

Note: Numbers are the percent of the population.

The U.S. population is 76% white (including Latinos who define themselves as white). The total U.S. population comprises: non-Hispanic white, 61%; black, 13.3%; Latino, 17.8%; Asian 5.7%; American Indian, 1.3% (U.S. Census 2017).

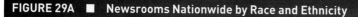

FIGURE 29A ■ Newsrooms Nationwide by Race and Ethnicity

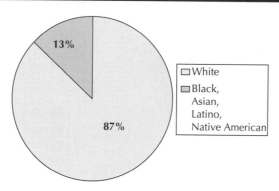

Source: Data from Unity, 2015.

Note: Numbers are the percent of the population.

FIGURE 29B ■ Race/Ethnicity in the Top 100 Films of 2014

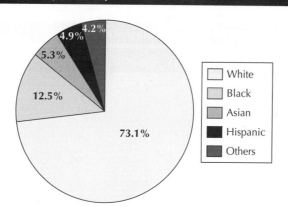

Source: USC Annenberg's Media Diversity & Social Change.

Note: These percentages have not changed since 2007.

The U.S. population is 76% white (including Latinos who define themselves as white). The total U.S. population comprises: non-Hispanic white, 61%; black, 13.3%; Latino, 17.8%; Asian 5.7%; American Indian, 1.3% (U.S. Census 2017).

FIGURE 30   ■   CEOs of Fortune 500 Companies by Race and Ethnicity

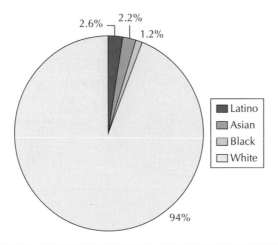

Source: Data from *Christian Science Monitor*, October 31, 2015.

Note: Numbers are the percent of the population.

FIGURE 31   ■   Other Occupations by Race and Ethnicity

	White	Black	Latino	Asian	Native American
Registered Nurses	80.4	8.9	3.4	5.5	0.4
Engineers	80.9	4.2	3.9	9.2	0.3
Police Supervisors	81.4	9.5	6.1	0.5	0.9
Police/Detectives	76.6	11.4	8.5	1.4	0.7
College Instructors	79.7	5.6	4.5	8.1	0.4
Judges/Hearing Examiners/JPs/Some Arbitrators	82.1	12.0	3.4	1.4	0.9
Clergy	81.8	8.4	3.9	4.1	0.7
Information Technology	73.8	7.6	5.1	11.4	0.3
School Teachers	81.8	9.0	5.7	1.8	0.5

Source: Data from U.S. Census Bureau 1 Percent Public Use Microdata Sample Surveys, *201*, 2000.

The U.S. population is 76% white (including Latinos who define themselves as white). The total U.S. population comprises: non-Hispanic white, 61%; black, 13.3%; Latino, 17.8%; Asian 5.7%; American Indian, 1.3% (U.S. Census 2017).

SECTION IX: GOVERNMENT

FIGURE 32 ■ **Racial/Ethnic Representation in the 115th Congress**

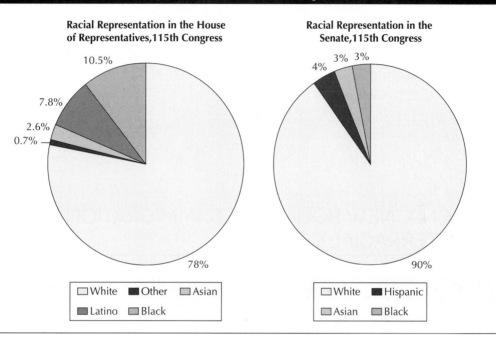

Racial Representation in the House of Representatives, 115th Congress

10.5%
7.8%
2.6%
0.7%
78%

☐ White   ■ Other   ☐ Asian
■ Latino   ☐ Black

Racial Representation in the Senate, 115th Congress

3% 3%
4%
90%

☐ White   ■ Hispanic
☐ Asian   ☐ Black

Source: Data from U.S. House of Representatives, House Press Gallery; U.S. Senate, Daily Press Gallery, Minority Senators, 2017.

FIGURE 33 ■ **Racial Representation in the Presidential Cabinet 2018**

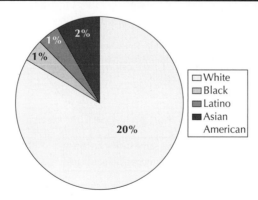

2%
1%
1%
20%

☐ White
☐ Black
■ Latino
■ Asian
  American

Source: House Press Gallery: *The President's Cabinet;* The White House.

The U.S. population is 76% white (including Latinos who define themselves as white). The total U.S. population comprises: non-Hispanic white, 61%; black, 13.3%; Latino, 17.8%; Asian 5.7%; American Indian, 1.3% (U.S. Census 2017).

FIGURE 34 ■ Race of Presidents as of 2011

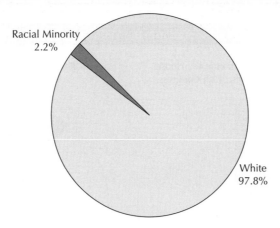

Racial Minority
2.2%

White
97.8%

SECTION X: NEW BOUNDARIES: IMMIGRATION AND INTERRACIAL COUPLES

FIGURE 35 ■ Interracial Married Couples 2015

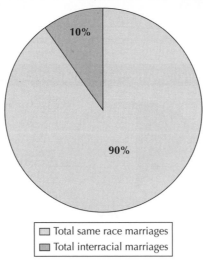

10%

90%

☐ Total same race marriages
☐ Total interracial marriages

Source: Data from Pew Research's Fact Tank report *Key facts about race and marriage, 50 years after* Loving v. Virginia.

The U.S. population is 76% white (including Latinos who define themselves as white). The total U.S. population comprises: non-Hispanic white, 61%; black, 13.3%; Latino, 17.8%; Asian 5.7%; American Indian, 1.3% (U.S. Census 2017).

FIGURE 36 ■ Ten Places with the Largest Two or More Races Population: 2010			
	Total Population	Two or More Races Population	
Place	Number	Rank	Number
New York, NY	8,175,133	1	325,901
Los Angeles, CA	3,792,621	2	175,635
Chicago, IL	2,695,598	3	73,148
Houston, TX	2,099,451	4	68,530
San Diego, CA	1,307,402	5	66,688
Urban Honolulu CDP, HI[1]	337,256	6	55,080
Phoenix, AZ	1,445,632	7	52,334
San Jose, CA	945,942	8	47,062
San Antonio, TX	1,327,407	9	45,531
Philadelphia, PA	1,526,006	10	43,070

Source: Data from U.S. Census Bureau, Census 2010 Restricting Data (Public Law 94–171) Summary File, Table P1.

[1] Urban Honolulu CDP, HI, is a census designated place (CDP). CDPs are the statistical counterparts of incorporated places and are delineated to provide data for settled concentrations of population that are identifiable by name but are not legally incorporated under the laws of the state in which they are located.

The U.S. population is 76% white (including Latinos who define themselves as white). The total U.S. population comprises: non-Hispanic white, 61%; black, 13.3%; Latino, 17.8%; Asian 5.7%; American Indian, 1.3% (U.S. Census 2017).

FIGURE 37 ■ Total Immigration to the United States from 1820 to 2000, by Decade

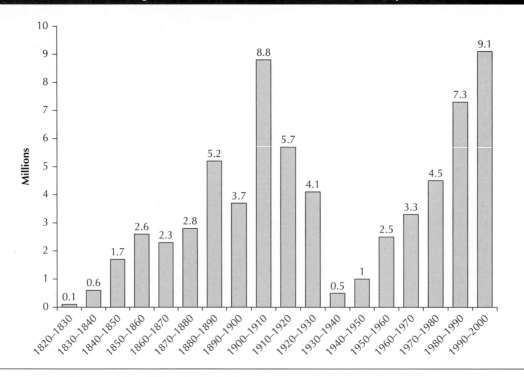

Source: Data from U.S. Immigration and Naturalization Service.

FIGURE 38 ■ Immigrant Share of Population

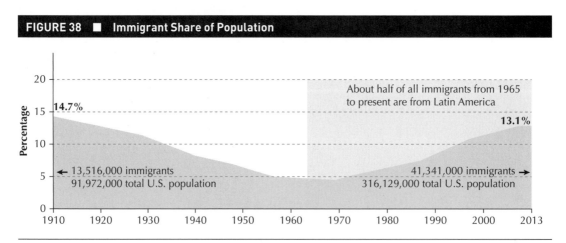

Source: U.S. Census Bureau, "Historical Census Statistics on the Foreign-Born Population of the United States: 1850–2000" and Pew Research Center tabulations of 2010 and 2013 American Community Survey (IPUMS).

The U.S. population is 76% white (including Latinos who define themselves as white). The total U.S. population comprises: non-Hispanic white, 61%; black, 13.3%; Latino, 17.8%; Asian 5.7%; American Indian, 1.3% (U.S. Census 2017).

NOTES AND REFERENCES

READING 2

References

Aptheker, Herbert, ed. 1974. *A Documentary History of the Negro People in the United States.* Secaucus, NJ: Citadel.

Boskin, Joseph. 1966. *Into Slavery: Radical Decisions in the Virginia Colony.* Philadelphia: Lippincott.

Catterall, Helen. 1937. *Judicial Cases Concerning American Slavery and the Negro.* 5 vols. Washington, DC: Negro University Press.

Davidson, Basil. 1961. *The African Slave Trade.* Boston: Little, Brown.

Donnan, Elizabeth, ed. 1965. *Documents Illustrative of the History of the Slave Trade to America.* 4 vols. New York: Octagon.

Elkins, Stanley. 1976. *Slavery: A Problem in American Institutional and Intellectual Life.* Chicago: University of Chicago Press.

Federal Writers Project. 1969. *The Negro in Virginia.* New York: Arno.

Franklin, John Hope. 1974. *From Slavery to Freedom: A History of American Negroes.* New York: Knopf.

Jordan, Winthrop. 1968. *White over Black: American Attitudes toward the Negro, 1550–1812.* Chapel Hill: University of North Carolina Press.

Morgan, Edmund S. 1975. *American Slavery, American Freedom: The Ordeal of Colonial Virginia.* New York: Norton.

Mullin, Gerald. 1974. *Flight and Rebellion: Slave Resistance in Eighteenth-Century Virginia.* New York: Oxford University Press.

Mullin, Michael, ed. 1975. *American Negro Slavery: A Documentary History.* New York: Harper & Row.

Phillips, Ulrich B. 1966. *American Negro Slavery: A Survey of the Supply, Employment and Control of Negro Labor as Determined by the Plantation Regime.* Baton Rouge: Louisiana State University Press.

Redding, J. Saunders. 1973. *They Came in Chains.* Philadelphia: Lippincott.

Stampp, Kenneth M. 1956. *The Peculiar Institution.* New York: Knopf.

Tannenbaum, Frank. 1963. *Slave and Citizen: The Negro in the Americas.* New York: Random House.

READING 3

Notes

1. *San Francisco Chronicle,* 14 September 1982, 19 May 1983. Ironically, the 1970 Louisiana law was enacted to supersede an old Jim Crow statute which relied on the idea of "common report" in determining an infant's race. Following Phipps's unsuccessful attempt to change her classification and have the law declared unconstitutional, a legislative effort arose which culminated in the repeal of the law. See *San Francisco Chronicle,* 23 June 1983.

2. The Mormon church, for example, has been heavily criticized for its doctrine of black inferiority.

3. Thomas F. Gossett notes:

   Race theory . . . had up until fairly modern times no firm hold on European thought. On the other hand, race theory and race prejudice were by no means unknown at the time when the English colonists came to North America. Undoubtedly, the age of exploration led many to speculate on race differences at a period when neither Europeans nor Englishmen were prepared to make allowances for vast cultural diversities. Even though race theories had not then secured wide acceptance or even sophisticated formulation, the first contacts of the Spanish with the Indians in the Americas can now be recognized as the beginning of a struggle between conceptions of the nature of primitive peoples which has not yet been wholly settled. (Thomas F. Gossett, *Race: The History of an Idea in America* [New York: Schocken Books, 1965], p. 16.)

Winthrop Jordan provides a detailed account of early European colonialists' attitudes about color and race in *White over Black: American Attitudes Toward the Negro, 1550–1812* (New York: Norton, 1977 [1968]), pp. 3–43.

4. Pro-slavery physician Samuel George Morton (1799–1851) compiled a collection of 800 crania from all parts of the world which formed the sample for his studies of race. Assuming that the larger the size of the cranium translated into greater intelligence, Morton established a relationship between race and skull capacity. Gossett reports that:

In 1849, one of his studies included the following results: The English skulls in his collection proved to be the largest, with an average cranial capacity of 96 cubic inches. The Americans and Germans were rather poor seconds, both with cranial capacities of 90 cubic inches. At the bottom of the list were the Negroes with 83 cubic inches, the Chinese with 82, and the Indians with 79. (Ibid., p. 74)

On Morton's methods, see Stephen J. Gould, "The Finagle Factor," *Human Nature* (July 1978).

5. Definitions of race founded upon a common pool of genes have not held up when confronted by scientific research which suggests that the differences *within* a given human population are greater than those between populations. See L. L. Cavalli-Sforza, "The Genetics of Human Populations," *Scientific American,* September 1974, pp. 81–89.

6. Arthur Jensen, "How Much Can We Boost IQ and Scholastic Achievement?" *Harvard Educational Review* 39 (1969):1–123.

7. Ernst Moritz Manasse, "Max Weber on Race," *Social Research* 14 (1947):191–221.

8. Quoted in Edward D. C. Campbell, Jr., *The Celluloid South: Hollywood and the Southern Myth* (Knoxville: University of Tennessee Press, 1981), pp. 168–70.

9. Marvin Harris, *Patterns of Race in the Americas* (New York: Norton, 1964), p. 56.

10. Ibid., p. 57.

11. After James Meredith had been admitted as the first black student at the University of Mississippi, Harry S. Murphy announced that he, and not Meredith, was the first black student to attend "Ole Miss." Murphy described himself as black but was able to pass for white and spent nine months at the institution without attracting any notice (Ibid., p. 56).

12. A. Sivanandan, "From Resistance to Rebellion: Asian and Afro-Caribbean Struggles in Britain," *Race and Class* 23(2–3) (Autumn–Winter 1981).

13. Gordon W. Allport, *The Nature of Prejudice* (Garden City, NY: Doubleday, 1958), pp. 184–200.

14. We wish to use this phrase loosely, without committing ourselves to a particular position on such social psychological approaches as symbolic interactionism, which are outside the scope of this study. An interesting study on this subject is S. M. Lyman and W. A. Douglass, "Ethnicity: Strategies of Individual and Collective Impression Management," *Social Research* 40(2) (1973).

15. Michael Billig, "Patterns of Racism: Interviews with National Front Members," *Race and Class* 20(2) (Autumn 1978):161–79.

16. "Miss San Antonio USA Lisa Fernandez and other Hispanics auditioning for a role in a television soap-opera did not fit the Hollywood image of real Mexicans and had to darken their faces before filming." Model Aurora Garza said that their faces were bronzed with powder because they looked too white. "I'm a real Mexican [Garza said] and very dark anyway. I'm even darker right now because I have a tan. But they kept wanting me to make my face darker and darker" (*San Francisco Chronicle,* 21 September 1984). A similar dilemma faces Asian American actors who feel that Asian character lead roles inevitably go to white actors

who make themselves up to be Asian. Scores of Charlie Chan films, for example, have been made with white leads (the last one was the 1981 *Charlie Chan and the Curse of the Dragon Queen*). Roland Winters, who played in six Chan features, was asked by playwright Frank Chin to explain the logic of casting a white man in the role of Charlie Chan: "The only thing I can think of is, if you want to cast a homosexual in a show, and get a homosexual, it'll be awful. It won't be funny . . . and maybe there's something there . . ." (Frank Chin, "Confessions of the Chinatown Cowboy," *Bulletin of Concerned Asian Scholars* 4(3) (Fall 1972)).

17. Melanie Martindale-Sikes, "Nationalizing 'Nigger' Imagery Through 'Birth of a Nation,'" paper prepared for the 73rd Annual Meeting of the American Sociological Association, 8 September 1978, San Francisco.

18. Jordan, *White over Black*, p. 95; emphasis added.

19. Historical focus has been placed either on particular racially defined groups or on immigration and the "incorporation" of ethnic groups. In the former case the characteristic ethnicity theory pitfalls and apologetics such as functionalism and cultural pluralism may be avoided, but only by sacrificing much of the focus on race. In the latter case, race is considered a manifestation of ethnicity.

20. The degree of antipathy for these groups should not be minimized. A northern commentator observed in the 1850s: "An Irish Catholic seldom attempts to rise to a higher condition than that in which he is placed, while the Negro often makes the attempt with success." Quoted in Gossett, op. cit., p. 288.

21. This analysis, as will perhaps be obvious, is essentially DuBoisian. Its main source will be found in the monumental (and still largely unappreciated) *Black Reconstruction in the United States, 1860–1880* (New York: Atheneum, 1977 [1935]).

22. Alexander Saxton argues that:

North Americans of European background have experienced three great racial confrontations: with the Indian, with the African, and with the Oriental. Central to each transaction has been a totally one-sided preponderance of power, exerted for the exploitation of nonwhites by the dominant white society. In each case (but especially in the two that began with systems of enforced labor), white workingmen have played a crucial, yet ambivalent, role. They have been both exploited and exploiters. On the one hand, thrown into competition with nonwhites as enslaved or "cheap" labor they suffered economically; on the other hand, being white, they benefited by that very exploitation which was compelling the nonwhites to work for low wages or for nothing. Ideologically they were drawn in opposite directions. *Racial identification cut at right angles to class consciousness.* (Alexander Saxton, *The Indispensable Enemy: Labor and the Anti-Chinese Movement in California* [Berkeley and Los Angeles: University of California Press, 1971], p. 1; emphasis added.)

23. Selig Perlman, *The History of Trade Unionism in the United States* (New York: Augustus Kelley, 1950), p. 52; emphasis added.

24. Whether southern blacks were "peasants" or rural workers is unimportant in this context. Some time during the 1960s blacks attained a higher degree of urbanization than whites. Before World War II most blacks had been rural dwellers and nearly 80 percent lived in the South.

25. See George Gilder, *Wealth and Poverty* (New York: Basic Books, 1981); Charles Murray, *Losing Ground* (New York: Basic Books, 1984).

26. A brilliant study of the racialization process in Britain, focused on the rise of "mugging" as a popular fear in the 1970s, is Stuart Hall et al., *Policing the Crisis* (London: Macmillan, 1978).

27. The case of Vincent Chin, a Chinese American man beaten to death in 1982 by a laid-off Detroit auto worker and his stepson who mistook him for Japanese and blamed him for the loss of their jobs, has been widely publicized in Asian American communities. On immigration conflicts and pressures, see Michael Omi, "New Wave Dread: Immigration and Intra-Third World Conflict," *Socialist Review* 60 (November–December 1981).

READING 4

Notes

1. Riley (2014).

2. Coates (2014).

3. U.S. Bureau of Labor Statistics (2014a).

4. Blau, Ferber, and Winkler (1998).

5. U.S. Census Bureau (2014).

6. U.S. Bureau of Labor Statistics (2014b).

7. Western and Wildeman (2009); Wakefield and Uggen (2010).

8. Massey and Denton (1993), 141–42; Duncan and Murnane (2011).

9. Bourdieu and Wacquant (1992), 199.

10. Loury (1977); see also Bourdieu (1986).

11. Xie and Gough (2011); see also Sanders and Nee (1987, 1992).

12. Murray (1984).

13. See Iceland (2013), ch. 5; Bureau of Justice Statistics (2011); and Patterson (2015), 106.

14. Martin et al. (2013).

15. E. Anderson (1999); Edin and Kefalas (2011).

16. McLanahan (2004); S. L. Brown (2010).

17. Hsin and Xie (2014); see also Zhou and Lee (2014); and Lee and Zhou (2014).

18. Sakamoto, Goyette, and Kim (2009).

19. Lamont and Lareau (1988), 164.

20. Bourdieu (1986); Kalmijn and Kraaykamp (1996).

21. Alba and Nee (2003), 11.

22. Alba and Nee (2003), 38.

23. Melvern (2004).

24. Parrillo (2012), 80.

25. Guinier and Torres (2009), 109–10.

26. Gallagher (2009), 100; see also Bonilla-Silva (2014).

27. Guinier and Torres (2009), 100–13.

28. Reiman (2009); Pager (2009).

29. Guinier and Torres (2009), 110.

References

Alba, Richard, and Victor Nee. 2003. *Remaking the American Mainstream: Assimilation and Contemporary Immigration.* Cambridge, MA: Harvard University Press.

Anderson, Elijah, 1999. *Code of the Street: Decency, Violence, and the Moral Life of the Inner City.* New York: Norton.

Blau, Francine D., Marianne A. Ferber, and Anne E. Winkler. 1998. *The Economics of Women, Men, and Work.* 3rd ed. Upper Saddle River, NJ: Prentice Hall.

Bonilla-Silva, Eduardo. 2014. *Racism without Racists: Color-Blind Racism and Persistence of Racial Inequality in America.* 4th ed. Lanham, MD: Rowman and Littlefield.

Bourdieu, Pierre. 1986. "The Forms of Capital." In *Handbook of Theory and Research for the Sociology of Education,* edited by John G. Richardson, 241–58. New York: Greenwood.

Bourdieu, Pierre, and Loic Wacquant. 1992. *An Invitation to Reflexive Sociology.* Chicago: University of Chicago Press.

Brown, Susan L. 2010. "Marriage and Child Well-Being: Research and Policy Perspectives." *Journal of Marriage and Family* 72:1059–77.

Bureau of Justice Statistics. 2011. *Homicide Trends in the United States, 1980–2009.* Washington, DC: U.S. Department of Justice.

Coates, Ta-Nehisi. 2014. "The Case for Reparations." *Atlantic,* June.

Duncan, Greg J., and Richard J. Murnane, eds. 2011. *Whither Opportunity? Rising Inequality, Schools, and Children's Life Chances.* New York: Russell Sage Foundation.

Edin, Kathryn, and Maria Kefalas. 2011. *Promises I Can Keep: Why Poor Women Put Motherhood before Marriage.* Berkeley: University of California Press.

Gallagher, Charles A. 2009. "Color-Blind Privilege: The Social and Political Functions of Erasing the Color Line in Post-Race America." In *Rethinking the Color Line,* edited by Charles A. Gallagher. 4th ed., 100–108. Boston: McGraw-Hill.

Guinier, Lani, and Gerald Torres. 2009. "The Ideology of Colorblindness." In *Rethinking the Color Line,* edited by Charles A. Gallagher. 4th ed., 109–13. Boston: McGraw-Hill.

Hsin, Amy, and Yu Xie. 2014. "Explaining Asian Americans' Academic Advantage over Whites." *Proceedings of the National Academy of Sciences of the United States of America* 111:8416–21.

Iceland, John. 2013. *Poverty in America: A Handbook.* 3rd ed. Berkeley: University of California Press.

Kalmijn, Matthijs, and Gerbert Kraaykamp. 1996. "Race, Cultural Capital, and Schooling: An Analysis of Trends in the United States." *Sociology of Education* 69 (1): 22–34.

Lamont, Michele, and Annette Lareau. 1988. "Cultural Capital: Allusions, Gaps and Glissandos in Recent Theoretical Developments." *Sociological Theory* 6 (2): 153–68.

Lee, Jennifer, and Min Zhou. 2014. "The Success Frame and Achievement Paradox: The Costs and Consequences for Asian Americans." *Race and Social Problems* 6:38–55.

Loury, Glenn C. 1977. "A Dynamic Theory of Racial Income Differences." In *Women, Minorities, and Employment Discrimination,* edited by Phyllis A. Wallace and Annette M. LaMond, 153–86. Lexington, MA: Heath.

Martin, Joyce A., Brady E. Hamilton, Michelle J. K. Osterman, Sally C. Curtin, and T. J. Mathews. 2013. "Births: Final Data for 2012." National Vital Statistics. December 30. www.cdc.gov/nchs/data/nvsr/nvsr62/nvsr62_09.pdf

Massey, Douglas S., and Nancy Denton. 1993. *American Apartheid: Segregation and the Making of the Underclass.* Cambridge, MA: Harvard University Press.

McLanahan, Sara. 2004. "Diverging Destinies: How Children Are Faring under the Second Demographic Transition." *Demography* 41 (4): 607–27.

Melvern, Linda. 2004. *Conspiracy to Murder: The Rwandan Genocide.* London: Verso.

Murray, Charles. 1984. *Losing Ground: American Social Policy, 1950–1980.* New York: Basic Books.

Pager, Devah. 2009. "The Mark of a Criminal Record." In *Rethinking the Color Line,* edited by Charles A. Gallagher. 4th ed., 246–49. Boston: McGraw-Hill.

Parrillo, Vincent N. 2012. *Understanding Race and Ethnic Relations.* 4th ed. Boston: Allyn and Bacon.

Patterson, Orlando. 2015. "The Nature and Dynamics of Cultural Processes." In *The Cultural Matrix: Understanding Black Youth,* edited by Orlando Patterson, 25–135.

Reiman, Jeffrey. 2009. ". . . and the Poor Get Prison." In *Rethinking the Color Line,* edited by Charles A. Gallagher. 4th ed., 234–45. Boston: McGraw-Hill.

Riley, Jason L. 2014. "Jesse, Al and Signs of Progress." *Wall Street Journal,* July 31. www.wsj.com/articles/poltical-diary-jesse-al-and-signs-of-progress-1406834202

Sakamoto, Arthur, Kimberly A. Goyette, and Chang Hwan Kim. 2009. "Socio-economic Attainments of Asian Americans." *Annual Review of Sociology* 35:255–76.

Sanders, Jimy M., and Victor Nee. 1987. "Limits of Ethnic Solidarity in the Enclave Economy." *American Sociological Review* 52:745–73.

——. 1992. "Problems in Resolving the Enclave Economy Debate." *American Sociological Review* 57:415–18.

U.S. Bureau of Labor Statistics. 2014a. "Earnings and Unemployment Rates by Educational Attainment." *Employment Projections.* Accessed September 4, 2014. www.bls.gov/emp/ep_table_001.htm

U.S. Bureau of Labor Statistics. 2014b. "Unemployed Persons by Marital Status, Race, Hispanic or Latino Ethnicity, Age and Sex." Table 24. *Labor Force Statistics from the Current Population Survey.* Accessed September 8, 2014. www.bls.gov/cps/cpsaat24.htm

U.S. Census Bureau. 2014. 2013 Current Population Survey. www.census.gov

Wakefield, Sara, and Christopher Uggen. 2010. "Incarceration and Stratification." *Annual Review of Sociology* 36:386–406.

Western, Bruce, and Christopher Wildeman. 2009. "The Black Family and Mass Incarceration." *Annals of the American Academy of Political and Social Science* 621 (1): 221–42.

Xie, Yu, and Margaret Gough. 2011. "Ethnic Enclaves and the Earnings of Immigrants." *Demography* 48:1293–1315.

Zhou, Min, and Jennifer Lee. 2014. "Assessing What Is Cultural about Asian Americans' Academic Advantage." *Proceedings of the National Academy of Sciences of the United States of America* 111 (23): 8321–22.

READING 5

Notes

1. All racialized social systems operate along white supremacist lines. See Charles W. Mills, *Blackness Visible* (Ithaca, NY: Cornell University Press, 1998).

2. I make a distinction between race and ethnicity. Ethnicity has a primarily sociocultural foundation, and ethnic groups have exhibited tremendous malleability in terms of who belongs. In contrast, racial ascriptions (initially) are imposed externally to justify the collective exploitation of a people and are maintained to preserve status differences. The distinction I make was part of a debate that appeared recently in the *American Sociological Review*. For specialists interested in this matter, see Bonilla-Silva, "The Essential Social Fact of Race," *American Sociological Review* 64, no. 6 (1999): 899–906.

3. Herbert Blumer was one of the first analysts to make this argument about systemic rewards received by the races ascribed the primary position in a racial order. See Herbert Blumer, "Reflections on Theory of Race Relations," pp. 3–21 in *Race Relations in World Perspective*, edited by A. W. Lind (Honolulu, HI: University of Hawaii Press, 1955). Du Bois's argument about the psychological wages of whiteness has been used recently by Manning Marable, *How Capitalism Underdeveloped Black America*; and by David Roediger, *The Wages of Whiteness*.

4. This point has been made by Michael Omi and Howard Winant, *Racial Formation in the United States*; Winant, *Racial Conditions*.

5. I am referring to cases such as Haiti. Nonetheless, recent research has suggested that even in such places, the abolition of slavery did not end the racialized character of the social formation. See Michel-Rolph Troillot, *Haiti, State Agency Nation: Origins and Legacy of Duvalierism* (New York: Monthly Review Press, 1990).

6. For a similar argument, see Floya Anthias and Nira Yuval-Davis, *Racialized Boundaries: Race, Nation, Gender, Colour, and the Anti-Racist Struggle* (London, England: Tavistock, 1992).

7. For an early statement on this matter, see Hubert M. Blalock, Jr., *Toward a Theory of Minority-Majority Group Relations* (New York: John Wiley and Sons, 1967). For a more recent statement, see Susan Olzack, *The Dynamics of Ethnic Competition and Conflict* (Stanford, CA: Stanford University Press, 1992).

8. Nineteenth-century nation-building processes throughout Latin America included the myth of racial democracy and color- or race-blindness. This facilitated the struggles for independence and the maintenance of white supremacy in societies wherein white elites were demographically insignificant. For discussions pertinent to this argument see the excellent collection edited by Michael Hanchard, *Racial Politics in Contemporary Brazil* (Durham and London: Duke University Press, 1999).

9. See my "The Essential Social Fact of Race," *American Sociological Review* 64, no. 6 (December 1999): 899–906.

10. On this point, see Warren Whatley and Gavin Wright, *Race, Human Capital, and Labor Markets in American History*, Working Paper #7 (Ann Arbor, MI: Center for Afroamerican and Africa Studies, University of Michigan, 1994). For an incisive discussion, see Samuel L. Meyers, Jr., "Measuring and Detecting Discrimination in the Post-Civil Rights Era," pp. 172–197 in *Race and Ethnicity in Research Methods*, edited by John H. Stanfield II and Rutledge M. Dennis (London: Sage Publications, 1993).

11. Michael Reich, "The Economics of Racism," in *Racial Conflict, Discrimination, and Power: Historical and Contemporary Studies*, edited by William Barclay,

Krishna Kumar, and Ruth P. Simms (New York: AMS Press, 1976), p. 224.

12. Omi and Winant, *Racial Formation in the United States*, 64.

13. On the invention of the white race, see Theodore W. Allen, *The Invention of the White Race,* Vol. I (London: Verso, 1994). On the invention of the "Indian" race, see Robert E. Berkhoffer, *The White Man's Indian* (New York: Vintage, 1978). On the invention of the black and white races, see Winthrop Jordan, *White over Black.*

14. A classic book on the ideological binary construction of the races in the United States is Thomas Gossett, *Race: The History of an Idea in America* (Dallas, TX: Southern Methodist University Press, 1963). For an analysis of an earlier period in the Americas, see Tzevetan Todorov, *The Conquest of America: The Question of the Other* (New York: Harper Colophon, 1984).

15. On this matter, I stated in my recent debate in the pages of the *American Sociological Review* with Mara Loveman that "'race,' like 'class' or 'gender,' is *always contingent* but is also *socially real*. Race operates 'as a shuttle between socially constructed meanings and practices, between subjective and lived, material reality' (Hanchard 1994:4)" (p. 901). Michael G. Hanchard, *Orpheus and Power* (Princeton, NJ: Princeton University Press, 1994).

16. This last point is an extension of Nicos Poulantzas' view on class. Races—as classes—are not an "empirical thing"; they denote racialized social relations or racial practices at all levels. Poulantzas, *Political Power and Social Classes* (London: Verso, 1982), p. 67.

17. For a full discussion, see my "The Essential Social Fact of Race." For a similar argument, see Teresa Amott and Julie Matthaei, *Race, Gender, and Work: A Multicultural Economic History of Women in the United States* (Boston, MA: South End Press, 1996).

18. Frederick Barth, "Introduction," pp. 9–38 in *Ethnic Groups and Boundaries: The Social Organization of Culture Difference,* edited by F. Barth (Bergen, Norway: Universitetsforlaget, 1969).

19. For the case of the Jews, see Robert Miles, *Racism After "Race Relations"* (London: Routledge, 1993). For the case of the Irish, see Allen, *The Invention of the White Race.*

20. For a recent excellent discussion on ethnicity with many examples from the United States, see Stephen Cornell and Douglas Hartmann, *Ethnicity and Race: Making Identities in a Changing World* (London: Pine Forge Press, 1998).

21. Roediger, *The Wages of Whiteness.* See also Noel Ignatiev, *How the Irish Became White* (New York: Routledge, 1995).

22. For identity issues among Caribbean immigrants, see the excellent edited collection by Constance R. Sutton and E. M. Chaney, *Caribbean Life in New York City: Sociocultural Dimensions* (New York: Center for Migration Studies of New York, 1987).

23. Barth, "Introduction," 17.

24. A few notable discussions on this matter are Ira Berlin, *Slaves Without Masters: The Free Negro in Antebellum South* (New York: Pantheon, 1975); John Hope Franklin, *From Slavery to Freedom: A History of the Negro Americans* (New York: Alfred Knopf, 1974); August Meir and Elliot Rudwick, *From Plantation to Ghetto* (New York: Hill and Wang, 1970).

25. The motivation for racializing human relations may have originated in the interests of powerful actors, but after social systems are racialized, all members of the dominant race participate in defending and reproducing the racial structure. This is the crucial reason why Marxist analysts (e.g., Cox, Reich) have not succeeded in successfully analyzing racism. They have not been able to accept the fact that after the phenomenon originated with the expansion of European capitalism into the New World, it acquired a life of its own. The subjects who were racialized as belonging to the superior race, whether or not they were members of the dominant class, became zealous defenders of the racial order.

26. Hillel Ticktin, *The Politics of Race: Discrimination in South Africa* (London: Pluto, 1991), p. 26.

27. The classic book on this is Paula Giddings, *When and Where I Enter: The Impact of Black Women*

on Race and Sex in America (New York: Bantam, 1984). See also Nancy Caraway, *Segregated Sisterhood: Racism and the Politics of American Feminism* (Knoxville, TN: University of Tennessee Press, 1991).

28. This argument is not new. Analysts of the racial history of the United States have always pointed out that most of the significant historical changes in this country's race relations were accompanied by some degree of overt violence. See Harold Cruse, *Rebellion or Revolution* (New York: William Morrow, 1968); Franklin, *From Slavery to Freedom*; and James W. Button, *Blacks and Social Change: Impact of the Civil Rights Movement in Southern Communities* (Princeton, NJ: Princeton University Press, 1989).

29. This point is important in literature on revolutions and democracy. On the role of violence in the establishment of bourgeois democracies, see Barrington Moore, Jr., *Social Origins of Dictatorship and Democracy* (Boston, MA: Beacon Press, 1966). On the pivotal role of violence in social movements, see Frances Fox Piven and Richard A. Cloward, *Poor People's Movements: Why They Succeed, How They Fail* (New York: Vintage, 1979).

30. The notion of relative autonomy comes from the work of Poulantzas (*Power and Social Classes*) and implies that the ideological and political levels in a society are partially autonomous in relation to the economic level; that is, they are not merely expressions of the economic level.

31. Paul Gilroy, *"There Ain't No Black in the Union Jack": The Cultural Politics of Race and Nation* (Chicago, IL: University of Chicago Press, 1991), p. 17.

32. See Ellis Cose, *The Rage of a Privileged Class: Why Are Middle-Class Blacks Angry? Why Should America Care?* (New York: HarperCollins, 1993); Lawrence Otis-Graham, *Member of the Club: Reflections on Life in a Racially Polarized World* (New York: HarperCollins, 1995).

33. In addition to the work by Joe R. Feagin and Hernán Vera already cited, see Lawrence Bobo, J. Kluegel, and R. Smith, "Laissez-Faire Racism:

The Crystallization of a Kinder, Gentler, Antiblack Ideology," and, particularly, Mary R. Jackman, *Velvet Glove: Paternalism and Conflict in Gender, Class and Race Relations* (Berkeley, CA: University of California Press, 1994).

34. Curiously, historian Eugene Genovese made a similar argument in his book *Red and Black*. Although he still regarded racism as an ideology, he stated that once it "arises it alters profoundly the material reality and in fact becomes a partially autonomous feature of that reality." *Red and Black: Marxian Explorations in Southern and Afroamerican History* (New York: Pantheon, 1971), p. 340.

35. Stuart Hall, "Race Articulation and Societies Structured in Dominance," in *Sociological Theories: Race and Colonialism,* edited by UNESCO (Paris: UNESCO, 1980), p. 336.

36. Actions by the Ku Klux Klan have an unmistakably racial tone, but many other actions (choosing to live in a suburban neighborhood, sending one's children to a private school, and opposing government intervention in hiring policies) also have racial undertones.

READING 6

Notes

1. Harvard School of Public Health, Boston, MA, USA.

2. Harvard University, Boston, MA, USA.

3. University of Cape Town, Cape Town, South Africa.

4. University of Washington-Bothell, Bothell, WA, USA.

References

Alexander, M. (2010). *The new Jim Crow: Mass incarceration in the age of colorblindness.* New York, NY: New Press.

Aronson, J., Burgess, D., Phelan, S. M., & Juarez, L. (2013). Unhealthy interactions: The role of stereotype threat in health disparities. *American Journal of Public Health, 103*(1), 50–56.

Barnes, L. L., de Leon, C. F. M., Lewis, T. T., Bienias, J. L., Wilson, R. S., & Evans, D. A. (2008). Perceived discrimination and mortality in a population–based study of older adults. *American Journal of Public Health, 98*(7), 1241–1247.

Barnes, L. L., Lewis, T. T., Begeny, C. T., Yu, L., Bennett, D. A., & Wilson, R. S. (2012). Perceived discrimination and cognition in older African Americans. *Journal of the International Neuropsychological Society, 18*(5), 856–865.

Blascovitch, J., Spencer, S. J., Quinn, D., & Steele, C. (2001). African Americans and high blood pressure: The role of stereotype threat. *Psychological Science, 12*(3), 225–229.

Bonilla-Silva, E. (1996). Rethinking racism: Toward a structural interpretation. *American Sociological Review, 62*(3), 465–480.

Braga, A. A., Papachristos, A., & Hureau, D. (2010). The concentration and stability of gun violence at micro places in Boston, 1980–2008. *Journal of Quantitative Criminology, 26*(1), 33–53.

Braveman, P. A., Cubbin, C., Egerter, S., Williams, D. R., & Pamuk, E. (2010). Socioeconomic disparities in health in the United States: What the patterns tell us. *American Journal of Public Health, 100,* S186–196.

Brondolo, E., Libby, D. J., Denton, E.-G., Thompson, S., Beatty, D. L., Schwartz, J., & Gerin, W. (2008). Racism and ambulatory blood pressure in a community sample. *Psychosomatic Medicine, 70*(1), 49–56.

Bryant, W. W. (2011). Internalized racism's association with African American male youth's propensity for violence. *Journal of Black Studies, 42*(4), 690–707.

Burgess, D., Warren, J., Phelan, S., Dovidio, J., & van Ryn, M. (2010). Stereotype threat and health disparities: What medical educators and future physicians need to know. *Journal of General Internal Medicine, 25*(Suppl. 2), S169–177.

Cell, J. W. (1982). *The highest stage of White supremacy: The origin of segregation in South Africa and the American South.* New York, NY: Cambridge University Press.

Chae, D. H., Lincoln, K. D., Adler, N. E., & Syme, S. L. (2010). Do experiences of racial discrimination predict cardiovascular disease among African American men? The moderating role of internalized negative racial group attitudes. *Social Science and Medicine, 71*(6), 1182–1188.

Chambers, E. C., Tull, E. S., Fraser, H. S., Mutunhu, N. R., Sobers, N., & Niles, E. (2004). The relationship of internalized racism to body fat distribution and insulin resistance among African adolescent youth. *Journal of the National Medical Association, 96*(12), 1594–1598.

Cooper, L. A., Roter, D. L., Carson, K. A., Beach, M. C., Sabin, J. A., Greenwald, A. G., & Inui, T. S. (2012). The associations of clinicians' implicit attitudes about race with medical visit communication and patient ratings of interpersonal care. *American Journal of Public Health, 102*(5), 979–987.

Cutler, D. M., & Glaeser, E. L. (1997). Are ghettos good or bad? *Quarterly Journal of Economics, 112,* 827–872.

Davis, J. A., & Smith, T. W. (1990). *General social surveys, 1972–1990 NORC ed.* Chicago, IL: National Opinion Research Center.

Deaux, K., Bikmen, N., Gilkes, A., Ventuneac, A., Joseph, Y., Payne, Y. A., & Steele, C. M. (2007). Becoming American: Stereotype threat effects in Afro-Caribbean immigrant groups. *Social Psychology Quarterly, 70*(4), 384–404.

Dirks, D., & Mueller, J. C. (2007). Racism and popular culture. In J. Feagin & H. Vera (Eds.), *Handbook of racial and ethnic relations* (pp. 115–129). New York, NY: Springer.

Dovidio, J. F., & Gaertner, S. L. (2004). Aversive racism. In M. Zanna (Ed.), *Advances in experimental social psychology* (Vol. 36, pp. 1–51). San Diego, CA: Academic Press.

Dumont, D. M., Brockmann, B., Dickman, S., Alexander, N., & Rich, J. D. (2012). Public health and the epidemic of incarceration. *Annual Review of Public Health, 33*(1), 325–339.

Earnshaw, V., Rosenthal, L., Lewis, J., Stasko, E., Tobin, J., Lewis, T., & Ickovics, J. (2013). Maternal experiences with everyday discrimination and infant birth weight: A test of mediators and moderators among young, urban women of color. *Annals of Behavioral Medicine, 45*(1), 13–23.

Factor, R., Williams, D. R., & Kawachi, I. (2013). The social resistance framework for understanding high-risk behavior among non-dominant minorities: Preliminary evidence. *American Journal of Public Health, 103*(12), 2245–2251.

Fischer, C. S., Hout, M., Jankowski, M. S., Lucas, S. R., Swidler, A., & Voss, K. (1996). *Inequality by design: Cracking the bell curve myth.* Princeton, NJ: Princeton University Press.

Fiske, S. T., Bergsieker, H. B., Russell, A. M., & Williams, L. (2009). Images of Black Americans. *Du Bois Review: Social Science Research on Race, 6*(1), 83–101.

Fuller-Rowell, T. E., Doan, S. N., & Eccles, J. S. (2012). Differential effects of perceived discrimination on the diurnal cortisol rhythm of African Americans and Whites. *Psychoneuroendocrinology, 37*(1), 107–118.

Galea, S., Tracy, M., Hoggatt, K. J., DiMaggio, C., & Karpati, A. (2011). Estimated deaths attributable to social factors in the United States. *American Journal of Public Health, 101*(8), 1456–1465.

Gee, G. C. (2002). A multilevel analysis of the relationship between institutional and individual racial discrimination and health status. *American Journal of Public Health, 92*(4), 615–623.

Gee, G. C., & Ford, C. L. (2011). Structural racism and health inequities. *Du Bois Review: Social Science Research on Race, 8*(1), 115–132.

Glaeser, E. L., & Vigdor, J. L. (2001). *Racial segregation in the 2000 Census: Promising news.* Washington, DC: Brookings Institution.

Glaeser, E. L., & Vigdor, J. (2012). The end of the segregated century: Racial separation in America's neighborhoods, 1890–2010. *Civic Report, 66.* Retrieved from http://www.manhattan-institute.org/html/cr_66.htm

Goff, P. A., Eberhardt, J. L., Williams, M. J., & Jackson, M. C. (2008). Not yet human: Implicit knowledge, historical dehumanization, and contemporary consequences. *Journal of Personality and Social Psychology, 94*(2), 292–306.

Haider, A. H., Janel, S. N. S., Cooper, L. A., Efron, D. T., Swoboda, S., & Cornwell, E. E., III. (2011). Association of unconscious race and social class bias with vignette-based clinical assessments by medical students. *JAMA: The Journal of the American Medical Association, 306*(9), 942–951.

Inzlicht, M., & Kang, S. K. (2010). Stereotype threat spillover: How coping with threats to social identity affects aggression, eating, decision making, and attention. *Journal of Personality and Social Psychology, 99*(3), 467–481.

Kessler, R. C., Mickelson, K. D., & Williams, D. R. (1999). The prevalence, distribution, and mental health correlates of perceived discrimination in the United States. *Journal of Health and Social Behavior, 40*(3), 208–230.

Kramer, M. R., Cooper, H. L., Drews-Botsch, C. D., Waller, L. A., & Hogue, C. R. (2010). Do measures matter? Comparing surface-density-derived and census-tract-derived measures of racial residential segregation. *International Journal of Health Geographies, 9*(29), 1–15.

Kramer, M. R., & Hogue, C. R. (2009). Is segregation bad for your health? *Epidemiologic Reviews, 31*(1), 178–194.

Kwate, N. O. A., & Meyer, I. H. (2011). On sticks and stones and broken bones: Stereotypes and African American health. *Du Bois Review: Social Science Research on Race, 8*(1), 191–198.

Lewis, T. T., Aiello, A. E., Leurgans, S., Kelly, J., & Barnes, L. L. (2010). Self-reported experiences of everyday discrimination are associated with elevated C-reactive protein levels in older African-American adults. *Brain, Behavior, and Immunity, 24*(3), 438–443.

Lewis, T. T., Barnes, L. L., Bienias, J. L., Lackland, D. T., Evans, D. A, & Mendes de Leon, C. F. (2009). Perceived discrimination and blood pressure in older African American and White adults. *Journals of Gerontology Series A: Biological Sciences and Medical Sciences, 64A*(9), 1002–1008.

Lewis, T. T., Everson-Rose, S., Powell, L. H., Matthews, K. A., Brown, C., Karavolos, K., & Wesley, D. (2006). Chronic exposure to everyday discrimination and coronary artery calcification in African-American women: The SWAN Heart Study. *Psychosomatic Medicine, 68,* 362–368.

Lewis, T. T., Kravitz, H. M., Janssen, I., & Powell, L. H. (2011). Self-reported experiences of discrimination and visceral fat in middle-aged African-American and Caucasian women. *American Journal of Epidemiology, 173*(11), 1223–1231.

Lewis, T. T., Troxel, W. M., Kravitz, H. M., Bromberger, J. T., Matthews, K. A., & Hall, M. H. (2012). Chronic exposure to everyday discrimination and sleep in a multiethnic sample of middle-aged women. *Health Psychology.* Advance online publication.

Lieberson, S. (1980). *A piece of the pie: Black and White immigrants since 1880.* Berkeley: University of California Press.

Massey, D. S., & Denton, N. A. (1993). *American apartheid: Segregation and the making of the underclass.* Cambridge, MA: Harvard University Press.

Mendez, D. D., Hogan, V. K., & Culhane, J. F. (2012). Stress during pregnancy: The role of institutional racism. *Stress and Health.* Advance online publication.

Morello-Frosch, R., & Jesdale, B. M. (2006). Separate and unequal: Residential segregation and estimated cancer risks associated with ambient air toxics in US metropolitan areas. *Environmental Health Perspectives, 114*(3), 386–393.

Mutz, D. C., & Goldman, S. K. (2010). Mass media. In J. F. Dovidio, M. Hewstone, P. Glick, & V. M. Esses (Eds.), *The Sage handbook of prejudice: Stereotyping and discrimination* (pp. 241–257). Thousand Oaks, CA: Sage.

Norton, M. I., & Sommers, S. R. (2011). Whites see racism as a zero-sum game that they are now losing. *Perspectives on Psychological Science, 6*(3), 215–218.

Nosek, B. A., Smyth, F. L., Hansen, J. J., Devos, T., Lindner, N. M., Ranganath, K. A., & Banaji, M. R. (2007). Pervasiveness and correlates of implicit attitudes and stereotypes. *European Review of Social Psychology, 18,* 36–88.

Orfield, G., Frankenberg, E., & Garces, L. M. (2008). Statement of American social scientists of research on school desegregation to the U.S. Supreme Court in *Parents v. Seattle School District* and *Meredith v. Jefferson County. Urban Review, 40*(1), 96–136.

Osypuk, T. L., & Acevedo-Garcia, D. (2010). Beyond individual neighborhoods: A geography of opportunity perspective for understanding racial/ethnic health disparities. *Health Place, 16*(6), 1113–1123.

Pager, D., & Shepherd, H. (2008). The sociology of discrimination: Racial discrimination in employment, housing, credit, and consumer markets. *Annual Review of Sociology, 34,* 181–209.

Pascoe, E. A., & Richman, L. S. (2009). Perceived discrimination and health: A meta-analytic review. *Psychological Bulletin, 135*(4), 531–554.

Pettigrew, T. F., & Meertens, R. W. (1995). Subtle and blatant prejudice in western Europe. *European Journal of Social Psychology, 25,* 57–75.

Pew Research Center. (2011). *Wealth gaps rise to record highs between Whites, Blacks and Hispanics.* Washington, DC: Author.

Pollack, C. E., Chideya, S., Cubbin, C., Williams, B., Dekker, M., & Braveman, P. (2007). Should health studies measure wealth? A systematic review. *American Journal of Preventive Medicine, 33*(3), 250–264.

Profant, J., & Dimsdale, J. E. (1999). Race and diurnal blood pressure patterns: A review and meta-analysis. *Hypertension, 33*(5), 1099–1104.

Sabin, J. A., Nosek, B. A., Greenwald, A. G., & Rivara, F. P. (2009). Physicians' implicit and explicit attitudes about race by MD race, ethnicity, and gender. *Journal of Health Care for the Poor and Underserved, 20*(3), 896–913.

Sampson, R. J. (1987). Urban Black violence: The effect of male joblessness and family disruption. *American Journal of Sociology, 93*(2), 348–382.

Schoen, D. E. (2012). *Race in America.* Retrieved from http://www.thedailybeast.com/content/dam/daily-beast/2012/04/06/Newsweek_DailyBeast_Race_In_America_Survey.pdf

Schuman, H., Steeh, C., Bobo, L., & Krysan, M. (1997). *Racial attitudes in America: Trends and interpretations* (Rev. ed.). Cambridge, MA: Harvard University Press.

Shih, M., Pittinsky, T. L., & Ambady, N. (1999). Stereotype susceptibility: Identity salience and shifts in quantitative performance. *Psychological Science, 10*(1), 80–83.

Smedley, B. D., Stith, A. Y., & Nelson, A. R. (2003). *Unequal treatment: Confronting racial and ethnic disparities in health care.* Washington, DC: National Academy Press.

Smith, T. W., Marsden, P. V., & Hout, M. (2011). *General Social Survey, 1972–2010.* Retrieved from Inter-university Consortium for Political and Social Research http://www.icpsr.umich.edu/icpsrweb/ICPSR/studies/31521

Steele, C. M. (1997). A threat in the air: How stereotypes shape intellectual identity and performance. *American Psychologist, 52*(6), 613–629.

Sternthal, M. J., Slopen, N., & Williams, D. R. (2011). Racial disparities in health: How much does stress really matter? *Du Bois Review, 8*(1), 95–113.

Talaska, C., Fiske, S., & Chaiken, S. (2008). Legitimating racial discrimination: Emotions, not beliefs, best predict discrimination in a meta-analysis. *Social Justice Research, 21*(3), 263–296.

Tesler, M. (2012). The spillover of racialization into health care: How President Obama polarized public opinion by racial attitudes and race. *American Journal of Political Science, 56*(3), 690–704.

Tomfohr, L., Cooper, D. C., Mills, P. J., Nelesen, R. A., & Dimsdale, J. E. (2010). Everyday discrimination and nocturnal blood pressure dipping in Black and White Americans. *Psychosomatic Medicine, 72*(3), 266–272.

Travis, J., & Waul, M. (2003). Prisoners once removed: The children and families of prisoners. In J. Travis & M. Waul (Eds.), *Prisoners once removed: The impact of incarceration and reentry on children, families, and communities* (pp. 1–32). Washington, DC: Urban Institute Press.

Tull, E. S., Cort, M. A., Gwebu, E. T., & Gwebu, K. (2007). Internalized racism is associated with elevated fasting glucose in a sample of adult women but not men in Zimbabwe. *Ethnicity and Disease, 17*(4), 731–735.

van Ryn, M., Burgess, D. J., Dovidio, J. F., Phelan, S. M., Saha, S., Malat, J., & Perry, S. (2011). The impact of racism on clinician cognition, behavior, and clinical decision making. *Du Bois Review, 8*(1), 199–218.

Verhaeghen, P., Aikman, S. N., & Van Gulick, A. E. (2011). Prime and prejudice: Co-occurrence in the culture as a source of automatic stereotype priming. *British Journal of Social Psychology, 50*(3), 501–518.

Viswanath, K. (2006). Public communications and its role in reducing and eliminating health disparities. In G. E. Thomson, F. Mitchell, & M. B. Williams (Eds.), *Examining the health disparities research plan of the National Institutes of Health: Unfinished business* (pp. 215–253). Washington, DC: Institute of Medicine.

Wallace, D. (2011). Discriminatory mass de-housing and low-weight births: Scales of geography, time, and level. *Journal of Urban Health, 88*(3), 454–468.

Washington Post Company. (2009). Washington Post–ABC News poll: Race relations. Retrieved from http://www.washingtonpost.com/wp-srv/politics/polls/postpoll_042609.html

Weisbuch, M., Pauker, K., & Ambady, N. (2009). The subtle transmission of race bias via televised nonverbal behavior. *Science, 326*(5960), 1711–1714.

Weisburd, D., Bushway, S., Lum, C., & Yang, S.-M. (2004). Trajectories of crime at places: A longitudinal study of street segments in the City of Seattle. *Criminology, 42*(2), 283–321.

White, K., & Borrell, L. N. (2011). Racial/ethnic residential segregation: Framing the context of health risk and health disparities. *Health and Place, 17*(2), 438–448.

White, K., Haas, J. S., & Williams, D. R. (2012). Elucidating the role of place in health care disparities: The example of racial/ethnic residential segregation. *Health Services Research, 47*(3, Part 2), 1278–1299.

Williams, D. R. (1997). Race and health: Basic questions, emerging directions. *Annals of Epidemiology, 7*(5), 322–333.

Williams, D. R. (2004). Racism and health. In K. E. Whitfield (Ed.), *Closing the gap: Improving the health of minority elders in the new millennium* (pp. 69–80). Washington, DC: Gerontological Society of America.

Williams, D. R. (2012). Miles to go before we sleep: Racial inequities in health. *Journal of Health and Social Behavior, 53*(3), 279–295.

Williams, D. R., & Collins, C. (2001). Racial residential segregation: A fundamental cause of racial disparities in health. *Public Health Reports, 116*(5), 404–416.

Williams, D. R., Gonzalez, H. M., Williams, S., Mohammed, S. A., Moomal, H., & Stein, D. J. (2008). Perceived discrimination, race and health in South Africa: Findings from the South Africa Stress and Health Study. *Social Science and Medicine, 67*(3), 441–452.

Williams, D. R., Jackson, J. S., Brown, T. N., Torres, M., Forman, T. A., & Brown, K. (1999). Traditional and contemporary prejudice and urban Whites' support for affirmative action and government help. *Social Problems, 46*(4), 503–527.

Williams, D. R., & Mohammed, S. A. (2009). Discrimination and racial disparities in health: Evidence and needed research. *Journal of Behavioral Medicine, 32*(1), 20–47.

Williams, D. R., Yu, Y., Jackson, J., & Anderson, N. (1997). Racial differences in physical and mental health: Socioeconomic status, stress, and discrimination. *Journal of Health Psychology, 2*(3), 335–351.

Williams, N. (2006). Where are the men? The impact of incarceration and reentry of African-American men and their children and families. *Community Voices: Healthcare for the Underserved.* Retrieved from http://www.communityvoices.org/uploads/wherearethemen2_00l08_00144.pdf

Wilson, W. J. (1987). *The truly disadvantaged.* Chicago, IL: University of Chicago Press.

READING 7

Notes

1. Rakesh, Kochhar, Richard Fry and Paul Taylor, *Wealth Gaps Rise to Record Highs Between Whites, Blacks, Hispanics.* Pew Research Center, July 2011. Data are from the Survey on Income and Program Participation.

2. Figure 1 presents median wealth values for each year depicted in the graph. All dollar values are in 2009 dollars.

3. Figure 2 presents the major factors yielded through Oaxaca decomposition analyses. The dependent variable, change in wealth over the 25-year study period, was transformed into its natural logarithm due to its skewed distribution. As such, these analyses were conducted only for households with positive wealth gain over 25 years. The variables in the analysis include change of marital status from married to single and vice versa, number of children, age, college degree, retired, unemployment (duration), average income over 25 years, inheritances and monetary supports, change from renting to owning and vice versa, homeownership (duration), and baseline wealth in 1984.

4. Figure 3 summarizes findings for median regression analyses conducted separately for white and African-American households. Median regressions are the appropriate approach for highly skewed dependent variables, in this case change

in wealth over 25 years. The variables in the median regression models include change of marital status from married to single and vice versa, number of children, age, college degree, retired, unemployment (duration), average income over 25 years, inheritances and monetary supports, change from renting to owning and vice versa, and homeownership (duration).

5. These analyses could be only conducted for households with positive wealth due to the need to transform the dependent variable into its natural logarithm. In this sample, 87% of white and 70% of African-American households had positive wealth growth during the study period.

6. Shapiro, Thomas, *The Hidden Cost of Being African American,* Oxford University Press, 2004.

7. Joint Center for Housing Studies analysis of American Housing Survey, 2009, tabulations of 2009 AHS.

8. Joint Center for Housing Studies, State of the Nation's Housing 2012.

9. IASP tabulations of Survey on Income and Program Participation, SIPP 2008, Wave 7.

10. Rakesh, Kochhar, Richard Fry, and Paul Taylor, *Wealth Gaps Rise to Record Highs Between Whites, Blacks, Hispanics.* Pew Research Center, July 2011.

11. Gruenstein Bocian, Debbie, Peter Smith, and Wei Li, *Collateral Damage: The Spillover Costs of Foreclosures.* Center For Responsible Lending, October 24, 2012.

12. Gruenstein Bocian, Debbie, Peter Smith, and Wei Li, ibid.

13. White and African-American wealth holdings are measured as the change of their wealth portfolios over the 25-year study period, comparing baseline wealth to wealth in 2009. The median 25-year change in wealth for white families in this group is $211,400 and $18,942 for African-Americans.

14. In real terms this means comparing whites at the 50th percentile to African-Americans at the 76th percentile.

15. The Project on Student Debt, *Student Debt and the Class of 2011*, October 2012.

16. The Project on Student Debt, ibid.

17. Martha J. Bailey and Susan M. Dynarski, "Inequality in Postsecondary Education" in *Whither Opportunity?* Edited by Greg J. Duncan and Richard J. Murnane, 2011.

18. Kornrich, Sobino, and Frank Furstenberg, "Investing in Children: Changes in Parental Spending on Children, 1972 to 2007," *Demography* 2012 Sep. 18.

READING 8

References

Adams, R. 1969. "The Unorthodox Race Doctrine of Hawaii." Pp. 81–90 in *Comparative Perspectives on Race Relations*, edited by M. Tumin. Boston: Little, Brown.

Ballhatchet, K. 1980. *Race, Sex, and Class Under the Raj.* London: Camelot.

Bennett, L., Jr. 1962. *Before the Mayflower: A History of the Negro in America, 1619–1962.* Chicago: Johnson.

Berry, B. 1963. *Almost White.* New York: Macmillan.

——. 1965. *Race and Ethnic Relations*, 3rd ed. New York: Houghton Mifflin.

Bilbo, T. G. 1947. *Take Your Choice: Separation or Mongrelization.* Poplarville, MS: Dream House Publishing.

Blalock, H. M., Jr. 1967. *Toward a Theory of Minority-Group Relations.* New York: Capricorn Books.

Blaustein, A. P., and C. C. Ferguson, Jr. 1957. *Desegregation and the Law.* New Brunswick, NJ: Rutgers University Press.

Burma, J. G. 1946. "The Measurement of Passing." *American Journal of Sociology* 52: 18–22.

Cannon, P. 1956. *A Gentle Knight: My Husband, Walter White.* New York: Rinehart.

Catterall, H. T., ed. 1926–1937. *Judicial Cases Concerning American Slavery and the Negro.* Vols. 1–5. Washington, DC: Carnegie Institute.

Daniel, G. R. 1992. "Beyond Black and White: The New Multiracial Consciousness." Pp. 333–341 in *Racially Mixed People in America,* edited by M. P. P. Root. Newbury Park, CA: Sage.

——. 2000. *More Than Black: Multiracial Identity and the New Racial Order.* Philadelphia: Temple University Press.

Davis, F. J. 1991. *Who Is Black? One Nation's Definition.* University Park: Pennsylvania State University Press.

——. 1995. "The Hawaiian Alternative to the One-Drop Rule." Pp. 115–131 in *American Mixed Race: The Culture of Microdiversity,* edited by Naomi Zack. Lanham, MD: Rowman and Littlefield.

Day, D. 1979. *The Adoption of Black Children: Counteracting Institutional Discrimination.* Lexington, MA: Lexington Books.

Dominguez, V. R. 1986. *White by Definition: Social Classification in Creole Louisiana.* New Brunswick, NJ: Rutgers University Press.

Durkheim, É. 1960. *The Division of Labor in Society.* Translated by G. Simpson. New York: Free Press.

Eckard, E. W. 1947. "How Many Negroes Pass?" *American Journal of Sociology* 52: 498–503.

Fernandez, C. A. 1995. "Testimony of the Association of Multiethnic Americans Before the Subcommittee on Census, Statistics, and Postal Personnel of the U.S. House of Representatives." Pp. 191–210 in *American Mixed Race: The Culture of Microdiversity*, edited by Naomi Zack. Lanham, MD: Rowman and Littlefield.

Foster, E. 1998. "Jefferson Fathered Slave's Last Child." *Nature,* November 5, pp. 27–28.

Gist, N. P., and R. Dean. 1973. *Marginality and Identity.* Leiden: Brill.

Graham, S. R. 1995. "Grassroots Advocacy." Pp. 185–189 in *American Mixed Race: The Culture of Microdiversity,* edited by N. Zack. Lanham, MD: Rowman and Littlefield.

Grosz, G. 1989. "From Sea to Shining Sea: A Current Listing of Interracial Organizations and Support Groups Across the Nation." *Interrace* 1: 24–28.

Gwaltney, J. L. 1980. *Drylongso: A Self-Portrait of Black America.* New York: Vintage.

Haizlip, S. T. 1994. *The Sweeter the Juice: A Family Portrait in Black and White.* New York: Simon and Schuster.

Haley, A. 1976. *Roots: The Saga of an American Family.* Garden City, NY: Doubleday.

Haley, A., and D. Stevens. 1993. *Queen.* New York: Avon.

Harris, M. 1964. *Patterns of Race in the Americas.* New York: Walker.

Hoetink, H. 1967. *Caribbean Race Relations: A Study of Two Variants.* London: Oxford University Press.

Howard, A. 1980. "Hawaiians." Pp. 449–452 in *Harvard Encyclopedia of American Ethnic Groups,* edited by S. Thernstrom. Cambridge, MA: Harvard University Press.

Jorge, A. 1979. "The Black Puerto Rican Woman in Contemporary American Society." Pp. 134–141 in *The Puerto Rican Woman,* edited by Edna Acosta-Belen. New York: Praeger.

Ladner, J. A. 1977. *Mixed Families: Adopting Across Racial Boundaries.* Garden City, NY: Anchor/Doubleday.

Lew, J. 2000. "Guidance on Aggregation and Allocation of Data on Race for Use in Civil Rights Monitoring and Enforcement," OMB Bulletin No. 00-02. Washington, DC: Office of Management and Budget.

Myrdal, G., R. Sterner, and A. M. Rose. 1944. *An American Dilemma.* New York: Harper and Row.

Nakashima, C. L. 1992. "An Invisible Monster: The Creation and Denial of Mixed-Race People in America." Pp. 162–178 in *Racially Mixed People in America,* edited by M. P. P. Root. Newbury Park, CA: Sage.

Nicholls, D. 1981. "No Hawks or Pedlars: Levantines in the Caribbean." *Ethnic and Racial Studies* 4: 415–431.

Ottley, R. 1943. *New World A-Coming.* Cleveland: World Publishing.

Page, C. 1996. *Showing My Color.* New York: Harper and Collins.

Reed, T. E. 1969. "Caucasian Genes in American Negroes." *Science* 165: 762–768.

Rose, A. M. 1956. *The Negro in America.* Boston: Beacon Press.

Russell, K., M. Wilson, and R. Hall. 1992. *The Color Complex: The Politics of Skin Color Among African Americans.* Orlando, FL: Harcourt Brace.

Solaun, M., and S. Kronus. 1973. *Discrimination Without Violence.* New York: John Wiley.

Stoddard, E. R. 1973. *Mexican Americans.* New York: Random House.

Trillin, Calvin. 1986. "American Chronicles: Black or White." *New Yorker,* April 14, pp. 62–78.

Valverde, K-L. C. 1992. "From Dust to Gold: The Vietnamese Amerasian Experience." Pp. 144–161 in *Racially Mixed People in America,* edited by M. P. P. Root. Newbury Park, CA: Sage.

Van Den Berghe, P. L. 1971. "Racial Segregation in South Africa: Degrees and Kinds." Pp. 379 in *South Africa: Sociological Perspectives,* edited by H. Adam. New York: Oxford University Press.

Vander Zanden, J. W. 1972. *American Minority Relations,* 3rd ed. New York: Ronald.

Wagley, C., ed. 1963. *Race and Class in Rural Brazil,* 2nd ed. Paris: UNESCO.

Watson, G. 1970. *Passing for White: A Study of Racial Assimilation in a South African School.* London: Tavistock.

White, W. 1948. *A Man Called White: The Autobiography of Walter White.* New York: Viking.

Williams, G. H. 1995. *Life on the Color Line: The True Story of a White Boy Who Discovered He Was Black.* New York: Dutton.

Williams, T. K. 1996. "Race as Process: Reassessing the 'What Are You?' Encounters of Biracial Individuals." Pp. 191–210 in *The Multiracial Experience,* edited by M. P. P. Root. Newbury Park, CA: Sage.

Williamson, J. 1980. *New People: Miscegenation and Mulattoes in the United States.* New York: Free Press.

READING 9

Notes

1. U.S. Congress, *American Indian Policy Review Commission: Final Report,* vol. 1 (Washington, D.C.: Government Printing Office, 1977), 3.

2. See, e.g., Haunani-Kay Trask, *From a Native Daughter: Colonialism and Sovereignty in Hawai'i*

(Monroe, Maine: Common Courage, 1993) and Roger MacPherson Furrer, ed., *He Alo a He Alo (Face to Face): Hawaiian Voices on Sovereignty* (Honolulu, Hawai'i: American Friends Service Committee–Hawai'i, 1993).

3. 3528 U.S. 495 (2000).

4. http://www.doi.gov/nativehawaiians/.

5. See S. James Anaya, "The Native Hawaiian People and International Human Rights Law: Toward a Remedy for Past and Continuing Wrongs," *Georgia Law Review* 28 (1994), 309–64.

6. Vine Deloria Jr., "The American Indian Image in North America," *Encyclopedia of Indians of the Americas*, vol. 1 (St. Clair Shores, Mich.: Scholarly Press, 1974), 43.

7. Paula D. McClain and Joseph Stewart Jr., "Can We All Get Along?" *Racial and Ethnic Minorities in American Politics* (Boulder, Colo.: Westview, 1998), 6, citing John Higham, *Strangers in the Land: Patterns of American Nativism, 1860–1925* (Westport, Conn.: Greenwood, 1963).

8. 180 U.S. 261 (1901).

9. Felix S. Cohen, *Handbook of Federal Indian Law*, reprint ed. (Albuquerque: University of New Mexico Press, 1972), 268.

10. Jack Utter, *American Indians: Answers to Today's Questions* (Lake Ann, Mich.: National Woodlands, 1993), 30–31.

11. William Quinn Jr., "Federal Acknowledgment of American Indian Tribes? The Historical Development of a Legal Concept," *American Journal of Legal History* 34 (October 1990): 331–63.

12. 56 *Federal Register* 47, 325 (1991).

13. 25 Code of Federal Regulations 83.7 (a)–(g) (1991).

14. 25 *U.S.C.* chapter 1, section 1, 961.

15. 25 *U.S.C.* chapter 1, 962.

16. William W. Quinn Jr., "Federal Acknowledgment of American Indian Tribes: Authority, Judicial Interposition, and 25 C.F.R. Sec. 83," *American Indian Law Review* 17 (Fall 1992): 48.

17. Quinn, "Federal Acknowledgment of American Indian Tribes," 52.

18. Felix Cohen, "The Erosion of Indian Rights, 1950–1953: A Case Study in Bureaucracy," *Yale Law Journal* 62 (February 1953): 352.

19. Letter from Carol A. Bacon, acting director of the Office of Tribal Services, Bureau of Indian Affairs, 3 December 1991. The author has a copy of the letter.

20. 108 Stat., 709.

21. See U.S. Congress, House, "A Bill to Provide for Administrative Procedures to Extend Federal Recognition to Certain Indian Groups, and for Other Purposes," 105th Cong., 2d sess., 1998, H. Rept. 1154. As of this writing—May 1999—none of these bills has become law.

22. Ellen Barry, "Agency Willing to Relinquish Power to Recognize Tribes," *Boston Globe,* 26 May 2000, B1.

23. 118 U.S. 948 (1998).

24. See, e.g., Trask, *From a Native Daughter,* and Anaya, "The Native Hawaiian People," 309.

25. Allogan Slagle, "Unfinished Justice: Completing the Restoration and Acknowledgment of California Indian Tribes," *American Indian Journal* 13, no. 4 (Fall 1989): 325–45.

26. William W. Quinn Jr., "The Southeast Syndrome: Notes on Indian Descendant Recruitment Organizations and Their Perceptions of Native American Culture," *American Indian Quarterly* 14, no. 2 (Spring 1990): 147–54.

27. Jackie J. Kim, "The Indian Federal Recognition Procedures Act of 1995: A Congressional Solution to an Administrative Morass," *The Administrative Law Journal of the American University* 9, no. 3 (Fall 1995): 899–932.

28. See http://www.doi.gov/bia/bar/indexq.htm for statistical details of the acknowledgment project's efforts.

29. Donald Fixico, *Termination and Relocation: Federal Indian Policy, 1945–1960* (Albuquerque: University of New Mexico Press, 1986).

30. 67 Stat., B132.

31. 110 Stat., 130.

32. N.C. Public Laws, 1953, chapter 874, p. 747.

33. 70 Stat., 254.

34. David E. Wilkins, "Breaking into the Intergovernmental Matrix: The Lumbee Tribe's Efforts to Secure Federal Acknowledgment," *Publius: The Journal of Federalism* 23 (Fall 1993): 123–42.

35. McClain and Stewart, *"Can We All Get Along?"* 6.

36. Bart Vogel, "Who Is an Indian in Federal Indian Law?" in *Studies in American Indian Law,* ed. Ralph Johnson (Pullman: Washington State University, 1970), 53.

37. C. Matthew Snipp, *American Indians: The First of This Land* (New York: Russell Sage Foundation, 1989), 34.

38. Snipp, First of This Land, 33.

39. Cohen, *Handbook,* 2.

40. Snipp, *First of This Land*, 33.

41. 29 Stat., 321.

42. Abdul G. Kahn, *Report on the Indian Definition Study* (Washington, D.C.: Department of Education, 1980).

43. Kahn, Indian Definition Study, 56.

44. Joane Nagel, *American Indian Ethnic Renewal: Red Power and the Resurgence of Identity and Culture* (New York: Oxford University Press, 1996), 243.

45. Brian Stackes, "Planned Bureau of Indian Affairs Regulations Stir Concerns Among Tribal Leaders," *Indian Country Today,* 18 August 2000, 1.

46. Russell Thornton, "Tribal Membership Requirements and the Demography of 'Old' and 'New' Native Americans," in *Changing Numbers, Changing Needs: American Indian Demography and Public Health,* ed. Gary D. Sandefur, Ronald R. Rindfuss, and Barney Cohen (Washington, D.C.: National Academy Press, 1996), 110–11.

47. See, e.g., Francis Paul Prucha, American Indian Treaties: *The History of a Political Anomaly* (Berkeley, Calif.: University of California Press, 1994) and Robert A. Williams Jr., *Linking Arms Together: American Indian Treaty Visions of Law and Peace, 1600–1800* (New York: Oxford University Press, 1997).

48. 16 Stat., 566.

49. 7 Stat., 391.

50. 7 Stat., 391.

51. Cesare Marino, "Reservations," in *Native America in the Twentieth Century: An Encyclopedia,* ed. Mary B. Davis (New York: Garland Publishing, Inc., 1996), 54–56.

52. Vine Deloria Jr. and Clifford M. Lytle, *American Indians, American Justice* (Austin: University of Texas Press, 1983), 58.

53. Deloria and Lytle, *American Indians,* 58.

54. John H. Moore, "The Enduring Reservations of Oklahoma," in *State & Reservation: New Perspectives on Federal Indian Policy,* ed. George Pierre Castile and Robert L. Bee (Tucson: University of Arizona Press, 1992), 92–109.

55. See Robert F. Heizer, *The Destruction of California Indians* (Lincoln: University of Nebraska Press, 1993) for a first-rate account of what these nations experienced from 1847 to 1865.

56. Title 18, *U.S. Code,* section 1151.

57. Council of Economic Advisers, *Changing America: Indicators of Social and Economic Well-Being by Race and Hispanic Origin* (Washington, D.C.: Government Printing Office, 1998), 4.

58. www.census.gov/prod/2001pubs.

59. Russell Thornton, *American Indian Holocaust and Survival: A Population History Since 1492* (Norman: University of Oklahoma Press, 1987).

60. www. census. gov /prod/ 2001 pubs.

61. Russell Thornton, "What the Census Doesn't Count," *New York Times,* 23 March 2001, A21.

62. C. Matthew Snipp, "The Size and Distribution of the American Indian Population: Fertility, Mortality, Migration, and Residence," in *Changing Numbers, Changing Needs: American Indian Demography and Public Health,* ed. Gary D. Sandefur, Ronald

R. Rindfuss, and Barney Cohen (Washington, D.C.: National Academy Press, 1996), 42–43.

63. Snipp, "The Size and Distribution," 39.

64. Snipp, *The First of This Land*, 171.

65. Snipp, *The First of This Land*, 165.

66. Lawrence H. Fuchs, *The American Kaleidoscope* (Hanover, N.H.: Wesleyan University Press, 1990), 329.

READING 10

Literature Cited

Ajrouch KJ, Jamal A. 2007. Assimilating to a white identity: the case of Arab Americans. *Int. Migr. Rev.* 41:860–79

Alba RD, Nee V. 2003. *Remaking the American Mainstream: Assimilation and Contemporary Immigration.* Cambridge, MA: Harvard Univ. Press

Albizu JA. 2007. Geolinguistic regions and diasporas in the age of satellite television. *Int. Commun. Gaz.* 69:239–61

Anderson B. 1991. *Imagined Communities: Reflections on the Origin and Spread of Nationalism.* London: Verso

Barth F. 1969. Introduction. In *Ethnic Groups and Boundaries: The Social Organization of Cultural Difference,* ed. F Barth, pp. 9–38. London: Allen & Unwin

Blau PM. 1977. *Inequality and Heterogeneity.* New York: Free Press

Bonacich E. 1973. A theory of middleman minorities. *Am. Sociol. Rev.* 37:583–94

Bruter M. 2003a. On what citizens mean by feeling 'European': perceptions of news, symbols and borderlessness. *F. Ethn. Migr. Stud.* 30:21–39

Bruter M. 2003b. Winning hearts and minds for Europe: the impact of news and symbols on civic and cultural European identity. *Camp. Polit. Stud.* 36:1148–79

Bruter M. 2005. *Citizens of Europe? The Emergence of a Mass European Identity.* London: Palgrave Macmillan

Burgess EM. 1981. Ethnic scale and intensity: the Zimbabwean experience. *Soc. Forces* 59:601–26

Calderon J. 1992. "Hispanic" and "Latino": the viability of categories for panethnic unity. *Lat. Am. Perspect.* 75:37–44

Chai S. 2005. Predicting ethnic boundaries. *Eur. Sociol. Rev.* 21:375–91

Chandra K. 2007. *Why Ethnic Parties Succeed: Patronage and Ethnic Head Counts in India.* New York: Cambridge Univ. Press

Cornell S. 1988. *The Return of the Native: American Indian Political Resurgence.* New York: Oxford Univ. Press

Cornell S. 1990. Land, labour and group formation: blacks and Indians in the United States. *Ethn. Racial Stud.* 13:368–88

Cornell S. 1996. The variable ties that bind: content and circumstance in ethnic processes. *Ethn. Racial Stud.* 19:265–89

Cornell S, Hartmann D. 2007. *Ethnicity and Race: Making Identities in a Changing World.* Newbury Park, CA: Pine Forge

Croucher S. 1997. *Imagining Miami: Ethnic Politics in a Postmodern World.* Charlottesville: Univ. Va. Press

Csepeli G, Simon D. 2004. Construction of Roma identity in Eastern and Central Europe: perception and self-identification. *J. Ethn. Migr. Stud.* 30:129–50

Dávila A. 2012. *Latinos, Inc.: The Marketing and Making of a People.* Berkeley: Univ. Calif. Press

De Genova N, Ramos-Zayas AY. 2003. *Latino Crossings: Mexicans, Puerto Ricans, and the Politics of Race and Citizenship.* New York: Routledge

De La Garza RO. 1992. From rhetoric to reality: Latinos and the 1988 election in review. In *From Rhetoric to Reality: Latino Politics in the 1988 Elections,* ed. RO De La Garza, L DeSipio, pp. 171–81. Boulder, CO: Westview

Dhingra P. 2007. *Managing Multicultural Lives: Asian American Professionals and the Challenge of Multiple Identities.* Stanford, CA: Stanford Univ. Press

Elbow G. 1997. Regional cooperation in the Caribbean: the Association of Caribbean States. *J. Geogr.* 96:13–22

Eriksen TH. 2002. *Ethnicity and Nationalism: Anthropological Perspectives.* London: Pluto

Espiritu YL. 1992. *Asian American Panethnicity: Bridging Institutions and Identities.* Philadelphia: Temple Univ. Press

Espiritu YL, Ong PM. 1994. Class constraints on racial solidarity among Asian Americans. In *The New Asian*

Immigration in Los Angeles and Global Restructuring, ed. PM Ong, E Bonacich, L Cheng, pp. 295–321. Philadelphia: Temple Univ. Press

Fligstein N. 2009. *Euroclash: The EU, European Identity, and the Future of Europe.* New York: Oxford Univ. Press

Fournier A. 2002. Mapping identities: Russian resistance to linguistic Ukrainisation in central and eastern Ukraine. *Eur.-Asia Stud.* 54:415–33

Fraga L, Garcia JA, Hero RE, Jones-Correa M, Martinez-Ebbers V, Segura G. 2009. *Latino Lives in America: Making It Home.* Philadelphia: Temple Univ. Press

Fraga L, Garcia JA, Hero RE, Jones-Correa M, Martinez-Ebbers V, Segura G. 2012. *Latinos in the New Millennium: An Almanac of Opinion, Behavior, and Policy Preferences.* New York: Cambridge Univ. Press

Gause FG III. 2011. Why Middle East Studies missed the Arab spring: the myth of authoritarian stability. *Foreign Aff.* 90:81–90

Gellner E. 2009. *Nations and Nationalism.* Ithaca, NY: Cornell Univ. Press

Georgiu M. 2012. Watching soap opera in the diaspora: cultural proximity or critical proximity? *Ethn. Racial Stud.* 35:868–87

Golash-Boza T, Darity W Jr. 2008. Latino racial choices: the effects of skin colour and discrimination on Latinos' and Latinas' racial self-identifications. *Ethn. Racial Stud.* 31:899–934

Haddad YH. 2004. *Not Quite American? The Shaping of Arab and Muslim Identity in the United States (A Charles Edmonson Historical Lecture).* Baylor, TX: Baylor Univ. Press

Hannan MT. 1979. The dynamics of ethnic boundaries in modern states. In *National Development and the World System,* ed. J Meyer, MT Hannan, pp. 253–75. Chicago: Univ. Chicago Press

Hanson JR. 1997. Ethnicity and the looking glass: the dialectics of national Indian identity. *Am. Indian Q.* 21:195–208

Harb Z, Bessaiso E. 2006. British Arab Muslim audiences and television after September 11. *J. Ethn. Migr. Stud.* 32:1063–76

Hechter M. 2000. *Containing Nationalism.* Oxford: Oxford Univ. Press

Hechter M, Levy M. 1994. Ethno-regional movements in the West. In *Nationalism,* ed. J Hutchinson, AD Smith, pp. 184–95. New York: Oxford Univ. Press

Hein J. 2006. *Ethnic Origins: The Adaptation of Cambodian and Hmong Refugees in Four American Cities.* New York: Russell Sage Found.

Hewstone M. 1996. Contact and categorization: social-psychological interventions to change intergroup relations. In *Foundations of Stereotypes and Stereotyping,* ed. CN Macrae, C Stagnor, M Hewstone, pp. 323–68. New York: Guilford

Hill M, Fee LK. 1995. *The Politics of Nation Building and Citizenship in Singapore.* New York: Routledge

Horowitz DL. 1985. *Ethnic Groups in Conflict.* Berkeley: Univ. Calif. Press

Itzigsohn J. 2004. The formation of Latino and Latina panethnic identities. In *Not Just Black and White: Historical and Contemporary Perspectives on Immigration, Race, and Ethnicity in the United States,* ed. N Foner, GM Fredrickson, pp. 197–216. New York: Russell Sage Found.

Itzigsohn J, Dore-Cabral C. 2000. Competing identities: race, ethnicity and panethnicity among Dominicans in the United States. *Social. Forum* 15:225–47

Itzigsohn J, Dore-Cabral C. 2001. The manifold character of panethnicity: Latino identities and practices among Dominicans in New York City. See Laó-Montes & Dávila 2001, pp. 1–54

Jamal A. 2005. The political participation and engagement of Muslim Americans: mosque involvement and group consciousness. *Am. Polit. Res.* 33:521–44

Jenkins R. 1994. Rethinking ethnicity: identity, categorization and power. *Ethn. Racial Stud.* 17:197–223

Jenkins R. 2008. *Rethinking Ethnicity: Arguments and Explorations.* London: Sage

Jones-Correa M, Leal DL. 1996. Becoming "Hispanic": secondary panethnic identification among Latin American-origin populations in the United States. *Hisp. J. Behav. Sci.* 18:214–54

Kao G, Joyner K. 2006. Do Hispanic and Asian adolescents practice panethnicity in friendship choices? *Soc. Sci. Q.* 87:972–92

Keyes CF. 1981. *Ethnic Change.* Seattle: Univ. Wash. Press

Kibria N. 2003. *Becoming Asian American: Second-Generation Chinese and Korean American Identities.* Baltimore, MD: Johns Hopkins Univ. Press

Kim AH, White MJ. 2010. Panethnicity, ethnic diversity, and residential segregation. *Am. J. Sociol.* 115:1558–96

Ladányi J, Szelényi I. 2006. *Patterns of Exclusion: Constructing Gypsy Ethnicity and the Making of an Underclass in Transitional Societies of Europe.* New York: Columbia Univ. Press

Laitin DD. 1986. *Hegemony and Culture: Politics and Change Among the Yoruba.* Chicago: Univ. Chicago Press

Laó-Montes A, Dávila AM, eds. 2001. *Mambo Montage: The Latinization of New York.* New York: Columbia Univ. Press

Lee S. 2004. Marriage dilemmas: partner choices and constraints for Korean Americans in New York City. In *Asian American Youth: Culture, Identity and Ethnicity,* ed. J Lee, M. Zhou, pp. 285–98. New York: Routledge

Lien P, Conway MM, Wong J. 2003. The contours and sources of ethnic identity choices among Asian Americans. *Soc. Sci. Q.* 84:461–81

Liu M, Geron K, Lai T. 2008. *The Snake Dance of Asian American Activism: Community, Vision, and Power in the Struggle for Social Justice, 1945–2000.* Lanham, MD: Lexington Books

Lopez D, Espiritu YL. 1990. Panethnicity in the United States: a theoretical framework. *Ethn. Racial Stud.* 13:198–224

Louie V. 2012. *Keeping the Immigrant Bargain: The Costs and Rewards of Success in America.* New York: Russell Sage Found.

Maeda DJ. 2009. *Chains of Babylon: The Rise of Asian America.* Minneapolis: Univ. Minn. Press

Martinez E. 1990. *500 Años Del Pueblo Chicano: 500 Years of Chicano History.* Albuquerque, NM: Southwest Community Resour.

Massey D, Sanchez M. 2010. *Brokered Boundaries: Creating Immigrant Identity in Anti-Immigrant Times.* New York: Russell Sage Found.

Masuoka N. 2006. Together they become one: examining the predictors of panethnic group consciousness among Asian Americans and Latinos. *Soc. Sci. Q.* 87:993–1011

Mellor N, Ayish M, Dajani N, Rinnawi K. 2011. *Arab Media.* Cambridge, UK: Polity

Mettam CW, Williams SW. 1998. Internal colonialism and cultural divisions of labour in the Soviet Republic of Estonia. *Nations Natl.* 4:363–88

Min PG. 2006. *Asian Americans: Contemporary Trends and Issues.* Thousand Oaks, CA: Sage

Mora GC. 2014a. Cross-field effects and ethnic classification: the institutionalization of Hispanic panethnicity. *Am. Sociol. Rev.* 79:183–210

Mora GC. 2014b. *Making Hispanics: How Activists, Bureaucrats, and Media Constructed a New American.* Chicago: Univ. Chicago Press

Nagata JA. 1979. *Malaysian Mosaic: Perspectives from a Poly-ethnic Society.* Vancouver, Can.: Univ. B.C. Press

Nagata JA. 1981. In defense of ethnic boundaries: the changing myths and charters of Malay identity. See Keyes 1981, pp. 87–118

Nagel CR. 2002. Constructing difference and sameness: the politics of assimilation in London's Arab communities. *Ethn. Racial Stud.* 25:258–87

Nagel J. 1986. The political construction of ethnicity. In *Competitive Ethnic Relations,* ed. S Olzak, J Nagel, pp. 93–112. Waltham, MA: Academic

Nagel J. 1995. American Indian ethnic renewal: politics and the resurgence of identity. *Am. Sociol. Rev.* 60:947–65

Naldi G. 1999. *The Organization of African Unity: An Analysis of Its Role.* New York: Bloomsbury

Nnoli O. 1978. *Ethnic Politics in Nigeria.* Enugu: Fourth Dimension

Nobles M. 2000. *Shades of Citizenship: Race and the Census in Modern Politics.* Stanford, CA: Stanford Univ. Press

Oboler S. 1995. *Ethnic Labels, Latino Lives: Identity and the Politics of (Re)Presentation in the United States.* Minneapolis: Univ. Minn. Press

Okamoto DG. 2003. Toward a theory of panethnicity: explaining Asian American collective action. *Am. Social. Rev.* 68:811–42

Okamoto DG. 2006. Institutional panethnicity: boundary formation in Asian-American organizing. *Soc. Forces* 85:1–25

Okamoto DG. 2007. Marrying out: a boundary approach to understanding the marital integration of Asian Americans. *Soc. Sci. Rev.* 36:1391–414

Okamoto DG. 2010. Organizing across ethnic boundaries in the post-civil rights era: Asian American panethnic coalitions. In *Strategic Alliances: Coalition Building and Social Movements,* ed. N Van Dyke, HJ McCammon, pp. 143–69. Minneapolis: Minn. Univ. Press

Okamoto DG. 2014. *Redefining Race: Asian American Panethnicity and Shifting Ethnic Boundaries.* New York: Russell Sage Found. In press

Okamoto DG, Gast MJ. 2013. Racial inclusion or accommodation? Expanding community boundaries among Asian American organizations. *Du Bois Rev.* 10:131–53

Olzak S. 1992. *The Dynamics of Ethnic Competition and Conflict.* Stanford, CA: Stanford Univ. Press

Olzak S. 2004. Ethnic and nationalist movements. In *The Blackwell Companion to Social Movements,* ed. D Snow, S Soule, H Kriesi, pp. 666–93. Malden, MA: Blackwell

Omi M, Winant H. 1994. *Racial Formation in the United States: From the 1960s to the 1990s.* New York: Routledge

Oropesa RS, Landale NS, Greif MJ. 2008. From Puerto Rican to pan-ethnic in New York City. *Ethn. Racial Stud.* 31:1315–39

Otis EM. 2001. The reach and limits of Asian panethnic identity: the dynamics of gender, race, and class in a community-based organization. *Qual. Sociol.* 24:349–79

Padilla FM. 1985. *Latino Ethnic Consciousness: The Case of Mexican Americans and Puerto Ricans in Chicago.* Notre Dame, IN: Univ. Notre Dame Press

Padilla FM. 1986. Latino ethnicity in the city of Chicago. In *Competitive Ethnic Relations,* ed. S Olzak, J Nagel, pp. 153–71. Orlando, FL: Academic

Pallares A. 2002. *From Peasant Struggles to Indian Resistance: The Ecuadorian Andes in the Late Twentieth Century.* Norman: Univ. Okla. Press

Park JZ. 2008. Second-generation Asian American pan-ethnic identity: pluralized meanings of a racial label. *Sociol. Perspect.* 51:541–61

Peled Y. 1998. Towards a redefinition of Jewish nationalism in Israel? The enigma of Shas. *Ethn. Racial Stud.* 21:703–27

Pettigrew TF, Tropp LR. 2011. *When Groups Meet: The Dynamics of Intergroup Contact.* New York: Psychology

Pew Res. Cent. 2007. *Muslim Americans: middle class and mostly mainstream.* Rep. Pew Res. Cent., May 22, Washington, DC. http://www.pewresearch.org/files/old-assets/pdf/muslim-americans.pdf

Portes A, MacLeod D. 1996. What shall I call myself? Hispanic identity formation in the second generation. *Ethn. Racial Stud.* 19:523–47

Portes A, Rumbaut RG. 2001. *Legacies: The Story of the Immigrant Second Generation.* Berkeley: Univ. Calif. Press

Portes A, Zhou M. 1993. The new second generation: segmented assimilation and its variants. *Ann. Am. Acad. Polit. Soc. Sci.* 530:74–96

Posner DN. 2004. The political salience of cultural difference: Why Chewas and Tumbukas are allies in Zambia and adversaries in Malawi. *Am. Polit. Sci. Rev.* 98:529–45

Prieto-Flores Ò, Sordé-Martí. 2011. The institutionalization of panethnicity from the grassroots standpoint in a European context: the case of Gitanos and Roma immigrants in Barcelona. *Ethnicities* 11:202–17

Qian Z, Blair SL, Ruf SD. 2001. Asian American interracial and interethnic marriages: differences by education and nativity. *Int. Migr. Rev.* 35:557–86

Read JG. 2008. Discrimination and identity formation in a post-9/11 era: a comparison of Muslim and Christian Arab Americans. In *Race and Arab Americans Before and After 9/11: From Invisible Citizens to Visible Subjects,* ed. A Jamal, NC Naber, pp. 305–17. Syracuse, NY: Syracuse Univ. Press

Reitz JG, Ashton MA. 1980. Ukrainian language and identity retention in urban Canada. *Can. Ethn. Stud.* 12:233–77

Ricourt M, Danta R. 2003. *Hispanas de Queens: Panethnicity in a New York City Neighborhood.* Ithaca, NY: Cornell Univ. Press

Rinnawi K. 2012. 'Instant nationalism' and the 'cyber Mufti': the Arab diaspora in Europe and the transnational media. *J. Ethn. Migr. Stud.* 38:1451–67

Rodriguez A. 1999. *Making Latino News: Race, Clan, and Language.* Thousand Oaks, CA: Sage

Rodríguez C. 2000. *Changing Race: Latinos, the Census, and the History of Ethnicity.* New York: NYU Press

Rodríguez JA. 1998. Becoming Latinos: Mexican Americans, Chicanos, and the Spanish myth in the urban southwest. *Western Hist. Q.* 29:165–85

Rosales FA. 2000. *Testimonio: A Documentary History of the Mexican American Struggle for Civil Rights.* Houston, TX: Arte Publico

Rosenfeld MJ. 2001. The salience of pan-national Hispanic and Asian identities in U.S. marriage markets. *Demography* 38:161–75

Roth WD. 2012. *Race Migrations: Latinos and the Cultural Transformation of Race.* Stanford, CA: Stanford Univ. Press

Sanders JM. 2002. Ethnic boundaries and identity in plural societies. *Annu. Rev. Sociol.* 28:327–57

Sandholtz W, Stone Sweet A. 1998. *European Integration and Supranational Governance.* Oxford: Oxford Univ. Press

Shankar LD, Srikanth R. 1998. *A Part, Yet Apart: South Asians in Asian America.* Philadelphia: Temple Univ. Press

Shiao JL. 1998. The nature of the nonprofit sector: professionalism versus identity politics in private policy definitions of Asian Pacific Americans. *Asian Am. Policy Rev.* 8:17–43

Shore C. 2000. *Building Europe: The Cultural Politics of European Integration.* New York: Routledge

Sinclair J. 1998. *Latin American Television: A Global View.* Oxford: Oxford Univ. Press

Sirin S, Bikmen N, Mir M, Fine M, Zaal M, Katsiaficas D. 2008. Exploring dual identification among Muslim-American emerging adults: a mixed methods study. *J. Adolesc.* 31:259–79

Smith AD. 1992. National identity and the idea of European unity. *Int. Aff.* 68:55–76

Smith AD. 2010. *Nationalism.* New York: Polity

Sommers LK. 1991. Inventing Latinismo: the creation of "Hispanic" panethnicity in the United States. *J. Am. Folklore* 104:32–53

Tefft SK. 1999. Perspectives on panethnogenesis: the case of the Montagnards. *Sociol. Spectr.* 19:387–400

Tienda M, Ortiz V. 1986. Hispanicity and the 1980 Census. *Soc. Sci. Q.* 67:3–20

Trottier RW. 1981. Charters of panethnic identity: indigenous American Indians and immigrant Asian Americans. See Keyes 1981, pp. 272–305

Tuan M. 1998. *Forever Foreigners or Honorary Whites? The Asian Ethnic Experience Today.* New Brunswick, NJ: Rutgers Univ. Press

Vargas Ramos C. 2011. Caribbeans in New York: political participation, strategic cooperation and the prospect for pan-ethnic political mobilization in the diaspora. *Caribbean Stud.* 39:65–103

Verkuyten M, Yildiz AA. 2007. National (dis)identification and ethnic and religious identity: a study among Turkish-Dutch Muslims. *Perspect. Soc. Psychol. Bull.* 33:1448–62

Vo LT. 2004. *Mobilizing an Asian American Community.* Philadelphia: Temple Univ. Press

Waldinger R. 2000. *Still the Promised City? African Americans and New Immigrants in Postindustrial New York.* Cambridge, MA: Harvard Univ. Press

Waters MC. 1994. Ethnic and racial identities of second generation black immigrants in New York City. *Int. Migr. Rev.* 28:795–820

Waters MC. 1999. *Black Identities: West Indian Immigrant Dreams and American Realities.* Cambridge, MA: Harvard Univ. Press

Wei W. 1993. *The Asian American Movement.* Philadelphia: Temple Univ. Press

Wimmer A. 2008. The making and unmaking of ethnic boundaries: a multilevel process theory. *Am. J. Sociol.* 113:970–1022

Winant H. 2000. Race and race theory. *Annu. Rev. Sociol.* 26:169–85

Wong J, Ramakrishnan SK, Lee T, Junn J. 2011. *Asian American Political Participation: Emerging Constituents and Their Political Identities.* New York: Russell Sage Found.

Yancey WL, Ericksen EP, Juliani RN. 1976. Emergent ethnicity: a review and reformulation. *Am. Sociol. Rev.* 41:391–403

Young C. 1976. *The Politics of Cultural Pluralism.* Madison: Univ. Wis. Press

Zia H. 2000. *Asian American Dreams: The Emergence of an American People.* New York: Farrar, Straus, & Giroux

READING 11

Notes

1. See *Racialization: Studies in Theory and Practice* by Karim Murji and John Solomos for an overview of the concept and how it is being employed. Aside from a few American contributors, the discussion appears to be taking place within European race scholarship.

2. Although they define it in their first edition of *Racial Formation in the United States,* the term does not appear in the revised 1994 version of the book.

References

Ahmed, Leila. 1992. *Women and Gender in Islam.* New Haven: Yale University Press.

Alsultany, Evelyn Azeeza. 2012. *Arabs and Muslims in the Media: Race and Representations after 9/11.* New York: New York University Press.

Amer, Mona and Joseph Hovey. 2007. "Sociodemographic Differences in Acculturation and Mental Health for a Sample of Second Generation & Early Immigrant Arab Americans." *Journal of Immigrant and Minority Health* 9:335–347.

Aranda, Elizabeth, and Guillermo Rebollo-Gil. 2004. "Ethnoracism and the 'Sandwiched' Minorities." *American Behavioral Scientist* 47(7): 910–927.

Banton, Michael. 1977. *The Idea of Race.* London: Tavistock.

Barot, Rohit and John Bird 2001. "Racialization: The Genealogy and Critique of a Concept." *Ethnic and Racial Studies* 21(4): 601-18.

Bayoumi, Moustafa. 2006. "Racing Religion." *The Centennial Review* 6(2): 267–293.

Bonilla-Silva, Eduardo. 2001. *White Supremacy & Racism in the Post-Civil Rights Era.* Boulder: Lynne Rienner.

Bonilla-Silva, Eduardo. 2004. "From Bi-racial to Tri-racial: Towards a New System of Racial Stratification in the USA." *Ethnic and Racial Studies* 27:931–950.

Bonilla-Silva, Eduardo. 2010. *Racism Without Racists: Color-Blind Racism and the Persistence of Racial Inequality in the United States.* Third Edition. Lanham, MD: Rowman & Littlefield Publishers, Inc.

Brodkin, Karen. 1998. *How Jews Became White Folks: And What That Says About Race in America.* New Brunswick, NJ: Rutgers University Press.

Cainkar, Louise A. 2008. "Thinking Outside the Box: Arabs and Race in the United States." Pp. 46–80 in *Race and Arab Americans Before and After 9/11: From Invisible Citizens to Visible Subjects,* edited by Amaney Jamal and Nadine Naber. Syracuse, NY: Syracuse University Press.

Cainkar, Louise A. 2009. *Homeland Insecurity: The Arab American and Muslim American Experience After 9/11.* New York City, NY: Russell Sage Foundation Publications.

Calvert, John C. M. 2007. "The Striving Shaykh: Abdullah Azzam and the Revival of Jihad." *Journal of Religion & Society* 2:83–102.

Cohen, Robin. 1994. *Frontiers of Identity: The British and the Others.* Harlow: Longman.

Cole, David. 2003. *Enemy Aliens.* New York City, NY: The New Press.

Du Bois, W.E.B. 1989. *The Souls of Black Folk.* New York: Bantam Books.

Fanon, Franz. 2004. *Wretched of the Earth.* Reprinted version. New York: Grove Press.

Frazier, Franklin. 1968a. "Sociological Theory and Race Relations." Pp. 30–42 in *E. Franklin Frazier on Race Relations,* edited by Franklin Edwards. Chicago: The University of Chicago Press.

Frazier, Franklin. 1968b. "Race Contacts and Social Structure." Pp. 43–61 in *E. Franklin Frazier on Race Relations,* edited by Franklin Edwards. Chicago: The University of Chicago Press.

Garner, Steve. 2009. "Ireland: From Racism without "Race" to Racism without Racists," *Radical History Review* 104:41–56.

Goldberg, David Theo. 2005. "Racial Americanization." Pp. 87–102 in *Racialization: Studies in Theory and Practice,* edited by Karim Murji and John Solomos. Oxford: Oxford University Press.

Goldschmidt, Henry. 2004. "Introduction: Race, Nation, and Religion." Pp. 3–34 in *Race, Nation, and Religion in the Americas,* edited by Henry Goldschmidt and Elizabeth McAlister. New York City, NY: Oxford University Press.

Gottschalk, Peter, and Gabriel Greenberg. 2007. *Islamophobia: Making Muslims the Enemy.* New York City, NY: Rowman & Littlefield Publishers, Inc.

Grosfoguel, Ramon, and Eric Mielants. 2006. "The Long-Duree Entanglement Between Islamophobia and Racism in the Modern/Colonial Capitalist/ Patriarchal World-System: An Introduction." *Human Architecture: Journal of the Sociology of Self-Knowledge* 5:1–12.

Halliday, Fred. 1999. "Islamophobia Reconsidered." *Ethnic and Racial Studies* 22(5): 892–902.

Ignatiev, Noel. 1996. *How the Irish Became White.* New York City, NY: Routledge.

Islamophobia: A Challenge for Us All. 1997. The Runnymede Trust.

Jamal, Amaney. 2008. "Conclusion: Arab American Racialization." Pp. 318–326 in *Race and Arab Americans Before and After 9/11: From Invisible Citizens to Visible Subjects,* edited by Amaney Jamal and Nadine Naber. Syracuse, NY: Syracuse University Press.

Kalmar, Ivan. 2009. "Anti-Semitism and Islamophobia: The Formation of a Secret." *Human Architecture: Journal of the Sociology of Self-Knowledge* 7:135–144.

Kibria, Nazli. 2011. *Muslims in Motion: Islam and National Identity in the Bangladeshi Diaspora.* New Jersey: Rutgers University Press.

Kushner, Tony. 2005. "Racialization and 'White European' Immigration." Pp. 207–226 in *Racialization: Studies in Theory and Practice,* edited by Karim Murji and John Solomos. Oxford: Oxford University Press.

Maira, Sunaina Marr. 2009. *Missing: Youth, Citizenship, and Empire after 9/11.* Durham, NC: Duke University Press Books.

Mandel, Daniel. 2001. "Muslims on the Silver Screen." *Middle East Quarterly* 8:19–30.

Meer, Nasar and Tariq Modood. 2010. "The Racialization of Muslims." Pp. 69–84 in *Thinking through Islamophobia: Global Perspectives,* edited by S. Sayid and Abdool Karim Vakil. New York: Columbia University Press.

Miles, Robert. 1993. *Racisms After 'Race Relations'.* London: Routledge.

Modood, Tariq. 2005. *Multicultural Politics: Racism, Ethnicity and Muslims in Britain.* Minneapolis: University of Minnesota Press.

Murji, Karim and John Solomos. 2005. "Introduction: Racialization in Theory and Practice." Pp. 1–28 in *Racialization: Studies in Theory and Practice,* edited by Karim Murji and John Solomos. Oxford: Oxford University Press.

Naber, Nadine. 2008. "Introduction." Pp. 1–45 in *Race and Arab Americans Before and After 9/11: From Invisible Citizens to Visible Subjects,* edited by Amaney Jamal and Nadine Naber. Syracuse, NY: Syracuse University Press.

Omi, Michael and Howard Winant. 1986. *Racial Formation in the United States: From the 1960s to the 1980s.* New York City, NY: Routledge.

Omi, Michael and Howard Winant. 1994. *Racial Formation in the United States: From the 1960s to the 1990s.* 2nd ed. New York City, NY: Routledge.

Park, Robert. 1950. *Race and Culture.* Glencoe: Free Press.

Peek, Lori Anne. 2011. *Behind the Backlash: Muslim Americans After 9/11.* Philadelphia: Temple University Press.

Pew Research Center for the People and the Press. Muslims Widely Seen As Facing Discrimination: Views of Religious Similarities and Differences, September 9, 2009, http://www.people-press.org/2009/09/09/muslims-widely-seenas-facing-discrimination/ accessed on January 4, 2013.

Rana, Junaid. 2007. "The Story of Islamophobia." *Souls* 9:148–161.

Rana, Junaid. 2011. *Terrifying Muslims: Race and Labor in the South Asian Diaspora.* Durham, NC: Duke University Press Books.

Razack, Sherene. 2008. *Casting out: The Eviction of Muslims from Western Law and Politics.* Toronto, ON: University of Toronto Press.

Shaheen, Jack G. 2008. *Guilty: Hollywood's Verdict on Arabs After 9/11.* New York City, NY: Olive Branch Press.

Shyrock, Andrew. 2008. "The Moral Analogies of Race: Arab American Identity, Color Politics, and the Limits of Racialized Citizenship." Pp. 81–113 in *Race and Arab Americans Before and After 9/11: From Invisible Citizens to Visible Subjects,* edited by Amaney Jamal and Nadine Naber. Syracuse, NY: Syracuse University Press.

Smith, Jane. 1999. *Islam in America.* New York: Columbia University Press.

Tehranian, John. 2008. *Whitewashed: America's Invisible Middle Eastern Minority.* New York City, NY: New York University Press.

Turner, James. 1978. "The Founding Fathers of American Sociology: An Examination of Their Sociological Theories of Race Relations." *Journal of Black Studies* 1(9): 3–14.

Wallerstein, Immanuel. 2006. *European Universalism: The Rhetoric of Power.* 1st ed. New York City, NY: New Press.

Williams, Rhys H. and Gira Vashi. 2007. "Hijab and American Muslim Women: Creating the Space for Autonomous Selves." *Sociology of Religion* 68:269–287.

READING 12

References

Abraham, Carolyn. 2006. "The New Science of Race." *Globe and Mail,* June 18, F1.

Bliss, Catherine. 2012. *Race Decoded: The Genomic Fight for Social Justice.* Stanford, CA: Stanford University Press.

Blumer, Herbert. 1958. "Race Prejudice as a Sense of Group Position." *The Pacific Sociological Review* 1:3–7.

Bobo, Lawrence D. 1988. "Group Conflict, Prejudice, and the Paradox of Contemporary Racial Attitudes." Pp. 85–114 in *Eliminating Racism: Profiles in Controversy,* edited by P. Katz and D. Taylor. New York: Plenum.

Bobo, Lawrence D. 1999. "Prejudice as Group Position: Microfoundations of a Sociological Approach to Racism and Race Relations." *Journal of Social Issues* 55:445–72.

Bobo, Lawrence and V. Hutchings. 1996. "Perceptions of Racial Group Competition: Extending Blumer's Theory of Group Position to a Multiracial Societal Context." *American Sociological Review* 61:951–72.

Bobo, Lawrence and James Kluegel. 1993. "Opposition to Race-targeting: Self-interest, Stratification Ideology, or Racial Attitudes?" *American Sociological Review* 58:443–64.

Bobo, Lawrence, J. R. Kleugel, and R. A. Smith. 1997. "Laissez-faire Racism: The Crystalization of a 'Kinder, Gentler' Anti-Black Ideology." Pp. 15–42 in *Racial Attitudes in the 1990s: Continuity and Change,* edited by S. A. Tuch and J. K. Martin. Westport, CT: Praeger.

Bonilla-Silva, Eduardo. 1997. "Rethinking Racism: Toward a Structural Interpretation." *American Sociological Review* 62:951–72.

Bonilla-Silva, Eduardo. 2010. *Racism without Racists: Color-blind Racism and Racial Inequality in Contemporary America.* 3rd ed. Lanham, MD: Rowman and Littlefield.

Bonilla-Silva, Eduardo. 2013. *"The Last Shall be First:* Best Books in the Race Field Since 2000." *Contemporary Sociology* 42:31–40.

Brodwin, Paul. 2005. "Genetic Knowledge and Collective Identity." *Culture, Medicine and Psychiatry* 29:139–43.

Cavalli-Sforza, Luca, Paolo Menozzi, and Alberto Piazza. 1994. *The History and Geography of Human Genes.* Princeton, NJ: Princeton University Press.

Dalmage, Heather. 2004. *The Politics of Multiracialism: Challenging Racial Thinking.* Albany, NY: SUNY Press.

Duster, Troy. 2011. "Ancestry Testing and DNA: Uses, Limits, and *Caveat Emptor.*" Pp. 99–115 in *Race and the Genetic Revolution: Science, Myth and Culture,* edited by Sheldon Krimsky and Kathleen Sloan. New York, NY: Columbia University Press.

Feagin, Joe R. 2009. *The White Racial Frame: Centuries of Framing and Counterframing.* New York: Routledge.

Fitzgerald, Kathleen J. 2007. *Beyond White Ethnicity: Developing a Sociological Understanding of Native American Identity Reclamation.* Lanham, MA: Rowman and Littlefield.

Fitzgerald, Kathleen J. 2013. "Genetic Ancestry Testing and Racial/Ethnic Identity Construction." Paper presented at the Association for Humanist Sociology Annual Meetings, Washington, DC.

Gallagher, Charles A. 1995. "White Reconstruction in the University." *Socialist Review* 24:165–87.

Gallagher, Charles A. 2003. "Playing the White Ethnic Card: Using Ethnic Identity to Deny Contemporary Racism." Pp. 145–58 in *White Out: The Continuing Significance of Racism,* edited by A. W. Doane and E. Bonilla-Silva. New York: Routledge.

Golbeck, Natasha and Wendy D. Roth. 2012. "Aboriginal Claims: DNA Ancestry Testing and Changing Concepts of Indigeneity." *Biomapping Indigenous Peoples: Towards an Understanding of the Issues* 1:415–32.

Gould, Stephen Jay. [1981] 1996. *The Mismeasure of Man, Revised and Expanded.* New York: W. W. Norton.

Graves, Joseph L. 2005. *The Race Myth: Why We Pretend Race Exists in America.* New York: A Plume Book.

Greely, Herny T. 2008. "Genetic Genealogy: Genetics Meets the Marketplace." Pp. 215–234 in *Revisiting Race in a Genomic Age,* edited by Barbara A. Koenig, Sandra Soo-Jim Lee, and Sarah S. Richardson. New Brunswick, NJ: Rutgers University Press.

Hackstaff, Karla B. 2009. "Who Are We? Genealogists Negotiating Ethno-racial Identities." *Qualitative Sociology* 32:173–94.

Haney-Lopez, Ian F. 2011. "Is the 'Post' in Post-racial the 'Blind' in Colorblind?" *Cardoza Law Review* 32:807–31.

Harris, Cherise A. and Nikki Khanna. 2010. "Black Is, Black Ain't: Biracials, Middle-class Blacks, and the Social Construction of Blackness." *Sociological Spectrum* 30:639–70.

Hochschild, Jennifer, Vesla Weaver, and Traci Burch. 2012. *Creating a New Racial Order: How Immigration, Multiracialism, Genomics, and the Young Can Remake Race in America.* Princeton, NJ: Princeton University Press.

Jackman, Mary. 1994. *The Velvet Glove: Paternalism and Conflict in Gender, Class and Race Relations.* Berkeley: University of California Press.

Jackson, John P. and Nadine M. Weidman. 2006. *Race, Racism and Science: Social Impact and Interaction.* New Brunswick, NJ: Rutgers University Press.

Jacobson, Matthew Frye. 1998. *Whiteness of a Different Color: European Immigrants and the Alchemy of Race.* Cambridge, MA: Harvard University Press.

Krimsky, Sheldon. 2011. "Introduction: How Science Embraced the Racialization of Human Populations." Pp. 1–12 in *Race and the Genetic Revolution: Science, Myth, and Culture,* edited by Sheldon Krimsky and Kathleen Sloan. New York, NY: Columbia University Press.

Leroi, Armond Marie. 2005. "A Family Tree in Every Gene." *New York Times,* March 14, A23.

Lewontin, Richard C. 1972. "The Apportionment of Human Diversity." *Evolutionary Biology* 6:381–98.

Lewontin, Richard C. 2012. "Is There a Jewish Gene?" *The New York Review of Books,* December 6, 2012.

Retrieved April 4, 2013 (http://www.nybooks.com/articles/archives/2012/dec/06/is-there-a-jewish-gene/?pagination=false).

Love, Bettina L. and Brandelyn Tosolt. 2010. "Reality or Rhetoric? Barack Obama and Postracial America." *Race, Gender and Class* 17:19–37.

Morning, Ann. 2008. "Reconstructing Race in Science and Society: Biology Textbooks, 1852–2002." *American Journal of Sociology* 114:S106–37.

Morning, Ann. 2011. *The Nature of Race: How Scientists Think and Teach about Human Difference.* Berkeley: University of California Press.

Nelson, Alondra. 2008. "The Factness of Diaspora: The Social Sources of Genetic Genealogy." Pp. 253–268 in *Revisiting Race in a Genomic Age,* edited by Barbara A. Koenig, Sandra Soo-Jim Lee, and Sarah S. Richardson. New Brunswick, NJ: Rutgers University Press.

Perry, Pamela. 2007. "White Universal Identity as a 'Sense of Group Position'." *Symbolic Interaction* 30:375–93.

Risch, Neal, Esteban Burchard, Elad Ziv, and Hua Tang. 2002. "Categorization of Humanis in Biomedical Research: Genes, Race and Disease." *Genome Biology* 3:1–12.

Roberts, Dorothy. 2011. *Fatal Invention: How Science, Politics, and Big Business Re-create Race in the Twenty-first Century.* New York, NY: The New Press.

Rockquemore, Kerry Ann and David L. Brunsma. 2002. *Beyond Black: Biracial Identity in America.* Thousand Oaks, CA: Sage.

Romano, Renee C. 2003. *Race Mixing: Black-white Marriage in Postwar America.* Cambridge, MA: Harvard University Press.

Root, Maria P. 2001. *Love's Revolution: Interracial Marriage.* Philadelphia, PA: Temple University Press.

Rosenberg, Noah H., Jonathan K. Pritchard, James L. Weber, Howard M. Cann, Kenneth K. Kidd, Lev A. Zhivotovsky, and Marcus W. Feldman. 2002. "Genetic Structures of Human Populations." *Science* 298:2381–85.

Saulny, Susan. 2011. "Race Remixed: Black? White? Asian? More Young Americans Choose All of the Above." *New York Times,* January 29. Retrieved April 5, 2013 (http://www.nytimes.com/2011/01/30/us/30mixed.html? ref=raceremixed&_r=0).

Shiao, Jiannbin Lee, Thomas Bode, Amber Beyer, and Daniel Selvig. 2012. "The Genomic Challenge to the Social Construction of Race." *Sociological Theory* 30:67–88.

Smedley, Audrey. 2007. *Race in North America: Origin and Evolution of a Worldview.* 3rd ed. Boulder, CO: Westview Press.

Smiley, Tavis and Cornel West. 2012. *The Rich and the Rest of Us: A Poverty Manifesto.* Carlsbad, CA: Smiley Books.

Spencer, Rainier. 2011. *Reproducing Race: The Paradox of Generation Mix.* Boulder, CO: Lynne Reiner.

Steinberg, Stephen. 2007. *Race Relations: A Critique.* Stanford, CA: Stanford University Press.

Swarns, Rachel. 2012. "Meet Your Cousin, the First Lady: A Family Story, Long Hidden." *The New York Times,* Sunday, June 17, 2012, A1, 10.

Sykes, Bryan. 2001. *The Seven Daughters of Eve: The Science That Reveals Our Genetic Ancestry.* New York: W. W. Norton.

Tallbear, Kimberly. 2008. "Native-American-DNA.com: In Search of Native American Race and Tribe." Pp. 235–252 in *Revisiting Race in a Genomic Age,* edited by Barbara A. Koenig, Sandra Soo-Jim Lee, and Sarah S. Richardson. New Brunswick, NJ: Rutgers University Press.

Thompson, Krissah. 2012. "Researchers Link Obama to Early Slave." *The Times-Picayune,* Tuesday, July 31, 2012, A2.

Wade, Nicholas. 2006. *Before the Dawn: Recovering the Lost History of Our Ancestors.* London, England: Penguin Press.

Walsh, Anthony and Ilhong Yun. 2011. "Race and Criminology in the Age of Genomic Science." *Social Science Quarterly* 92:1279–96.

Wellman, David. [1977] 1993. *Portraits of White Racism.* Cambridge, MA: Cambridge University Press.

READING 13

Notes

1. FUBU (For Us By Us) is a black-owned manufacturer of urban, hip-hop style clothing.

2. For an excellent overview of how the media construct a view of race relations that is overly optimistic, see Benjamin DeMott, *The Trouble with Friendship: Why Americans Can't Think Straight About Race* (New York: The Atlantic Monthly Press, 1995).

3. The Gallup Organization, "Black/White Relations in the U.S." (June 10, 1997):1–5; David Shipler, *A Country of Strangers: Blacks and Whites in America* (New York: Vintage Books, 1998).

4. For an insightful discussion of how neoconservative writers like Dinesh D'Souza distort history and contemporary race relations, see David Theo Goldberg, "The New Segregation," *Race and Society* 1, no. 1 (1998).

5. Dinesh D'Souza, *The End of Racism: Principles for a Multiracial Society* (New York: Free Press, 1995); Ellis Cose, *Color-Blind: Seeing Beyond Race in a Race-Obsessed World* (New York: Harper Collins, 1997).

6. David Moore, "Americans' Most Important Sources of Information: Local News," *The Gallup Poll Monthly,* 2–5 September 1995; David Moore and Lydia Saad, "No Immediate Signs That Simpson Trial Intensified Racial Animosity," *The Gallup Poll Monthly,* 2–5 October 1995; Kaiser Foundation, *The Four Americas: Government and Social Policy Through the Eyes of America's Multi-Racial and Multi-Ethnic Society* (Menlo Park, CA: Kaiser Family Foundation, 1995).

7. A. C. Nielsen, *Information Please Almanac* (Boston: Houghton Mifflin, 1997).

8. John Lewis and Sut Jhally, "Affirming Inaction: Television and the New Politics of Race," in *Marxism in the Postmodern Age: Confronting the New World Order,* edited by A. Callari, S. Cullenberg, and C. Biewener (New York: Guilford Press, 1995).

9. For an outstanding discussion of how color blindness is used politically by neoconservatives, see Amy Ansell, *New Right, New Racism: Race and Reaction in the United States* (New York: New York University Press, 1997); Howard Winant, *Racial Conditions: Politics, Theory, Comparisons* (Minneapolis: University of Minneapolis Press, 1994); Stephen Steinberg, *Turning Back: The Retreat from Racial Justice in American Thought and Policy* (New York: Beacon Press, 1995); Eduardo Bonilla-Silva, *White Supremacy and Racism in the Post-Civil Rights Era* (Boulder: Lynne Rienner Publishers); and Michael Omi, "Racism," in *The Making and Unmaking of Whiteness,* edited by Birget Brander Rasmussen, Eric Klineberg, Irene J. Nexica, and Matt Wray (Durham: Duke University Press, 2001).

10. Ruth Frankenberg, "The Mirage of an Unmarked Whiteness," in *The Making and Unmaking of Whiteness,* edited by Birget Brander Rasmussen, Eric Klineberg, Irene J. Nexica, and Matt Wray (Durham: Duke University Press, 2001).

11. David Theo Goldberg, *Racial Subjects: Writing on Race in America* (Thousand Oaks, CA: Routledge, 1997), 55; see also Charles Jaret, *Contemporary Racial and Ethnic Relations* (New York: HarperCollins, 1995), 265–270.

12. Leslie G. Carr, *Color-Blind Racism* (Thousand Oaks, CA: Sage Publications, 1997), 108; see also David Carroll Cochran, *The Color of Freedom: Race and Contemporary American Liberalism* (New York: State University of New York Press, 1999).

13. Mary Waters, *Ethnic Options: Choosing Identities in America* (Berkeley: University of California Press, 1990); Charles A. Gallagher, "Playing the Ethnic Card: Using Ethnic Identity to Negate Contemporary Racism," in *Deconstructing Whiteness, Deconstructing White Supremacy,* edited by Ashley Doane and Eduardo Bonilla-Silva (Lynne Rienner Publishers, forthcoming 2002).

14. Ashley W. Doane Jr., "Dominant Group Identity in the United States: The Role of 'Hidden' Ethnicity in Intergroup Relations," *The Sociological Quarterly* 38, no. 3 (1997): 378.

15. Joe Feagin and Melvin Sikes, *Living With Racism: The Black Middle Class Experience* (Boston: Beacon Press, 1994).

16. The Gallup Organization, "Black/White Relations in the U.S.," 10 June 1997, 1–5.

17. Kaiser Foundation, 1995.

18. Howard Schuman et al. (1997), 193.

19. U.S. Bureau of the Census, *Housing Vacancies and Home Ownership Annual Statistics* (Washington D.C.: U.S. Government Printing Office, 1999).

20. U.S. Bureau of the Census, *Asset Ownership of Households* (Washington D.C.: U.S. Government Printing Office, 1993); see also *Black Wealth/White Wealth: A New Perspective on Racial Inequality* (New York: Routledge, 1995).

21. John J. Macionis, *Sociology*, 7th ed. (Saddle River, NJ: Prentice Hall, 1999).

22. Diana B. Henriques, *New York Times,* 4 July 2001, p. A1.

23. U.S. Department of Health and Human Services, *National Center for Chronic Disease Prevention and Health Promotion,* 1998; Centers for Disease Control and Prevention, National Center for Health Statistics, *Monthly Vital Statistics Report* 46 (2001).

24. Feagin, 2000.

25. Karen Gullo, *The Atlanta Journal and Constitution,* 12 March 2001, p. A7.

26. Jim Abrams, *The Atlanta Journal and Constitution,* 2 December 2000, p. A9.

27. Laura Parker and Peter Eisler, *USA Today,* 6–8 April 2001, p. A1.

28. Frankenberg (2001), p. 76.

29. Lawrence Bobo and James R. Kluegel, "Status, Ideology, and Dimensions of Whites' Racial Beliefs and Attitudes: Progress and Stagnation," in *Racial Attitudes in the 1990s: Continuity and Change,* edited by Steven A. Tuch and Jack K. Martin (Westport, CT: Praeger, 1997), p. 95.

30. Carr (1997), p. x.

31. David Roediger, *The Wages of Whiteness: Race and the Making of the American Working Class* (New York: Verso Press, 1991), p. 137.

32. Cited in David Roediger, "The White Question," *Race Traitor* (Winter 1993): 104.

READING 14

Notes

1. I will use the terms "skin-lightening," "skin-whitening," and "skin-bleaching" interchangeably throughout the [reading]. Each term is commonly used throughout the literature, both scholarly and popular, and across various discourses on the topic. All three terms refer to the practice of chemically lightening the skin.

2. I use the term "Global South" to refer to developing nations, or Third World nations. Although there is much diversity within the Global South, many are former European colonies and consequently have particular economic and cultural relationships with the West.

References

Adebajo, S. (2002). An epidemiological survey of the use of cosmetic skin lightening cosmetics among traders in Lagos, Nigeria. *West African Journal of Medicine,* 21(1), 51–55.

American Society of Aesthetic Plastic Surgeons. (2010). Press center: Statistics (2000–2008). Retrieved from http://www.surgery.org/media/statistics.

American Society of Aesthetic Plastic Surgeons. (2010). Press center: Statistics (2009). Retrieved from http://www.surgery.org/media/statistics.

Ashikari, Mikiko. (2005). Cultivating Japanese whiteness: the "whitening" cosmetics boom and the Japanese identity. *Journal of Material Culture,* 10, 73–91.

Barnett, A. and Smith, Z. (2005, Oct. 16). Toxic creams for sale as thousands seek whiter skin. *The Observer.*

Barnier, B. (2009, Jan. 12). Senegal's fashion victims. ABC News. Retrieved from http://abcnews.go.com/International/story?id=6625808&page=1

Baumann, S. (2008). The moral underpinnings of beauty: A meaning-based explanation for light and dark complexions in advertising. *Poetics, 36*(1), 2–23.

Blay, Y. A. (2009). Ahoofe kasa!: Skin bleaching and the function of beauty among Ghanaian women. *JENdA: A Journal of Culture and African Women Studies,* 14.

Blum, V. (2005). *Flesh wounds: The culture of cosmetic surgery.* Berkeley, CA: University of California Press.

Boodman, S. (2007, May 29). Cosmetic surgery goes ethnic. *Washington Post.*

Bourdieu, P. (1984). *Distinction.* Cambridge: Harvard University Press.

Burke, T. (1996). *Lifebuoy men, lux women: Commodification, consumption, and cleanliness in modern Zimbabwe.* Durham, NC: Duke University Press.

Caldwell, K. (2007). *Negras in Brazil: Re-envisioning black women, citizenship, and the politics of identity.* New Brunswick, NJ: Rutgers University Press.

Campaign to rid streets of illegal bleaching products. (2007, Jan 19). Retrieved from http://www.jis.gov.jm/ health/html/20070118t090000-0500_11046_jis_cam- paign_to_rid_streets_of_illegal_bleaching_prod- ucts_begins_next_month_.asp

Charles, C.A.D. (2003). Skin bleaching, self-hate, and Black identity in Jamaica. *Journal of Black Studies,* 33(6):711–18.

Charles, C.A.D. (2009a). Skin bleachers' representa- tions of skin color in Jamaica. *Journal of Black Studies, 40(2),* 153–170.

Charles, C.A.D. (2009b). Liberating skin bleachers: From mental pathology to complex personhood. *JENdA: A Journal of Culture and African Women Studies,* 14.

Cortese, A. (1999). *Provocateur: Images of women and minorities in advertising.* Lanham, Maryland: Rowman & Littlefield.

Counter, S. A. and Buchanan, L. H. (2004). Mercury exposure in children: A review. *Toxicology and Applied Pharmacology,* 198(2), 209–230.

Davis, K. (1995). *Reshaping the female body: The dilemma of cosmetic surgery.* New York: Routledge.

del Giudice, P., and Yves, P. (2002). The widespread use of skin lightening creams in Senegal: A persistent public problem in West Africa. *International Journal of Dermatology,* 41(2), 69–72.

Fokuo, J. K. (2009). The lighter side of marriage: Skin- bleaching in post-colonial Ghana. *African and Asian Studies,* 8(1-2), 125–146.

Gabler, E. and Roe, S. (2010, May 18). Some skin- whitening creams contain toxic mercury, testing finds. *Chicago Tribune.*

Glenn, E. N. (2008). Yearning for lightness: Transnational circuits in the marketing and consumption of skin light- eners. *Gender & Society,* 22(3), 281–302.

Glenn, E. N. (Ed.). (2009). *Shades of difference: Why skin color matters.* Palo Alto, CA: Stanford University Press.

Harada, M., Nakachi, S., Tasaka, K., Sakashita, S., Muta, K., Yanagida, K., . . . & Ohno, H. (2001). Wide use of skin-lightening soap may cause mercurypoisoning in Kenya. *The Science of the Total Environment,* 269(1- 3), 183–187.

Hunter, M. (2002). "If you're light you're alright": Light skin color as social capital for women of color. *Gender & Society,* 16(2), 175–193.

Hunter, M. (2005). *Race, gender, and the politics of skin tone.* New York: Routledge.

International Society of Aesthetic Plastic Surgeons. (2010). *International survey on aesthetic/cosmetic procedures performed in 2009.* Retrieved from http:// www.isaps.org/uploads/news_pdf/Analysis_iSAPS_ Survey2009.pdf

James, J. (2009). In pictures: Natural African beauty. *BBC News,* July 20. Retrieved from http://news.bbc. co.uk/2/hi/africa/8148719.stm.

Kisule, H. A. (2008, Aug. 12). Skin bleaching thrives despite Ugandan government ban on dangerous cos- metics. *Women's International Perspective.* Retrieved from http://www.thewip.net/contributors/2008/08/ skin_bleaching_thrives_despite.html

Leonardo, Z. (2002). The souls of white folk: Critical pedagogy, whiteness studies, and globalization dis- course. *Race, Ethnicity & Education,* 5(1), 29–50.

Leong, S. (2006). Who's the fairest of them all? Television ads for skin-whitening cosmetics in Hong Kong. *Asian Ethnicity,* 7(2), 167–181.

Lewis, K., Robkin, N., Gaska, K., Njoki, L. C., Andrews, E., Jetha, K. (2009). The Tanzanian response to dangerous skin bleaching products and practices and the gendered politics of it all: A critical analysis. *JENdA: A Journal of Culture and African Women Studies* 14.

Mahe, A., Blanc, L., Halna, J., Keita, S., Sanogo, T., Bobin, P. (1993). An epidemiologic survey on the cosmetic use of bleaching agents by the women of Bamako. *Annales de Dermatologie,* 120(12), 870–873.

Mahe, A., Ly, F., & Gounongbe, A. (2004). The cosmetic use of bleaching products in Dakar, Senegal: Socioeconomic factors and claimed motivations. *Sciences Sociales Et Sante,* 22(2), 5–33.

Mire, A. (2001). Skin-bleaching: Poison, beauty, power, and the politics of the colour line. *Resources for Feminist Research,* 28(3-4), 13–38.

Mire, A. (2005). *Pigmentation and empire: The emerging skin whitening industry.* Retrieved 10 October 2006 from http://www.counterpunch.org/mire07282005.html

Mitchell, F. (2009, Nov 11). Sosa says he's preparing to endorse skin product. *Huffington Post.* Retrieved from http://www.chicagobreakingsports.com/2009/11/sosa-says-hes-preparing-toendorse-skin-product.html.

Ntshingla, F. (2005, Nov 27). Women buppies using harmful skin lighteners. *Sunday Times* (South Africa).

Olumide, Y. M., Akinkugbe, A. O., Altraide, D., Mohammed, T., Ahamefule, N., Ayanlowo, S., Onyekonwu, C., & Essen, N. (2008). Complications of chronic use of skin lightening cosmetics. *International Journal of Dermatology,* 47(4), 344–353.

Osuri, G. (2008). Ash-coloured whiteness: The transfiguration of Aishwarya Rai. *South Asian Popular Culture,* 6(2), 109–123.

Parameswaran, R., & Cardoza, K. (2009). Melanin on the margins: Advertising and the cultural politics of fair/light/white beauty in India. *Journalism & Communication Monographs,* 11(3), 213–274.

Perry, I. (2006). Buying white beauty. *Cardozo Journal of Law & Gender,* 12, 579–607.

Pierre, J. (2008). 'I like your colour!' Skin bleaching and geographies of race in urban Ghana. *Feminist Review,* 90(1), 9–29.

Rondilla, J. & Spickard, P. (2007). *Is lighter better? Skin-tone discrimination among Asian Americans.* Lanham, MD: Rowman & Littlefield.

Saraswati, L. A. (2010). Cosmopolitan whiteness: The effects and affects of skinwhitening advertisements in a transnational women's magazine in Indonesia. *Meridians,* 10(2), 15–41.

Skin Bleaching. (2005, April 12). Retrieved from http://www.ghanahealthservice.org/articles.php?nd=18&tt=Skin+Bleaching

Telles, E. E. (2006). *Race in another America: The significance of skin color in Brazil.* Princeton, NJ: Princeton University Press.

Thomas, L. (2009). "Skin lighteners in South Africa: Transnational entanglements and technologies of the self." In E. N. Glenn (Ed.) *Shades of difference: Why skin color matters.* Palo Alto, CA: Stanford University Press.

Winders, J., Jones, J. P. I., & Higgins, M. J. (2005). Making gueras: Selling white identities on late-night Mexican television. *Gender, Place and Culture,* 12(1), 71–93.

"Zambia: Ban sale of skin-bleaching creams-PHPF." (2010, March 31). *Lusaka Times.* Retrieved from http://www.lusakatimes.com/2010/03/31/ban-saleskinbleaching-creamsphpf/

READING 15

Notes

1. These categories are constructions, but they also contain populations experiencing all the pleasures and pains of being located in a hierarchy. And although I am often discussing constructions, I will forgo the practice of putting all racial, national, and related names and labels between quotes, except for unusual racial stereotypes.

2. The two races may not be called that openly, but ambiguous pejoratives have long been part of

the American vocabulary, for example *under-class* now, and *pauper* a century earlier (Gans 1995). Since races are social constructions, their names will depend in large part on who does the naming—and whose names become dominant in the public vocabulary.

3. Puerto Ricans are still often described as immigrants, even though they have been American citizens for a long time and their move from the island to the mainland is a form of interstate mobility. Racial, class, and linguistic considerations have undoubtedly influenced this labeling. The same dominant-race thinking led Irving Kristol and other neoconservatives to argue in the 1960s that blacks were similar enough to the white European immigrants to be able to adopt and act on immigrant values. They also assumed that blacks would then assimilate like immigrants, ignoring such facts as that blacks had originally come as slaves, not immigrants; had been here several centuries; and had not yet been allowed by whites to assimilate. Thirty years later, many whites ignore the same facts to propose the newest immigrants as role models for blacks.

4. Much less is said about black Hispanics, including Puerto Ricans, who suffer virtually all of the discriminatory and other injustices imposed on African-Americans.

5. Some highly placed whites are already worrying, for example in a *Time* cover story by William Henry III (1990), but then similar whites worried a century earlier what the then-arriving Catholic and Jewish newcomers would do to *their* country. The current worries are as meaningless as the old ones, since they are based on extrapolations of current patterns of immigration, not to mention current constructions of (nonwhite) race and (Hispanic) ethnicity.

6. Hacker (1996) notes, for example, that the term "white trash" is no longer in common use. Indeed, for reasons worth studying, the more popular term of the moment is "trailer trash," which nonetheless seems to be applied solely to poor whites.

7. In this respect, the United States differs from many other countries in the Western hemisphere, where blacks who have managed to become affluent are treated, within limits, as whites.

8. Not only might they perceive it more angrily than I am here doing, but they might be angrier about it than about the present hierarchy, simply because it is new but no great improvement. One result could be their constructions of new racial identities for themselves that depart drastically from the ones future nonblacks consider reasonable.

9. Being far fewer than Asians in number, South Asians are nationally not very visible now. Moreover, for religious and other reasons, South Asian immigrants have so far often been able to discourage their children from intermarrying.

10. My observations on multiracial constructions and people have benefited from many conversations with Valli Rajah.

11. Between 1970 and 1994, the number of people in interracial marriages grew from 676,000 to more than three million (Fletcher 1997). In 1990, biracial children made up 4 percent of all children, increasing from half a million in 1970 to about two million that year. The largest number were Asian-white children, followed by Native American-white and African American-white ones (Harrison and Bennett 1995).

12. Some observers currently estimate that 70 percent of all Japanese and Japanese-Americans are intermarried, mostly with whites. Since they came to the United States as families long before 1965, this estimate may supply a clue about what will happen to second-, third-, and later-generation descendants of other Asian-American populations.

13. Presumably class position will affect how other descendants of old Southern mulatto and creole populations (Dominguez 1986) will be classified.

14. In the political debates over the racial categories to be used in the Year 2000 Census, vocal multiracials preferred to be counted as and with various people of color. African-Americans and

other officially recognized racial groups also indicated their opposition to a multiracial category, being reluctant to reduce the power of their numbers or the federal benefits that now go to racial minorities (e.g., Holmes 1996).

15. Kohne (1996) reports that light-skinned biracial Columbia University students who identify as whites also apply for scholarships as blacks. But then, four decades earlier, I met Italian-Americans in Boston's West End who took Irish names in order to obtain jobs in Irish-dominated city hall.

16. The practice of quantifying racial bloods has a long history in Europe and the United States, thanks to both eugenics and slavery. Perhaps it will disappear when enough people have to start counting three or more races. However, people also still use blood fractions when they marry across religions, so that the notion of racial, ethnic, or religious "blood" is by no means obsolete.

17. They are also different, for "one and the same person may be considered white in the Dominican Republic or Puerto Rico . . . 'colored' in Jamaica, Martinique, or Curacao . . . [and] a 'Negro' in Georgia" (Hoetink 1967, xii).

18. This account is based mainly on the data summarized in Fiola 1990 and Skidmore 1992, the classic analysis of the Brazilian racial system in Skidmore 1993, Adamo's 1983 case study of race and class in Rio de Janeiro, and the sociopolitical analyses by Marx (1995, 1996). I am indebted to Anthony Marx for guiding me into the literature on Brazil, although there is still precious little social research, especially with current data, in English.

19. No one has so far paid much attention to who is constructed as exotic and why, except the multiracial people, mostly women, to whom it is applied. Some of them benefit because they are sought by industries that hire workers with exotic facial features; but women without these occupational interests resent such labeling because it turns them into sexual objects. Industries that employ workers with exotic features, facial and

otherwise, such as the fashion and entertainment industries, play an interesting, and probably unduly influential, role in the country's public racial construction.

20. Even now, at the close of the twentieth century, whites who argue that America is a "Christian" nation are pursuing a politics of identity as much as of religious dominance.

21. I am indebted to my Columbia University colleague, biologist Robert Pollack, for my understanding of this phenomenon.

22. Originally, people drew on nineteenth-century and earlier comparisons of apes and humans, with those determined to be closer to apes in facial appearance being thought inferior. Brain size was also used, at least until scientific research debunked its relevance, and the researchers also discovered that it did not correlate with status. The final blow was the discovery that the much maligned Neanderthalers had larger brains than *Homo sapiens.*

23. Ears have served mainly as anchors for adornment, although protruding ones have sometimes been brought surgically closer to the head.

24. Now that some young women show their navels or wear bathing suits with uncovered buttocks, these could become eligible for racial typing.

25. Constructionists in the social sciences and the humanities have so far mainly emphasized that races, like other human notions, are socially constructed, but social scientists have paid little attention to the actual construction process and its participants. What we know about that process comes mostly from scholars who analyze racial images over time, in literature or the popular culture, and have collected process information as part of their work.

26. Forced Chinese labor was also recruited for the cotton plantations, but the Chinese workers turned out to be inefficient cotton pickers and thus managed to avoid becoming slaves.

27. I am indebted to Roderick Harrison and especially Manuel de la Puente of the U.S. Bureau of

the Census for materials that clarified this set of responses.

28. Social scientists on the staff of the Census Bureau and the Bureau of Labor Statistics spend part of their time analyzing the large number of private races that people supply in answer to open-ended questions to produce the small number of public ones reported by the federal government.

29. For some similar practices by Jews in post-Holocaust Germany, see Rapaport 1997, 166–67.

30. For example, one of Waters's respondents explained that she traced her bad moods to "the Irish in me," while "all of the good things" were Italian (Waters 1990, 25). Embryo clinics are asked by some of their customers to supply sperm and egg donors of similar ethnic origin, in one case to obtain an "Irish background, or at least light hair and light eyes" (Kolata 1997, 34). As a result, ethnicity may be so racialized that it is not very voluntary, although voluntary ethnicity may also be used to achieve voluntarily chosen racial features.

31. Needless to say, traumatic and long-lasting economic decline is a more likely cause for a public recognition of class in America.

References

Adamo, Samuel C. 1983. "The Broken Promise: Race, Health and Justice in Rio de Janeiro, 1890–1940." Ph.D. diss., University of New Mexico.

Alba, Richard D. 1990. *Ethnic Identity*. New Haven: Yale University Press.

Dominguez, Virginia R. 1986. *White by Definition*. New Brunswick: Rutgers University Press.

Feagin, Joe R., and Michael P. Sykes. 1994. *Living with Racism*. Boston: Beacon.

Fields, Barbara J. 1990. "Slavery, Race and Ideology in the United States of America." *New Left Review* 15:95–108.

Fiola, Jan. 1990. "Race Relations in Brazil: A Reassessment of the 'Racial Democracy' Thesis." Occasional Papers Series no. 34. University of Massachusetts Latin American Studies Program, Amherst.

Fletcher, Michael A. 1997. "More Than a Black-White Issue." *Washington Post National Weekly Edition*, May 26, 34.

Frey, William H. 1996. "Immigration, Domestic Migration and Demographic Balkanization in America." *Population and Development Review* 22:741–63.

Gans, Herbert J. 1992. "Second Generation Decline: Scenarios for the Economic and Ethnic Futures of the Post-1965 American Immigrants." *Ethnic and Racial Studies* 15:173–92.

—. 1995. *The War against the Poor*. New York: Basic.

Gerber, Eleanor, and Manuel de la Puente. 1996. "The Development of and Cognitive Testing of Race and Ethnic Origin Questions for the Year 2000 Census." In Bureau of the Census, *1996 Annual Research Conference*. Washington: Government Printing Office.

Gitlin, Todd. 1995. *The Twilight of Common Dreams*. New York: Metropolitan.

Gordon, Milton M. 1964. *Assimilation in American Life*. New York: Oxford University Press.

Hacker, Andrew. 1996. Foreword to *The Coming Race War?* by Richard Delgado. New York: New York University Press.

Harrison, Roderick J., and Claudette Bennett. 1995. "Racial and Ethnic Diversity." In *State of the Union: America in the 1990s*, vol. 2, *Social Trends*, edited by Reynolds Farley. New York: Russell Sage Foundation.

Henry, William, III. 1990. "Beyond the Melting Pot." *Time*, April 9, 29–32.

Hoetink, Harry. 1967. *The Two Variants in Caribbean Race Relations*. London: Oxford University Press.

Holmes, Steven. 1996. "Census Tests New Category to Identify Racial Groups." *New York Times*, December 4, A25.

Ignatiev, Noel. 1995. *How the Irish Became White*. New York: Routledge.

Kalmijn, Matthijs. 1991. "Status Homogamy in the United States." *American Journal of Sociology* 93:496–523.

Kohne, Natasha G. 1996. "The Experience of Mixed-Race Women: Challenging Racial Boundaries." Unpublished senior thesis, Department of Sociology, Columbia University, New York.

Kolata, Gina. 1997. "Clinics Selling Embryos Made for 'Adoption.'" *New York Times,* November 23, 1, 34.

Loewen, James W. 1988. *The Mississippi Chinese.* 2d ed. Prospect Heights, Ill.: Waveland.

Marris, Peter. 1996. *The Politics of Uncertainty.* New York: Routledge.

Marx, Anthony W. 1995. "Contested Citizenship: The Dynamics of Racial Identity and Social Movements." *International Review of History* 40, supplement 3: 159–83.

—. 1996. "Race-Making and the Nation-State." *World Politics,* January, 180–208.

Mintz, Sidney W. 1989. *Caribbean Transformations.* New York: Columbia University Press.

Morganthau, Tom. 1995. "What Color Is Black?" *Newsweek,* February 12, 63–67.

Newman, Katherine. 1993. *Declining Fortunes.* New York: Basic.

Rapaport, Lynn. 1997. *Jews in Germany after the Holocaust.* Cambridge: Cambridge University Press.

Rodriguez, Clara E. 1989. *Puerto Ricans: Born in the U.S.A.* Boston: Unwin Hyman.

Roediger, David R. 1991. *Wages of Whiteness.* London: Verso.

Rumbaut, Ruben G. 1997. "Ties That Bind: Immigration and Immigrant Families in the United States." In *Immigration and the Family,* edited by Alan Booth, Ann C. Crouter, and Nancy Landale. Mahwah, N.J.: Erlbaum.

Sanjek, Roger. 1994. "Intermarriage and the Future of the Races in the United States." In *Race,* edited by Steven Gregory and Roger Sanjek. New Brunswick: Rutgers University Press.

Skidmore, Thomas L. 1992. "Fact and Myth: Discovering a Racial Problem in Brazil." Working paper 173. Helen Kellogg Institute for International Studies, University of Notre Dame.

—. 1993. *Black into White.* Durham: Duke University Press.

Stonequist, Everett V. 1937. *The Marginal Man.* New York: Scribner's.

Waters, Mary. 1990. *Ethnic Options: Choosing Identities in America.* Berkeley: University of California Press.

READING 17

References

1. https://www.nps.gov/articles/choctaw-indians-and-the-battle-of-new-orleans.htm

2. http://www.encyclopedia.com/places/united-states-and-canada/us-politicalgeography/houma

3. http://www.chitimacha.gov/history-culture/tribal-history

4. http://www.history.com/topics/exploration/hernando-de-soto

5. http://www.historymuseum.ca/virtual-museum-of-new-france/the-explorers/renerobert-cavelier-de-la-salle-1670-1687/

6. http://www.theadvocate.com/new_orleans/news/article_e26d8270-43e0-5354-b174-34b6a775d5f7.html

7. http://www.losislenos.org/history.html

8. http://musicrising.tulane.edu/learn/course/35/New-Orleans-and-Senegal-in-theAtlantic-World

9. http://www.nola.com/175years/index.ssf/2011/08/1855_free_people_of_color_fl_OU.html

10. http://gonola.com/2014/03/24/nola-history-the-new-orleans-haitian-connection.html

11. http://www.neworleansonline.com/neworleans/multicultural/multiculturalhistory/german.html

12. http://www.history.com/topics/new-orleans

13. http://www.history.com/topics/new-orleans

14. http://www.neworleansonline.com/neworleans/multicultural/multiculturalhistory/italian.html

15. http://www.neworleansonline.com/neworleans/multicultural/multiculturalhistory/irish.html

16. http://www.history.com/topics/new-orleans

17. https://stonecenter.tulane.edu/articles/detail/292/A-Latin-Americanists-Guideto-New-Orleans

18. http://www.neworleansonline.com/neworleans/multicultural/multiculturalhistory/vietnamese.html

19. http://www.neworleansonline.com/neworleans/multicultural/multiculturalhistory/

20. http://www.neworleansonline.com/neworleans/history/people.html

21. http://www.nola.com/politics/index.ssf/2010/04/slave_trade_in_new_orleans.html

22. https://www.nytimes.com/2015/02/10/us/history-of-lynchings-in-the-southdocuments-nearly-4000-names.html?_r=0

23. http://www.nola.com/news/baton-rouge/index.ssf/2015/02/lynchings_louisiana_report.html

24. http://www.pbs.org/wnet/supremecourt/antebellum/landmark_plessy.html

25. http://www.nola.com/politics/index.ssf/2011/05/first_freedom_riders_were_beat.html

26. https://www.washingtonpost.com/news/arts-and-entertainment/wp/2016/09/24/read-george-w-bushs-speech-at-the-african-american-museum-13-years-after-signing-the-bill-to-build-it/?utm_term=55ac80ad7ccd

27. http://www.crt.state.la.us/dataprojects/hp/nhl/attachments/Parish36/Scans/36117001.pdf

28. http://www.encyclopediavirginia.org/Lost_Cause_The#start_entry

29. 1718 to 1884 (when Robert E. Lee monument was dedicated) http://www.nola.com/politics/index.ssf/2015/06/lee_circle_by_another_name_a_c.html

30. 1865 to 1884 (when Robert E. Lee monument was dedicated) http://www.nola.com/politics/index.ssf/2015/06/lee_circle_by_another_name_a_c.html

31. https://www.ucs.louisiana.edu/~ras2777/amgov/stephens.html

32. https://www.washingtonpost.com/news/arts-andentertainment/wp/2016/09/24/full-transcript-of-president-obamas-speech-at-the-opening-ceremony-of-the-african-american-museum/?utm_term=.ffec0b1c5045

33. Pledge of Allegiance, http://www.ushistory.org/documents/pledge.htm

34. https://www.nps.gov/jazz/learn/historyculture/history_early.htm

35. https://www.washingtonpost.com/news/arts-and-entertainment/wp/2016/09/24/read-george-w-bushs-speech-at-the-africanamerican-museum-13-years-after-signing-the-bill-to-build-it/?utm_term=.55ac80ad7ccd

36. https://www.africa.upenn.edu/Articles_Gen/Letter_Birmingham.html

37. http://www.nola.com/politics/index.ssf/2017/05/terence_blanchard_confederate.html

38. https://en.wikipedia.org/wiki/John_F._Kennedy_High_School_(New_Orleans)

39. http://www.nola.com/politics/index.ssf/2017/05/terence_blanchard_confederate.html

40. http://www.nola.com/politics/index.ssf/2017/03/confederate_monuments_liberty.html

41. https://www.bestofneworleans.com/gambit/confederatemonumentandnbspupdate/Content?oid=2756084

42. 3 trial judges (Barbier, Griffin, Reese), 3 Fourth Circuit judges (Love, Jenkins, Edwards), 3 Fifth Circuit judges (Higginson, Higginbotham, Elrod), 4 Supreme Court justices (Johnson, Genovese, Clark, Weimer)

43. http://www.nola.com/politics/index.ssf/2015/12/confederate_monuments_lee_circ.html#incart_river_index

44. https://www.washingtonpost.com/posteverything/wp/2017/05/11/new-orleansmayor-why-im-taking-down-my-citys-confederate-monuments/?utm_term=.982c2fcfabc2

45. http://www.ca5.uscourts.gov/opinions/unpub/16/16-30107.0.pdf

46. http://www.nola.com/politics/index.ssf/2016/01/federal_judge_denies_restraini.html

47. http://www.nola.com/politics/index.ssf/2017/05/beauregard_monument_injunction_1.html

48. http://www.mandela.gov.za/mandela_speeches/1998/981029_trcreport.htm

49. http://www.bartleby.com/124/pres32.html

READING 19

Note

1. Of course, the politics of race do not map neatly on a right-left political continuum, as movements generally understood as progressive have adopted agendas that reinforce racial inequities, such as labor movements that support seniority systems that privilege white workers (Quadagno 1994). Even white-majority groups that self-identify on the left, claim heritage in the civil rights movement (Fleming and Morris 2014), and mobilize around opposition to racism have been shown to reproduce the racial inequities of the larger society in their dynamics and goals (Blee 2012; Hughey 2012; Polletta 2005; Polletta and Jasper 2001).

References

Abramowitz, Alan I. 2011. "Grand Old Tea Party: Partisan Polarization and the Rise of the Tea Party Movement." Pp. 195–211 in *Steep: The Precipitous Rise of the Tea Party,* edited by L. Rosenthal and C. Trost. Berkeley: University of California Press.

Adams, Josh and Vincent J. Roscigno. 2005. "White Supremacists, Oppositional Culture and the World Wide Web." *Social Forces* 84(2):759–78.

Allen, L. Dean II. 2000. "Promise Keepers and Racism: Frame Resonance as an Indicator of Organizational Vitality." *Sociology of Religion* 61:55–72.

Ansell, Amy Elizabeth. 1997. *New Right, New Racism: Race and Reaction in the United States and Britain.* New York: New York University Press.

Barkun, Michael. 1994. *Religion and the Racist Right: The Origins of the Christian Identity Movement.* Chapel Hill: University of North Carolina Press.

Bartkowski, John P. 2004. *The Promise Keepers: Servants, Soldiers. and Godly Men.* New Brunswick, NJ: Rutgers University Press.

Berbrier, Mitch. 2000. "The Victim Ideology of White Supremacists and White Separatists in the United States." *Sociological Focus* 33:175–91.

Blee, Kathleen M. 1991. *Women of the Klan: Racism and Gender in the 1920s.* Berkeley: University of California Press.

Blee, Kathleen M. 2000. "White on White: Interviewing Women in U.S. White Supremacist Groups." Pp. 93–110 in *Racing Research, Researching Race: Methodological Dilemmas in Critical Race Studies,* edited by F. W. Twine and J. Warren. New York: New York University Press.

Blee, Kathleen M. 2002. *Inside Organized Racism: Women in the Hate Movement.* Berkeley: University of California Press.

Blee, Kathleen M. 2010. "Trajectories of Action and Belief in U.S. Organized Racism." Pp. 239–65 in *Identity and Participation in Culturally Diverse Societies: A Multidisciplinary Perspective,* edited by A. E. Azzi, X. Chryssochoou, B. Klandermans, and B. Simon. London: Blackwell.

Blee, Kathleen M. 2012. *Democracy in the Making: How Activist Groups Form.* New York: Oxford University Press.

Blee, Kathleen M. and Kimberly A. Creasap. 2010. "Conservative and Right-wing Movements." *Annual Review of Sociology* 36:269–86.

Blee, Kathleen M. and Annette Linden. 2012. "Women in Extremist Right Parties and Movements: A Comparison of the Netherlands and the U.S." Pp. 98–114 in *Women of the Right: Comparisons and Interplay Across Borders,* edited by K. Blee and S. Deutch. University Park, PA: Penn State University Press.

Bonilla-Silva, Eduardo. 2009. *Racism without Racists: Color-blind Racism and the Persistence of Racial Inequality in the United States.* 3rd ed. New York: Rowman and Littlefield.

Brennan, Kevin and Sean Sullivan. 2011. "The Tea Party's Surprise: The Conservative Movement Has Helped Elect Blacks and Hispanics Who Faced Resistance from the Republican Establishment." *National Journal Magazine*, October 22. http://www.nationaljournal.com/magazine/tea-party-fuels-surge-of-minorities-into-office-20111020. Accessed 18 October 2014.

Burghart, Devin. 2014. "Special Report: The Status of the Tea Party Movement: Part One: The Tea Party in 2013." Kansas City, MO: Institute for Research and Education on Human Rights. Retrieved April 2, 2014 (http://www.irehr.org/issue-areas/tea-party-nationalism/tea-party-news-and-analysis/item/525-status-oftea-party-part-one).

Burghart, Devin and Leonard Zeskind. 2010. "Tea Party Nationalism: A Critical Examination of the Tea Party Movement and the Size, Scope and Focus of its National Factions." Kansas City, MO: Institute for Research and Education on Human Rights. Retrieved April 2, 2014 (http://www.irehr.org/images/stories/pdf/TeaPartyNationalism.pdf&chrome=true).

Burke, Meghan A. 2013. "Beyond Fear and Loathing: Tea Party Organizers' Continuum of Knowledge in a Racialized Social System." *Gender, Race, and Class* 20(1):93–109.

Chalmers, David. 1987. *Hooded Americanism: The History of the Ku Klux Klan.* 3rd ed. Durham, NC: Duke University Press.

Collins, Patricia Hill. 2000. *Black Feminist Thought: Knowledge, Consciousness, and the Politics of Empowerment.* New York: Routledge Classics.

Cunningham, David. 2012a. *Klansville, U.S.A.: The Rise and Fall of the Civil Rights-era Ku Klux Klan.* New York: Oxford University Press.

Cunningham, David. 2012b. "Mobilizing Ethnic Competition." *Theory and Society* 41(5):505–25.

della Porta, Donatella. 2013. *Clandestine Political Violence.* New York: Cambridge University Press.

Diamond, Sarah. 1998. *Not by Politics Alone: The Enduring Influence of the Christian Right.* New York: Guilford.

Dillard, Angela K. 2001. *Guess Who's Coming to Dinner Now? Multicultural Conservatism in America.* New York: NYU Press.

Disch, Lisa. 2011. "The Tea Party: A White Citizenship Movement?" Pp. 133–51 in *Steep: The Precipitous Rise of the Tea Party,* edited by L. Rosenthal and C. Trost. Berkeley: University of California Press.

Dobratz, Betty A. and Stephanie Shanks-Meile. 2000. *The White Separatist Movement in the United States: White Power, White Pride!* Baltimore: The Johns Hopkins University Press.

Durham, Martin. 2000. *The Christian Right, the Far Right and the Boundaries of American Conservatism.* Manchester, UK: Manchester University Press.

Durham, Martin. 2007. *White Rage: The Extreme Right and American Politics.* New York: Taylor & Francis.

Emory University. n.d. "Holocaust Denial on Trial." http://www.hdot.org/en/trial/index.html). Accessed 9 August 2014.

Ezekiel, Raphael S. 1996. *The Racist Mind: Portraits of American Neo-Nazis and Klansmen.* New York: Penguin.

Feagin, Joe R. 2006. *Systemic Racism: A Theory of Oppression.* New York: Routledge.

Fleming, Crystal and Aldon Morris. 2014. "Theorizing Ethnic and Racial Movements in the Global Age: Lessons from the Civil Rights Movement." *Sociology of Race and Ethnicity* 1(1):107–128.

Gardell, Mattias. 2003. *Gods of the Blood: The Pagan Revival and White Separatism.* Durham, NC: Duke University Press.

Hardisty, Jean. 1999. *Mobilizing Resentment: Conservative Resurgence from the John Birch Society to the Promise Keepers.* Boston: Beacon Press.

Hughey, Matthew W. 2010. "The (Dis) Similarities of White Racial Identities: The Conceptual Framework of 'Hegemonic Whiteness.'" *Ethnic and Racial Studies* 33(8):1289–309.

Hughey, Matthew W. 2012. *White Bound: Nationalists, Antiracists and the Shared Meaning of Race.* Stanford, CA: Stanford University Press.

Ignatiev, Noel. 2008. *How the Irish Became White.* New York: Routledge.

Irvine, Janice M. 2002. *Talk about Sex: The Battles over Sex Education in the United States.* Berkeley: University of California Press.

Kimmel, Michael. 2013. *Angry White Men: American Masculinity at the End of an Era.* New York: Nation Books.

Lassiter, Matthew D. 2007. *The Silent Majority: Suburban Politics in the Sunbelt South.* Princeton, NJ: Princeton University Press.

Lewis, Angela. 2005. "Black Conservatism in America." *Journal of African American Studies* 8(4):3–13.

Lienesch, Michael. 2007. *In the Beginning: Fundamentalism, the Scopes Trial, and the Making of the Antievolution Movement.* Chapel Hill: University of North Carolina Press.

Lio, Shoon, Scott Melzer, and Ellen Reese. 2008. "Constructing Threat and Appropriating 'Civil Rights': Rhetorical Strategies of Gun Rights and English Only Leaders." *Symbolic Interaction* 31(1):5–31.

Lowndes, Joseph. 2011. "The Past and Future of Race in the Tea Party Movement." Pp. 152–70 in *Steep: The Precipitous Rise of the Tea Party*, edited by L. Rosenthal and C. Trost. Berkeley: University of California Press.

McCright, Aaron M. and Riley E. Dunlap. 2003. "Defeating Kyoto: The Conservative Movement's Impact on U.S. Climate Change Policy." *Social Problems* 50(3):348–73.

McGirr, Lisa. 2001. *Suburban Warriors: The Origins of the New American Right*. Princeton, NJ: Princeton University Press.

McVeigh, Rory. 2009. *The Rise of the Ku Klux Klan: Right-wing Movements and National Politics.* Minneapolis: University of Minnesota Press.

McVeigh, Rory. 2014. "What's New about the Tea Party Movement?" Pp. 16–34 in *Understanding the Tea Party Movement*, edited by N. Van Dyke and D. S. Meyer. Surrey, UK, Ashgate.

McVeigh, Rory and David Cunningham. 2012. "Enduring Consequences of Right-wing Extremism: Klan Mobilization and Homicides in Southern Counties." *Social Forces* 90(3):843–62.

Miller-Idriss, Cynthia. 2012. *Blood and Culture: Youth, Right-wing Extremism, and Belonging in Contemporary Germany.* Durham, NC: Duke University Press.

Nagel, Joane. 2003. *American Indian Renewal: Red Power and the Resurgence of Identity and Culture.* New York: Oxford University Press.

Parker, Christopher S. and Matt A. Barreto. 2013. *Change They Can't Believe In: The Tea Party and Reactionary Politics in America.* Princeton, NJ: Princeton University Press.

Parker, Christopher S. and Christopher C. Towler. 2010. "2010 Multi-state Survey on Race and Politics—Attitudes towards Blacks, Immigrants and Gay Rights, by Tea Party Approval." University of Washington Institute for the Study of Ethnicity, Race and Sexuality. Retrieved April 2, 2014 (https://depts.washington.edu/uwiser/mssrp_table.pdt).

Polletta, Francesca. 2005. "How Participatory Democracy Became White: Culture and Organizational Choice." *Mobilization: An International Journal* 10(2):271–88.

Polletta, Francesca. 2006. *It Was Like a Fever: Storytelling in Protest and Politics.* Chicago: University of Chicago Press.

Polletta, Francesca and James M. Jasper. 2001. "Collective Identity and Social Movements." *Annual Review of Sociology* 27:283–305.

Prior, Francis B. 2014. "Quality Controlled: An Ethnographic Account of Tea Party Messaging and Action." *Sociological Forum* 29(2):301–17.

Quadagno, Jill. 1994. *The Color of Welfare: How Racism Undermined the War on Poverty.* New York: Oxford University Press.

Ribuffo, Leo P. 1983. *The Old Christian Right: The Protestant Far Right from the Great Depression to the Cold War.* Philadelphia: Temple University Press.

Rydgren, Jens. 2007. "The Sociology of the Radical Right." *Annual Review of Sociology* 33:241–62.

Shapira, Harel. 2013. *Waiting for José: The Minutemen's Pursuit of America.* Princeton, NJ: Princeton University Press.

Skocpol, Theda and Vanessa Williamson. 2012. *The Tea Party and the Remaking of Republican Conservatism.* New York: Oxford University Press.

Simi, Pete and Robert Futrell. 2010. *American Swastika: Inside the White Power Movement's Hidden Spaces of Hate.* Lanham, MD: Rowman & Littlefield.

Smith, Andrea. 2008. *Native Americans and the Christian Right: The Gendered Politics of Unlikely Alliances.* Durham, NC: Duke University Press.

Smith, Christian. 2003. *Moral, Believing Animals: Human Personhood and Culture.* New York: Oxford University Press.

Stem, Kenneth. 1996. *A Force upon the Plan: The American Militia Movement and the Politics of Hate.* New York: Simon & Schuster.

Twine, France Winddance and Jonathan Warren, eds. 2000. *Racing Research, Researching Race: Methodological Dilemmas in Critical Race Studies.* New York: New York University Press.

van Dyke, Nella and Sarah Soule. 2002. "Structural Social Change and the Mobilizing Effect of Threat: Explaining Levels of Patriot and Militia Organizing in the United States." *Social Problems* 49(4):497–520.

Vozella, Laura. 2013. "Jackson Keeps GOP Establishment at Arm's Length in VA Lieutenant Governor Campaign," *Washington Post*, September 3. http://www.washingtonpost.com/local/virgin-ia-politics/2013/09/03/936e7178-0ff84-11e3-85b6-d27422650fd5_story.html. Accessed 18 October 2014.

Yates, Elizabeth A. 2014. "Hosting the Tea Party: Grassroots Mobilization in a Conservative Bubble." Master's thesis, University of Pittsburgh.

Zeskind, Leonard. 2009. *Blood and Politics: The History of the White Nationalist Movement from the Margins to the Mainstream.* New York: Farrar, Straus and Giroux.

READING 20

Notes

1. Raphael Tardon, "Richard Wright Tells Us: The White Problem in the United States," *Action*, 24 Oct. 1946. Reprinted in Kenneth Kinnamon and Michel Fabre, *Conversations with Richard Wright* (Jackson, Miss., 1993), 99. Malcolm X and others used this same formulation in the 1960s, but I believe that it originated with Wright, or at least that is the earliest citation I have found so far.

2. This is also Toni Morrison's point in *Playing in the Dark: Whiteness in the Literary Imagination* (Cambridge, Mass., 1992).

3. Richard Dyer, "White," *Screen* 29 (fall 1988): 44.

4. I thank Michael Schudson for pointing out to me that since the passage of civil rights legislation in the 1960s whiteness dares not speak its name, cannot speak in its own behalf, but rather advances through a color-blind language radically at odds with the distinctly racialized distribution of resources and life chances in American society.

5. Walter Benjamin, "Madame Ariane: Second Courtyard on the Left," from *One-Way Street* (London, 1969), 98–99.

6. Richard Slotkin, *Gunfighter Nation: The Myth of the Frontier in Twentieth Century America* (New York, 1992); Eric Lott, *Love and Theft* (New York, 1993); David Roediger, *Wages of Whiteness* (New York, 1992); Michael Rogin, "Blackface White Noise: The Jewish Jazz Singer Finds His Voice," *Critical Inquiry* 18 (spring 1992).

7. Robin Kelley, *Hammer and Hoe* (Chapel Hill, N.C., 1990); Lizabeth Cohen, *Making a New Deal* (Cambridge, 1991); George Sanchez, *Becoming Mexican American* (New York, 1993); Edmund Morgan, *American Slavery, American Freedom* (New York, 1975); John Hope Franklin, *The Color Line: Legacy for the Twenty-first Century* (Columbia, Mo., 1993).

8. Alexander Saxton, *The Rise and Fall of the White Republic* (New York, 1992); Roediger, *Wages;* Michael Rogin, *Ronald Reagan, the Movie: And Other Episodes in Political Demonology* (Berkeley, 1987); Michael Rogin, "Blackface"; Michael Rogin, "'Democracy and Burnt Cork': The End of Blackface, the Beginning of Civil Rights," presented at the University of California Humanities Research Institute Film Genres Study Group, November 1992.

9. See Kenneth Jackson, *Crabgrass Frontier: The Suburbanization of the United States* (New York, 1985); and Douglas S. Massey and Nancy A. Denton, *American Apartheid: Segregation and the Making of the Underclass* (Cambridge, Mass., 1993).

10. I thank Phil Ethington for pointing out to me that these aspects of New Deal policies emerged out of political negotiations between the segregationist Dixiecrats and liberals from the North and West. My perspective is that white supremacy was not a gnawing aberration within the New Deal coalition but rather an essential point of unity between southern white and northern white ethnics.

11. Records of the Federal Home Loan Bank Board of the Home Owners Loan Corporation. City Survey

File, Los Angeles, 1939, Neighborhood D-53, National Archives, Washington, D.C., box 74, records group 195.

12. Massey and Denton, *American Apartheid,* 54.

13. John R. Logan and Harvey Molotch, *Urban Fortunes: The Political Economy of Place* (Berkeley, 1987), 182.

14. Ibid., 114.

15. Ibid., 130.

16. See Gary Gerstle, "Working-Class Racism: Broaden the Focus," *International Labor and Working Class History* 44 (fall 1993): 36.

17. Logan and Molotch, *Urban Fortunes,* 168–69.

18. Troy Duster, "Crime, Youth Unemployment, and the Black Urban Underclass," *Crime and Delinquency* 33 (Apr. 1987): 308.

19. Ibid., 309.

20. Massey and Denton, *American Apartheid,* 55.

21. Logan and Molotch, *Urban Fortunes,* 113.

22. Robert D. Bullard, "Environmental Justice for All," in *Unequal Protection: Environmental Justice and Communities of Color,* ed. Robert Bullard (San Francisco, 1994), 9–10.

23. Massey and Denton, *American Apartheid,* 61.

24. Gertrude Ezorsky, *Racism and Justice: The Case for Affirmative Action* (Ithaca, N.Y., 1991), 25.

25. Logan and Molotch, *Urban Fortunes,* 116.

26. Jim Campen, "Lending Insights: Hard Proof That Banks Discriminate," *Dollars and Sense* 191 (Jan.–Feb. 1991): 17.

27. Mitchell Zuckoff, "Study Shows Racial Bias in Lending," *The Boston Globe,* 9 October 1992, 1, 77, 78.

28. Paul Ong and J. Eugene Grigsby III, "Race and Life-Cycle Effects on Home Ownership in Los Angeles, 1970 to 1980," *Urban Affairs Quarterly* 23 (June 1988): 605.

29. Massey and Denton, *American Apartheid,* 108.

30. Gary Orfield and Carol Ashkinaze, *The Closing Door: Conservative Policy and Black Opportunity* (Chicago, 1991), 58, 78.

31. Logan and Molotch, *Urban Fortunes.*

32. Campen, "Lending Insights," 18.

33. Gregory Squires, "'Runaway Plants,' Capital Mobility, and Black Economic Rights," in *Community and Capital in Conflict: Plant Closings and Job Loss,* ed. John C. Raines, Lenora E. Berson, and David McI. Gracie (Philadelphia, 1982), 70.

34. Gertrude Ezorsky, *Racism and Justice: The Case for Affirmative Action* (Ithaca, N.Y., 1991), 15.

35. Orfield and Ashkinaze, *The Closing Door,* 225–26.

36. McClatchy News Service, "State Taxes Gouge the Poor, Study Says," *Long Beach Press-Telegram,* 23 April 1991, A1.

37. "Proposition 13," *UC Focus* (June–July 1993): 2.

38. William Chafe, *The Unfinished Journey* (New York, 1986), 442; Noel J. Kent, "A Stacked Deck: Racial Minorities and the New American Political Economy," *Explorations in Ethnic Studies* 14 (Jan. 1991): 11.

39. Kent, "Stacked Deck," 13.

40. Melvin Oliver and James Johnson, "Economic Restructuring and Black Male Joblessness in United States Metropolitan Areas," *Urban Geography* 12 (Nov.–Dec. 1991); Gerald David Jaynes and Robin M. Williams, Jr., eds., *A Common Destiny: Blacks and American Society* (Washington, D.C., 1989); Reynolds Farley and Walter R. Allen, *The Color Line and the Quality of Life in America* (New York, 1987); Melvin Oliver and Tom Shapiro, "Wealth of a Nation: A Reassessment of Asset Inequality in America Shows at Least 1/3 of Households Are Asset Poor," *Journal of Economics and Sociology* 49 (Apr. 1990); Jonathan Kozol, *Savage Inequalities: Children in America's Schools* (New York, 1991); Cornell West, *Race Matters* (Boston, 1993).

41. Orfield and Ashkinaze, *Closing Door,* 46.

42. Ibid., 206.

43. Bart Landry, "The Enduring Dilemma of Race in America," in Alan H. Wolfe, *America at Century's End* (Berkeley, 1991), 206; Franklin, *Color Line,* 36–37.

44. Kathleen Hall Jamieson, *Dirty Politics: Deception, Distraction, and Democracy* (New York, 1992), 100.

45. Mary Edsall and Thomas Byrne Edsall, *Chain Reaction* (New York, 1991).

46. Nathan Glazer makes this argument in *Affirmative Discrimination* (New York, 1975).

47. I borrow the term "overdetermination" here from Louis Althusser, who uses it to show how dominant ideologies become credible to people in part because various institutions and agencies independently replicate them and reinforce their social power.

48. Rogena Schuyler, "Youth: We Didn't Sell Them into Slavery," *Los Angeles Times*, 21 June 1993, B4.

49. Ibid.

50. Jim Newton, "Skinhead Leader Pleads Guilty to Violence, Plot," *Los Angeles Times*, 20 Oct. 1993, A1, A15.

51. Antonin Scalia, quoted in Cheryl I. Harris, "Whiteness as Property," *Harvard Law Review*, 106 (June 1993): 1767.

52. Ibid.

53. The rise of a black middle class and the setbacks suffered by white workers during deindustrialization may seem to subvert the analysis presented here. Yet the black middle class remains fragile, far less able than other middle-class groups to translate advances in income into advances in wealth and power. Similarly, the success of neo-conservatism since the 1970s has rested on securing support from white workers for economic policies that do them objective harm by mobilizing counter-subversive electoral coalitions against busing and affirmative action, while carrying out attacks on public institutions and resources by representing "public" space and black space. See Oliver and Shapiro, "Wealth of a Nation." See also Logan and Harvey, *Urban Fortunes*.

54. Johnny Otis, *Upside Your Head! Rhythm and Blues on Central Avenue* (Hanover, N.H., 1993).

55. Mobilizations against plant shutdowns, for environmental protection, against cutbacks in education spending, and for reproductive rights all contain the potential for pan-ethnic antiracist organizing, but, too often, neglect of race as a central modality for how issues of employment, pollution, education, or reproductive rights are experienced isolates these social movements from their broadest possible base.

56. Walter Benjamin, "Madame Ariane: Second Courtyard on the Left," from *One-Way Street* (London, 1969), 98, 99.

READING 21

Notes

1. Berry, "'Broad Is Da Road Dat Leads to Death'"; SMLIC Records.

2. "My dear serpent-killer," Fran Bowen to Jeffries Wyman, C12.2, November 25, 1845, CLM. I wish to thank Sowandé Mustakeem for providing a transcription of this letter.

3. "Jim's Revelations: Threatened by the Students, Be Prepared to Resign"; *Philadelphia Press*, December 8, 1882.

4. Washington, *Medical Apartheid*, 86–100, quoted material on 86–88.

5. Figure quoted is the CPI for the year 2014. See Samuel H. Williamson, "Seven Ways to Compute the Relative Value of a U.S. Dollar Amount, 1774 to Present," *Measuring Worth*, 2014, www.measuringworth.com/uscompare/, accessed September 5, 2014.

6. See Phineas T. Barnum, *The Life of P. T. Barnum: The World-Renowned Showman . . .* (New York: Redfield, 1855; repr.; Urbana: University of Illinois Press, 2000); Benjamin Reiss, *The Showman and the Slave: Death and Memory in Barnum's America* (Cambridge, MA: Harvard University Press, 2001); "P. T. Barnum, Joice Heth and Antebellum Spectacles of Race" *American Quarterly* 51, no. 1 (March 1999): 78–107; and Sappol, *A Traffic of Dead Bodies*, 92–93.

7. Quoted in Reiss, *The Showman and the Slave,* 129.

8. Reports from the New York Medico-Chirurgical Society (1857), NLM 16, 121–22. For other dissections of black men, see "Notes on the Dissection of a Negro," *Journal of Anatomy and Physiology* 13, no. 3 (1879): 382–86.

9. Jenifer L. Barclay, "The Greatest Degree of Perfection: Disability and the Construction of Race in Southern Slave Law," in "Locating African American Literature," ed. Rhondda Thomas and Angela Naimou, *South Carolina Review* 46, no. 2 (Spring 2014): 27–43.

10. Barney Stone, *Slave Narratives.* Indiana Narratives Supplement Series r, vol. 5 (Washington, DC: LOC/WPA, 1941), 186–87.

11. For a history of anatomy, see Sappol, *A Traffic of Dead Bodies,* chaps. 2 and 3, 44–97; and for contemporary conversations, see John C. McLachlan and Debra Patten, "Anatomy Teaching: Ghosts of the Past, Present and Future," *Medical Education* 40 (2006): 243–53.

12. Sappol, *A Traffic of Dead Bodies,* 103.

13. Shultz, quoting Sozinsky, in Shultz, *Body Snatching,* 14–15.

14. Daniel Drake, *Pioneer Physician of the Midwest* (Philadelphia: University of Pennsylvania Press, 1961), 71–72.

15. Blanton, *Medicine in Virginia in the Nineteenth Century,* 69.

16. Sappol, the primary author who identified this trade, is joined with a handful of other scholars who address this topic. See Sappol, *A Traffic of Dead Bodies.*

17. Some of the records used here do not identify the enslaved or free status of the deceased person, but they often identify race.

18. Tadman, *Speculators and Slaves,* esp. chap. 3, 47–82.

19. It is equally important to consider "agricultural calendars on both sides of the Atlantic." See Stephen D. Behrendt, "Seasonality in the Trans-Atlantic Slave Trade," *Slave Voyages,* http://www.slavevoyages.org/case/assessment/essays-seasonality-oi.faces, accessed November 10, 2014.

20. These references are for eighteenth- to nineteenth-century mortuary politics, to borrow from Vincent Brown. See Brown, *The Reaper's Garden;* Nudelman, John, *Browns Body;* and Marcha V. Pike and Janice Gray Armstrong, *A Time to Mourn: Expressions of Grief in Nineteenth Century America* (Stony Brook, NY: Museums at Stony Brook, 1980).

21. Shultz, *Body Snatching,* 30.

22. Craig Steven Wilder, *Ebony & Ivy: Race, Slavery, and the Troubled History of America's Universities* (New York: Bloomsbury Press, 2013).

23. Shultz, *Body Snatching,* 14.

24. Breeden, "Body Snatchers and Anatomy Professors," 321–45; Edward C. Halperin, "The Poor, the Black, and the Marginalized as the Source of Cadavers in United States Anatomical Education," *Clinical Anatomy* 20 (2007): 489–95; and David C. Humphrey, "Dissection and Discrimination: The Social Origins of Cadavers in America, 1760–1915," *Bulletin of the New York Academy of Medicine* 49, no. 9 (September 1973): 819–27.

25. Kinney, "'A Dictate of Both Interest and Mercy'?" 1–47; and Halperin, "The Poor, the Black, and the Marginalized."

26. Wilder, *Ebony & Ivy;* and Brian Altonen, "Timeline of Medical Schools," http://brianaltonenmph.com/6-history-of-medicine-and-pharmacy/hudson-valley-medical-history/the-post-war-years/the-early-medical-profession-in-new-york/part-6-a-period-of-change/a-timeline-of-medical-schools/, accessed August 7, 2014.

27. However, there is rich evidence of physicians discrediting the work of nontraditionally trained medicinal healers, in particular, African American women. Fett, *Working Cures;* and Savitt, *Medicine and Slavery.*

28. Lane Allen, "Grandison Harris, Sr.: Slave, Resurrectionist and Judge," *Bulletin of the Georgia Academy of Science* 34, no. 4 (September 1976): 192–99, quotes on 192 and 193.

29. Tommy L. Bagger, *Free Blacks in Norfolk, Virginia, 1790–1860: The Darker Side of Freedom* (Charlottesville: Biological Society of UVA, 1997), 129–30.

30. Allen, "Grandison Harris," 193.

31. "Record Book #1 of the Faculty of the Medical College of Georgia, October 17, 1833– November 18, 1852," Augusta, January 6, 1852, 151, GML. Values computed as CPI adjusted for 2014 dollars. See Berry Slave Value Database; and derived from Samuel H. Williamson, "Seven Ways to Compute the Relative Value of a U.S. Dollar Amount, 1774 to Present," *Measuring Worth*, 2015.

32. Tanya Telfair Sharpe, "Grandison Harris: The Medical College of Georgia's Resurrection Man," in *Bones in the Basement: Postmortem Racism in Nineteenth-Century Medical Training*, ed. Robert L. Blakely and Judith M. Harrington (Washington, DC: Smithsonian Institution Press, 1997), 212–13.

33. Staff, "Grave-Robbing Slave Had a Vital Role for Medical College of Georgia," *Augusta Chronicle*, August 1995. Article found on Ancestry.com, September 13, 2000. See also Sharpe, "Grandison Harris."

34. Allen, "Grandison Harris, Sr.," 192–99.

35. "Account Book #2 of the Dean of the Faculty of the Medical College of Georgia," GML, April 22, 1853, and May 14, 1853.

36. "Account Book #2 of the Dean of the Faculty of the Medical College of Georgia," GML, May 14, 1853; November 29, 1853; December 17, 1853; January 2, 1854; March/April 1854; July 14, 1854; November 15, 1854; December 4, 1854; February 6, 1855; March 16, 1855; March 27, 1855; May 5, 14, 23, 1855; October 29, 1855; November 16, 17, 1855; January 6, 1856; February 22, 1856; November 12, 22, 1856; December 15, 31, 1856; and February 6, 1857.

37. Augusta, February 15, 1858, "Record Book #2 of the Faculty of the Medical College of Georgia, December 14, 1852–April 14th, 1879," GML. Values computed in Berry Slave Value Database and derived from the CPI adjusted for 2014. See Samuel H. Williamson, "Seven Ways to Compute the Relative Value of a U.S. Dollar Amount, 1774 to Present," *Measuring Worth*, 2015, www.measuringworth.com/uscompare/, accessed February 9, 2015.

38. Warner and Edmonson, *Dissection*, 21, 65, and 134.

39. Annie Cheney, *Body Brokers: Inside America's Underground Trade in Human Remains* (New York: Broadway Books, 2006), especially the "Human Price List," xv. See also Scott Carney, *The Red Market: On the Trail of the World's Organ Brokers, Bone Thieves, Blood Farmers, and Child Traffickers* (New York: HarperCollins, 2010); and Mary Roach, *Stiff: The Curious Lives of Human Cadavers* (New York: W. W. Norton and Co., 2004).

40. Anatomical Donation Program, Mercer University, Macon, GA, https://medicine.mercer.edu/basic-macon/adp/, accessed February 7, 2015.

41. Barnum, *The Life of P. T. Barnum*, 176.

READING 22

References

Denton, N. A. (1994). Are African Americans still hyper-segregated? In R. D. Bullard, J. E. Grigsby, III, & C. Lee (Eds.), *Residential apartheid: The American legacy* (pp. 49–81). Los Angeles, CA: CAAS Publications, University of California.

Duncan, O. D., Cuzzort, R. P., & Duncan, B. (1961). *Statistical geography: Problems in analyzing areal data*. New York, NY: Free Press.

Duncan, O. D., & Duncan, B. (1955). A methodological analysis of segregation indices. *American Sociological Review, 20*, 210–217.

Hartman, C., & Squires, G. D. (Eds.). (2013). *From foreclosure to fair lending: Advocacy, organizing, occupy, and the pursuit of equitable credit*. New York, NY: New Village Press.

Jargowsky, P. A. (1997). *Poverty and place: Ghettos, barrios, and the American city*. New York, NY: Russell Sage Foundation.

Kochhar, R., Fry, R., & Taylor, P. (2011). *Twenty-to-one: Wealth gaps rise to record highs between whites, blacks and Hispanics*. Washington, DC: Pew Research Center.

Lieberson, S. (1981). An asymmetrical approach to segregation. In C. Peach, V. Robinson, & S. Smith (Eds.), *Ethnic segregation in cities* (pp. 61–82). London, UK: Croom Helm.

Logan, J. R., & Stults, B. J. (2011). *The persistence of segregation in the metropolis: New findings from the 2010 census* (Census brief prepared for Project US2010). Retrieved from http://www.s4.brown.edu/us2010/Data0Report/report2.pdf

Massey, D. S. (1990). American apartheid: Segregation and the making of the underclass. *American Journal of Sociology, 95*, 1153–1188.

Massey, D. S., & Brodmann, S. (2014). *Spheres of influence: The social ecology of racial and class inequality.* New York, NY: Russell Sage Foundation.

Massey, D. S., & Denton, N. A. (1988). The dimensions of residential segregation. *Social Forces, 67*, 281–315.

Massey, D. S., & Denton, N. A. (1989). Hypersegregation in U.S. metropolitan areas: Black and Hispanic segregation along five dimensions. *Demography, 26*, 373–393.

Massey, D. S., & Denton, N. A. (1993). *American apartheid: Segregation and the making of the underclass.* Cambridge, MA: Harvard University Press.

Massey, D. S., & Fischer, M. J. (2000). How segregation concentrates poverty. *Ethnic and Racial Studies, 23*, 670–691.

Peterson, R. D., & Krivo, L. J. (2010). *Divergent social worlds: Neighborhood crime and the racial-spatial divide.* New York, NY: Russell Sage Foundation.

Pettigrew, T. (1979). Racial change and social policy. *Annals of the American Academy of Political and Social Science, 441*, 114–131.

Quillian, L. (2012). Segregation and poverty concentration: The role of three segregations. *American Sociological Review, 77*, 354–379.

Rugh, J. S., Albright, L., & Massey, D. S. (Forthcoming). Race, space, and cumulative disadvantage: A case study of the subprime lending collapse. *Social Problems.*

Rugh, J. S., & Massey, D. S. (2010). Racial segregation and the American foreclosure crisis. *American Sociological Review, 75*, 629–651.

Sampson, R. J. (2012). *Great American city: Chicago and the enduring neighborhood effect.* Chicago, IL: University of Chicago Press.

Sharkey, P. (2013). *Stuck in place: Urban neighborhoods and the end of progress toward racial equality.* Chicago, IL: University of Chicago Press.

Small, M. (2004). *Villa Victoria: The transformation of social capital in a Boston barrio.* Chicago, IL: University of Chicago Press.

White, M. J. (1983). The measurement of spatial segregation. *American Journal of Sociology, 88*, 1008–1019.

Wilkes, R., & Iceland, J. (2004). Hypersegregation in the twenty-first century: An update and analysis. *Demography, 41*, 23–36.

Wilson, W. J. (1987). *The truly disadvantaged: The inner city, the underclass, and urban policy.* Chicago, IL: University of Chicago Press.

READING 24

Notes

1. Robert D. Bullard, 1994, *Dumping in Dixie: Race, Class and Environmental Quality.* Boulder, CO: Westview Press.

2. Robert D. Bullard, "Solid Waste Sites and the Black Houston Community," *Sociological Inquiry* 53 (Spring 1983):273–288.

3. U.S. General Accounting Office (1983), *Siting of Hazardous Waste Landfills and Their Correlation with Racial and Economic Status of Surrounding Communities,* Washington, DC: Government Printing Office.

4. Commission for Racial Justice (1987), *Toxic Wastes and Race in the United States,* New York: United Church of Christ.

5. Charles Lee, 1992, *Proceedings: The First National People of Color Environmental Leadership Summit,* New York: United Church of Christ Commission for Racial Justice.

6. Dana Alston, "Transforming a Movement: People of Color Unite at Summit against Environmental Racism," *Sojourner* 21 (1992), pp. 30–31.

7. William K. Reilly, "Environmental Equity: EPA's Position," *EPA Journal* 18 (March/April 1992): 18–19.

8. R. D. Bullard and B. H. Wright, "The Politics of Pollution: Implications for the Black Community," *Phylon* 47 (March 1986): 71–78.

9. Robert D. Bullard, "Race and Environmental Justice in the United States," *Yale Journal of International Law* 18 (Winter 1993): 319–335; Robert D. Bullard, "The Threat of Environmental Racism," *Natural Resources & Environment* 7 (Winter 1993): 23–26, 55–56.

10. Louis Sullivan, "Remarks at the First Annual Conference on Childhood Lead Poisoning," in Alliance to End Childhood Lead Poisoning, *Preventing Child Lead Poisoning: Final Report*, Washington, DC: Alliance to End Childhood Lead Poisoning, October, 1991, p. A-2.

11. Bill Lann Lee, "Environmental Litigation on Behalf of Poor, Minority Children, Matthews v. Coye: A Case Study," paper presented at the Annual Meeting of the American Association for the Advancement of Science, Chicago (February 9, 1992).

12. Ibid., p. 32.

13. Ibid.

14. Robert D. Bullard, "The Environmental Justice Framework: A Strategy for Addressing Unequal Protection," paper presented at Resources for the Future Conference on Risk Management, Annapolis, MD (November 1992).

15. Paul Mohai and Bunyan Bryant, "Race, Poverty, and the Environment," *EPA Journal* 18 (March/April 1993): 1–8; R. D. Bullard, "In Our Backyards," *EPA Journal* 18 (March/April 1992): 11–12; D. R. Wernette and L. A. Nieves, "Breathing Polluted Air," *EPA Journal* 18 (March/April 1992): 16–17; Patrick C. West, "Health Concerns for Fish-Eating Tribes?" *EPA Journal* 18 (March/April 1992): 15–16.

16. Marianne Lavelle and Marcia Coyle, "Unequal Protection," *National Law Journal* (September 21, 1992): S1–S2.

17. Robert D. Bullard, ed., *Confronting Environmental Racism: Voices from the Grassroots*, Boston: South End Press, 1993, chapter 1; Robert D. Bullard, "Waste and Racism: A Stacked Deck?" *Forum for Applied Research and Public Policy* 8 (Spring 1993): 29–35; Robert D. Bullard (ed.), *In Search of the New South—The Black Urban Experience in the 1970s and 1980s* (Tuscaloosa, AL: University of Alabama Press, 1991).

18. Florence Wagman Roisman, "The Lessons of American Apartheid: The Necessity and Means of Promoting Residential Racial Integration," *Iowa Law Review* 81 (December 1995): 479–525.

19. Joe R. Feagin, "A House Is Not a Home: White Racism and U.S. Housing Practices," in R. D. Bullard, J. E. Grigsby, and Charles Lee, eds., *Residential Apartheid: The American Legacy*, Los Angeles: UCLA Center for Afro-American Studies Publication, 1994, pp. 17–48.

20. Eric Mann, *L.A.'s Lethal Air: New Strategies for Policy, Organizing, and Action*, Los Angeles: Labor/Community Strategy Center, 1991, p. 31.

21. Jim Motavalli, "Toxic Targets: Polluters That Dump on Communities of Color Are Finally Being Brought to Justice," *E Magazine*, 4 (July/August 1997): 29–41.

22. Joe Bandy, "Reterritorializing Borders: Transnational Environmental Justice on the U.S./Mexico Border," *Race, Gender, and Class* 5 (1997): 80–103.

23. Bunyan Bryant and Paul Mohai, *Race and the Incidence of Environmental Hazards* (Boulder, CO: Westview Press, 1992); Bunyan Bryant, ed., *Environmental Justice*, pp. 8–34.

24. R. Pinderhughes, "Who Decides What Constitutes a Pollution Problem?" *Race, Gender, and Class* 5 (1997): 130–152.

25. Diane Takvorian, "Toxics and Neighborhoods Don't Mix," *Land Use Forum: A Journal of Law, Policy and Practice* 2 (Winter 1993): 28–31; R. D. Bullard, "Examining the Evidence of Environmental Racism," *Land Use Forum: A Journal of Law, Policy, and Practice* 2 (Winter 1993): 6–11.

26. For an in-depth examination of the Houston case study, see R. D. Bullard, 1987, *Invisible Houston:*

The Black Experience in Boom and Bust. College Station, TX: Texas A&M University Press, pp. 60–75.

27. Ruth Rosen, "Who Gets Polluted: The Movement for Environmental Justice," *Dissent* (Spring 1994): 223–230; R. D. Bullard, "Environmental Justice: It's More Than Waste Facility Siting," *Social Science Quarterly* 77 (September 1996): 493–499.

28. Commission for Racial Justice, *Toxic Wastes and Race in the United States,* pp. xiii–xiv.

29. U.S. General Accounting Office, *Siting of Hazardous Waste Landfills and Their Correlation with Racial and Economic Status of Surrounding Communities,* Washington, DC: U.S. General Accounting Office, 1983, p. 1.

30. Robert D. Bullard, ed., *Confronting Environmental Racism: Voices from the Grassroots,* Boston: South End, 1993; Robert D. Bullard, "The Threat of Environmental Racism," *Natural Resources & Environment* 7 (Winter 1993): 23–26; Bunyan Bryant and Paul Mohai, eds., *Race and the Incidence of Environmental Hazards,* Boulder, CO: Westview Press, 1992; Regina Austin and Michael Schill, "Black, Brown, Poor and Poisoned: Minority Grassroots Environmentalism and the Quest for EcoJustice," *The Kansas Journal of Law and Public Policy* 1 (1991): 69–82; Kelly C. Colquette and Elizabeth A. Henry Robertson, "Environmental Racism: The Causes, Consequences, and Commendations," *Tulane Environmental Law Journal* 5 (1991), 153–207; Rachel D. Godsil, "Remedying Environmental Racism," *Michigan Law Review* 90 (1991): 394–427.

31. Bullard and Feagin, "Racism and the City," pp. 55–76; Robert D. Bullard, "Dismantling Environmental Racism in the USA," *Local Environment* 4 (1999): 5–19.

32. W. J. Kruvant, "People, Energy, and Pollution," in D. K. Newman and Dawn Day, eds., *The American Energy Consumer,* Cambridge, Mass.: Ballinger, 1975, pp. 125–167; Robert D. Bullard, "Solid Waste Sites and the Black Houston Community," *Sociological Inquiry* 53 (Spring 1983): 273–288; United Church of Christ Commission for Racial Justice, *Toxic Wastes and Race in the United*

States, New York: Commission for Racial Justice, 1987; Dick Russell, "Environmental Racism," *The Amicus Journal* 11 (Spring 1989): 22–32; Eric Mann, *L.A.'s Lethal Air: New Strategies for Policy, Organizing, and Action,* Los Angeles: Labor/Community Strategy Center, 1991; D. R. Wernette and L. A. Nieves, "Breathing Polluted Air: Minorities Are Disproportionately Exposed," *EPA Journal* 18 (March/April 1992): 16–17; Bryant and Mohai, *Race and the Incidence of Environmental Hazards;* Benjamin Goldman and Laura J. Fitton, *Toxic Wastes and Race Revisited,* Washington, DC: Center for Policy Alternatives, NAACP, and United Church of Christ, 1994.

33. Myrick A. Freedman, "The Distribution of Environmental Quality," in Allen V. Kneese and Blair T. Bower (eds.), *Environmental Quality Analysis,* Baltimore: Johns Hopkins University Press for Resources for the Future, 1971; Michael Gelobter, "The Distribution of Air Pollution by Income and Race," paper presented at the Second Symposium on Social Science in Resource Management, Urbana, Illinois (June 1988); Gianessi et al., "The Distributional Effects of Uniform Air Pollution Policy in the U.S.," *Quarterly Journal of Economics* (May 1979): 281–301.

34. Patrick C. West, J. Mark Fly, and Robert Marans, "Minority Anglers and Toxic Fish Consumption: Evidence from a State-Wide Survey in Michigan," in Bryant and Mohai, *Race and the Incidence of Environmental Hazards,* pp. 100–113.

35. Robert D. Bullard, "Solid Waste Sites and the Black Houston Community," *Sociological Inquiry* 53 (Spring 1983): 273–288; Robert D. Bullard, *Invisible Houston: The Black Experience in Boom and Bust,* College Station, TX: Texas A&M University Press, 1987, chapter 6; Robert D. Bullard, "Environmental Racism and Land Use," *Land Use Forum: A Journal of Law, Policy & Practice* 2 (Spring 1993): 6–11.

36. United Church of Christ Commission for Racial Justice, *Toxic Wastes and Race;* Paul Mohai and Bunyan Bryant, "Environmental Racism: Reviewing the Evidence," in Bryant and Mohai, *Race and the Incidence of Environmental Hazards;* Paul Stretesky and Michael J. Hogan,

"Environmental Justice: An Analysis of Superfund Sites in Florida," *Social Problems* 45 (May 1998): 268–287.

37. Marianne Lavelle and Marcia Coyle, "Unequal Protection: The Racial Divide in Environmental Law," *National Law Journal,* September 21, 1992.

38. Agency for Toxic Substances Disease Registry, *The Nature and Extent of Lead Poisoning in Children in the United States: A Report to Congress,* Atlanta: U.S. Department of Health and Human Resources, 1988, pp. 1–12.

39. J. Schwartz and R. Levine, "Lead: An Example of the Job Ahead," *EPA Journal* 18 (March/April 1992): 32–44.

40. Centers for Disease Control and Prevention, "Update: Blood Lead Levels—United States, 1991–1994," *Mortality and Morbidity Weekly Report* 46, no. 7 (February 21, 1997): 141–146.

41. James L. Pinkle, D. J. Brody, E. W. Gunter, R. A. Kramer, D. C. Paschal, K. M. Glegal, and T. D. Matte, "The Decline in Blood Lead Levels in the United States: The National Health and Nutrition Examination Survey (NHANES)," *Journal of the American Medical Association* 272 (1994): 284–291.

42. Arnold W. Reitze, Jr., "A Century of Air Pollution Control Law: What Worked; What Failed; What Might Work," *Environmental Law* 21 (1991): 1549.

43. For an in-depth discussion of transportation investments and social equity issues, see R. D. Bullard and G. S. Johnson, eds., *Just Transportation: Dismantling Race and Class Barriers to Mobility.* Gabriola Island, BC: New Society Publishers, 1997.

44. Sid Davis, "Race and the Politics of Transportation in Atlanta," in R. D. Bullard and G. S. Johnson, *Just Transportation,* pp. 84–96; Environmental Justice Resource Center, *Sprawl Atlanta: Social Equity Dimensions of Uneven Growth and Development,* a report prepared for the Turner Foundation, Atlanta: Clark Atlanta University (January 1999).

45. D. R. Wernette and L. A. Nieves, "Breathing Polluted Air: Minorities Are Disproportionately Exposed," *EPA Journal* 18 (March 1992): 16–17.

46. CDC, "Asthma–United States, 1982–1992." *MMWR* 43 (1995): 952–955.

47. CDC, "Asthma Morality and Hospitalization among Children and Young Adults—United States, 1980–1993." *MMWR* 45 (1996): 350–353.

48. Anna E. Pribitkin, "The Need for Revision of Ozone Standards: Why Has the EPA Failed to Respond?" *Temple Environmental Law & Technology Journal* 13 (1994): 104.

49. CDC/NCHS, *Health United States* 1994, DHHS Pub. No. (PHS) 95–1232, Tables 83, 84, 86, 87.

50. CDC, "Asthma–United States, 1982–1992." *MMWR* 43 (1995): 952–955.

51. CDC, "Disabilities among Children Aged Less Than or Equal to 17 Years—United States, 1991–1992." *MMWR* 44 (1995): 609–613.

52. U.S. EPA, "Review of National Ambient Air Quality Standards for Ozone, Assessment of Scientific and Technical Information," OAQPS Staff Paper, Research Triangle Park, NC: EPA, 1996; Halûk Özkaynak, John D. Spengler, Marie O'Neil, Jianping Xue, Hui Zhou, Kathy Gilbert, and Sonja Ramstrom, "Ambient Ozone Exposure and Emergency Hospital Admissions and Emergency Room Visits for Respiratory Problems in Thirteen U.S. Cities," in American Lung Association, *Breathless: Air Pollution and Hospital Admissions/ Emergency Room Visits in 13 Cities,* Washington, DC: American Lung Association, 1996; American Lung Association, *Out of Breath: Populations-at-Risk to Alternative Ozone Levels,* Washington, DC: American Lung Association, 1995.

53. Centers for Disease Control and Prevention, National Center for Environmental Health, Division of Environmental Hazards and Health Effects, Air Pollution and Respiratory Branch, "Asthma Mortality and Hospitalization Among Children and Young Adults—United States, 1980–1993," *Morbidity and Mortality Weekly Report,* 45 (1996).

54. Centers for Disease Control, "Asthma: United States, 1980–1990," *MMWR* 39 (1992): 733–735.

55. Mary C. White, Ruth Etzel, Wallace D. Wilcox, and Christine Lloyd, "Exacerbations of Childhood

Asthma and Ozone Pollution in Atlanta," *Environmental Research* 65 (1994): 56.

56. R. D. Bullard, "The Legacy of Apartheid and Environmental Racism," *St. John's Journal of Legal Commentary* 9 (Spring 1994): 445–474.

57. Donald Schueler, "Southern Exposure," *Sierra* 77 (November/December 1992): 45.

58. Robert D. Bullard, "Ecological Inequities and the New South: Black Communities Under Siege." *Journal of Ethnic Studies* 17 (Winter 1990): 101–115; Donald L. Bartlett and James B. Steele, "Paying a Price for Polluters," *Time* (November 23, 1998), pp. 72–80.

59. Schueler, "Southern Exposure," p. 46.

60. Ibid., pp. 46–47.

61. James O'Byrne and Mark Schleifstein, "Drinking Water in Danger," *The Times Picayune,* February 19, 1991, p. A5.

62. Conger Beasley, "Of Poverty and Pollution: Keeping Watch in Cancer Alley," pp. 39–45.

63. Bartlett and Steele, "Paying a Price for Polluters," p. 77.

64. Conger Beasley, "Of Pollution and Poverty: Deadly Threat on Native Lands," *Buzzworm,* 2 (5) (1990): 39–45; Robert Tomsho, "Dumping Grounds: Indian Tribes Contend with Some of the Worst of America's Pollution," *The Wall Street Journal* (November 29, 1990); Jane Kay, "Indian Lands Targeted for Waste Disposal Sites," *San Francisco Examiner* (April 10, 1991); Valerie Taliman, "Stuck Holding the Nation's Nuclear Waste," *Race, Poverty & Environment Newsletter* (Fall 1992): 6–9.

65. Bradley Angel, *The Toxic Threat to Indian Lands: A Greenpeace Report*. San Francisco: Greenpeace, 1992; Al Geddicks, *The New Resource Wars: Native and Environmental Struggles Against Multinational Corporations*, Boston: South End Press, 1993.

66. Jane Kay, "Indian Lands Targeted for Waste Disposal Sites," *San Francisco Examiner* (April 10, 1991).

67. Ward Churchill and Winona la Duke, "Native America: The Political Economy of Radioactive Colonialism," *Insurgent Sociologist* 13 (1) (1983): 61–63.

68. Greenpeace, "The Logic Behind Hazardous Waste Export," *Greenpeace Waste Trade Update* (First Quarter 1992): 1–2.

69. Dana Alston and Nicole Brown, "Global Threats to People of Color," pp. 179–194 in R. D. Bullard, ed., *Confronting Environmental Racism: Voices from the Grassroots,* Boston: Southend Press, 1993.

70. Roberto Sanchez, "Health and Environmental Risks of the Maquiladora in Mexicali," *Natural Resources Journal* 30 (1) (1990): 163–186.

71. Beatriz Johnston Hernandez, "Dirty Growth," *The New Environmentalist* (August 1993).

72. T. Barry and B. Simms, *The Challenge of Cross Border Environmentalism: The U.S.-Mexico Case,* Albuquerque, NM: The Inter-Hemispheric Education Resource Center, 1994.

READING 25

Notes

1. Boston, John. 2003. "At Long Last, Going to Church Finally Pays." Online [cited 7 August 2003]. Available from http://www.the-signal.com/News/V iewStory.asp?storyID-2906.

2. Olson, Ted. 2004. "Fred Caldwell: Paying the Price for Unity." *Today's Christian,* July/August.

3. Excerpted from Emerson, Michael O. 2006. *People of the Dream: Multiracial Congregations in the United States.* Princeton, NJ: Princeton University Press, Chapter 2.

4. Hamilton, David L., and Tina K. Trolier. 1986. "Stereotype and Stereotyping: An Overview of the Cognitive Approach." In *Prejudice, Discrimination, and Racism,* eds. John F. Dovidio and Samuel L. Gaertner, 127–63, Orlando, FL: Academic Press, p. 188.

5. These seven biases are the result of several research works. See Hewstone, Miles, Jos Jaspers, and Mansur Lalljee. 1992. "Social Representations, Social Attribution and Social

Identity: The Intergroup Images of 'Public' and 'Comprehensive' Schoolboys." *European Journal of Social Psychology* 12:241–69; Hogg, Michael A., and Dominic Abrams. 1988. *Social Identifications: A Social Psychology of Intergroup Relations and Group Processes.* London: Routledge; Howard, John W., and Myron Rothbart. 1980. "Social Categorization and Memory for In-group and Out-group Behavior." *Journal of Personality and Social Psychology* 38:301–10; Linville, Patricia W., Peter Salovey, and Gregory W. Fischer. 1986. "Stereotyping and Perceived Distributions of Social Characteristics: An Application to Ingroup-Outgroup Perception." In *Prejudice, Discrimination, and Racism,* eds. John F. Dovidio and Samuel L. Gaertner, 165–208, Orlando, FL: Academic Press; Tajfel, Henri. 1978. "Social Categorization, Social Identity and Social Comparison." In *Differentiation Between Social Groups: Studies in the Social Psychology of Intergroup Relations,* ed. Henri Tajfel, 61–76, London: Academic Press; Taylor, S. E. 1981. "A Categorization Approach to Stereotyping." In *Cognitive Processes in Stereotyping and Intergroup Behavior,* ed. D. L. Hamilton, 83–114, Hillsdale, NJ: Erlbaum; Wilder, D. A. 1981. "Perceiving Persons as a Group: Categorization and Ingroup Relations." In *Cognitive Processes in Stereotyping and Intergroup Behavior,* ed. D. L. Hamilton, 213–57, Hillsdale, NJ: Erlbaum.

6. Niebuhr, Reinhold. 1932. *Moral Man and Immoral Society: A Study in Ethics and Politics.* New York & London: C. Scribner's.

7. Niebuhr 1932:xxii–xxiii.

8. Hechter, Michael. 1987. *Principles of Social Solidarity.* Berkeley: University of California Press, p. 41.

9. This section was excerpted from Emerson, Michael O., and Christian Smith. 2000. *Divided by Faith: Evangelical Religion and the Problem of Race in America.* New York: Oxford University, Chapter 8.

10. Hollinger, David. 1995. *Postethnic America: Beyond Multiculturalism.* New York: Basic Books.

11. Much but not all of this section is excerpted from Emerson, Michael O. 2006. *People of the Dream,* Chapters 4 and 7.

READING 26

Notes

1. A study funded by USA Swimming found that 58.2% of White children and adolescents were "skilled" swimmers as compared to 31.2% of Black children and adolescents (Irwin, Irwin, Martin, & Ross, 2010, p. 20). Another study calculated the annual drowning rate among Black children at 1.34 deaths per 100,000 population and the rate among White children at 0.48 deaths per 100,000 (Laosee, Gilchrist, & Rudd, 2012).

2. One exception is a 2010 article published in the *International Journal of Design and Nature and Ecodynamics* that contends there are physical explanations (different centers of gravity) for why the fastest runners in the world are Black and the fastest swimmers are White (Bejan, Jones, & Charles, 2010). For a critique of this argument, see Myers (2011).

3. The relationship between swimming ability and the risk of drowning is complicated and requires more thorough study (Brenner, Saluja, & Smith, 2003). The general consensus among scholars, doctors, and concerned organizations, however, is that swim lessons and swimming proficiency lower the risk of drowning deaths and that Black Americans are more likely to drown than Whites in part because they are less likely to know how to swim. In a 2011 article published in the *Journal of Black Studies,* a group of researchers who had undertaken a major study on minority swimming noted that "adequate swimming skills are considered a protective agent toward the prevention of drowning" and identified swimming ability as a "possible cause" for the drowning disparity between Blacks and Whites (Irwin, Irwin, Ryan, & Drayer, 2011). A 2010 technical report published by the American Academy of Pediatrics identified "poor swimming ability" as one of the "important factors" that may account for the drowning disparity between Blacks and Whites (Weiss, 2010). A 2009 study funded by the National Institute of Health found that swim lessons reduced the risk of drowning among children 1 to 4 years old by 88% and reduced the risk of drowning among children five to nineteen, although the reduction for the older age group was not "statistically significant."

The researchers who conducted the study concluded that the results for the older group were inconclusive because of the small sample size. They studied only 27 incidents of drowning for that group, of which seven knew how to swim (Brenner et al., 2009; "Swimming Lessons Do Not Increase Drowning Risk in Young Children," 2009). Finally, the explicit rationale behind USA Swimming's "Make a Splash" initiative and the "Constraints Impacting Minority Swimming Participation" study is that the higher drowning rate among Black Americans is caused in large part by their lower rates of swimming proficiency (Irwin et al., 2010, p. 3). None of this is conclusive, but it is the current consensus.

4. Although much less blatant and pervasive than in the past, Black Americans do still face potential racial discrimination in accessing swimming pools, as exemplified by the 2009 Valley Club incident in which a private swim club in suburban Philadelphia cancelled a lease agreement with an inner-city day camp after club members encountered Black and Latino campers in the pool. When pressed to explain why the club would not permit the campers back, club president John Duesler stated, "there was concern that a lot of kids would change the complexion . . . and the atmosphere of the club" (Gerhart, 2009; Tillman & Stendahl, 2009).

References

5,000 Negroes used Highland Park Pool this year. (1952, September 6). *Pittsburgh Courier*, p. 2.

1 Druid Hill Park city pool closed. (1956, July 24). *Baltimore Sun*, p. 13.

32 new pools to help Chicago keep its cool. (1968, March 13). *Chicago News*, "Swimming Pools—Chicago," clip file, Municipal Reference Collection, Harold Washington Library Center, Chicago, Illinois.

1500 troops go to area ready to shoot. (1966, July 16). *Chicago Tribune*, 1, p. 2.

2 Negro orphans jeered out of Baltimore pool. (1963, June 25). *New York Times*, p. 13.

Adieu to Grove Pool. (1957, October 29). *Kansas City Times*, p. 1.

Allen, R., & Nickel, D. (1969). The Negro and learning to swim: The buoyancy problem related to reported biological differences. *Journal of Negro Education, 38,* 408–409.

Attendance relatively small as city's public pools open. (1956, June 24). *Baltimore Sun*, p. 38.

Attner, P. (1972, May 31). Lack of pools hurts area swimming. *Washington Post*, p. D8.

Baltimore arrests 13 in racial dispute. (1962, September 4). *New York Times*, p. 26.

Baltimore reports attendance drop at integrated pools. (1956, August 27). *Washington Star*, p. B2.

Bejan, A., Jones, E., & Charles, J. (2010). The evolution of speed in athletics: Why the fastest runners are black and swimmers white. *International Journal of Design and Nature & Ecodynamics, 5,* 199–211.

Bigots hurl insults at race swimmer. (1962, August 11). *Pittsburgh Courier*, p. 1.

Birmingham keeps parks closed. (1962, March 17). *Chicago Defender*, p. 2.

Brenner, R., Saluja, G., & Smith, G. (2003). Swimming lessons, swimming ability, and the risk of drowning. *Injury Control and Safety Promotion, 10,* 211–215.

Brenner, R., Taneja, G., Haynie, D., Trumble, A., Qian, C., Klinger, R., & Klebanoff, M. (2009). Association between swimming lessons and drowning in childhood. *Archives of Pediatrics and Adolescent Medicine, 163,* 203–210.

Brozan, N. (1976, July 2). Swimming in the city. *New York Times*, p. 36.

Buyers plunge to get into swim as installation of pools widens. (1960, January 11). *New York Times*, p. 95.

Calverton will have new pool. (1965, June 26). *Washington Post*, p. D14.

Chevy Chase club explains stand on membership. (1962, January 17). *Washington Star*, p. A17.

City of Los Angeles Department of Parks and Recreation. (2006). *Pool assessment report*, pp. 2–3. Available from http://laparks.org

City pools open. (1974, June 23). *Los Angeles Times*, p. GB3.

Claiborne, R., & Francis, E. (2010). 6 teens drown while wading in Louisiana's Red River. *ABC News.* Available from http://abcnews.go.com

Close 4 Fla. pools over race issue. (1961, June 13). *Chicago Defender,* p. 3.

Close pool to avoid integration. (1961, July 6). *Chicago Defender,* p. 19.

Club in New Carrollton excludes Negro family. (1968, July 14). *Washington Star,* p. B4.

Collins, J. (2011, May 30). Public pools closing across country as cities struggle with budget cuts. *Huffington Post.* Available from http://www.huffingtonpost.com/201l/05/30/publicpools-closing-acro_n_868753.html

Community pool opens. (1960, August 13). *Washington Post,* p. D2.

Cool minipools for the hot summer. (1968, April). *American City,* pp. 81–83.

The cooperative family swim club. (1959). *Swimming Pool Data and Reference Annual,* p. 17.

County of Los Angeles Department of Parks and Recreation. (2005–2006). *Annual report,* p. 3. Available from http://file.lacounty.gov/dpr/cmsl_069242.pdf

County swimming pools to be free. (1975, April 3). *Los Angeles Times,* p. WS12.

Data on swimming pools. (1952, March). *Recreation, 45,* 575.

Dawson v. Mayor and City Council of Baltimore. (1955). 220 F. 2d 387.

Donihi, R. (1963, June 23). Young people take plunge into young summer. *Washington Post,* p. F5.

Estimated population of Los Angeles County. (2005). *Los Angeles Almanac.* Available from http://laalmanac.com

Fairfax club affirms barring of Negro family. (1965, July 30). *Washington Star,* p. C2.

Feelings vary on swim lessons. (1976, October 30). *Chicago Tribune,* p. 12.

Feinberg, L. (1968, December 14). Swim league spurns plea to integrate. *Washington Post,* p. B1.

Gerhart, A. (2009, July 11). Alleged prejudice starts probe at club. *Washington Post,* p. A2.

Goal: A pool for every neighborhood. (1967, July 19). *Chicago News,* "Swimming Pools—Chicago," clip file, Municipal Reference Collection, Harold Washington Library Center, Chicago, Illinois.

Grove Pool is closed. (1957, October 21). *Kansas City Times,* p. 3.

Guard patrol is cut in Chicago ghetto. (1966, July 18). *New York Times,* p. 17.

Harvey, B. (1962, May 27). Pools are opening. *Washington Post,* p. C5.

Here's how a westsider explains the outbreak. (1966, July 16–22). *Chicago Defender,* p. 7.

Hirsch, A. (1983). *Making the second ghetto: Race and housing in Chicago, 1940–1960.* New York, NY: Cambridge University Press.

How a swim club was born this year. (1964, September 5). *Washington Post,* p. E3.

Integrated Baltimore pool shut. (1956, July 23). *Washington Star,* p. B2.

Integration effort fails at Virginia City Pool. (1966, August 11). *Washington Star,* p. B3.

Integration vote fails at Bethesda swim club. (1966, August 2). *Washington Star,* p. B3.

Irwin, C., Irwin, R., Martin, N., & Ross, S. (2010). Constraints impacting minority swimming participation, phase II (presented to USA Swimming). Available from http://www.usaswimming.org

Irwin, C., Irwin, R., Ryan, T., & Drayer, J. (2011). The legacy of fear: Is fear impacting fatal and non-fatal drowning of African American children. *Journal of Black Studies, 42,* 561.

Irwin, R., Drayer, J., Irwin, C., Ryan, T., & Southall, R. (2008). *Constraints impacting minority swimming participation* (presented to USA Swimming). Available from http://www.usaswimming.org

Jackson, K. (1985). *Crabgrass frontiers: The suburbanization of the United States.* New York, NY: Oxford University Press, 241–243.

Jackson case ruling. (1971, June 17). *Chicago Defender*, p. 17.

James, F. (2010, August 3). Six teens' drowning a reminder of swimming disparity. *NPR*. Available from http://www.npr.org

Kuettner, A. (1963, August 31). Integration faces hardest going in recreation facilities. *Chicago Defender*, p. 9.

Laosee, O., Gilchrist, J., & Rudd, R. (2012). Drowning—United States, 2005–2009. *Morbidity and Mortality Weekly Report, 26*, 344.

Large splash being made by pool clubs. (1962, August 9). *Los Angeles Times*, p. G9.

Lindsay smiles his way through city. (1971, August 14). *New York Times*, p. 29.

Los Angeles County population growth. (2000). Available from http://www.laep.org

McKinley, J. (2011, July 7). Looking for a pool and coming up dry as cities shave budgets. *New York Times*, p. A13.

McKinley Pool in bad condition. (1962, March 30). *Washington Star*, p. A3.

Minor incidents at Paulson Pool to be stopped. (1953, July 4). *Pittsburgh Courier*, p. 1.

Murray, A. (1959, December 6). Co-op clubs offer swimming for families. *New York Times*, p. X31.

Myers, S., Jr. (2011). The economics of diversity: The efficiency vs. equity trade-off. In S. Chen (Ed.), *Diversity management: Theoretical perspectives and practical approaches* (pp. 55–70). New York: Nova Science.

Myers, S., Jr., & Cuesta, A. (2012). *Competitive swimming and racial disparities in drowning*. Retrieved from http://www.hhh.umn.edu/centers/rwc/pdf/CompetitiveswimmingAPPAM2012.pdf

Need for democracy cited here. (1945, September 1). *Pittsburgh Courier*, p. 1.

New pool group lets contract. (1962, April 21). *Washington Post*, p. D4.

O'Dowd, P. (2010, July 26). Amid heat wave, budget cuts force pool closures. *NPR All Things Considered*. Available from http://www.npr.org

Pangburn, W., & Allen, F. (1943). *Long range recreation plan, city of Baltimore, Maryland*. Baltimore, MD: Department of Public Recreation.

Pickets ask reopening of closed pool. (1963, July 6). *Washington Star*, p. A16.

Police get 12-hour duty in Westside uproar. (1966, July 16–22). *Chicago Defender*, p. 2.

Pool reopened after 23 years. (1988, July 7). *Los Angeles Sentinel*, p. A2.

The pools inadequate? The west side picture. (1966, July 16). *Chicago News*, "Swimming Pools—Chicago," clip file, Municipal Reference Collection, Harold Washington Library Center, Chicago, Illinois.

Pool under way at London Towne. (1969, April 19). *Washington Post*, p. 71.

Program rushed for slum youth. (1966, August 7). *New York Times*, p. 48.

Race riot in Chicago. (1960, July 31). *New York Times*, p. 15.

Robertson, C. (2010, August 4). 6 teenagers drown in river. *New York Times*, p. A12.

Rohrer, F. (2010, September 3). Why don't black Americans swim? *BBC News*. Available from http://www.bbc.co.uk

Sexton, C. (2012, May 25). Phoenix's city pools open once again. *The Republic*. Available from http://www.azcentral.com

Six outdoor pools for whites only. (1953, July 25). Baltimore *Afro-American*, p. 8.

Six teens drown in La. river. (2010, August 7). *Afro-American*. Available from http://afro.com

Six teens drown in Shreveport's Red River. (2010, August 3). *CNN*. Available from http://www.cnn.com

Skwine, B. (2009, June 21). The dead pool. *Philadelphia Weekly*. Available from http://www.philadelphiaweekly.com

Stengle, J. (2010, August 3). Red River drownings. Associated Press. Available from http://www.huffingtonpost.com

St. Louis Division of Parks and Recreation. (1949). *Annual report.* St. Louis, MO: Department of Public Welfare.

St. Louis Division of Parks and Recreation. (1954). *Annual report.* St. Louis, MO: Department of Public Welfare, p. 18.

St. Louis Division of Parks and Recreation. (1958). *Annual report.* St. Louis, MO: Department of Public Welfare, pp. 1–2.

Sugrue, T. (1996). *Origins of the urban crisis: Race and inequality in postwar Detroit.* Princeton, NJ: Princeton University Press.

Swimming lessons do not increase drowning risk in young children. (2009, March 2). *NIH News.* Retrieved from http://www.nih.gov/news/health/mar2009/nichd-02a.htm

Swimming pool sales making a bigger splash. (1971, October 23). *Philadelphia Evening Bulletin,* "Swimming Pools" clip file, Newspaper Clippings Collection, Urban Archives, Temple University, Philadelphia, Pennsylvania.

Tillman v. Wheaton-Haven Recreation Association. (1973). 410 U.S. 432–33.

Tillman, Z., & Stendahl, M. (2009, July 9). Montco club accused of racial discrimination. *Philadelphia Inquirer,* p. A1.

Troubled waters. (1989, August 3). *Detroit News,* p. B1.

Use of district pools cut in half since '48. (1959, July 19). *Washington Star,* p. C7.

Weiss, J. (2010). Technical report—Prevention of drowning. *Pediatrics, 126,* p. 254e. Available from http://pediatrics.aappublications.org

Wiese, A. (2005). *Places of their own: African American suburbanization in the twentieth century.* Chicago, IL: University of Chicago Press.

Wiltse, J. (2007). *Contested waters: A social history of swimming pools in America.* Chapel Hill: University of North Carolina Press.

Young Men's Christian Association. (1910). *Year book of the Young Men's Christian Associations of North America.* New York, NY: Author.

Young Men's Christian Association. (1935). *1935 year book and official rosters of the national council of the Young Men's Christian Associations of Canada and of the national council of the Young Men's Christian Associations of the United States of America.* New York, NY: Author.

Youngstown may close second pool. (1989, April 21). *Youngstown Vindicator,* p. 1.

READING 28

Notes

1. *Frontline*: The Plea, at www.pbs.org/wgbh/pages/frontline/shows/plea/four/patt.html; and Angela Davis, *Arbitrary Justice: The Power of the American Prosecutor* (New York: Oxford University Press, 2007), 50–52.

2. American Civil Liberties Union, *Stories of ACLU Clients Swept Up in the Hearne Drug Bust of November 2000* (Washington, DC: American Civil Liberties Union, Nov. 1, 2002), www.aclu.org/DrugPolicy/DrugPolicy.cfm?ID = 11160&c=80.

3. Human Rights Watch, Punishment and Prejudice: Racial Disparities in the War on Drugs, *HRW Reports,* vol. 12, no. 2 (May 2000).

4. Ibid.

5. Jeremy Travis, *But They All Come Back Facing the Challenges of Prisoner Reentry* (Washington, DC: Urban Institute Press, 2002), 28.

6. Ibid.

7. Ibid.

8. Marc Mauer and Ryan S. King, *Schools and Prisons: Fifty Years After* Brown *v.* of Education (Washington, DC: Sentencing Project, Apr. 2004), 3.

9. Marc Mauer, *The Changing Racial Dynamics of the War on Drugs* (Washington, DC: Sentencing Project, Apr. 2009).

10. See, e.g., U.S. Department of Health and Human Services, Substance Abuse and Mental Health Services Administration, *Summary of Findings from the 2000 National Household Survey on Drug Abuse,* NHSDA series H-13, DHHS pub. no. SMA

01-3549 (Rockville, MD: 2001), reporting that 6.4 percent of whites, 6.4 percent of blacks, and 5.3 percent of Hispanics were current illegal drug users in 2000; *Results from the 2002 National Survey on Drug Use and Health: National Findings*, NSDUH series H-22, DHHS pub. no. SMA 03-3836 (2003), revealing nearly identical rates of illegal drug use among whites and blacks, only a single percentage point between them; *Results from the 2007 National Survey on Drug Use and Health: National Findings*, NSDUH series H-34, DHHS pub. no. SMA 08-4343 (2007), showing essentially the same findings; and Marc Mauer and Ryan S. King, *A 25-Year Quagmire: The War on Drugs and Its Impact on American Society* (Washington, DC: Sentencing Project, Sept. 2007), 19, citing a study suggesting that African Americans have slightly higher rates of illegal drug use than whites.

11. See, e.g., Howard N. Snyder and Melissa Sickman, *Juvenile Offenders and Victims: 2006 National Report*, U.S. Department of Justice, Office of Justice Programs, Office of Juvenile Justice and Delinquency Prevention (Washington, DC: 2006), reporting that white youth are more likely than black youth to engage in illegal drug sales; Lloyd D. Johnson, Patrick M. O'Malley, Jerald G. Bachman, and John E. Schulenberg, *Monitoring the Future, National Survey Results on Drug Use, 1975–2006*, vol. 1, *Secondary School Students*, U.S. Department of Health and Human Services, National Institute on Drug Abuse, NIH pub. no. 07-6205 (Bethesda, MD: 2007), 32, stating "African American 12th graders have consistently shown lower usage rates than White 12th graders for most drugs, both licit and illicit"; and Lloyd D. Johnston, Patrick M. O'Malley, and Jerald G. Bachman, *Monitoring the Future: National Results on Adolescent Drug Use: Overview of Key Findings 2002*, U.S. Department of Health and Human Services, National Institute on Drug Abuse, NIH pub, no. 03-5374 (Bethesda, MD: 2003), presenting data showing that African American adolescents have slightly lower rates of illicit drug use than their white counterparts.

12. National Institute on Drug Abuse, *Monitoring the Future, National Survey Results on Drug Use, 1975–1999*, vol. 1, *Secondary School Students* (Washington, DC: National Institute on Drug Abuse, 2000).

13. U.S. Department of Health, *National Household Survey on Drug Abuse, 1999* (Washington, DC: Substance Abuse and Mental Health Services Administration, Office of Applied Studies, 2000), table G, p. 71, www.samhsa.gov/statistics/statistics.html.

14. Bruce Western, *Punishment and Inequality* (New York: Russell Sage Foundation, 2006), 47.

15. Ibid.

16. See Lynn Lu, "Prosecutorial Discretion and Racial Disparities in Sentencing: Some Views of Former U.S. Attorneys," *Federal Sentencing Reporter* 19 (Feb. 2007).

17. Douglas S. Massey and Nancy A. Denton, *American Apartheid: Segregation and the Making of the Underclass* (Cambridge, MA: Harvard University Press, 1993), 2.

18. For a discussion of possible replacement effects, see Robert MacCoun and Peter Reuter, *Drug War Heresies: Learning from Other Vices, Times, and Places* (New York: Cambridge University Press, 2001).

19. See Katherine Beckett, Kris Nyrop, Lori Pfingst, and Melissa Bowen, "Drug Use, Drug Possession Arrests, and the Question of Race: Lessons from Seattle," *Social Problems* 52, no. 3 (2005): 419–41; and Katherine Beckett, Kris Nyrop, and Lori Pfingst, "Race, Drugs and Policing: Understanding Disparities in Drug Delivery Arrests," *Criminology* 44, no. 1 (2006): 105.

20. Beckett, "Drug Use," 436.

21. Ibid.

22. Ibid.

23. David Cole, *No Equal Justice: Race and Class in the American Criminal Justice System* (New York: The New Press, 1999), 161.

24. Ibid., 162.

25. *City of Los Angeles v. Lyons*, 461 U.S. 95, 105 (1983).

26. See United States v. Brignoni-Ponce, 422 U.S. 873 (1975); and United States v. Martinez-Fuerte, 428 U.S. 543 (1976).

27. See Massey, *American Apartheid*.

28. For a thoughtful overview of these studies, see David Harris, *Profiles in Injustice: Why Racial Profiling Cannot Work* (New York: The New Press, 2002).

29. *State v. Soto*, 324 N.J. Super. 66, 69-77, 83-85, 734 A.2d 350, 352-56, 360 (N.J. Super. Ct. Law Div. 1996).

30. Harris, *Profiles in Injustice*, 80.

31. Ibid.

32. Jeff Brazil and Steve Berry, "Color of Drivers Is Key to Stops on I-95 Videos," *Orlando Sentinel*, Aug. 23, 1992; and David Harris, "Driving While Black and All Other Traffic Offenses: The Supreme Court and Pretextual Traffic Stops," *Journal of Criminal Law and Criminology* 87 (1997): 544, 561–62.

33. ACLU, *Driving While Black: Racial Profiling on our Nation's Highways* (New York: American Civil Liberties Union, 1999) 3, 27–28.

34. See www.aclunc.org, press release, "Oakland Police Department Announces Results of Racial Profiling Data Collection," May 11, 2001.

35. Al Baker and Emily Vasquez, "Number of People Stopped by Police Soars in New York," *New York Times*, Feb. 3, 2007.

36. Office of the Attorney General of New York State, *Report on the New York City Police Department's "Stop & Frisk" Practices* (New York: Office of the Attorney General of New York State, 1999), 95, 111, 121, 126.

37. Ibid., 117 n. 23.

38. Baker and Vasquez, "Number of People Stopped by Police Soars."

39. Ryan Pintado-Vertner and Jeff Chang, "The War on Youth," *Colorlines* 2, no. 4 (Winter 1999–2000), 36.

40. *Alexander v. Sandoval*, 532 U.S. 275 (2001).

READING 29
Notes

1. In March, 1988, approval of the LAPD's job performance was remarkably high for all groups: 80% for Latinos, 74% for whites, and 64% for blacks. Approval ratings declined substantially four days after the March 3, 1991 videotaped beating (51, 47, 26% respectively) and then eroded further in a March 20 poll (31, 41, 14% respectively) as a result of the repeated broadcast of a video of the beating (Weitzer 2002).

2. In 2009, the vast majority of Los Angeles residents approved of the LAPD's job performance: 68% of blacks, 76% of Latinos, and 81% of whites (Rubin 2009; see also Stone et al. 2009).

3. When asked, in a 1999 Gallup poll, whether they had ever been stopped by the police solely because of their race or ethnicity, black males aged 18–34 were much more likely to answer affirmatively (73%) than older black males (40%), same-age black females (38%), and same-age white males (11%). When asked generically about being stopped (rather than about racially-biased stops), one study found that blacks were twice as likely as whites to report being stopped in just the past year: 25% vs. 12%, respectively (Epp et al. 2014: 52).

4. This database is available at: http://www.theguardian.com/us-news/nginteractivc/2015/jun/01/the-counted-police-killings-us-database#.

5. Some of these studies find that minority officers treat citizens better than white officers, while other studies find the opposite (Sklansky 2006).

FURTHER READING

ACLU. 2015. *Stop and Frisk in Chicago*. American Civil Liberties Union.

Baker, A. 2015. Police unions, facing public anger, rethink how to address shootings. *New York Times*, April 19.

Brown, D. 2009. The time to impart lessons on authority: Parents teach truths to "post-racial" youth. *Washington Post*, July 30.

Brunson, R., & Weitzer, R. 2011. Negotiating unwelcome police encounters: The intergenerational transmission of conduct norms. *Journal of Contemporary Ethnography, 40,* 425–456.

Chanin, J. 2015. Examining the sustainability of pattern or practice police misconduct reform. *Police Quarterly, 18,* 163–192.

Christopher Commission. 1991. *Report of the Independent Commission on the Los Angeles Police Department.* Los Angeles: Commission.

Correll, J. 2007. Across the thin blue line: Police officers and racial bias in the decision to shoot. *Journal of Personality and Social Psychology, 92,* 1006–1023.

Epp, C., Maynard-Moody, S., & Haider-Markel, D. 2014. *Pulled Over.* Chicago: University of Chicago Press.

Fagan, J., Geller, A., Davies, G., & West, V. 2010. Street stops and broken windows revisited. In S. Rice & M. White (Eds.), *Race, Ethnicity, and Policing* (pp. 309–348). New York: NYU Press.

Greene, J. 1999. Zero tolerance: A case study of police policies and practices in New York City. *Crime and Delinquency, 45,* 171–187.

Howell, S., Perry, H., & Vile, M. 2004. Black cities, white cities: Evaluating the police. *Political Behavior, 26,* 45–68.

Jacob, H. 1971. Black and white perceptions of justice in the city. *Law and Society Review, 6,* 69–90.

Kane, R. 2002. The social ecology of police misconduct. *Criminology, 40,* 867–896.

Kindy, K. 2015. In 5 months, police fatally shoot 385. *Washington Post,* May 31.

Lawrence, R. 2000. *The Politics of Force: Media and the Construction of Police Brutality.* Berkeley: University of California Press.

Lowery, W. 2015. A softer approach to policing gains believers in Calif. City. *Washington Post,* May 8.

Mastrofski, S., Reisig, M., & McCluskey, J. 2002. Police disrespect toward the public: An encounter-based analysis. *Criminology, 40,* 519–551.

Moskos, P. 2008. Two shades of blue: Black and white in the blue brotherhood. *Law Enforcement Executive Forum, 8,* 57–86.

National Research Council. 2004. *Fairness and Effectiveness in Policing: The Evidence.* Washington DC: National Academies Press.

New York Times. 2014. Poll, August 19–20.

Pew Research Center. 2014. Poll, August 20–24.

Reaves, B. 2010. *Local Police Departments, 2007.* Washington, DC: Bureau of Justice Statistics.

Reaves, B. 2015. *Local Police Departments, 2013.* Washington, DC: Bureau of Justice Statistics.

Ross, C. 2014. Introducing the United States police-shooting database. Unpublished paper, University of California, Davis.

Rubin, J. 2009. LAPD gains new approval from the public. *Los Angeles Times,* June 22.

Sklansky, D. 2006. Not your father's police department: Making sense of the new demographics of law enforcement. *Journal of Criminal Law and Criminology, 96,* 1209–1242.

Skogan, W. 2006. Asymmetry in the impact of encounters with police. *Policing and Society, 16,* 99–126.

Skogan, W. 2008. Why reforms fail. *Policing and Society, 18,* 23–34.

Stone, C., Foglesong, T., & Cole, C. 2009. *Policing Los Angeles Under a Consent Decree: The Dynamics of Change at the LAPD.* Cambridge: Harvard Kennedy School.

Sykes, R., & Clark, J. 1975. A theory of deference exchange in police-civilian encounters. *American Journal of Sociology, 81,* 584–600.

Terrill, W., & Reisig, M. 2003. Neighborhood context and police use of force. *Journal of Research in Crime and Delinquency, 40,* 291–321.

Tyler, T., & Huo, Y. 2002. *Trust in the Law.* New York: Russell Sage.

Walker, S. 2012. Institutionalizing police accountability reforms: The problem of making police reforms endure. *St. Louis University Public Law Review, 32,* 57–92.

Wall Street Journal/NBC/Marist. 2013. Poll, September 15–16.

Washington Post. 2014. Poll, December 11–14.

Weitzer, R. 1999. Citizens' perceptions of police misconduct: Race and neighborhood context. *Justice Quarterly, 16,* 819–846.

Weitzer, R. 2002. Incidents of police misconduct and public opinion. *Journal of Criminal Justice, 30,* 397–408.

Weitzer, R. 2014. The puzzling neglect of Hispanic Americans in research on police-citizen relations. *Ethnic and Racial Studies, 37,* 1995–2013.

Weitzer, R., & Tuch, S. 2006. *Race and Policing in America: Conflict and Reform.* New York: Cambridge University Press.

Weitzer, R., Tuch, S., & Skogan, W. 2008. Police-community relations in a majority-black city. *Journal of Research in Crime and Delinquency, 45,* 398–428.

Wiley, M., & Hudik, T. 1974. Police-citizen encounters: A field test of exchange theory. *Social Problems, 22,* 119–127.

Wilson, R. 2015. Police accountability measures flood state legislatures after violent events. *Washington Post,* February 8.

Zernikeaug, K. 2014. Camden turns around with new police force. *New York Times,* August 31.

READING 30

Notes

1. For discussions of the effect of incarceration, see, e.g., J. Grogger, "The Effect of Arrests on the Employment and Earnings of Young Men," *Quarterly Journal of Economics* 110 (1995): 51–72; B. Western, "The Impact of Incarceration on Wage Mobility and Inequality," *American Sociological Review* 67, no. 4 (2002): 526–46.

2. This research is reported in D. Pager, "The Mark of a Criminal Record," *American Journal of Sociology* 108, no. 5 (2003): 937–75. IRP thanks the University of Chicago Press for permission to summarize the article.

3. See, for example, D. Neal and W. Johnson, "The Role of Premarket Factors in Black-White Wage Differences," *Journal of Political Economy* 104, no. 5 (1996): 869–95; S. Steele, *The Content of Our Character: A New Vision of Race in America* (New York: Harper Perennial, 1991).

4. The method of audit studies was pioneered in the 1970s with a series of housing audits conducted by the Department of Housing and Urban Development, and was modified and applied to employment by researchers at the Urban Institute in the early 1990s. M. Turner, M. Fix, and R. Struyk, *Opportunities Denied, Opportunities Diminished: Racial Discrimination in Hiring* (Washington, DC: Urban Institute Press, 1991).

5. Bureau of Labor Statistics, Local Area Unemployment Statistics. Last accessed March 2003. http://www.bls.gov/lau/ home.htm.

6. Over 90 percent of recent, entry-level job openings in Milwaukee were located in the outlying counties and suburbs, and only 4 percent in the central city. J. Pawasarat and L. Quinn, "Survey of Job Openings in the Milwaukee Metropolitan Area: Week of May 15, 2000," Employment and Training Institute Report, University of Wisconsin–Milwaukee, 2000.

7. M. Bendick, Jr., C. Jackson, and V. Reinoso, "Measuring Employment Discrimination through Controlled Experiments," *Review of Black Political Economy* 23 (1994): 25–48.

READING 32

Notes

1. Stephen Erie, *Rainbow's End* (Berkeley: University of California Press, 1988), 88–89.

2. Thomas Kessner, *Fiorella H. LaGuardia* (New York: McGraw-Hill, 1989); Charles Garrett, *The LaGuardia Years* (New Brunswick, NJ: Rutgers University Press, 1961).

3. A survey of the surviving members of the class indicates that 38 percent were Catholic and 36 percent Jewish, with Russia and Ireland the leading countries of origin of the respondents' grandparents (Richard Herrnstein et al., "New York City

Police Department Class of 1940: A Preliminary Report" [unpublished manuscript, Department of Psychology, Harvard University, n.d.]).

4. Nathan Glazer and Daniel P. Moynihan, *Beyond the Melting Pot* (Cambridge, MA: MIT Press, 1969).

5. Data on the ethnic composition of the fire department are from *Equal Employment Opportunity Statistics: Agency Full Report* (New York: New York City Department of Personnel, 1990); data on the religious composition are from Center for Social Policy and Practice in the Workplace, *Gender Integration in the Fire Department of the City of New York* (New York: Columbia University School of Social Work, 1988), p. 41.

6. Roger Waldinger, *Through the Eye of the Needle* (New York: New York University Press, 1986).

7. Heywood Broun and George Britt, *Christians Only* (New York: Vantage Press, 1931), 244.

8. Dominic Capeci, *The Harlem Riot of 1943* (Philadelphia: Temple University Press, 1977), 172.

9. Waldinger, *Through the Eye of the Needle*, 109–10. Employment data calculated from the census apply to employed persons twenty-five to sixty-four years old only. "Blacks" refers to native-born African Americans only. Data calculated from the Public Use Microdata Samples (U.S. Bureau of the Census, *Census of Population, 1940*, Public Use Microdata Samples [Computer file] [Washington, DC: U.S. Dept. of Commerce, Bureau of the Census, producer, 1983; Ann Arbor, MI: Inter-university Consortium for Political and Social Research, distributor, 1984]; U.S. Bureau of the Census, Census of Population, 1950, Public Use Microdata Samples [computer file] [Washington, DC: U.S. Dept. of Commerce, Bureau of the Census, and Madison: University of Wisconsin, Center for Demography and Ecology, producers, 1984; Ann Arbor, MI: Inter-university Consortium for Political and Social Research, distributor, 1984]).

10. Hasia Diner, *In the Almost Promised Land* (Westport, CT: Greenwood Press, 1977), presents a favorable account of the response among the Jewish trade union elite to the black influx into the garment industry; see chap. 6. Herbert Hill has offered a far more critical account in numerous writings, most important, "The Racial Practices of Organized Labor: The Contemporary Record," in *Organized Labor and the Negro*, edited by Julius Jacobson (New York: Doubleday, 1968), 286–337. For a judicious balancing of the issues, see Nancy Green, "Juifs et noirs aux etats-unis: La rupture d'une 'alliance naturelle,'" *Annales, E.S.C.*, 2 (March-April 1987):445–64.

11. Diane Ravitch, *The Great School Wars* (New York: Basic Books, 1974).

12. Roger Waldinger, "The Making of an Immigrant Niche," *International Migration Review* 28(1)(1994).

13. "The Debate Goes On," *Alumnus: The City College of New York* 87(1) (Winter 1992):8–11.

14. Emmanuel Tobier, "Population," in *Setting Municipal Priorities*, edited by Charles Brecher and Raymond Horton (New York: New York University Press, 1981), 24.

15. Data are from U.S. Bureau of the Census, *Occupations at the 1900 Census* (Washington, DC: GPO, 1904). See also Herman Bloch, *The Circle of Discrimination* (New York: New York University Press, 1969).

16. Data are from the U.S. Bureau of the Census, *Census of Population, 1940.*

17. Calculated from the U.S. Bureau of the Census, *Census of Population and Housing, 1990*, Public Use Microdata Sample (a Sample): 5-Percent Sample (computer file) (Washington, DC: U.S. Dept. of Commerce, producer, 1993; Ann Arbor, MI: Inter-university Consortium for Political and Social Research, distributor, 1993).

18. Colored Citizens' Non-Partisan Committee for the Reelection of Mayor Walker, *New York City and the Colored Citizen* (n.d. [1930?]), LaGuardia Papers, Box 3530, New York Municipal Archives.

19. Calculated from U.S. Bureau of the Census, *Census of Population, 1940*, Public Use Microdata Samples. Also see Edwin Levinson, *Black Politics in New York City* (New York: Twayne, 1974).

20. Ira Katznelson, *Black Men, White Cities* (New York: Oxford University Press, 1973), 82.

21. For a more detailed discussion of the Lindsay period, see Roger Waldinger, "The Ethnic Politics of Municipal Jobs," working paper no. 248, UCLA Institute of Industrial Relations, Los Angeles, 1993.

22. Raymond Horton, "Human Resources," in *Setting Municipal Priorities,* edited by Charles Brecher and Raymond Horton (New York: New York University Press, 1986). See also Roger Waldinger, "Changing Ladders and Musical Chairs," *Politics and Society* 15(4) (1986–87):369–402, and "Making of an Immigrant Niche."

23. City of New York, Citywide Equal Employment Opportunity Committee, *Equal Employment Opportunity in New York City Government, 1977–1987* (New York: Citywide Equal Employment Opportunity Committee, 1988), 6.

24. Data are from unpublished EEOC reports from the New York City Department of Personnel, New York Board of Education, New York City Transit Authority, and New York City Health and Hospitals Corporation.

25. City of New York, Mayor's Commission on Hispanic Concerns, *Report* (New York: Mayor's Commission on Hispanic Concerns, 1986), 109.

26. *1991 Korean Business Directory* (Long Island City, NY: Korean News, 1991).

27. Roger Waldinger, "Structural Opportunity or Ethnic Advantage: Immigrant Business Development in New York," *International Migration Review* 23(1) (1989):61.

28. Illsoo Kim, *The New Urban Immigrants* (Princeton, NJ: Princeton University Press, 1981), 51.

29. Pyong Gap Min, "Cultural and Economic Boundaries of Korean Ethnicity: A Comparative Analysis," *Ethnic and Racial Studies* 14(2) (1991):235.

30. Lucie Cheng and Yen Espiritu, "Korean Businesses in Black and Hispanic Neighborhoods," *Sociological Perspectives* 32(4) (1989):521.

31. Illsoo Kim, "The Koreans: Small Business in an Urban Frontier," in *New Immigrants in New York,* edited by Nancy Foner (New York: Columbia University Press, 1987), 238.

32. Tamar Jacoby, "Sonny Carson and the Politics of Protest," *NY:The City Journal* 1(4) (1991): 29–40.

READING 33

Notes

1. The research for this chapter was made possible by generous grants from the Russell Sage, Ford, Rockefeller, Spencer, and William T. Grant Foundations. A revised version of this chapter appears in Newman 1999.

2. There are further shades of gray below the line of the employed that distinguish those who are searching for work and those who have accepted their fate as nonworkers, with the latter suffering the greatest stigma of all.

3. For more on the moral structure associated with work and achievement of the American dream, see Hochschild 1995.

4. See Wilson 1996, Massey and Denton 1993, Hacker 1992, and Urban Institute 1991.

5. All names and identifying information have been changed to protect confidentiality.

6. Hochschild 1983 documents similar attempts in the airline industry. One airline holds a mandatory seminar for flight attendants to teach them "anger-desensitization" when dealing with rude and demeaning customers.

7. In areas experiencing exceptionally tight labor markets—including much of the Midwest in the late 1990s—wages for these jobs are climbing above the minimum-wage line.

8. This is one of the many reasons why increasing the minimum wage is so important. Ghettos have such impoverished job bases to begin with that they are almost always characterized by slack labor markets. Only when the labor supply outside ghetto walls has tightened down to almost impossible levels do we begin to see this tide lift inner-city boats. Eventually employers do turn to the workers who are low on their preference

queues (as we learned in the 1980s during the Massachusetts miracle), but these conditions are, sadly, rare and generally short-lived.

9. Indeed, over a five-month period in 1993 there were fourteen job applicants for every job opening at two different Burger Barns in Harlem (Newman and Lennon 1995).

10. The fact that Harlem residents rejected for these jobs hold these values is some evidence for the preexisting nature of this mind-set—although these rejects had already piled up work experience that may have contributed to the sharpening of this alternative critique.

11. It should be noted that women on welfare and women in low-wage jobs are not necessarily two distinct groups. Many women find it necessary to go back and forth between holding a low-wage job and relying solely on welfare, and many supplement one form of income with the other (not to mention other income from friends, family, and unreported work), since neither source alone provides enough money to support a family (see Edin 1994).

References

Edin, Kathryn. 1994. "The Myths of Dependency and Self-Sufficiency: Women, Welfare, and Low-Wage Work." Unpublished paper. Department of Sociology and Center for Urban Policy Research, Rutgers University.

Hacker, Andrew. 1992. *Two Nations.* New York: Ballantine.

Hochschild, Arlie. 1983. *The Managed Heart.* Berkeley: University of California Press.

Hochschild, Jennifer L. 1995. *Facing up to the American Dream.* Princeton: Princeton University Press.

Katz, Michael. 1989. *The Undeserving Poor.* New York: Pantheon.

Massey, Douglas S., and Nancy A. Denton. 1993. *American Apartheid.* Cambridge: Harvard University Press.

Newman, Katherine S. 1999. *No Shame in My Game: The Working Poor in the Inner City.* New York: Knopf/ Russell Sage Foundation.

Newman, Katherine S., and Chauncy Lennon. 1995. "The Job Ghetto." *American Prospect,* Summer, 66–67.

Urban Institute. 1991. *Opportunities Denied, Opportunities Diminished.* Report 91–9. Washington, DC: Urban Institute Press.

Wilson, William Julius. 1996. *When Work Disappears.* New York: Knopf.

READING 34

Notes

1. Unless otherwise noted, the following discussion is primarily based on these sources and the information provided by Liang Huan Ru, the former veteran union organizer in Brooklyn.

2. I use "Manhattan's Chinatown" because new Chinatowns have recently emerged in other boroughs of New York City, such as Queens and Brooklyn.

3. Abeles, Schwartz, Haechel & Silverblatt, Inc., *The Chinatown Garment Industry Study* (hereafter *Study*) (New York: International Ladies' Garment Workers' Union Local 23–25 and the New York Skirt and Sportswear Association, 1983), 55. For the sizes of the shops in Manhattan's Chinatown, see *Study,* 49–59.

4. See for example, the weekly special issue of the *Sing Tao Daily* (hereafter *STD*), March 8, 1998, 7.

5. My visit to the shop and interview with the shop owner.

6. One woman worker told me in an interview that it was so hot inside her shop in summer that sometimes she simply could not help crying while trying to rush out her work.

7. Experienced pressers began to lose this advantage in more and more Chinese garment shops in recent years, largely due to the increased competition from undocumented male workers. Unable to compete with the low wages accepted by the latter, they too had to face economic insecurity in the industry. I am indebted to a reminder from Liang Huan Ru, an organizer of UNITE! Local 23–25, and May Ying Chen, vice president of UNITE!, for this

piece of information. What, however, must be kept in mind is that while competition has mounted among pressers in recent years, women machine operators also faced competition from undocumented workers.

8. See Susan Glenn, *Daughters of the Shtetl: Life and Labor in the Immigrant Generation* (Ithaca, New York: Cornell University Press, 1990), 90–131, and Nancy Green, *Ready-to-Wear and Ready-to-Work: A Century of Industry and Immigrants in Paris and New York* (Durham: Duke University Press, 1997), 161–87.

9. The most recent case was the one at 446 Broadway in November 1997, in which a young woman employer closed her shop after withholding a large sum of money in back wages from her employees. The case was covered by most major newspapers inside and outside the Chinese community. See, for example, *New York Times*, December 14, 1997.

10. See "Opportunity at Work: The New York City Garment Industry" (New York: Community Service Society of New York, 1998), 39.

11. This observation has been supported by recent coverage in Chinese community newspapers. For example, as covered in *World Journal* (hereafter *WJ*) in 1996, the monthly income of an elderly couple who worked in a Chinese garment shop was $1,800 and $2,200, respectively. Given the depressed piece rates in the last two years and the seasonal nature of the industry, this observation, based on interviews with workers in Sunset Park, does not seem to be far away from reality.

12. Directly quoted from "Behind Closed Doors: A Look into the Underground Sweatshop Industry," a report by the New York State Assembly Sub-Committee on Sweatshops (New York, November 1997), 59–61.

13. Interview by the author on April 13, 1998.

14. See, for example, Bernard Wong, "The Role of Ethnicity in Enclave Enterprises: A Study of the Chinese Garment Factories in New York City," *Human Organization* 46 (2), 1987: 120–9.

15. "One country, two systems" is the Chinese state policy in Hong Kong after the former British colony was returned to China in 1997.

16. Cases like this are not unheard of in the Chinese garment industry in Manhattan's Chinatown as well as other boroughs of the city. See, for example, The Chinese Staff and Workers Association, *Zhi Gong Zhi Sheng* (January 1994).

17. I was told that this small number of workers from other ethnic groups were likely to have worked for the former owner of the shop and the Chinese employer employed them as part of the deal when he/she purchased the business. I was also told that some Chinese employers deliberately kept these workers to protect their businesses from harassment by Chinese gangsters, who tended not to attack shops with non-Chinese workers for fear that their illicit activities would be known beyond the Chinese community.

18. *STD*, December 19, 1997.

19. The "Hot Goods Bill" was signed into law on July 2, 1996. This bill has established "additional methods of obtaining restitution for unpaid apparel industry workers from contractors, manufacturers, and retailers." For a further discussion of this bill, see "Behind Closed Doors," 4.

20. The *Study* has reported that at the end of 1981, 28 percent of all Chinese shops in Chinatown had been in business for less than one year and close to half of them had been in operation for less than two years (p. 68). However, in the late 1990s, as many workers have pointed out, the Chinese garment shops in Sunset Park are often opened and closed down within months.

21. Taishan is a county in Guangdong Province. Immigrants from this county are also generally called "Cantonese."

22. Interview by the author on July 2, 1998.

23. Interview by the author on June 21, 1998.

24. Immigration status and whether one is living with their family have become important indexes because much of the Chinese community has chosen to believe that legal immigration and family life are the norms throughout the history of the community, however invalid this belief is.

25. For a summary of their arguments, see *STD*, April 22, 1998.

26. For different voices in the community, see, for example, the weekly special issues of *STD*, May 17, 1998, and June 28, 1998.

27. The estimate of 800 Chinese shops is based on an adding of the approximate 500 shops in Manhattan and the more than 300 shops in Brooklyn and other boroughs. More than 30,000 workers were estimated by the community press in the end of 1997. See *STD*, December 22, 1997.

28. These statistics are provided by the Research Department of the New York State Department of Labor.

29. In 1997, when the union signed a new contract with Chinese employers, the three Chinese contractors' associations represented only 406 shops in the city. This was later reported in most Chinese community newspapers. See, for example, *STD*, February 23, 1998.

30. This percentage of Chinatown union shops in 1997 is based on a comparison of the number of garment shops in the Chinatown area provided by the state labor department, which is not classified according to ethnicity, and the estimate of Chinatown union organizers and the Chinese newspapers. See, for example, *STD*, December 22, 1997, and April 29, 1998, and *WJ*, February 28, 1998.

31. These statistics are provided by the UNITE! Research Department. The estimated percentage of the local's Chinese membership in this study is consistent with the numbers provided by the local.

32. Green, *Ready-to-Wear*, 50.

33. See Nancy Green, "Sweatshop Migrations: The Garment Industry between Home and Shop," in *The Landscape of Modernity: Essays on New York City, 1900–1940*, eds. David Ward and Olivier Zunz (New York: Russell Sage Foundation, 1992), 213–32.

34. Mark Levitan, *Opportunity at Work: The New York City Garment Industry* (New York: Community Service Society of New York, 1998), 59.

35. One of the most active community-based labor organizations in New York's Chinatown in the last two decades is the Chinese Staff and Workers' Association.

READING 35

Notes

1. The authors are grateful to Glenn Bracey, Katisha Greer, and Krisen Lavelle for their helpful and insightful comments.

2. For two longer reviews of *Bamboozled*, see Barlowe (2003) and Epp (2003).

3. This quote is taken from the sketch, *Charlie Murphy's True Hollywood Stories*, "In the first (and easily the most popular sketch in the show so far—one that catapulted Chappelle to the level of phenomenon within days after airing), Charlie Murphy (Eddie Murphy's real-life brother) recounts supposed altercations between himself and the late funk musician Rick James, which took place during the height of his popularity in the early 1980s. Chappelle intersperses Murphy's retelling of his story with reenacted excerpts in which Chappelle plays the young Rick James and Murphy plays his younger self" (Wikipedia, 2005).

4. There have been numerous incidents of blackface parties at colleges across the United States (Mueller, Dirks, and Picca, forthcoming). One Swarthmore student stated, "I figured (obviously jokingly), that if I painted my face black, I would thus gain some super powers that would enable me to dance," explaining that dressing in blackface was a "spur of the moment thing." A Swarthmore history professor responded, "You don't inadvertently put on blackface, you inadvertently bang your shoulder on the way out the door'" (Nelson, 2002).

References

Barlowe, J. (2003). "You must never be a misrepresented people": Spike Lee's *Bamboozled*. *Canadian Review of American Studies*, 33, 1–16.

Baudrillard, J. (1981). *Simulacra and Simulation*. Ann Arbor: University of Michigan Press.

Baudrillard, J. (1989). *America*. Translated by C. Turner. London: Verso.

Bernstein, M. (1996). Nostalgia, ambivalence, irony: *Song of the South* and race relations in 1946 Atlanta. *Film History*, 8, 219–236.

Bogle, D. (2000 [1973]). *Toms, Coons, Mulattoes, Mammies, and Bucks: An Interpretive History of Blacks in American Films.* New York: Continuum.

Carrillo, K. J. (2003). Highly offensive: Karen Juanita Carrillo examines the ongoing currency of racist curios. Retrieved November 6, 2005 from: http://www .ferris.edu/news/jimcrowllinks/neWSliStlOffensive .htm.

Clinton, C. (1982). *The Plantation Mistress: Woman's World in the Old South.* New York: Pantheon.

Collins, P. H. (2001). *Black Feminist Thought: Knowledge, Consciousness, and the Politics of Empowerment.* New York: Routledge.

Collins, P. H. (2004). *Black Sexual Politics: African Americans, Gender, and the New Racism.* New York: Routledge.

Comedy Central (Producer). (2003). *Chappelle's Show* [Television series]. United States: Comedy Central.

Delgado, R. & Stephancic, J. (1992). Images of the outsider in American law and culture: Can free expression remedy systemic social ills? *Cornell Law Review, 77,* 1258–1297.

Deloria, P J. (1998). *Playing Indian.* New Haven, CT: Yale University Press.

Epp, M. H. (2003). Raising minstrelsy: Humour, satire and the stereotype in *The Birth of a Nation* and *Bamboozled. Canadian Review of American Studies,* 33, 17–35.

Farley, C. J. (2005, May l5). On the beach with Dave Chappelle. *Time Online Edition.* Retrieved October 19, 2005 from: http://www.time.com/tirne/arts/print-outl0,8816.1061415,00.html.

Feagin, J. R. (2000). *Racist America: Roots, Current Realities, and Future Reparations.* New York: Routledge.

Gayle, A., Jr. (1976). *The Way of the New World: The Black Novel in America.* New York: Doubleday Anchor.

Ghettopoly. (2002). *Ghettopoly.* Retrieved October 7, 2005 from: http://www.ghettopoly.com.

Grindstaff, L. (2004). *Reviving blackface: Talk shows as modern-day minstrelsy.* Paper presented at the International Communication Association meeting, May 27–31, New Orleans, LA.

Guerrero, E. (1993). *Framing Blackness: The African American Image in Film.* Philadelphia, PA: Temple University Press.

Haggis, P. (Director). (2005). *Crash* [Motion picture]. United States: Lions Gate Films.

Hodges, M. (2003, February 27). Bubble rap: How not to package a band. *Digital Korea Herald.* Retrieved November 6, 2005 from: http://wk.koreaherald.co.kr/ SITE/datalhtml_dir12003/021271200302270007 .asp.

hooks, b. (1996). *Reel to Real: Race, Sex, and Class at the Movies.* New York: Routledge.

hooks, b. (2004). *We Real Cool: Black Men and Masculinity.* New York: Routledge.

Kellner, D. (1995). *Media Culture: Cultural Studies, Identity and Politics between the Modern and the Postmodern.* New York: Routledge.

King, C. R. & Springwood, C. F. (2001). *Team Spirits: The Native American Mascots Controversy.* Lincoln, NE: University of Nebraska Press.

KOCCA (Korea Culture and Content Agency). (2003, February 25). Trouble bubbles up around pop group's look. Retrieved November 6, 2005 from: http:// www.kocca.or.kr/ctnews/eng/SITE/datalhtml_ dir12003/02/251200302250128.html.

Kramer, S. (Director). (1967). *Guess Who's Coming to Dinner?* [Motion picture]. United States: Stanley Kramer Productions.

Lee, S. (Director). (2000). *Bamboozled* [Motion picture]. United States: 40 Acres and a Mule Filmworks.

Lhamon, W. T., Jr. (1998). *Raising Cain: Blackface Jim Crow to Hip Hop.* Cambridge, MA: Harvard UP.

Lieff, Cabraser, Heimann & Bernstein, LLP. (2005). *$40 million paid to class members in December 2005 in Abercrombie & Fitch discrimination lawsuit settlement.* Retrieved January 10, 2006 from: http://www .afjustice.com.

McCurry, J. (2005, June 15). Japanese publisher defies Little Black Sambo protest. *The Guardian.* Retrieved

January 7, 2006 from: http://books.guardian.co.ukl-news/articles/0.6109.1506576.00.html.

Movie Revenues. (2006). Global film industry. Retrieved January 7, 2006 from: http://www.factbook.net/wbglobal_rev.htm.

Mueller, J. C., Dirks, D., & Picca, L. H. (forthcoming). Unmarking racism: Halloween costuming and engagement of the racial other. *Qualitative Sociology*.

Nelson, G. (2002, November 14). Collection on blackface raises larger race issues. *The Phoenix Online*. Retrieved June 1, 2004 from: http://www.sccs.swarthmore.edu/org/phoenix/2002/2002-11-07/news/l24l0.php.

Neupert, R. (2001). Trouble in watermelon land: George Pal and the Little Jasper cartoons. *Film Quarterly*, 55, 14–26.

Noriega, C. (2000). *Shot in America: Television, the State and the Rise of Chicano Cinema*. Minneapolis: University of Minnesota Press.

Noriega, C. (2001). *Race matters, media matters*. Viewing Race Project. Retrieved January 11, 2006 from: http://www.viewingrace.org/content.php?sec=essay&sub=1.

Pieterse, J. N. (1992). *White on Black: Images of Africa and Blacks in Western Popular Culture*. New Haven, CT: Yale University Press.

Pilgrim, D. (2000). Who was Jim Crow? The Jim Crow Museum of Racist Memorabilia. Retrieved June 1, 2004 from: http://www.ferris.edu/jimcrow/who.htm.

Pilgrim, D. (2001). New racist forms: Jim Crow in the 21st century. The Jim Crow Museum of Racist Memorabilia. Retrieved August 28, 2004 from: http://www.ferris.edu/jimcrow/newforms/.

Riggs, M. (Director). (1987). *Ethnic Notions* [Motion picture]. United States: Marlon Riggs.

Roediger, D. (1991). *The Wages of Whiteness: Race and the Making of the American Working Class*. New York: Verso.

Rosenberg, M. (2002, June 10). Take that, paleface! *The Nation*. Retrieved online January 6, 2006 from: http://www. thenation.com/doc/20020610/editors2.

Russell, K. K. (2001). *The Color of Crime: Racial Hoaxes, White Fear, Black Protectionism, Police Harassment, and Other Macroaggressions*. New York: New York University Press.

Schaffer, S. (1996). Disney and the imagineering of histories. *Postmodern Culture*, 6, 3. Retrieved January 7, 2006 from the ProjectMuse database.

Skal, D. J. (2002). *Death Makes a Holiday: A Cultural History of Halloween*. New York: Bloomsbury.

Strasburg, J. (2002, April 19). Abercrombie recalls T-shirts many found offensive. *San Francisco Chronicle*. Retrieved January 6, 2005 from: http://www.sfgate.com/cgi-bin/article.cgi?file=/c/a/2002/04/19/MN102999.DTL.

Strong, P. T. (2004). The mascot slot: Cultural citizenship, political correctness, and pseudo-Indian sports symbols. *Journal of Sport & Social Issues*, 28, 79–87.

Toll, R. C. (1974). *Blacking Up: The Minstrel Show in Nineteenth-Century America*. New York: Oxford University Press.

Trouillot, M. R. (1991). Anthropology and the savage slot: The poetics and politics of otherness. In R. G. Fox (Ed.), *Recapturing Anthropology: Working in the Present*. Santa Fe, NM: School of American Research Press.

Turner, P. A. (1994). *Ceramic Uncles and Celluloid Mammies: Black Images and Their Influence on Culture*. New York: Anchor.

Vera, H. & Gordon, A. M. (2003). *Screen Saviors: Hollywood Fictions of Whiteness*. Lanham, MD: Rowman & Littlefield.

Vera, H. & Gordon, A. M. (2005). On how to dissolve racial taboos. [Review of the motion picture *Guess Who?*] *Contexts*, 4, 68–69.

Walt Disney World. (2006). Splash Mountain. Retrieved January 7, 2006 from: http://disneyworld.disney.go.com/wdw/parks/attractionDetail?id=SplashMountainAttractionPage&bhcp=1.

Wasko, J. (2001). Is it a small world, after all? In J. Wasko, M. Phillips & E. R. Meehan (Eds.), *Dazzled by Disney?: The Global Disney Audiences Project* (pp. 3–30). London: Leicester University Press.

White, A. (1995). *The Resistance: Ten Years of Pop Culture That Shook the World.* New York: Overlook Hardcover.

Wilkinson, D. Y. (1974). Racial socialization through children's toys: A sociohistorical examination. *Journal of Black Studies, 5,* 96–109.

Williams, P. J. (1996). Metro Broadcasting, Inc. v. FCC: Regrouping in singular times. In K. Crenshaw, N. Gotanda, G. Peller, & K. Thomas (Eds.), *Critical Race Theory: The Key Writings That Formed the Movement.* New York: New Press.

World Wide Box Office. (2006). *Song of the South* world-wide sales. Retrieved January 6, 2006 from: http://worldwide boxoffice.com.

READING 36

Note

1. Term developed by bell hooks (1995) to describe the interlocking nature of domination and oppression.

References

Baker, R. K., & Ball, S. I. (Eds.). (1969). *Violence and the media.* Washington, DC: Government Printing Office.

Berger, P. L., & Luckmann, T. (1967). *The social construction of reality.* New York: Doubleday.

Blumer, H. (1969). *Symbolic interaction: Perspective and method.* Upper Saddle River, NJ: Prentice Hall.

Collins, P. H. (1991). *Black feminist thought: Knowledge, consciousness, and the politics of empowerment.* New York: Routledge.

Collins, P. (2004). *Black sexual politics: African Americans, gender, and the new racism.* New York: Routledge.

Comstock, G. A., Chaffee, S., Katzman, N., McCombs, M., & Roberts, D. (1978). *Television and human behavior.* New York: Columbia University Press.

Diawara, M. (1993). *Black American cinema.* New York: American Film Institute.

duCille, A. (1996). *Skin trade.* Cambridge, MA: Harvard University Press.

Emerson, R. A. (2002). "Where my girls at?" Negotiating Black womanhood in music videos. *Gender & Society, 16,* 115–135.

Fish, S. (1980). *Is there a text in this class? The authority of interpretive communities.* Cambridge, MA: Harvard University Press.

hooks, b. (1995). *Killing rage, ending racism.* New York: Holt.

Jordan, W. (1968). *White over Black: American attitudes toward the Negro, 1550–1812.* Chapel Hill: University of North Carolina Press.

McRobbie, A. (1982). Jackie: An ideology of adolescent femininity. In B. Waites, T. Bennet, & G. Martin (Eds.), *Popular culture: Past and present* (pp. 263–283). London: Open University Press.

Milkie, M. A. (1999). Social comparisons, reflected appraisals, and mass media: The impact of pervasive beauty images on Black and White girls' self-concepts. *Social Psychology Quarterly, 62,* 190–210.

Murray, D., Schwartz, J., & Lichter, S. R. (2001). *It ain't necessarily so: How the media remake our picture of reality.* New York: Penguin Books.

Pough, G. D. (2004). *Check it while I wreck it: Black womanhood, hip-hop culture, and the public sphere.* Boston: Northeastern University Press.

Rose, T. (1994). *Black noise rap music and Black culture in contemporary America.* New York: Wesleyan University Press.

Schaefer, R. T. (2005). *Race and ethnicity in the United States* (3rd ed.). Upper Saddle River, NJ: Prentice Hall.

Schiller, H. L. (1973). *The mind managers.* Boston: Beacon.

Slavery and the making of America. (2004). [Film]. New York: Ambrose.

READING 37

Notes

*Correspondence address: Bhoomi K. Thakore, Northwestern University Feinberg School of Medicine, 420 E. Superior St., Rubloff 650,

Chicago, IL 60611, USA. E-mail: Bhoomi.thakore@northwestern.edu

1. I use the umbrella term "South Asian" to fall in line with other scholars who discuss this larger group and identify the experiences of one as the experiences of all (e.g. Desai 2004; Davé 2013; Kibria 1998; Purkayastha 2005; Shankar 2008; Sharma 2010). Further, while Indians are only one part of the larger South Asian population, I argue that the media characterizations of Indians are similar to the media characterization of other South Asians in popular media. However, I use the terms somewhat interchangeably in this paper and discuss particular concepts as related to "Indians" where relevant.

2. While the original article by Rastogi addressed the increasing number of Indian characters on television, I contend that a similar case can be made for Indian characters in contemporary American films. Thus, I use the phrase "popular media" when discussing these images.

3. The exception to this is Mindy Kaling, formerly of *The Office,* and creator and star of the television show *The Mindy Project.* While she is darker, curvier, and shorter than other South Asian actresses in popular media, she was never chosen or cast by producers. As a writer on *The Office,* she created her role herself, and similarly cast herself in her own show. As a result, Kaling was able to break out of the White, heterosexual, male gaze (Mulvey 1975) reproduced by media producers.

References

Alba, Richard and Victor Nee. 2003. *Remaking the American Mainstream.* Cambridge, MA: Harvard University Press.

Alsultany, Evelyn. 2012. *Arabs and Muslims in the Media: Race and Representation after 9/11.* New York: New York University Press.

Bagdikian, Ben. 2004. *The New Media Monopoly.* Boston: Beacon Press.

Beltran, Mary. 2005. "The New Hollywood Racelessness: Only the Fast, Furious (and Multiracial) Will Survive." *Cinema Journal* 44(2): 50–67.

Bonilla-Silva, Eduardo. 1997. "Rethinking Racism: Toward a Structural Interpretation." *American Sociological Review* 62(3): 465–80.

Bonilla-Silva, Eduardo. 2004. "From Bi-Racial to Tri-Racial: Towards a New System of Racial Stratification in the USA." *Ethnic and Racial Studies* 27(6): 931–50.

Bourdieu, Pierre. 1999. *On Television.* P.P. Ferguson, trans. New York: The New Press.

Chito Childs, Erica. 2009. *Fade to Black and White: International Images in Popular Culture.* Lanham, MD: Rowman and Littlefield.

Collins, Patricia Hill. 2004. *Black Sexual Politics: African Americans, Gender, and the New Racism.* New York: Routledge.

Davé, Shilpa. 2013. *Indian Accents: Brown Voice and Racial Performance in American Television and Film.* Urbana: University of Illinois Press.

Desai, Jigna. 2004. *Beyond Bollywood: The Cultural Politics of South Asian Diasporic Films.* New York: Routledge.

Desai, Jigna. 2005. "Planet Bollywood: Indian Cinema Abroad." Pp. 55–71 in *East Main Street: Asian American Popular Culture.* New York: New York University Press.

Dhingra, Pawan. 2012. *Life Behind the Lobby: Indian American Motel Owners and the American Dream.* Stanford: Stanford University Press.

Feagin, Joe. 2001. *Racist America: Roots, Current Realities, and Future Reparation.* New York: Routledge.

Glenn, Evelyn Nakano. 2008. "Yearning for Lightness: Transnational Circuits in the Marketing and Consumption of Skin Lighteners." *Gender and Society* 22(3): 281–302.

Gray, Herman. 2004. *Watching Race: Television and the Struggle for Blackness.* Minneapolis: University of Minnesota Press.

Hall, Stuart. 1997. *Representation: Cultural Representations and Signifying Practices.* Thousand Oaks, CA: Sage.

Haller, William, Alejandro Portes, and Scott M. Lynch. 2011. "Dreams Fulfilled, Dreams Shattered:

Determinants of Segmented Assimilation in the Second Generation." *Social Forces* 89(3): 733–62.

Hunter, Margaret L. 2005. *Race, Gender, and the Politics of Skin Tone.* New York: Routledge.

Jacobs, Tom. 2012. Hollywood goes South Asian. *Salon,* August 30. Accessed July 7, 2013 (http://www.salon.com/2012/08/30/hollywoods_new_fascination_with_south_asians/).

Jefferson, Deana and Jayne E. Stake. 2009. "Appearance and Self-Attitudes of African American and European American Women: Media Comparisons and the Internalization of Beauty Ideals." *Psychology of Women Quarterly* 33(4): 396–409.

Jones, Dorothy. 1955. *The Portrayal of China and India on the American Screen, 1896–1955: The Evolution of Chinese and Indian Themes, Locales, and Characters as Portrayed on the American Screen.* Cambridge: MIT Center for International Studies.

Kibria, Nazli. 1998. "The Contested Meaning of 'Asian American': Racial Dilemmas in the Contemporary U.S." *Ethnic and Racial Studies* 21(5): 939–58.

Kim, Claire Jean. 1999. "The Racial Triangulation of Asian Americans." *Politics and Society* 27(1): 105–38.

Kitano, Harry and Roger Daniels. 2001. *Asian Americans: Emerging Minorities,* 3rd ed. Upper Saddle River, NJ: Pearson.

Koshy, Susan. 2002. "South Asians and the Complex Interstices of Whiteness." Pp. 29–50 in *White Women in Racialized Spaces,* edited by S. Najmi and R. Srikanth. Albany, NY: SUNY Press.

Lizardi, Geetika Tandon. 2011. Don't Hate Outsourced. *L.A. Times,* March 21. Accessed July 7, 2013 (http://articles.latimes.com/2011/mar/21/opinion/la-oe-lizardi-outsourced-20110321-22).

McChesney, Robert. 2004. *The Problem of the Media: U.S. Communication Politics in the 21st Century.* New York: Monthly Review Press.

McChesney, Robert. 2008. *The Political Economy of Media.* New York: Monthly Review Press.

Mistry, Reena. 1999. Can Gramsci's Theory of Hegemony Help Us Understand the Representation of Minorities in Western Television and Cinema? Accessed July 7, 2013 (http://www.theory.org.uk/ctr-rol6.htm).

Mulvey, Laura. 1975. "Visual Pleasure and Narrative Cinema." *Screen* 16(3): 6–18.

Nacos, Brigitte L. and Oscar Torres-Reyna. 2007. *Fueling Our Fears: Stereotyping, Media Coverage, and Public Opinion of Muslim Americans.* Lanham, MD: Rowman and Littlefield.

Omi, Michael and Howard Winant. 1994. *Racial Formation in the United States: From the 1960s to the 1990s,* 2nd ed. New York: Routledge.

Ono, Kent A. and Vincent T. Pham. 2009. *Asian Americans and the Media.* Cambridge, UK: Polity.

Prashad, Vijay. 2000. *The Karma of Brown Folk.* Minneapolis, MN: University of Minnesota Press.

Purkayastha, Bandana. 2005. *Negotiating Ethnicity: Second-Generation South Asian Americans Traverse a Translational World.* New Brunswick, NJ: Rutgers University Press.

Rangaswamy, Padma. 2007. "South Asians in Dunkin' Donuts: Niche Development in the Franchise Industry." *Journal of Ethnic and Migration Studies* 33(4): 671–86.

Rastogi, Nina. 2010. "Beyond Apu: Why Are There Suddenly So Many Indians on Television?" *Slate,* June 9. Accessed July 7, 2013 (http://www.slate.com/id/2255937/).

Rodriguez, Clara. 1997. *Latin Looks: Images of Latinas and Latinos in the U.S. Media.* Boulder, CO: Westview Press.

Selod, Saher and David G. Embrick. 2013. "Racialization and Muslims: Situating the Muslim Experience in Race Scholarship." *Sociology Compass* 7(8): 644–55.

Shankar, Shalini. 2008. *Desi Land: Teen Culture, Class and Success in Silicon Valley.* Durham, NC: Duke University Press.

Sharma, Nitasha Tamar. 2010. *Hip Hop Desis: South Asian Americans, Blackness, and a Global Race Consciousness.* Durham, NC: Duke University Press.

Stewart, Dodai. 2013. "Mindy Kaling Only Makes Out with White Guys on *The Mindy Project.*" *Jezebel,*

May 14. Accessed July 7, 2013 (http://jezebel.com/mindy-kaling-only-makes-out-with-white-guys-on-the-mind-504732390).

Takaki, Ronald. 1998. *Strangers from a Different Shore: A History of Asian Americans.* Rev. ed. Boston: Little, Brown and Company.

Tuan, Mia. 1999. *Forever Foreigners or Honorary Whites? The Asian Ethnic Experience Today.* New Brunswick: Rutgers University Press.

Vera, Hernán and Andrew Gordon. 2003. *Screen Saviors: Hollywood Fictions of Whiteness.* Lanham, MD: Rowman and Littlefield.

Webster, Yehudi O. 1992. *The Racialization of America.* New York: St. Martin's Press.

Wilson, Clint C., Felix Gutierrez, and Lena M. Chao. 2003. *Racism, Sexism and the Media: The Rise of Class Communication in Multicultural America,* 4th ed. Thousand Oaks, CA: Sage.

Wu, Frank. 2002. *Yellow: Race in America Beyond Black and White.* New York: Basic Books.

Zhou, Min and Yang Sao Xiong. 2007. "The Multifaceted American Experiences of the Children of Asian Immigrants: Lessons for Segmented Assimilation." *Ethnic and Racial Studies* 28(6): 1119–52.

READING 38

Notes

1. George W. Bush, "Address to a Joint Session of Congress and the American People," September 20, 2001, www.whitehouse.gov/newslreleases/2001/09/20010920-8.html.

2. See, for example, American-Arab Anti-Discrimination Committee, "Report on Hate Crimes and Discrimination against Arab Americans: The Post-September 11 Backlash" (Washington, DC: American-Arab Anti-Discrimination Committee Research Institute, 2003), www.adc.org/hate-crimes/pdf/2003_report_web.pdf.

3. Ibid.

4. For a summary of government initiatives after *9/11,* see Anny Bakalian and Mehdi Bozorgmehr,

Backlash 9/11: Middle Eastern and Muslim Americans Respond (Berkeley: University of California Press, 2009), 253–65.

5. I am building here on arguments made, for example, in the following: Howard Winant, *The New Politics of Race: Globalism, Difference, Justice* (Minneapolis: University of Minnesota Press, 2004); Jodi Melamed, "The Spirit of Neoliberalism: From Racial Liberalism to Neoliberal Multiculturalism," *Social Text,* no. 89 (2006): 1–24; and Eduardo Bonilla-Silva, *Racism without Racists: Color-Blind Racism and the Persistence of Racial Inequality in the United States,* 2nd ed. (New York: Rowman and Littlefield, 2006).

6. *Threat Matrix,* ABC, September 18, 2003–January 29, 2004; 24, FOX, season 6, January 14–May 21, 2007.

7. "Al-Fatiha," *Sleeper Cell,* Showtime, season 1, episode 1, December 4, 2005.

8. "Inter Arma Silent Leges," *The Practice,* ABC, season 6, episode 9, December 9, 2001.

9. "Bad to Worse," *The Practice,* ABC, season 7, episode 8, December 1, 2002.

10. For more on the history of representations of Arabs, see Jack G. Shaheen, *Reel Bad Arabs: How Hollywood Vilifies a People* (Northampton, MA: Interlink Publishing Group, 2001).

11. "Day 2," *24,* FOX, October 28, 2002–May 20, 2003.

12. "Day 4: 7am–8am," *24,* FOX, January 9, 2005.

13. Even post-9/11 films with positive representation of Arab and Muslim characters, such as *The Visitor* (2007) and *Sorry, Haters* (2005), are framed in the context of 9/11. *Little Mosque on the Prairie* (2007–2012), a sitcom televised by the Canadian Broadcasting Corporation, has not crossed over into the United States. Three sitcoms have been a departure from the 9/11 context: *Whoopi!* (NBC, 2003–4); *Aliens in America* (CW, 2007–8); and *Community* (NBC, 2009–present).

14. "Lifting the Veil," *CNN Newsnight,* November 20, 2001; "Free to Choose," "Unveiling Freedom," *CNN Newsnight,* December 3, 2001; "Under

the Veil," ABC, *Nightline*, October 26, 2006; Anna Mulrine, "Unveiled Threat: The Taliban Is Relentless in Its Oppression of Afghan Women," *U.S. News & World Report*, October 15, 2001, 32–34; Richard Lacayo, "Lifting the Veil," *Time*, December 3, 2001, 34–49; and "Beneath the Veil," *CNN Newsnight*, September 13, 2002.

15. See, for example, Richard Lacayo, Hannah Beech, Hannah Bloch, Matthew Forney, Terry McCarthy, Jeff Chu, Jeffrey Ressner, Alex Perry, Tim McGirk, and John F. Dickerson, "About Face," *Time*, December 3, 2001, www.time.com/time/magazine/article/0.9171.1001344.00.html; and David Van Bierna, Marguerite Michaels, and Nadia Mustafa, "Islam: In the U.S.: Freer, but Not Friedan," *Time*, December 3, 2001, www.time.com/time/magazine/article/0,9171, 100 1348,00.html#ixzzOr2vh2irx.

16. Lisa Beyer, "The Women of Islam," *Time*, November 25, 2001, www.time.com/time/world/article/0,8599, 185647,00.html.

17. Ibid.

18. Nonie Darwish, *Now They Call Me Infidel: Why I Renounced Jihad for America, Israel, and the War on Terror* (New York: Sentinel HC, 2006); and Darwish, *Cruel and Usual Punishment: The Terrifying Global Implications of Islamic Law* (Nashville, TN: Thomas Nelson, 2008).

19. Wafa Sultan, *A God Who Hates* (New York: St. Martin's Press, 2009).

20. Ayaan Hirsi Ali, *Infidel* (New York: Free Press, 2007).

21. "Crime and Punishment/Saudi Arabian Rape Case/Ali Interview," *Anderson Cooper 360*, CNN, November 29, 2007.

22. Moustafa Bayoumi, "The God That Failed: The Neo-Orientalism of Today's Muslim Commentators," in *Islamophobia/Islamophilia: Beyond the Politics of Enemy and Friend*, ed. Andrew Shryock (Bloomington: Indiana University Press, 2010), 79–93.

23. Sunaina Maira, "'Good' and 'Bad' Muslim Citizens: Feminists, Terrorists, and U.S. Orientalisms," *Feminist Studies* 35.3 (2009): 631–56.

24. Ibid.

READING 39

Notes

1. Many people have preferences about terms used to describe America's indigenous peoples. "American Indian" is commonly used, as is "Native American, Native, and Indian." These terms are used interchangeably in recognition of individual preferences, without disregarding the weight each word carries.

2. Lawsuits are currently underway to limit Heilman Breweries' use of the name Crazy Horse Liquor (Specktor, 1995). Several states have outlawed the sale of the beverage (Specktor, 1995). Also under review are important legal issues such as a tribe's sovereign power to exercise civil jurisdiction and the Witko family's right to protect the image of their ancestor.

References

Aaker, D., & A. L. Biel. (1993). *Advertising's role in building strong brands*. Mahwah, NJ: Lawrence Erlbaum.

Barthes, R. (1972). *Mythologies*. New York: The Noonday Press.

Berkhofer, R., Jr. (1979). *The White man's Indian: Images of the American Indian from Columbus to the present*. New York: Vintage Books.

Bird, S. E. (1996). Not my fantasy: The persistence of Indian imagery in *Dr. Quinn, Medicine Woman*. In S. E. Bird (Ed.), *Dressing in feathers: The construction of the Indian in American popular culture* (pp. 245–262). Boulder, CO: Westview Press.

Blalock, C. (1992). Crazy Horse controversy riles Congress: Controversies over Crazy Horse Malt Liquor and Black Death vodka. *Beverage Industry, 83*(9), 1–3.

Burnham, P. (1992, 27 May). Indians can't shake label as guides to good buys. *The Washington Times*, p. E1.

Champagne, D. (1994). *Native America: Portrait of the peoples*. Detroit: Visible Ink.

Cortese, A. J. (1999). *Provocateur: Images of women and minorities in advertising*. New York: Rowman & Littlefield Publishers, Inc.

Dotz, W., & Morton, J. (1996). *What a character! 20th century American advertising icons*. San Francisco: Chronicle Books.

Goings, K. W. (1994). *Mammy and Uncle Mose: Black collectibles and American stereotyping.* Bloomington, IN: Indiana University Press.

Graham, R. (1993, 6 January). Symbol or stereotype: One consumer's tradition is another's racial slur. *The Boston Globe,* p. 35.

Green, M. K. (1993). Images of American Indians in advertising: Some moral issues. *Journal of Business Ethics, 12,* 323–330.

Hall, S. (1997). *Representation: Cultural representations and signifying practices.* London: Sage.

Hill, R. (1992). The non-vanishing American Indian: Are the modern images any closer to the truth? *Quail* (May), 35–37.

Kates, S. M., & Shaw-Garlock, G. (1999). The ever-entangling web: A study of ideologies and discourses in advertising to women. *Journal of Advertising, 28*(2), 33–49.

Kern-Foxworth, M. (1994). *Aunt Jemima, Uncle Ben, and Rastus: Blacks in advertising yesterday, today, and tomorrow.* Westport, CT: Praeger.

Land O' Lakes. (2000). [On-line]. Available: http://www.landolakes.com.

Larson, C. (1937). Patent-medicine advertising and the early American press. *Journalism Quarterly, 14*(4), 333–339.

Lippmann, W. (1922/1961). *Public opinion.* New York: Macmillan & Company.

McCracken, G. (1993). The value of the brand: An anthropological perspective. In D. Aaker & A. L. Biel (Eds.), *Brand equity in advertising: Advertising's role in building strong brands.* Mahwah, NJ: Lawrence Erlbaum.

Merskin, D. (1998). Sending up signals: A survey of American Indian media use and representation in the mass media. *The Howard Journal of Communications, 9,* 333–345.

Metz, S., & Thee, M. (1994). Brewers intoxicated with racist imagery. *Business and Society Review, 89,* 50–51.

Mihesuah, D. A. (1996). *American Indians: Stereotypes and realities.* Atlanta, GA: Clarity Press.

Monitor Sugar Company. (2000). [On-line]. Available: http://members.aol.com/asga/mon.htm.

Morgan, H. (1986). *Symbols of America.* New York: Penguin Books.

Schmitt, B., & Simonson, A. (1997). *Marketing aesthetics: The strategic management of brands, identity, and image.* New York: The Free Press.

Sioux Honey Association. (2000). [On-line]. Available: http://www.suebeehoney.com.

Specktor, M. (1995, January 6). Crazy Horse exploited to peddle liquor. *National Catholic Reporter, 31*(10), 3.

Strickland, R. (1998). The celluloid Indian. *Oregon Quarterly* (Summer), 9–10.

van Dijk, T. A. (1996). *Discourse, racism, and ideology.* La Laguna: RCEI Ediciones.

Westerman, M. (1989, March). Death of the Frito bandito: Marketing to ethnic groups. *American Demographics, 11,* 28–32.

Williamson, J. (1978). *Decoding advertisements: Ideology and meaning in advertising.* New York: Marion Boyars.

READING 41

Notes

1. Tyrrell 1991, 1035; see also Lowenthal 1991.

2. Ringer 1983; de Tocqueville 1994 [1840]; Smith 1997.

3. Anno 13 Geo. II [1740], Cap. VII. See Kettner 1978.

4. The major exception was Charles I's concession of a Catholic colony in Maryland in 1632 (Baseler 1998, 56).

5. Klebaner 1958, 291–2; Baseler 1998; Kanstroom 2007, 45.

6. Baseler 1998, 80.

7. See Baseler 1998, 124–6.

8. Zolberg 2006, 79.

9. Baseler 1998, 227.

10. 1 Stat. 103, sec. 1.

11. Szajkowski 1970; Zolberg 2006, 83–7.

12. Zolberg 2006, 53–4.

13. Jacobson 1998.

14. Haney-López 1996, 61.

15. Ngai 2004, 41.

16. *Ozawa v. United States,* 260 U.S. 178 (1922).

17. Gordon 1945, 244.

18. *U.S. v. Bhagat Singh Thind,* 261 U.S. 204 (1923); Haney-López 1996, 67, 90–91.

19. *In re Rodriguez,* 81 Fed. (W.D. Tex. 1897); Hoffman 1974; Ngai 2004, 53–4.

20. Neuman 1993, 1870.

21. Act of Feb. 28, 1803, ch. 10, 2 Stat. 205.

22. 14 Stat. 27, sec. 1; U.S. Const, amend. XIV, §2; Dred Scott v. Sandford, 60 U.S. 393 (1857).

23. Hutchinson 1981, 57–8.

24. 16 Stat. 254, Sec. 7.

25. Miller 1975.

26. Saxton 1971; Hing 1993, 20–21; Briggs 2001, 35; Calavita 2001, 206; Tichenor 2002, 89; Zolberg 2006, 166.

27. Price 1974; Gyory 1998, 15; Briggs 2001.

28. *Congressional Record* 1882, 1482.

29. 1855 Cal. Stat. 194.

30. 1858 Cal. Stat. 295; 1862 Cal Stat. 462.

31. California Constitution [1879] Art. XIX.

32. 1891 Cal Stat. 185.

33. Lake and Reynolds 2008,176.

34. Zeidel 2004, 33.

35. "State of the Union Address," Theodore Roosevelt, Dec. 3,1907.

36. Bailey 1940.

37. Higham 1994.

38. 1819 Steerage Act, 3 Stat. 488; 1847 Passenger Act, 9 Stat. 128; 1855 Passenger Act, 10 Stat. 715; 1875 Page Law, 18 Stat. 477; 1882 Immigration Act, 22 Stat. 214, 1885 Contract Labor Law, 23 Stat. 332; 1891 Immigration Act, 26 Stat. 1084.

39. Ngai 2004, 18.

40. Totten 2008.

41. Banton 1987.

42. Jacobson 1998.

43. Higham 1994, 50–1; Tichenor 2002.

44. Zolberg 2006, 211.

45. Lake and Reynolds 2008, 62–3.

46. *Congressional Record* 28, 2817; Higham 1994, 142.

47. "President Grover Cleveland Veto Message," March 2, 1897.

48. "President William Howard Taft's Veto of a Literacy Test for Immigrants," February 14, 1913; "President Woodrow Wilson Veto Message," Jan. 28, 1915.

49. 39 Stat. 874.

50. Loescher and Scanlan 1986, xv.

51. Grant 1925.

52. Zeidel 2004.

53. Divine 1957, 62.

54. Divine 1957, 78–9.

55. Hoffman 1974; Hernández 2010.

References

Bailey, Thomas A. 1940. "The Root-Takahira Agreement of 1908." *Pacific Historical Review* no. 9 (1):19–35.

Banton, Michael. 1987. *Racial theories.* Cambridge: Cambridge University Press.

Baseler, Marilyn C. 1998. *"Asylum for mankind": America, 1607–1800.* Ithaca, NY: Cornell University Press.

Briggs, Vernon M. 2001. *Immigration and American unionism.* Ithaca, NY: Cornell University Press.

Calavita, Kitty. 2001. "Chinese exclusion and the open door with China: Structural contradictions and the 'chaos' of law, 1882–1910." *Social & Legal Studies* no. 10 (2):203–26.

de Tocqueville, Alexis. 1994 [1840]. *Democracy in America*. New York: Twayne Publishers.

Divine, Robert A. 1957. *American immigration policy, 1924–1952*. New Haven: Yale University Press.

Gordon, Charles. 1945. "The racial barrier to American citizenship." *University of Pennsylvania Law Review* no. 93 (3):237–58.

Grant, E. E. 1925. "Scum from the melting-pot." *American Journal of Sociology* no. 30 (6):641–51.

Gyory, Andrew. 1998. *Closing the gate: Race, politics, and the Chinese Exclusion Act*. Chapel Hill: University of North Carolina Press.

Haney-López, Ian. 1996. *White by law: The legal construction of race* (critical America). New York: New York University Press.

Hernández, Kelly Lytle. 2010. *Migra! A history of the U.S. Border Patrol*. Berkeley: University of California Press.

Higham, John. 1994. *Strangers in the land: Patterns of American nativism, 1860–1925*. New Brunswick, NJ: Rutgers University Press.

Hing, Bill Ong. 1993. *Making and remaking Asian America through immigration policy, 1850–1990*. Stanford, CA: Stanford University Press.

Hoffman, Abraham. 1974. *Unwanted Mexican Americans in the Great Depression: Repatriation pressures, 1929–1939*. Tucson: University of Arizona Press.

Hutchinson, Edward P. 1981. *Legislative history of American immigration policy, 1798–1965*. Philadelphia: University of Pennsylvania Press.

Jacobson, Matthew Frye. 1998. *Whiteness of a different color: European immigrants and the alchemy of race*. Cambridge, MA: Harvard University Press.

Kanstroom, Daniel. 2007. *Deportation nation: Outsiders in American history*. Cambridge, MA: Harvard University Press.

Kettner, James H. 1978. *The development of American citizenship, 1608–1870*. Chapel Hill: University of North Carolina Press.

Klebaner, Benjamin J. 1958. "State and local immigration regulation in the United States before 1882." *International Review of Social History* no. 3.

Lake, Marilyn, and Henry Reynolds. 2008. *Drawing the global colour line: White men's countries and the international challenge of racial equality*. Cambridge: Cambridge University Press.

Loescher, Gil, and John A. Scanlan. 1986. *Calculated kindness: Refugees and America's half-open door, 1945 to the present*. New York: Collier Macmillan.

Lowenthal, Abraham F. 1991. *Exporting democracy: The United States and Latin America*. Baltimore: Johns Hopkins University Press.

Miller, Floyd. 1975. *The search for a Black nationality: Black emigration and colonization, 1787–1863*. Urbana-Champaign: University of Illinois Press.

Neuman, Gerald L. 1993. "Lost century of American immigration law (1776–1875)." *Columbia Law Review* no. 93:1833.

Ngai, Mae M. 2004. *Impossible subjects: Illegal aliens and the making of modern America*. Princeton: Princeton University Press.

Price, Charles A. 1974. *The great white walls are built: Restrictive immigration to North America and Australasia, 1836–1888*. Canberra: Australian National University Press.

Ringer, Benjamin. 1983. *We the people and others: Duality and America's treatment of its racial minorities*. New York: Tavistock Publications.

Saxton, Alexander. 1971. *The indispensable enemy: Labor and the anti-Chinese movement in California*. Berkeley: University of California Press.

Smith, Rogers M. 1997. *Civic ideals: Conflicting visions of citizenship in U.S. history*. New Haven: Yale University Press.

Szajkowski, Zosa. 1970. *Jews and the French Revolutions of 1789, 1830 and 1848*. Newark, NJ: KTAV Publishing House.

Tichenor, Daniel J. 2002. *Dividing lines: The politics of immigration control in America*. Princeton, NJ: Princeton University Press.

Totten, Robbie. 2008. "National security and US immigration policy, 1776–1790." *Journal of Interdisciplinary History* no. 39 (1):37–64.

Tyrrell, Ian. 1991. "American exceptionalism in an age of international history." *The American Historical Review* no. 96: 1031–55.

Zeidel, Robert F. 2004. *Immigrants, progressives, and exclusion politics: The Dillingham Commission, 1900–1927.* DeKalb: Northern Illinois University Press.

Zolberg, Aristide. 2006. *A nation by design: Immigration policy in the fashioning of America.* Cambridge, MA: Harvard University Press.

READING 43

References

Adelman, Robert M., Hui-shien Tsao, Stewart E. Tolnay, and Kyle D. Crowder. 2001. "Neighborhood Disadvantage among Racial and Ethnic Groups: Residential Location in 1970 and 1980." *Sociological Quarterly* 42: 603–32.

Arthur, John A. 2000. *Invisible Sojourners: African Immigrant Diaspora in the United States.* New York: Praeger.

Dodoo, F. Nii-Amoo. 1999. "Black and Immigrant Labor Force Participation in America." *Race and Society* 2: 69–82.

Foerster, Amy. 2004. "Race, Identity, and Belonging: 'Blackness' and the Struggle for Solidarity in a Multiethnic Labor Union." *Social Problems* 51: 386–409.

Ho, Christine. 1991. *Salt-Water Trinnies: Afro-Trinidadian Immigrant Networks and Non-assimilation in Los Angeles.* New York: AMS Press.

James, Winston. 2002. "Explaining Afro-Caribbean Social Mobility in the United States: Beyond the Sowell Thesis." *Comparative Studies in Society and History* 44: 218–62.

Kasinitz, Philip. 1992. *Caribbean New York.* Ithaca, NY: Cornell University Press.

Kollehlon, Konia T., and Edward E. Eule. 2003. "The Socioeconomic Attainment Patterns of Africans in the United States." *International Migration Review* 37: 1163–90.

Logan, John R., and John Mollenkopf. 2003. *People and Politics in America's Big Cities.* New York: Drum Major Institute for Public Policy.

Rogers, Reuel R. 2004. "Race-Based Coalitions among Minority Groups: Afro-Caribbean Immigrants and African-Americans in New York City." *Urban Affairs Review* 39: 283–317.

Sowell, Thomas. 1978. "Three Black Histories." In *Essays and Data on American Ethnic Groups*, ed. Thomas Sowell. Washington, DC: Urban Institute.

Takyi, Baffour K. 2002a. "Africans in the Diaspora: Black-White Earnings Differences among America's Africans." *Ethnic and Racial Studies* 25: 913–41.

Takyi, Baffour K. 2002b. "The Making of the Second Diaspora: On the Recent African Immigrant Community in the United States of America." *Western Journal of Black Studies* 26: 32–43.

Waters, Mary. 1999. *Black Identities: West Indian Immigrant Dreams and American Realities.* Cambridge, MA: Harvard University Press.

READING 44

Notes

1. See William E. Leuchtenburg, "The American Perception of the Arab World." In George N. Atiyeh, ed., *Arab and American Cultures* (Washington, DC: American Enterprise Institute for Public Policy Research, 1977), p. 15.

2. Although it is possible to speak of several waves of Arab immigration to North America (e.g., 1880s to World War I, World War I to World War II, 1945 to 1967, 1968 to the present), there have been two main waves: from the 1880s to World War II and from World War II to the present. The major differences in the character and composition of the immigrant populations can be detected primarily between these two groups.

3. Unless otherwise indicated, references to the Arab community include the Arabs in Canada and those in the United States. Because of the much smaller numbers of Arabs in Canada, leadership on major issues usually has come from the Arab community in the United States.

4. See appendixes 1 and 2 in Gregory Orfalea, *Before the Flames: Quest for the History of Arab Americans* (Austin, TX: University of Texas Press, 1988), pp. 314–15. There were about 11,000 Arabs in Canada in 1931. For more on the subject of Arab immigration to Canada, see Baha Abu-Laban, *An Olive Branch on the Family Tree: The Arabs in Canada* (Toronto: McClelland and Stewart, 1980).

5. This is the official U.S. government figure cited in Philip Hitti's "The Emigrants," published in the 1963 edition of the *Encyclopedia of Islam* and reproduced in *Al-Hoda, 1898–1968* (New York: Al-Hoda Press, 1968), p. 133. A much larger estimate of 800,000 (Lebanese) was given by Ashad G. Hawie, *The Rainbow Ends* (New York: Theo. Gaus' Sons, 1942), pp. 149, 151.

6. This figure does not include the Arab community in Canada, which has fewer than 400,000 persons today. For estimates of Arab immigration to Canada, see Baha Abu-Laban, *An Olive Branch on the Family Tree: The Arabs in Canada* (Toronto: McClelland and Stewart, 1980) and Ibrahim Hayani's chapter in Michael Suleiman, ed., *Arabs in America: Building a New Future* (Philadelphia: Temple University Press, 1999). Philip M. Kayal gave the low estimate in 1974 for Arabs in the United States but provided a revised estimate much closer to the generally accepted figure in 1987. See his "Estimating Arab-American Population," *Migration Today* 2, no. 5 (1974): 3, 9, and "Report: Counting the 'Arabs' Among Us," *Arab Studies Quarterly* 9, no. 1 (1987): 98–104.

7. See Philip K. Hitti, *The Syrians in America* (New York: George H. Doran, 1924), p. 48; Alixa Naff, *Becoming American: The Early Arab Immigrant Experience* (Carbondale: Southern Illinois University Press, 1985), p. 83; Samir Khalaf, "The Background and Causes of Lebanese/Syrian Immigration to the United States before World War I," in Eric J. Hooglund, ed., *Crossing the Waters: Arabic-Speaking Immigrants to the United States before 1940* (Washington, DC: Smithsonian Institution Press, 1987), pp. 17–35; and Charles Issawi, "The Historical Background of Lebanese Emigration: 1800–1914," in Albert Hourani and Nadim Shehadi, eds., *The Lebanese in the World: A Century of Emigration* (London:

I.B. Tauris, 1992), pp. 13–31. See also Baha Abu-Laban, "The Lebanese in Montreal," in Albert Hourani and Nadim Shehadi, eds., *The Lebanese in the World: A Century of Emigration* (London: I.B. Tauris, 1992), pp. 227–42.

8. Charles Issawi, "The Historical Background of Lebanese Emigration: 1800–1914." In Albert Hourani and Nadim Shehadi, eds., *The Lebanese in the World: A Century of Emigration* (London: I.B. Tauris, 1992), p. 22.

9. Philip K. Hitti, *The Syrians in America* (New York: George H. Doran, 1924), pp. 49–50. See also Akram Fouad Khater, "'House' to 'Goddess of the House': Gender, Class, and Silk in 19th-Century Mount Lebanon," *International Journal of Middle East Studies* 28, no. 3 (1996): 325–48.

10. For an informed and intelligent discussion on this and related issues, see Louise Seymour Houghton's series of articles entitled "Syrians in the United States," *The Survey* 26 (1 July, 5 August, 2 September, 7 October, 1911), pp. 480–95, 647–65, 786–803, 957–68.

11. For an early account of Arab immigration to the United States and to North America in general, which cites religious persecution as the reason for migration, see Basil M. Kherbawi, "History of the Syrian Emigration," which is part seven of Kherbawi's *tarikh al-Wilayat al-Muttahida* (*History of the United States*) (New York: al Dalil Press, 1913), pp. 726–96, published in Arabic.

12. See Leila Tarazi Fawaz, An Occasion for War: Civil Conflict in Lebanon and Damascus in 1860 (Berkeley: University of California Press, 1995). See also Mikha'il Mishaqa, *Murder, Mayhem, Pillage and Plunder: The History of Lebanon in the 18th and 19th Centuries*. Translated by Wheeler M. Thackston, Jr. (Albany, NY: State University of New York Press, 1988).

13. See Louise Seymour Houghton's series of articles entitled "Syrians in the United States," *The Survey*, 26 (1911), pp. 480–95; and Alixa Naff, *Becoming American: The Early Arab Immigrant Experience* (Carbondale: Southern Illinois University Press, 1985), pp. 128–200. For Canadian statistics, see Baha Abu-Laban, *An Olive Branch on the Family*

Tree: The Arabs in Canada (Toronto: McClelland and Stewart, 1980).

14. *Kawkab America* (15 April 1892): 1, English section. The English titles of Arabic newspapers cited here are provided as originally used. The titles in parentheses are the transliterations used by the Library of Congress.

15. Even though *Kawkab America* was published for about seventeen years, only copies of the first four years are available; the others have been lost.

16. See Motaz Abdullah Alhourani, "The Arab-American Press and the Arab World: News Coverage in Al-Bayan and Al-Dalil" (master's thesis, Kansas State University, Manhattan, KS, 1993).

17. For a history of the organizational and political activities of Arabic-speaking groups in the United States during this period, see James Ansara, "The Immigration and Settlement of the Syrians" (master's thesis, Harvard University, Cambridge, MA, 1931).

18. Among these, the most important journal was *The Syrian World,* published and edited by Salloum Mokarzel. A useful publication is the *Annotated Index to the Syrian World, 1926–1932* by John G. Moses and Eugene Paul Nassar (Saint Paul, MN: Immigration History Research Center, University of Minnesota, 1994).

19. See Philip M. and Joseph M. Kayal, *The Syrian-Lebanese in America: A Study in Religion and Assimilation* (Boston, MA: Twayne Publishers, 1975).

20. A good account of the most prominent of these writers is provided by Nadira Jamil Sarraj, *Shu'ara' al-Rabitah al-Qalamiyah* (Poets of the Pen League) (Cairo, Egypt: Dar al-Ma'arif, 1964), published in Arabic.

21. See, for instance, Ameen Rihani, "To Syrians in the [American] Armed Forces," *As-Sayeh* (*al-Sa'ih*) (16 September 1918): 2, published in Arabic.

22. Advertisements and editorials in support of American Liberty bonds were found in most Arabic publications of that period, including *Al-Hoda* and *Meraat-ul-Gharb.*

23. See, in particular, *Syria before the Peace Conference* (New York: Syrian-Lebanese League of North America, 1919).

24. This was the view often voiced after French entrenchment in Syria and Lebanon in the late 1920s and the 1930s.

25. For a summary of these views, see "Editors and Arabian Newspapers Give Opinions on Zionism," *The Jewish Criterion* (5 July 1918): 16–17.

26. Among the more active participants in public lectures and writings on this issue were Ameen Rihani and F. I. Shatara. The Arab National League was established in 1936, and members spoke out on Palestine and other issues. For coverage of these and other activities related to the Palestine issue, see *Palestine & Transjordan* for that period. See also "A Communique from the Arab National League," *As-Sayeh* (6 August 1936): 9.

27. On the occupations of emigrant Arabs, especially in North America and specifically about those engaged in commerce, see Salloum Mokarzel, *Tarikh al-tijara al-Suriyya fi al-mahajir al-Amrikiyya* (*The History of Trade of Syrian Immigrants in the Americas*) (New York: Syrian-American Press, 1920), published in Arabic. On peddling activity, see Alixa Naff, *Becoming American: The Early Arab Immigrant Experience* (Carbondale: Southern Illinois University Press, 1985), pp. 128–200.

28. The Arabic press of the period was replete with such advice.

29. Edna Bonacich, "A Theory of Middleman Minorities," *American Sociological Review* 38 (1973): 591.

30. Prejudice against Arabs in America was widespread, and there was also some discrimination, especially in the southern United States. See, for instance, Nancy Faires Conklin and Nora Faires, "'Colored' and Catholic: The Lebanese in Birmingham, Alabama." In Eric J. Hooglund, ed., *Crossing the Waters: Arabic-Speaking Immigrants to the United States before 1940* (Washington, DC: Smithsonian Institution Press, 1987), pp. 69–84.

31. See, for instance, H. A. El-Kourie, "Dr. El-Kourie Defends Syrian Immigrants," *Birmingham Ledger* (20 September 1907) and "El-Kourie Takes Burnett to Task," *Age-Herald* (Birmingham, AL) (20 October 1907): 6.

32. In 1908, Canada issued the Order-in-Council, PC. 926, which severely restricted Asiatic immigration. Negative attitudes about "Syrians," mistaking them for "Turks," also were a factor in reducing the level of Arab immigration to Canada. See Baha Abu-Laban, "The Lebanese in Montreal." In Albert Hourani and Nadim Shehadi, eds., *The Lebanese in the World: A Century of Emigration* (London: I.B. Tauris, 1992), p. 229.

33. See Kalil A. Bishara, *The Origins of the Modern Syrian* (New York: Al-Hoda Publishing House, 1914), published in English and Arabic.

34. See *Ex Parte Dow*, 211 F. 486 (E.D. South Carolina 1914) and *In Re Dow*, 213 F. 355 (E.D. South Carolina 1914).

35. *Dow v. United States et al*, 26 F. 145 (4th Cir. 1915).

36. See Joseph W. Ferris, "Syrian Naturalization Question in the United States: Certain Legal Aspects of Our Naturalization Laws," Part II, *The Syrian World* 2, no. 9 (1928): 18–24.

37. *In Re Ahmed Hassan*, 48 F. Supp. 843 (E.D. Michigan 1942).

38. *Ex Parte Mohriez*, 54 F. Supp. 941 (D. Massachusetts 1944).

39. See the Arabic edition of *Al-Hoda, 1898–1968* (New York: Al-Hoda Press, 1968).

40. The Syrian Voice changed its name to The Syrian and Lebanonite Voice in the late 1930s.

41. See M[ichael A.] Shadid, "Syria for the Syrians," *Syrian World* 1, no. 8 (1927): 21–24, and see "'Syria for the Syrians' Again: An Explanation and a Retraction," *Syrian World* 3, no. 4 (1928): 24–28.

42. For an excellent early study of New York Arabs, see Lucius Hopkins Miller, "A Study of the Syrian Communities of Greater New York," *Federation* 3 (1903): 11–58.

43. This was the message often presented in *Al-Akhlaq* (al-Akhlaq) (*Character*) in the 1920s.

44. See the various articles in the Arabic press by Afifa Karam and Victoria Tannous.

45. This issue occupied the Arab community for a long time and was almost a weekly subject in the main newspapers until peddling activity dwindled in the late 1920s. See, for instance, Afifa Karam's (untitled) article about women peddlers and the *Kashshi* in *Al-Hoda* (14 July, 1903): 2.

46. See, for instance, Habib I. Katibah, "What Is Americanism?" *The SyrianWorld* 1, no. 3 (1926): 16–20; W. A. Mansur, "The Future of Syrian Americans," *The SyrianWorld* 2, no. 3 (1927): 11–17, and see "Modern Syrians' Contributions to Civilization," *The SyrianWorld* 4, no. 5 (1930): 7–14.

47. The question about whether to teach Arabic to their children was a controversial issue in the 1920s and hotly debated in two main journals, *The Syrian World* and *Al-Akhlaq*.

48. See Michael W. Suleiman, "A Community Profile of Arab-Americans: Major Challenges and Concerns," *Arab Perspectives* (September 1983): pp. 6–13.

49. See Ibrahim Abu-Lughod, ed., *The Arab-Israeli Confrontation of June, 1967: An Arab Perspective* (Evanston, IL: Northwestern University Press, 1970).

50. Michael W. Suleiman, "Arab-Americans and the Political Process." In Ernest McCarus, ed., *The Development of Arab-American Identity* (Ann Arbor: University of Michigan Press, 1994), pp. 37–60.

51. See "Dictionary of Races or Peoples." In *United States Reports of the Immigration Commission* (Washington, DC: Government Printing Office, 1911).

52. The details of these appeals are discussed in Michael W. Suleiman, "Early Arab-Americans: The Search for Identity." In Eric J. Hooglund, ed., *Crossing the Waters: Arabic-Speaking Immigrants to the United States before 1940* (Washington, DC: Smithsonian Institution Press, 1987), pp. 37–54.

53. C. P. Snow, *The Two Cultures and the Scientific Revolution* (Cambridge, England: Cambridge University Press, 1961).

54. This became a popular theme among many Arab-American writers. See, for instance, Abraham Mitry Rihbany, *A Far Journey* (Boston, MA: Houghton-Mifflin, 1914).

55. Abraham Mitrie Rihbany, *The Syrian Christ* (Boston, MA: Houghton-Mifflin, 1916).

56. See Evelyn Shakir, "Pretending to Be Arab: Role-Playing in Vance Bourjaily's 'The Fractional Man,'" MELUS 9, no. 1 (1982): 7–21. See also Vance Bourjaily, *Confessions of a Spent Youth* (New York: Bantam Books, 1961).

57. See, for instance, William Peter Blatty, *Which Way to Mecca, Jack?* (New York: Bernard Geis Associates, 1960).

58. See Ali Shteiwi Zaghel, "Changing Patterns of Identification among Arab Americans: The Palestine Ramallites and the Christian Syrian-Lebanese" (Ph.D. diss., Northwestern University, 1977).

59. Much has been written in this vein. For a lengthy bibliography, see Michael W. Suleiman, *The Arabs in the Mind of America* (Brattleboro, VT: Amana Books, 1988). For a Canadian-Arab activist's view, see Sheikh Muhammad Said Massoud, *I Fought as I Believed* (Montreal: Sheikh Muhammad Said Massoud, 1976).

60. Helen Hatab Samhan, "Politics and Exclusion: The Arab American Experience," *Journal of Palestine Studies* 16, no. 2 (1987): 11–28.

61. Nabeel Abraham, "Anti-Arab Racism and Violence in the United States." In Ernest McCarus, ed., *The Development of Arab-American Identity* (Ann Arbor, MI: University of Michigan Press, 1994), pp. 155–214.

62. For documentation, see, for instance, *1990 ADC Annual Report on Political and Hate Violence* (Washington, DC: American-Arab Anti-Discrimination Committee, 1991). For Canadian statistics, see Zuhair Kashmeri, *The Gulf Within: Canadian Arabs, Racism and the Gulf War* (Toronto: James Lorimer & Co., 1991).

63. Ronald Stockton, "Ethnic Archetypes and the Arab Image." In Ernest McCarus, ed., *The Development of Arab-American Identity* (Ann Arbor: University of Michigan Press, 1994), p. 120.

64. See the various essays and poems in Joanna Kadi, ed., *Food for Our Grandmothers: Writings by Arab-American and Arab-Canadian Feminists* (Boston, MA: South End Press, 1994).

65. See Louise Cainkar, "Palestinian Women in the United States: Coping with Tradition, Change, and Alienation" (Ph.D. diss., Northwestern University, 1988).

66. See Charlene Joyce Eisenlohr, "The Dilemma of Adolescent Arab Girls in an American High School" (Ph.D. diss., University of Michigan, 1988).

67. For an excellent study on Arab-American women, see Evelyn Shakir, *Bint Arab: Arab and Arab American Women in the United States* (Westport, CT: Praeger, 1997).

68. Joseph Massad, "Palestinians and the Limits of Racialized Discourse," *Social Text* 11, no. 1 (1993): 108.

69. The attempt has failed, at least so far. See the 16 September 1997 letter to Katherine K. Wellman of the Office of Management and Budget sent on Arab American Institute (AAI) stationery and signed by Helen Hatab Samhan (AAI), Samia El Badry (Census 2000 Advisory Committee), and Hala Maksoud, American-Arab Anti-Discrimination Committee.

70. Lisa Suhair Majaj, "Two Worlds: Arab-American Writing," *Forkroads* 1, no. 3 (1996): 64–80. See also different entries in Joanna Kadi, ed., *Food for Our Grandmothers: Writings by Arab-American and Arab-Canadian Feminists* (Boston, MA: South End Press, 1994).

71. See, for instance, Pauline Kaldas, "Exotic." In Joanna Kadi, ed., *Food for Our Grandmothers: Writings by Arab-American and Arab-Canadian Feminists* (Boston, MA: South End Press, 1994), pp. 168–69.

72. See Nabeel Abraham, "Arab-American Marginality: Mythos and Praxis." In Baha Abu-Laban and Michael W. Suleiman, eds., *Arab Americans: Continuity and Change* (Belmont, MA: AAUG Press, 1989), pp. 17–43.

73. See Michael W. Suleiman, "American Views of Arabs and the Impact of These Views on Arab Americans," *Al-Mustaqbal Al-Arabi* 16 (1993): 93–107, published in Arabic.

74. Milton Gordon states that the absence of a hostile attitude on the part of the host society is a key factor in the integration and assimilation of immigrants. See his *Assimilation in American Life: The Role of Race, Religion, and National Origins* (New York: Oxford University Press, 1964).

75. These attitudes were evident in a 1998 survey of Arabs active in U.S. politics, an analysis of which I plan to publish.

76. For analyses of some of the 1980 and 1990 U.S. census data, see John Zogby, *Arab America Today: A Demographic Profile of Arab Americans* (Washington, DC: Arab American Institute, 1990), and Samia El-Badry, "The Arab-American Market," *American Demographics* (January 1994): 22–27, 30. See also "CPH-L-149 Selected Characteristics for Persons of Arab Ancestry: 1990," U.S. Bureau of the Census, 1990 Census of Population and Housing, C-P-3-2, Ancestry of the Population in the United States: 1990.

77. Examples include Michael DeBakey in medicine (heart surgery); Elias Corey in chemistry (1990 Nobel Prize winner); Casey Kasem, Danny Thomas, and Paula Abdul in entertainment; Helen Thomas in journalism; Doug Flutie in sports (1984 Heisman Trophy winner); and Ralph Nader in consumer advocacy.

78. Casey Kasem, "We're Proud of Our Heritage," *Parade* (*Kansas City Star*) (16 January 1994): 1.

79. See Lisa Suhair Majaj, "Boundaries: Arab/American." In Joanna Kadi, ed., *Food for Our Grandmothers: Writings by Arab-American and Arab-Canadian Feminists* (Boston, MA: South End Press, 1994), pp. 65–84.

READING 45

Notes

1. The families of the teens were from twelve different countries including Jamaica (31 percent); Trinidad (21 percent); Guyana (16 percent); Barbados (10 percent); Haiti (10 percent); Grenada (5 percent); and a few each from the smaller islands of Montserrat, Saint Thomas, Anguilla, Saint Lucia, Dominica, and Nevis.

2. Middle class was defined as having at least one parent with a college degree or a professional or business position. Working class was defined as a parent with a low-skill job; poor were students whose parents were not currently employed.

References

Anderson, E. 1990. *Streetwise: Race, Class, and Change in an Urban Community.* Chicago: University of Chicago Press.

Feagin, J. R. 1991. "The Continuing Significance of Race—Antiblack Discrimination in Public Places." *American Sociological Review* 56(1): 101–116.

Foner, N. 1987. "The Jamaicans: Race and Ethnicity Among Migrants in New York City." In *New Immigrants in New York,* edited by N. Foner. New York: Columbia University Press.

Fordham, S. 1988. "Racelessness as a Factor in Black Students' School Success: Pragmatic Strategy or Pyrrhic Victory?" *Harvard Education Review* 58(1) (February).

Gans, H. J. 1992. "Second-Generation Decline: Scenarios for the Economic and Ethnic Futures of Post-1965 American Immigrants." *Ethnic and Racial Studies* 15 (April):173–192.

Kasinitz, P. 1992. *Caribbean New York: Black Immigrants and the Politics of Race.* Ithaca, NY: Cornell University Press.

Lieberson, A. 1980. *A Piece of the Pie: Blacks and White Immigrants Since 1980.* Berkeley: University of California Press.

Massey, D. 1990. "American Apartheid: Segregation and the Making of the Underclass." *American Journal of Sociology* 96(2) (September): 329–357.

Ogbu, J. U. 1990. "Minority Status and Literacy in Comparative Perspective." *Daedalus* 119(2) (Spring):141–168.

Portes, A., and M. Zhou. 1993. "The New Second Generation: Segmented Assimilation and Its Variants."

Annals of the American Academy of Political and Social Science 530 (November): 74–96.

Stafford, S. B. 1987. "Language and Identity: Haitians in New York City." In *Caribbean Life in New York City: Sociocultural Dimensions,* edited by C. R. Sutton and E. M. Chaney. New York: Center for Migration Studies.

Sutton, C. R., and S. P. Makiesky. 1975. "Migration and West Indian Racial and Ethnic Consciousness." In *Migration and Development: Implications for Ethnic Identity and Political Conflict,* edited by H. I. Safa and B. M. Du Toit. Paris: Mouton.

Warner, W. L., and L. Srole. 1945. *The Social Systems of American Ethnic Groups.* New Haven, CT: Yale University Press.

Woldemikael, T. M. 1989. *Becoming Black American: Haitian and American Institutions in Evanston, Illinois.* New York: AMS Press.

READING 46

Notes

1. In keeping with the U.S. Census Bureau definition, ethnicity refers to whether an individual is of Hispanic origin or not. Intermarriages are defined as marriages between Hispanic and non-Hispanic persons, or marriages between white, black, Asian, American Indian, or multiracial persons, or persons who report that they are some other race. Among all intermarried couples in 2015, 54% were in interethnic (Hispanic/non-Hispanic) marriages, and the remainder were in interracial marriages.

2. Asian Americans are an incredibly diverse group, with varying histories in the U.S. and very different demographic and economic profiles.

READING 47

Notes

1. "Over 93 percent of whites and of blacks marry within their own groups, in contrast to about 70 percent of Asians and of Hispanics and less than one-third of American Indians." Roderick

J. Harrison and Claudette E. Bennett, "Racial and Ethnic Diversity," in Reynolds Farley, ed., *State of the Union: America in the 1990s–Vol. Two: Social Trends* (1995), 165. When people of Latino and Asian ancestry marry exogamously, "their spouses are very likely to be white; interracial marriages in the United States [have seldom] involved the mixing of two minority groups" (Ibid.).

2. Reflecting on his marriage, Peter Norton once mused, "Other than sex itself, why do you want to spend your life in the company of a woman as opposed to a best male friend? Part of the answer has to do with the wonderful, bizarre, inexplicable differences between male psychology and female psychology. Well, in the same vein, why would you want to spend your life with a person from the same ethnic background? You miss the frisson" (quoted in David Owen, "The Straddler," *The New Yorker,* January 30, 1995).

3. Roxie Roker, the black actress who played Helen Willis, was herself married to a white man. The popular musician Lenny Kravitz is their son. See Lynn Norment, "Am I Black, White, or in Between?," *Ebony,* August 1995; "Roxie Roker, 66, Who Broke Barrier in Her Marriage on TV's *Jeffersons,*" *New York Times,* December 6, 1995.

4. Denise Nicholas, who played the character whom the sheriff married, actively shaped the public image of her role, particularly with respect to the interracial relationship. Nicholas felt that the characters "should either break [the relationship] off or get married because oftentimes, historically, interracial relationships were back-alley affairs, hidden and lied about, particularly in the South. It became really important to me that the [characters] do something dignified; I didn't want my character to be cheap" ("Denise Nicholas and Carroll O'Connor Wed on TV Drama 'In the Heat of the Night,'" *Jet,* May 9, 1994). It should be recalled that the basis for the television series was the film of the same name (1967), which featured a thoroughly bigoted white sheriff (played by Rod Steiger, in an Academy Award–winning performance).

5. ABC's hugely successful musical production starred Brandy as Cinderella and Paolo Montalban as the prince. Taking the role of Prince Charming's mother, the queen, was a black actress, Whoopi Goldberg, while the king was played by a white actor, Victor Garber. See Veronica Chambers, "The Myth of Cinderella," *Newsweek*, November 3, 1997; "Cinderella TV Music Special Produces Spectacular Rating for ABC," *Jet*, November 24, 1997.

6. Such depictions were no accident. When television producers sought guests for these programs, they advertised for people who had had *bad* experiences in or on account of interracial relationships. It was this bias that gave rise to episodes such as "Woman Disowned by Her Family for Dating a Black Man" on *Jenny Jones* and "Blacks and Blondes: White Girls Dating Black Guys for Sex, Style, and Status" on *Geraldo*.

7. Several months after *An American Love Story* aired, Cecily Wilson married a white union organizer whom she had met on a blind date. See "Weddings: Cecily Wilson, Gregory Speller," *New York Times*, May 7, 2000.

8. Fox has stated that she was surprised by some of her relatives' negative reactions to her interracial relationship, and surprised, too, by the regularity of the racial mistreatment her black lover suffered. In retrospect, she observes, "it was almost like I was deluded or something; I thought I was living in a different world than I was living in" (quoted in Paula Span, "Modern Family Life in Black and White: PBS Documentary Chronicles an Interracial Marriage," *Washington Post*, September 9, 1999).

9. Two excellent coming-of-age films that evoke the hazards and rewards of teenage interracial dating in the 1950s are Robert De Niro's *A Bronx Tale* (1993) and Barry Levinson's *Liberty Heights* (2000).

10. Although they failed to persuade the United States Census Bureau to offer the "multiracial" box for the 2000 census, multiracialist reformers have succeeded in convincing a number of state governments—including those of Georgia, Illinois, Florida, Indiana, Michigan, and Ohio—to require that such a box be provided on state forms that collect racial data. They have also managed to convince several important private institutions, among them Harvard University, to add a "multiracial" category alongside the other, more familiar and established, choices. See Tanya Kateri Hernandez, "'Multiracial' Discourse: Racial Classifications in an Era of Color-Blind Jurisprudence," *Maryland Law Review* 57 (1998): 97, 98 n. 4.

11. When the racial-classification issue was decided for the 2000 census, the person in charge of the supervisory agency was Franklin Raines, a black man married to a white woman. Franklin and Wendy Raines had two children who themselves faced this classification dilemma. See Julia Malone, "Facing the Racial Question: More Categories in the Census," *The Atlanta Journal and Constitution*, October 15, 1997.

12. Woods made his views known on Oprah Winfrey's television show soon after he won the prestigious Masters golf tournament. See Greg Couch, "Woods: I'm More Than Black," *Chicago Sun-Times*, April 22, 1997, p. 1.

13. In a satirical essay entitled "The Mulatto Millennium," Danzy Senna facetiously defined "Cablinasian" thus:

14. A rare exotic breed found mostly in California. This is the mother of all mixtures. . . . A show mulatto, with great performance skills, the Cablinasian will be whoever the crowd wants him to be, and can switch at the drop of a dime. Does not, however, answer to the name Black. . . . Note: If you spot a Cablinasian, please contact the Benetton Promotions Bureau. [In Claudine Chiawei O'Hearn, ed., *Half and Half: Writers on Growing up Biracial and Bicultural* (1998), 26.]

15. For a powerful defense of Woods's position, see Gary Kamiya, "Cablinasian Like Me," Salon.com, April 1997. For a critique, see Leonard Pitts, "Is There Room in This Sweet Land of Liberty for Such a Thing as 'Cablinasian'? Face It, Tiger: If They Say You're Black, Then You're Black," *Baltimore Sun*, April 29, 1997.

READING 48

Notes

1. Etienne Balibar and Immanuel Wallerstein, *Race, Nation, Class: Ambiguous Identities* (New York: Verso, 1991), 71.

2. Joe Feagin and Hernán Vera, *White Racism* (New York: Routledge, 1995), ix–x.

3. Abby L. Ferber, *White Man Falling: Race, Gender and White Supremacy* (New York: Rowman and Littlefield, 1998), 100.

4. Naomi Zack, *Race and Mixed Race* (Philadelphia: Temple University Press, 1994).

5. Mimi Abramowitz, *Regulating the Lives of Women: Social Welfare Policy from Colonial Times to the Present* (Boston: South End Press, 1996).

6. Ibid., 3.

7. Valerie Babb, *Whiteness Visible: The Meaning of Whiteness in American Literature and Culture* (New York: New York University Press, 1998), 76.

8. Grace Elizabeth Hale, *Making Whiteness: The Culture of Segregation in the South, 1890–1940* (New York: Vintage Books, 1998), 109.

9. See, for instance, Gail Folaron and McCartt Hess, "Placement Considerations for Children of Mixed African American and Caucasian Parentage," *Child Welfare League of America* 72, 3 (1993): 113–135.

10. See, for instance, Ferber, *White Man Falling.*

11. Ibid.

12. Ibid., 104.

13. Robert Merton, "Intermarriage and the Social Structure: Fact and Theory," *Psychiatry* 4 (1941): 361–374; see also Matthijs Kalmijn, "Trends in Black/White Intermarriage," *Social Forces* 72, 1 (1996): 119–146.

14. Merton, "Intermarriage"; Kingsley Davis, "Intermarriage in Caste Societies," *American Anthropologist* (September 1941): 388–395.

15. Ferber, *White Man Falling.*

16. Zack, *Race and Mixed Race*; Joel Williamson, *New People: Miscegenation and Mulattoes in the United States* (New York: New York University Press, 1984).

17. Ferber, *White Man Falling*, 103.

18. Kate Davy, "Outing Whiteness." *Theatre* 47, 2 (1995): 189–205.

19. Charles Gallagher, "White Reconstruction in the University," *Socialist Review* 24, 1 and 2 (1995): 165–188.

20. Cathy J. Cohen, "Contested Membership: Black Gay Identities and the Politics of AIDS," in *Queer Theory/Sociology,* ed. Steven Seidman (Cambridge, Mass.: Blackwell, 1996), 365.

21. Frantz Fanon, *Black Skin, White Masks* (New York: Grove), 83.

22. Ibid., 60.

23. Paul C. Rosenblatt, Terri A. Karis, and Richard D. Powell, *Multiracial Couples: Black and White Voices* (Thousand Oaks, Calif.: Sage, 1995), 155.

24. Michael Eric Dyson, "Essentialism and the Complexities of Racial Identity," in *Multiculturalism: A Critical Reader,* ed. David Theo Goldberg (Cambridge, Mass.: Blackwell, 1994), 222.

25. Rosenblatt et al., *Multiracial Couples,* 150.

26. Ibid., 151.

27. Ibid.

28. Gloria Wade-Gayles, *Rooted against the Wind* (Boston: Beacon, 1996), 110.

29. David Heer, "Negro-White Marriages in the United States," *Journal of Marriage and the Family* 28 (1966): 262–273; Kalmijn, "Trends"; Merton, "Intermarriage"; Davis, "Intermarriage in Caste Societies."

30. Although many people break up permanently, I interviewed individuals who eventually made the decision to commit to an interracial marriage.

31. Claudette Bennett, "Interracial Children: Implications for a Multiracial Category" (paper presented at the annual meeting of the American Sociological Association, Washington, D.C., 1995).

32. Rosenblatt et al., *Multiracial Couples,* 5.

READING 49

Notes

1. "A Methodological Note" in Drake and Cayton (1993 [1945]).

2. *Black Metropolis,* p. 127.

3. The strength and consequences of the tendency to racialize those of African descent in the United States is underscored by the persistent attempts of immigrants of African descent from the Caribbean and African continent to *emphasize* their cultural and linguistic differences from African Americans so as to escape the consequences of such racialization (Waters 1999).

4. OMB Directive 15 guidelines mandated federal agency compliance by 2003. As of 2006, the Education Department had not yet implemented the MOOM option. In August 2006, however, Education Department officials released a proposal for a plan to allow students to mark multiple racial categories that, if adopted, would comply with the federal guidelines.

5. The American College Personnel Association has an estimated 8,000 members.

6. Mavin Foundation has been quite involved in expanding the tracking and donation of bone marrow by mixed race people. They assert that mixed race people in need of bone marrow have difficulty finding matches because they are of mixed race.

7. Winant (1994) contrasts hegemony with domination. Rather than being silenced or repressed, hegemony incorporates opposition and difference (with modification) into the social order, as it robs opposition of its critical content.

References

Alba, R. (1990). *Ethnic Identity: The Transformation of White America.* New Haven, CT: Yale University Press.

Bakalian, A. (1993). *Armenian-Americans: From Being to Feeling Armenian.* New Brunswick, NJ: Transaction Publishers.

Bell, D. (1992). *Faces at the Bottom of the Well.* New York: Basic Books.

Benjamin, J. (1988). *The Bonds of Love: Psychoanalysis, Feminism and the Problem of Domination.* New York: Pantheon.

Blu, K. (1980). *The Lumbee Problem: The Making of an American Indian People.* Cambridge, UK: Cambridge University Press.

Comaroff, J. L. (1987). "Of Totemism and Ethnicity: Consciousness, Practice and the Signs of Inequality." *Ethnos* 52: 301–323.

Cose, E. (1992). *Rage of a Privileged Class: Why Do Prosperous Blacks Still Have the Blues?* New York: Harper Perennial.

DeMott, B. (1998 [1995]). *The Trouble with Friendship: Why Americans Can't Think Straight about Race.* New Haven: Yale University Press.

Drake, S. C. and H. Cayton. (1993 [1945]). *Black Metropolis: A Study of Negro Life in a Northern City.* Chicago: University of Chicago Press.

DuBois, W. E. B. ([1903] 1996). *The Souls of Black Folk. The Oxford W. E. B. DuBois Reader.* E. J. Sundquist. New York and Oxford, MI: Oxford University Press.

Espiritu, Y. L. (1992). *Asian American Panethnicity: Bridging Institutions and Identities.* Philadelphia: Temple University Press.

Files, J. (June 10, 2005). Report Describes Immigrants as Younger and More Diverse. *The New York Times:* 12.

Fordham, S. (1997). *Blacked Out.* Chicago, University of Chicago Press.

Gans, H. J. (1979). "Symbolic Ethnicity: The Future of Ethnic Groups and Cultures in America." *Ethnic and Racial Studies* 2: 1–20.

Lieberson, S. (1985). Unhyphenated Whites in the United States. *Ethnicity and Race in the U.S.A.: Toward the Twenty-first Century.* R. D. Alba. New York: Routledge: 159–180.

Nagel, J. (1995). "American Indian Ethnic Renewal: Politics and the Resurgence of Identity." *American Sociological Review* 60(6): 947–965.

Omi, M. and H. Winant. (1994). *Racial Formation in the United States: From the 1960s to the 1990s.* New York: Routledge.

Sanjek, R. (1994). Intermarriage and the Future of Races in the United States. *Race.* S. Gregory and R. Sanjek. New Brunswick, NJ: Rutgers University Press: 103–130.

Steinberg, S. (1989). *The Ethnic Myth: Race, Ethnicity, and Class in America.* Boston: Beacon Press.

Tuan, M. (1998). *Forever Foreigners or Honorary Whites? The Asian Ethnic Experience Today.* New Brunswick, NJ: Rutgers University Press.

Waters, M. (1990). *Ethnic Options: Choosing Ethnic Identities in America.* Berkeley: University of California Press.

Waters, M. C. (1999). *Black Identities: West Indian Immigrant Dreams and American Realities.* Cambridge, MA: Harvard University Press.

Winant, H. (1994). Racial Formation and Hegemony: Global and Local Developments. *Racism, Modernity and Identity on the Western Front.* A. Rattansi and S. Westwood. Cambridge, UK: Polity Press. 266–289.

READING 50

Notes

1. Brown, 1999, 9.

2. Price, 2003.

3. Sklar et al., 2001, 122.

4. Henry J. Kaiser Family Foundation, 2000, 1.

5. Ibid., 2.

6. Ibid., 4.

7. U.S. Department of Health and Human Services, 1998.

8. Shapiro, *Hidden Cost,* 2004, 52.

9. Sklar et al., 2001, 90.

10. Collins and Yeskel, 2000, 182.

11. Ibid.

12. Anderson et al., 2005, 1.

13. Root Cause, 2003.

14. Sklar et al., 2001, 118.

15. Phillips, 2001.

16. Boshara et al., 2004, 1.

17. Sklar et al., 2001, 118.

18. Muhammad et al., 2004, 7.

19. Woo, 2000, 104.

20. Shapiro, PowerPoint, 2004.

21. Sherradan, 1991, 3–7.

22. Brown, 1999, 17.

23. Shapiro, *Hidden Cost,* 2004, 185.

24. Ginsberg and Ochoa, 2003, B1.

25. Isbister, 1994, 2.

26. Ibid., 5.

27. Ibid.

28. Policy Link, 2003.

29. Ibid.

30. United for a Fair Economy, 2002.

31. Moreno, 1998, 6–7.

32. Ibid., 1.

33. Ibid., 17.

34. Orr, 2004, 14.

35. Spriggs, 2004, 18.

36. Muhammad et al., 2004, 17.

37. Agres, 2005, 37.

Society, Vol. 38(1) 49–66. Copyright 2014 SAGE Publications. Reprinted with permission.

READING 13

"Color-Blind Privilege: The Social and Political Functions of Erasing the Color Line in Post-Race America" by Charles A. Gallagher, from the RCG JOURNAL SPECIAL EDITION ON PRIVILEGE, Abby L. Ferber and Dena R. Samuels, co-editors, Vol. 10, No. 4, 2003.

READING 14

Excerpts from "Buying Racial Capital: Skin-Bleaching and Cosmetic Surgery in a Globalized World," by Margaret L. Hunter in *The Journal of Pan African Studies*, Volume 4, Number 4, June 2011. Reprinted with permission.

READING 15

Gans, Herbert J. "The Possibility of a New Racial Hierarchy in the Twenty-First Century United States." Reprinted from THE CULTURAL TERRITORIES OF RACE, edited by Michele Lamont. Copyright © 1999 University of Chicago and the Russell Sage Foundation. Reprinted by permission of the University of Chicago Press.

READING 16

"Race Prejudice as a Sense of Group Position" by Herbert Blumer, from THE PACIFIC SOCIOLOGICAL REVIEW 1, No. 1, Spring 1958: 3–7. Reprinted by permission of Dean S. Dorn for the Pacific Sociological Association.

READING 17

"Truth: Remarks on the Removal of Confederate Monuments in New Orleans," Mayor Mitchell J. Landriue. May 19, 2017.

READING 18

"Discrimination and the American Creed" by Robert K. Merton from DISCRIMINATION AND NATIONAL WELFARE, Edited by Robert M. MacIver. Copyright © 1949 by the Institute for Religious and Social Studies. Reprinted by permission of HarperCollins Publishers.

READING 19

Excerpts from "The Place of Race in Conservative and Far-right Movements," by Kathleen M. Blee and Elizabeth A.

Yates in *Sociology of Race and Ethnicity*, 2015, Vol. 1(1): 127–136. Reprinted with permission from The American Psychological Association.

READING 20

Lipsitz, George. "The Possessive Investment in Whiteness: Racialized Social Democracy and the 'White' Problem in American Studies." *American Quarterly* 47:3 (1995), 369–387. © 1995 The American Studies Association. Reprinted with permission of The Johns Hopkins University Press.

READING 21

Excerpts from "Postmortem: Death and Ghost Values," in *The Price for Their Pound of Flesh: The Value of the Enslaved, from Womb to Grave, in the Beginiing of a Nation* by Daina Ramey Berry. Copyright 2017 by Daina Ramey Berry. Reprinted with permission from Beacon Press.

READING 22

"A Research Note on Trends in Black Hypersegregation," by Douglas S. Massey and Jonathan Tannen in *Demography* (2015) 52: 1025–1034. © Population Association of America 2015. Reprinted with permission from Springer.

READING 23

"The Code of the Streets" by Elijah Anderson from *The Code of the Streets*. Originally in *The Atlantic Monthly* 273, No. 5, May 1994. Copyright © 1994 by Elijah Anderson. Reprinted with the permission of Elijah Anderson.

READING 24

"Environmental Justice in the 21st Century: Race Still Matters" by Robert D. Bullard, from PHYLON 49, No. 3–4 (2001): 151–171. Copyright © 2001 Phylon. Reprinted by permission.

READING 25

"Race, Religion, and the Color Line (Or Is That the Color Wall?)" by Michael O. Emerson. Reprinted by permission of the author.

READING 26

Excerpts from "The Black-White Swimming Disparity in America: A Deadly Legacy of Swimming Pool Discrimination," by Jeff Wiltse in *Journal of Sport and Social Issues*, 2014, Vol. 38(4), 366–389. Copyright 2014 SAGE Publications. Reprinted with permission.

READING 27

"How White Users Made Heroin a Public-Health Problem," by Andrew Cohen, in *The Atlantic*, April 12, 2015. Copyright © 2015 The Atlantic Media Co., as first published in The Atlantic Magazine. All rights reserved. Distributed by Tribune Content Agency, LLC.

READING 28

Excerpt from *The New Jim Crow: Mass Incarceration in the Age of Colorblindness* by Michelle Alexander. Copyright © 2010, 2012 by Michelle Alexander. Reprinted by permission of The New Press, www.thenewpress.com.

READING 29

"American Policing Under Fire: Misconduct and Reform," by Ronald Weitzer in *Sociology* (2015) 52: 475.480. Reprinted with permission from Springer.

READING 30

Pager, Devah. "The Mark of a Criminal Record" from IN FOCUS, The Newsletter for the Institute for Research on Poverty 23, No. 2 (Summer 2004). Copyright © 2004 by the Regents of the University of Wisconsin. Reprinted with permission.

READING 31

"Kristen v. Aisha; Brad v. Rasheed: What's in a Name and How It Affects Getting a Job" by Amy Braverman Puma, from "Why Brad and Kristen Beat Out Jermaine and Ebony." UNIVERSITY OF CHICAGO MAGAZINE 95 No. 3 (February 2003). Reprinted with permission.

READING 32

Waldinger, Robert, "When the Melting Pot Boils Over" in Michael Peter Smith and Joseph R. Feagin (eds) *The Bubbling Cauldron* (University of Minnesota Press, 1995) pp. 265–281. Copyright 1995 by the Regents of the University of Minnesota. Reprinted by permission.

READING 33

Newman, Katherine S. & Catherine Ellis, "'There's No Shame in My Game': Status and Stigma among Harlem's Working Poor." Reprinted from THE CULTURAL TERRITORIES OF RACE, edited by Michele Lamont. Copyright © 1999 University of Chicago and the Russell Sage Foundation. Reprinted by permission of the University of Chicago Press.

READING 34

Bao, Xiaolan. "Sweatshops in Sunset Park: A Variation of the Late Twentieth-Century Chinese Garment Shops in New York City" from *International Labor and Working-Class History*, Vol. 61, (April 2002), pp. 69–90. Copyright © 2002 The International Labor and Working-Class History Society. Reprinted with the permission of Cambridge University Press.

READING 35

Dirks, Danielle and Jennifer Mueller "Racism and Popular Culture." With kind permission from Springer Science+Business Media: *Handbook of the Sociology of Racial and Ethnic Relations*, edited by Hernan Vera and Joe Feagin. © Springer Science + Business Media, LLC 2007.

READING 36

Littlefield, Marci Bounds. "The Media as a System of Racialization: Exploring Images of African American Women and the New Racism" from American Behavioral Scientist 51, no. 5 (Jan. 2008): 675–685. Copyright 2008 SAGE Publications. Reprinted with permission.

READING 37

"Must-See TV: South Asian Characterizations in American Popular Media," by Bhoomi K. Thakore, in *Sociology Compass* 8/2 (2014): 149–156. With permission from John Wiley & Sons.

READING 38

Alsultany, Evelyn. "Arabs and Muslims in the Media after 9/11: Representational Strategies for a 'Postrace' Era," *American Quarterly*, Volume 65, Number 1, March 2013, pp. 161–169. © 2013 The American Sudies Association. Reprinted with permission of John Hopkins University Press.